The Ernst & Young Tax Guide 1994

Critical Acclaim . . .

"This is the best tax guide of the bunch . . . the most up-to-date guide . . . ."

USA Today

"Hard to beat . . . (Ernst & Young) experts elucidate each point, giving examples, definitions and strategies that you won't learn about from the IRS."

Money

"This book contains useable tax forms, perhaps saving a trip to the library or post office, and because it delays publication until December, it has more up-to-date information on tax changes than its competitors—or even the IRS."

Chicago Sun-Times

"Best of the commercially available guides . . . It is the only guide with the final version of federal tax forms."

New York Daily News

"Destined to become an 'old standard,' all written in plain English . . . If you can afford just one tax book, this could be the one."

Seattle Post-Intelligencer

"The text-with-commentary approach makes the book both authoritative and easy-to-use."

People

"The simplest tax guide to understand."

CBS This Morning

"The explanations, examples, and planning advice are top-drawer."

Orlando Sentinel

"Exceptionally detailed."

The Sunday Denver Post

"An excellent book, full of clear explanations, planning hints, tax savers and sample forms."

Atlanta Journal Constitution

"Our brand-name choice for filers with lots of questions for filing and planning situations . . . ."

Fort Worth Star-Telegram

". . . a veritable fountain of information . . ."

Milwaukee Sentinel

". . . the best of the bunch for return preparation."

Des Moines Register

Ask Ernst & Young

Questions and Answers About Your Taxes

Q. The new tax law passed in August raised my 1993 taxes. Is there anything I can do to ease the impact of these retroactive tax changes?

A. Yes, certain taxpayers may be able to defer payment of part of their additional 1993 tax to the extent that it is created by the retroactive increase in tax rates. See Chapter 1, *Filing Information,* for more information. You may also get a waiver of the estimated tax penalties if you have an underpayment of tax due to the 1993 tax law changes. See Chapter 5, *Tax Withholding and Estimated Taxes.*

Q. I receive social security. How will the new tax law affect me?

A. For 1993, up to one-half of your social security benefits can be subject to tax. In 1994, however, the new law taxes up to 85% of the benefits received. If your income is between $25,000 and $50,000, you may be able to do some tax planning that could reduce the amount of social security benefits that will be taxed. See Chapter 12, *Social Security and Equivalent Railroad Retirement Benefits.*

Q. Last year our adult child was unemployed and lived with us. Can we claim an exemption for that child?

A. Depending upon the child's age and income you may be eligible to claim an exemption for that child. It is a complicated matter, however, in Chapter 3, *Personal Exemptions and Deductions,* there are easy-to-use worksheets that will help in deciding whether or not you can claim the exemption.

Q. Is there an easy way to determine whether I should itemize my deductions or take the standard deduction?

A. No, the only way to be absolutely sure is to compute your itemized deductions and compare them against the standard deduction. Generally, if you own a home, make large charitable deductions, live in a state with a high income tax or had large medical expenses or casualty losses, the deductions will probably add up to more than the standard deduction. See "Should You Take the Standard Deduction or Should You Itemize Your Deductions?" on page 316.

Q. I work at home. Can I deduct part of my apartment expenses on my tax return?

A. If you are self-employed, and you set aside a portion of your apartment that is used *regularly* and *exclusively* as your principal place of business or as a place to meet and deal with your clients you probably can. If you are an employee you must meet stricter requirements such as the office being maintained for the convenience of your employer. See "Home Office" in Chapter 30, *Miscellaneous Deductions.*

Q. I was divorced last year and receive payments from my former spouse. Are these payments taxable to me?

A. Whether the payments you receive are taxable or not generally depends on the terms of the divorce decree or settlement. For example, if the payments were for child support they would not be taxable to you. See Chapter 19, *Alimony,* for a discussion of this topic.

Q. We rented out our beach house this last year for one week. The renter said that I didn't have to report the rent as income. Was he right?

A. Yes, if you only rented the beach house out for a week last year. If you use a dwelling unit as a home and rent it out for less than 15 days per year you do not have to report the rent as income. On the other hand, you cannot claim any rental expense deductions. See "Income and Deductions for Property Used as a Home" in Chapter 15, *Sale of Property.*

Q. If I give some old furniture and clothes to the Salvation Army can I take a deduction for them?

A. When you give property to a charity you can take a deduction equal to the fair market value of the property on the date of the gift. And there is the rub. What is the dollar value of the old furniture and the old clothes? What would someone be willing to pay for it? If no one wants to buy it, it has no dollar value and although you have indeed made a charitable gift there would be no deduction. See Chapter 25, *Contributions.*

The Ernst & Young Tax Guide 1994

By Ernst & Young

Peter W. Bernstein, *Editor*

John Wiley & Sons, Inc.
New York • Chichester • Brisbane • Toronto • Singapore

In the preparation of this book, every effort has been made to offer the most current, correct, and clearly expressed information possible. Nonetheless, inadvertent errors can occur, and tax rules and regulations often change.

Further, the information in the text is intended to afford general guidelines on matters of interest to taxpayers. The application and impact of tax laws can vary widely, however, from case to case, based upon the specific or unique facts involved. Accordingly, the information in this book is not intended to serve as legal, accounting, or tax advice. Readers are encouraged to consult with professional advisors for advice concerning specific matters before making any decision, and the author and publishers disclaim any responsibility for positions taken by taxpayers in their individual cases or for any misunderstanding on the part of readers.

The information in this book is based on the Internal Revenue Code as of November 30, 1993.

This book contains the text, charts, and figures from the Internal Revenue Service Publication 17, *Your Federal Income Tax* (rev. Nov. 1993).

ISBN: 0–471–59907–7
ISSN: 1059–809X

Text design by Cindy Geist

Manufactured in the United States of America

Revised Edition: January 1994
10 9 8 7 6 5 4 3 2 1

Table of Contents

For a summary of how the new tax law will affect your 1993 tax return, see Changes in the Tax Laws You Should Know About. For information about how the new law will affect your 1994 tax return, see Chapter 42, Planning Ahead for 1994 and Beyond.

Special Tables of Contents

SELF-EMPLOYED ENTREPRENEURS' TAX GUIDE

BUSINESS EXECUTIVES' TAX GUIDE

SENIOR CITIZENS' TAX GUIDE

MEMBERS OF THE ARMED FORCES' TAX GUIDE
(Including Veterans)

The Ernst & Young Tax Guide Editorial Board 1994

Chairman: Harvey B. Wishman

Atlanta

Tracy H. Brea
John D. Eadie
Alan Gotthardt
Stephanie A. Gruber
Gregory M. Guthrie
Herbert J. Harriott
Andrew D. Painter
Susan M. Parsons
Jim Tringas
Susan H. Walker

Chicago

Michael Beckerman
John Branstad
Steve Ciolino
Christine Franco
Virginia M. Johnson
Dennis Madsen
Kristine Martz
Susan L. Young

Dallas

Walter Coppinger
Barbara J. Raasch
J. David Thach III
William W. Thorburn
Justin E. Way

MetroPark/Hackensack

Marie E. Corwin
Donald A. Culp
Steven M. Kates
Gary P. Lubowiecki
Cheryl Spielman

Milwaukee

Steven Ayers
Anthony J. Berndt
Michael E. Friedman
Sherri T. Hiller
Alan L. Keltner
Thomas J. McCutcheon
Arthur T. Phillips
Lisa M. Waite
Randall J. Wichinski

New York

Paul Allutto
Donald J. Andres
Kevin Leifer
John Martinkat
Kurt C. Neidhardt
Paul J. Stroud

Providence

Christopher Bartlett
Edward T. Broadmeadow
Charlene K. Butler
Stephen B. Forman
Edward P. Pieroni

Walnut Creek

Robert W. Call
Stephen R. Nadeau

Washington

Donald Anderson
Lorraine Bell
Anthony L. Brady
Diane C. Carruthers
Gary N. Cohen
James B. Conley
Robert B. Coplan
David J. Kautter
Robert A. Midler
S. Theodore Reiner
Paul R. Schultz

Special thanks to Ray J. Groves, Chairman of Ernst & Young; William J. Lipton, Vice Chairman–Tax Services; Herbert J. Lerner, National Director–Tax Policy and Standards; Richard S. Bobrow, National Director–Technical and Industry Tax Services; Robert J. Garner, National Director–Personal Financial Counseling; Patrice Ingrassia; Howard Freedman; and Alan Meister.

Special Acknowledgments: Cornelia Carter, Georgina Woods, Susan Barry, Glen Haley, and Julia Willard

Ernst & Young is the nation's leading professional services firm, providing tax, accounting, and management consulting services to thousands of individuals as well as businesses of all sizes. This book draws upon the experience of many of the firm's professionals for its content.

How to Use This Guide

The Ernst & Young Tax Guide 1994 is an easy-to-use, step-by-step guide to preparing your own tax return. It has been designed with you, the reader, in mind, and its format should help highlight information to save you time and money. To make sure you have the most up-to-date tax information available, we have, unlike other tax guides, waited until the beginning of December before going to press.

The book explains, in clear and simple English, important aspects of the tax laws that affect you. It covers what you need to know about your taxes—from how to file your return to how to lower the tax you'll pay next year. Throughout the book, you will find hundreds of examples illustrating how the tax law works. Sample tax forms and schedules show you how to fill out your return line by line. Here are some of the book's special features and how to use them:

- **Two Books-In-One.** *The Ernst & Young Tax Guide 1994* is really two books. The first book is the official Internal Revenue Service tax guide, Publication 17, *Your Federal Income Tax,* which is reproduced here. Published annually, it contains the IRS's position on many of the tax questions taxpayers face. The second book is the Ernst & Young guide. Here are comments, explanations, and tax-saving tips on what the IRS tells you—and doesn't tell you. It's no surprise that the IRS doesn't tell you everything, and what it does say often favors the U.S. government. Courts and tax professionals frequently disagree with IRS opinions. The Ernst & Young text provides you with this additional material. The two books have been spliced together to give you the most well-rounded tax guide on the market. The IRS text appears in black throughout the book. Ernst & Young's comments appear in the blue boxes or in blue type.

- **TaxSavers, TaxPlanners, TaxAlerts, and Tax Organizers.** One of the book's biggest attractions is the over 400 *TaxSavers, TaxPlanners, TaxAlerts,* and *TaxOrganizers* that you'll find appropriately placed throughout the text. *TaxSavers* are tips that help you slash your tax bill this year and next—legally. *TaxPlanners* outline strategies that help you plan better for the upcoming year. *TaxAlerts* point out taxes and regulations that have just changed or may change in the near future and they give you important current filing advice about things you will want to consider as you prepare your returns. *TaxOrganizers,* new to the book this year, point out things you need to do now to make it easier to file your taxes later.

- **Tax Forms You Can Use.** *The Ernst & Young Tax Guide 1994* is the only tax guide that contains official tax forms that you can use. You'll find many of the federal tax forms that you need in Part VI, along with tax tables and tax rate schedules. Simply tear the forms out and fill them in. It's perfectly acceptable to send your completed forms from this book to the IRS (don't forget to make a copy of them for your files). A listing of all the tax forms that appear in the book can be found in the Table of Contents.

- **Special Tables of Contents.** We've taken great pains to ensure that this book is clearly organized for easy access. If you can't find the section you want in the regular Table of Contents, look over the *Special Tables of Contents.* All told, there are eight of these—one each for families, homeowners, investors in stocks and bonds, investors in real estate, self-employed entrepreneurs, business executives, senior citizens, and members of the armed forces. Each *Special Table of Contents* contains a listing of the major tax issues for members of that group and tells where you can find the answers in the book.

- **Easy-to-Find References to Form 1040**. In the front of this book, you'll find a Form 1040, each line of which is indexed to the page in the book where you can find the specific information you need to complete that item.

We have drawn from the tax experience of scores of Ernst & Young partners and staff from all parts of the United States to create this tax guide. Among the major accounting firms, only Ernst & Young publishes a complete tax guide that is available to the general public. It provides the most complete and most up-to-date tax information of any tax guide published. You also might find of interest three additional Ernst & Young books: *The Ernst & Young Tax-Saving Strategies Guide 1994, The Ernst & Young New York, New Jersey, Connecticut State Tax Guide 1994,* and *Ernst & Young's Guide to the New Tax Law,* a complete explanation of the just-passed tax legislation.

Changes in the Tax Law You Should Know About

A Summary of 1993 Tax Developments

The most significant changes in the tax law in 1993 were those enacted in the Omnibus Budget Reconciliation Act of 1993 (the 1993 Tax Act). The new law included increases in tax rates retroactive to January 1, 1993. At the same time, some tax benefits were extended retroactively to June 30, 1992. These and other important changes and adjustments are summarized below.

New Tax Rates for 1993

The 1993 Tax Act created two new income tax rates for higher-income individuals retroactively to January 1, 1993. The two new rates are in addition to the three existing rates of 15%, 28%, and 31%.

A fourth tax bracket of 36% applies to taxable income exceeding the following amounts based on filing status:

- $115,000 (single)
- $127,500 (head of household)
- $140,000 (married filing jointly)
- $70,000 (married filing separately)

In addition, a 10% surtax applies to certain high-income taxpayers. It is computed by applying a 39.6% rate to taxable income in excess of the following amounts:

- $250,000 (all individuals, except married filing separately)
- $125,000 (married filing separately)

Long-term capital gains continue to be subject to a maximum rate of 28%. See Chapter 31, *How to Figure Your Tax,* and the *Tax Rate Tables* in Chapter 47.

Deferral of Additional 1993 Taxes

Certain taxpayers may be able to defer payment of part of their additional 1993 taxes. See Chapter 1, *Filing Information.*

Waiver of Estimated Tax Penalty

If you have an underpayment of tax due to 1993 tax law changes, you may be able to get a waiver of the estimated tax penalty. See Chapter 5, *Tax Withholding and Estimated Tax.*

Taxation of Social Security Benefits

For tax years beginning after 1993, a higher percentage of social security benefits will be subject to income tax for certain higher-income recipients of social security benefits. In general, recipients of social security benefits whose income exceeds $44,000 for married individuals ($34,000 for unmarried individuals) will be liable for tax on up to 85% of their social security benefits. Under the prior law, only up to 50% of social security benefits were subject to tax. See Chapter 31, *How to Figure Your Tax.*

Medicare Tax

For 1993, the Medicare tax does not apply to wages and other earned income above $135,000. After 1993, the dollar limit on wages and self-employment income subject to the 1.45% Medicare tax (2.9% for self-employed individuals) will be eliminated for wages and other earned income.

Self-employed Health Insurance

The special rule that allows self-employed individuals to deduct 25% of health insurance premiums from gross income was reinstated retroactively to June 30, 1992. See Chapter 22, *Medical and Dental Expenses.*

Alternative Minimum Tax (Individuals)

The alternative minimum tax (AMT) rates have increased retroactively to January, 1993. There are two AMT rates: a 26% rate applies to the first $175,000 of alternative minimum taxable income (AMTI), and a 28% rate applies to AMTI in excess of $175,000 ($87,000 for married individuals filing separately). Under prior law, the AMT rate was a flat 24%. The exemption amounts have been increased to $45,000 (married filing jointly), $33,750 (single and heads of household), and $22,500 (married filing separately and estates and trusts). You may also be able to report alternative minimum tax on Form 1040a. See Chapter 31, *How to Figure Your Tax.*

Gifts of Appreciated Property

The 1993 Tax Act enables taxpayers to recognize a charitable contribution deduction for the full fair market value of appreciated long-term capital gain property for both regular and AMT purposes.

For contributions of tangible personal property (such as works of art), the new rules are retroactive to July 1, 1992. For contributions of all other property (such as stock or real estate), the new rules are retroactive to contributions made after December 31, 1992. See Chapter 25, *Contributions.*

Charitable Contributions

If you make a contribution of $250 or more after 1993, you generally must have a written acknowledgment from the organization in order to deduct the contribution. See Chapter 25, *Contributions.*

Luxury Tax

The new tax law repealed the 10% luxury excise tax on higher-price airplanes, boats, furs, and jewelry, retroactively for sales after 1992.

However, the new tax law did not repeal the luxury tax on automobiles that cost more than $30,000. The $30,000 threshold amount will be indexed for inflation effective for automobiles purchased after August 10, 1993, the date the new law was enacted.

Moving Expense Deduction

The 1993 Tax Act makes a number of changes to the rules for deducting moving expenses. The changes are effective for expenses incurred after 1993. The changes include:

- The distance between a taxpayer's new job must be at least 50 miles farther from the former residence than his or her former job for moving expenses to be deductible. Under the prior law, the new job only had to be 35 miles farther from the former home.
- Deductible moving expenses only include the expense of transporting the taxpayer (and members of his or her household) to the new residence as well as the cost of moving household goods and personal effects. Deductible moving expenses will no longer include: 1) the cost of meals; 2) the costs of pre-move house-hunting trips; 3) the costs of temporary living expenses; 4) the costs incident to the purchase or lease of your old residence; and 5) the costs incident to the purchase or lease of your new residence.
- Reimbursed moving expenses are excluded from income. Expenses that qualify as moving expenses that are not paid or reimbursed by your employer or are no longer deducted as an itemized deduction are now allowable as a deduction in calcu-

lating your adjusted gross income. See Chapter 27, *Moving Expenses*.

Travel Away From Home

You cannot deduct business travel expenses paid or incurred after 1992 for assignments away from home that last for more than one year at a single location. These assignments are no longer considered temporary. See Chapter 28, *Car Expenses and Other Employee Business Expenses*.

Standard Mileage Rate

For 1993, the standard mileage rate for the business use of a car is 28 cents a mile for all business miles. See Chapter 28, *Car Expenses and Other Employee Business Expenses*.

Credit for Electric Vehicle

You may be allowed a 10% tax credit if you placed an electric vehicle in service after June 30, 1993. See Chapter 35, *Other Credits*.

Business Meals and Entertainment

For 1993, subject to certain exceptions (e.g., expenses treated as compensation and included in gross income), the deduction for meals and entertainment expenses is still limited to 80% of the amount incurred. Starting in 1994, the deductible portion of business meals and entertainment expenses is 50%. See Chapter 28, *Car Expenses and Other Employee Business Expenses*.

Club Dues

Starting in 1994, generally, no deduction is allowed for club dues. This rule applies to luncheon clubs as well as all social clubs. Specific business expenses (e.g., meals) incurred at a club are deductible only to the extent that they otherwise satisfy current law standards for deductibility. See Chapter 30, *Miscellaneous Deductions*.

Small Business Equipment Expensing Election

For 1993 in lieu of depreciation, a taxpayer with a sufficiently small amount of annual investment in tangible personal property can elect to deduct up to $17,500 of the cost of qualifying property placed in service for the tax year. See Chapter 36, *If You are Self-Employed*.

Qualified Retirement Plan Benefits and Contributions

The annual compensation limit that can be taken into account for purposes of benefits and contributions under qualified retirement plans is $235,840 in 1993. Beginning in 1994 the compensation cap has been reduced to $150,000. See Chapter 11, *Retirement Plans, Pensions and Annuities*.

Passive Activity Loss Liberalization

Beginning in 1994, active real estate professionals (defined as working more than half of their time in real estate with a minimum of 750 hours and at least a 5% ownership in their employer if they are an employee) are able to offset passive losses against all of their income. See Chapter 13, *Other Income*.

Real Estate Taxes

For homes sold after 1992, the information reported to the IRS and seller of the home on Form 1099-S, Proceeds from Real Estate Transactions, must include the part of any real estate tax that is treated as tax imposed on the buyer. See Chapter 16, *Selling Your Home*

Refunds of Home Mortgage Interest

New box 3 of Form 1098, Mortgage Interest Statement, will show certain mortgage interest refunded to you during 1993 that you paid in a prior year. See Chapter 24, *Interest Expense*.

Seller-financed Mortgage Transactions

Beginning in 1993, a new law requires that taxpayer identification numbers must be reported to the IRS in seller-financed mortgage transactions. See Chapter 16, *Selling Your Home*.

Employer-provided Parking

Beginning in 1993, there is a limit on the exclusion for employer-provided parking to $155 per month. Partners in a partnership, however, cannot benefit from any exclusion for employer-provided parking under this provision. See Chapter 28, *Car Expenses and Other Employee Business Expenses*.

Back-up Withholding

Beginning in 1993, the back-up withholding rate for interest and dividends increases from 20% to 31%.

Withholding on Gambling Winnings

An increase in the rate of withholding on gambling winnings from 20% to 28% took effect in 1993. However, while under prior law, withholding was required on gambling winnings of $1,000 or more, currently withholding is only required on winnings of $5,000 or more. See Chapter 5, *Tax Withholding and Estimated Tax*.

Employer-provided Educational Assistance

The exclusion of employer-provided educational assistance from wages has been retroactively extended through December 31, 1994. See Chapter 6, *Wages, Salaries, and Other Earnings*.

Tax Rates for Estates and Gifts

For individuals who died after 1992 and transfers made after the same date, the new tax law reinstates the top statutory estate tax rates that were in effect prior to their reduction on January 1, 1993. The top statutory rates are 53% on estates over $2.5 million but not over $3 million and 55% on estates of $3 million or higher. See "Planning Your Estate" in Chapter 42, *Planning Ahead for 1994 and Beyond*.

INFLATION ADJUSTMENTS

Filing Requirements

Generally, the amount of income you can have before you are required to file a return has been increased. See Chapter 1, *Filing Information*.

Personal exemption. The amounts for personal and dependent exemptions are indexed for inflation annually. For 1993 the amount for each exemption is $2,350. However, your exemption amount could be phased out if you have high income. See Chapter 3, *Personal Exemptions and Dependents*.

Standard Deduction

The standard deduction for 1999 has increased. See Chapter 20, *Standard Deduction*.

Retirement Benefits. Cost-of living-adjustments are applied annually to the dollar limitations on benefits and contributions to retirement plans, such as 401(k) plans. The maximum amount you could contribute to a 401k plan in 1993 was $8,994. See Chapter 11, *Retirement Plans, Pensions, and Annuities*.

Limit on Itemized Deductions

Some of your itemized deductions may be limited if your adjusted gross income is more than $108,450 ($54,225 if you are married filing separately). See Chapter 21, *Limit on Itemized Deductions*.

Social Security wage base

The amount of wages and self-employment income subject to the social security tax increased from $55,500 in 1992 to $57,600 in 1993. See Chapter 31, *How to Figure Your Tax*.

FORMS UPDATE

Expanded Form 1040EZ

If you are married filing a joint return and have no dependents, you may be able to file Form 1040EZ for 1993. See Chapter 1, *Filing Information*.

Electronic Filing of Federal and State Returns

If you live in certain areas of the country, you may be able to electronically file both your federal and state returns. See Chapter 1, *Filing Information*.

How to Avoid 25 Common Errors

1. Most importantly, check your math.
2. Double-check that your social security number has been correctly written on the return.
3. Include your social security number on each page of the return so that, if a page is misplaced by the IRS, it can be reattached.
4. Check that you have claimed all of your dependents, such as elderly parents who may not live with you.
5. Include on the return the social security numbers for all dependents who are 1 year old and over.
6. If you received a state tax refund, make sure you have not included too much of your refund in your income. State tax refunds may not be taxable if you did not get a tax benefit from deducting them. If, for example, you used the standard deduction in the year in which the taxes were paid, you do not have to include the refund in income this year.
7. Recheck your basis in the shares you sold this year, particularly shares of a mutual fund. Income and capital gains dividends that were automatically reinvested in the fund over the years increase your basis in the mutual fund and thus reduce a gain or increase a loss that you have to report.
8. If your income exceeds $45,000 and you have large deductions or other items that are specially treated, check to see if you are subject to the alternative minimum tax.
9. Fill out Form 8606, *Nondeductible IRA Contributions,* for your contributions to an IRA account, even if you don't claim any deduction for the contribution.
10. Claim the additional standard deductions if you are blind or 65 years of age or older.
11. Be sure that your Form W-2 and all 1099s are correct. If they're wrong, have them corrected as soon as possible so that the IRS's records agree with the amounts you show on your return.
12. If you are married, check to see if filing separate returns rather than a joint return is more beneficial.
13. If you are single and have a dependent who lives with you, check to see if you qualify for the lower tax rates available to a head of household or surviving spouse with a dependent child.
14. Recheck that you have used the correct column in the Tax Rate Table or the right Tax Rate Schedule for your filing status.
15. If you worked for more than one employer, be sure to claim a credit for any overpaid social security taxes withheld from your wages.
16. Only a portion of your social security benefits is taxable. If your income does not exceed a certain amount, none of it may be taxable.
17. Check last year's tax return to see if there are any items that carry over to this year, such as charitable contributions or capital losses that exceeded the amount you were previously able to deduct.
18. If you can be claimed as a dependent on someone else's return do not claim a personal exemption on your return.
19. If you did not pay enough taxes during the year, complete Form 2210, *Underpayment of Estimated Tax,* to calculate the underpayment penalty. You may come up with a lower penalty amount than the IRS would.
20. Attach all Copy Bs of your W-2 forms to your return in order to avoid correspondence with the IRS.
21. Write your social security number on the face of any checks made out to the IRS. You should also put the form number and tax year on the check. Be sure to sign your check.
22. Make sure to sign and date your return. If you are filing a joint return, be sure that your spouse also signs as required.
23. Don't miss deadlines: December 31—set up a Keogh plan; April 15—make your IRA contribution; April 15—file your return or request an extension. Check the tax calendar periodically.
24. If you regularly get large refunds, you're having too much withheld and, in effect, giving an interest-free loan to the IRS. Changing the number of allowances you claim on a W-4 form will increase your take-home pay.
25. Keep records of all documents you send to the IRS. Use certified mail for all important correspondence to the IRS. And don't forget to keep your records in good shape so that you can find answers to any IRS questions about your return.

50 of the Most Easily Overlooked Deductions

The following list will serve as a reminder of some deductions you can easily overlook when you prepare your return. It is not intended to be all-inclusive, nor applicable to everyone. The circumstances of your situation will determine whether you qualify. See the page reference following each item for a complete explanation.

1. Accounting fees for tax preparation services and IRS audits (p. 464)
2. Alcoholism and drug abuse treatment (p. 326)
3. Amortization of premium on taxable bonds (p. 465)
4. Appreciation on property donated to a charity (p. 371)
5. Breach-of-employment-contract damages (p. 455)
6. Business gifts of $25 or less per recipient (p. 455)
7. Casualty loss (p. 378)
8. Cellular telephones (p. 456)
9. Cleaning and laundering services when traveling (p. 413)
10. Commissions on sale of property (p. 396)
11. Contact lenses (p. 326)
12. Contraceptives, if bought with a prescription (p. 326)
13. Contributions to public parks (p. 362)
14. Cost of a nondependent student who is living with you (p. 366)
15. Depreciation of home computers (p. 456)
16. Dues to labor unions (p. 461)
17. Employee educational expenses (p. 444, 455)
18. Employee's moving expenses, including those related to house-hunting, selling your old home or settling an unexpired lease, and travel (including lodging and meals) (p. 398)
19. Employee contributions to state disability fund (p. 338)
20. Employment agency fees (p. 460)
21. Fees for a safe-deposit box to hold investments (e.g., stock certificates) (p. 464)
22. Foreign taxes paid (p. 338)
23. Gambling losses to the extent of gambling gains (p. 465)
24. Appraisal fees for charitable donations or casualty losses. (p. 463)
25. Hearing devices (p. 326)
26. Hospital services fees (laboratory work, therapy, nursing services, and surgery) (p. 326)
27. Impairment-related work expenses for a disabled individual (p. 331)
28. IRA trustee's administrative fees billed separately (p. 464)
29. Lead paint removal (p. 326)
30. Medical transportation, including standard mileage deduction (p. 326)
31. Mortgage prepayment penalties (p. 353)
32. Orthopedic shoes (p. 326)
33. Out-of-pocket expenses relating to charitable activities, including the standard mileage deduction (p. 366)
34. Passport fee for a business trip (p. 455)
35. Penalty on early withdrawal of savings (p. 127)
36. Points on a home mortgage and certain refinancings (p. 350)
37. Real estate taxes associated with the purchase or sale of property (p. 339)
38. Résumé-preparation cost associated with looking for a new job in your present occupation (p. 461)
39. Seeing-eye dog (p. 326)
40. Self-employment tax (p. 342)
41. Special equipment for the disabled (p. 327)
42. Special foods diet (p. 330)
43. Special schools (p. 331)
44. State personal property taxes on cars (p. 342)
45. Theft or embezzlement losses (p. 380)
46. Trade or business tools with life of 1 year or less (p. 461)
47. Tuition fee for medical care (p. 327)
48. Uniforms and work clothes not suitable as ordinary wearing apparel (p. 461)
49. Wigs essential to mental health (p. 327)
50. Worthless stock or securities (p. 229)

FORM 1040 LINE-BY-LINE

(16)

Form 1040

Department of the Treasury—Internal Revenue Service

U.S. Individual Income Tax Return (T) 19**93**

If you need more information, turn to page shown in circle.

IRS Use Only—Do not write or staple in this space.

For the year Jan. 1–Dec. 31, 1993, or other tax year beginning _____, 1993, ending _____, 19___   OMB No. 1545-0074

Label

(See instructions on page 12.)

Use the IRS label. Otherwise, please print or type.

LABEL HERE

Your first name and initial | Last name

If a joint return, spouse's first name and initial | Last name

Home address (number and street). If you have a P.O. box, see page 12. | Apt. no.

City, town or post office, state, and ZIP code. If you have a foreign address, see page 12.

Your social security number

Spouse's social security number   (16)

For Privacy Act and Paperwork Reduction Act Notice, see page 4.

Presidential Election Campaign

(17) (See page 12.)   (28)

Do you want $3 to go to this fund? . . . .

If a joint return, does your spouse want $3 to go to this fund? . . .

| | Yes | No |

Note: Checking "Yes" will not change your tax or reduce your refund.

Filing Status

(See page 12.)

Check only one box.

(29) **1** ☐ Single

(31) **2** ☐ Married filing joint return (even if only one had income)

(33) **3** ☐ Married filing separate return. Enter spouse's social security no. above and full name here. ▶ _____

4 ☐ Head of household (with qualifying person). (See page 13.) If the qualifying person is a child but not your dependent, enter this child's name here. ▶ _____

(35) **5** ☐ Qualifying widow(er) with dependent child (year spouse died ▶ 19___). (See page 13.)

Exemptions

(See page 13.)

(37) (37)

(38)

If more than six dependents, see page 14.

6a ☐ **Yourself.** If your parent (or someone else) can claim you as a dependent on his or her tax return, **do not** check box 6a. But be sure to check the box on line 33b on page 2

b ☐ **Spouse**

c Dependents:

(1) Name (first, initial, and last name)	**(2)** Check if under age 1	**(3)** If age 1 or older, dependent's social security number	**(4)** Dependent's relationship to you	**(5)** No. of months lived in your home in 1993

No. of boxes checked on 6a and 6b _____

No. of your children on 6c who:
• lived with you _____
• didn't live with you due to divorce or separation (see page 15) _____

Dependents on 6c not entered above _____

(48) **d** If your child didn't live with you but is claimed as your dependent under a pre-1985 agreement, check here ▶ ☐

(89) **e** Total number of exemptions claimed . . . . (102)

Add numbers entered on lines above ▶ ☐

Income

(108)

Attach Copy B of your Forms W-2, W-2G, and 1099-R here.

(126)

(128)

(189) (300)

If you did not get a W-2, see page 10.

(157) (292)

(138)

If you are attaching a check or money order, put it on top of any Forms W-2, W-2G, or 1099-R.

(93)

(172)

(179)

7 Wages, salaries, tips, etc. Attach Form(s) W-2 (81) | **7**

8a **Taxable** interest income (see page 16). Attach Schedule B if over $400 | **8a**

b **Tax-exempt** interest (see page 17). DON'T include on line 8a | **8b**

9 Dividend income. Attach Schedule B if over $400 . . . . | **9**

10 Taxable refunds, credits, or offsets of state and local income taxes (see page 17) . . | **10**

11 Alimony received (529) . . . . (267) | **11**

12 Business income or (loss). Attach Schedule C or C-EZ . . | **12**

13 Capital gain or (loss). Attach Schedule D . . . . . | **13**

14 Capital gain distributions not reported on line 13 (see page 17) . | **14**

15 Other gains or (losses). Attach Form 4797 . . . . (292) | **15**

16a Total IRA distributions . | 16a | (179) | **b** Taxable amount (see page 18) | **16b** (157)

17a Total pensions and annuities | 17a | | **b** Taxable amount (see page 18) | **17b**

18 Rental real estate, royalties, partnerships, S corporations, trusts, etc. Attach Schedule E | **18**

19 Farm income or (loss). Attach Schedule F (186) (187) (181) (173) | **19**

20 Unemployment compensation (see page 19) . . . . | **20**

21a Social security benefits | 21a | | **b** Taxable amount (see page 19) | **21b**

22 Other income. List type and amount—see page 20 . . . . | **22**

23 Add the amounts in the far right column for lines 7 through 22. This is your **total income** ▶ | **23**

Adjustments to Income

(282)

(283)

(533)

(See page 20.)

(535)

(127)

(300)

24a Your IRA deduction (see page 20) . . . . | 24a

b Spouse's IRA deduction (see page 20) . . (6) | 24b

25 One-half of self-employment tax (see page 21) . | 25

26 Self-employed health insurance deduction (see page 22) | 26

27 Keogh retirement plan and self-employed SEP deduction | 27

28 Penalty on early withdrawal of savings . . | 28

29 Alimony paid. Recipient's SSN ▶ _____ (536) | 29

30 Add lines 24a through 29. These are your **total adjustments** . . . . ▶ | **30**

Adjusted Gross Income

31 Subtract line 30 from line 23. This is your **adjusted gross income.** *If this amount is less than $23,050 and a child lived with you, see page EIC-1 to find out if you can claim the "Earned Income Credit" on line 56* . . . . ▶ | **31**

Cat. No. 11320B   (471)

Form **1040** (1993)

Tax Computation

(See page 23.)

32 Amount from line 31 (adjusted gross income) . . . . | **32** |

33a Check if: ☐ **You** were 65 or older, ☐ Blind; ☐ **Spouse** was 65 or older, ☐ Blind.
Add the number of boxes checked above and enter the total here . . . . ▶ **33a** ☐

b If your parent (or someone else) can claim you as a dependent, check here . ▶ **33b** ☐

c If you are married filing separately and your spouse itemizes deductions or you are a dual-status alien, see page 24 and check here . . . . . ▶ **33c** ☐

34 Enter the larger of your:
{ **Itemized deductions** from Schedule A, line 26, **OR**
Standard deduction shown below for your filing status. **But if you checked any box on line 33a or b**, go to page 24 to find your standard deduction. If you checked **box 33c**, your standard deduction is zero.
● Single—$3,700　　● Head of household—$5,450
● Married filing jointly or Qualifying widow(er)—$6,200
● Married filing separately—$3,100 } | **34** |

35 Subtract line 34 from line 32 . . . . | **35** |

36 If line 32 is $81,350 or less, multiply $2,350 by the total number of exemptions claimed on line 6e. If line 32 is over $81,350, see the worksheet on page 25 for the amount to enter . | **36** |

37 **Taxable income.** Subtract line 36 from line 35. If line 36 is more than line 35, enter -0- | **37** |

38 Tax. Check if from **a** ☐ Tax Table, **b** ☐ Tax Rate Schedules, **c** ☐ Schedule D Tax Worksheet, or **d** ☐ Form 8615 (see page 25). Amount from Form(s) 8814 ▶ **e** _____ | **38** |

If you want the IRS to figure your tax, see page 24.

39 Additional taxes (see page 25). Check if from **a** ☐ Form 4970 **b** ☐ Form 4972 . . | **39** |

40 Add lines 38 and 39 . . . . ▶ | **40** |

Credits

(See page 25.)

41 Credit for child and dependent care expenses. Attach Form 2441 | **41** |
42 Credit for the elderly or the disabled. Attach Schedule R . . | **42** |
43 Foreign tax credit. Attach Form 1116 . . . . . . | **43** |
44 Other credits (see page 26). Check if from **a** ☐ Form 3800 **b** ☐ Form 8396 **c** ☐ Form 8801 **d** ☐ Form (specify) _____ | **44** |
45 Add lines 41 through 44 . . . . | **45** |
46 Subtract line 45 from line 40. If line 45 is more than line 40, enter -0- . . . . . ▶ | **46** |

Other Taxes

47 Self-employment tax. Attach Schedule SE. Also, see line 25. . . . . | **47** |
48 Alternative minimum tax. Attach Form 6251 . . . . | **48** |
49 Recapture taxes (see page 26). Check if from **a** ☐ Form 4255 **b** ☐ Form 8611 **c** ☐ Form 8828 | **49** |
50 Social security and Medicare tax on tip income not reported to employer. Attach Form 4137 | **50** |
51 Tax on qualified retirement plans, including IRAs. If required, attach Form 5329 . . | **51** |
52 Advance earned income credit payments from Form W-2 . . . . | **52** |
53 Add lines 46 through 52. This is your **total tax** . . . . ▶ | **53** |

Payments

Attach Forms W-2, W-2G, and 1099-R on the front.

54 Federal income tax withheld. If any is from Form(s) 1099, check ▶ ☐ | **54** |
55 1993 estimated tax payments and amount applied from 1992 return . | **55** |
56 **Earned income credit.** Attach Schedule EIC . . . . | **56** |
57 Amount paid with Form 4868 (extension request) . . . . | **57** |
58a Excess social security, Medicare, and RRTA tax withheld (see page 28) . | **58a** |
b Deferral of additional 1993 taxes. Attach Form 8841 . . | **58b** |
59 Other payments (see page 28). Check if from **a** ☐ Form 2439 **b** ☐ Form 4136 . . . | **59** |
60 Add lines 54 through 59. These are your **total payments** . . . . ▶ | **60** |

Refund or Amount You Owe

61 If line 60 is more than line 53, subtract line 53 from line 60. This is the amount you **OVERPAID**. ▶ | **61** |
62 Amount of line 61 you want **REFUNDED TO YOU**. . . . . ▶ | **62** |
63 Amount of line 61 you want **APPLIED TO YOUR 1994 ESTIMATED TAX** ▶ | **63** |
64 If line 53 is more than line 60, subtract line 60 from line 53. This is the **AMOUNT YOU OWE**. For details on how to pay, including what to write on your payment, see page 29 . . | **64** |
65 Estimated tax penalty (see page 29). Also include on line 64 | **65** |

Sign Here

Keep a copy of this return for your records.

Under penalties of perjury, I declare that I have examined this return and accompanying schedules and statements, and to the best of my knowledge and belief, they are true, correct, and complete. Declaration of preparer (other than taxpayer) is based on all information of which preparer has any knowledge.

▶ Your signature | Date | Your occupation

▶ Spouse's signature. If a joint return, BOTH must sig | Date | Spouse's occupation

Paid Preparer's Use Only

Preparer's signature ▶ | Date | Check if self-employed ☐ | Preparer's social security no.

Firm's name (or yours if self-employed) and address ▶ | E.I. No. | ZIP code

xx

When to File Your State Tax Returns

State	Filing Date*	Taxpayer's Assistance	Where to Order Forms From
Alabama	April 15	(205) 323-6387	Alabama Department of Revenue Income Tax Forms, P.O. Box 327470 Montgomery, AL 36132-7470
Arizona	April 15	(602) 255-3381	Arizona Department of Revenue 1600 West Monroe, Phoenix, AZ 85007
Arkansas	May 15	(800) 882-9275	State Income Tax Forms P.O. Box 3628, Little Rock, AR 72203-3628
California	April 15	(800) 852-5711	Franchise Tax Board Tax Forms Request Unit, P.O. Box 307 Rancho Cordova, CA 95741-0307
Colorado	April 15	(303) 534-1209	Colorado Department of Revenue 1375 Sherman Street, Denver, CO 80261
Connecticut	April 15	(203) 566-7033	Taxpayer Services Division Department of Revenue Services, 92 Farmington Avenue Hartford, CT 06105
Delaware	April 30	(302) 577-3310 within Deleware 800-292-7826	Division of Revenue Route 113, DuPont Highway, Georgetown, DE 19947
District of Columbia	April 15	(202) 727-6103	Department of Finance & Revenue Municipal Center, 300 Indiana Avenue, N.W., Room 1046 Washington, D.C. 20001
Georgia	April 15	(404) 656-4071	Atlanta Regional Office 322 Plaza Level, West Tower, Floyd Building Atlanta, GA 30334
Hawaii	April 20	(800) 933-4321	Hawaii District Office P.O. Box 1377, Hilo, HI 96721-1377
Idaho	April 15	(208) 334-3660	Tax Commission 3131 W. State Street, P.O. Box 56, Boise, ID 83756-0201
Illinois	April 15	(217) 782-3336	Illinois Department of Revenue P.O. Box 19010, Springfield, IL 62794-9010
Indiana	April 15	(317) 232-2240	Indianapolis Downtown Office 100 N. Senate Avenue, Indianapolis, IN 46204-2253
Iowa	April 30	(515) 281-3114	Taxpayer Services Section Iowa Department of Revenue, Hoover State Office Bldg., 4th Floor Des Moines, IA 50319
Kansas	April 15	(913) 296-0222	Kansas Income and Inheritance Tax Bureau Box 12001, Topeka, KS 66612-2001
Kentucky	April 15	(502) 564-3658	Property and Mail Services Section 859 East Main Street Revenue Cabinet, Frankfort, KY 40620
Louisiana	May 15	(504) 925-4611	Department of Revenue and Taxation 330 N. Ardenwood Drive, Baton Rouge, LA 70821
Maine	April 15	(207) 773-7895	Bureau of Taxation State Office Building, Room 500, Augusta, ME 04332-1067
Maryland	April 15	(301) 974-3981	Income Tax Division Annapolis, MD 21411-0001
Massachusetts	April 15	(617) 727-4545	Massachusetts Department of Revenue Forms Supply, 100 Cambridge Street, Boston, MA 02204

State	Filing Date*	Taxpayer's Assistance	Where to Order Forms From
Michigan	April 15	(800) 487-7000	Michigan Department of Treasury Treasury Building, 430 W. Allegan Street Lansing, MI 48922
Minnesota	April 15	(612) 296-3781	Minnesota Tax Forms Mail Station 7131, St. Paul, MN 55146-7131
Mississippi	April 15	(601) 359-1088	State Tax Commission Woolfolk State Office Bldg., Room 107, Jackson, MS 39205
Missouri	April 15	(314) 751-7191	Missouri Department of Revenue Truman State Office Bldg., Room 330 Jefferson City, MO 65105
Montana	April 15	(406) 444-2837	Montana Department of Revenue Income Tax Division, P.O. Box 5805, Helena, MT 59604
Nebraska	April 15	(402) 471-5729	Nebraska Department of Revenue P.O. Box 94818, Lincoln, NE 68509-4818
New Jersey	April 15	(609) 588-2000	Division of Taxation Taxpayer Information Service, 50 Barrack Street, CN 269 Trenton, NJ 08646-0269
New·Mexico	April 15	(505) 841-8000	Taxation & Revenue Department First National Bank Bldg. East 5301 Central, NE, P.O. Box 8485 Albuquerque, NM 87198-8485
New York State & New York City	April 15	(518) 438-8581	NYS Tax Department Taxpayer Assistance Bureau, W.A. Harriman Campus Albany, NY 12227
North Carolina	April 15	(800) 222-9965	North Carolina Department of Revenue Secretary of Revenue 2 S. Salisbury Street, P.O. Box 25000 Raleigh, NC 27640
North Dakota	April 15	(701) 224-3450	Office of the State Tax Commissioner State Capitol, 600 E. Boulevard Avenue Bismarck, ND 58505-0599
Ohio	April 15	(614) 846-6712	Ohio Department of Taxation P.O. Box 2476, Columbus, OH 43266-0076
Oklahoma	April 15	(405) 521-3108	Tax Commission 2501 Lincoln Boulevard, Oklahoma City, OK 73194-0009
Oregon	April 15	(503) 243-2833	Oregon Department of Revenue P.O. Box 14999, Salem, OR 97309-0990
Pennsylvania	April 15	(814) 946-7310	Revenue District Office Cricket Field Plaza, 615 Howard Avenue Altoona, PA 16601-4867
Rhode Island	April 15	(401) 277-2905	Rhode Island Division of Taxation One Capital Hill, Providence, RI 02908-5810
South Carolina	April 15	(803) 737-4661	South Carolina Tax Commission Attention: Forms, P.O. Box 125, Columbia, SC 29214
Utah	April 15	(801) 530-4848	Utah State Tax Commission Heber M. Wells Building, 160 East Third South Salt Lake City, UT 84134-0200
Vermont	April 15	(802) 828-2865	Vermont Department of Taxes 109 State Street, Montpelier, VT 05609-1401
Virginia	May 1	(804) 367-8055	Virginia Department of Taxation Form Request Unit, P.O Box 1317 Richmond, VA 23210-1317
West Virginia	April 15	(304) 348-3333	Department of Tax and Revenue Taxpayer Services Division, P.O. Box 3784 Charleston, WV 25337
Wisconsin	April 15	(608) 266-2772	Department of Revenue 4638 University Avenue Madison, WI 53702

*For calendar-year taxpayers.

1994 Tax Calendar

Date in 1994	Action Required
January 18	Final estimated tax payment for 1993 due if you did not pay your income tax (or enough of your income tax) for that year through withholding. Use Form 1040ES.
January 31	If you did not pay your last installment of estimated tax by January 18, file your income tax return for 1993 on this date, thereby avoiding any penalty for late payment of the last installment. Use Form 1040 or 1040A.
	Employers of household employees (like a nanny or a housekeeper) must file Form 942 for the fourth quarter of the prior year.
February 15	File a new Form W-4 to adjust your withholding allowances, if necessary.
March 1	Farmers and fishermen must file their 1993 income tax return (Form 1040) to avoid an underpayment penalty for the last quarter of 1993 if they were required to pay estimated tax on January 18.
April 15	File your income tax return for 1993 (Forms 1040, 1040A, or 1040 EZ) and pay any tax due.
	Make your IRA contribution.
	If you are not extending your return, make your Keogh contribution if you have self-employment income.
	For an automatic 4-month extension, file Form 4868 and pay any tax that you estimate will be due. Then file Form 1040 or 1040A by August 15. If you get an extension, you can't file Form 1040EZ.
	Pay the first installment of your 1994 estimated tax if you are not paying your 1994 income tax (or enough of it) through withholding tax. Use Form 1040ES.
	If you made any taxable gifts during 1993 (more than $10,000 per donee), file a gift tax return for that year (Form 709 or 709-A) and pay any tax due. For an automatic 4-month extension, file Form 4868. (You can use one Form 4868 to file for both your income tax and gift tax extensions.)
May 2	Employers of household employees must file Form 942 for the first quarter of 1994.
June 15	Pay the second installment of 1994 estimated tax.
June 30	Individuals who have signature authority or other authority over certain bank, securities, or other financial accounts in a foreign country must file Form TDF 90-22-1.
August 1	Employers of household employees must file Form 942 for the second quarter of 1994.
August 15	If you filed for an automatic 4-month extension to file your 1993 income tax return, file Form 1040 or Form 1040A and pay any tax, interest, and penalties due. Also make your Keogh contribution if it has not already been made. If you want an additional extension, file Form 2688.
	If you filed for an automatic 4-month extension to file your gift tax return for 1993, file it and pay any tax, interest, and penalties due. If you want an additional extension, file Form 2688.
September 15	Pay the third installment of your 1994 estimated tax.
October 17	If you were given an automatic 4-month extension and an additional 2-month extension for your 1993 income tax return, file Form 1040 or Form 1040A and pay any tax, interest, and penalty due and any gift tax return if due.
	Last day to make a Keogh contribution for calendar year 1993 if you were granted an additional extension of time to file your tax return.
October 31	Employers of household employees must file Form 942 for the third quarter of 1994.
December 31	Last day to establish a Keogh (H.R. 10) plan for 1994.

Individual Tax Organizer

The following schedules should help you organize the data you need to prepare your 1993 federal income tax return. They are intended only to provide general guidelines and should not be regarded as all-inclusive.

TAXPAYER INFORMATION

PERSONAL DATA

Your name _____

Your spouse's name _____

Social security number _____ Spouse's _____

Marital status at year-end: ☐ Married ☐ Single ☐ Widowed after 1990 ☐ Divorced ☐ Married but separated

DEPENDENT CHILDREN

Name (address if different from yours)	Social security number if at least 1 year old on December 31, 1993	Date of birth	Did you provide more than half of support?	Married filing a joint return?	Full-time student for 5 months or more?	Income over $2,350

OTHER DEPENDENTS

Name (address if different from yours)	Social security number	Relationship	Months lived in your home	Is dependent's income over $2,350	Did you provide more than half of support?

PAYMENTS AND REFUNDS OF INCOME TAXES

	Federal		State		City	
	Date paid	Amount	Date paid	Amount	Date paid	Amount
1993 estimated payments, including overpayment credited from 1992 return:						
Tax refunds received in 1993[1]						

1. Do not include interest received on refunds or paid on deficiencies. Detail these amounts in the interest sections of this organizer.

COMPENSATION

Indicate recipient: H—Husband; W—Wife.

H W	Employer name	Gross earnings	Federal income tax withheld	FICA	State tax withheld	City tax withheld

INTEREST INCOME

Report all interest received by you or for your account on Forms 1099-INT or other statements of total interest received. Failure to record any such income could result in a notice from the IRS.

If the amount of interest reported on Forms 1099-INT includes interest accrued on bonds at the time of purchase, adjustments can be made.

If you invested in a tax-exempt municipal bond fund, note the fund's schedule of percentage income related to each state.

H W J		Amount
	Savings accounts, credit unions, and certificates of deposit:	
	U.S. Savings Bonds and other U.S. government securities:	
	Corporate bonds:	
	Other interest[1]:	
	Tax-exempt interest:	
	Interest received on tax refunds:	

1. If you received interest income from seller-financed mortgages, you will need the payer's name and address.

DIVIDEND INCOME

Indicate ownership: H—Husband; W—Wife; J—Joint.

Report all dividends received by you or for your account on Forms 1099-DIV or other information statements received. Failure to record any such income could result in a notice from the IRS.

H W J	Name of corporation [identify foreign corporation with (F)]	Indicate T (taxable), C (capital gain), or N (nontaxable)	Dividends received	U.S. taxes withheld

SALE OR PURCHASE OF RESIDENCE

Did you sell your residence during the year or within the last two years? ☐ Yes ☐ No
If you answered "Yes," see Chapter 16, *Selling Your Home*.

SALE OF STOCKS AND BONDS

Indicate H-Husband; W-Wife; or J-Joint.

Note: Gross proceeds from sales reported here should reconcile with Forms 1099-B received from your broker. You should explain any discrepancies to prevent an IRS inquiry stemming from their matching program.

H W J	Description (include number of shares, common or preferred, and par value of bonds)	Date		Gross sales price[1]	Cost or other basis plus expenses of sale[2]	Gain or (loss)[3]
		Acq.	Sold			

1. List proceeds of sale or cash received in lieu of fractions on receipt of stock rights or stock dividends.

2. The basis of stock should be decreased by all nontaxable dividends and increased by any reinvested dividends.

3. Have you acquired stock, securities, contracts, or options to sell or   ☐ Yes   ☐ No
   acquire stock or securities substantially identical to stock or securities
   sold at a loss within a period beginning 30 days prior to and ending 30
   days after the date of sale? If "Yes," see the discussion of "Wash
   Sale" in Chapter 15, *Sale of Property*.

OTHER TRANSACTIONS

Did you exchange securities for other securities or exchange any investment property for any other property? Did any security held by you or any amounts due you become worthless during the year? Did you sell your vacation home or other property during the year? Did you realize a gain or a loss on property, in whole or in part, by destruction, theft, seizure, or condemnation (including the threat or imminence thereof)? Did you engage in any commodity transactions (including open positions on December 31) during the year? Did you engage in any transactions involving traded options?

If you answered "Yes" to any of these questions, read the applicable portions of this book.

SALE OF OTHER PROPERTY

H W J	Description	Date		Gross sales price	Cost of other basis, plus expenses of sale	Depreciation or depletion	Gain or (loss)
		Acq.	Sold				

INSTALLMENT SALES

Did you make sales during the year for which the receipt of all or part of
the sales price was deferred until future years?   ☐ Yes   ☐ No
    If yes, discuss with your tax advisor

Did you collect on any installment obligations from sales made prior to   ☐ Yes   ☐ No
1993?

For more information, see Chapter 15, *Sale of Property*.

RENT AND ROYALTY INCOME

	Property A		Property B	
Did you actively participate in the operation of the rental activity during the year?	☐ Yes	☐ No	☐ Yes	☐ No
Location and description of property[1]				
Gross rents and royalties received				
Expenses				

1. If property has been used by you or your family as a personal residence, indicate the total days
   held for rent but not rented, days rented, and days used by you or your family.

PARTNERSHIPS (P), SMALL BUSINESS CORPORATIONS (S), AND ESTATES AND TRUSTS (E/T)

Retain all Forms K-1 or other information relating to entity listed below.

P S E/T	H W J	Name	Tax shelter registration number	I.D. number	Income or (loss)

PENSION AND ANNUITY INCOME

Did you receive any payments from a retirement plan?	☐ Yes	☐ No

If yes, provide the amount received during the year and any taxes withheld. _____

Did you roll over a profit-sharing or retirement plan distribution into another plan?	☐ Yes	☐ No

What was the starting date of your annuity? _____

What is the amount received in the current taxable year? _____

Did you receive any IRA distributions during the year?	☐ Yes	☐ No

OTHER INCOME

Description	Amount
Alimony or legal separation payments received	
Disability payments	
Other tax refunds not shown elsewhere	
Unemployment insurance compensation	
Social security benefits	
Other[1] (describe)	

1. The types of other income include, but are not limited to, net income from self-employment, director's fees, prizes, cancellation of debts, gambling winnings, jury fees, punitive damages, receiver's fees, and certain tuition paid by an employer. Also, include gross income from oil and gas working interests, as well as any expenses relating to them.

Did you receive any income from a foreign source?	☐ Yes	☐ No
Did you own shares in a mutual fund that retained your share of capital gains and paid the tax on it?	☐ Yes	☐ No
Did you have any income from farm property?	☐ Yes	☐ No
Did you own Series EE Savings Bonds?	☐ Yes	☐ No
Did you have any bartering income?	☐ Yes	☐ No

DEDUCTIONS

ADJUSTMENTS TO INCOME

Alimony or legal separation payments made in current taxable year _____

Recipient's last name _____ and social security no. _____-____-_____

Penalties for early withdrawal of savings _____

Individual Retirement Arrangements (IRAs)¹   Amount

Did you contribute to your own IRA?	☐ Yes	☐ No	_____
Did you participate in a retirement plan maintained by your employer?	☐ Yes	☐ No	_____
Did your spouse contribute to his/her own IRA?	☐ Yes	☐ No	_____
Did your spouse participate in a retirement plan maintained by his/her employer?	☐ Yes	☐ No	_____
Did you and your spouse contribute to a spousal IRA?	☐ Yes	☐ No	_____

Self-employed Keogh (HR-10) plan   Yours   Spouse's

Amount contributed   _____ _____

Did you or your spouse receive any disability payments?   ☐ Yes   ☐ No   _____

1. Depending on your (and your spouse's) income level and whether you (or your spouse) are an active participant in an employer-maintained retirement plan, your IRA deduction may be limited.

MEDICAL EXPENSES

Note: You will qualify for a federal deduction only if your total unreimbursed medical expenses exceed 7.5% of your adjusted gross income.

List even if reimbursed	Amount
Medical or health insurance premiums (including amounts paid by payroll deductions)	
Medicare premiums	
Prescription drugs and insulin	
Doctors and dentists	
Hospitals	
Other medical expenses	
Reimbursements for medical expenses through insurance or other sources	

Note: If you are divorced or separated, have a child, and paid medical expenses for that child, include these amounts whether or not you are entitled to the dependency exemption.

TAXES

Item	Amount
Real estate taxes	
Personal property	
Vehicle licenses (allowed in some states). State of	
State or local income taxes (if not listed elsewhere)	
Other taxes (not including income taxes and other taxes listed elsewhere)	
State disability tax	

Note: Foreign income taxes paid or withheld should be listed by country.

INTEREST EXPENSES

Item	Payee	Amount
Home mortgage paid to financial institutions		
Home mortgage paid to individuals[1]		
Mortgage points on principal residence[2]		
Prepayment penalty on loans		
Brokerage accounts		
Investment interest		
Other (itemize)		

1. Furnish name(s) and address(es).

2. Include only points, including loan origination fees, on the purchase or improvement of your principal residence.

For more information, see Chapter 24, *Interest Expense*.

CHARITABLE CONTRIBUTIONS

In addition to outright gifts of cash or property, deductible contributions also include out-of-pocket expenses incurred for charity, for example, transportation (automobile mileage may be claimed at 12 cents per mile), meals and lodging away from home, and cost and upkeep of special uniforms and equipment required in the performance of donated services.

If you have sold any property to a charity for less than the property's fair market value, you will need details.

For more information, see Chapter 25, *Contributions*.

Cash Contributions

Recipient	Amount[1]

If total noncash contributions have a value in excess of $500, you will need the following information:
the name and address of the donee; the date of the gift; a description of the property, how it was acquired by you, and when it was acquired by you; your tax basis; its value at the time of the donation and how the value was ascertained. Indicate (√) if any property was held by you for less than 1 year.

If you made noncash contributions of property in excess of $5,000 in value, use Form 8283, *Noncash Charitable Contributions*, with Section B, *Appraisal Summary*, completed.   □ Yes   □ No

CASUALTY LOSSES

Note: You will qualify for a deduction for a personal casualty loss only if it exceeds 10% of your adjusted gross income. See Chapter 26, *Nonbusiness Casualty and Theft Losses*, for details.

Casualty losses include such items as losses from automobile collisions; damage from storms, fires, and floods; and damage from vandalism, theft, and other casualties.

Describe the casualty loss and its approximate date and location. _____

_____

_____

Indicate (√) type of property: _____ business _____ investment _____ personal

OTHER DEDUCTIONS

Note: In general, you will qualify for a federal deduction only if your total other miscellaneous deductions exceed 2% of your adjusted gross income.

Item	Amount	Item	Amount
Investment expenses: Automobile expense		Educational expense (to maintain or improve skills required by employer)	
Investment counsel fees		Entertainment[1]	
Safe-deposit box		Tax advice/return fees	
Dues and subscriptions		Union dues	
Telephone		Dues for professional organizations	
IRA fees		Business publications	
Other		Office-in-home expenses[2]	
		Other	

1. Only 80% of entertainment expenses are deductible.

2. See Chapter 30, *Miscellaneous Deductions.*

MOVING EXPENSES IN CONNECTION WITH EMPLOYMENT

Have you incurred moving expenses in connection with starting work at a new permanent location? See Chapter 27, *Moving Expenses.*   ☐ Yes   ☐ No

EMPLOYEE BUSINESS EXPENSES

Were you reimbursed for any business expenses incurred in connection with the performance of services for your employer?   ☐ Yes   ☐ No

If yes, answer the following questions:

A. Are you required to return reimbursement to the extent it exceeds expenses?   ☐ Yes   ☐ No

B. Are you required to submit itemized supporting documentation to your employer?   ☐ Yes   ☐ No

If you answered yes to the above questions and your reimbursement does not exceed your expenses, you are generally not required to report the reimbursement and expenses on your return. However, if your reimbursement does not equal your expenses, or if you answered no to questions A and/or B, report below the total reimbursements and expenses for the year. Certain other business expenses, even if not reimbursed, may also be deductible.

Employee business expenses   Amount

Total amount reimbursed. (Do not include any amounts that were reported to you as wages in box 10 of Form W-2.)

Do you have substantiation (described below) for travel and entertainment expenses?   ☐ Yes   ☐ No

Information that must be available includes

- Amounts spent
- Dates of departure and return for each trip and the number of days spent on business
- Dates of entertainment
- Places of entertainment or travel

- Dates and descriptions of business gifts
- Business purposes of the travel, entertainment, or business gifts
- Business relationships with the persons entertained or to whom gifts were made

AUTOMOBILE EXPENSES

Mileage information	Automobile 1	Automobile 2
Number of months used for business during the year	_____	_____
Total mileage (include personal miles)	_____	_____
Business mileage portion of the total mileage	_____	_____
Commuting mileage portion of the total mileage	_____	_____

Total actual expenses (business and personal for months used for business)

_____

_____

Automobile Depreciation

Year, make, model	Cost	Date acquired
Automobile _____	_____	_____

Do you have adequate or sufficient evidence to justify the deduction for the vehicles?   ☐ Yes   ☐ No

If yes, is the evidence written?   ☐ Yes   ☐ No

CHILD CARE CREDIT

If you incurred any expenses for child or dependent care so that you and your spouse could be gainfully employed or attend an educational institution as a full-time student, complete the table below.

Did your employer provide or reimburse you for the cost of child or dependent care?   ☐ Yes   ☐ No

If so, the credit must be reduced by the amount excluded from your income through your employer's dependent care assistance program.

Name of child or dependent	Name, address, and social security number or FEIN of person or organization providing care	Relationship, if any	Period of care		Amount paid
			From	To	

1. Did you pay more than $50 per quarter to an individual for services provided in your home?   ☐ Yes   ☐ No

2. Did you file an employment tax return?   ☐ Yes   ☐ No

FOREIGN INCOME TAXES

List foreign source income and foreign income taxes paid

Country	Income		Taxes Paid	
	Type	Amount	Date paid	Amount

Income and Expense Records You Should Keep—Some Suggestions That Could Come in Handy

Income	Records
Wages, salaries	Form W-2
Interest income	1099-INT, 1099-OID or Substitute 1099, such as broker statement or year-end account summary
Dividend income	1099-DIV or Substitute 1099 such as broker statement or year-end account summary
State tax refunds	Form 1099-G, state income tax return
Self-employment income	Sales slips, invoices, receipts, sales tax reports, business books and records
Capital gains and losses	1099-B or Substitute 1099, such as broker statement or year-end account summary showing proceeds from sales of securities or other capital assets. Records must also show your cost or other basis and the expenses of the sale. Your records must show when and how an asset was acquired (including property received as a gift or inheritance), how the asset was used, and when and how it was disposed of. To support the basis of securities, you should keep old account statements, buy/sell execution records, stock dividend and stock split information, and dividend reinvestment records (see Chapter 15, *Sale of Property*).
IRA distributions	1099-R, year-end account summary
Pension and annuities	1099-R, records of contributions
Rents	Checkbook, receipts and cancelled checks, and other books and records
Partnerships, S corporations	Schedule K-1, record of unused passive activity losses
Estates, trusts	Schedule K-1
Social security benefits	Form SSA-1099
Royalties	1099-MISC
Unemployment Compensation	1099-G
Alimony	Divorce settlement papers
Miscellaneous income	1099-MISC and other records of amounts receicved

Expense	Records
Self-employment expense	Bills, cancelled checks, receipts, bank statements, all business books and records
IRA contribution	Year-end account summary, deposit receipt
Keogh contribution	Year-end account summary, deposit receipt
Alimony	Divorce settlement papers, cancelled alimony checks
Medical and dental expense	Bills, cancelled checks, receipts, pay stubs if employer withholds medical insurance from wages
Taxes	Cancelled checks, mortgage statements, receipts, Form W-2
Interest expense	Bank statements, mortgage statements (Form 1098), cancelled checks
Charitable contributions	Cancelled checks, receipts, detailed description of noncash property contributed
Miscellaneous deductions	Receipts, cancelled checks, or other documentary evidence (See Chapters 27 through 30.)
Casualty and theft losses	Description of property, photograph of damaged property, receipts, cancelled checks, policy and insurance reports.
Exemptions	Birth certificates, social security numbers

Credits	Records
Child and dependent care	Receipts, cancelled checks and name, address and identification number of care provider
Estimated taxes	Cancelled checks
Foreign taxes	Form 1099 DIV
Withheld taxes	Forms W-2 and 1099

I | The Income Tax Return

The five chapters in this part provide basic information on the tax system. They take you through the first steps of filling out a tax return—such as deciding what your filing status is, how many exemptions you can take, and which form to file. They also discuss recordkeeping requirements, electronic filing, certain penalties, and the two methods used to pay tax during the year: withholding and estimated tax.

Chapter 1 Filing Information
Chapter 2 Filing Status
Chapter 3 Personal Exemptions and Dependents
Chapter 4 Decedents
Chapter 5 Tax Withholding and Estimated Tax

1 | Filing Information

Introduction

Unlike the other certainty in life, paying taxes is the one for which you may obtain an extension. Besides explaining when you must file your tax return and what to do if you are unable to get it prepared on time, this chapter provides an introduction to the basic framework within which you file your federal income tax return. It answers a lot of the elementary questions about the procedures and calculations involved in determining your income tax.

This chapter discusses such items as who is required to file and who should file even though he or she is not required to do so. It tells you which forms to use, how to go about preparing your tax return once you have obtained the correct forms, and where to mail your tax return once it has been completed. In addition, the chapter informs you about the penalties that may be imposed if you do not pay your taxes on time and instructs you on what to do if you discover that a previous tax return is in error. The chapter also explains what the different accounting methods are and which method may be used in preparing your return.

Important Changes for 1993

Filing requirements. Generally, the amount of income you can receive before you are required to file a return has been increased.
Expanded Form 1040EZ. If you are married filing a joint return and have no dependents, you may be able to file Form 1040EZ for 1993. See *Which Form Should I Use?*, later.
Presidential election campaign fund. Beginning with your 1993 return, the amount you may designate to go to this fund is $3. See *Presidential Election Campaign Fund*, later.
Deferral of additional 1993 taxes. You may be able to elect to defer part of your additional 1993 taxes that are solely due to the rate increases reflected in the 1993 tax rate schedules. See *Amount You Owe*, later.

Important Reminders

Installment agreement. If you cannot pay the full amount due with your return, you may ask to make monthly installment payments. See *Installment Agreement*, later, under *Amount You Owe*.
Combat zone service. You are allowed additional time to take care of tax matters if you are a member of the Armed Forces who served in the Persian Gulf Area combat zone, or if you are not a member of the Armed Forces but served in the combat zone in support of the Armed Forces. You are allowed additional time for filing your tax returns, paying your taxes, and filing claims for refund. See *Extensions Related to Combat Zone*, later, under *When Do I Have To File?*
Change of address. If you change your address for any reason, you should use Form 8822, *Change of Address*, to notify the IRS. See *Change of Address*, later, under *What Happens After I File?*
Electronic filing. You may want to take advantage of filing your return electronically instead of on a paper form. Electronic filing can shorten the time for processing returns to within 3 weeks. See *Electronic Filing*, later, under *Where Do I File?*
Computerized returns. You may want to take advantage of filing your return on a personal computer. This return, called Form 1040PC, can be processed faster and more accurately than the regular tax return. See *Computerized Returns*, later, under *Where Do I File?*

This chapter discusses:

- Whether you have to file a return,
- Which form to use,
- When, how, and where to file your return,
- What happens if you pay too little or too much tax,
- What records you should keep and how long you should keep them, and
- How you can change a return that has already been filed.

This chapter covers the requirements for filing a tax return. It refers you to other chapters for specific information on the income, deductions, and credits that you include on your return.

Do I Have to File a Return?

If you are a citizen or resident of the United States or a resident of Puerto Rico, you must file a federal income tax return if the filing requirements for any of the following categories apply to you:

- Individuals—In General
    Surviving Spouses, Executors, Administrators, or Legal Representatives
    U.S. Citizens Living Outside the U.S.
    Residents of Puerto Rico
    Individuals With Income From U.S. Possessions
- Dependents
- Children Under Age 14

- Self-Employed Persons
- Aliens

The filing requirements apply even if you do not owe tax.

Note. Even if you are not required to file a return, it may be to your advantage to file a tax return. See *Who Should File,* later.

One return. File only *one* federal income tax return regardless of how many jobs you had, how many Forms W–2 you received, or how many states you lived in during the year.

Individuals—In General

If you are a U.S. citizen or resident, your filing requirement depends on three factors:

1) Your gross income,
2) Your filing status, and
3) Your age.

However, you must file a return if your situation is one of those discussed later under *Other Situations When You Must File.*

Gross income. This includes all income you receive in the form of money, goods, property, and services that is not exempt from tax. Common types of income are discussed in the chapters in Part Two of this publication.

Community property. If you are married and live with your spouse in a community property state, half of any income described by state law as community income may be considered to be yours. See Publication 555, *Federal Tax Information on Community Property,* for more information.

Self-employed individuals. If you are self-employed, your gross income includes the amount on line 7 of Schedule C (Form 1040), *Profit or Loss From Business,* or line 1 of Schedule C–EZ (Form 1040), *Net Profit From Business.* See *Self-Employed Persons,* later, for more information about your filing requirements.

Filing status. Your filing status depends on whether you are single or married and on your family situation. Your filing status is determined on the last day of your tax year, which is December 31 for most taxpayers. See Chapter 2, *Filing Status,* for an explanation of each filing status.

Age. If you are 65 or older at the end of the year, the requirement to file a return may be different for you. You can generally have a higher amount of gross income than other taxpayers before you are required to file. You are considered 65 on the day before your 65th birthday. For example, if your 65th birthday was on January 1, 1994, you are considered 65 for 1993. See *Table 1–1,* below.

Example

You are 65 years old and earned $7,100 of **taxable income** last year. Your husband, who is 66 years old, received a **pension** of $4,000, all of which was **taxable income.** You and your husband legally separated on December 28. If you had been living together at the end of the year, you would not have had to file an income tax return, since your combined income was less than $12,300. But, since you are living apart and your gross income was more than $6,950, you must file a return.

Filing requirements chart for most taxpayers. Generally, if you are a U.S. citizen or resident, you must file a tax return if your gross income for the year is at least as much as the amount shown for your filing status and age in *Table 1–1.* If your parent (or

Table 1-1. **1993 Filing Requirements Chart for Most Taxpayers**

To use this chart, first find your marital status at the end of 1993. Then, read across to find your filing status and age at the end of 1993. You must file a return if your gross income was at least the amount shown in the last column. Gross income means all income you received in the form of money, goods, property, and services that is not exempt from tax, including any gain on the sale of your main home (even if you may exclude or postpone part or all of the gain).

Also, see *Table 1-2* and *Table 1-3* for other situations when you must file.

Marital Status	Filing Status	Age*	Gross Income
Single (including divorced and legally separated)	Single	under 65	$6,050
		65 or older	$6,950
	Head of household	under 65	$7,800
		65 or older	$8,700
Married with a child and living apart from your spouse during the last 6 months of 1993	Head of household	under 65	$7,800
		65 or older	$8,700
Married and living with your spouse at end of 1993 (or on the date your spouse died)	Married, joint return	under 65 (both spouses)	$10,900
		65 or older (one spouse)	$11,600
		65 or older (both spouses)	$12,300
	Married, separate return	any age	$2,350
Married, not living with your spouse at the end of 1993 (or on the date your spouse died)	Married, joint or separate return	any age	$2,350
Widowed before 1993 and not remarried in 1993	Single	under 65	$6,050
		65 or older	$6,950
	Head of household	under 65	$7,800
		65 or older	$8,700
	Qualifying widow(er) with dependent child	under 65	$8,550
		65 or older	$9,250

*If you were age 65 on January 1, 1994, you are considered to be age 65 at the end of 1993.

someone else) can claim you as a dependent, do not use this chart. See *Dependents,* later.

Surviving Spouses, Executors, Administrators, or Legal Representatives

You must file a final return for a decedent (a person who died) if:

- You are the surviving spouse, executor, administrator, or legal representative, and
- The decedent met the filing requirements at the date of death.

For more information on rules for decedents, see Chapter 4, *Decedents.*

U.S. Citizens Living Outside the U.S.

If you are a U.S. citizen living outside the United States, you must file a return if you meet the filing requirements. For more information on special tax rules that may apply to you, get Publication 54, *Tax Guide for U.S. Citizens and Resident Aliens Abroad.* It is available at most U.S. embassies and consulates, or you can order it using the order blank at the end of this publication.

Explanation
For more information about U.S. citizens living abroad, see Chapter 38, *U.S. Citizens Working Abroad.*

Residents of Puerto Rico

Generally, if you are a U.S. citizen and a resident of Puerto Rico, you must file a U.S. income tax return if you meet the filing requirements. This is in addition to any legal requirement you may have to file an income tax return for Puerto Rico.

If you are a resident of Puerto Rico for the entire year, gross income does not include income from sources within Puerto Rico, except for amounts received as an employee of the United States or a United States agency. If you receive income from Puerto Rican sources that is not subject to U.S. tax, the income level for your requirement to file a U.S. income tax return is lower than the applicable amount in *Table 1–1* or *Table 1–2*. See Publication 570, *Tax Guide for Individuals With Income From U.S. Possessions,* for further information.

Individuals With Income From U.S. Possessions

If you had income from Guam, the Northern Mariana Islands, American Samoa, the Virgin Islands, or Puerto Rico, special rules may apply in determining whether you must file a U.S. federal income tax return. In addition, you may have to file a return with the individual island government. See Publication 570 for more information.

Dependents

If you are a dependent (one who meets the **dependency tests** in Chapter 3), the requirement to file a return generally depends on:

- The amount of your earned and unearned income,
- The amount of your gross income,
- Whether you are single or married,
- Whether you are 65 or older, and
- Whether you are blind.

You also must file if your situation is one of those discussed later under *Other Situations When You Must File.* See *Table 1–2* to determine whether a dependent must file a return.

Earned income. This is salaries, wages, tips, professional fees, and other amounts received as pay for work actually done. For this purpose, earned income also includes any part of a scholarship that you must include in income. See *Scholarship and Fellowship Grants* in Chapter 13, *Other Income.*

Unearned income. This is income that does not meet the definition of earned income. It includes investment-type income such as interest, dividends, and capital gains. It also includes unemployment compensation, taxable social security benefits, pensions, and annuities. Distributions of interest, dividends, capital gains, and other unearned income from a trust are also unearned income to a beneficiary of the trust.

Responsibility of parent. If a dependent child with taxable income cannot file an income tax return, a parent, guardian, or other legally responsible person must file it for the child. If the child cannot sign the return, the filer must sign the child's name followed by the words "By (your signature), parent (or guardian) for minor child."

If a child's tax is not paid, the parent or guardian is liable for the income tax on salaries and wages of the child.

Child's income. Amounts a child earns by performing services are his or her gross income. This is true even if under local law the child's parents have the right to the earnings and may actually have received them.

Explanation
For more details about **dependents,** see Chapter 3, *Personal Exemptions and Dependents.*

Children Under Age 14

If a child's only income is interest and dividends (including Alaska Permanent Fund dividends) and certain other conditions are met, a parent can elect to include the child's income on the parent's return. If this election is made, the child is not required to file a return. See *Parent's Election to Report Child's Unearned Income,* in Chapter 32, *Tax on Investment Income of Certain Minor Children.* Also see Publication 929, *Tax Rules for Children and Dependents.*

Self-Employed Persons

You are self-employed if you:

- Carry on a trade or business as a sole proprietor.
- Are an independent contractor.
- Are a member of a partnership.
- Are in business for yourself in any other way.

Self-employment can include work in addition to your regular full-time business activities. It also includes certain part-time work that you do at home or in addition to your regular job.

Examples
A person who delivers newspapers would be subject to self-employment tax. A woman working at home in a cottage industry—making quilts or pillows, for example—would be subject to self-employment tax.

In some instances, it is to your advantage to report income from self-employment, since, if you do not al-

Table 1-2. **1993 Filing Requirements Chart for Dependents**

See Chapter 3 to find out if someone can claim you as a dependent.

If your parent (or someone else) can claim you as a dependent, and any of the four situations listed below applies to you, you must file a return. In this chart, **unearned income** includes taxable interest and dividends. **Earned income** includes wages, tips, and taxable scholarship and fellowship grants.
Caution: If your gross income was $2,350 or more, you generally cannot be claimed as a dependent unless you were under 19 **or** under 24 and a full-time student. For details, see *Gross Income Test* in Chapter 3.

1. Single dependents under 65 and not blind.—You must file a return if—

Your unearned income was:	and	the total of that income plus your earned income was:
$1 or more		more than $600
$0		more than $3,700

2. Single dependents 65 or older or blind.—You must file a return if—

• Your **earned income** was more than $4,600 ($5,500 if 65 or older **and** blind), or

• Your **unearned income** was more than $1,500 ($2,400 if 65 or older **and** blind), or

• Your **gross income** was more than the **total** of your earned income (up to $3,700) **or** $600, whichever is larger, **plus** $900 ($1,800 if 65 or older **and** blind)

3. Married dependents under 65 and not blind.—You must file a return if—

• Your **earned income** was more than $3,100, or

• You had any **unearned income** and your gross income was more than $600, or

• Your **gross income** was at least $5 and your spouse files a separate return on Form 1040 and itemizes deductions.

4. Married dependents 65 or older or blind.—You must file a return if—

• Your **earned income** was more than $3,800 ($4,500 if 65 or older **and** blind), or

• Your **unearned income** was more than $1,300 ($2,000 if 65 or older **and** blind), or

• Your **gross income** was more than the **total** of your earned income (up to $3,100) **or** $600, whichever is larger, **plus** $700 ($1,400 if 65 or older **and** blind), or

• Your **gross income** was at least $5 and your spouse files a separate return on Form 1040 and itemizes deductions.

ready qualify, you will then become eligible for social security benefits.

Filing Requirements for Self-Employed Persons

You must file Form 1040 if your gross income is at least as much as the filing requirement amount for your filing status and age *or* if your net earnings from self-employment are $400 or more. See *Table 1-1*, shown earlier.

Gross income. For purposes of the filing requirements, your gross income includes all income you receive in the form of money, goods, property, and services that is not exempt from tax. This includes the gross income amount on line 7 of Schedule C (Form 1040), *Profit or Loss From Business*, or line 1 of Schedule C–EZ (Form 1040), *Net Profit From Business*.

If you are self-employed in a business that provides services (where products are not a factor), then the gross income on line 7 of Schedule C (or line 1 of Schedule C–EZ) is gross receipts from that business. If you are self-employed in a business involving manufacturing, merchandising, or mining, the gross income on line 7 of Schedule C is the total sales from that business less cost of goods sold, plus any income from investment and incidental or outside operations or sources.

Net earnings of $400 or more. You must file a tax return if you had net earnings of $400 or more from self-employment. Net earnings from self-employment generally is the net income (gross income minus deductible business expenses) from your business or profession. The $400 net earnings figure applies regardless of your age.

Your net earnings are reduced by a 7.65% deduction that is used to figure self-employment tax. Multiply your net earnings by 0.9235 for the 7.65% deduction (100% − 7.65% = 92.35% or 0.9235).

Minimum income. You must have $433.13 or more of net earnings from self-employment before reduction by the 7.65% deduction to be subject to self-employment tax (.9235 × $433.13 = $400). If your net earnings are less than $433.13 before the 7.65% reduction, you do not have to pay the tax.

Self-employment tax. If your net earnings from self-employment are $400 or more, you must pay self-employment tax. This tax is comparable to the social security and Medicare tax withheld from an employee's wages.

The combined self-employment tax rate for 1993 is 15.3%. The 15.3% rate is a total of 12.4% for social security and 2.9% for Medicare. Use **Schedule SE** (Form 1040), *Self-Employment Tax*, to figure your tax. Attach it to Form 1040. A copy of this schedule is shown in Chapter 39, *Foreign Citizens Living in the United States*.

Table 1-3. **Other Situations When You Must File a 1993 Return**

If any of the four conditions listed below apply, you must file a return.

1. You owe any special taxes, such as:

   - Social security or Medicare tax on tips you did not report to your employer. (See Chapter 7.)

   - Uncollected social security, Medicare, or railroad retirement tax on tips you reported to your employer. (See Chapter 7.)

   - Uncollected social security, Medicare, or railroad retirement tax on your group-term life insurance.

   - Alternative minimum tax. (See Chapter 31.)

   - Tax on a qualified retirement plan, including an individual retirement arrangement (IRA). (See Chapter 18.)

   - Tax from recapture of investment credit or a low-income housing credit you claimed in a previous year. (See the instructions for Form 4255, *Recapture of Investment Credit* or Form 8611, *Recapture of Low-Income Housing Credit).*

   - Recapture tax on the disposition of a home purchased with a federally-subsidized mortgage. (See Chapter 16.)

2. You received any advance earned income credit (EIC) payments from your employer. This amount should be shown in box 9 of your Form W-2. (See Chapter 35.)

3. You had net earnings from self-employment of at least $400. See ("Self-Employed Persons.")

4. You had wages of $108.28 or more from a church or qualified church-controlled organization that is exempt from employer social security and Medicare taxes. (See Publication 533, *Self-Employment Tax.*)

Maximum income. No more than $57,600 of your combined wages, tips, and net earnings in 1993 is subject to any combination of the 12.4% social security part of self-employment tax, social security tax, or railroad retirement tax.

No more than $135,000 of your combined wages, tips, and net earnings in 1993 is subject to any combination of the 2.9% Medicare part of self-employment tax, social security tax, or railroad retirement tax.

TAXSAVER

In prior years, there was an advantage for a self-employed person whose earnings were slightly over the maximum tax base to employ a spouse in the business to lower his or her self-employment tax. The spouse's wages were not subject to social security taxes or self-employment tax. Now, however, the spouse's wages are subject to social security taxes. A self-employed person who has previously employed his or her spouse for this reason should consider terminating this practice.

Explanation

You are able to deduct one-half of your self-employment tax for the year in calculating your adjusted gross income. For details see Chapter 23, *Taxes You May Deduct.*

Self-employment tax has two parts: old age, survivor, and disability insurance (OASDI) and Medicare hospital insurance (HI). (The comparable social security tax with-

held on an employee's wages consists of these same two parts.) In 1993, there are two separate income limits for the application of OASDI and HI. The cap on self-employment income subject to OASDI is $57,600. The limit on wages and self-employment income subject to HI is $135,000.

Foreign organizations or governments. If you are a U.S. citizen who works in the United States for an international organization, a foreign government, or a wholly owned instrumentality of a foreign government, and if your work is exempt from social security and Medicare taxes, you must pay self-employment tax on earnings from services performed in the United States.

Employees of churches. If you work for a church or a qualified church-controlled organization that elected exemption from social security and Medicare taxes, you will have to pay self-employment tax if you are paid $108.28 or more in a year by the church organization. See Publication 533 for more information.

Aliens

Your status as an alien—resident, nonresident, or dual-status—determines how you file your income tax return.

The rules used to determine if you are a resident or nonresident alien are discussed in Publication 519, *U.S. Tax Guide for Aliens.*

Resident aliens. If you are a resident alien for the entire year, you must file a tax return following the same rules that apply to U.S. citizens. Use the forms discussed in this publication.

Nonresident aliens. If you are a nonresident alien, the rules and tax forms that apply to you may be different from those that apply to U.S. citizens. See Publication 519 to find out if U.S. income tax laws apply to you and which forms you should file.

Dual-status taxpayers. If you were a resident alien for part of the tax year and a nonresident alien for the rest of the year, you are a dual-status taxpayer. Different rules apply for the part of the year you were a resident of the United States and the part of the year you were a nonresident. For information on dual-status taxpayers, see Publication 519.

Joint return. If you are an alien and you were married to a person who was a U.S. citizen or resident on the last day of the tax year, you may be able to file a joint return with your spouse. See Publication 519.

Explanation

For more information about foreign citizens living in the United States, see Chapter 39, *Foreign Citizens Living in the United States.*

Other Situations When You Must File

You may need to file a tax return even if your gross income is **less** than the amount shown earlier in *Tables 1–1* and *1–2.* You must file a return if any of the situations in *Table 1–3* apply.

Who Should File

Even if you are not required to file, you should file a federal income tax return to get money back if:

- You had income tax withheld from your pay, or
- You qualify for the earned income credit. See Chapter 35, *Other Credits,* for more information.

Which Form Should I Use?

You must use one of three forms to file your return—Form 1040EZ, Form 1040A, or Form 1040. *Table 1–4* may help you decide which form to use.

Form 1040EZ

If you are single or married filing jointly, you may be able to use the simpler Form 1040EZ.

You can use Form 1040EZ if all of the following apply.

- Your filing status is single or married filing jointly.
- You (and your spouse if married filing a joint return) were not 65 or older or blind.
- You do not claim any dependents.
- Your taxable income is less than $50,000.
- Your income is only from wages, salaries, tips, taxable scholarship and fellowship grants, and taxable interest of $400 or less.
- You did not receive any advance earned income credit (EIC) payments.
- If you were a nonresident alien at any time in 1993, your filing status is married filing jointly.
- If you are married filing jointly and either you or your spouse worked for more than one employer, the total wages of that person were not over $57,600.

- You do not itemize deductions, claim any adjustments to income or tax credits, or owe any taxes other than the amount from the Tax Table.

You must meet all of these requirements to use Form 1040EZ. If you do not meet all of them, you must use Form 1040A or Form 1040.

TAXPLANNER

Even though it might be easier for you to file Form 1040EZ, you should carefully review your situation before doing so, especially if your income is close to the Form 1040EZ maximum level of $50,000. Check what deductions you may be able to claim if you itemize them. (You cannot claim **itemized deductions** on Form 1040EZ.) If you have deductions that can be itemized and you do not claim them, you could be significantly overpaying your tax.

Form 1040A

If you do not qualify to use Form 1040EZ, you may be able to use Form 1040A.

You can use Form 1040A if:

- Your income is *only* from wages, salaries, tips, IRA distributions, pensions and annuities, taxable social security and railroad retirement benefits, taxable scholarship and fellowship grants, interest, dividends (except for Alaska Permanent Fund dividends), and unemployment compensation.
- Your taxable income is less than $50,000.
- Your only adjustment to income is the deduction for contributions to an IRA.
- You do not itemize your deductions.
- Your only taxes are the amount from the Tax Table, alternative minimum tax, and (if you received any) advance earned income credit (EIC) payments.
- Your only credits are:
  a) The credit for child and dependent care expenses (see Chapter 33, *Child Care and Dependent Care Credit*).
  b) The credit for the elderly or the disabled (see Chapter 34, *Credit for the Elderly or Disabled*).
  c) The earned income credit (see Chapter 35, *Other Credits*).

If you file Form 1040A, you can claim estimated tax payments for 1993 and the exclusion of interest from Series EE U.S. savings bonds issued after 1989.

If you do not meet all of the above requirements, you cannot use Form 1040A. For example, you may want to claim itemized deductions, which you cannot claim on Form 1040A. Check the list under *Form 1040* to see if you are required to use Form 1040.

TAXALERT

An expanded Form 1040A, introduced in 1990, lets you report most retirement income, including pension and annuity payments, taxable social security and railroad retirement benefits, and payments from your IRA. Furthermore, it allows you to claim the credit for the elderly or the disabled and report your estimated tax payments. If you have been filing a Form 1040 because of these items, you can qualify for the easier-to-file Form 1040A.

Table 1-4. Which Tax Forms Can I Use?

Caution: You must file Form 1040 if you had a foreign account or were a grantor of, or transferor to, a foreign trust.	1040EZ	1040A	1040
Filing Status			
Single [1,2]	•	•	•
Married filing jointly [2]	•	•	•
Any other [1]		•	•
Exemptions			
None	•	•	•
For you (and your spouse if married)	•	•	•
Any others		•	•
Income			
Total taxable income under $50,000	•	•	•
Total taxable income $50,000 or more			•
Wages and salaries	•	•	•
Tips[3]	•	•	•
Scholarships and fellowships	•	•	•
Interest ($400 or less)[4]	•	•	•
Interest (over $400)[4]		•	•
Dividends[5]		•	•
Pensions, annuities, IRAs		•	•
Unemployment compensation		•	•
Taxable social security benefits		•	•
Taxable railroad retirement benefits		•	•
Self-employment income			•
Received as a partner in a partnership			•
Rents and royalties			•
Taxable state and local tax refunds			•
Capital gains			•
Sale of your home			•
Alimony			•
Any other			•
Adjustments to Income			
None	•	•	•
IRA contributions		•	•
Any other			•
Itemized Deductions			
None	•	•	•
Any itemized deductions			•
Other Taxes			
None	•	•	•
Advance earned income credit payments		•	•
Alternative minimum tax		•	•
Lump-sum distributions			•
Accumulation distribution of trusts			•
Self-employment tax			•
Uncollected social security and Medicare tax			•
Any other			•
Tax Credits			
None	•	•	•
Earned income credit		•	•
Credit for child and dependent care expenses		•	•
Credit for the elderly or the disabled		•	•
Any other			•
Payments			
Federal income tax withheld	•	•	•
Excess social security and Medicare tax withheld		•	•
Excess railroad retirement tax withheld		•	•
Tax paid with filing extension request	•	•	•
Estimated tax payments		•	•
Any other			•

[1] You must file Form 1040 if you are a resident alien who was a nonresident at any time during 1993.

[2] You must file Form 1040A or Form 1040 if you (or your spouse, if married) were 65 or older or blind.

[3] You must file Form 1040 if you received tips of $20 or more in any month that you did not report to your employer, or your Form W-2 shows an amount for allocated tips in box 7.

[4] You must file Form 1040 if you received or paid accrued interest on securities transferred between interest payment dates, or you elect to report your child's interest on your return.

[5] You must file Form 1040 if you received nontaxable dividends, capital gain distributions, or Alaska Permanent Fund dividends, or you elect to report your child's dividends on your return.

Be aware that you still cannot claim itemized deductions on Form 1040A. If you have deductions that can be itemized, you may be better off continuing to file a Form 1040.

Form 1040

Form 1040 is used to report more types of income, deductions, and credits than you can include on either Form 1040EZ or Form 1040A.

You may have received Form 1040A or Form 1040EZ in the mail because of the return you filed last year. If your situation has changed this year, it may be to your advantage to file Form 1040 instead. You may pay less tax by filing Form 1040 because you can take itemized deductions, adjustments to income, and some credits that you cannot take on Form 1040A or Form 1040EZ.

You must use Form 1040 if:

- Your taxable income is $50,000 or more.
- You itemize your deductions.
- You received or paid accrued interest on securities transferred between interest payment dates.
- You received nontaxable dividends, capital gain distributions, or Alaska Permanent Fund dividends.
- You are required to complete Part III of Schedule B (Form 1040) because:

    You were a grantor of, or transferor to, a foreign trust that existed during 1993, or

    At any time during the year you had an interest in, or signature or other authority over, a bank, securities, or other financial account in a foreign country. **Note.** If the combined value of the foreign account(s) is $10,000 or less during all of 1993, or if the account(s) was with a U.S. military banking facility operated by a U.S. financial institution, you may be able to use Form 1040A or Form 1040EZ.

- You had income *other* than wages, salaries, tips, IRA distributions, pensions and annuities, taxable social security and railroad retirement benefits, taxable scholarship and fellowship grants, unemployment compensation, interest, or dividends. This includes gain from the sale of your home or other property, barter income, alimony income, taxable refunds of state and local income taxes, and self-employment income (including farm income).
- You sold or exchanged capital assets or business property.
- You claim adjustments to gross income for payments for self-employed health insurance, the deduction for self-employment tax, payments to a Keogh or SEP plan, the penalty on early withdrawal of savings, alimony paid, certain required repayments of supplemental unemployment benefits, jury pay turned over to your employer, qualified performing artists' expenses, and other allowable adjustments to income.
- Your Form W–2 shows uncollected employee tax (social security and Medicare tax) on tips or group-term life insurance in box 13. See Chapter 7, *Income from Tips.*
- You received $20 or more in tips in any one month, and you did not report all of these tips to your employer. See Chapter 7.
- You must pay tax on self-employment income. See Schedule SE (Form 1040), *Self-Employment Tax,* and Chapter 36, *If You Are Self-Emloyed: How to File Schedule C.*

- You have to repay an investment credit or a low-income housing credit you claimed in a previous year.
- You have to recapture tax on the disposition of a home purchased with a federally-subsidized mortgage. See Chapter 16, *Selling Your Home.*
- You have to pay tax on an excess golden parachute payment.
- You claim credits against your tax for any of the following:

    Mortgage interest credit

    Foreign tax credit

    Any general business credit

    Credit for prior year minimum tax

    Credit for fuel from a nonconventional source

    Credit for federal tax on fuels

    Qualified electric vehicle credit

    Regulated investment company credit
- You file any of the following:

    Form 2119, *Sale of Your Home* (when filed in the year of sale)

    Form 2555, *Foreign Earned Income*

    Form 2555–EZ, *Foreign Earned Income Exclusion*

    Form 4563, *Exclusion of Income for Bona Fide Residents of American Samoa*

    Form 4970, *Tax on Accumulation Distribution of Trusts*

    Form 4972, *Tax on Lump-Sum Distributions* (See Chapter 11, *Retirement Plans, Pensions, and Annuities.*)

    Form 5329, *Return for Additional Taxes Attributable to Qualified Retirement Plans (Including IRAs), Annuities, and Modified Endowment Contracts*

    Note: If you are filing only because you owe tax on an IRA or a qualified retirement plan, you only have to file Form 5329. (See Chapters 11, *Retirement Plans, Pensions, and Annuities,* and 18, *Individual Retirement Arrangements* (IRAs).)

    Form 8271, *Investor Reporting of Tax Shelter Registration Number*

    Form 8814, *Parents' Election To Report Child's Interest and Dividends*

When Do I Have To File?

April 15, 1994, is the due date for filing your 1993 income tax return if you use a calendar year. If you use a fiscal year (a year ending on the last day of any month except December, or a 52–53 week year), your income tax return is due by the 15th day of the 4th month after the close of your fiscal year.

When the due date for doing *any* act for tax purposes—filing a return, paying taxes, etc.—falls on a Saturday, Sunday, or legal holiday, you can do that act on the next business day.

Filing on time. Your return is filed on time if it is properly addressed and postmarked no later than the due date. The return must have sufficient postage. If you send a return by registered mail, the date of the registration is the postmark date. The registration is evidence that the return was delivered. If you send a return by certified mail and have your receipt postmarked by a postal employee, the date on the receipt is the postmark date. The postmarked certified mail receipt is evidence that the return was delivered.

Filing late. If you do not file your return by the due date, you may have to pay a failure-to-file penalty and interest. See *Penalties,* later.

Nonresident alien. If you are a nonresident alien and earn wages that are subject to U.S. income tax withholding, your 1993 U.S. income tax return (Form 1040NR) is due by:

- April 15, 1994, if you file on a calendar year basis, or
- The 15th day of the 4th month after the end of your fiscal year if you file on a fiscal year basis.

If you do not earn wages that are subject to U.S. income tax withholding, your return is due by:

- June 15, 1994, if you file on a calendar year basis, or
- The 15th day of the 6th month after the end of your fiscal year, if you file on a fiscal year basis.

Get Publication 519, *U.S. Tax Guide for Aliens,* for more filing information.

Filing for a decedent. If you must file a final return as an executor, administrator, legal representative, or surviving spouse of a taxpayer who died during the year (a decedent), the income tax return is due by the 15th day of the 4th month after the end of the deceased taxpayer's normal tax year. See *Final Return for the Decedent* in Chapter 4, *Decedents.* In most cases, for a 1993 return, this will be April 15, 1994.

Extensions

There are three types of extensions that may apply to your return. These are:

- Time to file,
- Time to file and pay, and
- Related to service in a combat zone.

Each extension is discussed separately.

Extensions of Time To File

If you are not able to file your return by the due date, you may be able to get an automatic 4–month extension of time to file your 1993 tax return. To get the automatic extension, you must file **Form 4868,** *Application for Automatic Extension of Time To File U.S. Individual Income Tax Return.*

Any extension of time granted for filing your 1993 calendar year income tax return also extends the time for filing a 1993 gift tax return.

Example. If your return is due on April 15, 1994, you will have until August 15, 1994, to file.

Caution: You may not be eligible. If you want the IRS to figure your tax, you cannot use the automatic extension of time to file. If you are under a court order to file by the regular due date, you also cannot use the automatic extension of time to file.

When to file Form 4868. You must file Form 4868 by April 15, 1994, with the Internal Revenue Service Center for your area. If you are filing a fiscal year return, file Form 4868 by the regular due date for your return. You can file Form 1040EZ, Form 1040A or Form 1040 any time before the 4–month extension period ends.

TaxSaver

An extension of time to file will not be valid if it does not show a "proper" estimate of tax liability. A proper estimate is based on all the facts and information you have at the time of filing. If your estimate is found to be improper, your extension will be invalid and you will be subject to failure-to-file penalties. See *Penalties*, later.

Some tax experts contend that you should request the maximum extension allowed for filing your return, arguing that your chances of an audit are reduced, since IRS field agents will have less time to conduct the audit. Other tax experts contend that you're better off filing on April 15, since that way you get lost in the crowd. Both theories are oversimplifications of IRS procedures.

TaxAlert

A recent IRS notice provides some relief to taxpayers unable to pay the amount owed with the filing of Form 4868. Under this notice, Form 4868 may be filed and an automatic 4–month extension obtained even though the tax properly estimated to be due is not paid in full when the form is filed. No late filing penalty will be assessed under these circumstances. However, it is still required that the tax liability shown on Form 4868 be properly estimated based on the information available to the taxpayer. Further, unless at least 90% of the taxpayer's actual tax liability was paid prior to the original due date of the return through withholding or estimated payment, a late payment penalty of 1/2% per month will be assessed for each month from the original due date to the date of payment plus the regular rate of interest under payments.

An extension of time to file is not an extension of time to pay. You must make an accurate estimate of your tax for 1993. If your find you cannot pay the full amount due with Form 4868, you can still get the extension. You will owe interest on the unpaid amount.

You also may be charged a penalty for paying the tax late unless you have reasonable cause for not paying your tax when due. See *Penalties,* later.

Interest and penalties are assessed (charged) from the original due date of the return, which, for most taxpayers, is April 15.

Caution: If you plan to elect the deferral of additional 1993 taxes, see *Payment of first installment* under *Amount You Owe,* later.

When you file your return. Enter any payment you made with Form 4868 on line 57, Form 1040. If you file Form 1040EZ or Form 1040A, include in the total on line 7 of Form 1040EZ or line 28d of Form 1040A the amount paid with Form 4868. Also write "Form 4868" and the amount paid in the space to the left of line 7 or line 28d.

Extensions beyond the automatic 4–month extension. If you qualify for the 4–month extension and you later find that you are not able to file within the 4–month extension period, you may be able to get 2 more months to file, for a total of 6 months.

You can apply for an extension beyond the 4–month extension either in a letter or by filing **Form 2688,** *Application for Additional Extension of Time To File U.S. Individual Income Tax Return.* You should request the extension early so that, if refused, you still will be able to file on time. Except in cases of undue hardship, Form 2688 or a request by letter will not be accepted until you have first used Form 4868 to get an automatic 4–month extension. Form 2688 or your letter will not be considered if you file it after the extended due date.

To get an extension beyond the automatic 4–month extension, you must give all the following information:

- The reason for requesting the extension.
- The tax year to which the extension applies.
- The length of time needed for the extension.
- Whether another extension of time to file has already been requested for this tax year.

You may sign the request for this extension, or it may be signed by your attorney, CPA, enrolled agent, or a person with a power of attorney. If you are unable to sign the request because of illness or for another good reason, a person in close personal or business relationship to you can sign for you, stating why you could not sign the request.

Explanation

Generally, only causes that are beyond your control will be acceptable as reasons for an additional extension. In addition to personal sickness or injury and to a death or serious illness in your immediate family, some acceptable reasons, drawn from IRS proceedings and court cases, include the following:

1. You have a substantial number of security transactions (approximately 200) during the taxable year, some quite complex, and there has not been sufficient time to gather and analyze all the required information.
2. You have invested in oil properties and received the information from the operators too late to complete your return adequately by the due date.
3. You have a complicated deduction problem with your medical expenses that is under study by your tax advisors, and it may not be resolved in time to prepare your tax return adequately.
4. You sold securities in the taxable year that you had held for some years, and you have not as yet been able to determine the tax basis of such securities. You have checked your records but may have to go back to old records of your broker to determine the correct figures.
5. A partnership on the accrual basis in which you are a member initiated a profit-sharing plan at the end of the tax year, the contribution to which depends on approval of the plan by the IRS. Such approval has not yet been received.
6. Any other situation in which there is a "reasonable cause"—for example, the destruction by fire or other casualty of your business records, or a lack of funds to pay the tax when you can demonstrate that this lack occurred despite the exercise of ordinary business care and prudence.

If your application for this extension is approved, you will be notified by the IRS. Attach the notice to your return when you file it.

If an extension is granted and the IRS later determines that the statements made on your request for this extension are false and misleading and an extension would not have been granted at the time based on the true facts, the extension is null and void. You will have to pay the failure-to-file penalty (discussed later).

If your application for this extension is not approved, you must file your return by the extended due date of the automatic extension. You may be allowed to file within 10 days of the date of the notice you get from the IRS if the end of the 10–day period is later than the due date. The notice will tell you if the 10–day grace period is granted.

No further extensions. An extension of more than 6 months will not be granted if you are in the United States. However, if you are outside the United States and meet certain tests, you may be granted a longer extension. See *Filing Requirements* in Publication 54 for more information.

Extensions of Time To File and Pay

You are allowed an automatic 2–month extension (until June 15, 1994, if you use a calendar year) to file your 1993 return and pay any federal income tax that is due if you are a U.S. citizen or resident and on the regular due date of your return:

- You are living outside of the United States and Puerto Rico, and your main place of business or post of duty is outside the United States and Puerto Rico, *or*
- You are in military or naval service on duty outside the United States and Puerto Rico.

However, if you pay the tax due after the original due date, interest will be charged from the original due date until the date the tax is paid.

See *When To File* in Publication 54 for more information.

Note. If you served in a combat zone, see *Extensions Related to Combat Zone,* later, for special rules that apply to you.

Married taxpayers. If you file a joint return, only one spouse has to qualify for this automatic extension to apply. If you and your spouse file separate returns, this automatic extension applies only to the spouse who qualifies.

How to receive the extension. To use this special automatic extension, you must attach a statement to your return explaining what situation qualified you for the extension.

Extensions beyond the automatic 2–month extension. If you are unable to file your return within the automatic 2–month extension period, you may be able to get an additional 2–month

Table 1-5.   **When to File Your 1993 Return** (For U.S. citizens and residents who file returns on a calendar year)

	For Most Taxpayers	For Certain Taxpayers Outside the U.S.
No extension requested	April 15, 1994	June 15, 1994
Form 4868 filed (1st extension)	August 15, 1994	August 15, 1994
Form 2688 filed after filing Form 4868 (2nd extension)	October 17, 1994	October 17, 1994

extension of time to file your return, for a total of 4 months. You must file Form 4868 by the end of the automatic extension period (usually June 15, 1994) to get this additional 2–month extension.

This additional 2–month extension of time to file is **not** an extension of time to pay. You must make an accurate estimate of your tax for 1993. If you cannot pay the full amount due with Form 4868 you can still get the extension. You will owe interest on the unpaid amount and may be charged a penalty for paying the tax late. See *Penalties,* later.

Extensions beyond 4 months. If you are still unable to file your return within the 4–month extension, you may be able to get an extension for 2 more months, for a total of 6 months. See *Extensions beyond the automatic 4–month extension,* earlier.

No further extensions. An extension of more than 6 months will generally not be granted. However, if you are outside the United States and meet certain tests, you may be granted a longer extension. See *Filing Requirements* in Publication 54 for more information.

TAXPLANNER

An extension of time to file is not an extension of time to pay. If you are unable to pay the full amount of tax due with your tax return because of financial hardship, you should still file the tax return along with a "good faith" payment of as much of the tax due as you can afford to pay. You should complete Form 9465 to request the privilege of paying the remaining tax in installments. This form should be attached to the front of the return when it is filed. You can expect a decision back from the IRS within 30 days regarding your installment request; however, **you will still be subject to interest and the failure-to-pay penalty on the unpaid tax.**

The IRS will continue to send you a bill for the unpaid tax, interest, and penalty until the total amount is paid. After the tax is completely paid, you can request in writing that the penalty be waived due to reasonable cause because of financial hardship. The IRS has total discretion in waiving penalties and may require you to prove your financial hardship.

If your tax return is already in the formal collection process (i.e., you have been contacted by an IRS official regarding a delinquent tax liability) and you are unable to pay the tax due, you may request an installment agreement with the IRS officer. If he or she agrees, the installment agreement is made using Form 433-D, and you will be required to provide financial information. You may need to seek professional tax advice if this is the case.

Extensions Related to Combat Zone

If you served in the Armed Forces in the Persian Gulf Area combat zone, the deadline for filing your tax return, paying any tax that you may owe, and filing a claim for refund is automatically extended. The deadline is also extended if you served in the combat zone in support of the Armed Forces, even though you were not a member of those forces. This category includes Red Cross personnel, accredited correspondents, and civilians under the direction of the Armed Forces in support of the Armed Forces.

For purposes of the deadline extension, the Persian Gulf Area became a combat zone on August 2, 1990. See Publication 945, *Tax Information for Those Affected by Operation Desert Storm,* for more information on these and other benefits.

Length of extension period. Your deadline for filing your return, paying any tax that is due, and for filing a claim for refund is extended for at least 180 days after the later of:

1) The last day you are in a combat zone (or the last day the area qualifies as a combat zone), or
2) The last day of any continuous qualified hospitalization for injury from service in the combat zone.

In addition to the 180 days, your deadline is also extended by the number of days you had left to file when you entered the Persian Gulf Area combat zone. For example, you have 3½ months (January 1 – April 15, 1994) to file your 1993 tax return. Any days of this 3½–month period that are left when you entered the combat zone (or the entire 3½ months if you entered the combat zone before January 1, 1994) are added to the 180 days to find the end of your time extension for filing your 1993 return.

How Do I Prepare the Forms?

This section explains how to get ready to fill in your tax return, including when to report your income and expenses. It also explains how to complete certain sections of the form. You may find *Table 1–6,* shown later, helpful when you prepare your return.

In most cases, the IRS will mail you either Form 1040, Form 1040A, or Form 1040EZ with related instructions, based on what you filed last year. Before you fill in your return, look over the forms to see if you need additional forms or schedules.

If you have not received a tax return package in the mail, or if you need other forms, you can order them. You can get most forms and publications you need from the IRS Forms Distribution Center for your state by using the order blank at the end of this publication or by calling the toll-free number 1–800–TAX–FORM (1–800–829–3676).

Form W–2. If you are an employee, you should receive Form W–2 from your employer. You will need the information from this form before you prepare your return.

If you do not receive Form W–2 by February 1, contact your employer. If you still do not get the form by February 15, the IRS can help you by requesting the form from your employer.

Substitute tax forms. You cannot use your own version of a tax form unless it meets the requirements explained in Publication 1167, *Substitute Printed, Computer-Prepared, and Computer-Generated Tax Forms and Schedules.*

Explanation

The tax forms provided in the back of this book meet these requirements.

Tax help on videotape. A videotape of tax return instructions is available in either English or Spanish at participating libraries.

When Do I Report My Income and Expenses?

You must figure your taxable income on the basis of a tax year. A "tax year" is an annual accounting period used for keeping your records and reporting your income and expenses. You must account for your income and deductions in a way that clearly shows your taxable income. The way you account is called an accounting method. This section explains which accounting periods and methods you can use.

Table 1-6. 6 Steps for Preparing Your Return

1—Get all of your records together for income and expenses.
2—Get all forms, schedules, and publications that you need.
3—Fill in your return.
4—Check your return to make sure it is correct.
5—Sign and date your return.
6—Attach all required forms and schedules.

Accounting Periods

Most individual tax returns cover a *calendar year*—the 12 months from January 1 through December 31. This is one accounting period. Another accounting period is the *fiscal year.* A regular fiscal year is a 12–month period that ends on the last day of any month except December. A 52–53 week fiscal year varies from 52 to 53 weeks and ends on a particular day of the week.

You must choose your accounting period when you file your first income tax return. It cannot be longer than 12 months.

Changing your accounting period. To change your accounting period, you generally must get permission from the IRS. If you want to change your accounting period, get **Form 1128,** *Application To Adopt, Change, or Retain a Tax Year.* Form 1128 must be filed on or before the 15th day of the second calendar month of the requested accounting period. The new period cannot be used until you receive approval from IRS. A fee is charged to request a change in your accounting period.

Example. Last year, you were an employee and filed your income tax return on a calendar year basis. On July 1 this year you quit your job and open your own repair shop. For business reasons, you want to file your income tax return on a fiscal year basis from July 1 to June 30. To change your accounting period, complete and submit Form 1128 by August 15.

TaxPlanner

To operate on a fiscal year accounting basis, you must keep your books and records based on that fiscal year. Since most individual taxpayers keep their personal financial records on a calendar year basis, it is easier to use a calendar year period.

It is virtually impossible for an individual to secure permission to change to a fiscal year accounting period without justification. Usually the justification must be that you are involved in a cyclical business from which self-employment or partnership income flows. Furthermore, in most cases, that income has to be your sole or principal source of income.

Additional information. For more information on accounting periods, see Publication 538, *Accounting Periods and Methods.*

Accounting Methods

Your accounting method is the way you account for your income and deductions. Most taxpayers use either the cash method or an accrual method. You choose a method when you first file a return.

Cash method. If you use this method, report all items of income in the year in which you actually or constructively receive them. Deduct all expenses in the year you pay them. This is the method most individual taxpayers use.

Explanation

Accounting methods are important, because they determine when you recognize income and when you deduct expenses for tax purposes. The cash method allows you more flexibility and control over your tax liability.

Individuals who do not own and operate their own business must use the cash method. However, the IRS will not permit you to use the cash method if you own your own business and if inventories of unsold goods or materials are on hand at the end of the year.

TaxAlert

Recently, IRS officials have expressed the view that you may not use the cash method for any substantial business activity, even one providing only personal or professional services. The law does not support this view. Nevertheless, in conducting audits, the IRS has been more aggressive in urging taxpayers to change to the accrual method of accounting.

TaxPlanner

Generally, most taxpayers who expect to be in the same tax bracket from one year to the next and who want to reduce their current tax bill as much as possible should attempt to defer income to a subsequent year and to take deductions in the current year. (If you suspect you might be in a higher tax bracket in a subsequent year, however, you would want to do just the opposite.)

You might consider lumping together your deductions in a single year. For example, in some states and cities, you may pay property, state, and local income taxes in either December or January, giving you the opportunity to pay two years' worth of these taxes in a single calendar year. You can also control when you make charitable contributions. To some extent, you can also control when you make interest payments on a mortgage.

Constructive receipt. Income is constructively received when it is credited to your account, or is set apart in any way that makes it available to you. You do not need to have physical possession of it. For example, dividends or interest credited to your bank account on December 31, 1993, are taxable income to you in 1993 if you could have withdrawn them in 1993 (even if the amount is not entered in your passbook or withdrawn until 1994).

Garnisheed wages. If your employer uses your wages to pay your debts, or if your wages are attached or garnisheed, the full amount is constructively received by you. You must include these wages in income for the year you would have received them.

Brokerage and other accounts. Profits from a brokerage account, or similar account, are fully taxable in the year you earn them. This is true even if:

1) You do not withdraw the earnings,
2) The credit balance in the account may be reduced or eliminated by losses in later years, or
3) Current profits are used to reduce or eliminate a debit balance from previous years.

Example

You sold your ABC Company stock on December 15, 1993, realizing a gain of $5,000. You did not withdraw the cash in your account until January 5, 1994. The gain is taxable income to you for 1993.

Debts paid for you. If another person cancels or pays your debts (but not as a gift or loan), you have constructively received the amount and must include it in your gross income for the year.

Example

Your new employer pays the balance of the mortgage due on your home that is not covered by the selling price so you can move to Florida to work for him. The payments are not intended to be a gift or a loan to you. The amount your employer pays on the mortgage is income to you in the year that he pays it.

Payment to third party. If a third party is paid income from property you own, you have constructively received the income. It is the same as if you had actually received the income and paid it to the third party.

Payment to an agent. Income received by an agent for you is income constructively received by you in the year the agent receives it. If you indicate in a contract that your income is to be paid to another person, you must include the amount in your gross income when the other person receives it.

Explanation

The IRS considers you to have received income in the year that your agent receives it, but, if a person who is not your agent or creditor receives your income, then you do not have to consider that amount as income until you personally obtain it. The key question is whether you can control the receipt of the income during the year. If you can, the income is taxable to you in that year.

Example

ABC Company mailed you a $500 dividend check on December 8, 1993. The post office inadvertently delivered the check on December 31 to Mr. Wheat on the other side of town. You didn't receive the check until January 5, 1994, since Mr. Wheat was not your agent. You should carefully explain this turn of events when you prepare your return, because the IRS document-matching program will have a Form 1099 from ABC Company that lists the $500 as having been paid to you in 1993.

TAXPLANNER

It is possible to structure a sale of property so that the sale funds are deposited in an escrow account and then disbursed to you a year later. The advantage to you in this arrangement is that you have the security of knowing that the sale proceeds exist but, at the same time, you're able to defer taxes on the funds until they become income to you, a year later. To do this, the escrow arrangement must be agreed on by both the buyer and the seller. The arrangement must follow other specific guidelines as well. You will need to seek professional advice.

Check received or available. A valid check you received or that was made available to you before the end of the tax year is constructively received by you in that year, even if you do not cash the check or deposit it in your account until the next year.

No constructive receipt. There may be facts to show that you did not constructively receive income.

Example. Alice Johnson, a teacher, agreed to her school board's condition that, in her absence, she would receive only the difference between her regular salary and the salary of a substitute teacher hired by the school board. Therefore, Alice did not constructively receive the amount by which her salary was reduced to pay the substitute teacher.

Explanation

The IRS does not consider you to have paid an expense if you use a note in lieu of cash to make the payment. In this case, you have only made a promise to pay sometime in the future. However, the IRS considers you to have made a payment if you use cash borrowed from a third party to pay an expense.

Example

If you give a note to your doctor promising to pay him for medical services already rendered, you have not yet paid the expense in the IRS's eyes. However, if you borrow money from your bank and use the cash to pay your doctor, you have paid the expense for tax purposes. Similarly, if you pay by credit card, you have made the payment for tax purposes. Paying by credit card is just like borrowing from a third party.

Exception

Individual Retirement Arrangements. If you qualify for a tax-deductible contribution, you may take a deduction for a contribution to an Individual Retirement Arrangement (IRA) in one year, even though you do not make the actual cash contribution to your account until the following year; that is, you may file your tax return showing a deduction for a contribution to your IRA, although you have not yet made the contribution. The deduction is valid as long as you make the contribution on or before April 15 of the following year. For more information, see Chapter 18, *Individual Retirement Arrangements (IRAs)*.

Accrual method. If you use this method, you report income when you earn it, whether or not you receive it. You deduct your expenses when you incur them, rather than when you pay them.

Income paid in advance. Prepaid income is generally included in gross income in the year you receive it. Your method of accounting does not matter as long as the income is available to you. Prepaid income includes rents or interest received in advance and compensation for services to be performed later.

If, under an agreement, you receive advance payment for services to be performed by the end of the next tax year, you can defer these payments from income until you earn them by performing the service. You *must* be an accrual method taxpayer to defer advance payments. You cannot defer them beyond the year after the year you receive them. For more information, get Publication 538.

Example

You are the owner of a home construction company. In December 1993, a customer paid you $10,000 to supervise the building of a residence, but the residence will not be built until 1994. You will not perform any service until then. If your company keeps its records and reports its earnings using the accrual method, you can delay reporting the $10,000 until 1994. If your company uses the cash method of accounting, you must report the income in 1993.

Changing your accounting method. Once you have chosen your accounting method, you ordinarily cannot change it without the permission of the IRS. However, you can use a different method for each business you have.

Example. You work for a salary and use the cash method to report that income on your tax return. You open a gift shop and continue to work for a salary. Even though you use the cash method for your salary, you can use an accrual method for reporting income from your gift shop.

Explanation

If you run a gift shop, you may be required to use the accrual method of accounting. Whenever the sale of merchandise produces income, as it does in any store, you will have goods on hand to sell to customers. If you maintain an inventory, you are required to use the accrual method of accounting to record purchases and sales.

How to change. If you want to change your accounting method, get Form 3115, *Application for Change in Accounting Method.* In general, Form 3115 must be filed within 180 days after the beginning of the year of change. A fee is charged to request a change in your accounting method.

Exception

If you use the cash method of accounting, you must include all the income from the sale of property at the time cash and notes are received. If you use the accrual method of accounting, you include all the income from the sale of property as income when the sale takes place. Under both methods, income from the sale of property would generally be recognized in the year of the sale.

Additional information. For more information on accounting methods, get Publication 538.

Address Label

After you have completed your return, peel your address label off the cover of your tax return package and place it in the address area of the Form 1040, Form 1040A, or Form 1040EZ you send to the IRS. If you have someone prepare your return, give that person your label to use.

The coding on the label is used by the IRS in processing your return. The label helps to correctly identify accounts. It also saves processing costs and speeds up processing so that refunds can be issued sooner.

Correcting the label. Make necessary name and address changes on the label. If you have an apartment number that is not shown on the label, please write it in. If you and your spouse file a joint return and maintain separate homes, choose one address to enter on your return. If the label is for a joint return and the social security numbers are not listed in the same order as the first names, change the numbers to show the correct order. If your social security number is not correct, or if you changed your name, see the discussion under *Social Security Number,* later.

No label. If you did not receive a tax return package with a label, print or type your name, address, and social security number in the spaces provided at the top of Form 1040 or Form 1040A. If you are married filing a separate return, do not enter your spouse's name in the space at the top. Instead, enter his or her name in the space provided on line 3.

If you file Form 1040EZ and you do not have a label, print (do not type) this information in the spaces provided.

P.O. box. If your post office does not deliver mail to your street address and you have a P.O. box, write your P.O. box number on the line for your present home address instead of your street address.

Foreign address. If your address is outside the United States or its possessions or territories, enter the information on the line for "City, town or post office, state, and ZIP code" in the following order:

1) City,
2) Province or state,
3) Foreign postal code, and
4) Name of foreign country.

Do not abbreviate the name of the country.

TaxAlert

You are not excused from filing a return because you have not received the proper forms from the IRS. In addition to any IRS office (check the telephone book), you may usually obtain the necessary forms at your local post office or bank. Forms that you can use to file your return are provided at the back of this book.

Social Security Number

You must show your social security number (SSN) on your return. If the number shown on the address label on the tax return package you received in the mail is wrong, mark through it. Correct it on the label. If you did not receive a return with a label, enter your number in the space provided on the return.

If you are married and you did not receive a tax return package with a label, enter the social security numbers for both you and your spouse, whether you file jointly or separately.

Name change. If you changed your name because of marriage, divorce, etc., make sure you immediately notify your Social Security Administration (SSA) office so the name on your tax return is the same as the one the SSA has on its records. This may prevent delays in issuing your refund and safeguard future social security benefits.

Dependent's social security number. If you claim an exemption for a dependent who is at least *1 year old* by December 31, 1993, you must list the dependent's SSN on Form 1040 or Form 1040A. The social security number requirement applies to *all dependents* (not just your children) claimed on the tax return who are at least 1 year old.

TaxAlert

You must have a social security number for a dependent who is at least 1 year old by December 31. Failure to get one may delay the processing of your return.

No social security number. If you or your dependent who is at least 1 year old does not have an SSN, file a **Form SS–5** with your local SSA office. If you are a U.S. citizen, you must show proof of age, identity, and citizenship with your Form SS–5. If you are 18 or older, you must appear in person.

Form SS–5 is available at any SSA office. If you have any questions about which documents you can use as proof of age, identity, or citizenship, contact your SSA office.

It usually takes about 2 weeks to get an SSN. If you or your dependent will not have a number by the time you are ready to file your tax return, ask the SSA to give you a receipt. If you or your dependent does not receive a number by the time you are ready to file, you should file your return and enter *"Applied for"* in the space provided for the number. If SSA gave you a receipt, attach a copy to your return.

Nonresident alien dependents. If you claim dependents who are residents of Mexico or Canada, they must have SSNs. You can apply for an SSN with either the Social Security Administration or a U.S. consulate or embassy. See *Social Security Number for Dependents* in Chapter 3, *Personal Exemptions and Dependents,* for more information.

Nonresident alien spouse. If your spouse is a nonresident alien and you file a joint return, your spouse must get an SSN. If your spouse does not receive an SSN by the time you are ready to file, follow the instructions explained earlier under *No social security number.*

If you file a separate return and your spouse does not have an SSN or any income, enter "NRA" in the space provided for your spouse's number.

Penalty for not providing social security number. If you do not include your social security number or the number of your spouse or dependent as required, you may have to pay a penalty. See the discussion on *Penalties,* later, for more information.

SSN on correspondence. If you write to the IRS about your tax account, be sure to include your SSN in your correspondence. Because your SSN is used to identify your account, this helps the IRS respond to your correspondence promptly.

Presidential Election Campaign Fund

This fund was set up to help pay for presidential election campaigns. You may have $3 of your tax liability go to this fund by checking the *Yes* box on Form 1040, Form 1040A, or Form 1040EZ. If you are filing a joint return, your spouse may also have $3 go to the fund. If you check *Yes,* it will not change the tax you pay or the refund you will receive.

Rounding Off Dollars

You may round off cents to whole dollars on your return and schedules. If you do round to whole dollars, you must round all amounts. To round, drop amounts under 50 cents and increase amounts from 50 to 99 cents to the next dollar. For example, $1.39 becomes $1 and $2.50 becomes $3.

If you have to add two or more amounts to figure the amount to enter on a line, include cents when adding the amounts and round off only the total.

Example. You receive two W–2 forms: one showing wages of $5,000.55 and one showing wages of $18,500.73. On Form 1040, line 7, you would enter $23,501 ($5,000.55 + $18,500.73 = $23,501.28) instead of $23,502 ($5,001 + $18,501).

Additional Schedules

Depending on the form you file and the items reported on your return, you may have to complete additional schedules and attach them to your return.

Form 1040EZ. There are no additional schedules to file for Form 1040EZ.

Form 1040A. If you file Form 1040A, you must complete and attach any of the following four schedules that apply.

- Schedule 1 to report your *interest income* or *dividend income* if either amount is more than $400, you claim the *exclusion of interest* from Series EE U.S. savings bonds, you received interest or dividends as a nominee, or you received a Form 1099–INT for tax-exempt interest.
- Schedule 2 to take the *credit for child and dependent care expenses.*
- Schedule 3 to take the *credit for the elderly or the disabled.*
- Schedule EIC to take the *earned income credit.*

Form 1040. If you file Form 1040, attach the necessary schedules or forms, such as:

- Schedule A to *itemize your deductions.*
- Schedule B to report over $400 in *interest or dividends* (including capital gain and nontaxable distributions), to answer the *foreign accounts* and *foreign trusts* questions, or if any of the following apply to you:
    - You claim the exclusion of interest from Series EE U.S. savings bonds,
    - You received interest or dividends as a nominee,
    - You received a Form 1099–INT for tax-exempt interest,
    - You reduce your interest income for amortizable bond premium or for accrued interest on a bond bought between interest payment dates, or
    - You received a Form 1099–OID showing a larger amount of original issue discount than you are required to report as income.
- Schedule C or Schedule C–EZ to report profit or loss subject to self-employment tax from a *business* you operated or a *profession* you practiced as a sole proprietor, and to report wages and expenses you had as a statutory employee.
- Schedule D to report *capital gains and losses.*
- Schedule E to report income or loss from *rental real estate, royalties, partnerships, estates, trusts, S corporations, and REMICs (residual interests).*
- Schedule EIC to claim the *earned income credit.*
- Schedule F to report *farm income and expenses.*

- Schedule R to claim the **credit for the elderly or the disabled.**
- Schedule SE to figure **self-employment tax.**

Foreign financial accounts and foreign trusts. You must complete Part III of Schedule B (Form 1040) if:

1) You received more than $400 in either interest or dividends, or
2) You had a foreign account or were the grantor of, or transferor to, a foreign trust.

If you checked *Yes* to the question on line 11a, Part III of Schedule B, you must file Form TD F 90–22.1, *Report of Foreign Bank and Financial Accounts,* by June 30, 1994, with the Department of the Treasury at the address shown on the form. Form TD F 90–22.1 is not a tax return, so do not attach it to your Form 1040. Be sure to file your Form 1040 with the IRS. You can get Form TD F 90–22.1 by using the order blank at the end of this publication.

For more information, see the instructions for Part III of Schedule B (Form 1040).

Assembling your return. Attach all forms and schedules behind Form 1040 in order of the "Attachment Sequence Number" shown in the upper right corner of the form or schedule. Attach all other statements or attachments at the end of your return, even if they relate to another form or schedule.

> ### TaxPlanner
>
> If you fail to organize your return according to the prescribed sequence numbers, the IRS, upon receipt of your return, will disassemble it and put it back together in the proper order. This procedure may result in the loss of a page of your return, causing some delay in its processing.

Form W–2. Form W–2, *Wage and Tax Statement,* is a statement from your employer of the wages and other compensation paid to you and the taxes withheld from your pay. You should have a Form W–2 from each employer. Be sure to attach the first copy or copy B of Form W–2 in the place indicated on the front of your return. For more information, see *Form W–2* in Chapter 5, *Tax Withholding and Estimated Tax.*

Signatures

You must sign and date your return. If you file a joint return, both you and your spouse must sign the return, even if only one of you had income.

Enter your occupation in the space provided in the signature section. If you file a joint return, enter both your occupation and your spouse's occupation.

If you prepare your own return, leave the space under your signature blank. If another person prepares your return and does not charge you, that person should not sign your return.

Paid preparer. Generally, anyone who is paid to prepare, assist in preparing, or review your tax return must sign it and fill in the other blanks in the paid preparer's area of your return. Paid preparers of Form 1040EZ must sign the return and provide all other required information at the bottom of the form below the area for the taxpayer's signature.

If the preparer is self-employed (that is, not employed by any person or business to prepare the return), he or she should check the self-employed box in the *Paid Preparer's Use Only* space on Form 1040 or Form 1040A.

Signature stamps and labels are not acceptable. The preparer must give you a copy of your return in addition to the copy filed with the IRS.

If you have questions about whether a preparer must sign your return, please contact any IRS office.

> ### TaxAlert
>
> A person who is paid to prepare all or a substantial portion of your income tax return must sign it. In addition, the IRS says that a tax consultant who is paid to review a tax return that you have already prepared and signed is also considered a tax return preparer and must sign it.
>
> If an individual who prepares your return refuses to sign it, you are probably dealing with someone you should not rely on. While you could still file the return, you should probably consider using another tax preparer. If you have to pay the first preparer, you should report the matter to the IRS.

Someone else can sign for you. You can appoint an agent to sign your return if you are:

1) Unable to sign the return because of disease or injury,
2) Absent from the United States for a continuous period of at least 60 days before the due date for filing your return, or
3) Given permission to do so by the IRS district director in your district.

Power of attorney. A return signed by an agent in any of these cases must have a power of attorney (POA) attached that authorizes the agent to sign for you. You can use a POA that states that the agent is granted authority to sign the return, or you can use Form 2848, *Power of Attorney and Declaration of Representative.* Part I of Form 2848 must state that the agent is granted authority to sign the return.

Unable to sign. If the taxpayer is mentally incompetent and cannot sign the return, it must be signed by a court-appointed representative who can act for the taxpayer.

If the taxpayer is mentally competent but physically unable to sign the return or POA, a valid "signature" is defined under state law. It can be anything that clearly indicates the taxpayer's intent to sign. For example, the taxpayer's "X" with the signatures of two witnesses might be considered a valid signature under a state's law.

Spouse unable to sign. If your spouse is unable to sign for any reason, see *Signing a Joint Return,* in Chapter 2, *Filing Status.*

Child's return. If a child is required to file a tax return but cannot sign the return, the child's parent, guardian, or another legally responsible person must sign the child's name, followed by the words "By (signature), parent (or guardian) for minor child."

Refunds

When you complete your return, you will determine if you paid more income tax than you owed. If so, you can get a refund of the amount you overpaid or, if you file Form 1040 or Form 1040A, you can choose to apply all or part of the overpayment to your next year's (1994) estimated tax.

Follow the instructions in your tax forms package to complete the entries to claim your refund and/or to apply your overpayment to your 1994 estimated tax.

Note. You cannot have your overpayment applied to your 1994 estimated tax if you file Form 1040EZ.

Explanation

If you choose to apply all or part of your overpayment to your next year's estimated tax, the estimated tax installment payment is considered made on April 15. Your first installment may be reduced accordingly. See Chapter 5, *Tax Withholding and Estimated Tax.*

Overpayment less than one dollar. If your overpayment is less than one dollar, you will not receive a refund unless you request it on a separate statement attached to your return.

Cashing your refund check. U.S. Government checks must be cashed within 12 months of the date they are issued. Checks not cashed within 12 months will be canceled and the proceeds returned to the IRS. Cash your tax refund check soon after you receive it.

If your check has been canceled, you can apply to the IRS to have it reissued.

Amount You Owe

When you complete your return, you will determine if you have paid the full amount of tax that you owe. If you owe additional tax, you should pay it with your return. If you owe less than one dollar, you need not pay it.

If the IRS figures your tax for you, you will receive a bill for any tax that is due. You should pay this bill within 30 days (or by the due date of your return, if later). See *Tax Figured by IRS* in Chapter 31, *How to Figure Your Tax.*

If you do not pay your tax when due, you may have to pay a failure-to-pay penalty. See *Penalties,* later. For more information about your balance due, see Publication 594, *Understanding the Collection Process.*

TAXALERT

To the extent you owe additional 1993 income taxes because of the new higher tax rates, you can elect on your 1993 income tax return to pay the additional 1993 tax in three equal installments. The installments are due each year on April 15 for calendar year taxpayers, beginning on April 15, 1994. No interest or underpayment of estimated tax penalty will be charged on the payments due that are attributable to the retroactive tax rate increase.

It is important to note that the ability to elect the installment payment provision only applies to tax increases that are a result of the increase in the regular tax rates and the application of the surtax. It does not include the increase in the alternative minimum tax rates. Therefore, if your 1993 tax liability is higher than it would have been under the old law due to the increase in the alternative minimum tax rates, that increase cannot be paid in three installments. It must be paid in full on April 15, 1994.

Example

Greg's 1993 federal tax liability is determined to be $70,038. Greg calculates that his 1993 federal tax liability would have been $65,552 under the tax rates in effect under the prior law. At first glance, it looks as if Greg can elect to pay the difference of $4,486 in three installments. However, Greg's 1993 alternative minimum tax is $68,600. Because the $68,600 is greater than the $65,552, he can only elect to pay $1,438 ($70,038 − $68,600) over three installments. If his 1993 alternative minimum tax had been under $65,552, he would have been able to pay the entire $4,486 in three installments.

Deferral of additional 1993 taxes. You may be able to elect to defer two-thirds of your additional 1993 taxes that are solely due to the rate increases reflected in the 1993 tax rate schedules. No interest or penalties are due on the deferred tax if paid on time.

If you make this election, you pay the additional 1993 taxes in three equal installments. You must pay the first installment by the due date of your 1993 return (without regard to extensions); the second installment by the date that is one year after that due date; and the third installment by the date that is 2 years after that due date. For calendar year taxpayers, those dates are April 15, 1994, April 17, 1995, and April 15, 1996. If you do not pay any installment on time, the entire unpaid tax will be due immediately upon notice and demand from the IRS.

Making the election. To make this election, you must complete **Form 8841,** *Deferral of Additional 1993 Taxes,* attach it to your original 1993 return, and file it by the due date (including extensions). You can use Form 8841 only if you do not owe alternative minimum tax for 1993 and your taxable income on Form 1040, line 37, exceeds the amount shown below for your filing status:

Married filing separately	$ 70,000
Single	$115,000
Head of household	$127,500
Married filing jointly	$140,000
Qualifying widow(er)	$140,000

Payment of first installment. You will be treated as having timely paid the first installment of your additional 1993 taxes only if your total tax payments made by April 15, 1994, are at least:

90% of your total tax (line 53, Form 1040), *minus*
Two-thirds of your additional 1993 taxes (line 26, Form 8841).

Interest

You will have to pay interest on any tax you owe that is not paid by the due date of your return. Interest is charged even if you get an extension of time for filing.

Note. If you choose to have the IRS figure your tax for you, interest cannot start earlier than the 31st day after the IRS sends you a bill. For information on this choice, see *Tax Figured by IRS* in Chapter 31, *How to Figure Your Tax.*

Interest on penalties. Interest is charged on the failure-to-file penalty, the accuracy-related penalty, and the fraud penalty from the due date of the return (including extensions) to the date of payment. Interest on other penalties starts on the date of notice and demand, but is not charged on penalties paid within 10 days from the date of the notice.

Interest due to IRS error or delay. All or part of any interest you were charged for a deficiency or payment can be forgiven if the interest is due to an error or delay by an officer or employee of the IRS in performing a ministerial act. This is a procedural or mechanical act that occurs during the processing of a taxpayer's case.

The interest can be forgiven only if you are not responsible in any important way for the error or delay and the IRS has notified you in writing of the deficiency or payment. For more information, get Publication 556, *Examination of Returns, Appeal Rights, and Claims for Refund.*

TaxPlanner

If you owe additional tax, it is *not* a good idea to file your return by January 31. As long as you have planned well and have paid enough in estimated taxes to avoid a penalty, you would be better off keeping any other tax you owe in your savings account, where it will earn interest for 2½ months, rather than paying your tax bill early.

How to Pay
If you pay by check or money order, make it out to *Internal Revenue Service.* Please write your correct name, address, social security number, daytime telephone number, and tax year and form number on the front of your check or money order.

For example, if you file Form 1040 for 1993 and you owe additional tax, write your name and address, social security number, daytime telephone number, and *1993 Form 1040* on your check or money order. If you file an amended return (Form 1040X) for 1992 and you owe tax, write your name and address, social security number, daytime telephone number, and *1992 Form 1040X* on the front of your check or money order. Be sure to attach your payment on top of any Forms W–2, 1099–R, etc. on the front of your return.

Your tax is not paid until your check or money order is paid (IRS receives the funds from your bank, etc.).

Do not mail cash with your return. If you pay cash at an IRS office, keep the receipt as part of your records.

Do not include any estimated tax payment in your check or money order that is payment for your 1993 income tax return. Mail the estimated tax payment separately to the address shown in the Form 1040–ES instructions. The address for mailing estimated tax payments is different from the address for sending your tax return.

Installment Agreement
If you cannot pay the full amount due with your return, you may ask to make monthly installment payments. However, you will be charged interest and a late payment penalty on the tax not paid by the due date even if your request to pay in installments is granted. To limit the interest and penalty charges, pay as much of the tax as possible with your return. But before requesting an installment agreement, you should consider other less costly alternatives, such as a bank loan.

To ask for an installment agreement, attach to the front of your return either a completed **Form 9465,** *Installment Agreement Request,* or your own written request. You can get Form 9465 by calling 1–800–TAX–FORM (1–800–829–3676). A written request should include your name, address, social security number, the amount owed, the amount paid with your return, and the amount and date you can pay each month. It should also include the tax year and the form number (Form 1040, Form 1040A, or Form 1040EZ). You should receive a response to your request for installments within 30 days. But if you file your return after March 31, it may take longer for a reply.

Gift To Reduce the Public Debt
You can make a contribution (gift) to reduce the public debt. If you wish to do so, enclose a *separate* check in the envelope with your income tax return, and make it payable to *Bureau of the Public Debt.* You can deduct this gift on next year's tax return if you

itemize your deductions. Please do not add it to any tax you owe. If you owe tax, include a separate check for the tax payable to *Internal Revenue Service.*

Where Do I File?
After you complete your return, you must send it to the IRS. You can mail it or you may be able to file it electronically.

Mailing Your Return
If an addressed envelope came with your tax forms package, you should mail your return using that envelope.

If you do not have an addressed envelope or if you moved during the year, mail your return to the Internal Revenue Service Center for the area where you now live. The street address of the Service Center is not needed. A list of Service Center addresses is shown on the inside back cover of this publication.

Electronic Filing
You may be able to have your return filed electronically instead of on a paper form. The electronic filing method can be used by many tax return preparers and other professional filers (who do not prepare returns but use this method to file returns already completed by taxpayers). These preparers and filers can send tax return information over telephone lines to an Internal Revenue Service Center. They will charge you for this service, but you will normally receive your refund sooner, and you may be able to have it deposited directly into your savings or checking account.

Electronic filing is available to preparers in all 50 states. Also, in some states, they can file an electronic state return simultaneously with the federal return.

Federal/State electronic filing is offered statewide in Indiana, Kansas, Louisiana, Mississippi, New Mexico, New York, North Carolina, South Carolina, Utah, West Virginia, and Wisconsin. It is also offered in limited programs in Arkansas, Colorado, Connecticut, Delaware, Idaho, Iowa, Kentucky, Maine, Michigan, Missouri, Nebraska, Oklahoma, and Oregon. In these states, check with your preparer to see whether you can participate in this program.

Advantages. Electronic filing can shorten the time for processing returns to within 3 weeks. Electronic filing uses automation to replace most of the manual steps needed to process paper returns. As a result, processing for electronic returns is faster and more accurate. However, errors on the return or problems with its transmission can delay processing.

Example
You expect a $3,000 refund. If you can receive your refund in 3 weeks by filing electronically instead of 3 months by filing a paper form, you could save money by investing the refund sooner. Assuming you can earn 7% after tax on your money, you might save $45. However, the company that files your return electronically will usually charge you a separate fee for this service. This should be considered in your decision to file electronically.

TaxAlert
Several states participated in electronic filing last year and more are expected this year. Check with your state to see if electronic filing is available.

Table 1-7. **Benefits of Filing Electronically**

Accuracy	• Computer programs can quickly catch mistakes before they become problems
Acknowledgement	• Receipt of return and any errors are transmitted back to the electronic filer fast (usually the next day)
Fast Refund	• Generally issued within three weeks
File Now, Pay Later	• File early and send balance due by April 15
Simultaneous Federal/State Filing	• Tax information for both state and federal returns can be sent together to IRS (see *Where Do I File?* for a list of participating states)

As with a paper return, you are responsible for making sure your return contains accurate information and is filed on time. Electronic filing does not affect your chances of an IRS examination of your return.

Form 8453. Your preparer will ask you to sign Form 8453, *U.S. Individual Income Tax Declaration for Electronic Filing.* Both spouses must sign if a joint return is being filed. Your preparer will file the form with the IRS. Your signature on the declaration form:

- Certifies that the information on Form 8453 is correct and corresponds to the information on your return,
- Authorizes your preparer to file your return electronically,
- Authorizes the IRS, if you elect direct deposit, to deposit your refund directly into your checking or savins account or inform your preparer if the direct deposit will not be made, and
- Authorizes the IRS to disclose to the preparer when your refund was sent and the reasons for any delay in the processing of your return or refund.

Your preparer will give you the required preparer-signed copy of your return, including a copy of the completed Form 8453. This material is for your records. Do not mail this copy to the IRS; if you do, your refund may be delayed.

Balance due. If you have a balance due with your return, you must make a full payment of any tax due on or before April 15, 1994 to avoid penalties and interest. Mail the payment with **Form 9282**, *Form 1040 Electronic Payment Voucher,* which will be provided by the preparer.

Explanation: Composition of an Electronic Return

In total, an electronic return contains the same information as a comparable return filed entirely on paper documents.

An electronic return consists of:

1. Electronic portion of return—Data transmitted to the IRS electronically
2. Nonelectronic portion of return—Paper documents (filed with the IRS at a later date) that contain information that cannot be electronically transmitted, such as taxpayer signatures, documents prepared by third parties, and so on.

Electronic Portion of Return

For 1993 returns, most forms and schedules, including Form 1040 and Form 1040A, can be transmitted electronically and are considered the "electronic portion" of the return.

Nonelectronic Portion of Return

Some parts of your return *cannot* be filed electronically, including the following:

- Form 8453, U.S. Individual Income Tax Declaration for Electronic Filing, required for all electronic returns
- Copy B Forms W-2, W-2G, or 1099-R, which would normally be attached to the front of a paper return
- Other information documents that are voluntarily being included with the return by the taxpayer as supporting material

Exclusions from Electronic Filing

The following are some of the types of returns that are excluded from electronic filing:

Decedent returns, including joint returns filed by surviving spouses

Returns with a power of attorney currently in effect for the refund to be sent to a third party

Returns subject to community property rules with filing status "Married Filing Separately"

Returns with social security numbers within the range 900-00-0000 through 999-99-9998. These are temporary social security numbers.

Refunds. You can have a refund check mailed to you, or you can elect to have your refund deposited directly to your savings or checking account.

Direct deposit. To choose direct deposit of your refund, complete Part II of Form 8453. Your signature in Part III gives IRS your authorization to deposit the refund. Your signature also gives IRS permission to notify your preparer whether the direct deposit request will be honored.

Errors in direct deposit information will cause delays in processing your refund. Review the information carefully. Make sure the "routing transit number" (RTN) of your financial institution contains 9 digits. Your return will be rejected if there are fewer than 9 digits. If this occurs, your electronic filer will be notified.

Your request for direct deposit may not be honored if one of the following occurs:

• You owe federal tax, a student loan, child support, or debts to other federal agencies.
• The IRS has certain special processing needs. (IRS will notify you and a paper check will be sent to you.)

Once an electronic return has been accepted by IRS, you cannot cancel the direct deposit election nor can you change your RTN or bank account number.

Explanation: Direct Deposit

Direct Deposit refunds will usually be issued 2 to 3 weeks from the date the electronic return is accepted. However, the Treasury Department does not guarantee that a refund will be issued by a specific date or for the anticipated amount.

The following conditions may delay refunds and/or change refund amounts. Direct Deposit elections generally will not be honored in these cases:

1. Taxpayer owes back taxes, either individual or business.
2. Taxpayer owes delinquent child support.
3. Taxpayer has a certain delinquent debt, such as student loans, and so on.
4. The last name and social security number of the primary taxpayer must be the same as on last year's return, or the return will be delayed at least 1 week for rematching.
5. The estimated tax payments reported on the return do not match the estimated tax payments recorded on the IRS master file. This generally occurs when:
   a. The spouse made separate payments and filed a joint return, or vice versa; or
   b. The return was filed before the January 17, 1994 estimated tax payment was credited to the taxpayer's account.
6. The taxpayer has a Schedule E claiming a deduction for a questionable tax shelter.
7. The taxpayer is claiming a blatantly unallowable deduction.

TAXPLANNER

A refund anticipation loan (RAL) is a loan made to you based on your expected refund. The loan is a contract between you and a financial institution. Generally, the financial institution will require that you sign an authorization that permits the institution to debit your account after the refund has been credited to it. You can expect to pay a fee to the electronic filer, who with your permission submits information to the financial institution, and a fee to the financial institution. These fees are in addition to the tax preparation fee and electronic filing fee. Generally, Direct Deposit takes 2 to 3 weeks before you receive your refund. An RAL could speed up the time for you to have your money by about 2 weeks but at a relatively high "interest cost." For example, if your expected refund is $1,000 and the fee is $30, the "interest cost" to you for the 2 weeks' use of the money comes to over 75% on an annualized basis.

Tele-Tax information. For more information on electronic filing, a recorded message is available on the Tele-Tax system. The Tele-Tax number for your area is located near the end of this publication. You can also call toll-free 1–800–TAX–1040 (1–800–829–1040) for more information. Ask for electronic filing information.

Refund inquiries. The IRS will notify your preparer of the date your electronic return was accepted for processing. If you do not receive your refund within 3 weeks after the return was accepted by IRS, you can call Tele-Tax Automated Refund Information. The Tele-Tax number for your area is listed at the back of this publication. Before you call Tele-Tax, please have the following information from your return available:

• The first social security number shown on the return,
• Your filing status, and
• The exact amount of your refund.

If the Tele-Tax recording tells you the date your refund was issued, you should receive the refund within a week of that date. If you do not receive the refund by the end of that week, contact your IRS office. See the telephone numbers listed under *Call the IRS With Your Tax Question* at the back of this publication.

If Tele-Tax has no information on your return, contact your preparer for the date IRS accepted your return. If your return was accepted more than 3 weeks ago, contact your local IRS office. Explain that you filed your return electronically and that Tele-Tax has no information on it. Also, provide the first social security number shown on your return and the date the IRS accepted your return.

Computerized Returns

Almost anyone who files a tax return can now file a Form 1040PC return. Form 1040PC is prepared on a personal computer that automatically prints the return in a three column "answer sheet" format. It prints the line numbers, dollar amounts, and when called for, brief descriptions. For example, a lengthy 11-page return requiring forms and schedules can print out to a two-page Form 1040PC return.

Form 1040PC tax preparation software is checked and accepted by the IRS. It can be processed faster and more accurately than the regular tax return. Software packages are available at many computer software stores. They are not available from the IRS. For more information, call the Tele-Tax number for your area listed near the end of this publication.

Explanation

You may now use Form 1040PC tax preparation software to file your tax return with the IRS. The software automatically prints the return in a three column "answer sheet" format that is accepted by the IRS. Form 1040PC tax preparation software is available at many computer software stores.

What Happens After I File?

After you send your return to IRS, you may have some questions. This section discusses some concerns that you may have about recordkeeping, your refund, and errors on your return.

What Records Should I Keep?

You must keep records so that you can prepare a complete and accurate income tax return. The law does not require any special form of records. However, you should keep all receipts, canceled checks or other proof of payment, and documentation to support any deductions or credits you claim.

If you file a claim for refund, you must be able to prove by your records that you have overpaid your tax.

> **TaxPlanner**
>
> See the detailed listing of tax records to keep on page xxxii at the end of the Ernst & Young Tax Organizer in the front of this book.

How long to keep records. You must keep your records for as long as they are important for any Internal Revenue law.

Keep records that support an item of income or a deduction appearing on a return until the period of limitations for the return runs out. (A period of limitations is the limited period of time after which no legal action can be brought.) Usually this is 3 years from the date the return was filed, or 2 years from the date the tax was paid, whichever date is later. Returns filed before the due date are treated as filed on the due date.

If income that should have been reported on your return was not reported, and it is more than 25% of the income shown on the return, the period of limitations does not run out until 6 years after the return was filed. If a return is false or fraudulent with intent to evade tax, or if no return is filed, an action can generally be brought at any time.

In property transactions, the basis of new or replacement property may depend on the basis of the old property. Keep the records of transactions relating to the basis of property for as long as they are important in figuring the basis of the original or replacement property. See Chapter 14, *Basis of Property,* for information on determining basis.

Copies of returns. You should keep copies of tax returns you have filed and the tax return package as part of your records. They may be helpful in amending filed returns or preparing future ones.

If you need a copy of a prior year tax return, you can obtain it from the IRS. Use **Form 4506.** There is a charge for a copy of a return, which must be paid with Form 4506.

You can also use Form 4506 to request a tax return transcript showing most lines from your original return, including accompanying forms and schedules.

Tax account information only. If you need a statement of your tax account showing any later changes that you or the IRS made to the original return, you will need to request tax account information.

Do not use Form 4506 for tax account information. Instead, contact your local IRS office. You should have your name, social security number or employer identification number (if applicable), tax period, and form number available. You will receive the following information **free** of charge:

- Type of return filed
- Filing status
- Federal income tax withheld
- Tax shown on return
- Adjusted gross income
- Taxable income
- Self-employment tax
- Number of exemptions

- Amount of refund
- Amount of earned income credit

> **TaxPlanner**
>
> We recommend that you keep all your cancelled checks for 6 years. It would be wise to keep your income tax returns permanently. You should keep documents showing your basis in a piece of property for as long as you own that piece of property. If you sell a piece of property, you should keep your records showing your basis in the old property for at least 6 years after the sale.
>
> If you do not keep the requisite records, it may be impossible for you to prove that you incurred deductible expenses or to establish your basis for gain or loss. Without such proof, the IRS can deny you a deduction. If you acquire property from an estate or by gift, it is advisable to secure a copy of the valuation of the estate or of the gift tax return so that you can determine the donor's basis in the property that you have been given. Knowing the donor's basis, you can easily determine your gain or loss when you sell the property. See Chapter 14, *Basis of Property,* for more details on determining gains and losses from the sale of property.
>
> **Example**
>
> Your parents buy a house for you as a wedding present. You sell the house 10 years later. The only record of the initial transaction is in the county real estate records. You believe there were other costs associated with the purchase, but you cannot find any records of them. If you claim the additional unsupported costs and the IRS examines your return for the year of the sale, it's likely that those costs will not be allowed. If you claim the additional costs and do not disclose on your return the lack of records to substantiate them, you could be subject to a penalty.

For more information on recordkeeping, get Publication 552, *Recordkeeping for Individuals.*

Interest on Refunds

If you are due a refund, you may also be entitled to receive interest on your overpayment. The interest rates are adjusted quarterly.

If the refund is made within 45 days after the due date of your return, no interest will be paid. If you file your return after the due date (including extensions), no interest will be paid if the refund is made within 45 days after the date you filed. If the refund is not made within this 45–day period, interest will be paid from the due date of the return or from the date you filed, whichever is later.

For determining whether you are entitled to any interest on a refund, your return will be treated as filed when all of the following steps are completed:

1) It is filed on a permitted form,
2) It contains information that identifies you,
3) It is signed by you, and
4) It contains sufficient information for mathematical verification of the tax liability shown on the return.

Accepting a refund check does not change your right to claim an additional refund and interest. File your claim within the applicable period of time. See *Amended Returns and Claims for Refund,* later. If you do not accept a refund check, no more interest will be paid on the amount of the overpayment included in the check.

Interest on erroneous refund. All or part of any interest you were charged on an erroneous refund generally will be forgiven. Any interest charged for the period before demand for repayment was made will be forgiven unless:

1) You, or a person related to you, caused the erroneous refund in any way, or
2) The refund is more than $50,000.

For example, if you claimed a refund of $100 on your return, but the IRS made an error and sent you $1,000, you would not be charged interest for the time you held the $900 difference. You must, however, repay the $900 when requested by the IRS.

Offset Against Debts

If you are due a refund but have not paid certain obligations, all or part of your overpayment of tax may be used to pay all or part of the past-due amount. This includes past-due income tax, other federal debts (such as student loans), and child and spousal support payments. The IRS will notify you if the refund you claimed has been offset against your debts.

Joint return and injured spouse. When a joint return is filed and only one spouse is obligated to pay past-due child and spousal support or a federal debt, the spouse who is not obligated for the debt can be considered an *injured spouse.* An injured spouse can obtain a refund for his or her share of the overpayment that would otherwise be used to pay the past-due amount.

To be considered an injured spouse, you must:

1) File a joint return,
2) Have received income (such as wages, interest, etc.),
3) Have made tax payments (such as federal income tax withheld from wages or estimated tax payments),
4) Report the income and tax payments on the joint return, and
5) Have an overpayment, all or part of which may be applied against the past-due amount.

If you are an injured spouse, you can obtain your portion of the joint refund by completing **Form 8379,** *Injured Spouse Claim and Allocation.* Follow the instructions on the back of the form.

Note. Refunds that involve community property states must be divided according to local law. If you live in a community property state in which all community property is subject to the debts of either spouse, your entire refund is subject to offset. You do not qualify for injured spouse status.

Change of Address

If you move, always notify in writing the Internal Revenue Service Center where you filed your last return, or the Chief, Taxpayer Service Division, in your local IRS district office. You can use **Form 8822,** *Change of Address,* to notify us of your new address. If you move after filing your return and you are expecting a refund, also notify the post office servicing your old address. This will help to forward your check to your new address.

Be sure to include your social security number (and the name and social security number of your spouse, if you filed a joint return) in any correspondence with the IRS.

Past-Due Refund

If you do not get your refund within 8 weeks after filing your return, call your IRS office or write to the Service Center where you filed your return. Be sure to include your name, address, daytime telephone number, and social security number (and the name and social security number of your spouse, if you filed a joint return) in any letter you send to the IRS. Also have the social security number(s) available if you call the IRS.

Telephone service for tax refund information. You may be able to call a telephone number for your area to find out the status of your income tax refund. For details on how to use this telephone service, see *What Is Tele-Tax?,* at the end of this publication. Please wait 8 weeks after filing your 1993 tax return before using this service. However, if you filed your return electronically, see *Where Do I File?,* earlier, for information about refund inquiries when you file an electronic return.

What If I Made a Mistake?

If there is an error on your tax return, you may have to pay one or more penalties. If you discover an error, you can file an amended return or claim for refund.

Penalties

The law provides penalties for failure to file returns or pay taxes as required.

Civil Penalties

If you do not file your return and pay your tax by the due date, you may have to pay a penalty. You may also have to pay a penalty if you substantially understate your tax, file a frivolous return, or fail to supply your social security number. If you provide fraudulent information on your return, you may have to pay a civil fraud penalty.

Filing late. If you do not file your return by the due date (including extensions), you may have to pay a *failure-to-file* penalty. The penalty is based on the tax not paid by the due date (without regard to extensions). The penalty is usually 5% for each month or part of a month that a return is late, but not more than 25% of your tax.

Fraud. If your failure to file is due to fraud, the penalty is 15% for each month or part of a month that your return is late, up to a maximum of 75% of your tax.

Return over 60 days late. If you file your return more than 60 days after the due date or extended due date, the minimum penalty is the lesser of $100 or 100% of the balance of tax due.

Exception. You will not have to pay the penalty if you show that you failed to file on time because of reasonable cause and not because of willful neglect.

Paying tax late. You will have to pay a *failure-to-pay* penalty of ½ of 1% of your unpaid taxes for each month, or part of a month, after the due date that the tax is not paid. This penalty does not apply during the extension period available by filing Form 4868, *Application for Automatic Extension of time To File U.S. Individual Income Tax Return,* if you paid at least 90% of your actual tax liability before the original due date of your return through withholding on wages, estimated tax payments, or a payment sent in with Form 4868.

If a notice of intent to levy is issued, the rate will increase to 1% at the start of the first month beginning at least 10 days after the day that the notice is issued. If a notice and demand for immediate payment is issued, the rate will increase to 1% at the start of the first month beginning after the day that the notice and demand is issued.

This penalty cannot be more than 25% of your unpaid tax. You will not have to pay the penalty if you can show that you had a good reason for not paying your tax on time. This failure-to-pay penalty is added to interest charges on late payments.

Combined penalties. If both the failure-to-file penalty and the failure-to-pay penalty (discussed earlier) apply in any month, the 5% (or 15%) failure-to-file penalty is reduced by the failure-to-pay penalty. However, if you file your return more than 60 days after the due date or extended due date, the minimum penalty is the lesser of $100 or 100% of the balance of tax due.

Accuracy-related penalty. You may have to pay an accuracy-related penalty if:

1) There is any underpayment of tax on your return due either to "negligence" or to "disregard" of rules or regulations, or
2) You substantially understate your income tax.

The penalty is equal to 20% of the underpayment. Each term is discussed later.

The penalty will not be figured on any part of an underpayment on which a fraud penalty (discussed later) is charged.

Negligence or disregard. The term "negligence" includes a failure to make a reasonable attempt to comply with the tax law or to exercise ordinary and reasonable care in preparing a return. Negligence also includes failure to keep adequate books and records. The term "disregard" includes any careless, reckless, or intentional disregard.

The penalty is based on the part of the underpayment due to negligence or disregard of rules or regulations, not on the entire underpayment on the return.

TAXPLANNER

The IRS has a comprehensive program to compare the amounts of income reported as paid by payers on Form 1099 series information returns with the amounts of income reported by the payees in their income tax returns. If this document-matching program discloses apparently underreported income, you will receive a notice of additional tax due that likely will include imposition of a 20% negligence penalty. If you receive an information return showing income paid to you that through no fault of your own you did not receive in 1993 or that for some reason is not taxable to you, you should nevertheless report as income on your return the entire amount shown by the information return and subtract from that the amount you believe to be erroneous. Following this procedure usually will avoid automatic generation of the IRS notice and the inconvenience and frustration of corresponding with the IRS to get the matter resolved.

Adequate disclosure. The penalty for negligence or disregard of rules or regulations may be avoided if you adequately disclose a nonfrivolous position on the return or can show reasonable cause and good faith for the tax treatment of a particular item.

To make this adequate disclosure, see *Disclosure statement,* later.

Substantial understatement of income tax. You understate the tax if the tax shown on your return is less than the correct tax. You substantially understate your tax if the understatement is more than the larger of 10% of the correct tax or $5,000. However, the penalty is reduced to the extent that there is:

1) Substantial authority, or
2) Adequate disclosure.

Substantial authority. If there is substantial authority for the tax treatment of an item, the item is treated as if it were shown properly on the return. For tax shelter items, this exception applies only if you reasonably believed that the tax treatment was more likely than not the correct treatment.

Whether there is or was substantial authority depends on the facts and circumstances. Consideration will be given to court opinions, Treasury regulations, revenue rulings, revenue procedures, and notices and announcements issued by the IRS and published in the *Internal Revenue Bulletin* that involve the same or similar circumstances as yours.

Disclosure statement. Except in the case of a tax shelter item, the understatement may also be reduced if you have adequately disclosed the relevant facts about the tax treatment of the item. To make this disclosure, use **Form 8275,** *Disclosure Statement.*

In cases of substantial overstatement only, items that meet the requirements of Revenue Procedure 92-23, 1992-13 I.R.B. 21 (or later update), are considered adequately disclosed on your return without filing Form 8275. This revenue procedure is updated annually.

Use **Form 8275–R,** *Regulation Disclosure Statement,* to disclose items or positions contrary to regulations. You cannot use Form 8275 for this purpose.

Explanation

The IRS explanation of the penalty for substantial understatement and how to avoid it oversimplifies a very complex situation.

Under regulations issued by the IRS, the following items may generally be considered substantial authority:

- Internal Revenue Code and other statutory provisions
- Temporary and final IRS regulations
- Court cases
- Administrative pronouncements (including revenue rulings and revenue procedures)
- Tax treaties and regulations issued as a result of a treaty
- Congressional intent as reflected in committee reports, joint explanatory statements of managers included in conference committee reports, and statements made in Congress by one of a bill's managers prior to enactment of a bill
- General explanations of tax legislation prepared by the Joint Committee on Taxation (the Blue Book).
- Proposed IRS regulations
- Information or press releases, notices, announcements, and any other similar documents published by the IRS in the Internal Revenue Bulletin
- Private letter rulings, technical advice memoranda, actions on decisions, and general counsel memoranda after they have been released to the public, if they are dated after December 31, 1984

Reasonable cause. You will not have to pay a penalty if you show a good reason (reasonable cause) for giving special tax treatment to a particular item.

Penalty for frivolous return. You may have to pay a penalty of $500 if you file a frivolous return. A frivolous return is one that does not include enough information to figure the correct tax or that contains information clearly showing that the tax you reported is substantially incorrect.

You will have to pay the penalty if you filed this kind of return because of a frivolous position on your part or a desire to delay or interfere with the administration of federal income tax laws. This includes altering or striking out the preprinted language above the space provided for your signature.

This penalty is added to any other penalty provided by law.

Explanation

Congress enacted this penalty to attack a great variety of tax protest activities, including:

1. Irregular tax forms not in processible form
2. References to spurious constitutional arguments as a basis for not completing tax forms
3. Unallowable deductions claimed as a protest against military expenses
4. Deliberate use of incorrect Tax Tables
5. Presentation of clearly inconsistent information, such as a taxpayer who lists only two dependents while claiming 99 exemptions for withholding purposes

TaxAlert

Unlike most other penalties, the penalty for filing a frivolous return is not based on your tax liability. The penalty for filing a frivolous return will be assessed immediately and added to many other penalties.

The penalty must be paid in full upon notice and demand from IRS even if you protest the penalty.

Fraud penalty. If there is any underpayment of tax on your return due to fraud, a penalty of 75% of the underpayment due to fraud will be added to your tax.

Joint return. The fraud penalty on a joint return does not apply to a spouse unless some part of the underpayment is due to the fraud of that spouse.

Penalty for failure to supply social security number. If you do not include your social security number or the social security number of another person, including your dependent, where required on a return, statement, or other document, (other than returns or statements related to interest, dividends, or patronage dividends), you will be subject to a penalty of $50 for *each* failure. You will also be subject to the penalty of $50 if you do not give your social security number to another person when it is required on a return, statement, or other document.

For example, if you have a bank account that earns interest, you must give your social security number to the bank. The number must be shown on the Form 1099–INT or other statement the bank sends you. If you do not give the bank your social security number, you will be subject to the $50 penalty. (You also may be subject to "backup" withholding of income tax. See Chapter 5, *Tax Withholding and Estimated Tax.*)

You will not have to pay the penalty if you are able to show that the failure was due to reasonable cause and not willful neglect.

Penalty for failure to furnish tax shelter registration number. A person who sells (or otherwise transfers) to you an interest in a tax shelter must give you the tax shelter registration number or be subject to a $100 penalty. If you claim any deduction, credit, or other tax benefit because of the tax shelter, you must **Form 8271**, *Investor Reporting of Tax Shelter Registration Number,* to

your return to report this number. You will have to pay a penalty of $250 for each failure to report a tax shelter registration number on your return. The penalty can be excused if you have a reasonable cause for not reporting the number.

Criminal Penalties

You may be subject to criminal prosecution (brought to trial) for actions such as:

1) Tax evasion.
2) Willful failure to file a return, supply information, or pay any tax due.
3) Fraud and false statements.
4) Preparing and filing a fraudulent return.

TaxAlert

In addition to any of the other penalties discussed in this section, you can be charged a penalty for paying your tax with a bad check. The penalty may not be imposed if you submit a bad check in good faith and with reasonable cause to believe that it will be paid. The penalty is 2% of the amount of the check or, if the check is less than $750, the lesser of $15 or the amount of the check.

Amended Returns and Claims for Refund

You should correct your return if, after you have filed it, you find that:

1) You did not report some income,
2) You claimed deductions or credits you should not have claimed,
3) You did not claim deductions or credits you could have claimed, or
4) You should have claimed a different filing status. (You cannot change your filing status from married filing jointly to married filing separately after the due date of the original return. However, an executor may be able to make this change for a deceased spouse.)

If you need a copy of your return, see *Copies of returns* under *What Records Should I Keep?,* earlier in this chapter.

Form 1040X. Use Form 1040X, *Amended U.S. Individual Income Tax Return,* to correct the Form 1040, Form 1040A, or Form 1040EZ you have already filed.

Completing Form 1040X. On Form 1040X, write your income, deductions, and credits as you originally reported them on your return, the changes you are making, and the corrected amounts. Then figure the tax on the corrected amount and the amount you owe or your refund. If you owe tax, pay the full amount with Form 1040X using *Form 1040X Payment-Voucher.* The tax owed will not be subtracted from any amount you had credited to your estimated tax. If you overpaid tax, a refund will be sent separately from any refund shown on your original return.

Filing Form 1040X. After you finish your Form 1040X, check it to be sure that it is complete. Do not forget to show the year of your original return and explain all changes you made. Be sure to attach any forms or schedules needed to explain your changes. Mail your Form 1040X to the Internal Revenue Service Center serving the area where you now live (as shown in the instructions to the form).

A separate form must be filed for each tax year or period involved.

Time for filing a claim for refund. Generally, you must file your claim for a credit or refund within 3 years from the date your original return was filed or within 2 years from the date the tax was paid, whichever is later. Returns filed before the due date (without regard to extensions) are considered to have been filed on the due date (even if the due date was a Saturday, Sunday, or legal holiday).

If the last day for claiming a credit or refund is a Saturday, Sunday, or legal holiday, the claim is considered timely if it is filed on the next business day.

If you do not file a claim within this period, you may not be entitled to a credit or a refund.

Note. If you did not file an original return, you must file a claim for refund within 2 years from the time the tax was paid.

Limit on amount of refund. If you file your claim within 3 years after the date you filed your return, the credit or refund cannot be more than the part of the tax paid within the 3 years (plus any extension of time for filing your return) before you filed the claim.

Tax paid. Payments made before the due date (without regard to extensions) of the original return are considered paid on the due date. Examples include federal income tax withheld from wages and estimated income tax.

Example 1. You made estimated tax payments of $500 and got an automatic extension of time to August 15, 1990, to file your 1989 income tax return. When you filed your return on that date, you paid an additional $200 tax. On August 15, 1993, you filed an amended return and claimed a refund of $700. Because you filed within the 3 years plus the 4–month extension period, you received a refund of $700.

Example 2. The situation is the same as in Example 1, except you filed your return on October 31, 1990, 2½ months after the extension period ended. You paid an additional $200 on that date. On October 26, 1993, you filed an amended return and claimed a refund of $700. Although you filed your claim within 3 years from the date you filed your original return, the refund was limited to $200. The estimated tax of $500 was paid before the 3 years plus the 4–month extension period.

If you file a claim after the 3–year period, but within 2 years from the time you paid the tax, the credit or refund cannot be more than the tax you paid within the 2 years immediately before you file the claim.

Example. You filed your 1989 tax return on April 16, 1990. You paid taxes of $500. On November 4, 1991, after an examination of your 1989 return, you had to pay an additional tax of $200. On May 3, 1993, you file a claim for a refund of $300. However, your refund will be limited to the $200 you paid during the 2 years immediately before you filed your claim.

Exceptions for special types of refunds. If you file a claim for one of the items listed below, the dates and limits discussed earlier (under *Time for filing a claim for refund* and *Limit on amount of refund*) may not apply. These special types of refunds are:

- A bad debt.
- A worthless security.

- Foreign tax paid or accrued.
- Net operating loss carryback.
- Carryback of certain tax credits.
- A claim based on an agreement with the Service extending the period for assessment of tax.
- An injured spouse claim.

Processing claims for refund. It often takes 2 to 3 months to process a claim. Your claim may be accepted as filed or may be subject to examination. If a claim is examined, the procedures are the same as in the examination of a tax return.

However, you should request in writing that your claim be immediately rejected if:

> You are filing a claim for a credit or refund based solely on contested income tax or on estate tax or gift tax issues considered in your previously examined returns, and
> You want to take your case to court instead of appealing it within the IRS.

You must file a timely claim with the IRS before going to court.

A notice of claim disallowance will then be promptly sent to you. You have 2 years from the date of mailing of the notice of disallowance to file a refund suit in the United States District Court having jurisdiction or in the United States Claims Court.

TAXPLANNER

The IRS routinely shares information with most states that have state income taxes. If you file an amended federal tax return showing a balance due, you can avoid interest on tax due to the state and any penalties by taking the initiative and filing amended state tax returns when that is appropriate.

Reduced refund. Your refund may be reduced by an additional tax liability that has been assessed against you.

Also, your refund may be reduced by amounts you owe for past-due child support or debts to another federal agency. The IRS will notify you if this happens. The refund procedures discussed in this chapter will not be available to you to get back the reduction. However, if you are the spouse of a person who owes past-due amounts for these obligations and the reduced refund relates to an overpayment on a joint return, you may be able to get a refund of your share of the overpayment before or after it is used to pay the past-due amount. See *Offset Against Debts,* earlier.

Affect on state tax liability. If your return is changed for any reason, it may affect your state income tax liability. This includes changes made as a result of an examination of your return by the IRS. Contact your state tax agency for more information.

2 | Filing Status

Introduction

*One of the first things to determine in preparing your income tax return is your filing status. There are five possible choices: **single, married filing jointly, married filing separately, unmarried head of household,** and **qualifying widow or widower** with dependent child.*

*Your choice of filing status dictates which Tax Table or Tax Rate Schedule you will use in calculating your tax liability; whether you may claim an **exemption** for a **dependent** or whether you may be claimed as a dependent; and how much income you can have before you are taxed at all.*

This chapter helps you decide which filing status you should choose so that you pay the least amount of tax.

This chapter discusses which filing status you should use. There are five filing statuses to choose from:

This chapter discusses which filing status you should use. There are five filing statuses to choose from:

- Single
- Married Filing Jointly
- Married Filing Separately
- Head of Household
- Qualifying Widow(er) With Dependent Child

If more than one filing status applies to you, choose the one that will give you the lowest tax.

Your filing status is a category that identifies you based on your marital and family situation. State law governs whether you are married, divorced, or legally separated under a decree of divorce or separate maintenance.

Explanation

If your filing status changes during the year, you may not file under one status for one part of that year and under a second status for the remainder of the year. The law requires that your filing status for the entire year be determined by your status on the last day of the tax year.

Your filing status is an important factor in determining whether you are required to file (see Chapter 1, *Filing Information*), the amount of your standard deduction (see Chapter 20, *Standard Deduction*), and your correct amount of tax (see Chapter 31, *How to Figure Your Tax*). Your filing status is also important in determining whether you can take other deductions and credits.

You must indicate your filing status by checking the appropriate box on line 1 of Form 1040EZ or on lines 1 through 5 of Form 1040 or Form 1040A.

There are different tax rates for different filing statuses. To determine your correct amount of tax, use the column in the Tax Table or Tax Rate Schedule in your forms package that applies to your filing status.

Useful Items

You may want to see:

Publication

☐ **501** Exemptions, Standard Deduction, and Filing Information
☐ **519** U.S. Tax Guide for Aliens
☐ **555** Federal Tax Information on Community Property

Form (and Instructions)

☐ **1040X** Amended U.S. Individual Income Tax Return

Single

Your filing status is *single* if you are unmarried or separated from your spouse by a divorce or separate maintenance decree, and you do not qualify for another filing status. However, if you were considered married for part of the year and lived in a community property state (listed under *Married Filing Separately),* special rules may apply in determining your income and expenses. See Publication 555 for more information.

Your filing status may be single if you were widowed before January 1, 1993, and did not remarry in 1993. However, you may be able to use another filing status that will give you a lower tax. See *Head of Household* and *Qualifying Widow(er) With Dependent Child* to see if you qualify.

You may file Form 1040EZ (if you have no dependents and are under 65 and not blind), Form 1040A, or Form 1040. Show your filing status as single by checking the box on line 1. Use the *Single* column of the Tax Table, or *Schedule X* of the Tax Rate Schedules, to figure your tax.

Married Filing Jointly

You may choose *married filing jointly* as your filing status if you are married and both you and your spouse agree to file a joint return. On a joint return, you report your combined income and deduct your combined allowable expenses.

If you and your spouse decide to file a joint return, your tax may be lower than the tax for the other filing statuses. Also, your standard deduction (if you do not itemize deductions) may be higher, and you may qualify for tax benefits that do not apply to other filing statuses. You may file a joint return even if one of you had no income or deductions. If you and your spouse each have income, you may want to figure your tax both on a joint return and on separate returns (using the filing status of married filing separately). Choose the method that gives you the lower tax.

If you file as married filing jointly, you may use Form 1040EZ, Form 1040A, or Form 1040. You select this filing status by checking the box on line 1 of Form 1040EZ or line 2 on Form 1040A or Form 1040. You figure your tax by using the *Married filing jointly* column of the Tax Table, or *Schedule Y–1* of the Tax Rate Schedules.

Married Taxpayers

You are considered married for the whole year if on the last day of your tax year you are either:

1) Married and living together as husband and wife,
2) Living together in a **common law marriage** that is recognized in the state where you now live or in the state where the common law marriage began,
3) Married and living apart, but not legally separated under a decree of divorce or separate maintenance, or
4) Separated under an interlocutory (not final) decree of divorce. For purposes of filing a joint return, you are not considered divorced.

Explanation

Marriage tax penalty. Marriage partners who earn approximately the same income may pay more tax if they file a joint return or file separate married returns than they would if they could file two single returns. This is known as "the marriage tax penalty."

Example

John and Mary were both employed during the year. Mary had a **gross income** of $30,000, and John earned $28,000. If John and Mary were wed before the end of the year, their joint tax liability after deducting personal exemptions and the standard deduction would be $8,391. However, if they postponed their marriage until next year, their combined tax liabilities for the current year, filing as single taxpayers, would be as follows:

Mary's tax	$3,833
John's tax	3,293
Total	$7,126

Thus, there is a marriage tax penalty of $1,265. One possible solution would be to delay getting married.

Explanation

Singles' tax penalty. A single person earning the same **taxable income** as a married person whose spouse has comparatively little taxable income will pay substantially more income tax than the married person. In other words, if you marry somebody with little or no taxable income, your tax decreases. This is known as "the singles' tax penalty."

Example

Assume the same facts as in the above example, except that John only had $300 of interest income. If John and Mary were married before December 31, 1993, their joint tax liability on the gross income $30,300 would be $2,910. If they married after the end of the year, their combined tax liabilities in the current year, filing as singles taxpayers, would be as follows:

Mary's tax:	$3,833
John's tax:	0
Total:	$3,833

Thus, there is a singles' tax penalty of $923. One possible solution would be to get married quickly.

TAXSAVER 1

When to get married. If you are contemplating a winter marriage and one of you has more income than the other, choose December instead of January if you want to save on your taxes. If you have similar incomes, choose January.

TAXSAVER 2

If you are at least 55 years old and you are planning to marry someone else who is at least 55, and if both of you own principal residences with low tax bases, both of you should consider selling prior to marriage. In this way, both of you may get the one-time, $125,000 tax-free **exclusion** that is available to all individuals 55 and older who sell their homes. For this exclusion, a taxpayer's filing status is determined as of the date of the sale. If you both sell your homes on December 30 while still unmarried, you will qualify for two one-time exclusions. If you then marry on December 31, you may file a joint return for that year. For more details, see Chapter 16, *Selling Your Home.*

Spouse died during the year. If your spouse died during the year, you are considered married for the whole year for filing status purposes.

If you did not remarry before the end of the tax year, you may file a joint return for yourself and your deceased spouse. See *Final Return for the Decedent* in Chapter 4, *Decendents.* For the next 2 years, you may be entitled to the special benefits described later under *Qualifying Widow(er) With Dependent Child.*

If you remarried before the end of the tax year, you may file a joint return with your new spouse. Your deceased spouse's filing status is married filing separately for that year.

Married persons living apart. If you live apart from your spouse and meet certain tests, you may be **considered unmarried.** Therefore, you may file as head of household even though you are not divorced or legally separated. See *Head of Household,* later, for more information. If you qualify to file as head of household instead of as married filing separately, your standard deduction will be higher. Also, your tax may be lower, and you may be able to claim the earned income credit. See Chapter 35, *Other Credits,* for information on the earned income credit.

Divorced persons. If you are divorced under a final decree by the last day of the year, you are considered unmarried for the whole year.

Exception. If you obtain a divorce in one year for the sole purpose of filing tax returns as unmarried individuals, and at the time of divorce you intended to and did remarry each other in the next tax year, you and your spouse must file as married individuals.

Annulled marriages. If you obtain a court decree of annulment, which holds that no valid marriage ever existed, and you do not remarry, you must file as single or head of household, whichever applies, for that tax year. You also must file amended returns claiming single or head of household status for all tax years affected by the annulment that are not closed by the statute of limitations for filing a tax return. The statute of limitations generally does not expire until 3 years after your original return was filed. For information on when and how to file an amended return, see *Amended Returns and Claims for Refund* in Chapter 1, *Filing Information.*

Explanation

Invalid divorces. This is a very confusing subject, because courts in different geographic locations disagree with each other. Furthermore, the courts and the IRS have interpreted the law differently.

Generally, you may *not* file a joint return with your second spouse unless the marital relationship with your first spouse has been severed.

While terminating a marriage is usually a matter of obtaining a divorce from a foreign or a domestic court, it is not always that straightforward. When a particular state's law does not recognize the validity of a divorce decree acquired in another jurisdiction, the IRS and the courts disagree over the status of the divorce.

The Second and Third Circuit Courts of Appeals adhere to the so-called rule of validation. Basically, this rule specifies that a divorce in any court's jurisdiction must be recognized for the purposes of tax law. Consequently, under the rule of validation, a valid joint return may be filed with a second spouse. However, the IRS, the Tax Court, and the Ninth Circuit Court of Appeals do not support the rule of validation. Instead, they maintain that a second court possessing jurisdiction may declare a prior divorce invalid. Thus, a return filed jointly by a party of the invalid divorce and a subsequent marriage partner may not be valid. Nevertheless, neither these courts nor the IRS will challenge the validity of a divorce decree until a court of competent jurisdiction has declared the divorce invalid.

Prisoners of war. You are still considered to be married if your spouse is a prisoner of war (POW) or is listed as missing in action (MIA). Even if you subsequently discover that your spouse died in action or in captivity in a prior year, you cannot alter your married filing status on prior income tax returns.

TAXSAVER

When to get divorced. December is the better month to get divorced if spouses have similar incomes. In this way, you can file single returns for the entire year. January is the better month to get divorced if one spouse has considerably more income than the other and you both want to save on taxes.

Questions have arisen about a year-end tax-motivated divorce followed by immediate remarriage, actions that are designed to control an individual's marital status at the close of the year for tax purposes. The IRS contends that such divorce-remarriage schemes are shams and should be disregarded for tax purposes. According to the IRS, individuals retain their married status when:

1. A divorce under the laws of a foreign jurisdiction is obtained late in the year
2. At the time of the divorce the parties intend to remarry
3. The remarriage occurs in January of the next year

However, a divorce followed by cohabitation is not necessarily a sham. The IRS has recognized such arrangements and has allowed individuals to claim single filing status as long as they say that they intend to remain divorced and not remarry each other.

Filing a Joint Return

Both you and your spouse must include all your income, exemptions, and deductions on your joint return.

Accounting period. Both of you must use the same accounting period, but you may use different accounting methods. See *Accounting Periods* and *Accounting Methods* in Chapter 1, *Filing Information.*

Joint responsibility. Both of you may be held responsible, jointly and individually, for the tax and any interest or penalty due on your joint return. One spouse may be held responsible for all the tax due even though all the income was earned by the other spouse.

Exception. Under certain circumstances, you may not have to pay the tax, interest, and penalties on a joint return. You must establish that you did not know, and had no reason to know, that there was a substantial understatement of tax that resulted because your spouse:

1) Omitted a gross income item, or
2) Claimed a deduction, credit, or property basis in an amount for which there is no basis in fact or law.

When the facts and circumstances are considered, it also must be unfair to hold you liable for the tax due. One consideration in determining your responsibility for any tax, interest, and penalties is whether you significantly benefited from the substantial understatement of tax. Normal support received from your spouse is not a significant benefit. Being later divorced or deserted by your spouse may be another consideration.

This exception applies only if your spouse's action resulted in an understatement of tax of more than $500.

In addition, if the tax understatement resulted from claiming a deduction, credit, or basis, the exception applies only if the additional tax, interest, and penalties are more than:

1) 10% of your adjusted gross income (AGI) for the preadjustment year, if your AGI was $20,000 or less, or
2) 25% of your AGI for the preadjustment year, if your AGI was more than $20,000.

Your preadjustment year is your most recent tax year ending before a deficiency notice was mailed. If you were married to a different person at the end of the preadjustment year, your AGI includes your new spouse's income, whether or not you filed a joint return for that year.

For purposes of this exception, community property rules do not apply to items of gross income (other than gross income from property).

Divorced taxpayer. You may still be held jointly and individually responsible for any tax, interest, and penalties due on a joint return filed before your divorce. This responsibility applies even if your divorce decree states that your former spouse will be responsible for any amounts due on previously filed joint returns.

Signing a joint return. For a return to be considered a joint return, both husband and wife must sign the return. If your spouse died before signing the return, see *Signing the return* in Chapter 4, *Decedents.*

Spouse away from home. If your spouse is away from home, you should prepare the return, sign it, and send it to your spouse to sign so that it can be filed on time.

Injury or disease prevents signing. If your spouse cannot sign because of disease or injury and tells you to sign, you may sign your spouse's name in the proper space on the return followed by the words "By (your name), Husband (or Wife)." Be sure to also sign in the space provided for your signature. Attach a dated statement, signed by you, to the return. The statement should include the form number of the return you are filing, the tax year, the reason your spouse cannot sign, and that your spouse has agreed to your signing for him or her.

Signing as guardian of spouse. If you are the guardian of your spouse who is mentally incompetent, you may sign the return for your spouse as guardian.

Other reasons spouse cannot sign. If your spouse cannot sign the joint return for any other reason, you may sign for your spouse only if you are given a valid power of attorney (a legal document giving you permission to act for your spouse). Attach the power of attorney to your tax return. You may use Form 2848, *Power of Attorney and Declaration of Representative.*

TaxAlert

Contrary to the IRS's assertion, the failure of one spouse to sign a return will not prevent a finding that the return was a joint return. If the facts of the case support the conclusion that the nonsigning spouse gave tacit consent to a joint filing, then a valid joint return exists.

Even when a spouse's signature is forged, a valid joint return can exist. In one case, the IRS challenged the return of a husband who, due to marital difficulties, had an unknown person forge his wife's signature. Even though his wife testified in court that she would not have signed a joint return under any circumstances, the court ruled that the joint return was valid. The court reasoned that the wife's refusal to sign was unrelated to the joint filing status claim. Furthermore, since the couple had always filed jointly in the past and the wife did nothing to indicate her disapproval of her husband's intention to continue to file jointly, the court said she had no grounds to complain after the filing was made. The court's message is: the presence or absence of an authentic signature does not constitute conclusive evidence of the intent to file jointly or singly. In addition, the refusal to sign does not necessarily mean that the intent to file a joint return was nonexistent.

Spouse in combat zone. If your spouse is unable to sign the return because he or she is serving in a combat zone, such as the Persian Gulf Area, and you do not have a power of attorney or other statement, you may sign your joint return if you attach your own signed, written statement to your return that explains that your spouse is serving in the combat zone. When you file, write *"Desert Storm"* at the top of your return and on the envelope in which you mail it. For more information on special tax rules for persons who are serving in a combat zone, get Publication 945, *Tax Information for Those Affected by Operation Desert Storm.*

Nonresident alien or dual-status alien. A joint return generally cannot be made if either spouse is a nonresident alien at any time during the tax year. However, if at the end of the year one spouse was a nonresident alien or dual-status alien married to a U.S. citizen or resident, both spouses may choose to file a joint return. If you do file a joint return, you and your spouse are both taxed as U.S. citizens or residents for the entire tax year. See *Nonresident Spouse Treated as a Resident* in Chapter 1 of Publication 519.

TaxPlanner

You may file a joint return and use the more beneficial joint tax rates if you fall into either of the following two categories:

1. As of the close of the tax year, you are a nonresident alien married to a citizen or resident of the United States.
2. You are a nonresident alien at the beginning of the tax year but a resident of the United States at the close of the tax year (i.e., a dual-status taxpayer) and you are married to a citizen or resident of the United States at the end of the tax year.

The catch is that a joint return requires that the worldwide income of both spouses for the entire year be included in taxable income.

Generally, not filing jointly means that separate returns are required. Only the worldwide income of a U.S. citizen and the worldwide income of an alien while a U.S. resident would be included in each person's taxable income. As a result, the alien spouse's income while a nonresident would be excluded. However, the more burdensome married filing separately tax rates must be used. For more information, see Chapter 39, *Foreign Citizens Living in the United States.*

Married Filing Separately

You may choose **married filing separately** as your filing status if you are married. This method may benefit you if you want to be responsible only for your own tax or if this method results in less tax than a joint return. If you and your spouse do not agree to file a joint return, you may have to use this filing status.

If you live apart from your spouse and meet certain tests, you may be **considered unmarried** and file as head of household. This is true even though you are not divorced or legally separated. If you qualify to file as head of household, instead of as married filing separately, your tax may be lower, you may be able to claim the earned income credit, and your standard deduction will be higher. The head of household filing status allows you to choose the standard deduction even if your spouse chooses to itemize deductions. See *Head of Household,* later, for more information.

Unless you are required to file separately, you may want to figure your tax both ways (on a joint return and on separate returns). Do this to make sure you are using the method that results in the lower combined tax. However, you will generally pay more combined tax on separate returns than you would on a joint return because the tax rate is higher for married persons filing separately.

If you file a separate return, you generally report only your own income, exemptions (you may not split an exemption), credits, and deductions on your individual return. You may file a separate return and claim an exemption for your spouse if your spouse had no gross income and was not a dependent of another person. However, if your spouse had any gross income, or was the dependent of someone else, you may not claim an exemption for him or her on your separate return.

If you file as married filing separately, you may use Form 1040A or Form 1040. Select this filing status by checking the box on line 3 of either form. You must also write your spouse's social security number and full name in the spaces provided. Figure your tax by using the *Married filing separately* column of the Tax Table or *Schedule Y–2* of the Tax Rate Schedules.

Separate Returns

Special rules apply when filing a separate return.
Community property states. If you live in Arizona, California, Idaho, Louisiana, Nevada, New Mexico, Texas, Washington, or Wisconsin and file separately, your income may be considered separate income or community income for income tax purposes. See Publication 555.
If you file a separate return:

1) Your spouse should itemize deductions if you itemize deductions, because he or she cannot claim the standard deduction. However, see *Married persons living apart,* earlier, and Chapter 20, *Standard Deduction.*
2) You cannot take the credit for child and dependent care expenses in most instances.
3) You cannot take the earned income credit.
4) You cannot exclude any interest income from series EE U.S. Savings Bonds that you used for higher education expenses.
5) You cannot take the credit for the elderly or the disabled unless you lived apart from your spouse for all of 1993.
6) You may have to include in income part of your social security benefits (including any equivalent railroad retirement benefits) you received in 1993.

TaxSaver

Consider filing separate returns:

1. If you suspect that your spouse owes the IRS money. If you file a joint return, you will both be liable for any tax due.
2. If you can obtain a larger benefit from a deduction for a net operating loss against separate rather than joint income.

3. If you or your spouse have significant medical or miscellaneous expenses or casualty losses, a larger deduction may be obtained, since only medical expenses exceeding 7.5%, miscellaneous expenses exceeding 2%, and casualty losses exceeding 10% of adjusted gross income are deductible. Thus, the lower your adjusted gross income, the more medical or miscellaneous expenses or casualty losses will be deductible.
4. If you are getting divorced. Overall tax savings will result when a high-bracket taxpayer deducts his or her alimony payment and an ex-spouse includes that alimony payment in his or her income at a lower marginal rate.
5. If neither you nor your spouse-to-be may itemize deductions (see Chapters 20–30). The standard deduction for a single person in 1993 is $3,700. Two single individuals filing separately could claim two standard deductions totaling $7,400. That is $1,200 more more than the $6,200 standard deduction for a married couple. If neither of you can itemize your deductions, postponing your marriage until the following tax year will enable you to generate an additional $1,200 of income, tax free.
6. If both husband and wife have similar income and deductions.
7. If a spouse wishes to be responsible for only his or her tax liability.

Consider filing a joint return:

1. If only one spouse has income.
2. If, as of the close of the tax year, you are a nonresident alien married to a citizen or resident of the United States, or you are a nonresident alien at the beginning of the tax year but a resident of the United States at the close of the year and you are married to a U.S. citizen or resident of the United States at the end of the year.

Individual Retirement Arrangements (IRAs). If you make contributions to your Individual Retirement Account, your IRA deduction may be subject to a phaseout rule. The phaseout rule applies if either you or your spouse was covered by an employer retirement plan, you and your spouse file separate returns, and you lived together during the year. See *Deductible Contributions* in Chapter 18, *Individual Retirement Arrangements (IRAs).*
Passive activity losses. You may generally offset a loss from a rental real estate activity of up to $25,000 against your nonpassive income if you actively participate in the activity. However, married persons filing separate returns who lived together at any time during the year may not claim this offset for a loss from a rental real estate activity. Married persons filing separate returns who lived apart at all times during the year, are each allowed a $12,500 maximum offset for rental real estate activities. See *Limits on Rental Losses* in Chapter 10, *Rental Income and Expenses.*

Joint Return After Separate Returns
You may change your filing status by filing an amended return using Form 1040X, *Amended U.S. Individual Income Tax Return.*
If you or your spouse (or each of you) files a separate return, you

may change to a joint return any time within 3 years from the due date of the separate return or returns. This does not include any extensions. A separate return includes a return filed by you or your spouse claiming married filing separately, single, or head of household filing status. If the amount paid on your separate returns is less than the total tax shown on the joint return, you must pay the additional tax due on the joint return when you file it.

Separate Returns After Joint Return

Once you file a joint return, you cannot choose to file separate returns for that year after the due date of the return.

> **Explanation**
> If a husband and wife fail to file for a particular year, they may still file a joint return for that period, even if the return is as much as 3 years overdue. However, once the IRS has notified each spouse individually that he or she has not filed a return that is more than 3 years overdue, they cannot file a joint return.

Exception. A personal representative for a decedent may change from a joint return elected by the surviving spouse to a separate return for the decedent. The personal representative has one year from the due date of the return to make the change. See Chapter 4, *Decedents,* for more information on filing a return for a decedent.

Head of Household

You may be able to file as *head of household* if you are unmarried or considered unmarried on the last day of the year. In addition, you must have paid more than half the cost of keeping up a home for you and a qualifying person for more than half the year. If you qualify to file as head of household, your tax rate will be lower than the rates for single or married filing separately. You will also receive a higher standard deduction than if you file as single or married filing separately. (You can claim the standard deduction only if you do not itemize deductions.)

If you file as head of household, you may use either Form 1040A or Form 1040. Indicate your choice of this filing status by checking the box on line 4 of either form. You figure your tax by using the *Head of a household* column of the Tax Table or *Schedule Z* of the Tax Rate Schedules.

Considered Unmarried

You are considered unmarried on the last day of the tax year if you meet **all** of the following tests.

1) You file a separate return.
2) You paid more than half the cost of keeping up your home for the tax year.
3) Your spouse did not live in your home during the last 6 months of the tax year.
4) Your home was, for more than half the year, the main home of your child, stepchild, adopted child, or foster child whom you can claim as a dependent. However, you can still meet this test if you cannot claim your child as a dependent only because:
   a) You state in writing to the noncustodial parent that he or she may claim an exemption for the child, or
   b) The noncustodial parent provides at least $600 support for the dependent and claims an exemption for the dependent under a pre-1985 divorce or separation agreement.

The rules to claim a dependent are explained in Chapter 3, *Personal Exemptions and Dependents.*

Note. If you were considered married for part of the year and lived in a community property state (listed earlier under *Married Filing Separately*), special rules may apply in determining your income and expenses. See Publication 555 for more information.

Qualifying Person

Each of the following individuals is considered a qualifying person.

1) Your child, grandchild, stepchild, or adopted child who is:
   a) Single. This child does not have to be your dependent. However, a foster child must be your dependent. See Chapter 3, *Personal Exemptions and Dependents,* for more information on dependents.
   b) Married. This child must qualify as your dependent. However, if your married child's other parent claims him or her as a dependent under the special rules for a *Noncustodial parent* discussed in Chapter 3 under *Support Test for Divorced or Separated Parents,* the child does not have to be your dependent.

If the qualifying person is your child but not your dependent, enter that child's name in the space provided on line 4 of Form 1040 or Form 1040A.

2) Any relative listed below whom you claim as a dependent. However, if your dependent parent does not live with you, a special rule applies. See *Father or mother,* later.

Parent	Brother-in-law
Grandparent	Sister-in-law
Brother	Son-in-law
Sister	Daughter-in-law, or
Half brother	Half sister
Stepbrother	If related by blood:
Stepsister	Uncle
Stepmother	Aunt
Stepfather	Nephew
Mother-in-law	Niece
Father-in-law	

> **Explanation**
> A person does not qualify as the head of a household for tax purposes when he or she lives alone with numerous pet cats and dogs. The IRS's reasoning is that a pet does not qualify as a dependent.

You are related by blood to an uncle or aunt if he or she is the brother or sister of your father or mother.

You are related by blood to a nephew or niece if he or she is the child of your brother or sister.

Note. A dependent can qualify only one taxpayer to use the head of household filing status for any tax year.

Dependents. If the person you support is required to be your dependent, you do not qualify as a head of household if you can only claim the dependent under a multiple support agreement. See *Multiple Support Agreement* in Chapter 3, *Personal Exemptions and Dependents.*

Explanation

Foster child. You qualify as head of household if you meet the rules above and you can claim your foster child as a dependent. See Chapter 3.

Father or mother. You may be eligible to file as head of household even if your dependent parent does not live with you. You must pay more than half the cost of keeping up a home that was the main home for the *entire year* for your mother or father. You are keeping up a main home for your dependent father or mother if you pay more than half the cost of keeping your parent in a rest home or home for the elderly.

TAXPLANNER

If you are providing some support for your parents—but less than half of their total support—you should investigate targeting your support payments so that you can qualify as a head of household by establishing one of your parents as a dependent. For example, when you are providing funds to your parents for their support, some type of notation should be made on your check that specifically states *for whom* the money is being provided. In this fashion, you can clearly demonstrate that the 50% support requirement has been satisfied for at least one of your parents.

Temporary absences. You are considered to occupy the same household despite the temporary absence due to special circumstances of either yourself or the other person. Temporary absences due to special circumstances include those due to illness, education, business, vacation, and military service. It must be reasonable to assume that you or the other person will return to the household after the temporary absence, and you must continue to maintain a household in anticipation of the return.

Temporary absences. You are considered to occupy the same household despite the temporary absence due to special circumstances of either yourself or the other person. Temporary absences due to special circumstances include those due to illness, education, business, vacation, and military service. It must be reasonable to assume that you or the other person will return to the household after the temporary absence, and you must continue to maintain a household in anticipation of the return.

Examples

One court has held that a man still qualified as head of a household even though he temporarily moved out of his home after becoming legally separated. The court believed that the man had always intended to return to his home (and, in fact, he did return). The court was also aware that he had been awarded custody of his child.

Another court has held that a man could not claim that he was the head of the household that he maintained for his son where he himself did not live because of fear of his son.

Note: If your child or stepchild is absent from the home less than 6 months under a custody agreement, the absence is considered temporary.

Death or birth. If the individual who qualifies you to use head of household filing status is born or dies during the year, you still may be able to claim that filing status. You must have provided more than half of the cost of keeping up a home that was the individual's main home for more than half the year, or, if less, the period during which the individual lived.

Example. You are unmarried. Your mother lived in an apartment by herself. She died on September 2, 1993. The cost of the upkeep of her apartment for the year until her death was $6,000. You paid $4,000 and your brother paid $2,000. Your brother made no other payments towards your mother's support. Your mother had no income. Since you paid more than half the cost of keeping up the apartment for your mother from January 1, 1993, until her death, and she qualifies as your dependent, you may file as a head of household.

Explanation

Except when you are supporting and maintaining your parents, who do not have to live with you, the IRS says that you cannot qualify as head of household unless you live in the home that you are supporting and maintaining. However, some courts have said that you can maintain more than one home and still claim head of household status. The household that qualifies you as a head of household need not be your principal place of abode, but it must be the home where you and members of your household live for an adequate period of time.

Examples

A woman who owned two homes, hundreds of miles apart, could still claim to be head of household at the home that was the principal place of residence of her adopted son, though she spent only 40% of her time there. For both homes, however, she paid more than half the cost of upkeep.

A man could not claim to be head of household, although he paid 80–90% of the household expenses and was a member of a nearby church, because he did not spend a substantial amount of time at the house. He only visited his sisters at the house, either when he was in town on business during the week or when he stopped by for Sunday dinner. The house was owned by his sisters.

A woman who spent 85% of her time in one house and 15% in another house that was the principal residence of her daughter and grandchildren was not allowed to claim head of household status. In this case, the houses were less than 2 miles apart and the woman stayed over at her daughter's only when either she or her daughter was ill. Besides, the daughter, not her mother, rented the house, although the daughter used money given to her by her mother to pay the rent.

The case of the two-family house. In this case, a husband, wife, and their children lived in one of the house's units and the wife's mother and unwed sister lived in the other unit. The home contained some common areas but also some partitioned areas for the private use of each family unit. A court upheld the wife's mother's claim of head of household status based on her support of her unwed daughter. Even though the mother paid less than half of the total household expenses, she did pay more than half of the expenses attributable to her and her daughter.

Nonresident alien spouse. You are considered unmarried for head of household purposes if your spouse was a nonresident alien at any time during the year, and you do not choose to treat your nonresident spouse as a resident alien. Your spouse is not considered your relative. You must have another qualifying relative and meet the other tests to be eligible to file as a head of household. However, you are considered married if you have chosen to treat your spouse as a resident alien. See *Nonresident Spouse Treated as a Resident* in Chapter 1, *Filing Information,* of Publication 519.

Dual-status and nonresident alien taxpayers. These taxpayers may not claim head of household status.

Keeping Up a Home

You are keeping up a home only if **you pay more than half** of the cost of its upkeep. You may determine whether you paid more than half of the cost of keeping up a home by using the *Cost of Maintaining a Household* worksheet, later.

Costs you include. Include such costs as rent, mortgage interest, taxes, insurance on the home, repairs, utilities, and food eaten in the home.

Costs you do not include. Do not include the cost of clothing, education, medical treatment, vacations, life insurance, transportation, or the rental value of a home you own. Also, do not include the value of your services or those of a member of your household.

State AFDC (Aid to Families with Dependent Children). State AFDC payments you use to keep up your home do not count as amounts you paid. They are amounts paid by others that you must include in the total cost of keeping up your home to figure if you paid more than half.

Include or exclude the costs previously mentioned only to figure whether you are keeping up a home. Do not claim them as deductions on your return unless they are otherwise deductible. See *Support Test* in Chapter 3, *Personal Exemptions and Dependents,* for expenses you can use to figure if a person qualifies as your dependent.

Cost of Maintaining a Household

	Amount You Paid	Total Cost
Property taxes	$	$
Mortgage interest expense		
Rent		
Utility charges		
Upkeep and repairs		
Property insurance		
Food consumed on the premises		
Other household expenses		
Totals	$	$
Minus total amount you paid		( )
Amount others paid		$

If you paid more than others paid, you meet the requirement of maintaining a household.

Qualifying Widow(er) With Dependent Child

If your spouse died in 1993, you may use married filing jointly as your filing status for 1993 if you would otherwise qualify. See *Married Filing Jointly,* earlier.

You may be eligible to use *qualifying widow(er) with dependent child* as your filing status for 2 years following the year of death of your spouse. For example, if your spouse died in 1992, and you have not remarried, you may be able to use this filing status for 1993 or 1994. The rules to file as a qualifying widow(er) with dependent child are explained in more detail later.

This filing status entitles you to use joint return tax rates and the highest standard deduction amount (if you do not itemize deductions). This status does not authorize you to file a joint return.

Indicate your filing status by checking the box on line 5 of either Form 1040A or Form 1040 (you may not file Form 1040EZ). Write the year your spouse died in the space provided on line 5. You figure your tax by using the *Married filing jointly* column of the Tax Table or *Schedule Y–1* of the Tax Rate Schedules.

Eligibility rules for filing as a qualifying widow(er) with dependent child. You are eligible to file as a qualifying widow(er) with dependent child if you meet all of the following tests.

1) You were entitled to file a joint return with your spouse for the year your spouse died (it does not matter whether you actually filed a joint return).
2) You did not remarry before the end of the tax year.
3) You have a child, stepchild, adopted child, or foster child who qualifies as your dependent for the year.
4) You paid more than half the cost of keeping up a home that is the main home for you and that child for the entire year, except for temporary absences. See *Temporary absences* and *Keeping Up a Home,* discussed earlier under *Head of Household.*

Note. As mentioned earlier, this filing status is only available for 2 years following the year of death of your spouse.

Example. John Reed's wife died in 1991. John has not remarried. He has continued during 1992 and 1993 to keep up a home for himself and his dependent child. For 1991 he was entitled to file a joint return for himself and his deceased wife. For 1992 and 1993 he may file as qualifying widower with a dependent child. After 1993 he may file as head of household if he qualifies.

Death or birth. If the dependent who qualifies you to use qualifying widow(er) with dependent child filing status is born or dies during the year, you still may be able to claim that filing status. You must have provided more than half of the cost of keeping up a home that was the dependent's main home during the entire part of the year he or she was alive.

3 | Personal Exemptions and Dependents

Introduction

In 1993, you are entitled to a $2,350 **deduction** *for yourself, your spouse, and each person you support who otherwise qualifies as a dependent. Each year the amount of the personal exemption is adjusted for inflation. This chapter tells you what specific qualifications you have to meet to take these deductions. It informs you about the special rules and procedures that apply to divorced and separated couples with children, widows and widowers, and residents of* **community property** *states. Perhaps, most importantly, this chapter suggests when it might not be a good idea to take a deduction, even though you qualify for it.*

To qualify as your **dependent** *, a person must meet five tests, all of which are explained in great detail in this chapter:*

1. *The person must be either a relative or a full-time member of your household.*
2. *The person must be a citizen or resident of the United States or a resident of Canada or Mexico.*
3. *The person must not file a* **joint return** *with another person.*
4. *The person must receive over half of his or her* **support** *from you.*
5. *The person must have less than $2,350 in* **gross income** *for the year, unless he or she is your child and is either under age 19 or a full-time student under age 24.*

The original intent of personal **exemptions** *for dependents was to provide tax relief so that even the poorest citizen would be left with enough money after taxes to support self and family. Obviously, a $2,350 deduction these days can save the taxpayer only a small portion of the income necessary to live, even at a subsistence level. Ironically, the higher your income level and the higher your* **marginal tax rate** *, the greater economic benefit you derive from these—or, for that matter, any—deductions. A $2,350 deduction is worth $353 to a married couple filing a joint return with a* **taxable income** *of $20,000 and a marginal tax rate of 15%. The same $2,350 deduction is worth $729 to a married couple filing a joint return with a taxable income over $90,000 and a marginal tax rate of 31%. (Once your adjusted gross income reaches a certain threshold, figuring out what the exemption is worth is more complicated. This chapter explains this in more detail.)*

Also explained are the rules that phase out the value of your personal exemptions if your adjusted gross income exceeds certain amounts: $162,700 for married persons filing jointly, $135,600 for heads of household, $108,450 for single taxpayers, and $81,350 for married persons filing separate returns.

Figuring out who should claim whom as a dependent can be a difficult matter involving considerable tax planning. For example, when parents are divorced, the custodial parent may sign a declaration permitting the noncustodial parent to claim the exemption for the dependent child. Consequently, if the noncustodial parent is in a higher tax bracket, a greater tax benefit can be obtained. Either parent is entitled to claim the medical expenses paid for the child, even if that parent cannot claim the child as a dependent.

Important Changes for 1993

Exemption amount. The amount you may deduct as an exemption has increased from $2,300 in 1992 to $2,350 in 1993.

Exemption phaseout. In 1993 you will lose all or part of the benefit of your exemptions if your adjusted gross income goes above a certain level. The income level ranges from $81,350 (for married filing separately) to $162,700 (for married filing jointly) depending upon your filing status. See *Phaseout of Exemptions,* later.

Important Reminder

Social security numbers for dependents. If you claim a dependent on a tax return, you have to list the dependent's social security number if he or she is age *one or older.* If you do not provide a dependent's social security number when it is required, or if you list an incorrect number, you may be subject to a $50 penalty.

This chapter discusses exemptions. The following topics will be explained:

- Personal exemptions — You generally can take one for yourself and, if you are married, one for your spouse.
- Dependency exemptions — You must meet five dependency tests for each dependent you claim. If you are entitled to claim an exemption for a dependent, that dependent cannot claim a personal exemption on his or her own tax return.
- Phaseout of exemptions — You get less of a deduction when your taxable income goes above a certain amount.
- Social security number (SSN) requirement for dependents — You must list an SSN for any dependent age one or older.

Exemptions are amounts that reduce your taxable income. For 1993, each exemption is worth $2,350. How you claim an exemption on your tax return depends on which form you file.

If you file Form 1040EZ, you are allowed an exemption for yourself (and your spouse if married filing a joint return), unless someone else can claim you (or your spouse if married filing a joint return) as a dependent. The exemption amount is combined with the standard deduction amount and entered on line 5.

If you file Form 1040A or Form 1040, follow the instructions for the form. The total number of exemptions you can claim is the total in the box on line 6e. Also complete line 21 (Form 1040A) or line 36 (Form 1040) by multiplying the total number of exemptions shown in the box on line 6e by $2,350.

Caution. If your adjusted gross income is $81,350 or more, see *Phaseout of Exemptions,* later.

Useful Items

You may want to see:

Form (and Instructions)

☐ **2120** Multiple Support Declaration
☐ **8332** Release of Claim to Exemption for Child of Divorced or Separated Parents

Exemptions

There are two types of exemptions: personal exemptions and dependency exemptions. While these are both worth the same amount, different rules apply to each type.

Personal Exemptions

You are generally allowed one exemption for yourself and, if you are married, one exemption for your spouse. These are called personal exemptions.

Your Own Exemption

You may take one exemption for yourself unless you can be claimed as a dependent by another taxpayer.

Single persons. If another taxpayer is entitled to claim you as a dependent, you may not take an exemption for yourself. This is true even if the other taxpayer does not actually claim your exemption.

Married persons. If you file a joint return, you may take your own exemption. If you file a separate return, you may take your own exemption only if another taxpayer is not entitled to claim you as a dependent.

Your Spouse's Exemption

Your spouse is never considered your dependent. You may be able to take one exemption for your spouse only because you are married. See *Separate return* later.

TAXPLANNER

An exemption for your spouse is available only if you are married to that person on the last day of your tax year. Our advice for tax-conscious lovers is: December weddings are generally better than January weddings. As for divorces, January is generally better than December.

A common-law marriage is recognized for federal tax purposes if it is recognized by the state where it was entered into. To determine if you are married in common law may require legal advice.

Other tax considerations may make a year-end wedding inadvisable. If bride and groom have equal incomes, single tax rates may be more beneficial than married tax rates. For more advice about taxes and marriage, see Chapter 2, *Filing Status.*

Joint return. If your spouse had *any gross income,* as defined in Chapter 1, *Filing Information,* you may claim his or her exemption only if you file a joint return.

Explanation

Filing a joint return with your spouse will prevent anyone else from claiming him or her as a dependent, even if that person was otherwise entitled to do so. However, your spouse's parents may be able to claim your spouse as a dependent if you do not file a joint return.

Example
John and Mary attended college for 6 months during 1993 and were married in November that year. John earned $10,000 and Mary earned $2,700 during 1993. If the newlyweds file a joint income tax return, they will owe $270 in taxes. However, Mary's parents will then be unable to claim their daughter as a dependent, even though they provided more than half her support that year.

If John and Mary file as "married, filing separately," Mary will owe no tax and John will owe $683. In addition, Mary's parents, who are in the 31% tax bracket, will be entitled to claim Mary as a dependent, giving them a tax benefit of $729. Thus, if the newlyweds file separate returns, their overall tax liability combined with that of Mary's parents will be reduced by $316 (the $729 tax savings to Mary's parents less the additional $413 tax John and Mary incur by filing separate returns). If John's parents also provided half of his support in 1993 and can claim him as a dependent, the combined tax liability for everybody involved will be even lower.

Separate return. If you file a separate return, you may claim the exemption for your spouse only if your spouse had *no gross income* and was not the dependent of another taxpayer. This is true even if the other taxpayer does not actually claim your spouse's exemption. This is also true if your spouse is a nonresident alien.

Death of spouse. If your spouse died during the year, you may generally claim your spouse's exemption under the rules just explained in *Joint return* and *Separate return*.

If you remarried during the year, you may not take an exemption for your deceased spouse.

If you are a surviving spouse without gross income and you remarry, you may be claimed as an exemption on both the final separate return of your deceased spouse and the separate return of your new spouse whom you married in the same year. If you file a joint return with your new spouse, you may be claimed as an exemption only on that return.

Final decree of divorce or separate maintenance during the year. If you obtain a final decree of divorce or separate maintenance by the end of the year, you may not take your former spouse's exemption. This rule applies even if you provided all of your former spouse's support.

TaxPlanner
If you're getting divorced near the end of 1993, it may be better to postpone the divorce until January of 1994. In that way, you can claim an exemption for your spouse as well as use the married filing jointly tax rates.

Exemptions for Dependents

You are allowed one exemption for each person you can claim as a dependent. This is called a dependency exemption.

A person is your dependent if *all five* of the dependency tests, discussed later, are met. You may take an exemption for your dependent even if your dependent files a return. However, see *Joint Return Test* later in this chapter.

If your dependent files a tax return, that dependent cannot claim

his or her own exemption. For information on filing requirements for dependents, see *Dependents* in Chapter 1, *Filing Information*.

Child born alive. If your child was born alive during the year, and the dependency tests are met, you may take the full exemption. This is true even if the child lived only for a moment. Whether your child was born alive depends on state or local law. There must be proof of a live birth shown by an official document, such as a birth certificate. You may not claim an exemption for a stillborn child.

TaxPlanner
You can take a dependency exemption for 1993 for a child born on or before December 31, 1993, but not for a baby born January 1, 1994. Plan accordingly!

Death of dependent. If your dependent died during the year and otherwise qualified as your dependent, you can take his or her exemption.

Example. Your dependent mother died on January 15. You can take a full exemption for her on your return.

Housekeepers, maids, or servants. If these people work for you, you cannot claim them as dependents.

Dependency tests. The following five tests must be met for a person to be your dependent:

1) Member of Household or Relationship Test
2) Citizenship Test
3) Joint Return Test
4) Gross Income Test
5) Support Test

Member of Household or Relationship Test

To meet this test, a person must live with you for the entire year as a member of your household or be related to you. If at any time during the year the person was your spouse, you may not claim that person as a dependent. See *Personal Exemptions,* earlier.

Explanation
For an unrelated person to qualify as your dependent, he or she must live with you at your principal place of residence—not merely at a house that you maintain for the entire year.

Temporary absences. You are considered to occupy the same household despite the temporary absence due to special circumstances of either yourself or the other person. Temporary absences due to special circumstances include those due to illness, education, business, vacation, and military service.

If the person is placed in a nursing home for an unspecified period of time to receive constant medical care, the absence is considered temporary.

Death or birth. A person who died during the year, but was a member of your household until death, will meet the member of household test. The same is true for a child who was born during the year and was a member of your household for the rest of the year. The test is also met if a child would have been a member except for any required hospital stay following birth.

Test not met. A person does not meet the member of household test if at any time during your tax year the relationship between you and that person violates local law.

Relatives not living with you. A person related to you in any of the following ways does not have to live with you for the entire year as a member of your household to meet this test.

> Your child, grandchild, great grandchild, etc. (a legally adopted child is considered your child)
>
> Your stepchild
>
> Your brother, sister, half brother, half sister, stepbrother, or stepsister
>
> Your parent, grandparent, or other direct ancestor, but not foster parent
>
> Your stepfather or stepmother
>
> A brother or sister of your father or mother
>
> A son or daughter of your brother or sister
>
> Your father-in-law, mother-in-law, son-in-law, daughter-in-law, brother-in-law, or sister-in-law

Any of the above relationships that were established by marriage are not ended by death or divorce.

Explanation

A dependent must be *either* a relative described above or a full-time resident in your principal residence. Your child qualifies as a relative, even if the child is illegitimate.

While your stepchild, stepfather, and stepmother all qualify as relatives, their blood relations do not. Even so, their blood relations may qualify as your dependents if they are full-time residents in your home.

While your spouse's brother and/or sister qualify as relatives to you, their spouses do not.

Example

Amy is married to Oliver. Amy's sister Laura, along with Laura's husband, Stephen, are relatives of Amy, but only Laura is a relative of Oliver. If Amy and Oliver file a joint tax return, Laura and Stephen may both be claimed as dependents (as relatives) if they otherwise qualify. But if Amy and Oliver file married but separate returns, Stephen would not be considered a relative of Oliver and could only be claimed as a dependent by Oliver if Stephen was a full-time resident in Oliver's personal residence.

Adoption. Before legal adoption, a child is considered to be your child if he or she was placed with you for adoption by an authorized agency. Also, the child must have been a member of your household. If the child was not placed with you by such an agency, the child will meet this test only if he or she was a member of your household for your entire tax year.

Example

George and Karen are married. Peggy, a 5-year-old orphan, is placed by an authorized adoption agency in their home in July 1993. She is a member of the household for the rest of the year. Even though Peggy was not a resident of their household for 12 months during 1993, and even though she was not legally adopted by George and Karen until 1994, she may be claimed as George and Karen's dependent for 1993. However, if Peggy had not been placed in George and Karen's home by an authorized adoption agency,

George and Karen would not be able to claim her as a dependent.

Foster individual. A foster child or adult must live with you as a member of your household for the entire year to qualify as your dependent.

However, if a state, one of its political subdivisions, or a tax-exempt child-placing agency makes payments to you as a foster parent, you may not take the child as your dependent. Your expenses are incurred on behalf of the agency that made payments to you. Expenses you incur in excess of nontaxable payments you receive are allowed as charitable contributions. You may deduct these contributions on Schedule A (Form 1040) if you itemized deductions. If you receive taxable payments, your expenses may be deductible as business expenses. See *Foster-care providers* under *Income Not Taxed* in Chapter 13, *Other Income,* and *Foster parents* in Chapter 25, *Contributions.*

Cousin. Your cousin will meet this test only if he or she lives with you as a member of your household for the entire year. A cousin is a descendant of a brother or sister of your father or mother and does not qualify under the relationship test.

Joint return. If you file a joint return, you do not need to show that a dependent is related to both you and your spouse. You also do not need to show that a dependent is related to the spouse who provides support.

For example, your spouse's uncle who receives more than half his support from you may be your dependent, even though he does not live with you. However, if you and your spouse file *separate returns,* your spouse's uncle can be your dependent only if he is a member of your household and lives with you for your entire tax year.

Citizenship Test

To meet the citizenship test, a person must be a U.S. citizen or resident, or a resident of Canada or Mexico for some part of the calendar year in which your tax year begins.

Explanation

Residents of Puerto Rico do not meet the citizenship test unless they are also U.S. citizens.

If you are not a U.S. citizen, then you are considered an alien. Aliens are classified as **nonresident** aliens and **resident** aliens. For more information get Publication 519, *U.S. Tax Guide for Aliens.*

Children's place of residence. Children usually are citizens or residents of the country of their parents.

If you were a U.S. citizen when your child was born, the child may be a U.S. citizen although the other parent was a nonresident alien and the child was born in a foreign country. If so, and the other dependency tests are met, the child is your dependent and you may take the exemption. It does not matter if the child lives abroad with the nonresident alien parent.

Example

The IRS ruled that a U.S. citizen living in England since the age of 9, who subsequently married an Englishwoman, could not claim their son, who was born in England, as a dependent. The foreign-born child of a U.S. citizen and a nonresident alien is *not* a citizen or resident of the United States unless the American parent lived in the United States for 10 years before the child's birth. At least 5 of those 10 years must have been subsequent to age 14.

If you are a U.S. citizen living abroad who has legally adopted a child who is not a U.S. citizen or resident, and the other dependency tests are met, the child is your dependent and you may take the exemption if your home is the child's main home and the child is a member of your household for your entire tax year.

Foreign students place of residence. Foreign students brought to this country under a qualified international education exchange program and placed in American homes for a temporary period generally are not U.S. residents and do not meet the citizenship test. They may not be claimed as dependents. However, if you provided a home for a foreign student, you may be able to take a charitable contribution deduction. See *Expenses Paid for Student Living With You* in Chapter 25, *Contributions.*

Explanation
For more information about taxes for aliens, see Chapter 39, *Foreign Citizens Living in the United States.*

Joint Return Test

Even if the other dependency tests are met, you are generally not allowed an exemption for your dependent if he or she files a joint return.

Example. You supported your daughter for the entire year while her husband was in the Armed Forces. The couple files a joint return. Even though all the other tests are met, you may not take an exemption for your daughter.

Exception. If the other dependency tests are met, you may take an exemption for your married dependent who files a joint return if:

1) Neither your dependent nor your dependent's spouse is required to file a return,
2) Neither your dependent nor your dependent's spouse would have a tax liability if they filed separate returns, and
3) They only file a joint return in order to get a refund of tax withheld.

Example. Your son and his wife each had less than $2,000 of wages and no unearned income. Neither is required to file a tax return. Taxes were withheld from their income, so they file a joint return to get a refund. You are allowed exemptions for your son and daughter-in-law if the other dependency tests are met.

Gross Income Test

Generally, you may not take an exemption for a dependent if that person had gross income of $2,350 or more for the year. This test does not apply if the person is your child and is either under age 19, or a student under age 24, as discussed later.

If you file on a fiscal year basis, the gross income test applies to the calendar year in which your fiscal year begins.

Gross income. All income in the form of money, property, and services that is not exempt from tax is gross income.

In a manufacturing, merchandising, or mining business, gross income is the total net sales minus the cost of goods sold, plus any miscellaneous income from the business.

Gross receipts from rental property are gross income. You may not deduct taxes, repairs, etc., to determine the gross income from rental property.

Gross income includes a partner's share of the gross, not a share of the net, partnership income.

Example
Mark's father retired 5 years ago and receives over half of his support from Mark. The father is a partner in a real estate partnership, and his share of gross rental income from the partnership is $2,500 before expenses. After expenses, his net rental income is $200. Mark may not claim his father as a dependent, because his father's share of the partnership's gross rental income exceeds the $2,350 exemption amount.

Gross income also includes all unemployment compensation and certain scholarship and fellowship grants. Scholarships received by degree candidates that are used for tuition, fees, supplies, books, and equipment required for particular courses are not included in gross income. For more information, see Chapter 13, *Other Income.*

Tax-exempt income, such as certain social security payments, is not included in gross income. See *Income Not Taxed* in Chapter 13, *Other Income.*

Explanation
Gross income also includes: (1) gross profit from self-employment, (2) the full gain from the sale of stock or real estate, and (3) the gain on the sale of a personal residence, even if the gain is deferred by the purchase of a replacement home or is partially exempt due to the age of the homeowner.

Gross income does *not* include: (1) tax-free municipal bond interest and (2) gifts received from others.

TAXSAVER
Since tax-free municipal bond interest is not included in gross income, a person who may possibly be claimed by another as a dependent may be better off holding municipal bonds rather than taxable bonds.

Example
Widower Harry, 63 years old, lives with his son and daughter-in-law. His only source of income is from the $35,000 he has to invest. If he invests in a bond yielding 8%, he would receive $2,800 of taxable income. Since that is less than his $3,700 standard deduction, Harry would not have any tax liability. However, Harry's son would not be able to claim his father as a dependent, because Harry would have more than $2,350 in gross income.

If Harry invests $20,000 in the 8% bond and $15,000 in a 6% tax-free municipal bond, his annual income would be $2,500 ($1,600 + $900), $300 less than if he put all his money in a bond. His son would now be able

Figure 3-A. Can You Claim a Dependency Exemption?

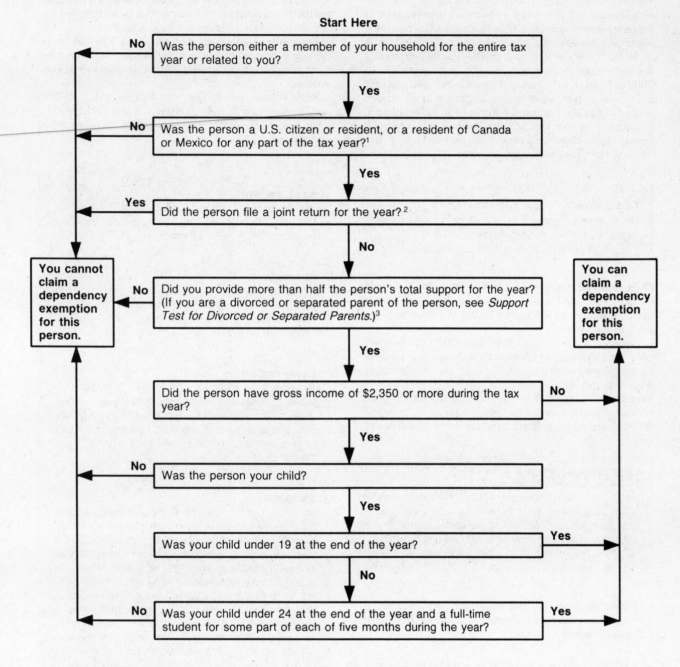

[1] If the person was your legally adopted child and lived in your home as a member of your household for the entire tax year, answer "yes" to this question.

[2] If neither the person nor the person's spouse is required to file a return but they file a joint return to claim a refund of tax withheld, you may answer "no" to this question.

[3] Answer "yes" to this question if you meet the multiple support requirements under *Multiple Support Agreement*.

to claim his father as a dependent, since Harry's gross income ($1,600) would be less than $2,350. However, Harry would now have to file a tax return since his total income is more than $600, the filing requirement threshold for dependents (see Chapter 1, *Filing Information*).

The tax benefit to his son should be compared with Harry's lower yield and increased tax to see which is more beneficial.

For this gross income test, gross income does not include income received by a permanently and totally disabled individual at a sheltered workshop. The availability of medical care must be the main reason the individual is at the workshop. Also, the income must come solely from activities at the workshop that are incident to this medical care. A sheltered workshop is a school operated by certain tax-exempt organizations, or by a state, a U.S. possession, a political subdivision of a state or possession, the United States, or the District of Columbia, that provides special instruction or training designed to alleviate the disability of the individual.

Child defined. For purposes of the gross income test, your child is your son, stepson, daughter, stepdaughter, a legally adopted child, or a child who was placed with you by an authorized placement agency for your legal adoption. A foster child who was a member of your household for your entire tax year is also considered your child. See *Foster individual,* earlier.

Exception

The gross income exception for children is not available for a son-in-law or daughter-in-law.

Child under 19. If your child is under 19 at the end of the year, the gross income test does not apply. Your child may have any amount of income and still be your dependent if the other dependency tests are met.

Example. Marie Grey, 18, earned $2,400. Her father provided more than half her support. Marie may be claimed as a dependent because the gross income test does not apply and the other dependency tests were met.

Student under age 24. If your child is a student, the gross income test does not apply if the child is under age 24 at the end of the calendar year. The other dependency tests must still be met.

TaxPlanner

You are not allowed an exemption for a child who is age 24 or older whose gross income is not less than the exemption amount. However, if you can't claim an exemption for your child because of this new rule, the child can claim the exemption on his or her return.

Student defined. To qualify as a student your child must be, during some part of each of 5 calendar months during the calendar year (not necessarily consecutive):

1) A full-time student at a school that has a regular teaching staff, course of study, and regularly enrolled body of students in attendance, or
2) A student taking a full-time, on-farm training course given by a school described in (1) above or a state, county, or local government.

Full-time student defined. A full-time student is a person who is enrolled for the number of hours or courses the school considers to be full-time attendance.

School defined. The term "school" includes elementary schools, junior and senior high schools, colleges, universities, and technical, trade, and mechanical schools. It does *not* include on-the-job training courses, correspondence schools, and night schools.

Example. James Clay, 22, attends college as a full-time student. During the summer, James earned $2,700, which he spent for his support. His parents provided more than $2,700 toward his support and the other dependency tests were met. On their return, they may take the exemption for James as a dependent.

Vocational high school students. People who work on "co-op" jobs in private industry as a part of the school's prescribed course of classroom and practical training are considered full-time students.

Night school. Your child is not a full-time student while attending school only at night. However, full-time attendance at a school may include some attendance at night as part of a full-time course of study.

Explanation
In order to qualify for the full-time student exemption, the child must be enrolled in an institution in which education is the primary purpose.

Example
A hospital providing programs for interns and residents does not qualify. However, a division of the hospital whose primary purpose is the education of students rather than on-the-job training may qualify.

Explanation
The gross income exception for full-time students is designed to allow students to work to help pay their way through school without jeopardizing their parents' dependency deduction. However, the parents must continue to provide over half of the child's support to take the deduction.

Example
Mr. and Mrs. Johnson's 22-year-old unmarried son, Robert, graduated from college in June 1993 and got a job for the remainder of the year that paid him $10,000 in taxable income. Since Robert was a full-time student for at least 5 months during 1993, he is exempt from the gross income test. Nevertheless, Mr. and Mrs. Johnson will not be able to take a $2,350 deduction for Robert as their dependent unless they can prove that they provided half of Robert's support during the entire year. If they are entitled to take the deduction for him, Robert is not entitled to claim an exemption for himself on his return.

Assuming the exemption for Robert is more valuable on his parents' return than on Robert's own return, Robert's parents should document that they did furnish over half their son's support during the year by paying for his tuition and room and board while he was in school. Robert should have used as large a portion of his income as possible for things that do not constitute support. The more money he saved and invested in 1993, the better. Then Mr. and Mrs. Johnson would be entitled to claim Robert as a dependent and take a $2,350 deduction.

On the other hand, if Mr. and Mrs. Johnson are subject to the personal exemption phaseout, they may want to make sure that they can't claim Robert as a dependent since it does them no good. In 1993, the personal exemption phaseout begins at $162,700 for joint returns. If Mr. and Mrs. Johnson have a taxable income of $288,000, they would receive no benefit from having Robert as a dependent. They should then plan not to provide over 50% of Robert's support.

Explanation
The gross income of a married couple residing in a community property state is generally split equally between each spouse for the purposes of the dependency deduction.

Example
Henry Smith provides more than 50% of the support for his son Jim and his daughter-in-law Jan, both of whom are over 19. Jim has no income and is not a student during 1993. Jan earns $5,000. Assuming that the other four dependency tests are met, Henry Smith may claim his son Jim as a dependent in a common-law state. In a community property state, however, Henry could *not* claim Jim as a dependent, since each spouse is treated as having gross income of $2,500 (half of $5,000).

Support Test

You must provide more than half of a person's total support during the calendar year to meet the support test. You figure whether you have provided more than half by comparing the amount you contributed to the person's support with the entire amount of support the person received from all sources. This amount includes the person's own funds used for support. You may not include in your contribution any part of your child's support that is paid for by the child with the child's own wages, even if you pay the wages. See *Total Support,* later. For exceptions to the support test, see *Multiple Support Agreement* and *Support Test for Divorced or Separated Parents,* later.

A person's own funds are not support unless they are actually spent for support.

Example. Your mother received $2,400 in social security benefits and $300 in interest. She paid $2,000 for lodging, $400 for recreation, and $300 for life insurance premiums.

Even though your mother received a total of $2,700, she spent only $2,400 for her own support. Life insurance premiums are not support items. If you spent more than $2,400 for her support and no other support was received, you have provided more than half of her support.

Cost determines support. The total cost, not the period of time you provide the support, determines whether you provide more than half of the support.

Explanation
You may be able to claim someone as a dependent even though you provide support for less than half the year. Support depends on the amount spent, not the length of time over which it is spent. As long as you provide over 50% of the total amount of a person's support for a year, you may claim that person as a dependent.

Year support is provided. The year you provide the support is the year you pay for it, even if you do so with borrowed money that you repay in a later year.

Explanation
Only the amount actually spent on support is relevant to the support test. The funds made available for support purposes are not relevant until actually used.

Example 1
The income of a trust for the benefit of a minor was not spent for the minor's support. The parent who provided the funds for the child's support may claim the dependency deduction.

Example 2
According to a court ruling, an individual could claim a dependency deduction for his grandmother even though she received state old age assistance payments that exceeded the amounts spent by the grandson. The grandmother did not spend all of the payments received from the state for her support. The amount of the state payments that she did spend for her support was less than what was provided to her by her grandson.

If you use a fiscal year to report your income, you must provide more than half of the dependent's support for the calendar year in which your fiscal year begins.

TaxPlanner
You should maintain complete records of expenditures made to support anyone whom you intend to claim as a dependent. Take particular pains to maintain records of support for children of divorced parents and for children who are attending college.

The IRS has established guidelines so that members of a commune can determine who is entitled to deduct whom as a dependent. For additional information, see IRS Publication 555.

Armed Forces dependency allotments. Both the part of the allotment contributed by the government and the part withheld from your military pay are considered provided by you in figuring whether you provide more than half of the support. If your allotment is used to support persons other than those you name, you may take the exemptions for them if they otherwise qualify as dependents.

Example. You are in the Armed Forces. You authorize an allotment for your widowed mother that she uses for the support of herself and your sister. If it provides more than half of their support, you may take an exemption for each of them, even though you authorize the allotment only for your mother.

Tax-exempt military quarters allowances. These allowances are treated the same way as dependency allotments in figuring support. Both the allotment of pay and the tax-exempt basic allowance for quarters are considered as provided by you for support.

Tax-exempt income. In figuring a person's total support, include tax-exempt income, savings, and borrowed amounts used to support that person. Tax-exempt income includes certain social security benefits, welfare benefits, nontaxable life insurance proceeds, Armed Forces family allotments, nontaxable pensions, and tax-exempt interest.

Example 1. You provide $2,000 for your mother's support during the year. She has taxable income of $600, nontaxable social security benefit payments of $1,800, and tax-exempt interest of $200. She uses all these for her support. You may not claim your mother as a dependent because the $2,000 you provide is not more than half of her total support of $4,600.

Example 2. Your daughter takes out a student loan of $2,500 and uses it to pay her college tuition. She is personally responsible for the loan. You provide $2,000 toward her total support. You may not claim your daughter as a dependent because you provide less than half of her support.

Social security benefit payments. If a husband and wife each receive social security benefit payments that are paid by one check made out to both of them, half of the total paid is considered to be for the support of each spouse, unless they can show otherwise.

If a child receives social security benefits and uses them toward his or her own support, the payments are considered as provided by the child.

State benefit payments (welfare, food stamps, housing, etc.). These types of payments are considered as support provided by the state. They are included in determining the total support of the recipient. For example, AFDC (Aid to Families with Dependent Children) is support provided by the state. However, payments based on the needs of the recipient will not be considered as used entirely for that person's support if it is shown that part of the payments were not used for that purpose.

Home for the aged. If you make a lump-sum advance payment to a home for the aged to take care of your relative for life and the payment is based on that person's life expectancy, the amount of your support each year is the lump-sum payment divided by the relative's life expectancy. Your support also includes any other amounts that you provided during the year.

Example
Jane's mother resides in a senior citizens' home that is supported and operated by a church. It cost the church $6,000 last year to support Jane's mother. For Jane to claim her mother as a dependent, she must prove that she has provided more than $6,000 additional support for her mother, over and above the $6,000 provided by the church.

Total Support
To figure if you provided more than half of the support of a person, you must first determine the total support provided for that person. Total support includes amounts spent to provide food, lodging, clothing, education, medical and dental care, recreation, transportation, and similar necessities.

Explanation
Money that is not included in gross income, such as certain social security benefits, veterans' benefits, and so on, must be considered in determining support. For example, an amount borrowed by the person, or by you, and spent for support must be included in total support.

Explanation
Here's a quick list of broad areas in which expenditures constitute support. For more details see the text below.

Lodging, including utilities and telephone
Room and board at a college or private school
Clothing, laundry, and dry cleaning
Education, including tuition, books and supplies, and music and dancing lessons
Medical expenses, including doctor, dentist, and health insurance premiums
Transportation, including purchase of a car, its maintenance, and gas
Child care, including baby-sitters, nursery school, and summer camp
Entertainment, including movies, theater, spending money, toys, and vacations
Charitable contributions on behalf of a dependent
Wedding costs
Payments to an institution for the care of an elderly parent

Generally, the IRS maintains that only expenditures necessary for essential support—basic food, housing, clothing, education, health, and transportation—qualify toward the 50% support test. The courts have been more lenient, allowing expenditures for dancing lessons, summer camp, vacations, and wedding receptions to count toward support.

Generally, the amount of an item of support is the amount of the expense incurred in providing that item. Expenses that are not directly related to any one member of a household, such as the cost of food for the household, must be divided among the members of the household. If the item is property or lodging, the amount of such item is its fair rental value.

Example. Your parents live with you, your spouse, and your two children in a house you own. The fair rental value of your parents' share of lodging is $2,000 a year, which includes furnishings and utilities. Your father receives a nontaxable pension of $4,200, which he spends equally for items of support such as clothing, transportation, and recreation, for your mother and himself. Your total food expense for the household is $6,000. Your heat and utility bills amount to $1,200. Your mother has hospital and medical expenses of $600, which you pay during the year. Figure your parents' total support as follows:

	Support provided	
	Father	Mother
Fair rental value of lodging	$1,000	$1,000
Pension spent for their support	2,100	2,100
Share of food (1/6 of $6,000)	1,000	1,000
Medical expenses for mother		600
Parents' total support	$4,100	$4,700

Since you provided different amounts to each parent, you must figure the dependency status of each parent separately. You provide $2,000 ($1,000 lodging, $1,000 food) of your father's total support of $4,100—less than half. You provide $2,600 to your mother ($1,000 lodging, $1,000 food, $600 medical)—more than half of her total support of $4,700. You may claim your mother as a dependent, but not your father. Heat and utilities are included in the fair rental value of the lodging, so these are not considered separately.

Lodging defined. Lodging is the fair rental value of the room, apartment, or house in which the person lives. It includes a reasonable allowance for the use of furniture and appliances, and for heat and other utilities.

Fair rental value defined. This is the amount you could reasonably expect to receive from a stranger for the same kind of lodging. It is used in place of rent or taxes, interest, depreciation, paint, insurance, utilities, cost of furniture and appliances, etc. In some cases, fair rental value may be equal to the rent paid.

If you are considered to provide the total lodging, determine the fair rental value of the room the person uses, or a share of the fair rental value of the entire dwelling if the person has use of your entire home. If you do not provide the total lodging, the total fair rental value must be divided depending on how much of the total lodging you provide. If you provide only a part and the person supplies the rest, the fair rental value must be divided between the two of you according to the amount each of you provides.

Example. Your parents live rent free in a house you own. It has a fair rental value of $5,400 a year furnished, which includes a fair rental value of $3,600 for the house and $1,800 for the furniture. This does not include heat and utilities. The house is completely furnished with furniture belonging to your parents. You pay $600 for their utility bills. Utilities are not usually included in rent for houses in the area where your parents live. Therefore, you consider the total fair rental value of the lodging to be $6,000 ($3,600 fair rental value of the unfurnished house, $1,800 allowance for furnishings provided by your parents, and $600 cost of utilities) of which you are considered to provide $4,200 ($3,600 + $600).

Person living in his or her own home. The total fair rental value of a person's home that he or she owns is considered support contributed by that person.

If you help to keep up the home by paying interest on the mortgage, real estate taxes, fire insurance premiums, ordinary repairs, or other items directly related to the home, or give someone cash to pay those expenses, reduce the total fair rental value of the home by those amounts in figuring that person's own contribution.

Example. You provide $6,000 cash for your father's support during the year. He lives in his own home, which has a fair rental value of $6,600 a year. He uses $800 of the money you give him to pay his real estate taxes. Your father's contribution for his own lodging is $5,800 ($6,600 &minus $800 for taxes).

Living with someone rent free. If you live with a person rent free in his or her home, you must reduce the amount you provide for support by the fair rental value of lodging he or she provides you.

Property. Property provided as support is measured by its fair market value.

Capital expenses. Capital items, such as furniture, appliances, and cars, that are bought for a person during the year may be included in total support under certain circumstances.

The following examples show when a capital item is or is not support.

Example 1. You buy a $200 power lawn mower for your 13-year-old child. The child is given the duty of keeping the lawn trimmed. Because a lawn mower is ordinarily an item you buy for personal and family reasons that benefits all members of the household, you cannot include the cost of the lawn mower in the support of your child.

Example 2. You buy a $150 television set as a birthday present for your 12-year-old child. The television set is placed in your child's bedroom. You include the cost of the television set in the support of your child.

Example 3. You pay $5,000 for a car and register it in your name. You and your 17-year-old daughter use the car equally. Because you own the car and do not give it to your daughter but merely let her use it, you cannot include the cost of the car in your daughter's total support. However, you can include in your daughter's support your out-of-pocket expenses of operating the car for her benefit.

Example 4. Your 17-year-old son, using personal funds, buys a car for $4,500. You provide all the rest of your son's support — $4,000. Since the car is bought and owned by your son, the car's fair market value ($4,500) must be included in his support. The $4,000 support you provide is less than half of his total support of $8,500. You cannot claim your son as a dependent.

entire $4,500 to buy the car. However, if the parents had contributed $251 toward the car's purchase, they would then have contributed more than half of their son's support and could claim the son as a dependent and get a $2,350 deduction. Assuming that the parents were in the 31% tax bracket, the deduction was worth $729 to them. The moral of the story is: Contributing to the purchase of a car or a trip in the year in which your child graduates from school may make good tax sense if the contribution ensures you one more year in which you can claim your child as a dependent.

Medical insurance premiums. Medical insurance premiums you pay, including premiums for supplementary Medicare coverage, are included in the total support you provide.

Medical insurance benefits. These benefits, including basic and supplementary Medicare benefits, are not part of support.

Tuition payments and allowances under the GI Bill. Amounts veterans receive under the GI Bill for tuition payments and allowances while they attend school are included in total support.

Example. During the year, your son receives $2,200 from the government under the GI Bill. He uses this amount for his education. You provide the rest of his support — $2,000. You may not claim your son as your dependent because you did not provide more than half of his total support of $4,200.

Other support items. Other items may be considered as support depending on the facts in each case. For example, if you pay someone to provide child care or disabled dependent care, you may include these payments as support, even if you claim a credit for them. For information on the credit, see Chapter 33, *Child and Dependent Care Credit.*

If you contribute support to a household other than the one in which you live and that household includes more than one person who may qualify as your dependent, you may earmark portions of your support funds for specific persons. This will enable you to prove that you have provided more than 50% of the support for a certain member or members of the household. Without written corroboration, it is likely that the monies contributed will be prorated among all the members of the household, which could result in your losing a dependency exemption.

Example

You provide $5,000 of support for your parents. They live in their own apartment and spend $6,000 annually on their joint support.

Unless you have specifically designated who your money is for, the IRS will assume that half of the money was intended for each parent. Therefore, you have not provided more than 50% of the support for either parent.

If you establish in writing that over $3,000 of your funds spent on support are for one of your parents and the balance is for the other, you will be able to claim one dependency deduction.

Do Not Include in Total Support

The following items are not included in total support:

1) Federal, state, and local income taxes paid by persons from their own income.
2) Social security and Medicare taxes paid by persons from their own income.
3) Life insurance premiums.
4) Funeral expenses.
5) Scholarships received by your child if your child is a full-time student. (If a child is committed to a state training school because of antisocial behavior, the value of the room, board, and education provided is not a scholarship. It must be included in support.)

Explanation

Savings should not be included in total support.

Example

If a child puts his or her entire after-tax earnings from a part-time job in a savings account or purchases common stock, the child is not considered to have spent any earnings toward self-support.

This is an important point to remember in the year in which a child graduates from school and gets a job for the rest of the year. Whether or not the parents may claim the child as a dependent hinges on whether or not their support payments—tuition, room and board, graduation presents, and so on—exceed the child's earnings that are not put into savings or used to pay taxes.

6) Survivors' and Dependents' Educational Assistance payments used for support of the child who receives them.

Multiple Support Agreement

Sometimes no one provides more than half of the support of a person. Instead, two or more persons, each of whom would be able to take the exemption but for the support test, together provide more than half the person's support.

When this happens, you may agree that any one of you who individually provides more than 10% of the person's support, but *only one,* may claim an exemption for that person. Each of the others must sign a written statement agreeing not to claim the exemption for that year. The statements must be filed with the income tax return of the person who claims the exemption. **Form 2120,** *Multiple Support Declaration,* is used for this purpose.

Example 1. You, your sister, and your two brothers provide the entire support of your mother for the year. You provide 45%, your sister 35%, and your two brothers each provide 10%. Either you or your sister may claim an exemption for your mother. The other must sign a Form 2120 or a written statement agreeing not to take an exemption for her. Because neither brother provides more than 10% of the support, neither can take the exemption. They do not have to sign a Form 2120 or the written statement.

Example 2. You and your brother each provide 20% of your mother's support for the year. The remaining 60% of her support is provided equally by two persons who are not related to her. She does not live with them. Because more than half of her support is provided by persons who cannot claim her as a dependent, no one may claim the exemption.

Example 3. Your father lives with you and receives 25% of his support from social security, 40% from you, 24% from his brother,

Table 3-1. **Worksheet for Determining Support**

Income

1) Did the person you supported receive any income, such as wages, interest, dividends, pensions, rents, social security, or welfare? (If yes, complete lines 2, 3, 4, and 5)	☐ Yes ☐ No
2) Total income received	$
3) Amount of income used for support	$
4) Amount of income used for other purposes	$
5) Amount of income saved	$
(The total of lines 3, 4, and 5 should equal line 2)	

Expenses for Entire Household (where the person you supported lived)

6) Lodging (Complete item a or b)	
a) Rent paid	$
b) If not rented, show fair rental value of home. If the person you supported owned the home, include this amount in line 20.	$
7) Food	$
8) Utilities (heat, light, water, etc. not included in line 6a or 6b)	$
9) Repairs (not included in line 6a or 6b)	$
10) Other. Do not include expenses of maintaining home, such as mortgage interest, real estate taxes, and insurance.	$
11) Total household expenses (Add lines 6 through 10)	$
12) Total number of persons who lived in household	

Expenses for the Person You Supported

13) Each person's part of household expenses (line 11 divided by line 12)	$
14) Clothing	$
15) Education	$
16) Medical, dental	$
17) Travel, recreation	$
18) Other (specify)	
	$
19) Total cost of support for the year (Add lines 13 through 18)	$
20) Amount the person provided for own support (line 3, plus line 6b if the person you supported owned the home)	$
21) Amount others provided for the person's support. Include amounts provided by state, local, and other welfare societies or agencies.	$
22) Amount you provided for the person's support (line 19 minus lines 20 and 21)	$
23) 50% of line 19	$

If line 22 is more than line 23, you meet the support test for the person. If the person meets the other dependency tests, you may claim an exemption for that person. If line 23 is more than line 22, you may still be able to claim an exemption for that person under a multiple support agreement. See *Multiple Support Agreement* in this chapter.

and 11% from a friend. Either you or your uncle may take the exemption for your father. A Form 2120 or a written statement from the one not claiming the exemption must be attached to the return of the one who takes the exemption.

TAXPLANNER

The multiple support agreement provides a tax-planning opportunity that should not be overlooked. If more than one individual provides at least 10% of the support of a dependent, and if no one individual provides over 50%

support, an individual in a higher tax bracket may take the deduction, even if that individual did not provide the most support for the dependent.

Example

Four adult children jointly furnish all of the support for their elderly father. The marginal tax rate for three of the children is 15%, but the fourth child is in the 31% bracket. Therefore, the fourth child should be designated as the one to claim the dependency deduction under the multiple support agreement, even if he or she is providing less support than the other three. The $2,350 deduction is worth $729 to the fourth child but is worth only $353 to any of the other children, since they are taxed at 15%.

Support Test for Divorced or Separated Parents

The support test for a child of divorced or separated parents is based on special rules that apply only if:

1) The parents are divorced or legally separated under a decree of divorce or separate maintenance, or separated under a written separation agreement, or lived apart at all times during the last 6 months of the calendar year,
2) One or both parents provide more than half of the child's total support for the calendar year, and
3) One or both parents have custody of the child for more than half of the calendar year.

"Child" is defined earlier under the *Gross Income Test.*
Exceptions. This discussion does not apply in any of the following situations:

1) A third party, such as a relative or friend, provides half of the child's support or more,
2) The child is in the custody of a person other than the parents for half of the year or more,
3) The support of the child is determined under a multiple support agreement, as discussed earlier, or
4) The parents are separated under a written separation agreement or are living apart, but they file a joint return for the tax year.

Custodial parent. The parent who has custody of the child for the greater part of the year (the custodial parent) is generally treated as the parent who provides more than half of the child's support. It does not matter whether the custodial parent actually provided more than half of the support. The noncustodial parent is the parent who has custody of the child for the shorter part of the year or who does not have custody at all.
Custody. Custody is usually determined by the terms of the most recent decree of divorce or separate maintenance, or a later custody decree. If there is no decree, use the written separation agreement. If neither a decree nor agreement establishes custody, then the parent who has the physical custody of the child for the greater part of the year is considered to have custody of the child. This also applies if the validity of a decree or agreement awarding custody is uncertain because of legal proceedings pending on the last day of the calendar year.

If the parents are divorced or separated during the year and had joint custody of the child before the separation, the parent who has custody for the greater part of the rest of the year is considered to have custody of the child for the tax year.

Example 1. Under the terms of your divorce, you have custody of your child for 10 months of the year. Your former spouse has custody for the other 2 months. You and your former spouse provide the child's total support. You are considered to have provided more than half of the support of the child. However, see *Noncustodial parent,* below.

Example 2. You and your former spouse provided your child's total support for 1993. You had custody of your child under your 1990 divorce decree, but on August 31, 1993, a new custody decree

granted custody to your former spouse. Because you had custody for the greater part of the year, you are considered to have provided more than half of your child's support.
Noncustodial parent. The noncustodial parent will be treated as providing more than half of the child's support if:

1) The custodial parent signs a written declaration that he or she will not claim the exemption for the child, and the noncustodial parent attaches this written declaration to his or her return,
2) A decree or agreement went into effect after 1984 and it unconditionally states that the noncustodial parent can claim the child as a dependent, or
3) A decree or agreement executed before 1985 provides that the noncustodial parent is entitled to the exemption, and he or she provides at least $600 for the child's support during the year, unless the pre-1985 decree or agreement is modified after 1984 to specify that this provision will not apply.

Example. Under the terms of your 1982 divorce decree, your former spouse has custody of your child. The decree specifically states that you are entitled to the exemption. You provide at least $600 in child support during the calendar year. You are considered to have provided more than half of the child's support.

Written declaration. The custodial parent should use **Form 8332,** *Release of Claim to Exemption for Child of Divorced or Separated Parents,* or a similar statement, to make the written declaration to release the exemption to the noncustodial parent. The noncustodial parent must attach the form or statement to his or her tax return.

The exemption may be released for a single year, for a number of specified years (for example, alternate years), or for all future years, as specified in the declaration. If the exemption is released for more than one year, the original release must be attached to the return of the noncustodial parent for the first year of such release, and a copy of the release must be attached to the return for each succeeding taxable year for which the noncustodial parent claims the exemption.

Children who didn't live with you. If you are claiming a child who didn't live with you under the rules for children of divorced or separated parents, enter the number of children who did not live with you (or who lived with their other parent for the greater part of the year) on the line to the right of line 6c of your Form 1040 or Form 1040A labeled "No. of your children on 6c who didn't live with you due to divorce or separation."

Then you must either:

1) Check the box on line 6d of your Form 1040 or Form 1040A if your divorce decree or written separation agreement was in effect before 1985 and it states that you can claim the child as your dependent, or
2) Attach Form 8332 or a similar statement to your return. If your divorce decree or separation agreement went into effect after 1984 and it unconditionally states that you can claim the child as your dependent, you may attach a copy of the following pages from the decree or agreement instead of Form 8332:
   a) Cover page (write the other parent's social security number on this page),
   b) The page that unconditionally states you can claim the child as your dependent, and
   c) Signature page showing the date of the agreement.

Enter the total number of children who did not live with you for reasons other than divorce or separation on the line labeled "Dependents on 6c not entered above." Include your dependent children who were not U.S. citizens and who lived in Canada or Mexico during 1993.

Figure 3-B. Support Test for Children of Divorced or Separated Parents

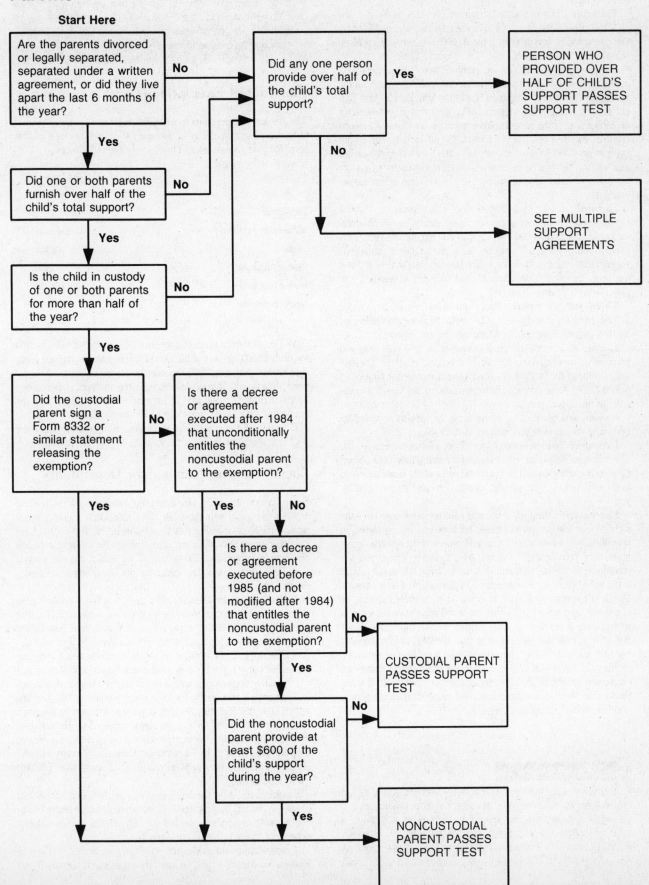

Child support. All child support payments actually received from the noncustodial parent are considered used for the support of the child.

Example. The noncustodial parent provides $1,200 for the child's support. This amount is considered as support provided by the noncustodial parent even if the $1,200 was actually spent on things other than support.

Support payments for an earlier year. If support payments made this year are not more than the amount required of the noncustodial parent, the amount of support provided by that parent is not reduced by any payment of support that parent owed for an earlier year. If the support payments are more than the amount required for this year, any payment for an earlier year is not support provided by the noncustodial parent for either the earlier year or for this year. It is reimbursement to the custodial parent for amounts paid for the support of the children in an earlier year.

Example. Under your divorce decree, you must pay $400 a month to your former spouse for the support of your two children. Last year you paid $4,000 instead of $4,800 due for the year. This year, if you pay the full amount, the entire $4,800 is considered support that you provided. If you also pay any part of the $800 you owe from last year, that amount is not included as support provided by you in either year.

Third–party support. Support provided by a third party for a divorced or separated parent is not included as support provided by that parent. However, see *Remarried parent,* below.

Example. You are divorced. During the whole year, you and your child live with your mother in a house she owns. The fair rental value of the lodging provided by your mother for your child is $1,000. The home provided by your mother is not included in the amount of support you provide.

Remarried parent. If you remarry, the support provided by your new spouse is treated as provided by you.

Example. You have two children from a former marriage who live with you. You have remarried and are living in a home owned by your present spouse. The fair rental value of the home provided to the children by your present spouse is treated as provided by you.

Home jointly owned. If you and your former spouse have the right to use and live in the home, each of you is considered to provide half of your child's lodging. However, if the divorce decree gives only you the right to use and live in the home, you are considered to provide your child's entire lodging. It does not matter if the legal title to the home remains in the names of both parents.

Medical expenses. A child of divorced or separated parents or of parents who live apart during the last 6 months of the year, is treated as a dependent of both parents for the medical expense deduction if the child receives more than half of his or her support from the parents. Thus, a parent can deduct medical expenses he or she paid for the child even though the other parent claims an exemption for the child. This special rule does not apply if more than half of the child's support is treated as received from a person under a multiple support agreement.

> **TAXPLANNER**
>
> Generally, the parent in the higher tax bracket should be designated as the parent to claim the dependency exemption for a child, assuming that the parent meets all the tests for claiming the dependency deduction. However, if the person with the highest tax bracket is subject to the phaseout of the personal exemption, the dependency exemption may not benefit that person.
> *Note:* The child care credit and medical expense deductions may be claimed whether or not you can claim the child as a dependent.

Phaseout of Exemptions

The amount you can claim as a deduction for exemptions is phased out once your adjusted gross income (AGI) goes above a certain level for your filing status. These levels are as follows:

Filing Status	AGI Level Which Reduces Exemption Amount
Married filing separately	$ 81,350
Single	108,450
Head of household	135,600
Married filing jointly	162,700
Qualifying widow(er)	162,700

You must reduce the dollar amount of your exemptions by 2% for each $2,500, or part of $2,500 ($1,250 if you are married filing separately), that your AGI exceeds the amount shown above for your filing status. If your AGI exceeds the amounts shown above by more than $122,500 ($61,250 if married filing separately), the amount of your exemptions will be reduced to zero.

If your AGI exceeds the level for your filing status, use *Table 3–2* in this chapter to figure the amount of your 1993 exemptions.

Social Security Number for Dependents

If you claim a dependent who is at least *one year old* by the end of your tax year, you must list the dependent's social security number (SSN) on your Form 1040 or Form 1040A. If you do not list the dependent's SSN when required or if you list an incorrect SSN, you may be subject to a $50 penalty. This penalty may be waived if you can show reasonable cause for not providing your dependent's SSN.

No social security number. If a person whom you expect to claim as a dependent on your return does not have an SSN, either you or that person should apply for an SSN as soon as possible by filing **Form SS–5,** *Application for a Social Security Card* with the Social Security Administration (SSA). Information about applying for an SSN and Form SS–5 is available at your local SSA office.

It usually takes about 2 weeks to get an SSN. If your dependent will not have a number by the time you are ready to file your tax return, ask the SSA to give you a receipt. When you file your return, write *"Applied for"* in the space provided for the number. If the SSA gave you a receipt, attach a copy of it to your return.

Dependents living in Mexico or Canada. Taxpayers who claim dependents living in Mexico or Canada must have SSNs for these dependents.

To obtain SSNs for these dependents, complete Form SS–5 and check the "Other" box for line 3, Citizenship. Attach a statement to explain that the SSN is needed for income tax purposes for a dependent living in Mexico or Canada.

A dependent living in **Mexico** may apply for an SSN at the U.S. Embassy in Mexico City or at any U.S. consulate in Mexico. If you

Table 3-2. **Deduction for Exemptions Worksheet**

Use this worksheet only if the amount on Form 1040, line 32, is more than the dollar amount shown on line 3 below for your filing status. If the amount on Form 1040, line 32, is equal to or less than the dollar amount shown on line 3, multiply $2,350 by the total number of exemptions claimed on Form 1040, line 6e, and enter the result on line 36.

1. Multiply $2,350 by the total number of exemptions claimed on Form 1040, line 6e ....   1. _____

2. Enter the amount from Form 1040, line 32 ....   2. _____

3. Enter on line 3 the amount shown below for your filing status:

   • Married filing separately, enter $81,350

   • Single, enter $108,450

   • Head of household, enter $135,600   3. _____

   • Married filing jointly or Qualifying widow(er), enter $162,700

4. Subtract line 3 from line 2. If zero or less, stop here; enter the amount from line 1 above on Form 1040, line 36. ....   4. _____

   Note: *If line 4 is more than $122,500 (more than $61,250 if married filing separately),* **stop here;** *you* cannot *take a deduction for exemptions. Enter -0- on Form 1040, line 36.*

5. Divide line 4 by $2,500 ($1,250 if married filing separately). If the result is not a whole number, round it up to the next higher whole number ....   5. _____

6. Multiply line 5 by 2% (.02), and enter the result as a decimal amount ....   6. _____

7. Multiply line 1 by line 6 ....   7. _____

8. **Deduction for exemptions.** Subtract line 7 from line 1. Enter the result here and on Form 1040, line 36. ....   8. _____

claim a dependent who lives in Mexico, enter "MX" instead of a number in column (5) of line 6c of your Form 1040 or Form 1040A.

A dependent living in **Canada** may apply for an SSN at the American Embassy in Ottawa or at a consulate. Those living near the U.S. border may also apply at a SSA office in a nearby American city. If you claim a dependent who lives in Canada, enter "CN" instead of a number in column (5) of line 6c of your Form 1040 or Form 1040A.

4 | Decedents

Introduction

The death of an individual causes special income tax problems that are likely to be unfamiliar and puzzling to the survivors. Among other things, the decedent's will and local inheritance laws can create a bewildering array of questions about how income is to be allocated and which **deductions** *may be claimed and by whom. This chapter helps you sort out such questions. It is most helpful to a survivor who has to deal with a relatively uncomplicated situation and a small estate. Where the assets are large and the situation is complex, professional assistance is recommended.*

As a general rule, you should remember that taxes are just as certain after death as they are during life. If the decedent realizes income, it must be reported—on the decedent's final tax return, by his or her estate, or by the heirs. Similarly, items that are deductible during life continue to be deductible after death. The questions are how and by whom. This chapter discusses the rules on these matters.

Death is not without its tax benefits. The most important one concerns the cost basis of **capital assets.** *(See Chapter 14, Basis of Property, for a complete discussion of* **basis.***) Generally such* **assets** *get a new cost basis at death, and usually the figure is the* **fair market value** *of the property at the date of death. Thus, if your grandfather owned an apartment building solely in his name and he willed it to you, you would look to the fair market value at the date of death to determine your cost basis for* **depreciation** *or to figure your gain or loss on sale. It wouldn't matter that your grandfather bought the building for $100 in 1923.*

If you own income-producing property, it's important to consider how you hold title to it—whether, for example, you are the sole owner or whether your spouse (or your heir) is a joint tenancy owner. How you hold title to income-producing property will determine both income taxes and estate taxes due after your death. See Planning Your Estate, in Chapter 42, Planning Ahead for 1994 and Beyond, for details.

This chapter discusses the tax responsibilities of the person(s) who is in charge of the property of a decedent (person who died). It covers the following topics:

- What individual income tax return(s) must be filed
- Who must file the return
- When and where the return must be filed
- Who must pay any tax that is due
- What income tax, if any, a survivor owes on inherited income or property

This chapter does not discuss the requirements for filing an income tax return of an estate (Form 1041). For information on Form 1041, see *Income Tax Return of an Estate–Form 1041* in Publication 559, *Survivors, Executors, and Administrators.* This chapter also does not discuss the requirements for filing an estate tax return (Form 706). For information on Form 706, see Publication 448, *Federal Estate and Gift Taxes.*

Useful Items

You may want to see:

Publication

☐ **559** Survivors, Executors, and Administrators

Form (and Instructions)

☐ **56** Notice Concerning Fiduciary Relationship
☐ **1310** Statement of Person Claiming Refund Due a Deceased Taxpayer
☐ **4810** Request for Prompt Assessment Under Internal Revenue Code Section 6501(d)

Personal Representatives

A personal representative of an estate can be an executor, an administrator, or anyone who is in charge of the decedent's property.

The surviving spouse may or may not be the personal representative, depending on the terms of the decedent's will or the court appointment.

Generally, an *executor* (or executrix) is named in a decedent's will to administer the estate (property and debts left by the decedent) and distribute properties as the decedent has directed. An *administrator* (or administratrix) is usually appointed by the court if no will exists, if no executor was named in the will, or if the named executor cannot or will not serve. In general, an executor and an administrator perform the same duties and have the same responsibilities. For simplicity, the term *personal representative* will be used throughout this chapter.

Duties. The primary duties of a personal representative are to collect all of the decedent's assets, pay the creditors, and distribute the remaining assets to the heirs or other beneficiaries.

The personal representative must also:

- Notify the IRS that he or she is acting as the personal representative,
- File any income tax return that is due, and
- Make sure that any income tax that is due is paid.

You can use **Form 56,** *Notice Concerning Fiduciary Relationship,* to notify the IRS.

For more information on the duties and responsibilities of the personal representative, see *Duties* under *Personal Representatives* in Publication 559.

Explanation
Publication 559, a voluminous and valuable booklet, is recommended for those who wish to specialize in the handling of decedents' tax matters.

Final Return for the Decedent

The same filing requirements that apply to individuals (income, age, and filing status) determine if a final income tax return must be filed for the decedent and whether Form 1040, Form 1040A, or Form 1040EZ should be used. Filing requirements are discussed in Chapter 1, *Filing Information.*

If none of the filing requirements are met, but the decedent had tax withheld or paid estimated tax, a final return should be filed to get a refund. A final return should also be filed if the decedent was entitled to a refundable credit such as the earned income credit. See Chapters 35, *Other Credits,* for additional information on refundable credits.

Methods of accounting. The method of accounting used by the decedent generally determines what income you must include and what deductions you can take on the final return. Generally, individuals use one of two methods of accounting: cash or accrual.

Cash method. If the decedent used the cash method of accounting, which most people use, report only the items of income that the decedent actually or constructively received before death and deduct only the expenses the decedent paid before death. For an exception for certain medical expenses not paid before death, see *Medical costs,* later, under *Deductions.*

Explanation
Actual or constructive receipt of income includes items such as uncashed payroll checks and uncashed **dividend** checks if they were received or were available to the decedent before death.

Example
If the decedent's payroll check for June 1 through June 15 is available on Wednesday, June 15, but she fails to pick it up and dies on Thursday, June 16, the income is included in the decedent's final return. However, if the decedent would not have been paid until Friday, June 17—that date appears on the check and that is the first day it could have been picked up—the income is reported as part of the estate and *not* on the final Form 1040. In the latter case, the income is called *income in respect of the decedent* and is discussed in the following section.

If the decedent was married and lived in a **community property** state—Arizona, California, Idaho, Louisiana, Nevada, New Mexico, Texas, or Washington—half of the combined income and expenses of husband and wife up to the date of death may be attributable to the decedent. Wisconsin has a "marital property" law that is similar to community property law.

TAXSAVER

The person filing the decedent's final return may elect to include as income on that return all of the U.S. Savings Bond interest that had accumulated but had not been reported. If the decedent otherwise had low **taxable income** to report on her final return, this return could be the best one in which to recognize the interest income. To determine whether or not this is advantageous, you have to compare the tax rate of the decedent on the final return with the tax rate of the recipient of the bonds. (For a further discussion of this point, see Chapter 8, *Interest Income.*)

Accrual method. If the decedent used an accrual method of accounting, report only those items of income that the decedent accrued, or earned, before death. Deduct those expenses the decedent was liable for before death, regardless of whether the expenses were paid.

Additional information. For more information on the cash and accrual methods, see *Accounting Methods* in Chapter 1, *Filing Information.*

Who must file the return? The personal representative of the decedent is responsible for filing any income tax returns and making sure that any income tax that is due is paid. This includes the final income tax return of the decedent (for the year of death) and any returns not filed for preceding years.

Example. Roberta Russell died on February 5, 1994, before filing her 1993 tax return. Her personal representative must file her 1993 tax return as well as her final tax return for 1994.

Explanation
If the decedent had not yet filed a return for the previous year, the executor, administrator, or survivor should prepare the return just as the decedent would have. The

only difference is that the executor signs the return. See *Signing the Return,* later.

For the year of death, the decedent's final return covers income received and deductions paid during the period from January 1 through the date of death.

Exception. Under certain circumstances, a surviving spouse may be able to file a joint final return or joint returns for preceding years for which returns have not yet been filed. See *Joint return,* later.

TaxSaver

A surviving spouse may be able to reduce the tax on his or her income by filing a **joint return** with the decedent. Even if a taxpayer died on January 1 with no income earned by that date, the availability of joint tax rates to the surviving spouse could be very beneficial.

Filing the return. When you file a return for the decedent, either as the personal representative or as the surviving spouse, you should write "DECEASED," the decedent's name, and the date of death across the top of the tax return. This same information should be included on any Form 1040X, *Amended U.S. Individual Income Tax Return,* that you file for the decedent.

If the decedent and surviving spouse are filing a joint return, you should write the name and address of the decedent and the surviving spouse in the name and address space. If a joint return is not being filed, write the decedent's name in the name space and the personal representative's name and address in the remaining space.

Example. John Doe died early in 1993. The top of his final return is filled in as shown later.

Signing the return. If a personal representative has been appointed, the personal representative must sign the return. If a joint return is filed, the surviving spouse must also sign it. If no personal representative has been appointed by the due date for filing the return, the surviving spouse (on a joint return) should sign the return and write in the signature area "Filing as surviving spouse." See *Joint return,* later.

If no personal representative has been appointed and if there is no surviving spouse, the person in charge of the decedent's property must file and sign the return as "personal representative."

Example. Assume in the John Doe example above that Mrs. Doe is filing as a surviving spouse. She signs their final joint return as shown later.

Claiming a refund. Generally, a person who is filing a return for a decedent and claiming a refund must file **Form 1310,** *Statement of Person Claiming Refund Due a Deceased Taxpayer,* with the return. However, if you are a surviving spouse filing a joint return with the decedent, you do not have to file Form 1310. If you are a court appointed or certified personal representative filing Form 1040, Form 1040A, or Form 1040EZ for the decedent, you also do not have to file Form 1310, but you must attach to the return a copy of the court certificate showing your appointment.

Example. Joe Brown died on January 14, 1994, before filing his 1993 tax return. On April 4, 1994, you are appointed the personal representative for Joe's estate, and you file his Form 1040 for 1993 showing a refund due. You do not need to attach Form 1310 to claim the refund, but you must attach to his return a copy of the court certificate to show that you are the appointed personal representative of Joe's estate.

TaxPlanner

To make sure that refunds are not delayed, it is recommended that Form 1310 be attached to *any* return, joint or otherwise, filed for a decedent.

When and where to file. The final return is due by the date the decedent's return would have been due had death not occurred. The final return for a calendar year taxpayer is generally due by April 15 of the year following the year of death. However, when the due date for filing tax returns falls on a Saturday, Sunday, or legal holiday, you can file on the next business day.

You can mail the decedent's final income tax return to the Internal Revenue Service Center for the area where you live. See *Where to File* near the end of this publication.

Request for prompt assessment of tax. As the personal representative for the decedent's estate, you must see to it that any additional taxes that the decedent may owe are paid. The IRS usually has 3 years after the filing of a return to charge any additional tax that may be due. Returns filed before the due date are treated as filed on the due date.

You can shorten the time that the IRS has to charge the decedent's estate any additional tax by requesting a prompt assessment of the decedent's income taxes. This request reduces the time the IRS has to charge any additional tax from 3 years from the date the return is filed to 18 months from the date the IRS receives the request. This may permit a quicker settlement of the tax responsibilities of the estate and earlier distribution of the decedent's assets, such as money and property, to the beneficiaries.

You can make the request for any tax years for the decedent that are still subject to additional tax charges, even if the returns were filed before the decedent's death.

Note. Requesting this prompt assessment will not shorten the time the IRS has to charge any additional tax if it can be charged beyond the 3 years from the date the return was filed or due. For example, additional tax can still be charged because of a substantial understatement of income or if a fraudulent return was filed.

How to request. You can use **Form 4810,** *Request for Prompt Assessment Under Internal Revenue Code Section 6501(d),* for making this request. If Form 4810 is not used, you must clearly indicate that you are requesting a prompt assessment under Section 6501(d) of the Internal Revenue Code and specify the year(s) involved. You must file the request separately from any other document. Send it to the IRS office where the decedent's return was filed.

TaxPlanner

A representative of a decedent's estate may be held personally liable by the IRS for later-discovered tax deficiencies if the representative has not retained enough of the estate's assets to pay those deficiencies. Therefore, many cautious representatives are slow to distribute the estate's assets to the heirs. A request for prompt assessment may shorten the period in which the IRS may blame the representative for not paying enough tax.

Joint return. Generally, the personal representative and the surviving spouse can file a joint return for the decedent and the surviving spouse. However, the surviving spouse alone can file the joint return if:

DECEASED   JOHN J. DOE   February 28, 1993

Form **1040**

Department of the Treasury—Internal Revenue Service
U.S. Individual Income Tax Return (T) **1993**

IRS Use Only—Do not write or staple in this space.

For the year Jan. 1–Dec. 31, 1993, or other tax year beginning _____ , 1993, ending _____ , 19___   OMB No. 1545-0074

Label

(See instructions on page 12.)

Use the IRS label. Otherwise, please print or type.

L A B E L   H E R E

Your first name and initial: John J.   Last name: Doe

Your social security number: 765 00 4321

If a joint return, spouse's first name and initial: Jane M.   Last name: Doe

Spouse's social security number: 123 00 4567

Home address (number and street). If you have a P.O. box, see page 12.: 1992 Oak St.   Apt. no.

City, town or post office, state, and ZIP code. If you have a foreign address, see page 12.: Sheridan   WY   82801

For Privacy Act and Paperwork Reduction Act Notice, see page 4.

Presidential Election Campaign
(See page 12.)

Do you want $3 to go to this fund? . . . .   Yes ✓ No

If a joint return, does your spouse want $3 to go to this fund? . . . .   Yes ✓ No

Note: *Checking "Yes" will not change your tax or reduce your refund.*

Sign Here

Keep a copy of this return for your records.

Under penalties of perjury, I declare that I have examined this return and accompanying schedules and statements, and to the best of my knowledge and belief, they are true, correct, and complete. Declaration of preparer (other than taxpayer) is based on all information of which preparer has any knowledge.

Your signature ▶ _____   Date _____   Your occupation _____

Spouse's signature. If a joint return, BOTH must sign. ▶ Jane M. Doe Filing as surviving spouse   Date 4-1-94   Spouse's occupation Engineer

Paid Preparer's Use Only

Preparer's signature ▶ _____   Date _____   Check if self-employed ☐   Preparer's social security no.

Firm's name (or yours if self-employed) and address ▶ _____   E.I. No. _____   ZIP code _____

1) The decedent did not file a return for that year, and
2) No personal representative is appointed before the due date for filing the return of the surviving spouse.

This also applies to the return for the preceding year if the decedent died after the close of the preceding tax year and before the due date for filing that return. The final joint return must show the decedent's income before death and the surviving spouse's income for the entire year.

TaxPlanner

If you are a surviving spouse and are filing a joint return with the decedent, you are not relieved of the obligation to make estimated tax payments because of the death. Since the **IRS** may not agree with the computation you use to determine the estimated tax payments required from you as the surviving spouse, it's best to make payments sufficient to avoid any penalties and the aggravation of dealing with the IRS.

If the surviving spouse remarried before the end of the year in which the decedent died, a final joint return with the deceased spouse cannot be filed. The filing status of the deceased spouse is then married filing separately.

TaxSaver

If the decedent was married, it is important to calculate whether the tax on a joint return would be less than the total tax on two separate returns.

Ordinarily, a joint return would save you more tax, as it does for most married couples, but only a complete computation will tell you for sure. Remember, the joint return will include all of the income and deductions of the survivor for the entire year but those of the decedent are included only up to the date of death. If property was owned jointly with the surviving spouse, all of the income after death would have to be reported in the joint return, since it, along with the ownership of the property, passed to the surviving spouse. However, if the property was not owned jointly and passed to an executor at death, the subsequent income on that property would be reported on the income tax return for the estate for which the executor is responsible and not on the joint return.

Change to joint return. If a separate return was filed by or for the decedent, and the due date for filing that return has expired, that return can be changed to a joint return only by the personal representative on behalf of the decedent. The surviving spouse must also agree to the change. For more information, see *Joint Return After Separate Returns* in Chapter 2, *Filing Status.*

Change to separate return. If the surviving spouse files a joint return with the decedent and a personal representative is later appointed by the court, the personal representative can change the joint return election. The personal representative has one year from the due date of the return to file a separate return for the decedent. The joint return would then become the separate return of the surviving spouse. The decedent's items would be excluded, and the tax liability would be refigured on the separate return.

How to Report Certain Income

This section explains how to report certain types of income on the final return. The rules on income discussed in the other chapters of this publication also apply to a decedent's final return. See Chapters 6, *Wages, Salaries and Other Earnings,* through 17, *Reporting Gains and Losses,* if they apply.

Interest and Dividend Income (Forms 1099)

Payers of interest and dividends report amounts on Forms 1099 using the name and identification number of the person to whom the account is payable. After a person's death, the Forms 1099 must reflect the new owner's (the estate's or beneficiary's) name and identification number. As the personal representative, you must furnish this information to the payers.

For example, if an interest-bearing account becomes part of the estate, you must provide the estate's name and identification number to the payer so that the Form 1099–INT, *Interest Income,* can reflect the correct payee information. If the interest-bearing account is transferred to a surviving joint owner, you must provide the survivor's name and identification number to the payer.

You should receive Forms 1099 for the decedent that report amounts of interest and dividends earned prior to death. The estate or beneficiary should receive separate Forms 1099 that report the amounts earned after death and that are payable to them.

If you receive Forms 1099 that include both income earned before the date of death (reportable on the decedent's final return) and income earned after the date of death (reportable by the estate or other recipient), then you will need to request new Forms 1099. You should contact the payers to ask them for corrected Forms 1099 that properly identify the recipient of the income (by name and identification number) and the correct amounts.

If you are unable to contact the payer or if you do not receive the corrected forms on time, prepare the decedent's final return as follows.

1) Report the total amounts shown on Forms 1099–INT and 1099–DIV, *Dividends and Distributions,* on Schedule 1 (Form 1040A), or on Schedule B (Form 1040).
2) On the appropriate schedule and part (several lines above lines 2 and/or 6), enter a "subtotal" of the combined amounts of all of the interest or dividends listed.
3) Below this subtotal, write "Nominee Distribution" and show the amount of any interest or dividends included on the Forms 1099 that belongs to another recipient. Subtract it from the subtotal.
4) Report the net result on the proper line of the part of the income schedules being used (lines 2 and/or 6), and follow the directions shown for that line to carry the amount forward to the front of the return.

TaxPlanner

No matter how hard you try, you will not get the payers of dividends and interest to reflect properly the amounts paid to the decedent prior to death and the amounts that are paid to the decedent's successor in interest. It is therefore imperative that you follow the instructions under "How to Report" carefully in order to avoid bothersome inquiries from the IRS.

Example

Marty died on June 30, 1993. Marty owned 50 shares of ABC Corporation and 75 shares of XYZ Corporation, both of which paid a $1 per share quarterly dividend on February 1, May 1, August 1, and November 1. Upon Marty's death, all shares were transferred to his estate. XYZ Corporation has properly issued two Forms 1099-DIV. One Form 1099-DIV identifies Marty as the recipient of $150 (the dividends paid to Marty prior to death, from January 1, 1993 to June 30, 1993), and the other identifies Marty's estate as the recipient of $150 (the dividends paid to the estate, from July 1, 1993 to December 31, 1993). ABC Corporation, however, issued only one Form 1099-DIV, naming Marty as the recipient of the entire year's dividend ($200).

On Marty's final return, you must report total dividends as indicated on all Forms 1099-DIV issued in Marty's name ($150 from XYZ Corporation and $200 from ABC Corporation) on line 5, Part II of Form 1040, Schedule B. Several lines above line 6, write "Subtotal" and enter $350. Below this subtotal, write "Nominee Distribution" and enter $100 (the dividends paid by ABC Corporation to Marty's estate). Subtract the nominee distribution from the subtotal and report the net result of $200 on line 6.

TaxOrganizer

You should make sure you keep a copy of the Forms 1099 that you receive in the mail.

For information on how to report interest income from Series EE or Series E Savings Bonds, see *Decedents* under *U.S. Savings Bonds* in Chapter 8, *Interest Income.* Chapters 8 and 9, *Dividends and Other Corporate Distributions,* have more information about interest and dividend income.

Note: If the decedent received interest or dividends as a nominee (that is, in the decedent's name, but the interest actually belongs to someone else), you generally must give the actual owner a Form 1099.

TaxOrganizer

Form 1099 accompanied by Form 1096, *Annual Summary and Transmittal of U.S. Information Returns,* must be filed by February 28, 1994.

Capital Loss

A capital loss sustained by a decedent during his or her last tax year can be deducted only on the final return filed for the decedent. The capital loss limits discussed in Chapter 17 still apply in this situation. The loss cannot be deducted by the estate or carried over to following years.

Business Income

This section discusses some of the business income which may have to be included on the final return.

Partnership income. If the decedent was a partner, his or her death generally does not close the partnership's tax year. See *Closing of Partnership Year* under *Liquidation of Partner's Interest* in Publication 541, *Tax Information on Partnerships,* for how to treat partnership income if the partnership year does end with the death of a partner.

As the personal representative, you must include on the final return the decedent's share of partnership income for the partnership's tax year that ends within or with the decedent's last tax year (year ending on the date of death).

Do not include on the final return the decedent's share of partnership income for a partnership's tax year that ends after the date of death. In this case, partnership income earned up to and including the date of death is income in respect of the decedent, which is discussed later in this chapter. Income earned after the date of death to the end of the partnership's tax year is income to the estate or successor in interest (beneficiary).

Explanation

For income tax purposes, partnership income or loss is considered to arise on the last day of the partnership's tax year. If a partner dies on October 15 but the partnership's tax year ends on December 31, then the deceased partner's final individual income tax return will not include any partnership income.

The partnership income would have to be reported by the partner's successor in interest, usually the estate. Tax rates for an estate may be higher than tax rates for the joint return that the decedent may have been entitled to file. Also, the decedent's deductions and **exemptions** would not apply to the estate but would appear on the decedent's final return. The result is that the decedent's deductions and exemptions would be wasted. This could be especially costly if the partnership was the decedent's main source of income.

Example

A partner in a law firm died on December 1, 1993. His partnership income for the year ending December 31, 1993, of $100,000 will be included in his estate's income tax return. During the year and prior to his death, the decedent had **itemized deductions** of $20,000 and was entitled to the personal exemption of $2,350. If he had no other income during 1993, the $22,350 of deductions and exemptions would be useless; there would be nothing to apply them against on the decedent's final return.

A member of a tax-shelter partnership has the same problem in reverse. The decedent presumably invested in the tax shelter to have losses to write off against income. However, the tax losses for the year of death will not appear on the final return but will go to the estate, where they may be wasted.

TAX**SAVER**

Planning for partnership interests can save substantial amounts of income tax. For example, a partner should investigate the possibility of appointing his or her spouse as successor in interest to the partnership so that the income or loss for the year of death can flow onto the survivor's return and thus onto the joint return.

There is another way of ensuring the immediate transfer of the partnership interest to the spouse upon the partner's death so that the income or loss can be reported on the joint return. The spouses may own the partnership interest in joint tenancy. Be sure to check that the partnership will permit this. Also, if the executor has the assets and the legal authority to make a distribu-

tion to the spouse, all or a portion of the partnership income can be transferred to the final joint return. Prompt action may be necessary.

S corporation income. If the decedent was a shareholder in an S corporation, you must include on the final return the decedent's share of S corporation income for the corporation's tax year that ends within or with the decedent's last tax year (year ending on the date of death). The final return must also include the decedent's pro rata share of the S corporation's income for the period between the end of the corporation's last tax year and the date of death.

The income for the part of the S corporation's tax year after the shareholder's death is income to the estate or other person who has acquired the stock in the S corporation.

Example

Julia Jones was a 20% partner in XYZ partnership and a 20% shareholder in ABC Corporation, an S corporation. The tax year for both the partnership and the corporation ends on December 31. Julia died on October 1, 1993. Had she lived, Julia would have earned $100,000 of ordinary income in 1993 from the partnership and another $100,000 of ordinary income from the corporation.

Julia's final tax return for 1993 will not include any taxable income from the XYZ partnership, because the end of the partnership's tax year is after October 1. However, Julia's return will include $75,068 (274 days/ 365 days × $100,000) of income from the S corporation. The remaining $24,932 of S corporation income will be included in the tax return of whoever is the owner of Julia's stock from October 1, 1993 through December 31, 1993.

Self-employment income. You must include on the final return the self-employment income that the decedent actually or constructively received or accrued, depending on the decedent's accounting method. For self-employment tax purposes only, the decedent's self-employment income will include the decedent's distributive share of a partnership's income or loss through the end of the month in which death occurred. For more information on how to compute the decedent's self-employment income, see Publication 533, *Self-Employment Tax.*

Deductions, Credits, and Exemptions

Generally, the rules for deductions, credits, and exemptions that apply to individuals also apply to the decedent's final income tax return. On the final return, claim deductible items that were paid before the decedent's death (or accrued, if the decedent reported deductions on an accrual method).

Deductions

All of the deductions that are discussed in this publication also apply to the final return as long as the decedent was eligible for the deduction at the time of death.

You can generally choose to claim itemized deductions or the standard deduction on the final return. See *Standard deduction,* later, for instances when you cannot choose the standard deduction or when the amount of the standard deduction may be limited.

If you have a choice, you should figure the amount of the decedent's itemized deductions before you decide whether to itemize or claim the standard deduction to be sure that you are using the method that gives you the lower tax.

Itemized deductions. If the total of the decedent's itemized deductions are more than the decedent's standard deduction, the federal income tax will generally be less if you claim itemized deductions on the final return. See Chapters 22 through 30 for the types of expenses that are allowed as itemized deductions.

Note. The amount you can deduct for most itemized deductions is limited if adjusted gross income is more than $108,450 ($54,225 if married filing separately). See Chapter 21, *Limit on Itemized Deductions,* for more information.

Medical costs. If you itemize deductions on the final return, you may be able to deduct medical expenses of the decedent even though they were not paid before the date of death. See *Decedents* in Chapter 22, *Medical and Dental Expenses,* for an explanation of how this election can be made.

TaxSaver 1

The executor may elect to claim certain medical and dental expenses as deductions on the estate tax return or as deductions on the decedent's final income tax return. The tax should be computed both ways to see which results in more tax savings.

If the executor makes the election to include the medical and dental expenses on the decedent's income tax return rather than on the federal estate tax return, he or she must attach a statement to the income tax return stating that he or she has not claimed the amount as an estate tax deduction and that the estate waives the right to claim the amount as a deduction.

TaxSaver 2

Net operating losses (or carryover losses) from business operations and **capital losses** (or carryover losses) of the decedent may not be carried over to the returns of executors or heirs. However, if a joint return is filed for the year of death, these losses may be used to offset the survivor's income for the entire year. In this case, it may be advantageous for the surviving spouse to incur **capital gains** and/or other income and to offset them with the capital losses and/or net operating losses that cannot be carried forward past the year of the spouse's death.

Example

Your husband died on June 30, 1993, with $10,000 in **short-term capital losses** in his personal account. Because the maximum capital loss that can be deducted in a year is $3,000, only $3,000 of those losses will be allowed on your 1993 joint return, with no carryover of the remaining $7,000. However, you could incur an additional $7,000 in gains before the end of the year and use your deceased husband's remaining $7,000 of losses to offset the gains by filing a joint return. If you waited until a later year to incur those gains, they would be fully taxable, unless you had incurred other losses to offset them.

TaxSaver 3

When death is expected, proper planning can save tax dollars. Deductible expenses, such as interest expense, accounting fees, and the like, that are due near the date of death may be paid before death or after death. Choose the time offering the greater tax benefit. If you arrange to pay the expenses before death, they are deductible on the decedent's final Form 1040 if deductions are itemized. If you arrange to pay them after death, they are deductible on the estate's income tax return.

Unrecovered investment in pension. If the decedent was receiving a pension or annuity and died without a surviving annuitant, you can take a deduction on the decedent's final return for the amount of the decedent's investment in the pension or annuity contract that remained unrecovered at death. The deduction is a miscellaneous itemized deduction that is not subject to the 2% of adjusted gross income limit. See Chapter 30, *Miscellaneous Deductions.*

Standard deduction. You can generally claim the full amount of the standard deduction on the decedent's final return. However, you cannot use the standard deduction if the surviving spouse files a separate return and itemizes deductions. In that event, you must also itemize deductions on the decedent's final return.

The amount of the standard deduction for a decedent's final return is the same as it would have been had the decedent continued to live. However, if the decedent was not 65 or older at the time of death, the higher standard deduction for age cannot be claimed.

If another taxpayer can claim the decedent as a dependent, the amount you can claim for the decedent's standard deduction may be limited. See Chapter 20, *Standard Deduction,* for more information on how to determine the amount of the standard deduction.

Credits

Any of the tax credits that are discussed in this publication also apply to the final return if the decedent was eligible for the credits at the time of death. These credits are discussed in Chapters 33 through 36 of this publication.

Tax withheld and estimated payments. There may have been income tax withheld from the decedent's pay, pensions, or annuities before death, and the decedent may have paid estimated income tax. To get credit for these tax payments, you must claim them on the decedent's final return. For more information, see *Credit for Withholding and Estimated Tax* in Chapter 5, *Withholding and Estimated Tax.*

Exemptions

You can claim the full amount of the personal exemption on the decedent's final return unless the decedent can be claimed as a dependent by another taxpayer. In that case, the decedent's own exemption amount on the final return is zero. See Chapter 3, *Personal Exemptions and Dependents,* for more information on this limit and on other dependency exemptions that may be allowed on the final return.

Explanation

Exemption allowances, the standard deduction, and itemized deductions are not prorated over that part of the year during which a now deceased taxpayer was alive. However, exemptions claimed for **dependents** could be a problem if the decedent did not live long enough during the year to provide the required amount of support. In most situations, potential problems will be alleviated if the surviving spouse files a joint return with the decedent.

Tax Effect on Others

This section contains information about the effect of an individual's death on the income tax liability of others: the survivors (including the widow or widower), the beneficiaries, and the estate. Any survivor or beneficiary should coordinate the filing of his or her own tax return with the personal representative handling the decedent's estate. The personal representative can coordinate filing status, exemptions, income, and deductions so that the final return and the income tax returns of the survivors, beneficiaries, and estate are all filed correctly.

Survivors

If you are a survivor, you may qualify for certain benefits when filing your own income tax return. This section addresses some issues that may apply to you.

Inherited property. Property received as a gift, bequest, or inheritance is not included in your income. However, if the property you receive in this manner later produces income, such as interest, dividends, or rentals, then that income is taxable to you. If the gift, bequest, or inheritance you receive is the income from property, that income is taxable to you.

If you inherited the right to receive income in respect of the decedent, see *Income in Respect of the Decedent,* later.

TaxAlert

Fees received by an executor or administrator for duties performed for an estate are includable in the gross income of the executor or administrator.

However, a bequest to the executor is not treated as income. It is merely a gift to an heir who also happens to be serving as executor.

Joint return by surviving spouse. A surviving spouse can file a joint return with the decedent for the year of death as long as the survivor has not remarried before the end of that year. See *Joint return,* earlier.

If there is a dependent child, the surviving spouse may also be entitled to use the standard deduction amount and the tax rates that apply to joint returns for the 2 following years. See *Qualifying Widow(er) With Dependent Child* in Chapter 2 for information on how to qualify.

Explanation

After the 2 years pass, you may qualify as a **head of household** and you may be able to use the Tax Table and Tax Rate Schedules for head of household. While

---

not as beneficial as joint return rates, they are better than those for single persons. See Chapter 2, *Filing Status,* for more details.

The decedent as a dependent. If the decedent qualified as your dependent for the part of the year before death, you can claim the full exemption amount for the dependent on your tax return.

Income in Respect of the Decedent

All gross income that the decedent had a right to receive and that is not properly includible on the decedent's final return is called income in respect of the decedent. Instead of being reported on the final return of the decedent, the income is included, for the tax year when received, in the gross income of:

1) The decedent's estate, if the estate acquires the right to receive the income from the decedent,
2) The person who acquires the right to the income directly from the decedent without going through the estate, or
3) Any person to whom the estate properly distributes the right to receive the income.

Example 1. Thornton Jones owned and operated an orchard, and he used the cash method of accounting. He sold and delivered $2,000 worth of fruit to a customer, but he did not receive payment before his death. When the estate was settled, payment had still not been made, and the estate gave the right to receive the payment to his niece. When she collects the $2,000, she must include it in her income. It is not reported on the final return of the decedent nor on the estate's income tax return.

Example 2. If, in Example 1, Thornton Jones had used the accrual method of accounting, the income from the fruit sale must be included on his final return. Neither his estate nor his niece will report the income when the money is later paid.

Example 3. Mary Smith was entitled to a large salary payment at the time of her death. It was to be paid in five yearly payments. Her estate, after collecting two payments, distributes the right to the remaining payments to you, the beneficiary. None of the payments would be included on the decedent's final return. The estate must include in its gross income, as income in respect of the decedent, the two payments it received. You must include in your gross income each of the three remaining payments as you receive them.

Transferring your right to income. If you transfer your right to receive income in respect of a decedent, you must include in your income the larger of:

1) The amount you receive for the right, or
2) The fair market value of the right at the time of the transfer. Fair market value is defined in Chapter 14, *Basis of Property,* under *Other Basis.*

Giving your right to income as a gift. If you give your right to receive income in respect of a decedent as a gift, you must include in your gross income the fair market value of the right at the time you make the gift.

Example

Tom has a right to receive a payment of $10,000 that represents income in respect of his deceased father. He makes a gift of his right to receive the money. He would immediately have to recognize the $10,000 as income on his tax return.

Type of income. The character, or type, of income that you receive in respect of a decedent is generally the same as it would have been had the decedent continued to live and had received it. For example, if the income would have been a long-term capital gain to the decedent, it will be a long-term capital gain to you.

Interest on certificates of deposit (CDs). Interest on CDs that is not received by the date of death but that is earned between the date of the last interest payment and the date of death is interest income in respect of the decedent. Interest income earned on the account after the decedent's death that becomes payable on CDs after death is not income in respect of a decedent. Such interest is ordinary income that belongs to the respective recipients and must be included in their gross income.

Installment payments. If the decedent had sold property using the installment method and you receive the right to collect the payments after the date of death, the payments you collect are income in respect of the decedent. You will use the same gross profit percentage that the decedent used to figure the part of each payment that represents profit. Include in your income the same profit the decedent would have included had death not occurred. See Publication 537, *Installment Sales,* for more information on the installment method.

Explanation

Payments from an installment sale can consist in whole or in part of (1) principal payment, (2) capital gain, and (3) interest income.

Sale or exchange. If you sell or exchange an installment obligation that you received from a decedent, the rules explained in Publication 537 for figuring the gain or loss on the disposition will apply. However, your basis in the obligation is the same as the decedent's basis, adjusted for all installment payments you received before the sale or exchange.

Example

Andrew sold some undeveloped real estate held as an investment in 1991 for $120,000, receiving a note payable in four annual installments of $30,000 each plus interest. Andrew's basis in the land was $40,000. Andrew died before the first installment was due, and the note was transferred to Helen, Andrew's heir. Helen collected the first installment of the note, $30,000, in 1992. When Helen was in need of additional cash in early 1993, she sold the note to a bank for its fair market value of $90,000. For 1992, Helen must recognize gain on the payment she received. Using the same gross profit percentage as the decedent's ($80,000/$120,000), she would recognize a $20,000 gain, computed as follows:

$$\$30,000 \times \$80,000/\$120,000 = \$20,000$$

For 1993, Helen must recognize gain on the disposition of the installment obligation. The gain is the difference between her basis and the fair market value at the time of the disposition. Her basis in the obligation is the same as Andrew's ($40,000) less the payment of principal received by her in 1992 ($10,000). Hence, her gain is computed as follows:

$$\$90,000 - (\$40,000 - \$10,000) = \$60,000$$

Whether the gain recognized by Helen on her tax return is **ordinary income** or capital gain depends on what it would have been to Andrew had he lived to collect the payments.

Other income. For examples of other income situations concerning decedents, see *Specific Types of Income in Respect of a Decedent* in Publication 559.

Deductions in Respect of the Decedent

Deductions in respect of the decedent are items, such as business expenses, income-producing expenses, interest, and taxes, for which the decedent was liable, but which are not deductible on the decedent's final income tax return. When paid, these expenses may be deducted by:

1) The estate, or
2) If the estate is not liable for the expenses, the person who, because of the decedent's death, acquired the decedent's property subject to that liability.

Explanation

Deductions in respect of the decedent are items that would normally be deductible by the decedent except that he or she had not paid them before death. Typical examples are real estate taxes, state income taxes, and interest expense.

TaxSaver

Expenses in respect of a decedent are *also* deductible on the estate tax return of the decedent. The reason is that the estate tax and the income tax are two different taxes with two entirely unrelated sets of rules. Taking a deduction on one return does not preclude taking the same deduction on the other return. When death is anticipated, planning the best possible use of double deductions may yield significant tax savings. A professional who specializes in this area should be consulted.

Example

When Oscar died in 1993, he owed accrued interest of $100. The marginal estate tax rate for Oscar's estate is 50%, and the estate's marginal *income* tax rate is 28%. The deduction on the estate tax return is worth $50 (50% of $100), and the deduction on the estate's income tax return is worth $28. Consequently, $78 of the $100 liability is recovered through tax savings.

On the other hand, less tax savings would be realized if Oscar had paid the $100 of interest before he died. He would have been able to take the interest deduction on his personal income tax return, paying $28 less in taxes, assuming he was in the 28% bracket. When he died, he would have been net out-of-pocket $72, his estate would be $72 less, and therefore his estate tax would be reduced by $36 (50% of $72). Thus, if he had paid the expense, his total tax savings would have been $64—$28 of income tax and $36 of estate tax—instead of the $78 tax saved because he had not paid the interest before he died, thus allowing the double deduction.

Federal estate tax deduction. Income that a decedent had a right to receive is included in the decedent's gross estate and is subject to estate tax. This income in respect of a decedent is also taxed when received by the estate or beneficiary. However, an income tax deduction is allowed to the person (or estate) receiving the income. If you must include in your gross income an amount of income in respect of a decedent, then you can claim a deduction for part of any estate tax paid. The deduction must be claimed in the same tax year that the income is included in your gross income.

You can claim the deduction only as a miscellaneous itemized deduction on Schedule A (Form 1040). This deduction is not subject to the 2% limit on miscellaneous itemized deductions as discussed in Chapter 30, *Miscellaneous Deductions*.

If the income is capital gain income, then in figuring the maximum capital gain rate or any net capital loss limitation, the amount of the gain must be reduced, but not below zero, by the amount of any estate tax deduction attributable to such gain.

For more information, see *Estate Tax Deduction* in Publication 559.

Explanation

The deduction for federal estate tax attributable to income in respect of a decedent is complex. The good news is that the question does not arise if there is no federal estate tax on the decedent's estate. If the amount that each individual can leave tax-free—$600,000 after 1986—and the marital deduction are large enough to eliminate any federal estate tax liability, there cannot be an income tax deduction for federal estate tax.

If the estate is large enough that there is some federal estate tax, the recipient of income in respect of a decedent may be entitled to an itemized deduction on his or her income tax return.

To determine the amount that can be deducted, you must first determine if the income and deductions in respect of the decedent result in net income. If so, you must then calculate the additional estate tax attributable to the net income in respect of the decedent.

To determine whether the items in respect of the decedent result in net income, you must deduct the total amount of deductions in respect of the decedent that appear on the estate tax return from the total amount of income in respect of the decedent that appear on that return. To calculate the additional estate tax, you must compare the actual estate tax with the estate tax that would have been paid if the net income in respect of a decedent had not been included. This amount is the deduction. The recipient's claim to the deduction is in the same proportion as his or her share in the total income in respect of the decedent.

Example

Assume that the estate tax return shows that the estate received salary income in respect of a decedent of $2,500 and had a deduction in respect of a decedent of $500 for unpaid real estate tax. The net of these two amounts is $2,000. Recomputation of the estate tax with $2,000 removed from the return shows that the estate tax caused by including these items is $680. If you, as one of two heirs of the estate, collect half of the $2,500 salary, you will be entitled to an income tax itemized deduction of half the $680, or $340.

5 | Tax Withholding and Estimated Tax

Introduction

*April 15 is the date by which most people file their income tax return for the previous year, but it is not the day most people actually pay their taxes. The bulk of your taxes is paid during the year, either by your employer's withholding money from your paycheck or by your making **estimated tax** payments every quarter. The tax system operates on a pay-as-you-go policy that generally requires that at least 90% of your tax liability be paid during the year.*

The tax law imposes severe penalties if you underwithhold or underpay your estimated taxes. Furthermore, the 1993 Tax Act modified the rules for how certain taxpayers must figure their estimated taxes. Yet it is clearly not in your best interest to overwithhold or overpay estimated taxes, as the U.S. government does not pay interest on such overpayments. Therefore, it is essential that you estimate your tax liability as accurately as possible so that you neither underpay nor overpay your taxes. This chapter helps you do just that.

*Salaries and wages are subject to withholding by your employer regardless of the amount you are paid, the frequency of payment, or the form of payment. Nevertheless, you are entitled to reduce the amount of withholding by filing a completed Form W–4 with your employer. This form takes into account not only your marital status, personal **exemptions,** and **dependents,** but also your estimated **deductions** and tax credits. Form W–4 may prove especially beneficial if you have large mortgage deductions or tax-shelter investments.*

*Estimated tax payments cover sources of income not subject to withholding— **self-employment** income, **interest, dividends, capital gains,** and **trust and estate** income. While generally your tax withholding and estimated payments have to cover 90% of your tax liability for you to avoid paying some stiff penalties, this is not always the case. This chapter discusses all the important exceptions.*

Tax Law Changes

1993. There are several changes in the tax law that might affect your 1993 return. You must consider these changes in computing your tax and any underpayment penalty for 1993. You will also need to consider many of these items when you figure your estimated tax for 1994. These changes are briefly discussed under *Changes Effective in 1993*.

1994. There are also several changes in the tax law that will not become effective until 1994. You will need to consider these changes when you figure your estimated tax for 1994. These changes are briefly discussed under *Changes Effective in 1994*.

Changes Effective in 1993

You should consider the items in this section when figuring your tax and any underpayment penalty for 1993. Unless an item applies only to 1993, you should also consider it when figuring your estimated tax for 1994. For more information on important tax changes, see Publication 553, *Highlights of 1993 Tax Changes*.

Excess social security, Medicare, or railroad retirement tax withholding. You will have excess social security or tier 1 railroad retirement tax withholding for 1993 only if your wages from two or more employers exceeded $57,600. You will have excess Medicare tax withholding only if your wages from two or more employers exceeded $135,000. See *Credit for Excess Social Security Tax, Medicare Tax, or Railroad Retirement Tax Withheld* in Chapter 35, *Other Credits*.

Waiver of penalty for underpayment of estimated tax. If you underpaid your 1993 estimated tax, you may be eligible for a waiver of the penalty for underpayment of estimated tax.

Extension of expired tax items. The following items previously expired and have now been extended:

- Deduction for 25% of the health insurance costs of self-employed individuals—costs paid through December 31, 1993,
- Exclusion for employer-provided educational assistance—amounts paid through December 31, 1994,
- Targeted jobs credit—employees who begin work through December 31, 1994,
- Research and experimentation credit—expenses paid or incurred through June 30, 1995, and
- Low-income housing credit—made permanent.

Charitable contribution of capital gain property. The amount of appreciation with respect to a charitable contribution of capital gain property is no longer treated as a tax preference item. For more information, see Publication 909, *Alternative Minimum Tax for Individuals.*

Increase in tax rates. The tax rate for certain taxpayers has increased to 36%. In addition, certain taxpayers will be subject to a new surtax.

Installment payments of 1993 tax. Certain taxpayers may be able to elect to pay any additional 1993 tax due to new tax rates in three installments. This is explained in Chapter 1, *Filing Information.*

Alternative minimum tax. The alternative minimum tax rates and exemption amounts have changed. For more information, see Publication 909.

Disaster area losses. The rules concerning the treatment of some disaster area losses have changed. See Publication 547, *Nonbusiness Disasters, Casualties, and Thefts.*

Changes Effective in 1994

You should consider the items in this section when you figure your income tax withholding or estimated tax for 1994. Remember to also consider the items that apply from *Changes Effective in 1993.* For more information on important tax changes, see Publication 553, *Highlights of 1993 Tax Changes.*

Personal exemption. For 1994, the personal exemption amount for you, your spouse, and each dependent has increased to $2,450.

Phaseout of personal exemptions. Your deduction for personal exemptions is reduced by 2% for each $2,500 ($1,250 if you are married filing separately), or part of that amount, by which your adjusted gross income exceeds an amount based on your filing status. The amounts for 1994 are:

Single	$111,800
Married filing jointly or qualifying widow(er)	$167,700
Married filing separately	$ 83,850
Head of household	$139,750

Standard deduction. Individuals who do not itemize deductions have an increased standard deduction for 1994. For more information, see Publication 505, *Tax Withholding and Estimated Tax.*

Education Savings Bond Program. For 1994, you may be able to claim an interest exclusion under the Education Savings Bond Program. This exclusion applies only if your modified adjusted gross income is less than $61,900 ($100,350 if you are married filing jointly).

Reduction of itemized deductions. For 1994, certain itemized deductions are reduced by 3% of your adjusted gross income that exceeds $111,800 ($55,900 if you are married filing separately). The reduction cannot be more than 80% of your affected deduc-

tions. Itemized deductions subject to the reduction are those other than medical expenses, investment interest, casualty and theft losses, or gambling losses. This reduction does not apply when computing alternative minimum tax, nor does it apply to estates or trusts.

Earned income credit. Beginning in 1994, the rules to determine eligibility for the credit and the rules for computing the credit will change. For more information see Publication 553.

Self-employment tax. Beginning in 1994, the Medicare (hospital insurance) part of the self-employment tax is 2.9% of all net earnings. The social security (old-age, survivor, and disability insurance) part of the tax is 12.4% of net earnings up to a certain amount. See Publication 505.

Medicare withholding. Previously, there was a limit on the amount of wages subject to Medicare withholding. Beginning in 1994, there will no longer be a limit.

Rental real estate passive loss rules. Beginning in 1994, new rules will apply to passive losses relating to rental real estate activities. For more information, see Publication 553.

Business meals, entertainment, and club dues. Beginning in 1994, new rules will reduce the deduction for business meals and entertainment and eliminate the deduction for club dues. For more information, see Publication 553.

Moving expenses. Beginning in 1994, new rules will reduce the amount you deduct as moving expenses. For more information, see Publication 553.

Estimated tax rules. Beginning in 1994, new rules will apply for figuring the amount of estimated tax you need to pay in order to avoid the estimated tax penalty. See *Estimated Tax,* later.

TAX ALERT

The 1993 Tax Act modified the rules for how certain taxpayers must figure their estimated taxes. Effective for estimated tax payments applicable to tax years beginning after 1993, if your previous year's adjusted gross income was $150,000 or less ($75,000 or less if married filing separately) you can avoid paying a penalty by making estimated tax payments equal to 100% of your tax liability for the *last* taxable year. If your previous year's adjusted gross income exceeds $150,000, you must pay 110% of the prior year's liability in order to avoid penalties. All taxpayers can avoid penalties for underpayment of tax if at least 90% of their *current* tax liability is paid through withholding and estimated tax payments.

Example

Jill Kennedy's 1994 income tax liability is $60,000. Her adjusted gross income in 1993 was $180,000, while her 1993 tax liability was $40,000. Kennedy will avoid an underpayment penalty in 1994 if the total amount of tax withheld and estimated tax payments made for 1994 exceeds 110% of her 1993 liability, or $44,000, because her adjusted gross income exceeded $150,000.

Taxability of social security and railroad retirement benefits. Beginning in 1994, certain taxpayers will need to include 85% of benefits received in taxable income. For more information, see Publication 553.

Withholding on supplemental wages. Beginning in 1994, your employer may withhold income tax from any supplemental wages (such as bonuses and overtime) at a flat rate of at least 28%. See *Supplemental Wages,* later.

Important Reminders

Special rule regarding estimated tax payments — limit on the use of prior year's tax. Certain taxpayers (other than farmers and fishermen) may not be able to use 100% of their 1993 tax to figure their 1994 estimated tax payments. See Chapter 2 of Publication 505 if your 1993 adjusted gross income was more than $150,000 (more than $75,000 if you were married filing separately).

Underpayment penalty. A similar special rule applies to the underpayment penalty. For 1993, if your 1993 adjusted gross income (AGI) was more than $75,000 (more than $37,500 if you are married filing separately) **AND** your 1993 AGI exceeded your 1992 AGI by more than $40,000 ($20,000 if married filing separately), see Chapter 4 of Publication 505.

Claiming withholding and estimated tax payments. When you file a federal income tax return, be sure to take credit for all federal income tax and excess social security, Medicare, or railroad retirement taxes withheld from your salary, wages, pensions, etc., and any backup withholding shown on Forms 1099. Also take credit for all estimated tax payments you made for that year. For example, all estimated tax payments made for tax year 1993 should be claimed on the tax return you file for the 1993 tax year. You should file a return and claim these credits even if you do not owe tax. See *Credit for Withholding and Estimated Tax,* later in this chapter.

This chapter discusses how to pay your tax as you earn or receive income during the year. In general, the federal income tax is a pay-as-you-go tax. There are two ways to pay as you go:

- *Withholding.* If you are an employee, your employer probably withholds income tax from your pay. Tax may also be withheld from certain other income — including pensions, bonuses, commissions, and gambling winnings. In each case, the amount withheld is paid to the Internal Revenue Service (IRS) in your name.
- *Estimated tax.* If you do not pay your tax through withholding, or do not pay enough tax that way, you might have to pay estimated tax. People who are in business for themselves generally will have to pay their tax this way. You may have to pay estimated tax if you receive income such as dividends, interest, rent, royalties, and unemployment compensation. Estimated tax is used to pay not only income tax, but self-employment tax and alternative minimum tax as well.

This chapter explains both of these methods. In addition, it explains:

- *Credit for withholding and estimated tax.* When you file your 1993 income tax return, take credit for all the income tax withheld from your salary, wages, pensions, etc., and for the estimated tax you paid for 1993.
- *Underpayment penalty.* If you did not pay enough tax in 1993 either through withholding or by making estimated tax payments, you will have an underpayment of estimated tax, and you may have to pay a penalty. The IRS usually can compute this penalty for you. See *Underpayment Penalty,* near the end of this chapter.

Useful Items

You may want to see:

Publication

- ☐ **505** Tax Withholding and Estimated Tax
- ☐ **553** Highlights of 1993 Tax Changes
- ☐ **919** Is My Withholding Correct for 1994?

Form (and Instructions)

- ☐ **W-4** Employee's Withholding Allowance Certificate
- ☐ **W-4P** Withholding Certificate for Pension or Annuity Payments
- ☐ **W-4S** Request for Federal Income Tax Withholding From Sick Pay
- ☐ **1040-ES** Estimated Tax for Individuals
- ☐ **2210** Underpayment of Estimated Tax by Individuals and Fiduciaries

Withholding

Income tax is withheld from the following kinds of income:

Salaries and wages. Income tax is withheld from the pay of most employees. Your pay includes bonuses, commissions, and vacation allowances, in addition to your regular pay. It also includes reimbursements and other expense allowances paid under a nonaccountable plan. See *Supplemental Wages,* later.

Military retirees. Military retirement pay is treated in the same manner as regular pay for income tax withholding purposes, even though it is treated as a pension or annuity for other tax purposes.

Household workers. If you are a household worker, you can ask your employer to withhold income tax from your pay. Tax is withheld only if you want it withheld and your employer agrees to withhold it. If you do not have enough income tax withheld, you may have to make estimated tax payments, as discussed later under *Estimated Tax.*

Farmworkers. Income tax is generally withheld from your cash wages for work on a farm unless your employer:

1) Pays you cash wages of less than $150 during the year, and
2) Pays cash wages to all employees totaling less than $2,500 during the year.

If you receive cash wages not subject to withholding or noncash wages, you can ask your employer to withhold income tax. If your employer does not agree to withhold tax, or if not enough is withheld, you may have to make estimated tax payments, as discussed later under *Estimated Tax.*

Explanation

Generally, withholding is required on wages, regardless of the amount of wages paid, the frequency of payment, the form of payment (cash, check, stock, or other property), or the manner in which the wage is computed (hourly, weekly, yearly, or even as a percentage of employer profits).

For more information about household workers, see Chapter 37, *What to Do if You Employ Domestic Help*.

Tips. The tips you receive and report to your employer while working as an employee are counted in with your regular wages to figure the amount withheld.

Taxable fringe benefits. Your employer will withhold income tax from most taxable fringe benefits paid to you either at a flat 20% rate or at your regular rate of withholding.

Sick pay. Income tax is withheld from sick pay you receive from your employer or an agent of your employer, just as it is from your salaries and wages. If you receive sick pay from someone who is not acting as an agent of your employer, such as an insurance company, you can usually arrange to have income tax withheld from the sick pay. A special rule covers sick pay paid to you under certain union agreements.

Pensions and annuities. Income tax is generally withheld from your pension or annuity. In certain cases, however, you can choose not to have it withheld.

Gambling winnings. Income tax is withheld from certain gambling winnings at a flat 28% rate.

Withholding on Salaries and Wages

The amount of income tax withheld from your regular pay depends on two things:

1) The amount you earn, and
2) The information you give your employer on **Form W–4.**

Form W–4 includes three types of information that your employer will use to figure your withholding:

1) Whether to withhold at the single rate or at the lower married rate,
2) How many withholding allowances you claim (each allowance reduces the amount withheld), and
3) Whether you want an additional amount withheld.

If your income is low enough that you will not have to pay income tax for the year, you may be exempt from withholding. See *Exemption From Withholding,* later.

New job. When you start a new job, you must fill out Form W–4 and give it to your employer. Your employer should have copies of the form. If you later need to change the information you gave, you must fill out a new form.

If you start working after the beginning of the year, or if you work only part of the year, too much tax may be withheld. You may be able to avoid overwithholding if your employer agrees to use the part-year method. See *Part-year method* in Chapter 1 of Publication 505 for more information.

Changing your withholding. Events during the year may change your marital status or the exemptions, adjustments, deductions, or credits you expect to claim on your return. When this happens, you may need to give your employer a new Form W–4 to change your withholding status or allowances.

You *must* give your employer a new Form W–4 within 10 days after:

1) Your divorce, if you have been claiming married status, or
2) Any event that decreases the withholding allowances you can claim.

Generally, you can submit a new Form W–4 at any time you wish to change your withholding allowances for any other reason.

If events in 1994 will decrease your withholding allowances for 1995, you must give your employer a new Form W–4 by December 1, 1994. If the event occurs in December 1994, submit a new Form W–4 within 10 days.

Explanation
You must file a new Form W–4 when it becomes reasonable for you to expect that the estimated deductions or credits you claim on your existing Form W–4 will be less than you anticipated. Conversely, you may file a new Form W–4 when it becomes reasonable to expect that your estimated deductions or credits will be more than you claim on your existing form. Examples of situations that might warrant that you file a new Form W–4 include, (1) buying or selling a house, (2) refinancing or paying off a home mortgage, (3) moving to a different city, or (4) a substantial increase in medical costs.

Cumulative wage method. If you change your withholding allowances during the year, too much or too little tax may have been withheld for the period before you made the change. You may be able to compensate for this if your employer agrees to use the cumulative wage withholding method for the rest of the year. You must request in writing that your employer use this method.

To be eligible, you must have been paid for the same kind of payroll period (weekly, biweekly, etc.) since the beginning of the year.

Checking your withholding. After you have given your employer a Form W–4, you can check to see whether the amount of tax withheld from your pay is too little or too much. See *Getting the Right Amount of Tax Withheld,* later. If too much or too little tax is being withheld, you should give your employer a new Form W–4 to change your withholding.

Example
Tom is a bachelor living in an apartment. His annual income is $35,000, and he claims the standard deduction when he files his income tax return. He is currently claiming two allowances on his Form W-4. In March of 1993, Tom buys a house. As a result of the increased deductions resulting from the purchase, he will itemize his deductions on his 1993 federal income tax return. He estimates that the deductions will total $11,500 and will be made up of mortgage interest, points, real estate tax, and state income tax. He revises his Form W-4 (see completed example) to reflect the change in his status to claim 5 allowances for the remainder of the year.

Completing Form W–4
The following discussions explain how to complete your Form W–4.

Marital status (line 3). The tax rates for married people filing a joint return are lower than those for single people. Therefore, there is a lower married withholding rate for people who can use the tax rates for joint returns. Everyone else must have tax withheld at the higher single rate.

You must claim *single* status if either of the following applies.

1993 Form W-4

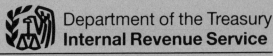

Department of the Treasury
Internal Revenue Service

Purpose. Complete Form W-4 so that your employer can withhold the correct amount of Federal income tax from your pay.

Exemption From Withholding. Read line 7 of the certificate below to see if you can claim exempt status. *If exempt, complete line 7; but do not complete lines 5 and 6.* No Federal income tax will be withheld from your pay. Your exemption is good for one year only. It expires February 15, 1994.

Basic Instructions. Employees who are not exempt should complete the Personal Allowances Worksheet. Additional worksheets are provided on page 2 for employees to adjust their withholding allowances based on itemized deductions, adjustments to income, or two-earner/two-job situations. Complete all worksheets that apply to your situation. The worksheets will help you figure

the number of withholding allowances you are entitled to claim. However, you may claim fewer allowances than this.

Head of Household. Generally, you may claim head of household filing status on your tax return only if you are unmarried and pay more than 50% of the costs of keeping up a home for yourself and your dependent(s) or other qualifying individuals.

Nonwage Income. If you have a large amount of nonwage income, such as interest or dividends, you should consider making estimated tax payments using Form 1040-ES. Otherwise, you may find that you owe additional tax at the end of the year.

Two-Earner/Two-Jobs. If you have a working spouse or more than one job, figure the total number of allowances you are entitled to claim on

all jobs using worksheets from only one Form W-4. This total should be divided among all jobs. Your withholding will usually be most accurate when all allowances are claimed on the W-4 filed for the highest paying job and zero allowances are claimed for the others.

Advance Earned Income Credit. If you are eligible for this credit, you can receive it added to your paycheck throughout the year. For details, get Form W-5 from your employer.

Check Your Withholding. After your W-4 takes effect, you can use **Pub. 919,** Is My Withholding Correct for 1993?, to see how the dollar amount you are having withheld compares to your estimated total annual tax. Call 1-800-829-3676 to order this publication. Check your local telephone directory for the IRS assistance number if you need further help.

Personal Allowances Worksheet

For 1993, the value of your personal exemption(s) is reduced if your income is over $108,450 ($162,700 if married filing jointly, $135,600 if head of household, or $81,350 if married filing separately). Get Pub. 919 for details.

A Enter "1" for **yourself** if no one else can claim you as a dependent . . . . **A** _____

B Enter "1" if:
- You are single and have only one job; or
- You are married, have only one job, and your spouse does not work; or
- Your wages from a second job or your spouse's wages (or the total of both) are $1,000 or less.

. . **B** _____

C Enter "1" for your **spouse.** But, you may choose to enter -0- if you are married and have either a working spouse or more than one job (this may help you avoid having too little tax withheld) . . . . **C** _____

D Enter number of **dependents** (other than your spouse or yourself) whom you will claim on your tax return . . . . . **D** _____

E Enter "1" if you will file as **head of household** on your tax return (see conditions under **Head of Household,** above) . **E** _____

F Enter "1" if you have at least $1,500 of **child or dependent care expenses** for which you plan to claim a credit . . **F** _____

G Add lines A through F and enter total here. **Note:** *This amount may be different from the number of exemptions you claim on your return* ▶ **G** _____

For accuracy, do all worksheets that apply.
- If you plan to **itemize or claim adjustments to income** and want to reduce your withholding, see the Deductions and Adjustments Worksheet on page 2.
- If you are **single** and have **more than one job** and your combined earnings from all jobs exceed $30,000 OR if you are **married** and have a **working spouse or more than one job,** and the combined earnings from all jobs exceed $50,000, see the Two-Earner/Two-Job Worksheet on page 2 if you want to avoid having too little tax withheld.
- If **neither** of the above situations applies, **stop here** and enter the number from line G on line 5 of Form W-4 below.

-------------------- **Cut here and give the certificate to your employer. Keep the top portion for your records.** --------------------

| Form **W-4**
Department of the Treasury
Internal Revenue Service | **Employee's Withholding Allowance Certificate**
▶ **For Privacy Act and Paperwork Reduction Act Notice, see reverse.** | OMB No. 1545-0010
1993 |

| **1** Type or print your first name and middle initial | Last name | **2** Your social security number |

| Home address (number and street or rural route) | **3** ☐ Single ☐ Married ☐ Married, but withhold at higher Single rate.
Note: *If married, but legally separated, or spouse is a nonresident alien, check the Single box.* |
| City or town, state, and ZIP code | **4** If your last name differs from that on your social security card, check here and call 1-800-772-1213 for more information . . . . . ▶ ☐ |

5 Total number of allowances you are claiming (from line G above or from the worksheets on page 2 if they apply) . | **5** _____

6 Additional amount, if any, you want withheld from each paycheck . . . . | **6** $ _____

7 I claim exemption from withholding for 1993 and I certify that I meet **ALL** of the following conditions for exemption:
- Last year I had a right to a refund of **ALL** Federal income tax withheld because I had **NO** tax liability; **AND**
- This year I expect a refund of **ALL** Federal income tax withheld because I expect to have **NO** tax liability; **AND**
- This year if my income exceeds $600 and includes nonwage income, another person cannot claim me as a dependent.

If you meet all of the above conditions, enter "EXEMPT" here . . . . ▶ | **7** _____

Under penalties of perjury, I certify that I am entitled to the number of withholding allowances claimed on this certificate or entitled to claim exempt status.

Employee's signature ▶   Date ▶ _____ , 19___

| **8** Employer's name and address (Employer: Complete 8 and 10 only if sending to the IRS) | **9** Office code (optional) | **10** Employer identification number |

Cat. No. 10220Q

1) **You are single.** If you are divorced, or separated from your spouse under a court decree of separate maintenance, you are considered single.

2) **You are married, but you are neither a citizen nor a resident of the United States,** or your spouse is neither a citizen nor a resident of the United States. However, if one of you is a citizen or a resident, you can choose to have the other treated as a resident. You can then file a joint return and claim married status on your Form W-4. See *Nonresident Spouse Treated as a Resident* in Chapter 1 of Publication 519, *U.S. Tax Guide for Aliens,* for more information.

You can claim *married* status if either of the following applies.

1) **You are married and neither you nor your spouse is a nonresident alien.** You are considered married for the whole year even if your spouse died during the year.

2) **You expect to be able to file your return as a qualifying widow or widower.** You usually can use this filing status if your spouse died within the previous two years and you provide a home for your dependent child. However, you must file a new Form W-4 showing your filing status as single by December 1 of the last year you are eligible to file as qualifying widow or widower. See *Qualifying Widow(er) With Dependent Child* in Chapter 2, *Filing Status.*

Some married people find that they do not have enough tax withheld at the married rate. This can happen, for example, when both spouses work. Therefore, even if you qualify for the married rate, you can still choose to have tax withheld at the higher single rate.

Withholding allowances (line 5). The more allowances you claim on Form W-4, the less income tax your employer will withhold. You will have the most tax withheld if you claim "0" allowances. The number of allowances you can claim depends on:

1) How many exemptions you can take on your tax return,
2) Whether you have income from more than one job,
3) What deductions, adjustments to income, and credits you expect to have for the year, and
4) Whether you will file as head of household.

If you are married, it also depends on whether your spouse also works and claims any allowances on his or her own Form W-4. If you both work, you should figure your combined allowances on one Form W-4 worksheet, You then should divide the allowances among the Forms W-4 you each file with every employer. See *Two jobs,* later.

Form W-4 worksheets. Form W-4 has worksheets to help you figure how many withholding allowances you can claim. The worksheets are for your own records. Do not give them to your employer.

You are not required to use the worksheets if you use a more accurate method of withholding. See *Alternative method of figuring withholding allowances* under *Completing Form W-4 and Worksheets* in Chapter 1 of Publication 505 for more information.

TaxPlanner 1

The tax withheld from your salary or wage based on the revised Form W-4 that you file with your employer should be appropriate for your circumstances on an annual basis. However, the new withholding is effective only for pay periods after you file the form, and the total tax withheld for any given year may be significantly less than your actual tax liability. You should estimate your annual tax, as explained later in this chapter, and compare that estimate to the year-to-date tax withheld plus the amounts expected to be withheld based on your revised Form W-4. If that comparison shows a substantial gap, it would be appropriate to file a new Form W-4, claiming fewer allowances or requesting a larger additional amount to be withheld in order to narrow that gap.

TaxPlanner 2

You are liable for severe penalties if you complete a Form W-4 with false information in an attempt to reduce your withholding below the amount you are legally allowed. The form should be filled out carefully and accurately so that the amount of your withholding is the least you are legally allowed but enough to avoid underpayment penalties.

On the other hand, contrary to the belief of many taxpayers, there is *not* a penalty for overwithholding. With the appearance of the new W-4 forms, so much emphasis has been put on the accuracy of various worksheets that some taxpayers may have *increased* their withholding more than they actually want. If you are more comfortable claiming fewer exemptions than you are entitled to so that you can get a nice refund when you file your return, feel free to do so.

TaxPlanner 3

Your Form W-4 should be reviewed periodically as your sources and levels of income change and as your deductible expenses and credits increase or decrease.

Withholding and estimated tax. Before you figure your withholding allowances, use your estimated adjustments, deductions, and tax credits to reduce the amount of estimated tax you must pay. The *Deductions and Adjustments Worksheet* on page 2 of Form W-4 does this for you. But if you use an alternative method of figuring withholding allowances, take into account only the amount of these items remaining after you have reduced the estimated tax you must pay to zero.

Example 1

You have an estimated net loss from a partnership of $2,000, which you would report on Schedule E of your Form 1040. You are not required to make any payments of estimated tax. You may use your $2,000 partnership loss to figure the number of withholding allowances you may claim on your Form W-4.

Example 2

You have an estimated net loss from business of $3,000, which you would report on Schedule C. You would also otherwise be required to make payments of estimated tax on your **alimony** income of $3,000. You may not use your business loss to figure your withholding allowances.

Example 3

You have an estimated net loss from your farm of $5,000, which you would report on Schedule F. You would otherwise be required to make payments of estimated tax on rental income of $4,000. To figure your withholding allowances, you may include only $1,000 of your farm loss ($5,000 estimated net loss minus $4,000 income subject to estimated tax).

Example 4

You expect to have itemized deductions of $15,000, which you would report on Schedule A. You also expect to have $9,000 of self-employment income on which you would otherwise have to pay estimated tax. To figure your withholding allowances for Form W-4, you should include only $6,000 of your itemized deductions ($15,000 total itemized deductions minus the $9,000 self-employment income subject to estimated tax). This will allow you to withhold through your salary any estimated tax due on your self-employment income. However, if your wages are below $135,000, you will still be subject to self-employment tax on the $9,000 income.

Rules relating to when you may properly claim withholding allowances. For the purpose of figuring your withholding allowances for estimated deductions and estimated tax credits, *estimated* means the dollar amount of each item you reasonably expect to claim on your 1994 return. That dollar amount should be no more than the sum of

1. The amount of each item shown or expected to be shown on your 1993 return that you also reasonably expect to show on your 1994 return, plus
2. Additional amounts that you can determine for each item for 1994

Additional amounts that can be determined are amounts that are not included in (1) and that can be shown to result from identifiable events in 1993 or 1994. Amounts can be shown to result from identifiable events if the amounts relate to payments already made during 1994, to binding obligations to make payments (including payments of taxes) during 1994, and to other events or transactions that have been started and that you can prove at the time you file your Form W-4.

Amounts disallowed by the Internal Revenue Service. Generally, to figure your withholding allowances for 1994, you should not include any amount shown on your 1993 return that has been disallowed by the IRS. If you have not yet filed your 1993 return, you should not include any amount shown on your 1992 return that has been disallowed by the IRS.

Two jobs. If you have income from two jobs at the same time, or if both you and your spouse are employed and you expect to file a joint return, complete only one set of Form W-4 worksheets. Then split your allowances between the Forms W-4 for each job. You cannot claim the same allowances with more than one employer at the same time. You can claim all your allowances with one employer and none with the other, or divide them in any other way you wish.

If both you and your spouse are employed and you expect to file a joint return, figure your withholding allowances using your combined income, adjustments, deductions, exemptions, and credits. Use only one set of worksheets. You can divide your total allowances in any way you wish, but you cannot claim an allowance that your spouse also claims.

If you and your spouse expect to file separate returns, figure your allowances separately based on your own individual income, adjustments, deductions, exemptions, and credits.

Example

Bill and Alice are married. Both are employed and expect to file a joint return. When they combine their expected salary and other income, and then total their expected deductions and credits on a Form W-4 worksheet, they determine that they are entitled to claim 26 allowances. Bill and Alice must each file separate W-4 forms with their respective employers but may allocate the 26 allowances any way they like. Bill could claim 24 allowances and Alice could claim 2, for example, or each could claim 13 allowances.

Personal Allowances Worksheet. Use the *Personal Allowances Worksheet* on page 1 of Form W-4 to figure your withholding allowances for exemptions. Add the special allowance for only one job, the allowance for head of household status, and the allowance for the child and dependent care credit (if they apply) to your total allowances.

Special allowance (worksheet line B). You can claim the special allowance if any of the following apply.

1) You are single, and you have only one job at a time.
2) You are married, you have only one job at a time, and your spouse does not work.
3) Your wages from a second job or your spouse's wages (or the total of both) are $1,000 or less.

Example

John and Mary are married and plan to file a joint return. John's wages from his only employer are $55,000. Mary's wages from her only employer are $1,000. Since Mary's wages are $1,000 or less, John may claim a special allowance.

Head of household (worksheet line E). You can claim one additional withholding allowance if you expect to file as head of household on your tax return. To find out whether you qualify, see *Head of Household* in Chapter 2, *Filing Status*.

Child and dependent care credit (worksheet line F). You can claim one additional withholding allowance if you expect to have at least $1,500 of qualifying child or dependent care expenses that you plan to claim a credit for on your tax return. For information on this credit, see Chapter 33, *Child and Dependent Care Credit*.

Instead of using line F, you can choose to figure allowances for the child and dependent care credit (and other credits you expect to claim on your return) as explained next.

Deductions and Adjustments Worksheet. To adjust your withholding allowances for deductions, adjustments to income, and tax credits, use the *Deductions and Adjustments Worksheet* on page 2 of Form W-4. Chapter 1 of Publication 505 explains this worksheet.

Nonwage income. You may need to reduce the number of withholding allowances you would otherwise claim if you expect to receive taxable nonwage income. This includes interest, dividends, net rental income, unemployment compensation, alimony received, gambling winnings, prizes and awards, hobby income, capital gains, royalties, and partnership income.

Two-Earner/Two-Job Worksheet. You may need to complete this worksheet if you have two jobs or a working spouse. You should also use this worksheet to figure additional withholding if you expect to owe an amount other than income tax, such as self-employment tax.

For more information about Form W–4 and a filled-in example, see Chapter 1 of Publication 505.

Getting the Right Amount of Tax Withheld

In most situations, the tax withheld from your pay will be close to the tax you figure on your return if:

1) You accurately complete all the Form W–4 worksheets that apply to you, and
2) You give your employer a new Form W–4 when changes occur.

But because the worksheets and withholding methods do not account for all possible situations, you may not be getting the right amount withheld. This is most likely to happen in the following situations.

1) You are married and both you and your spouse work.
2) You have more than one job at a time.
3) You have nonwage income, such as interest, dividends, alimony, unemployment compensation, or self-employment income.
4) You will owe additional amounts with your return, such as self-employment tax.
5) Your withholding is based on obsolete Form W–4 information for a substantial part of the year.

To make sure you are getting the right amount of tax withheld, get Publication 919. It will help you compare the total tax to be withheld in 1994 with the tax you can expect to figure on your return. It also will help you determine how much additional withholding is needed each payday to avoid owing tax when you file your return. If you do not have enough tax withheld, you may have to make estimated tax payments, as explained under *Estimated Tax,* later.

TAXPLANNER

Overwithholding amounts to giving the government a portion of your salary as an interest-free loan. Nevertheless, underwithholding may subject you to stiff nondeductible penalties. It is therefore essential that you estimate your tax liability as accurately as possible so that you neither underwithhold nor overwithhold.

Rules Your Employer Must Follow

The following are some of the withholding rules that can affect how you fill out your Form W–4 and how you handle problems that may arise. For other rules, see *Rules Your Employer Must Follow* in Chapter 1 of Publication 505.

Putting a new Form W–4 into effect. When you start a new job, your employer should give you a Form W–4 to fill out. Your employer will use the information you give on the form to figure your withholding, beginning with your first payday.

If you later fill out a new Form W–4, your employer can put it into effect as soon as it is practical to do so. The deadline for putting it into effect is the start of the first payroll period ending 30 or more days after you turn it in.

Withholding without a Form W–4. If you do not give your employer a completed Form W–4, your employer must withhold at the highest rate—as if you were single and claimed no allowances.

Repaying withheld tax. If you find you are having too much tax withheld because you did not claim all the withholding allowances you are entitled to, you should give your employer a new Form W–4. Your employer cannot repay you any of the tax withheld under your old Form W–4.

However, if your employer has withheld more than the correct amount of tax for the Form W–4 you have in effect, you do not have to fill out a new Form W–4 to have your withholding lowered to the correct amount. Your employer can repay you the amount that was incorrectly withheld. If you are not repaid, you will receive credit on your tax return for the full amount actually withheld.

Exemption From Withholding

If you claim exemption from withholding, your employer will not withhold federal income tax from your wages. The exemption applies only to income tax, not to social security or Medicare tax.

You can claim exemption from withholding for 1994 only if **both** the following situations apply.

1) For 1993 you had a right to a refund of all federal income tax withheld because you had no tax liability.
2) For 1994 you expect a refund of all federal income tax withheld because you expect to have no tax liability.

Use *Figure 5-A* in this chapter to help you decide whether you can claim exemption. Do not use the chart if you are 65 or older or blind, or if you will itemize deductions or claim dependents or tax credits on your 1994 return. These situations are discussed later.
Student. If you are a student, you are not automatically exempt. See Chapter 1 to see if you must file a return. If you work only part time or only during the summer, you may qualify for exemption from withholding.

Example 1. You are a high school student and expect to earn $2,500 from a summer job. You do not expect to have any other income during 1994, and your parents will be able to claim you as a dependent on their tax return. You worked last summer and had $375 federal income tax withheld from your pay. The entire $375 was refunded when you filed your 1993 return. Using *Figure 5-A,* you find that you **can** claim exemption from withholding.

Example 2. The facts are the same as in Example 1, except that you have a savings account and expect to have $20 interest income in 1994. Using *Figure 5-A,* you find that you **cannot** claim exemption from withholding because your unearned income will be $1 or more and your total income will be more than $600.
Age 65 or older or blind. If you are 65 or older or blind, use one of the worksheets in Chapter 1 of Publication 505, under *Exemption From Withholding,* to help you decide whether you can claim exemption from withholding. Do not use either of those worksheets if you will itemize deductions or claim dependents or tax credits on your 1994 return—see the following discussion instead.
Itemizing deductions or claiming dependents or tax credits. If you had no tax liability for 1993 and you will itemize your deductions or claim dependents or tax credits on your 1994 return, use the 1994 Estimated Tax Worksheet in Form 1040–ES (or see Chapter 2 of Publication 505) to figure your 1994 expected tax liability. You can claim exemption from withholding only if your total expected tax liability (line 13c of the worksheet) is zero.
Claiming exemption. To claim exemption, you must give your employer a Form W–4. Write in the word "EXEMPT" on line 7.

Your employer must send the IRS a copy of your Form W–4 if you claim exemption from withholding and your pay is expected to usually be more than $200 a week. If it turns out that you do not qualify for exemption, the IRS will send both you and your employer a written notice.

TaxPlanner

You should not be concerned if, by all reasonable expectations, your deductions and credits entitle you to 10 or more allowances, even though your employer must send a Form W-4 to the IRS. If you are entitled to 10 or more allowances, you should claim them. However, if you do claim 10 or more allowances, preserve your Form W-4 worksheets and supporting papers. They may be needed to satisfy the IRS that you are entitled to the allowances you are claiming.

If you claim exemption, but later your situation changes so that you will have to pay income tax after all, you must file a new Form W–4 within 10 days after the change. If you claim exemption in 1994, but you expect to owe income tax for 1995, you must file a new Form W–4 by December 1, 1994.

TaxSaver

Many students and retired persons who expect to have no federal income tax liability work part-time in occupations in which they receive tips. To avoid unnecessary income tax withholding, you may file a Form W-4 with your employer, certifying that you had no federal income tax liability last year and expect to have none this year as well.

An exemption is good for only one year. You must give your employer a new Form W–4 by February 15 each year to continue your exemption.

Supplemental Wages
Supplemental wages include bonuses, commissions, overtime pay, and certain sick pay. Your employer or other payer of supplemental wages may withhold income tax from these wages at a flat rate of at least 28%. The payer can also figure withholding using the same method used for your regular wages.

Also see *Withholding on Sick Pay,* later.

Expense allowances. Reimbursements or other expense allowances paid by your employer under a nonaccountable plan are treated as supplemental wages.

Reimbursements or other expense allowances paid under an accountable plan are treated as paid under a nonaccountable plan to the extent they are more than your proven expenses. However, this does not apply if you return the excess payments within a reasonable period of time.

For more information about accountable and nonaccountable expense allowance plans, see *Reimbursements* in Chapter 28, *Car Expenses and Other Employee Business Expenses.*

Penalties
You may have to pay a penalty of $500 if:

1) You make statements or claim withholding allowances on your Form W–4 that reduce the amount of tax withheld, and
2) You have no reasonable basis for such statements or allowances at the time you prepare your Form W–4.

There is also a criminal penalty for willfully supplying false or fraudulent information on your Form W–4 or for willfully failing to supply information that would increase the amount withheld. The penalty upon conviction can be either a fine of up to $1,000 or imprisonment for up to one year, or both.

These penalties will apply if you deliberately and knowingly falsify your Form W–4 in an attempt to reduce or eliminate the proper withholding of taxes. A simple error — an honest mistake — will not result in one of these penalties. For example, a person who has tried to figure the number of withholding allowances correctly, but claims seven when the proper number is six, will not be charged a W–4 penalty.

Withholding on Tips

The tips you receive while working on your job are considered part of your pay. You must include your tips on your tax return on the same line as your regular pay. However, tax is not withheld directly from tip income, as it is from your regular pay. Nevertheless, your employer will take into account the tips you report when figuring how much to withhold from your regular pay.

See Chapter 7, *Income from Tips,* for information on reporting your tips to your employer. For more information on the withholding rules for tip income, see Publication 531, *Reporting Tip Income.*

Figuring the amount to withhold. The tips you report to your employer are counted as part of your income for the month you report them. Your employer can figure your withholding in either of two ways:

1) By withholding at the regular rate on the sum of your pay plus your reported tips, or
2) By withholding at the regular rate on your pay plus an amount equal to 20% of your reported tips.

Not enough pay to cover taxes. If your regular pay is too low for your employer to withhold all the tax (including social security tax, Medicare tax, or railroad retirement tax) due on your pay plus your tips, you may give your employer money to cover the shortage.

If you do not give your employer money to cover the shortage, your employer will first withhold as much social security tax, Medicare tax, or railroad retirement tax as possible, up to the proper amount, and then withhold income tax up to the full amount of your pay. If not enough tax is withheld, you may have to make estimated tax payments. When you file your return, you also may have to pay any social security tax, Medicare tax, or railroad retirement tax your employer could not withhold.

Allocated tips. Your employer should not withhold income tax, social security tax, Medicare tax, or railroad retirement tax on any allocated tips. Withholding is based only on your pay plus your *reported tips.* Your employer should refund to you any incorrectly withheld tax. See *Tip Allocation* in Chapter 7, *Income from Tips,* for more information.

Withholding on Taxable Fringe Benefits

The value of certain noncash fringe benefits you receive from your employer is considered part of your pay. Your employer generally must withhold income tax on these benefits from your regular pay for the period the benefits are paid or considered paid.

For information on taxable fringe benefits, see *Fringe Benefits* under *Employee Compensation* in Chapter 6, *Wages, Salaries and Other Earnings.*

Your employer can choose not to withhold income tax on the value of your personal use of a car, truck, or other highway motor vehicle provided by your employer. Your employer must notify you if this choice is made.

When benefits are considered paid. Your employer can choose to treat a fringe benefit as paid by the pay period, by the quarter, or on some other basis as long as the benefit is considered paid at least once a year. Your employer can treat the benefit as

Figure 5-A. Exemption From Withholding on Form W-4

NOTE: **Do not use this chart** if you are 65 or older or blind, or if you will itemize your deductions or claim dependents or tax credits. Instead, see the discussions in this chapter under *Exemption From Withholding*.

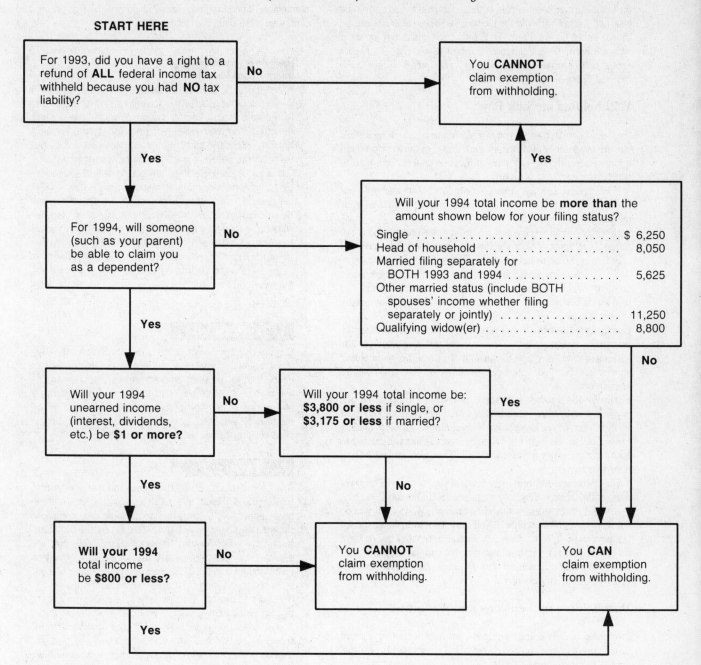

being paid on one or more dates during the year, even if you get the entire benefit at one time.

Special rule. Your employer can choose to treat a benefit provided during November or December as paid in the next year. Your employer must notify you if this rule is used.

Example. Your employer treats the value of benefits paid from November 1, 1992, through October 31, 1993, as paid to you in 1993. To determine the total value of benefits paid to you in 1994, your employer will add the value of any benefits paid in November and December of 1993 to the value of any benefits paid in January through October of 1994.

Exceptions. Your employer cannot choose when to withhold

tax on certain benefits. These benefits are transfers of either real property or personal property of a kind normally held for investment (such as stock). Your employer must withhold tax on these benefits at the time of transfer.

How withholding is figured. Your employer may either add the value of a fringe benefit to your regular pay and figure income tax withholding on the total or withhold 20% of the benefit's value.

If the benefit's actual value cannot be determined when it is paid or treated as paid, your employer may use a reasonable estimate. Your employer must determine the actual value of the benefit by January 31 of the next year. If the actual value is more than the estimate, your employer must pay the IRS any additional withhold-

ing tax required. Your employer has until April 1 of that next year to recover from you the additional tax paid to the IRS for you.
How your employer reports your benefits. Your employer must report on Form W–2, *Wage and Tax Statement,* the total of the taxable fringe benefits paid or treated as paid to you during the year and the tax withheld for the benefits. These amounts can be shown either on the Form W–2 for your regular pay or on a separate Form W–2. For more information, see *How To Report Fringe Benefits* under *Fringe Benefits* in Chapter 6, *Wages, Salaries and Other Earnings.*

Withholding on Sick Pay

"Sick pay" is a payment to you to replace your regular wages while you are temporarily absent from work due to sickness or personal injury. To qualify as "sick pay," it must be paid under a plan to which your employer is a party.

If you receive sick pay from your employer or an agent of your employer, income tax must be withheld just as it is from your regular pay.

However, if you receive sick pay from a third party who is not acting as an agent of your employer, income tax will be withheld only if you choose to have it withheld. See *Form W–4S,* later.

If you receive payments under a plan in which your employer does not participate (such as an accident or health plan where you paid all the premiums), the payments are not sick pay and usually are not taxable.

Union agreements. If you receive sick pay under a collective bargaining agreement between your union and your employer, the agreement may determine the amount of income tax withholding on sick pay. See your union representative or your employer for more information.

Form W–4S. If you choose to have income tax withheld from sick pay paid by a third party, such as an insurance company, you must fill out Form W–4S, *Request for Federal Income Tax Withholding From Sick Pay.* Its instructions contain a worksheet you can use to figure the amount you want withheld. They also explain restrictions that may apply.

Give the completed form to the payer of your sick pay. The payer must withhold according to your directions on the form.

If you do not request withholding on Form W–4S, or if you do not have enough tax withheld, you may have to make estimated tax payments. If you do not pay enough estimated tax or have enough income tax withheld, you may have to pay a penalty. See *Who Must Make Estimated Tax Payments* and *Underpayment Penalty,* later in this chapter.

Withholding on Pensions and Annuities

Income tax usually will be withheld from your pension or annuity distributions, unless you choose not to have it withheld. This rule applies to distributions from:

1) An individual retirement arrangement (IRA),
2) A life insurance company under an endowment, annuity, or life insurance contract,
3) A pension, annuity, or profit-sharing plan,
4) A stock bonus plan, and
5) Any other plan that defers the time you receive compensation.

This rule does not apply to eligible rollover distributions, discussed later.

The amount withheld depends on whether you receive payments spread out over more than one year (periodic payments) or whether you receive all the payments within one year (nonperiodic payments).

Nontaxable part. A part of your pension or annuity may not be taxable. See Chapter 11, *Retirement Plans, Pensions and Annuities,* for information on figuring the nontaxable part. Income tax will not be withheld from the part of your pension or annuity that is nontaxable. Therefore, the tax withheld will be figured on, and cannot be more than, the taxable part.

TaxAlert

A distribution made after December 31, 1992, that is eligible for direct rollover treatment (see Chapter 11, *Retirement Plans, Pensions, and Annuities*), but is not directly rolled over is subject to mandatory 20% withholding unless the participant's eligible rollover distributions for the year are expected to be less than $200.

If a participant elects to have a portion of a distribution transferred in a direct rollover and the remainder distributed to him, only the portion that is distributed will be subject to the 20% withholding. A plan administrator will not be liable for tax, interest, or penalties for failure to withhold if it reasonably relied on information about the participant's plan received from the participant.

Note: Hardship distributions from qualified plans are not excluded from the mandatory 20% income tax withholding.

TaxPlanner

If property other than cash is distributed, withholding must still occur. However, if the distribution consists of cash or other property and securities of the company withholding need not exceed the sum of the cash and fair market value of property received. Consequently, no mandatory withholding occurs where the distribution consists only of securities of the company.

TaxAlert

A written explanation of the direct rollover option and related rules (including the rules governing withholding) must generally be provided to participants not more than 90 days and no less than 30 days before the distribution date. For a series of periodic payments that are eligible for direct rollover, an initial timely notice must be given and an additional notice must be provided at least annually for as long as the payments continue.

Failure to provide such notice could cause the plan to become disqualified under the Internal Revenue Code. The IRS has issued a model notice that plan administrators are allowed to customize by deleting any portions that do not apply to the plan and adding additional information that is not inconsistent with the model notice.

Periodic Payments
Withholding from periodic payments of a pension or annuity is figured in the same way as withholding from salaries and wages. To tell the payer of your pension or annuity how much you want withheld, fill out **Form W–4P,** *Withholding Certificate for Pension or Annuity Payments,* or a similar form provided by the payer. Follow the rules discussed under *Withholding on Salaries and Wages,* earlier, to fill out your Form W–4P.

The withholding rules for pensions and annuities differ from those for salaries and wages in the following ways.

1) If you do not fill out a withholding certificate, tax will be withheld as if you were married and were claiming three withholding allowances.
2) Your certificate will not be sent to the IRS regardless of the number of allowances you claim on it.
3) You can choose not to have tax withheld, regardless of how much tax you owed last year or expect to owe this year. You do not have to qualify for exemption. See *Choosing Not to Have Income Tax Withheld,* later.
4) Tax will be withheld as if you were single and claiming no withholding allowances if:
   a) You do not give the payer your social security number (in the required manner), or
   b) The IRS notifies the payer, before any payment or distribution is made, that you gave it an incorrect social security number.

Note. Military retirement pay generally is treated in the same manner as wages and not as a pension or annuity for income tax withholding purposes. Military retirees should use Form W–4, not Form W–4P.

TaxAlert

If a series of periodic payments began prior to January 1, 1993, you determine whether post-December 31, 1992 payments are a series of substantially equal periodic payments over a specified period by taking into account all payments, including payments made before January 1, 1993. If the post-December 31, 1992 payments are not a series of substantially equal periodic payments, they will be subject to the direct rollover rules, including mandatory 20% withholding.

Nonperiodic Payments

Tax will be withheld at a 10% rate on any nonperiodic payments you receive.

Because withholding on nonperiodic payments does not depend on withholding allowances or whether you are married or single, you cannot use Form W–4P to tell the payer how much to withhold. But you can use Form W–4P to specify that an additional amount be withheld. You can also use Form W–4P to choose not to have tax withheld or to revoke a choice not to have tax withheld. See *Choosing Not to Have Income Tax Withheld,* later.

Note. The 10% rate of withholding on nonperiodic payments is less than the lowest tax rate (15%). Therefore, you may need to use Form W–4P to ask for additional withholding. If you do not have enough tax withheld, you may need to make estimated tax payments, as explained later.

Eligible Rollover Distributions

Distributions you receive that are eligible to be rolled over tax free into qualified retirement or annuity plans are subject to a 20% withholding tax.

An *eligible rollover distribution (ERD)* is any distribution from a qualified pension or tax-sheltered annuity other than:

1) A minimum required distribution, or
2) One of a series of substantially equal periodic pension or annuity payments made over:
   a) Your life (or your life expectancy) or the joint lives of you and your beneficiary (or your life expectancies), or
   b) A specified period of 10 or more years.

The withholding rules for non-ERD distributions are discussed earlier under *Periodic Payments* and *Nonperiodic Payments*.

A distribution is subject to withholding if it is not substantially equal to the periodic payments.

For example, upon retirement you receive 30% of your accrued pension benefits in the form of a single-sum distribution with the balance payable in annuity form. The 30% distribution is an ERD subject to 20% withholding. The annuity payments are periodic payments subject to withholding only if you choose to have withholding taken out.

The payer of a distribution must withhold at a 20% rate on any part of an ERD that is not rolled over directly to another qualified plan. You cannot elect not to have withholding on these distributions.

If tax is withheld on the ERD, it will be withheld only on the taxable part. You must either:

1) Contribute to the new plan (within 60 days from the date of the distribution) an amount equal to the taxable part of the total ERD, including the amount withheld, or
2) Include in your income for the year of the distribution any amount withheld for which you did not make a matching contribution to the new plan.

The matching contribution to cover the withheld amount must be in addition to the rollover of all the taxable part that you actually received.

Therefore, if the amount you actually received is less than the taxable part of the ERD and you do not:

1) Roll over the entire amount received, and
2) Also contribute to the new plan an amount sufficient to bring the total of the rollover plus the additional amount contributed up to an amount equal to that taxable part,

you must include any difference in your income.

If the amount you actually received is more than the taxable part of the total ERD, you cannot roll over more than the taxable part. If you roll over an amount equal to the taxable part, you do not have to include any of the amount withheld in your income. If you roll over less than the taxable part, you must include in your income the difference between the amount you roll over and the taxable part.

Exception to withholding rule. The only way to avoid withholding on an ERD is to have it directly rolled over from the employer's plan to a qualified plan or IRA. This direct rollover is made only at your direction. You must first make sure that the receiving trustee agrees to accept a direct rollover. The transferor trustee must allow you to make such a rollover and provide to you, within a reasonable period of time, written instructions on how to do so. You must also follow spousal consent and other participant and beneficiary protection rules.

Additional information. For more information on distributions from and taxation of qualified retirement plans and annuities, see Chapter 11, *Retirement Plans, Pensions and Annuities*. For information on IRAs, see Chapter 18, *Individual Retirement Arrangements (IRAs)*.

TaxSaver

If you receive an eligible rollover distribution from which the mandatory 20% withholding tax has been withheld, and you then decide you wish to roll the distribution over to an IRA within the allowed 60 days, you must come up with the 20% that was withheld from other funds within the 60 day period in order to roll the entire balance over. Otherwise the 20% which has been withheld will be treated as a taxable distribution and ineligible for rollover.

Choosing Not to Have Income Tax Withheld

You can choose not to have income tax withheld from your pension or annuity, whether the payments are periodic or nonperiodic. This rule does not apply to eligible rollover distributions. The payer will tell you how to make this choice. If you use Form W–4P, check the box on line 1 to make this choice. This choice will stay in effect until you decide you want withholding.

The payer will ignore your request not to have income tax withheld if:

1) You do not give the payer your social security number (in the required manner), or
2) The IRS notifies the payer, before any payment or distribution is made, that you gave it an incorrect social security number.

TAXPLANNER

You should choose to have no tax withheld from nonperiodic payments (total distributions within 1 year) from an employer pension or profit-sharing plan if you intend to defer taxation by putting the money directly into an Individual Retirement Arrangement (IRA).

If you choose not to have any income tax withheld from your pension or annuity, or if you do not have enough withheld, you may have to make estimated tax payments. See *Estimated Tax,* later.

If you do not pay enough tax either through estimated tax or withholding, you may have to pay a penalty. See *Underpayment Penalty,* later in this chapter.

Outside United States. If you are a U.S. citizen or resident alien and you choose not to have tax withheld from pension or annuity benefits, you must give the payer of the benefits a home address in the United States or in a U.S. possession. Otherwise, the payer must withhold tax. For example, the payer would have to withhold tax if you provide a U.S. address for a nominee, trustee, or agent to whom the benefits are to be delivered, but do not provide your own home address in the United States or in a U.S. possession.

Revoking a choice not to have tax withheld. If you want to revoke your choice not to have tax withheld, the payer of your pension or annuity will tell you how. If the payer gives you Form W–4P, write "Revoked" by the checkbox on line 1 of the form.

If you get periodic payments and do not complete the rest of the form, the payer will withhold tax as if you were married and claiming three allowances. If you want tax withheld at a different rate, you must complete the rest of the form.

Notice required of payer. The payer of your pension or annuity is required to send you a notice telling you about your right to choose not to have tax withheld.

Withholding on Gambling Winnings

Income tax is withheld from certain kinds of gambling winnings. The amount withheld from proceeds (the amount of your winnings minus the amount of your bet) paid after 1992 is 28%.

Gambling winnings of more than $5,000 from the following sources are subject to income tax withholding:

1) Any sweepstakes, wagering pool, or lottery, and
2) Any other wager, if the proceeds are at least 300 times the amount of the bet.

It does not matter if payment is in cash, property, or as an annuity. Proceeds not in money shall be taken into account at their fair market value.

Gambling winnings from bingo, keno, and slot machines are not subject to income tax withholding. If you receive gambling winnings not subject to withholding, you may need to make estimated tax payments. (See *Estimated Tax,* later.)

If you do not pay enough tax through withholding or estimated tax payments, you may be subject to a penalty. (See *Underpayment Penalty,* later.)

Form W–2G. If a payer withholds income tax from your gambling winnings, you should receive a Form W–2G, *Certain Gambling Winnings,* showing the amount you won and the amount withheld. Report your winnings on line 22 of Form 1040 and report the tax withheld on line 54 of Form 1040. Gambling losses are deductible only to the extent that they offset gambling winnings. You must use Schedule A of Form 1040 to deduct your losses and to deduct state tax withholding.

TAXPLANNER

Gambling losses are deductible, but only to the extent that you have gambling winnings to offset the losses and only if you itemize your deductions. It's very important to keep accurate records to document both your winnings and your losses.

Backup Withholding

Banks and other businesses that pay you certain kinds of income must file an information return (Form 1099) with the IRS. The information return shows how much you were paid during the year. It also includes your name and taxpayer identification number (TIN). Your TIN is either a social security number or an employer identification number.

These payments generally are not subject to withholding. However, "backup" withholding is required in certain situations. And, backup withholding can apply to most kinds of payments that are reported on Form 1099.

Payments made to you are subject to backup withholding at a flat 31% rate in the following situations.

1) You do not give the payer your TIN in the required manner.
2) The IRS notifies the payer that the TIN you gave is incorrect.
3) You are required, but fail, to certify that you are not subject to backup withholding.
4) The IRS notifies the payer to start withholding on interest or dividends because you have underreported interest or dividends on your income tax return. The IRS will do this only after it has mailed you four notices over a 120-day period.

See *Backup Withholding* in Chapter 1 of Publication 505 for more information.

Penalties. There are civil and criminal penalties for giving false information to avoid backup withholding. The civil penalty is $500. The criminal penalty, upon conviction, is a fine of up to $1,000, or imprisonment of up to one year, or both.

Estimated Tax

Estimated tax is the method used to pay tax on income that is not subject to withholding. This includes income from self-employment, unemployment compensation, interest, dividends, alimony, rent, gains from the sale of assets, prizes, and awards. You also may have to pay estimated tax if the amount of income tax being withheld from your salary, pension, or other income is not enough. To figure and pay estimated tax, use **Form 1040–ES,** *Estimated Tax for Individuals.*

Estimated tax is used to pay both income tax and self-employment tax, as well as other taxes and amounts reported on Form 1040. If you do not pay enough tax through withholding or by making estimated tax payments, you may be charged a penalty. If you do not pay enough by the due date of each payment period (see *When to Pay Estimated Tax,* later), you may be charged a penalty even if you are due a refund when you file your tax return. For information on when the penalty applies, see *Underpayment Penalty,* later.

Who Must Make Estimated Tax Payments

If you had a tax liability for 1993, you may have to pay estimated tax for 1994.

General rule. You must make estimated tax payments for 1994 if you expect to owe at least $500 in tax for 1994 after subtracting your withholding and credits, and you expect your withholding and credits to be less than the smaller of:

1) 90% of the tax to be shown on your 1994 tax return, or
2) 100% of the tax shown on your 1993 tax return. The return must cover all 12 months.

TAXALERT

The 1993 Tax Act modified the rules for how certain taxpayers must figure their estimated taxes. Effective for estimated tax payments applicable to tax years beginning after 1993, if your previous year's adjusted gross income was $150,000 or less ($75,000 or less if married filing separately), you can avoid underpayment penalties buy calculating your estimated payments as 100% of your prior year's tax. If your previous year's adjusted gross income exceeds $150,000, you must pay 110% of last year's liability to avoid penalties. The new law retains the rule that taxpayers can avoid penalties for underpayment of tax if at least 90% of their *current* tax liability is paid through withholding and estimated tax payments.

Note. If all your 1994 income will be subject to income tax withholding, you probably do not need to make estimated tax payments.

Exceptions. There are exceptions to the general rule if you are a farmer or fisherman or your 1993 adjusted gross income was more than $150,000 ($75,000 if you were married filing separately). See Chapter 2 of Publication 505 for more information.

To whom the rules apply. The estimated tax rules apply to:

• U.S. citizens and residents,
• Residents of Puerto Rico, the Virgin Islands, Guam, the Commonwealth of the Northern Mariana Islands, and American Samoa, and
• Nonresident aliens (use Form 1040–ES(NR)).

If you also receive salaries or wages, you can avoid having to make estimated tax payments by asking your employer to take more tax out of your earnings. To do this, file a new Form W–4 with your employer.

No tax liability last year. You do not have to pay estimated tax for 1994 if you meet all three of the following conditions:

1) You had no tax liability for your 1993 tax year,
2) You were a U.S. citizen or resident for the whole year, and
3) Your 1993 tax year covered a 12-month period.

You had no tax liability for 1993 if your total tax (defined later under *Required annual payment*) was zero or you were not required to file an income tax return.

Married taxpayers. To figure whether you must make estimated tax payments for 1994, apply the rules discussed here to your 1994 separate estimated income. If you can make joint estimated tax payments, you can apply these rules on a joint basis.

You and your spouse can make joint payments of estimated tax even if you are not living together.

You and your spouse cannot make joint estimated tax payments if you are separated under a decree of divorce or separate maintenance. Also, you cannot make joint estimated tax payments if either spouse is a nonresident alien or if you have different tax years.

Whether you and your spouse make joint estimated tax payments or separate payments will not affect your choice of filing a joint tax return or separate returns for 1994.

Change from 1993 separate returns to 1994 joint return. If you plan to file a joint return with your spouse for 1994, but you filed separate returns for 1993, your 1993 tax is the total of the tax shown on your separate returns. You filed a separate return for 1993 if you filed as single, head of household, or married filing separately.

Change from 1993 joint return to 1994 separate return. If you plan to file a separate return for 1994, but you filed a joint return with your spouse for 1993, your 1993 tax is your share of the tax on the joint return. You file a separate return for 1994 if you file as single, head of household, or married filing separately. To figure your share, first figure the tax both you and your spouse would have paid had you filed separate returns for 1993 using the same filing status as for 1994. Then multiply your joint tax liability by the following fraction:

$$\frac{\text{Your separate tax liability}}{\text{Both spouses' separate tax liabilities}}$$

Example. Joe and Phyllis filed a joint return for 1993 showing taxable income of $48,000 and a tax of $8,650. Of the $48,000 taxable income, $40,000 was attributable to Joe and $8,000 was attributable to Phyllis. For 1994, they file married filing separately. Joe figures his share of the tax on the 1993 joint return as follows:

Tax on $40,000 based on a separate return	$ 8,809
Tax on $8,000 based on a separate return	1,204
Total	$10,013
Joe's portion of total ($8,809 ÷ $10,013)	88%
Joe's share of joint return tax	
($8,650 × 88%)	$ 7,612

Aliens. Resident and nonresident aliens are required to make estimated tax payments. Resident aliens should follow the rules in this chapter unless noted otherwise. Nonresident aliens should get **Form 1040–ES(NR),** *U.S. Estimated Tax for Nonresident Alien Individuals.*

Figure 5-B. Do You Have To Pay Estimated Tax?

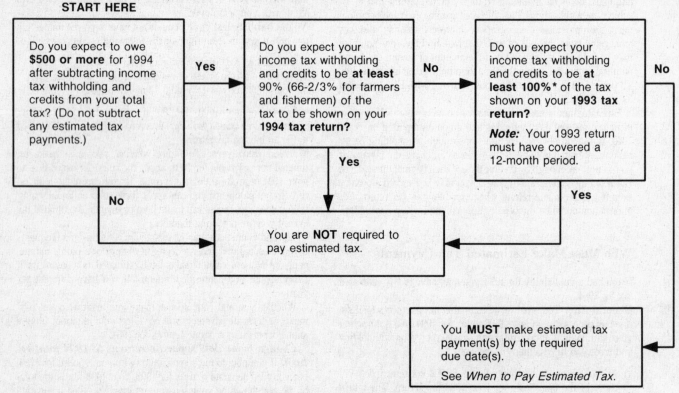

*110% If less than two-thirds of your gross income for 1993 or 1994 is from farming or fishing and your 1993 adjusted gross income was more than $150,000 ($75,000 if you were married filing separately)

How to Figure Estimated Tax

To figure your estimated tax for 1994, you must figure your expected adjusted gross income, taxable income, and taxes and credits for the year.

When figuring your 1994 estimated tax, it may be helpful to use your income, deductions, and credits for 1993 as a starting point. Use your 1993 federal tax return as a guide. You will also need Form 1040–ES to figure and pay your estimated tax for 1994. You must be careful to make adjustments both for changes in your own situation and for recent changes in the tax law. For 1994, there are several important changes in the law. These changes are discussed under *Tax Law Changes* at the beginning of this chapter.

Form 1040–ES includes a worksheet to help you figure your estimated tax. Keep the worksheet for your records.

For complete information and examples on how to figure your estimated tax for 1994, see Chapter 2 of Publication 505.

Expected adjusted gross income. Your expected adjusted gross income for 1994 is your expected total income minus your expected adjustments to income. Include all the income you expect to receive during the year, even income that is subject to withholding. However, do not include income that is tax exempt. Be sure to subtract all the adjustments to income you expect to take on your 1994 tax return. These are the adjustments shown on the 1993 Form 1040, that you included in the total on line 30. On the 1993 Form 1040A, these are the adjustments on lines 15a and 15b.

If you are self-employed, you can use *Worksheet 2.1* in Chapter 2 of Publication 505 to figure your deduction for one-half your self-employment tax.

Expected taxable income. Reduce your expected adjusted gross income by either your expected itemized deductions or your standard deduction and by a $2,450 deduction for each exemption. For information on the 1994 standard deduction amounts and a possible limit on your itemized deductions, see Publication 505 or the instructions for Form 1040–ES.

Expected taxes and credits. After you have figured your expected taxable income, figure your expected income tax. Use the 1994 Tax Rate Schedules near the end of Publication 505 or in the Form 1040–ES instructions. See Chapter 32, *Tax on Investment Income of Certain Minor Children,* for the special tax computation to use for a child under age 14 who has more than $1,200 of investment income.

Add your expected additional taxes from Form 4970, *Tax on Accumulation Distribution of Trusts,* and Form 4972, *Tax on Lump-Sum Distributions.* Subtract your expected credits. These are the credits shown on the 1993 Form 1040 that you included in the total on line 45. On the 1993 Form 1040A, these are the total credits on line 24c. If your credits are more than your taxes, use "–0–" as the result.

Add your expected self-employment tax and other taxes (see Chapter 2 of Publication 505). Other taxes are those shown on lines 48, 49 (other than from Form 8828), and 51 of the 1993 Form 1040, plus advance earned income credit payments on line 52 and any write-in amounts on line 53. Do not include uncollected social security, Medicare, or railroad retirement tax. On the 1993 Form 1040A, include as "other tax" any advance earned income credit payments on line 26.

Finally, subtract your expected earned income credit and fuel tax credit (from Form 4136). The result is your expected total tax for 1994.

Required annual payment. You figure the total amount you must pay for 1994 through withholding and estimated tax payments on lines 14a through 14c of the 1994 Estimated Tax Worksheet. The result is your required annual payment. It is the *smaller* of:

1) 90% of your total expected tax for 1994, or
2) 100% of the total tax shown on your 1993 return. (The return must cover all 12 months.)

Exceptions. If you are a farmer or fisherman, or your 1993 adjusted gross income was more than $150,000 ($75,000 if you were married filing separately), your required annual payment may be different. See *Required Annual Payment* in Chapter 2 of Publication 505.

TaxAlert

The 1993 Tax Act modified the rules for how certain taxpayers must figure their estimated taxes. Effective for estimated tax payments applicable to tax years beginning after 1993, if your previous year's adjusted gross income was $150,000 or less ($75,000 or less if married filing separately), you can avoid underpayment penalties by calculating your estimated payments as 100% of your prior year's tax. If your previous year's adjusted gross income exceeds $150,000, you must pay 110% of last year's liability to avoid penalties. The new law retains the rule that taxpayers can avoid penalties for underpayment of tax if at least 90% of their *current* tax liability is paid through withholding and estimated tax payments.

Total tax for 1993. Your 1993 total tax on Form 1040 is the amount on line 53 reduced by the total of the amounts on lines 50 and 56, any credit from Form 4136 included on line 59, any uncollected social security, Medicare, or railroad retirement tax included on line 53, any tax from Form 5329 (other than Part II) included on line 51, and any tax from Form 8828 included on line 49. On Form 1040A, it is line 27 reduced by line 28c. On Form 1040EZ, it is line 8.

Total estimated tax payments. Figure the total amount you must pay for 1994 through estimated tax payments on lines 15 and 16 of the 1994 Estimated Tax Worksheet. Subtract your expected withholding from your required annual payment. You usually must pay this difference in four equal installments. (See *When to Pay Estimated Tax* and *How to Figure Each Payment,* later.)

If your total expected tax on line 13c, minus your expected withholding on line 15, is less than $500, you are not required to make estimated tax payments.

Withholding. Your expected withholding for 1994 (line 15 of the 1994 Estimated Tax Worksheet) includes the income tax you expect to be withheld from all sources (wages, pensions and annuities, etc.). It also includes excess social security and railroad retirement tax you expect to be withheld from your wages.

For information on excess social security or tier 1 railroad retirement tax withholding for 1994, see Publication 505.

TaxPlanner

A convenient way to figure your estimated tax is to list all your sources of income from last year. Then enter the estimated income from each source for *this* year. Add to this list all new sources of income that you expect this year. Repeat this procedure for all deductions and exemptions. If your itemized deductions are more than the standard deduction, use your itemized deductions. Then compute your estimated tax liability for 1994 based on your estimated taxable income.

To your estimated tax liability, add any additional taxes, including self-employment taxes, that you expect to pay for the current year. Then subtract the various tax credits you expect to claim for the current year, and also subtract the income tax you expect to have withheld. The remaining tax liability is your estimated tax.

If your estimated tax exceeds $500, equal estimated tax payments generally have to be made on April 15, June 15, September 15, and January 15. Special exceptions, described later in this chapter, may reduce or eliminate this requirement.

When to Pay Estimated Tax

For estimated tax purposes, the year is divided into four payment periods. Each period has a specific payment due date. If you do not pay enough tax by the due date of each of the payment periods, you may be charged a penalty even if you are due a refund when you file your income tax return. The following chart gives the payment periods and due dates for 1994 estimated tax payments.

For the period:	Due date:
Jan. 1* through Mar. 31	April 15
April 1 through May 31	June 15
June 1 through Aug. 31	September 15
Sept. 1 through Dec. 31	January 15 next year**

*If your tax year does not begin on January 1, see *Fiscal year taxpayers,* later.

**See *January payment,* later.

Saturday, Sunday, holiday rule. If the due date for making an estimated tax payment falls on a Saturday, Sunday, or legal holiday, the payment will be on time if you make it on the next day that is not a Saturday, Sunday, or legal holiday. Thus, a payment due January 15, 1995, will be on time if you make it on or before January 17, 1995.

January payment. If you file your 1994 return by January 31, 1995, and pay the rest of the tax you owe, you are not required to make your estimated tax payment that would be due on January 15, 1995.

Fiscal year taxpayers. If your tax year does not start on January 1, your payment due dates are:

The 15th day of the 4th month of your fiscal year,
The 15th day of the 6th month of your fiscal year,
The 15th day of the 9th month of your fiscal year, and
The 15th day of the 1st month after the end of your fiscal year.

You do not have to make the last payment listed above if you file your income tax return by the last day of the first month after the end of your fiscal year and pay all the tax you owe with your return.

When to Start

You do not have to make estimated tax payments until you have income on which you will owe the tax. If you have income subject to estimated tax during the first payment period, you must make your first payment by the due date for the first payment period. You can pay all your estimated tax at that time, or you can pay it in four installments. If you choose to pay in installments, make your first payment by the due date for the first payment period. Make your remaining installments by the due dates for the later periods.

If you first have income subject to estimated tax during a later payment period, you must make your first payment by the due date for that period. You can pay your entire estimated tax by the due date for that period, or you can pay it in installments by the due date for that period and the due dates for the remaining periods. The following chart shows when to make installment payments:

If you first have income on which you must pay estimated tax:	Make a payment by:	Make later installments by:
On or before March 31	April 15	June 15 September 15 January 15 next year*
After March 31 and before June 1	June 15	September 15 January 15 next year*
After May 31 and before Sept. 1	September 15	January 15 next year*
After August 31	January 15 next year*	(Not applicable)

*See *January payment,* and *Saturday, Sunday, holiday rule* under *When to Pay Estimated Tax,* earlier.

After making your first estimated tax payment, changes in your income, adjustments, deductions, credits, or exemptions may make it necessary for you to refigure your estimated tax. Pay the unpaid balance of your amended estimated tax by the next payment due date after the change or in installments by that date and the due dates for the remaining payment periods.

Example

In April, 1994, John figured that his estimated tax for 1994 would be $12,000. Accordingly, he made his first 1994 quarterly estimated payment of $3,000 on April 15, 1994, and his second quarterly estimated payment of $3,000 on June 15, 1994. In August, John purchased a new home, and his monthly mortgage payments increased dramatically. Since John could deduct his mortgage interest payments, he reduced his third and fourth quarterly estimated payments due on September 15, 1994, and January 16, 1995, respectively.

To determine how much you should pay by each payment due date, see *How to Figure Each Payment,* next.

How to Figure Each Payment

You should pay enough estimated tax by the due date of each payment period to avoid a penalty for that period. If you do not pay enough each payment period, you may be charged a penalty even if you are due a refund when you file your tax return. See *Underpayment Penalty,* later in this chapter.

Regular Installment Method

If you must pay estimated tax beginning with the payment due April 15, 1994, you can figure your required payment for each period by dividing your total estimated tax payments (line 16 of the 1994 Estimated Tax Worksheet) by 4. Use this method only if your required annual payment stays the same throughout the year. (Under certain circumstances, your required payment may be less. See *Annualized Income Installment Method,* later.)

Amended estimated tax. If you refigure your estimated tax during the year, or if your first payment is due after April 15, 1994, figure your required payment for each remaining payment period using the following worksheet.

1. Amended total estimated tax payments _____

2. Multiply line 1 by:

  .50 if next payment is due

    June 15, 1994.

  .75 if next payment is due

    September 15, 1994.

  1.00 if next payment is due

    January 17, 1995 .... _____

3. Estimated tax payments for all previous periods .... _____

4. **Next required payment:** Subtract line 3 from line 2 and enter the result (but not less than zero) here and on your payment-voucher for your next required payment .... _____

If the payment on line 4 is due January 17, 1995, **stop here.** Otherwise, go on to line 5.

5. Add lines 3 and 4 .... _____

6. Subtract line 5 from line 1 and enter the result (but not less than zero) .... _____

7. **Each following required payment:** If the payment on line 4 is due June 15, 1994, enter one-half of the amount on line 6 here and on the payment-vouchers for your payments due September 15, 1994, and January 17, 1995. If the amount on line 4 is due September 15, 1994, enter the full amount on line 6 here and on the payment-voucher for your payment due January 17, 1995 .... _____

Example. Early in 1994, you figure your estimated tax is $1,800. You make estimated tax payments on April 15 and June 15 of $450 each ($1,800 ÷ 4).

On July 16, you sell investment property at a gain. Your refigured estimated tax is $3,600. Your required estimated tax payment for the third payment period is $1,800, figured as follows.

1. Amended total estimated tax payments $3,600

2. Multiply line 1 by:

  .50 if next payment is due

    June 15, 1994.

  .75 if next payment is due

    September 15, 1994.

  1.00 if next payment is due

    January 17, 1995 2,700

3. Estimated tax payments for all previous periods 900

4. **Next required payment:** Subtract line 3 from line 2 and enter the result (but not less than zero) here and on your payment-voucher for your next required payment $1,800

If the payment on line 4 is due January 17, 1995, **stop here.** Otherwise, go on to line 5.

5. Add lines 3 and 4 2,700

6. Subtract line 5 from line 1 and enter the result (but not less than zero) 900

7. **Each following required payment:** If the payment on line 4 is due June 15, 1994, enter one-half of the amount on line 6 here and on the payment-vouchers for your payments due September 15, 1994, and January 17, 1995. If the amount on line 4 is due September 15, 1994, enter the full amount on line 6 here and on the payment-voucher for your payment due January 17, 1995 .... $900

If your estimated tax does not change again, your required estimated tax payment for the fourth payment period will be $900.

Note. If your estimated tax payment for a previous period is less than one-fourth of your amended estimated tax, you may be charged a penalty for underpayment of estimated tax for that period when you file your tax return. To avoid the penalty, you must show that the total of your withholding and estimated tax payment for the period was at least as much as your annualized income installment. Complete Form 2210 and Schedule B — *Annualized Income Installment Method,* and attach the form and Schedule B to your tax return. See *Form 2210,* later, under *Underpayment Penalty,* for more information.

Annualized Income Installment Method
If you do not receive your income evenly throughout the year (for example, your income from a repair shop you operate is much larger in the summer than it is during the rest of the year), your required estimated tax payment for one or more periods may be less than the amount figured using the regular installment method.

To see if you can pay less for any period, complete the *1994 Annualized Estimated Tax Worksheet (Worksheet 2.11)* in Chapter 2 of Publication 505.

Note. If you use the annualized income installment method to figure your estimated tax payments, you *must* attach to your tax return a completed Form 2210 and Schedule B (Form 2210). See *Form 2210* under *Underpayment Penalty,* later.

Explanation
The following discusses in detail how to compute your annualized income installment.

Figure your installment for each payment period as follows:

1. Figure your adjusted gross income (AGI), alternative minimum taxable income (AMTI), and adjusted self-employment income (SEI) for the months in 1994 ending before the due date of the payment period. (Your AGI is your actual total taxable income minus your actual adjustments to income for the months in the period.)
2. Multiply each of the amounts in step (1) by
   a) 4, if the payment due date is April 15.
   b) 2.4, if the payment due date is June 15.
   c) 1.5, if the payment due date is September 15.
   d) 1, if the payment due date is January 16, 1995. These amounts are your annualized AGI, AMTI, and SEI.
3. Determine the greater of your

a) Actual itemized deductions for the months in the period multiplied by the same figure used in step (2), or
b) Standard deduction for the year.
4. Multiply your exemptions by $2,450 (the 1994 exemption amount).
5. Add the amounts from steps (3) and (4), and subtract the total from your annualized AGI determined in step (2). This amount is your annualized taxable income.
6. Figure the appropriate tax on your annualized taxable income [from step (5)] and on your annualized AMTI and SEI [from step (2)].
7. Total the amounts figured in step (6).
8. Add any additional taxes that you may owe because of events that occurred during the months in 1994 ending before the due date of the payment period. "Additional taxes" are the ones listed on line 39 of the 1993 Form 1040.
9. Subtract from this total any nonrefundable credits that you may be able to claim because of events that occurred during the months in 1994 ending before the due date of the payment period. These are the credits that make up the total on line 46 of the 1993 Form 1040. If these credits are more than the total of step (7) plus additional taxes figured in step (8), use zero as the result and go on to the next step.
10. Add to the result of step (9) any of the taxes listed below that you may owe because of events that occurred during the months in 1994 ending before the due date of the payment period:
    a) Tax from recapture of an investment credit.
    b) Tax on premature distributions from retirement plans (Form 5329, Part II only).
    c) Section 72 penalty taxes.
    d) Excise tax on golden parachute payments.
11. Add any advance earned income credit payments received during the months in 1994 ending before the due date of the payment period.
12. Subtract the following credits that apply to your situation for the months in 1994 ending before the due date of the payment period:
    a) Credit for federal tax on gasoline and special fuel.
    b) Earned income credit.
13. Multiply the result of step (12) by
    a) 22.5%, if the payment due date is April 15.
    b) 45%, if the payment due date is June 15.
    c) 67.5%, if the payment due date is September 15.
    d) 90%, if the payment due date is January 16, 1995.
14. Figure the total estimated tax you had to pay by the due date of each of the preceding payment periods. This is the total of the lower of the required installment or the annualized income installment for each payment period.
15. Subtract the step (14) amount from the step (13) amount.

If the annualized income installment for the payment period is less than the required installment, you only need to pay the annualized income installment.

When you pay the annualized income installment, for the next payment period, you must add the difference between the required installment for that subsequent payment period (as increased) and the annualized income installment for the previous payment period to the required installment for the next payment period.

Estimated Tax Payments Not Required

You do not have to make estimated tax payments if your withholding in each payment period is at least one-fourth of your required annual payment or at least your required annualized income installment for that period. You also do not have to make estimated tax payments if you will pay enough through withholding to keep the amount you owe with your 1994 return under $500.

How to Pay Estimated Tax

There are two ways to make estimated tax payments:

1) By crediting an overpayment on your 1993 return to your 1994 estimated tax, and
2) By sending in your payment with a payment-voucher from **Form 1040–ES.**

Crediting an Overpayment

When you file your Form 1040 or Form 1040A for 1993 and you have an overpayment of tax, you can apply part or all of it to your estimated tax for 1994. On line 63 of Form 1040, or line 31 of Form 1040A, write the amount you want credited to your estimated tax rather than refunded. The amount you have credited should be taken into account when figuring your estimated tax payments. You can use all the credited amount toward your first payment, or you can spread it out in any way you choose among any or all of your payments.

Once you have asked that an overpayment be credited to your estimated tax for the next year, you cannot have that amount refunded to you. You also cannot use that overpayment in any other way.

Explanation

An overpayment that is applied to your estimated tax payment for the current year is considered to have been paid on time even if you are granted an extension and file your previous year's tax return after April 15.

Example

If you get a legal extension on your tax return from April 15 to August 15 and you actually file your return in July, you can apply any overpayment you may have made in the previous year to your estimated tax payments that were due on April 15 and June 15.

Using the Payment-Vouchers

Each payment of estimated tax must be accompanied by a payment-voucher from Form 1040–ES. If you made estimated tax payments last year, you should receive a copy of the 1994 Form 1040–ES in the mail. It will have payment-vouchers preprinted with your name, address, and social security number. Using the preprinted vouchers will speed processing, reduce the chance of error, and help save processing costs.

If you did not pay estimated tax last year, you will have to get a copy of Form 1040–ES from the IRS. Do so by calling toll-free 1–800–TAX–FORM (1–800–829–3676). After you make your first payment, the IRS will mail to you a Form 1040–ES package with preprinted vouchers. Follow the instructions in the package to make sure you use the vouchers correctly.

Use the addressed envelopes that came with your Form 1040–ES package. If you use your own envelope, make sure you mail your payment-vouchers to the address shown in the Form 1040–ES instructions for the place where you live. *Do not* use the address shown in the Form 1040 or Form 1040A instructions.

Explanation

The following explanation discusses in detail how to use the payment voucher.

1. Enter your Social Security number, name, and address on the voucher. If this information is preprinted on the voucher, make any corrections that are necessary. Use the preprinted voucher if you have one.

   If you are making joint estimated tax payments, your spouse's name and Social Security number should be included on the voucher. If you make joint payments and you have different last names, separate them with an "and"—for example, "John Brown and Mary Smith."

2. On line 1 of the voucher, enter the amount you are paying. If you credited an overpayment on last year's return to your estimated tax for this year, subtract the amount of the overpayment that you want to apply to this payment from the amount you need to pay for the period. The result is the amount you should pay with the voucher. Enter only this amount on line 1 of the voucher. If the amount is zero, you do not have to send in a voucher.
3. If you use a fiscal year as your tax year, enter the date your fiscal year ends on line 2 of the voucher.
4. Tear off the voucher at the perforation.
5. Enclose (but do not staple or otherwise attach) your check or money order with the voucher. Make your check or money order payable to Internal Revenue Service. Write your Social Security number and "1994 Form 1040–ES" on your check or money order.
6. Fill in the Record of Estimated Tax Payments on your Form 1040–ES package so that you will have a record of your payments.
7. Mail the voucher to the Internal Revenue Service Center for the place where you live. Use the addressed envelope that comes with your voucher or the address for your state shown in the Form 1040–ES package.

Change of address. You must notify the IRS if you are making estimated tax payments and you changed your address during the year. You must send a clear and concise written statement to the IRS Center where you filed your last return and provide all of the following:

1) Your full name (and your spouse's full name),
2) Your signature (and spouse's signature),
3) Your old address (and spouse's old address if different),
4) Your new address, and

5) Your social security number (and spouse's social security number).

You can use Form 8822, *Change of Address,* for this purpose.

You can continue to use your old pre-printed payment-vouchers until the IRS sends you new ones. However, *DO NOT* correct the address on the old voucher or the address on the envelope.

Credit for Withholding and Estimated Tax

When you file your 1993 income tax return, take credit for all the income tax and excess social security, Medicare, or railroad retirement tax withheld from your salary, wages, pensions, etc. Also, take credit for the estimated tax you paid for 1993. These credits are subtracted from your tax. You should file a return and claim these credits even if you do not owe tax.

If you had two or more employers and were paid wages of more than $57,600 during 1993, too much social security, Medicare, or railroad retirement tax may have been withheld from your wages. See *Credit for Excess Social Security Tax, Medicare Tax, or Railroad Retirement Tax Withheld* in Chapter 35, *Other Credits.*

Withholding

If you had income tax withheld during 1993, you should receive a statement by January 31, 1994, showing your income and the tax withheld. Depending on the source of your income, you will receive:

Form W-2, *Wage and Tax Statement,*
Form W-2G, *Certain Gambling Winnings,* or
A form in the 1099 series.

Forms W-2 and W-2G. You file these forms file with your income tax return. You should get at least two copies of each form you receive. Attach Copy B to the front of your federal income tax return. Copy C is for your records. You should also receive copies to file with your state and local returns.

Example

Ted Taxpayer is employed by ABC Company, Inc. His Form W-2, box 2 reflects that he had $10,675.50 in federal tax withheld by ABC Company on wages of $46,958. His state income tax of $2,817.48 withheld for the state of Georgia is reflected in box 18 on the same amount of wages. Box 13 indicates (Code D—Code definitions can be found on the back of the W-2 form) that Ted contributed $2,546.21 to his company's 401(k) plan. That amount of income was not included in the federal or state wages, but it is included in determining how much was withheld from Ted's income for social security and Medicare purposes. Refer to boxes 3 and 5. The Social Security tax withheld is in box 4, and the Medicare tax withheld is in box 6. Box 14 shows any other deductions that were made from Ted's income and that he contributed $325.61 to the United Way. The pension plan box is checked in box 15 and lets Ted (and the IRS) know that he is covered by a pension plan and therefore may be limited in his ability to make deductible IRA contibutions.

Form W-2 reproduction:

a Control number 012345	Void

b Employer's identification number 58-2345 790	1 Wages, tips, other compensation 46,958	2 Federal income tax withheld 10,675.50

c Employer's name, address, and ZIP code: ABC Company, Inc. 1400 Main Street Anytown, GA 91221

3 Social security wages 49,504.21	4 Social security tax withheld 2,911.40
5 Medicare wages and tips 49,504.21	6 Medicare tax withheld 717.81
7 Social security tips	8 Allocated tips

d Employee's social security number 357-34-5454 | 9 Advance EIC payment | 10 Dependent care benefits

e Employee's name, address, and ZIP code: Ted Taxpayer 237 East Street Anytown, GA 90210

11 Nonqualified plans | 12 Benefits included in Box 1
13 See Instrs. for Box 13: D 2,546.21 | 14 Other: UN Way 325.61
15 Statutory employee / Deceased / Pension plan [X] / Legal rep / 942 emp / Subtotal / Deferred compensation

16 State GA, Employer's state I.D. No. 23574 9-Q | 17 State wages, tips etc 46,958 | 18 State income tax 2,817.48 | 19 Locality name | 20 Local wages, tips etc | 21 Local income tax

Department of the Treasury—Internal Revenue Service

Form **W-2** Wage and Tax Statement **1993**
Copy B To Be Filed With Employee's FEDERAL Tax Return

This information is being furnished to the Internal Revenue Service.

OMB No. 1545-0008

Form W-2

Your employer should give you a Form W-2 for 1993 by January 31, 1994. You should receive a separate Form W-2 from each employer you worked for.

If you stop working before the end of the year, your employer can give you your Form W-2 any time after you leave your job but no later than January 31 of the following year (or the next day that is not a Saturday, Sunday, or holiday if January 31 is a Saturday, Sunday, or holiday). If you ask for the form, your employer must give it to you within 30 days after receiving your written request or within 30 days after your final wage payment, whichever is later.

If you have not received your Form W-2 by January 31, 1994, you should ask your employer for it. If you do not receive it by February 15, call the IRS toll-free telephone number for your area. The number is listed in the Form 1040, Form 1040A, and Form 1040EZ instructions. You will be asked to give your employer's name, address, and telephone number, and, if known, your employer's identification number. You will also be asked for your address, social security number, daytime telephone number, dates of employment, and your best estimate of your total wages and federal income tax withheld.

Form W-2 shows your total pay and other compensation and the income tax, social security tax, and Medicare tax that was withheld during the year. Take credit for the federal income tax withheld on:

Line 54 if you file Form 1040,
Line 28a if you file Form 1040A, or
Line 7 if you file Form 1040EZ.

Form W-2 is also used to report any taxable sick pay you received and any income tax withheld from your sick pay.

Form W-2G

If you had gambling winnings, the payer may have withheld 28% as income tax. If tax was withheld, the payer will give you a Form W-2G showing the amount you won and the amount of tax withheld. Report the amounts you won on line 22 of Form 1040. Take credit for the tax withheld on line 54 of Form 1040. If you had gambling winnings, you must use Form 1040; you cannot use Form 1040A or Form 1040EZ. See *Deductions Not Subject To the 2% Limit* in Chapter 30, *Miscellaneous Deductions,* for information on how to deduct gambling losses.

The 1099 Series

Most forms in the 1099 series are not filed with your return. Keep these forms for your records. There are several different forms in this series, including:

Form 1099-B, *Proceeds From Broker and Barter Exchange Transactions,*
Form 1099-DIV, *Dividends and Distributions,*
Form 1099-G, *Certain Government Payments,*
Form 1099-INT, *Interest Income,*
Form 1099-MISC, *Miscellaneous Income,*
Form 1099-OID, *Original Issue Discount,*
Form 1099-R, *Distributions From Pensions, Annuities, Retirement or Profit-Sharing Plans, IRAs, Insurance Contracts, etc.,*
Form SSA-1099, *Social Security Benefit Statement,* and
Form RRB-1099, *Payments by the Railroad Retirement Board.*

Attach Form 1099-R to your return if Box 4 shows federal income tax withholding. Include the amount withheld in the total on line 54 of Form 1040 or line 28a of Form 1040A. Check the box next to the total.

For some types of income reported on forms in the 1099 series, you may not be able to use Form 1040A or Form 1040EZ. See the instructions to these forms for details.

If you were subject to backup withholding on income you received during 1993, include the amount withheld, as shown on your Form 1099, in the total on line 54 of Form 1040, or line 28a of Form 1040A. Check the box next to this total.

Form Not Correct

If you receive a form with incorrect information on it, you should ask for a corrected form. The corrected Form W-2G or Form 1099 you receive will be marked "CORRECTED." A special form, Form W-2c, *Statement of Corrected Income and Tax Amounts,* is used to correct a Form W-2.

Form Received After Filing

If you file your return and you later receive a form for income that you did not include on your return, you should report the income and take credit for any income tax withheld by filing Form 1040X, *Amended U.S. Individual Income Tax Return.* See *Amended Returns and Claims for Refund* in Chapter 1, *Filing Information.*

Separate Returns

If you are married but file a separate return, you can take credit only for the tax withheld from your own income. Do not include any amount withheld from your spouse's income. However, different rules may apply if you live in a community property state.

Community property states. Arizona, California, Idaho, Louisiana, Nevada, New Mexico, Texas, Washington, and Wisconsin are community property states. If you live in a community property state and file a separate return, you and your spouse must each report half of all community income in addition to your own separate income. Each of you takes credit for half of all taxes withheld on the community income. If you were divorced during the year, each of you generally must report half the community income and can take credit for half the withholding on that community income for the period before the divorce.

For more information on these rules, and some exceptions, see Publication 555, *Federal Tax Information on Community Property.*

Fiscal Years

If you file your tax return on the basis of a fiscal year (a 12-month period ending on the last day of any month except December), you must follow special rules, described below, to determine your credit for federal income tax withholding.

During your fiscal year, one calendar year will end and another will begin. You can claim credit on your tax return only for the tax withheld during the calendar year ending in your fiscal year. You cannot claim credit for any of the tax withheld during the calendar year beginning in your fiscal year. You will be able to claim credit for that withholding on your return for next year.

However, if income tax has been withheld from your income under the backup withholding rule, take credit for it on your tax return for the fiscal year in which you received the payment.

Explanation

Employees on a fiscal year may suffer a delay in utilizing their credit from withheld taxes. See Chapter 39, *Foreign Citizens Living in the United States,* for an example.

For a more detailed discussion of how to take credit for withholding on a fiscal year return, see *Fiscal Years* in Chapter 3 of Publication 505.

Estimated Tax

Take credit for all your estimated tax payments for 1993 on line 55 of Form 1040 or line 28b of Form 1040A. Include any overpayment from 1992 that you had credited to your 1993 estimated tax. You must use Form 1040 or Form 1040A if you paid estimated tax. You cannot use Form 1040EZ.

Name changed. If you changed your name, and you made estimated tax payments using your old name, attach a brief statement to the front of your tax return indicating:

1) When you made the payments,
2) The amount of each payment,
3) Which IRS address you sent the payments to, and
4) Your name when you made the payments and your social security number.

The statement should cover payments you made jointly with your spouse as well as any you made separately.

Separate Returns

If you and your spouse made separate estimated tax payments for 1993 and you file separate returns, you can take credit only for your own payments.

If you made joint estimated tax payments, you must decide how to divide the payments between your returns. One of you can claim all of the estimated tax paid and the other none, or you can divide it in any other way you agree on. If you cannot agree, you must divide the payments in proportion to each spouse's individual tax as shown on your separate returns for 1993.

Divorced Taxpayers

If you made joint estimated tax payments for 1993, and you were divorced during the year, either you or your former spouse can claim all of the joint payments, or you each can claim part of them. If you cannot agree on how to divide the payments, you must divide them in proportion to each spouse's individual tax as shown on your separate returns for 1993.

If you claim any of the joint payments on your tax return, enter your former spouse's social security number in the space provided on the front of Form 1040 or Form 1040A. If you divorced and remarried in 1993, enter your present spouse's social security number in that space and write your former spouse's social security number, followed by "DIV," to the left of line 55, Form 1040, or line 28b, Form 1040A.

Underpayment Penalty

If you did not pay enough tax either through withholding or by making estimated tax payments, you will have an underpayment of estimated tax and you may have to pay a penalty. However, you will **not** generally have to pay a penalty for 1993 if any of the following situations applies to you.

- The total of your withholding and estimated tax payments was at least as much as your 1992 tax, you are not subject to the special rule limiting use of prior year's tax, and all required estimated tax payments were on time.

timated tax payments was at least as much as your previous year's tax. However, if your previous year's adjusted gross income exceeds $150,000, you must pay 110% of last year's liability in order to avoid penalties. The new law retains the rule that taxpayers can avoid penalties for underpayment of tax if at least 90% of their current tax liability is paid through withheld taxes and estimated tax payments.

Example

In 1994, Bob anticipates salary income of $325,000, interest and dividend income of $50,000, capital gains of $25,000, and partnership income from his 50% interest in Limited Partnership of $64,000. (Bob has no available losses to shelter this partnership income.) His modified adjusted gross income will therefore be $464,000. Bob's 1993 adjusted gross income was $220,000. Because Bob's 1993 adjusted gross income exceeded $150,000, Bob would pay 110% of the prior year's tax to avoid an underpayment penalty.

- The tax balance on your return is no more than 10% of your total 1993 tax, and all required estimated tax payments were on time.
- Your total 1993 tax minus your withholding is less than $500.
- You did not owe tax for 1992.

Special rules apply if you are a farmer or fisherman. See *Farmers and Fishermen* in Chapter 4 of Publication 505 for more information.

IRS can figure the penalty for you. If you think you owe the penalty but you do not want to figure it yourself when you file your tax return, you may not have to. Generally, the IRS will figure the penalty for you and send you a bill. However, you must complete Form 2210 and file it with your return if you check any of the boxes in Part 1 of the form. See *Reasons for filing* later in this section.

General Rule

In general, you may owe a penalty for 1993 if the total of your withholding and estimated tax payments did not equal at least the *smaller* of:

1) 90% of your 1993 tax, or
2) 100% of your 1992 tax. (Your 1992 return must cover a 12-month period.) This rule may not apply if you meet the conditions under the *Special rule,* later.

Because the penalty is figured separately for each payment period, you may owe a penalty for an earlier payment period even if you later paid enough to make up the underpayment. If you did not pay enough tax by the due date of each of the payment periods, you may owe a penalty even if you are due a refund when you file your income tax return.

be withheld during the current year must be paid in estimated installments throughout the year. However, certain taxpayers may have to use 110% of last year's tax to calculate their estimated tax.

Example

Elizabeth West's 1993 tax return indicates that her 1993 tax liability (including self-employment tax and alternative minimum tax) was $14,000. In 1994, Elizabeth estimates that her tax liability will jump to $24,000 due to several contemplated stock sales that should result in a substantial capital gain. Elizabeth's withholding on her 1994 salary is expected to be $13,000.

Since her withholding of $13,000 during 1994 is not expected to exceed her 1993 tax of $14,000, she should increase her withholding by $1,000 during the year. Even though she will have paid less than 90% of her tax liability for 1994, she will avoid an underpayment penalty because she has paid an amount at least equal to her 1993 tax. If she made this determination early enough in the year, she could accomplish the same result by making four quarterly estimated tax payments of $250.

However, Elizabeth will have to pay an additional $10,000 ($24,000 − $14,000) when she files her 1994 tax return by April 17, 1995. Nevertheless, she will have had the use of this money from the time she sold her stock until the time she filed her 1994 tax return.

Example. You did not make estimated tax payments during 1993 because you thought you had enough tax withheld from your wages. Early in January 1994, you made an estimate of your total 1993 tax. You then realized that your withholding was $2,000 less than the amount needed to avoid a penalty for underpayment of estimated tax.

On January 11, you made an estimated tax payment of $3,000, the difference between your withholding and your estimate of your total tax. Your final return shows your total tax to be $50 less than you originally figured, so you are due a refund.

You do not owe a penalty for your payment due January 15, 1994. However, you will owe a penalty through January 11 for your underpayments for the earlier payment periods.

Special rule. You may not be able to use the general rule to avoid the underpayment penalty if you meet *all* of the conditions below.

- *Condition 1.* You are not a farmer or fisherman.
- *Condition 2.* You made an estimated tax payment for 1990, 1991, or 1992, or you were charged a penalty for not paying estimated taxes in any of those years. Do not include withholding or a credit from your prior year's tax as a payment of estimated tax.
- *Condition 3.* Your 1993 AGI (line 31 of your Form 1040) is more than $75,000 ($37,500 if married filing separately).
- *Condition 4.* Your 1993 modified AGI (line 31 of your 1992 Form 1040) by more than $40,000 ($20,000 if married filing separately).

If you meet all four conditions, you must use a special rule to determine what your required annual payment was for 1993.

For a definition of "modified AGI" and more information on the special rule, see Chapter 4 of Publication 505.

Minimum required each period. You will owe a penalty for any 1993 payment period for which your estimated tax payment plus your withholding for the period and overpayments for previous periods was less than the *smaller* of:

1) 22.5% of your 1993 tax, or
2) 25% of your 1992 tax. (Your 1992 return must cover a 12-month period.)

If you miss a payment or you paid less than the minimum required in a period, you may be charged an underpayment penalty from the date the amount was due to the date the payment is made. **Change from 1992 separate returns to 1993 joint return.** If you file a joint return with your spouse for 1993, but you filed separate returns for 1992, your 1992 tax is the total of the tax shown on your separate returns. You filed a separate return in 1992 if you filed as single, head of household, or married filing separately.

Change from 1992 joint return to 1993 separate return. If you file a separate return for 1993, but you filed a joint return with your spouse for 1992, your 1992 tax is your share of the tax on the joint return. You filed a separate return in 1993 if you filed as single, head of household, or married filing separately. To figure your share, first figure the tax both you and your spouse would have paid had you filed separate returns for 1992, using the same filing status as in 1993. Then multiply your joint tax liability by the following fraction:

$$\frac{\text{Your separate tax liability}}{\text{Both spouses' separate tax liabilities}}$$

Example. Lisa and Chris filed a joint return for 1992 showing taxable income of $48,000 and a tax of $8,793. Of the $48,000 taxable income, $40,000 was attributable to Lisa and $8,000 was attributable to Chris. In 1993, they file married filing separately. Lisa figures her share of the tax on the 1992 joint return as follows:

Tax on $40,000 based on a separate return	$ 8,880
Tax on $8,000 based on a separate return	1,204
Total	$10,084
Lisa's portion of total ($8,880 ÷ $10,084)	88%
Lisa's share of joint return tax	
($8,793 × 88%)	$ 7,738

Form 2210. In most cases, you do not need to file Form 2210. The IRS will figure the penalty for you and send you a bill. If you want to figure your penalty, complete Part I, Part II, and either Part III or Part IV of Form 2210. *Do not* file Form 2210 unless you are required to file, as explained later under *Reasons for filing*. If you use Form 2210, you cannot file Form 1040EZ.

On Form 1040, enter the amount of your penalty on line 65. If you owe tax on line 64, add the penalty to your tax due and show your total payment on line 64. If you are due a refund, subtract the penalty from the overpayment you show on line 61.

On Form 1040A, enter the amount of your penalty on line 33. If you owe tax on line 32, add the penalty to your tax due and show your total payment on line 32. If you are due a refund, subtract the penalty from the overpayment you show on line 29.

Reasons for filing. You may be able to lower or eliminate your penalty if you file Form 2210. You *must* file Form 2210 with your return if any of the following applies.

1) You request a waiver. (See *Waiver of Penalty,* later.)
2) You use the annualized income installment method.
3) You use your actual withholding for each payment period for estimated tax purposes.
4) You base any of your required installments on the tax shown on

your 1992 return and you filed or are filing a joint return for either 1992 or 1993 but not for both years.

5) You meet all of the conditions listed under *Special rule* earlier under *Underpayment Penalty*.

For help in completing Form 2210, including illustrated examples, see Chapter 4 of Publication 505.

Annualized income installment method. If you did not receive your income evenly throughout the year (for example, your income from a repair shop you operated was much larger in the summer than it was during the rest of the year), you may be able to lower or eliminate your penalty by figuring your underpayment using the *annualized income installment method.* Under this method, your required installment for one or more payment periods may be less than one-fourth of your required annual payment.

To figure your underpayment using this method, complete Schedule B of Form 2210. Also check the box on line 1b in Part I of Form 2210. You must file the form and Schedule B with your return. This method is explained in Chapter 4 of Publication 505.

TAXPLANNER

The annualized income installment method works to your advantage in the following two situations: (1) your rate of income is relatively greater toward the end of the year than at the beginning of the year, and (2) you are able to deduct fewer expenses toward the end of the year than you could at the beginning of the year.

Example

Jim Smith files a joint return for 1993 with two dependency exemptions. The following facts exist:

1. Jim's 1993 tax liability was $17,980.
2. The amount of 1993 tax withheld was $13,000.
3. No estimated tax payments were made.
4. Jim's 1992 tax liability was $15,000.

Jim was required to pay either 90% of his actual 1993 tax (90% of $17,980 = $16,182) or 100% of his 1992 tax ($15,000), whichever was less. Therefore, it appears that Jim had an underpayment of estimated tax of $500 for each quarter ($15,000 × 25% = $3,750 less 25% × $13,000 = $3,250).

Nevertheless, Jim is not subject to the underpayment penalty for the first three estimated tax payments because of the annualized income method. Here is why.

After deducting all of his deductible expenses, Jim Smith received income during 1993 in the following amounts:

	Actual taxable income	Annualized taxable income	Annualized tax
January through March	$10,000	$40,000	$ 6,403
January through May	20,000	48,000	8,643
January through August	40,000	60,000	12,003
January through December	80,000	80,000	17,603

For the period January through March, Jim's tax liability for his annualized taxable income is $6,403. Note that 90% of $6,403 is $5,763. One-quarter of $5,763—$1,441—should have been paid-in through withholding or estimated tax by April 15. Since Jim's withholding

amounted to $13,000 for the year, a quarter of that, or $3,250, is considered paid by April 15. Therefore, according to the annualized income installment method, there is no underpayment penalty for the April 15 payment date.

For the period January through May, Jim's tax liability for his annualized taxable income is $8,643. Note that 90% of this amount is $7,779. Half of $7,779—$3,889—should have been paid through withholding or estimated tax by June 15. Since Jim's withholding amounted to $13,000 for the year, half of that, or $6,500, is considered paid by June 15. Therefore, there is no underpayment penalty for the June 15 payment date.

For the period January through August, Jim's tax liability for his annualized taxable income is $12,003. Note that 90% of this amount is $10,803. Three-quarters of $10,803—$8,102—should have been paid through withholding or estimated tax by September 15. Since three-quarters of Jim's withholding, or $9,750, is considered paid by September 15, there is no underpayment penalty for the September payment date.

Jim does have an underpayment of estimated tax of $2,000 for the fourth quarter, which is calculated by using his actual 1992 tax of $15,000 less the amount withheld by December 31, 1993, of $13,000. The underpayment penalty on $2,000 for the period January 16, 1994, to April 17, 1995, will be considerably less than the penalties based on the $500 quarterly underpayments calculated from the quarterly due dates through April 15, 1994.

Actual withholding method. Instead of using one-fourth of your withholding to figure your payments, you can choose to establish how much was actually withheld on or before the due dates and use those amounts. You can make this choice separately for the tax withheld from your wages and for all other withholding.

Using your actual withholding may result in a smaller penalty if most of your withholding occurred early in the year.

If you use your actual withholding, you must check the box on line 1c, Part I of the Form 2210. Complete Form 2210 and file it with your return.

Short method for figuring the penalty. You may be able to use the short method in Part III of Form 2210 to figure your penalty for underpayment of estimated tax. If you qualify to use this method, it will result in the same penalty amount as the regular method, but with fewer computations.

You can use the short method *only* if you meet one of the following requirements.

1) You made no estimated tax payments for 1993. It does not matter whether you had income tax withholding.
2) You paid estimated tax on all four due dates in equal installments. You must have paid the same amount on each of the following dates:
   April 15, 1993,
   June 15, 1993,
   September 15, 1993, and
   January 18, 1994.

If you do not meet either requirement, figure your penalty using the regular method in Part IV, Form 2210.

Note. If you use the short method in Part III, you cannot use the annualized income installment method or the actual withholding method.

If, late in the year, it appears that you will have underpaid the year's taxes because previous estimated tax payments proved insufficient to meet your actual tax liability, you might correct the situation by greater withholding for the rest of the year. You may consider amounts withheld from your salary as being spread evenly throughout the year.

Example

In November, Jim Smith revises his earlier estimate. He now believes that his tax liability for the year will reach $20,000. With his current withholding allowances, however, only $17,000 will be withheld from his salary for the year. He will be subject to a penalty, since less than 90% of his tax liability for the current year will be paid. The penalty will apply even if he makes a $1,000 fourth-quarter estimated tax payment, since he failed to make any other quarterly estimated tax payments.

If Jim Smith changes his withholding allowances by filing a revised Form W–4 with his employer that increases his withholding by $1,000 during the period from November to December, he will not have to pay a penalty, since total withholding for the year is considered to have been paid evenly throughout the year.

Exceptions

Generally, you do not have to pay an underpayment penalty if any of the following conditions apply:

- Your total tax due is less than $500,
- You had no tax liability last year, or
- Your underpayment was created or increased by the provisions of the Revenue Reconciliation Act of 1993.

Less Than $500 Due
You do not owe a penalty if the total tax shown on your return minus the amount you paid through withholding (including excess social security, Medicare, and railroad retirement tax withholding) is less than $500.

Total tax for 1993. For 1993, your total tax on Form 1040 is the amount on line 53 reduced by the total of the following amounts:

1) Any recapture of a federal mortgage subsidy from Form 8828 included on line 49,
2) Any social security or Medicare tax on tips not reported to your employer on line 50,
3) Any tax on an IRA or a qualified retirement plan from Form 5329 (other than Part II) included on line 51,
4) Any uncollected social security, Medicare, or railroad retirement tax included on line 53,
5) Any earned income credit on line 56, and
6) Any credit for federal tax on fuels from Form 4136 included on line 59.

Note. If you were able to defer payment of part of your 1993 tax due to the increase in the tax rates, see Publication 505.

Your total tax on Form 1040A for 1993 is the amount on line 27 minus the amount on line 28c. Your total tax on Form 1040EZ for 1993 is the amount on line 8.

No Tax Liability Last Year
You do not owe a penalty if you had no tax liability last year and you were a U.S. citizen or resident for the whole year. For this rule to apply, your tax year must have included all 12 months of the year.

You had no tax liability for 1992 if your total tax was zero or you were not required to file an income tax return.

Example. Ray, who is single and age 50, was unemployed for most of 1992. He earned $1,700 in wages before he was laid off, and he received $2,500 in unemployment compensation afterwards. He had no other income. Even though he had gross income of $4,200, he did not have to pay income tax because his gross income was less than the filing requirement for a single person under age 65 ($5,900 for 1992). He filed a return only to have his withheld income tax refunded to him. In 1993, Ray began regular work as an independent contractor. Ray made no estimated tax payments in 1993. Even though he did owe tax at the end of the year, Ray does not owe the underpayment penalty for 1993 because he had no tax liability for 1992.

Total tax for 1992. For 1992, your total tax on Form 1040 is the amount on line 53 reduced by the total of the following amounts:

1) Any recapture of a federal mortgage subsidy from Form 8828 included on line 49,
2) Any social security or Medicare tax on tips not reported to your employer on line 50,
3) Any tax on an IRA or a qualified retirement plan from Form 5329 (other than Part II) included on line 51,
4) Any uncollected social security, Medicare, or railroad retirement tax included on line 53,
5) Any earned income credit on line 56, and
6) Any credit for federal tax on fuels from Form 4136 included on line 59.

Your total tax on Form 1040A for 1992 is the amount on line 27 minus the amount on line 28c. Your total tax on Form 1040EZ for 1992 is the amount on line 7.

Waiver of Penalty

The IRS can waive the penalty for underpayment if:

1) You did not make a payment because of a casualty, disaster, or other unusual circumstance, and it would be inequitable to impose the penalty,
2) You retired (after reaching age 62) or became disabled during the tax year a payment was due or during the preceding tax year, and both the following requirements are met:
   a) You had reasonable cause for not making the payment, and
   b) Your underpayment was not due to willful neglect, or
3) The underpayment was caused by provisions of the Revenue Reconciliation Act of 1993 (for periods before April 16, 1994).

To claim any of these waivers, follow the procedures explained in the instructions for Form 2210.

II | Income

The chapters in this part discuss many kinds of income. They explain what income is and is not taxed. The following chart lists some of the topics covered in this part. It is divided into (1) items you generally must include in income and (2) items you generally do not include in income. See Chapters 14–17 for information on gains and losses that are reported on Schedule D (Form 1040). Nonbusiness casualty and theft losses are discussed in Chapter 26, *Nonbusiness Casualty and Theft Losses.*

Chapters 18 and 19 discuss two deductions that are used to figure adjusted gross income—the deduction for alimony you pay and the deduction for payments to an individual retirement arrangement (IRA). Other deductions used to figure adjusted gross income are the deductions for self-employment tax (see Chapter 23, *Taxes You May Deduct*), for self-employed health insurance (see Chapter 22, *Medical and Dental Expenses*), for payments to a Keogh retirement plan or self-employed SEP (see Publication 560, *Retirement Plans for the Self-Employed*), and for a penalty on early withdrawal of savings (see Chapter 8, *Interest Income*).

You can also write in certain deductions in figuring adjusted gross income on Form 1040. These write-in deductions are limited to the following:

- Amortization of the costs of forestation or reforestation (see Publication 535, *Business Expenses*), and
- Expenses of certain performing artists (see Chapter 28, *Car Expenses and Other Employee Business Expenses*),
- Certain required repayments of supplemental unemployment benefits (see Chapter 6, *Wages, Salaries, and Other Earnings*),
- Foreign housing deduction (see Chapter 37, *U.S. Citizens Working Abroad,* and Publication 54, *Tax Guide for U.S. Citizens and Resident Aliens Abroad*),
- Jury duty pay given to your employer (see Chapter 13, *Other Income*).

INCOME

INCOME GENERALLY INSLUDES:

Alimony (Chapter 13, *Other Income*)

Bartering income (Chapter 13, *Other Income*)

Cancelled debt income (Chapter 13, *Other Income*)

Dividends (Chapter 9, *Dividends and Other Corporate Distributions*)

Gain on the sale of personal items, such as a car (Chapter 13, *Other Income*)

Gambling winnings (Chapter 13, *Other Income*)

Income from an activity not for profit (Chapter 13, *Other Income*)

Interest (Chapter 8, *Interest Income*)

Part of social security benefits and equivalent railroad retirement benefits (Chapter 12, *Social Security and Equivalent Railroad Retirement Benefits*)

Pensions and annuities (Chapter 11, *Retirement Plans, Pensions, and Annuities*)

Recoveries of amounts previously deducted (Chapter 13, *Other Income*)

Rental income (Chapter 10, *Rental Income and Expenses*)

Royalties (Chapter 13, *Other Income*)

Tips (Chapter 7, *Income from Tips*)

Wages, salaries, and other earnings (Chapter 6, *Wages, Salaries, and Other Earnings*)

Your share of estate and trust income (Chapter 13, *Other Income*)

Your share of partnership or S Corporation income (Chapter 13, *Other Income*)

INCOME GENERALLY DOES NOT INCLUDE:

Accident and health insurance proceeds (Chapter 13, *Other Income*)

Gifts and inheritances (Chapter 13, *Other Income*)

Housing allowance for members of the clergy (Chapter 6, *Wages, Salaries, and Other Earnings*)

Interest on state and local government obligations (Chapter 8, *Interest Income*)

Life insurance proceeds (Chapter 13, *Other Income*)

Military allowances (Chapter 6, *Wages, Salaries, and Other Earnings*)

Part of scholarship and fellowship grants (Chapter 13, *Other Income*)

Part of social security benefits and equivalent railroad retirement benefits (Chapter 12, *Social Security and Equivalent Railroad Retirement Benefits*)

Veterans' benefits (Chapter 6, *Wages, Salaries, and Other Earnings*)

Welfare and other public assistance benefits (Chapter 13, *Other Income*)

Workers' compensation and similar payments for sickness and injury (Chapter 13, *Other Income*)

6 | Wages, Salaries, and Other Earnings

Introduction

*Ask most people how much they get paid, and, if they are willing to admit anything, they'll tell you what their salary is. Usually, there's more to income than that. The way the IRS sees it, "**gross income** means all income from whatever source derived." That means that not only is your salary subject to tax but so also are many of the fringe benefits that you might receive—everything from basic medical insurance and employer-provided discounts to a company car. This chapter spells out in greater detail items of compensation that are taxable.*

*Some fringe benefits you receive from your employer are tax-free. For example, the cost of the first $50,000 of coverage in a group term life insurance plan will be tax-free if all **employees** in the plan are treated in the same way. And, if your employer, in a moment of detached and disinterested generosity, presents you with a Rolls Royce as a gift, there's a chance that you will not have to pay taxes on it. This chapter prepares you—in a tax sense—for that golden moment.*

Important Changes for 1993

Employer-provided educational assistance. The exclusion from gross income and wages of qualified employer-provided educational assistance is extended retroactively from June 30, 1992, through December 31, 1994. For more information, see Chapter 5 of Publication 535, *Business Expenses.*

Employer-provided transportation. Beginning in 1993, the value of employer-provided transportation, such as a vanpool, transit pass, or qualified parking, can be excluded from an employee's gross income up to certain limits. For more information on fringe benefits, see *Fringe Benefits,* later.

Important Reminder

Interest. Interest received on dividends left on deposit with the Department of Veterans Affairs is nontaxable income. See *Veterans,* later.

This chapter discusses wages, salaries, fringe benefits, and other compensation received for services as an employee. The topics include:

- Bonuses and awards
- Unemployment compensation
- Disability income
- Special rules for certain employees
- Military

The chapter also explains what income is included in the employee's gross income and what is not included.

Explanation
One of the most important decisions you have to make in determining your correct taxable income is what payments to include. A taxable payment is not limited to cash. It may be property, stock, or other **assets.** Also, you must include in your gross income the fair market value of payments in kind.

Example 1
Your employer provides you with a car that is used for both personal and business purposes. The value of the personal use of the car is included in earnings taxable to you.

Example 2
You assist a group of investors in purchasing a piece of **real estate.** In consideration of your services, the investors award you an unconditional percentage of ownership in the acquired asset. You have invested none of your personal funds. The fair market value of your ownership interest is considered as wages taxable to you in the year the transfer is completed.

Example 3
A farmer receives 50 bushels of wheat as a payment in kind. Unless specifically excluded under a government

program, the farmer has income to the extent of the fair market value of the wheat.

Useful Items

You may want to see:

Publication

☐ **503**   Child and Dependent Care Expenses
☐ **505**   Tax Withholding and Estimated Tax
☐ **525**   Taxable and Nontaxable Income
☐ **917**   Business Use of a Car

Employee Compensation

This section explains many types of employee compensation. The subjects are arranged in alphabetical order followed by *Fringe Benefits, Disability Income,* and *Pension and Annuity Contributions,* which are explained in greater detail.

Explanation

All compensation for personal services, no matter what the form of payment, must be included in gross income. Such compensation is subject to taxes in the year received, unless the taxpayer reports income on the accrual basis.

Advance commissions and other earnings. If you receive advance commissions or other amounts for services to be performed in the future, and you are a cash method taxpayer, you must include these amounts in your income in the year you receive them.

If you repay unearned commissions or other amounts in the same year in which you received them, reduce the amount to include in your income by the repayment. However, if you repay the unearned commissions or other amounts in a later tax year, you can deduct the repayment as an itemized deduction on your Schedule A (Form 1040), or you may be able to take a credit for that year. See *Repayments* in Chapter 13, *Other Income.*

Explanation

In some cases, an advance payment of a commission or salary may be considered a loan, thus permitting you to delay paying tax on that amount. If the loan is repaid, you will not have to recognize any taxable income. If the loan is forgiven, you will recognize the amount of the loan as compensation in the year in which it was forgiven. Commissions and salaries are considered to be income when they are paid to you or when they are applied as a reduction to your loan account.

The key question is: When may a payment be characterized as a loan? Generally, for a transaction to be considered a loan, a debtor-creditor relationship must exist at the outset. In other words, the lending party

expects and will eventually receive monetary repayment. Payment in return for a future obligation to render services is *not* a loan. Thus, an advance on your wages is not a loan. Whether a payment is or is not a loan is usually a question of fact, requiring a review of each case's unique circumstances.

Example

If you receive an advance of your January 1994 salary on December 31, 1993, you will have taxable income in 1993.

TaxSaver

Generally, you should take advantage of your employer's 401(k) plan. Your contribution to the plan will not be included in your taxable wages. See Chapter 11, *Retirement Plans, Pensions, and Annuities,* for more information about these plans.

TaxPlanner

You may wish to consider a loan from your employer's qualified pension or annuity plan rather than an advance on your next year's salary. Loans are not considered taxable income to the borrower under most circumstances. See Chapter 11, *Retirement Plans, Pensions, and Annuities,* for rules regarding loans from an employer's qualified pension or annuity plan.

Back pay awards. Amounts you are awarded in a settlement or judgment for back pay, including unpaid life insurance premiums and unpaid health insurance premiums, are included in your gross income. They should be reported to you by your employer on Form W-2, *Wage and Tax Statement.*

Explanation

If you received an amount in settlement or judgment for back wages and liquidated damages (e.g., under The Age Discrimination in Employment Act or Equal Pay Act), see *Court awards and damages* in Chapter 13, *Other Income.* Either all or a portion of the award may be excludable from your taxable income.

Bonuses and awards. Amounts paid to you for outstanding work, such as bonuses or awards, are income shown on your Form W-2. These include prizes such as vacation trips for meeting sales goals. If a prize or award is in goods or services, you must include the fair market value of the goods or services in your income. However, if your employer merely promises to pay you a bonus or award at some future time, it is not taxable until you receive it or it is made available to you. If you receive an award for length of service or safety achievement, see *Employee achievement awards* in Chapter 13, *Other Income.*

Child-care providers. If you provide child care, either in the child's home or in your home or other place of business, the pay you receive must be included in your income. If you provide the care in the child's home, you may be an employee. If you provide the care in your home or other place of business, you may or may not be an employee. You are an employee if you are subject to the will and control of your employer as to what you are to do and how you are to do it.

Babysitting. The rules for child-care providers also apply to anyone who periodically babysits for relatives or neighborhood children.

If you are an employee, you should receive a Form W–2 if your pay is subject to social security and Medicare taxes or would be subject to the withholding of income tax if one exemption were claimed. Include your pay on line 7 of Form 1040 or Form 1040A, or on line 2 of Form 1040EZ, even if you do not receive a Form W–2.

If you are not an employee, you are probably self-employed and must include the payments you receive on Schedule C (Form 1040), *Profit or Loss From Business,* or Schedule C-EZ (Form 1040), *Net Profit From Business,* if you qualify.

Government cost-of-living allowances. These allowances are generally not included in the income of federal civilian employees, including federal court employees stationed in Alaska, Hawaii, or outside the 48 contiguous states or the District of Columbia.

Allowances and differentials that increase your basic pay as an incentive for taking a less desirable post of duty are part of your compensation and must be included in your income. For example, your compensation includes Foreign Post, Foreign Service, and Overseas Tropical salary differentials. For more information, get Publication 516, *Tax Information for U.S. Government Civilian Employees Stationed Abroad.*

Holiday gifts. If your employer gives you a turkey, ham, or other item of nominal value at Christmas or other holidays, the value of the gift is not income. However, if your employer gives you cash, a gift certificate, or similar item that you can easily exchange for cash, the value of the gift is extra salary or wages regardless of the amount involved.

Explanation
Government cost-of-living allowances paid to federal civilian employees are tax-exempt only for those employees whose compensation is set by statute.

Interview expenses. If an employer asks you to appear for an interview and pays you an allowance, or reimburses you for your transportation and other travel expenses, you include in your income on line 22, Form 1040, only the amount you receive that is more than your actual expenses.

Moving expense allowances or reimbursements. Your employer must include these amounts in your salary or wages for the tax year in which paid. See *How to Report* in Chapter 27, *Moving Expenses.*

Property purchased from employer. If your employer allows you to buy property below its fair market value as compensation for your services, you must include in your income as wages the difference between the property's fair market value and the amount you paid for it.

Example
Your employer offers to sell you a parcel of land worth $5,000 for a bargain price of $3,500. You would have to include the $1,500 that the company, in effect, gave you as income for the year. In turn, your cost **basis** for the property would be $5,000, not the $3,500 you actually paid for it.

This example shows the importance of putting a reasonable value on the property you receive from your employer. The lower the value is, the less income you report.

Property received for services. If you receive property for your services, you generally must include its value in your gross income as wages. Property for services includes shares of corporate stock you receive from your employer. You must include the fair market value of this property in the year you receive it. However, you may not have to include the value of the property in your income in the year received, if the property is both nontransferable and subject to a substantial risk of forfeiture. For details, see *Restricted Property Received for Services* in Publication 525.

Explanation
A substantial risk of forfeiture occurs when your ownership of property is conditional on the performance of substantial services in the future. When you complete these services or when the property may be legally transferred by you, whichever is earlier, you must recognize as income the difference between the fair market value of the property on that date and the amount, if any, you paid for it.

TaxSaver
If you expect the value of the property to appreciate, you may choose to recognize the income generated by the property before any restrictions on your ownership are lifted. Then, if the property increases in value from the time you have recognized it as income to the time the risk of forfeiture is removed, it will not be taxed at that time. Instead, the tax on that appreciation will be deferred until the property is sold. You may make this choice even if you pay an amount for the property at least equal to its fair market value and therefore recognize zero taxable income currently. You must decide no later than 30 days after you receive the property if you are going to recognize the income while the property is still subject to restrictions.

If you recognize the income and then are forced to forfeit the property, you may deduct as a loss the amount you originally paid for the property. If you believe that the chances you have of forfeiting the property are high, then you should avoid recognizing the income up front.

Example 1
On December 10, 1993, your employer sold you a share of stock for $10 that had a fair market value of $110. The stock is subject to a substantial risk of forfeiture until April 1, 1995. Because the stock might have to be forfeited, you do not have to include the difference between your purchase price and the fair market value of the stock in your 1993 taxable income.

Assume you did not recognize the income immediately. On April 1, 1995, the fair market value of your share of stock is $210. You must include $200 ($210 − $10) in your taxable income in 1995. Assuming you are in the 31% tax bracket, your tax is $62.

However, if you chose to recognize the income on the stock immediately, you would include $100 ($110 −

$10) in your taxable income for 1993 and would incur tax of $31 if you were in the 31% tax bracket. Having made that choice, you owe no more tax until you sell the stock, at which time you will owe tax on the excess of the selling price over your $110 tax basis for the stock.

Example 2
Assume the same facts as in Example 1, except that, after you recognized the income from the property in your 1993 income, you had to forfeit your claim to the property. You may deduct only the $10 you paid for the stock as a **capital loss.** Since you will have paid $31 of tax on your "gain," your net after-tax loss will be $38. You do *not* get to claim a loss on the *income* you previously reported.

Dividends you receive on restricted stock are extra compensation to you. Restricted stock is stock you received from your employer and did not include in your income because it was nontransferable and subject to forfeiture. Your employer should include these payments on your Form W–2.

Dividends you receive on stock you chose to include in your income in the year transferred are treated the same as any other dividends. Report them on line 9, Form 1040. For a discussion of dividends, see Chapter 9, *Dividends and Other Earnings.*

Get Publication 525 for information on how to treat dividends reported on both your Form W–2 and Form 1099–DIV.

Severance pay. Amounts you receive as severance pay are taxable. A lump-sum payment for cancellation of your employment contract is income in the tax year you receive it and must be reported with your other salaries and wages.

Accrued leave payment. If you are a federal employee and receive a lump-sum payment for accrued annual leave when you retire or resign, this amount will be included on your Form W–2.

If you resign from one agency and are reemployed by another agency, you may have to repay part of your lump-sum annual leave payment to the second agency. You can reduce gross wages by the amount you repaid in the same tax year in which you received it. You should attach to your tax return a copy of the receipt or statement furnished by the agency to which repayment is made to explain the difference between the wages on the return and the wages on your Forms W–2.

Employer provided outplacement services. If you receive employer-provided outplacement services, such as training in resumé writing and interview techniques, in lieu of higher severance pay, you must include the amount of the unreduced severance pay in income.

Sick pay. Amounts you receive from your employer while you are sick or injured are part of your salary or wages. Report the amount you receive on line 7, Form 1040; line 7, Form 1040A; or line 2, Form 1040EZ. You must include in your income payments made by any of the following:

1) Your employer.
2) A welfare fund.
3) A state sickness or disability fund.
4) An association of employers or employees.
5) An insurance company, if your employer paid for the plan.

However, if you paid the premiums on an accident or health insurance policy, the benefits you receive under the policy are not taxable.

Railroad sick pay. If you receive sick pay under the Railroad Unemployment Insurance Act, these payments are taxable and you must include them in your income. However, you do not include them in your income to the extent they are for an on-the-job injury.

If you received income because of a disability, see *Disability Income,* later.

Social security and Medicare taxes paid by employer. If you and your employer have an agreement that your employer pays your social security and Medicare taxes without deducting them from your gross wages, you must report the amount of tax paid for you as taxable wages on your tax return. You must also treat the payments as wages for figuring your social security and Medicare taxes and your social security and Medicare benefits. However, these payments are not treated as social security and Medicare wages if you are a household worker or a farm worker.

Stock appreciation rights. If your employer grants you a stock appreciation right, do not include it in your income until you exercise the right. When you exercise (use) the right, you are entitled to a cash payment equal to the amount by which the fair market value of the corporation's stock on the date of exercise has increased over the fair market value on the date the right was granted. You include the cash payment in your income in the year you exercise the right.

Explanation
Stock appreciation rights (SARs) are rights awarded to an employee by a corporation that enable the employee to benefit over a certain period of time from the appreciation in value of the employer's stock without the employee actually owning the stock.

Example
You are given 10 SARs when your company's stock is valued at $25 per share. You may exercise your SARs at any time during a 24-month period. In the first 6 months after the SARs are awarded, the company's stock rises to $50 per share. However, you do not exercise your SARs, because you expect the stock to continue to appreciate in value. Even though you have an unrealized gain of $250 [($50 less $25) × 10 SARs], you do not include it in gross income, because the SARs have not been exercised.

Eighteen months after the SARs are issued, the company stock is selling for $85 per share. You exercise your SARs, and the company pays you $600 [($85 less $25) × 10 SARs]. The $600 gain must now be included in your gross income.

Stock options. You usually have taxable income when you receive or exercise a nonstatutory option to buy stock (or other property) as payment for your services. However, if your option is a statutory stock option (an incentive stock option or an option granted under an employee stock purchase plan) special rules generally delay the tax until you sell or exchange your shares of stock. For details, get Publication 525.

Explanation
A stock option gives you the right to buy a company's stock at a specified price within a designated time period. Generally, stock options are awarded to you by your employer as an alternative method of compensation. The option itself is not taxed when it is granted to you. The amount of income and the year when it is included

in your taxable income depend on the type of option granted. There are two basic types of stock options: nonqualified stock options and incentive stock options.

Nonqualified stock options. Generally, nonqualified stock options are those *not accorded* favorable or preferred tax treatment by a specific provision of the Internal Revenue Code.

A nonqualified stock option is not taxable to you at the time the option is granted, unless the *option* is traded through a public stock exchange. Rather, you are taxed when the option is exercised on the difference between the fixed option price and the fair market value of the stock on the date you exercise your option. This amount is taxed at ordinary income rates. The basis of the stock received is generally its fair market value on the date you exercise the option. If the stock appreciates thereafter, that gain will be taxable as a capital gain when you sell it.

An advantage of the nonqualified stock option is that you do not have to invest any personal funds when the option is granted or while the option is outstanding. However, if you decide to exercise the option, you will need funds to pay the option price *and* the income tax that will be levied on your gain.

Incentive stock options. Generally, incentive stock options enable you to take advantage of a specific provision of the Internal Revenue Code.

Incentive stock options are not taxable to you at the time the option is granted, nor do you pay tax when the option is exercised. Furthermore, if you do not dispose of the stock within two years after the option is granted, and you hold the stock for over a year after you exercise the option, any gain will be taxed as a long-term capital gain. However, if you sell the stock within 1 year after the date you exercised the option, the stock loses its preferential treatment and any gain is taxed to you as ordinary income.

The spread between the option price and the fair market value of the stock upon exercise of the incentive stock option may be taxed indirectly if you are subject to alternative minimum tax. For a discussion of the alternative minimum tax, see Chapter 31, *How to Figure Your Tax.*

TaxAlert

Net capital gains, the excess of net long-term capital gain over net short-term capital loss, is taxed at a maximum marginal rate of 28%, while ordinary income can be taxed at the maximum marginal rate, currently 39.6%.

TaxPlanner

You can use stock swaps to finance the exercise of stock options by giving the company stock equal in value to the price of the option.

TaxSaver

Employee stock purchase plans. Many companies have stock purchase plans that offer participating employees the opportunity to buy company stock. Employees usually contribute to the plan by authorizing payroll deductions, which are not excludable from gross income.

As an employee, you do not have to pay any tax when the plan's trustee exercises the option and purchases company stock. The stock is merely credited to your account within the plan.

At some future time, you may request to receive the stock purchased for your account. On distribution, if you immediately sell the stock, any gain will be taxed as ordinary income. The gain will generally be determined by the sale price less the amount you contributed to the plan to buy the stock. Your company should be able to provide you with all relevant information.

However, if after receiving the stock you hold it long enough to meet the long-term capital gain holding period, any gain will be treated as a long-term capital gain. Again, if you have a capital loss carryover, the fact that the sale is characterized as a capital gain could still result in a tax benefit for you.

Unemployment compensation. You must include in your income all unemployment compensation you receive. You should receive a Form 1099–G showing the unemployment compensation paid to you. Generally, you enter unemployment compensation on line 12, Form 1040A, or line 20, Form 1040. You may be liable for estimated tax if you receive unemployment compensation. For more information on estimated tax, see Chapter 5, *Tax Withholding and Estimated Tax.*

Types of unemployment compensation. Unemployment compensation generally includes any amount received under an unemployment compensation law of the United States or of a state. It includes:

1) Benefits paid by a state or the District of Columbia from the Federal Unemployment Trust Fund.
2) Unemployment insurance benefits.
3) Railroad unemployment compensation benefits.
4) Disability payments from a government program paid as a **substitute** for unemployment compensation (amounts received as workers' compensation for injuries or illness are **not** unemployment compensation).
5) Trade readjustment allowances under the Trade Act of 1974.
6) Benefits under the Airline Deregulation Act of 1978.
7) Unemployment assistance under the Disaster Relief Act Amendments of 1974.

Governmental program. If you contribute to a governmental unemployment compensation program, and your contributions are not deductible, amounts you receive under the program are not included as unemployment compensation until you recover your contributions.

Supplemental unemployment benefits. Benefits received from a company-financed fund (to which the employees did not contribute) are not unemployment compensation. They are taxable as wages subject to income tax withholding but not subject to social security, Medicare, or federal unemployment taxes. Report these payments on line 7 of Form 1040 or Form 1040A.

You may have to repay some of your supplemental unemployment benefits to qualify for trade readjustment allowances under the Trade Act of 1974. If you repay supplemental unemployment benefits in the same year you receive them, reduce the total benefits by the amount you repay. However, if you repay the benefits in a later year, you must include the full amount of the benefits received in your income for the year you received them.

Deduct the repayment in the later year as an adjustment to gross income. Include the repayment on line 30, Form 1040, and put "Sub-pay TRA" and the amount on the dotted line next to line 30. If the amount you repay in a later year is more than $3,000, you may be able to take a credit against your tax for the later year instead of deducting the amount repaid. For more information on this, see the discussion on *Repayments* in Chapter 13, *Other Income.*

Private unemployment fund. Unemployment benefit payments from a private fund to which you voluntarily contribute are taxable only if the amounts you receive are more than your total payments into the fund. Report the taxable amount on line 22, Form 1040.

Payments by a union. Benefits paid to you as an unemployed member of a union out of regular union dues are included in your gross income on line 22, Form 1040.

Guaranteed annual wage. Payments you receive from your employer during periods of unemployment, under a union agreement that guarantees you full pay during the year, are taxable as wages.

State employees. Payments can be made by a state to its employees who are not covered by the state's unemployment compensation law. If the payments are similar to benefits under that law, they are fully taxable. Report these payments on line 22, Form 1040.

Fraud. Fraudulently obtained unemployment compensation is fully taxable and you report it on line 22, Form 1040.

Repayment of unemployment compensation benefits. If you repaid in 1993 unemployment compensation benefits you received in 1993, subtract the amount you repaid from the total amount you received and enter the difference on line 20, Form 1040, or on line 12, Form 1040A. Also, enter "Repaid" and the amount you repaid on the dotted line next to line 20 or next to line 12. If, in 1993, you repaid unemployment compensation that you included in gross income in an earlier year, you may deduct the amount repaid on Schedule A (Form 1040), line 20. See *Repayments* in Chapter 13, *Other Income.*

Union benefits and dues. Amounts deducted from your pay for union dues, assessments, contributions, or other payments to a union cannot be excluded from your salary or wages. You must include them in your income as wages.

You may be able to deduct some of these payments as a miscellaneous deduction subject to the 2% limit if they are related to your job and if you itemize your deductions on Schedule A (Form 1040). You may deduct them whether you paid them directly to the union or had them deducted from your pay. See *Union Dues and Expenses* in Chapter 30.

Strike and lockout benefits. Benefits paid to you by a union from union dues as strike or lockout benefits, including both cash and the fair market value of other property, are usually included in your income as wages. You can exclude these benefits from your income only when the facts show that the union intended them as gifts to you.

Explanation

While strike and lockout benefits are generally taxable, the Supreme Court and the IRS have indicated that such payments may be considered tax-free gifts if the following conditions exist:

1. Payments are given to both union and nonunion strikers.
2. The amount and form of the benefit are dependent on individual need.

3. No conditions are attached to the receipt of the payments.
4. The payments are dependent on the lack of unemployment compensation or other types of government assistance.

Withholding. Amounts withheld from your pay for income tax, social security tax, Medicare tax, or savings bonds are considered received by you. They will be included in your wages on Form W–2. The same generally is true of amounts withheld for taxable fringe benefits, pensions, insurance, union dues, and other assessments. For more information on withholding, get Publication 505.

If your employer uses your wages to pay your debts, or if your wages are attached or garnisheed, the full amount is considered received by you. Also included in your wages are fines or penalties withheld from your pay.

Explanation

If you perform services and decide that payment for them should be made to another person, the monies remitted to the third party are taxable to you. The IRS and the courts have long held that "fruits" of a taxpayer's labor are attributable to the "tree" that grew them.

Furthermore, you may not render services and then ask your employer to hold the funds in an attempt to control artificially when the wages will be included in your taxable income.

Example

You are due compensation for work you performed. You advise the payer to hold the money because you will not require the funds immediately. The payer credits the payment due you on the company books. You do not request the money until after the close of the tax year in which the services were rendered.

The IRS may hold that you were in **constructive receipt** of the funds before year's end. The compensation may have to be included in your income for the year in which the payment could have been received, even though you were not actually paid until later.

TAXPLANNER

You will have a problem with the IRS if you ask your employer *after* you have performed the work to withhold funds in an attempt to control artificially when the wages will be included in your taxable income. If you make arrangements to defer receipt of income *prior* to commencing work, you will not have a problem.

However, if your employer forces you to take your bonus in a later year, then it is not taxable to you until the year in which you receive it.

Example

If at the beginning of the year you arrange to have your employer pay you your year-end bonus over a 5-year period, the IRS will not claim that you were in constructive receipt of the entire bonus at year's end. You may even arrange to have your employer add interest to your deferred bonus. You must, however, make these arrangements prior to performance of the work for which the bonus will be paid.

Fringe Benefits

The value of fringe benefits you receive from your employer is taxable and must be included in your income as compensation, unless the benefits are specifically excluded by law or you pay fair market value for them.

Some of the benefits you must report in your income include your personal use of an employer-provided car or aircraft or a membership in a country club.

Generally, your employer determines the amount of your fringe benefits and includes this amount on your Form W–2. For more information on how an employer determines taxable fringe benefits, see Publication 535, *Business Expenses.*

Transportation

Beginning in 1993, the value of employer-provided transportation, such as a vanpool, transit pass, or qualified parking, can be excluded from an employee's gross income up to certain limits. A qualified transportation fringe is:

1) Transportation in a commuter highway vehicle between the employee's home and work place,
2) A transit pass, or
3) Qualified parking.

Cash reimbursement by the employer for these expenses under a bona fide reimbursement arrangement is also excludable. However, cash reimbursement for a transit pass is allowed only if a voucher or similar item which may be exchanged only for a transit pass is not readily available for direct distribution to the employee.

Exclusion limit. The exclusion for commuter highway vehicle transportation and transit pass fringe benefits cannot exceed a total of $60 a month, regardless of the total value of both benefits.

The exclusion for the qualified parking fringe benefit cannot exceed $155 a month, regardless of its value.

If the benefits have a value in excess of these limits, the excess must be included in the employee's income.

Commuter highway vehicle. This is a highway vehicle that seats at least six adults (not including the driver). At least 80% of the vehicle's mileage must reasonably be expected to be for transporting employees between their homes and work place and at least half of the vehicle's seating capacity must be (not including the driver's) occupied by employees.

Transit pass. This is any pass, token, farecard, voucher, or similar item entitling a person to ride mass transit (whether public or private) free or at a reduced rate or in a commuter highway vehicle operated by a person in the business of transporting persons for compensation.

Qualified parking. This is parking provided to an employee on or near the employer's place of business. It also includes parking provided on or near a location from which the employee commutes to work in a commuter highway vehicle or carpool. It does not include parking on or near the employee's residence.

More information. For more information on fringe benefits, see Chapter 4 of Publication 535, *Business Expenses.*

Group Life Insurance Premiums

Bought for employees. Generally, the cost of up to $50,000 of group-term life insurance coverage that is provided to you by your employer is not included in your income. However, you must in-clude in your income the cost of insurance that is more than the cost of $50,000 of insurance, reduced by the amount you pay towards the purchase of the insurance.

Form W–2. The amount included in your income is reported as part of your wages on Form W–2 and is shown separately on the form. If you paid any part of the cost of the insurance and the payment qualifies to reduce the amount otherwise included in your income, the reduced amount would be shown on Form W–2. See *Your payment,* later.

Retired employees. If you are retired, you must generally include in income the cost of payments for insurance coverage that are for more than $50,000. However, certain retired employees do not have to include these amounts in income. For more information, get Publication 525.

Group-term life insurance. This insurance is term life insurance protection (insurance for a fixed period of time) that:

1) Provides a general death benefit that is excluded from income,
2) Is provided to a group of employees,
3) Is provided under a policy carried by the employer, and
4) Provides an amount of insurance for each employee based on a formula that prevents individual selection.

Your payment. If you pay any part of the cost of the insurance, your entire payment reduces, dollar for dollar, the amount your employer would otherwise include in your income. However, you cannot reduce the amount to include in your income by:

1) Payments for coverage in a different tax year, or
2) Payments not taxed to you because of the exceptions discussed below.

Example

Your employer, ABC Company, pays the premiums on your $150,000 group term life insurance policy. You are 40 years old. Every $1,000 worth of coverage costs $2.04. Since under law only $50,000 worth of coverage may be excluded from your income, the cost of the additional $100,000 of life insurance, or $204, has to be included in your income, even though your employer covers the cost.

If you pay any amount of the $204 directly, you may reduce, dollar for dollar, the amount of the premium that would otherwise be included in your income. Thus, if you paid $50, only $154 ($204 − $50) of the premium would be included in your income.

Permanent benefits. If your group-term life insurance policy includes permanent benefits, such as a paid-up or cash surrender value, you must include in your income, as wages, the cost of the permanent benefits, reduced by the amount you pay for them. Your employer should be able to tell you the amount to include in your income.

Accidental or other death benefits. If you receive accidental or other death benefits from a policy that does not provide general death benefits (travel insurance, for example), these benefits are not included as group-term life insurance coverage.

Exceptions. You are not taxed on the cost of group-term life insurance if any of the following apply:

1) You are disabled and have ended your employment;
2) Your employer is the beneficiary of the policy for the entire period the insurance is in force during the tax year; or
3) The only beneficiary is a qualified charitable organization (defined in Chapter 25) for the entire period the insurance is in force

during the tax year. You are not entitled to a deduction for a charitable contribution by naming a charitable organization as the beneficiary of your policy.

Entire cost taxed. You are taxed on the entire cost of group-term life insurance protection provided by your employer through a qualified employees' trust, such as a pension trust or a qualified annuity plan.

You are also taxed on the entire cost of the group-term life insurance coverage provided by your employer if you are a key employee and your employer's plan discriminates in favor of key employees.

Life insurance agents. Full-time life insurance agents who are considered employees for social security and Medicare tax withholding purposes are treated as employees in applying the provisions relating to group-term life insurance under a policy carried by their employer.

One employer. If you have only one employer and you were insured at any time during the tax year for more than $50,000 under a group-term life insurance policy, your income from this source is shown as other compensation on the Form W-2 you receive.

Two or more employers. If two or more employers provide you group-term life insurance coverage totaling more than $50,000, you must figure how much to include in your income for the cost of all coverage that is more than $50,000. You must include the cost of life insurance provided to you during the tax year, regardless of when your employers paid the premiums.

You figure the cost for each month of coverage by multiplying the number of thousands of dollars of insurance coverage, less $50,000 of insurance (both figured to the nearest tenth), by the cost from the following table. You must prorate the cost if less than a full month of coverage is involved.

COST PER $1,000 OF PROTECTION
FOR ONE MONTH

Age	Cost
Under 30	8 cents
30 through 34	9 cents
35 through 39	11 cents
40 through 44	17 cents
45 through 49	29 cents
50 through 54	48 cents
55 through 59	75 cents
60 through 64	$1.17
65 through 69	$2.10
70 and older	$3.76

Example. You are 51 years old and work for Employers A and B. Both employers provide group-term life insurance coverage for you. Your coverage with Employer A is 35,000, and your coverage with Employer B is $45,000. You pay premiums of $50 a year under the Employer B group plan. You figure the amount to include in your income as follows:

Employer A coverage (in thousands)	$	35
Employer B coverage (in thousands)		45
Total coverage (in thousands)	$	80
Minus: Exclusion (in thousands)		50
Excess amount (in thousands)	$	30

Multiply by cost per $1,000 per month, age 51 (from table)		.48
Cost of excess insurance for 1 month		$ 14.40
Multiply by number of full months coverage at this cost		12
Cost of excess insurance for tax year		$172.80
Minus: Premiums you paid		50.00
Cost to include in your income as wages		$122.80

For information on employer payments for group-term life insurance, get Publication 535.

How To Report Fringe Benefits

The amount of your taxable fringe benefits is shown on your Form W-2.

Employer-provided car. If your employer provides a car (or other highway motor vehicle) to you, your personal use of the car is usually a taxable noncash fringe benefit.

Your employer must determine the actual value of this fringe benefit to include in your income. Your employer determines this value by either of the following methods:

1) The actual value of your personal use of the car, or
2) The actual value of the car as if you used it entirely for personal purposes (100% income inclusion).

If your employer includes 100% of the value in your income, you may deduct the value of your business use of the car as long as you itemize your deductions. You figure the value of this business use on Form 2106, *Employee Business Expenses.*

Certain employer-provided transportation can be excluded from gross income. See the discussion on *Transportation,* earlier.

Accounting period. You must use the same accounting period your employer uses to report your taxable fringe benefits and to claim any related deductions. Your employer has the option to report taxable fringe benefits by using either of the following rules:

1) The general rule: value the benefit for a full calendar year (January 1–December 31), or
2) The special accounting period rule: treat the value of benefits provided during the last two months of the calendar year (or any shorter period) as paid during the following calendar year.
   a) Under this rule, each year your employer includes the value of benefits provided the last 2 months of the prior year and the first 10 months of the current year.
   b) If your employer uses this rule to determine the amount to include in your income, you must use the same accounting period to claim an employee business deduction (for use of a car, for example).

Your employer does not have to use the same accounting period for each fringe benefit, but is required to use the same period for all employees who receive a particular benefit.

Form W-2. Your employer reports your taxable fringe benefits in box 1 (Wages, tips, other compensation) and, if applicable, box 3 (Social security wages) and box 5 (Medicare wages) of Form W-2. The total value of your fringe benefits should also be shown in box 12. The value of your fringe benefits may be added to your other compensation on one Form W-2, or you may receive a separate Form W-2 showing just the value of your fringe benefits in box 1 with a notation in box 12.

Disability Income

Generally, if you retire on disability you must report your pension or annuity as income. There is a tax credit for people who are permanently and totally disabled. For information on this credit and the definition of permanent and total disability, see Chapter 34, *Credit for the Elderly or the Disabled.*

Disability pensions. Generally, you must report as income any amount you receive for your disability through an accident or health insurance plan paid for by your employer. If both you and your employer pay for the plan, only the amount you receive for your disability that is due to your employer's payments is reported as income. However, certain payments may not be taxable. Your employer should be able to give you specific details about your pension plan and tell you the amount you paid for your disability pension. In addition to disability pensions and annuities, you may be receiving other payments for sickness and injury. See *Other Sickness and Injury Benefits* in Chapter 13, *Other Income.*

Cost paid by you. If you pay the entire cost of a health or accident insurance plan, do not include any amounts you receive for your disability as income on your tax return. If your plan reimbursed you for medical expenses you deducted in an earlier year, you may have to include some, or all, of the reimbursement in your income. See *Reimbursement in a later year* in Chapter 22, *Medical and Dental Expenses.*

Accrued leave payment. If you retire on disability, any lump-sum payment you receive for accrued annual leave is a salary payment. The payment is not a disability payment. You must report it as wages in the tax year you receive it.

Retirement and profit-sharing plans. Any payments you receive from a retirement or profit-sharing plan that does not provide for disability retirement are not payments from an accident or health plan. Therefore, do not report them as disability income. The payments are taxable and should be reported as a pension or annuity. See *Disability Income* in Chapter 11, *Retirement Plans, Pensions, and Annuities.*

Military disability pensions. Generally, you must report these disability pensions as income. But certain military and government disability pensions are not taxable. For more information, see *Military and Certain Government Disability Pensions* in Chapter 11, *Retirement Plans, Pensions, and Annuities.*

How to report. If you retired on disability, payments you receive are taxed as wages until you reach minimum retirement age. Minimum retirement age generally is the age at which you can first receive a pension or annuity were you not disabled. You must report your taxable disability payments on line 7, Form 1040, or on line 7, Form 1040A, until you reach minimum retirement age.

Beginning on the day after you reach minimum retirement age, payments you receive are taxable as a pension. Report the payments on lines 17a and 17b of Form 1040, or on lines 11a and 11b of Form 1040A. The rules for reporting pensions are explained in *How to Report* in Chapter 11, *Retirement Plans, Pensions, and Annuities.*

Pension and Annuity Contributions

Generally, you cannot exclude from income amounts you pay into a pension plan through payroll deductions.

Contributions to Federal Thrift Savings Fund. Federal employees can choose to make contributions, from their salaries, to the Federal Thrift Savings Fund. Contributions are not included in income. Your salary before contributions are taken out is used for purposes of figuring social security and Medicare taxes and benefits. Payments from the fund are taxable as a distribution from a qualified pension or annuity plan.

Employer's contributions to qualified plan. Generally, your employer's contributions to a qualified pension plan for you are not included in income at the time contributed. However, employer contributions that are made out of funds that would otherwise have been paid to you as salary, except that you entered into a salary reduction agreement with your employer (elective deferral), are excluded from income only up to a limit.

For 1993, you cannot set aside more than a total of $8,994 for all elective deferrals. If you set aside more than $8,994, the excess is included in your gross income that year. Contributions to tax-sheltered annuities are subject to a higher limit. Get Publication 571, *Tax-Sheltered Annuity Programs for Employees of Public Schools and Certain Tax-Exempt Organizations,* for more information.

Explanation

Payments by your employer toward the purchase of a tax-sheltered annuity for you may be excluded from your income if (1) your rights to the annuity may not be forfeited or transferred to another person and (2) you sign an irrevocable agreement with a life of at least 1 year with your employer saying that, in return for the employer's contribution toward your annuity, you will either pass up a raise or take a reduction in salary.

There is a limit to how much your employer may contribute toward your annuity that may be excluded from your income. This maximum amount is determined at the end of the year and is calculated as follows: [20% × (your annual salary) × (number of years you have worked for the qualified employer)] minus the aggregate amount of excludable contributions made on your behalf by your employer for all prior years.

Example

Your annual salary is $20,000. You have been teaching in the same public school system for 10 years. Your employer contributes $4,000 for your annuity contract this year. You have excluded $37,000 from your income for prior annuity contract purchases by your employer. You figure how much of your employer's $4,000 contribution may be excluded from your income this year as follows:

20% × $20,000	$ 4,000
Multiplied by your years of service	× 10
	$40,000
Minus the total contributions made by your employer in past years	($37,000)
Maximum amount that can be excluded from your income this year	$ 3,000

Therefore, of the $4,000 your employer contributes to your annuity this year, $1,000 must be included in your taxable income.

Note: If your employer did not contribute the maximum amount allowed by law in prior years, the law permits catch-up contributions.

There are further limitations on the aggregate amount you can exclude if you have more than one tax-sheltered annuity or other elective deferral arrangement.

The cost of life insurance coverage included in an employer's plan may be income if the proceeds of the policy are payable directly or indirectly to your beneficiary. See *Group Life Insurance Premiums,* earlier, under *Fringe Benefits.*

Amounts actually distributed or made available to you generally are taxable, unless they are eligible for a tax-free rollover and are rolled over (within 60 days after receipt) to another qualified plan or to an individual retirement account or annuity. If you elect an eligible rollover distribution to be paid directly to you (even if you plan to roll over the distribution), the payer must withhold part of the distribution for income tax. You can avoid withholding if you choose a direct transfer to another qualified retirement plan. Your employer may be able to tell you how the amount you received is taxed. See Chapters 11, *Retirement Plans, Pensions, and Annuities* and 18, *Individual Retirement Arrangements (IRAs).*

Employer's contributions to nonqualified plan. If your employer pays into a nonqualified plan for you, you generally must include the contributions in your income as wages for the tax year in which the contributions are made. Report this income on line 7 of Form 1040 or Form 1040A, or on line 2 of Form 1040EZ. However, if your interest is not transferable and is subject to a substantial risk of forfeiture (you have a good chance of losing it), you need not include the amount of the contribution or premium in your income. When your interest becomes transferable or is no longer subject to a substantial risk of forfeiture, you must include the value in your income.

Explanation

Participating employees may defer taxation on an employer's contributions into their individual accounts or for their vested benefits in qualified plans until some future date of distribution. Additionally, the tax on the income the account generates may be deferred until the money is distributed to the employee.

The same deferred taxation is allowed under a nonqualified plan as long as the employee's interest in the plan is not transferable and is subject to substantial risk of forfeiture. However, when either of these restrictions is no longer met, the value of the account will immediately become taxable to the employee. (Whether a plan is qualified or nonqualified depends on whether or not certain statutory requirements are satisfied.)

See Chapter 11, *Retirement Plans, Pensions, and Annuities,* for suggestions about what to do when you receive distributions from qualified plans.

Railroad retirement annuities. If you received railroad retirement tier 1 benefits that are more than the "social security equivalent benefit," or tier 2 or vested dual benefits, these payments are treated as pension or annuity income and are taxable under the rules explained in Chapter 11, *Retirement Plans, Pensions, and Annuities.*

Special Rules for Certain Employees

This section deals with special rules for people in certain types of employment. It includes members of the clergy, people working for foreign employers, military personnel, veterans, ACTION and Peace Corps volunteers, and statutory employees.

Clergy

If you are a member of the clergy, you must include in your income offerings and fees you receive for marriages, baptisms, funerals, masses, etc., in addition to your salary. If the offering is made to the religious institution, it is not taxable to you.

If you are a member of a religious organization and you give your outside earnings to the organization, you still must include the earnings in your income. However, you may be entitled to a charitable contribution deduction for the amount paid to the organization. **Rental value of a home.** Do not include in your income the rental value of a home (or utility expenses) provided to you as part of your pay for your duties as an ordained, licensed, or commissioned minister. However, you must include the rental value of the home, and related allowances, as earnings from self-employment on Schedule SE (Form 1040) if you are subject to the self-employment tax.

Housing allowance. A housing allowance paid to you as part of your salary is not income to the extent you use it, in the year received, to provide a home or to pay utilities for a home with which you are provided. The amount of the housing allowance that you can exclude from your income cannot be more than the reasonable compensation for your services as a minister. The church or organization that employs you must officially designate the payment as a housing allowance before the payment is made. A definite amount must be designated; the amount of the housing allowance cannot be determined at a later date.

If you are employed and paid by a local congregation, a resolution by a national church agency of your denomination does not effectively designate a housing allowance for you. The local congregation must officially designate the part of your salary that is to be a housing allowance. However, a resolution of a national church agency can designate your housing allowance if you are directly employed by the agency. If no part has been officially designated, you must include your total salary in your income.

Expenses of providing a home include rent, house payments, furniture payments, costs for a garage, and utilities. They do not include the cost of food or servants.

Homeowner. If you own your home, or are buying it, you can exclude your housing allowance from your income if you spend it for the down payment on the home, for mortgage payments, or for interest, taxes, utilities, repairs, etc. However, you cannot exclude more than the fair rental value of the home plus the cost of utilities, even if a larger amount is designated as a housing allowance. Fair rental value of a home includes the fair rental value of furnishings in it.

Interest and taxes on your home. You can deduct the qualified mortgage interest and real estate taxes you pay on your home even if you use nontaxable housing allowance funds to make the payments. See Chapters 23, *Taxes You May Deduct* and 24, *Interest Expense.*

Explanation

To qualify for the exclusions from gross income, you must be ordained, commissioned, or licensed as a minister and must be employed by a religious organization to perform ministerial functions. A Jewish rabbi or cantor qualifies as a member of the clergy if he or she has been appropriately ordained according to the faith's customs.

Exception

An ordained minister may not claim the exclusions from gross income when the crux of his or her ministry consists of preachings against communism for a nonreligious, tax-exempt organization. Such a message is not religious, because anticommunism is not an adopted tenet of his or her faith.

Sham churches. The IRS has been cracking down on individuals who declare themselves clergy of newly established churches, arrange to have all their income paid to the church, and then have the church pay their living expenses. The object of such individuals is to take advantage of a church's tax-exempt status and shield income from taxation. Individuals who set up sham churches may be subject to criminal sanctions.

Teachers or administrators. If you are a minister employed as a teacher or administrator by a church school, college, or university, you are, for purposes of the housing exclusion, performing ministerial services. However, if you perform services as the head of a religious department, or as a teacher or administrator on the faculty of a nonchurch college, and if your specific duties involve no religious functions, you cannot exclude from your income a housing allowance or the value of a home that is provided to you.

If you live in qualified campus housing as an employee of an educational institution, do not include the value of that housing in your income if you pay rent equal to or greater than the fair rental value of the housing.

If you serve as a "minister of music" or "minister of education," or serve in an administrative or other function of your religious organization, but are not authorized to perform all of the religious duties of an ordained minister in your church, even though you are commissioned as a "minister of the gospel," you cannot exclude from your income a housing allowance or the value of a home provided to you.

Theological students. You cannot exclude a housing allowance from your income if you are a theological student serving a required internship as an assistant pastor, unless you are ordained, commissioned, or licensed as a minister.

Traveling evangelists. You can exclude amounts received from out-of-town churches for evangelistic services if you are an ordained minister, if those amounts are designated as a housing allowance, and you actually use them to maintain your permanent home.

Retired members of the clergy. The rental value of a home provided rent free by your church for your past services is not income if you are a retired minister. In addition, a housing allowance paid to you is not income to the extent you spend it for utilities, maintenance, repairs, and similar expenses that are directly related to providing a home.

The general convention of a national religious denomination can designate a housing allowance for retired ministers, if the local congregations authorize the general convention to establish and maintain a unified pension system for all retired clergy members of the denomination for their past services to the local churches.

A surviving spouse of a retired minister cannot exclude a housing allowance from income. It must be reported on lines 17a and 17b of Form 1040, or on lines 11a and 11b of Form 1040A.

Pension. A pension or retirement pay for a member of the clergy is usually treated the same as any other pension or annuity. (See Chapter 11, *Retirement Plans, Pensions, and Annuities.*) If you are not expected to perform any further services, payments from the congregation may be gifts. They are not taxable if they are based solely on your financial needs and the financial capacity of the congregation. If these payments are made under a legal agreement, an established plan, or because of past practice, they do not qualify as nontaxable gifts.

Members of religious orders. If you are a member of a religious order who has taken a vow of poverty, the amounts you earn for services you perform which you renounce and turn over to the order may or may not be included in your income.

Services performed for the order. If you are performing the services as an agent of the order in the exercise of duties required by the order, you do not include in your income the amounts you turn over to the order.

If your order directs you to perform services for another agency of the supervising church or an associated institution, you are considered to be performing the services as an agent of the order. Any wages you earn as an agent of an order that you turn over to the order are not included in your gross income.

Example. You are a member of a church order and have taken a vow of poverty. You renounce any claims to your earnings and turn over to the order any salaries or wages you earn. You are a registered nurse, so your order assigns you to work in a hospital that is an associated institution of the church. However, you remain under the general direction and control of the order. You are considered to be an agent of the order and, therefore, any wages you earn at the hospital that you turn over to your order are not included in your gross income.

Services performed outside the order. If you are directed to work outside the order, the work will not constitute the exercise of duties required by the order unless the services you perform meet both of the following requirements:

1) The services are the kind that are ordinarily the duties of members of the order, and
2) The services are part of the duties that are required to be exercised for, or on behalf of, the religious order as its agent.

If the legal relationship of employer and employee exists between you and a third party, the services you perform for the third party will not be considered directed or required of you by the order. Amounts you receive for these services are included in your gross income, even if you have taken a vow of poverty.

Example. Mark Brown is a member of a religious order and has taken a vow of poverty. He renounces all claims to his earnings and turns over his earnings to the order.

Mark is a school teacher. He was instructed by the superiors of the order to get a job with a private tax-exempt school. Mark became an employee of the school, and, at his request, the school made the salary payments directly to the order.

Because Mark is an employee of the school, he is performing services for the school rather than as an agent of the order. Therefore, the wages Mark earns working for the school are included in his gross income.

Foreign Employer

Special rules apply if you work for a foreign employer.
U.S. citizen. If you are a U.S. citizen who works for a foreign government, an international organization, a foreign embassy, or any foreign employer, you must include your salary in your income.

Social security and Medicare taxes. You are exempt from social security and Medicare taxes if you are employed in the United States by an international organization or a foreign government. However, you must pay self-employment tax on your earnings from services performed in the United States, even though you are not self-employed. This rule also applies if you are an employee of a qualifying wholly-owned instrumentality of a foreign government.

Non-U.S. citizen. If you are not a U.S. citizen, or if you are a U.S. citizen but also a citizen of the Philippines, and you work for an international organization in the United States, your salary from that source is exempt from tax. If you work for a foreign government in the United States, your salary from that source is exempt from tax if your work is like the work done by an employee of the United States in that foreign country and if the foreign government gives an equal exemption for the salary of the U.S. employee.

Alien status. If you are an alien and give up your right to this exemption (by filing a waiver under section 247(b) of the Immigration and Nationality Act to keep your immigrant status), you are not entitled to the exemption from the date you give it up, unless you get the exemption from a treaty, consular agreement, or international agreement.

Pensions. This exemption applies only to employees' wages, salaries, and fees. Pensions received by former employees living in this country do not qualify for this exemption.

Employment abroad. For information on income earned abroad, get Publication 54, *Tax Guide for U.S. Citizens and Resident Aliens Abroad.*

Military

Payments you receive as a member of a military service generally are taxable except for certain allowances. Report them as wages. For additional information on military pay, see Publication 3, *Tax Information for Military Personnel (Including Reservists Called to Active Duty).*

Taxable Income
Taxable income includes the following items.
Wages. Military pay taxed as wages includes:

- Active duty pay,
- Reserve training pay,
- Reenlistment bonus,
- Armed services academy pay,
- Amounts received by retired personnel serving as instructors in junior ROTC programs,
- Lump-sum payments upon separation or release from active duty, and
- Student loan repayments from the General Educational Loan Repayment Program.

Military retirement pay. If this retirement pay is based on age or length of service, it is taxable and must be included on lines 17a and 17b of Form 1040, or on lines 11a and 11b of Form 1040A.

Nontaxable Income
Qualified military benefits you receive are not taxable. The following amounts are nontaxable.

- Annual round trip for dependent students
- Burial and death services (interment allowances)
- Combat zone compensation and combat-related benefits (limited amount for commissioned officers)
- Death gratuities
- Defense counseling
- Dental benefits
- Dependent education
- Disability benefits
- Educational assistance
- Emergency assistance
- Evacuation allowances
- Family counseling
- Family separation allowances
- Group-term life insurance
- Housing allowances

- Medical benefits
- Moving and storage
- Overseas cost-of-living allowances
- Premiums for survivor and retirement protection plans
- Professional education
- Quarters allowances
- Subsistence allowances
- Temporary lodging in conjunction with certain orders
- Travel for consecutive overseas tours
- Travel for consecutive overseas tours for dependents
- Travel in lieu of moving dependents during ship overhaul or inactivation
- Travel of dependents to a burial site
- Travel to a designated place in conjunction with reassignment in a dependent-restricted status
- Uniform allowance

Note. Personal use of a vehicle cannot be excluded from income as a qualified military benefit.

Combat zone exclusion. If you are a member of the U.S. Armed Forces who serves in a combat zone, you may exclude certain pay from your income. For more information, get Publication 945, *Tax Information for Those Affected by Operation Desert Storm.*

Veterans

Veterans' benefits under any law, regulation, or administrative practice that was in effect on September 9, 1986, and administered by the Department of Veterans Affairs (VA), are not included in gross income. The following amounts paid to veterans or their families are not taxable:

- Education, training, or subsistence allowances.
- Disability compensation and pension payments for disabilities.
- Grants for homes designed for wheelchair living.
- Grants for motor vehicles for veterans who lost their sight or the use of their limbs.
- Veterans' pensions paid either to the veterans or to their families.
- Veterans' insurance proceeds and dividends paid either to veterans or their beneficiaries, including proceeds of a veteran's endowment policy paid before death.
- Interest on insurance dividends you leave on deposit with the VA.

Rehabilitative program payments. VA payments to hospital patients and resident veterans for their services under the VA's therapeutic or rehabilitative programs are included as income other than wages on line 22, Form 1040.

Volunteers

The tax treatment of amounts you receive as a volunteer worker for the Peace Corps, ACTION, or similar agency is covered in the following discussions.

Peace Corps
If you are a Peace Corps volunteer or volunteer leader, some amounts you receive may be exempt from tax.
Taxable allowances. Taxable allowances must be included in your income and reported as wages. These include:

- Cash allowances received during training.
- Allowances paid to your spouse and minor children while you are training in the United States.

- The part of living allowances designated by the President, under the Peace Corps Act, as basic compensation.
- Allowances for personal items such as domestic help, laundry and clothing maintenance, entertainment and recreation, transportation, and other miscellaneous expenses.
- Leave allowances.
- Readjustment allowances or "termination payments." These are considered received by you when credited to your account.

Example. Gary Carpenter, a Peace Corps volunteer, gets $175 a month during his period of service, to be paid to him in a lump sum at the end of his tour of duty. Although the allowance is not available to him until the end of his service, Gary must include it in his income on a monthly basis as it is credited to his account. **Nontaxable allowances.** These allowances include travel and living allowances for basic necessities, such as housing, utilities, food, clothing, and household supplies.

ACTION
ACTION participants perform services in antipoverty programs and Older American volunteer programs. Some amounts these participants receive are taxable and others are exempt from tax. **VISTA.** If you are a VISTA volunteer, you must include meals and lodging allowances paid to you in your income as wages.

Explanation
VISTA volunteers do not benefit from the same gross income exclusions as do members of the Peace Corps.

University Year for Action program. If you receive a stipend as a full-time student for service in the University Year for Action program, you must include the stipend in your income as wages.

Older American programs. Do not include in your income amounts you receive for supportive services or reimbursements for out-of-pocket expenses from the following programs:

- Retired Senior Volunteer Program (RSVP),
- Foster Grandparent Program, and
- Senior Companion Program.

Other Volunteer Programs
If you receive amounts for supportive services or are reimbursed for out-of-pocket expenses under either of the following volunteer programs, you do not include these amounts in your gross income:

- Service Corps of Retired Executives (SCORE), and
- Active Corps of Executives (ACE).

Volunteer tax counseling. You do not include in your income any reimbursements you receive for transportation, meals, and other expenses you have in training for, or actually providing, volunteer federal income tax counseling for the elderly (TCE).

You can deduct as a charitable contribution your unreimbursed out-of-pocket expenses in taking part in the volunteer income tax assistance (VITA) program.

Statutory Employees

Statutory employees are considered self-employed independent contractors for purposes of reporting income and expenses on their tax returns. If you are a statutory employee, get Publication 525 for more information.

Explanation
For more information about who qualifies as a statutory employee and the tax benefits of being a statutory employee, see Chapter 36, *If You Are Self-Employed.*

7 | Income from Tips

Introduction

*Tips are one of the least-reported types of income. Not surprisingly, the IRS is cracking down. In the past, employers reported to the IRS only the income from tips that their **employees** reported to them. Now the IRS says that certain employers should "assume" that their employees are receiving a certain amount of income from tips. That assumed amount now has to be reported to the IRS. Nevertheless, employee reporting requirements and employer withholding requirements have not changed. This chapter spells out the details.*

The consequences of not reporting income from tips can be severe. Individuals who underreport may face criminal and civil penalties, and their future social security benefits on retirement may be reduced.

This chapter discusses the tax rules for people who receive tips, such as waiters, waitresses, other food service employees, hairdressers, cab drivers, and casino dealers. It includes:

- What records of tips you should keep,
- When and how to report tips to your employer,
- What taxes your employer must withhold from your tips,
- How to treat tips you did not report to your employer, and
- Whether tip allocation affects you and how to report your tips if your employer allocates tips.

All tips you receive are taxable income and are subject to federal income tax. You must include in gross income tips you receive directly from customers, tips from charge customers that are paid to you by your employer, and your share of any tips you receive under a tip-splitting arrangement.

Withholding tax on tips. Cash tips of $20 or more that you receive in a month while working for any one employer are subject to withholding of income tax, social security or railroad retirement tax, and Medicare tax. Report the tips you receive to your employer so that the correct amount of these taxes can be determined. This is explained under *Withholding on Tips by Employer,* later in this chapter.

Social security or railroad retirement benefits. Your tips and other pay are used to determine the amount of social security or railroad retirement benefits you or your family may receive if you retire, become disabled, or die. Also, your tip income will be considered in determining your eligibility for Medicare benefits at age 65 or if you become disabled. You can get information about these benefits from Social Security or Railroad Retirement Board offices. Noncash tips are not counted as wages for social security or Medicare purposes.

Your future benefits can be figured correctly only if the Social Security Administration (SSA) has your correct information. To make sure that you have received credit for all your earnings, you should request a statement of your earnings from SSA at least every other year. You can get information on how to receive a statement of your earnings by calling 1–800–SSA–1213. When you get the statement from SSA, you should check it to be sure it includes all of your earnings.

Explanation

Numerous courts have held that all tips are subject to tax because they are additional compensation received for normal services performed and are not tax-free gifts from the customer to the employee. Tips are subject to both income tax and social security tax.

An arbitrary fixed charge that your employer adds to the customer's bill is not a tip or gratuity subject to tip reporting and withholding requirements. Even if it is called a tip, the amount an employee is guaranteed from his or her employer is additional wage compensation.

TAXPLANNER

If it is not customary to tip for a type of service, the IRS may be willing to concede that additional payments received for normal services may not be tips and may, indeed, be tax-free gifts from the customer. You would have to prove that the services performed did not extend beyond the minimum requirements of the job and that you work in an industry in which extra compensation is not traditional.

This claim would be impossible to sustain in all but the most unusual circumstances. The IRS and the courts generally presume that amounts received for performing services are taxable as compensation.

Useful Items

You may want to see:

Publication

☐ **531** Reporting Tip Income
☐ **1244** Employee's Daily Record of Tips and Report to Employer

Form (and Instructions)

☐ **4137** Social Security and Medicare Tax on Unreported Tip Income

Reporting Tips

You must report all tips as wages on Form 1040, Form 1040A, or Form 1040EZ. This includes the value of tips not paid in cash, such as passes, tickets, goods, or services. If you received tips of $20 or more in a month and you did not report all of them to your employer, you must file Form 1040 and Form 4137. You cannot file Form 1040A or Form 1040EZ. If you are a railroad employee and you did not report tips of $20 or more, contact your employer.

Explanation
All voluntary payments received from customers are taxable to the employee. This includes the **fair market value** of any noncash items given to employees.

Example
Tokens given to blackjack dealers in gambling casinos are taxable as income from tips to the dealers.

Service charges. A club, hotel, or restaurant may require customers who use its dining or banquet rooms to pay a service charge, which is given to the waiters or waitresses and other employees. Your share of this service charge is not a tip, but it is part of your wages paid by the employer. You should not include your share of the service charge in your report of tips to your employer. Your employer should not include your share of the service charge in tips paid to you, but should include it in your wages.

Tip splitting. If you split tips with fellow employees (such as waiters giving a part of their tips to busboys), include only your share of the tips in your report to your employer. "Tip splitting" may be referred to also as "tip sharing" or "tip pooling."

Example
A club does not permit its members to tip its employees but adds 10% to each member's restaurant charges. This additional amount is set aside in a fund and is disbursed monthly to all employees. Since the employer controls the allocation of the funds, they are additional wages, not tips.

However, if a headwaiter receives one lump-sum payment to be distributed to all waiters and waitresses, then the payments are income from tips. The headwaiter would include in his income only the amount he retained, not the total he distributed.

Daily Record of Tips

You must keep a **daily record** or **other documentation** to prove the amount of tip income you report on your return.
Daily record. Your daily record must show the following:

- Your name and address,
- Your employer's name, and
- The establishment's name.

Also show for each workday:

- The amount of cash tips you receive directly from customers or from other employees,
- Tips from credit card charge customers when paid to you by your employer,
- The amount of tips you paid out to other employees through tip splitting, etc., and
- The names of the other employees to whom you paid tips.

Make the entries in your daily record on or near the date you receive the tip income. Your records should show the date each entry is made.
Other documentation. If you do not keep a daily record of tips, you must maintain other documentation of the tip income you receive. This other documentation must be as credible and reliable as a daily record. This other documentation can be:

- Documentary records that show tips added to checks by customers and paid over to you, or
- Amounts paid for food or beverages on which you generally would receive a tip.

Examples of documentary records are:

- Copies of restaurant bills,
- Credit card charges, or
- Charges under any other arrangement containing amounts added by customers as tips.

Which form to use. You can use *Form 4070–A, Employee's Daily Record of Tips,* to record your tips.
Form 4070–A can be found only in Publication 1244, *Employee's Daily Record of Tips and Report to Employer.* You can get Publication 1244 from the IRS or your employer.
Your personal records. You should keep your daily tip record and a copy of the written reports you give your employer with your personal records.

When to Report Tips to Employer

You must give your employer a written report of your tips for each month by **the 10th day** of the next month. This report is required for each month that you receive tips of $20 or more while working for that employer.
Saturday, Sunday, holiday rule. If the 10th day of the month falls on a Saturday, Sunday, or legal holiday, you can give your employer the report on the next day that is not a Saturday, Sunday, or legal holiday.
Example. You must report tips of $20 or more you receive during March 1994 to your employer by Monday, April 11, 1994.

How to Report Tips to Employer

The following discussions refer only to tips paid by cash, credit card, and check.

Less than $20 in tips in one month. If you receive less than $20 in tips while working for one employer during a month, you do not have to report them to that employer. But you must include the tips in gross income on your income tax return. You do not have to pay social security tax, Medicare tax, or railroad retirement tax on these tips.

$20 or more in tips in one month. If you receive tips of $20 or more in a month while working for any one employer, you must report the total amount of your tips to that employer.

Example 1. You work for Watson's Restaurant during the month and receive $75 in tips. Because your tips are more than $20 for the month, you must report the $75 to your employer.

Example 2. You work for Watson's Restaurant during the month and receive $17 in tips. In that same month you work for Parkview Restaurant and get $14 in tips. Even though your tips total $31, you do not have to report tips to either employer because you received less than $20 in tips from each job. However, you should keep a record of the $31 because you must report it as income on your tax return.

Explanation
The amount of tips you report to your employer is treated as income subject to withholding in the month after it has been reported.

Example
If you earn $75 in tips in October, you must report that amount to your employer by November 10. In November your employer will treat you as having an additional $75 of compensation subject to federal income tax withholding and social security tax.

If you earn only $15 in tips in October, you do not have to report anything to your employer. You pay federal income tax on the tips when you report them on your tax return. The $15 is never subject to social security tax.

Your tip report to your employer should cover only one calendar month. But, your employer may require you to report your tips more often than once a month. For example, you may be required to report your tips weekly. In this case, you must make your report on the dates set by your employer.

When you stop working for your employer, you should report your tips of $20 or more to your employer at that time. If you do not report the tips when you stop working, you must give a statement to your employer either before your final payday or by the 10th day following the month you receive the tips, whichever is earlier.

Tips are treated as paid to you when you make the written report to your employer. However, if you make no report to your employer, tips are treated as paid to you when you receive them.

Example 1. During December 1993, you received $300 in tips. On January 10, 1994, you reported the tips to your employer. Your December 1993 tips will be treated as paid to you in January 1994, the time you made the report to your employer. You must report the $300 on your 1994 income tax return.

Example 2. If during December 1993 your tips were only $18, you would not have to make a report to your employer. In this case your tips are treated as paid in December 1993, the time you actually received them. You must report the $18 on your 1993 income tax return.

TaxSaver
If you earn income from tips in December, 1993, but do not report it to your employer until January, 1994, you may defer recognizing that income until you file your 1994 tax return.

To report tips to your employer, you can use **Form 4070,** *Employee's Report of Tips to Employer.* This form, available only in Publication 1244, tells you what information you must report. If you do not use Form 4070, your report should include the following.

- The amount of tips,
- Your employer's name and address,
- Your name, address, social security number,
- The month (or shorter period) covered,
- Your signature, and
- The date of the report.

TaxPlanner
You are not required to complete Form 4070-A as long as you have an alternative method of recording your tips. The IRS issues the form merely to help employees keep track of their income from tips.

Complete records, however, are essential, particularly if you must later substantiate a claim that you did not receive all the tips your employer alleges were allocated to you.

Publication 1244 contains several copies of both Form 4070 and Form 4070–A for your use.

Withholding on Tips by Employer

Your employer must withhold income tax, social security or railroad retirement tax, and Medicare tax on the tips you report. Your employer usually deducts the withholding due on tips from your regular wages. However, you do not have to have income tax withheld if you can claim exemption from withholding. You can claim exemption only if you had no income tax liability last year and expect none this year. See *Exemption From Withholding* in Chapter 5, *Tax Withholding and Estimated Tax* for more information.

TaxSaver
Many students and retired persons who expect to have no federal income tax liability work part-time in occupations in which they receive tips. To avoid unnecessary income tax withholding, you may file a Form W–4 with your employer, certifying that you had no federal income tax liability last year and expect to have none this year as well.

Employer's recordkeeping. Your employer may withhold an estimated amount from your wages to cover the tax on your tips.

Your employer also may require your written tip reports more than once a month and deduct the taxes due on your reported tips even though they do not yet total $20. If this is done, your employer must adjust the amount of taxes withheld from time to time, based on the actual amount of tips you report.

Form W–2. The Form W–2, *Wage and Tax Statement,* which you get from your employer, includes your reported tips.

- Box 1 includes your total wages, other compensation, and the tips you reported.
- Box 3 is your social security wages not including tips.
- Box 7 is your social security tips, the tips you reported to your employer.
- Box 5 is your Medicare wages and tips, which for most persons will be the sum of boxes 3 and 7. Your Medicare wages will be higher if your wages and tips are more than $57,600.

Any tips that are allocated to you (discussed later) are shown in box 8. Allocated tips are not included in boxes 1, 5, and 7. Any errors you find in these amounts should be brought to your employer's attention as soon as possible so you can obtain a corrected form.

Giving your employer money for taxes. Your regular pay may not be enough for your employer to withhold all the tax due on your regular pay plus reported tips. You can give your employer money to pay this withholding tax up to the close of the calendar year.

If your wages and any money you provide are not enough to pay all of your withholding taxes, the amounts will be applied in the following order. Your employer will first withhold from your wages all taxes due on your regular wages. This includes withholding for state and local income tax. Next, your employer will withhold from the balance of your wages taxes due on your reported tips. Social security and Medicare tax on reported tips will be withheld before any income tax will be withheld. Any taxes that remain unpaid should be collected by the employer out of your next paycheck.

You may pay estimated tax instead of giving your employer extra money. See Chapter 5, *Tax Withholding and Estimated Tax,* for information on estimated tax.

Uncollected employee social security and Medicare tax on tips. Box 13 (code A) on your Form W–2 will show the amount of social security tax on tips that your employer was unable to withhold and for which you did not give your employer extra money to pay the tax.

Box 13 (code B) will show the amount of Medicare tax on tips that your employer was unable to withhold and for which you did not give your employer extra money to pay the tax.

You must file Form 1040 to report the amount of uncollected tax on tips from Box 13 (code A and B), Form W–2, and pay it with your return, even if you do not otherwise have to file a return. Include the amount of uncollected tax in the total on line 53 of Form 1040. On the dotted line next to line 53, write "Uncollected Tax" and show the amount.

Limit on social security, Medicare, and railroad retirement tax. There are limits on the amount of social security, Medicare, and railroad retirement tax that your employer withholds from your wages and reported tips. If you worked for two or more employers in 1993, and you earned more than $57,600 ($42,900 if you are a railroad employee), you may have overpaid one or more of these taxes. You may be eligible for a credit for excess social security tax, Medicare tax, or railroad retirement tax, discussed in Chapter 35, *Other Credits.*

TAXALERT

Beginning in 1994, there will no longer be a limit on the amount of wages and reported tips subject to Medicare tax. Your entire wages and reported tips are subject to Medicare tax in 1994.

No limit for withholding of income tax. Unlike the social security, Medicare, and railroad retirement taxes, there is no dollar limit on the income tax withheld on wages and tips. The income tax withheld by your employer will either decrease what you owe at the end of the year or increase your refund when you file your return.

Tips Not Reported to Employer

If you received tips of $20 or more in any month while working for one employer, but did not report all of them to your employer, you must figure your social security and Medicare tax on the tips not reported. You should use **Form 4137** and attach it to Form 1040. See *Social Security and Medicare Tax on Unreported Tip Income (Form 4137),* later.

Employees subject to the Railroad Retirement Act. If you received tips of $20 or more in any month while working for a railroad employer and did not report them to your employer, do not use Form 4137. Instead, see *Employees subject to the Railroad Retirement Act,* in Publication 531.

Explanation

Tips received while working at a job covered by the Railroad Retirement Tax Act or while working for most state or local governments or for some nonprofit organizations are not subject to social security tax and should not be included on Form 4137.

Penalty for failure to report tips. If you do not report tips to your employer as required, you may be subject to a penalty equal to 50% of the employee social security or railroad retirement tax and Medicare tax, in addition to the tax that you owe.

If you did not report tips to your employer as required, you should attach a statement to your return explaining why you did not report them.

Reasonable cause. The penalty will not be charged if such failure is due to reasonable cause and not willful neglect.

Tip Allocation

Large food or beverage establishments are required to report certain additional information about tips to the IRS.

To make sure that employees are correctly reporting tips, employers must keep records to verify amounts reported by employees. Certain employers must allocate tips if the percentage of tips reported by employees falls below a required minimum percentage of gross sales. To "allocate tips" means to assign an additional amount as tips to each employee whose reported tips are below the required percentage.

How the rules work. If the rules on tip allocation apply to your employer's establishment, your employer must allocate the difference between 8% (or some lower acceptable percentage) of the total sales and the amount of total reported tips among all tipped employees. However, no allocation will be made to you if you report tips at least equal to your share of 8% of total sales.

If the customers do not tip 8% on the average, either your employer or a majority of the directly-tipped employees may petition to have the allocation percentage reduced from 8%. However, it cannot be reduced below 2%.

Allocated tips on Form W-2. Your employer will report the amount of tips allocated to you on your Form W–2 (in Box 8), separately from your wages and reported tips. Your employer bases withholding only on wages and reported tips. Your employer *should not withhold* income, social security, railroad retirement, or Medicare taxes from the allocated amount. Any incorrectly withheld taxes should be refunded to you by your employer.

Allocated tips you must report as income. You must report as income on Form 1040, line 7, at least the amount of allocated tips shown on your Form(s) W–2 unless you have adequate records that prove you received a smaller amount. If you have records, you **must** report as income the amount of tips your records show you actually received, even if this amount is more or less than the allocated tips. The IRS may determine that you received a larger amount of tip income than reflected by the tip allocation.

For more information on these requirements, see *Tip Allocation* in Publication 531.

Explanation

The reporting requirements apply only to what an *employer* must report to the IRS. You still report to your employer only the amount of tips you actually received. Income tax and Social Security withholding are calculated only on the amount of tips actually received and reported by the employee. The allocated amount is included in a special box on your Form W–2, but you do not have to include this amount as income if you can substantiate that your income from tips was less.

The 8% allocation is neither a minimum nor a maximum amount of income from tips. The employer needs to report only a guideline amount to help the IRS.

Example

The following example shows how a food and beverage establishment might determine what amount to include in the special box provided on each employee's Form W–2.

Jack's is a large food and beverage establishment that for one payroll period had gross receipts of $100,000 and reported tips of $6,200. Directly tipped employees reported $5,700, while indirectly tipped employees reported $500.

Directly tipped employees	Gross receipts for payroll period	Tips reported
Amos	$ 18,000	$1,080
Bob	16,000	880
Charlie	23,000	1,810
Dave	17,000	800
Ed	12,000	450
Frank	14,000	680
	$100,000	$5,700

The allocation computations would be as follows:

1. Total tips to be allocated: $100,000 (gross receipts) × 0.08 = $8,000
2. Tips reported by indirectly tipped employees = $500
3. Tips to be allocated to directly tipped employees: $8,000 − $500 (indirect employees tips) = $7,500
4. Allocation of tips to directly tipped employees:

	Directly tipped share of 8% gross	Gross receipts ratio		Employee share of 8% gross
Amos	$7,500 ×	18,000/100,000	=	$1,350
Bob	7,500 ×	16,000/100,000	=	1,200
Charlie	7,500 ×	23,000/100,000	=	1,725
Dave	7,500 ×	17,000/100,000	=	1,275
Ed	7,500 ×	12,000/100,000	=	900
Frank	7,500 ×	14,000/100,000	=	1,050
				$7,500

5. Calculation of tip shortfall of directly tipped employees:

	Employee share 8% gross	Tips reported		Employees shortfall
Amos	$1,350 −	$1,080	=	$ 270
Bob	1,200 −	880	=	320
Charlie	1,725 −	1,810	=	—
Dave	1,275 −	800	=	475
Ed	900 −	450	=	450
Frank	1,050 −	680	=	370
	Total shortfall			$1,885

Since Charlie has no reporting shortfall, there is no allocation to him.

6. Total tips reported, including reported tips of indirectly tipped employees: $8,000 − $6,200 (total tips reported) = $1,800 (amount allocable among shortfall employees)
7. Allocation of tip shortfall among directly tipped employees:

	Allocable amount	Shortfall ratio		Amount of allocation
Amos	$1,800 ×	270/1885	=	$258
Bob	1,800 ×	320/1885	=	305
Dave	1,800 ×	475/1885	=	454
Ed	1,800 ×	450/1885	=	430
Frank	1,800 ×	370/1885	=	353
		Total		$1,800

These are the amounts the employer must report on the employees' W–2s in Box 7.

The reporting requirements for employers are only guidelines and apply only to large food or beverage establishments. Nevertheless, the courts have imposed "industry averages" on taxpayers who had no records or inadequate records.

Example

In a series of cases, the courts held that average tips for taxi drivers come to 10% of gross income. A court was willing to accept a 2% figure for tips only when the driver produced daily logs that showed the amounts of fares and tips. The court believed that the records were true and accurate.

The courts have held that the average tips for barbers and hairdressers range from 2% to 8%.

To estimate the tip income of waiters and waitresses, the IRS has used various methods, based on the total sales of the restaurant. While the courts often adjust the IRS determination, they usually accept any reasonable method the IRS uses.

Our advice is: Maintain adequate records of all amounts that you actually receive.

Social Security and Medicare Tax on Unreported Tip Income (Form 4137)

Report on line 1 of Form 4137 *all* of the tips you received. This includes tips you reported to your employer, unreported tips, and allocated tips that you must report as income. Report on line 2 the amount of tips you reported to your employer and on line 4 the amount of tips you did not report because the total was less than $20 in a calendar month. These amounts are subtracted from the amount on line 1. The balances on lines 9 and 14 are the unreported tips subject to social security and Medicare tax figured on Form 4137.

Note: Only include cash, check, and charge tips when completing Form 4137. The value of tips not paid in cash or by check or charge card are not counted as wages for social security and Medicare tax purposes.

Be sure to complete Schedule U on the bottom of Form 4137. Schedule U is used by the Social Security Administration to credit your social security and Medicare accounts.

Attach Form 4137 to Form 1040. Enter the tax on line 50 of Form 1040. You may not use Form 1040EZ or Form 1040A.

Note: Do not include on line 50, Form 1040, any amount of uncollected social security tax and Medicare tax due on tips you did report to your employer. This amount, if any, is shown in Box 13 on Form W–2. Instead, see *Uncollected employee social security and Medicare tax on tips* under *Withholding on Tips by Employer* for the method of paying these taxes.

8 | Interest Income

Introduction

Interest income is a significant portion of all income earned by Americans. The government takes pains to make sure that all such income is reported by taxpayers. That's why payers of interest, like banks, are required to report to the government the amounts of interest they pay out and to whom. If you do not supply your proper tax identification number—usually your social security number—to a payer of interest, tax will automatically be withheld.

Some investments permit you to delay reporting interest income. Such investments may boost the after-tax rate of return on your money, because you pay tax on the income in a year—a retirement year, for example—when your tax rate is lower. This chapter helps you sort through some of the strategies for postponing taxes on interest income.

Important Changes for 1993

Market discount rules changed for certain taxable bonds. Bonds issued before July 19, 1984, are subject to the rules for market discount bonds if you purchased them after April 30, 1993. For more information, see *Market discount bonds* later in this chapter.

Market discount rules changed for certain tax-exempt bonds. When you redeem or dispose of tax-exempt bonds that you bought after April 30, 1993, any gain from market discount is taxable as ordinary income. For tax-exempt bonds that you bought before May 1, 1993, the gain from market discount is capital gain. For more information, see *Market discount bonds* later in this chapter.

Tax exemption continued for qualified mortgage bonds and qualified small issue bonds. The interest on qualified mortgage bonds and qualified small issue bonds was scheduled to become taxable on bonds issued after June 30, 1992. Instead, the exemption from tax on these bonds has been extended, and interest on these bonds continues to be exempt from tax. For more information about tax-exempt bonds, see *State or Local Government Obligations* later in this chapter.

Important Reminders

Reporting interest on seller-financed mortgage. If an individual buys his or her home from you in a sale that you finance, you must report the buyer's name, address, and social security number on line 1 of either Schedule B (Form 1040) or Schedule 1 (Form 1040A). If you do not, you may have to pay a $50 penalty. The buyer may have to pay a $50 penalty if he or she does not give you this information.

The buyer must report your name, address, and social security number (or employer identification number) on Schedule A (Form 1040). You must give this information to the buyer. If you do not, you may have to pay a $50 penalty.

For more information about reporting interest income, see *How to Report Interest Income* later in this chapter.

Education Savings Bond Program. You may be able to exclude from income interest on qualified U.S. savings bonds that you redeem if you pay qualified higher educational expenses. These are expenses for tuition and required fees at an eligible educational institution (college or eligible vocational school) for you, your spouse, or your dependent. A "qualified U.S. savings bond" is a Series EE savings bond that is *issued after December 31, 1989,* to an individual 24 years of age or older.

Reporting tax-exempt interest. You must show on your tax return the amount of any tax-exempt interest you received or accrued during the tax year. This is an information-reporting requirement and does not convert tax-exempt interest to taxable interest. For more information, see *How to Report Interest Income.*

This chapter discusses:

- Different types of interest income,
- What interest is taxable and what interest is nontaxable,
- When to report interest income, and
- How to report interest income on your tax return.

In general, any interest that you receive or that is credited to your account and can be withdrawn is taxable income. (It does not have to be entered in your passbook.) Exceptions to this rule are discussed later in this chapter.

As an important part of your records, you should keep a list showing sources and amounts of interest received during the year.

You may be able to deduct expenses you have in earning this income on Schedule A (Form 1040) if you itemize your deductions. See Chapter 30.

Useful Items

You may want to see:

Publication

- ☐ **525** Taxable and Nontaxable Income
- ☐ **537** Installment Sales
- ☐ **550** Investment Income and Expenses
- ☐ **925** Passive Activity and At-Risk Rules
- ☐ **1212** List of Original Issue Discount Instruments

Form (and Instructions)

☐ **Schedule B (Form 1040)**   Interest and Dividend Income
☐ **Schedule 1 (Form 1040A)**   Interest and Dividend Income for Form 1040A Filers
☐ **1099**   1993 Instructions for Forms 1099, 1098, 5498, and W–2G
☐ **3115**   Application for Change in Accounting Method
☐ **8815**   Exclusion of Interest From Series EE U.S. Savings Bonds Issued After 1989
☐ **8818**   Optional Form To Record Redemption of Series EE U.S. Savings Bonds Issued After 1989

General Information

A few items of general interest are covered here.

Passive activity income and losses. There are tax rules which limit the amount of losses and tax credits from passive activities that you can claim. Generally, you can use losses from passive activities only to offset income from passive activities. You generally cannot use passive activity losses to offset your other income, such as your wages or your *portfolio income* (that is, any gross income from interest, dividends, etc., that is not derived in the ordinary course of a trade or business). For more information about determining and reporting income and losses from passive activities, see Publication 925.

> **Explanation**
> For more information about passive activity gains and losses, see Chapter 13, *Other Income.*

Tax on investment income of a child under age 14. Part of a child's investment income may be taxed at the parent's tax rate. This may happen if the child is under age 14, has more than $1,200 of investment income (such as taxable interest and dividends), and either parent is alive at the end of the year. If these requirements are met, **Form 8615,** *Tax for Children Under Age 14 Who Have Investment Income of More Than $1,200,* must be completed and attached to the child's tax return. If these requirements are not met, Form 8615 is not required and the child's income is taxed at his or her own tax rate.

However, the parent can choose to include the child's interest and dividends on the parent's return if certain requirements are met. Use **Form 8814,** *Parents' Election To Report Child's Interest and Dividends,* for this purpose.

> **Explanation**
> You may only elect to include your child's income on your return if (1) your child's income consists solely of interest and dividends and is between $500 and $5,000, (2) your child made no estimated tax payments, (3) your child had no backup withholding, and (4) your child did not have any overpayment of tax shown on his or her 1992 return applied to the 1993 return. You may still need to file a state income tax return for your child.

For more information about the tax on investment income of children and the parents' election, see Chapter 32, *Tax on Investment Income of Certain Minor Children.*

Beneficiary of an estate or trust. Interest, dividends, or other investment income you receive as a beneficiary of an estate or trust is generally taxable income. You should receive a **Schedule K–1** (Form 1041), *Beneficiary's Share of Income, Deductions, Credits, etc.,* from the fiduciary. Your copy of Schedule K–1 and its instructions will tell you where to report the items from Schedule K–1 on your Form 1040.

Backup withholding. To ensure that income tax is collected on interest and other types of income that generally are not subject to withholding, backup withholding will apply in certain circumstances.

Under backup withholding, when you open a new account you must certify under penalties of perjury that your social security number is correct and that you are not subject to backup withholding. If you fail to make this certification, backup withholding may begin immediately on your new account or investment, and 31% of the interest paid on your account will be withheld. Your payer will give you a **Form W–9,** *Request for Taxpayer Identification Number and Certification,* or a similar form, to make this certification. Backup withholding may also be required if the Internal Revenue Service (IRS) has determined that you underreported your interest or dividend income. For more information, see *Backup Withholding* in Chapter 5, *Tax Withholding and Estimated Tax.*

Social security number. You must give your name and social security number to any person required by federal tax law to make a return, statement, or other document that relates to you. This includes payers of interest. If you are married and the funds in a joint account belong to you, you should give your social security number to the payer of the interest. If the funds in the account belong to both you and your spouse, you may give either your number or your spouse's number. But the number you provide must correspond with the name listed first on the account. You must give the payer the correct social security number if the number being used is wrong.

Penalty. If you do not give your social security number to the payer of interest, you may have to pay a penalty. See *Penalty for failure to supply social security number* under *Penalties* in Chapter 1, *Filing Information.* Backup withholding also may apply. See *Backup Withholding* in Chapter 5, *Tax Withholding and Estimated Tax.*

> **TAXPLANNER**
> If you change your name because of marriage, divorce, or any other reason, it is important to notify the Social Security Administration promptly. Otherwise, the IRS may believe it has discovered a reporting discrepancy that you will have to explain. In addition, some taxpayers who fail to notify the government of a name change do not receive credit for taxes they have paid.

Joint accounts. In a joint account, two or more persons, such as you and your spouse, hold property that pays interest, as *joint tenants, tenants by the entirety, or tenants in common.* That property can include a savings account or bond. Each person receives a share of any interest from the property. Each person's share is determined by local law.

> **Explanation**
> Whether or not a person receives a share of any interest from a property depends on state law and the intentions of the parties.

Many people open a joint bank account with a friend or a relative so that the friend or relative may inherit the property more easily upon the owner's death. No immediate transfer of property interest is intended. In these circumstances, the interest income should be reported solely by the owner.

Example 1

If two brothers, Tom and Bill, have a joint brokerage account in which all the funds were contributed by Tom, with no intention of conferring any immediate benefit on Bill, all of the income should be reported by Tom.

Example 2

If a husband and wife own bonds as joint tenants, tenants by the entirety, or tenants in common, and they file separate tax returns, each should include his or her share of the income.

Example 3

If a parent does not transfer bonds to her child but uses joint tenancy so that ownership of the bonds will pass automatically to the child in case of her death, the income belongs to the parent. The parent's social security number should be used, and all income should be reported on the parent's return. The same applies to joint savings accounts, other bank accounts, and certificates of deposit.

If a parent does intend to transfer some or all of her bonds to a child, a proportionate amount of interest should be included in both of their tax returns. Either person's social security number may be used.

Note: Bonds, savings accounts, and the like that are in the name of a parent or other adult as custodian under the state's Uniform Gifts to Minors Act should use the *child's* social security number.

TAXPLANNER

Since only one social security number will be recorded by the payer of interest, the IRS's document-matching program may issue deficiency notices when interest income is split between two or more returns. This situation arises because the tax return with the social security number shown on the payer's records may not include the full amount of the interest paid. To reduce the chance of receiving an IRS deficiency notice, show both the full amount of the interest paid and a subtraction for "amount attributable to others" on Schedule B (Form 1040) in the section used for reporting distributions of income.

The person who receives the other part of the interest needn't worry. Although that person includes on his or her return an amount for which he or she does not receive a Form 1099–INT, the IRS rarely questions returns where income in excess of that computed by the government is reported.

Income from property given to a child. Property you give as a parent to your child under the Model Gifts of Securities to Minors Act, the Uniform Gifts to Minors Act, or any similar law, is a true gift for federal gift tax purposes.

Income from property transferred under these laws is taxable to

the child unless it is used in any way to satisfy a legal obligation of support of that child. The income is taxable to the person having the legal obligation to support the child (parent or guardian) to the extent that it is used for the child's support.

Savings account with parent as trustee. Interest income, derived from a savings account opened for a child who is a minor but placed in the name, and subject to the order, of the parents as trustees, is taxable to the child, if, under the law of the state in which the child resides:

1) The savings account legally belongs to the child, and
2) The parents are not legally permitted to use any of the funds to support the child.

Form 1099–INT. Interest income is generally reported to you on Form 1099–INT, *Interest Income,* or a similar statement, by banks, savings and loans, and other payers of interest. This form shows you the interest you received during the year. Keep this form for your records. You do not have to attach it to your tax return.

Report on your tax return the total amount of interest income that is shown on any Form 1099–INT that you receive for the tax year. You must report all of your taxable interest income even if you do not receive a Form 1099–INT.

Explanation

The IRS contends that the figures shown on Form 1099 represent the correct amount of interest income paid to you. You have the burden of proof to demonstrate otherwise. If you have a valid reason for claiming that the correct amount is different—write on your return the amount shown on Form 1099 and then immediately show a subtraction (or addition) with an explanation for the adjustment. If you notice an error in the amount of interest stated, you should request that the payor issue a corrected Form 1099.

Example

You buy a bond on April 1, 1993 which pays interest once a year on December 31. Because you bought the bond between the interest payment dates, you pay, in addition to the bond, $400 for "purchased interest" (i.e. money to reimburse the seller for the interest earned between January 1, 1993 and April 1, 1993). On December 31, 1993, you receive a $3,000 interest payment which represents interest for the period January 1, through December 31, 1993. Since you did not earn the interest from January 1 through April 1, 1993, you should not have to pay income tax on this amount. Therefore, on Schedule B (Form 1040), you should report as follows:

XYZ Corporation interest	$3,000
Less amount of purchased interest	(400)

See *Bonds Sold Between Interest Dates* later in this chapter.

TAXORGANIZER

You should keep copies of each Form 1099-INT you receive in the mail.

Reporting backup withholding. If backup withholding is deducted from your interest income, the payer must give you a Form 1099–INT that indicates the amount withheld. The Form

1099–INT will show any backup withholding as "Federal income tax withheld."

Nominees. Generally, if someone receives interest as a nominee for you, that person will give you a Form 1099–INT showing the interest they received on your behalf.

If you receive a Form 1099–INT that includes amounts belonging to another person, see the discussion on nominee distributions, later, under *How to Report Interest Income.*

Incorrect amount. If you receive a Form 1099–INT that shows an incorrect amount (or other incorrect information), you should ask the issuer for a corrected form. The corrected Form 1099–INT you receive will be marked "CORRECTED."

Interest on Form 1099–OID. Reportable interest income may also be shown on Form 1099–OID, *Original Issue Discount.* For more information about amounts shown on this form, see *Original Issue Discount (OID),* later in this chapter.

TaxOrganizer

You should keep copies of each Form 1099-OID you receive in the mail.

Accuracy-related penalty. A 20% accuracy-related penalty may be charged for underpayments of tax due to negligence or disregard of rules and regulations or substantial understatement of tax. For more information on the penalty and any applicable interest, see *Penalties* in Chapter 1, *Filing Information.*

Explanation

Interest on the penalty will run from the time the return was due until the penalty is paid. Nevertheless, Congress and the IRS are taking a hard line on failure to report income for which you receive (or know you should have received) a Form 1099. They assume that you know that you own the stock or other asset and, therefore, that you should know there is some income to report, whether you receive the information from the payer or not. The negligence penalty will be automatically assessed, and you will have the almost impossible burden of persuading the IRS that you weren't negligent.

TaxSaver

Carefully compare your tax return with all your stocks, bonds, bank accounts, and other holdings, and be sure you've accounted for everything. Then double-check your memory—penalties and interest can add up if you don't.

Individual Retirement Arrangements (IRAs). Interest that you earn on an IRA is tax-deferred. You generally do not include it in your income until you make withdrawals from the IRA. Nor is it included in the amount to be reported as tax-exempt interest. See Chapter 18, *Individual Retirement Arrangements (IRAs).*

TaxPlanner

Interest earned in a **Keogh plan** (see Chapter 18, *Individual Retirement Arrangements (IRAs),* for details),

in a **qualified pension** or profit-sharing plan, or on your own voluntary contribution to a qualified profit-sharing plan is not taxable as long as you make no withdrawal.

The income earned must be reported and taxed when withdrawals are made. Nevertheless, it's possible to time your withdrawals so that they occur when you are in a lower tax bracket. In addition, some of these plans permit the income to be taxed at special low rates if withdrawn in a lump sum. See Chapter 11, *Retirement Plans, Pensions, and Annuities.*

Exempt-interest dividends you receive from a regulated investment company (mutual fund) are not included in your taxable income. (However, see *Information reporting requirement,* next.) You will receive a notice from the mutual fund telling you the amount of the tax-exempt-interest dividends that you received. Exempt-interest dividends are not shown on Form 1099–DIV or Form 1099–INT.

Information reporting requirement. Although these dividends are not taxable, you must show them on your tax return if you are required to file. This is an information reporting requirement and does *not* convert the exempt-interest dividend to taxable income. See *How to Report Interest Income,* later. Also, exempt-interest dividends may be treated as tax-exempt interest on specified private activity bonds, which is a "tax preference item" that may be subject to the alternative minimum tax. See *Alternative Minimum Tax* in Chapter 31 for more information. Publication 550 contains a discussion on private activity bonds, under *State or Local Government Obligations.*

TaxSaver

Investment income that is exempt from federal tax may still be taxable on your state tax return. This includes interest and dividends paid or accrued to you on state, municipal, or any other type of obligation. However, in most states, there are also certain federally tax-exempt bonds that are also not taxable at the state level. Be sure to check your state filing requirements before you invest in federally tax-exempt obligations.

Interest income on frozen deposits. A frozen deposit is an account from which you are unable to withdraw funds because:

1) The financial institution is bankrupt or insolvent, or
2) The state where the financial institution is located has placed limits on withdrawals because other banks in the state are bankrupt or insolvent.

Exclude from your gross income interest credited during 1993 on frozen deposits that you could not withdraw by the end of 1993.

Amount to exclude. The amount of interest you must exclude from gross income in 1993 is the interest that was credited on the frozen deposits minus the sum of:

1) The net amount you withdrew from these deposits during 1993, and
2) The amount you could withdraw as of the end of 1993 (not reduced by any penalty for premature withdrawals of a time deposit).

If you receive a Form 1099–INT for interest income on deposits that were frozen at the end of 1993, see *Frozen deposits* later under

How to Report Interest Income, for information about reporting this interest income exclusion on your 1993 tax return.

The interest you excluded from your income in 1993 must be reported in the later tax year when you can withdraw it from your account.

Example. $100 of interest was credited on your frozen deposit during the year. You withdrew $80 but could not withdraw any more as of the end of the year. Your net amount withdrawn was $80. You must exclude $20. You must include $80 in your income for the year.

Interest on VA dividends. Interest on insurance dividends that you leave on deposit with the Department of Veterans Affairs (VA) is *not* taxable. This includes interest paid on dividends on converted United States Government Life Insurance and on National Service Life Insurance policies.

Taxable Interest

Taxable interest includes interest you receive from bank accounts, loans you make to others, and interest from most other sources. The following are some other sources of taxable interest.

Dividends that are actually interest. Certain distributions commonly referred to as dividends are actually interest. You must report as interest so-called "dividends" on deposits or on share accounts in:

> Cooperative Banks
> Credit Unions
> Domestic Building and Loan Associations
> Domestic Savings and Loan Associations
> Federal Savings and Loan Associations
> Mutual Savings Banks

Money market funds. Generally, amounts you receive from money market funds should be reported as dividends, not as interest.

Money market certificates, savings certificates, and other deferred interest accounts. If you open any of these accounts, and interest is paid at fixed intervals of one year or less during the term of the account, you must include this interest in your income when you actually receive it or are entitled to receive it without paying a substantial penalty. The same is true for accounts that mature in one year or less and give a single payment of interest at maturity. If interest is deferred for more than one year, see *Original Issue Discount (OID),* later.

Money borrowed to invest in money market certificate. The interest you pay on money borrowed from a bank or savings institution to meet the minimum deposit required for a money market certificate from the institution and the interest you earn on the certificate are two separate items. You must report the total interest you earn on the certificate in your income. You may deduct the interest you pay, as investment interest subject to certain limits, only if you itemize deductions.

Example. You deposit $5,000 with a bank and borrow $5,000 from the bank to make up the $10,000 minimum deposit required to buy a 6–month money market certificate. The certificate earns $575 at maturity in 1993, but you receive only $265, which represents the $575 you earned minus $310 interest charged on your $5,000 loan. The bank gives you a Form 1099–INT for 1993 showing the $575 interest you earned. The bank also gives you a statement showing that you paid $310 interest for 1993. You must include the $575 in your income. You may deduct $310 on Schedule A (Form 1040) if you itemize your deductions, subject to the investment interest expense limit.

Gift for opening account. The fair market value of "gifts" or services you receive for making long-term deposits or for opening accounts in savings institutions is interest. Report it in income in the year you receive it.

Example. In 1993, you open a savings account at your local bank. The account earns $20, which is credited as interest. You also receive a $10 calculator. If no other interest is credited to your account during 1993, the Form 1099–INT you receive would show $30 interest income for 1993.

Interest on insurance dividends. Interest on insurance dividends that you leave on deposit with an insurance company, that is credited annually, and that can be withdrawn annually, is taxable to you when the interest is credited to your account. However, if you can only withdraw it on the anniversary date of the policy (or other specified date), the interest is taxable in the year in which that date occurs.

dend on deposit with the insurance company, any interest you receive on it should be included as part of your **gross income,** just as it would be if you had invested the money elsewhere.

If you receive Form 1099–INT from an insurance company every year, you may have an untapped source of cash at your disposal. This form usually indicates that insurance dividends paid in prior years are accumulating in a savings account paying *passbook* rates—about 3% these days. This money might be better invested in money market funds paying higher rates. To find out if you have money you did not know about, contact your insurance agent.

Prepaid insurance premiums. Any increase in the value of prepaid insurance premiums, advance premiums, or premium deposit funds is interest if it is applied to the payment of premiums due on insurance policies or made available for you to withdraw. Your insurance company must give you a Form 1099–INT showing the interest you earned for the year if you had $10 or more of interest income from that company.

U.S. obligations. Interest on U.S. obligations, such as U.S. Treasury bills, notes, and bonds, issued by any agency or instrumentality of the United States, is taxable for federal income tax purposes, but is exempt from all state and local income taxes.

Explanation

Interest income on U.S. obligations is not subject to *state and local* income tax. If your state has a high income tax rate, investing in U.S. obligations, rather than in instruments taxable at the state level, could mean a significant tax saving overall. Nevertheless, interest paid on tax refunds made by the federal government is taxable by both the state and the federal governments.

Treasury bills are issued at a discount and generally have 13–week, 26–week, and 52–week maturity periods. The difference between the discounted price you pay for the bills and the face value you receive at maturity is interest income. Report this interest income when the bill is paid at maturity.

Treasury notes range in maturity periods from 1 to 10 years. Maturity periods for Treasury bonds are longer than 10 years. Both notes and bonds generally pay interest every 6 months. Report this interest for the year paid. For more information, see *U.S. Treasury Bills, Notes, and Bonds* in Publication 550.

Explanation

The paragraph above discusses interest income only when a Treasury bill is held until maturity. When a Treasury bill is sold before maturity, the difference between the purchase price and the selling price may be part interest and part **short-term capital gain** or loss.

Example

You buy a $10,000 Treasury bill for $9,760 exactly 100 days before maturity. Thirty days later, you sell the bill for $9,850.

For tax purposes, you have earned a pro rata portion of the discount as interest income for the time you held the bill: 30/100 × ($10,000 − $9,760) = $72. The other $18 you receive over and above the purchase price is a short-term capital gain.

U.S. Treasury bills are relatively short-term investments. Their maturity dates vary from a week to a year. Since the interest income in most cases is reported at maturity—unless the bill is sold beforehand—purchasing Treasury bills with a maturity date falling in the following year offers cash basis taxpayers an opportunity to postpone interest income from one year to the next. However, if you borrow money to acquire Treasury bills, your interest expense deduction may be deferred. See Chapter 24, *Interest Expense,* for an explanation.

For information on Series EE and Series HH Savings Bonds, see *U.S. Savings Bonds,* later.

Interest on tax refund. Interest you receive on tax refunds is taxable income.

Interest on condemnation awards. If the condemning authority pays you interest to compensate you for a delay in paying an award, the interest is taxable.

Explanation

The interest on the award is taxable even if the condemning authority is a state or local government. The logic is as follows: The interest arises out of the government's eminent domain activities and not through the exercise of its borrowing power.

Installment sale payments. Certain deferred payments you receive under a contract for the sale or exchange of property provide for interest that is taxable. If little or no interest is provided for in certain contracts with payments due more than one year after the date of sale, each payment due more than 6 months after the date of sale will be treated as containing interest. These unstated interest rules apply to certain payments received on account of a **seller-financed** sale or exchange of property. See *Unstated Interest* in Publication 537, *Installment Sales.*

Explanation

Congress has clamped down on a device that was used with great success. The idea was to sell a piece of real estate at an inflated price in order to receive a larger long-term capital gain and, in turn, agree to accept deferred payments carrying a low interest rate. The strategy was to give up interest income taxed at ordinary rates and replace it with a larger long-term capital gain taxed at a lower rate.

Under legislation effective for debt instruments issued after December 31, 1984, payments must be made on a current basis, and certain tests are applied to determine if the interest rate is appropriate. If it isn't, some of each payment is recharacterized as interest. Because the rules are very complex, you should obtain professional assistance when you are negotiating a deal and making the necessary computations.

The rules are not applicable to sales of less than $250,000, the sale of your principal residence, or sales for less than $1 million of a farm used by the seller as a farm.

However, in these situations, the IRS has the authority to recharacterize a transaction if the stipulated interest rate falls below the published federal rate. In such cases, the IRS would reduce the amount of the capital gain and increase the interest income.

Interest on annuity contract. Accumulated interest on an annuity contract you sell before its maturity date is taxable.

Usurious interest. Usurious interest is taxable unless state law automatically changes it to a payment on the principal. Usurious interest is interest charged at an illegal rate.

Accrued interest on bonds. If you sell bonds between interest payment dates, the accrued interest paid to you is taxable. See *Bonds Sold Between Interest Dates,* later.

Bonds traded flat. If you purchase bonds when interest has been defaulted or when the interest has accrued but has not been paid, that interest is not income and is not taxable as interest if later paid. Such payments are returns of capital which reduce the remaining cost basis. Interest which accrues after the date of purchase, however, is taxable interest income for the year in which received or accrued. See *Bonds Sold Between Interest Dates,* later, for more information.

Interest on below-market loans. A below-market loan is a loan on which no interest is charged or on which interest is charged at a rate below the applicable federal rate. See *Below-Market Loans* in Publication 550 for more information.

U.S. Savings Bonds

You may earn interest on U.S. Savings Bonds in one of two ways. On some bonds, interest is paid at stated intervals by interest checks or coupons. Other bonds are issued at a discount and pay all interest at redemption or maturity. The interest on the latter is the difference between what you pay for the bond and its redemption or maturity value.

This section provides information on different types of U.S. Savings Bonds, how to report the interest income on these bonds, and how to treat transfers of these bonds.

Cash-basis taxpayers. If you use the cash method of accounting, as most individual taxpayers do, you generally report the interest on U.S. Savings Bonds when you receive it. The cash method of accounting is explained in Chapter 1, *Filing Status* under *Accounting Methods.*

Accrual-basis taxpayers. If you use an accrual method of accounting, you must report interest on U.S. Savings Bonds each year as it accrues. You cannot postpone reporting interest until you receive it or the bonds mature. Accrual methods of accounting are explained in Chapter 1, *Filing Status* under *Accounting Methods.*

Series HH Bonds. These bonds are issued at face value. Interest is paid twice a year by check or by direct deposit to your bank account. If you are a cash-basis taxpayer, you must report interest on these bonds as income in the year you receive it.

Series HH Bonds were first offered in 1980. Before 1980, *Series H Bonds* were issued. Series H Bonds are treated the same as Series HH Bonds. If you are a cash-basis taxpayer, you must report the interest when you receive it.

Series EE Bonds. These bonds are issued at a discount. You pay less than the face amount for the bonds. The face amount is payable to you at maturity. The difference between the purchase price and the redemption value is taxable interest.

Series EE Bonds were first offered in 1980. Before 1980, *Series E Bonds* were issued. If you own either Series EE or Series E Bonds and use the cash method of reporting income, you can:

1) Postpone reporting the interest until the earlier of the year you cash the bonds or the year in which they finally mature (*method 1*), or
2) Choose to report the increase in redemption value as interest each year (*method 2*).

Change from method 1. If you want to change your method of reporting the interest from method (1) to method (2), you can do so without permission from the IRS. However, in the year of change you must report all interest accrued to date and not previously reported for all such bonds.

Once you choose to report the interest each year, you must continue to do so for all Series EE or Series E Bonds you own and for any you get later, unless you request permission to change, as discussed next.

Change from method 2. To change from method (2) to method (1), complete **Form 3115,** *Application for Change in Accounting Method,* and attach it to your income tax return for the year of change. Type or print at the top of page 1 of the Form 3115 "*Filed Under Rev. Proc. 89–46.*" You must file your return by the due date (including extensions). You must identify the savings bonds for which you are requesting this change in accounting method.

Permission for the change is automatically granted if you attach to Form 3115 a statement that you agree to report all interest on the bonds acquired:

Table 8-1. **Who Pays Tax on U.S. Savings Bond Interest**

How Bond Is Purchased	Who Must Pay Tax on Bond Interest
You use your funds to buy a bond in your name and the name of another person as co-owners.	You
You buy a bond in the name of another person, who is the sole owner of the bond.	The person for whom you bought the bond
You and another person buy a bond as co-owners, each contributing part of the purchase price.	Each of you, in proportion to the amount you and the other co-owner each paid
You and your spouse, who live in a community property state, buy a bond that is community property.	If you file separate returns, each of you generally pays tax on one-half.

1) During the year of change and for all subsequent tax years, when the interest is realized upon disposition, redemption, or final maturity, whichever is earlier, and
2) Before the year of change, when the interest is realized upon disposition, redemption, or final maturity, whichever is earlier, with the exception of any interest income previously reported in prior tax years.

Explanation

Series E and Series EE Bonds are unique investments from a tax viewpoint. Since you, as a cash method taxpayer, may decide not to report the increase in value of the bonds as income each year and instead may decide to report the interest income when the bonds are cashed in or when they reach final maturity (whichever is earlier), you can—to an unusual extent—control when the income is recognized. The best time to redeem the bonds is a year in which you have a low income and a low tax rate.

Few people choose to report income annually rather than at sale or maturity, but, if you do, you would report as income the increase in the redemption value of each bond each year. All you must do is file a tax return reporting the income. It would be advantageous to report the income annually only if you had an income so low that your personal **exemption** and itemized deductions or standard deduction might otherwise be wasted. The most likely people to choose this option are children age 14 and over and retired people, both of whom may have low taxable incomes. (Under the Tax Reform Act of 1986, income received by children under age 14 may be taxed at their parents' rate.) Remember, once you choose to report the income each year, you must obtain permission from the IRS to change your reporting method.

Example

A 70-year-old unmarried man with only $1,500 of other income might wish to report his savings bond interest each year, since his first $6,950 of income (his standard deduction and exemption) is tax-free in 1993. If he holds the bonds and reports all the income in the year they mature, his taxable income in that year might be more than $6,950, and he would therefore pay tax unnecessarily.

Explanation

When held for 5 years or longer, Series EE Bonds become eligible to receive a market-based interest rate, retroactive to the first day of the month of issue. They receive interest at either 85% of the average return on marketable Treasury securities with 5 years remaining to their maturity or the minimum guaranteed rate in effect when the bond is issued or extended. The current guaranteed minimum rate on newly purchased Series EE bonds is 4%.

Millions of Series E and H bonds continue to be held by the public. Most are still earning interest due to extended maturity rates. Some, however, have reached their final maturity and should be exchanged or redeemed.

Series HH Bonds may be obtained in exchange for outstanding eligible Series EE Bonds and Series E Bonds having a combined redemption value of $500 or more. Owners who have deferred reporting interest earned on the bonds that they plan to exchange may continue to defer the interest until the year in which the Series HH Bonds received in exchange are redeemed, reach final maturity, or are otherwise disposed of.

Although Series H Bonds cannot be exchanged for Series HH Bonds (nor can Series E Bonds be exchanged for Series EE Bonds), the redemption proceeds can be reinvested in new series bonds. However, any previously tax-deferred interest must be reported for federal income tax purposes in the year of redemption.

Note. If you plan to redeem Series EE bonds in the same year that you pay for higher education expenses, you **should** use method (1). See *Education Savings Bond Program* later for more information.

Bonds held beyond maturity. If you hold the bonds beyond the original maturity period, and if you have chosen to report the interest each year, you must continue to do so unless you get permission to change your method of reporting. If you have chosen to postpone reporting the interest, you need not include the interest in income for the year of original maturity. Report it in the year you redeem the bonds or the year in which the extended maturity period ends, whichever is earlier. The original maturity period has been extended on all Series E Bonds.

The extended maturity period of Series E Bonds issued between May 1941 and November 1965 ends 40 years from their issue dates. The Department of the Treasury has announced that no further extension will be given to these bonds. Therefore, if you have postponed reporting interest on Series E Bonds purchased in 1953, you must report the interest on your 1993 return, unless you trade your Series E Bonds for Series HH Bonds.

Co-owners. If you buy a U.S. Savings Bond issued in your name and another person's name as co-owners, such as you and your child or you and your spouse, interest on the bond is taxable to the co-owner who bought the bond. If you used your funds to buy the bond, you must pay the tax on the interest. This is true even if you let the other co-owner redeem the bond and keep all the proceeds. Under these circumstances, since the other co-owner will receive a Form 1099–INT at the time of redemption, the other co-owner must provide you with another Form 1099–INT showing the amount of interest from the bond that is taxable to you. The co-owner who redeemed the bond is a "nominee." See *Nominee distributions and accrued interest (Form 1040),* later, under *How to Report Interest Income,* for more information about how a person who is a nominee reports interest income belonging to another person.

If you and the other co-owner each contribute part of the purchase price, interest on the bond is taxable to each of you, in proportion to the amount each of you paid.

If you and your spouse live in a community property state and hold bonds as community property, one-half of the interest is considered received by each of you. If you file separate returns, each of you must report one-half the bond interest. For more information about community property, see Publication 555, *Federal Tax Information on Community Property.*

These rules are also contained in *Table 8–1.*

Ownership transferred. If you bought Series EE or Series E Bonds **entirely with your own funds** and have them reissued in your co-owner's name or beneficiary's name alone, you must include in your gross income for the year of reissue all interest that you earned on such bonds and have not previously reported. But, if the bonds were reissued in your name alone, you do not have to report the interest accrued at that time. This same rule applies when bonds are transferred between spouses incident to divorce.

Explanation

If you make a gift of Series E or Series EE Bonds to a child, remember that it is not possible to transfer the obligation of reporting the interest income that has already accumulated.

Example

John has Series EE Bonds bought for $500 on January 1, 1987, that mature on January 1, 1997, for $1,000. He makes a gift of these bonds on January 1, 1993. He must report $250 of income in 1993. When the bond matures in 1997, the person who received the bond will report only $250 of income. The amounts of interest are determined by tables issued by the government.

Purchased jointly. If you buy Series EE or Series E Bonds *jointly* with a co-owner and have them reissued in the co-owner's name alone, you must include in your gross income for the year of reissue your share of all the interest earned on the bonds that you have not previously reported. At the time of reissue, the former co-owner does not have to include in gross income his or her share of the interest earned that was not reported before the transfer. This interest, however, as well as all interest earned after the reissue, is income to the former co-owner.

This income reporting rule also applies when the bonds are reissued in the name of your former co-owner and a new co-owner. But the new co-owner will report only his or her share of the interest earned after the transfer.

If bonds that you and a co-owner bought *jointly* are reissued to each of you separately in the same proportion as your contribution to the purchase price, neither you nor your co-owner has to report at that time the interest earned before the bonds were reissued.

Example. You and your spouse each spent an equal amount to buy a $1,000 Series EE Savings Bond. The bond was issued to you as co-owners. You both postpone reporting interest on the bond. You later have the bond reissued as two $500 bonds, one in your name and one in your spouse's name. At that time neither you nor your spouse has to report the interest earned to the date of reissue. But if you bought the $1,000 bond entirely with your own funds, you must report half the interest earned to the date of reissue. This is the previously postponed interest earned on the $1,000 bond that is attributable to the $500 bond issued to your spouse.

Transfer to a trust. If you own Series EE or Series E Bonds and transfer them to a trust, giving up all rights of ownership, you must include in your income for that year the interest earned to the date of transfer, if you have not already reported it. However, if you are considered the owner of the trust and if the increase in value both before and after the transfer continues to be taxable to you, you can continue to postpone reporting the interest earned each year. You must include the total interest in your income when the bonds are cashed or finally mature, whichever is earlier.

Explanation

If you transfer the bonds to a revocable trust, of which you are considered the owner, you may continue to defer reporting the income. Many individuals use a revocable trust as a substitute for a will. A revocable trust is not required to pay federal income tax on income earned in the trust. Instead, you will be taxed on the interest from the bond you transferred to such a trust. For more details, consult your tax advisor.

The same rules apply to previously unreported interest on Series EE or Series E Bonds if the transfer to a trust consisted of Series HH or Series H Bonds you got in a trade for the Series EE or Series E Bonds. See *Savings bonds traded,* later.

Decedents. The manner of reporting interest income on Series EE or Series E Bonds, after the death of the owner, depends on the accounting and income reporting method previously used by the decedent. If the bonds transferred because of death were owned by a person who used an accrual method, or who used the cash method and had chosen to report the interest each year, the interest earned in the year of death up to the date of death must be reported on that person's final return. The person who acquires the bonds includes in income only interest earned after the date of death.

If the transferred bonds were owned by a decedent who used the cash method, who had not chosen to report the interest each year, and who bought the bonds entirely with his or her own funds, all interest earned before death must be reported in one of the following ways:

1) The surviving spouse or personal representative (executor, administrator, etc.) who files the final income tax return of the decedent can choose to include on that return all of the interest earned on the bonds before the decedent's death. The person who acquires the bonds then includes in income only interest earned after the date of death, or

2) If the choice in (1) is not made, the interest earned up to the date of death is income in respect of a decedent. It should not be included in the decedent's final return. All of the interest earned both before and after the decedent's death is income to the person who acquires the bonds. If that person uses the cash method and does not choose to report the interest each year, he or she can postpone reporting any of it until the bonds are cashed or finally mature, whichever is earlier. In the year that person reports the interest, he or she can claim a deduction for any federal estate tax paid that was for the part of the interest included in the decedent's estate.For more information on income in respect of a decedent, see Chapter 4, *Decedents.*

TaxPlanner

If the final income tax return of the decedent shows a low amount of taxable income, it would be better to include the interest income from the date of purchase of the bonds through the date of death, the choice described in (1). Otherwise, the IRS says that the interest income must be reported by the person who receives the bonds, the choice described in (2).

However, there is a third option. If the bonds are in the name of the decedent alone, their ownership passes to the executor or administrator of the estate. The estate is a separate taxable entity that files its own income tax return. If the estate has a low amount of taxable income, it might be advisable for the executor to redeem the bonds.

A point to remember is this: The unique method by

which interest from U.S. Savings Bonds is taxed gives you an opportunity to reduce income tax by selecting the person or entity with the lowest tax rate to receive the income.

Example 1

Your uncle, a cash method taxpayer, died and left you a $1,000 Series E Bond. He bought the bond for $750 and chose not to report the interest each year. At the date of death, interest of $200 had accrued on the bond and its value of $950 was included in your uncle's estate. Your uncle's executor did not choose to include the $200 accrued interest in your uncle's final income tax return.

You are a cash method taxpayer and do not choose to report the interest each year as it is earned. If you cash the bond when it reaches maturity value of $1,000, you will report $250 interest income—the difference between the maturity value of $1,000 and the original cost of $750. Also, you may deduct in that year any federal estate tax you paid (as a miscellaneous itemized deduction not subject to the 2% AGI limit), because the $200 interest was included in your uncle's estate. See Chapter 4, *Decedents.*

Example 2

If, in Example 1, the executor had chosen to include the $200 accrued interest in your uncle's final return, you would report only $50 as interest when you cashed the bond at maturity. This $50 is the interest earned after your uncle's death.

Example 3

Your aunt died owning Series H Bonds that she got in a trade for Series E Bonds. (See *Savings bonds traded.*) You were the beneficiary of these bonds. Your aunt used the cash method and did not choose to report the interest on the Series E Bonds each year as it accrued. Your aunt's executor did not choose to include on her final return any interest earned before her death.

The income in respect of a decedent is the sum of the unreported interest on the Series E Bonds and the interest, if any, payable on the Series H Bonds but not received as of the date of your aunt's death. You must report any interest received during the year as income on your return. The part of the interest that was payable but not received before your aunt's death is income in respect of the decedent and may qualify for the estate tax deduction. For when to report the interest on the Series E Bonds traded, see *Savings bonds traded,* next.

Savings bonds traded. If you traded Series E Bonds for Series H Bonds, or traded Series EE or Series E Bonds for Series HH Bonds, you did not realize taxable income unless you received cash in the trade. Any cash you received is income to the extent of the interest earned on the bonds traded. When your Series HH or Series H Bonds mature, or if you dispose of them before maturity, you report as interest the difference between their redemption value and your cost. Your cost is the sum of your cost of the traded Series EE or Series E Bonds plus any amount you had to pay at the time of the trade.

Example. You trade Series E Bonds with a redemption value of $2,723 for Series HH Bonds. You get $2,500 in Series HH Bonds and $223 in cash. You must report the $223 as taxable income in

the year of the trade to the extent that you did not report interest on the Series E Bonds you traded.

$500 minimum value. Series EE or Series E Bonds that you want to trade must have a current redemption value of $500 or more. To figure the current redemption value of the bonds to be traded, you must add the accrued interest to their original purchase price.

Choice to report interest in year of trade. You can choose to treat all of the accrued interest on the Series EE or Series E Bonds traded for Series HH Bonds as income in the year of the trade.

Form 1099–INT for U.S. Savings Bonds interest. When you cash a bond, the bank or other payer that redeems it must give you a Form 1099–INT if the interest part of the payment you receive is $10 or more. Box 3 of your Form 1099–INT should show the interest as the difference between the amount you received and the amount paid for the bond. However, your Form 1099–INT may show more interest than you are required to include on your income tax return. For example, this may happen if:

1) You chose to report the increase in the redemption value of the bond each year. The interest shown on your Form 1099–INT will not be reduced by amounts previously included in income.
2) You received a bond from a decedent. The interest shown on your Form 1099–INT will not be reduced by any interest reported by the decedent before death, or on the decedent's final return, or by the estate on the estate's income tax return.
3) Ownership of a bond was transferred. The interest shown on your Form 1099–INT will not be reduced by interest that accrued prior to the transfer.
4) You redeemed a bond on which you were named as a co-owner but for which you did not use your funds to buy the bond. (See *Co-owners,* earlier in this chapter, for more information about the reporting requirements.)
5) You received a taxable distribution of bonds from a retirement or profit-sharing plan. The interest shown on your Form 1099–INT will not be reduced by the interest portion of amounts taxable as a distribution from a retirement or profit-sharing plan and not taxable as interest. (These amounts are generally shown on Form 1099–R, *Distributions From Pensions, Annuities, Retirement or Profit-Sharing Plans, IRAs, Insurance Contracts, etc.*)

For information on including the correct amount of interest on your return for (1), (2), (3), and (4) above, see *How to Report Interest Income,* later. Publication 550 includes examples showing how to report these amounts.

If you received a taxable distribution of bonds from a retirement or profit-sharing plan ((5), above), see *Interest from U.S. Savings Bonds* under *How to Report Interest Income* in Publication 550 for information on how to report the interest.

Note. U.S. Savings Bond interest is exempt from state and local taxes. The Form 1099–INT you receive will indicate the amount that is for U.S. Savings Bond interest in Box 3. Do not include this amount on your state or local income tax return.

Explanation

When you redeem U.S. Savings Bonds, the government assumes that the difference between the issue price and the redemption amount is interest paid to you entirely at that time, even though some of the interest may already have been reported by you or someone else. The government will therefore issue a Form 1099–INT to you for the full amount.

As discussed later in the IRS text, you should show the full amount on Schedule B (Form 1040) and also show a subtraction for the amount that is not taxable to you. This will help you to avoid IRS deficiency notices.

Education Savings Bond Program. You may be able to exclude from income all or part of the interest you receive on the redemption of qualified U.S. Savings Bonds during the year if you pay qualified higher educational expenses during the same year. This exclusion is known as the *Education Savings Bond Program.*

Married taxpayers who file separate returns *do not* qualify for this exclusion.

Qualified U.S. Savings Bonds. A qualified U.S. Savings Bond is a Series EE U.S. Savings Bond *issued after December 31, 1989.* The bond must be issued either in your name (sole owner) or in your and your spouse's name (co-owners). You must be at least 24 years old before the bond's issue date.

The date a bond is issued may be earlier than the date the bond is purchased because bonds are issued as of the first day of the month in which they are purchased. You may designate any individual (including a child) as a beneficiary of the bond (payable on death).

Eligible expenses. Qualified higher educational expenses are tuition and fees required for you, your spouse, or your dependent (for whom you can claim an exemption) to attend an eligible educational institution. Eligible expenses do not include expenses for room and board or for courses involving sports, games, or hobbies that are not part of a degree program.

Eligible educational institutions. These institutions include most public and nonprofit universities and colleges and certain vocational schools that are eligible for federal assistance.

Amount excludable. If the total redemption proceeds (interest and principal) from the qualified U.S. Savings Bonds you redeem during the year are not more than your qualified higher educational expenses for the year, you can exclude all of the interest. If the proceeds are more than the expenses, you will be able to exclude only part of the interest.

To determine the excludable amount, multiply the interest part of the redemption proceeds by a fraction. The numerator (top part) of the fraction is the qualified higher educational expenses you paid during the year. The denominator (bottom part) of the fraction is the total redemption proceeds you received during the year.

Example. In April 1993, Mark and Joan, a married couple, cashed qualified Series EE U.S. Savings Bonds they bought in January 1990. In 1993, they helped pay for their daughter's college tuition. They received proceeds of $5,800, representing principal of $5,000 and interest of $800. The qualified higher educational expenses they paid during 1993 totaled $4,000. They can exclude $552 ($800 × ($4,000 ÷ $5,800)) of interest in 1993.

Exclusion reduced for certain benefits. Before you figure your interest exclusion, you must reduce your qualified higher educational expenses by certain benefits the student may have received. These benefits include qualified scholarships that are exempt from tax and any other nontaxable payments (other than gifts, bequests, or inheritances) received for educational expenses, such as veterans' educational assistance benefits and employer-provided educational assistance benefits. See Publication 520, *Scholarships and Fellowships,* for more information on qualified scholarships.

Modified adjusted gross income limit. The interest exclusion is phased out if your modified adjusted gross income (modified AGI) is:

- $45,500 to $60,500 for taxpayers filing single, head of household, or qualifying widow(er) with dependent child, and
- $68,250 to $98,250 for married taxpayers filing jointly.

You do not qualify for the interest exclusion if your modified AGI is more than the upper limit for your filing status.

Modified AGI, for purposes of this exclusion, is adjusted gross income (line 16 of Form 1040A or line 31 of Form 1040) figured *before* the interest exclusion, and modified by adding back any:

1) Foreign earned income exclusion,
2) Foreign housing exclusion or deduction,
3) Exclusion for income from certain U.S. possessions, and
4) Exclusion for income from sources within Puerto Rico.

If you do not have any of these items, your modified AGI is your adjusted gross income before the interest exclusion.

If you have investment interest expense attributable to royalty income, see *Education Savings Bond Program* in Publication 550.

Form 8815. Use Form 8815, *Exclusion of Interest From Series EE U.S. Savings Bonds Issued After 1989,* to figure your exclusion and to compute your modified AGI.

Recordkeeping. If you claim the interest exclusion, you must keep a written record of the Series EE U.S. Savings Bonds issued after 1989 that you redeem. Your written record must include the serial number, issue date, face value, and redemption proceeds of each bond. You may use **Form 8818,** *Optional Form To Record Redemption of Series EE U.S. Savings Bonds Issued After 1989,* to keep this information.

You should also keep bills, receipts, canceled checks, or other documentation that shows you paid qualified higher educational expenses during the year.

Verification by IRS. Only Series EE U.S. Savings Bonds issued after December 31, 1989, qualify for this exclusion. If you claim the exclusion, IRS will check it by using bond redemption information from Department of the Treasury records.

Bonds Sold Between Interest Dates

When bonds are sold between interest dates, part of the sales price represents interest accrued to the date of sale. The seller must report this interest in gross income. The purchaser must treat this amount as a capital investment and deduct it from the next interest payment as a return of capital. To do this, the purchaser must:

1) Report the total interest payment as taxable interest on line 1 of Schedule B (Form 1040), and
2) Show the accrued interest separately and subtract it from the total interest reported. See *Nominee distributions and accrued interest (Form 1040),* later under *How to Report Interest Income,* for information about making this adjustment.

Explanation
Usually, interest on a bond is paid every 6 months. When a bond is sold between interest payment dates, the seller is entitled to payment from the buyer—in addition to payment for the bond itself—for the interest earned since the issuer's last interest payment. This extra payment—often called "purchased interest" on a broker's statement—is interest income to the seller of the bond, reportable for tax purposes as of the date of the sale. The buyer of the bond should record the purchased interest separately from the price of the bond in his or her

Minus: Annual $1,000 interest exclusion	1,000
Amount included in gross income	**$ 2,750**

records. The purchased interest partially offsets the first interest payment made to the buyer.

If the purchased interest is paid in 1993 but the first interest payment is not received until 1994, the buyer should report the purchased interest as an adjustment to interest income in 1994, not in 1993.

Example 1

On April 1, 1993, John bought from George a $10,000 bond yielding 10%. Interest on the bond is paid on January 1 and July 1 of each year. John paid $10,250—$10,000 in principal plus $250 for interest earned from January 1 to April 1. Thus, George received $250 of interest income on April 1, 1993. John received his first interest check on July 1, 1993. Half of that $500 represented a payment of purchased interest, and the other half represented interest income.

Example 2

Assume the same facts as above, except that John bought the bond from George on October 1, 1993. John received his interest check for $500 on January 1, 1994. As before, half of it represented repayment of purchased interest, and the other half represented interest income. However, John may *not* deduct the $250 of purchased interest for 1993 but must wait until 1994. On the other hand, George will report his $250 of interest income on his 1993 return, since he received it on October 1, 1993.

If the bond is an original issue discount (OID) debt instrument, see *Original Issue Discount (OID)*, later, to determine the OID you must include in income. Also, see *Original issue discount (OID)*, under *How to Report Interest Income*, for information on how to report OID on your income tax return.

If the bond has market discount, see *Market discount bonds*, later under *Original Issue Discount (OID)*, for information about the accrued market discount that must be recognized as interest income.

Insurance Received in Installments

If insurance proceeds are payable to you because your spouse died before October 23, 1986, and you receive the proceeds in installments, you can exclude up to $1,000 a year of the interest included in the installments. This $1,000 interest exclusion is in addition to the part of each installment that you do not include in income because it is a recovery of the lump sum payable at death. (See *Life Insurance Proceeds* in Chapter 13.) If you later remarry, you can continue to take the $1,000 interest exclusion. If your spouse died after October 22, 1986, you do not qualify for the $1,000 interest exclusion.

Example. Fern Green, a widow whose husband died in June 1986, chooses to receive the proceeds of her husband's $75,000 life insurance policy in ten yearly installments of $11,250. The payments are based on a guaranteed interest rate. She will include $2,750 in income each year. She figures this as follows:

Fixed payment	$11,250
Minus: Amount of insurance principal	
($75,000 ÷ 10)	7,500
Interest included in installment	$ 3,750

Annuity. If you buy an annuity with life insurance proceeds, the annuity payments you receive are taxed as pension and annuity income, not as interest income. See Publication 939, *Pension General Rule (Nonsimplified Method)*, for information on taxation of pension and annuity income.

Additional information. For more information about the tax treatment of insurance proceeds, see *Life Insurance Proceeds* in Publication 525, *Taxable and Nontaxable Income*.

Original Issue Discount (OID)

A long-term debt instrument, such as a bond, note, or other evidence of indebtedness, generally has original issue discount (OID) when the instrument is issued for a price that is less than its stated redemption price at maturity (principal amount). The amount of OID is the difference between the principal amount and the issue price of the instrument. OID is a form of interest; however, you report OID as it accrues, whether or not you receive any payments from the bond issuer. All long-term debt instruments that pay no interest prior to maturity are presumed to be issued at a discount. Zero-coupon bonds are one example of such instruments.

The OID rules do not apply to short-term obligations (those with a fixed maturity date of one year or less from date of issue). See *Discount on Short-Term Obligations* in Publication 550.

De minimis OID. You can disregard the discount and treat it as zero if it is less than one-fourth of 1% (.0025) of the stated redemption price at maturity, multiplied by the number of full years from the date of original issue to maturity. This small discount is known as "de minimis OID."

Example 1. You bought a 10–year bond, with a stated redemption price at maturity of $1,000, issued at $980 and having OID of $20. One-fourth of 1% of $1,000 (stated redemption price) times 10 (number of full years from the date of original issue to maturity) equals $25. Because the $20 discount is less than $25, you can disregard reporting the OID.

Example 2. Assume the same facts as in Example 1, except that the bond was issued at $950. The OID is $50. Because the $50 discount is not less than the $25 figured in Example 1, you must report the OID.

Form 1099–OID. The issuer of the debt instrument (or your broker, if you held the instrument through a broker) should give you Form 1099–OID, *Original Issue Discount*, or a similar statement, if the total OID for the calendar year is $10 or more. Form 1099–OID shows the amount of OID for the period in 1993 that you held the bond. It also will show the stated interest that you must include in your income. A copy of Form 1099–OID will be sent to the IRS. Do not file your copy with your return. Keep it for your records. See *Recomputation of OID shown on Form 1099–OID*, later in this discussion and also *Original issue discount (OID)*, later under *How to Report Interest Income*, for more information.

Nominee. If someone is the holder of record (the registered owner) of an OID instrument that belongs to you and receives a Form 1099–OID on your behalf, that person must give you a Form 1099–OID.

Debt instrument bought at premium. If you bought at a premium a debt instrument that was originally issued at a discount, you do not have to report any OID as ordinary income. *Premium* means a purchase price that exceeds the stated redemption price of the instrument at maturity. When you sell or redeem an instrument bought at a premium, the difference between the sale or redemption price and your purchase price is a capital gain or loss.

Premium is not the same as "acquisition premium," discussed later.

Exceptions to the OID rules. The OID rules discussed in this chapter for publicly offered, long-term instruments do not apply to the following debt instruments:

1) Tax-exempt obligations (however, see *Stripped tax-exempt obligations* under *Stripped Bonds and Coupons* in Publication 550),
2) U.S. Savings Bonds,
3) Short-term debt instruments (those which have fixed maturity dates of not more than one year from the date of issue),
4) Obligations issued by an individual before March 2, 1984, and
5) Loans between individuals, if:
   a) The lender is not in the business of lending money,
   b) The amount of the loan, plus the amount of any outstanding prior loans, is $10,000 or less, and
   c) Avoiding any federal tax is not one of the principal purposes of the loan.

Explanation

The IRS interpretation is misleading with respect to tax-exempt obligations issued after September 3, 1982, and acquired after March 1, 1984. Even though interest on such obligations is tax-free, the OID rules will apply in determining the basis of the security in the event of sale, exchange, or maturity. (See the discussion later in this chapter.)

In addition, under the Technical and Miscellaneous Revenue Act of 1988, the original issue discount on a stripped tax-exempt bond may be treated as taxable interest if the stripped bond is sold at a discount rate that is higher than the original issue.

Debt instruments issued after 1954 and before May 28, 1969 (or before July 2, 1982, if a government instrument). For these instruments, you pay no tax on the OID until the year you sell, exchange, or redeem the instrument. If a gain results, and if the instrument is a capital asset, the amount of the gain equal to the OID is taxed as ordinary interest income. The balance of the gain is capital gain. If there is a loss on the sale of the instrument, the entire loss is a capital loss and no reporting of OID is required.

Corporate debt instruments issued after May 27, 1969, and before July 2, 1982. If you hold these debt instruments as capital assets, you must include a part of the discount in your gross income each year that you own the instruments. Your basis in the instrument is increased by the amount of OID that you include in your gross income.

Include in your gross income the total OID from Form 1099–OID. Box 1 shows the OID on the debt instrument for the part of the year you owned it. In certain cases, you cannot use the amount in Box 1. Instead, you must figure the correct OID to report. See *Recomputation of OID shown on Form 1099–OID,* later, for more information.

Explanation

The IRS explanation about bonds issued before and after July 1, 1982, is correct. However, the Deficit Reduction Act of 1984 extended these rules to debt instruments issued by individuals after March 1, 1984. This

will affect individuals who borrow and lend at a discounted rate.

The current law also makes original issue discount the general rule with regard to obligations issued after July 18, 1984, and purchased in the open market. (This law also applies to bonds issued before July 19, 1984 and purchased after April 30, 1993.) Under the prior law, the difference between the purchase price and ultimate proceeds on the sale or redemption of a debt instrument was treated as a capital gain. Now, however, if you sell property after December 31, 1984, or buy a bond in the marketplace that was issued after July 18, 1984, or a bond issued prior to July 1984 and purchased after April 30, 1993, you must determine whether there is original issue discount and, if so, how much. Some of that amount will be included in your ordinary income each year. You will need professional help to make this calculation. For more information, see *Market Discount Bonds* later in this chapter.

Example

Assume that Jim purchases a publicly traded 6% $1 million bond that was issued after December 31, 1984, for $900,000. The bond has a maturity of 10 years at the time of purchase. Jim will also receive $60,000 in interest each year.

The computation of the amount of original issue discount to be included is as follows:

Post 7/1/82 debt
With coupon

Face value	$1,000,000
Purchase price	$900,000
Length of term	10
Coupon rate	6%

Period	Beginning basis	Total payment	OID portion	Interest portion	Ending basis
1	$900,000	$69,533	$9,533	$60,000	$909,533
2	909,533	69,634	9,634	60,000	919,166
3	919,166	69,736	9,736	60,000	928,902
4	928,902	69,839	9,839	60,000	938,740
5	938,740	69,943	9,943	60,000	948,683
6	948,683	70,048	10,048	60,000	958,732
7	958,732	70,155	10,155	60,000	968,886
8	968,886	70,262	10,262	60,000	979,148
9	979,148	70,371	10,371	60,000	989,519
10	989,519	70,481	10,481	60,000	1,000,000
		$700,000	$100,000	$600,000	

The total interest income recognized for the first year will be $69,533 ($60,000 interest and $9,533 of OID). Further special computations will be required if the obligation is sold prior to maturity. Professional advice is *absolutely essential* for anyone who needs to make special OID computations.

TAXPLANNER

A zero-coupon bond is one that is purchased at a substantial discount and pays no interest during its life.

If you buy a zero-coupon bond, you do not bear the investment risk entailed in reinvesting interest payments received over the life of the bond, because there are no such payments. Moreover, since the issue price and the maturity value have been derived from compound interest tables, you may figure what the precise return on your investment will be if the bond is held until it matures. This is true *only* of zero-coupon bonds.

A word of caution: Because you do not receive the interest until a zero-coupon bond matures, prices during the holding period can be very volatile as market interest rates change. The longer the maturity is, the more volatile is the price.

Even though the interest on a zero-coupon bond is not paid until maturity, it is included in income each year. Consequently, taxable zero-coupon bonds are not popular with individuals who pay substantial amounts of tax, because they must report as income the annual increase in the value of the bonds. However, such bonds may be of interest to you for your Individual Retirement Arrangement or Keogh plan [see Chapter 18, *Individual Retirement Arrangements* (IRAs)], because you do not pay tax on the bonds' earnings in these accounts. The advantage is that you lock in an interest rate.

On the other hand, nontaxable zero-coupon bonds—such as zero-coupon municipal bonds—may be attractive to individuals in a high tax bracket for the obvious reasons that interest rates are locked in and taxes are avoided. In this case, you increase your cost basis on the bonds each year by the amount of the original issue discount applicable to that year, even though you don't pay any federal tax on the income.

Example

Assume that Jennifer purchases a 10-year $100,000, nontaxable zero-coupon bond on June 28, 1993, for $50,000. The chart below illustrates how the basis of the bond increases over the life of the bond.

Post 7/1/82 debt
Zero-coupon

Face value	$100,000	
Purchase price	$50,000	
Length of term	10	

Period	Beginning Basis	OID	Ending Basis
1	$50,000	$3,589	$53,589
2	53,589	3,846	57,435
3	57,435	4,122	61,557
4	61,557	4,418	65,975
5	65,975	4,735	70,711
6	70,711	5,075	75,786
7	75,786	5,439	81,225
8	81,225	5,830	87,055
9	87,055	6,248	93,303
10	93,303	6,697	100,000
		$50,000	

The new method for determining original issue discount illustrated above is applicable to tax-exempt bonds. The annual increase in basis is determined accordingly. However, the new original issue discount computation is *not* the method used for a tax-exempt bond issued before September 4, 1982, and acquired before March 2, 1984. Instead, a rule is used that allocates the discount proportionately over the life of the bonds. The result of this is illustrated as follows:

Example

Assume the same facts as in the previous example except that the bond was purchased on July 1, 1982. The following chart illustrates how the basis of the bond increased under prior tax law.

Pre 7/1/82 debt
Zero-coupon

Face value	100,000	
Purchase price	50,000	
Length of term	10	

Period	Beginning Basis	OID	Ending Basis
1	50,000	5,000	55,000
2	55,000	5,000	60,000
3	60,000	5,000	65,000
4	65,000	5,000	70,000
5	70,000	5,000	75,000
6	75,000	5,000	80,000
7	80,000	5,000	85,000
8	85,000	5,000	90,000
9	90,000	5,000	95,000
10	95,000	5,000	100,000
		50,000	

This is not the way interest actually accrued, and the consequence is an inflated basis for these bonds in their early years. The bizarre result: You may be able to sell these bonds and report a large capital loss even though there is no real economic loss.

Debt instruments issued after July 1, 1982, and before January 1, 1985. If you hold these debt instruments as capital assets, you must include a part of the discount in your gross income each year and increase your basis by the amount included.

Include in your gross income the OID from Box 1 of Form 1099–OID. In certain cases, you cannot use the amount in Box 1. Instead, you must figure the correct OID to report. See *Recomputation of OID shown on Form 1099–OID,* later.

Debt instruments issued after December 31, 1984. If you hold these debt instruments, the OID reporting rules, in general, are similar to those for debt instruments issued after July 1, 1982. However, you report the total applicable OID (based on the number of days in the accrual period) regardless of whether you hold that debt instrument as a capital asset. Your basis in the instrument is increased by the amount of OID that you include in your gross income. The method for determining the reportable discount on any OID instrument issued after 1984 is based on an accrual period of 6 months. For more information about determining reportable OID for these debt instruments, see *Debt Instruments Issued After December 31, 1984,* in Publication 1212.

Recomputation of OID shown on Form 1099–OID. You must recompute the OID shown in Box 1 of Form 1099–OID if any of the following apply:

1) You bought the debt instrument after its original issue and paid an acquisition premium (as explained in *Acquisition premium,* later),
2) The debt instrument is a stripped bond or a stripped coupon (these include certain zero coupon instruments), or
3) You received the Form 1099–OID as a "nominee" recipient.

For each of these situations, see Publication 1212 for detailed information and examples on figuring the amount of OID to report on your income tax return. The rules for figuring OID are broken down in Publication 1212 to reflect the specific computations that apply to corporate long-term OID debt instruments issued before July 2, 1982, and to all long-term OID debt instruments issued after July 1, 1982.

If you bought the debt instrument at a market discount, see *Market discount bonds,* later, for information about including market discount in income.

Reporting correct amount of OID. If you are reporting OID in an amount greater or less than the amount shown on Form 1099–OID, see *Original issue discount (OID)* at the end of this chapter, for information about reporting the correct amount of OID on Schedule B (Form 1040).

Acquisition premium. If you bought a debt instrument for more than the original issue price plus accumulated OID from the date of issue, that excess amount (or acquisition premium) reduces the amount of discount includible in your income. See *Computation of reportable OID* in Publication 1212 for information about figuring this reduction.

REMIC regular interests. If you own a regular interest in a real estate mortgage investment conduit (REMIC), you will receive a Form 1099–OID and an additional written statement from your broker. Form 1099–OID shows the amount of OID and interest, if any, that accrued to you for the period you held the regular interest. You will not need to make any adjustments to the amounts reported even if you held the regular interest for only a portion of the calendar year. The additional written statement should also contain enough information to enable you to figure your accrual of market discount or amortizable bond premium. See *REMICs* in Publication 550 for more information.

If a Form 1099–OID is not received. If you had OID for 1993 but did not receive a Form 1099–OID, see Publication 1212 which lists total OID on certain debt instruments. If your debt instrument is not listed in Publication 1212, consult the issuer for further information about the OID that accrued for 1993.

Recomputation of periodic interest shown on Form 1099–OID. If you disposed of a corporate debt instrument or acquired it from another holder during 1993, see *Bonds Sold Between Interest Dates,* earlier, for information about the treatment of periodic interest that may be shown in Box 2 of Form 1099–OID for that instrument. See *Nominee distributions and accrued interest (Form 1040)* under *How to Report Interest Income,* later, for information about reporting the correct amount of interest on Schedule B (Form 1040).

Stripped bonds and stripped coupons. Special rules apply to the sale and purchase of stripped bonds and stripped coupons after July 1, 1982. These rules also cover the treatment of zero coupon U.S. Treasury-backed securities. See *Rules for Figuring OID on Stripped Bonds and Stripped Coupons* in Publication 1212 for more information.

Explanation

Stripped coupon bonds are coupon bonds that have been separated into component parts. The coupons represent claims for interest payments, which are paid on a periodic basis. The bond itself represents the claim for the repayment of the principal, which occurs at some future time.

Example

A 10-year, $10,000, 9% bond (interest paid semi-annually) was issued on January 1, 1993, for $10,000. On April 1, 1993, when the bond had a market price of $9,900, the coupons were stripped from the bond so that they and the bond became separate assets that could be bought and sold in the marketplace. In other words, the holder could have sold the right to receive $450 semiannually for the next 9¾ years and could have independently sold the right to receive the $10,000 on January 1, 2003.

Assume that the right to receive 20 semiannual payments is worth $4,100 and the right to receive $10,000 on January 1, 2003, is worth $5,800. The tax treatment to buyer and to seller is as follows:

The seller

1. Include the accrued interest income of $225 from January 1, 1993, through April 1, 1993, in income.
2. Increase your basis by the $225 to $10,225.
3. Allocate the basis, using **fair market value,** to the coupons [($4,100 ÷ $9,900) × $10,225 = $4,235)] and the bond [($5,800 ÷ $9,900) × $10,225 = $5,990)].
4. Compare the proceeds for what you sell—either the coupons or the bond—with the basis figured above to determine if you've had a gain or a loss.
5. The difference between the basis of what is not sold and the amount that will be received over time is considered an original issue discount (OID). That amount is treated as earned over the life of the asset. Thus, if the coupons were retained, the difference between their basis ($4,235) and the amount that will be received over time ($450 semiannually for 10 years, or $9,000) would be the original issue discount.

In this example, $4,765 in interest income must be included on your returns over the 10 years. The amount to be included in your income for each year is figured by performing a complicated computation, for which you will probably require professional assistance.

Similarly, if the bond were retained, the difference between its basis ($5,990) and the proceeds ($10,000) would be its original issue discount. Again, complicated computations are required to determine the amount included in your income each year.

The purchaser

The difference between what you pay and what you will receive over time is the original issue discount. A special computation is necessary to figure how much you should include in income each year.

Certificates of deposit (CDs) and similar deposit arrangements. If you purchase a CD or a similar deposit arrangement and the receipt of interest is postponed for more than one year, you must include in income each year a part of the total interest due and report it in the same way as other original issue discount (OID).

Examples of such deposit arrangements with banks, building and loan associations, etc., include:

Certificates of deposit
Time deposits
Bonus plans
Savings certificates
Deferred income certificates
Bonus savings certificates
Growth savings certificates

Interest subject to penalty for early withdrawal. If you deposit money in one of the arrangements listed above that has a term of one year or less, and you lose part of the interest because you withdraw funds before the end of the term, you must include all the interest in income at the end of the term. However, you can deduct the entire penalty, even if it exceeds your interest income, on line 28 of Form 1040.

Explanation

A time deposit with a penalty for early withdrawal is one of the few investments that permits you to defer the recognition of income to a subsequent year. Other examples are U.S. Savings Bonds and U.S. Treasury bills.

Example. On October 1, 1992, you invested $10,000 in a savings certificate that was to pay you $10,600 on April 1, 1993. Because you withdrew part of the principal or interest before April 1, the bank charged you a penalty of $300. For 1993, you must report as income the entire $600 accrued interest. However, you can deduct, as an adjustment to gross income, the $300 penalty.

Bearer certificates of deposit. These are not issued in the depositor's name and, therefore, are transferable from one individual to another. They are issued by banks for a certain period, usually a number of years. Interest is not usually paid until the certificates are redeemed by the bank at the end of this period.

Banks are required to provide the IRS and the person redeeming the bearer certificate with a Form 1099–INT.

Certificates of deposit issued after 1982 are generally required to be in registered form. For more information about this requirement, see *Obligations issued in bearer form* in Chapter 15, *Sale of Property.*

For more information about interest income from certificates of deposit, see *Original Issue Discount (OID)* in Publication 550.

Market discount bonds. A market discount bond is any bond having market discount except:

1) Short-term obligations (those with fixed maturity dates of up to one year from the date of issue),
2) Tax-exempt obligations that you bought before May 1, 1993,
3) U.S. Savings Bonds, and
4) Certain installment obligations.

Market discount arises when the value of a debt obligation decreases after its issue date, generally because of an increase in interest rates. If you buy a bond on the secondary market, it may have market discount.

If you dispose of a market discount bond, you generally must recognize the gain as taxable interest income up to the amount of the bond's *accrued market discount,* if:

1) The bond was issued after July 18, 1984, or
2) You purchased the bond after April 30, 1993.

The rest of the gain is capital gain if the bond was a capital asset. For more information about the tax treatment of market discount, see *Market Discount Bonds* in Publication 550.

Discount on short-term obligations. Certain holders of short-term obligations are required to accrue and include the discount on such obligations in current income. See *Discount on Short-Term Obligations* in Publication 550 for more information.

REMIC regular interests. If you are the holder of a regular interest in a real estate mortgage investment conduit (REMIC), or an interest in a collateralized debt obligation (CDO), that interest is considered to be a debt instrument for income tax purposes, whether or not it is in the form of a debt instrument. Accordingly, the OID, market discount, and income-reporting rules that apply to bonds and other debt instruments apply to such interests with certain modifications. For more information, see *REMICs and Other CDOs* in Publication 550.

State or Local Government Obligations

Generally, interest on obligations of state or local governments is tax exempt. This includes obligations of a state or one of its political subdivisions, the District of Columbia, a possession of the United States, or one of its political subdivisions, used to finance governmental operations. This includes interest on certain obligations issued after 1982 by an Indian tribal government treated as a state.

If you receive a Form 1099–INT for interest paid on a tax-exempt obligation, see *Tax-exempt interest income* under *How to Report Interest Income.*

Explanation

Assume that an issue of tax-exempt municipal bonds was sold to the public at par (face value) at an interest rate lower than the rate demanded by today's investors. Since the interest rate on these bonds is lower than the rate demanded by today's investors, the bonds are trading in the marketplace at a substantial discount from par. This is a market discount. If you buy these bonds now and subsequently realize a gain either when you sell them or when they reach maturity, you must report the gain as taxable interest income up to the amount of the bonds' accrued market discount and the remaining portion as capital gain if the bond was a capital asset. Similarly, if you realize a capital loss on municipal bonds, it is deductible.

The rule with regard to bonds bought at a premium is different. If you buy a bond for $11,000 that will mature for $10,000 and you hold it until maturity, you may not claim a capital loss or any kind of deduction, because the tax law requires that you **amortize** the premium over the life of the bond.

TaxSaver

While most municipal bond interest is not subject to federal tax, capital gain income and accretion of market discount is. You should be aware of this when you are deciding which bonds to buy.

Example

A $10,000, 10-year tax-exempt municipal bond, yielding 8% purchased at par, will provide $800 of tax-free interest each year, and there will be no capital gain on maturity. The total earned for the 10 years is $8,000.

Similarly, a $12,000, 10-year tax-exempt municipal bond with a 5.2% coupon ($624 interest per year) purchased on May 2, 1993, at $10,000 will yield a total of $8,240 over the life of the bond—$624 of tax-free interest each year plus $200 of taxable interest income each year if the bond is held to maturity. This represents the market discount accretion. But the taxable interest income will be subject to tax of up to 39.6%, so the net earnings for the 10 years may be reduced to as little as $7,448.

TAXPLANNER

When you are determining whether to invest in tax-exempt securities, compare the net after-tax income from a tax-exempt investment with a similar taxable investment.

Equivalent Yield Needed from a Taxable Bond

Tax-Exempt Yield	Your Combined Federal, State & Local Marginal Tax Bracket						
	28%	31%	33%	36%	39.6%	42%	46%
4.00	5.56	5.80	5.97	6.25	6.62	6.90	7.41
4.50	6.25	6.52	6.72	7.03	7.45	7.76	8.33
5.00	6.94	7.25	7.46	7.81	8.28	8.62	9.26
5.50	7.64	7.97	8.21	8.59	9.11	9.48	10.19
6.00	8.33	8.70	8.96	9.38	9.93	10.34	11.11
6.50	9.03	9.42	9.70	10.16	10.76	11.21	12.04
7.00	9.72	10.15	10.45	10.94	11.59	12.07	12.96

Interest on arbitrage bonds issued by state or local governments after October 9, 1969, and interest on private activity bonds generally is *taxable.*

For more information on whether such interest is taxable or tax exempt, see *State or Local Government Obligations* in Publication 550.

Information reporting requirement. If you received or accrued any tax-exempt interest income (such as interest on certain state and municipal bonds), you must show that interest on your tax return if you are required to file. This is an information reporting requirement and does not convert tax-exempt interest to taxable interest. See *How to Report Interest Income,* later.

When to Report Interest Income

When you report your interest income depends on whether you use the cash method or an accrual method of reporting income.

Cash method. If you use this method, you generally report your interest income in the year in which you actually or constructively receive it. Most individual taxpayers use this method. However, there are special rules for OID and certain U.S. Savings Bonds. See *U.S. Savings Bonds,* and *Original Issue Discount (OID),* earlier.

Example. On September 1, 1991, you loaned $2,000 at 12% a year. The note stated that principal and interest would be due on August 31, 1993. In 1993, you received $2,480 ($2,000 principal and $480 interest). If you use the cash method, you must include in income on your 1993 return the $480 interest you received in 1993.

Constructive receipt. You constructively receive income when it is credited to your account or made available to you. You do not need to have physical possession of it. For example, you are considered to receive interest, dividends, or other earnings on any deposit or account in a bank, savings and loan, or similar financial institution, or interest on life insurance policy dividends left to accumulate, when they are credited to your account and subject to your withdrawal. This is true even if they are not yet entered in your passbook.

You constructively receive income on the deposit or account even if you must:

1) Make withdrawals in multiples of even amounts,
2) Give a notice to withdraw before making the withdrawal,
3) Withdraw all or part of the account to withdraw the earnings, or
4) Pay a penalty on early withdrawals, unless the interest you are to receive on an early withdrawal or redemption is substantially less than the interest payable at maturity.

You constructively receive interest when it is credited to your account under a long-term savings plan that does not let you withdraw interest until a specified date, if the plan lets you freely withdraw your deposits of principal.

Accrual method. If you use an accrual method, you report your interest income when you earn it, whether or not you have received it.

Example. If, in the previous example, you use an accrual method, you must include the interest in your income as you earn it. You would report the interest as follows: 1991, $80; 1992, $240; and 1993, $160.

Coupon bonds. Interest on coupon bonds is taxable in the year the coupon becomes due and payable. It does not matter when you mail the coupon for payment.

How to Report Interest Income

Generally, you report all of your taxable interest income on line 8a, Form 1040; line 8a, Form 1040A; or line 3, Form 1040EZ.

You cannot use Form 1040EZ if any of the following are true.

1) Your interest income is more than $400.
2) You are excluding interest under the Education Savings Bond Program.
3) You received interest as a nominee (that is, in your name but the interest actually belongs to someone else).
4) You received a Form 1099–INT for U.S. Savings Bond interest that includes amounts you reported before 1993. (See *Interest from U.S. Savings Bonds,* later, for how to report this interest.)

Instead, you must complete the schedules for Form 1040A or Form 1040, as described later. In addition, you must use Form 1040 under certain circumstances described later.

Form 1099–INT. Your taxable interest income, except for interest from U.S. Savings Bonds and Treasury obligations, is shown in Box 1 of Form 1099–INT. Add this amount to any other taxable interest income you received.

If you had any tax-exempt interest income, or exempt-interest dividends from a mutual fund, you should report the total of this tax-exempt income on line 8b of Form 1040A or Form 1040. If you file Form 1040EZ, write "TEI" in the space to the right of the words "Form 1040EZ" on line 3. After "TEI," show the amount of your tax-exempt interest, but do not add tax-exempt interest in the total on Form 1040EZ, line 3.

If you forfeited interest income because of the early withdrawal of a time deposit, the deductible amount will be shown on Form 1099–INT in Box 2 (early withdrawal penalty). If an amount ap-

☐ CORRECTED (if checked)

PAYER'S name, street address, city, state, and ZIP code	Payer's RTN (optional)	OMB No. 1545-0112 **19**93 **Interest Income**

PAYER'S Federal identification number	RECIPIENT'S identification number	1 Interest income not included in box 3 $	**Copy B For Recipient**

RECIPIENT'S name

| 2 Early withdrawal penalty $ | 3 Interest on U.S. Savings Bonds and Treas. obligations $ |

Street address (including apt. no.)

4 Federal income tax withheld $

City, state, and ZIP code

5 Foreign tax paid | 6 Foreign country or U.S. possession

Account number (optional) $

This is important tax information and is being furnished to the Internal Revenue Service. If you are required to file a return, a negligence penalty or other sanction may be imposed on you if this income is taxable and the IRS determines that it has not been reported.

Form **1099-INT**   (Keep for your records.)   Department of the Treasury - Internal Revenue Service

pears in Box 2, you should file Form 1040 and report this amount on line 28 (penalty on early withdrawal of savings).

Box 3 of Form 1099–INT shows the amount of interest income you received from U.S. Savings Bonds, Treasury bills, Treasury notes, and Treasury bonds. Include the amount shown in Box 3 in your total taxable interest income, unless it includes an amount previously included in interest income. If you are redeeming U.S. Savings Bonds you bought after 1989 **and** you have qualified educational expenses, see *Form 8815,* later. If part of the amount shown in Box 3 was previously included in interest income, see *Interest from U.S. Savings Bonds,* next.

Box 4 of Form 1099–INT (federal income tax withheld) will contain an amount if you were subject to backup withholding. You may be subject to backup withholding if, for example, you did not furnish your social security number to a payer. Report the amount from Box 4 on Form 1040A, line 28a, or on Form 1040, line 54 (federal income tax withheld), and check the box.

If there are entries in Boxes 5 and 6 of Form 1099–INT, you must file Form 1040. Report the amount shown in Box 5 (foreign tax paid) on **Form 1116,** *Foreign Tax Credit,* unless you deduct this amount on Schedule A of Form 1040 as "Other taxes." For more information on the credit and deduction, see Publication 514, *Foreign Tax Credit for Individuals.*

TaxSaver

Whenever possible, it is better to claim a credit on Form 1116 rather than claiming a deduction on Schedule A, since a tax credit is a dollar-for-dollar reduction against your tax liability. Because of the complicated computations, however, you should consult your tax advisor.

Interest from U.S. Savings Bonds. If you received a Form 1099–INT for U.S. Savings Bond interest, the form may show interest you are not required to report. See *Form 1099–INT for U.S. Savings Bonds interest,* earlier, under *U.S. Savings Bonds.*

If you have qualified education expenses (as discussed earlier under *Education Savings Bond Program*), see *Form 8815,* later, for information on your interest exclusion.

You should show on line 1, Part I of Schedule B (Form 1040), or

on line 1, Part I of Schedule 1 (Form 1040A), all the interest shown on your Form 1099–INT.

If Form 1099–INT includes interest you previously reported, make the following adjustment. On Schedule B, several lines above line 2, enter a subtotal of all interest listed on line 1. If you use Form 1040A, enter this subtotal several lines above line 2, Part I of Schedule 1. Below the subtotal write "U.S. Savings Bond Interest Previously Reported," and enter amounts previously reported or interest accrued prior to receiving the bond. (To figure the amount to enter for interest reported or being reported as a taxable distribution from a retirement or profit-sharing plan, see *Interest from U.S. Savings Bonds* in Publication 550.) Subtract these amounts from the subtotal and enter the result on line 2 of Schedule B (Form 1040) or on line 2, Part I of Schedule 1 (Form 1040A).

Form 8815. Use Form 8815, *Exclusion of Interest From Series EE U.S. Savings Bonds Issued After 1989,* to figure your interest exclusion when you redeem bonds and pay qualified higher educational expenses during the same year.

For more information on the exclusion and qualified higher educational expenses, see the earlier discussion under *Education Savings Bond Program.*

You must show your total interest from Series EE Savings Bonds issued after 1989 on line 6 of Form 8815 and on line 1 of either Schedule 1 (Form 1040A) or Schedule B (Form 1040). After completing Form 8815, enter the result from line 14 (Form 8815) on line 3 of Schedule 1 (Form 1040A) or line 3 of Schedule B (Form 1040).

Form 1040A

You must complete Part I of Schedule 1 (Form 1040A), if you file Form 1040A and:

1) Your taxable interest income totals more than $400,
2) You are claiming the interest exclusion under the Education Savings Bond Program, or
3) You received, as a nominee, interest that actually belongs to someone else. (See *Nominee distributions (Form 1040A),* later, for how to report this interest.)

List each payer's name and the amount of interest income received from each payer. If you received a Form 1099–INT or Form 1099–

OID from a brokerage firm, list the brokerage firm as the payer. Attach Schedule 1 to your return.

However, you must use Form 1040 instead of Form 1040A if:

- You are reporting OID in an amount more or less than the amount shown on Form 1099–OID,
- You received or paid accrued interest on securities transferred between interest payment dates,
- You acquired taxable bonds after 1987 and choose to reduce interest income from the bonds by any amortizable bond premium (see *Bond Premium Amortization* in Publication 550), or
- You forfeited interest income because of the early withdrawal of a time deposit.

Reporting interest on seller-financed mortgage. If an individual buys his or her home from you in a sale that you finance, you must report the buyer's name, address, and social security number on line 1 of Schedule 1 (Form 1040A). If you do not, you may have to pay a $50 penalty. The buyer may have to pay a $50 penalty if he or she does not give you this information.

The buyer must report your name, address, and social security number (or employer identification number) on Schedule A (Form 1040). You must give this information to the buyer. If you do not, you may have to pay a $50 penalty.

Nominee distributions (Form 1040A). If the total interest income you list on line 1, Part I of Schedule 1 (Form 1040A), includes any amount that you received as a nominee for the real owner, show that amount separately below a subtotal of all interest income listed. Identify the amount as "Nominee Distribution," and subtract it from the interest income subtotal. Report the result on line 2, Part I of Schedule 1.

For more information, see *Nominee distributions and accrued interest* later under *Form 1040.*

Tax-exempt interest income (Form 1040A). If you received any tax-exempt interest, such as from state or local governmental obligations, do not include this income on line 8a. Instead, enter your tax-exempt interest on line 8b. Also include on line 8b any exempt-interest dividends received from a mutual fund or other regulated investment company.

Interest earned on an individual retirement arrangement (IRA) is tax deferred rather than tax exempt. Do not include such amount in tax-exempt interest.

If you are completing Part I of Schedule 1, include the tax-exempt interest on line 1 only if you received a Form 1099-INT for that interest. Several lines above line 2, put a subtotal of all interest income. Below this subtotal, write "Tax-Exempt Interest," and show the amount of this interest. Subtract this amount from the subtotal, and write the result on line 2 of Part I. Be sure to show the tax-exempt interest on line 8b.

If you redeemed Series EE U.S. Savings Bonds and you have qualified educational expenses, complete and attach Form 8815. Enter the result from line 14 of Form 8815 on line 3 of Schedule 1. Subtract the amount on line 3 from the amount on line 2. Enter the result on line 4 of Schedule 1 and on line 8a of Form 1040A. See *Education Savings Bond Program* and *Form 8815* earlier for more information.

Frozen deposits (Form 1040A). Even if you receive a Form 1099-INT for interest on deposits that you could not withdraw at the end of 1993, you must exclude these amounts from your gross income, as explained earlier under *General Information.* Do not include this income on line 8a. If you are completing Part I of Schedule 1, include on line 1 the interest shown on Form 1099-INT. Several lines above line 2, put a subtotal of all interest income. Below this subtotal, write "Frozen Deposits," and show the amount

of interest that you are excluding. Subtract this amount from the subtotal and write the result on line 2 of Part I.

Form 1040

You must complete Schedule B of Form 1040 if any of the following are true.

1) Your taxable interest income is more than $400.
2) You are claiming the interest exclusion under the Education Savings Bond Program.
3) You received a Form 1099–INT for tax-exempt interest. (See *Tax-exempt interest income (Form 1040),* later, for how to report this interest.)
4) You received, as a nominee, interest that actually belongs to someone else. (See *Nominee distributions and accrued interest (Form 1040),* later, for how to report this interest.)
5) You received a Form 1099–INT for interest on a bond that you bought between interest payment dates. (See *Nominee distributions and accrued interest (Form 1040),* later, for how to report this interest.)
6) You are reporting OID in an amount more or less than the amount shown on Form 1099–OID. (See *Original issue discount (OID),* later, for how to report your OID.)
7) You choose to reduce your interest income from a bond by the amount of amortizable bond premium. (For more information about this choice, see *Bond Premium Amortization* in Publication 550.)

On Schedule B, list each payer's name and the amount received from each.

First, report on line 1, Part I of Schedule B, any interest income from seller-financed mortgages. (For more information about reporting this income, see *Reporting interest on seller-financed mortgage,* next.)

Next, report on line 1, Part I of Schedule B (Form 1040), all other taxable interest you received. Include the total amount of interest income that is shown in Box 1 and Box 3 of any Form 1099–INT or in Box 1 and Box 2 of any Form 1099–OID that you receive for the tax year, and other interest income received for which you did not receive a Form 1099. List each payer's name and the amount of interest received from each. If you received a Form 1099–INT or Form 1099–OID from a brokerage firm, list the brokerage firm as the payer. If you received more than $400 in taxable interest, you must also complete Part III of Schedule B (Form 1040). See *Foreign financial accounts and foreign trusts,* discussed in Chapter 1.

If you redeemed Series EE U.S. Savings Bonds and you have qualified educational expenses, complete and attach Form 8815. Enter the result from line 14 of Form 8815 on line 3 of Schedule B. See *Education Savings Bond Program* and *Form 8815* earlier for more information.

Reporting interest on seller-financed mortgage. If an individual buys his or her home from you in a sale that you finance, you must report the buyer's name, address, and social security number on line 1 of Schedule B (Form 1040). If you do not, you may have to pay a $50 penalty. The buyer may have to pay a $50 penalty if he or she does not give you this information.

The buyer must report your name, address, and social security number (or employer identification number) on Schedule A (Form 1040). You must give this information to the buyer. If you do not, you may have to pay a $50 penalty.

Tax-exempt interest income (Form 1040). If you received any tax-exempt interest income (such as interest on certain state and municipal bonds), you must report the total amount of that interest on line 8b of Form 1040. Also report on line 8b any exempt-interest dividends that you received from a mutual fund or other regulated investment company. Do not include this interest in your taxable interest income on line 8a.

If you are completing Part I of Schedule B (Form 1040), report tax-exempt interest on line 1 only if you received a Form 1099–INT for that interest. Several lines above line 2, put a subtotal of all interest income listed on line 1. Below this subtotal, write "Tax-Exempt Interest," and show the amount of interest that you are excluding. Subtract this amount from the subtotal and enter the result on line 2. Be sure to also show the tax-exempt interest on Form 1040, line 8b.

Interest earned on an individual retirement arrangement (IRA) is tax deferred rather than tax exempt. Do not include such amount in tax-exempt interest.

Frozen deposits (Form 1040). Even if you receive a Form 1099–INT for interest on deposits that you could not withdraw at the end of 1993, you must exclude these amounts from your gross income, as explained earlier under *General Information.* Do not include this income on line 8a. If you are completing Part I of Schedule B, include the full amount of interest shown on your Form 1099–INT on line 1. Several lines above line 2, put a subtotal of all interest income. Below this subtotal, write "Frozen Deposits," and show the amount of interest that you are excluding. Subtract this amount from the subtotal and write the result on line 2, Part I of Schedule B.

Nominee distributions and accrued interest (Form 1040). If the total interest income you list on line 1, Part I of Schedule B, includes any amount that you received as a nominee for the real owner or that reflects accrued interest paid on a bond that you bought between interest payment dates, show that amount separately below a subtotal of all interest income listed. Identify the amount as "Nominee Distribution," or "Accrued Interest," as appropriate, and subtract it from the interest income subtotal. Report the result on line 2, Part I of Schedule B.

Interest on a joint account. If you receive a Form 1099–INT which shows your taxpayer identification number and names two or more recipients or includes amounts belonging to another person, you must file a Form 1099–INT with the IRS to show the proper distributions of the amounts shown. Complete a Form 1099–INT and **Form 1096,** *Annual Summary and Transmittal of U.S. Information Returns,* and file both forms with your Internal Revenue Service Center. Give the other person(s) Copy B of the Form 1099–INT which you filed as a nominee. On Form 1099–INT and Form 1096, you should be listed as the "Payer." Prepare one Form 1099–INT for each other owner and show that person as the "Recipient." You are not required, however, to file Form 1099–INT to show payments for your spouse. For more information about the reporting requirements and the penalties for failure to file (or furnish) certain information returns, see *1993 Instructions for Forms 1099, 1098, 5498, and W–2G.*

Example. You receive a Form 1099–INT for 1993 that shows a total of $1,500 of interest income earned on a savings account that you hold jointly with your sister. You each have agreed to share the yearly interest income in proportion to the amount that each of you has invested, even though your identification (social security) number was submitted to the bank for its recordkeeping purposes. Your sister has deposited 30% of the amount invested in this account. As a result, you received as a nominee the amount of interest income belonging to your sister. For 1993, this amount is $450, or 30% of the total interest of $1,500.

You must provide your sister with a Form 1099–INT no later than January 31, 1994, showing $450 of interest income that she earned for 1993. You must also send a copy of the nominee Form 1099–INT, along with Form 1096, to the Internal Revenue Service Center no later than February 28, 1994. Show your own name, address, and identification number as the "Payer" on the Form 1099–INT. Provide the same information for your sister in the blocks provided for identification of the "Recipient."

When you prepare your own 1993 federal income tax return, report the total amount of interest income, $1,500, on line 1, Part I of Schedule B (Form 1040), and identify the name of the bank which paid this interest. Show the amount belonging to your sister, $450, as a subtraction from the subtotal of all interest on Schedule B and identify this subtraction as a "Nominee Distribution." (Your sister will report the $450 of interest income on her own tax return, if she is required to file a return, and identify you as the payer of that amount.)

Original issue discount (OID). If you are reporting OID in an amount greater or less than the amount shown on Form 1099–OID, or other written statement (such as for a REMIC regular interest), include the full amount of OID shown on your Form 1099–OID or other statement on line 1, Part I of Schedule B (Form 1040). If the OID to be reported is less than the amount shown on Form 1099–OID, follow the earlier reporting rules for nominee distributions or accrued interest, as applicable, so that you will report only the OID you are required to report. Below the subtotal, write "OID Adjustment," and show the OID you are not required to report. If the OID to be reported is greater than the amount shown on Form 1099–OID, show the additional OID separately below a subtotal of all interest income listed. Identify the amount as "OID Adjustment," and add it to the interest income subtotal.

Market discount. Report as interest any gain on the sale (or other disposition) of certain market discount bonds, to the extent of the accrued market discount. See *Market discount bonds,* under *Original Issue Discount (OID)* earlier.

Penalty on early withdrawal of savings. If you withdraw funds from a time savings account before maturity, you may be charged a penalty. You must report the gross amount of interest paid or credited to your account during the year, without subtracting the penalty. You deduct the penalty on line 28, Form 1040. Deduct the entire penalty even if it exceeds your interest income. The Form 1099–INT or similar statement given to you by the financial institution will show the gross amount of interest and the penalty.

Sample returns. The sample return in Chapter 44, *Sample Form 1040A,* has an example of reporting interest income on Form 1040A. The sample return in Chapter 45, *Sample Form 1040,* has an example of reporting interest income on Form 1040.

9 | Dividends and Other Corporate Distributions

Introduction

*Most people think they know what **dividends** are. The problem is that the term is popularly used to describe a large number of items that the **IRS** does not consider to be dividends. "Dividends" paid by an insurance company to its policyholders are considered by the IRS to be a return of premiums, not dividends. "Dividends" paid by a savings and loan association to its depositors are considered to be interest, not dividends. This chapter discusses only distributions from corporations (including **mutual funds**) made to an individual because he or she owns stock in that corporation.*

*Most dividends paid out by a corporation are taxable. The question is **how** they are taxed. Some are fully taxable. Others, like dividends paid in stock rather than cash, are not taxable except in certain circumstances.*

*Just because a dividend is paid in cash doesn't mean that it is taxable. Some cash distributions represent a partial return of purchase price. Also, cash is sometimes distributed with an otherwise nontaxable **stock dividend.** In both these cases and others, the IRS might perceive no income, some **ordinary income,** some **capital gain** income, or some combination of categories. This chapter helps sort out the intricacies of dividends and other corporate distributions.*

*This chapter also discusses dividend reinvestment plans that reinvest the dividends in the stock generating them. These plans are provided by companies for all their shareholders and should not be confused with retirement plans run by employers for the benefit of their **employees.***

Important Reminder

Dividends received in January. Any dividend declared by a regulated investment company (mutual fund) or real estate investment trust (REIT) in October, November, or December and payable to you in such a month, but actually paid during January of the following calendar year, is treated as paid to you in the earlier year.

This chapter discusses the tax treatment of:

- Dividend income,
- Capital gain distributions,
- Nontaxable distributions, and
- Other distributions you may receive from a corporation or a mutual fund.

This chapter also explains how to report dividend income on your tax return.

Dividends are distributions of money, stock, or other property paid to you by a corporation. You also may receive dividends through a partnership, an estate, a trust, or an association that is taxed as a corporation. However, some amounts you receive that are called dividends are actually interest income. See *Dividends that are actually interest* under *Taxable Interest* in Chapter 8.

Most distributions that you receive are paid in cash (or check). However, you may receive distributions such as additional stock, stock rights, other property, or services. These distributions are also discussed in this chapter.

Explanation
An interest-free loan or below-market-rate loan by a corporation to a stockholder may result in dividend income to the stockholder.

Useful Items

You may want to see:

Publication

☐ **514** Foreign Tax Credit for Individuals
☐ **550** Investment Income and Expenses
☐ **564** Mutual Fund Distributions
☐ **925** Passive Activity and At-Risk Rules

Form (and Instructions)

☐ **Schedule B (Form 1040)** Interest and Dividend Income
☐ **Schedule 1 (Form 1040A)** Interest and Dividend Income for Form 1040A Filers
☐ **1099** 1993 Instructions for Forms 1099, 1098, 5498, and W–2G

General Information

This section discusses general rules on dividend income.

Passive activity income and losses. There are tax rules which limit the amount of losses and tax credits from passive activities that you can claim. Generally, you can use losses from passive activities only to offset income from passive activities. You generally cannot use passive activity losses to offset your other income, such as your wages or your portfolio income. *Portfolio income* is any gross income from interest, dividends, etc., that is not derived in the ordinary course of a trade or business. For more information about determining and reporting income and losses from passive activities, see Publication 925.

Tax on investment income of a child under age 14. Part of a child's investment income may be taxed at the parent's tax rate. This may happen if the child is under age 14, has more than $1,200 of investment income (such as taxable interest and dividends), and either parent is alive at the end of the year. If these requirements are met, **Form 8615,** *Tax for Children Under Age 14 Who Have Investment Income of More Than $1,200,* must be completed and attached to the child's tax return. If these requirements are not met, Form 8615 is not required and the child's income is taxed at his or her own tax rate.

However, parents can choose to include their child's gross income on their return if certain requirements are met. Use **Form 8814,** *Parents' Election To Report Child's Interest and Dividends,* for this purpose.

Explanation

After 1988, you may elect to include your child's income on your return. For you to do so, your child must have unearned income between $500 and $5,000, consisting solely of interest and dividends. You should not make the election if estimated payments were made in your child's name or if your child is subject to backup withholding. (See explanation of backup withholding below.)

For more information about the tax on investment income of children and the parents' election, see Chapter 32, *Tax on Investment Income of Certain Minor Children.*

Beneficiary of an estate or trust. Interest, dividends, or other investment income you receive as a beneficiary of an estate or trust is generally taxable income. You should receive a **Schedule K–1** (Form 1041), *Beneficiary's Share of Income, Deductions, Credits, etc.,* from the fiduciary. Your copy of Schedule K–1 and its instructions will tell you where to report the items from Schedule K–1 on your Form 1040.

Backup withholding. To ensure that income tax is collected on dividends and other types of income that generally are not subject to withholding, backup withholding will apply in certain circumstances.

Under backup withholding, when you open a new account you must certify under penalties of perjury that your social security number is correct and that you are not subject to backup withholding. If you fail to make this certification, backup withholding may begin immediately on your new account or investment, and 31% of the amount paid on your account or investment will be withheld. Your payer will give you a **Form W–9,** *Request for Taxpayer Identification Number and Certification,* or a similar form, to make this certification. Backup withholding may also be required if the Internal Revenue Service (IRS) has determined that you underreported your interest or dividend income. For more information, see *Backup Withholding* in Chapter 5, *Tax Withholding and Estimated Tax.*

Form 1099–DIV. Most corporations use Form 1099–DIV, *Dividends and Distributions,* to show you the distributions you received from them during the year. Keep this form with your records. You do not have to attach it to your tax return. Even if you do not receive Form 1099–DIV, you must report all of your taxable dividend income.

Explanation

The Form 1099 that you receive must be examined carefully. If you receive a Form 1099–DIV, you have received dividends during the year on stock you own. If you receive a Form 1099–INT, you have received interest on a savings account, even though the description on the form may say "dividends."

Reporting tax withheld. If tax is withheld from your dividend income, the payer must give you a Form 1099–DIV that indicates the amount withheld.

Nominees. If someone receives distributions as a nominee for you, that person will give you a Form 1099–DIV, which will show distributions they received on your behalf.

Explanation

A nominee is someone who in his or her name and with his or her social security or federal identification number receives income that belongs to another person. Form 1099 is used by the nominee to report the amount and type of income to the owner.

You should cite the source of such income on your tax return as the nominee, not the original payer.

Example

Brokerage Firm A collects your dividend from XYZ Corporation and reports the income to you on Form 1099. You should show the dividend as being received from Brokerage Firm A, *not* from XYZ Corporation.

If you receive a Form 1099–DIV that includes amounts belonging to another person, see *Nominees,* later under *How to Report Dividend Income,* for more information.

Form 1099–MISC. Certain substitute payments in lieu of dividends or tax-exempt interest that are received by a broker on your behalf must be reported to you on Form 1099–MISC, *Miscellaneous Income,* or a similar statement. See *Reporting substitute payments* under *Short Sales* in Publication 550 for more information about reporting such substitute payments.

Incorrect amount. If you receive a Form 1099 that shows an incorrect amount (or other incorrect information), you should ask the issuer for a corrected form. The corrected Form 1099 you receive will be marked"CORRECTED."

Accuracy-related penalty. A 20% accuracy-related penalty can be charged for underpayments of tax due to negligence or disregard of rules and regulations or substantial understatement of tax. For more information on the penalty and any applicable interest, see *Penalties* in Chapter 1, *Filing Information.*

Explanation

Congress and the IRS are taking a hard line on failure to report income for which you receive (or know you should have received) a Form 1099. They assume you know you own stock or other assets and therefore should know there is some income to report, whether or not you receive the information from the payer. The negligence penalty will automatically be assessed, and you will have the almost impossible burden of persuading the IRS that you were not negligent.

TAXSAVER

Carefully compare your tax return with all your stocks, bonds, bank accounts, and other holdings to be sure you've accounted for everything. Then double-check your memory—penalties and interest can add up if you don't.

Social security number. You must give your name and social security number to any person required by federal tax law to make a return, statement, or other document that relates to you. This includes payers of dividends. If you are married and the funds in a joint account belong to you, you should give your social security number to the payer of the dividends. If the funds in the account belong to both you and your spouse, you may give either your number or your spouse's number. But the number you provide must correspond with the name listed first on the account. You must give the payer the correct social security number if the number being used is wrong.

Explanation

There are many technical problems if stock is jointly registered in two or more names. You should not assume that any income earned is earned jointly. Rather, in cases where no immediate gift transfer of the property is intended, the income should be reported by the owner. (See *Joint accounts,* Chapter 8, *Interest Income,* for a complete discussion of this matter.)

TAXPLANNER

Since only one Social Security number will be recorded by the corporation paying the dividend, the IRS's docu-

ment-matching program may issue deficiency notices when the income is split between two or more returns. This situation arises because the income tax return with the Social Security number shown on the company's records may not include the full amount of the dividend paid.

To reduce the chance of receiving an IRS deficiency notice, show both the full amount of the dividend paid and a subtraction for "amount attributable to others" on Schedule B (Form 1040) in the section used for reporting dividends.

The person who receives the other part of the dividend needn't worry. Although that person includes on his or her return an amount for which he or she does not receive a Form 1099–DIV, the IRS rarely questions returns when income in excess of that computed by the government is reported. (See the discussion regarding *nominees* later in this chapter and *Joint accounts* in Chapter 8, *Interest Income,* for a further discussion of this matter.)

Penalty. If you do not give your social security number to the payer of dividends, you may have to pay a penalty. See *Penalty for failure to supply social security number* under *Penalties* in Chapter 1, *Filing Information.* Backup withholding also may apply. See *Backup Withholding* in Chapter 5, *Tax Withholding and Estimated Tax.*

Dividends received in January. If a regulated investment company (mutual fund) or real estate investment trust (REIT) declares a dividend (including any exempt-interest dividend) in October, November, or December and that dividend is payable to you on a specified date in such month, you are considered to have received the dividend on December 31 even though the company or trust actually pays the dividend during January of the following calendar year. Therefore, you report the amount in the year of declaration.

Ordinary Dividends

Ordinary (taxable) dividends are the most common type of distribution from a corporation. They are paid out of the earnings and profits of a corporation and are ordinary income to you. You can assume that any dividend you receive, whether on common or preferred stock, is an ordinary dividend unless the paying corporation tells you otherwise.

Money market funds. Report amounts you receive from money market funds as dividend income. These amounts generally are not interest income and should not be reported as interest.

TAXPLANNER

Dividends paid from money market funds are reported as *dividends*—not interest—even though they represent income the money market fund received on certificates of deposit and other interest-bearing securities. These dividends *must* be shown in the dividend section of Schedule B (Form 1040). If they are not, you're likely to receive a notice from the IRS requesting an explanation.

However, dividends paid or credited by a mutual savings bank, building and loan association, or savings and

loan association are considered *interest*—not dividends—for income tax reporting purposes. The Form 1099 that you receive from these organizations generally instructs you on how to report the income.

Dividends on capital stock. Dividends on the capital stock of organizations, such as savings and loan associations, are ordinary dividends. They are not interest. You should report them with your dividend income.

Stock certificate in two or more names. If two or more persons, such as a husband and wife, hold stock as *joint tenants, tenants by the entirety, or tenants in common,* each person receives a share of any dividends from the stock. Each person's share is determined by local law.

Explanation

As indicated above and in the preceding chapter, each person receives a portion of the income as determined by his or her contribution to the purchase price and/or by the intention of the parties.

Dividends used to buy more stock. The corporation in which you own stock may have a *dividend reinvestment plan.* This plan lets you choose to use your dividends to buy more shares of stock in the corporation instead of receiving the dividends in cash. If you are a member of this type of plan and you use your dividends to buy more stock at a price equal to its fair market value, you must report the dividends as income.

If you are a member of a dividend reinvestment plan that lets you buy more stock at a price less than its fair market value, you must report as income the fair market value of the additional stock on the dividend payment date.

You also must report as income any service charge subtracted from your cash dividends before the dividends are used to buy the additional stock. But you may be able to deduct the service charge. See Chapter 30, *Miscellaneous Deductions,* for more information about deducting expenses of producing income.

In some dividend reinvestment plans, you can invest more cash to buy shares of stock at a price less than fair market value. If you choose to do this, you must report as income the difference between the cash you invest and the fair market value of the stock you buy. When figuring this amount, use the fair market value of the stock on the dividend payment date.

Explanation

Dividend reinvestment plans—even those in which employees may make voluntary contributions—should not be confused with retirement plans that invest in company stock. Dividend reinvestment plans are open to all stockholders. Dividends are immediately reinvested in the stock generating them.

Dividend reinvestment plans may cause confusion. For example, some plans permit you to reinvest in shares at a discount, usually about 5%. The amount of the dividend taxable to you and that must be reported includes the discount.

Example

Stock of Company X is selling for $10. You are entitled to $20 in dividends on the stock you hold. Since you are in a qualified dividend reinvestment plan that includes a 5% discount, your dividends will buy 2.105 shares of stock. You will report $21.05 of dividend income.

TaxPlanner 1

Unless you're very careful, you're likely to get an IRS deficiency notice when you take advantage of a dividend reinvestment plan if you hold the shares that are producing the dividends. Problems can occur if you receive two Forms 1099. One will report the dividends paid on shares you hold. The other Form 1099 will report the discount and the dividends paid on the shares held in the plan. Be sure to reconcile the amounts and report the correct total.

Any service charge paid on a dividend reinvestment plan may be taken as an **itemized deduction** on Schedule A of Form 1040 (subject to the 2% of adjusted gross income limitation explained in Chapter 30, *Miscellaneous Deductions*). You should not offset your dividend income with the service charge. If you do, you may receive a notice from the IRS.

TaxPlanner 2

When you sell shares acquired in a dividend reinvestment plan, you compute the gain or loss in the same fashion that you normally would by subtracting your cost from the proceeds of the sale. Usually your only record of the shares' cost is the annual statement issued by the administrator of the dividend reinvestment plan. It is imperative to keep these statements as a permanent part of your records. Most dividend reinvestment plans charge a fee for recreating records.

TaxSaver

Dividend reinvestment plans that permit you to invest at less than market price may be a very good deal. In effect, you earn a higher yield because you are receiving "extra" shares.

Public utility stock reinvestment plans. If you own stock in a qualified domestic public utility and chose to receive your dividends in common stock, rather than in cash, you must include in your gross income the total value of such stock dividends.

Pre-1986 stock dividend exclusion. If after 1981 and before 1986, you chose to receive your dividends from the public utility stock in the form of more stock, you could choose to exclude the value of the dividend from your income. You had to make this choice on your return for the year in which you would have included the dividends in income.

If you excluded the value of stock dividends from income, your basis in that stock is zero.

Capital Gain Distributions

These distributions or dividends are paid by *regulated investment companies, mutual funds, and real estate investment trusts.* A Form 1099–DIV or the mutual fund statement will tell you the amount you are to report as a capital gain distribution. Report capital gain distributions as long-term capital gains on your tax return regardless of how long you have owned the stock in the mutual fund. Those distributions that are not derived in the ordinary course of a trade or business are treated as portfolio income and are not considered as income from a passive activity (see *Passive activity income and losses,* earlier).

Undistributed capital gains. In addition to the amounts you receive, you must report as long-term capital gains any amounts that the investment company or mutual fund credited to you as capital gain distributions, even though you did not actually receive them. (This income is not reported to you on Form 1099–DIV.)

Form 2439. You can take a credit on your return for any tax that the investment company or mutual fund has paid for you on the undistributed capital gains. The company or fund will send you Form 2439, *Notice to Shareholder of Undistributed Long-Term Capital Gains,* showing the amount of the undistributed long-term capital gain and the tax that was paid. Take this credit by entering the amount of tax paid and checking box a on line 59, Form 1040. Attach Copy B of Form 2439 to your return.

Basis adjustment. Increase your basis in the stock by the difference between the amount of undistributed capital gain that you report and the amount of the tax paid for you by the fund. Keep Copy C of Form 2439 as part of your records to show increases in the basis of your stock.

Explanation

An investment company or mutual fund may elect to treat some or all of the capital gain it incurs during the year as distributed to its shareholders in proportion to their stockholdings, even though no cash is distributed. The stockholders are then able to claim as a credit, on a proportional basis, the amount of tax paid by the corporation on that capital gain. In addition, each stockholder increases his or her basis in the stock.

Example

ABC Mutual Fund elects to treat all of its 1993 capital gain as an undistributed capital gain. *The shareholders receive no cash distribution.* Each shareholder reports his or her share of capital gain and tax paid on his or her behalf by ABC Mutual Fund. These amounts are shown on the Form 2439 that each shareholder receives.

If your share of the capital gain is $1,200 and your share of the tax is $408, the $1,200 is included as capital gain income and the $408 is claimed as a credit on your individual return. Increase your basis in the stock by $792, the net amount not distributed to you.

Note. You must report any undistributed long-term gains shown on Form 2439 in addition to any capital gain distributions reported on Form 1099–DIV.

Real estate investment trusts (REITs). You will receive a Form 1099–DIV or similar statement from the REIT showing the capital gain distributions you must include in your income. You report the capital gain distributions as long-term capital gain regardless of how long you owned stock in the REIT.

Additional information. For more information on the treatment of distributions from mutual funds and regulated investment companies, see Publication 564, *Mutual Fund Distributions.*

Nontaxable Distributions

You may receive a return of capital or a tax-free distribution of more shares of stock or stock rights. These distributions are not treated the same as ordinary dividends or capital gain distributions.

Return of Capital

A return of capital is a distribution that is not paid out of the earnings and profits of a corporation. It is a return of your investment in the stock of the company. You should receive a Form 1099–DIV or other statement from the corporation showing you what part of the distribution is a return of capital. If you do not receive such a statement, you report the distribution as an ordinary dividend.

Basis adjustment. A return of capital reduces the basis of your stock and is not taxed until your basis in the stock is fully recovered. If you buy stock in a corporation in different lots at different times, reduce the basis of your earliest purchases first.

When the basis of your stock has been reduced to zero, report any return of capital that you receive as a capital gain. Whether you report it as a long-term or short-term capital gain depends on how long you have held the stock. See *Holding Period* in Chapter 15, *Sale of Property.*

Example. You bought stock in 1986 for $100. In 1988, you received a return of capital of $80. You did not include this amount in your income, but you reduced the basis of your stock. Your stock now has an adjusted basis of $20. You receive a return of capital of $30 in 1993. You use $20 of this amount to reduce your basis to zero. You report the other $10 as a long-term capital gain for 1993. You must report as a long-term capital gain any return of capital you receive on this stock in later years.

TaxOrganizer

It is extremely important to keep accurate records of nontaxable dividends. Most people do not realize that a nontaxable dividend is usually considered a return of purchase price and then a capital gain once your cost has been recovered. Keep in mind that even nontaxable dividends become subject to tax at some point.

Liquidating distributions. Liquidating distributions, sometimes called liquidating dividends, are distributions you receive during a partial or complete liquidation of a corporation. These distributions are, at least in part, one form of a return of capital. They may be paid in one or more installments. You will receive a Form 1099–DIV from the corporation showing you the amount of the liquidating distribution.

Any liquidating distribution you receive is not taxable to you until you have recovered the basis of your stock. After the basis of your stock has been reduced to zero, you must report the liquidating distribution as a capital gain (except in certain instances with regard to collapsible corporations). Whether you report the gain as a long-term or short-term capital gain depends on how long you have held the stock. See *Holding Period* in Chapter 15.

Stock acquired at different times. If you acquired stock in the same corporation in more than one transaction, you own more than one block of stock in the corporation. If you receive distributions from the corporation in complete liquidation, you must divide the distribution among the blocks of stock you own in the following proportion: the number of shares in that block over the total number of shares you own. Divide distributions in partial liquidation among that part of the stock that is redeemed in the partial liquidation. After the basis of a block of stock is reduced to zero, you must report the part of any later distribution for that block as a capital gain.

Distributions less than basis. If the total liquidating distributions you receive are less than the basis of your stock, you may have a capital loss. You can report a capital loss only after you have received the final distribution in liquidation that results in the redemption or cancellation of the stock. Whether you report the loss as a long-term or short-term capital loss depends on how long you held the stock. See *Holding Period* in Chapter 15, *Sale of Property.*

Example 1
You own stock in XYZ Corporation with a basis of $100. You received liquidating distributions of $60 in 1991, $50 in 1992, and $40 in 1993. You reported no gain in 1991, a gain of $10 in 1992, and a gain of $40 in 1993.

Example 2
You own stock in XYZ Corporation with a basis of $100. You received liquidating distributions of $90: $60 in 1992 and $30 in 1993. You reported the $10 loss in 1993.

Distributions of Stock and Stock Rights

Distributions by a corporation of its own stock are commonly known as stock dividends. Stock rights (also known as "stock options") are distributions by a corporation of rights to subscribe to the corporation's stock. Generally, stock dividends and stock rights are not taxable to you, and you do not report them on your return.

Taxable stock dividends and stock rights. Distributions of stock dividends and stock rights are taxable to you if:

1) You or any other shareholder has the choice to receive cash or other property instead of stock or stock rights,
2) The distribution gives cash or other property to some shareholders and an increase in the percentage interest in the corporation's assets or earnings and profits to other shareholders,
3) The distribution is in convertible preferred stock and has the same result as in (2),
4) The distribution gives preferred stock to some common stock shareholders and gives common stock to other common stock shareholders, or
5) The distribution is on preferred stock. (This requirement, however, does not apply if the distribution is made on convertible preferred stock solely to take into account a stock dividend, stock split, or a similar event that would otherwise result in reducing the conversion right.)

In addition, any transaction having the effect of increasing your proportionate interest in the corporation's assets or earnings and profits may be taxable to you, even though no stock or stock rights are actually distributed.

Explanation
A number of transactions have the effect of increasing your proportionate interest in a corporation—for exam-

ple, a change in the conversion ratio on certain classes of stock or a change in the redemption price of certain securities. If such a transaction occurs, you will be informed by the corporation.

The term "stock" includes rights to acquire such stock, and the term "shareholder" includes a holder of rights or of convertible securities.

Basis. If you receive taxable stock dividends or stock rights, include their fair market value at the time of the distribution in your income. This amount is your basis in the stock or stock rights received. If you receive stock dividends or stock rights that are not taxable to you, see *Stocks and Bonds* under *Basis of Investment Property* in Chapter 4 of Publication 550 for information on how to figure their basis.

Fractional shares. You may not own enough stock in a corporation to receive a full share of stock if the corporation declares a stock dividend. However, with the approval of the shareholders, the corporation may set up a plan in which no fractional shares are issued, but are sold, and the cash proceeds are given to the shareholders. Any cash you receive for fractional shares under such a plan is treated as an amount realized on the sale of the fractional shares. You must determine your gain or loss and report it as a capital gain or loss on Schedule D (Form 1040). Your gain or loss is the difference between the cash you receive and the basis of the fractional shares sold.

Example. You own one share of common stock that you bought on January 3, 1990, for $100. The corporation declared a common stock dividend of 5% on June 30, 1993. The fair market value of your stock at the time the stock dividend was declared was $200. You were paid $10 for the fractional-share stock dividend under a plan described in the above paragraph. You figure your gain or loss as follows:

Fair market value of old stock	$200.00
Fair market value of stock dividend (cash received)	10.00
Fair market value of old stock and stock dividend	$210.00
Basis (cost) of old stock after the stock dividend	
(($200 ÷ $210) × $100)	$ 95.24
Basis (cost) of stock dividend	
(($10 ÷ $210) × $100)	4.76
Total	$100.00
Cash received	$ 10.00
Basis (cost) of stock dividend	4.76
Gain	$ 5.24

Because you had held the share of stock more than one year at the time the stock dividend was declared, your gain on the stock dividend is a long-term capital gain.

Explanation
It is *not* true that all amounts received with regard to fractional shares are treated as capital gains, as described in the IRS text.

If a company declares a dividend in full shares only and makes a cash payment in lieu of the fractional share to which a stockholder is entitled, the amount received in cash is dividend income, which is taxed as ordinary income.

Generally, a company tells you what kind of payment you have received. If you receive "cash in lieu of a fractional share," the payment is taxable as a dividend. If you receive "cash paid for a fractional share," the payment is a capital gain or loss, as discussed in the IRS text.

Other Distributions

You may receive any of the following distributions during the year.

Exempt-interest dividends. Exempt-interest dividends you receive from a regulated investment company (mutual fund) are not included in your taxable income. (However, see *Information reporting requirement,* next.) You will receive a notice from the mutual fund telling you the amount of the exempt-interest dividends you received. Exempt-interest dividends are not shown on Form 1099–DIV or Form 1099–INT. See *Gains and Losses* in Publication 564 for information about the loss treatment of mutual fund stock on which you received exempt-interest dividends.

Information reporting requirement. Although these dividends are not taxable, you must show them on your tax return if you are required to file. This is an information-reporting requirement and does not convert exempt-interest dividends to taxable income. See *How to Report Interest Income* in Chapter 8, *Interest Income.*

Also, exempt-interest dividends may be treated as tax-exempt interest from private activity bonds, which is a "tax preference item" that may be subject to the alternative minimum tax. See *Alternative Minimum Tax* in Chapter 31, *How to Figure Your Tax,* for more information.

Dividends on insurance policies. Dividends you receive on insurance policies are a partial return of the premiums you paid. Do not include them in your gross income until they are more than the total of all net premiums you paid for the contract. However, you must report as taxable income the interest paid or credited on dividends that are left with an insurance company. See Chapter 8, *Interest Income,* for treatment of interest income.

Dividends on veterans' insurance. Dividends you receive on veterans' insurance policies are not taxable. In addition, do ***not*** report as taxable income interest on dividends left with the Department of Veterans Affairs. See *Veterans* in Chapter 6, *Wages, Salaries, and Other Earnings,* for more information about veterans' benefits.

Patronage dividends. Patronage dividends you receive in money from a cooperative organization are generally included in your income.

Do not include in your income patronage dividends you receive on:

1) Property bought for your personal use, or
2) Capital assets or depreciable property bought for use in your business. But you must reduce the basis (cost) of the items bought. If the dividend is more than the adjusted basis of the assets, you must report the excess as income.

These rules are the same whether the cooperative paying the dividend is a taxable or tax-exempt cooperative.

Explanation

Patronage dividends are amounts paid by a cooperative organization to one of its patrons (1) on the basis of the quantity or quality of business done with the patron, (2) pursuant to a written obligation in existence before the cooperative received the amounts paid into it by the patron, and (3) determined by reference to net earnings. In other words, patronage dividends amount to a return of some of the amounts a patron spent with a cooperative. Patronage dividends usually occur with farm cooperatives. Any "refund" or "discount" to the patron is income.

However, if the purchase leading to receipt of the dividend was neither deductible nor considered a capital expense, the dividend really amounts to a discount or a rebate, which is not considered income.

Alaska Permanent Fund Dividends. Do not report these amounts as dividends. Instead, report these amounts on line 22 of Form 1040.

How to Report Dividend Income

Generally, you can use either Form 1040 or Form 1040A to report your dividend income. However, you must use Form 1040 if you receive capital gain distributions or return of capital distributions. You cannot use Form 1040EZ if you receive any dividend income.

Form 1099–DIV. If you owned stock on which you received more than $10 in gross dividends and other distributions, you should receive a Form 1099–DIV.

Box 1a of Form 1099–DIV shows the amount of gross dividends and other distributions you received on stock. Box 1a is the total of boxes 1b, 1c, 1d, and 1e.

Box 1b of Form 1099–DIV shows your ordinary dividends. This amount is included in box 1a. If you do not need to file Schedule B (Form 1040), or Schedule 1 (Form 1040A), add together the amounts shown in boxes 1b and 1e and enter the total on line 9 (Form 1040 or Form 1040A). Also see the paragraph later about box 1e.

Box 1c of Form 1099–DIV shows your capital gain distributions. You report these capital gains on line 5 of Schedule B (Form 1040). You cannot file Form 1040A. Since these capital gains are included in the amount shown in box 1a of Form 1099–DIV, you enter them on line 5 of Schedule B. Then you subtract them out on line 7 of Schedule B. You must also report these capital gains on line 14, Part II of Schedule D (Form 1040). However, if you do not need to complete Schedule D for any other capital transactions, report them directly on line 14 of Form 1040.

Box 1d of Form 1099–DIV shows your nontaxable distributions. Since this amount is included in the amount shown in box 1a of Form 1099–DIV, you enter it on line 5 of Schedule B (Form 1040). You then subtract it out on line 8 of Schedule B. Amounts shown in box 1d are usually a return of capital that reduces your basis in the stock. Once you have received an amount equal to your cost or other basis, these distributions are taxable to you as a capital gain even if the payer lists them as nontaxable.

If you own stock in a nonpublicly-offered regulated investment company, your pro rata share of that fund's allocable investment expenses is shown in box 1e of Form 1099–DIV. This amount is also included in box 1a of Form 1099–DIV. You must include this amount as income on your tax return. You can deduct these expenses as a miscellaneous itemized deduction subject to the 2% of

☐ CORRECTED (if checked)

PAYER'S name, street address, city, state, and ZIP code	**1a** Gross dividends and other distributions on stock (Total of 1b, 1c, 1d, and 1e) $	OMB No. 1545-0110 **1993**	**Dividends and Distributions**
	1b Ordinary dividends $		

PAYER'S Federal identification number	RECIPIENT'S identification number	**1c** Capital gain distributions $	**2** Federal income tax withheld $	**Copy B For Recipient**
RECIPIENT'S name		**1d** Nontaxable distributions $	**3** Foreign tax paid $	This is important tax information and is being furnished to the Internal Revenue Service. If you are required to file a return, a negligence penalty or other sanction may be imposed on you if this income is taxable and the IRS determines that it has not been reported.
Street address (including apt. no.)		**1e** Investment expenses $	**4** Foreign country or U.S. possession	
City, state, and ZIP code		**Liquidation Distributions**		
Account number (optional)		**5** Cash $	**6** Noncash (Fair market value) $	

Form **1099-DIV**   (Keep for your records.)   Department of the Treasury - Internal Revenue Service

adjusted gross income limit only if you itemize your deductions on Schedule A (Form 1040).

Box 2 of Form 1099–DIV shows the amount of "Federal income tax withheld" if you were subject to backup withholding. You may be subject to backup withholding if, for example, you failed to furnish your social security number to a payer. Report this amount on Form 1040A, line 28a, or on Form 1040, line 54, and check the box.

Box 3 of Form 1099–DIV shows the amount of foreign taxes withheld (paid) on dividends and other distributions, and box 4 identifies the foreign country or U.S. possession that did the withholding. If there are entries in these boxes, fill out Form 1040 and **Form 1116**, *Foreign Tax Credit*. However, do not complete Form 1116 if you claim this amount as "Other taxes" on Schedule A. For more information on the credit and deduction, see Publication 514, *Foreign Tax Credit for Individuals*.

Box 5 of Form 1099–DIV shows distributions of cash from corporations in partial or complete liquidation. Box 6 shows the fair market value of noncash distributions. If there are entries in these boxes, see *Liquidating distributions* under *Dividends and Other Corporate Distributions* in Publication 550.

Dividends received on restricted stock. Restricted stock is stock that you get from your employer for services you perform and that is nontransferable and subject to a substantial risk of forfeiture. You do not have to include the value of the stock in your income when you receive it. However, if you get dividends on the restricted stock, you must include them in your income as wages, not dividends.

Your employer should include these dividends in the wages shown on your Form W–2. If you also get a Form 1099–DIV for these dividends, list them on line 5, Part II of Schedule B (Form 1040), with any other dividends you received. Enter a subtotal of all your dividend income several lines above line 6. Below the subtotal, write "Dividends on restricted stock reported as wages on line 7, Form 1040," and enter the amount of the dividends included in your wages on line 7, Form 1040. Subtract this amount from the subtotal and enter the result on line 6, Part II of Schedule B.

Election. You can choose to include in gross income the value of restricted stock as compensation for services. If you make this choice, the dividends are treated as any other dividends.

If you receive both a Form 1099–DIV and a Form W–2 showing these dividends, do not include the dividends in your wages reported on line 7, Form 1040. List the dividends on line 5, Part II of Schedule B, along with your other dividends (if the amount of dividends received from all sources is more than $400). Attach a statement to your Form 1040 explaining why the amount shown on line 7 of your Form 1040 is different from the amount shown on your Form W–2.

Dividends on stock sold. If stock is sold, exchanged, or otherwise disposed of after a dividend is declared, but before it is paid, the owner of record (usually the payee shown on the dividend check) must report the dividend. Even if the purchase price of the stock goes up because of the amount of the anticipated dividend, the owner of record must report such dividend.

dividend income on Schedule B (Form 1040). If the repayment is greater than $3,000, however, you may save taxes by recomputing your tax for the prior year. Consult your tax advisor.

Stock sold short. If you borrow stock to make a short sale, you may have to pay the lender an amount to replace the dividends distributed while you maintain your short position. Your treatment of the payment depends on the kind of distribution for which you are reimbursing the lender of the stock.

If your payment is made for a liquidating distribution or nontaxable stock distribution, or if you buy more shares equal to a stock distribution issued on the borrowed stock during your short position, you have a capital expense. You must add the payment to the cost of the stock sold short. See *Short Sales* in Publication 550 for more information about the tax treatment of short sales.

Example

Ben feels that the market value of XYZ Corporation stock is going to decline, so he sells XYZ stock to Sally. However, Ben does not hold any XYZ stock, so to effect the transaction, Ben's broker borrows XYZ stock from another customer, Robert, to deliver to Sally. Sally is now the stockholder of record.

XYZ Corporation will pay any and all dividends on this stock directly to Sally. However, Robert is entitled to the money, since he merely lent his shares to Ben. Ben, not XYZ Corporation, will pay Robert the amount of the dividend. Ben may deduct the payment as an itemized deduction on Schedule A if he borrows the stock for more than 45 days and has not diminished his risk of loss by, for example, holding an option to buy substantially similar stock. Robert enters that amount on page 1 (Form 1040) as income from Ben.

If Ben returns the stock within 45 days, he will not be able to claim a deduction. The amount paid to Robert increases the basis of the stock sold.

Expenses related to dividend income. You may deduct expenses related to dividend income only if you itemize your deductions on Schedule A (Form 1040). See Chapter 30, *Miscellaneous Deductions,* for general information about deducting expenses of producing income.

Explanation

Expenses that may be deducted include custody fees, investment advisory fees, depositary fees (which are usually applicable to foreign dividends), and service charges relating to dividend income. A more complete discussion of these items appears in Chapter 30, *Miscellaneous Deductions*.

Form 1040A

Report your total dividends on line 9, Form 1040A. You also must list each payer's name and the amount of dividends received from each payer in Part II of Schedule 1 (Form 1040A) and attach it to your Form 1040A, if:

1) The amount on line 9 is more than $400, or
2) You received, as a nominee, dividends that actually belong to someone else. (See *Nominees (Form 1040A),* next, for how to report these dividends.)

If you received a Form 1099–DIV from a brokerage firm, list the brokerage firm as the payer. However, you must use Form 1040 instead of Form 1040A if you had capital gain distributions or return of capital distributions.

Exempt-interest dividends, which are treated as interest, should be reported on line 8b. See *How to Report Interest Income* in Chapter 8, *Interest Income*.

Nominees (Form 1040A). If you received dividends as a nominee (that is, the dividends are in your name but actually belong to someone else), include them on line 5 of Schedule 1. Several lines above line 6, put a subtotal of all dividend income listed on line 5. Below this subtotal, write "Nominee Distribution" and show the amounts received as a nominee. Subtract the total of your nominee distributions from the subtotal. Enter the result on line 6 of Part II.

See *Nominees (Form 1040),* later, for more information.

Form 1040—Total Dividends of $400 or Less

Report only the total of your ordinary dividends from box 1b of Form 1099–DIV and any investment expenses from box 1e of Form 1099–DIV on line 9, Form 1040, if:

1) Your total dividends, including capital gain and nontaxable distributions, are $400 or less, and
2) You did not receive, as a nominee, dividends that actually belong to someone else.

Explanation

Even if your dividends are less than $400, you must report them and, to the extent that they are not excluded, pay tax on them.

Capital gain distributions. Report capital gain distributions (box 1c of Form 1099–DIV) on line 14, Part II of Schedule D (Form 1040). If you do not need Schedule D to report any other capital gains or losses, enter your capital gain distributions on line 14, Form 1040.

Note: Report your capital gain distributions on Schedule D and use the *Schedule D Tax Worksheet* to figure your tax if your taxable income (Form 1040, line 37) is more than: $89,150 if married filing jointly or qualifying widow(er); $53,500 if single; $76,400 if head of household; or $44,575 if married filing separately.

Nontaxable (return of capital) distributions. Some distributions are nontaxable because they are a return of your cost. You report return of capital distributions (box 1d of Form 1099–DIV) as a capital gain only when your basis in the stock has been reduced to zero. If the basis of your stock is zero, report any return of capital distributions you receive on line 1, Part I of Schedule D, if you held the stock one year or less. Report them on line 9, Part II of Schedule D, if you held the stock for more than one year.

Explanation

It is not true that a return of capital distribution is reported only after the basis of the stock has been reduced to zero, since, as seen below, all such distributions are reported on Schedule B (Form 1040). The IRS's comment means only that no reporting on Schedule D (Capital Gains and Losses) is required unless your tax basis has been reduced to zero.

Form 1040—Total Dividends of More Than $400

You must fill in Part II of Schedule B and attach it to your return, if:

1) Your total dividends, including capital gain and nontaxable distributions, are more than $400, or
2) You received, as a nominee, dividends that actually belong to someone else. (See *Nominees (Form 1040),* later, for how to report these dividends.)

If your total dividends are more than $400, you must also complete Part III of Schedule B.

You must report all of your dividend income (box 1a of Form 1099–DIV) on line 5, Part II of Schedule B. You must include on this line all the ordinary dividends, capital gain distributions, and return of capital distributions you receive. You should list the name of the payer and the amount of income for each distribution you receive. If your securities are held by a brokerage firm (in "street name"), list the name of the brokerage firm that is shown on Form 1099–DIV as the payer. If your stock is held by a nominee who is the owner of record, and the nominee credits or pays you dividends on the stock, you should show the name of the nominee and the dividends you received or were credited for. You should enter on line 6 the total of the amounts listed on line 5. However, if you hold stock as a nominee, see *Nominees (Form 1040),* later.

TAXSAVER

Foreign dividends. Foreign governments often withhold tax on dividends from foreign corporations before you receive them. For example, if you are a stockholder in a Canadian company that declares a $100 dividend, you might receive only $85 because of a $15 Canadian withholding tax. Nevertheless, the $100 must be reported. The $15 of foreign taxes may be claimed either as a foreign tax credit using Form 1116 or as an itemized deduction on Schedule A (Form 1040). It's generally preferable to take the tax credit. For more on this subject, see Chapter 23, *Taxes You May Deduct.*

Capital gain distributions. You enter on line 7, Part II of Schedule B, any amount shown on line 5 that is a capital gain distribution. You also enter this amount on line 14, Part II of Schedule D (Form 1040). If you do not need to use Schedule D to report any other gains or losses, do not use it. Instead, show your capital gain distributions on line 14, Form 1040.

Note: Report your capital gain distributions on Schedule D and use the *Schedule D Tax Worksheet* to figure your tax if your taxable income (Form 1040, line 37) is more than: $89,150 if married

filing jointly or qualifying widow(er); $53,500 if single; $76,400 if head of household; or $44,575 if married filing separately.

Nontaxable (return of capital) distributions. You enter on line 8, Part II of Schedule B, any amount from line 5 that you received as a return of capital distribution. However, after the basis of your stock has been reduced to zero, you must also show this amount on line 1, Part I of Schedule D, if you held the stock one year or less. Show it on line 9, Part II of Schedule D, if you held the stock for more than one year.

Completing Schedule B. Add the amounts shown on lines 7 and 8, and enter the total on line 9. Subtract the amount on line 9 from the amount on line 6. The difference, if any, is your taxable ordinary dividends. Enter this amount on line 10, Part II of Schedule B, and on line 9, Form 1040. If you had over $400 of dividends, you must also complete Part III of Schedule B. See *Foreign financial accounts and foreign trusts* under *Additional Schedules* in Chapter 1, *Filing Information,* for more information.

Nominees (Form 1040). Include on line 5, Part II of Schedule B (Form 1040), all dividends you received. This includes dividends you received, as a nominee, that actually belong to another person (such as your child), even if you later distributed some or all of this income to others. Enter a subtotal of all your dividend income listed on line 5 several lines above line 6. Below the subtotal, write "Nominee Distribution," and show the amounts received as a nominee. Subtract these distributions from the subtotal, and enter the result on line 6.

If you receive a Form 1099–DIV on which your taxpayer identification number is shown, and two or more recipients are named, or amounts belonging to another person are included, you must file a Form 1099–DIV with the IRS to show the proper distributions of the amounts shown. Complete a **Form 1096,** *Annual Summary and Transmittal of U.S. Information Returns,* and file both forms with the Internal Revenue Service Center. Give the other person Copy B of the Form 1099–DIV that you filed as a nominee. On Form 1099–DIV and Form 1096, you should be listed as the "Payer." On Form 1099–DIV, the other owner should be listed as the "Recipient." You are not required, however, to file a Form 1099–DIV to show payments for your spouse. For more information about the reporting requirements and the penalties for failure to file (or furnish) certain information returns, see *1993 Instructions for Forms 1099, 1098, 5498, and W–2G.*

TAXPLANNER

The complexity of paperwork involved in serving as a nominee makes it clear that you should avoid doing so unless absolutely necessary. If you are a nominee and fail to file the appropriate returns, you could be penalized by the IRS.

Liquidating distributions. You will receive Form 1099–DIV from the corporation showing the amount of the liquidating distribution. Generally, this is treated as the sale or exchange of a capital asset and you should report it on Schedule D (Form 1040).

Sample returns. The sample return in Chapter 44, *Sample Form 1040A,* has an example of reporting dividend income on Form 1040A. The sample return in Chapter 45, *Sample Form 1040,* has an example of reporting dividend income on Form 1040.

10 | Rental Income and Expenses

Introduction

Rent is the income received for allowing another person to use property that you own. This income is customarily received in cash. If, in lieu of paying all or part of the rent in cash, a tenant provides you with certain services, the value of the services is rental income to you.

You may deduct any expenses directly incurred to repair or to maintain your rental property. However, certain other expenses may not be deducted in the year in which you pay for them; rather, they must be **capitalized** *and deducted over a period of years. You may also deduct any* **depreciation** *taken on your rental property. Depreciation is a noncash expense claimed in order to deduct each year a small part of what you originally paid for the property.*

For many, depreciation is a confusing subject. The methods by which you figure a property's depreciation to get your tax deduction generally bear little resemblance to a property's physical life. A car may be fully depreciated in 5 years for tax purposes, but, with a little luck, it will last far longer. Fully depreciated property may be depreciated again if it changes ownership. In many cases, there may be tax incentives for you to get rid of a piece of property, even though it is in the same physical shape as when you bought it.

There are a variety of methods by which you may depreciate property and calculate your tax deduction, and all are explained in this chapter. In 1981, Congress adopted the **Accelerated Cost Recovery System (ACRS).** *In some ways, ACRS narrowed a taxpayer's options, but, at the same time, it offered new opportunities for tax savings. Then, in 1986, Congress made some additional changes and adopted the* **Modified Accelerated Cost Recovery System (MACRS).** *This chapter delves into all the complexities of ACRS and MACRS and outlines strategies that will enable you to benefit from them.*

Typically, you will do better taking a current **deduction** *rather than capitalizing an expense and depreciating an item over time. But, since there are no hard and fast rules as to what must be considered a deductible expense and what must be capitalized, there are plenty of opportunities to be appropriately aggressive and save on your taxes. This chapter explains the rules and the opportunities for tax savings.*

If your deductions exceed your rental income, the amount of rental loss you can claim may be limited.

This chapter discusses rental income and expenses. It covers the following topics:

- Rental income
- Rental expenses
- Vacation homes and other dwelling units
- Depreciation
- Limits on rental losses
- How to report your rental income and expenses

If you sell or otherwise dispose of your rental property, see Publication 527, *Residential Rental Property.*

If you have a loss from damage to, or from theft of, rental property, see Chapter 26 of Publication 334, *Tax Guide for Small Business.*

If you rent out a condominium or a cooperative apartment, some special rules apply to you even though you receive the same tax treatment as other owners of rental property. See Publication 527 for more information.

Useful Items

You may want to see:

Publication

☐ **334**   Tax Guide for Small Business
☐ **527**   Residential Rental Property
☐ **534**   Depreciation
☐ **535**   Business Expenses
☐ **544**   Sales and Other Dispositions of Assets
☐ **909**   Alternative Minimum Tax for Individuals
☐ **925**   Passive Activity and At-Risk Rules
☐ **946**   How To Begin Depreciating Your Property

Form (and Instructions)

☐ **4562**   Depreciation and Amortization
☐ **8582**   Passive Activity Loss Limitations
☐ **Schedule E (Form 1040)**   Supplemental Income and Loss

Rental Income

Rental income is any payment you receive for the use or occupation of property.

You generally must include in your gross income all amounts you receive as rent.

In addition to amounts you receive as normal rent payments, there are other amounts that may be rental income.

Advance rent. Advance rent is any amount you receive before the period that it covers. Include advance rent in your rental income in the year you receive it regardless of the period covered or the method of accounting you use.

Example. You sign a 10–year lease to rent your property. In the first year, you receive $5,000 for the first year's rent and $5,000 as rent for the last year of the lease. You must include $10,000 in your income in the first year.

Explanation
Some taxpayers have attempted to circumvent the rule requiring advance rent to be included in current income by structuring the payment as a "loan." The courts have generally disallowed this technique. As a general rule, if such a loan is to be repaid out of future rental proceeds, the loan will probably be considered advance rent.

Security deposits. Do not include a security deposit in your income when you receive it if you plan to return it to your tenant at the end of the lease. But, if during any year, you keep part or all of the security deposit because your tenant does not live up to the terms of the lease, include the amount you keep in your income for that year.

If an amount called a security deposit is to be used as a final payment of rent, it is advance rent. Include it in your income when you receive it.

Explanation
Generally, when the landlord's obligation to return the security deposit is limited, and when the landlord exercises complete control over the deposit, it is considered advance rent.

The courts have held that a security deposit should be considered income in the year in which it is received if a landlord has the option either to refund a security deposit or to apply it to a future year's rent. The courts' reasoning is that the landlord has unrestricted use of the money.

In cases in which the landlord is required by law to pay interest on the security deposit, the deposit generally is not considered advance rent.

TAXPLANNER
Landlords often forget whether they have treated a security deposit as a true security deposit or as advance rent. If this happens, the landlord will not be sure how to treat the refund and/or application of the security deposit at the end of the term of the lease. Be sure to note in your records exactly how you are treating the amount for tax purposes so that the tax returns for the year in which the security deposit is returned and/or applied will be easy to prepare.

TAXSAVER
When drawing up a rental agreement, word it so that the security deposit is an amount *equal to* 1 month's rent and not an amount *in lieu of* the last month's rent. This helps ensure deferred recognition of the security deposit as income until such time as you determine it should not be refunded.

Payment for canceling a lease. If your tenant pays you to cancel a lease, the amount you receive is rent. Include the payment in your income for the year you receive it regardless of your method of accounting.

Explanation
Additionally, the courts have ruled that any payments you receive as consideration for modifying the terms of an existing lease must be treated as **ordinary income.** However, certain expenses incurred as a result of the cancellation or modification of a lease may be currently deductible. For example, attorney fees attributable to the *lessee's* forfeiture and termination of a lease would be currently deductible. On the other hand, if the lessor caused the termination, the expense would usually be amortized over a period of time. You should consult your tax advisor.

TAXSAVER
A payment for cancellation of a lease may be very large, depending on the time left on the lease and the agreement of the parties. As with most types of income to cash basis taxpayers, arranging for the receipt of this payment in a year in which you have a lower **marginal tax rate** may save you taxes.

Expenses paid by tenant. If your tenant pays any of your expenses, these payments are rental income. You must include them in your income. You can deduct those expenses if they are deductible rental expenses.

Explanation

When a tenant pays to have capital improvements constructed on the landlord's property and these improvements are *not* made in lieu of rent or other required payments, the value of these improvements is *not* income to the landlord, either when made or on termination of the lease, even though the landlord keeps the improvements.

Example

Susan rents an apartment to Pam. Pam, at her own expense, constructs a wall to separate the dining area from the living room. At the end of the lease, Pam vacates the apartment, leaving the wall. Susan does not record income at any time, even though she may benefit from the capital improvement.

If Susan must incur an expense to remove the wall and restore the property, it is either deducted from income or capitalized, depending on factors discussed later in this chapter. See *Rental Expenses*.

TAXPLANNER

It would be unusual for an expense paid by a tenant that is the responsibility of the landlord not to be deductible by the landlord as well. But such expenses do exist. Consider, for example, a building code violation fine incurred for some change made in the tenant's space by the tenant without the landlord's consent. The fine is imposed on the landlord, but the violation is the tenant's fault. The tenant pays the penalty, but the landlord still has to declare that amount as income, and, in this case, the landlord probably will not be able to deduct the amount of the fine as an expense. Most penalties are not deductible. If this is a possibility, a clause in the lease making the payment of such a penalty the responsibility of the tenant when the tenant is at fault would probably keep the payment by the tenant from being income to the landlord.

Property or services. If you receive property or services, instead of money, as rent, include the fair market value of the property or services in your rental income.

Explanation

Examples of types of income treated as rental income but not mentioned in the IRS text include the following:

1. Amounts received from an insurance company under a policy that reimburses a property owner for rent lost because of a fire or other casualty affecting the rental property.
2. Amounts received by subletting a property to another individual. If you did receive such income, you would be able to deduct the rent you are paying to the landlord as an expense. However, you are still not the owner and therefore would not be able to depreciate the property.

If the services are provided at an agreed upon or specified price, that price is the fair market value in the absence of evidence to the contrary.

Rental of property also used as a home. If you rent property that you also use as your home and you rent it for less than 15 days during the tax year, do not include the rent you receive in your gross income. You cannot deduct rental expenses. However, you can deduct allowable interest, taxes, and casualty and theft losses as itemized deductions on Schedule A of Form 1040. See *Personal Use of Vacation Homes and Other Dwelling Units,* later.

TAXSAVER

This is one of the very few instances in which the IRS considers income to be nontaxable. You should be on the lookout for opportunities to rent property for less than 15 days to take advantage of this tax loophole. Residents of Augusta, Georgia, for example, have an annual opportunity to rent their houses for a short period during the Masters Golf Tournament.

If you own a part interest in rental property, you must report your part of the rental income from the property.

Rental Expenses

This part discusses repairs and certain other expenses of renting property that you ordinarily can deduct from your gross rental income. It includes information on the expenses you can deduct if you rent part of your property, or if you change your property to rental use. Depreciation, which you can also deduct from your gross rental income, is discussed later.

If you own a part interest in rental property, you can deduct your part of the expenses that you paid.

TAXSAVER

You may deduct expenses on your rental property during a period in which it is *not* being rented as long as it is actively being held out for rent. This applies to a period between rentals, as well as to the period during which a property is being marketed as a rental property for the first time.

The IRS can disallow these deductions if you are unable to show you were actively seeking a profit and had a reasonable expectation of achieving one. The deduction cannot be disallowed just because your property is difficult to rent.

Example

You own a house in a high crime area. You intend to rent the house, but it languishes on the market for a long time. As long as you can demonstrate that you have been actively trying to rent the house (i.e. newspaper clippings advertising the property for rent), you may deduct depreciation, repairs, and other expenses.

When to deduct. You generally deduct your rental expenses in the year you pay or incur them.

Vacant rental property. If you hold property for rental purposes, you may be able to deduct your ordinary and necessary expenses for managing, conserving, or maintaining the property while the property is vacant. However, you cannot deduct any loss of rental income for the period the property is vacant.

Pre-rental expenses. You can deduct your ordinary and necessary expenses for managing, conserving, or maintaining rental property from the time you make it available for rent.

Expenses for rental property sold. If you sell property you held for rental purposes, you can deduct the ordinary and necessary expenses for managing, conserving, or maintaining the property until it is sold.

Personal use of rental property. If you sometimes use your rental property for personal purposes, you must divide your expenses between rental and personal use. Also, your rental expense deductions may be limited. See *Personal Use of Vacation Homes and Other Dwelling Units,* later.

Repairs and Improvements

You can deduct the cost of repairs that you make to your rental property. You cannot deduct the cost of improvements. You recover the costs of improvements by taking depreciation (explained later).

Separate the costs of repairs and improvements, and keep accurate records. You will need to know the cost of improvements when you sell or depreciate your property.

Repairs. A repair keeps your property in good operating condition. It does not materially add to the value of your property or substantially prolong its life. Repainting property inside or out, fixing gutters or floors, fixing leaks, plastering, and replacing broken windows are examples of repairs.

If you make repairs as part of an extensive remodeling or restoration of your property, the whole job is an improvement.

Improvements. An improvement adds to the value of your property, prolongs its useful life, or adapts it to new uses. Putting a recreation room in an unfinished basement, paneling a den, adding a bathroom or bedroom, putting decorative grillwork on a balcony, putting up a fence, putting in new plumbing or wiring, putting in new cabinets, putting on a new roof, and paving a driveway are examples of improvements.

Explanation
The examples given by the IRS are not necessarily improvements that must be capitalized. If a so-called improvement does not prolong useful life or add to value, it is deductible currently as a repair.

Example
The cost of a new roof that merely maintains the property and does not extend the useful life of the building may be currently deductible, even though the amount spent is rather large and its usefulness extends beyond the current tax year.

The cost of new plumbing or wiring or the repaving (but not the original paving) of a driveway may be currently deductible, notwithstanding the IRS's view. You should consult with your tax advisor in making this determination.

If you make an improvement to property before you begin renting it, add the cost of the improvement to the basis of the property.

Basis is explained later under *Modified Accelerated Cost Recovery System (MACRS).*

Other Expenses

Other expenses you can deduct from your gross rental income include advertising, janitor and maid service, utilities, fire and liability insurance, taxes, interest, commissions for the collection of rent, ordinary and necessary travel and transportation, and other expenses discussed below.

Explanation
While commissions paid to collect rent are deductible, commissions paid to obtain long-term rentals (greater than a one-year-period) must be capitalized and **amortized** over the life of the lease. Commissions paid to acquire the rental property must be capitalized as part of the basis of that property and recovered when the property is depreciated.

Points paid to acquire a mortgage on the rental property must be amortized over the life of the mortgage.

Other deductible expenses connected to renting include legal costs for dispossessing a tenant, property management fees, and pest control fees.

The "ordinary and necessary travel and transportation" category includes, of course, local transportation. It also covers the cost of meals and lodging on trips to inspect rental property located outside the immediate area. However, for the cost of nonlocal transportation and some other expenses to be deductible, the *primary* purpose of the trip must be to take care of the rental property. (See Chapter 28, *Car Expenses and Other Employee Business Expenses,* for a discussion of how to deduct expenses when you use your personal automobile in your trade or business.)

Example
If you make a 1-week trip to Florida and spend 1 day inspecting your rental property, *no* nonlocal transportation expenses are deductible. If, on the other hand, 6 of the 7 days are used to repair and attend to the property, *all* nonlocal transportation expenses are deductible. In both cases, local transportation expenses incurred traveling to and from the property are deductible.

Salaries and wages. You can deduct reasonable salaries and wages you pay to your employees. You can also deduct bonuses you pay to your employees if, when added to their regular salaries or wages, the total is not more than reasonable pay.

You can deduct reasonable wages you pay to your dependent child if your child is your bona fide employee. However, you cannot deduct the cost of meals and lodging for the child.

Rental payments for property. You can deduct the rent you pay for property that you use for rental purposes. If you buy a leasehold for rental purposes, you can deduct an equal part of the cost each year over the term of the lease.

Example 1
If you pay $1,100 rent for property and collect $1,200 in rent from a third party for the same property, you may

deduct the $1,100 you pay. Your profit from the rental activity is $100.

Example 2

If you buy a 10–year lease on property from someone for $1,000, you have to pay the rent that the former owner of the lease had to pay. In turn, you report as income any rent you receive on the property. You may amortize the cost of the lease over 10 years, deducting $100 each year.

Rental of equipment. You can deduct the rent you pay for equipment that you use for rental purposes. However, in some cases, lease contracts are actually purchase contracts. If so, you cannot deduct these payments. You can recover the cost of purchased equipment through depreciation.

Explanation

A lease with an option to buy may be a purchase contract. Generally, if the sum of the rental payments on a lease with an option to buy amounts to a substantial part of what would be the purchase price, and if the option period is clearly less than the useful life of the property, the transaction is treated as a sale. Income is recognized under the installment sale rules. (See Chapter 15, *Sale of Property,* for details.)

If the lease is treated as a sale, there may be unwanted tax consequences for the landlord. The payments that the landlord receives will be proceeds from the sale of property, and he or she will report the gain on the installment method. The landlord may also have to report imputed interest income (see Chapter 13, *Other Income*). Consequently, the landlord might have more income and fewer deductions than expected.

TaxPlanner

The rules in this area are complex, but a careful drafting of a property agreement will reduce or eliminate the likelihood that the IRS will consider the lease a sale. Professional help should be obtained.

Insurance premiums. You can deduct insurance premiums you pay. If you pay the premiums for more than one year in advance, each year you can deduct the part of the premium payment that will apply to that year. You continue to deduct your premium in this manner for as long as the insurance is in effect. You cannot deduct the total premium in the year you pay it.

Local benefit taxes. Generally, you cannot deduct charges for local benefits that increase the value of your property, such as for putting in streets, sidewalks, or water and sewer systems. These charges are nondepreciable capital expenditures. You must add them to the basis of your property. You can deduct local benefit taxes if they are for maintaining, repairing, or paying interest charges for the benefits.

TaxSaver

Whether or not you are offering property for rent, it is important to keep a file on the assessments you pay for sewers, streets, and the like. These add to your cost basis in the property and are important in determining your gain or loss if you ever sell the property. In addition, if you do rent the property out, the increase in your cost basis for any special assessment increases your depreciation deduction.

Charges for services. You can deduct charges you pay for services provided for your rental property, such as water, sewer, and trash collection.

Travel expenses. You can deduct the ordinary and necessary costs of traveling away from home if the primary purpose of the trip was to collect rental income or to manage, conserve, or maintain your rental property. You must properly allocate between rental and nonrental activities. For information on travel expenses, see Chapter 28, *Car Expenses and Other Employee Business Expenses.*

To deduct travel expenses, you must keep records that follow the rules in Chapter 28, *Car Expenses and Other Employee Business Expenses.*

Local transportation expenses. You can deduct your ordinary and necessary local transportation expenses if you incur them to collect rental income or to manage, conserve, or maintain your property.

Generally, if you use your personal car, pickup truck, or light van for rental activities, you can deduct local transportation expenses using one of two methods: actual expenses or the standard mileage rate. The standard mileage rate for 1993 is **28 cents a mile** for all business miles.

To deduct car expenses under either method, you must follow certain rules. These rules are discussed in Chapter 28, *Car Expenses and Other Employee Business Expenses.*

In addition, you must complete Part V of Form 4562 and attach it to your tax return.

Tax return preparation. You can deduct, as a rental expense, the part of tax return preparation fees you paid to prepare Part I of Schedule E. You can also deduct, as a rental expense, any expense you paid to resolve a tax underpayment related to your rental activities. Thus, on your 1993 Schedule E (Form 1040), you can deduct fees paid in 1993 to prepare your 1992 Schedule E (Form 1040).

Renting Part of Your Property

If you rent part of your property, you must divide certain expenses between the part of the property used for rental purposes and the part of the property used for personal purposes as though you actually had two separate pieces of property.

You can deduct a part of some expenses, such as mortgage interest and property taxes, as a rental expense. You can deduct the other part, subject to certain limitations, only if you itemize your deductions. You can also deduct as a rental expense a part of other expenses that normally are nondeductible personal expenses, such as expenses for electricity, a second telephone line, or painting the outside of your house.

You do not have to divide the expenses that belong only to the rental part of your property. If you paint a room that you rent, or if you pay premiums for liability insurance in connection with renting a room in your home, your entire cost is a rental expense. You can deduct depreciation, discussed later, on the part of the property used for rental purposes as well as on the furniture and equipment you use for these purposes.

How to Divide Expenses

If an expense is for both rental use and personal use, such as mortgage interest or the heat for the entire house, you must divide the expense between the rental use and the personal use. You can use any reasonable method for dividing the expense. The two most common methods are one based on the number of rooms in your home and one based on the square footage of your home.

Allocating costs. Dividing certain expenses based on the number of people involved may be the proper method to use. For example, if you provide meals to tenants, the most accurate method of dividing food costs between rental and personal expenses may be one based on the total number of people eating the food. Or, if you rent an apartment and your tenants have unrestricted use of your second telephone line, dividing the monthly charge for that line by the number of people using it may be the best method to use.

Limits on Deductions for Rental Expenses

If you rent out part of your property and you also use that or another part of the same property for personal purposes during the year, your deductions for rental expenses for the property may be limited. See *Personal Use of Vacation Homes and Other Dwelling Units,* later, for more information.

Property Changed to Rental Use

If you change your home, apartment, or other property, or a part of it, to rental use at any time other than at the beginning of your tax year, you must divide yearly expenses, such as depreciation, taxes, and insurance, between rental use and personal use.

You can deduct as rental expenses only the part of the expense that is for the part of the year the property was used or held for rental purposes.

You cannot deduct depreciation or insurance for any property or part of property held for personal use. However, you can deduct the allowable part of the interest and tax expenses for personal use as an itemized deduction on Schedule A (Form 1040).

Example. You moved from your home in May 1993 and started renting it out on June 1, 1993. You can deduct as rental expenses seven-twelfths of your yearly expenses, such as taxes and insurance.

You can deduct as rental expenses, starting with June, the amounts you pay for items generally billed monthly, such as utilities.

Information on depreciation. See *Personal home changed to rental use,* later, under *Modified Accelerated Cost Recovery System (MACRS)* for information about how to figure your deduction for depreciation.

Other limits. If you change property to rental use and later use part or all of it for personal purposes, there are other rules that apply to how much of your rental expenses you can deduct. These rules are explained later under *Personal Use of Vacation Homes and Other Dwelling Units.*

Not Rented For Profit

If your rental of a property is an activity that you do not carry on to make a profit, you can deduct your rental expenses only up to the amount of your rental income. You cannot carry forward any of your rental expenses that are more than your rental income. For more information about the rules for an activity not engaged in for profit, see Chapter 1 of Publication 535.

Where to report. Report your rental income on line 22, Form 1040. Deduct your mortgage interest, real estate taxes, and casualty losses on the appropriate lines of Schedule A (Form 1040).

You claim your other expenses, subject to the rules explained in Chapter 1 of Publication 535, as miscellaneous itemized deductions on line 20 of Schedule A. You can deduct these expenses only if they, together with certain other miscellaneous itemized deductions, total more than 2% of your adjusted gross income. For more information about miscellaneous deductions, see Chapter 30, *Miscellaneous Deductions.*

Personal Use of Vacation Homes and Other Dwelling Units

If you have any personal use of a vacation home or other dwelling unit that you rent out, you must divide your expenses between the rental use and the personal use. See *Figuring Days of Personal Use* and *How to Divide Expenses,* later.

If you use the dwelling unit as a home and you rent it for fewer than 15 days during the year, you do not have to include any of the rent in your income, and you cannot deduct any of the rental expenses. If you rent out the dwelling unit for 15 or more days, you must include the rent in your income and, if you have a net loss, you may not be able to deduct all of the rental expenses. See *How to Figure Your Income and Deductions,* later.

Explanation
In general, the tax rules governing the rental of vacation homes and other dwelling units are the same as those governing any rental property. The allowable methods of depreciation, the types of deductible expenditures, and the types of expenditures that should be capitalized are all determined in the same way for both categories of rental property. However, if you or a member of your family use the vacation home or dwelling unit during the year, the amount of deductible expenses may be limited by special rules.

Here's an easy way to figure out whether or not you have to follow the special rules for reporting rental income outlined later:

Step 1. Determine the number of days the property was rented at **fair market value** during the year. If this number is less than 15, STOP. You may not deduct any rental expenses, and you do not report any rental income. (*Note:* You may always deduct qualified residence interest, taxes, **casualty losses,** and theft losses if you itemize deductions. To do so, simply take the deduction for the entire amount of these items on Schedule A of Form 1040.) If the number of days rented is 15 or more, you must report rental income. Proceed to Step 2.

Step 2. Determine the number of days you personally use the property. If this number does not exceed the greater of (a) 14 days or (b) 10% of the number of days for which the property was rented at fair market value, you are not subject to any special rules. After completing Step 3, you determine your rental income or loss in the same way you would for any type of rental property.

If your personal use of the property exceeds the limits above, you *are* subject to special rules limiting the amount of deductible expenses. After completing Step 3, you determine your rental income or loss using the rules discussed in this section.

Step 3. Allocate *all* expenses between the rental period and the period in which you use the property personally, using the method described in the following section. Expenses allocated to the period of personal use are not deductible, except for interest, taxes, and casualty and theft losses (see Step 1). Then determine your rental income or loss, either using the general rules for rental property or the special rules regarding vacation homes, whichever is appropriate.

Dwelling unit. The rules in this section apply to vacation homes and other dwelling units. A dwelling unit includes a house, apartment, condominium, mobile home, boat, or similar property. A dwelling unit has basic living accommodations, such as sleeping space, a toilet, and cooking facilities. A dwelling unit does not include property used solely as a hotel, motel, inn, or similar establishment.

Property is used solely as a hotel, motel, inn, or similar establishment if it is regularly available for occupancy by paying customers and is not used by an owner as a home during the year.

Explanation
A dwelling unit must provide basic living accommodations, such as sleeping space, a restroom, and cooking facilities. The Tax Court has ruled that a mini-motor home qualifies as a dwelling unit.

An outbuilding used in conjunction with the main building to provide living accommodations, such as a garage, a barn, or a greenhouse, constitutes part of the main dwelling unit. When renting one of these outbuildings, you may deduct expenses only to the extent you have income. You may not deduct a rental loss. This is so because the outbuilding is not considered separate from the main building that is being used as a personal residence or vacation home.

"Rental pools" and "time shares." "Rental pools" are agreements under which two or more vacation homes are made available for rent by their owners, who agree to share "at least substantially part of the rental income from the homes regardless [of] which of the vacation homes are actually rented." Under proposed IRS regulations, special rules apply when you are computing income, expense, and personal use days.

Also, under proposed IRS regulations, individuals owning a "time share" that they rent are to treat their rental income and expense separately with respect to their unit. Consult your tax advisor.

Example. You rent out a room in your home that is always available for occupancy by paying customers. You do not use the room yourself, and you only allow paying customers to use the room. The room is used solely as a hotel, motel, inn, or similar establishment and is therefore not a dwelling unit.

Dwelling Unit Used as Home

You use a dwelling unit as a home during the tax year if you use it for personal purposes more than the greater of:

1) 14 days, or
2) 10% of the total days it is rented to others at a fair rental price.

See *Figuring Days of Personal Use,* later.

If a dwelling unit is used for personal purposes on a day it is rented at a fair rental price, do not count that day as a day of rental in applying (2) above. Instead, count it as a day of personal use in applying (1) and (2) above.

Example. You own a cottage at the shore. You rent it out at a fair rental price from June 1 through August 31, a total of 92 days. The tenant who rented the cottage for the month of July was unable to use it from July 4 through July 8. The tenant allowed you to use the cottage for those 5 days. The tenant did not ask for a refund of or a reduction in the rent. Your family used the cottage for 3 of those days.

To determine the number of days the cottage was rented at a fair rental price, do not count those 3 days you used it for personal purposes. The cottage was rented at a fair rental price for 89 days (92 − 3).

Fair rental price. A fair rental price for your property generally is an amount that a person who is not related to you would be willing to pay. The rent you charge is not a fair rental price if it is substantially less than the rents charged for other properties that are similar to your property.

Ask yourself the following questions when comparing another property with yours.

Is it used for the same purpose?
Is it approximately the same size?
Is it in approximately the same condition?
Does it have similar furnishings?
Is it in a similar location?

If any of the answers are no, the properties probably are not similar.

Examples. The following examples show how to determine whether you used your rental property as a home.

Example 1. You converted the basement of your home into an apartment with a bedroom, a bathroom, and a small kitchen. You rent the apartment at a fair rental price to college students during the regular school year. You rent to them on a 9-month (273 days) lease.

During the summer, your brothers stay with you for a month (30 days) and live in the apartment rent free.

Your basement apartment is used as a home because you use it for personal purposes for 30 days. That is more than the greater of 14 days or 10% of the total days it is rented.

Example 2. You rent out the guest bedroom in your home at a fair rental price during the local college's homecoming, commencement, and football weekends (a total of 27 days). Your sister-in-law stays in the room, rent free, for the last three weeks (21 days) in July.

The room is used as a home because you use it for personal use for 21 days. That is more than the greater of 14 days or 10% of the total days it is rented.

Figuring Days of Personal Use

A day of personal use of a dwelling unit is any day that it is used by:

1) You or any other person who has an interest in it, unless you rent it to another owner as his or her main home under a shared equity financing agreement (defined later),
2) A member of your family or a member of the family of any other person who has an interest in it, unless the family member uses the dwelling unit as his or her main home and pays a fair rental price. Family includes only brothers and sisters, half-brothers and half-sisters, spouses, ancestors (parents, grandparents, etc.) and lineal descendants (children, grandchildren, etc.),
3) Anyone under an arrangement that lets you use some other dwelling unit, or
4) Anyone at less than a fair rental price.

Main home. If the other owner or member of the family in (1) or (2) above has more than one home, his or her main home is the one lived in most of the time.

Shared equity financing agreement. This is an agreement under which two or more persons acquire undivided interests for more than 50 years in an entire dwelling unit, including the land, and one or more of the co-owners is entitled to occupy the unit as his or her main home upon payment of rent to the other co-owner or owners.

Donation of use of property. You use a dwelling unit for personal purposes if:

You donate the use of the unit to a charitable organization,
The organization sells the use of the unit at a fund-raising event, and
The purchaser uses the unit.

Examples

The following examples show how to determine days of personal use.

Example 1. You and your neighbor are co-owners of a condominium at the beach. You rent the unit out to vacationers whenever possible. The unit is not used as a main home by anyone. Your neighbor uses the unit for two weeks every year.

Because your neighbor has an interest in the unit, both of you are considered to have used the unit for personal purposes during those two weeks.

Example 2. You and your neighbors are co-owners of a house under a shared equity financing agreement. Your neighbors live in the house and pay you a fair rental price.

Even though your neighbors have an interest in the house, the days your neighbors live there are not counted as days of personal use by you. This is because your neighbors rent the house as their main home under a shared equity financing agreement.

Example 3. You own a rental property that you rent to your son. Your son has no interest in this dwelling unit. He uses it as his main home. He pays you a fair rental price for the property.

Your son's use of the property is not personal use by you because your son is using it as his main home, he has no interest in the property, and he is paying you a fair rental price.

Example 4. You rent your beach house to Marcia. Marcia rents her house in the mountains to you. You each pay a fair rental price.

You are using your house for personal purposes on the days that Marcia uses it because your house is used by Marcia under an arrangement that allows you to use her house.

Example 5. You rent an apartment to your mother at less than a fair rental price. You are using the apartment for personal purposes on the days that your mother rents it.

Days Not Counted as Personal Use

Some days you spend at the dwelling unit are not counted as days of personal use.

Repairs and maintenance. Any day that you spend working substantially full time repairing and maintaining your property is not counted as a day of personal use. Do not count such a day as a day of personal use even if family members use the property for recreational purposes on the same day.

Use as home before or after renting. When determining if you used your property as a home, the following special rule applies. Do not count days on which you used the property as your main home either before or after renting it or offering it for rent in the following circumstances:

1) You rented or tried to rent the property for 12 or more consecutive months, or
2) You rented or tried to rent the property for a period of less than 12 consecutive months and the period ended because you sold or exchanged the property.

This special rule does not apply when dividing expenses between rental and personal use.

Explanation
If the dwelling unit is rented and you are a guest of the occupant for a brief visit, this will not constitute personal use. Of course, the longer the visit is, the more likely the IRS is to claim you were an occupant rather than a visitor. Certainly, 1 or 2 days should be no problem.

How to Divide Expenses

If you use a dwelling unit for both rental and personal purposes, you must divide your expenses between the rental use and the personal use. For purposes of dividing your expenses:

1) Any day that the unit is rented at a fair rental price is a day of rental use even if you have personally used the unit for that day, and

2) A unit is not considered used for rental during the time that it is held out for rent but not actually rented.

Example. You offer your beach cottage for rent from June 1 through August 31 (92 days). Your family uses the cottage during the last 2 weeks in May (14 days). During 1993, you were unable to find a renter for the first week in August (7 days). The person who rented the cottage for July allowed you to use it over a weekend (2 days) without any reduction in or refund of rent. The cottage was not used at all before May 17 or after August 31.

The cottage was used for rental a total of 85 days (92 − 7). The days it was held out for rent but not rented (7 days) are not days of rental use. For purposes of dividing expenses, the July weekend on which you used it (2 days) is rental use because you received a fair rental price for the weekend.

You used the cottage for personal purposes for 14 days (the last 2 weeks in May).

The total use of the cottage was 99 days (14 days personal use + 85 days rental use). Therefore, you use 85/99 (86%) of these expenses as rental expenses.

TaxSaver

The Tax Court allows you to use a different allocation formula for interest and taxes than the one the IRS describes above. Under the Tax Court formula, interest and taxes are allocated in the ratio of days rented to days in the year instead of in the ratio of days rented to days used. Using the Tax Court ratio results in a smaller amount of interest and taxes being allocated to the rental property, which creates the potential for you to deduct a larger amount of your other rental expenses.

Example

You own a cabin, which you rented for June and July, lived in for 1 month, and tried to rent the rest of the year. Your rental income for the 2 months was $2,800. Your total expenses for the cabin were as follows:

Interest	$1,500
Taxes	900
Utilities	750
Maintenance	300
Depreciation	1,200

	IRS method	Tax Court method
1) Gross rental income	$2,800	$2,800
2) Minus:		
a) Part of interest for rental use		
($1,500 × 2/3)	1,000	
($1,500 × 61/365)		251
b) Part of taxes for rental use		
($900 × 2/3)	600	
($900 × 61/365)		150
3) Gross rental income that is more than the interest and taxes for rental	$1,200	$2,399
4) Minus:		
a) Part of utilities for rental use	500	500
b) Part of maintenance for rental use	200	200
5) Gross rental income that is more than the interest, taxes, and operating expenses for rental use	$ 500	$1,699
6) Minus: Depreciation limited to the part for rental use ($1,200 × 2/3 = $800) or line 5, whichever is less	500	800
7) Net rental income	$ −0−	$ 899

Both the IRS method and the Tax Court method allocate interest expense and real estate taxes partly to Schedule E (for determining net rental income) and partly to Schedule A (for personal itemized deductions). But examine how these allocations affect Schedule A.

Total interest paid is $1,500. Since the IRS method allocates $1,000 to the rental activity, the $500 balance is allocated to Schedule A. The Tax Court method allocates only $251 to the rental activity, leaving $1,249 for a deduction on Schedule A. Similarly, the IRS method allocates $600 of the $900 in real estate taxes to the rental activity, leaving $300 for Schedule A. The Tax Court method allocates only $150 to the rental activity, leaving $750 for Schedule A.

	Schedule A		Additional itemized deduction per Tax Court method
	Tax Court method	IRS method	
Interest	$1,249	$500	$ 749
Real estate taxes	750	300	450
			$1,199

Under the Tax Court method, you end up with additional deductions of $1,199, but you also have an additional net rental income of $899. The difference is that you reduce your taxable income by $300 more than under the IRS method. This conclusion assumes that you had enough other itemized deductions to make itemizing worthwhile.

Under the Tax Reform Act of 1986, the concept illustrated above is even more important. Rental income is considered to be passive income and, as such, can be used to offset passive losses. For more details, see Chapter 24, *Interest Expense.*

How to Figure Your Income and Deductions

How you figure your rental income and deductions depends on how much personal use you made of the property and how many days the property was rented.

General Rule

If you do not use a dwelling unit as a home, you divide your expenses between personal use and rental use based on the number of days it was used for each purpose.

Your deductible rental expenses can be more than your gross rental income. However, see *Limits on Rental Losses,* later.

Where to report. Report the rental income and all of the rental expenses on Schedule E (Form 1040), *Supplemental Income and Loss.*

You can deduct allowable interest, taxes, and casualty losses for the personal use of the property on Schedule A (Form 1040) if you itemize deductions.

Income and Deductions for Property Used as a Home

If you use a dwelling unit as a home during the year (as explained earlier), how you figure your rental income and deductions depends on how many days the unit was rented.

Rented fewer than 15 days. If you use a dwelling unit as a home and you rent it for fewer than 15 days during the year, you do not report any of the rental income. Also, you cannot deduct any expenses as rental expenses.

However, you can deduct your allowable interest, taxes, and casualty and theft losses on Schedule A (Form 1040) if you itemize deductions.

Rented 15 days or more. If you use a dwelling unit as a home and rent it for 15 days or more during the year, you include all your rental income in your gross income. You must divide your expenses between the personal use and the rental use based on the number of days used for each purpose. If you had a net profit from the rental property for the year; that is, if your rental income is more than the total of your rental expenses, including depreciation), deduct all of your rental expenses. However, if you had a net loss, you may not be able to deduct all of your rental expenses.

Use *Table 10–1* to figure your deductible expenses.

Explanation

The IRS explanation is correct as far as it goes. However, four areas require clarification:

1. The starting point in determining your rental income is gross rental income, which is defined by the IRS as the gross rent received less expenses incurred to obtain tenants, such as advertising and real estate agent's fees. This definition is important, because it enables you to deduct this type of expense *before* taking deductions for interest, taxes, and casualty losses, which might be enough to reduce your rental income to zero. The result may be a larger *total* deduction. The key point is: Start with gross rent received, deduct your expenses to obtain tenants, and then proceed through the deduction process described above.

2. The total amount of a casualty or theft loss allocated to the rental period is deductible. Ordinarily, a personal casualty or theft loss is deductible only to the extent that it is more than $100 and more than 10% of your **adjusted gross income,** but this is not the case when you are dealing with rental property. (See Chapter 26, *Nonbusiness Casualty and Theft Losses,* for further details.)

3. Your basis in the vacation home or other dwelling unit is reduced only by the amount of depreciation actually allowed as a deduction, not by the amount of depreciation allocated to the rental period. This, in effect, decreases any gain you have to recognize if you subsequently sell the property. For more details on sales of **depreciable assets,** see *Depreciation,* later in this chapter.

4. Although the deductions for operating expenses and depreciation may not reduce income below zero, the deductions for interest and real estate taxes may.

TaxSaver

When you personally use a dwelling unit for more than 14 days or more than 10% of the number of days it is rented at fair market value, it is generally to your advantage to use the Tax Court formula for computing the amount of interest and taxes allocable to the rental period. Doing so usually allows you a greater *total* deduction, since interest, taxes, and casualty losses may be deducted on Schedule A, even if they are disallowed on Schedule E.

However, when your personal use of the dwelling is less than both 15 days and 10% of the number of days it is rented at fair market value, it is to your advantage to use the IRS method of allocating interest and taxes, because the net loss on the rental property will be allowed if your personal use is not substantial. (This assumes that the passive loss rules will not limit your net loss.) In this case, the IRS method does not reduce your total deduction; instead, it decreases your rental income (or increases your rental loss) and hence decreases your adjusted gross income.

Decreasing your adjusted gross income can be important, for the following reasons:

1. For 1993, if your adjusted gross income is in excess of $108,450, your total itemized deductions will be reduced by 3% of the excess of your adjusted gross income over $108,450. Therefore, a reduction in adjusted gross income will reduce the effect of this limitation.

2. The amounts of certain itemized deductions, such as medical expenses, casualty losses, and most miscellaneous itemized deductions, are determined by reference to your adjusted gross income. Decreasing your adjusted gross income potentially increases your itemized deductions for these items.

3. Many states use adjusted gross income as the starting point in computing state taxable income. Using the IRS method may reduce your state tax liability.

4. If you are subject to alternative minimum tax, this method will reduce your alternative minimum taxable income.

5. A reduction in adjusted gross income may reduce the taxable amount of social security payments.

6. If you are a participant in a qualified pension plan, a decrease in your adjusted gross income may increase the deductibility of your IRA.

Table 10-1. **Worksheet for Figuring the Limit on Rental Deductions for a Dwelling Unit Used as a Home**

Use this worksheet only if you answer "yes" to all of the following questions.
- Did you use the dwelling unit as a home this year? (See *Dwelling Unit Used as a Home*.)
- Did you rent the dwelling unit 15 days or more this year?
- Are the total of your rental expenses and depreciation more than your rental income?

1. Enter rents received . . . . _____

2. a. Enter the rental portion of deductible home mortgage interest (see instructions) . . . . _____
   b. Enter the rental portion of real estate taxes . . . . _____
   c. Enter the rental portion of deductible casualty and theft losses (see instructions) . . . . _____
   d. Enter indirect rental expenses (see instructions) . . . . _____
   e. **Fully deductible rental expenses.** Add lines 2a–2d . . . . _____

3. Subtract line 2e from line 1. If zero or less, enter zero . . . . _____

4. a. Enter the rental portion of expenses directly related to operating or maintaining the dwelling unit (such
      as repairs, insurance, and utilities) . . . . _____
   b. Enter the rental portion of excess mortgage interest (see instructions) . . . . _____
   c. Add lines 4a and 4b . . . . _____
   d. **Allowable operating expenses.** Enter the smaller of line 3 or line 4c . . . . _____

5. Subtract line 4d from line 3. If zero or less, enter zero . . . . _____

6. a. Enter the rental portion of excess casualty and theft losses (see instructions) . . . . _____
   b. Enter the rental portion of depreciation of the dwelling unit . . . . _____
   c. Add lines 6a and 6b . . . . _____
   d. **Allowable excess casualty and theft losses and depreciation.** Enter the smaller of line 5 or line 6c . . . . _____

7. a. **Operating expenses to be carried over to next year.** Subtract line 4d from line 4c . . . . _____
   b. **Excess casualty and theft losses and depreciation to be carried over to next year.** Subtract line
      6d from line 6c . . . . _____

Enter the amounts on **lines 2e, 4d, and 6d** on the appropriate lines of Schedule E (Form 1040), Part I.

Worksheet Instructions

Follow these instructions for the worksheet above. If you were unable to deduct all your expenses last year, including operating expenses, casualty and theft losses, and depreciation, because of the rental income limit, add these unused amounts to your expenses for this year.

Line 2a. Figure the mortgage interest on the dwelling unit that you could deduct on Schedule A (Form 1040) if you had not rented the unit. **Do not** include interest on a loan that did not benefit the dwelling unit. For example, **do not** include interest on a home equity loan used to pay off credit cards or other personal loans, buy a car, or pay college tuition. Include interest on a loan used to buy, build, or improve the dwelling unit, or to refinance such a loan. Enter the rental portion of this interest on line 2a of the worksheet.

Line 2c. Figure the casualty and theft losses related to the dwelling unit that you could deduct on Schedule A (Form 1040) if you had not rented the dwelling unit. To do this, complete Section A of Form 4684, treating the losses as personal losses. On line 17 of

Form 4684, enter 10% of your adjusted gross income figured **without** your rental income and expenses from the dwelling unit. Enter the rental portion of the result from line 18 of Form 4684 on line 2c of this worksheet. **Note:** Do **not** file this Form 4684 or use it to figure your personal losses on Schedule A. Instead, figure the personal portion on a separate Form 4684.

Line 2d. Enter the total of your rental expenses that are not directly related to operating or maintaining the dwelling unit. These include interest on loans used for rental activities other than to buy, build, or improve the dwelling unit. Also include rental agency fees, advertising, office supplies, and depreciation on office equipment used in your rental activity.

Line 4b. On line 2a, you entered the mortgage interest you could deduct on Schedule A if you had not rented out the dwelling unit. Enter on line 4b of this worksheet the mortgage interest you could not deduct on Schedule A because it is **more than** the limit on home mortgage interest. **Do not** include interest on a loan

that did not benefit the dwelling unit (as explained in the line 2a instructions).

Line 6a. To find the rental portion of excess casualty and theft losses you can deduct, follow these steps. Use the Form 4684 you prepared for line 2c of this worksheet.

A. Enter the amount from line 10 of Form 4684 . . . . _____
B. Enter the rental portion of (A).. _____
C. Enter the amount from line 2c of the worksheet . . . . _____
D. Subtract (C) from (B). Enter the result here and on line 6a of the worksheet . . . . _____

Allocating the limited deduction. If you cannot deduct all of the amount on line 4c or 6c this year, you can allocate the allowable deduction in any way you wish among the expenses included on line 4c or 6c. Enter the amount you allocate to each expense on the appropriate line of Schedule E, Part I.

Depreciation

When you use your property to produce income, such as rents, the law generally allows you to recover (get back) some or all of what you paid for the property through tax deductions. You do this by "depreciating" the property; that is, by deducting some of your cost on your tax return each year.

Several factors determine how much depreciation you can deduct. The main factors are: (1) your basis in the property, and (2) the recovery period for the property.

You can deduct depreciation only on the part of your property

used for rental purposes. Depreciation reduces your basis for figuring gain or loss on a later sale or exchange. You may have to use **Form 4562,** *Depreciation and Amortization,* to figure and report your depreciation. See *How to Report Rental Income and Expenses,* later.

You should claim the correct amount of depreciation each tax year. If you did not deduct depreciation in earlier years, you cannot deduct the unclaimed depreciation in the current or any later tax year. You also must still reduce your basis in the property by the amount of depreciation that you should have deducted. However, you may be able to claim the depreciation on an amended return

(Form 1040X) for the earlier year. See *Amended Returns and Claims for Refund* in Chapter 1 for more information.

Land. You can never depreciate land. This generally includes the cost of clearing, grading, planting, and landscaping because these expenses are all part of the cost of land.

Depreciation Systems

There are three ways to figure depreciation. The depreciation system you use depends on the type of asset and when the asset was placed in service. For *tangible property* you use:

1) MACRS if placed in service after 1986,
2) ACRS if placed in service after 1980 but before 1987, or
3) Straight line or an accelerated method of depreciation, such as the declining balance method, if placed in service before 1981.

Explanation

Depreciation may perhaps be best understood as a way of deducting the cost of an expenditure over many years. Depreciation is calculated in the same way whether you report income on the **cash** or the **accrual method**.

The period of time over which you depreciate your property has long been the subject of controversy. Different taxpayers, often in the same business, have depreciated the same type of property over widely different periods. Efforts to bring more uniformity to the write-off period resulted in the introduction of the Accelerated Cost Recovery System (ACRS). ACRS was replaced with MACRS (Modified ACRS) by the Tax Reform Act of 1986. Most tangible personal property can be depreciated. Artwork is an exception. It cannot be depreciated, because no useful life can be established.

Tangible property is any property that you can see and touch. This includes automobiles, buildings, and equipment.

If you placed property in service before 1993, continue to use the same method of figuring depreciation that you used in the past. If you need information about any other method of depreciation, see Publication 534, *Depreciation*.

Section 179 election. You cannot claim the section 179 deduction for property used in rental activities.

Cannot be more than basis. The total of all your yearly depreciation deductions cannot be more than your cost or other basis of the property. For this purpose, the total depreciation must include any depreciation that you were allowed to claim, even if you did not claim it.

Cooperative apartments. If you are a tenant-stockholder in a cooperative housing corporation and you rent your cooperative apartment to others, you may deduct your share of the corporation's depreciation. See *Cooperative apartments* in Publication 527 for information on how to figure your depreciation deduction.

Explanation

To qualify as a cooperative housing corporation, four tests must be met:

1. There is only a single class of stock outstanding.
2. Each stockholder must be entitled (solely because he or she owns stock) to occupy a house or an apartment owned or leased by the corporation.

3. There are no distributions to a stockholder that are not out of the corporation's earnings, except for partial or complete liquidation.
4. At least 80% of the corporation's gross income is received from the tenant–stockholders.

If you are a tenant–stockholder in a co-op, you compute your depreciation deduction in the following manner:

1. Compute depreciation for all of the depreciable property owned by the corporation, using the following method:
   a) Multiply your cost per share for the corporation stock by the total number of shares outstanding.
   b) Add the total mortgage indebtedness on the property as of the date you purchased your stock to the amount computed in (a).
   c) From the amount determined in (b), subtract the part of the mortgage indebtedness (existing on the date you purchased your stock) allocable to non-depreciable property, such as land. The result is the depreciable basis of the corporation's property.
   d) Compute the depreciation, using the basis calculated in (c) and one of the allowable methods of depreciation discussed later.
2. From the amount of depreciation computed in (1), subtract depreciation on any rental space owned by the corporation that may not be lived in by tenant–stockholders.
3. Divide the number of shares of stock in the corporation you own by the total number of shares outstanding (including shares held by the corporation).
4. Multiply the amount calculated in (2) by the percentage determined in (3). This is your depreciation deduction, which is limited to the adjusted basis of your stock in the corporation.

If you rent your co-op, you may also deduct other rental expenses, such as repairs, maintenance, commissions, and insurance fees, as well as depreciation. Whether or not you rent your co-op, you may deduct your share of the corporation's deductible interest and taxes.

Modified Accelerated Cost Recovery System (MACRS)

The modified accelerated cost recovery system (MACRS) applies to all tangible property placed in service during 1993.

MACRS consists of two systems that determine how you depreciate your property. The main system is called the *General Depreciation System (GDS).* The second system is called the *Alternative Depreciation System (ADS).* GDS is used to figure your depreciation deduction for property used in most rental activities, unless you elect ADS.

To figure your MACRS deduction, you need to know the following information about your property:

1) Its recovery period,
2) Its placed-in-service date, and
3) Its depreciable basis.

Excluded property. You cannot use MACRS for certain personal property placed in service before 1987 (before August 1, 1986, if election made) that is transferred after 1986 (after July 31, 1986, if election made). Generally, if you acquired the property from a related party, or if you or a related party used the property before 1987, you cannot use MACRS. Property that does not come under MACRS must be depreciated under ACRS or one of the other methods of depreciation, such as straight line or declining balance. In addition, you may elect to exclude certain property from the application of MACRS. See Publication 534 for more information.

Personal home changed to rental use. You must use MACRS to figure the depreciation on property you used as your home and changed to rental property in 1993.

Recovery Periods Under GDS

Each item of property that can be depreciated is assigned to a property class. The recovery period of a piece of property depends on the class the property is in. The property classes are:

3–year property,
5–year property,
7–year property,
10–year property,
15–year property,
20–year property,
Nonresidential real property, and
Residential rental property.

The class to which property is assigned is determined by its class life. Class life is discussed in Publication 534.

Under GDS, tangible property that you placed in service during 1993 in your rental activities generally falls into one of the following classes. Also see *Table 10–2* in this chapter. The other recovery classes are discussed in Publication 534.

1) *5–year property.* This class includes computers and peripheral equipment, office machinery (typewriters, calculators, copiers, etc.), automobiles, and light trucks.

Depreciation on automobiles, certain computers, and cellular telephones is limited. See Chapter 4 of Publication 534.

2) *7–year property.* This class includes office furniture and equipment (desks, files, etc.), and appliances, carpets, furniture, etc. used in residential rental property. This class also includes any property that does not have a class life and that has not been designated by law as being in any other class.

3) *15–year property.* This class includes roads and shrubbery (if depreciable).

4) *Residential rental property.* This class includes any real property that is a rental building or structure (including a mobile home) for which 80% or more of the gross rental income for the tax year is from dwelling units. A dwelling unit is a house or an apartment used to provide living accommodations in a building or structure, but does not include a unit in a hotel, motel, inn, or other establishment where more than half of the units are used on a transient basis. If you live in any part of the building or structure, the gross rental income includes the fair rental value of the part you live in. This property is depreciated over *27.5 years.*

Additions or improvements to property. Treat additions or improvements you make to any property as separate property items for depreciation purposes. The recovery period for an addition or improvement begins on the later of:

1) The date the addition or improvement is placed in service, or
2) The date the property to which the addition or improvement is placed in service.

The class and recovery period of the addition or improvement is the one that would apply to the underlying property if it were placed in service at the same time as the addition or improvement.

Example. You own a residential rental house that you have been renting out since 1980 and are depreciating under ACRS. If you put an addition onto the house, and you place the improvement in service after 1986, you use MACRS for the addition. Under MACRS, the addition would be depreciated as residential rental property.

When to begin depreciation. You can begin to depreciate property when you place it in service in your trade or business or for the production of income. Property is considered placed in service in a rental activity when it is ready and available for a specific use in that activity.

Basis

To deduct the proper amount of depreciation each year, you must first determine your basis in the property you intend to depreciate. The basis used for figuring depreciation is your original basis in the property increased by any improvements made to the property. Your original basis is usually your cost. However, if you acquire the property in some other way, such as by inheriting it, getting it as a gift, or building it yourself, you may have to figure your original basis in another way. Other adjustments could also affect your basis. See Chapter 14, *Basis of Property.*

Example

You use an old truck in your business with an unrecovered cost of $6,000. You trade it in for a new truck and pay an additional $9,000 in cash. You subsequently spend $1,000 to have a heavy-duty component added. Your unadjusted basis is $16,000: the unrecovered cost of the old truck ($6,000) plus the cash paid for the new truck ($9,000) and the heavy-duty component ($1,000). Although you have one adjusted basis for your new truck, you may have to use one method of depreciation for the $6,000 unrecovered cost of the old truck and another method of depreciation for the $10,000. (See the antichurning rules later in this chapter.)

Figuring MACRS Depreciation Under GDS

You can figure your MACRS depreciation under GDS in one of two ways. The deduction is the same both ways. You can either:

1) Actually compute the deduction using the applicable depreciation method and convention over the recovery period of the property, or
2) Use the percentage from the optional MACRS tables.

If you actually compute the deduction, the depreciation method you use depends on the class of the property.

5-, 7-, or 15-year property. For property in the 5- or 7–year class, you use the double (200%) declining balance method over 5 or 7 years and a half-year convention or the mid-quarter convention, if applicable. These conventions are explained later. For property in the 15–year class, you use the 150% declining balance method over 15 years and a half-year convention.

You can also choose to use the 150% declining balance method for property in the 5–, 7–, or 15–year class over its ADS recovery period. See *Figuring MACRS Depreciation Under ADS,* later, for the ADS recovery periods. You make this election on Form 4562. In Part II, column (f), enter "150 DB."

Change from either declining balance method to the straight line method in the first tax year that the straight line method gives you a larger deduction.

Table 10-2. **MACRS Recovery Periods for Property Used in Rental Activities**

Type of property	MACRS Recovery Period to use	
	General Depreciation System	Alternative Depreciation System
Computers and their peripheral equipment	5 years	5 years
Office machinery, such as: typewriters calculators copiers....................	5 years	6 years
Automobiles	5 years	5 years
Light trucks	5 years	5 years
Office furniture and equipment, such as: desks files	7 years	10 years
Appliances, such as: stoves refrigerators	7 years	12 years
Carpets	7 years	12 years
Furniture used in rental property	7 years	12 years
Any property that does not have a class life and that has not been designated by law as being in any other class	7 years	12 years
Roads	15 years	20 years
Shrubbery	15 years	20 years
Residential rental property (buildings or structures) and structural components such as furnaces, water pipes, venting, etc.	27.5 years	40 years
Improvements and additions, such as a new roof......................	The recovery period of the property to which the addition or improvement is made, determined as if the property were placed in service at the same time as the improvement or addition.	

You can also choose to use the straight line method with a half-year or mid-quarter convention for 5–, 7–, and 15–year property. The choice to use the straight line method for one item in a class of property applies to all property in that class that is placed in service during the tax year of the election. You elect the straight line method on Form 4562. In Part II, column (f), enter"S/L." Once you make this election, you cannot change to another method.

Residential rental property. You must use the straight line method and a mid-month convention (explained later) for residential rental property.

Declining Balance Method

To figure your MACRS deduction, first determine your declining balance rate from the table in the next column. However, if you elect to use the 150% declining balance method for 5– or 7–year property, figure the declining balance rate by dividing 1.5 (150%) by the ADS recovery period for the property.

Multiply the adjusted basis of the property by the declining balance rate, and apply the applicable convention to figure your depreciation for the first year. In later years, use the following steps to figure your depreciation.

1) Adjust your basis by subtracting the amount of depreciation allowable for the earlier years.

2) Multiply your adjusted basis in (1) by the same rate used in the first year.

Follow these steps each year that you use the declining balance method. See *Conventions,* later, for information on depreciation in the year you dispose of property.

Declining balance rates. The following table shows the applicable declining balance rate for each class of property and the first year for which the straight line method will give an equal or greater deduction. (The rates for 5– and 7–year property are based on the 200% declining balance method.)

Class	Declining Balance Rate	Year
5	40.00%	4th
7	28.57%	5th
15	10.00%	7th

Straight Line Method

To figure your MACRS deduction under the straight line method, you must figure a new depreciation rate for each tax year in the recovery period. For any tax year, figure the straight line rate by dividing the number 1 by the years remaining in the recovery period at the beginning of the tax year. Multiply the unrecovered basis of the property by the straight line rate. You must figure the depreciation for the first year using the applicable convention. (See *Conventions,* later.) If the remaining recovery period at the beginning of the tax year is less than 1 year, the straight line rate for that tax year is 100%.

Example. Using the straight line method for property with a 5–year recovery period, the straight line rate is 20% (1 ÷ 5) for the first tax year. After applying the half-year convention, the first year rate is 10% (20% ÷ 2).

At the beginning of the second year, the remaining recovery period is 4½ years because of the half-year convention. The straight line rate for the second year is 22.22% (1 ÷ 4.5).

To figure your depreciation deduction for the second year:

1) Subtract the depreciation taken in the first year from the basis of the property, and
2) Multiply the remaining basis in (1) by 22.22%.

Residential rental property. In the first year you claim depreciation for residential rental property, you can only claim depreciation for the number of months the property is in use, and you must use the mid-month convention (explained later). Also, for the first year of depreciation under ADS, you must use the mid-month convention (explained later) to figure your depreciation deduction.

Conventions

In the year that you place property in service or in the year that you dispose of property, you are only allowed to claim depreciation for only part of the year. The part of the year (or convention) depends on the class of the property.

A half-year convention is used to figure the deduction for property used in rental activities other than residential rental property. However, under a special rule, a mid-quarter convention may have to be used. For residential rental property, use a mid-month convention in all situations.

Half-year convention. The half-year convention treats all property placed in service, or disposed of, during a tax year as placed in service, or disposed of, in the middle of that tax year.

A half year of depreciation is allowable for the first year property is placed in service, regardless of when the property is placed in service during the tax year. For each of the remaining years of the recovery period, you will take a full year of depreciation. If you hold the property for the entire recovery period, a half year of depreciation is allowable for the year following the end of the recovery period. If you dispose of the property before the end of the recovery period, a half year of depreciation is allowable for the year of disposition.

Mid-quarter convention. Under a mid-quarter convention, all property placed in service, or disposed of, during any quarter of a tax year is treated as placed in service, or disposed of, in the middle of the quarter.

A mid-quarter convention must be used in certain circumstances for property used in rental activities, other than residential rental property. This convention applies if the total basis of such property that is placed in service in the last 3 months of a tax year is more than 40% of the total basis of all such property you place in service during the year.

Do not include in the total basis any property placed in service and disposed of during the same tax year.

Example. During 1993, John Joyce purchased the following items to use in his rental property:

A dishwasher for $400, which he placed in service in January;
Used furniture for $100, which he placed in service in September; and
A refrigerator for $500, which he placed in service in October.

John uses the calendar year as his tax year. The total basis of all property placed in service in 1993 is $1,000. The $500 basis of the refrigerator placed in service during the last 3 months of his tax year exceeds $400 (40% × $1,000). Therefore, John must use the mid-quarter convention for all three items. The dishwasher, refrigerator, and used furniture are 7–year property under GDS.

Mid-month convention. Under a mid-month convention, residential rental property placed in service, or disposed of, during any month is treated as placed in service, or disposed of, in the middle of that month.

Explanation

Under the modified MACRS rules, a "half-year convention" is used on business personal property placed in service or removed from service during the year. For example, a calendar year taxpayer who has been in business all year computes his or her depreciation as if all property had been acquired on July 1.

If the taxable year is less than 12 months (usually in the case of a new business), the property will be treated as in service during half of the short tax year.

If more than 40% of your business personal property is placed in service in the last 3 months of your full tax year, a special averaging convention applies. This is called a mid-quarter convention and requires property placed in service during any quarter of a tax year to be treated as placed in service at the midpoint of such quarter.

Dispositions of business personal property result in a half-year of depreciation.

Residential and nonresidential real property are treated as placed in service (or taken out of service) in the middle of the month.

Note that you may also need to compute alternative minimum tax depreciation for purposes of computing your alternative minimum taxable income. See Chapter 31, *How To Figure Your Tax,* for additional information.

Optional Tables

You can use *Table 10–3* to compute annual depreciation under MACRS. The percentages in Tables A, B, and C make the change from declining balance to straight line in the year that straight line will yield a larger deduction. See *Declining Balance Method,* earlier.

If you elect to use the straight line method for 5–, 7–, or 15–year property, or the 150% declining balance method for 5– or 7–year property, use the tables in *Appendix A* of Publication 534.

How to use the tables. The following section explains how to use the optional tables. Figure the depreciation deduction by multiplying your unadjusted basis in the property by the percentage shown in the appropriate table. Your ***unadjusted basis*** is your depreciable basis without reduction for depreciation previously claimed. The tables show the percentages for the first 6 years.

Tables A, B, and C. These tables take the half-year and mid-quarter conventions into consideration in figuring percentages. Use Table A for 5–year property, Table B for 7–year property, and Table C for 15–year property. Use the percentage in the second column (half-year convention) unless you must use the mid-quarter convention (explained earlier). If you must use the mid-quarter convention, use the column that corresponds to the calendar year quarter in which you placed the property in service.

Table 10-3. Optional MACRS TABLES

Table 10-3-A. MACRS 5-Year Property

Year	Half-year convention	Mid-quarter convention			
		First quarter	Second quarter	Third quarter	Fourth quarter
1	20.00%	35.00%	25.00%	15.00%	5.00%
2	32.00	26.00	30.00	34.00	38.00
3	19.20	15.60	18.00	20.40	22.80
4	11.52	11.01	11.37	12.24	13.68
5	11.52	11.01	11.37	11.30	10.94
6	5.76	1.38	4.26	7.06	9.58

Table 10-3-B. MACRS 7-Year Property

Year	Half-year convention	Mid-quarter convention			
		First quarter	Second quarter	Third quarter	Fourth quarter
1	14.29%	25.00%	17.85%	10.71%	3.57%
2	24.49	21.43	23.47	25.51	27.55
3	17.49	15.31	16.76	18.22	19.68
4	12.49	10.93	11.97	13.02	14.06
5	8.93	8.75	8.87	9.30	10.04
6	8.92	8.74	8.87	8.85	8.73

Table 10-3-C. MACRS 15-Year Property

Year	Half-year convention	Mid-quarter convention			
		First quarter	Second quarter	Third quarter	Fourth quarter
1	5.00%	8.75%	6.25%	3.75%	1.25%
2	9.50	9.13	9.38	9.63	9.88
3	8.55	8.21	8.44	8.66	8.89
4	7.70	7.39	7.59	7.80	8.00
5	6.93	6.65	6.83	7.02	7.20
6	6.23	5.99	6.15	6.31	6.48

Table 10-3-D. Residential Rental Property (27.5-year)

	Use the row for the month of the taxable year placed in service.					
	Year 1	Year 2	Year 3	Year 4	Year 5	Year 6
Jan.	3.485%	3.636%	3.636%	3.636%	3.636%	3.636%
Feb.	3.182	3.636	3.636	3.636	3.636	3.636
March	2.879	3.636	3.636	3.636	3.636	3.636
Apr.	2.576	3.636	3.636	3.636	3.636	3.636
May	2.273	3.636	3.636	3.636	3.636	3.636
June	1.970	3.636	3.636	3.636	3.636	3.636
July	1.667	3.636	3.636	3.636	3.636	3.636
Aug.	1.364	3.636	3.636	3.636	3.636	3.636
Sept.	1.061	3.636	3.636	3.636	3.636	3.636
Oct.	0.758	3.636	3.636	3.636	3.636	3.636
Nov.	0.455	3.636	3.636	3.636	3.636	3.636
Dec.	0.152	3.636	3.636	3.636	3.636	3.636

Example 1. You purchased a stove and refrigerator and placed them in service on February 1, 1993. Your basis in the stove is $300, and your basis in the refrigerator is $500. Both are 7–year property. Using the half-year convention column in Table B, you find the depreciation percentage for year 1 is 14.29%. Your 1993 depreciation deduction on the stove is $43 ($300 × .1429). Your 1993 depreciation deduction on the refrigerator is $71 ($500 × .1429).

Using the half-year convention for year 2, you find your depreciation percentage is 24.49%. Therefore, your 1994 depreciation deduction will be $73 ($300 × .2449) for the stove and $122 ($500 × .2449) for the refrigerator.

Example 2. Assume the same facts in Example 1, except you buy the refrigerator in October 1993 instead of February. You must use the mid-quarter convention column to figure depreciation on the stove and refrigerator. The basis of the refrigerator ($500), placed in service in the last 3 months of the tax year, is more than 40% of the total basis of all property ($800) placed in service during the year.

Because you placed the stove in service in February, you use the first quarter column of Table B and find that the depreciation percentage for year 1 is 25%. Your 1993 depreciation deduction on the stove is $75 ($300 × .25).

Because you placed the refrigerator in service in October, you use the fourth quarter column of Table B and find that the depreciation percentage for year 1 is 3.57%. Your depreciation deduction on the refrigerator is $18 ($500 × .0357).

Table D. Use this table for residential rental property. Find the row for the month that you placed the property in service. Use the percentages listed for that month for your depreciation deduction. The mid-month convention is considered in the percentages used in the tables.

Example. You purchased a single family rental house and placed it in service on February 1, 1993. Your basis in the house is $80,000. Using Table D, you find that the percentage for property placed in service in February of year 1 is 3.182%. Your 1993 depreciation deduction is $2,546 ($80,000 × .03182).

Figuring MACRS Depreciation Under ADS

If you choose, you can use the ADS method for most property. Under ADS, you use the straight line method of depreciation.

Table 10–2 shows the recovery periods for property used in rental activities that you depreciate under ADS. See *Appendix B* in Publication 534 for other property. If your property is not listed, it is considered to have no class life.

Use the mid-month convention for residential rental property. For all other property, use the half-year or mid-quarter convention.
Election. You choose to use ADS by entering the depreciation on line 15, Part II of Form 4562.

The election of ADS for one item in a class of property generally applies to all property in that class that is placed in service during the tax year of the election. However, the election applies on a property-by-property basis for residential rental property.

Once you choose to use ADS, you cannot change your election.

Explanation
The antichurning rules, as they are called, are designed to prevent you from taking undue advantage of the new, faster depreciation deduction rates by engaging in transactions in which the real and beneficial ownership interest in the property does not really change. For property originally acquired after 1980 and before 1986, rather than switching to MACRS, you must continue to use the previous method of depreciation only if MACRS will yield greater depreciation deductions in the first year. For property originally acquired prior to 1980, you must continue to use the previous method of accounting in all cases.

Example 1
You own your residence, which you bought in 1975. In 1993, you move out and convert the house to rental property. Although you first put it to business use in 1993, you cannot use MACRS, because the property was actually acquired prior to 1980.

Example 2
In 1984, John and Mary acquired assets that they held as community property during their married life. John died in 1987, and his property was included in his estate, which resulted in his half being revalued to current fair market value. John's half of the property can be written off under MACRS, but the IRS says that the antichurning rules prevent Mary from using MACRS on her revalued half, because there was no change of ownership, the property was placed in service after 1980 and before 1982, and the MACRS yields a greater first-year deduction.

Other Rules About Depreciable Property

In addition to the rules about what methods you can use, there are other rules you should be aware of with respect to depreciable property.
If you dispose of depreciable property at a profit, you may have to report, as ordinary income, all or part of the profit. See Chapter 2 of Publication 527.

Explanation
When you sell an asset for more than your unrecovered cost, you face the problem of recapture, that is, reporting all or part of your gain as ordinary income as opposed to capital gain. If you sell tangible personal property at a gain, your recapture is the lower of your gain or the previous amount of depreciation.

Example

	Case 1	Case 2
1) Cost	$1,000	$1,000
2) Depreciation previously claimed	(600)	(600)
3) Unrecovered cost	$ 400	$ 400
4) Selling price	$ 900	$1,200
5) Gain on sale (4 − 3)	$ 500	$ 800
6) Recapture ordinary income (lower of 2 or 5)	(500)	(600)
7) Possible capital gain (5 − 6)	$ –0–	$ 200

TAXPLANNER

The Tax Reform Act of 1986 eliminated the distinction between capital gains and ordinary income tax rates through 1990. However, the 1993 Tax Act imposes a maximum rate of 39.6% on ordinary income while keeping the capital gains rate at 28%. Thus, the depreciation recapture may be taxed at a higher rate at the time of the sale.

Additional tax on preference items. If you use accelerated depreciation, you may have to file **Form 6251,** *Alternative Minimum Tax — Individuals.* Accelerated depreciation includes MACRS and ACRS and any other method that allows you to deduct more depreciation than you could deduct using a straight line method. For more information, see Publication 909, *Alternative Minimum Tax for Individuals.*

Limits on Rental Losses

Rental real estate activities are generally considered passive activities and the amount of loss you can deduct is limited. Generally, you cannot deduct losses from rental real estate activities unless you have income from other passive activities. See *Passive Activity Limits,* later.

Losses from passive activities are first subject to the *at-risk rules.* At-risk rules limit the amount of deductible losses from holding most real property placed in service after December 31, 1986.
Exception. If your rental losses are less than $25,000 ($12,500 if married filing separately), the passive activity limits probably do

not apply to you. See *Losses From Rental Real Estate Activities,* later.

Property used as a home. If you used the rental property as a home during the year, the passive activity rules do not apply to you. Instead, you must follow the rules explained earlier under *Personal Use of Vacation Homes and Other Dwelling Units.*

At-Risk Rules

The at-risk rules place a limit on the amount you can deduct as losses from activities often described as tax shelters. Holding real property (other than mineral property) placed in service before 1987 is not subject to the at-risk rules.

Generally, any loss from an activity subject to the at-risk rules is allowed only to the extent of the total amount you have at risk in the activity at the end of the tax year. You are considered at risk in an activity to the extent of cash and the adjusted basis of other property you contributed to the activity and certain amounts borrowed for use in the activity. See Publication 925, *Passive Activity and At-Risk Rules,* for more information.

Passive Activity Limits

You generally cannot offset income, other than passive income, with losses from passive activities. Nor can you offset taxes on income, other than passive income, with credits resulting from passive activities.

In general, any rental activity is a passive activity. For this purpose, a rental activity is an activity from which you receive income mainly for the use of tangible property, rather than for services.

Use **Form 8582,** *Passive Activity Loss Limitations* to figure the amount of any passive activity loss for the current year for all activities and the amount of the passive activity loss allowed on your tax return.

> **Explanation**
> For more about Passive Activities see Chapter 13, *Other Income.*
>
> **TaxAlert**
> Beginning in 1994, rental activities will not be considered passive activities if certain conditions are met. See Publication 553, *Highlights of 1993 Tax Changes,* for more information.

Losses From Rental Real Estate Activities
You can deduct up to $25,000 ($12,500 if married filing separately and living apart from your spouse the entire year) of losses from rental real estate activities in which you *actively participated* during the tax year. This allows you to deduct up to $25,000 of otherwise unallowable losses from rental real estate activities against other income (nonpassive income). The $25,000 ($12,500) figure is reduced if your adjusted gross income is more than $100,000 ($50,000 if married filing separately and living apart from your spouse the entire year).

If you lived with your spouse at any time during the year and are filing a separate return, you cannot use this special offset to reduce your nonpassive income or tax on nonpassive income.

Active participation. You actively participate in a rental real estate activity if you own at least 10% of the rental property and you make management decisions in a significant and bona fide sense. Management decisions include approving new tenants, deciding on rental terms, approving expenditures, and similar decisions. For these purposes, you are considered to own any portion of the property owned by your spouse.

See Publication 925 for more information on the passive loss limits, including information on the treatment of unused disallowed passive losses and credits and the treatment of gains and losses realized on the disposition of a passive activity.

How to Report Rental Income and Expenses

Report rental income on your return for the year you actually or constructively receive it (if you are a cash-basis taxpayer). You are considered to constructively receive income when it is made available to you, for example, by being credited to your bank account.

For more information about when you constructively receive income, see *Accounting Methods* in Chapter 1.

Expenses carried over. If you could not deduct all of your 1992 rental expenses because you used your property as a home, treat the part you could not deduct in 1992 as a 1993 rental expense. Deduct the expenses carried over to 1993 only up to the amount of your 1993 gross rental income, even if you did not use the property as your home in 1993.

Where to report. Where you report rental income and expenses, including depreciation, depends on whether you provide certain services to your tenant.

If you rent out buildings, rooms, or apartments, and provide only heat and light, trash collection, etc., you normally report your rental income and expenses in Part I of Schedule E (Form 1040), *Supplemental Income and Loss.* However, see *Not Rented For Profit,* earlier.

If you provide additional services that are primarily for your tenant's convenience, such as regular cleaning, changing linen, or maid service, you report your rental income and expenses on **Schedule C** (Form 1040), *Profit or Loss From Business* or **Schedule C–EZ,** *Net Profit From Business.* For information, see Publication 334. You also may have to pay self-employment tax on your rental income. See Publication 533, *Self-Employment Tax.*

Form 1098. If you paid $600 or more of mortgage interest on your rental property, you should receive a Form 1098, *Mortgage Interest Statement,* or a similar statement showing the interest you paid for the year. If you and at least one other person (other than your spouse if you file a joint return) were liable for, and paid interest on the mortgage, and the other person received the Form 1098, report your share of the interest on line 13 of Schedule E. Attach a statement to your return showing the name and address of the other person. In the left margin of Schedule E, next to line 13, write "See attached."

Schedule E

Use Part I of Schedule E (Form 1040) to report your rental income and expenses. List your total income, expenses, and depreciation for each rental property. Be sure to answer the question on line 2. On line 20 of Schedule E (Form 1040), show the depreciation you are claiming.

You must complete and attach Form 4562 for rental activities *only if* you are claiming:

- Depreciation on rental property placed in service during 1993, or

- Depreciation on any rental property that is listed property (such as a car), regardless of when it was placed in service, or
- Any automobile expenses (actual or the standard mileage rate).

Otherwise, figure your depreciation on your own worksheet. You do not have to attach these computations to your return.

If you have more than three rental or royalty properties, complete and attach as many Schedules E as are needed to list the properties. Complete lines 1 and 2 for each property. However, fill in the "Totals" column on only one Schedule E. The figures in the "Totals" column on that Schedule E should be the combined totals of all Schedules E. If you need to use page 2 of Schedule E, use page 2 of the same Schedule E you used to enter the combined totals in Part I.

Example. Eileen Green owns a townhouse that she rents out. She receives $1,100 a month rental income. Her rental expenses for 1993 are as follows:

Fire insurance (1–year policy)	$ 200
Mortgage interest	5,000
Fee paid to real estate company for collecting monthly rent	572
General repairs	175
Real estate taxes imposed and paid in 1993	800

Eileen bought the property and placed it in service on January 1, 1993. Her basis for depreciation of the townhouse is $65,000. She is using MACRS with a 27.5–year recovery period. On April 1, 1993, Eileen bought a new dishwasher for the rental property at a cost of $425. She uses the MACRS method with a 7–year recovery period.

Eileen uses the percentage for "January" in *Table 10–3–D* to figure her deduction for the townhouse. She uses the percentage under "Half-year convention" in *Table 10–3–B* to figure her deduction for the dishwasher. She must report the depreciation on Form 4562.

Eileen figures her net rental income or loss for the townhouse as follows:

Total rental income received		
($1,100 × 12)		$13,200
Minus Expenses:		
Fire insurance	$ 200	
Mortgage interest	5,000	
Real estate fee	572	
General repairs	175	
Real estate taxes	800	
Total expenses		6,747
Balance		$ 6,453
Minus Depreciation:		
On townhouse ($65,000 × 3.485%)	$2,265	
On dishwasher ($425 × 14.29%)	61	
Total depreciation		2,326
Net rental income for townhouse		$ 4,127

11 | Retirement Plans, Pensions, and Annuities

Introduction

No matter how welcome retirement may be, you're liable to encounter a host of challenging tax dilemmas that you've never before faced. For starters, the chances are good that you will have some difficulty projecting your tax liabilities. Your income will most likely be different from what it has been, and the way in which you calculate your tax will be different, too. If your **pension** *payments are not subject to mandatory withholding rules (effective for distributions made in 1993 and in subsequent years), you may have to start making* **estimated tax** *payments. You'll have to puzzle over the complicated withdrawal stipulations for an* **Individual Retirement Arrangement (IRA)** *and possibly for a* **Keogh plan,** *a pension plan for the* **self-employed.** *Perhaps, most important, if you are entitled to any* **lump-sum distributions,** *you will have to make the difficult decision as to whether to roll over the funds and defer the tax or to pay the tax currently but at the low rates permitted by* **5-year averaging** *or 10-year income averaging, if you are eligible. This chapter helps guide you through this maze of complicated decisions.*

Most retirement payments are taxable—whether they come from your IRA, an employee pension plan, or a disability pension. However, the tax code is full of special provisions that may help you reduce your tax. Although the Tax Reform Act of 1986 eliminated the extra personal exemption for taxpayers who are over 65 or blind, such taxpayers will be entitled to an additional standard deduction amount of $700 for 1993. Furthermore, there is a disability credit, a credit for the elderly, and ways in which you may roll over cash distributions into other retirement plans. Many of these tax-deferral techniques are discussed in this chapter.

This chapter tells you how to report income you receive from an employee pension plan and a disability pension. [IRAs are discussed in Chapter 18, Individual Retirement Arrangements (IRAs)]. You'll also find comments about distributions from company profit-sharing and stock bonus plans. The chapter aims to make your retirement as carefree—and as tax-free—as possible.

The 1986 tax law made significant changes in the taxation of distributions from qualified retirement plans. These changes were generally effective starting in 1987. In addition, there are several significant changes involving rollovers and withholding on eligible rollover distributions that are effective for distributions made in 1993 and thereafter. Details about the changes are discussed later in this chapter.

This chapter discusses the tax treatment of amounts you receive from:

- Employee pensions and annuities,
- Disability retirement, and
- Purchased annuities.

If you are retired from the Federal Government (either regular or disability retirement), see Publication 721, *Tax Guide to U.S. Civil Service Retirement Benefits.* Also see Publication 721 if you are the survivor or beneficiary of a federal employee or retiree who died.

Information on amounts you receive from an individual retirement arrangement (IRA), as well as general information on IRAs, is in Chapter 18, *Individual Retirement Arrangements (IRAs)*.

Useful Items

You may want to see:

Publications

- ☐ **559** Survivors, Executors, and Administrators
- ☐ **575** Pension and Annuity Income (Including Simplified General Rule)
- ☐ **721** Tax Guide to U.S. Civil Service Retirement Benefits
- ☐ **939** Pension General Rule (Nonsimplified Method)

Forms and Instructions

- ☐ **W–4P** Withholding Certificate for Pension or Annuity Payments
- ☐ **4972** Tax on Lump-Sum Distributions
- ☐ **5329** Additional Taxes Attributable to Qualified Retirement Plans (Including IRAs), Annuities, and Modified Endowment Contracts

Employee Pensions and Annuities

Generally, if you did not pay any part of the cost of your employee pension or annuity and your employer did not withhold part of the cost of the contract from your pay while you worked, the amounts you receive each year are fully taxable. You must report them on your income tax return.

If you paid part of the cost of your annuity, you are not taxed on the part of the annuity you receive that represents a return of your cost. The rest of the amount you receive is taxable. You use either the **General Rule** or the **Simplified General Rule** to figure the taxable and nontaxable parts of your pension or annuity.

If your annuity starting date was **before** July 2, 1986, and you recovered your cost under the **Three-Year Rule,** you cannot use the General Rule or the Simplified General Rule because your payments are fully taxable.

Changing the method. If your annuity starting date is after July 1, 1986, you can change the way you figure your pension cost recovery exclusion. You can change from the General Rule to the Simplified General Rule, or the other way around. Make the change by filing amended returns for all your tax years beginning with the year in which your annuity starting date occurred. You must use the same method for all years. Generally, you can make the change only within 3 years from the due date of your return *for the year in which you received your first annuity payment.* You can make the change later if the date of the change is within 2 years after you paid the tax for that year.

If your annuity starting date was before July 2, 1986, you cannot choose the Simplified General Rule at any time.

More than one program. If you receive benefits from more than one program, such as a pension plan and a profit-sharing plan, you must figure the taxable part of each separately. Make separate computations even if the benefits from both are included in the same check. For example, benefits from one of your programs could be fully taxable, while the benefits from your other program could be taxable under the General Rule or the Simplified General

Rule. Your former employer or the plan administrator should be able to tell you if you have more than one program.

Railroad retirement benefits. Part of the railroad retirement benefits you receive is treated like social security benefits, and part is treated like an employee pension. For information about railroad retirement benefits treated as an employee pension, see *Railroad Retirement* in Publication 575, *Pension and Annuity Income (Including Simplified General Rule)*.

Credit for the elderly or the disabled. If you receive a pension or annuity, you may be able to take the credit for the elderly or the disabled. See Chapter 34, *Credit for the Elderly or the Disabled,* for information about this credit.

Explanation

Since this credit is designed to help only those taxpayers with very modest resources, you are ineligible if you receive substantial social security benefits or have substantial **adjusted gross income.**

Withholding and estimated tax. The payer of your pension, profit-sharing, stock bonus, annuity, or deferred compensation plan will withhold income tax on the taxable parts of amounts paid to you. You can choose not to have tax withheld except for amounts paid to you that are eligible rollover distributions. See *Eligible rollover distributions* under *Rollovers,* later. You make this choice by filing Form W–4P, *Withholding Certificate for Pension or Annuity Payments.*

For payments other than eligible rollover distributions, you can tell the payer how to withhold by filing Form W–4P. If an eligible rollover distribution is paid directly to you, 20% will generally be withheld. There is no withholding on a direct rollover of an eligible rollover distribution. See *Direct rollover option* under *Rollovers,* later. If you choose not to have tax withheld or you do not have enough tax withheld, you may have to pay estimated tax.

For more information, see *Withholding on Pensions and Annuities* and *Estimated Tax* in Chapter 5, *Tax Withholding and Estimated Tax.*

TaxAlert

As of January 1, 1993, the payor of your pension, profit-sharing, stock bonus, annuity, or deferred compensation plan is required to withhold an amount equal to 20% of any designated distribution that is an **eligible rollover distribution,** unless you elect to have that distribution paid *directly* to an **eligible retirement plan.** An eligible rollover distribution is any taxable distribution of all or a portion of an employee's balance in a qualified plan or tax-sheltered annuity arrangement. The exceptions to this are: (1) any distribution that is one of a series of substantially equal periodic payments made over the life or life expectancy of the employee (or the joint lives or life expectancies of the employee and the employee's designated beneficiary) or made over a period of ten years or more, (2) required minimum distributions for individuals who have attained age 70-1/2, and (3) certain corrective and deemed distributions. An **eligible retirement plan** is generally another **qualified retirement plan,** an **individual retirement account (IRA),** or an **individual retirement annuity.**

If the payment made to you is not an eligible rollover distribution, the payor will withhold income tax on the taxable amounts paid to you. However, withholding from these payments is not mandatory and you can tell the payor how to withhold by filing Form W-4P, *Withholding Certificate for Pension or Annuity Payments.* If you choose not to have tax withheld, you may have to pay estimated tax.

For more information, see *Withholding on Pensions and Annuities* and *Estimated Tax* in Chapter 5, *Tax Withholding and Estimated Tax.*

Loans. If you borrow money from an employer's qualified pension or annuity plan, a tax-sheltered annuity program, a government plan, or from a contract purchased under any of these plans, you may have to treat the loan as a distribution. This means that you may have to include in income all or part of the amount borrowed. Even if you do not have to treat the loan as a distribution, you might not be able to deduct the interest on the loan in some situations. For details, see *Loans Treated as Distributions* in Publication 575. For information on the deductibility of interest, see Chapter 24, *Interest Expense.*

Exception

A loan will not be considered a distribution to the extent that the loan (when added to the outstanding balance of all other loans maintained by the employer) does not exceed the lesser of (1) $50,000 or (2) the greater of either $10,000 or one-half of the participant's vested accrued benefits under the plan.

Effective for loans made after December 31, 1986, the $50,000 limit is reduced by the excess of the participant's highest outstanding loan balance during the preceding 12-month period, over the outstanding balance at the date of the new loan.

In addition, the exception does not apply unless the loan by its terms must be repaid within 5 years and requires level repayments made not less frequently than quarterly over the term of the loan.

The 5-year rule (above) does not apply to loans made after December 31, 1986, in connection with the purchase of a principal residence of a participant.

TaxAlert

Interest on a loan from an employee plan is only deductible under the general loan interest rules (discussed in Chapter 24, *Interest Expense*). This is the case as long as the loans are not made to key employees or secured by amounts attributable to employee salary reduction amounts. (For years after 1990, personal loan interest is not deductible.)

Check with your plan administrator to determine whether Department of Labor regulations will affect your plan loans currently or plan loans that you intend to make.

TaxPlanner

Plan loans are a good way to provide for children's college expenses, a housing down payment, or any other family need. The interest paid helps your account grow at an attractive rate if the plan credits interest paid on the loan to your account.

Elective deferrals. Some retirement plans allow you to choose (elect) to have part of your pay contributed by your employer to a retirement fund, rather than have it paid to you. You do not pay tax on this money until you receive it in a distribution from the fund.

Elective deferrals generally include elective contributions to cash or deferred arrangements (known as *section 401(k) plans*), section 501(c)(18) plans, salary reduction simplified employee pension (SEP) plans, and tax-sheltered annuities provided for employees of tax-exempt organizations and public schools.

TaxPlanner 1

The benefits of section 401(k) plans are substantial. The elective deferrals are not subject to federal, state (except for Pennsylvania), and local income taxes until they are withdrawn. Earnings on the elective deferrals are also not subject to income tax until they are withdrawn. An employer-matching contribution program, which is deductible to the employer within certain limits, can encourage employees to make elective contributions. Finally, on withdrawal, a lump-sum distribution can avoid immediate income tax or excise tax if it is deposited in a rollover account. For more information, see *Rollovers* later in this chapter.

TaxPlanner 2

The benefits of section 403(b) plans (tax-sheltered annuities, or TSA plans) are important to employees of tax-exempt organizations and public schools who (except for certain grandfathered organizations) are not able to participate in section 401(k) plans. The elective deferrals are not subject to federal income tax, most state income taxes, and most local income taxes until they are withdrawn. Earnings on elective deferrals are also not subject to income tax until they are withdrawn. Rollovers are permitted for qualifying distributions to help avoid immediate income tax or excise taxes, if applicable.

For information on the tax treatment of elective deferrals, including their limits, see *Elective deferrals* under *Excess Contributions, Deferrals, and Annual Additions* in Publication 575. For information about tax-sheltered annuities, see Publication 571, *Tax-Sheltered Annuity Programs for Employees of Public Schools and Certain Tax-Exempt Organizations.*

H.R. 10 (Keogh) plans. Keogh plans are retirement plans that can only be set up by a sole proprietor or a partnership (but not a partner). They can cover self-employed persons, such as the sole proprietor or partners, as well as regular (common-law) employees.

Distributions from these plans are usually fully taxable. If you have an investment (cost) in the plan, however, your pension or annuity payments are taxed under the General Rule or the Simplified General Rule.

Deferred compensation plans of state and local governments and tax-exempt organizations. If you participate in one of these plans (known as *section 457 plans*), you will not be taxed currently on your pay that is deferred under the plan. You or your beneficiary will be taxed on this deferred pay only when it is distributed or otherwise made available to either of you.

Distributions of deferred pay are not eligible for 5- or 10-year averaging, rollover treatment, or the death benefit exclusion, all discussed later. Distributions are, however, subject to the tax for failure to make minimum distributions, discussed later.

For information on these deferred compensation plans and their limits, see *Section 457 plans—deferred compensation plans of state and local governments and tax-exempt organizations* under *Excess Contributions, Deferrals, and Annual Additions* in Publication 575.

Cost

Before you can figure how much, if any, of your pension or annuity benefits is taxable, you must determine your cost in the plan (your investment). Your total cost in the plan includes everything that you paid. It also includes amounts your employer paid that you were required to include in your income at the time paid. Cost does not include any amounts you deducted or excluded from income.

From this total cost paid or considered paid by you, subtract any refunds of premiums, rebates, dividends, unpaid loans, or other tax-free amounts you received before the later of the annuity starting date or the date on which you received your first payment. If you use the General Rule to figure the tax treatment of your payments, you must also subtract from your cost the value of any refund feature in your contract.

The *annuity starting date* is the later of the first day of the first period that you receive a payment from the plan or the date on which the plan's obligation became fixed.

Your employer or the organization that pays you the benefits (plan administrator) should show your cost in Box 5 of your Form 1099-R.

Foreign employment. If you worked in a foreign country before 1963 and your employer paid into your retirement plan, a part of those payments may be considered part of your cost. For details, see *Foreign employment* under *Investment in the Contract (Cost)* in Publication 575.

Explanation

Your cost includes contributions by your employer if you were required to include the amounts in your gross income. If you were employed abroad before 1963, your cost also includes amounts contributed by your employer before 1963 that would have been excludable from your gross income if paid directly to you.

Simplified General Rule

If you can use the Simplified General Rule, it will probably be simpler and more beneficial than the General Rule, discussed later, in figuring the taxability of your annuity.

Who can use it. You may be able to use the Simplified General Rule if you are a retired employee or if you are receiving a survivor annuity as the survivor of a deceased employee. You can use it to figure the taxability of your pension *only* if:

- Your annuity starting date is after July 1, 1986,
- The annuity payments are for either (a) your life, or (b) your life and that of your beneficiary,
- The annuity payments are from a qualified employee plan, a qualified employee annuity, or a tax-sheltered annuity, and
- At the time the payments began, either you were under age 75 or the payments were guaranteed for fewer than 5 years.

If you are not sure whether your retirement plan is a qualified plan (that meets certain Internal Revenue Code requirements), ask your employer or plan administrator.

If you are a survivor of a deceased retiree, you can use the Simplified General Rule if the retiree used it.

Amount of exclusion. If your annuity starting date was after July 1, 1986, and before January 1, 1987, you continue to take your monthly exclusion for as long as you receive your annuity.

If your annuity starting date is after 1986, the total you can exclude over the years is limited to your cost.

In both cases, any unrecovered cost at your or the last annuitant's death is allowed as a miscellaneous itemized deduction in the last tax year. This deduction is not subject to the 2%-of-adjusted-gross-income limit. The deduction is taken on the final return of the decedent.

How to use it. If you meet the conditions and you choose the Simplified General Rule, use the following worksheet to figure your taxable pension. In completing this worksheet, use your age at the birthday preceding your annuity starting date. Be sure to keep a copy of the completed worksheet; it will help you figure your 1994 taxable pension.

Worksheet for Simplified General Rule

1. Total pension received this year. Also add this amount to the total for Form 1040, line 17a, or Form 1040A, line 11a $ _____

2. Your cost in the plan (contract), at annuity starting date, plus any death benefit exclusion* .... _____

3. Age at annuity starting date: Enter:

55 and under	300
56 – 60	260
61 – 65	240
66 – 70	170
71 and over	120 ....

4. Divide line 2 by line 3.. _____

5. Multiply line 4 by the number of months for which this year's payments were made...................................... _____

   NOTE: If your annuity starting date is **before 1987,** enter the amount from line 5 on line 8 below. Skip lines 6, 7, 10, and 11.

6. Any amounts previously recovered tax free in years after 1986 .... _____

7. Subtract line 6 from line 2 .... _____

8. Enter the smaller of line 5 or line 7 .... _____

9. **Taxable pension for year.** Subtract line 8 from line 1. Enter the result, but not less than zero. Also add this amount to the total for Form 1040, line 17b, or Form 1040A, line 11b.. $ _____

   NOTE: If your Form 1099-R shows a larger taxable amount, use the amount on line 9 instead of the amount from Form 1099-R.

10. Add lines 6 and 8.. _____

11. Balance of cost to be recovered. Subtract line 10 from line 2 .... $ _____

*Statement for death benefit exclusion

Cost in plan (contract) .... $ _____

Death benefit exclusion... _____

Total (enter on line 2 above) .... $ =======

Signed: _____

Date: _____

KEEP FOR YOUR RECORDS

Example. Bill Kirkland, age 65, began receiving retirement benefits under a joint and survivor annuity to be paid for the joint lives of he and his wife, Kathy. He received his first annuity payment in January 1993. He had contributed $24,000 to the plan and had received no distributions before the annuity starting date. Bill is to receive a retirement benefit of $1,000 a month, and Kathy is to receive a monthly survivor benefit of $500 upon Bill's death.

Bill chooses to use the Simplified General Rule computation. He fills in the worksheet as follows:

Worksheet for Simplified General Rule

1. Total pension received this year. Also add this amount to the total for Form 1040, line 17a, or Form 1040A, line 11a $12,000

2. Your cost in the plan (contract) at annuity starting date, plus any death benefit exclusion* $24,000

3. Age at annuity starting date: Enter:

     55 and under   300

     56 – 60   260

     61 – 65   240

     66 – 70   170

     71 and over   120 240

4. Divide line 2 by line 3... 100

5. Multiply line 4 by the number of months for which this year's payments were made........................... 1,200

NOTE: If your annuity starting date is **before 1987,** enter the amount from line 5 on line 8 below. Skip lines 6, 7, 10, and 11.

6. Any amounts previously recovered tax free in years after 1986 0

7. Subtract line 6 from line 2 24,000

8. Enter the smaller of line 5 or line 7 1,200

9. **Taxable pension for year.** Subtract line 8 from line 1. Enter the result, but not less than zero. Also add this amount to the total for Form 1040, line 17b, or Form 1040A, line 11b.................................. $10,800

NOTE: If your Form 1099-R shows a larger taxable amount, use the amount on line 9 instead of the amount from Form 1099-R.

10. Add lines 6 and 8.. 1,200

11. Balance of cost to be recovered. Subtract line 10 from line 2 .... $22,800

*Statement for death benefit exclusion

Cost in plan (contract) .... $ _____

Death benefit exclusion... _____

Total (enter on line 2 above) .... $ =======

Signed: _____

Date: _____

KEEP FOR YOUR RECORDS

Bill's tax-free monthly amount is $100 (see line 4 of the worksheet). If he lives to collect more than 240 monthly payments, he will have to include the full amount of the additional payments in his gross income.

If Bill dies before collecting 240 monthly payments and Kathy begins receiving monthly payments, she will also exclude $100 from each payment until her payments, when added to his, total 240 payments. If she dies before 240 payments are made, a miscellaneous itemized deduction will be allowed for the unrecovered cost on her final income tax return. This deduction is not subject to the 2%-of-adjusted-gross-income limit.

Death benefit exclusion. If you are a beneficiary of a deceased employee or former employee, you may qualify for a death benefit exclusion of up to $5,000. This exclusion is discussed later in this chapter. If you choose the Simplified General Rule and you qualify for the death benefit exclusion, you increase your cost in the pension or annuity plan by the allowable death benefit exclusion. Your cost is on line 2 of the worksheet.

The payer of the annuity cannot add the death benefit exclusion to the cost for figuring the nontaxable and taxable part of payments reported on Form 1099-R. Therefore, the Form 1099-R taxable amount will be larger than the amount you will figure for yourself. Report on your return the smaller amount that you figure. You must attach a signed statement to your income tax return stating that you are entitled to the death benefit exclusion in making the Simplified General Rule computation. Or you may use the statement shown at the bottom of the worksheet. You must attach this statement to your return every year until you fully recover the cost in the pension or annuity plan.

Example. Diane Greene, age 48, began receiving a $1,500 monthly annuity in 1993 upon the death of her husband. She received 10 payments in 1993. Her husband had contributed $25,-000 to his qualified employee plan. Diane is entitled to a $5,000 death benefit exclusion for the annuity payments. She adds that amount to her husband's contributions to the plan, making her total cost in the plan $30,000.

Diane chooses to use the Simplified General Rule. She fills out the worksheet as follows:

Worksheet for Simplified General Rule

1. Total pension received this year. Also add this amount to the total for Form 1040, line 17a, or Form 1040A, line 11a $15,000

2. Your cost in the plan (contract) at annuity starting date, plus any death benefit exclusion* 30,000

3. Age at annuity starting date: Enter:

     55 and under   300

     56 – 60   260

     61 – 65   240

     66 – 70   170

     71 and over   120 300

4. Divide line 2 by line 3 100

5. Multiply line 4 by the number of months for which this
   year's payments were made 1,000

   NOTE: If your annuity starting date is **before 1987,** enter
   the amount from line 5 on line 8 below. Skip lines 6, 7,
   10, and 11.

6. Any amounts previously recovered tax free in years after
   1986 0

7. Subtract line 6 from line 2 30,000

8. Enter the smaller of line 5 or line 7 1,000

9. **Taxable pension for year.** Subtract line 8 from line 1.
   Enter the result, but not less than zero. Also add this
   amount to the total for Form 1040, line 17b, or Form
   1040A, line 11b $14,000

   NOTE: If your Form 1009-R shows a larger taxable amount,
   use the amount on line 9 instead of the amount from
   Form 1099-R.

10. Add lines 6 and 8 1,000

11. Balance of cost to be recovered. Subtract line 10 from line
    2 .... $29,000

    *Statement for death benefit exclusion

    Cost in plan (contract) $25,000

    Death benefit exclusion 5,000

    Total (enter on line 2 above) $30,000

    Signed: *Diane Greene*

    Date: 4-14-94

    KEEP FOR YOUR RECORDS

In completing Form 1099–R, the payer of the annuity chooses to report the taxable part of the annuity payments using the Simplified General Rule. However, since the payer does not adjust the investment in the contract by the death benefit exclusion, the payer figures the tax-free part of each monthly payment to be $83.33, as follows:

$$\frac{\text{Total investment: } \$25,000}{\text{Expected payments: } 300} = \$83.33 \quad \begin{array}{l}\text{(Monthly return}\\ \text{of investment)}\end{array}$$

However, Diane figures a $100 monthly tax-free amount (see line 4 of the worksheet). Because of this difference in the computations, the Form 1099–R given by the payer to Diane shows a greater taxable amount than what she figures for herself. She should report on line 17b of Form 1040 or line 11b of Form 1040A only the smaller taxable amount based on her own computation. She must attach a signed statement to her income tax return stating that she is entitled to the death benefit exclusion in making the Simplified General Rule computation.

General Rule

You must use the General Rule to figure the taxability of your pension or annuity if your annuity starting date is after July 1, 1986, and you do not qualify for, or you do not choose, the Simplified General Rule (explained earlier). You must also use the General Rule if your annuity starting date was before July 2, 1986, and you did not qualify to use the Three-Year Rule. (The three-year rule was repealed.)

Under the General Rule, a part of each payment is nontaxable because it is considered a return of your cost. The remainder of each payment (including the full amount of any later cost-of-living increases) is taxable. Finding the nontaxable part is very complex and requires you to use actuarial tables. For a full explanation and the tables you need, get Publication 939, *Pension General Rule (Nonsimplified Method).*

The nontaxable amount remains the same even if the total payment increases. If your annuity starting date was before 1987, you continue to exclude the same nontaxable amount from each annuity payment for as long as you receive your annuity. If your annuity starting date is after 1986, your total exclusion over the years cannot be more than your cost of the contract reduced by the value of any refund feature.

If your annuity starting date is after July 1, 1986, and you (or a survivor annuitant) die before the cost is recovered, a miscellaneous itemized deduction is allowed for the unrecovered cost on your, or your survivor's, final income tax return. The deduction is not subject to the 2%-of-adjusted-gross-income limit.

Explanation

The purpose of the General Rule is to let you recover your investment in the annuity by allowing you, in effect, a tax **deduction** each year against the amount you receive.

Old General Rule. For annuities that started prior to 1987, this deduction was determined in advance and remains the same no matter how long you live. Consequently, you will generally recover either more or less than your actual cost.

If you live longer than your life expectancy, you win in two ways: You receive much more in annuity payments than the insurance company thought your investment would require, *and* your taxes are reduced, because your cost recovery deductions will total more than your actual investment in the annuity.

If you live a shorter period than your life expectancy, you lose in two ways: You will have received less in payments than your investment would have produced over your normal life expectancy, *and* you will have reported more taxable income than you should have, because you will not have recovered all your cost before death.

IRS Publication 575 tells you how to compute your expected return and exclusion percentage. However, usually you do not have to bother doing the arithmetic. The information on how much income to include in taxable income and how much to exclude is routinely provided by your employer, both to you and to the IRS.

New General Rule. For annuities that start in 1987, the exclusion percentage will only be used until you have recovered your cost. Once you have recovered your cost, any amount that you receive after that will be fully taxable. If you die before recovering your cost, a deduction for the unrecovered cost will be allowed on your final return filed for the year of your death. Your executor would report this as a miscellaneous itemized deduction *not* subject to the 2% of adjusted gross income limitation.

Survivors

If you receive a survivor annuity because of the death of a retiree who had reported the annuity under the Three-Year Rule, include the total received in income. (The retiree's cost has already been recovered tax free.)

If the retiree was reporting the annuity payments under the General Rule, apply the same exclusion percentage as the retiree used to your initial payment called for in the contract. The resulting tax-free amount will then remain fixed. Any increases in the survivor annuity are fully taxable.

If the retiree had chosen to report the annuity under the Simplified General Rule, the monthly tax-free amount remains fixed. You continue to use the same monthly tax-free amount for your survivor payments.

If the annuity starting date is after 1986, the total exclusion over the years cannot be more than the cost minus (if the General Rule is used) the value of any refund feature.

If you are the survivor of an employee or former employee who died before receiving any annuity payments, you must figure the taxable and nontaxable parts of your annuity payments. You may qualify to add up to $5,000 to the decedent's cost to be recovered tax free. This *death benefit exclusion* is treated as an addition to the cost of the annuity. See *Death benefit exclusion,* earlier, under *Simplified General Rule.*

Estate tax. If your annuity was a joint and survivor annuity that was included in the decedent's estate, an estate tax may have been paid on it. You can deduct, as a miscellaneous itemized deduction, the part of the total estate tax attributable to the annuity. This deduction is not subject to the 2%-of-adjusted-gross-income limit. The deceased annuitant must have died after the annuity starting date. This amount cannot be deducted in one year. It must be deducted in equal amounts over your remaining life expectancy.

Explanation

The deduction for an annuity that is included in the decedent's estate has become very rare. Since the exemptions for estate tax have been greatly increased and the marital deduction is now unlimited, it is unusual for any estate tax to be paid on a joint and survivor annuity. However, some people do qualify.

Example

Alexander dies while receiving an annuity worth $10,000. Alexander's beneficiary will receive $1,000 per year for the next 15 years. The estate tax figured with the annuity included is $4,500 more than when figured without the annuity.

The recipient may claim an itemized deduction (not subject to the 2% of adjusted gross income limitation) each year of $300 ($1,000/$15,000 × $4,500). In this computation, the $15,000 represents the total dollars that will be received over the 15-year period.

No deduction is allowed, however, for the portion of the estate tax that is attributable to the tax on excess accumulations in a retirement account.

How to Report

If you file Form 1040, report your total annuity on line 17a and the taxable part on line 17b. If your pension or annuity is fully taxable, enter it on line 17b; do not make an entry on line 17a.

If you file Form 1040A, report your total annuity on line 11a and the taxable part on line 11b. If your pension or annuity is fully taxable, enter it on line 11b; do not make an entry on line 11a.

More than one annuity. If you receive more than one annuity and at least one of them is not fully taxable, enter the total amount received from *all* annuities on line 17a, Form 1040, or line 11a, Form 1040A, and enter the taxable part on line 17b, Form 1040, or line 11b, Form 1040A. If all the annuities you receive are fully taxable, enter the total of all of them on line 17b, Form 1040, or line 11b, Form 1040A.

Explanation

If you receive a lump-sum distribution and, to avoid the current tax, decide to roll it over into another retirement vehicle, such as an IRA, you still are required to show the total amount received on line 17. However, on line 17 you would show the taxable amount as zero.

Joint return. If you file a joint return and you and your spouse each receive one or more pensions or annuities, report the total of the pensions and annuities on line 17a, Form 1040, or line 11a, Form 1040A, and report the taxable part on line 17b, Form 1040, or line 11b, Form 1040A.

Death Benefit Exclusion

If you are the beneficiary of a deceased employee or former employee, the pension or annuity you get because of that person's death may qualify for a death benefit exclusion. This exclusion cannot be more than $5,000.

If you are eligible for the exclusion, add it to the cost or unrecovered cost of the annuity when you figure your cost at the annuity starting date.

If you are the survivor under a joint and survivor annuity, the exclusion applies only if either:

1) The decedent died before receiving, or becoming entitled to receive, retirement pension or annuity payments, or
2) The decedent received disability income payments that were not treated as pension or annuity income (the decedent had not reached minimum retirement age).

For more information on the death benefit exclusion, see *Payments to beneficiaries of deceased employees (death benefit exclusion)* under *Life Insurance Proceeds* in Chapter 13, *Other Income,* and *Death benefit exclusion* under *Investment in the Contract (Cost)* in Publication 575.

Explanation

Chapter 13, *Other Income,* discusses an application of the $5,000 death benefit exclusion. Typically, the exclusion arises when an employer makes a payment to the family of a deceased employee that was not required to be made to the decedent. The first $5,000 may be excluded from income. Generally, the exclusion does not apply to amounts that the employee, immediately before death, had a right to receive while living. It does apply to lump-sum distributions from a qualified pension, annuity, stock bonus, or profit-sharing plan, or from certain tax-sheltered annuities.

The $5,000 amount applies, regardless of the number of employers paying death benefits or the number of beneficiaries.

Lump-Sum Distributions

Lump-sum distributions you receive from a qualified retirement plan (an employer's qualified pension, stock bonus, or profit-sharing plan) may be given special tax treatment. A qualified plan is a plan that meets certain requirements of the Internal Revenue Code. For information on a distribution you receive that includes employer securities, see *Distributions of employer securities* under *Lump-Sum Distributions* in Publication 575.

Explanation

Employer securities distributed as part of a lump-sum distribution may have increased in value after they were purchased by the trust that is making the distribution. This increase is called "net unrealized appreciation." It is not taxed at the time of the lump-sum distribution.

If you later sell these securities, any gain is taxed as a **long-term capital gain**—up to the amount of your net unrealized appreciation. Any gain above this amount is a long-term capital gain if the employee holds the stock for more than 1 year prior to selling it. You may also elect not to use this treatment on your tax return and instead treat the capital gain (net unrealized appreciation) as part of your lump-sum distribution.

You may not claim a loss if you receive stock that is worth less than your total contributions to the plan. You may claim a loss when you sell the stock if it is sold for less than the amount of your own after-tax employee contributions allocated to the shares of stock sold.

Example

Assume that Widget Company's pension trust used the company's contribution for Sarah Jones to purchase 100 shares of Widget Company common stock at $10 per share on January 15, 1987. These securities were given to Sarah Jones as part of a lump-sum distribution on January 1, 1993, when their value had risen to $15 per share. Sarah is taxed on the $10 per share that was contributed by Widget, but she is not taxed on the net unrealized appreciation of $5 per share on January 1, 1993.

If Sarah sold the 100 shares of Widget Company stock on January 12, 1993, for $25 per share, the $500 gain [($15 − $10) × 100 shares] attributed to net unrealized appreciation would be taxed as long-term capital gain. The gain of $1,000 [($25 − $5 − $10) × 100 shares] would be taxed as a short-term capital gain, since Sarah held the securities for less than 1 year from the distribution date.

If Sarah had made her own after-tax contributions of $1,700 to the pension trust and received Widget Company stock valued at only $1,000 at the time of the lump-sum distribution, she could not have claimed a loss at that time. However, if she later sold the stock, she would compare her proceeds with $1,700 to determine if she had a gain or a loss on the sale.

TaxPlanner

There is no mandatory 20% withholding requirement for employer securities distributed in an eligible rollover distribution after December 31, 1992. See *Rollovers,* later in this chapter. Therefore, it may be beneficial under some circumstances for you to receive an eligible rollover distribution consisting of employer securities or employer securities and cash, rather than all cash.

Distributions that qualify. A lump-sum distribution must be paid within a single tax year. It is the distribution of a plan participant's *entire balance,* from all of the employer's qualified pension plans, all of the employer's qualified stock bonus plans, or all of the employer's qualified profit-sharing plans. (The participant's entire balance does not include deductible voluntary employee contributions or certain forfeited amounts.)

The distribution must be paid:

1) Because of the plan participant's death,
2) After the participant reaches age 59½,
3) Because the participant, if an employee, separates from service, or
4) After the participant, if a self-employed individual, becomes totally and permanently disabled.

TaxPlanner

If you change jobs after December 31, 1993, and plan to participate in your new employer's plan, you may want to consider a "plan-to-plan" transfer to the new plan if your new employer cooperates. If an amount is transferred from one qualified plan to another, no amount will be required to be withheld on the amount transferred from your old employer's plan. While there is nothing in the law that requires your new employer to accept transferred amounts, some employers may do this as an accommodation to new employees.

TaxAlert

As of January 1, 1993, a qualified plan must allow participants the option of a direct rollover to other qualified plans or an IRA. Like plan-to-plan transfers, however, there is nothing in the law that requires your new employer to accept these amounts. If the new employer's plan will not accept these amounts, they could be transferred directly from your old employer's plan to an IRA.

Tax treatment. You can recover your *cost* in the lump sum tax free. Also, you may be entitled to special tax treatment for the remaining part of the distribution.

In general, your *cost* consists of:

1) The plan participant's total nondeductible contributions to the plan,
2) The total of the plan participant's taxable costs of any life insurance contract distributed,
3) Any employer contributions that were taxable to the plan participant, and
4) Repayments of loans that were taxable to the plan participant.

You must reduce this cost by amounts previously distributed tax free.

Capital gain treatment. If the plan participant reached age 50 before 1986 (was born before 1936), you can choose to treat a portion of the taxable part of a lump-sum distribution as a capital gain that is taxable at a 20% (.20) rate. This treatment applies to the portion you receive for the participation in the plan before 1974. You can choose this treatment only once for any plan participant. Use Form 4972, *Tax on Lump-Sum Distributions,* to make this choice.

Special averaging method. If the plan participant reached age 50 before 1986 (was born before 1936), you can elect special averaging of the ordinary income portion of the distribution. (This also includes the capital gain portion of the distribution if you do not choose capital gain treatment for it.) To qualify, you must elect to use special averaging on all lump-sum distributions received in the tax year.

To use special averaging for a distribution you receive for your own participation in the retirement plan, you must have been a participant in the plan for at least 5 full tax years. You can only make one lifetime election to use this method for any plan participant.

Explanation

You must have been a participant in the plan for at least 5 years *before* the taxable year in which the distribution is made to use special averaging.

If you choose the special averaging method, you generally figure your tax, using Form 4972, as though the distribution were received over 5 years.

However, you can treat the distribution as though it were received over 10 years instead of 5 years, provided you apply the special 1986 tax rates to it. Form 4972 shows how to make this computation. The Form 4972 Instructions contain a special 1986 tax rate schedule that you must use in making the 10–year averaging computation.

Form 1099–R. If you receive a total distribution from a plan, you should receive a Form 1099–R, *Distributions From Pensions, Annuities, Retirement or Profit-Sharing Plans, IRAs, Insurance Contracts, etc.* If the distribution qualifies as a lump-sum distribution, box 3 shows the capital gain, and box 2a minus box 3 is the ordinary income. If you do not get a Form 1099–R, or if you have questions about it, contact your plan administrator.

TaxORGANIZER

If you receive *any* distibution from a qualified plan after 1990, you should receive a Form 1099-R from the plan administrator or its agent. This form has been changed to incorporate new codes for direct rollovers (discussed below).

Explanation

The great attraction of a lump-sum distribution is its special tax treatment. Compared to reporting the lump sum as ordinary income, using the special tax treatment usually results in considerable tax savings.

The special tax treatment of a lump-sum payment has three aspects. First, you subtract the amount of your contributions to the plan. This leaves the amount of the distribution that is taxable, a part of which may be treated as a long-term capital gain. If you so choose and you qualify, the balance of the distribution may be taxed under the 5-year or 10-year averaging method (see explanation below).

The capital gain portion and the ordinary income por-

---

tion of the distribution are stated separately on Form 1099-R. This form is required to be given to you by your employer by January 31 of the year following the distribution. The capital gain amount should be in the same proportion to the total taxable distribution as the number of months you were an active participant in a qualified plan before 1974 bears to the total number of months you actively participated in the plan. For persons born before January 1, 1936, the amount treated as a capital gain can be taxed at 20%.

Five- or ten-year averaging. The rest of your lump-sum distribution may be taxed under the 5- or 10-year averaging method. In using the 5-year or 10-year averaging method, you assume that your income was received by 5 different individuals (10 for 10-year averaging) in the current year and that each of these individuals had *no* other income. As a result, most of the income is taxed at the lowest rates on the single taxpayer Tax Rate Schedule. The tax for these fictional individuals is then added up and becomes your tax.

TaxSAVER

Five- or ten-year averaging. The 5-year or 10-year averaging method may be so beneficial to you that you elect to have the long-term capital gain portion of the distribution included in the 5-year or 10-year averaging computation rather than to have it taxed as long-term capital gain. The tax should be figured both ways to see which is lower. You are not eligible to make this election if in any previous tax year you received a lump-sum distribution and treated any part of it as long-term capital gain.

Note: Distributions from IRAs do not qualify for long-term capital gain treatment or 5- or 10-year averaging. Except in the case of death, any distribution to an employee with less than 5 years' participation in a qualified plan prior to the distribution year is not eligible for the 5-year or 10-year averaging method.

TaxPLANNER

Plan-to-plan transfers have certain advantages over rollovers, discussed below. One advantage is that your periods of service for both employers would be counted by the plans for purposes of the 5-year or 10-year averaging computation.

Life insurance proceeds. An employee's life insurance proceeds paid in a lump sum under an insurance contract on the death of an employee usually are not taxable. However, any amounts you received that are larger than the face amount of the life insurance are taxable to the extent of the excess. Life insurance proceeds are discussed in Chapter 13, *Other Income.*

Rollovers

Generally, a rollover is a tax-free distribution to you of cash or other assets from a qualified retirement plan that you transfer to an **eligible retirement plan.** However, see *Direct rollover,* later.

An eligible retirement plan is an IRA, a qualified employee retirement plan, or a qualified annuity plan. See Chapter 18, *Individual Retirement Arrangements (IRAs),* for information on rollovers from IRAs.

In general, the most you can roll over is the part that would be taxable if you did not roll it over. You cannot roll over your contributions, other than your deductible employee contributions. You do not pay tax on the amount that you rolled over. The amount you roll over, however, is generally taxable later when it is paid to you or your survivor.

You must complete the rollover by the 60th day following the day on which you receive the distribution. (This 60–day period is extended for any time the amount distributed is in a frozen deposit in a financial institution.) For all rollovers to an individual retirement arrangement (IRA), you must irrevocably elect rollover treatment by written notice to the trustee or issuer of the IRA.

Eligible rollover distributions. Generally, you can roll over any part of the taxable portion of most nonperiodic distributions from a qualified retirement plan, unless it is a required minimum distribution.

Direct rollover option. You can choose to have the administrator of your old plan transfer the distribution directly from your old plan to the new plan (if permitted) or IRA. If you decide to make a tax-free rollover, it is generally to your advantage to choose this direct rollover option. Under this option, the plan administrator would not withhold tax from your distribution.

Withholding tax. If you choose to have the distribution paid to you, it is taxable in the year distributed unless you roll it over to a new plan or IRA within 60 days. The plan administrator must withhold income tax of 20% on the taxable distribution paid to you. (See *Withholding on Pensions and Annuities* in Chapter 5.) This means that, if you decide to make a tax-free rollover of the entire distribution, your contribution to the new plan or IRA must include other money (for example, from savings or amounts borrowed) to replace the amount withheld. The administrator should give you a written explanation of your distribution options within a reasonable period of time before making an eligible rollover distribution.

Explanation

Remember, if you do not wish to include the property received as part of a distribution in the rollover, you cannot roll over cash in place of the property received (such as stock) unless the actual property is sold. The proceeds from the bona fide sale may then be included in the rollover. If the plan in which you participate makes eligible rollover distributions, the plan administrator (usually the employer) is required by law to give you a written explanation of how the rollover rules work.

Generally, an **eligible rollover distribution** means any distribution of all or any portion of an employee's balance in a qualified plan. Eligible rollover distributions do not include the following:

- Required minimum distributions (for example, distributions required to be made to individuals who have attained the age of 70-1/2);
- Distributions that are part of a series of substantially equal payments that are received at least annually over the life or life expectancy of the employee (or the joint lives or life expectancies of the employee and the employee's designated beneficiary) or made over a period of at least 10 years;
- Distributions not includable in gross income (for example, distributions that represent a return of an employee's after-tax contributions);
- Certain corrective distributions made because of

the plan's violation of the Internal Revenue Code's limitations;
- Loans treated as distributions because they violate the Internal Revenue Code's plan loan rules;
- Loans in default that are treated as distributions; and
- Certain dividends paid on employer securities.

Eligible rollover distributions made after December 31, 1992 can be rolled over in one of two ways. First, you can transfer funds in a **direct rollover** where the plan trustee transfers some or all of your eligible rollover distribution directly to the trustee of an eligible retirement plan.

TAXPLANNER

A **direct rollover** may be accomplished by wire transfer, by mailing a check to the trustee of the recipient plan, or even by providing you with a check and instructing you to deliver it to an eligible retirement plan. However, the check must be made payable only to the trustee or custodian of the eligible retirement plan, not to you.

Explanation

You cannot be precluded from dividing an eligible rollover distribution by electing to make a direct rollover of a portion of the distribution and to receive a distribution of the remaining portion. However, your employer may preclude you from electing to have a portion of an eligible rollover distribution paid on a direct rollover if that portion is less than $500.

TAXPLANNER

Employers may, but need not, exclude eligible rollover distributions that are less than $200 from the direct rollover option. The $200 de minimis rule also applies to the mandatory 20% withholding requirement. However, amounts of $200 or less may still be eligible for rollover by you within 60 days after receipt (see discussion below).

An employer is not required to allow employees to have a direct rollover paid to more than one recipient plan. Therefore, if you wish to diversify an IRA investment, for example, you can subsequently roll over a distribution to another IRA or utilize an IRA trustee-to-trustee transfer.

The withholding requirement can be avoided and a distribution received currently simply by having amounts transferred directly to an IRA and then immediately withdrawing them from the IRA.

TAXALERT

Plan administrators are required to give plan participants a written notice explaining the direct rollover option and related tax rules. You may consider the decision whether to have your benefits paid in a direct rollover or paid directly to you for at least 30 days after you receive this notice, unless you waive this right.

Explanation

There is a second way amounts can be rolled over. If your funds are not transferred in a direct rollover (for example, where the plan trustee has made the check payable to you) you may nonetheless roll over some or all of your eligible rollover distribution to an eligible retirement plan. You must complete the rollover by the 60th day following the day on which you receive the distribution. In this case, 20% of the distribution will be withheld as income tax by the plan administrator making the distribution, and in order to rollover the full distribution, you will have to use other funds to make up the 20% withheld. If you do not make up the amount withheld, you will be taxed on the amount withheld and may also owe a 10% early distribution tax on such amount. See *Tax on Early Distributions* later in this chapter.

Deductible voluntary employee contributions. If you receive an eligible rollover distribution from your employer's qualified plan of part of the balance of your accumulated deductible voluntary contributions, you can roll over tax free any part of this distribution. The rollover can be either to an IRA or to certain other qualified plans.

TAXSAVER 1

One of the most difficult decisions you have to make when you near retirement is what to do with your qualified pension or profit-sharing plan. There are usually four choices:

1. **Lump-sum distribution.** You pay tax based on either 5-year or 10-year income averaging (discussed above) and retain the rest of the distribution to invest as you see fit.
2. **Annuity.** The qualified plan pays you and/or your surviving spouse an annuity, the value of which is determined by how much of an annuity the lump-sum distribution would have bought from an insurance carrier based on your life expectancy. When you and your spouse die, nothing further is paid. If your plan requires that a joint and survivor annuity be offered to married participants, then, in order to elect out of the annuity alternative, your spouse must consent to another form of distribution, such as a lump-sum distribution.
3. **Rollover to an IRA.** There is no income tax required to be withheld on any portion of an eligible rollover distribution made after December 31, 1992, that is rolled over directly to an eligible retirement plan. The principal continues to earn income without tax until it is withdrawn. Withdrawals are taxed at ordinary income rates and are required to begin not later than April 1 of the calendar year following the calendar year in which the employee attains age 70½. Withdrawals are to be made over the life of such employee or over the lives of such employee and a designated beneficiary (or over a period not extending beyond the life expectancy of such employee or the joint life expectancy of such employee and a designated beneficiary).

4. **Retention in the plan.** If you have more than $3,500 in the plan, the plan must permit you to leave your account balance in the qualified plan until you reach age 62 or a stipulated normal retirement age, if earlier. This may be advantageous if you don't need the money right away, depending on the investment return of the plan. If you have less than $3,500 in the plan, the plan may require that you receive your account balance in a lump sum whether or not you consent.

Example

You have $100,000 in the company's qualified plan, and you will reach the retirement age of 65 shortly. You may have the following options, depending on the plan's distribution provisions:

1. You may take a lump-sum distribution of $100,000. In 1993 you will pay a 10-year income-averaging tax of $14,471 (or $15,000 under 5-year averaging) and be left with a fund of $85,529. Any income you earn on this money will be subject to normal tax rules.
2. You and your spouse may receive a joint and survivor annuity of $12,000 every year through the year of death of the last to die. Each payment will be subject to tax at ordinary rates, which may be as high as 39.6% in 1993 and afterwards, depending on which bracket you're in. The total that you and/or your spouse will receive will depend on your life spans and your actual marginal tax rates in each year that you live. This is the joint and 100% survivor annuity option. Most plans permit more than one annuity option. As an alternative, if your plan permits, you could elect to receive more during your lifetime and have your spouse receive less upon your death, so long as your spouse receives no less than 50% of the amount you receive.
3. You may roll over the entire amount into an IRA. You will have to begin receiving payments, which will be taxed at ordinary income rates, no later than April 1 of the year following the year you reach age 70½.
4. The plan invests solely in a guaranteed insurance contract that has a fixed rate of 8.5% for 1993. This rate may be so attractive that you may elect to defer the receipt of your account balance until a later year, if you qualify.
5. No current tax is paid or withheld if the entire amount is rolled over to a qualified plan of a new employer. (Remember that while a qualified plan is required to offer the direct rollover option, there is no requirement that another qualified plan accept such rollovers.) You will pay tax when withdrawals occur, based on special averaging or an annuity. There are rules restricting certain participants from using this option. These rules are explained below.
6. If you will be self-employed during the year in which you retire, you can roll over your qualified pension plan into a Keogh plan. The virtue of rolling over your pension into a Keogh plan instead of an IRA is that you can be taxed using the 5-year or 10-year averaging method (discussed above) when you withdraw the money from the account. You cannot use the 5-year or 10-year averaging method if you roll over your

pension plan into an IRA. Many people find it easy to arrange to be self-employed in the year in which they retire. If the plan-to-plan transfer is done properly, you can preserve your pretransfer service from the old plan for purposes of the 5-year minimum participation requirement.

In this example, the choice between options 1, 2, 3, and 4 is tricky and requires analysis under various assumptions of interest rates, life expectancy, medical expenses, current needs, and tax rates. Professional help is necessary and well worth the cost.

Methods 5 and 6 may also save you time and keep your investments consolidated in one account while preserving your option to be taxed using the 5-year or 10-year averaging method. Consult your tax advisor if you think you qualify for these two alternatives.

Rollover by surviving spouse or other beneficiary. You may be entitled to roll over to an IRA part or all of a retirement plan distribution you receive as the surviving spouse of a deceased employee. You cannot roll it over to another qualified retirement plan. The rollover rules apply to you as if you were the employee. However, a beneficiary other than the employee's surviving spouse cannot roll over a distribution.

For more information on the rules for rolling over distributions see Publication 575.

Explanation

If you have not designated a beneficiary for any salary that because of death you will not collect, the money will generally be paid into your estate. In that case, it would be reported as income on the estate's income tax return. Any distribution attributable to an employee that is paid to the employee's surviving spouse is treated in the same manner as if the spouse were the employee. The same rule applies if any distribution attributable to an employee is paid to a spouse or a former spouse as an "alternate payee" under a qualified domestic relations order (QDRO). A distribution made to the surviving spouse of an employee (or an alternate payee under a QDRO) after December 31, 1992, is an eligible rollover distribution if it meets the requirements explained above. For further details, consult your tax advisor.

Bond Purchase Plans

The Department of the Treasury stopped issuing U.S. Retirement Plan Bonds after April 30, 1982. They were a special series of interest-bearing bonds that retirement plans could buy.

If your plan bought retirement bonds, you can cash them at any time. A beneficiary can cash them after the participant's death. Interest on the bonds stops 5 years after the owner of the bonds dies. They may be cashed at any Federal Reserve Bank branch or at the office of the Treasurer of the United States.

If a retirement bond is distributed from a bond purchase plan to you as an employee or beneficiary and you cash in the bond, you are taxed on the amount received minus your cost (normally, any voluntary nondeductible employee payments used to buy that bond). However, you can defer the tax on the amount received by rolling it over to an IRA as discussed under *Rollovers* in Chapter

18, *Individual Retirement Arrangements (IRAs)*. You can also roll it over to a qualified employer plan (but later distributions of the rollover amount do not qualify for 5- or 10-year averaging or capital gain treatment covered earlier).

Tax on Early Distributions

Distributions you receive from your **qualified retirement plan or deferred annuity contract** before you reach age 59½, and amounts you receive when you cash in retirement bonds before you are age 59½, are usually subject to an additional tax of 10%. The tax applies to the taxable part of the distribution.

For this purpose, a **qualified retirement plan** means:

1) A qualified employee retirement plan,
2) A qualified annuity plan,
3) A tax-sheltered annuity plan for employees of public schools or tax-exempt organizations, or
4) An individual retirement arrangement (IRA).

Exceptions to tax. The additional tax does not apply to distributions that are:

1) Made to a beneficiary or to the estate of the plan participant or annuity holder on or after his or her death,
2) Made because you are totally and permanently disabled,
3) Made as part of a series of substantially equal periodic (at least annual) payments over your life expectancy or the joint life expectancy of you and your beneficiary,
4) Made to you after you separated from service if the separation occurred during or after the calendar year in which you reached age 55,
5) Made to you, to the extent you have deductible expenses for medical care (the medical expense that exceeds 7.5% of your adjusted gross income) whether or not you itemize deductions for the tax year,
6) Made to alternate payees under qualified domestic relations orders,
7) Made to you if, as of March 1, 1986, you separated from service and began receiving benefits from the qualified plan under a written election designating a specific schedule of benefit payments,
8) Made to you to correct excess deferrals, excess contributions, or excess aggregate contributions,
9) Allocable to cost in a deferred annuity contract before August 14, 1982,
10) From an annuity contract under a qualified personal injury settlement,
11) Made under an immediate annuity contract, or
12) Made from a deferred annuity contract purchased by your employer upon the termination of a qualified employee retirement plan or qualified annuity that is held by your employer until you separate from the service of the employer.

TAXSAVER

Note that the 10% excise tax also does not apply in the year of distribution if you roll over a qualifying distribution (or make a direct rollover of an eligible rollover distribution after December 31, 1992). This is because the tax is applied only to taxable distributions. This helps to make rollovers an even more attractive alternative.

The exception in (3) applies to distributions from qualified employee plans **only** if the payments begin after you separate from service. The exceptions in (4), (5), (6), and (7) apply only to distributions from qualified employee plans. Exceptions (9) through (12) apply only to distributions from deferred annuity contracts.

Explanation

In addition to the exceptions stated above, the tax on early distributions does not apply to distributions that are made consisting of dividends on employer securities from an Employee Stock Ownership Plan (ESOP)

This exception does not apply to IRA distributions.

TAXORGANIZER

On Form 1099-R, distributions should be coded by the payer without regard to whether a rollover is made or anticipated. Thus, for purposes of 1099-R reporting, a rollover that is planned or has already occurred should not be considered an exception to the early distribution penalty.

Example

If Ben Jones withdraws the total balance in his qualified plan, informs the IRA trustees that the funds will be rolled over, is under age 59½, and meets no other exception under the early distribution rules, the Form 1099-R should contain a code 1, "early premature distribution, no known exception." If Mr. Jones then rolls over his distribution, he should properly report the rollover on his federal income tax return to avoid the early (premature) distribution penalty.

Reporting tax or exception. If distribution code 1 is shown in box 7 of Form 1099-R, *Distributions From Pensions, Annuities, Retirement or Profit-Sharing Plans, IRAs, Insurance Contracts, etc.,* multiply the taxable part of the early distribution by 10% and enter the result on line 51 of Form 1040 and write "No" on the dotted line.

However, if you owe this tax and also owe any other additional tax on a distribution, you must file Form 5329, *Additional Taxes Attributable to Qualified Retirement Plans (Including IRAs), Annuities, and Modified Endowment Contracts,* to report the taxes.

If you qualify for an exception to the 10% tax and distribution code 2, 3, or 4 is shown in box 7 of Form 1099-R, you do not need to report the exception. However, if the code is not shown, or the code shown is incorrect, you must file Form 5329.

Tax on Excess Distributions

If *retirement distributions* over $150,000 are made to you during the calendar year, you are subject to a 15% excise tax on the amount over $150,000. The tax is offset by any 10% early distribution tax that applies to the excess distribution. (See the preceding discussion.)

Retirement distributions. Retirement distributions include distributions from qualified employee retirement plans, qualified annuity plans, tax-sheltered annuities, and individual retirement arrangements (IRAs).

Exceptions to tax. The tax on excess distributions does not apply to the following distributions:

1) Distributions after death,
2) Distributions paid to your spouse or former spouse under a qualified domestic relations order that are includible in the income of the payee (the distributions are included in determining your spouse's or former spouse's excess distributions),
3) Distributions attributable to the employee's investment in the contract,
4) Distributions to the extent rolled over tax free,
5) Retirement distributions of annuity contracts, the value of which are not included in gross income at the time of the distribution (other than distributions under, or proceeds from the sale or exchange of, such contracts),
6) Retirement distributions of excess deferrals (and income allocable to them), and
7) Retirement distributions of excess contributions (and income allocable to them) under section 401(k) plans or IRAs, or excess aggregate contributions (and income on them) under qualified plans. The aggregate contributions relate to highly compensated employees and the plan will figure the excess.

Combining distributions. If distributions for you are made to you and others, you must combine the distributions in figuring the amount of excess distributions for the year.

Lump-sum distributions. A different limit applies to a lump-sum distribution for which you choose special averaging or capital gain treatment. In this case, the $150,000 annual amount increases five times to $750,000. You must figure a separate tax on the lump-sum distribution over $750,000.

Special grandfather election. If you made a special "grandfather election" on your 1987 or 1988 return, you can exclude from the tax a prorated part of a distribution that is related to your accrued benefits on August 1, 1986. To have made this special choice, your accrued benefit as of August 1, 1986, must have exceeded $562,500. For more information, see the instructions for Part IV of Form 5329.

Form 5329. You must file a Form 5329 if you receive excess distributions from a qualified retirement plan, whether or not you owe tax.

TAXPLANNER

There is a 15% excise tax on what Congress has called excess distributions and excess accumulations. In general, amounts in excess of $750,000 for lump-sum distributions and $150,000 for other distributions are considered excess distributions. Transition rules increase these amounts for individuals with large accrued benefits on August 1, 1986. Any excess retirement accumulation that remains at your death can result in a 15% excise tax. Additionally, a 10% excise tax is imposed on premature distributions from IRAs and premature distributions from qualified retirement plans (see the following.)

Tax for Failure to Make Minimum Distribution

Your qualified retirement plan must distribute to you your entire interest in the plan, or begin to make minimum distributions to you by no later than April 1 of the year following the calendar year in which you reach age 70½. It does not matter whether you have retired. This rule applies to qualified employee retirement plans, qualified annuity plans, deferred compensation plans under section 457, tax-sheltered annuity programs (for benefits accruing after 1986), and IRAs.

You reach age 70½ on the date that is 6 calendar months

after the date of your 70th birthday. For example, if your 70th birthday was on July 1, 1992, you were age 70½ on January 1, 1993. Your required beginning date is April 1, 1994. If your 70th birthday was on June 30, 1992, you were age 70½ on December 30, 1992, and your required beginning date was April 1, 1993.

Exceptions. The above rule does not apply to governmental plans or church plans. Nor does it apply to any individual (unless a 5% owner) who reached age 70½ before 1988.

In these cases, distributions must begin no later than April 1 of the calendar year following the later of:

1) The calendar year in which you reach age 70½, or
2) The calendar year in which you retire.

5% owners. If you are a 5% (or more) owner of the company maintaining the plan, distributions to you must begin by April 1 of the calendar year after the year in which you reach 70½, regardless of when you retire.

Minimum distributions. These are regular periodic distributions that are large enough to use up the entire interest over your life expectancy or over the joint life expectancies of you and a designated surviving beneficiary (or over a shorter period).

Additional information. For more information on this rule, see *Tax on Excess Accumulation* in Publication 575.

Tax on failure to distribute. If you do not receive these required minimum distributions, you, as the payee, are subject to an excise tax. The tax equals 50% of the difference between the amount that was required to be distributed and the amount that was distributed during the tax year. You can get this excise tax excused if you establish that the shortfall in distributions was due to reasonable error and that you are taking reasonable steps to remedy the shortfall.

TaxAlert

Because the penalty for failure to receive required minimum distributions is severe, you must take steps to ensure that you receive these amounts on a timely basis. Many financial institutions do not inform their IRA holders when it is time to begin receiving distributions.

State insurer delinquency proceedings. You might not receive the minimum distribution because of state insurer delinquency proceedings for an insurance company. If your payments are reduced below the minimum due to these proceedings, you should contact your plan administrator. Under certain conditions, you will not have to pay the excise tax.

Form 5329. You must file a Form 5329 if you owe a tax because you did not receive a minimum required distribution from your qualified retirement plan.

Disability Income

Generally, if you retire on disability, you must report your pension or annuity as income.

If you were 65 or older at the end of the tax year, or if you were under 65, retired on permanent and total disability, and you received taxable disability income, you may be able to claim the credit for the elderly or the disabled. See Chapter 34 for more information about the credit.

Taxable Disability Pensions and Annuities

Whether you must report your disability pension or annuity as income depends on your pension plan's financing method.

Generally, you must report as income any amount you receive for your disability through an accident or health insurance plan that is paid for by your employer. However, certain payments may not be taxable to you. A discussion of these payments appears in Chapter 13 under *Other Sickness and Injury Benefits*.

No employee contributions. If the plan does not say that you must pay a specific part of the cost of the disability pension, your employer is considered to provide the disability pension. You must report on your return all payments you receive.

Employee contributions. If the plan says that you must pay a specific part of the cost of your disability pension, any amounts you receive that are due to your payments to the disability pension are not taxed. You do not report them on your return. They are treated as benefits received under an accident or health insurance policy that you bought. You generally must include in income the rest of the amounts you receive that are due to your employer's payments.

Plan details. Your employer should be able to give you specific details about your pension plan and to tell you the amount, if any, you paid for your disability pension.

Accrued leave payment. If you retired on disability, any lump-sum payment you received for accrued annual leave is a salary payment. The payment is not a disability payment. You should report it as wages in the year you received it.

Worker's compensation. If part of your disability pension is worker's compensation, you do not pay tax on that part. If you die, your survivor does not pay tax on the part of a survivor's benefit that represents a continuation of the worker's compensation.

How to report. You must report all your taxable disability income on line 7, Form 1040, or line 7, Form 1040A, until you reach minimum retirement age.

If you made contributions to your pension or annuity plan, your payments are taxable under the General Rule or Simplified General Rule (discussed earlier) beginning with the day after you reach *minimum retirement age.*

Generally, minimum retirement age is the age at which you may first receive a pension or annuity if you are not disabled.

Explanation

The principal ways in which disability income may qualify for exclusion from your income are as follows:

1. The income is attributable to payments you made for disability insurance.
2. You receive payments for a combat-related injury. For more information, see *Military and Certain Government Disability Pensions,* below.
3. You receive disability payments from the Veterans Administration directly or indirectly. For more information, see below.

Military and Certain Government Disability Pensions

Generally, you must report disability pensions as income. But certain military and government disability pensions are not taxable. If your disability pension is taxable, you may be able to take the credit for the elderly or the disabled. See Chapter 34 for more information about the credit.

Members of government services. Generally, you must report on your return any disability payments you receive for personal injuries or sickness resulting from active service in the armed forces of any country or in the National Oceanic and Atmospheric Administration, the Public Health Service, or the Foreign Service. However, do not include payments in income if they are based on percentage of disability, and:

1) You were entitled to receive a disability payment before September 25, 1975, or
2) You were a member of a government service or its reserve component, or were under a binding written commitment to become a member, on September 24, 1975, or
3) You receive disability payments for a ***combat-related injury,*** or
4) You would be entitled to receive disability compensation from the Department of Veterans Affairs (VA) if you filed an application for it.

A combat-related injury is a personal injury or sickness that:

1) Directly results from armed conflict,
2) Takes place while you are engaged in extra-hazardous service,
3) Takes place under conditions simulating war, including training exercises such as maneuvers, or
4) Is caused by an instrumentality of war.

Disability based on years of service. If you receive a disability pension based on years of service, you generally must include it in your income. But do not include in income the part of your pension that you could have excluded under the rules explained above if the pension had been based on percentage of disability. You must include the rest of your pension in income.

Terrorist attack. You do not include disability payments in income if you receive them for injuries directly resulting from a violent attack that occurred while you were a U.S. government employee performing official duties outside the United States. For your disability payments to be tax exempt, the Secretary of State must determine that the attack was a terrorist attack.

VA disability benefits. Disability benefits you receive from the VA are tax free. If you are a military retiree and receive your disability benefits from other than the VA, exclude from income the amount of disability benefits equal to the VA benefits to which you are entitled.

If you retire from the armed services (based on years of service) and at a later date are given a retroactive service-connected disability rating by the VA, exclude from income for the retroactive period the part of your retirement pay you would have been entitled to receive from the VA during that period. However, you must include in income any lump-sum readjustment payment you received on release from active duty, even though you are later given a retroactive disability rating by the VA.

Purchased Annuities

If you purchased an annuity contract from a commercial organization, such as an insurance company, you must use the General Rule to figure the tax-free part of each annuity payment. For more information, get Publication 939, *Pension General Rule (Nonsimplified Method).*

Sale of annuity. Gain on the sale of an annuity contract before its maturity date is ordinary income to the extent that the gain is due to interest accumulated on the contract. You do not recognize gain or loss on an exchange of an annuity contract solely for another annuity contract.

See *Transfers of Annuity Contracts* in Publication 575 for more information about exchanges of annuity contracts.

Explanation
Purchased annuities are subject to the General Rule. If you sell an annuity before its maturity date, the insurance company determines the amount of interest income and provides you with that information.

TAXSAVER
Annuities are popular investments, because the amount you contribute grows over time through the accumulation of interest. The interest income is not currently taxable to you and is reported as income only in later years, when payments are made from the annuity. The taxable payments are most likely to be made after you've retired. Therefore, an annuity may be a good way in which to earn income and defer taxes. Nowadays, it is more important than ever to investigate the financial strength and credit rating of the insurance company issuing the annuity.

12 | Social Security and Equivalent Railroad Retirement Benefits

Introduction

Social security income and equivalent railroad retirement benefits used to be tax-free. That's no longer the case. Now, you may have to pay income tax on amounts you receive.

Figuring out whether the benefits you receive are taxable is not easy. You will be required to puzzle through complicated rules, obtain information, and make numerous computations. This chapter will simplify your task. Among other things, it includes worksheets to help you make the necessary calculations.

This chapter discusses the taxability of any social security or equivalent tier 1 railroad retirement benefits you may have received. It also explains:

- How to figure whether your benefits are taxable,
- How to use the social security benefits worksheet,
- How to report your taxable benefits on Form 1040 and Form 1040A (with examples), and
- How to treat repayments that are more than the benefits you received during the year.

Note. This chapter does not discuss the tax rules that apply to railroad retirement benefits that are not subject to the social security equivalent portion of tier 1 benefits (including special guaranty benefits). The tax rules that apply to these benefits, tier 2 benefits, vested dual benefits, and supplemental annuity benefits, are discussed in Publication 575, *Pension and Annuity Income (Including Simplified General Rule)*.

Also not discussed are the tax rules that apply to foreign social security benefits. These benefits are taxable as a pension or annuity unless exempt from U.S. tax under a treaty. For example, social security benefits received by a U.S. citizen or resident from the United Kingdom are taxable under the tax rules discussed in Publication 575.

Useful Items

You may want to see:

Publication

- ☐ **505** Tax Withholding and Estimated Tax
- ☐ **575** Pension and Annuity Income (Including Simplified General Rule)
- ☐ **590** Individual Retirement Arrangements (IRAs)
- ☐ **915** Social Security Benefits and Equivalent Railroad Retirement Benefits

---

Taxation of Benefits

In figuring if any of your benefits are taxable, use the amount shown in box 5 of the Form SSA–1099 or Form RRB–1099 you received. If you received more than one form, add together the amount in box 5 of each form.

Form SSA–1099. If you received or repaid social security benefits during 1993, you will receive Form SSA–1099, *Social Security Benefit Statement.* An IRS Notice 703 will be enclosed with your Form SSA–1099. This notice includes a worksheet you can use to determine if any of your benefits may be taxable. Keep this notice for your own records. Do **not** mail it to either the IRS or the SSA.

Every person who received social security benefits will receive a Form SSA–1099, even if the benefit is combined with another person's in a single check. If you receive benefits on more than one social security record, you may get more than one Form SSA–1099.

Explanation

Social security payments from prior years received during 1993 may or may not be taxed, depending on your income level in the prior year. If they are taxable, you have a choice of how to compute the tax, which is explained later in the section on lump-sum benefits.

Form RRB–1099. If you received or repaid the social security equivalent portion of tier 1 railroad retirement benefits or special guaranty benefits during 1993, you will receive Form RRB–1099, *Payments by the Railroad Retirement Board.*

Each beneficiary will receive his or her own Form RRB–1099. If you receive benefits on more than one railroad retirement record, you may get more than one Form RRB–1099.

Who is taxed. The person who has the legal right to receive the benefits must determine if the benefits are taxable. For example, if you and your child receive benefits, but the check for your child is made out in your name, you must use only your portion of the benefits in figuring if any part is taxable to you. The portion of the benefits that belongs to your child must be added to your child's other income to see if any of those benefits are taxable.

Explanation

You will be able to determine your child's portion of the benefits by referring to forms provided by the Social Security Administration.

TaxOrganizer

You should keep copies of your Form(s) SSA-1099 and RRB-1099 that you received in the mail.

Are Any of Your Benefits Taxable?

If the only income you received during 1993 was your social security or equivalent tier 1 railroad retirement benefits, your benefits are generally not taxable and you probably do not have to file a return.

Base amount. If you received income during 1993 in addition to social security or equivalent tier 1 railroad retirement benefits, your benefits are generally not taxable if your income is not more than the following *base amounts*:

- $25,000 if you are single, head of household, or qualifying widow(er) with dependent child.
- $25,000 if you are married, do not file a joint return, and *did not* live with your spouse at any time during 1993.
- $32,000 if you are married and file a joint return.
- $–0– if you are married, do not file a joint return, and *did* live with your spouse at any time during 1993.

Explanation

Your social security benefits and railroad retirement benefits are taxed only if your combined income is more than $32,000 if you are married, filing jointly or more than $25,000 if you are single. If you are married filing separately and you lived with your spouse any time during the year, your base amount is $0. Your combined income in most cases is the total of your adjusted gross income, tax-exempt interest, one-half of your social security benefits, and excluded foreign source income.

TaxSaver

The amount of your combined income is what triggers the tax on your social security benefits. If you expect your combined income to exceed the base amount— $32,000 if you are filing a joint return, $25,000 if you are filing single—you may wish to consider the following strategies:

- *Deferring the recognition of income* by investing in U.S. Savings Bonds. If you never cash in the bonds, your heirs will recognize the income.
- *Staggering the recognition of income* so that you have alternating years of low and high income. With the right combination of figures, you could arrange to have your social security income taxed only in alternate years. Consider cashing in U.S. Savings Bonds, making withdrawals from **IRAs,** and selling appreciated property for capital gains in alternate years. You might also schedule the dates of maturity of U.S. Treasury bills to fall in alternate years.

Caution – New 85% rate for 1994. Beginning in 1994, a new higher 85% inclusion rate may increase the amount of your social security and equivalent tier 1 railroad retirement benefits to be included in taxable income.

The new 85% rate will apply only to income (the amount on line 7 of Worksheet 1 or 1A, provided later) that exceeds $44,000 for married persons filing jointly or $34,000 for unmarried individuals or married persons filing separately who do not live with their spouse at any time during the year. The 50% rate will continue to be used to figure the taxable part of excess income between the existing level ($25,000 or $32,000) and the new higher level.

If you are married filing separately and you live with your spouse at any time during 1994, your base amount will be zero. In that case, your gross income will include the lesser of:

- 85% of your social security or equivalent railroad retirement benefits received, or
- 85% of your income on line 7 of the worksheet.

If you expect the new rules will increase your taxable benefit for 1994, you should take that increase into account when you figure your 1994 estimated tax. For more information on the 85% rate, see Publication 553, *Highlights of 1993 Tax Changes*.

Joint return. If you are married and file a joint return for 1993, you and your spouse must combine your incomes and your benefits when figuring if any of your combined benefits are taxable. Even if your spouse did not receive any benefits, you must add your spouse's income to yours when figuring if any of your benefits are taxable.

You can use the worksheet in the following example, substituting your own amounts, to figure whether your income is more than the base amount for your filing status. A similar worksheet is included in your Form SSA–1099 or Form RRB–1099 package.

Example. You and your spouse are filing a joint return for 1993, and you both received social security benefits during the year. In January 1994, you received a Form SSA–1099 showing net benefits of $6,600 in box 5. Your spouse received a Form SSA–1099 showing $2,400 in box 5. You also received a taxable pension of $10,000 and interest income of $500 during 1993. You did not have any tax-exempt interest in 1993. Your benefits are not taxable for 1993 because your income, as figured in the following worksheet, is not more than your base amount ($32,000).

A Write in the amount from *box 5* of all your Forms SSA–1099 and RRB–1099. Include the full amount of any lump-sum benefit payments received in 1993, for 1993 and earlier years, if you choose to report the full amount for the 1993 tax year. (If you received more than one form, combine the amounts from box 5 and write in the total.) .... A. $9,000

Note: *If the amount on line A is zero or less, stop here; none of your benefits are taxable this year.*

B Divide line A by 2 and write in the result.. B. 4,500

C Add your taxable pensions, wages, interest, dividends, and other taxable income and write in the total .... C.   10,500

D Write in any tax-exempt interest, such as interest on municipal bonds .... D.   –0–

E Add lines B, C, and D and write in the total .... E.   15,000

Note: *If the amount on line E is not more than the* **base amount** *for your filing status, none of your benefits are taxable this year.*

Repayments. Any repayment of benefits you made during 1993 is automatically subtracted from the gross benefits you received in 1993. It does not matter if the repayment you made in 1993 was for a benefit you received before 1993. Your gross benefits are shown in box 3 of Form SSA–1099 or RRB–1099 and your repayments are shown in box 4. The amount in box 5 shows your net benefits for 1993 (box 3 minus box 4). This is the amount you will use to figure if any of your benefits are taxable.

How Much Is Taxable?

Your social security or equivalent tier 1 railroad retirement benefits may be taxable, depending on the amount of your income in addition to these benefits and on your filing status.

If your benefits are taxable, you can generally figure the taxable amount by using Worksheet 1 (for Form 1040 filers) or Worksheet 1A (for Form 1040A filers), provided at the end of this chapter.

Special worksheets for IRA deduction and taxable benefits. If you made contributions to an individual retirement arrangement (IRA) for 1993 and if your IRA deduction is limited because you or your spouse is covered by a retirement plan at work, you must use the special worksheets in Appendix B of Publication 590 to figure your IRA deduction and taxable benefits to be reported on your return.

Limit on taxable benefits. Before you figure the amount of your taxable benefits, read *How To Report,* later, and the following examples, which you can use as a guide to figure taxable benefits. You will find that the amount of taxable benefits cannot be more than 50% of the total net benefits (amounts received minus amounts repaid) received during the year.

TaxAlert

Beginning in 1994, a new higher 85% inclusion rate may increase the amount of your social security and equivalent tier 1 railroad retirement benefits to be included in taxable income. See *Caution – New 85% rate for 1994* under *Base amount,* earlier.

Explanation

Tax-exempt income is *not* taxable, even if you receive social security benefits. It is merely one of the items taken into consideration in determining if any of your social security benefits are taxable.

Lump-sum benefits. If you received a lump-sum (or retroactive) payment of benefits during 1993 that includes benefits you should have received before 1993, it will be included in box 3 of your Form SSA–1099 or Form RRB–1099.

Special election. Generally, you include a lump-sum benefit payment in total benefits for the year in which you receive it.

However, if you receive a lump-sum benefit payment in 1993 that includes benefits for one or more earlier years, you can figure whether any part of those earlier year benefits are taxable based on the earlier year's income. If that method gives you a lower taxable benefit, you can choose to treat the earlier benefits as received in the earlier year. In that case, any part of the earlier year benefits that is taxable is then added to your taxable benefits for the current year and the total is included in your current year's income.

For more information on lump-sum benefits and what worksheets to complete, see Publication 915.

Estimated tax. Tax is not withheld on social security benefits. This means that you may have to make estimated tax payments during the year if these benefits are taxable and you do not have enough taxes withheld from other income. See Chapter 5 for more information on estimated tax.

How To Report

After you figure your taxable benefits on one of the worksheets at the end of the chapter or in Publication 915, report your taxable benefits on Form 1040 or Form 1040A. You *cannot* use Form 1040EZ. Report your net benefits (the amount in box 5 of your Form SSA–1099 or RRB–1099) on line 21a, Form 1040, or line 13a, Form 1040A. Report the taxable part (from the last line of the worksheet) on line 21b, Form 1040, or line 13b, Form 1040A.

Worksheets. To help you figure your taxable benefits, use the worksheet in the Form 1040 or Form 1040A instruction package, as long as you are not required to use the Publication 590 worksheets (see *Special worksheets for IRA deduction and taxable benefits,* earlier). Publication 915 also has worksheets you can use. However, if you are not required to use the worksheets in Publication 590 and you take the U.S. savings bond interest exclusion, the foreign earned income exclusion, the foreign housing exclusion or deduction, the exclusion of income from U.S. possessions, or the exclusion of income from Puerto Rico by bona fide residents of Puerto Rico, you *must* use the worksheets in Publication 915.

Lump-sum payment. If you received a lump-sum benefit payment in 1993 that includes benefits for one or more earlier years and choose to treat the payment as if it were received in those years, you *must* use the worksheets in Publication 915. Otherwise, you should treat the amount as if it were fully attributable to 1993 and include it in your total benefits received during that year.

Examples

Following are a few examples you can use as a guide to figure the taxable part of your benefits.

Example 1. George White is single and files Form 1040 for 1993. He received the following income in 1993:

Fully taxable pension	$18,600
Wages from part-time job	9,400
Interest income	990
Total	$28,990

George also received social security benefits during 1993. The Form SSA–1099 he received in January 1994 shows $7,200 in box 3; $1,220 in box 4; and $5,980 in box 5. To figure his taxable benefits, George completes the worksheet shown here (for Form 1040 filers).

Table 12-1. **Where to Report Social Security and Equivalent Railroad Retirement Benefits**

Note: You cannot use Form 1040EZ to report taxable benefits.

	Form 1040	Form 1040A
Net Benefits (Box 5 of Forms SSA–1099 or RRB–1099)	Line 21a	Line 13a
Taxable Amount (From last line of the worksheet*)	Line 21b	Line 13b

* See *How to Report* in this chapter to decide what worksheet you should use and where to find it.

Social Security and Equivalent Railroad Retirement Benefits Worksheet (Keep for your records)

Check only one box

☑ **A.** Single, Head of household, or Qualifying widow(er) with dependent child.

☐ **B.** Married filing a joint return.

☐ **C.** Married not filing a joint return and lived with your spouse at any time during the year.

☐ **D.** Married not filing a joint return and **DID NOT** live with your spouse at any time during the year.

1. Enter the total amount from **box 5** of **ALL** your **Forms SSA–1099 and Forms RRB–1099** (if applicable) 5,980

Note: *If line 1 is zero or less, stop here; none of your benefits are taxable. Otherwise, go on to line 2.*

2. Divide line 1 by 2 2,990

3. Add the amounts on Form 1040, lines 7, 8a, 8b, 9 through 15, 16b, 17b, 18 through 20, and line 22. Do not include here any amounts from box 5 of Forms SSA–1099 or RRB–1099 28,990

4. Add lines 2 and 3 31,980

5. Enter the amount from Form 1040, line 30 .... –0–

6. Subtract line 5 from line 4 31,980

7. Enter: $25,000 if you checked

box **A** or **D,** or

$32,000 if you checked

box **B,** or

–0– if you checked box **C** 25,000

8. Subtract line 7 from line 6. Enter the result, but not less than zero 6,980

Note: *If line 8 is zero, stop here. None of your benefits are taxable. Do not enter any amounts on Form 1040, lines 21a or 21b. If you checked box D, however, enter –0– on line 21b and write "D" to the left of line 21a. If line 8 is more than zero, go on to line 9.*

9. Divide line 8 by 2 3,490

10. **Taxable benefits.**

• First, enter on Form 1040, line 21a, the amount from line 1 above.

• Then, enter the **smaller** of line 2 or line 9 here and on Form 1040, line 21b 2,990

The amount on line 10 of George's worksheet shows that $2,990 of his social security benefits are taxable. On line 21a of his Form 1040, George enters his net benefits of $5,980. On line 21b, he enters his taxable part of $2,990.

Example 2. Ray and Alice Hopkins file a joint return on Form 1040A for 1993. Ray is retired and receives a fully taxable pension of $15,500. Ray also receives social security benefits and his Form SSA–1099 for 1993 shows net benefits of $5,600 in box 5. Alice worked during the year and had wages of $14,000. She made a deductible payment to her IRA account of $1,000. Ray and Alice have two savings accounts. The Forms 1099–INT they received showed they had a total of $250 in interest income for 1993. They complete the worksheet below for Form 1040A filers and find that none of Ray's social security benefits are taxable.

Social Security and Equivalent Railroad Retirement Benefits Worksheet (Keep for your records)

Check only one box

☐ **A.** Single, Head of Household, or Qualifying widow(er) with dependent child.

☑ **B.** Married filing a joint return.

☐ **C.** Married not filing a joint return and lived with your spouse at any time during the year.

☐ **D.** Married not filing a joint return and **DID NOT** live with your spouse at any time during the year.

1. Enter the total amount from **box 5** of **ALL** your **Forms SSA–1099 and Forms RRB–1099** (if applicable) 5,600

Note: *If line 1 is zero or less, stop here; none of your benefits are taxable. Otherwise, go on to line 2.*

2. Divide line 1 by 2 2,800

3. Add the amounts on Form 1040A, lines 7, 8a, 8b, 9, 10b, 11b, and 12. Do not include here any amounts from box 5 of Forms SSA–1099 or RRB–1099 29,750

4. Add lines 2 and 3 32,550

5. Enter the amount from Form 1040A, line 15c.................. 1,000

6. Subtract line 5 from line 4 31,550

Worksheet 1. **Social Security and Equivalent Railroad Retirement Benefits**
(Keep for your records)

Check only one box:

☐ **A.** Single, Head of household, or Qualifying widow(er) with dependent child
☐ **B.** Married filing a joint return
☐ **C.** Married not filing a joint return and lived with your spouse at any time during the year
☐ **D.** Married not filing a joint return and **DID NOT** live with your spouse at any time during the year

---

1. Enter the total amount from box 5 of ALL your Forms SSA–1099 and RRB–1099 (if applicable) .... 1. _____
   Note: *If line 1 is zero or less, stop here; none of your SSA or equivalent tier 1 RRB benefits are taxable. Otherwise, go on to line 2.*
2. Divide line 1 by 2 .... 2. _____
3. Add the amounts on your 1993 Form 1040, lines 7, 8a, 8b, 9 through 15, 16b, 17b, 18 through 20, and line 22. Do not include any amounts from box 5 of Forms SSA–1099 or RRB–1099 here .... 3. _____
4. Enter the amount of any U.S. savings bond interest exclusion, foreign earned income exclusion, foreign housing exclusion, exclusion of income from U.S. possessions, or exclusion of income from Puerto Rico by bona fide residents of Puerto Rico that you claimed .... 4. _____
5. Add lines 2, 3, and 4 .... 5. _____
6. Enter the amount from your 1993 Form 1040, lines 24 through 29, plus any write-in amounts on line 30 (other than the foreign housing deduction) .... 6. _____
7. Subtract line 6 from line 5 .... 7. _____
8. Enter:
       $25,000 if you checked Box **A** or **D**, or
       $32,000 if you checked Box **B**, or
       –0– if you checked Box **C** .... 8. _____
9. Subtract line 8 from line 7, but do not enter less than zero. .... 9. _____
   Note: *If line 9 is zero, stop here. None of your SSA or equivalent tier 1 RRB benefits are taxable. Do not enter any amounts on Form 1040, lines 21a or 21b, unless you checked Box D above. If you checked Box D, enter –0– on line 21b and write "D" to the left of line 21a. If line 9 is more than zero, go on to line 10.*
10. Divide line 9 by 2 .... 10. _____
11. **Taxable benefits.**
    • First, enter on Form 1040, line 21a, the amount from line 1 above.
    • Then, compare the amounts on lines 2 and 10 above, and enter the **smaller** of the two amounts on this line. Also enter this amount on Form 1040, line 21b (unless you make the lump-sum election for benefits attributable to earlier year(s)) .... 11. _____

Note: *Use this worksheet whether or not you received a lump-sum payment. If you received a lump-sum payment in this year that was for an earlier year, see Lump-Sum Benefits, earlier. As that discussion suggests (under special election), if this worksheet shows that part of your benefits is taxable, complete Worksheets 2 and 3 in Publication 915 to see whether you can report a lower taxable benefit.*

7. Enter: $25,000 if you checked
       box **A** or **D**, or
       $32,000 if you checked
       box **B**, or
       –0– if you checked box **C** 32,000

8. Subtract line 7 from line 6. Enter the result, but not less than zero .... –0–

Note: *If line 8 is zero, stop here. None of your benefits are taxable. Do not enter any amounts on Form 1040A, lines 13a or 13b. If you checked box D, however, enter –0– on line 13b and write "D" to the left of line 13a. If line 8 is more than zero, go on to line 9.*

9. Divide line 8 by 2 .... _____

10. **Taxable benefits.**
    • First, enter on Form 1040A, line 13a, the amount from line 1 above.
    • Then, enter the **smaller** of line 2 or line 9 here and on Form 1040A, line 13b .... _____

Repayments More Than Gross Benefits

In some situations, your Form SSA–1099 or Form RRB–1099 will show that the total benefits you repaid (box 4) is more than the gross benefits (box 3) you received. If this occurred, your net benefits in box 5 will be a negative figure and none of your benefits will be taxable. If you receive more than one form, a negative figure in box 5 of one form is used to offset a positive figure in box 5 of another form. If you have any questions about this negative figure, contact your local Social Security Administration office or your local Railroad Retirement Board field office.

Joint return. If you and your spouse file a joint return, and your Forms SSA–1099 or RRB–1099 show that your repayments are more than your gross benefits, but your spouse's are not, subtract the amount in box 5 of your form from the amount in box 5 of your spouse's form to get your net benefits when figuring if your combined benefits are taxable.

Example. John and Mary file a joint return for 1993. John received Form SSA–1099 showing $3,000 in box 5. Mary also received Form SSA–1099 and the amount in box 5 was ($500). John and Mary will use $2,500 ($3,000 − $500) as the amount of their

Worksheet 1A (for 1040A filers).   **Social Security and Equivalent Railroad Retirement Benefits**
(Keep for your records)

Check only one box:

☐ **A.** Single, Head of household, or Qualifying widow(er) with dependent child
☐ **B.** Married filing a joint return
☐ **C.** Married not filing a joint return and lived with your spouse at any time during the year
☐ **D.** Married not filing a joint return and **DID NOT** live with your spouse at any time during the year

---

1. Enter the total amount from box 5 of ALL your Forms SSA–1099 and RRB–1099 (if
applicable)... **1.** _____
   Note: *If line 1 is zero or less, stop here; none of your SSA or equivalent tier 1 RRB benefits
   are taxable. Otherwise, go on to line 2.*

2. Divide line 1 by 2 .... **2.** _____

3. Add the amounts on your 1993 Form 1040A, lines 7, 8a, 8b, 9, 10b, 11b, and 12. Do not
include here any amounts from box 5 of Forms SSA–1099 or RRB–1099 .... **3.** _____

4. Enter the amount of any U.S. savings bond interest exclusion from Schedule 1, line 3, that
you claimed .... **4.** _____

5. Add lines 2, 3, and 4.. **5.** _____

6. Enter the amount from Form 1040A, line 15c .... **6.** _____

7. Subtract line 6 from line 5 .... **7.** _____

8. Enter:
   $25,000 if you checked Box **A** or **D**, or
   $32,000 if you checked Box **B**, or
   –0– if you checked Box **C** .... **8.** _____

9. Subtract line 8 from line 7, but do not enter less than zero....................... **9.** _____
   Note: *If line 9 is zero, stop here. None of your SSA or equivalent tier 1 RRB benefits are
   taxable. Do not enter any amounts on Form 1040A, lines 13a or 13b, unless you checked
   Box D above. If you checked Box D, enter –0– on line 13b and write "D" to the left of line
   13a. If line 9 is more than zero, go on to line 10.*

10. Divide line 9 by 2 .... **10.** _____

11. **Taxable benefits.**
    • First, enter on Form 1040A, line 13a, the amount from line 1 above.
    • Then, compare the amounts on lines 2 and 10 above, and enter the **smaller** of the two
    amounts on this line. Also enter this amount on Form 1040A, line 13b (unless you make
    the lump-sum election for benefits attributable to earlier year(s)) .... **11.** _____

Note: *Use this worksheet whether or not you received a lump-sum payment. If you received a lump-sum payment in this year that was
for an earlier year, see Lump-Sum Benefits, earlier. As that discussion suggests (under special election), if this worksheet shows
that part of your benefits is taxable, complete Worksheets 2 and 3A in Publication 915 to see whether you can report a lower
taxable benefit.*

net benefits when figuring if any of their combined benefits are taxable.

Explanation

Social security benefits are determined on a cash basis, just like most other income of individuals. Accordingly, repayments of prior-year amounts reduce current-year amounts.

Repayment of benefits received in an earlier year. If the sum of the amount shown in box 5 of all of your Forms SSA–1099 and RRB–1099 is a negative figure and all or part of this negative figure is for benefits you included in gross income in an earlier year, you can take an itemized deduction on Schedule A, Form 1040, for the amount of the negative figure that represents those benefits.

This deduction, *if $3,000 or less,* is subject to the 2%-of-adjusted-gross-income limit that applies to certain miscellaneous itemized deductions and is claimed on line 20, Schedule A (Form 1040).

TAXALERT

For 1993, if your adjusted gross income exceeds $108,450, certain itemized deductions claimed on your return may be phased out. See Chapter 30, *Miscellaneous Deductions,* for further details.

If this deduction is more than $3,000, you should figure your tax two ways:

1) Figure your tax for 1993 with the itemized deduction. This more-than-$3,000 deduction is *not* subject to the 2%-of-adjusted-gross-income limit that applies to certain miscellaneous itemized deductions.

2) Figure your tax for 1993 without the deduction. If a portion of the negative figure represents a repayment of 1984 benefits, you must first recompute your 1984 tax, reducing your 1984 social security benefits by that portion. Recompute your 1985, 1986, etc., tax in the same manner, using any portion of the negative figure that represents a repayment of benefits for those years. Reduce your 1993 tax, figured without the deduction, by the

total decrease in your 1984, 1985, 1986, etc., tax as recomputed. Compare the tax figured in methods (1) and (2). Your tax for 1993 is the smaller of the two amounts. If method (1) results in less tax, take the itemized deduction on line 25, Schedule A (Form 1040). If method (2) results in less tax, claim a credit for the applicable amount on line 59 of Form 1040 and write "I.R.C. 1341" in the margin to the left of line 59. If both methods produce the same tax, deduct the repayment in full on line 25, Schedule A (Form 1040).

Explanation
This confusing computation allows you to reduce your current tax by the *greater* of two amounts: (1) what you paid in tax in the prior year because of including the amount in income or (2) the amount of tax you would save by taking the deduction this year.

13 | Other Income

Introduction

Your salary, interest you earn, **dividends,** *a gain from the sale of your house—all of these, of course, are* **taxable income.**

Unfortunately, so are a lot of other things: a debt forgiven by a friend, jury pay, a free trip you receive from a travel agency for organizing a group of tourists, **royalties** *you earn on a book. All of these are taxable income to you, too.*

The general rule is that anything that enriches you should be included in your **gross income,** *unless it is specifically excluded by the tax law.*

Indeed, some things are excluded from taxation. You don't have to pay income tax on life insurance proceeds that you receive because of the death of the insured. Most gifts and inheritances are tax-free income. The value of the vegetables you grow in your garden and eat yourself is not taxable. This chapter tells you what kind of income is taxable, what kind of income is not taxable, and how you can tell the difference. It also discusses how you can expense up to $17,500 for property you use in your trade or business.

This chapter includes a discussion on passive activity losses. Passive investments include all rental activities, all limited partnerships, and those other businesses in which the taxpayer is not involved in the operations on a regular, continuous, and substantial basis.

This chapter discusses many kinds of income and explains whether they are taxable or nontaxable.

- Income that is taxable must be reported on your tax return and is subject to tax.
- Income that is nontaxable may have to be shown on your tax return but is not subject to tax.

You must include on your return all income you receive in the form of money, property, and services unless the tax law states that you do not include them. Some items, however, are only partly excluded from income. They are listed and discussed briefly in this chapter.

Useful Items

You may want to see:

Publication

- ☐ **501** Exemptions, Standard Deduction, and Filing Information
- ☐ **520** Scholarships and Fellowships
- ☐ **525** Taxable and Nontaxable Income
- ☐ **544** Sales and Other Dispositions of Assets
- ☐ **550** Investment Income and Expenses

Miscellaneous Taxable Income

This section begins with brief discussions of numerous income items, arranged in alphabetical order. These discussions are followed by discussions of other taxable income items which are discussed in greater detail as follows:

> Bartering
> Recoveries (including state income tax refunds)
> Repayments
> Royalties

Note. When you report miscellaneous taxable income on line 22 of Form 1040, write a brief description of the income on the dotted line next to line 22.

Activity not for profit. You must include on your return income from an activity not for profit. An example of this type of activity would be a hobby or a farm you operate mostly for recreation and pleasure. Enter this income on line 22 of Form 1040. Deductions for expenses related to the activity are limited. They cannot total more than the income you report, and can be taken only if you itemize deductions on Schedule A (Form 1040). See *Not-for-Profit Activities* in Publication 535, *Business Expenses,* for information on whether an activity is considered carried on for a profit.

Explanation
An activity will be presumed to have been for profit if it results in a profit in at least 3 out of 5 consecutive tax

years. However, for the breeding, training, showing, or racing of horses, the activity must result in a profit in at least 2 out of 7 consecutive tax years. If the activity meets this test, it is presumed to be carried on for profit, and the limits will not apply.

If you have engaged in an activity for less than 3 years, you can postpone the determination that the activity is not for profit by filing Form 5213, *Election to Postpone Determination*. Get Publication 535, *Business Expenses*, for more information.

It is possible that the IRS may treat you as engaged in a profit-making activity, even if you do not have a profit for 3 or more years during a period of 5 consecutive tax years. The IRS determines the activity's status—for profit or as a hobby—by considering the facts and circumstances surrounding the case. Some factors that will be considered include the following:

1. The manner in which you carry on the activity. For example, do you conduct your actions in a business-like manner?
2. The expertise possessed by you and your advisors.
3. The time and effort you expend in carrying on the activity.
4. Any expectation you have that **assets** used in the activity may appreciate in value.
5. Prior success in similar or dissimilar activities.
6. Your history of income or loss with respect to the activity.
7. The amount of occasional profits, if any, that you earn through the activity.
8. Your financial status. For example, that you do not have substantial income from other sources may indicate that you are engaging in the activity for profit.
9. Elements of personal pleasure or recreation.

TAXPLANNER

If an activity does show a profit for any 3 of 5 consecutive years (2 of 7 years for horse farms), there is a presumption by law that you are engaged in the activity for profit. The IRS has the burden of proving that the activity is only a hobby. However, if you do not meet the 3-year test and the IRS determines that the activity is a hobby, then you have the burden of proving your profit motive.

You would normally not file Form 5213, *Election to Postpone Determination with Respect to the Presumption That an Activity Is Engaged in for Profit,* until the IRS has examined records from one of the early years in which you engaged in the activity and has concluded that it is a hobby. Then, to prevent the IRS from assessing a tax on the years under examination, you should file Form 5213.

However, by filing the form, you agree to extend the period for which the IRS may collect additional taxes by disallowing the losses until 2 years after the examination period is over.

Also, by filing, you virtually guarantee that the IRS will carefully examine all years during the period under examination. Since the IRS previously concluded that the activity is a hobby, it is virtually certain to reach the same conclusion again.

Alaska oil royalties. If you were a resident of Alaska and qualified to receive a payment from Alaska's mineral income fund (Alaska Permanent Fund dividends), you must report this amount on line 22, Form 1040. The state of Alaska will send you a Form 1099–MISC which shows this amount. The IRS will also receive a copy of this form.

Alimony. Include in your income on line 11, Form 1040, any alimony payments you receive. Amounts you receive for child support are not income to you. Alimony and child support payments are discussed in Chapter 19, *Alimony*.

TAXPLANNER

While alimony payments you receive are taxable, property settlements arising out of divorce are not. You should bear this in mind when considering the tax consequences of a divorce. See Chapter 19, *Alimony*, for more details.

Allowances and reimbursements. If you receive travel, transportation, or other business expense allowances or reimbursements from your employer, or you are reimbursed for the business use of your car, see Chapter 28, *Car Expenses and Other Employee Business Expenses*. If you are reimbursed for moving expenses, see Chapter 27, *Moving Expenses*.

Canceled debt. A canceled debt, or a debt paid for you by another person, is generally income to you and must be reported on line 22, Form 1040.

A discount offered by a financial institution for the prepayment of a mortgage loan is income from the cancellation of a debt. However, you have no income from the cancellation of a debt if the cancellation, or the payment by another person, is intended by the other person as a gift to you.

If your debt is canceled in a bankruptcy case (title 11) or when you are insolvent, do not include the canceled debt in your gross income. Get Publication 908, *Bankruptcy and Other Debt Cancellation*.

TAXALERT

The 1993 Tax Act changes the rules about how certain real property business debts can be treated. Under prior law, if you were solvent (i.e. not in bankruptcy) and you wished to discharge certain business real property debts, the amount of the debt discharged would be counted as gross income to you. Under the new tax law, if you are a solvent taxpayer, you can elect to exclude from your income the discharge of qualified real property business indebtedness. The amount that can be excluded from income cannot exceed the basis of the depreciable real property. In addition, the amount excluded from your income is considered a reduction in the basis of the property. If you subsequently dispose of the property, the amount of the reduction in the basis of the property is treated as depreciation for purposes of computing how much ordinary income must be recaptured in order to calculate your tax.

There are certain limitations on the amount of debt that you can discharge and exclude from your income. The amount you may exclude from your income may not exceed the principal amount of the debt (immediately before the discharge) of the real property that is security for the debt. For this purpose, the fair market value of the property is reduced by the outstanding principal amount of any other qualified real property business indebtedness secured by the property. You should consult with your tax advisor.

Example

Assume on July 1, 1993, Christine owns a building worth $150,000, used in her trade or business, that is subject to a first mortgage debt of $110,000 and a second mortgage debt of $90,000. Christine agrees with her second mortgagee to reduce the second mortgage debt to $30,000, resulting in a discharge of indebtedness income in the amount of $60,000. Assuming that Christine has sufficient basis in business real property to absorb the reduction, Christine can elect to exclude $50,000 of that discharge from her gross income. Why $50,000? The $50,000 amount is the excess of her combined mortgage debts ($200,000) over the fair market value of the estate ($150,000) immediately before the discharge of the indebtedness. However, $10,000, the amount of the debt relief over the excluded amount in this example, would be considered income to Christine in 1993 and therefore subject to tax. The logic here is that because of the discharge of the indebtedness, Christine gained $10,000 in equity in the property at its current fair market value.

TAXSAVER

Proceed cautiously if the financial institution that holds your mortgage offers you a substantial discount on your loan balance in exchange for a prepayment on it. While this might at first appear very attractive, remember that you will have to pay ordinary income tax on the amount of the discount offered, which may considerably reduce any advantage to you. Your money might be put to better use in investments with a high after-tax yield or in paying off expensive consumer credit.

TAXPLANNER

Family members often make interest-free or below-market interest loans to one another. The IRS may recharacterize these loans as arm's-length transactions and impute interest income to the lender and interest expense to the borrower, which is then reported on their respective tax returns. You should consult your tax advisor about how to report any below-market loan transactions.

Cancellation of student loan. You do not have income if your student loan is canceled because you agreed to certain conditions to obtain the loan and then performed the services required. Under the terms of the loan you must be required to work for a specified period of time in certain professions for one of a broad class of employers. To qualify, the loan must have been made by:

1) The government—federal, state, or local, or an instrumentality, agency, or subdivision thereof,
2) A tax-exempt public benefit corporation that has assumed control of a state, county, or municipal hospital, and whose employees are considered public employees under state law, or
3) An educational organization under an agreement with an entity

described in (1) or (2) that provided the funds to the institution to make the loan.

Cancellations of student loans under section 465 of the Higher Education Act of 1965 also are not income.

Court awards and damages. To determine if settlement amounts you receive by compromise or judgment must be included in your income, you must consider the item that the settlement replaces. Include the following as ordinary income:

1) Interest on any award.
2) Compensation for lost wages or lost profits.
3) Punitive damages awarded in cases not involving physical injury or sickness. Report this income on line 22, Form 1040.
4) Amounts received in settlement of pension rights (if you did not contribute to the plan).
5) Damages for:
   a) Patent or copyright infringement,
   b) Breach of contract, or
   c) Interference with business operations.

Do not include as your income compensatory damages for the following:

1) Personal injury or sickness (whether received in a lump sum or installments).
2) Damage to your character.
3) Alienation of affection.
4) Surrender of custody of a minor child.

Explanation

The legal expense that you incur in the process of getting a damage award may be claimed as an itemized deduction (subject to the 2% of adjusted gross income floor) only if the award is included in your gross income. If the award is only partially included in your gross income, you may deduct only a proportional amount in legal fees. Thus, if the entire award is excluded from your gross income, none of your legal fees are deductible.

TAXSAVER

A technique now being used in large personal-injury cases is the so-called structured settlement, in which the defendant's insurance company offers an **annuity** to the injured party instead of a **lump-sum distribution.** The IRS has ruled that the entire amount of the annuity payments may be excluded from the recipient's gross income, even though the recipient is, in effect, receiving interest.

Estate and trust income. An estate or trust, unlike a partnership, may have to pay federal income tax. If you are a beneficiary of an estate or trust, you are taxed on your share of its income. However, there is never a double tax. Estates and trusts file their returns on Form 1041, *U.S. Fiduciary Income Tax Return,* and report your share of the income on Schedule K–1 of Form 1041.

Current income required to be distributed. If you are the beneficiary of a trust that must distribute all of its current income, you must report your share of the distributable net income whether or not you have actually received it.

Current income not required to be distributed. If you are the beneficiary of an estate or trust and the fiduciary has the choice of whether to distribute all or part of the current income, you must report all income that is required to be distributed to you, whether or not it is actually distributed, plus all other amounts actually paid or credited to you, to the extent of your share of distributable net income.

Explanation

Many people find this area very confusing, and for good reason. Gifts and inheritances are not gross income to the recipient. However, money or property that you inherit may earn some interest, dividends, or rent while the estate is being settled. It is that income that must be reported either by you or by the estate. Ordinarily, the executor of the estate files an income tax return for the estate, reporting the income, but he or she may shift the tax burden of that income to the beneficiaries if the property has already been distributed to them.

How to report estate and trust income. Each item of income is treated the same for you as for the estate or trust. If it is dividend income for the trust, it is the same for you.

The fiduciary of the estate or trust must tell you the type of items making up your share of the estate or trust income and any credits you are allowed on your individual income tax return.

Losses. Losses of estates and trusts generally are not deductible by the beneficiaries.

Exception

There are significant exceptions to the rule that losses of estates and trusts are not deductible by the beneficiaries. When an estate or a trust terminates, the beneficiaries are frequently allowed a deduction for certain expenses that the estate or trust had but was unable to use as a deduction. These items are (1) net operating loss carryovers, (2) certain excess deductions in the year of termination, and (3) **capital loss carryovers.**

When an estate is terminated, it is not unusual for the attorney's and executor's fees to be paid in the year in which the estate is closed. If such expenses and the net operating loss carryover exceed the estate's income for that year, the excess is deductible by the beneficiaries. This deduction may be claimed only by itemizing deductions on Schedule A (Form 1040). These deductions are subject to the 2% rule on miscellaneous itemized deductions. This means that they are only deductible to the extent that the expenses exceed 2% of adjusted gross income.

A capital loss carryover from an estate or a trust may be used in the beneficiaries' current or subsequent returns to reduce capital gains and/or to generate a deduction subject to the limitation that only $3,000 of capital losses in excess of capital gains may be deducted each year.

When to report estate and trust income. You must include your share of the estate or trust income on your return for your tax year in which the last day of the estate or trust tax year falls.

The trustee of the trust or estate will provide you with a Form K-1 that tells you each item of income and where it should be reported on your return.

TaxSaver

It may be a good idea if you are the beneficiary of a trust to inform the trustee of your tax situation so that all possible tax-saving alternatives can be explored. Amounts that are *not* required to be distributed currently, according to the terms of the trust, may sometimes be distributed at the discretion of the trustee. There may be substantial tax advantages to the timing, amounts, and methods of such distributions. You and the trustee should consult with a professional who specializes in this area.

Grantor trust. Income earned by a grantor trust is taxable to the grantor, not the beneficiary. This rule applies if the property put into the trust will revert (be returned) to the grantor or the grantor's spouse. Generally, for transfers after March 1, 1986, a trust is a grantor trust if the grantor has a reversionary interest valued (at the date of transfer) at more than 5% of the value of the transferred property. For transfers in trust made before March 2, 1986, a trust was a grantor trust if it was expected that the property would revert to the grantor within 10 years.

Fees. Include all fees for your services in your gross income. Examples of these fees are amounts you receive for services as:

1) A corporate director,
2) An executor or administrator of an estate,
3) A notary public, or
4) An election precinct official.

If these payments total $600 or more for the year, the payer must report these fees to the IRS on Form 1099–MISC. You will receive a copy of Form 1099–MISC.

Self-employment income. Report these payments on Schedule C (Form 1040), *Profit or Loss From Business,* or Schedule Schedule C-EZ (Form 1040), *Net Profit From Business,* as self-employment income.

Exception. If you are not in the trade or business of being an executor (for instance, you are the executor of a friend's or relative's estate), do not include these amounts on Schedule C or Schedule C-EZ (Form 1040).

Form W–2. If you receive a Form W–2 showing corporate director fees, report these fees on line 7 of Form 1040 or Form 1040A, or on line 2 of Form 1040EZ.

Explanation

Self-employment income. Some of the fees mentioned above, such as corporate director fees and notary public fees, are self-employment income. For both employees and self-employed individuals, the 1993 wage base is $57,600 for Old-Age, Survivor, and Disability Insurance (OASDI) and $135,000 for Medicare. Thus, if a person earns self-employment income of $135,000 or more, he or she will pay the maximum 1993 self-employment tax of $11,057.40 [i.e., $57,600 × 15.3%, plus ($135,000 − $57,600) × 2.9%]. The self-employment tax rate is 15.3%.

If you receive such fees and your other compensation subject to FICA (social security) tax is less than $135,000, you have to pay self-employment tax on the amount up to $135,000 less the compensation subject to FICA. If your other compensation subject to FICA is more than $135,000, you do not have to pay any additional self-employment tax.

Fees are self-employment income only if you present yourself as being in the trade or business that produces the fees. Therefore, unless you *regularly* appear as a witness, act as an executor or trustee, or judge elections, the fees earned will not be self-employment income subject to self-employment tax.

Clergy fees. Fees received by clergy for performing funerals, marriages, baptisms, or other services must be included in gross income.

TaxAlert

Beginning in 1994, the 2.9% Medicare tax will not have a wage base. That is, all wages and self-employment income will be subject to the Medicare tax. You may want to evaluate your 1993 tax position to see if there are some tax-saving advantages to accelerating income and/or deferring deductions.

TaxPlanner

Any business that pays you more than $600 in fees should provide you with a Form 1099. A copy of this form should also be filed with the **IRS** by the business. Individual payers are not required to file this form. However, you are not excused from your responsibility to report the income just because you do not receive a Form 1099.

Professional fees—fees received by a doctor, lawyer, and so on—should be shown on Schedule C, *Profit or Loss from Business, not* in the Miscellaneous Income section on line 22 of Form 1040. Otherwise, the IRS's document-matching program may generate unwarranted notices, suggesting that you have underpaid your tax.

Explanation

Sole proprietorship (self-employment) income. Unlike a partnership or a regular corporation, a sole proprietorship is not a separate entity. In a sole proprietorship, you and your business are one and the same. You report gross profit or loss for the year from the sole proprietorship on Form 1040, Schedule C, and it becomes part of your adjusted gross income. In addition to owing income tax on such income, you, as the sole proprietor, will usually be liable for self-employment tax, and you may also be required to make payments of estimated taxes. A net loss from the business can generally be deducted in computing your adjusted gross income.

Your profit (or loss) is computed as income less your allowable deductions. Income includes cash, property, and services received by the business from all sources, unless specifically excluded under the tax code. Allowable deductions include all necessary and ordinary expenses incurred in connection with the business. For sole proprietorships in the business of selling goods or inventory, the primary expense will be the cost of goods sold. The cost of goods sold represents the cost of materials, labor, and overhead included in the inventory sold during the year. Other expenses that you deduct on Schedule C include salaries and wages, interest on

loans used in the business, rent, depreciation, bad debts, travel and entertainment, insurance, real estate taxes, and so on. See Chapter 36, *If You Are Self-Employed,* for further information.

If you operate your own business or have other self-employment income, such as babysitting or selling crafts, see these other publications for more information:

- Publication 334, *Tax Guide for Small Business*
- Publication 535, *Business Expenses*
- Publication 533, *Self-Employment Tax*

TaxSaver

An important note: If you receive fees that are self-employment income, you may contribute to a **Keogh plan.** See Chapter 18, *Individual Retirement Arrangements (IRAs),* for details.

Free tour. A free tour you receive from a travel agency for organizing a group of tourists must be included in your income on line 22, Form 1040, or on Schedule C or Schedule C-EZ (Form 1040), at the fair market value of the tour. You cannot deduct your expenses in serving as the voluntary leader of the group at the group's request.

Gambling winnings. You must include your gambling winnings in income on line 22, Form 1040.

If you itemize your deductions on Schedule A (Form 1040), you can deduct gambling losses you had during the year, but only up to the amount of your winnings. See Publication 529, *Miscellaneous Deductions,* for information on recordkeeping.

Lotteries and raffles. Winnings from lotteries and raffles are gambling winnings. In addition to cash winnings, you must include in your income bonds, cars, houses, and other noncash prizes at their fair market value.

Note. If you win a state lottery prize payable in installments, you must include in your gross income the annual payments and any amount you receive designated as "interest" on the unpaid installments.

Form W-2G. You may have received a Form W-2G showing the amount of your gambling winnings and any tax withheld. Include the amount from box 1 on line 22 of Form 1040. Be sure to include any amount from box 2 on line 54 of Form 1040.

Explanation

While a winner of the Canadian government lottery does not have to pay Canadian tax on the winnings, a U.S. citizen or resident who wins does have to pay U.S. tax on the amount. Citizens and residents of the United States have to report all income, including foreign income.

TaxPlanner

Since you may not win money gambling until late in the year and you may deduct gambling losses only up to the amount of your winnings, you should plan ahead by saving racetrack tickets, lottery tickets, and so forth on which you did not win. In that way, if you do win, you will be able to itemize your gambling losses. Keeping a diary of gambling losses incurred during the entire year is also a good idea. These losses are deducted as miscellaneous itemized deductions but are not subject to the 2% of adjusted gross income floor.

Hobby losses. Losses from a hobby are not deductible from other income. A hobby is an activity from which you do not expect to make a profit. See *Activity not for profit,* earlier.

Note. If you collect stamps, coins, or other items as a hobby for recreation and pleasure, and you sell any of the items, your gain is taxable as a capital gain. (See Chapter 17.) However, if you sell items from your collection at a loss, you cannot deduct a net loss.

Explanation
While a *net* loss from the sale of stamps, coins, or other items that you collect for a hobby may not be deducted, a loss from the sale of these items may be offset against a gain from the sale of similar items occurring in the same year.

Example
You sell several stamps at a gain of $1,000. You may offset up to $1,000 in losses from the sale of other stamps against this gain. The result is that there is no taxable gain.

TaxSaver
If you are planning to sell an item in your collection that has appreciated in value and your collection also contains an item that has decreased in value, you should sell both in the same year to incur the least amount of tax. In short, clean out the junk to establish losses in a year when you have gains.

Illegal income. Illegal income, such as stolen or embezzled funds, must be included in your gross income on line 22, Form 1040, or on Schedule C or Schedule C-EZ (Form 1040).

Explanation
It is not necessary for the activity that produces income to be legal for the income to be taxable. Income from illegal activities, such as embezzlement, drug dealing, bookmaking, and bootlegging, is taxable. Al Capone, the notorious Chicago bootlegger during Prohibition, was convicted of income tax evasion on his bootlegging income.

Embezzlement income is taxable in the year in which the funds are stolen. If the embezzler pays back the stolen funds in a later year, he or she can claim a deduction in the year of repayment.

Indian fishing rights. If you are a member of a qualified Indian tribe that has fishing rights secured by treaty, executive order, or an Act of Congress as of March 17, 1988, do not include in your income amounts you receive from activities related to those fishing rights. The income is not subject to income tax, self-employment tax, or employment taxes.

Investment clubs. An investment club is a group of friends, neighbors, business associates, or others who pool limited or stated amounts of funds to invest in stock or other securities. The club may or may not have a written agreement, charter, or by-laws. Usually the group operates informally with members pledging a regular amount to be paid into the club monthly. Some clubs have a committee that gathers information on securities, selects the most promising, and recommends that the club invest in them. Other clubs rotate the investigatory responsibilities among all their members. Most require all members to vote for or against all investments, sales, exchanges, or other transactions.

How the income from an investment club is reported on your tax return depends on how the club operates. Most clubs operate as partnerships and are treated as such for federal tax purposes. Others operate as corporations, trusts, or associations taxed as corporations.

For more information about investment clubs, get Publication 550.

Explanation
Members of an investment club should include their share of each type of the club's income on their returns. For example, dividends are reported on Schedule B, Part II, line 5, and capital gains are reported on Schedule D.

The expenses incurred by the club to produce or to collect income, to manage investment property, or to determine any tax due are also reported separately. You may deduct your share of these items on Schedule A as a miscellaneous deduction if you itemize your deductions.

Note: These expenses—along with some others— have to exceed 2% of your adjusted gross income to be deductible as miscellaneous itemized deductions.

TaxAlert
Depending on how your investment club is organized, it may be required to file a separate partnership, corporation, or trust tax return. For more details, consult your tax advisor.

Jury duty. Jury duty pay you receive must be included in your income on line 22, Form 1040.

If you are required to give the pay to your employer because your employer continues to pay your salary while you serve on the jury, you can deduct the amount turned over to your employer as an adjustment to your income. Include the amount you repay your employer on line 30, Form 1040, and write "Jury pay" and the amount on the dotted line next to line 30.

Explanation
Jury fees. This item is often overlooked. Just because a fee is paid by a government body does not mean that it is not subject to tax. However, the Tax Court has ruled that the mileage allowance received by a juror to cover the cost of transportation between the court and his or her home is not included in income. In addition, if you are required to give your jury pay to your employer, you can claim a deduction for the amount paid over. You can claim this deduction whether or not you itemize your deductions.

Kickbacks. You must include in your income on line 22, Form 1040, or on Schedule C or Schedule C-EZ (Form 1040), kickbacks, side commissions, push money, or similar payments you receive.

Example. You are a car salesperson and help arrange car insurance for buyers. Insurance brokers pay back part of their commissions to you for referring customers to them. You must include the kickbacks in your income.

Note received for services. If your employer gives you a note as payment for your services, you must include the fair market value (usually the discount value) of the note in your income as wages for the year you receive it. When you later receive payments on the note, part of each payment is a recovery of the fair market value that you previously included in your income. Do not include that part in your income again. Include the rest of the payment in your income in the year of payment.

Explanation

The fair market value of a note is extremely difficult to determine, unless the note may be sold to a third party, and even then its worth may be difficult to determine.

If the issuer of the note is insolvent, the fair market value of the note is zero. In this case, any money you subsequently get from the issuer is taxed as ordinary income in the year in which you receive it. Similarly, if the value of the note is less than its face value, any amount that you subsequently receive from the issuer that is greater than the recognized value of the note is taxed as ordinary income the year in which it is received.

A note's fair market value may be less than its face amount if, based on the facts and circumstances at the time the note is issued, it is uncertain that you will be able to collect the face amount. A note may also be considered to be worth less than its face amount if the interest rate that it pays is below the market rate and if the collateral pledged against the note is limited.

If you think the note you receive may be worth more or less than its face value, consult your tax advisor about how to report the transaction.

Prizes and awards. If you win a prize in a lucky number drawing, television or radio quiz program, beauty contest, or other event, you must include it in your income. For example, if you win a $50 prize in a photography contest, you must report this income on line 22, Form 1040.

Employee cash awards or bonuses. Cash awards or bonuses given to you by your employer for good work or suggestions generally must be included in your income. However, certain employee awards can be excluded from your income. See *Employee achievement awards,* later.

Goods or services. Prizes and awards in goods or services must be included in income at their fair market value. If you refuse to accept a prize, do not include its value in your income.

Explanation

Fair market value is the price at which property would be exchanged between a willing buyer and a willing seller when neither party is compelled to buy or to sell. When merchandise is received as a prize, fair market value is the suggested retail price, unless some other measure of fair market value can be readily ascertained. Other ways to measure fair market value that have been approved by the courts include the following:

1. **Resale value.** The Tax Court has ruled that, in some cases, the fair market value of an item is what you could realize by selling it.
2. **Value to the recipient.** If you receive a prize that is not something you would ordinarily purchase, the Tax Court has said that you may discount the value of the prize.

Example 1

An individual received a new car as an award from her employer. The Tax Court ruled that the amount to be considered as income was not what the employer had paid for the car but how much the recipient would have realized by selling the car immediately after it was received.

Example 2

Taxpayers received two first-class cruise tickets from a game show. The tickets were nontransferable and had to be used within 1 year. The Tax Court found that the tickets were not something that the taxpayers would normally have acquired but were a luxury that would otherwise have been beyond their means. Accordingly, the Tax Court permitted an amount less than the retail price of the tickets in the taxpayers' gross income.

There is no standardized technique to determine the amount to be included in gross income in cases similar to these. Our advice is this: If you believe that you can justify a value less than normal retail price, it may be worthwhile to include the lower amount in taxable income.

Pulitzer, Nobel, and other prizes. If you were awarded a Pulitzer, Nobel, or other prize in recognition of past accomplishments (in religious, charitable, scientific, artistic, educational, literary, or civic fields) you do not include this prize in your income if you meet *all* of the following requirements.

1) You were selected without any action on your part to enter the contest or proceeding.
2) You are not required to perform substantial future services as a condition to receiving the prize or award.
3) The prize or award is transferred directly to a governmental unit or tax-exempt charitable organization as designated by you.

Get Publication 525 for more information about the conditions that apply to the transfer.

Sale of personal items. If you sell an item that you owned for personal use, such as a car, refrigerator, furniture, stereo, jewelry, or silverware, a gain is taxable as a capital gain reported on Schedule D (Form 1040). You cannot deduct a loss.

However, if you sell an item that you held for investment, such as gold or silver bullion, coins, or gems, a gain is taxable as a capital gain and a loss is deductible as a capital loss.

Bartering

Bartering is an exchange of property or services. You must include in your income, at the time received, the fair market value of property or services you receive in bartering. If you exchange services with another person and you both have agreed ahead of time as to the value of the services, that value will be accepted as fair market value unless the value can be shown to be otherwise.

Report this income on Schedule C or Schedule C-EZ (Form 1040).

Explanation

The IRS explanation is correct in stating that, if you exchange your property and/or services for the property and/or services of another, you have taxable income. However, when you exchange property for property, you generally recognize income only to the extent that the fair market value of the property you receive exceeds your **adjusted basis** in the property you give up. The proper way of determining gain on exchanges of property and your **basis** in the property you receive is discussed in Chapters 14, *Basis of Property*, and 15, *Sale of Property*.

Example 1. You are a self-employed attorney and perform legal services for a client, a small corporation. The corporation gives you shares of its stock as payment for your services. You must include in income the fair market value of the shares on Schedule C or Schedule C-EZ (Form 1040) in the year that you receive them.

Example 2. You are self-employed and a member of a barter club. The club uses "credit units" as a means of exchange. It adds credit units to your account for goods or services you provide to members, which you can use to purchase goods and services offered by other members of the barter club. The club subtracts credit units from your account when you receive goods or services from other members. You must include in income the value of credit units that are added to your account, even though you may not actually receive goods or services from other members until a later tax year.

Example 3. You own a small apartment building and an artist gives you a work of art that the artist created in return for 6 months' rent-free use of an apartment. You must report as rental income on Schedule E (Form 1040) the fair market value of the art work, and the artist must report as income on Schedule C or Schedule C-EZ (Form 1040) the fair rental value of the apartment.

Barter exchange. If you exchanged property or services through a barter exchange, you should receive Form 1099–B or a similar statement. You should receive the statement by January 31, 1994, and it will generally show the value of cash, property, services, credits, or scrip you received from exchanges during the year. The IRS will also get a copy of Form 1099–B.

Backup withholding. The income you receive from bartering is generally not subject to withholding. However, backup withholding will apply in certain circumstances to ensure that income tax is collected on this income.

If you join a barter exchange, you must certify under penalties of perjury that your social security or employer identification number is correct and that you are not subject to backup withholding. If you do not make this certification, backup withholding may begin immediately. The barter exchange will give you a Form W–9, *Request for Taxpayer Identification Number and Certification,* or a similar form, for you to make this certification. For more information, see *Backup Withholding* in Chapter 5.

Reporting the tax withheld. If tax is withheld from your barter income, the barter exchange must give you a Form 1099–B, or similar statement, that indicates the amount of tax withheld.

Partnership Income

A partnership is not a taxable entity. The income, gains, losses, credits, and deductions of a partnership are "passed through" to the partners based on each partner's distributive share of these items.

Explanation

Your distributive share of the partnership losses is limited to the adjusted basis of your interest in the partnership at the end of the partnership year in which the losses took place. To determine the adjusted basis of your interest in the partnership, begin with your initial investment and your initial share of partnership liabilities and make the following adjustments:

Additions to basis

1. Your distributive share of the partnership's taxable income
2. Your share of any tax-exempt income earned by the partnership
3. Your share of the excess of partnership deductions for depletion over the basis of partnership property subject to depletion
4. Any additional capital you contribute
5. Your share of any increase in partnership liabilities

Subtractions from basis

1. Any cash distributions you receive
2. The basis which you take in any property distributed to you by the partnership
3. Your share of oil and gas depletion claimed by the partnership
4. Your distributive share of partnership losses
5. Your share of nondeductible, noncapital expenditures made by the partnership
6. Your share of any decrease in partnership liabilities

The partnership agreement usually covers the distribution of profits, losses, and other items. However, if there is no agreement for sharing a specific item of gain or loss, generally each partner's distributive share is figured according to the partner's interest in the partnership.

In addition, **special "at-risk" rules apply** to a partnership engaged in any activity.

You may deduct your share of a partnership loss from any activity only up to the total amount that you have at risk in the activity at the end of the partnership's tax year.

The amount you have at risk in an activity is the cash and the adjusted basis of other property you contributed to the activity. Also, you have at risk any amounts borrowed for use in the activity for which you are either personally liable or have pledged property, except property used in the activity, as security.

Generally, you are not at risk for

1. Any nonrecourse loans used to finance the activity, to acquire property used in the activity, or to acquire your interest in the activity, unless they are secured by property not used in the activity
2. Amounts for which you are protected against loss by

guarantees, stop-loss agreements, or other similar arrangements
3. Amounts borrowed from interested or related parties if your partnership is engaged in certain activities

For more information on the at-risk rules, see Publication 536, *Net Operating Losses and the At-Risk Limits.*

In addition to the factors discussed above, your amount at risk is affected by the operating results of the activity itself. Income from the activity increases the amount you have at risk. Losses from the activity decrease the amount you have at risk. The at-risk amount is determined at the end of each tax year. Any loss in excess of that amount is disallowed for that year. It may, however, be carried over to future years and, to the extent that you subsequently have amounts at risk, it may be deducted in those years.

Under prior law, a partnership engaged in real estate activity was not subject to the at-risk rules. The Tax Reform Act of 1986 extended the at-risk rules to include real estate activities placed in service after December 31, 1986, but makes exceptions for third-party nonrecourse debt from commercial lenders and certain other parties.

In addition to the at-risk rules, the income from real estate partnerships is also subject to the passive activity rules. See the discussion, *Passive Activity Losses and Tax Shelters,* at the end of this chapter. Also, consult your tax advisor for further information.

The partnership must file a return on Form 1065, *U.S. Partnership Return of Income,* and send Schedule K–1 to each partner. In addition, the partnership will send each partner a copy of the *Partner's Instructions for Schedule K–1 (Form 1065),* to help each partner report his or her share of the partnership's income, credits, deductions, and tax preference items. Do not attach Schedule K–1 (Form 1065) to your Form 1040 (unless you are required to file it with Form 8271). Keep it for your records.

Explanation
When to report partnership income. Partnership income is treated as paid to you on the last day of the partnership year. Generally, you must include your distributive share of partnership items on your return for your tax year in which the last day of the partnership year falls. If you receive income from a partnership other than in your capacity as a partner, however, you must report the income in the year in which it was received. For instance, if you sell property to your partnership at a gain, the gain is generally included in income when you receive the sale proceeds, regardless of when your partnership's tax year ends.

Estimated tax payments. A partner must take into account his or her share of the partnership's income or deductions to date at *each* estimated tax payment date. Often this information is not readily available. If you are a member of a partnership, you may protect yourself from underpayment penalties by basing your payments on one of the exceptions described in Chapter 5, *Tax Withholding and Estimated Tax.* For example, you might base your estimated tax payments on last year's tax.

For most other tax purposes, however, partnership income or loss is deemed to come into existence on the last day of the partnership's tax year. Thus, if a partner dies before the partnership's year ends, the income or loss for the whole year is included in the income tax return of the partner's estate or in the return of the person who succeeds to the decedent's interest.

Similarly, if a partner moves from one state to another, and if the states involved follow federal rules, the partnership income or loss should be reported in the state income tax return for the state in which the partner resides when the partnership's year ends.

Sale of partnership interest. If you have a gain or a loss from the sale or exchange of a partnership interest, it is treated as a gain or a loss from the sale of a capital asset. The gain or loss is the difference between the amount you receive and the adjusted basis of your interest in the partnership. If you are relieved of any debts of the partnership, you must include these debts in the amount you receive.

However, you may have ordinary income as well as capital gain or loss on the sale of your partnership interest if the sale involves uncollected accounts receivable or inventory items that have increased in value. Consult your tax advisor for further help.

For an example of how to report partnership items, see Chapter 45, *Sample Form 1040.*

For more information on partnerships, get Publication 541, *Tax Information on Partnerships.*

S Corporation Income

In general, an S corporation does not pay tax on its income. Instead, the income and expenses of the corporation are "passed through" to the shareholders.

An S corporation must file a return on Form 1120S, *U.S. Income Tax Return for an S Corporation,* and send Schedule K–1 (Form 1120S) to each shareholder. In addition, the S corporation will send each shareholder a copy of the *Shareholder's Instructions for Schedule K–1 (Form 1120S)* to help each shareholder report his or her share of the S corporation's income, credits, and deductions. Do not attach Schedule K–1 (Form 1120S) to your Form 1040 (unless you are required to file it with Form 8271). Keep it for your records.

Explanation
Shareholder's return. Generally, S corporation distributions are a nontaxable return of your basis in the corporation's stock. However, in certain cases, part of the distributions may be taxable as a dividend, or as a long-term or short-term capital gain, or as both. The corporation's distributions may be in the form of cash or property.

All current-year income or loss and other tax items are taxed to you at the corporation's year end. Generally, these items passed through to you as a shareholder will increase or decrease the basis of your S corporation stock as appropriate. Dividends are paid only from prior year earnings (generally retained earnings from years prior to 1983 or prior to becoming an S corporation).

Generally, property (including cash) distributions, except dividend distributions, are considered a return of capital to the extent of your basis in the stock of the corporation. Distributions in excess of basis are treated as a gain from the sale or exchange of property.

You should receive from the S corporation in which you are a shareholder a copy of the *Shareholder's Instructions for Schedule K–1* (Form 1120S), together with a copy of Schedule K–1 (Form 1120S), showing your share of the income, credits, and deductions of the S corporation for the tax year. Your distributive share of the items of income, gain, loss, deduction, or credit of the S corporation must be shown separately on your Form 1040. The character of these items generally is the same as if you had realized or incurred them personally.

Individuals form an S corporation to get the legal benefits of a corporation, such as limited liability, while retaining the tax benefits of an individual. Usually, an S corporation does not pay federal income tax. One exception is a tax on certain gains that is paid by the S corporation, but normally the individual owners of the corporation pay tax or accrue tax benefits on their personal returns based on the corporation's profits and losses.

Income from an S corporation is included in an individual's return as if the S corporation did not exist. Dividends that the S corporation receives are included as dividends on your return on Schedule B (Form 1040). Capital gains are included as capital gains on Schedule D (Form 1040). Types of income from an S corporation that are not treated specially on an individual's return are combined and included on Schedule E (Form 1040). If you have losses from a subchapter S corporation when you are not an active participant in the corporation's business activities, your losses will be subject to the passive activity limitations. See the section on Passive Activity Losses and Tax Shelters at the end of this chapter.

Generally, an S corporation must have its tax year end on December 31. However, under certain circumstances, an S corporation may operate on a **fiscal year**; that is, its tax year may end on a date other than December 31. Your return should include all S corporation income for its operating year that ends within your tax year.

Example

If your S corporation's year ends on October 31, your return for 1993 will include the income items for the corporation's entire year that ended October 31, 1993, even though that means including two months of 1992.

Deducting losses. You may deduct any losses of the S corporation for the year up to the amount of your basis.

Basis in an S corporation. Your basis in an S corporation at the end of a year is your investment (stock and loans), with the following adjustments:

Additions to basis

1. Your distributive share of the S corporation's separately and nonseparately stated taxable income.
2. Your share of tax-exempt income earned by the S corporation.

3. Any additional capital that you contribute.
4. Deductions for depletion in excess of the basis of the property.
5. A loan to the corporation directly from the shareholder. However, a guarantee of a third-party loan by a shareholder does not qualify as an addition to basis.

Subtractions from basis

1. Generally, any cash distributed and the fair market value of property distributed (other than taxable dividends) reduce your basis, but not below zero.
2. Your distributive share of the S corporation's separately and nonseparately stated items of loss and deduction.
3. Your share of nondeductible, noncapital expenditures made by the S corporation.
4. Your share of the deductions for depletion for any oil and gas property held by the S corporation to the extent that the deduction does not exceed the proportionate share of the property's adjusted basis allocated to you.

Example 1

Your basis in an S corporation is $20,000. The corporation makes a distribution to you of $30,000 in cash or property. You would have a gain of $10,000.

Example 2

Your basis in an S corporation is $20,000. If it reports losses of $30,000, you may deduct only $20,000 for the year. The other $10,000 worth of losses is carried over until you have more basis.

All you need to prepare your individual tax return is the Form K-1 provided by the S corporation. It tells you what the numbers are and where to put them on your Form 1040.

TAXPLANNER

An S corporation is just one of several alternatives to consider as a vehicle to conduct economic activities, but it does offer some of the best features of a regular corporation, a partnership, and a sole proprietorship.

1. As in a regular corporation, the stockholders of an S corporation are normally immune from liabilities in excess of their investment.
2. Like a regular corporation, the S corporation structure is convenient for transferring equity to children as part of your estate planning and the gradual transition of management and control to your heirs or successors. As shareholders, the children then report their proportionate share of S corporation income and losses on their respective tax returns.
3. Like a partnership or sole proprietorship, the S corporation permits the investors to deduct operating losses. Just as important, profits are not taxed twice, as they are in a regular corporation. A regular corporation itself pays taxes, and so do the individuals who receive a share of those profits when dividends are paid. An S corporation is, except in certain circumstances, exempt from taxes—at least at the federal level.

For more information on S corporations and their shareholders, get Publication 589, *Tax Information on S Corporations.*

Recoveries

A recovery is a return of an amount you deducted or took a credit for in an earlier year. Generally, you must include all or part of the recovered amounts in your income in the year the recovery is received. The most common recoveries are refunds, reimbursements, and rebates of deductions itemized on Schedule A (Form 1040). Non-itemized deduction recoveries include such items as payments you receive on previously deducted bad debts, reimbursements not included on your Form W–2 for an employee business expense deducted before 1987, and recoveries on items for which you previously claimed a tax credit.

Federal income tax refund. Refunds of federal income taxes are not included in your income because they are never allowed as a deduction from income.

Interest. Interest on any of the amounts you recover must be reported as interest income in the year received.

Recovery and expense in same year. If the refund or other recovery and the deductible expense occur in the same year, the refund or recovery reduces the deduction and is not reported as income.

Recovery attributable to 2 or more years. If you receive a refund or other recovery from one item, such as a real estate tax rebate, that is for amounts you paid in 2 or more separate years, you must allocate, on a pro rata basis, the recovered amount between the years in which it was paid.

This allocation is necessary to determine the amount of recovery attributable to any earlier years and to determine the amount, if any, of your allowable deduction for this item for the current year. For information on how to compute the allocation, see *Recoveries* in Publication 525.

Tax benefit rule. If you did not derive a tax benefit from your prior year deduction, you do not have to include the amount you received this year in income. This could happen if you were subject to the alternative minimum tax or had credits that reduced your tax liability to zero. For more information, get Publication 525.

Itemized Deduction Recoveries

If you recover any amount that you deducted in an earlier year on Schedule A (Form 1040), you must determine how much, if any, of the recovery to include in your income.

Due to changes in the tax law, different computations are needed for the recovery of items deducted after 1986 or before 1987. The discussions in this section apply to recovery of items deducted after 1986. If you recovered an item deducted before 1987, contact your local IRS office for assistance, or see a tax practitioner.

Standard deduction. To determine if amounts deducted in 1992 and recovered in 1993 must be included in your income, you must know the standard deduction for your filing status in 1992. Standard deduction amounts for 1992 are in Publication 525.

Form 1099–G. If you received a state or local income tax refund in 1993, you may receive a statement, Form 1099–G, *Certain Government Payments,* from the payer of the refund (or credit or offset) by January 31, 1994. The IRS will also receive a copy of the Form 1099–G.

Report any interest you received on state or local income tax refunds on line 8a of Form 1040.

No earlier year deduction. If you did not itemize deductions in the year for which you received the recovery, do not include any of the recovery amount in your income.

Explanation
Although the amount of a state tax refund should not be included in gross income if you did not itemize your deductions that year, any interest you receive on federal or state refunds is taxable.

TaxPlanner
The IRS correctly points out that the recovery of certain amounts you deducted is not income if you did not itemize your deductions in the year in which you paid these expenses. However, if the payer of the refund submits a Form 1099 or Form 1099–G to the IRS, we suggest that you *both* include the item in income and subtract it out on the same line. You should also put a statement in your return explaining why the item does not represent taxable income. This may prevent an inquiry from the IRS.

If you were subject to the alternative minimum tax in 1992, you may not have obtained any benefit for all or part of your state income tax deduction. This is because state income taxes are not deductible for purposes of computing the alternative minimum tax. (The alternative minimum tax is explained in Chapter 31, *How to Figure Your Tax.*) You will want to compute carefully the amount of the refund you received in 1993 that did not give you any tax benefit in 1992. Attach a statement in your return explaining why the item does not represent taxable income.

This will require a "with-and-without" computation. If your prior-year tax was not lower *with* the deduction, you did not receive a benefit and, therefore, the refund is *not* taxable income when received.

If, in 1992, you itemized your deductions and had your itemized deductions scaled back due to a high adjusted gross income, a portion of your refund may not have to be included in your income for 1993.

The amount of a refund that would be included in income is the difference between (1) the prior year's allowed itemized deductions and (2) the deductions that would have been claimed had you paid the correct amount of tax in the prior year and had no refund (number 2 above is determined by taking the greater of the itemized deductions that were allowed or the standard deduction).

Example
Tracy had $505,250 of AGI in 1992, paid $40,000 in state income taxes during 1992, and had no other itemized deductions. Tracy had $12,000 of itemized deductions disallowed (3% × $400,000). She received a $5,000 state tax refund in 1993. If Tracy had only paid in the correct $35,000 of state taxes in 1992, she would still have had $12,000 in itemized deductions disallowed. She received a tax benefit to the extent of the $5,000 difference between her $28,000 deduction ($40,000 less $12,000) for 1992 and the $23,000 1992 deduction she would have claimed had she paid in the correct tax in 1992 ($35,000 less $12,000). Thus, the entire $5,000 state tax refund ($28,000 less $23,000) is includible in Tracy's 1993 income.

Recovery limited to deduction. You do not include in your income any amount of your recovery that is more than the amount you deducted in the earlier year. The amount you include in your income is limited to the smaller of:

1) The amount deducted on Schedule A (Form 1040), or
2) The amount recovered.

Example. During 1992 you paid $1,200 for medical expenses. From this amount you subtracted $1,000, which was 7.5% of your adjusted gross income. Your taxable income for 1992 was $9,000. Your actual medical expense deduction was $200. In 1993, you received a $500 reimbursement from your medical insurance for your 1992 expenses. The only amount of the $500 reimbursement that must be included in your income in 1993 is $200—the amount actually deducted.

Explanation

Sometimes you get some money back in a year after you paid and deducted it (e.g., a refund of state income tax or real estate tax). To the extent that you got a tax benefit in the earlier year, and *only* to that extent, you must include the refund in income. No special computation is necessary if your other itemized deductions were greater than the standard deduction for that prior year—you just include the whole refund in income. If your other itemized deductions were less than the standard deduction, you have to determine the amount of the refund that gave you a tax benefit.

Total recoveries included in income. The total amount recovered in 1993 is included in your income if certain requirements are met. The recoveries included in your income will not be more than the amount deducted. See *Tax benefit rule,* earlier.

Amounts deducted **after 1986** will be included in your income if:

1) The recoveries are equal to or less than the amount by which your itemized deductions exceeded the standard deduction for your filing status in the earlier year, and
2) Your taxable income in the earlier year was –0– or more.

Where to report. Enter your state and local income tax refund on line 10, Form 1040, and the total of all other recoveries as other income on line 22, Form 1040.

Example. In 1992, you filed a joint return. Your taxable income was $20,000. The standard deduction for your filing status was $6,000, and you had itemized deductions of $7,000. In 1993, you received the following recoveries for amounts deducted in 1992:

Medical expenses	$200
State and local income tax refund	400
Real estate tax rebate	325
Total recoveries	**$925**

None of the recoveries were more than the deductions taken in 1992.

Because your total recoveries are less than the amount your itemized deductions exceeded the standard deduction ($7,000 – 6,000 = $1,000), and your 1992 taxable income was –0– or more ($20,000), you must include your total recoveries in your income in

1993. Report the state and local income tax refund of $400 on line 10, Form 1040, and the balance of your recoveries, $525, on line 22, Form 1040.

Total recoveries not included in income. The total recovery that must be included in your income is limited to the itemized deductions amount that reduced your tax in the earlier year. (See *Tax benefit rule,* earlier.)

You are generally allowed to claim the standard deduction if you do not itemize your deductions. Only your itemized deductions that are more than your standard deduction are subject to the recovery rule. Therefore, include in your income the smaller of:

1) Your recoveries, or
2) The amount by which your itemized deductions exceeded the standard deduction.

Example. You filed a joint return in 1992. Your itemized deductions were $7,000. The standard deduction that you could have claimed was $6,000. In 1993 you recover $2,400 of your 1992 itemized deductions. None of the recoveries were more than the actual deductions in 1992. Include $1,000 of the recoveries in your 1993 income. This is the smaller of your recoveries ($2,400) or the amount your itemized deductions exceeded the standard deduction ($7,000 – 6,000 = $1,000).

Other recoveries. See *Recoveries* in Publication 525 if:

1) You had a negative taxable income in the prior year.
2) You have recoveries from items other than itemized deductions.
3) You were required to itemize deductions in the prior year for which you received the recovery.
4) You received a recovery for an item for which you claimed a tax credit (other than investment credit or foreign tax credit) in a prior year.
5) You were subject to the alternative minimum tax, or you had credits that reduced your tax liability to zero, in the year the deduction was claimed.
6) Your last payment of 1992 estimated state income tax was made in 1993.
7) Your itemized deductions for 1992 were limited as discussed in Chapter 21.

Repayments

If you had to repay an amount that you had included in your income in an earlier year because at that time you thought you had an unrestricted right to it, you can deduct the amount repaid from your income in the year in which you repay it.

Type of deduction. The type of deduction you are allowed in the year of repayment depends on the type of income you included in the earlier year. For instance, if you repay an amount that you previously reported as a capital gain, deduct the repayment as a capital loss.

Repayment $3,000 or less. If the amount you repaid was $3,000 or less, deduct it from your income in the year you repaid it. If you reported it as wages, unemployment compensation, or other ordinary income, enter it on line 20, Schedule A (Form 1040). If you reported it as a capital gain, deduct it on Schedule D (Form 1040).

Repayment over $3,000. If the amount you repaid was more than $3,000, you can take a deduction for the amount repaid, or you can take a credit against your tax. Follow the steps below and compare the results. Use the method (credit or deduction) that results in less tax.

1) Figure your tax for 1993 claiming a deduction for the repaid amount.
2) Figure your tax for 1993 *without* deducting the amount you repaid. Then,
   a) Refigure your tax from the earlier year without including in income the amount you repaid in 1993.
   b) Subtract the tax in (a) from the tax shown on your return for the earlier year.
   c) Then subtract the answer in (b) from the tax for 1993 figured without the deduction.

How you treat the repayment on your 1993 return depends on which answer above results in less tax.

- If the answer in Step (1) is less tax, deduct the amount repaid on the same form or schedule on which you previously reported it. For example, if you reported it as self-employment income, deduct it on Schedule C or Schedule C-EZ (Form 1040), or if you reported it as wages, deduct it on line 25 of Schedule A (Form 1040).
- If the answer in Step (2) is less tax, claim a credit on line 59, Form 1040, and write "I.R.C. 1341" on the dotted line next to line 59.

An example of this computation can be found in Publication 525.

Example

For tax year 1992 you were married with no **dependents.** You filed a **joint return** with your spouse, claimed two **exemptions,** and reported adjusted gross income of $100,000. Your taxable income after deductions and exemptions was $90,000. Your return showed a tax liability of $20,659, which you paid. In 1993, you had to return $5,000 that you had received and had included in your 1992 gross income because you had a claim to such income. Your marital and filing status were the same in 1993 as in 1992, and your taxable income after taking normal deductions is now $82,000. Your tax liability for this amount would be $18,163. Under Method 1 (see IRS text), you take an additional $5,000 deduction on your 1993 return for the amount you repaid and figure your tax liability on $77,000, which is $16,763. Under Method 2, you figure the amount of the decrease in tax for 1992, which you may claim as a credit on your 1993 return, as follows:

Taxable income for 1992 on which tax previously determined was based	$90,000
Minus: Income you claim	5,000
Taxable income as adjusted	$85,000
Amount of decrease in tax for 1992:	
Tax as previously determined	$20,659
Tax as refigured (on $85,000)	19,153
Decrease in tax	$ 1,506

Your tax liability under Method 2 is $16,657 (your normal 1993 tax liability of $18,163 minus the $1,506 credit for the decrease in 1992 tax as figured above). You must use Method 2 to figure your 1993 tax, because

the tax liability figured this way, $16,657, is less than $16,763, the liability figured under Method 1. If, by using Method 2, your credit is more than your tax, the excess is refunded to you or applied to your account.

Royalties

Royalties from copyrights, patents, and oil, gas, and mineral properties are taxable as ordinary income.

You generally report royalties on Part I, Schedule E (Form 1040). However, if you hold an operating oil, gas, or mineral interest, or are in business as a self-employed writer, inventor, artist, etc., report gross income and expenses on Schedule C or Schedule C-EZ (Form 1040).

Explanation

Income from a working interest in an oil or gas property is reported on Schedule C and is generally subject to self-employment tax, even though you may not actively participate in the operations that produce the income. Such income, however, is not eligible for IRA or Keogh plan contributions, since it is not earned by personal services you performed.

Copyrights and patents. Royalties from copyrights on literary, musical, or artistic works, and similar property, or from patents on inventions, are amounts paid to you for the right to use your work over a specified period of time. Royalties are generally based on the number of units sold, such as the number of books, tickets to a performance, or machines sold.

Oil, gas, and minerals. Royalty income from oil, gas, and mineral properties is the amount you receive when natural resources are extracted from your property. The royalties are based on units, such as barrels, tons, etc., and are paid to you by a person or company who leases the property from you.

Depletion. If you are the owner of an economic interest in mineral deposits or oil and gas wells, you can recover your investment through the depletion allowance. For information on this subject, see Chapter 13 of Publication 535, *Business Expenses.*

Explanation

Two methods are used to compute the depletion allowance: cost depletion and percentage depletion.

Cost depletion. The first step in computing the cost depletion deduction is to estimate the number of units (barrels, tons, etc.) that you will be able to extract from the property. This estimate is revised annually. You then divide this amount into your adjusted basis in the property. This gives you your cost per unit. Each year your depletion deduction is computed by multiplying the cost per unit by the number of units you extracted and sold during that year. Each year you reduce your basis in the property by the amount of depletion deducted. Once this basis has been reduced to zero, you may no longer claim cost depletion.

Percentage depletion. To compute the percentage depletion allowance, you take a percentage of the gross income from the property. Different percentage rates are specified for different types of property. If you are not an independent producer or a royalty owner, this deduction is limited to 50% of the taxable income from the property, computed before the deduction for depletion is claimed. However, if you are an independent producer or a royalty owner, the deduction is limited to the lesser of 65% of your total taxable income (computed without regard to any **net operating loss** or capital loss carrybacks) or 50% of the taxable income from the property (computed before the deduction for depletion is claimed). Any part of the percentage depletion allowance disallowed because of the 65% limitation may be carried over into future years. Unlike cost depletion, you may claim percentage depletion, even though your basis in the property has been reduced to zero.

Example

A small independent producer of crude oil invests $1 million in an oil well. Her geologists estimate that the well will yield 1 million barrels of oil. During 1993, she pumped 75,000 barrels of oil and sold 60,000 of them at $30 per barrel. The oil cost $15 per barrel to produce.

The permissible rate for percentage depletion for an independent producer of crude oil is 15%. The independent oil producer computes her depletion allowance as follows:

Cost Depletion Method

Sales (60,000 × $30)	$1,800,000
Less: Production costs (60,000 × $15)	900,000
Income	$ 900,000
Cost Depletion:	
Depletable cost per unit ($1,000,000 ÷ 1,000,000 = $1)	
Cost depletion (60,000 × $1)	$ 60,000

Percentage Depletion Method

Gross income from property	$1,800,000	
Percentage depletion ($1,800,000 × 15%)	$ 270,000	(A)
Limitation (50% of the $900,000 income computed above from the property)	$ 450,000	(B)
Percentage depletion, lesser of A or B	$ 270,000	

Since percentage depletion is more advantageous than cost depletion, the independent oil producer may use percentage depletion on her oil well. However, there is a further limitation—percentage depletion may not exceed 65% of taxable income computed without depletion. Professional help is advisable.

Coal and iron ore. Under certain circumstances, you can treat amounts you receive from the disposal of coal and iron ore as payments from the sale of a capital asset, rather than as royalty income. For information about gain or loss from the sale of coal and iron ore, get Publication 544.

Interest in the property sold. If you sell your complete interest in the oil, gas, or mineral rights, the amount you receive is considered payment for the sale of your property, not royalty

income. Under certain circumstances, the sale is subject to capital gain or loss treatment on Schedule D (Form 1040). For information on capital gain or loss, see Chapter 15, *Sale of Property*.

Also, you can report the sale as an installment sale if you are to receive at least one payment after the tax year in which the sale took place. For more information, get Publication 537, *Installment Sales*.

Explanation

The sale of most items producing royalty income is treated as a capital transaction. However, this is not true for copyrights and other property created by your personal efforts. The purpose of this exception is to prevent people such as authors from receiving capital gain treatment for their literary efforts. For more information about installment sales, see Chapter 15, *Sale of Property*.

Part of future production sold. If you own mineral property but sell part of the future production, you generally treat the money you receive from the buyer at the time of the sale as a loan from the buyer. Do not include it in your income or take depletion based on it.

When production begins, you include all the proceeds in your income, deduct all the production expenses, and deduct depletion from that amount to arrive at your taxable income from the property.

Your payments for the buyer's share of the proceeds are treated as a loan repayment. The buyer will treat the share as a return of capital that is not included in your income or subject to a depletion allowance. Any interest factor received by the buyer will be treated as ordinary income not subject to the allowance for depletion.

Retained interest. If you retain a royalty, an overriding royalty, or a net profit interest in a mineral property for the life of the property, you have made a lease or a sublease, and any cash you receive for the assignment is ordinary income subject to a depletion allowance.

Explanation

If you are paid royalties or bonuses for the production of oil before production actually begins, you do not qualify for a depletion allowance in the year in which the advance royalty or bonus is included in your income, but you will be entitled to a depletion allowance in the year in which production begins. You should consult your tax advisor for further clarification of this point.

Income Not Taxed

You generally should not report the following items on your return. Some of the items, however, are only partly excluded from your income. A discussion of other totally and partly excluded items follows this list.

Accident and health insurance proceeds
"Black lung" benefits
Casualty insurance and other reimbursements (Chapter 26, *Nonbusiness Casualty and Theft Losses*)
Child support payments (Chapter 19, *Alimony*)
Damages awarded for physical injury or sickness
Employment agency fees (Chapter 30, *Miscellaneous Deductions*)

Federal Employees' Compensation Act payments

Government cost-of-living allowances for civilian employees stationed outside the continental U.S. (other than Alaska) (Chapter 6, *Wages, Salaries, and Other Earnings*)

Interest on state or local government obligations (Chapter 8, *Interest Income*)

Meals and lodging

Members of the clergy housing allowance (Chapter 6)

Military allowances (Chapter 6)

Scholarship and fellowship grants

Social security benefits and equivalent railroad retirement benefits (Chapter 12, *Social Security and Equivalent Railroad Retirement Benefits*)

Supplemental security income

Veterans' benefits (Chapter 6)

Welfare benefits

Workers' compensation

Campaign contributions. These contributions are not income to a candidate unless they are diverted to his or her personal use. To be exempt from tax, the contributions must be spent for campaign purposes or kept in a fund for use in future campaigns. However, interest earned on bank deposits, dividends received on contributed securities, and net gains on sales of contributed securities are taxable and must be reported on Form 1120–POL, *U.S. Income Tax Return for Certain Political Organizations.* Excess campaign funds transferred to an office account must be included in the officeholder's income on line 22, Form 1040, in the year transferred.

Cash rebates. A cash rebate you receive from a dealer or manufacturer of an item you buy is not income.

Example. You buy a new car for $9,000 cash and receive a $400 rebate check from the manufacturer. The $400 is not income to you. Your cost is $8,600. This is your basis on which you figure gain or loss if you sell the car, and depreciation if you use it for business.

Explanation
The IRS realistically views rebates as another way of offering a price reduction to induce you to buy a product. Similarly, the "dividends" that a life insurance company pays you are a reduction of your premium rather than an addition to your gross income.

Employee achievement awards. You can exclude from income employee achievement awards you receive only if your employer can deduct them. To be deducted by your employer, and excluded by you, the awards must meet all the following requirements:

1) Be given for length of service or safety achievement.
2) Be tangible personal property other than cash, gift certificates, or equivalent items.
3) Be given under conditions and circumstances that do not create a significant likelihood of the payment of disguised compensation.
4) Be given as part of a meaningful presentation.
5) Be no more than the specified dollar limits.

Dollar limits. There are limits to the total awards you can exclude in one year. Awards from nonqualified plans are limited to $400, and total awards, from both qualified and nonqualified plans, are limited to $1,600. The cost to your employer is the determining factor for these limits. Amounts over the limits cannot be deducted by your employer and must be included in your income.

Qualified plan award. A qualified plan award is one you are awarded as part of an established written plan by your employer that does not discriminate in favor of highly compensated employees. An award will not be considered a qualified plan award if the average cost of all employee achievement awards given by your employer during the tax year is more than $400. In determining average cost, awards of nominal value are not taken into account.

Example. Ben Green received three employee achievement awards during 1993: a nonqualified plan award of a watch valued at $250, and two qualified plan awards of a stereo valued at $1,000 and a set of golf clubs valued at $500. Assuming that the requirements for qualified plan awards are otherwise satisfied, each award by itself would be excluded from his income. However, since the total value of the awards is more than $1,600, Ben must include the excess of $150 ($1,750 − $1,600) in his income.

Energy conservation subsidies. For taxable years beginning after 1992, residential customers can exclude from gross income any subsidy provided, either directly or indirectly, by public utilities for the purchase or installation of an energy conservation measure with respect to a dwelling unit.

Energy conservation measure. This includes installations or modifications that are primarily designed to reduce consumption of electricity or natural gas, or improve the management of energy demand with respect to a dwelling unit.

Dwelling unit. This includes a house, apartment, condominium, mobile home, boat, or similar property. If a building or structure contains both dwelling and other units, any subsidy must be properly allocated.

Foster-care providers. Payments you receive from a state, political subdivision, or tax-exempt child-placement agency for providing foster care to qualified individuals in your home are not included in your income. You cannot deduct the related expenses. However, you must include in your income payments received for the care of more than 5 individuals age 19 and older.

A qualified foster individual is a person who:

1) Is living in a foster family home, and
2) Was placed there by:
   a) An agency of a state or one of its political subdivisions, or
   b) A tax-exempt child placement agency licensed by a state, if the individual is under age 19.

TaxPlanner
If a foster child lives with you in your home for the entire year, you are entitled to claim the child as a dependent if you provide more than half of his or her support. This is often the case when you care for the children of relatives. If you receive payments from an outside agency and the payments are clearly less than the child's expenses, it may be worthwhile for you to calculate whether you are in fact providing more than half the child's support. (See Chapter 33, *Child and Dependent Care Credit*, for details.)

Difficulty-of-care payments. These payments are not included in your income. These are additional payments made to foster-care providers of physically, mentally, or emotionally handicapped individuals by a state, political subdivision, or tax-exempt child placement agency that are designated as difficulty-of-care payments. A state must determine that the additional compensation is needed. You must include in your income difficulty-of-care payments received for more than:

1) 10 children under age 19, and
2) 5 individuals age 19 and older.

Maintaining space in home. If you are paid by a placement agency to maintain space in your home for foster-care individuals, or if you receive payments that you must include in your income, you are in business as a foster-care provider and you are self-employed. You must include these payments in your income. You can deduct expenses related to these payments.

Report the income and expenses on Schedule C or Schedule C-EZ (Form 1040) and net business income on Schedule SE (Form 1040). See *Home Office* in Chapter 30.

For more information on foster care, get Publication 501.

Gifts and inheritances. Property you receive as a gift, bequest, or inheritance is not included in your income. However, if property you receive this way later produces income such as interest, dividends, or rentals, that income is taxable to you. If property is given to a trust and the income from it is paid, credited, or distributed to you, that also is income to you. If the gift, bequest, or inheritance is the income from the property, that income is taxable to you.

Items given to you as an incentive to enter into a business transaction are not gifts. For example, items such as small appliances or dinnerware given to you by a bank as an incentive to make a deposit are interest income to you and must be reported at their fair market value.

Interest on frozen deposits. In general, you must exclude from your income the amount of interest earned on a frozen deposit. A deposit is frozen if, at the end of the calendar year, you cannot withdraw any part of the deposit because:

1) The financial institution is bankrupt or insolvent, or
2) The state where the institution is located has placed limits on withdrawals because other financial institutions in the state are bankrupt or insolvent.

Excludable amount. The amount of interest you must exclude from gross income for the year is the interest that was credited on the frozen deposit for that tax year minus the sum of:

1) The net amount withdrawn from the deposit during that year, and
2) The amount that could have been withdrawn at the end of that tax year (not reduced by any penalty for premature withdrawals of a time deposit).

In the year the interest becomes withdrawable, you must include in your income the part of the interest that was excluded.

Example. For tax year 1993, Bill and Joan Smith had interest income of $1,500 credited to their account. The account is with a bank that has been insolvent since 1985. The Smiths were not able to withdraw any money from this frozen account. They must exclude the $1,500 of interest credited to this account from their 1993 gross income.

Interest on qualified savings bonds. You can exclude from your income the interest from qualified U.S. savings bonds you redeem if you pay qualified higher educational expenses in the same year. "Qualified higher educational expenses" are those you pay for tuition and required fees at an eligible educational institution for you, your spouse, or your dependent. A "qualified U.S. savings bond" is a Series EE savings bond issued after December 31, 1989, to an individual 24 years of age or older. For more information on this exclusion, see Chapter 8.

Living expenses paid by insurance. Do not include in income amounts you receive under an insurance policy for additional living expenses you and your family had because you lost the use of your home by fire, storm, or other casualty. The amount you exclude from income is limited to your extra living expenses that are more than the normal expenses you would have had. Extra living expenses, for this purpose, include only those to keep you and your family at the same standard of living you had before the loss.

Sale of home. If you are 55 or older and sell your main home, you may be able to exclude from income all or part of any gain from the sale. See Chapter 16, *Selling Your Home.*

Explanation
If you file a joint return and the home you sold was owned in **joint tenancy, tenancy by the entirety,** or as **community property,** the age requirement for exclusion of gains from your income is satisfied if either spouse has reached his or her 55th birthday.

Transporting schoolchildren. Do not include in your income a school board mileage allowance for taking children to and from school if you are not in the business of taking children to school. You cannot deduct expenses for providing this transportation.

Utility rebates. If you are a customer of an electric utility company and you participate in the utility's energy conservation program, you may receive on your monthly electric bill, either:

1) A reduction in the purchase price of electricity furnished to you (rate reduction), or
2) A nonrefundable credit against the purchase price of the electricity.

The amount of the rate reduction or nonrefundable credit is not included in your income.

Life Insurance Proceeds

Life insurance proceeds paid to you because of the death of the insured person are not taxable unless the policy was turned over to you for a price. This applies even if the proceeds were paid under an accident or health insurance policy or an endowment contract.

Proceeds not received in installments. If death benefits are paid to you in a lump sum or other than at regular intervals, include them in your gross income only to the extent they are more than the amount payable to you at the time of the insured person's death. If the benefit payable at death is not specified, you include the benefit payments in your income to the extent they are more than the present value of the payments at the time of death.

Proceeds received in installments. If you receive life insurance proceeds in installments, you can exclude part of each installment from your income.

To determine the excluded part, you must divide the amount held by the insurance company (generally the total lump sum payable at the death of the insured person) by the number of installments to be paid. Include anything over this excluded part in your income as interest. For more information, get Publication 525.

Surviving spouse. If your spouse died before October 23, 1986, and insurance proceeds are payable to you because of the death of your spouse, and you receive them in installments, you can exclude up to $1,000 a year of the interest included in the installments. This is in addition to the part of each installment that is excluded as a recovery of the lump sum payable at death. If you remarry, you can continue to take the exclusion.

If your spouse died after October 22, 1986, you cannot exclude any interest payments included in the installment payments.

See *Insurance Received in Installments* in Chapter 8.

Interest option on insurance. If an insurance company pays you only interest on proceeds from life insurance left on deposit with them, the interest you are paid is taxable.

If your spouse died before October 23, 1986, and you chose to receive only the interest from your insurance proceeds, the $1,000 interest exclusion for a surviving spouse does not apply. If you later decide to receive the proceeds from the policy in installments, you can take the interest exclusion from the time you begin to receive the installments.

Surrender of policy for cash. If you surrender a life insurance policy for cash, you must include in income any proceeds that exceed the amount of premiums that you paid.

Reporting. If you received a Form 1099–R, report these amounts on lines 17a and 17b of Form 1040, or lines 11a and 11b of Form 1040A.

Endowment proceeds. Endowment proceeds paid in a lump sum to you at maturity are taxable only if the proceeds are more than the cost of the policy. Add any amounts that you previously received under the contract and excluded from your income to the lump-sum payment to find how much of the total is a return of your cost and how much is an excess over your cost. Include any excess over your cost in your income.

Endowment proceeds that you choose to receive in installments instead of a lump-sum payment at the maturity of the policy are taxed as an annuity as explained in Publication 575, *Pension and Annuity Income (Including Simplified General Rule)*. For this treatment to apply, you must choose to receive the proceeds in installments before receiving any part of the lump sum. This election must be made within 60 days after the lump-sum payment first became payable to you.

TAXSAVER

There are a number of ways in which insurance proceeds may be paid. The choice may have been made by the deceased, or the choice may belong to the recipient of the proceeds. In either case, proper planning may save tax dollars and increase wealth.

Generally, the insured should not decide how the insurance benefits are to be paid, unless he or she is worried that the beneficiary, be it a child or a spouse, might squander the money. Absent that, determining the method of payment should be left to the beneficiary, who, after the death of the insured, is in the best position to consider potential investments, as well as tax benefits.

When initially enacted, the $1,000 exclusion was a substantial sum. But, over the years, inflation took its toll, and, in the Tax Reform Act of 1986, Congress terminated the exclusion for deaths after October 22, 1986.

Explanation

Endowment contracts, much like whole life insurance contracts, require you, as the owner, to pay annual premiums in return for a certain sum of cash that is paid when you reach a specified age or on death. Unless you choose to receive the endowment proceeds in installments, the excess of the proceeds over the cost of the policy is taxable in the year of maturity, *even if the proceeds are not received until a later year.* The excess of the proceeds are taxed as ordinary income, not as capital gain. The cost of the endowment contract is the total amount of the premiums you paid for it, not its cash value at the time of maturity or when you surrender it.

However, if you agree to take the proceeds as an annuity within 60 days after the lump-sum payment becomes available and before you receive any cash, you are not considered to have received the lump sum for tax purposes. The lump sum is taxed as an annuity; that is, you are taxed on the amounts as you receive them each year.

The Technical and Miscellaneous Revenue Act of 1988 includes a provision designed to discourage the use of a life insurance contract as a tax shelter. For certain contracts entered into or materially changed after June 21, 1988, you may be required to treat distributions first as income and then as recovery of investment. Distributions are defined for this purpose to include a loan. In certain circumstances, an additional 10% tax will be imposed on the amount that is includable in gross income. Consult your tax advisor to determine if you are subject to this provision.

Payments to beneficiaries of deceased employees (death benefit exclusion). The first $5,000 of payments made by or for an employer because of an employee's death can be excluded from the income of the beneficiaries. The payments need not be made as the result of a contract. The amount excluded for any deceased employee cannot be more than $5,000 regardless of the number of employers or the number of beneficiaries.

This exclusion also covers payments of the balance to the credit of a deceased employee under a stock bonus, pension, or profit-sharing plan, as long as they are received during one tax year of the beneficiary.

Example. William Smith was an officer of a corporation at the time of his death last year. The board of directors voted to pay Mr. Smith's salary to his widow for the remainder of the year for his past services. During the year the corporation made payments of $18,000 to the widow. She can exclude from her income the first $5,000 she received, but must include the remaining $13,000 on line 22, of her Form 1040.

Self-employed individuals. The death benefit exclusion also applies to lump-sum distributions paid on behalf of self-employed individuals, if paid under a qualified pension, profit-sharing, or stock bonus plan.

Payments not qualifying. Any amount the deceased employee (or self-employed individual) had a guaranteed right to receive had death not occurred cannot be excluded as a tax-free death benefit. If the deceased employee was receiving a retirement annuity, and the beneficiary continues to receive payments under a joint and survivor annuity option, these payments do not qualify for the death benefit exclusion. However, if the deceased employee had retired on disability and at the time of death had not reached minimum retirement age, payments to the beneficiary may qualify for the death benefit exclusion. Minimum retirement age generally is the age at which an individual can receive a pension or annuity were that individual not disabled.

Paid in installments. Death benefits paid in installments over a period of years are annuity payments. If you are the beneficiary of an employee who died while still employed, the pension or annuity you receive may qualify for the death benefit exclusion. This exclusion is limited to $5,000 and generally applies to the amount by which the present value of the annuity (explained in Publication 575), figured as of the date of the employee's death, is more than the larger of:

1) The employee's contributions to the plan, or
2) The amount the employee had a guaranteed right to receive.

If you are eligible for the exclusion, add it to the cost or unrecovered cost of the annuity in figuring, at the annuity starting date, the investment in the contract.

Treatment of annuity payments to beneficiaries of employees and the death benefit exclusion are discussed in Chapter 11, *Retirement Plans, Pensions, and Annuities.*

Deceased public safety officers. If you are a surviving dependent of a public safety officer (law enforcement officer or firefighter) who died in the line of duty, do not include in your income the death benefit payable to you by the Bureau of Justice Assistance.

Welfare and Other Public Assistance Benefits

Do not include in your income the benefit payments from a public welfare fund, such as payments due to blindness. Payments from a state fund for the victims of crime should not be included in the victims' incomes if they are in the nature of welfare payments. Do not deduct medical expenses that are reimbursed by such a fund.

Payments for age and residency. If the state of Alaska makes payments to its citizens who meet certain age and residency tests, and the payments are not based on need, the payments are not welfare benefits. Include them in gross income on line 22, Form 1040.

Employment Opportunities for Handicapped Individuals Act. Persons with disabilities who are employed in community service activities under this Act do not include in income the allowances or reimbursements paid to them under the Act. Compensation received for services performed under this Act are includible in gross income.

Disaster Relief Act of 1974. Grants made under this Act to help victims of natural disasters are not included in income. Do not deduct casualty losses or medical expenses that are specifically reimbursed by these disaster relief grants. Disaster unemployment assistance payments under the Act are unemployment benefits that are taxable. See *Unemployment compensation* in Chapter 6, *Wages, Salaries, and Other Earnings.*

Mortgage assistance payments. Payments made under section 235 of the National Housing Act for mortgage assistance are not included in the homeowner's gross income.

Interest paid for the homeowner under the mortgage assistance program cannot be deducted.

Payments to reduce cost of winter energy. Payments made by a state to qualified people to reduce their cost of winter energy use are not taxable.

Other Sickness and Injury Benefits

In addition to welfare or insurance benefits, you may receive other payments for sickness and injury. *Table 13–1* gives a general overview of some of these payments.

Workers' compensation. Amounts you receive as workers' compensation for an occupational sickness or injury are fully exempt from tax if they are paid under a workers' compensation act

Table 13-1. **Are Your Sickness and Injury Benefits Taxable?**

This table is intended as a general overview. Additional rules may apply depending on your situation. For more information about your benefits, see the discussion, "Other Sickness and Injury Benefits," in this chapter.	
Type of Benefit	**General Rule**
Workers' Compensation	Not taxable if paid under a workers' compensation act or a statute in the nature of a workers' compensation act and paid due to a work related sickness or injury. However, payments received after returning to work are taxable.
Federal Employees' Compensation Act (FECA)	Not taxable if paid because of personal injury or sickness. However, payments received as "continuation of pay" for up to 45 days while a claim is being decided and pay received for sick leave while a claim is being processed are taxable.
Compensatory Damages	Not taxable if received for injury or sickness.
Accident or Health Insurance Benefits	Not taxable if you paid the insurance premiums.
Disability Benefits	Not taxable if received for loss of income or earning capacity due to an injury covered by a "no-fault" automobile policy.
Compensation for Permanent Loss or Loss of Use of a Part or Function of Your Body, or for Permanent Disfigurement	Not taxable if paid due to the injury. The payments must be figured without regard to any period of absence from work.
Reimbursements for Medical Care	Not taxable—but the reimbursement may reduce your medical expense deduction.

or a statute in the nature of a workers' compensation act. The exemption also applies to your survivor(s) if the payments otherwise qualify as workers' compensation. The exemption from tax, however, does not apply to retirement benefits you receive based on your age, length of service, or prior contributions to the plan, even though you retired because of occupational sickness or injury.

Note. If part of your workers' compensation reduces your social security or equivalent railroad retirement benefits received, that part is considered social security (or equivalent railroad retirement) benefits and may be taxable. For more information, see Publication 915, *Social Security Benefits and Equivalent Railroad Retirement Benefits.*

Return to work. If you return to work after qualifying for workers' compensation, payments you continue to receive while assigned to light duties are taxable. Report these payments as wages on line 7 of Form 1040 or Form 1040A, or on line 2 of Form 1040EZ.

Federal Employees' Compensation Act (FECA). Payments made under this Act for personal injury or sickness, including payments to beneficiaries in case of death, are not taxable. However, amounts are taxable that are received under this Act as "continuation of pay" for up to 45 days while a claim is being decided. Report this income on line 7 of Form 1040 or Form 1040A, or on line 2 of Form 1040EZ. Also, pay for sick leave while a claim is being processed is taxable and must be included in your income as wages.

You can deduct the amount you spend to "buy back" sick leave for an earlier year to be eligible for nontaxable FECA benefits for that period. It is a miscellaneous deduction subject to the 2% limit on Schedule A (Form 1040). If you "buy back" sick leave in the same year you use it, the amount reduces your taxable sick leave pay. Do not deduct it separately.

Other compensation. Many other amounts you receive as compensation for injury or illness are not taxable. These include:

- **Compensatory damages** received for injury or illness (however, punitive damages in cases not involving physical injury or sickness are taxable),
- **Benefits received under an accident or health insurance policy** attributable to premiums you paid,
- **Disability benefits** received for loss of income or earning capacity as a result of injuries under a "no-fault" automobile policy, and
- **Compensation received for permanent loss** or loss of use of a part or function of your body, or for your permanent disfigurement. This compensation must be figured only on the injury and not on the period of your absence from work. These benefits are exempt from tax even though your employer pays for the accident and health plan that provides these benefits.

Reimbursement for medical care. A reimbursement for medical care is generally not taxable. However, this reimbursement may reduce your medical expense deduction. For more information, see Chapter 22.

Scholarship and Fellowship Grants

If you receive a scholarship or fellowship grant, you may be able to exclude from income all or part of the amounts you receive.

Qualified scholarships. Only a candidate for a degree can exclude amounts received as a qualified scholarship. A qualified scholarship is any amount you receive that is for:

1) Tuition and fees to enroll at or attend an educational organization, or

2) Fees, books, supplies, and equipment required for courses at the educational institution.

Amounts used for room and board **do not** qualify.

Payments for services. All payments you receive for services must be included in income, even if the services are a condition of receiving the grant and are required of all candidates for the degree. This includes amounts received for teaching and research. Include these payments on line 7 of Form 1040 or Form 1040A, or on line 2 of Form 1040EZ. Get Publication 520 for information on how to report the taxable portion of scholarships and fellowship grants.

VA payments. Allowances paid by the Department of Veterans Affairs are not included in your gross income. These allowances are not considered scholarship or fellowship grants.

Prizes. Scholarship prizes won in a contest are not scholarships or fellowships if you do not have to use the prizes for educational purposes. You must include these amounts in your gross income on line 22, Form 1040, whether or not you use the amounts for educational purposes.

Qualified tuition reductions. These reductions are excluded from your income. A qualified tuition reduction is the amount of reduction in tuition for education (below the graduate level) furnished to an employee of an educational institution (or certain other persons) provided certain requirements are met. However, graduate students who engage in teaching or research activities for the educational institution may qualify for this exclusion. For more information, get Publication 520.

Passive Activity Losses and Tax Shelters

Explanation

Investments that yield tax benefits are sometimes called "tax shelters." In some cases, Congress has concluded that the loss of revenue is an acceptable side effect of special tax provisions designed to encourage taxpayers to make certain types of investments. In many cases, however, losses from tax shelters produce little or no benefit to society, or the tax benefits are exaggerated beyond those intended. Those cases are referred to as "abusive tax shelters."

An investment that is considered a tax shelter is subject to restrictions, including the requirement that it be registered, unless it is a projected income investment.

Passive activity losses and credits. The passive activity loss and credit rules limit the amount of losses and credits that can be claimed from such activities and limit the amount that can offset nonpassive income, such as certain portfolio income from investments.

Beginning in 1987, individuals, estates, trusts, certain closely held corporations, and personal service corporations are prohibited from deducting losses in excess of income generated by passive activities. In addition, credits from passive activities are generally limited to the tax allocable to such activities. Passive activity losses that are not deductible in the current year are suspended and carried forward to offset passive activity income generated in future years. Similar treatment applies to excess credits.

A passive activity involves the conduct of any trade or business in which the taxpayer does not materially participate. A taxpayer is treated as a material participant only if the individual is involved in the operations of the activity on a regular, continuous, and substantial basis. The participation of the taxpayer's spouse is taken into account when making this determination. Rental activities are considered passive activities, regardless of the degree of participation. However, special rules apply to some activities. Losses attributable to limited partnership interests are considered passive, except where regulations provide otherwise. In general, working interests in any oil or gas property held directly or through an entity that does not limit the taxpayer's liability is *not* considered passive, whether or not the taxpayer is a material participant.

Example 1

Three brothers own a hardware store as partners. Two of them consider it their full-time job, since it is their only source of income. The third brother lives 200 miles away and is consulted only on major issues. The two brothers who work at the store meet the material participation test. The third brother has a passive investment.

Example 2

Bonnie owns a one-sixteenth interest in four different racehorses. She does not own the stables where the horses are trained and fed. She is not involved in the daily care of the horses. She pays her fair share of the costs, and her advice is considered on when and where the horses are to run. Bonnie has significant salary income from a full-time job and from managing her portfolio. Bonnie is probably not a material participant.

Example 3

Andrea ia a limited partner in a partnership. She is not a material participant.

Example 4

Chris owns rental property. He has a passive investment.

Example 5

Herbert and Diane Morris are married, file a joint return, and have combined wages of $135,000 in 1993. They own interests in the following business activities. They are at risk for all of their investment in the activities.

1. Activity A is rental real estate activity. Herbert and Diane actively participate in Activity A and are 100% owners of the activity. Activity A's net loss for 1993 is $10,000. The prior-year unallowed losses for Activity A are $8,000.
2. Activity B is a trade or business partnership. Herbert and Diane own a 10% interest in Activity B and do not materially participate in this activity. In 1993, their distributive share of the partnership loss is $2,000 and their share of prior-year unallowed losses for the partnership is $1,200.
3. Activity C is a rental real estate activity. Herbert and Diane do not actively participate in the activity. In 1993, their distributive share of income from the activity is $5,000. Activity C has no prior-year unallowed losses.

See Filled in Form 8582 on page 200.

Exception

The passive loss rules do not apply to certain real estate rental activities in which an individual taxpayer actively participates. For this purpose, active participation requires a lesser amount of involvement than does material participation. A taxpayer is considered *not* to have actively participated in the rental activity, however, if, at any time during the tax year, the individual owns less than a 10% interest in the activity. In general, active participants in real estate rental activities may deduct up to $25,000 of the passive losses and the "deduction equivalent" of credits arising from the real estate rental activities each tax year against income from nonpassive sources (e.g., salary). The $25,000 maximum deduction is reduced by 50% of the amount by which the taxpayer's adjusted gross income exceeds $100,000. Thus, this deduction is completely phased out for individuals with adjusted gross incomes of $150,000 or more. For this purpose, adjusted gross income is determined without regard to taxable social security benefits, IRA contribution deductions, and any passive activity loss.

Example 1

Ron's adjusted gross income for purposes of rental real estate losses is $120,000. Ron has rental losses of $30,000. Since his income is over $100,000 by $20,000, he cannot deduct $10,000 of the first $25,000 of real estate loss. Ron is limited to deducting $15,000. This leaves Ron with total disallowed real estate losses of $15,000. This $15,000 is added to any other passive losses Ron may have.

Example 2

Jean and Bill anticipate filing a joint return for 1993. They think they will have salary income of $200,000, interest income of $10,000 from a $100,000 corporate bond, and a $10,000 loss from an actively managed rental property. The rental property has a mortgage of $100,000 at 10% interest. If Jean and Bill take no action, none of the rental loss will be allowed, since 100% of passive losses are disallowed, according to the phase-in rules described above. Their adjusted gross income would be $210,000 ($200,000 + $10,000 − $0).

Jean and Bill should consider selling their corporate bond and paying off their real estate mortgage. If they do this, their adjusted gross income will be $200,000 ($200,000 + 0 − 0), or $10,000 less.

TAXALERT

Beginning in 1994, certain real estate professionals will be able to offset passive losses against all of their income. You qualify for this special rule if you work for more than half your time in real estate, spending a minimum of 750 hours during the year, and have at least a 5% ownership in your employer if you are an employee. An independent contractor providing realtor services would qualify.

Example

During 1994, a self-employed real estate developer earned $100,000 in development fees from projects the developer spent 1,200 hours developing. In addition the developer incurred rental real estate losses of $200,000 from properties which the developer spent over 800 hours managing during 1994. The developer performs no other personal services during the year, and has no other items of income or deduction. Since the developer (1) materially participated in the rental real estate activity, (2) performed more than 750 hours in real property trades or businesses, and (3) performed more than 50% of the developer's total personal service hours in real estate trades or businesses in which the developer materially participated, the developer will have a net operating loss of $100,000 to carry back (and the excess to carry forward) to offset any source of income.

Explanation

Interest expense on a passive investment. If you borrowed money to purchase a passive investment, any interest on the loan will be considered part of your passive investment loss.

TAXPLANNER

You should try to realign your personal finances so that you maximize your interest expense deductions. If you are in a real estate limited partnership, you may be able to have all the partners contribute additional capital so that the passive loss is reduced or limited. Your capital contribution could come from your other investments or from a mortgage on a personal residence. If you have untapped appreciation in your personal residence, you can borrow against it and deduct the interest cost subject to certain limitations. Make sure, however, that any mortgage does not exceed the limits applicable to your situation, since such disallowed interest would be considered nondeductible personal interest.

Previously disallowed losses (but not credits) are recognized in full when the taxpayer disposes of his or her entire interest in the passive activity in a fully taxable transaction. However, suspended losses are not deductible when the taxpayer sells the interest to a related party. Rather, the losses remain with the individual (and may offset passive income) until the related purchaser disposes of the interest in a taxable transaction to an unrelated person. Various other types of dispositions trigger suspended losses, including abandonment, death of the taxpayer, gifts, and installment sales of entire interests, although special rules apply.

Recent legislation clarified that a sale in a taxable year beginning before January 1, 1987, reported on the installment method and included in income after December 31, 1986, would be considered income from a passive activity.

Example

Bob disposes of rental property in 1986 under the installment sale method and properly reports $2,000 of taxable gain in his 1986 through 1993 tax returns. Bob may treat the 1987 through 1993 gains as income from a passive activity and may offset other passive losses in these years.

Form 8582 — Passive Activity Loss Limitations

Form **8582**
Department of the Treasury
Internal Revenue Service

Passive Activity Loss Limitations

▶ See separate instructions.
▶ Attach to Form 1040 or Form 1041.

OMB No. 1545-1008

1993

Attachment Sequence No. 88

Name(s) shown on return: Herbert and Diane Morris

Identifying number: 100308888

Part I — 1993 Passive Activity Loss

Caution: *See the instructions for Worksheets 1 and 2 on page 7 before completing Part I.*

Rental Real Estate Activities With Active Participation (For the definition of active participation see Active Participation in a Rental Real Estate Activity on page 3 of the instructions.)

1a Activities with net income (from Worksheet 1, column (a))	1a		
b Activities with net loss (from Worksheet 1, column (b))	1b (10,000)		
c Prior year unallowed losses (from Worksheet 1, column (c))	1c (8,000)		
d Combine lines 1a, 1b, and 1c		1d	<18,000>

All Other Passive Activities

2a Activities with net income (from Worksheet 2, column (a))	2a 5,000		
b Activities with net loss (from Worksheet 2, column (b))	2b (2,000)		
c Prior year unallowed losses (from Worksheet 2, column (c))	2c (1,200)		
d Combine lines 2a, 2b, and 2c		2d	1,800

3 Combine lines 1d and 2d. If the result is net income or zero, see the instructions for line 3. If this line is net income or zero, see the instructions for line 3. Otherwise, go to line 4. If the losses, go to line 4. Otherwise, enter -0- on line 9 and go to line 10 ... 3 | <16,200>

Part II — Special Allowance for Rental Real Estate With Active Participation

Note: *Enter all numbers in Part II as positive amounts. (See instructions on page 7 for examples.)*

4 Enter the smaller of the loss on line 1d or the loss on line 3	4	<16,200>
5 Enter $150,000. If married filing separately, see the instructions	5	150,000
6 Enter modified adjusted gross income, but not less than zero (see instructions)	6	135,000
Note: *If line 6 is equal to or greater than line 5, skip lines 7 and 8, enter -0- on line 9, and then go to line 10. Otherwise, go to line 7.*		
7 Subtract line 6 from line 5	7	15,000
8 Multiply line 7 by 50% (.5). **Do not enter more than $25,000.** If married filing separately, see instructions	8	7,500
9 Enter the smaller of line 4 or line 8	9	7,500

Part III — Total Losses Allowed

10 Add the income, if any, on lines 1a and 2a and enter the total	10	5,000
11 **Total losses allowed** from all passive activities for 1993. Add lines 9 and 10. See the instructions to find out how to report the losses on your tax return	11	12,500

For Paperwork Reduction Act Notice, see separate instructions.

Cat. No. 63704F

Form **8582** (1993)

Form 8582 (1993)

Page 2

Caution: *The worksheets are not required to be filed with your tax return and may be detached before filing Form 8582. Keep a copy of the worksheets for your records.*

Worksheet 1—For Form 8582, Lines 1a, 1b, and 1c (See instructions on page 7.)

Name of activity	Current year		Prior year	Overall gain or loss	
	(a) Net income (line 1a)	(b) Net loss (line 1b)	(c) Unallowed loss (line 1c)	(d) Gain	(e) Loss
Activity A		<10,000>	<8,000>		<18,000>
Total. Enter on Form 8582, lines 1a, 1b, and 1c ▲		<10,000>	<8,000>		

Worksheet 2—For Form 8582, Lines 2a, 2b, and 2c (See instructions on page 7.)

Name of activity	Current year		Prior year	Overall gain or loss	
	(a) Net income (line 2a)	(b) Net loss (line 2b)	(c) Unallowed loss (line 2c)	(d) Gain	(e) Loss
Activity B	5,000	<2,000>	<1,200>		<3,200>
Activity C				5,000	
Total. Enter on Form 8582, lines 2a, 2b, and 2c ▲	5,000	<2,000>	<1,200>		

Worksheet 3—Use this worksheet if an amount is shown on Form 8582, line 9 (See instructions on page 8.)

Name of activity	Form or schedule to be reported on	(a) Loss (See instructions.)	(b) Ratio (See instructions.)	(c) Special allowance (See instructions.)	(d) Subtract column (c) from column (a) (See instructions.)
Activity A	Sch E	18,000	1.00	7,500	10,500
Total ▲		18,000	1.00	7,500	10,500

Worksheet 4—Allocation of Unallowed Losses (See instructions on page 8.)

Name of activity	Form or schedule to be reported on	(a) Loss (See instructions.)	(b) Ratio (See instructions.)	(c) Unallowed loss (See instructions.)
Activity A	Sch E	10,500	.766423	6668
Activity B	Sch E	3,200	.233577	2032
Total ▲		13,700	1.00	8,700

Worksheet 5—Allowed Losses (See instructions on page 8.)

Name of activity	Form or schedule to be reported on	(a) Loss (See instructions.)	(b) Unallowed loss (See instructions.)	(c) Allowed loss (See instructions.)
Activity A	Sch E	18,000	6668	11,332
Activity B	Sch E	3,200	2,032	1,168
Total ▲		21,200	8,700	12,500

Form **8582** (1993)

14 | Basis of Property

Introduction

The gain or loss you realize on the disposition of property—whether through sale or exchange—is measured by the difference between the selling price and your **basis.** *In many cases, the basis of an* **asset** *is no more than your cost. However, if you acquire property in exchange for services, by inheritance, or in exchange for other property, different factors besides cost are likely to have a crucial bearing on determining your tax basis.*

This chapter tells you how to calculate the basis of property. Particular attention is given to some of the more complicated situations that may arise. You'll learn, for instance, how to calculate your basis in a particular piece of property by referring to other assets you already hold.

To help you determine which expenditures increase your basis in a piece of property and which do not, comprehensive lists of allowable—but often overlooked—expenditures are provided.

This chapter discusses how to figure your basis in property and covers the following topics:

- Cost basis of property you purchase.
- Adjustments to basis after you acquire property.
- Property you acquire because of a casualty or condemnation.
- Property you receive in exchange for your services.
- Business or investment property you acquire in an exchange or trade-in.
- Property you receive as a gift.
- Property transferred to you because of a divorce.
- Property you inherit.
- Stocks, bonds, and mutual funds in which you invest.

Basis is a way of measuring your investment in property for tax purposes. Use the basis of property to figure the deductions for depreciation, amortization, depletion, and casualty losses. Also use it to figure gain or loss on the sale or other disposition of property. You must keep accurate records of all items that affect the basis of property so you can make these computations.

Explanation

This chapter does not reflect the provisions of the law that deal with bankruptcy. If any of your debts were cancelled by a creditor or were discharged because you became bankrupt, the basis of your assets might be affected. For information about the effect these provisions may have on basis, see Publication 908, *Bankruptcy and Other Debt Cancellation.*

Publication 908, *Bankruptcy and Other Debt Cancellation*, discusses the technical rules related to bankruptcy, but here are several key points to remember:

1. How a debt arose determines how the debt is taxed if it is forgiven. For example, a personal loan from a relative, when it was unrelated to a business or an investment, is not taxed if it is forgiven. Instead, it is considered a gift. If the amount is over $10,000, the person forgiving the loan might have to file a gift tax return and pay gift tax.

2. A loan for a business purpose forgiven for business reasons is taxed. Alternatively, instead of paying tax on a forgiven loan, the IRS permits you to reduce the basis of your assets by an amount equal to the debt that was forgiven. The result is that you are not able to deduct as much in depreciating the asset. Thus, if it is sold before it is fully depreciated, you have either a larger gain or a smaller loss on the asset than you would if you paid the tax directly. After 1986, a *solvent* taxpayer may make this election only if the loan is "purchase money debt," in which case, the forgiveness is treated as a purchase price adjustment of the related asset.

3. If you declare personal bankruptcy, you are not taxed on any debt you owe that is forgiven or cancelled. You also are not taxed on any debt you owe that is forgiven or cancelled if a business you own goes into bankruptcy. However, you may be required to reduce the **net operating loss** carryforwards and **tax credit carryforwards** that otherwise would be available in subsequent years to offset income and reduce your income tax liability. One strategy to avoid losing these tax benefits is to reduce the basis of depreciable and nondepreciable property by an amount equal to the debt forgiven.

Useful Items

You may want to see:

Publication

- ☐ **448** Federal Estate and Gift Taxes
- ☐ **525** Taxable and Nontaxable Income
- ☐ **537** Installment Sales
- ☐ **550** Investment Income and Expenses
- ☐ **551** Basis of Assets
- ☐ **564** Mutual Fund Distributions
- ☐ **917** Business Use of a Car

Cost Basis

The basis of property you buy is usually its cost. The cost is the amount of cash and debt obligations you pay for it and the fair market value of other property or services you provide in the transaction. Your cost also includes amounts you pay for:

1) Sales tax charged on the purchase,
2) Freight charges to obtain the property,
3) Installation and testing charges,
4) Excise taxes,
5) Legal and accounting fees (when required to be capitalized),
6) Revenue stamps,
7) Recording fees, and
8) Real estate taxes (if assumed for the seller).

In addition, the cost basis of real estate and business assets will include other items.

TaxAlert

If you perform services for an entity and in exchange receive stock or a partnership interest, the fair market value of what you receive is treated as compensation. Your basis in the stock or partnership interest is equal to the amount of compensation reported by you, increased by the amount, if any, paid for the stock or interest. For more information, see Chapter 6, *Wages, Salaries, and Other Earnings*.

TaxSaver

If you receive an equity interest in a business in exchange for services rendered, you should consider discounting its value. You may do this if the shares are not marketable and/or if they represent only a minority holding.

Loans with low or no interest. If you buy property on any time-payment plan that charges little or no interest, the basis of your property is your stated purchase price, less the amount considered to be unstated interest. You generally have unstated interest if your interest rate is less than the applicable federal rate.

For more information, see *Unstated Interest* in Publication 537.

Explanation

If you buy personal property or educational services by contract and carrying charges are separately stated but interest cannot be ascertained, the IRS assumes that interest is being charged at the rate of 6% per annum on the average unpaid balance of the contract during the tax year. (Other types of contracts in which no interest is provided generally require a 9% interest rate.) Your tax basis is determined by subtracting the interest from the total contract cost of the property. You may deduct the interest in the year in which it is, in effect, being paid. But see Chapter 24, *Interest Expense*, for possible limitations on your deductions.

Real Property

If you buy real property, certain fees and other expenses you pay are part of your basis in the property. Real property is land and generally anything erected on, growing on, or attached to land. For example, a building is considered real property.

Assumption of a mortgage. If you buy property and assume an existing mortgage on the property, your basis includes the amount you pay for the property in cash plus the unpaid mortgage you assume.

Settlement fees and other costs. Legal and recording fees are some of the settlement fees or closing costs that are included in the basis of property. Some others are:

1) Abstract fees,
2) Charges for installing utility services,
3) Surveys,
4) Transfer taxes,
5) Title insurance, and
6) Any amounts the seller owes that you agree to pay, such as back taxes or interest, recording or mortgage fees, charges for improvements or repairs, and sales commissions.

Explanation

If the real property is used in your trade or business or as a rental, you may no longer elect to deduct transfer taxes in lieu of adding them to your basis.

You must reasonably allocate these fees or costs between land and improvements, such as a building, to figure the basis for depreciation of the improvements. Settlement fees do not include amounts placed in escrow for the future payment of items such as taxes and insurance.

Explanation

The following costs increase your tax basis:

1. Interest on debt incurred to finance the construction or production of real property, long-lived personal property, and other tangible property requiring more than 2 years (1 year in the case of property costing more than $1 million) to produce or construct or reach a productive stage. Additionally, interest incurred to finance property produced under a long-term contract increases your tax basis to the extent

that income is not reported under the percentage-of-completion method.

These rules do not *apply* to interest incurred during the construction of real property to be used as your principal residence or second home. (For a definition of principal residence, see Chapter 16, *Selling Your Home*. But see Chapter 24, *Interest Expense*, for other rules affecting how much interest you may be able to deduct on a residence.)

2. The costs of defending or perfecting a title, architect's fees, and financing and finder's fees. Points, usually up-front payments on a mortgage charged to purchasers or borrowers, may be deducted as interest. See Chapter 24, *Interest Expense*, for more information and the timing of the deduction.

3. Certain start-up costs for a business. These include legal fees for the drafting of documents, accounting fees, and other similar expenses directly associated with the organization of a business. The costs of organizing a partnership, such as the expenses incurred in raising capital, putting together a prospectus, and paying commissions on the sale of investment units, also increase your basis, as does the cost of investigating the creation or acquisition of an active trade or business. See Chapter 36, *If You Are Self-Employed*, for further information.

Some taxpayers who are starting a new business try to deduct the expenses incurred before the business actually begins. The IRS, however, may not accept these as current **deductions,** and it may either require that you deduct the expenses over a number of years or decide that the expenses should increase your basis in the business. The IRS allows you to amortize certain business start-up and organizational costs over 60 months if an election statement providing certain information is included in a tax return that you file on a timely basis. If you currently neither deduct nor amortize an expense, the tax benefit is obtained when the entity is sold or ceases operation. Therefore, it is important to include the election with your tax return for the year in which the costs are first incurred.

Unlike costs of organizing a partnership or starting up its business, costs of selling partnership interests (syndication costs) may not be amortized or deducted. (For further discussion, see *Adjusted Basis*, following.)

TAXSAVER 1

Increasing your tax basis by as much as possible subsequently reduces the amount of gain or increases the amount of loss realized when you dispose of the property.

TAXALERT

Individuals do not derive any tax benefit from **realizing a loss** related to the disposition of personal property. Personal property includes any property that is not considered an investment (such as a refrigerator), as well as any property that is not used in a trade or business.

TAXSAVER 2

If you pay interest and taxes on unimproved real estate but cannot deduct these expenses because you do not itemize your deductions, consider treating them as **capital expenditures,** which increase your basis and reduce your gain on sale.

Example

Jane rents an apartment and has few **itemized deductions.** She borrows money to purchase an unimproved lot in Florida. She incurs $1,000 in interest expense on the borrowed funds and pays $100 in real estate taxes in each of the 5 years she holds the property. If Jane elects to capitalize the interest and taxes, she increases her basis by $5,500 over the 5 years.

TAXORGANIZER

You should keep a copy of the closing statement you receive when you are either buying or selling real property.

Expenses paid to obtain a mortgage. Most deductible expenses may be deducted in full in the tax year in which you pay them. If you pay a deductible expense to obtain a mortgage, however, you generally must capitalize and deduct the expense ratably over the term of the mortgage. Do not add the expense, such as points (such as prepaid interest), to the basis of the related property.

Points on home mortgage. Special rules may apply to an amount you pay as points to obtain a mortgage for your main home. If that amount meets certain requirements, you can deduct it in full as points for the year in which you pay it. For more information, see *Points* in Publication 936, *Home Mortgage Interest Deduction*.

Nondeductible expenses. Any nondeductible expenses you pay to purchase real property, such as an appraisal fee for your home or other nonbusiness, you generally add to the basis of the property. Other expenses, such as fire insurance premiums, cannot be added to the basis of the property.

Real estate taxes. If you buy real property and agree to pay taxes the seller owed on it, treat the taxes you pay as part of the cost. You cannot deduct them as taxes paid.

If you reimburse the seller for taxes the seller paid for you, you can usually deduct that amount. Do not include that amount in the cost of the property.

Explanation

If you are the seller, you are entitled to a deduction for real estate taxes paid for you by the buyer. However, you must include this amount in figuring the proceeds you clear from the sale of the house. This increases the gain—or decreases the loss—you recognize on the sale.

Adjusted Basis

Before figuring any gain or loss on a sale, exchange, or other disposition of property, or figuring allowable depreciation, depletion, or amortization, you must usually make certain adjustments (increases and decreases) to the basis of the property. The result of these adjustments to the basis is the adjusted basis.

Increases to Basis

Increase the basis of any property by all items properly added to a capital account. This includes the cost of any improvements having a useful life of more than one year and amounts spent after a casualty to restore the damaged property. Other items added to the basis of property include the cost of extending utility service lines to the property and legal fees, such as the cost of defending and perfecting title.

Explanation

It is important to distinguish between expenditures that constitute additions to basis and those that constitute repairs. If the asset is used in a trade or a business, repairs are deductible but do not increase its basis. If the asset is personal, the costs of repairs are not deductible and do not increase the asset's basis. (For a more complete discussion of this matter, see Chapter 10, *Rental Income and Expenses*.)

As noted by the IRS, your basis in property is reduced by money you receive as a return of capital. See Chapter 9, *Dividends and Other Corporate Distributions*, for further details.

Example

You buy land and a building for $25,000 for use as a parking lot. You pay $3,000 to have the building torn down, and you sell some of the materials you salvage from it for $5,000. You figure your adjusted basis in the property by taking your $25,000 initial cost, adding the $3,000 you spent for tearing down the building, and subtracting the $5,000 you received for the materials you salvaged. Your adjusted basis for the lot is $23,000. The money you received from the sale of the salvaged materials is not income, and the cost of tearing down the building is not deductible.

Improvements. Add the cost of improvements that increase the value of property, lengthen its life, or adapt it to a different use to your basis in the property. For example, putting a recreation room in your unfinished basement, adding another bathroom or bedroom, putting up a fence, putting in new plumbing or wiring, installing a new roof, or paving your driveway are improvements. Add their costs to your basis in your property.

TaxSaver

When you sell your home, your gain or loss is measured by the difference between the price you receive on the sale and your basis. Any improvements you have made will have increased your basis and now will decrease your tax liability. It is important that you keep adequate records of all improvements.

Among the improvements and other costs that increase your basis are the following:

1. Replacing the roof
2. Installing permanent storm windows
3. Installing new plumbing
4. Installing a new heating or air conditioning system
5. Installing a new furnace
6. Restoring a run-down house
7. Landscaping; adding new trees, shrubs, or lawn
8. Building a swimming pool, tennis court, or sauna
9. Constructing or improving a driveway
10. Constructing walks
11. Constructing patio and decks
12. Constructing walls
13. Payment of real estate commissions
14. Payment of legal fees stemming from improvements, zoning, and so on
15. Payment of closing costs
16. Cost of appliances

Many of the items listed above, such as real estate commissions and closing costs, appear on the closing statement you receive when you purchase the property.

TaxOrganizer

You should keep a copy of all invoices you receive for improvements that increase your basis in real property.

Assessments for local improvements. Add assessments for improvements such as streets and sidewalks, which increase the value of the property assessed, to the basis of the property. Do not deduct them as taxes. For example, if your city puts in a paved sidewalk along the street in front of your home and assesses you and the other affected landowners for the cost of the sidewalk, you must add the assessment to the basis of your property. However, you can deduct as taxes assessments you pay for maintenance or repair or meeting interest charges on the improvements.

Explanation

For further discussion of assessments and how to treat them, see Chapter 23, *Taxes You May Deduct*.

Decreases to Basis

Decrease the basis of your property by any items that represent a return of capital or a deferred gain. These include:

1) The section 179 deduction,
2) The deduction for clean-fuel vehicles and clean-fuel refueling property,
3) Nontaxable corporate distributions,
4) Recognized losses on involuntary exchanges,
5) Deductions previously allowed (or allowable) for amortization, depreciation, and depletion,
6) Exclusions from income of subsidies for energy conservation measures (see *Energy conservation subsidies*, in Chapter 13, *Other Income*),
7) Credit for qualified electric vehicles,
8) Gain from the sale of your old home on which tax was postponed, and
9) Casualty and theft losses.

Casualties and thefts. If you have a casualty or theft loss, decrease the basis of your property by the amount of any insurance or other reimbursement you receive and by any deductible loss not covered by insurance. However, increase your basis for amounts you spend after a casualty to restore the damaged property. For

Table 14-1. **Examples of Increases and Decreases To Basis**

This chart shows some common examples of items that increase or decrease basis. Usually, you must make these adjustments to basis before you can figure any gain or loss on a sale, exchange, or other disposition of property, or figure allowable depletion, or amortization.

Increases to Basis	Decreases to Basis
Capital improvements: • Putting an addition on your home • Replacing an entire roof • Paving your driveway • Installing central air conditioning • Rewiring your home	Exclusion from income of subsidies for energy conservation measures: • Amount of the exclusion
Assessments for local improvements: • Water connections • Sidewalks • Roads	Casualty or theft losses: • Insurance reimbursements • Casualty or theft loss deductions
Casualty Losses: • Restoring damaged property	Easements: • Amount received for granting an easement
	Credit for qualified electric vehicles: • Amount of the credit
	Gain from the sale of your old home on which tax was postponed • Amount of gain
	Residential energy credit: • Amount of the credit if the cost of the energy item was previously added to the basis of your home
	Section 179 deduction: • Amount of the deduction
	Deduction for clean-fuel vehicles and clean-fuel vehicle refueling property: • Amount of the deduction
	Depreciation: • The greater of the depreciation deduction that decreased your tax liability for any year or the deduction you could have taken under the depreciation method that you selected
	Corporate distributions: • Nontaxable amount

more information, see Chapter 26, *Nonbusiness Casualty and Theft Losses*.

Easements. The amount you receive for granting an easement is usually considered to be from the sale of an interest in your real property. It reduces the basis of the affected part of the property. If the amount received is more than the basis of the part of the property affected by the easement, reduce your basis to zero and treat the excess as a recognized gain.

Residential energy credit. The residential energy credit is no longer available. However, if in the past you were allowed the credit, decrease the basis of your home by the credit if you added the cost of the energy items to the basis of your home.

Explanation
The residential energy credit expired on December 31, 1985.

Section 179 deduction. If you take the section 179 deduction for part of the cost of property, decrease the basis of the property by the amount of the section 179 deduction. Make this adjustment to determine the basis for figuring depreciation. Therefore, if you take the section 179 deduction, your depreciation deduction will be less.

Explanation
For more information on the section 179 deduction, see Chapter 36, *If You Are Self-Employed: How to File Schedule C.*

Depreciation. Decrease the basis of your property by the depreciation you could have deducted on your tax returns under the method of depreciation you selected. If you deducted more depreciation than you should have, decrease your basis as follows. Decrease it by an amount equal to the depreciation you should have deducted, as well as by the part of the excess depreciation you deducted that reduced your tax liability for any year.

However, if you deducted less depreciation than you could have under the method you selected, decrease your basis by the amount that you could have deducted.

Credit for qualified electric vehicles. If you claim the credit for qualified electric vehicles you must reduce the basis of the property on which you claimed the credit. For more information on this credit, see Chapter 15 in Publication 535.

Deduction for clean-fuel vehicle and clean-fuel vehicle refueling property. If you take either the deduction for clean-fuel vehicles or clean-fuel vehicle refueling property, or both, you decrease the basis of the property by the amount of the deduction. For more information on these deductions, see chapter 15 in Publication 535, *Business Expenses.*

Exclusion from income of subsidies for energy conservation measures. If you received a subsidy from a public utility company for the purchase or installation of any energy conservation measure, you can exclude it from income. If you exclude the subsidy from income, reduce the basis of the property on which you received the subsidy, by the amount of the subsidy. For more information on this subsidy, see Publication 525, *Taxable and Nontaxable Income.*

Adjusted Basis Example

You owned a duplex used as rental property that cost you $40,000. The $40,000 cost was allocated $35,000 for the building and $5,000 for the land. You added an improvement to the duplex that cost $10,000. On February 1, 1992, the duplex was damaged by fire. Up to that time you had been allowed depreciation of $23,000. You sold the salvage for $1,300 and collected $19,700 from your insurance company. You deducted a casualty loss of $1,000 on your 1992 income tax return. You spent $19,000 of the insurance proceeds for restoration of the duplex, which was completed in 1993. The adjusted basis of the duplex, after the restoration, is figured as follows:

Original cost of duplex		$35,000
Addition to duplex		10,000
Total cost of duplex		$45,000
Minus: Depreciation		23,000
Adjusted basis before casualty		$22,000
Minus: Casualty loss	$ 1,000	
Insurance proceeds	19,700	
Salvage proceeds	1,300	22,000
Adjusted basis after casualty		$ –0–
Add: Cost of restoring duplex		19,000
Adjusted basis after restoration		$19,000

Your basis in the land is its original cost of $5,000.

Other Basis

There are many times when you cannot use cost as a basis. In these cases the fair market value or the adjusted basis of certain property may be important. Fair market value is discussed next, adjusted basis is discussed earlier.

Fair market value (FMV). FMV is the price at which the property would change hands between a buyer and a seller, neither being required to buy or sell, and both having reasonable knowledge of all necessary facts. Sales of similar property, on or about the same date, may be helpful in figuring the FMV of the property.

Property received for services. If you receive property for your services, include the property's FMV in income. The amount you include in income becomes your basis.

Restricted property. If you receive property for your services and the property is subject to certain restrictions, your basis in the property is its FMV when you can transfer it or when it is not subject to a substantial risk of forfeiture. For more information, see *Restricted Property Received for Services,* in Publication 525.

Bargain purchases. A bargain purchase is a purchase of an item for less than its FMV. If your employer lets you purchase goods or other property at less than FMV, include the difference between the purchase price and the property's FMV in your income. Your basis in the property is its FMV, that is, your purchase price plus the amount you include in your income. If this difference represents a qualified employee discount, you do not include the difference in income. However, your basis in the property is still its FMV. See *Qualified Employee Discount* in Chapter 4 of Publication 535.

Business use of a company car, parking at or near your business premises, business periodicals, and any other property or service provided by your employer can be excluded from your taxable income if you would be allowed to take a business deduction had you paid for the benefit yourself.

Other nontaxable fringe benefits from employers include free medical services, reimbursement of medical expenses, gifts of $25 or less, payments of premiums for up to $50,000 of group term life insurance coverage, tuition given to children of university employees, dinner money, and meals furnished to employees on the employer's business premises.

Taxable exchanges. A taxable exchange is one in which the gain is taxable or the loss is deductible. If you receive property in exchange for other property in a taxable exchange, the basis of the property you receive is usually its FMV at the time of the exchange.

Involuntary Exchanges

If you acquire property as a result of an involuntary exchange, such as a casualty, theft, or condemnation, you may figure the basis of the replacement property you acquire using the basis of the property exchanged.

Similar or related property. If you receive property that is similar or related in service or use to the property exchanged, the new property's basis is the same as the old property's basis on the date of the exchange with the following adjustments:

Decreased by–
1) Any loss recognized on the exchange, and
2) Any money received that was not spent on similar property.

Increased by–
1) Any gain recognized on the exchange, and
2) Any cost of acquiring replacement property.

Not similar or related property. If you receive money or other property that is not similar or related in service or use to the old property, and you buy new property that is similar or related in service or use to the old property, the basis of the new property is the cost of the new property, decreased by the amount of gain that is not recognized on the exchange.

TaxSaver

You can elect to exclude the gain if within 2 years following the year in which the involuntary gain was realized you buy new property that is similar or related in service or use to the old property. If this election is made, gain will be recognized to the extent that the gain realized exceeds the cost of the replacement property. The basis of the new property is the cost of the new property, decreased by the amount of gain that is not recognized.

The 1993 Tax Act has extended the replacement period for your principal residence or any of its contents if it is converted involuntarily as a result of a disaster. The new replacement period is extended to four years after the close of the first year in which conversion is realized. This provision is effective for property in areas that the President declared disaster areas on or after September 1, 1991.

Example. The state condemned your property. The property had an adjusted basis of $26,000, and the state paid you $31,000 for it. You realized a gain of $5,000 ($31,000 − $26,000). You bought new property that is similar in use to the old property for $29,000. You recognize a gain of $2,000 ($31,000 − $29,000), the unspent part of the payment from the state. Your gain not recognized is $3,000, the difference between the $5,000 realized gain and the $2,000 recognized gain. The basis of the new property is figured as follows:

Cost of new property	$29,000
Minus: Gain not recognized	3,000
Basis of new property	**$26,000**

Allocating the basis. Allocate the basis among parts of the new property you acquire as a result of an involuntary exchange. This allocation usually is based on the ratios of each part's FMV to the whole new property's FMV.

If you buy more than one piece of replacement property, allocate your basis among the properties based on their respective costs. If, in the previous example, the state had condemned unimproved real property, and the new property you bought was improved real property with both land and buildings, you would make an allocation. Take the new property's $26,000 basis and allocate between land and buildings based on their fair market values.

TaxPlanner

When you buy more than one asset for a single amount, such as land with buildings or the operating assets of a business, your costs must be reasonably allocated among the different assets. While the IRS may always question whether or not you have allocated these costs fairly, it is unlikely to do so if the allocation has been contractually agreed to by the parties involved, particularly if you and the seller have adverse interests. Therefore, it may often be to your advantage to have the allocation spelled out in the purchase agreement.

If you are acquiring a trade, business, or investment asset, a favorable allocation of costs may have tax advantages. For example, raw land may not be depreciated, but buildings may. A favorable allocation between land and building enables you to claim more depreciation. The 1993 Tax Act provides that the costs of specified intangible assets (such as goodwill, covenant-not-to-compete, franchise, etc.) will be amortized over a 15-year period. Thus, while you can now amortize costs allocated to certain intangible assets, allocating more cost to operating assets instead may create a tax advantage because of the more rapid depreciation methods available for equipment.

The new tax law also provides that if you dispose of a specified intangible asset that was acquired in a transaction, but you retain other specified intangible assets acquired in the same transaction, you may not claim a loss as a result of the disposition. Instead, the bases of the retained specified intangible assets are increased by the amount of the unrecognized loss.

For information about asset allocations, see Chapter 36, *If You Are Self-Employed: How To File Schedule C.*

A provision of the Tax Reform Act of 1986 that is still in effect mandates that the residual method must be used to allocate the purchase price of acquired assets.

Under the residual method, the amount allocated to the value of goodwill and going concern value is the excess of the purchase price over the fair market value of the tangible assets and the other identifiable intangible assets.

For certain types of acquisitions of assets used in a trade or a business, the buyer and seller must file Form 8594 with the IRS, showing how the purchase price was allocated among various classes of assets. For more information, consult your tax advisor.

Nontaxable Exchanges

A nontaxable exchange is an exchange in which any gain is not taxed and any loss cannot be deducted. In a nontaxable exchange, business or investment property is exchanged solely for like-kind or like-class property, stock is exchanged solely for stock of the same corporation, or property is exchanged for securities of a controlled corporation. The basis of property you receive in a nontaxable exchange is usually the same as the basis of the property you exchanged. See *Nontaxable Trades* in Chapter 15, *Sale of Property*.

Explanation

In general, all gains and losses realized on sales and other dispositions of property are taxable, but an exception is made when business or investment property is traded or exchanged for "like-kind" property. In this case, the newly acquired property is viewed as a continuation of the investment in the original property, so the tax basis does not change. The reason to make such tax-free exchanges is not to avoid taxes but to defer them while realizing some other investment aims. (For more details on nontaxable exchanges, see Chapter 15, *Sale of Property*.)

Partially nontaxable exchange. A partially nontaxable exchange is an exchange in which you receive unlike property or money in addition to like-kind or like-class property.

The basis of property you receive is usually the same as the basis of the property exchanged **decreased** by any money you received and any loss recognized on the exchange; and then **increased** by any additional costs incurred, and any gain recognized on the exchange.

Allocate the basis among the properties, other than money, you received in the exchange. In making this allocation, the basis of the unlike property is its fair market value on the date of exchange. The remainder is the basis of the like-kind or like-class property.

Example. You trade in an old truck, which has an adjusted basis of $1,700, for a new one costing $6,800. The dealer allows you $2,000 on the old truck, and you pay $4,800. This is a nontaxable exchange, and the basis of the new truck is $6,500, that is, the adjusted basis of the old one, $1,700, increased by the additional cost, $4,800. If you sell your old truck to a third party for $2,000 and then buy the new one from the dealer, you have a taxable gain on the sale, and the basis of the new truck is the price you pay the dealer for it.

Trade-in or sale and purchase. If a sale and purchase are a single transaction, you cannot increase the basis of property for depreciation by selling your old property outright to a dealer and then buying the new property from the same dealer. If the sale to the dealer of your old property and your purchase from that dealer of the new property are dependent on each other, you are considered to have traded in your old property. Treat the transaction as an exchange no matter how it is carried out.

Example. You are a salesperson and use one of your cars 100% for business. You have used this car in your sales activities for 2 years and have depreciated it. Your adjusted basis in the car is $2,600, and its FMV is $3,100.

You are interested in a new car with a listed retail price of $8,695, which usually sells for $8,000. If you trade your old car and $4,900 for the new one your basis for depreciation for the new car would be $7,500 ($4,900 plus $2,600 basis of your old car). However, you want a higher basis for depreciating the new car, so you agree to pay the dealer $8,000 for the new car if he will pay you $3,100 for your old car.

Since the sale and purchase are dependent on each other, you are treated as if you had exchanged your old car for the new one. Your basis for depreciating the new car is $7,500, which is the same as it would be if you had traded the old car.

For information about the trade of a car used partly for business, see Publication 917.

Property Received as a Gift

To figure the basis of property you receive as a gift, you must know its adjusted basis to the donor just before it was given to you, its FMV at the time it was given to you, and any gift tax paid on it.

Explanation

If a gift tax return was filed, you should examine it for information on the donor's tax basis.

FMV less than donor's adjusted basis. If the FMV of the property was less than the donor's adjusted basis, your basis for gain on its sale or other disposition is the same as the donor's adjusted basis plus or minus any required adjustment to basis during the period you held the property (see *Adjusted Basis* earlier). Your basis for loss on its sale or other disposition is its FMV at the time you received the gift plus or minus any required adjustment to basis during the period you held the property (see *Adjusted Basis* earlier).

Example. You received an acre of land as a gift. At the time of the gift, the acre had an FMV of $8,000. The donor's adjusted basis was $10,000. After you received the property, no events occur that would increase or decrease your basis in it. If you later sell the property for $12,000, you have a $2,000 gain because you must use the donor's adjusted basis ($10,000) at the time of the gift as your basis to report a gain. If, however, you sell the property for $7,000, you have a loss of $1,000 because you must use the FMV ($8,000) at the time of the gift to report a loss.

If the sales price is between $8,000 and $10,000, you have neither a gain nor a loss. For instance, if the sales price was $9,000 and you computed for a gain using the donor's adjusted basis ($10,000), you would get a loss of $1,000. If you then computed for a loss using the FMV ($8,000), you would get a gain of $1,000.

Example

Owen owns a building in which his adjusted basis is $40,000. The fair market value of the building, however, is only $30,000. Owen gives the building to Jim. Jim's basis is $40,000—Owen's adjusted basis—for determining depreciation and for computing a gain on the sale of the building. Jim's basis is $30,000—the fair market value at the time of the gift—for computing a loss on a sale of the building.

Note: If the fair market value of the building increases to $35,000, Jim may sell the property without recognizing a gain or a loss. His proceeds of $35,000 would be greater than the basis used for computing a loss on the sale and less than the basis used for computing a gain on the sale.

TAXPLANNER

If the fair market value of property that you intend to give as a gift is less than your adjusted basis in the property, you might want to sell the property and then make a gift of the proceeds. In this way, you recognize a loss on the sale of the property. This could provide you with a tax savings. The recipient of the gift will receive the same amount of value, but in cash rather than property. Had the recipient received property, he or she would not be able to deduct the loss you had on the property when the recipient sold it, because the recipient's basis in the property for computing a loss is the property's fair market value at the time the gift is made.

Nonbusiness and business property. If you hold the gift as nonbusiness property, the only kind of loss you can deduct is a personal casualty loss on the property. If you hold the gift as business property, your basis for figuring any depreciation, depletion, or amortization deduction, as the same as the donor's adjusted basis plus or minus any required adjustments to basis while you hold the property. However, if the property was nonbusiness property that you converted (all or part) to business property, a special rule applies to your basis for depreciation. See *Property Changed to Business or Rental Use,* later.

FMV equal to or greater than donor's adjusted basis. If the FMV of the property was equal to or greater than the donor's adjusted basis, your basis is the same as the donor's adjusted basis at the time you received the gift. Increase your basis by all or part of the gift tax paid, depending on the date of the gift.

Also, for figuring gain or loss from a sale or other disposition of the property of figuring depreciation, depletion, or amortization deductions on business property, you must increase or decrease your basis (the donor's adjusted basis) for any required adjustments to basis while you held the property, as pointed out in the preceding discussion.

Gift received before 1977. If you received a gift before 1977, increase your basis in the gift by the gift tax paid on it. (Your basis in the gift is the donor's adjusted basis.) However, do not increase your basis above the FMV of the gift when it was given to you.

Example 1. You were given a house in 1976 with an FMV of $21,000. The donor's adjusted basis was $20,000. The donor paid a gift tax of $500. Your basis is $20,500, the donor's adjusted basis plus the gift tax paid.

Example 2. If, in Example 1, the gift tax paid had been $1,500, your basis would be $21,000. This is the donor's adjusted basis plus the gift tax paid, limited to the FMV of the house at the time you received the gift.

Gift received after 1976. If you received a gift after 1976, increase your basis in the gift by the part of the gift tax paid that

is due to the net increase in value of the gift. (Your basis in the gift is the donor's adjusted basis.) Figure the increase by multiplying the gift tax paid on the gift by a fraction. The numerator (top part) of the fraction is the net increase in value of the gift, and the denominator (bottom part) is the amount of the gift. The net increase in value of the gift is the FMV of the gift minus the donor's adjusted basis.

Example. In 1993 you received a gift of property from your mother that had an FMV of $50,000. Her adjusted basis was $20,000. She paid a gift tax of $9,000 on the property. For figuring depreciation, depletion, amortization, and gain or loss, your basis is $25,400, figured as follows:

Fair market value	$50,000
Minus: Adjusted basis	20,000
Net increase in value	$30,000
Gift tax paid	$ 9,000
Multiplied by ($30,000 ÷ $50,000)	.60
Gift tax due to net increase in value	$ 5,400
Adjusted basis of property to your mother	20,000
Your basis in the property	$25,400

Property Transferred From a Spouse

The basis of property transferred to you or transferred in trust for your benefit by your spouse, or by your former spouse if the transfer is incident to divorce, is the same as the transferor's adjusted basis of the property. However, adjust your basis for any gain recognized by the transferor on a property transferred in trust. This rule applies only to a property transfer in which the liabilities assumed, plus the liabilities to which the property is subject, are more than the adjusted basis of the property transferred.

If the property transferred is a Series E or EE United States savings bond, the transferor must include in income the interest accrued to the date of transfer. The transferee's basis in the bond immediately after the transfer is equal to the transferor's adjusted basis in the bond increased by the interest income includible in the transferor's income.

The transferor must supply you with records necessary to determine the adjusted basis and holding period of the property as of the date of the transfer. For more information regarding the transfer of property between spouses, see Chapter 15, *Sale of Property.*

Inherited Property

Your basis in property you inherit is usually its FMV at the date of the decedent's death. If a federal estate tax return has to be filed, your basis in property you inherit can be its FMV at the alternate valuation date if the estate qualifies and elects to use alternate valuation. If a federal estate tax return does not have to be filed, your basis in the property is its appraised value at the date of death for state inheritance or transmission taxes.

Explanation

The alternate valuation date is the earlier of the date 6 months after death and the date on which the estate's assets are distributed, sold, exchanged, or disposed of. Alternate valuation may be elected only if it is necessary to file an estate tax return. Furthermore, use of the alternate valuation date must result in a decrease in the estate tax. The election must be made for all property included in the estate.

TAXSAVER

Choosing an alternate valuation date may be helpful in reducing estate tax if the market value of the assets in the estate is declining. However, if this is the case, the tax basis of those assets must also be reduced; this means increased income taxes in the future if the market value of the assets rises and they are then sold. Thus, the decision to elect the alternate valuation date to reduce estate tax should be balanced against a possible increase in future income taxes.

Your basis in inherited property may also be figured under the special farm or closely held business real property valuation method, if chosen for estate tax purposes. See Publication 448 for information on valuation methods for estate tax purposes.

For more information about the basis of inherited property, such as property held by a surviving tenant and qualified joint interest in property held by a husband and wife, see *Inherited Property* in Publication 551.

Explanation

If a decedent used property that he or she owned for farming, trade, or business purposes at the date of death, the executor of the decedent's estate may, under most conditions, choose the special-use valuation method for that property. This means that the property is included in the decedent's estate at the value based on its *current use* and not at the value based on what its most lucrative use might be. For example, if the land is being used for farming, its value is figured on its worth as farmland and not on what it might be worth if used for industrial purposes.

The following conditions must be met before you use the special-use valuation method:

1. The decedent must have been a resident or a citizen of the United States.
2. The property must pass to a qualified heir, meaning an ancestor of either the decedent or his or her spouse or one of their lineal descendants.
3. The property must be located in the United States and must be used in a trade or a business.
4. The property must have been used by the decedent in a trade or a business for 5 of the past 8 years. The 8-year period is measured from the earliest of the decedent's death, disablement, or retirement.
5. The value of the real and personal property used in the farm or closely held business must form at least one-half of the decedent's gross estate. (Gross estate is the total amount of the decedent's assets.)
6. At least one-quarter of the value of the gross estate must be qualified real property. (Livestock and farm machinery are not considered qualified real property. Real estate is.)

The maximum amount that the special-use method can decrease the value of the estate is $750,000.

TAXSAVER

In community property states, the basis of the surviving spouse's one-half share of the community property will also receive a step-up in basis, normally to its fair market value, at the date of the decedent spouse's death.

TAXORGANIZER

If you receive property by inheritance, you should request a copy of the estate tax return from the executor of the estate to determine your basis in the inherited property.

Property Changed to Business or Rental Use

When you hold property for personal use and change it to business use or use it to produce rent, you must figure the basis for depreciation. An example of this would be renting out your former main home.

Basis for depreciation. The basis for depreciation equals the lesser of:

1) The FMV (defined earlier under *Other Basis*) of the property on the date of the change, or
2) Your adjusted basis on the date of the change. Adjusted basis is your cost or other basis (the donor's adjusted basis if you received the property as a gift) of the property, plus the cost of permanent improvements or additions since you acquired it, minus deductions for any casualty losses claimed on earlier years' income tax returns and other decreases to basis.

Example. Several years ago you paid $60,000 to have your house built on a lot that cost you $10,000. Before changing the property to rental use last year, you paid $20,000 for permanent improvements to the house and claimed a $2,000 casualty loss deduction to the house. Because land is not depreciable, you can include only the cost of the house when figuring the basis for depreciation.

Your adjusted basis in the house when you change its use is $78,000 ($60,000 + $20,000 &minus $2,000). On the date of the change in use, your property has an FMV of $80,000, of which $15,000 is for the land and $65,000 is for the house. The basis for depreciation on the house is the FMV at the date of the change ($65,000) because it is less than your adjusted basis ($78,000).

Sale of property. If you later sell or dispose of the property, the basis of the property to be used will depend on whether you are figuring gain or loss.

Gain. The basis for gain is your adjusted basis when you sell the property. Adjusted basis is your cost or other basis, plus the cost of any permanent improvements or additions, less depreciation allowed or allowable, deductions for casualty losses claimed on prior years' returns, and other decreases to basis, such as amounts received for easements or rights-of-way.

Loss. Figure the basis for loss using the smaller of your adjusted basis or the FMV of the property at the time of the change to business or rental use. Adjust this amount for improvements and additions you made after the change, and by the depreciation, allowed or allowable, and casualty loss deductions you claimed after the change.

Example. You sell your house, which you had changed to rental property after using it as your home. When you changed it to rental use, it had an FMV of $33,000 and an adjusted basis of $35,000. In your case the original cost of your house and the adjusted basis were the same, as there were no increases or decreases to basis since its purchase. You claimed $3,000 depreciation, figured under the straight line method, while renting it.

Your adjusted basis at the time of the sale, for figuring **gain,** is $32,000 ($35,000 − $3,000). This was your original cost less depreciation.

Your adjusted basis at the time of the sale, for figuring **loss,** is $30,000 ($33,000 − $3,000). This was the FMV, when you changed it to rental use, less depreciation. In this example, FMV must be used because it was smaller than the adjusted basis at the time you changed the house to rental use.

If the sales price is between $30,000 and $32,000, you have neither a gain nor a loss on the sale.

Stocks and Bonds

The basis of stocks or bonds you own generally is the purchase price plus the costs of purchase such as commissions and recording or transfer fees. If you acquired stocks or bonds other than by purchase, your basis is usually determined by FMV or the donor's adjusted basis, as previously discussed.

The basis must be adjusted for certain events that occur after purchase. For example, if you receive additional stock from nontaxable stock dividends or stock splits, reduce the basis of your original stock. Also reduce your basis when you receive nontaxable distributions because these are a return of capital.

Example. In 1991, you bought 100 shares of XYZ stock for $1,000 or $10 a share. In 1992, you bought 100 shares of XYZ stock for $1,600 or $16 a share. In 1993, XYZ declared a 2-for-1 stock split. You now have 200 shares of stock with a basis of $5 a share and 200 shares with a basis of $8 a share.

Other basis. There are other ways to determine the basis of stocks or bonds depending on how you acquired them. Some ways in which you can acquire stock are by automatic investment programs, dividend reinvestment plans, and stock rights. For detailed information, see Publication 550.

Identifying shares. If you buy and sell securities at different times in varying quantities and you cannot definitely identify the securities you sell, the basis of those sold is figured under the first-in first-out method—that is, the first securities you acquired are the first sold.

TaxPlanner

If your portfolio consists of various lots of the same stock acquired at different times and at different costs, some care must be exercised when a sale of a portion of these shares is contemplated. For example, assume that you own five different lots of ABC Motors stock acquired at different times and ranging in cost basis between $40 and $80 per share. If the stock is currently selling for $60 per share and you sell a lot with a basis of $40 per share, you recognize a gain; on the other hand, if you sell a lot having a basis of $80 per share, you sustain a loss. The situation may be far more complicated if the company has paid **stock dividends** or has split its stock one or more times.

It may be advisable to take any shares that you receive as the result of a stock dividend or a stock split and combine them with the shares that gave rise to the dividend or split. Have your broker convert all such re-

lated stock certificates into one certificate. Thus, each block of stock having a distinguishable cost basis is separately maintained. Although you are certainly not required to do this, it simplifies your recordkeeping task and makes it much easier for you to compute your gain or loss when you sell the shares.

TaxOrganizer

You should keep a copy of your broker confirmation statement as a record for your cost basis in the shares of stock you have purchased during the year.

Identification. You make an adequate identification if you deliver to your broker or agent certificates for securities that you purchased on a certain date or for a specific price.

If you left the security certificates with your broker or other agent, an adequate identification is made if you:

1) Tell your broker the particular security to be sold or transferred at the time of the sale or transfer, and
2) Receive a written confirmation of this from your broker or other agent within a reasonable time.

Explanation

Your instructions to your broker need not be in writing. Even if stock certificates from a different lot are actually delivered to the transfer agent, you may consider the stock sold as you specified, provided that you identified the shares to be sold and received written confirmation of your orders.

If you bought securities in different lots at different times and you hold a single certificate for these securities, you make an adequate identification if you:

1) Tell your broker the particular security to sell or transfer when you deliver the certificate to your broker, and
2) Receive a written confirmation of this from your broker or other agent within a reasonable time.

TaxPlanner

Incentive stock options. If the shares you are selling were acquired by exercising an Incentive Stock Option (ISO) with previously owned employer shares, special rules will apply in determining the basis of the ISO shares.

The sale or transfer of stock acquired through the exercise of an ISO within 2 years of the option's grant date and within 1 year of the option's exercise date is known as a "disqualifying disposition." If the sale constitutes a disqualifying disposition of the ISO shares, the lowest basis shares are considered to be sold first, regardless of your effort to identify and sell specific shares. For more information, see Chapter 6, *Wages, Salaries, and Other Earnings*, and Publication 525, *Taxable and Nontaxable Income.*

Charitable contributions. If you own several blocks of appreciated shares, it is generally to your advantage to give away those shares with the lowest tax basis.

When you make a contribution of the stock, you should be especially careful to designate which shares are being contributed. Let your stockbroker or transfer agent and the charity know the date you purchased the shares that you are now donating. It's important to take these steps at the time you are making the gift.

TaxAlert

The 1993 Tax Act provides that unrealized gains from contributions of appreciated property will no longer be subject to the alternative minimum tax. (The new law has repealed the provision, which treated the untaxed appreciation deducted as a charitable contribution as a tax preference item for the purpose of calculating the alternative minimum tax.) For more information, see Chapter 25, *Contributions*.

Mutual fund shares. You can choose to use the average basis of shares you own in a regulated investment company (mutual fund) if:

1) You acquired the shares at different times and prices, and
2) You left the shares on deposit in an account kept by a custodian or agent. For more information, see *Basis of Shares* in Publication 564.

Explanation
For further discussion, see Chapter 17, *Reporting Gains and Losses*.

Premiums on bonds. If you buy a taxable bond at a premium and choose to amortize the premium paid, reduce the basis of the bond by the amount of the amortized premium. See *Bond Premium Amortization* in Chapter 3 of Publication 550 for more information. Although you cannot take a deduction for the premium on tax-exempt bonds, you must amortize the premium and decrease your basis in the bonds by the amount of the amortizable bond premium.

Example
Elizabeth buys a Stowe, Vermont, tax-exempt bond for $1,130. The bond has a face value of $1,000 and a maturity of 3 years. Each year, one-third of the premium must be amortized ($130 ÷ 3 years = $43.33 per year). Thus, Elizabeth's basis at the end of the first year is $1,087 ($1,130 − $43); $1,044 ($1,087 − $43) at the end of the second year; and $1,000 at the end of the third year. However, Elizabeth may not claim the amortization as a deduction on her tax return.

If the bond had been taxable rather than tax-exempt, Elizabeth would have had the option of amortizing the premium. Had she not done so, her basis would have remained unchanged and, therefore, she would have recognized a capital loss. However, if she had chosen to amortize the premium, she would have been able to use the amortization to reduce her interest income. Her

basis would have been adjusted, as it was in the case of a tax-exempt bond.

Original issue discount (OID) on debt instruments. You must increase your basis in an OID debt instrument by the amount of OID that you included in income for that instrument. See *Original Issue Discount* in Chapter 8.

Tax-exempt bonds. OID on tax-exempt bonds is not taxable. However, there are special rules for determining basis on tax-exempt OID bonds issued after September 3, 1982, and acquired after March 1, 1984. See Chapter 1 of Publication 550.

Explanation
For further discussion of original issue discount, including some recent changes in the law, see Chapter 8, *Interest Income*.

Automatic investment service and dividend reinvestment plans. If you take part in an automatic investment service, your cost basis per share of stock, including fractional shares, bought by the bank or other agent is your proportionate share of the agent's cost of all shares purchased at the same time plus the same share of the brokerage commission paid by the agent. If you take part in a **dividend** reinvestment plan and you receive stock from the corporation at a discount, your cost is the full fair market value of the stock on the dividend payment date. You must include the amount of the discount in your income as an additional dividend.

Special rules apply in determining the basis of stock you acquired through a **stock dividend** or a **stock right**. **Stock dividends** are distributions by a corporation of its own stock. Usually, stock dividends are not taxable to the shareholder. However, for exceptions to this rule, see Chapter 9, *Dividends and Other Corporate Distributions*. If stock dividends are not taxable, you must allocate your basis for the stock between the old and the new stock in proportion to the fair market value of each on the date of the distribution of the new stock.

New and old stock identical. If the new stock you received as a dividend is the same as the old stock on which the dividend is declared, both new and old shares probably have equal fair market values and you can divide the adjusted basis of the old stock by the number of shares of old and new stock. The result is your basis for each share of stock.

Example
You owned one share of common stock that you bought for $45. The corporation distributed two new shares of common stock for each share you held. You then had three shares of common stock, each with a basis of $15 ($45 ÷ 3). If you owned two shares before the distribution, one bought for $30 and the other for $45, you would have six shares after the distribution: three with a basis of $10 each and three with a basis of $15 each.

Explanation
New and old stock not identical. If the new stock you received as a nontaxable dividend is not the same as the

old stock on which the dividend was declared, the fair market values of the old stock and the new stock will probably be different, so you should allocate the adjusted basis of your old stock between the old stock and the new stock in proportion to the fair market values of each on the date of the distribution of the new stock.

Example 1

This example shows how to account for stock splits and stock dividends.

	Block 1		
	Shares	Total cost	Cost per share
Jan. 15, 1976	100	$3,000	$ 30
2 for 1 stock split	100	–0–	
Dec. 31, 1976	200	$3,000	$ 15
Nov. 30, 1982 10% stock dividend	20		
Dec. 31, 1982	220	$3,000	$13.636

	Block 2		
	Shares	Total cost	Cost per share
Nov. 30, 1982 10% stock dividend	100 10	$2,000	$ 20
Dec. 31, 1982	110	$2,000	$18.182

The original cost of each block of stock must be divided by the number of shares on hand at any given date to arrive at basis per share.

Example 2

This example shows how to account for nontaxable stock dividends with a fair market value that is different from the value of the original stock held.

	Shares	Total cost	Cost per share	Total fair market value (FMV)	FMV per share
Feb. 7, 1992 Purchased common stock	100	$14,000	$14	$14,000	$14
Aug. 30, 1992 10% stock dividend of preferred stock. Fair market value of original stock is $22 per share.	10			$ 1,000	$10

100 shares × $14 = $14,000   Cost of originating stock

100 shares × $22 = $22,000   Market value of original stock

10 shares × $10 = $ 1,000   Market value of preferred stock

$22,000/$23,000 × $14,000 = $13,391   Cost of original stock apportioned to such stock

$1,000/$23,000 × $14,000 = $609   Cost of original stock apportioned to the preferred stock

Explanation

If your stock dividend is taxable on receipt, the original basis of your new stock is its fair market value on the date of distribution. Your holding period is determined from the date of distribution.

Stock rights are rarely taxable when you receive them. For more information, see Chapter 9, *Dividends and Other Corporate Distributions*.

If you receive stock rights that are taxable, the basis of the rights is their fair market value at the time of distribution.

If you receive stock rights that are not taxable and you allow them to expire, they have no basis.

If you exercise or sell the nontaxable stock rights and if, at the time of distribution, the rights had a fair market value of 15% or more of the fair market value of the old stock, you must divide the adjusted basis of the stock between the stock and the stock rights. Use a ratio of the fair market value of each to the total fair market value of both at the time of distribution of the rights. If the fair market value of the stock rights is less than 15%, their basis is zero unless you choose to allocate a part of the basis of the old stock to the rights. You make this allocation on your return for the tax year in which the rights are received.

Basis of new stock. If you exercise the stock rights, the basis of the new stock is its cost plus the basis of the stock rights exercised. The holding period of the new stock begins on the date on which you exercised the stock rights.

Example

You own 100 shares of Tan Company stock, which cost you $22 per share. The Tan Company gave you 10 stock rights that would allow you to buy 10 additional shares of stock at $26 per share. At the time the rights were distributed, the stock had a market value of $30, without the rights, and each right had a market value of $3. The market value of the stock rights is less than 15% of the market value of the stock, but you choose to divide the basis of your stock between the stock and the rights. You figure the basis of the rights and the basis of the old stock as follows:

100 shares × $22 = $2,200, basis of old stock

100 shares × $30 = $3,000, market value of old stock

10 rights × $3 = $30, market value of rights

30/3,030 × $2,200 = $21.78, basis of rights

3,000/3,030 × $2,200 = $2,178.22, new basis of old stock

If you sell the stock rights, the basis for figuring gain or loss is $2.178 per right. If you exercise the stock rights, the basis of the new stock you receive is $28.178 per share, the subscription price paid ($26), plus the basis of the stock rights exercised ($2.178 each). The remaining basis of the 100 shares of old stock for figuring gain or loss on a later sale is $2,178.22, or $21.7822 per share.

Explanation

Other basis rules. There are many other special rules you must follow in determining your basis in certain types of property. Here are some examples:

If you receive stock of one corporation in exchange for stock of another corporation in certain types of corporate reorganizations, your basis in the stock received will be equal to the basis of the stock you exchanged.

Certain types of tax credits may reduce basis in whole or in part. For example, if you claim rehabilitation credits on a building, the basis of the property is reduced by the amount of the credit.

If you lease real property on which the lessee makes improvements and the value of such improvements is excluded from income, your basis in the improvements is zero.

If you sell property to charity in a bargain sale, your basis for determining the gain from the sale is reduced by the ratio of the total basis of the property to its fair market value.

For more information, you should consult your tax advisor.

15 | Sale of Property

Introduction

Any time you sell or exchange a piece of property at a gain—whether it be your house, a stock you own, or something you use in your trade or business—you usually have to pay taxes on the transaction. That, of course, doesn't mean that sales and exchanges should be avoided, but the manner in which you choose to dispose of an **asset** *may determine how much you will have to pay in taxes. This chapter describes the various options available to you and the tax consequences of each.*

The Tax Reform Act of 1986 changed some of the tax considerations in selling or exchanging property. The law eliminated the long-term capital gain exclusion and limited your ability to defer tax by using an installment sale. These and other changes are pointed out at appropriate places in this chapter. In addition, for some taxpayers, the gap between the maximum tax rate for ordinary income (now 39.6%) and the maximum tax rate for capital gains (28%) just got wider. The new 1993 Tax Act added two new tax brackets for higher income taxpayers. Therefore, the distinction between ordinary gain and capital gain will be more important to your future tax planning.

Since the amounts involved in sales and exchanges of property are often quite large relative to other items that make up your income, this chapter merits careful attention. It not only spells out how you determine the way in which various transactions are taxed but also offers suggestions about how to minimize or defer the tax burdens that you may incur.

In addition, this chapter discusses **bad debts.** *When a borrower cannot repay a loan, it is known as a bad debt. Some loans are made in connection with a trade or a business, some are made for purely personal reasons, and still others are made to make a profit. All sorts of rules have to be followed, and not every bad debt qualifies for a deduction. This chapter spells out what kind of documentation you need to prove that the money you lost was a bona fide debt and that there is no chance of repayment—the two conditions that must be met for you to take a deduction.*

Important Change for 1993

Rollover provided for gain from sale of publicly traded securities. You may be able to postpone reporting part or all of your capital gain from publicly traded securities sold after August 9, 1993, if you buy certain replacement property within 60 days of the sale and meet certain other requirements. The replacement property must be common stock or a partnership interest in a specialized small business investment company. The amount of gain you can postpone may be limited. For more information, see *Rollover of Gain* later in this chapter.

Important Reminder

Holding period. The holding period for a long-term capital gain or loss generally is more than one year. The holding period for a short-term capital gain or loss generally is one year or less.

This chapter discusses the tax consequences of selling or trading investment property. It explains:

- What is a sale or trade,
- When you have a nontaxable trade,
- What to do with a related party transaction,
- Whether the property you sell is a capital asset or a noncapital asset,
- Whether you have a capital or ordinary gain or loss from the sale of property,
- How to determine your holding period, and
- When you can make a tax-free rollover of a gain from selling certain securities.

Sales not discussed in this publication. Certain sales or trades of property are discussed in other IRS publications. They include, for example, installment sales, covered in Publication 537, *Installment Sales,* and transfers of property at death, covered in Publication 559, *Survivors, Executors, and Administrators.*

Publication 544, *Sales and Other Dispositions of Assets,* provides information about various types of transactions involving business property, including dispositions of assets used in a trade or business or for the production of income.

Publication 550, *Investment Income and Expenses,* provides more detailed discussion about sales and trades of investment property. Publication 550 includes information about the rules covering nonbusiness bad debts, straddles, section 1256 contracts, puts and calls, commodity futures, short sales, and wash sales. It also discusses investment-related expenses.

Publication 925, *Passive Activity and At-Risk Rules,* discusses the rules that limit losses and credits from passive activities as well as the rules that apply to the disposition of an interest in a passive activity.

If you sell your home, different tax rules apply. These rules are discussed in Chapter 16.

Note: Beginning in 1998, you may have to pay tax on only one-half of your gain from the sale or exchange of **qualified small business stock.** This applies only to stock issued after August 10, 1993, and held by you for more than 5 years. You must have acquired the stock at its original issue, directly or through an underwriter, in one of the following ways:

1) In exchange for money or other property (not including stock), or
2) As compensation for services performed (other than services performed as an underwriter of the stock).

For more information, see Publication 553, *Highlights of 1993 Tax Changes.*

TaxSaver

The new 1993 Tax Act provides that a noncorporate taxpayer who holds qualified small business stock (QSBS) for more than five years can exclude from gross income 50% of any gain realized from the sale or exchange of the stock. This exclusion is limited to the greater of:

1. 10 times the taxpayer's basis in the stock; or
2. $10 million in gain from all of the taxpayer's transactions in stock of that corporation (held for more than five years).

The rules for determining whether stock is "qualified small business stock" can be summarized as follows:

- The stock must be newly issued stock.
- The stock cannot be acquired in exchange for other stock.
- The issuing corporation must be a C corporation, but may not be a cooperative, Domestic International Sales Corporation (DISC), former DISC, Real Estate Investment Trust (REIT), Regulated Investment Company (RIC), Real Estate Mortgage Investment Conduit (REMIC), a corporation having a possessions tax credit election in effect and may not own a subsidiary who has a possessions tax credit election in effect.
- At least 80% of the corporation's assets must be used in the active conduct of a qualifed trade or business, or in the start-up of a future qualified trade or business.
- A qualified trade or business is any business other than one involving the performance of services in the fields of health, law, engineering, architecture, accounting, actuarial science, performing arts, consulting, athletics, financial services, brokerage services, or any other trade or business where the principal asset of the business is the reputation or skill of one or more employees. A qualified trade or business also cannot involve the businesses of banking, insurance, financing, leasing, investing, or similar businesses, farming, or certain businesses involving natural resource extraction or production, and businesses operating a hotel, motel, restaurant, or similar business.
- The corporation may not have greater than $50 million in gross assets (i.e., the sum of cash plus the aggregate fair market value of other corporate property) at the time the qualified small business stock is issued. If the corporation meets this test at the time of issuance of the stock, a subsequent event that violates this rule will not disqualify stock that previously qualified.

Note: Another provision of the 1993 Tax Act provides that, under certain circumstances, the gain on the sale of publicly traded securities will not be taxed if the proceeds from the sale are used to acquire common stock in a specialized small business investment company (SSBIC) within a 60-day period. See Publication 553, *Highlights of 1993 Tax Changes,* for a detailed description of these additional requirements.

Useful Items

You may want to see:

Publication

☐ **504** Divorced or Separated Individuals
☐ **550** Investment Income and Expenses
☐ **564** Mutual Fund Distributions

Form (and Instructions)

☐ **Schedule D (Form 1040)** Capital Gains and Losses
☐ **8824** Like-Kind Exchanges

Sales and Trades

Sales and trades (or exchanges) of assets generally result in taxable gains or deductible losses, although some trades of property are nontaxable.

Form 1099–B. If you sold property such as stocks, bonds, or certain commodities through a broker, you should receive Form 1099–B, *Proceeds From Broker and Barter Exchange Transactions,* or an equivalent statement from the broker. You should receive the statement by January 31, 1994, showing the gross proceeds from sales during 1993. The Internal Revenue Service (IRS) will also get a copy of Form 1099–B from the broker.

If you receive a Form 1099–B or equivalent statement, you must complete Schedule D of Form 1040.

Unstated interest and imputed principal rules for sales or exchanges. For information about the unstated interest rules applicable to certain payments received on account of a ***seller-financed*** sale or exchange of property, and about the imputed principal rules applicable to any debt instrument issued on account of such transactions, see Publication 537.

What is a Sale or Trade?

A sale is generally a transfer of property for money only or for a promise to pay money, such as a mortgage or note. A trade is a transfer of property in return for other property or services and may be taxed in the same way as a sale.

Sale and purchase. Ordinarily, a transaction is not a trade when you voluntarily sell property for cash and immediately buy similar property to replace it. Such a sale and purchase are two separate transactions.

Example

You sell your car to your brother and buy a new one from a dealer. You have entered into two separate transactions.

Redemption of stock. A redemption of stock is treated as a sale or trade and is subject to the capital gain or loss provisions unless the redemption is a dividend or other distribution on stock.

Dividend vs. sale or trade. Whether a redemption is treated as a sale, trade, dividend, or other distribution depends on the circumstances in each case. Both direct and indirect ownership of stock will be considered. The redemption is treated as a sale or trade of stock if:

1) The redemption is not essentially equivalent to a dividend (see Chapter 9),
2) There is a substantially disproportionate redemption of stock,
3) There is a complete redemption of all the stock of the corporation owned by the shareholder, or
4) The redemption is a distribution in partial liquidation of a corporation.

Redemption or retirement of bonds. A redemption or retirement of bonds or notes at their maturity is a sale or trade that you must report on Schedule D (Form 1040) whether or not you realize gain or loss on the transaction.

However, if the issuer has merely extended the maturity date of its notes, during which period some of the noteholders have agreed not to redeem their notes until all the other notes are retired or their retirement is provided for, neither a trade nor a closed or completed transaction has occurred. Under these circumstances, you do not figure gain or loss.

Surrender of stock. A surrender of stock by a dominant shareholder, who retains control of the corporation, is treated as a contribution to capital rather than as an immediate loss deductible from taxable income. The surrendering shareholder must reallocate his or her basis in the surrendered shares to the shares he or she retains.

Exceptions

While an exchange is generally taxable, the following "exchanges" are not:

- The extension of the maturity date of promissory notes

- The exercise of an option to convert a bond into stock of the issuing corporation, if the conversion privilege is provided for in the bond
- The conversion of security interests to stock in the same corporation subsequent to certain reorganizations (one example: the exchange of common stock for preferred stock)

TAXPLANNER

You may save taxes by carefully planning major sales and exchanges. It may be better to wait until after the end of the year before finalizing a sale so that a gain may be deferred until the next year or so that more losses may be realized in the current year. Professional advice should be obtained before, not after, a major transaction.

Explanation

Estates. The transfer of property of a decedent to the executor or administrator of the estate, or to the heirs or beneficiaries, generally is not a sale or exchange. No taxable gain or deductible loss results from the transfer.

Easements. Granting or selling an easement usually is not a taxable sale of property. Instead, the amount received for the easement is subtracted from the **basis** of the property. If only a part of an entire tract of property is permanently affected by the easement, only the basis of that part is reduced by the amounts received. Any amount received that is more than the basis of the property to be reduced is a taxable gain. The transaction is reported as if it were a sale of the property.

If you transfer a perpetual easement for consideration, the transaction will be treated as a sale of property.

Life estate, etc. The entire amount you realize from disposing of a life interest in property, an interest in property for a set number of years, or an income interest in a trust is a taxable gain if you first got the interest as a gift, inheritance, or transfer in trust. Your basis in the property is considered to be zero. This rule does not apply if all interests in the property are disposed of at the same time.

Example 1

Your father dies, leaving his farm to you for life, with a remainder interest to your younger brother. You decide to sell your life interest in the farm. The entire amount you receive is a taxable gain, and your basis in the farm is disregarded.

Example 2

The facts are the same as in Example 1, except that your younger brother joins you in selling the farm. Since the entire interest in the property is conveyed, your taxable gain is the amount by which your share of the proceeds is more than your adjusted basis in the farm.

Note: In Example 2, each brother's gain is computed by allocating the tax basis between them. The basis for the entire property—the **fair market value** at the date of the decedent's death—is adjusted for **depreciation** and improvements. Then, using actuarial tables, you compute the value of the life interest and of the **remainder interest** at the date of sale.

The younger brother could sell his remainder interest

in the property independently of his brother, using his separate basis in computing his gain or loss on the sale. However, the older brother may not get the benefit of his basis in the property if he sells his life interest separately. The moral of the story is: Sometimes you save on taxes if you get along with your brother.

Sale versus lease. Just because a document says that it is a lease does not necessarily make it a lease for tax purposes. The rules are very complicated and not completely clear. Professional help is advisable. See Publication 544, *Sales and Other Dispositions of Assets.*

Installment sales. Some sales are made under a plan that provides for part or all of the sales price to be paid in a later year. These are called "installment sales." If you finance the buyer's purchase of your property instead of having the buyer get a loan or mortgage from a bank, you probably have an installment sale.

You report your gain on an installment sale only as you actually receive the payment. You are taxed only on the part of each payment that represents your profit on the sale. In this way, the installment method of reporting income relieves you of paying tax on income that you have not yet collected.

The first step in using the installment method is to find what portion of each installment payment represents a gain. This is determined by calculating the gross profit percentage, which is your gross profit divided by the contract price. Apply this percentage to all payments you receive in a year.

Gross profit is the selling price less the adjusted basis of the property sold. The selling price includes any cash you receive, the fair market value of the property received from the buyer, plus the amount of any existing mortgage on the property.

Contract price is the selling price less any mortgage encumbrance on the property. However, if the amount of the mortgage is more than the adjusted basis of the property, then the selling price is reduced only by the adjusted basis, so the gross profit percentage is 100%.

Example

In 1978, Able bought some commercial **real estate** for $100,000. He put $20,000 cash down and took out a mortgage for $80,000. By 1993, Able had reduced the mortgage to $40,000 and had an adjusted basis in the real estate of $85,000 (original cost, less depreciation, plus improvements). Able sold the real estate to Baker for $190,000. To pay Able, Baker assumed the rest of the mortgage and made three installment payments of $50,000 each.

Able figures his gross profit as follows:

Selling price	$190,000
Less adjusted tax basis	85,000
Gross profit	$105,000

Able figures his contract price as follows:

Selling price	$190,000
Less mortgage assumed	40,000
Contract price	$150,000

Able's gross profit percentage is 70% (gross profit divided by contract price). Every year in which Able collects a part of the contract price from Baker, he must report 70% as a gain, until he has reported the entire contract amount.

TaxSaver 1

Using the installment sale method may spread out your gain over several years and may result in a lower total tax on your gain.

By taking only a portion of the gain into income each year, you may avoid reaching a higher tax bracket. Even if you are already in the highest bracket, use of the installment sale method may still be beneficial, since taxes may be deferred to later years.

A disadvantage of the installment sale method is that, if you are the seller, you do not obtain the sale proceeds immediately and therefore cannot reinvest them elsewhere.

TaxSaver 2

Installment sale treatment is not obligatory. You may elect not to follow the installment sale rules, in which case, your total gain is recognized in the year of the sale.

While it is generally advantageous to defer recognition of a gain or part of a gain by using the installment sale method, under certain circumstances, accelerating recognition may result in overall tax savings. For example, if you expect your income in future years to be much higher than it is now or if you currently have a **capital loss** that may be offset by a gain, you may want to recognize your gain immediately.

The Tax Reform Act of 1986 limited the ability to defer tax by using the installment method for sales of certain kinds of property. For example, the installment method may no longer be used for sales of publicly traded stocks or securities. However, you may sell other types of property, such as real property used in your business or for rental, under an installment sale and be able to defer the tax on the gain.

If you decide not to use the installment sale reporting method, indicate this decision on either Schedule D (Form 1040) or Form 4797 by the date your tax return for the year of the sale is due. (Schedule D is used to report sales of capital assets. Form 4797 is used to report sales of trade or business property and other noncapital assets.) Once you decide not to use the installment sale method, you may change your decision only with the consent of the IRS.

If you choose not to use the installment method and you are a **cash basis** taxpayer, remember that you may discount the value of any installment payments that you are to receive at a later date. Therefore, the total gain on the sale you report should be discounted, because you do not receive the total payment at the time of the sale.

TaxAlert

Sales at a loss do not qualify for installment sale reporting. Also, under changes made by the Revenue Act of 1987, sales by dealers or by persons who regularly sell personal property on the installment basis no longer qualify for the installment method.

Explanation

The gain you have from an installment sale will be treated as **capital gain** if the property you sold was a capital asset (discussed later). However, if you took depreciation **deductions,** including the section 179 deduction, on the asset, part of your gain may be treated as **ordinary income.**

Example

On January 31, 1993, Susan sells property for $4,000 on which she has a $1,000 gain. Half of the gain is taxable at ordinary rates.

If Susan receives the initial $2,000 payment in 1993, she is receiving one-half the proceeds and so must report one-half of the gain, or $500. Since the ordinary income portion must be reported first, the entire $500 is treated as an **ordinary gain.** When Susan receives the second $2,000 payment, she reports the second half of the gain, $500, as a capital gain.

Explanation

The 1984 Deficit Reduction Act changed some of the rules regarding the reporting of income on installment sales after June 6, 1984. Now, any depreciation claimed on personal property must be recaptured as ordinary income in the year of sale, even if there are no payments received in the year of sale. The depreciation recapture for real property is generally limited to the amount by which the depreciation claimed exceeds the amount available under the straight-line method of depreciation. The adjusted basis of the property being sold is increased by the amount of recaptured income that you include in your gross income in the year of sale, so that the gain recognized in future years is decreased.

Example

Assume that Sam sells tangible personal property to Betty in 1992 for $100,000 to be paid in installments over 5 years, beginning in 1993. Interest is payable at market rates. The property was originally purchased for $30,000. Because of depreciation, it has an adjusted basis of $20,000. There is a gain of $80,000 ($100,000 − $20,000), of which $10,000 is recaptured income to be reported on Sam's current-year return.

The $10,000 that is included in Sam's income in the year of sale is added to the $20,000 adjusted basis to figure how much income Sam must report using the installment method. Therefore, Sam's gross profit is $70,000 ($100,000 − $30,000). Sam's gross profit percentage is 70%.

On each of the $20,000 payments that Sam receives from 1993 through 1997, $14,000 would be included in his income ($20,000 × 70%).

Explanation

The installment sale rules contain a number of very important limitations.

Sales to a spouse or an 80% controlled entity. If you sell depreciable property to your spouse or to a partnership or corporation of which you own 80% or more, you must report all of the gain in the year of the sale, despite any installment payment schedules set up under the sale agreement. The same rule may also apply to the sale of property to a trust of which you (or your spouse) is a beneficiary.

Sales to other relatives. If you sell property, other than marketable securities, to a related person on an installment basis and that person resells (or makes a gift of) the property within 2 years, you have to recognize any additional gain in the year of the resale.

If you sell marketable securities to a related person and that person resells the property, you have to recognize any additional gain, unless the sale takes place after you have received all the installment payments due to you. There is no 2-year cutoff date as with other kinds of property, noted above. See the special rules regarding publicly traded property, below.

A related person includes your spouse, children, grandchildren, and parents. A related person is also any partnership in which you are a partner, any estates and trusts of which you are a beneficiary, any grantor trusts of which you are treated as an owner, and any corporation in which you own at least half of the total value of the stock.

The normal 3-year statute of limitations for tax assessments by the IRS is extended for resales of installment property by a related person. In these cases, the statute of limitations will not expire until 2 years after you report to the IRS that a resale took place.

Nontaxable trades. Special rules apply to the exchange of like-kind property, which is tax-free. However, nonlike-kind property included in the exchange is taxable. The installment method may be used for the nonlike-kind property. For a further discussion of this subject, see *Nontaxable Trades.*

Like-kind exchanges. Changes made by the Omnibus Budget Reconciliation Act of 1989 provide that, in like-kind exchanges involving related parties, both parties must hold the property for more than 2 years. This rule is applicable to both parties to the transaction, even though only one party avails himself or herself of like-kind treatment. Also, real property located in the United States and real property located outside the United States no longer qualify as property of a like kind. These changes are effective for transfers after July 10, 1989, unless the transfer is pursuant to a written binding contract in effect on that date.

Disposing of installment obligations. If you sell property on an installment basis and then later dispose of the installment note, you may have to report a gain or a loss. Generally, the amount of your gain or loss is equal to the difference between your basis in the installment note and the amount you receive when you dispose of the note.

Example

Toni sells real estate on an installment basis for a $200,000 note receivable and has a $120,000 gross profit from the sale. After she collects $100,000 (and reports a profit of $60,000, half her gross profit), she sells the remaining $100,000 note receivable to a bank for $95,000. Toni reports a $55,000 profit in the year of the sale of the note (the remaining $60,000 of gross profit less the $5,000 loss on the sale of the note).

Explanation

A "disposition" for this purpose is not limited to a sale of the installment note. For example, if you make a sale of property after December 31, 1988, for more than $150,000, and you assign the installment obligation as collateral security for a loan, the IRS will treat this as a disposition. This is because you would have deferred the gain on the sale while obtaining the use of the money through a loan.

Publicly traded property. The installment method cannot be used for sales of publicly traded property, including stock or securities that are traded on an established securities market.

Repossessing property sold under the installment method. If you sell property on an installment plan, you may have to repossess it if, for example, the buyer defaults on his or her obligation. When repossession takes place, you may have to report a gain or a loss. You follow different rules for determining your gain or loss, depending on whether the property being repossessed is personal property or real property.

Personal property. If you repossess personal property sold under an installment plan, you must compare the fair market value of the property recovered with your basis in the installment notes plus any expenses you had in connection with repossession. Under the installment method, your basis is the face value of the note still outstanding less the amount of unreported profit on the original sale. (If you did not use the installment reporting method, your basis is the value of the property at the time of the original sale less payments of principal received to date.)

Your gain or loss is of the same character (short term or long term) as the gain or loss realized on the original sale if you used the installment method. If you did not, any gain resulting from repossession is treated as ordinary income. Any loss is an **ordinary loss** if the property is business property. If it is nonbusiness property, any loss resulting from repossession is treated as a short-term capital loss.

Real property. If you have to repossess your former residence because the buyer defaults and you elected to exclude $125,000 of the gain or you deferred recognition of the gain by acquiring a replacement home (see Chapter 16, *Selling Your Home,* for details), no gain or loss is recognized if you resell the house within 1 year of repossession. If the property is not resold within 1 year, you may have to recognize the gain. You may never deduct a loss on repossession, because you may not deduct losses on property used primarily for personal purposes.

Computing your gain or loss on repossessed real property. Generally, you compute your gain or loss on property you repossess by subtracting (1) the amount of taxable gain you previously reported on the installment sale from (2) the total amount of payments you received under the installment sale prior to repossession. Your basis in the repossessed property is your adjusted basis at the time of the original sale.

The total gain you may report on an installment sale and repossession is limited to the gross profit you expected on the installment sale less repossession costs.

Example

Linda Smith sold a building that was not her personal residence to Ann Carter in 1988 for $100,000, payable in 10 annual installments. Linda's basis in the building was $70,000, and no mortgage was outstanding. The expected gross profit in the sale was $30,000, and the gross profit percentage was 30%.

In 1993, Ann failed to pay the sixth installment. By then, Linda had recognized $15,000 of gain from the $50,000 in payments received. She repossessed the building, incurring legal fees of $1,000 in the process. Linda's gain is computed as follows:

Gain	
Payments received	$50,000
Less: Taxable gain already reported on sale	15,000
Gain subject to limitation	$35,000

Limitation on gain	
Gross profit expected on installment sale	$30,000
Less: Repossession costs	1,000
Less: Taxable gain already reported on sale	15,000
Limitation	$14,000

Linda must report a $14,000 gain on repossession. Her basis in the reacquired building is $49,000, figured by taking $70,000 (her original adjusted basis) and subtracting $21,000 ($35,000 − $14,000), the amount of gain on repossession unrecognized because of the limitation on gain.

TAXPLANNER

Computing interest on installment sales. Special rules may apply regarding the amount of interest to be recognized on installment sales of more than $3,000.

If the amount of interest is not specifically stated in the sales agreement or if the stated interest is at an unrealistically low rate, you must calculate "unstated" or "imputed" interest. In general, you have "unstated" interest if (1) the sum of all payments due more than 6 months after the date of sale exceeds (2) the present value of such payments and the present value of any interest payment provided for in the contract. Present value is determined by using a so-called testing rate compounded semiannually. If there is unstated interest, you are required to *impute* interest using the testing rate. The testing rate is calculated by using the applicable federal rate (AFR). The AFR is based on average market yields of U.S. obligations. The AFR may be the short-, medium-, or long-term rate that U.S. obligations are yielding, depending on the length of the contract.

The testing rate is equal to *110% of the AFR* at the time the sale is made. If unstated interest results using the testing rate, then interest must be computed using the testing rate, compounded semiannually.

The rate used to impute interest cannot exceed 9% for sales of property after June 30, 1985, that involve borrowings of $2.8 million or less, except for sales of new property eligible for the investment credit.

Example

On June 1, 1993, Nicholas and Alexandra sell their limousine for $45,000, to be paid in three annual installments of $15,000 each on June 1, 1993, 1994, and 1995. No interest is stated in the sales contract. Their basis in the car is $35,000.

Since $30,000, the sum of the payments due more than 6 months after the sale, exceeds $26,314, the present value of such payments discounted at 9% semiannually, there is unstated interest.

The imputed interest over the 3 years is $3,686 (9% compounded semiannually). This amount must be subtracted from the selling price when the gain on the sale is computed:

Stated selling price	$45,000
Less: Unstated interest	3,686
Adjusted selling price	$41,314
Less: Basis	35,000
Gain on sale	$ 6,314
Gross profit percentage: ($6,314 ÷ $41,314)	15.3%

Imputed interest is important to consider for two reasons: (1) It alters the amount of gain on a sale, and (2) it is deductible as an interest expense by the buyer, subject to limitations (See Chapter 24, *Interest Expense*), and must be reported as interest income by the seller.

Note: If all of the installment payments are due within 1 year after the date of sale, it is not necessary to figure your imputed interest. Additionally, payments received within the first 6 months of a sale have no imputed interest. The AFR will be determined by the IRS every month.

TaxOrganizer

You should keep a copy of your sales agreements, loan agreements, and closing statements associated with any installment sale.

How to Figure a Gain or Loss

You figure gain or loss on a sale or trade of property by comparing the amount you realize with the adjusted basis of the property.
Gain. Gain is the amount you realize from a sale or trade minus the adjusted basis of the property you transfer.
Loss. Loss is the adjusted basis of the property minus the amount you realize.
Adjusted basis. The adjusted basis of property is your original cost or other original basis properly adjusted (increased or decreased) for certain items. See Chapter 14 for more information about determining the adjusted basis of property.
Amount realized. The amount you realize from a sale or trade of property is everything you receive for the property. This includes the money you receive plus the fair market value of all property or services you receive.
Fair market value. Fair market value is the price at which the property would change hands between a buyer and a seller, neither being forced to buy or sell and both having reasonable knowledge of all the relevant facts.

TaxPlanner

An appraisal by a qualified person is usually accepted by both the courts and the IRS as the fair market value. The appraiser should be familiar with valuation methods accepted in the particular field (real estate, art objects, equipment and machinery, etc.). For real estate, a local appraiser is better qualified than an out-of-towner. In other fields, prior experience in the field is more important. It may be prudent to obtain an appraisal at the date of the transaction, just in case it is needed later.

TaxOrganizer

You should keep a copy of your appraisal report of any property sold in order to verify its value.

The fair market value of notes or other evidence of indebtedness you receive as a part of the sale price is usually the best amount you can get from selling them to, or discounting them with, a bank or other buyer of such debt instruments.
Debt paid off. An indebtedness against the property, or against you, that is paid off as a part of the transaction, or that is assumed by the buyer, must be included in the amount realized. This is true even if neither you nor the buyer is personally liable for the debt. For example, if you sell or trade property that is subject to a nonrecourse loan, the amount you realize includes the full amount of the note assumed by the buyer even though the amount of the note exceeds the fair market value of the property.

Example 1

You sell property to a buyer who pays you $20,000 cash and assumes an existing mortgage on the property of $8,000. You bought the property for $6,000 and added improvements costing $10,000. Your selling expenses were $1,400. Your gain on the sale is figured as follows:

Amount realized		
Cash	$20,000	
Mortgage assumed by buyer	8,000	$28,000
Minus: Adjusted basis		
Cost	$ 6,000	
Improvements	10,000	
Total	$16,000	
Plus: Selling expenses	1,400	17,400
Gain		**$10,600**

Example 2

You exchange property with an adjusted basis of $7,000 for other property with a fair market value of $10,000. Your gain is $3,000 ($10,000 − $7,000). If you also received a mortgage or trust note for $6,000 that has a discount value of $4,000, your gain is $7,000 ($10,000

+ \$4,000 − \$7,000). But in some cases your gain may not be taxable.

Payment of cash. If you trade property for other property and in addition pay cash, the amount you realize is the fair market value of the property you receive. Determine your gain or loss by subtracting your adjusted basis (the cash you pay plus the adjusted basis of the property you traded in) from the amount you realize.

Example 1. You sell stock that you had pledged as security for a bank loan of \$8,000. Your basis in the stock is \$6,000. The buyer pays off your bank loan and pays you \$20,000 in cash. The amount realized is \$28,000 (\$20,000 + \$8,000). Your gain is \$22,000 (\$28,000 − \$6,000).

Example 2. You trade A Company stock with an adjusted basis of \$7,000 for B Company stock with a fair market value of \$10,000, which is your amount realized. Your gain is \$3,000 (\$10,000 − \$7,000). If you also receive a note for \$6,000 that has a discount value of \$4,000, your gain is \$7,000 ((\$10,000 + \$4,000) − \$7,000).

Explanation

If you receive a mortgage or a trust note, payments include some interest income in addition to principal.

Example

Assume that a \$10,000 installment note with a discounted value of \$8,000 is given by an individual to a cash basis taxpayer in payment for property with a basis of \$7,000. The taxpayer recognizes \$1,000 (\$8,000 − \$7,000) as a capital gain. As each installment is paid, eight-tenths (\$8,000 ÷ \$10,000) of the payment is a return of principal and two-tenths is interest income.

Explanation

If you are an **accrual basis** taxpayer—and most people are not—use the full face value of the note in computing your gain or loss on the sale. Consequently, payments on the note are returns of principal.

If you are a cash basis taxpayer, and if the installment note is given by a corporation and the discounted value of the note is used to compute your gain on the sale of a capital asset, the income to be recognized is a capital gain. If the note is given by an individual, the income is taxable as ordinary income.

Example

A cash basis taxpayer sells a capital asset to a corporation in exchange for a \$10,000 note with an interest rate of 9%. Because current interest rates are more than 9% or because of the corporation's low credit status, the note has a discounted value of \$8,000, 80% of its face value. The taxpayer uses the \$8,000 value to compute gain or loss on the sale. When the corporation later pays the note, the \$2,000 difference, which must be reported as income, is treated as a capital gain. If an individual had issued the note, the \$2,000 gain to the taxpayer realized on payment of the note would be taxed as ordinary income.

Explanation

Property used partly for business. If you sell or exchange property that you used for both business and personal purposes, the gain or loss on the sale or exchange must be figured as though you had sold two separate pieces of property. You must divide the selling price, selling expenses, and the basis between the business and personal parts. Depreciation is deducted from the basis of the business part. Gain or loss realized on the business part of the property may be treated as capital gain or loss, or as ordinary gain or loss (see Publication 544, *Sales and Other Dispositions of Assets*). Any gain realized on the personal part of the property is a capital gain. A loss on the personal part is not deductible.

Example

You sold a house in 1993 for \$57,000. You bought the house in 1974 for \$30,000 and used two-thirds of it as your home and rented out the other third. Depreciation totaling \$4,000 (straight-line method) was allowed for the rented part during the period in which you owned the property. Your expenses in connection with selling the house were \$3,600. The sale resulted in a gain of \$11,800 on the rented part of the property and a gain of \$15,600 on the personal part, figured as follows:

	Rented part	Personal part
1) Cost	\$10,000	\$20,000
2) Minus: Depreciation	4,000	–0–
3) Adjusted basis	\$ 6,000	\$20,000
4) Selling price	\$19,000	\$38,000
5) Minus: Adjusted basis (line 3)	6,000	20,000
6) Gain	\$13,000	\$18,000
7) Minus: Expenses of sale	1,200	2,400
8) Net gain	\$11,800	\$15,600

The gain applicable to the personal part may be deferred if you qualify under the rules discussed in Chapter 16, *Selling Your Home.* The gain on the rented part may not be deferred but is taxable in 1993 as capital gain or as ordinary gain, depending on your other section 1231 transactions (see Publication 544, *Sales and Other Dispositions of Assets*). See Chapter 17, *Reporting Gains and Losses,* for a brief discussion of section 1231 property.

TaxOrganizer

You should keep a copy of the following in order to compute your net gain on the sale of property: costs for improvements to property, selling costs, and closing statements for the purchase and sale of property.

No gain or loss. You may be required to use a basis for figuring gain different from that used for figuring loss. In this case, you may not have a gain or loss. See *Other Basis* in Chapter 14. In these situations, if you use the basis for figuring a gain and figure a loss, and then use the basis for figuring a loss and figure a gain, you will have neither a gain nor a loss.

Example. You receive a gift of investment property having an adjusted basis of $10,000 at the time of the gift. The fair market value at the time of the gift is $9,000. You later sell the property for $9,500. You have neither gain nor loss. Your basis for figuring gain is $10,000, and $10,000 minus $9,500 results in a $500 loss. Your basis for figuring loss is $9,000, and $9,500 minus $9,000 results in a $500 gain.

TaxSaver

If you plan to give away a capital asset that has depreciated in value, consider selling it and giving away the proceeds instead, particularly if the would-be recipient of the property would likely sell it in the immediate future. By selling, you realize a capital loss and the consequent tax savings. At the same time, the would-be recipient of the property, who might have been unable to claim a capital loss because he or she would have had a different basis in the property, receives assets of the same value, only in cash instead of property.

Nontaxable Trades

Certain trades or exchanges are nontaxable. This means that any gain from the exchange is not taxed, and any loss cannot be deducted. In other words, even though you may realize a gain or loss on the exchange, it will not be recognized for tax purposes. The property you get generally has the same basis as the adjusted basis of the property you gave up.

If you traded business property or depreciable investment property, see Publication 544.

Like-kind exchanges. If you traded business or investment property for other business or investment property of a like kind, you must postpone tax on the gain or postpone deducting the loss until you sell or dispose of the property you receive. To be nontaxable, a trade must meet all six of the following conditions:

1) The property must be business or investment property. You must hold both the property you trade and the property you receive for business or investment purposes. Neither property may be used for personal purposes, such as your home or family car.
2) The property must not be property held for sale. The property you trade and the property you receive must not be property you sell to customers, such as merchandise. It must be property held for investment or property held for productive use in your trade or business.
3) There must be an exchange of like-kind property. The exchange of real estate for real estate and the exchange of personal property for similar personal property are exchanges of like-kind property. The trade of an apartment house for a store building, or a panel truck for a pickup truck, are like-kind exchanges. The exchange of a piece of machinery for a store building is not a like-kind exchange.
4) The property must not be stocks, bonds, notes, choses in action, certificates of trust or beneficial interest, or other securities or evidence of indebtedness or interest, including partnership interests. However, you can have a nontaxable exchange of corporate stocks, as discussed later under *Corporate stocks*.
5) The property must meet the identification requirement. The property to be received must be identified on or before the day

that is 45 days after the date of transfer of the property given up in the exchange.
6) The exchange must meet the completed transaction requirement. The property must be received on or before the earlier of:
   a) The 180th day after the date on which you transfer the property given up in the transfer, or
   b) The due date, including extensions, for your tax return for the year in which the transfer of the property given up occurs.

Explanation

The term "like-kind" refers to a property's nature or character, not its grade or quality. With real estate, for example, the location of the property and whether or not it has been improved are factors that affect only grade or quality, not its nature. Property held for productive use in a trade or a business may be exchanged for property held for investment.

Examples

Like-kind exchanges include the following:

- Improved for unimproved real estate when exchanged by a person who does not deal in real estate.
- A used car for a new one to be used for the same purpose.

The following are *not* considered like-kind exchanges:

- Personal property (such as a boat) for real property.
- Gold numismatic coins for gold bullion. The IRS ruled that an investment in gold coins was an investment in the coins themselves, while the investment in bullion was an investment in the world gold market.
- Gold bullion for silver bullion.
- Male livestock for female livestock.
- U.S. real property for real property located outside the United States.

TaxAlert

For exchanges after April 10, 1991, depreciable, tangible personal property may be exchanged for either like-kind or "like-class" property and may qualify for **like-kind exchange treatment**. Like-class properties are depreciable, tangible personal properties within the same "general asset classes" as defined in the Standard Industrial Classification Manual (See Publication 544, *Sales and Other Dispositions of Assets*).

For exchanges of multiple properties after April 10, 1991, you are not required to make a property-by-property comparison if you

1. Separate the properties into two or more exchange groups, or
2. Transfer or receive more than one property within a single exchange group.

Partially nontaxable exchange. If, in addition to like-kind property, you receive cash or nonlike-kind property, and the above conditions are met, you have a partially nontaxable trade. You are taxed on the gain you realize, but only to the extent of the cash and the fair market value of the nonlike-kind property you receive. You cannot deduct a loss.

Example

You exchange real estate held for investment that has an adjusted basis of $8,000 for other real estate that you want to hold for investment. The real estate you receive has a fair market value of $10,000, and you also receive $1,000 in cash. Although the total gain realized on the transaction is $3,000, only $1,000 (cash received) is included in your income.

TAXSAVER 1

Assume that you are to receive property that is worth less than the property you are to give up and that you expect to make improvements on the new property. Rather than receive money or unlike property from the other owner to make up the difference in value, you might ask her to make the improvements on her property before the transfer. In that way, you reduce the amount of unlike property included in the exchange and therefore reduce the amount of tax you have to pay on the transfer. What is the incentive for the other owner? Making the improvement might induce you to make the deal.

TAXSAVER 2

If the amount of liabilities you assume in an exchange is less than the amount of liabilities you give up, the difference is treated as cash received. Consequently, if you assume a mortgage that is less than the mortgage you had been carrying on the exchanged property, you recognize gain as if you had received cash for the difference.

If you receive cash but assume more debt than you were relieved of, you cannot offset the cash received with the debt assumed. In this case, you should have the buyer pay down some of the debt you are assuming rather than paying you the cash directly. You may be able to borrow the difference against the property at a later date.

Like-kind property and nonlike-kind property transferred. If you give up nonlike-kind property in addition to the like-kind property, you must recognize gain or loss only on the nonlike-kind property you give up. The gain or loss is the difference between the adjusted basis of the nonlike-kind property and its fair market value. See Chapter 1 of Publication 544 for more information about partially nontaxable exchanges.

Like-kind property and money transferred. If conditions (1) – (6) are met, you have a nontaxable trade even if you pay money in addition to transferring property in exchange for like-kind property.

Basis. To figure the basis of the property received, see *Nontaxable Exchanges,* in Chapter 14, *Basis of Property.*

How to report. You must report the exchange of business or investment like-kind property on **Form 8824,** *Like-Kind Exchanges.* If you figure a recognized gain or loss on Form 8824, report it on Schedule D of Form 1040 (or Form 4797, *Sales of Business Property,* whichever applies).

For exchanges you report on Schedule D, enter any gain or loss from Form 8824 on line 4 or line 12 of Schedule D. (See Chapter 17 to determine whether to use line 4 or line 12.) If one or more exchanges involved a related party, write "Related Party Like-Kind Exchange" at the top of Schedule D.

To compute any partial gains or losses and for more information on like-kind exchanges, see the instructions for Form 8824. For more information on how to report the sale of business property, see Publication 544.

TAXSAVER

A like-kind exchange is a useful planning tool in deferring tax on appreciated property if you intend to reinvest in a similar property within a relatively short period. The IRS has issued final regulations relating to deferred like-kind exchanges that affect property transferred on or after June 10, 1991. No gain or loss is recognized in a deferred like-kind exchange if you meet the following requirements:

1. You must follow specific procedures to identify replacement property within 45 days after relinquishing the old property.
2. You must receive the replacement property within 180 days after relinquishing the old property.
3. You must structure the exchange to comply with one or more of the "guidelines" described in the final regulations. The reason for this step is that, if the exchange does not fall within one of the guidelines, then the exchange could be subject to scrutiny by the IRS.

Taxpayers should design their transactions to comply with one of the following IRS guidelines:

1. You cannot have an immediate ability or unrestricted right to receive money or other property pursuant to the security or guarantee arrangement. However, the replacement property may be secured or guaranteed before you actually receive like-kind replacement property by one or more of the following:
   a. Mortgage, deed of trust, or other security interest in property.
   b. Standby letter of credit meeting certain specifications and a guarantee of a third party.
2. You may not have an immediate ability or unrestricted right to receive, pledge, borrow, or otherwise obtain the benefits of the cash or cash equivalent held in an escrow account or qualified trust. However, the replacement property may be secured by cash or a cash equivalent if the cash or cash equivalent is held in a qualified escrow account or in a qualified trust.
3. You may not have an immediate ability or unrestricted right to receive, pledge, borrow, or otherwise obtain the benefits of money or other property held by a qualified intermediary. However, you may use a "qualified intermediary" in a deferred exchange if the qualified intermediary is unrelated to you (see the IRS final regulations for details). A qualified intermediary may be an escrow or title company.

More than one IRS guideline can be used in the same deferred exchange, but the terms and conditions of each must be separately satisfied. You should consult your tax advisor if you are contemplating a like-kind exchange.

Transfers of property between spouses or incident to divorce. Generally, no gain or loss is recognized on a transfer of property from an individual to (or in trust for the benefit of) a spouse, or a former spouse if incident to a divorce. This nonrecognition rule does not apply if the recipient-spouse or former spouse is a nonresident alien. The rule also does not apply to a transfer in trust to the extent the adjusted basis of the property is less than the amount of the liabilities assumed and liabilities on the property.

Any transfer of property to a spouse or former spouse on which gain or loss is not recognized is treated by the transferee as acquired by gift and is not considered a sale or exchange. The transferee's basis in the property will be the same as the adjusted basis of the transferor immediately before the transfer. This carryover basis rule applies whether the adjusted basis of the transferred property is less than, equal to, or greater than its fair market value at the time of transfer. This rule applies for purposes of determining loss as well as gain. Any gain recognized on a transfer in trust increases the basis.

A transfer of property is incident to a divorce if the transfer occurs within one year after the date on which the marriage ends, or if the transfer is related to the ending of the marriage.

For more information, see Publication 504.

Explanation

The Technical and Miscellaneous Revenue Act of 1988 enacted two provisions regarding transfers of property between spouses. For transfers of property incident to divorce to a former spouse who is a nonresident alien, gain or loss may be recognized to the spouse who transferred the property based on the fair market value of the property transferred.

The law also provides that a transfer of stock between spouses or incident to divorce will not cause income to be recognized to the spouse who transferred the property if the stock was acquired by exercising an incentive stock option. The same results occur even if the spouse who transferred the property did not hold the stock for the required holding period. For more information on the tax treatment of incentive stock options, see *Stock Options* in Chapter 6, *Wages, Salaries, and Other Earnings*.

Corporate stocks. The following trades of corporate stocks generally do not result in a taxable gain or a deductible loss.

Stock for stock of the same corporation. You can exchange common stock for common stock or preferred stock for preferred stock in the same corporation without having a recognized gain or loss. This is true for a trade between two persons as well as a trade between a stockholder and a corporation.

In some instances, you can trade common stock for preferred stock, preferred stock for common stock, or stock in one corporation for stock in another corporation without having a recognized gain or loss. These trades must be part of mergers, recapitalizations, transfers to controlled corporations, bankruptcies, corporate divisions, corporate acquisitions, or other corporate reorganizations.

Convertible stocks and bonds. You will not have a recognized gain or loss if you convert bonds into stock or preferred stock into common stock of the same corporation according to a conversion privilege in the terms of the bond or the preferred stock certificate, except where gain is specifically required to be recognized.

Property for stock of a controlled corporation. If you transfer property to a corporation solely in exchange for stock in that corporation, and immediately after the trade you are in control of the corporation, you ordinarily will not recognize a gain or loss. This rule applies both to individuals and to groups who transfer property to a corporation. It does not apply if the corporation is an investment company.

However, if you had a gain from the disposition of depreciable property from this transaction, you may be taxed on part of the gain. See *Dispositions of Depreciable Property* in Publication 544 for more information.

For this purpose, to be in control of a corporation, you or your group of transferors must own, immediately after the exchange, at least 80% of the total combined voting power of all classes of stock entitled to vote, and at least 80% of the outstanding shares of each class of nonvoting stock of the corporation. See Chapter 1 of Publication 544 for information about other exchanges for corporate stocks.

If this provision applies to you, you must attach to your return a complete statement of all facts pertinent to the exchange.

Additional information. For more information on trades of stock, see *Nontaxable Trades* in Publication 550.

Explanation

The statement must include the following information:

- A description of the property transferred, with its cost or other basis
- The kind of stock received, including the number of shares and fair market value
- The principal amount and fair market value of any securities received
- The amount of money received, if any
- A description of any liabilities assumed by the corporation in the transaction, including the corporate business reason for the assumption

Generally, when you transfer property to a corporation that you alone will control in exchange for its stock, no gain or loss is recognized. "Control" means that you or your group of investors own at least 80% of the outstanding voting stock and at least 80% of the shares of all other classes of outstanding stock. However, if you receive property other than stock, then you may have to recognize a gain equal to that additional property's value. Moreover, if the property you transfer to the corporation has been depreciated, all or a portion of your gain may be ordinary income rather than a capital gain.

Under changes made by the Omnibus Budget Reconciliation Act of 1989, property must be transferred to the controlled corporation solely in exchange for stock. After 1989, it is no longer possible to receive securities in such a transfer tax-free. Therefore, securities are treated as "other property," and gain will be recognized to the extent of their value.

Example

You transfer machinery with an adjusted basis of $10,000 and a fair market value of $25,000 to a corporation that you and your associates will control in exchange for stock worth $20,000 and $5,000 in cash. You realize a $15,000 gain on the transfer of the machinery.

The transfer would have been tax-free if all you had received in return was stock. However, you have to report a gain of $5,000 for the cash received. Furthermore, if you previously claimed $5,000 or more in depreciation on the machinery, all of the $5,000 you received is treated as ordinary income under the depreciation recapture rules. For a complete discussion of depreciation, see Chapter 10, *Rental Income and Expenses*.

Explanation

There has been much litigation over the issue of momentary control—a situation that arises when investors hold the required 80% of stock only briefly and then dispose of a portion of it. Generally, momentary control is not sufficient to ensure preferential tax treatment if there was an agreement or prearranged plan for subsequent disposition of the stock acquired in the exchange.

Condemnations and involuntary exchanges. Condemnation is the process by which private property is legally taken by governments or certain entities, such as public utilities, in exchange for money or property.

If the condemnation award you receive is more than your adjusted basis in the condemned property, you have a gain. This gain may be postponed if you receive similar property instead of cash or if replacement property is purchased with the cash you receive. If you purchase replacement property, it must be put to a use similar to that of the original property. It also must be purchased within 2 years from the close of the first year in which any part of the gain on condemnation is realized. For business real property, the purchase must be made within 3 years.

If the condemnation award you receive is less than your basis in the property, you have a loss. This loss is not deductible if the property was your residence. Your loss, however, may be deducted if the property was used in a trade or a business or for the production of income. See Publication 549, *Condemnations and Business Casualties and Thefts*.

Insurance policies and annuities. You will not have a recognized gain or loss if you trade:

1) A life insurance contract for another life insurance contract or for an endowment or an annuity contract,
2) An endowment contract for an annuity contract, or for another endowment contract that provides for regular payments beginning at a date not later than the beginning date under the old contract, or
3) An annuity contract for another annuity contract.

The insured or annuitant must stay the same as under the original contract. Exchanges of contracts not included in this list, such as an annuity contract for an endowment contract, or an annuity or endowment contract for a life insurance contract, are taxable.

U.S. Treasury notes or bonds. You can trade certain issues of U.S. Treasury obligations for other issues, designated by the Secretary of the Treasury, with no gain or loss recognized on the trade. See *U.S. Treasury Notes or Bonds* under *Nontaxable Trades* in Publication 550 for information about the tax treatment of income from these investments. For other information on Treasury notes or bonds, write to:

Bureau of the Public Debt
U.S. Department of Treasury Customer Inquiry Section
Room 429
Washington, D.C. 20239–1000

Related Party Transactions

Special rules apply to the sale or trade of property between related parties.

TAXPLANNER

Special rules are imposed on taxpayers who try to avoid taxation on property gains by passing the property on to a trust. A special tax is imposed on a trust when the trust sells appreciated property within 2 years of having received it. The property may have been acquired by gift, through a bargain purchase, or as a transfer from another trust. The trust's gain is taxed at the highest rate that the donor of the property would have had to pay had he or she reported the gain on the sale in the same year in which the trust did.

Exception

This special tax is not imposed on a sale or an exchange that occurs within 2 years of the transfer of property if the sale or exchange takes place after the death of the donor of the property.

The purpose of the special tax is to prevent the grantor from taking advantage of a lower tax bracket in a trust. The law assumes, except in the case of death, that, if the property is sold within 2 years, this was the plan all along.

Like-kind exchanges. Generally, if you trade business or investment property for other business or investment property of a like kind, no gain or loss is recognized. See *Like-kind exchanges* discussed earlier under *Nontaxable Trades*.

This rule also applies to exchanges of property between related parties, defined next under *Loss on sale or trade of property*. However, if either related party disposes of the like-kind property within 2 years after the exchange, the gain or loss on the exchange must be recognized. Each related person must report any gain or loss not recognized on the original exchange on the tax return filed for the year in which the later disposition occurred.

These rules generally ***do not apply*** to:

Dispositions due to the death of either related person,
Involuntary conversions (see Chapter 1 of Publication 544), or
Exchanges or dispositions whose main purpose is not the avoidance of federal income tax.

The 2–year period does not include the period during which the holder's risk of loss is substantially diminished by:

The holding of a put on the property,
The holding by another person of a right to acquire the property, or
A short sale or any other transaction.

Loss on sale or trade of property. You cannot deduct a loss on the sale or trade of property, other than a distribution in complete liquidation of a corporation, if the transaction is directly or indirectly between you and the following related parties:

1) Members of your family — this includes only your brothers and sisters, half-brothers and half-sisters, spouse, ancestors (parents, grandparents, etc.), and lineal descendants (children, grandchildren, etc.).
2) A corporation in which you directly or indirectly own more than 50% in value of the outstanding stock (see *Constructive ownership of stock,* later).
3) A tax-exempt charitable or educational organization that is directly or indirectly controlled, in any manner or by any method, by you or by a member of your family, whether or not this control is legally enforceable.

In addition, a loss on the sale or trade of property is not deductible if the transaction is directly or indirectly between the following related parties:

1) A grantor and fiduciary, or the fiduciary and beneficiary, of any trust,
2) Fiduciaries of two different trusts, or the fiduciary and beneficiary of two different trusts, if the same person is the grantor of both trusts,
3) A trust fiduciary and a corporation of which more than 50% in value of the outstanding stock is directly or indirectly owned by or for the trust, or by or for the grantor of the trust,
4) A corporation and a partnership if the same persons own more than 50% in value of the outstanding stock of the corporation and more than 50% of the capital interest, or the profits interest, in the partnership,
5) Two S corporations if the same persons own more than 50% in value of the outstanding stock of each corporation,
6) Two corporations, one of which is an S corporation, if the same persons own more than 50% in value of the outstanding stock of each corporation,
7) Two corporations that are members of the same controlled group (under certain conditions, however, such losses are not disallowed but must be deferred),
8) Two partnerships if the same persons own, directly or indirectly, more than 50% of the capital interests or the profits interests, or
9) A partnership and a person who owns, directly or indirectly, more than 50% of the capital interest, or the profits interest, in the partnership.

If you sell or trade to a related party a number of blocks of stock or pieces of property in a lump sum, you must figure the gain or loss separately for each block of stock or piece of property. The gain on each item may be taxable. However, you cannot deduct the loss on any item. Also, you cannot reduce gains from the sales of any of these items by losses on the sales of any of the other items.

Indirect transactions. These include sales through a stock exchange. You cannot deduct your loss on the sale of stock through your broker if, for example, under a prearranged plan a related person or entity buys the same stock that you had owned.

Constructive ownership of stock. In determining whether a person ***directly or indirectly*** owns any of the outstanding stock of a corporation, the following rules apply.

Rule 1. Stock directly or indirectly owned by or for a corporation, partnership, estate, or trust is considered owned proportionately by or for its shareholders, partners, or beneficiaries.

Rule 2. An individual is considered to own the stock that is directly or indirectly owned by or for his or her family. Family includes only brothers and sisters, half-brothers and half-sisters, spouse, ancestors, and lineal descendants.

Rule 3. An individual owning, other than by applying rule 2, any stock in a corporation is considered to own the stock that is directly or indirectly owned by or for his or her partner.

Rule 4. When applying rule 1, 2, or 3, stock constructively owned by a person under rule 1 is treated as actually owned by that person. But stock constructively owned by an individual under rule 2 or 3 is not treated as owned by that individual for again applying either rule 2 or 3 to make another person the constructive owner of the stock.

Property received from a related party. If you sell or trade at a gain property that you acquired from a related party, you recognize the gain only to the extent it is more than the loss previously disallowed to the transferor. This rule applies only if you are the original transferee and you acquired the property by purchase or exchange. This rule does not apply if the transferor's loss was disallowed because of the wash sale rules, described in Publication 550 under *Wash Sales.*

Example 1. Your brother sells you stock with a cost basis of $10,000 for $7,600. Your brother cannot deduct the loss of $2,400. Later, you sell the same stock to an unrelated party for $10,500, thus realizing a gain of $2,900 ($10,500 − $7,600). Your reportable gain is $500: the $2,900 gain minus the $2,400 loss not allowed to your brother.

Example 2. If in *Example 1,* you sold the stock for $6,900 instead of $10,500, your recognized loss is only $700 ($7,600 basis minus $6,900). You cannot deduct the loss that was not allowed to your brother.

Explanation
Transactions between a trust and the relative of a trust beneficiary may be indirect related-party transactions. Similarly, the sale of stock by one spouse followed by the purchase by the other spouse of an equal number of the same corporation's shares is an indirect sale between related parties, even though both spouses deal through brokers on the New York Stock Exchange. However, if there is a significant time lapse between the two transactions—a month or more—the transactions are not considered linked.

Gain on sale or trade of depreciable property. The capital gain provisions do not apply, and your gain is ordinary income, if:

1) You have a recognized gain on the sale or trade of property, including a leasehold or a patent application, that is depreciable property in the hands of the party who receives it, and
2) The transaction is between you and a controlled entity, or you and a trust in which you or your spouse is a beneficiary.

See Chapter 2 in Publication 544 for more information.

Capital or Ordinary Gain or Loss

This section discusses the tax treatment of different types of investment transactions. For information about transactions that are not discussed here, refer to those IRS publications described at the beginning of this chapter.

If you have a taxable gain or a deductible loss from a transaction, it may be either a capital gain or loss or an ordinary gain or loss, depending on the circumstances. Generally, a sale or trade of a capital asset (defined later) results in a capital gain or loss. A sale or trade of a noncapital asset generally results in ordinary gain or loss. Depending on the circumstances, a gain or loss on a sale or trade of property used in a trade or business may be treated as either capital or ordinary, as explained in Publication 544. In some situations, part of your gain or loss may be a capital gain or loss and part may be an ordinary gain or loss.

Character of gain or loss. It is important for you to properly distinguish or classify your gains and losses as either ordinary or capital gains or losses. You also need to classify your capital gains and losses as either short-term or long-term. The correct classification helps you figure the limit on capital losses and your proper tax if you can use the *Schedule D Tax Computation* explained in Chapter 17, *Reporting Gains and Losses.*

For information about determining whether your capital gain or loss was short-term or long-term, see the discussion under *Holding Period,* later in this chapter.

Capital Assets and Noncapital Assets

For the most part, everything you own and use for personal purposes, pleasure, or investment is a **capital asset.** Some examples are:

• Stocks or bonds held in your personal account
• A house owned and used by you and your family
• Household furnishings
• A car used for pleasure or commuting
• Coin or stamp collections
• Gems and jewelry
• Gold, silver, or any other metal

The following items are **noncapital assets:**

1) **Property held mainly for sale to customers** or property that will physically become a part of the merchandise that is for sale to customers;
2) **Depreciable property** used in your trade or business, even though fully depreciated;
3) **Real property** used in your trade or business;
4) **A copyright, a literary, musical, or artistic composition, a letter or memorandum,** or similar property:
   a)   That you created by your personal efforts,
   b)   That was prepared or produced for you as a letter, memorandum, or similar property, or
   c)   That you acquired under circumstances (for example, by gift) entitling you to the basis of a person who created the property or for whom it was prepared or produced;
5) **Accounts or notes receivable** acquired in the ordinary course of a trade or business, or for services rendered as an employee, or from the sale of any of the properties described in (1); and
6) **U.S. Government publications** that you received from the government free or for less than the normal sales price, or that you acquired under circumstances entitling you to the basis of someone who received the publications free or for less than the normal sales price.

Property Held for Personal Use

Property held for personal use is a capital asset. Gain from a sale or exchange of that property is a capital gain. Losses from sales and exchanges of that property are not deductible, unless they result from personal casualties or thefts as discussed in Chapter 26, *Nonbusiness Casualty and Theft Losses.*

Example
You bought a car for personal use and later sold it for less than you paid for it. The loss is not deductible. However, if you had sold it for more than you paid for it, the gain would be taxable. A loss would be deductible only if, or to the extent that, the car was used for busi-

ness. If it was sold at a loss, the loss would be deductible. If the car had been stolen, you would have had a theft loss.

Caution: In determining the amount of the loss, what you paid for the car would have to be reduced by any depreciation allowed as a deduction. This would reduce the amount of the loss you could claim.

Explanation
While losses on personal property generally are not deductible, losses associated with a trade or a business may be. However, property originally held for personal use may be converted to business use under certain circumstances (and vice versa). There are very few court cases in this area, and those that exist do not provide much guidance about how long property must be rented before it is considered converted to business use. Each case depends on the specific facts and circumstances. In general, if a residence has been rented for a period of years, there is strong evidence that it has been converted to rental property.

Examples
In one case, a residence was rented out for several months under a bona fide lease. The property could not be reoccupied by the owner during the term of the lease. The owner's motive for leasing the house was to make money. The court held that the property had been converted to rental use.

In another case, a building was remodeled to make it fit for business purposes. This was considered to be strong evidence that the property was being converted to rental use.

Note: There are no clear-cut guidelines for what constitutes conversion to business use. However, simply listing the property with a rental agent is not sufficient. The guidelines in Chapter 16, *Selling Your Home*, may be helpful.

Investment Property
Investment property is a capital asset. Any gain or loss from its sale or exchange is generally a capital gain or loss.

Gold, silver, stamps, coins, gems, etc. These are capital assets except when they are held for sale by a dealer. Any gain or loss you have from their sale or trade generally is a capital gain or loss.

TAXPLANNER
If you collect gold, silver, stamps, antiques, and the like, you should be aware that losses from the sale or trade of such property generally are not deductible. In order to claim a loss, you must be able to show that your primary purpose in collecting the property was to make a profit. Furthermore, you must show that you were not collecting the items purely as a hobby or for personal enjoyment. Obviously, there may be a very fine line between a hobby and a profit-making activity.

Example
The Tax Court did *not* allow a taxpayer to deduct a loss on the sale of antiques he used to furnish his home. The

taxpayer argued that he was speculating on large increases in the value of the antiques. The Tax Court emphasized his personal use of the antiques and noted that most of the taxpayer's sales of antiques were merely a means of financing the acquisition of more antiques.

Stocks, stock rights, and bonds. All of these (including stock received as a dividend) are capital assets except when held for sale by a securities dealer. However, if you own small business stock, see *Losses on Small Business Stock* in Publication 550.

Worthless securities. Stocks, stock rights, and corporate or government bonds with interest coupons or in registered form, which became worthless during the tax year, are treated as though they were capital assets sold on the last day of the tax year if they were capital assets in your hands. To determine whether they are long-term or short-term capital assets, you are considered to have held the stocks or securities until the last day of the year in which they became worthless. See *Holding Period,* later.

If you are a cash-basis taxpayer and make payments on a negotiable promissory note that you issued for stock that became worthless, you can deduct these payments as losses in the years you actually make the payments. Do not deduct them in the year the stock became worthless.

How to report loss. Report worthless securities on line 1 or line 9 of Schedule D (Form 1040), whichever is applicable. In columns (c) and (d), write "Worthless."

Filing a claim for refund. If you do not claim a loss for a worthless security on your original return for the year it becomes worthless, you can file a claim for a credit or refund due to the loss. Use Form 1040X, *Amended U.S. Individual Income Tax Return.* You must file it within 7 years from the date your original return for that year had to be filed, or 2 years from the date you paid the tax, whichever is later. For more information about filing a claim, see *Amended Returns and Claims for Refund* in Chapter 1, *Filing Information.*

Explanation
A security is considered worthless when it has no recognizable value. You should be able to establish that the worthless security had value in the year preceding the year in which you take the deduction and that an identifiable event reduced the value to zero, causing the loss in the year in which you deduct it. A drop in the value of a stock, even though substantial, does not constitute worthlessness. The courts have held that, if stock is sold for a very nominal sum (e.g., less than 1 cent per share), that is proof of worthlessness.

TaxPlanner
The deduction for a worthless security must be taken in the year in which it becomes worthless, even if it is sold for a nominal sum in the following year. If you do not learn that a security has become worthless until a later year, you should file an amended return for the year in which it became worthless. Since it may be difficult to determine exactly when a stock becomes worthless, the capital loss deduction should be claimed in the earliest year in which such a claim may be reasonably made.

If you hold securities that seem to be on the verge of worthlessness, it may be easier to sell them now and take your capital loss without waiting for proof of worthlessness.

When securities are bought on credit, the timing of the deduction for worthlessness depends on the type of debt you have incurred. If the stock is purchased by giving the seller a note and the stock becomes worthless before the note is paid off, you may deduct the loss only as you make the payments on the note. However, if you borrow the funds from a third party, you may deduct the loss in the year in which the stock becomes worthless. In either case, an accrual basis taxpayer takes the deduction in the year in which the security becomes worthless.

TaxOrganizer
You should keep any documents indicating the date on which the security becomes worthless. Examples of sufficient documentation are bankruptcy documents and financial statements.

Discounted debt instruments. Treat your gain or loss on the sale, redemption, or retirement of a bond or other evidence of indebtedness originally issued at a discount as follows.

Treat gains on *short-term federal, state, or local government obligations* as ordinary income up to the ratable share of the acquisition discount. This treatment applies to obligations that have a fixed maturity date not more than one year from the date of issue. However, this treatment does not apply for state or local government obligations with tax-exempt interest. Any gain in excess of the ratable share of the acquisition discount is capital gain. Any loss is capital loss. *Acquisition discount* is the excess of the stated redemption price at maturity over your basis in the obligation.

However, do not treat such gains as income to the extent you previously included the discount in income. This amount increases your basis in the obligation. See *Discount on Short-Term Obligations* in Publication 550 for more information.

Treat gains on *short-term nongovernment obligations* (whether or not tax exempt) as ordinary income up to the ratable share of original issue discount (OID). This treatment applies to obligations that are not short-term government obligations and that have a fixed maturity date of not more than one year from the date of issue.

However, to the extent you previously included the discount in income, you do not have to include it in income again. This amount increases your basis. See *Discount on Short-Term Obligations* in Publication 550 for more information.

Long-term debt instruments issued after 1954, and before May 28, 1969 (or before July 2, 1982, if a government issue). If you sell, exchange, or redeem for a gain one of these debt instruments, the part of your gain due to the original issue discount (OID) is interest income at the time of the sale or redemption. The balance of the gain is capital gain. If, however, there was an intention to call the debt instrument before maturity, the entire amount of OID is treated as ordinary income at the time of sale. This treatment of taxable gain also applies to corporate instruments issued after May 27, 1969, under a written commitment that was binding on that date and thereafter.

See *Original Issue Discount (OID)* in Chapter 8, *Interest Income,* for information on OID.

Long-term corporate debt instruments issued after May 27, 1969, and government instruments issued after July 1, 1982. If you hold one of these debt instruments, you must include a part of the OID in your gross income each year that you own the instrument. Your basis in the instrument is increased by the amount of OID that you have included in your gross income. See *Original Issue Discount (OID)* in Chapter 8, *Interest Income,* for information about the OID that you must report on your tax return.

If you sell or exchange the debt instrument before it reaches maturity, your gain on the sale is a capital gain, provided the debt instrument was a capital asset. Any amount that you receive on the retirement of a debt instrument is treated in the same way as if you had sold or exchanged that instrument.

However, if at the time the instrument was originally issued there was an intention to call it before its maturity, your gain on the sale of the instrument is ordinary income to the extent of the entire OID reduced by any amounts of OID previously includible in your income. The rest of the gain is capital gain.

See *Capital or Ordinary Gain or Loss* in Publication 550 for more information about the tax treatment on the sale or redemption of discounted debt instruments.

Explanation

Any interest income recognized on the sale of a market discount bond is to be added to your cost in order to compute any capital gain on the bond.

See Chapter 8, *Interest Income*, for a more detailed discussion of original-issue discount (OID) income.

Tax-exempt state and local government bonds. If these bonds were originally issued at a discount before September 4, 1982, and you acquired them before March 2, 1984, treat your part of the OID as tax-exempt interest. Do not include it in income.

However, any gain from market discount is taxable on disposition or redemption of tax-exempt bonds. If you bought the bonds before May 1, 1993, the gain from market discount is capital gain. If you bought the bonds after April 30, 1993, the gain from market discount is ordinary income.

You figure the market discount by subtracting the price you paid for the bond from the sum of the original issue price of the bond and the amount of accumulated OID from the date of issue that represented interest to any earlier holders.

Example

On March 1, 1984, Kathy bought a $10,000 tax-exempt state government bond for $9,000 that was originally issued at $8,500 on September 3, 1982. Kathy must treat her part of the original issue discount (OID) as tax-exempt interest. The accumulated OID from the date of issue to the date Kathy purchased the bond was $600. On August 15, 1993, Kathy sold the bond for $9,800. Kathy must report a $100 capital gain on the sale. The market discount in the bond is the original issue price ($8,500) plus the accumulated OID from the date of issue that represented interest to any earlier holders ($600) and minus the price Kathy paid for the bond ($9,000). As a result, the market discount is $100 ($9,100–$9,000). The remaining difference of $700 ($9,800–$9,100)) is treated as tax-exempt interest.

You must accrue OID on tax-exempt state and local government bonds issued after September 3, 1982, and acquired after March 1, 1984. Your adjusted basis at the time of disposition is figured by adding accrued OID to your basis. You must accrue OID on tax-exempt obligations under the same method used for OID on corporate obligations issued after July 1, 1982.

A loss on the sale or other disposition of a tax-exempt state or local government bond is deductible as a capital loss.

Example

On March 2, 1984, Julie bought a $10,000 tax-exempt state government bond for $9,100 that was originally issued at $8,500 on September 4, 1982. On August 15, 1993, Julie sold the bond for $9,800. Julie previously accrued $500 of OID tax-exempt interest over the period she held the bond. Julie must report a $200 capital gain on the sale of the bond ($9,800 − ($9,100 + $500)).

Notes of individuals. If the evidence of indebtedness you bought at a discount was issued by an individual, its retirement generally will not be given capital gain treatment. But if you sell the discounted instrument to someone other than the original borrower, any gain is a capital gain as long as it was not acquired in the ordinary course of your trade or business for services rendered or from the sale of inventory. In figuring your adjusted basis in the note, do not reduce your original basis by any interest payments or by the part of the principal payments you received that is taxable discount income.

Example. You bought a $10,000 note of an individual for $6,000 on which no payments had been made. You receive principal payments totaling $4,000. Then you sell the note for $3,800. Only 60% ($6,000/$10,000) of the $4,000 is a return of your investment. The balance is discount income. You reduce your cost by $2,400 ($4,000 × 60%) to figure your adjusted basis. Your capital gain is $200, figured as follows:

Selling price of note		$3,800
Minus adjusted basis of note:		
Cost of note	$6,000	
Minus return on investment	2,400	3,600
Capital gain		**$ 200**

The OID rules discussed in Chapter 8, under *Original Issue Discount (OID),* apply to obligations issued by individuals after March 1, 1984. The OID rules will not apply to loans between individuals in amounts of $10,000 or less (including the outstanding amounts of prior loans) if the lender is not in the business of lending money, except if a principal purpose of the loan is to avoid federal tax.

Obligations issued in bearer form. Generally, any loss on a registration-required obligation held in bearer form is not deductible. Any gain on the sale or other disposition of such obligation is ordinary income, unless the issuer was subject to a tax on the issuance of the obligation.

A registration-required obligation is any obligation except an obligation:

1) That is issued by a natural person,
2) That is not of a type offered to the public,
3) That has a maturity at the date of issue of not more than 1 year, or
4) That was issued before 1983.

Explanation

There are other kinds of sales or trades that many interests enter into. Some of these transactions are discussed below. The tax rules are very complicated. Professional advice should be obtained if you plan to invest in any of these transactions.

Short sales. A short sale occurs when the seller borrows the property delivered to the buyer and, at a later date, either buys substantially identical property and delivers it to the lender or makes delivery out of such property held by the seller at the time of the sale. The holding period on a short sale is usually determined by the length of time the seller actually holds the property that is eventually delivered to the lender to close the short sale.

Example

Even though you do not own any stock in the Ace Corporation, you contract to sell 100 shares of it, which you borrow from your broker. After 13 months, when the price of the stock has fallen, you buy 100 shares of Ace Corporation stock and immediately deliver them to your broker to close out the short sale. Your gain is treated as a short-term capital gain, because your holding period for the delivered property is less than 1 day.

Explanation

Long and short positions. If you have held substantially identical property to the property sold short for 1 year or less on the date of the short sale, the following two rules apply:

1. Any gain on closing of the short sale is a short-term gain
2. The holding period of the substantially identical property begins on the date of the closing of the short sale or on the date of the sale, gift, or other disposition of this property, whichever comes first

These two rules also apply if you acquire substantially identical property after the originating short sale and before the closing of the short sale.

Example

On February 6, 1992, you bought 100 shares of Able Corporation stock for $1,000. On July 6, 1992, you sold short 100 shares of similar Able stock for $1,600. On November 6, 1992, you purchased 100 more shares of Able stock for $1,800 and used them to close the short sale. On this short sale, you realized a $200 short-term capital loss.

On February 7, 1993, you sold for $1,800 the stock originally bought on February 6, 1992. Although you have actually held this stock for more than 1 year, by using rule 2, the holding period is treated as having begun on November 6, 1992, the date of the closing of the short sale. The $800 gain realized on the sale is therefore a short-term capital gain.

TaxAlert

Short sales take away the tax benefits of long-term holding periods with respect to any substantially identical stock held in a long position, unless you have already met the long-term holding requirement at the time you make the short sale.

Treatment of losses. If, on the date of a short sale of a capital asset, you have held substantially identical property for more than 1 year, any loss you have on the short sale is treated as a long-term capital loss, even though the property used to close the sale was held for 1 year or less.

TaxOrganizer

You should keep a copy of your broker confirmation statement for the purchase of any securities or options. Also, keep a copy of the Form 1099-B provided by your broker for any sales of securities or options.

TaxPlanner 1

Short sales against the box. Selling short against the box means that you are selling borrowed securities while owning substantially identical securities that you later deliver to close the short sale. Many investors with unrealized profits near year's end may want to consider a short sale against the box, which locks in profit while delaying the recognition of a gain.

Example

Jane Doe owned 100 shares of XYZ Corporation. Near the end of 1992, she borrowed from her broker another 100 shares of XYZ, which she then sold short. In 1993, she delivered her original 100 shares to close out her short position. Any gain or loss realized on the sale at year's end was locked in; it was not recognized until 1993, the year in which the short position was closed out.

TaxPlanner 2

Purchasing put options. Acquiring a put option means that you are buying an option contract to sell 100 shares of stock at a set price during a specific time period. Investors who own appreciated securities that they are not yet ready to sell because of tax reasons often buy put options as a way of protecting their securities against possible price declines.

If the stock price subsequently increases, you obtain the benefit of the price increase less the cost of the put, which expires as worthless. If the stock price declines, however, you may either sell your shares at the put option price or sell the put option separately.

Example

Jim Smith purchased 100 shares of XYZ stock in July, 1992 at $25 per share. The selling price in November, 1992 was $55. Jim could have sold his shares in November and realized a $30 per-share gain, but it would have been taxed in 1992. Since Jim believed that the stock still had some upward potential and also wanted to postpone recognizing the gain, he bought a put option with an expiration date in March, 1993, giving him the right to sell his stock at $55 per share. He locked in his gain and limited his loss to the cost of the put option.

Tax treatment of put options

1. If you sell the put—in lieu of exercising it—the gain or loss is a short-term or long-term capital gain or loss, depending on how long the put has been held.
2. If you neither sell nor exercise the put, the expiration is treated as a sale or an exchange of the put on the expiration date. Whether the loss you incur is a short-term or long-term capital loss depends on how long the put has been held.
3. If you exercise the put, its cost increases your basis in the underlying securities and thus is included in computing your gain or loss at the time of the securities' sale. Whether the gain or loss is short-term or long-term usually depends on the holding period of the underlying stock at the time the put option was acquired.

TAXPLANNER 3

Stock index options. Unlike a put option, which is based on shares in a specific company, a stock index option represents a group of stocks. For example, an index option is available that is keyed to Standard & Poor's 500 stock averages. Investors use stock index options to reduce portfolio exposure to general market or industry fluctuations and to improve their return on investment. Stock index options may also be used to protect current paper gains (gains you have "on paper" but have not yet realized) and to save taxes when a taxpayer owns appreciated stock that has not been held long enough to qualify for long-term capital gain treatment.

If you expect the stock market to go down, you might purchase stock index put options. If the market does go down, the put options gain in value, perhaps offsetting the loss in any appreciated stock you might hold.

TAXPLANNER 4

Writing covered call options. If you have stock that has appreciated in value but want (1) to defer the gain until the following year and (2) to provide yourself with protection from market declines, consider writing a covered call option with an expiration date next year. A covered call is the selling of an option to purchase shares that you own at a specified price within a set time frame. If the purchaser of the call doesn't exercise it until next year (or lets it lapse), both the amount you receive from selling the call and the proceeds from disposition of the stock are not reported until the following year.

One disadvantage is: You give up the opportunity to benefit from a price increase in the stock you own above the option exercise price.

Example

Bill purchased 100 shares of XYZ stock for $20 per share on December 21, 1991. On December 22, 1992, the stock was selling for $50 per share, but Bill wanted to defer the gain until 1993 and protect himself against a market decline. Bill wrote a covered call option, agreeing to sell his 100 shares for $50 per share at any time within the next 3 months. He received $3 per share for selling this call option. Bill has acquired protection

against a market decline, because he now has $3 per share in the bank. If the person who bought the option does not exercise it, Bill reports the $3 per share as a short-term capital gain in 1993. If the option is exercised, the $3 per share is added to the $50 per share exercise price.

If the stock had continued to appreciate, Bill could have bought other shares of the stock in the open market to deliver against the call, or he could have chosen to purchase, or buy back, the option. A short-term loss would have been realized when the option position was closed in either of these two ways.

Explanation

Wash sales. Losses from wash sales or exchanges of stocks or securities are not deductible. However, the gain from these sales is taxable. Commodity futures contracts are not stock or securities and are not covered by the wash sale rule. Any position of a straddle acquired after June 23, 1981, however, is covered by the wash sale rule. This includes futures contracts. See Publication 550, *Investment Income and Expenses.*

A wash sale occurs when you sell stock or securities and, within 30 days before or after the sale, you buy, acquire in a taxable exchange, or acquire a contract or option to buy substantially identical stock. The substantially identical stock may be acquired by subscription for newly issued stock as well as by buying old stock. However, the unallowable loss is added to the basis of the newly acquired stock or security.

Example

You buy 100 shares of X stock for $1,000. At a later date, you sell these shares for $750. Then, within 30 days of the sale, you acquire 100 shares of the same stock for $800. Your loss of $250 on the sale is not deductible. However, the unallowed loss ($250) is added to the cost of the new stock ($800) to get the basis of the new stock ($1,050).

Explanation

For purposes of the wash sale rule, a short sale is considered complete on the date on which the short sale is entered into if on that date

1. You own (or, on or before that date, you enter into a contract or option to acquire) stock or securities identical to those sold short, and
2. You later deliver such stock or securities to close the short sale

Otherwise, a short sale is not considered complete until the property is delivered to close the sale.

Example

On June 3, you buy 100 shares of stock for $1,000. You sell short 100 shares of the stock for $750 on October 7. On October 8, you buy 100 shares of the same stock for $750. You close the short sale on November 18 by delivering the shares bought on June 3. The $250 loss ($1,000 − $750) is not deductible, because the date of entering into the short sale (October 7) is deemed to be the date of sale for wash sale purposes and substantially identical stock was purchased within 30 days from the date of the sale. Therefore, the wash sale rule applies, and the loss is not deductible.

Explanation

Options. Gain or loss from the sale or exchange of a purchased option to buy or sell property that is a capital asset in your hands, or would be if you acquired it, is a capital gain or loss.

If you do not exercise an option to buy or sell, and you have a loss, the option is treated as having been sold or exchanged on the date that it expired.

The capital asset treatment does not apply

1. To a gain from the sale or exchange of an option, if the gain from the sale of the property underlying the option would be ordinary income, or
2. To a dealer in options, if the option is part of inventory, or
3. To a loss from failure to exercise a fixed-price option acquired on the same day on which the property identified in the option was acquired; such loss is not deductible.

If you grant an option on stocks, securities, commodities, or commodity futures and it is not exercised, the amount you receive (if you are not in the business of granting options) is treated as a short-term capital gain reportable on Schedule D (Form 1040), regardless of the classification of the property in your hands. If the option is exercised, you add the option payment to other amounts you receive to figure the amount you realize on the sale of the property. The classification of your gain or loss is then determined by the type of property you sold.

Your holding period for property acquired under an option to purchase begins on the day after the property was acquired, not the day after the option was acquired.

Commodity futures. A commodity future is a contract for the sale or purchase of some fixed amount of a commodity at a future date for a fixed price. The contracts are treated as either (1) hedges to ensure against unfavorable price changes in a commodity bought or sold in the course of business or (2) capital investments.

Gains and losses on hedging contracts for a commodity purchased in the ordinary course of a trade or a business to ensure the price of, and an adequate supply of, the commodity for use in the business are treated as ordinary business gains and losses.

Straddles. A straddle is a position that offsets an interest an investor has in personal property other than stock. It may take the form of a futures contract, an option, or cash. The purpose of a straddle is to reduce an individual's risk of property loss.

Example

Karen bought an option to have 5,000 bushels of wheat delivered to her in June, 1993. At the same time, she bought an option to deliver 5,000 bushels of wheat in July, 1993. Karen has a straddle.

Explanation

Complex rules established in 1981 for the treatment of straddles are designed to prevent the deferral of income and the conversion of ordinary income and capital gains.

Example 1

ABC stock is selling at $30. Peter purchases two options on ABC. He purchases a call to buy 100 shares of the stock for $25 per share and a put to sell 100 shares of the stock for $35 per share. As long as the stock does not stay at $30, one of the options will produce a gain and the other one will produce a loss.

Assume that by the end of the year the price of ABC is $34. The value of the call should have increased by $400, and the value of the put should have declined by $400. Under prior law, Peter could have repurchased the call and recognized the loss on his tax return, while the gain on the put could have been deferred to the following year.

Under current law, Peter cannot recognize the loss on the call until he recognizes the offsetting gain on the put.

Example 2

James purchases 100 shares of BCD stock on August 2, 1992, at $40 per share. On November 1, the BCD sells at $46 per share. James sells a call due in February, 1993 for $100. In December, the stock is selling for $50, and James repurchases the call for $400. James has a $300 short-term loss, which under prior law was deductible. Also, when he sells BCD in the following year, he could have a long-term gain. The loss cannot be deducted until the year in which the call is closed. The holding period of BCD stock is also changed. If James sells BCD in February, 1993 for $50 per share, he would have a short-term gain of $700 to report (the $1,000 gain on the stock minus the $300 loss on the call).

A note of caution: There are many special terms, rules, and exceptions to learn if you want to try your luck on these investment strategies. You should study the markets and the tax law very carefully.

TAXALERT

The 1993 Tax Act provides that specific types of capital gains can be treated as ordinary income for certain additional financial transactions. Certain gains from the sale of any "conversion transaction" entered into after April 30, 1993 can now be treated as ordinary income.

A conversion transaction occurs when substantially all of the expected return from an investment is attributable to the time value of the net investment. In addition, if the transaction falls within one of the following classifications, it will be considered a conversion transaction:

1. acquiring property, and on a contemporaneous basis, contracting to sell the same property for a determined price;
2. certain straddles;
3. any transaction that is marketed as or sold as producing capital gains; or
4. other transactions that the U.S. Treasury Department will describe in future regulations.

A special rule exempts options dealers and commodities traders from the above provisions, but anti-abuse rules prevent limited partners or entrepreneurs from unduly profiting by this exception.

The amount of gain that can be considered ordinary income will not exceed the amount of interest that would have accrued on your net investment in the property at a rate equal to 120% of the applicable Federal rate for the period of time you held the investment. This amount is then reduced by the amount of ordinary income that was recognized from the conversion transaction and any interest expense in connection with purchasing the property.

Example

Suzanne acquires stock for $10,000 on January 1, 1994, and on that same day agrees to sell it to Rick for $11,500 on January 1, 1996. Assume that the applicable Federal rate is 5%. On January 1, 1996, Suzanne delivers the stock to Rick in exchange for $11,500. If the transaction was not a conversion transaction, Suzanne would have recognized a $1,500 capital gain ($11,500–$10,000).

However, the 1993 Tax Act considers this arrangement as a conversion transaction. Thus, $1,236 of her gain would be recharacterized as ordinary income (120% of 5% compounded for two years, applied to an investment of $10,000).

Computation of Ordinary Gain	
Investment	$10,000
Applicable Rate (120% × 5%)	6%
	600
Investment	10,000
Amount After First Year	10,600
Applicable Rate (120% × 5%)	6%
	636
Amount After First Year	10,600
	11,236
Investment	(10,000)
Ordinary Income	$1,236

The difference between the ordinary income and the appreciation, $264 ($1,500–$1,236), is classified as a long-term capital gain.

Additional requirements are imposed on conversion transactions with respect to built-in losses, options dealers, commodities traders, and limited partners and limited entrepreneurs in an entity that deals in options or trades in commodities.

Since the application of these rules are complex, you should consult your tax advisor when considering a potential conversion transaction.

Explanation

Sale of business. The sale of a business is not usually the sale of one asset. If you sell your business or your interest in a business and need more information, see Publication 544, *Sales and Other Dispositions of Assets.*

Cancelling a sale of real property. If you sell real property to an individual and the sales contract gives the buyer the right to return the property to you for the amount paid, you may not have to recognize gain or loss on the sale. You will not recognize gain or loss if the property is returned to you within the same tax year as the sale. However, if the property is returned to you in a future tax year, you must recognize gain or loss in the year of the sale. In the year in which the property is returned to you, your new basis in the property will be equal to the amount you give back to the buyer.

Lease cancelled or sold. If a tenant receives payments for the cancellation of a lease on property used as the tenant's home, a gain is taxed as a capital gain but any loss is not deductible. If the lease was used in the tenant's trade or business, gain or loss may be capital or ordinary, as explained in Publication 544, *Sales and Other Dispositions of Assets.*

Payments received by a landlord for cancellation of a lease are ordinary income and not capital gains.

Subleases. When you transfer leased property under an arrangement in which the new occupant takes over your monthly lease payments and also pays you an amount each month for relinquishing use of the property, a sublease has been entered into and payments you receive are ordinary income.

Repossession of real property. If real property that is a capital asset in your hands is repossessed by the seller under the terms of the sales contract or by foreclosure of a mortgage, you may have a capital gain or loss. The gain or loss is the difference between your adjusted basis in the property (purchase price with adjustments) and the full amount of your obligation cancelled, plus any money received, in exchange for the property. Losses on repossessions of property held for personal use, however, are not deductible. See Publication 537, *Installment Sales.* Also see the discussion of installment sales in this chapter.

Subdivision of land. If you own a tract of land and, in order to sell or exchange it, you subdivide it into individual lots or parcels, you may receive capital gains treatment on at least a part of the proceeds if you meet the following four conditions:

1. You are not a dealer in real estate.
2. You have not made any major improvement on the tract while you held it that substantially enhances the value of the lot or parcel sold, and no such improvement will be made as part of the contract of sale with the buyer. A substantial improvement is generally one that increases the value of the property by more than 10%. Some improvements that are considered substantial are structural work on commercial and residential buildings, laying down hard-surface roads, and installing utility services.
3. You have held the land for at least 5 years, unless you got it by inheritance or devise.
4. You did not previously hold the tract or any lot or parcel on such tract mainly for sale to customers in the ordinary course of your trade or business (unless the tract previously would have qualified for this treatment), and, during the same tax year in which the sale occurred, you were not holding any other land for sale to customers in the ordinary course of trade or business.

Gain on sale of lots. If your land meets these tests, the gain realized on the sale or exchange will be treated in the following manner:

If you sell less than six lots or parcels from the same tract, the entire gain is a capital gain. In figuring the number of lots or parcels sold, two or more adjoining lots sold to a single buyer in a single sale are counted as only one parcel.

When you sell or exchange the sixth lot or parcel from the same tract, the amount by which 5% of the selling price is more than the expenses of the sale is treated as ordinary income, and the rest of any gain will be a capital gain. Five percent of the selling price of all lots sold or exchanged from the tract in the tax year in which the sixth lot is sold or exchanged, and in later years, is treated as ordinary income.

If you sell the first six lots of a single tract in 1 year, to the extent of gain, the lesser of 5% of the selling price of each lot sold or the gain is treated as ordinary income. On the other hand, if you sold the first three lots in a single tract in 1 year and the next three lots in the following year, the 5% rule would apply only to the gains realized in the second year.

The selling expenses of the sale must first be deducted from the part of the gain treated as ordinary income, and any remaining expenses must be deducted from the part treated as a capital gain. You may not deduct the selling expenses from other income as ordinary business expenses.

Example 1

You sold five lots from a single tract last year. This year, you sell the sixth lot for $20,000. Your basis for this lot is $10,000, and your selling expenses are $1,500. Your gain is $8,500, all of which is capital gain, figured as follows:

Selling price		$20,000
Minus:		
Basis	$10,000	
Expense of sale	1,500	11,500
Gain from sale of lot		$ 8,500
5% of selling price	$ 1,000	
Minus: Expense of sale	1,500	
Gain reported as ordinary income		–0–
Gain reported as capital gain		$ 8,500

Because the selling expenses are more than 5% of the selling price, none of the gain is treated as ordinary income.

Example 2

Assume in Example 1 that the selling expenses are $800. The amount of gain is $9,200, of which $200 is ordinary income and $9,000 is capital gain, figured as follows:

Selling price		$20,000
Minus:		
Basis	$10,000	
Expense of sale	800	10,800
Gain from sale of lot		$ 9,200
5% of selling price	$ 1,000	
Minus: Expense of sale	800	
Gain reported as ordinary income		200
Gain reported as capital gain		$ 9,000

Explanation

Loss on sale of lots. The 5% rule does not apply to losses. If you sell a lot at a loss, it will be treated as a capital loss if you held it for investment.

For more information on subdivision of land, see Publication 544, *Sales and Other Dispositions of Assets*.

Inventions. An invention is usually a capital asset in the hands of the inventor, whether or not a patent has been applied for or has been obtained. The inventor is the individual whose efforts created the property and who qualifies as the original and first inventor or joint inventor.

If you are an inventor and transfer all substantial rights to patent property, you may get special tax treatment, as described below, if the transfer is not to your employer or to a related person.

If, for a consideration paid to the inventor, you acquire all the substantial rights to patent property before the invention is reduced to practice (tested and operated successfully under operating conditions), you may, when you dispose of your interest, get special tax treatment, if you are not the employer of the inventor or related to the inventor (as described later). However, if you buy patent property after it is reduced to practice, it may be treated as either a capital or a noncapital asset, depending on the circumstances.

Special tax treatment. If you are the inventor or an individual who acquired all the substantial rights to the patent property before the invention was reduced to practice, and you transfer all the substantial rights or an undivided interest in all such rights, the transfer will be treated as a sale or an exchange of a long-term capital asset. This rule applies even if you have not held the patent property for more than 1 year and whether or not the payments received are made periodically during the transferee's use of the patent or are contingent on the productivity, use, or disposition of the property transferred.

Courts have enforced the substantial rights requirement very strictly. Generally, a patent seller must be able to show that any rights he or she retains are insubstantial in order to treat the sale of rights in the patent property as a long-term capital gain.

The U.S. Courts of Appeals for the Sixth, Seventh, and Ninth Circuits have overturned lower court rulings that allowed patent owners transferring exclusive rights to impose geographical limitations within the United States on the person purchasing the patent. However, the official IRS position is that a transfer of all substantial rights may be limited to one or more countries.

Payment for the patent may be received by the seller in a lump sum, as an installment sale, as a fixed percentage of all future profits from the patent, or as a fee per item produced. All these methods qualify for capital gains treatment, even if the total amount of payment is uncertain.

Transfers between related parties. The special tax treatment does not apply if the transfer is either directly or indirectly between you and certain related parties.

Copyrights. Literary, musical, or artistic compositions, or similar property, are not treated as capital assets if your personal efforts created them or if you got the property in such a way that all or part of your basis in the property is determined by reference to a person whose personal efforts created the property (e.g., if you got the property as a gift). The sale of such property, whether or not it is copyrighted, results in ordinary income.

However, if you get such property, or a copyright to it, in any other way, the amounts you got for granting the exclusive use or right to exploit the work throughout the life of the copyright are treated as being received from the sale of property. It does not matter if the payment is a fixed amount or a percentage of receipts from the sale, performance, exhibition, or publication of the copyright work, or an amount based on the number of copies sold, performances given, or exhibitions made. It also does not matter if the payment is made over the same period as that covering the grantee's use of the copyrighted work.

Loss on deposits in an insolvent or bankrupt financial institution. If you can reasonably estimate your loss on a deposit because of the bankruptcy or insolvency of a qualified financial institution, you can choose to treat the amount as either a casualty loss or an ordinary loss in the current year. Either way, you claim the loss as an itemized deduction. Otherwise, you can wait until the year of final determination of the actual loss and treat the amount as a nonbusiness bad debt (discussed later under *Nonbusiness Bad Debts*) in that year.

If you claim a casualty loss, attach **Form 4684,** *Casualties and Thefts,* to your return. Each loss must be reduced by $100. Your total casualty losses for the year are reduced by 10% of your adjusted gross income.

If you claim an ordinary loss, report it as a miscellaneous itemized deduction on line 20 of Schedule A (Form 1040). The maximum amount you can claim is $20,000 ($10,000 if you are married filing separately) reduced by any expected state insurance proceeds. Your loss is subject to the 2% of adjusted gross income limit. You cannot choose to claim an ordinary loss if any part of the deposit is federally insured.

You cannot choose either of these methods if:

You own at least 1% of the financial institution,
You are an officer of the institution, or
You are related to such an owner or officer.

If the actual loss that is finally determined is more than the amount deducted as an estimated loss, you can claim the excess loss as a bad debt. If the actual loss is less than the amount

deducted as an estimated loss, you must include in income (in the final determination year) the excess loss claimed.

TaxPlanner

Whether you elect to claim a casualty or an ordinary loss in the year in which the requirements for the election are met will depend on a number of factors. First, you must compare the available **casualty loss deduction** (after reducing your loss by $100 plus 10% of your adjusted gross income) to your **ordinary loss deduction** (after adding the loss to other miscellaneous itemized deductions and reducing the total by 2% of adjusted gross income). The ordinary loss election is available on deposits of up to $20,000 ($10,000 if you are married and file a separate return). The $20,000 limitation applies to each financial institution, not each deposit or each tax year. This is important if you hold deposits in more than one institution.

The election to claim an ordinary loss, once made, cannot be revoked unless you obtain the consent of the IRS.

You should also consider whether it is better to forgo either election and claim the entire amount as a **capital loss** from a nonbusiness bad debt (see *Nonbusiness Bad Debts,* following). This might be advisable if you have sufficient capital gain income with which to offset the capital loss. Consult with your financial advisor when you're considering these elections.

Example

Judy Porter estimates that she has incurred a total loss of her $30,000 bank account with an insolvent financial institution. Her account is not federally insured. Judy's adjusted gross income (AGI) is $70,000, and she has no miscellaneous itemized deductions. Judy wants to review the tax consequences of electing to claim the estimated loss as either a casualty loss or an ordinary loss, which is treated as a miscellaneous itemized deduction.

The net deduction available under each method is as follows:

	Casualty loss	Ordinary loss
Estimated loss	$ 30,000	$ 20,000*
$100 casualty loss limitation	(100)	n/a
10% AGI limitation	(7,000)	n/a
2% AGI limitation	n/a	(1,400)
Net deduction available	$ 22,900	$ 18,600

* Limited to $20,000 per institution.

In addition, if the loss actually sustained by Judy exceeds the amount deducted as an estimated loss, she can claim the excess loss as a bad debt in the year in which that loss is finally determined. Thus, if Judy elects to treat the estimated loss as an ordinary loss and she determines in a subsequent year that her entire balance of $30,000 was lost, she could claim an additional $10,000 deduction for bad debts. This would increase her cumulative deductions under this alternative to a total amount of $28,600.

Sale of annuity. The part of any gain on the sale of an annuity contract before its maturity date that is attributable to interest accumulated on the contract is ordinary income.

Nonbusiness Bad Debts

If someone owes you money that you cannot collect, you have a bad debt. You may be able to deduct the amount owed to you when you figure your tax for the year the debt becomes worthless. For a bad debt to qualify for the deduction, the debt must be genuine. A debt is genuine if it arises from a debtor-creditor relationship based on a valid and enforceable obligation to repay a fixed or determinable sum of money.

Bad debts that you did not get in the course of operating your trade or business are nonbusiness bad debts. To be deductible, nonbusiness bad debts must be totally worthless. You cannot deduct a partially worthless nonbusiness bad debt.

Unpaid salaries, wages, etc. To deduct a bad debt, you must have a basis in it — that is, you already included the amount in your income or you loaned out your cash. For example, you cannot claim a bad debt deduction for court-ordered child support not paid to you by your former spouse. If you are a cash-basis taxpayer, and most individuals are, you cannot take a bad debt deduction for expected income. Examples include unpaid salaries, wages, rents, fees, interest, dividends, etc., unless you previously included the amount in income.

business bad-debt treatment is limited to those situations in which the taxpayer derives his or her main source of income from credit transactions. Whether or not you are in a trade or business is a question of fact. The greater the regularity of the activity, however, the more likely that a trade or business exists.

Example

You occasionally lend money to individuals starting new businesses. That is an investment activity, not a trade or a business.

2. **You make a loan to a corporation in which you are an employee and a stockholder.** You are allowed a business bad-debt deduction if the loan was made primarily to protect your salary. If the loan was made primarily to protect your investment, it is considered a nonbusiness loan. The larger your investment is in a company and the smaller your salary is from it, the greater the chance that a court will determine that a loan you make to the company is for nonbusiness purposes.

TaxPlanner 1

If you make advances to a corporation you own, the IRS may attempt to recharacterize the advances as equity capital rather than bona fide loans. This might postpone a deduction for a bad debt until the year in which your stock is wholly worthless. Therefore, it is important that you properly document advances you make to the corporation as bona fide loans. Generally, written, interest-bearing instruments with fixed repayment terms will qualify as bona fide debt.

TaxPlanner 2

If you want a loan to a family member to be considered a bona fide debt, you should document the transaction so that it is clear that both parties expect and intend repayment of the loan.

A child may borrow money from his or her parents for a business venture. To indicate that the borrowed money is not intended as a gift, the parents should draft a note saying who owes whom money. (The parties might check with a lawyer about the exact form the note should take.) If the note calls for partial payments of the debt, each payment should be made on time. This provides evidence that a legitimate creditor-debtor relationship exists. To further support their status as creditors, parents may consider investigating the business in which the child is investing the borrowed money. An arm's length lender typically makes such an investigation.

It's also a good idea for the note from the parents to provide that the money be repaid with interest. Charging interest provides another bit of evidence that the loan between parents and child is a valid arm's length transaction. Failure to charge adequate interest can also have important gift and income tax consequences. For details, see Chapter 8, *Interest Income.*

Example 1

Gail lends her son $20,000, which the son then invests in a new business venture. Gail draws up a note that provides for a specific repayment schedule and a stated rate of interest. Collateral is also established on the note to provide Gail with some security. Later, before any payments on the note have been made, the son's business venture fails. Despite repeated efforts to collect the debt, Gail is able to recover only a small amount based on the collateral established at the time of the loan.

Gail may take a bad-debt deduction of $20,000, less the amount of collateral she recovered. Gail's son may deduct his loss as a business loss.

Example 2

Assume the same facts as in Example 1 except that Gail does not document the loan. No note is drawn up, and no specific provisions are made about when her son will repay the loan. If the son's business venture fails, he may deduct his loss. The mother, however, may not take a bad-debt deduction.

Explanation

Loans in your business. If you are in a business or a profession, you may have bad debts that come from loans you make to your clients. If you are not in the business of lending money and the loans have no close relationship to your business or profession, these bad debts are nonbusiness bad debts.

Mechanics' and suppliers' liens. Workers and material suppliers sometimes file liens against property because of debts owed by a builder or a contractor. If you pay off such a lien to avoid foreclosure and loss of your property, you are entitled to repayment from the builder or contractor. If the debt is uncollectible, you may take a deduction for a bad debt.

Insolvency of contractor. You can take a bad-debt deduction for the amount you deposit with a contractor if the contractor becomes insolvent and you are unable to recover (collect) your deposit. If the deposit is for work that is not related to your trade or business, it is a nonbusiness bad-debt deduction.

Secondary liability on home mortgage. If you sell your home and the purchaser assumes your mortgage, you may remain secondarily liable for repayment of the mortgage loan. If the purchaser defaults on the loan, you may have to make up the difference if the house is then sold for less than the amount outstanding on the mortgage. You can take a bad-debt deduction for the amount you pay to satisfy the mortgage if you cannot collect it from the purchaser.

Corporate securities that become worthless are generally deductible as capital losses. This includes shares of stock, stock rights, bonds, debentures, notes, or certificates, as explained in Chapter 17, *Reporting Gains and Losses.*

TaxPlanner

Frequently, it is difficult to establish the year in which a corporate security becomes worthless. One guide is a publication called *Capital Changes Reporter,* published by Commerce Clearing House. The section called

"Worthless Securities" provides a current list of companies whose securities have lost their value.

It is even more difficult to determine when a closely held business becomes worthless. It is not necessary for the company to declare bankruptcy. If you are aware that a company is insolvent, you may be able to take a loss. If the business continues to operate and has more than nominal assets, however, it may be only temporarily insolvent. If that is the case, you may not be able to take a loss.

Explanation
Recovery of a bad debt. Any amount recovered for a bad debt deducted in a previous year generally must be included in your income in the year in which the amount was recovered. However, you may exclude the amount recovered up to the amount of the deduction that did not reduce your income subject to tax in the year deducted. Recovery of amounts deducted in previous years is discussed in Chapter 13, *Other Income*.

Example
In 1991 Bill had a $25,000 **long-term capital gain,** a $25,000 bad-debt loss, and other deductions totaling $2,480. Bill had no **taxable income** for 1991.

In 1993, Bill recovered the entire $25,000 debt. To figure how much he should include in his 1993 income, see the calculations below.

	1991 with bad debt	1991 without bad debt
Income:		
Net long-term capital gain	$25,000	$25,000
Bad-debt loss	(25,000)	
Adjusted gross income	–0–	$25,000
Less:		
Standard deductions	–0–	$3,000
Personal exemption	–0–	$1,950
Taxable income	–0–	$20,050

The calculations show that Bill's 1991 taxable income was reduced by $20,050 by including the bad debt. Therefore, $20,050 is included in Bill's taxable income for 1993, the year in which he collected the $25,000 debt.

Explanation
Business bad debts. There are two crucial differences in the treatment of business bad debts and nonbusiness bad debts:

1. Business bad debts are treated as **ordinary losses,** which may be deducted directly from gross income. Nonbusiness bad debts are short-term capital losses and should be shown on Schedule D along with your short-term and long-term gains and losses from other sources. The maximum capital loss that you may use to offset your other income each year is $3,000. See Chapter 17, *Reporting Gains and Losses*, for further information.

2. A business bad debt may be just *partially* worthless and still give rise to a tax deduction. A nonbusiness bad debt has to be totally worthless.

Example
Janet Jones, an accrual basis taxpayer, performs some plumbing work for XYZ Corporation and sends them an invoice for $20,000 in 1992. In 1993, Janet learns that XYZ Corporation will not be able to pay the entire amount of the bill. She may claim a bad-debt deduction for the amount of the invoice that is worthless.

Explanation
Some businesses use the **reserve method** of computing bad-debt expense in keeping their books. Under this method, an estimate of accounts expected to be uncollectible is computed, based on prior years' experience, and the amount is placed in reserve as bad-debt expense.

The reserve method is no longer allowed for tax purposes, except for certain financial institutions. Therefore, a business bad debt will be allowed only if it is **specifically charged off** the taxpayer's books during the year. Therefore, if you own a business with a large number of accounts receivable, to maximize your allowable tax deduction, you should carefully review old accounts at year end to make sure all worthless accounts are written off.

Guarantees. If you guarantee payment of another person's debt and then have to pay it off, you may be able to take a bad-debt deduction for your loss. It does not matter in what capacity you make the guarantee, whether as guarantor, endorser, or indemnitor.

To qualify for a bad-debt deduction, the guarantee must either be entered into with a profit motive or be related to your trade or business or employment.

A worthless debt qualifies as a *nonbusiness bad debt* if you can show that your reason for making the guarantee was to protect your investment or to make a profit. If you make the guarantee as a favor to friends and are not given anything in return, it is considered a gift and you may not take a deduction.

You are justified in taking the deduction if you can show that you *expected* to receive something in return at a future time. The expectation must be reasonable.

Example 1
A taxpayer who ran a successful car rental operation loaned money to her brother-in-law to assist him in starting his own car rental business. The taxpayer received a promissory note due 1 year after the date of the loan, with a stated rate of interest. The brother-in-law's business venture was a flop, and the taxpayer eventually took a bad-debt deduction. The court allowed the deduction, pointing out that, at the time the loan was made, the brother-in-law was solvent and there was a reasonable expectation that the rental business would serve as a source of repayment.

Example 2
A taxpayer loaned his brother-in-law about $2,000 over a 2–year period to help him support the taxpayer's sister

and her children. During the entire period, the brother-in-law was low on cash and his business was failing. There was no record of the loan or any understanding about how it would be repaid. The court ruled that the taxpayer could not take a bad-debt deduction, because there was no reasonable expectation that the loan would be repaid. Instead, the court said that the $2,000 "loan" should be considered a gift.

How to report bad debts. Deduct nonbusiness bad debts as short-term capital losses on Schedule D (Form 1040), *Capital Gains and Losses*. There are limits on how much of your capital losses may be deducted. For a discussion of these limits, see Chapter 17.

In Part I, line 1 of Schedule D, enter the name of the debtor and "statement attached," in column (a), and the amount of the bad debt in column (f). Use a separate line for each bad debt.

For each bad debt, attach a statement to your return that contains:

1) A description of the debt, including the amount, and the date it became due,
2) The name of the debtor, and any business or family relationship between you and the debtor,
3) The efforts you made to collect the debt, and
4) Why you decided the debt was worthless. For example, you could show that the borrower has declared bankruptcy, or that legal action to collect would probably not result in payment of any part of the debt.

Filing a claim for refund. If you do not deduct a bad debt on your original return for the year it becomes worthless, you can file a claim for a credit or refund due to the bad debt. Use Form 1040X, *Amended U.S. Individual Income Tax Return*. You must file it within 7 years from the date your original return for that year had to be filed, or 2 years from the date you paid the tax, whichever is later. For more information about filing a claim, see *Amended Returns and Claims for Refund* in Chapter 1, *Filing Information*. **Additional information.** For more information, see *Nonbusiness Bad Debts* in Publication 550.

For information on business bad debts, see Chapter 14 of Publication 535.

Losses on Small Business Stock

You can deduct as an ordinary loss, rather than as a capital loss, your loss on the sale, trade, or worthlessness of certain stock you own in a small business corporation or certain stock in a small business investment company. Gain on this stock is capital gain and is reported on Schedule D (Form 1040) if the stock is a capital asset in your hands. See *Losses on Small Business Stock* and *Losses on Small Business Investment Company Stock* in Publication 550.

Explanation
While individuals who own certain stock in a small business investment company may be allowed to deduct as an ordinary loss a loss on the sale, exchange, or worthlessness of their stock, the amount that may be claimed is subject to an annual limit of $50,000 ($100,000 on **joint returns**) per taxpayer.

Ordinary loss treatment is generally available only to the original owner. If you obtain stock in a small business corporation or investment company through pur-

chase, gift, inheritance, or the like, you may not claim ordinary losses. Similarly, if small business stock is owned through a partnership, to claim a loss, you must have been a partner when the stock was issued. If you were not a partner at such time and the partnership later distributed the stock to the partners, you may not take an ordinary loss deduction.

To qualify for ordinary loss treatment, you must own section 1244 stock. This is the stock of a small business corporation or investment company with total capital of under $1 million that meets a *passive income test.* To meet this test, the aggregate of any gross receipts generated over the last 5 years by royalties, rents, **dividends,** interest, annuities, and sales of stock or securities must be less than 50% of total gross receipts taken in by the corporation in the 5-year period. In addition, the corporation's stock must have been issued for money or property other than securities. Stock that is convertible into other securities of the corporation is not treated as section 1244 stock.

TAXPLANNER

The loss limitation of $50,000 per taxpayer is an annual limitation. Therefore, if you are considering a sale of section 1244 stock that is expected to produce a loss of over $50,000, you should consider structuring the transaction so that stock sales will take place in more than 1 year.

Example
Craig, a bachelor, has owned 10,000 shares of qualified small business stock for several years. The stock has a basis of $150,000. He plans to dispose of the stock but expects to realize only $50,000 on the sale. If he sells all 10,000 shares in 1993, he will recognize a $100,000 loss in 1 year. Only $50,000 will be deductible as an ordinary loss. The other $50,000 will be treated as a long-term capital loss. The long-term capital loss can be offset against other capital gains, but the excess can be deducted at the rate of only $3,000 per year.

If Craig sells 5,000 shares in 1993 and 5,000 shares in 1994 and receives the same price, he will still have a total loss of $100,000. Yet, since $50,000 of the loss will be recognized in 1993 and the other $50,000 in 1994, Craig may treat both losses as ordinary losses, which makes the total $100,000 loss fully deductible.

Craig should use Form 4797 to report the section 1244 loss as a sale of a noncapital asset.

Holding Period

If you sold or traded investment property, you must determine whether any capital gain or loss is a short-term or long-term capital gain or loss by determining your holding period.

Long term or short term. If you hold investment property *more than one year,* any capital gain or loss is a *long-term* capital gain or loss. If you hold the property *one year or less,* any capital gain or loss is a *short-term* capital gain or loss.

To figure how long you held the investment property, begin counting on the date after the day you acquired the property. The same date of each following month is the beginning of a new month regardless of the number of days in the preceding month. The day you disposed of the property is part of your holding period.

Example. If you buy investment property on February 3, 1993, you start counting on February 4. The 4th of each following month is the beginning of a new month. If you sell the property on February 3, 1994, your holding period is not more than one year and you will have a short-term capital gain or loss. If you sell it on February 4, 1994, your holding period is more than one year and you will have a long-term capital gain or loss.

Securities traded on established market. For securities traded on an established securities market, your holding period begins the day after the *trading date* you bought the securities, and ends on the trading date you sold them. Ignore the settlement date for holding period purposes.

Example. You are a cash-basis, calendar-year taxpayer. You sold stock at a gain on December 28, 1993. According to the rules of the stock exchange, the sale was closed by delivery of the stock 5 trading days after the sale, on January 5, 1994. You received payment of the sales price on that same day. Report your gain on your 1993 return, even though you received the payment in 1994. The gain is long term or short term depending on whether you held the stock more than one year. Your holding period ended on December 28 (the trading date). If you had sold the stock at a loss, you would also report it on your 1993 return.

TaxSaver

If you sell stock at the end of the year, your December statement from your broker may not reflect the sale. The broker may not record the transaction until the closing date, which could be the following year. To avoid the penalties associated with underreporting, be sure to examine your January statement as well. You should also receive Form 1099-B from your broker. This form should list all your sales for the year based on the trade date.

Nontaxable trades. If you acquire investment property in a trade for other investment property and your basis for the new property is determined, in whole or in part, by your basis in the old property, your holding period of the new property begins on the day following the date you acquired the old property. Chapter 14, *Basis of Property,* discusses basis.

Property received as a gift. If you receive a gift of property and your basis is determined by the donor's basis, your holding period is considered to have started on the same day as the donor's holding period. See *Property Received as a Gift* in Chapter 14, *Basis of Property.*

If your basis is determined by the fair market value of the property, your holding period starts on the day after the date of the gift.

Inherited property. If you inherit investment property and your basis for it is:

1) Determined with reference to its fair market value at the date of the decedent's death,
2) Determined with reference to its fair market value at the alternate valuation date, or
3) The decedent's adjusted basis (for appreciated property),

your capital gain or loss on any later disposition of such property is treated as a long-term capital gain or loss. You are considered to have held the property for more than one year, even if you dispose of it within one year after the decedent's death. See *Inherited Property* in Publication 551, *Basis of Assets.*

Real property bought. To figure how long you have held real property bought under an unconditional contract, begin counting on the earlier of the day after you received title to it, or the day after you took possession and assumed the burdens and privileges of ownership. However, taking delivery or possession of real property under an option agreement is not enough to start the holding period. The holding period cannot start until there is an actual contract of sale. The holding period of the seller cannot end before that time.

Mutual fund stock. If you received exempt-interest dividends on mutual fund stock that you held 6 months or less and sold at a loss, you cannot claim the part of the loss that is equal to or less than the exempt-interest dividends. You must report the rest of the loss as a short-term capital loss.

See Publication 564, *Mutual Fund Distributions,* for more information on mutual fund distributions.

Real estate investment trust (REIT). If you received a capital gain distribution on REIT stock that you held 6 months or less and sold at a loss, you report as a long-term capital loss the part of the loss that is equal to, or less than, the long-term capital gain distribution. This rule does not apply to dispositions of stock under a periodic liquidation plan. See *Capital Gain Distributions* in Chapter 9 for information on capital gain distributions.

Automatic investment service and dividend reinvestment plans. If you take part in a plan to buy stock through a bank or other agent, the date the bank or other agent buys the stock is your purchase date for figuring the holding period of that stock. In determining your holding period for shares bought by the bank or agent, full shares are considered bought first and any partial shares are considered bought last. If a full share or a partial share was bought over a period of more than one purchase date, your holding period for that share is a split holding period. A part of the share is considered to have been bought on each date that stock was bought by the bank or other agent with the proceeds of available funds.

Nontaxable stock dividend. The holding period for new stock you received as a nontaxable stock dividend begins on the same day as the holding period of the old stock. This rule also applies to stock acquired in a "spin-off," which is a distribution of stock or securities in a controlled corporation.

Nontaxable stock rights. Your holding period for nontaxable stock rights begins on the same day as the holding period of the underlying stock. The holding period for stock acquired through the exercise of stock rights begins on the date the right was exercised.

Rollover of Gain

This section discusses the tax-free rollover of certain gains from the sale of publicly traded securities. If you buy certain replacement property and make the choice described in this section, you postpone part or all of your gain. You postpone the gain by adjusting the basis of the replacement property as described in *Basis of replacement property,* later. This postpones your gain until the year you dispose of the replacement property.

You qualify to make this choice if you meet the following tests:

1) You sell publicly traded securities at a gain after August 9, 1993. Publicly traded securities are securities traded on an established securities market.
2) Your gain from the sale is a capital gain.
3) During the 60-day period beginning on the date of the sale, you buy replacement property. This replacement property must be either common stock or a partnership interest in a *specialized small business investment company (SSBIC)* (any part-

nership or corporation licensed by the Small Business Administration under Section 301(d) of the Small Business Investment Act of 1958, as in effect on May 13, 1993).

Amount of gain postponed. If you make the choice described in this section, you must recognize gain only up to the following amount:

1) The amount realized on the sale, *minus*
2) The cost of any common stock or partnership interest in an SSBIC that you bought during the 60-day period beginning on the date of sale (and did not previously take into account).

If this amount is less than the amount of your gain, you can postpone the rest of your gain, subject to the limit described next. If this amount is more than the amount of your gain, you must recognize the full amount of your gain.

Limit on gain postponed. The amount of gain you can postpone each year is limited to the smaller of:

1) $50,000 ($25,000 if you are married and file a separate return), or
2) $500,000 ($250,000 if you are married and file a separate return), *minus* the amount of gain you postponed for all earlier years.

Basis of replacement property. You must subtract the amount of postponed gain from the basis of your replacement property.

How to report gain. If you choose to postpone gain, report the entire gain realized from the sale on line 1 or line 9 of Schedule D (Form 1040), whichever is appropriate. Directly below the line on which you report the gain, enter "SSBIC Rollover" in column (a) and enter the amount of gain postponed in column (f).

Also attach a schedule showing:

1) How you figured the postponed gain,
2) The name of the SSBIC in which you purchased common stock or a partnership interest,
3) The date of that purchase, and
4) Your new basis in that SSBIC stock or partnership interest.

16 | Selling Your Home

Introduction

*Your home is probably the most valuable **asset** you own and may increase in value. Consequently, you may have a significant gain—and lots of taxes to pay—when you sell it. With careful planning, you may defer many of these taxes and avoid others altogether. Alternatively, due to the recent downturn in the real estate market in many parts of the country, some homes will be sold at a loss. Unfortunately, a loss on the sale of your home is generally not deductible. This chapter tells you what you should and shouldn't do when you're considering selling your home.*

You may, for example, want to fix up your home before putting it on the market. Such expenses may be deducted from the selling price of the house, which may reduce the gain you recognize and the taxes you pay on the sale if the sales proceeds are not all reinvested in a new principal residence. The repairs, however, must be done within a 90-day period that ends on the date on which the contract to sell your home is made.

Your home is probably your best tax shelter. The tax system continues to give many breaks to homeowners. You may deduct the cost of real estate taxes and, subject to certain limitations, the cost of interest paid on your mortgage. (See Chapter 24, Interest Expense, for an explanation of the limitations on deducting home mortgage interest.) If you're 55 or older, up to $125,000 of the gain on the sale may be completely exempt from taxes. In addition, by reinvesting the proceeds in a new principal residence, if the cost of such new residence exceeds the selling price of the old residence, you may defer the entire gain you realize on the sale of your residence. Some states continue to allow various types of residential energy conservation and solar energy tax credits against your state income tax liability. Refer to your state's tax return instruction guide to determine if such credits are available.

Any gain you are required to recognize on the sale of a home will be treated as long-term capital gain if the home was held for more than one year. Currently, the maximum tax rate applicable to net capital gains is significantly lower than the top tax rate applicable to ordinary income.

Important Changes for 1993

Additional Form 1099–S information. For homes sold after 1992, the information reported (generally by the settlement agent) to the IRS and seller of the home on Form 1099–S, *Proceeds From Real Estate Transactions*, must include the part of any real estate tax that is treated as tax imposed on the buyer. See *Real estate taxes* under *New Home,* later in this chapter.

Basis of home. Beginning in 1993, you must generally reduce the basis of your home by an amount equal to any part of a public utility subsidy you received (directly or indirectly) that is excluded from income. This rule applies to any public utility subsidy you receive after 1992 for the purchase or installation of an energy conservation measure for your home. See *Adjusted Basis* under *Basis,* later in this chapter.

Important Reminders

Change of address. If you change your mailing address, be sure to notify the IRS using Form 8822, *Change of Address*. Mail it to the Internal Revenue Service Center for your old address (addresses for the Service Centers are on the back of the form).

Seller-financed mortgages. If you sold your home and hold a note, mortgage, or other financial agreement, you may have to report the buyer's address and social security number (SSN) when you report the interest income. See *Installment sale* under *How and When to Report,* later.

Abandonment, foreclosure, or repossession. If your home was abandoned, foreclosed on, or repossessed, you have a sale or disposition that you should report on Form 2119, *Sale of Your*

Home. If the disposition resulted in a gain, also report it on Schedule D (Form 1040).

You should receive **Form 1099–A,** *Acquisition or Abandonment of Secured Property,* from the lender who acquired the property. This form will have the information you need to determine whether you have a capital gain or loss, or ordinary income from a canceled debt on the abandonment, foreclosure, or repossession. See *Foreclosure, Repossession, or Abandonment* in Chapter 2 of Publication 544, *Sales and Other Dispositions of Assets,* for more information.

Combat zone service. The replacement period for postponing tax on any gain from the sale of your home is suspended if you served in the Persian Gulf Area combat zone. For this suspension, the area is considered a combat zone beginning August 2, 1990. See *Time Allowed for Replacement* under *Postponement of Gain,* later, for more information.

Form 1099–S. The law requires that transactions involving the sale of most residential real estate property be reported to the IRS on Form 1099–S, *Proceeds From Real Estate Transactions.* Real estate brokers are prohibited from charging any customer separately for preparing Form 1099–S.

Maximum tax rate on capital gains. A taxable gain on the sale of your home is a capital gain. The maximum tax rate on a net capital gain is 28%. See *How and When to Report,* later.

Qualified mortgage bonds and mortgage credit certificates. If you sell your main home that was purchased or improved with federally subsidized financing, you may have to recapture part of the subsidy. See *Recapture of Federal Subsidy,* later.

Home sold with undeducted points. If you have not deducted all the points you paid to secure a mortgage on your old home, you may be able to deduct the remaining points in the year of the sale. See *Mortgage ending early* under *Points* in Chapter 24 of this publication.

This chapter discusses the tax treatment of the sale of your main home. It covers the following topics:

- How to treat any gain or loss from selling your main home,
- How to postpone paying tax on all or part of the gain from selling your main home,
- How you can exclude all or part of the gain if you are age 55 or older, and
- How to report the sale on Form 2119.

In certain cases, you must postpone paying tax on the gain from the sale of your main home if you buy or build a new main home within specific time limits. You must report the sale of your main home using Form 2119, *Sale of Your Home.* This is true whether you sell the home at a gain or a loss and whether or not you buy another main home. You must file Form 1040 with Form 2119 for the year of sale, even if you are not otherwise required to file a return.

If you exchange your home for other property, the exchange is treated as the sale of your home. The same rules for reporting a sale apply to reporting an exchange. (See *Trading homes* under *Old Home,* later.) However, if you transfer your home to your spouse, or former spouse incident to your divorce, no gain or loss is recognized on the transfer. Therefore, the rules in this chapter do not apply. See *Property Settlements* in Publication 504, *Divorced or Separated Individuals,* for more information.

Useful Items

You may want to see:

Publication

- ☐ **521** Moving Expenses
- ☐ **523** Selling Your Home
- ☐ **530** Tax Information for First-Time Homeowners
- ☐ **551** Basis of Assets

Form (and Instructions)

- ☐ **Schedule D (Form 1040)** Capital Gains and Losses
- ☐ **1040X** Amended U.S. Individual Income Tax Return
- ☐ **2119** Sale of Your Home
- ☐ **8822** Change of Address
- ☐ **8828** Recapture of Federal Mortgage Subsidy

Gain or Loss On the Sale

If you sell your main home, you may be able to postpone paying tax on all or part of the gain from the sale. If you have a loss on the sale, you cannot deduct it.

Gain on sale. You ***must postpone*** the tax on all the gain from the sale if you buy a new home and the purchase price of the new home is at least as much as the adjusted sales price of the old home. You will generally be subject to tax on all or part of the gain if you do not buy a new home, or if the purchase price of the new home is less than the adjusted sales price of the old home. However, if you are age 55 or older, you may qualify to exclude the gain as explained later.

Loss on sale. You ***cannot*** deduct a loss on the sale of your home. It is a personal loss. However, you must report the sale on Form 2119. The loss has no effect on the basis of your new home.

TAXSAVER

While you cannot deduct a loss on the sale of your home, if you own a house as an investment (and do not use it for personal purposes) you may be able to deduct any loss realized.

Example

Tom bought a house in 1985. From 1985 to 1990, Tom lived in the house with his mother. In 1990, Tom died and bequeathed the house to his mother. Tom's mother continued to live in the house until 1993, at which time she sold it at a loss. She cannot deduct the loss because it is a loss from the sale of a personal residence. Assume instead that Tom bequeathed the house to his friend Carmine, and Carmine held the house as an investment (and did not use it for personal purposes) from 1990 to 1993. If Carmine sold the house at a loss in 1993, he would have a deductible loss, because it is generated from the sale of property held for investment, and not from the sale of a personal residence. See Chapter 17, *Reporting Gains and Losses,* for limitations on deductibility of capital losses and for the treatment of losses from the sale of property used in a trade or business.

Joint ownership. If you and your spouse sell your jointly owned home and file a joint return, you figure and report your gain or loss as one taxpayer. If you file separate returns, each of you must figure and report your own gain or loss according to your ownership interest in the home. Your ownership interest is determined by state law.

If you and a joint owner other than your spouse sell your jointly owned home, each of you must figure and report your own gain or loss according to your ownership interest in the home. Each of you applies the rules discussed in this chapter on an individual basis.

Purchase price at least as much as sales price. Your entire gain on the sale of your home is not taxed at the time of the sale if, within *2 years before or 2 years after* the sale, you buy and live in another home that costs at least as much as the adjusted sales price (described later) of the old home. If you are on active duty in the Armed Forces, if you served in a combat zone, or if your tax home is outside the U.S., the 2-year period after the sale may be suspended. See *People Outside the U.S.* and *Members of the Armed Forces* under *Time Allowed for Replacement,* later.

Explanation
The new home may be a cooperative apartment, a condominium, a single-family home, a trailer, a houseboat, or almost any other type of residence. However, if you buy a multiple-family dwelling, only the part that you personally use should be included in figuring the amount of the gain that you may defer on sale or exchange. A newly constructed home also qualifies as a replacement residence.

Purchase price less than sales price. If the purchase price of your new home is less than the adjusted sales price of your old home and you buy and live in the new home within 2 years before or 2 years after the sale, the gain taxed in the year of the sale is the lesser of:

1) The gain on the sale of the old home, or
2) The amount by which the adjusted sales price of the old home is more than the purchase price of the new home.

TaxSaver
If you purchase a new home for a price that is less than the sales price of your old home you should make any improvements to the new home within two years of the sale of the old home. To the extent these improvements add to the home's value or extend its useful life, they will be considered part of the cost of the new home and thus decrease the amount of gain required to be recognized.

You need not use the same funds received from the sale of your old home to buy or build your new home. For example, you can use less cash than you received, increase the amount of your mortgage loan, and still postpone the tax on your gain.

Recapture of Federal Subsidy

If you financed your home under a federally subsidized program (loans from tax-exempt qualified mortgage bonds or loans with mortgage credit certificates), you may have to recapture all or part of the benefit you received from that program when you sell or otherwise dispose of your home. You recapture the benefit by increasing your federal income tax for the year of the sale. The postponement and exclusion of gain provisions discussed later in this chapter do not apply to this recapture tax.

The recapture tax is figured on **Form 8828.** If your mortgage loan is subject to the recapture rules, you must file Form 8828 even if you do not owe a recapture tax.

Loans subject to recapture rules. The recapture of the subsidy applies to loans provided after 1990 that:

1) Came from the proceeds of qualified mortgage bonds issued after August 15, 1986, or
2) Were based on mortgage credit certificates issued after December 31, 1990.

The recapture also applies to assumptions of these loans.

If your mortgage loan is subject to this recapture rule, you should have received a notice containing information that you need to figure the recapture tax.

When the recapture applies. The recapture of the federal mortgage subsidy applies only if you meet *all* of the following conditions.

1) You sell or otherwise dispose of your home at a gain,
2) Your income for the year of disposition exceeds that year's adjusted qualifying income for your family size for that year (related to the income requirements a person must meet to qualify for the federally subsidized program), and
3) You dispose of your home during the first 9 years after the date you closed your mortgage loan.

When recapture does not apply. The recapture does *not* apply if any of the following situations apply to you:

- The mortgage was secured solely as a qualified home improvement loan not in excess of $15,000,
- The home is disposed of as a result of your death,
- You dispose of the home more than 9 years after the date you closed your mortgage loan,
- You transfer the home to your spouse, or to your former spouse incident to a divorce, where no gain is included in your income,
- You dispose of the home at a loss, or
- Your home is destroyed by a casualty, and you repair it or replace it on its original site within 2 years after the destruction.

See Publication 523 for information on reporting this recapture tax.

Postponement of Gain

Generally, you *must* postpone tax on the gain on the sale of your main home if you buy a new main home within the replacement period and it costs at least as much as the adjusted sales price of the old home. However, if you are age 55 or older and meet certain qualifications, no tax applies to the extent you elect to exclude the gain. See *Exclusion of Gain,* later.

This section explains the time allowed for replacement, how to determine the taxable gain, if any, and how to report the sale.

You may want to use the *Worksheet for Postponement of Gain* when you read the examples in this chapter. This worksheet appears later in this chapter as *Table 16–1.*

TaxSaver
There may be unusual circumstances under which you want to **recognize the gain** you realize on selling your home when the proceeds of sale are being reinvested in

a new home. To do this, you must delay buying the new residence until after the expiration of the statutory replacement period.

The tax on the gain is *postponed, not forgiven.* You subtract any gain that is not taxed in the year you sell your old home from the cost of your new home. This gives you a lower basis in the new home. If you sell the new home in a later year and again replace it, you continue to postpone tax on your gain.

Example. You sold your home in 1993 for $90,000 and had a $5,000 gain. Within the time allowed for replacement, you bought another home for $103,000. The $5,000 gain will not be taxed in 1993 (the year of sale), but you must subtract it from the $103,000. This makes the basis of your new home $98,000. If you later sell the new home for $110,000, and you do not buy and live in a replacement home within the allowed time, you will be subject to tax on the $12,000 gain ($110,000 − $98,000) in the year of that sale.

Main Home

Usually, the home in which you live is your main home. The home you sell and the one you buy to replace it must both qualify as your main home. *Property used partly as your home and partly for business or rental* and *Home changed to rental property* are discussed later under *Old Home.*

Your main home can be a houseboat, a mobile home, a cooperative apartment, or a condominium.

Fixtures (permanent parts of the property) generally are part of your main home. Furniture, appliances, and similar items that are not fixtures generally are not part of your main home.

Explanation
The IRS relies on the law of the state in which your property is located to determine whether a particular item is a fixture. The general rule is: Items that are easily movable are not fixtures.

Land. You may sell the land on which your main home is located, but not the house itself. In this case, you cannot postpone tax on any gain you have from the sale of the land.

Example. You sell the land on which your main home is located. Within the replacement period, you buy another piece of land and move your house to it. This sale is not considered a sale of your main home, and you cannot postpone tax on any gain on the sale.

More than one home. If you have more than one home, only the sale of your main home qualifies for postponing the tax. If you have two homes and live in both of them, your main home is the one you live in most of the time.

Example 1. You own and live in a house in town. You also own beach property, which you use in the summer months. The town property is your main home; the beach property is not.

Example 2. You own a house, but you live in another house that you rent. The rented home is your main home. However, if a house you own is your main home, you can temporarily rent it out before its sale without changing its character as your main home.

Explanation
If you own more than one property, it is important to determine which is your principal, or main, residence.

The IRS will not issue a ruling on whether or not a home qualifies as a principal residence. The gain on the sale of your principal residence may be deferred, but the gain on the sale of your nonprincipal residence or rental property is taxed in the year of the sale.

To determine which is your principal residence, the IRS considers the following: where you vote, the address you use on your tax returns, the address you claim to be your residence in other financial dealings, where your children go to school, where you work, where your car is registered, and where you belong to social and religious groups.

That the property is currently rented or has been rented in the past does not mean that you may not consider it to be your principal residence. For example, a property that is rented out for a brief period while you are away or while you are trying to sell it should not affect the property's status as your principal residence.

Example 1
In one case, a taxpayer had occupied a house as his principal residence, but, when he married, he and his wife moved to a rented house. The taxpayer's mother continued to live in the house. Later, the taxpayer sold the house to his mother and used the proceeds to purchase a new home within the statutory period allowed to defer a gain. The Tax Court did not allow him to defer the gain, ruling that the house he sold was not his principal residence at the time of sale.

Example 2
A taxpayer attempted to sell his home when he was transferred to another city. Due to a weak real estate market, the taxpayer had to rent the old home for various lengths of time, before he sold it 3 years later. After vacating his old home, the taxpayer rented a home for 2 years before purchasing a new home 1 year prior to the sale of his old home. The Tax Court ruled that the old home was his principal residence at the time of the sale, even though he had vacated his old residence 3 years prior to the sale, with no intention of returning. The court held that, based on the facts and circumstances of this particular case, the taxpayer's primary intent was to sell his old home upon vacating it. The court felt that the rentals of the old home were necessitated by the exigencies of the real estate market and were ancillary to sales efforts. One key factor that influenced the court's decision was that the taxpayer left the old home vacant for periods of time, between rental periods, in order to facilitate the sale of the home.

Example 3
A member of Congress owned a house in Washington, D.C., and also maintained a residence in his home district, which he used occasionally. The IRS ruled that his Washington, D.C. home was his principal residence, since that was where he and his family lived most of the time.

Example 4
If you live in one home for the summer months and live in a different residence during the other 9 months of the year, you may not claim your summer home as your principal residence.

Figure 16-A. An Illustration of the Time Allowed for Replacement

This illustrates the time period during which you can replace your main home and postpone tax on the gain from sale. It does not apply if you served in the Persian Gulf Area combat zone. *Caution: The dates in this chart are for illustration purposes only. Your dates may be different.*

	If you sold your former home on June 30, 1993:	
	Your time for replacement begins on:	Your time for replacement ends on or before:
Most taxpayers	June 30, 1991 (2 years before sale)	June 30, 1995 (2 years after sale)
Certain people outside the U.S. and members of the Armed Forces [1]	June 30, 1991 (2 years before sale)	June 30, 1997 (4 years after sale)
Certain members of the Armed Forces stationed overseas [2]	June 30, 1991 (2 years before sale)	June 30, 2001 (8 years after sale)

[1] Your 2-year replacement period after the sale can be suspended while you live and work outside the U.S. or are on extended active duty in the Armed Forces. However, your replacement period, plus any period of suspension, cannot exceed 4 years after the date of sale of your old home. See *People Outside the U.S.* or *Members of the Armed Forces.*

[2] Your 2-year replacement period after the sale can be suspended while you are stationed outside the U.S. or required to live in on-base quarters after returning from a tour of duty outside the U.S. However, your replacement period, plus any period of suspension, cannot exceed 8 years after the date of sale of your old home. See *Overseas military assignment* under *Members of the Armed Forces.*

Example 5

Lisa was unable to sell her home until 4 years after she vacated it because her former spouse, Paul, refused to sell his interest in the home. Lisa lived in an apartment that she rented during the 4 years subsequent to vacating her old home because it was Lisa's intention to sell the home immediately upon moving out. Under facts identical to these, the Tax Court ruled that the home qualified as her principal residence at the time of the sale.

Time Allowed for Replacement

You must buy (or build) and live in another house within *2 years before or 2 years after* the date of sale of your old home to postpone the tax on the gain from the sale.

Example. On April 27, 1993, before you sell your old home, you buy and move into a new home that you use as your main home. You have until April 27, 1995, a period of 2 years, to sell your old home and postpone tax on any gain.

Explanation

Your replacement residence may be either a purchased home or a newly constructed home, but it must be *bought and occupied* within 2 years before or after the sale of your old home. Key terms to remember are "bought," "occupied," and "2 years."

Occupancy test. You must physically live in the replacement home as your main home within the required period. If you move furniture or other personal belongings into the new home but do not actually live in it, you have not met the occupancy test.

No added time beyond the specified period is allowed. To postpone gain on the sale of your home, you must replace the old home and occupy the new home within the specified period. You are not allowed any additional time, even if conditions beyond your control keep you from doing it. For example, destruction of the new home while it was being built would not extend the replacement period. However, there may be a suspension of time, discussed later, for people outside the U.S. or members of the Armed Forces.

TaxAlert

Warning: This rule is inviolate. Taxpayers have tried to extend the replacement period by citing circumstances beyond their control, such as severe weather that prevented the completion of the new house's construction and depressed market conditions that prevented the sale of an old home—all to no avail. If you want to defer tax on the gain from your old home, make absolutely sure you occupy the new home as your principal residence in time.

If you do not replace the home in time and you had postponed gain in the year of sale, you must file an amended return for the year of sale. You must include in your income the entire gain on the sale of your old home. Also, if you began building your new home within the specified period, but for any reason were unable to live in it within 2 years, no more time for occupancy is allowed. You must report your entire gain on an amended return for the year of the sale. See *Amended Return,* later.

If you file an amended return and pay the tax you originally deferred, you also owe the IRS interest. However, you may control when you pay the interest to some degree by anticipating your failure to replace your old home in time and filing an amended return early. Interest paid to the IRS will be considered consumer interest and will not be allowed as a deduction. See Chapter 24, *Interest Expense*, for more details.

The tax law also stipulates that interest you pay to the IRS on an underpayment will be at a rate 1% greater than what the IRS will give you on a refund. Therefore, if you are not entirely certain that you will reinvest the gain from the sale of your old home in another home within the specified time period, your best strategy may be to include the gain in income at the time of the sale and thus avoid any IRS interest charges. If you do reinvest the funds in another home, you can file a refund claim on Form 1040X.

People Outside the U.S.

The replacement period after the sale of your old home is suspended while you have your tax home (the place where you live and work) outside the U.S. This suspension applies only if your stay abroad begins before the end of the 2-year replacement period. The replacement period, plus the period of suspension, is limited to *4 years* after the date of sale of your old home.

Example

You sold your home on May 14, 1993. This began your replacement period. On September 14, 1993, you were transferred to a foreign country. You have used 4 months of your replacement period. From September 14, 1993, to June 14, 1995, when you return to the United States, your replacement period will be suspended. Your replacement period starts again when you return on June 14, 1995, and you have until February 14, 1997 (20 months), to buy and live in your new home.

Note: If you are married, this suspension of the replacement period lasts while either you or your spouse has a tax home outside the United States, provided that you both used the old and the new home as your principal home.

For more information, see *People Outside the U.S.* in Publication 523. For a discussion of tax home, see Chapter 28.

Nonmilitary service in a combat zone in support of the Armed Forces. The running of the replacement period (including the suspension if you live and work outside the U.S.) is suspended for any period you served in the Persian Gulf Area combat zone in support of the Armed Forces, plus 180 days, even though you were not a member of those forces. This includes Red Cross personnel, accredited correspondents, and civilians under the direction of the Armed Forces in support of those forces.

The rules for suspending the running of the replacement period and for applying that suspension to your spouse are the same as the suspension rules explained later under *Members of the Armed Forces* and its discussion, *Military service in a combat zone.*

Members of the Armed Forces

The replacement period after the sale of your old home is suspended while you serve on extended active duty in the Armed Forces. You are on extended active duty if you are serving under a call or order for more than 90 days or for an indefinite period. The suspension applies only if your service begins before the end of the 2-year replacement period. The replacement period, plus any period of suspension, is limited to *4 years* after the date you sold your old home. For more information, see *Members of the Armed Forces* in Publication 523.

Example 1

You sold your home on April 1, 1993. This began your replacement period. You joined the armed forces on July 1, 1993. You have used 3 months of your replacement period (April, May, and June). From July 1, 1993, to June 30, 1995, when you will be discharged, your replacement period is suspended. Your replacement period starts again after your discharge on June 30, 1995, and you have until April 1, 1997 (21 months), to buy and live in your new home. This is a total replacement period of 2 years—3 months before you joined the armed forces and 21 months after your discharge.

Example 2

You are a regular member of the armed forces and sold your home on July 1, 1993. Your tax on the gain from the sale of the old home may be postponed only if you buy, or build, and live in another home by July 1, 1997.

Overseas military assignment. The suspension of the replacement period after the sale of your old home is extended for up to an additional 4 years while you are stationed outside the U.S. This also applies while you are required to live in on-base quarters following your return from a tour of duty outside the U.S. In this case, you must be stationed at a remote site where the Secretary of Defense has determined that adequate off-base housing is not available.

The suspension can continue for up to one year after the last day you are stationed outside the U.S. or the last day you are required to reside in government quarters on base. However, the replacement period, plus any period of suspension, is limited to *8 years* after the date of sale of your old home.

If you qualify for the time suspension for members of the Armed Forces and have already filed an income tax return reporting gain from the sale of a home that can be further postponed, you can file Form 1040X to claim a refund. See *Amended Return,* later.

Example

You are a regular member of the armed forces and sell your home on August 1, 1993. During 4 years from August 1, 1993, you serve outside the United States. On returning from serving outside the United States, you are required to live in on-base housing, because the Secretary of Defense determined that off-base housing is not available at a remote site. The time to replace your home is suspended while you are serving outside the United States or required to reside in on-base housing. Your replacement period plus your period of suspension cannot last beyond August 1, 2001.

Explanation

Spouse in armed forces. If your spouse is in the armed forces and you are not, the suspension applies to you if you own the old home. Both of you must have used the old home and the new home as your principal home. However, if you are divorced or legally separated while the replacement period is suspended, the suspension ends for you on the day after the date of the divorce or legal separation.

Military service in a combat zone. The running of the replacement period (including any suspension) is suspended for any period you served in the Persian Gulf Area combat zone. For this suspension, the designation of the area as a combat zone is effective August 2, 1990.

If you performed military service in an area outside the combat zone that was in direct support of military operations in the combat zone *and* you received special pay for duty subject to hostile fire or imminent danger, you are treated as if you served in the combat zone.

This suspension ends 180 days after the later of:

1) The last day you were in the combat zone (or, if earlier, the last day the area qualified as a combat zone), or
2) The last day of any continuous hospitalization (limited to 5 years if hospitalized in the U.S.) for an injury sustained while serving in the combat zone.

For more information on extension of the replacement period, see *Military service in a combat zone* in Publication 523. For more information on other tax benefits available to those who served in a combat zone, get Publication 945, *Tax Information for Those Affected by Operation Desert Storm*.

Amended Return

If you sell your old home and do not plan to replace it, you must include the gain in income for the year of sale. If you later change your mind, buy or build and live in another home within the replacement period, and meet the requirements to postpone gain, you will have to file an amended return (Form 1040X) for the year of sale to claim a refund. For information on the time allowed for filing an amended return, see Chapter 1, *Filing Information*.

Extended replacement period. If you have an extended replacement period because you have your tax home outside the U.S. or are a member of the Armed Forces, the replacement period may go beyond the last date you can file an amended return claiming a refund for the year of sale. If there is a possibility you may change your mind and buy another home during the extended replacement period, you should file a *protective claim* for refund of the tax you paid on the gain. File this claim on Form 1040X at the same time you file the return for the year of sale or anytime within the period allowed for filing an amended return.

Protective claim. To file a protective claim for refund, use Form 1040X and its instructions. However, you may leave lines 1 through 23 blank on the front of the form if you do not know the amount of your postponed gain at the time you file it. In *Part II* of the form:

1) Write "Protective Claim,"
2) Explain that you paid tax on the gain from the sale of your old home,
3) State the amount of the gain you reported on your original return,
4) State that you have an extended replacement period and why this extended period applies to your particular situation, and
5) State that you are filing this protective claim because during your extended replacement period you may buy (or build) a new main home.

Basis

Your basis in your home is determined by how you acquired it. Your basis is its cost if you bought it or built it. If you acquired it in some other way, its basis is either its fair market value when you received it or the adjusted basis of the person you received it from.

While you owned your home, you may have made adjustments (increases or decreases) to the basis. This adjusted basis is used to figure gain or loss on the sale of your home.

You can find more information on basis and adjusted basis in Chapter 14.

Adjusted Basis

Adjusted basis is your basis *increased* or *decreased* by certain amounts.

Increases to basis. This includes any:

1) Improvements.
2) Additions.
3) Special assessments for local improvements.
4) Amounts spent after a casualty to restore damaged property.

TaxOrganizer

The following documentation should be maintained to support the basis in your home upon sale:

- Receipts for all the above listed increases to basis.
- Closing statement from purchase of home to support all transfer taxes, attorney's fees, and other fees (survey, inspection, appraisal).
- Annual statements from cooperative housing corporations (COOPS) regarding maintenance payments used to reduce the indebtedness owed by the corporation.

Decreases to basis. This includes any:

1) Gain from the sale of your old home on which tax was postponed.
2) Insurance reimbursements for casualty losses.
3) Deductible casualty losses not covered by insurance.
4) Payments received for easement or right-of-way granted.
5) Depreciation allowed or allowable if you used your home for business or rental purposes.
6) Residential energy credit (generally allowed from 1977 through 1987) claimed for the cost of energy improvements that you added to the basis of your home.
7) Energy conservation subsidy excluded from your gross income because you received it (directly or indirectly) from a public utility after December 31, 1992, for the purchase or installation of any energy conservation measure.

Energy conservation measure. This is any installation or modification primarily designed to reduce the amount of electricity or natural gas or improve the management of energy for a home.

No effect on basis. Items that you cannot deduct from, or add to, your basis include:

1) Certain settlement fees or closing costs. These include:
   - Fire insurance premiums.
   - Mortgage insurance premiums.
   - Rent for occupancy of the house before closing.
   - Charges for utilities or other services relating to occupancy of the house before closing.
2) The cost of repairs.
3) Any item that you deducted as a moving expense. See *Home-Related Expenses* in Chapter 27, *Moving Expenses*.

Improvements. These are costs that add to the value of your home, prolong its useful life, or adapt it to new uses. You add the cost of improvements to the basis of your property.

Examples. Putting a recreation room in your unfinished basement, adding another bathroom or bedroom, putting up a fence, putting in new plumbing or wiring, putting on a new roof, or paving your driveway are improvements you add to basis.

For a list of some other examples of improvements, see *Table 1, Examples of Improvements* in Publication 523.

TaxSaver

The Tax Court has held that shrubbery and trees may qualify as improvements to be added to the basis of the taxpayer's property.

Repairs. These are costs that maintain your home in good condition. They do not add to its value or prolong its life, and you do not add them to the basis of your property.

Examples. Repainting your house inside or outside, fixing your gutters or floors, repairing leaks or plastering, and replacing broken window panes are examples of repairs.

Recordkeeping. You should keep records of your home's purchase price and purchase expenses. You should also save receipts and other records for all improvements, additions, and other items that affect the basis of your home. This includes any Form 2119 that you filed to report postponement of gain from the sale of a previous home.

Ordinarily, you must keep records for 3 years after the due date for filing your return for the tax year in which you sold, or otherwise disposed of, your home. But if you use the basis of your old home in figuring the basis of your new one, such as when you sell your old home and postpone tax on any gain, you should keep those records longer. Keep those records as long as they are needed for tax purposes.

TaxPlanner

If you lose your original receipts, other documents may be used to substantiate the cost of improvements to your home. Cancelled checks, contracts, before and after photographs, and building permits may be acceptable to the IRS. If all documentation is lost, you should figure your basis by getting estimates of the cost of similar improvements made at the same time you made yours.

For more information on basis and adjusted basis, see Chapter 14, *Basis of Property*.

Old Home

Gain or loss on the sale of your old home is figured on Part II of Form 2119. To figure the gain or loss, you must know the selling price, the amount realized, and the adjusted basis.

You use Part IV of Form 2119 to figure the adjusted sales price, the taxable gain, and the postponed gain.

Selling price. The selling price (line 4 of Form 2119) is the total amount you receive for your home. It includes money, all notes, mortgages, or other debts assumed by the buyer as part of the sale, and the fair market value of any other property you receive.

If you received a Form 1099–S, *Proceeds From Real Estate Transactions*, the total amount you received for your home (except for the fair market value of any other property or services you received or will receive) should be shown in box 2. If you received or will receive any other property or services as part of the sale, the value of these items is not shown on Form 1099–S. However, box 4 of that form should be checked.

Employer reimbursement. You may have to sell your home because of a job transfer. If your employer pays you for a loss on the sale or for your selling expenses, do **not** include the payment (reimbursement) as part of the selling price. Include it in your gross income as wages on line 7 of Form 1040. For more information, see *How to Report* in Chapter 27, *Moving Expenses*.

TaxSaver

If during 1993 you sold your home directly to your employer at **fair market value,** no portion of the proceeds is treated as additional compensation. Any tax on your gain is deferred if you reinvest the proceeds in another home. However, if your home was sold to your employer at an amount above fair market value, part of the proceeds would be treated as compensation or ordinary income.

Option to buy. If you grant an option to buy your home and the option is exercised, add the amount you receive for the option to the sales price of your home. If the option is not exercised, you must report the amount as ordinary income in the year the option expires. Report this amount on line 22 of Form 1040.

Selling expenses. Selling expenses (line 5 of Form 2119) include commissions, advertising, and legal fees. Loan charges paid by the seller, such as loan placement fees or "points," are usually a selling expense.

Explanation

The following items are also considered selling expenses: (1) broker's fees, (2) fees for drafting a contract of sale, (3) fees for drafting the deed, (4) escrow fees, (5) geological surveys, (6) maps, (7) title insurance, (8) recording fees, (9) abstracts of title, (10) title certificate, (11) title opinion, and (12) title registration.

Moving expenses. If your move was job-related, some expenses of selling your home may be deducted as moving expenses. However, you cannot decrease the amount realized on the sale of your home by the real estate commission or similar expenses you deduct as a moving expense. See Chapter 27, *Moving Expenses*.

Amount realized. The amount realized (line 6 of Form 2119) is the selling price minus selling expenses.

Gain. Your gain on the sale (line 8 of Form 2119) is the amount realized minus the adjusted basis of the home (line 7 of Form 2119). See *Basis*, discussed earlier, to figure the adjusted basis of your property. Also, the *Instructions for Form 2119* has a worksheet to help you figure the adjusted basis of your old home.

Fixing-up expenses. Fixing-up expenses (line 16 of Form 2119) are decorating and repair costs that you paid to sell the old home. For example, the costs of painting the home, planting flowers, and replacing broken windows are fixing-up expenses. These expenses must:

1) Be for work done during the 90-day period ending on the day you sign the contract of sale with the buyer.
2) Be paid no later than 30 days after the date of sale.
3) Not be deductible in arriving at your taxable income.
4) Not be used in figuring the amount realized.
5) Not be capital expenditures or improvements.

Note. You deduct fixing-up expenses from the amount realized *only* in figuring the part of the gain that you postpone. You *cannot* deduct them in figuring the actual gain on the sale of the old home. If the amount realized does not exceed the cost of your new home, you postpone your entire gain. In this case, you do not need to figure your fixing-up expenses.

Adjusted sales price. Use the adjusted sales price of your old home (line 18 of Form 2119) to figure the part of your gain that you can postpone. The adjusted sales price is the amount realized minus any exclusion you claim (line 14 of Form 2119) and minus any fixing-up expenses you might have. Compare the adjusted sales price with the cost of your new home to find the amount of gain that you can postpone.

Example. Your old home had a basis of $55,000. You signed a contract to sell it on December 17, 1992. On January 7, 1993, you sold it for $71,400. Selling expenses were $5,000. During the 90-day period ending December 17, 1992, you had the following work done. You paid for the work on February 4, 1993—within 30 days after the date of sale.

Inside and outside painting	$800
New venetian blinds and new water heater	$900

Within the required time, you bought and lived in a new home that cost $64,600. The amount of gain on which tax is postponed, is not postponed, and the basis of your new home, are as follows:

Gain Realized

a) Selling price of old home	$71,400	
b) Minus: Selling expenses	5,000	
c) Amount realized on sale		$66,400
d) Basis of old home	$55,000	
e) Add: Improvements (blinds and heater)	900	
f) Adjusted basis of old home		55,900
g) Gain realized [(c) minus (f)]		$10,500

Gain Taxed in 1993

h) Amount realized on sale	$66,400	
i) Minus: Fixing-up expenses (painting)	800	
j) Adjusted sales price		$65,600
k) Minus: Cost of new home		64,600
l) Excess of adjusted sales price over cost of new home		$ 1,000
m) Gain taxed in 1993 [lesser of (g) or (l)]		$ 1,000

Gain Not Taxed in 1993

n) Gain realized [line (g)]	$10,500	
o) Minus: Gain taxed in 1993 [line (m)]	1,000	
p) Gain not taxed in 1993		$ 9,500

Adjusted Basis of New Home

q) Cost of new home [line (k)]	$64,600	
r) Minus: Gain not taxed in 1993 [line (p)]	9,500	
s) Adjusted basis of new home		$55,100

Explanation

In the above example, although you spent $1,700 refurbishing your house and all the expenditures were incurred and paid for within the time period required for them to be classified as fixing-up expenses, only the cost of the interior and exterior painting qualifies as fixing-up expenses. The cost of the new blinds and water heater represents capital improvements and must be added to your basis, thereby reducing the gain on the sale of the house. The fixing-up expenses reduce the amount you realized from the sale.

TAXSAVER

If a portion of the gain on the sale of your home may not be postponed, subtracting fixing-up expenses from the amount realized means a smaller portion of the gain is taxed currently and a larger portion of your tax is deferred (see the example above). However, when the cost of your new home is high enough to defer your entire gain, fixing-up expenses provide no tax benefit.

Example

Assume the same facts as in the IRS example above, except that your new home costs $70,000 (the line numbers in this example correspond to the line numbers in the IRS example above):

j)	Adjusted sales price	$65,600
k)	Cost of new home	70,000
l)	Gain not postponed [(j) minus (k)]	–0–
m)	Gain postponed [(g) minus (l)]	$10,500
n)	Cost of new home	$70,000
o)	Minus: Gain postponed [(g) minus (l)]	10,500
p)	Basis of new home	$59,500

Note: The $800 of fixing-up expenses does not affect the gain recognized, since the entire gain is deferred. The fixing-up expenses have no effect on the basis of the new home.

Trading homes. If you trade your old home for another home, treat the trade as a sale and a purchase.

Example. You owned and lived in a home that had a basis of $41,000. A real estate dealer accepted your old home as a trade-in and allowed you $50,000 toward a new house priced at $80,000. You are considered to have sold your old home for $50,000 and to have had a gain of $9,000 ($50,000 − $41,000). Because you re-placed it with a new home costing more than the sales price of the old one, you must postpone the tax on the gain. The basis of your new home is $71,000 ($80,000 cost minus $9,000 gain that is not currently taxed).

If the dealer had allowed you $27,000 and assumed your unpaid mortgage of $23,000 on your old home, $50,000 would still be considered the sales price of the old home (the trade-in allowed plus the mortgage assumed).

Property used partly as your home and partly for business or rental. You may use part of your property as your home and part of it for business or to produce income. Examples are a work-ing farm on which your house is located, an apartment building in which you live in one unit and rent out the others, or a store building with an upstairs apartment in which you live. If you sell the whole property, you postpone only the tax on the part used as your home. This includes the land and outbuildings, such as a garage for the home, but not those for the business or the produc-tion of income. For more information, see *Property used partly as your home and partly for business or rental* in Publication 523.

Example

You own a four-unit apartment house. You live in one unit and rent three units. You sell the apartment house, and buy and live in a new home. Your records show the following:

Apartment house

Cost	$ 80,000
Capital improvements	20,000
	$100,000
Minus: Depreciation (on three rented units only)	40,000
Adjusted basis	$ 60,000
Selling price	$120,000
Selling expense	8,000
New home: Purchase price	$ 70,000

Because one-fourth of the apartment building is your home, you figure the gain on which tax is postponed as follows:

	Personal (1/4)	Rental (3/4)
1) Selling price	$30,000	$90,000
2) Selling expense	2,000	6,000
3) Amount realized (adjusted sales price)	$28,000	$84,000
4) Basis (including improvements)	$25,000	$75,000
5) Depreciation	–0–	40,000
6) Adjusted basis	$25,000	$35,000
7) Gain [(3) minus (6)]	$ 3,000	$49,000
8) Gain not postponed		$49,000
9) Gain postponed	$ 3,000	

The gain of $49,000 on the three-fourths of the build-ing that was rental property is subject to tax in the year

of sale. This gain is reported on Form 4797, *Gains and Losses from Sales or Exchanges of Assets Used in a Trade or Business and Involuntary Conversions.* The tax is postponed on the gain on the one-fourth that was your home, because the $28,000 adjusted sales price of this one-fourth was less than the $70,000 cost of your new home. The basis of the new home is $67,000 ($70,000 cost minus $3,000 postponed gain).

TAXSAVER

If improvements have been made solely to rental units, their cost should be specifically allocated to the rental part of the property. This allocation will decrease the gain on the business portion of the property, which is taxable in the year of sale.

Keep detailed records of improvements. Be careful to specify whether the improvements were made exclu-sively to either the business or the personal portion of the residence, or whether they improved the residence as a whole.

Example

Jane Smith purchases a two-family house. The two units in the house are identical. Jane rents one out and uses the other as her personal residence. The house costs $80,000—$20,000 for the land and $60,000 ($30,000 per unit) for the building. Jane remodels the kitchen in the rental unit. The job costs $10,000, which is added to the basis of the rental unit, increasing it to $40,000. Once the unit is rented, depreciation may be claimed on this $40,000 basis.

When the property is sold, the selling price must be apportioned between the business and personal por-tions of the residence. If, at the time of sale, the adjusted basis of the rental unit, including the amount allocated to land, is $28,000, and if $60,000 of the selling price is allocated to the rental unit, there is currently a taxable gain of $32,000. Without the $10,000 kitchen expense, the adjusted basis would be only $18,000, increasing the currently taxable gain to $42,000.

Explanation

The apportionment of the selling price between the busi-ness and personal portions of a house should be based upon the relative fair market value of each portion. Sub-stantial improvements made to each portion of the prop-erty should be considered in determining the amount of the selling price that is allocated to each part.

Consequently, the allocation of the sales price, as well as the allocation of the cost of the improvements, may affect the amount of gain to be deferred or taxed upon the sale of property used partly as your principal home. Evidence to support a particular allocation of the sales price can include a real estate broker's appraisal or the negotiated terms of the sales contract.

Business use of your home. If, in the year of sale, you are entitled to deduct expenses for the business use of your home, you cannot postpone the gain on the part of the home used for business. In figuring the amount of gain on which you can postpone tax, you must make an allocation for the business-use part of the home. For information on how to figure the business part, see *Business Part of Home Expenses* in Publication 587, *Business Use of Your Home*.

Explanation

The following examples indicate that the use of your principal home at the time at which it is sold determines if you may postpone the tax on all or only part of your gain. If your principal home was used partly for a business purpose in prior years, you can still defer the tax on your home as long as your home was not used partly for business in the year of the sale.

Prior use of your home for business, however, will decrease the adjusted basis of the property and, thereby, could increase the amount of postponed gain on the home.

Example 1

Bill Brown, a doctor, purchased a home in January, 1981 for $70,000 and lived in it as his principal home until December 1993. Bill used part of his home exclusively on a regular basis to see his patients in the normal course of his medical practice. From 1981 to 1993, Bill claimed a deduction on his returns for the business use of his home. In December, 1993, Bill sold his home for $120,000 and purchased a new principal home for $140,000. In figuring the amount of gain he may postpone, Bill must make an allocation for the business part of his home. He will postpone only the tax on the part of the gain that is for the personal-use part of his home.

Example 2

In 1972, Susan Jones bought a home for $40,000 and lived in it as her principal home. Susan is a school teacher and uses part of her den to correct papers and prepare her lessons. On Susan's returns for years 1972 through 1976, she was allowed a deduction for the business use of her home. However, for 1977 and later years, she was not allowed this deduction, because she did not use her den exclusively for business purposes, nor was it for the convenience of her employer. However, Susan continued to use part of her den to correct papers and prepare her lessons. In November, 1993, Susan sold her home for $80,000 and purchased a new principal home for $90,000. Because Susan was not allowed a deduction for the business use of her den on her 1993 return, she does not have to make any allocation in figuring the amount of gain she will postpone. Susan may postpone the entire gain on the sale of the old home.

Note: Although Susan will postpone the entire gain, in figuring the amount of her gain, she will have to adjust the basis of her old home by any depreciation claimed in years 1972 through 1976 for the business use of her home.

Home changed to rental property. You cannot postpone tax on the gain on rental property, even if you once used it as your home. The rules explained in this chapter generally will not apply to its sale. Gains are taxable and losses are deductible as explained in Publication 527, *Residential Rental Property*. The basis of the property is determined as explained under *Property Changed to Business or Rental Use* in Chapter 14, *Basis of Property*.

You have not changed your home to rental property if you

temporarily rented out your old home before selling it, or your new home before living in it, as a matter of convenience or for another nonbusiness purpose. You can postpone the tax on the gain from the sale if you meet the requirements explained earlier under *Postponement of Gain*. For information on how to treat the rental income you receive, see Chapter 10, *Rental Income and Expenses*.

If you place your home with a real estate agent for rent or sale and it is *not* rented, it is not considered business property or property held for the production of income. The rules explained in this chapter apply to the sale of the home.

Explanation

The IRS distinguishes between the temporary use of your home as a rental property and its permanent conversion to rental use.

If you temporarily rent your home, it remains your principal residence and you may defer any gain on its sale according to the rules discussed in this chapter. However, if you move into another residence and rent out your former principal residence for more than a temporary period, the IRS will consider your former residence as income-producing property. Any gain on the sale of income-producing property is taxable, and any loss may be tax deductible.

Courts have classified some property as held for business use even though no income has been received from it when, for example, the property is listed for rent with real estate agents but no suitable tenant can be found. In determining the property's status, courts pay particular attention to the type and duration of efforts made to produce income through the property.

TAXPLANNER

If you buy a new principal home and then have trouble selling your old home, you should carefully consider the tax and economic consequences of renting out your old place. How you are taxed will generally depend on whether your intent is to rent temporarily while continuing your efforts to sell the old home or whether you permanently convert your old home to income-producing rental property. If your intent is to rent temporarily, it is best to rent the house on a month-to-month basis. However, if you must offer a longer-term lease to attract reliable tenants, be sure to document your motives. It may be helpful to obtain a statement from your real estate broker confirming that adverse market conditions have affected your ability to attract buyers at reasonable prices, and that a longer-term lease is necessary to obtain a responsible tenant. You should keep in mind that the two-year period to sell your home begins running when you purchase the new home.

Except as discussed in Note 2 following Example 1 below, the IRS and the courts have not allowed taxpayers to treat their former principal home as rental property and also to defer the gain realized upon the sale of the property. Generally, the IRS will not seriously challenge your effort to defer the gain from the sale of your principal home (see *Postponement of Gain,* earlier in this chapter). The IRS has, however, disallowed depreciation, insurance, maintenance, and other rental deductions that can offset other types of taxable income.

Example 1

You contract to purchase a new principal residence on May 1, 1993. Your intention is to sell your old home as soon as possible and defer the tax on the $30,000 gain you expect to realize from the sale. However, the real estate market turns sour and your agent cannot get you any good offers on your old home. Financial considerations force you to rent your former home while continuing efforts to sell it. On July 1, 1993, you occupy your new principal home and rent your former home on a month-to-month basis for the remainder of 1993.

The monthly cash flow from your rental property is shown below:

1) Monthly rental income		$ 800
2) Minus: Monthly mortgage interest	$600	
3) Minus: Monthly property taxes	150	
4) Total interest and taxes		750
5) Net cash flow available to defray other costs of maintaining the rental property [(1) minus (4)]		$ 50
6) Minus: Other estimated monthly expenses, consisting of:		
a) Property insurance	$35	
b) Utilities	30	
c) Repairs and maintenance	50	
d) Gardening	60	
7) Total other expenses		175
8) Net cash flow		$ − 125

You can expect to incur a loss of $125 for each month you are required to rent the home. Since your intention is to sell your former residence within the 2-year period that began on July 1, 1993, and postpone the tax on any gain from the sale, the IRS will not permit you to deduct the loss of $125 per month on your 1993 tax return.

However, the IRS will allow you to deduct expenses up to the amount of rental income you receive from the property. Interest expense and property taxes attributable to the rental must be deducted first. Therefore, in this example, only $50 of the other monthly expenses could be deducted against rental income. The rental activity for the year should be reported on Part I of Schedule E (Form 1040).

Note 1: Generally, each month's mortgage payment includes an interest charge and a loan repayment amount. The portion of each mortgage payment that reduces the mortgage principal outstanding will further increase your out-of-pocket costs, because, whether you rent the property or not, the repayment of the mortgage loan will not be tax deductible.

Note 2: Based upon essentially the same facts as described in Example 1, the Ninth Circuit Court of Appeals overturned the IRS's position that you cannot deduct rental-related expenses (including depreciation) in excess of rental income and also defer recognition of a gain on the sale of your former principal residence. According to the court ruling, you would be entitled to deduct monthly losses (as shown in Example 2 below) *and* defer the capital gain from the sale of your former principal residence if it is sold within the requisite 2-year period. However, deductions in excess of income may be limited under other rules dealing with passive losses and personal use of a house for more than 14 days in a year. See Chapter 10, *Rental Income and Expenses*.

The ruling only applies in the Ninth Circuit, which includes Alaska, Arizona, California, Guam, Hawaii, Idaho, Montana, Nevada, Oregon, and Washington. Courts outside the Ninth Circuit are not bound by the decision. Furthermore, the IRS might continue to pursue the matter. Taxpayers, both within and outside of the jurisdiction of the Ninth Circuit Court of Appeals who are considering relying on the court ruling, should consult their tax advisors.

Example 2

Instead of temporarily renting your former residence (as in Example 1), you decide to hold it for long-term investment and to convert it to a rental property. You could generate a tax-deductible loss as follows:

1) Monthly rental income		$ 800
2) Minus: Monthly expenses consisting of		
a) Mortgage interest	$600	
b) Property taxes	150	
c) Property insurance	35	
d) Utilities	30	
e) Repairs and maintenance	50	
f) Gardening	60	
g) Depreciation	250	
3) Total tax-deductible expenses		1,175
4) Monthly tax-deductible loss on rental property		$ − 375

Because your intention was to convert your former principal home to an income-producing property and the facts support this intention, the excess of the tax-deductible expenses over the rental income ($375) may be used to offset taxable income derived from other sources. However, unless your former home subsequently becomes your principal home, you will not be able to defer the taxes on any gain you realize when you sell the property. For more details about the tax treatment of a gain or a loss from the sale of rental property, see Chapter 15, *Sale of Property*. For more details about depreciation, see Chapter 10, *Rental Income and Expenses*.

Your ability to deduct the loss described in Example 2 may be limited because of special rules that apply to losses from real estate rental activities. See the section on tax shelters and passive activity losses in Chapter 13, *Other Income*.

Condemnation. If your home is condemned for public use and you have a gain, you can postpone the tax on the gain in one of two ways. You can postpone the tax under the rules explained in this chapter or under those discussed under *Involuntary Conversions* in Chapter 1 of Publication 544, *Sales and Other Dispositions of Assets*.

TAXSAVER

If you can't replace your residence within the 2-year period, you may apply to the IRS for an extension of time.

The condemnation rules differ from the principal-residence rules in this respect. It's at the IRS's discretion to issue an extension, so the fact that you apply for one does not mean it will be granted. Generally, taxpayers must show unusual or extenuating circumstances to get these types of extensions.

Explanation

If your home is condemned for public use and you have a gain, it may be treated either as an involuntary conversion or as a voluntary sale. For all practical purposes, the only difference between the two alternatives lies in how long you have to find a new home and thus how long you may defer your gain.

Involuntary conversion. If you choose to report the gain on **condemnation** as an involuntary conversion, the gain is deferred only if, after the condemnation is under way, you reinvest in another home that you use as your personal residence. The new residence must be purchased within the period that begins either on the date of the conversion (the date on which the property is actually taken by requisition or condemnation) or on the date on which you receive notice of the condemnation proceedings, whichever is earlier, and terminates 2 years after the end of the first tax year in which you realize the gain.

Example

John Jones's residence was condemned in 1989. In that same year, he received $50,000 as payment for his residence from the condemning authority. The $50,000 was more than his adjusted cost basis for the home, therefore giving him a gain. Jones claimed that the property was worth $200,000, but the condemning authority believed it was worth $50,000. Jones sued to try to collect the full $200,000. The suit was settled in 1993, and Jones collected an additional $75,000.

Jones's first gain was realized in 1989, so the replacement period started at that time and expired in 1991. Thus, the $75,000 would be taxed in 1993, unless Jones had requested an extension of time to acquire replacement property or had, in fact, already made the replacement. Additionally, if Jones did not report on his 1989 return the amount he received in excess of his basis, he would have to file an amended return.

Explanation

Voluntary sale. As in the previous case, if you elect to treat the condemnation of your residence as a voluntary sale, the gain is deferred only if the old home and your new home both qualify as your principal residence. You must attach a statement to your tax return indicating that you are electing to treat the disposition of your old residence as a sale. Once you file the statement, you may not revoke it. Your new residence must be purchased and occupied within a 4-year period, beginning 2 years before and ending 2 years after the sale of your old residence. If you don't meet the deadline, you have to file an amended tax return. The gain from your residence is then included in your income for the year of sale and is subject to tax.

Example

You purchased a new residence in March, 1993 and planned to sell your old home. Prior to moving, you received a notice that your old home had been condemned for public use. Assume that you realized a gain on that condemnation and chose to treat it as an involuntary conversion (see above). You would not have been allowed to postpone recognizing that gain by treating the new residence as replacement property, because you had acquired it before you received notice of the condemnation proceedings. But assume that you chose to treat the condemnation as a voluntary sale. You would have been allowed to defer the gain, since the replacement period included the 2 years prior to the "sale."

If it would take you more than 2 years to acquire a replacement residence, use the involuntary conversion rules, which may allow you as much as 3 years to find a new home.

Gain on casualty. The tax on a gain from a fire, storm, or other casualty cannot be postponed under the rules explained in this chapter, but may be postponed under the rules explained in Publication 547, *Nonbusiness Disasters, Casualties, and Thefts*.

Explanation

For a complete discussion of this matter, see Chapter 26, *Nonbusiness Casualty and Theft Losses*.

New Home

Use the *purchase price of your replacement home* to figure the gain taxed and the gain on which tax is postponed on the sale of your old home. Purchase price includes costs incurred within the replacement period (beginning 2 years before and ending 2 years after the date of sale) for the following items:

1) Buying or building the home.
2) Rebuilding the home.
3) Capital improvements or additions.

You cannot consider any costs incurred before or after the replacement period. However, if you are a person outside the U.S. or a member of the Armed Forces, you can include in the purchase price any costs incurred during the suspension period.

TaxSaver

Even if your new home is not complete and not fully paid for, the full gain may still be deferred if you have moved into your new home and the total costs incurred for it within the 2-year period after the sale of your old home exceed the amount you realized on the old house you sold.

Example

Helen Smith sold her home on Lake Shore Drive for $250,000 on June 6, 1991. Two days later, she purchased a brownstone for $210,000. Helen moved into an apartment while having a new roof and various major structural repairs performed on the brownstone. The total cost of this work was $90,000. Helen moved into the brownstone on May 6, 1993. Since Helen had moved in and invested more than $250,000 ($210,000 + $90,000) by June 6, 1993, she could defer the gain realized on the sale of the old residence.

New home outside the U.S. If your new home is outside the U.S., you still may qualify to postpone your gain from the sale of your old home that is in the U.S. You must buy or build and live in the new home within the time allowed for replacement.

Debts on the new property. The price of a new home includes the debts it is subject to when you buy it (purchase-money mortgage or deed of trust) and the face amount of notes or other liabilities you give for it.

Temporary housing. If a builder gives you temporary housing while your new home is being finished, you must reduce the contract price to arrive at the cost of the new home. To figure the amount of the reduction, multiply the contract price by a fraction. The numerator is the value of the housing and the denominator is the sum of the value of the housing plus the value of the home.

Settlement fees or closing costs. When buying your home, you may have to pay settlement fees or closing costs in addition to the contract price of the property. Some of the settlement fees or closing costs that you can include in the basis of your property are:

1) Abstract fees,
2) Charges for installing utility services,
3) Legal fees (including title search and preparing documents),
4) Recording fees,
5) Surveys,
6) Transfer taxes,
7) Title insurance, and
8) Any amounts the seller owes that you agree to pay, such as back taxes or interest, recording or mortgage fees, charges for improvements or repairs, and sales commissions.

Settlement fees do not include amounts placed in escrow for the future payment of items such as taxes and insurance.

If you itemize your deductions in the year you buy the house, you can deduct some of the costs you paid at closing, such as real estate taxes, mortgage interest, and "points" that are deductible as interest. For more information, see Chapters 23 and 24, *Taxes You May Deduct* and, *Interest Expenses,* respectively.

Real estate taxes. If you agree to pay taxes the seller owed on your new home (that is, taxes up to the date of sale), the taxes you pay are treated as part of the cost. You cannot deduct them as taxes paid. If the seller paid taxes for you (that is, taxes beginning with the date of sale), you can still deduct the taxes. If you do not reimburse the seller for your part of the taxes, you must reduce your basis in your new home by the amount of those taxes. For more information, see *Settlement or closing costs* under *Basis* in Publication 530.

Note: For homes sold after 1992, the information reported (generally by the settlement agent) to the IRS and seller of the home on Form 1099–S, *Proceeds From Real Estate Transactions* , must include the part of any real estate tax that is treated as tax imposed on the buyer. For more information, see *Property taxes* under *Old Home* in Publication 523.

You cannot deduct, or add to your basis, certain settlement fees or closing costs. These include fire insurance premiums, mortgage insurance premiums, charges for the use of utilities, rent for occupancy before closing, and other fees or charges for services concerning occupancy of the house.

Investment in retirement home. You have not purchased a replacement home if you sell your home and invest the proceeds in a retirement home project that gives you living quarters and personal care, but does not give you any legal interest in the property. Therefore, you must include in income any gain on the sale of your home. However, if you are 55 or older, see *Exclusion of Gain,* later in this chapter.

Explanation
The IRS takes the position that the purchase of the right to live in a retirement home is a contract for future support, not an interest in **real property.** However, if you reinvest the proceeds from the sale of your home in a dwelling unit located in a retirement community, you may defer paying taxes on any gain you might have had, just as if you had bought a new home anywhere else.

Allocation between you and your spouse. You or your spouse may have owned the old home separately, but title to the new one is in both your names as joint tenants. Or, you and your spouse may have owned the old home as joint tenants, and either you or your spouse owns the new home separately. In both of these cases, you can postpone the gain from the sale of the old home.

You and your spouse can divide the postponed gain, which reduces the basis of the new home, if both of you meet the following requirements:

1) You used the old home as your main home and you use the new home as your main home.
2) You sign a statement that says: "We agree to reduce the basis of the new home by the gain from selling the old home."

Both of you must sign the statement. You can make the statement in the bottom margin of Form 2119 or on a sheet attached to your tax return. If both of you do not sign the statement, you must report the gain in the regular way without allocation.

Example 1. You sell your home that is owned separately by you, but both you and your spouse use it as your main home. The adjusted sales price is $98,000, the adjusted basis is $86,000, and the gain on the sale is $12,000. Within 2 years you and your spouse buy a new home for $100,000. The title is held jointly and, under state law, you each have a one-half interest. If you both sign the statement to reduce the basis of the new home, you postpone the gain on the sale as if you had owned both the old and new homes jointly. You and your spouse will each have an adjusted basis of $44,000 ($50,000 cost minus $6,000 postponed gain) in the new home.

If you both do not sign the statement, your entire gain of $12,000 will be currently taxed. This is because the adjusted sales price of the old home ($98,000) is greater than your part of the cost of the new home ($50,000). You and your spouse will each have a basis of $50,000 in the new home.

Example 2. Assume in Example 1 that you and your spouse owned the old home jointly and each had a one-half interest under state law. Your spouse buys the new home with separate funds and takes title individually. If you both sign the statement, you and your spouse postpone the $12,000 gain from the sale of the old home. Your spouse will have an adjusted basis of $88,000 ($100,000 cost minus $12,000 postponed gain) in the new home.

If you both do not sign the statement, you will be taxed on your share of the gain on the old home, but your spouse will postpone tax on his or her share of the gain. This is because the cost of the new home was more than your spouse's share of the adjusted sales price of the old home. Your spouse's basis in the new home will be $94,000 ($100,000 cost minus $6,000 postponed gain).

Example 3. Assume in Example 1 that you own the old home individually and your spouse owns the new home individually. If you both sign the statement, you postpone the $12,000 gain from the sale of the old home. Your spouse will have an adjusted basis in the new home of $88,000.

If you both do not sign the statement, your entire gain will be taxed and your spouse's basis in the new home will be $100,000. **Deceased spouse.** For sales after 1984, if your spouse dies after you sell your old home and before you purchase a new home, you can postpone the gain from the sale of the old home if the basic requirements are met, and:

1) You were married on the date your spouse died, and
2) You use the new home as your main home.

This applies whether title to the old home is in one spouse's name or held jointly.

If you sold your home and did not postpone the entire gain on the sale because of the death of your spouse (but otherwise qualified to do so under the rules explained in this chapter), you can file an amended return (Form 1040X) to postpone the entire gain. See Chapter 1, *Filing Information,* for the time allowed to file an amended return.

Explanation

The preceding three examples illustrate what happens when married taxpayers filing joint returns consent to allocate the gain from the sale of a main home between them. However, under prior law, this provision did not apply in the case of a spouse who died after the date of sale of the old home and before the date of purchase of the new home. Now, pursuant to the Technical and Miscellaneous Revenue Act of 1988, a surviving spouse may qualify for nonrecognition of gain when such spouse occupies the new home within the 24-month replacement period.

TaxSaver

The expanded nonrecognition of gain provision described above applies to sales of old residences after December 31, 1984. Thus, for sales after 1984, it is possible to claim a tax refund by filing amended tax returns in cases in which the maximum postponement of gain was not available due to the death of a spouse and the expiration of the statute of limitations does not bar you from amending the tax return.

Separate homes replaced by single home. If you and your spouse had two separate gains from the sales of homes that had been your separate main homes before your marriage, you can postpone the tax on both gains. You must jointly purchase a new replacement home, and one-half the amount of the cost of the new home must be at least as much as the adjusted selling price of each of your old homes.

Each spouse must individually satisfy the requirements for postponing gain. Each spouse's share of the cost of the new home is the portion equal to his or her interest in the home under state law (generally one-half). This share of the cost must be equal to or greater than the adjusted sales price of his or her old home.

Example. You sold your old home in April 1993 for an adjusted sales price of $90,000. Your spouse sold her old home in June 1993 for an adjusted sales price of $110,000. You each realized a gain from your sale. Before the end of 1993, you jointly purchased a new replacement home at a cost of $200,000. Under state law, you each have a one-half interest in the new home.

You postpone your gain since you are treated as purchasing a replacement home for $100,000 (½ of $200,000).

There is tax on $10,000 of your spouse's gain at the time of the sale. This is the amount by which the adjusted sales price of her former home is more than her $100,000 share of the cost of the replacement home.

Report the sales of the old homes on separate Forms 2119.

Explanation

Commuter marriages. The IRS has not addressed the situation in which a wife and a husband live in different cities. Since the IRS has stated that a taxpayer may have only one principal residence, presumably, the time spent in each residence would determine which one constitutes a principal residence.

Title to new home not held by either you or your spouse. You cannot postpone the tax on the gain from the sale of your old home if you reinvest the proceeds from the sale in a new home in which neither you nor your spouse holds any legal interest. For example, if someone else (such as your child) holds the title to the new home, you cannot postpone the gain from the sale.

Home replaced by two homes of spouses living apart. If you and your spouse have agreed to live apart, and you each buy and live in separate replacement homes, the postponement provisions apply separately to your gain and to your spouse's gain.

Example. You and your spouse bought a home in 1984. You owned the property jointly and used it as your main home. In 1993, you agreed to live apart, and sold the home for $98,000. The gain on the sale was $20,000. Under state law, each of you is entitled to one-half of the proceeds of the sale. Therefore, each of you had a $10,000 gain from the sale of your home.

Before the end of 1993, you and your spouse individually bought and lived in separate homes. The cost of each new home, $71,000 and $75,000 respectively, was more than your respective shares of the adjusted sales price of the old home. You and your spouse must postpone the tax on the $20,000 gain on the old home.

Your new home has an adjusted basis of $61,000 ($71,000 minus ½ of the $20,000 gain postponed). Your spouse's new home has an adjusted basis of $65,000 ($75,000 minus ½ of the $20,000 gain postponed).

You report the sale of your home on two Forms 2119 as if two separate properties were sold. You each report half of the sales price. See *Divorce after sale* under *How and When to Report,* later.

Inheritance or gift. If you receive any part of your new home as a gift or an inheritance, you cannot include the value of that part in the cost of the new home when figuring the gain taxed in the year of sale and the gain on which tax is postponed. However, you include the basis of that part in your adjusted basis to determine any gain when you sell the new home.

Example. Your father died in 1993 and you inherited his home. Its basis to you is $62,000. You spent $14,000 to modernize the home, resulting in an adjusted basis to you of $76,000.

When your father died, you owned a home that you bought in 1989 for $60,000. Assume that within 2 years of inheriting your father's home you sell your old home for $65,000, at a gain of $5,000. You have fixing-up expenses of $200 on your old home.

To find the gain taxed in the year of the sale, you compare the adjusted sales price of the old home, $64,800 ($65,000 − $200), with the $14,000 you invested in your new home. The $5,000 gain is fully taxed because the adjusted sales price of the old home is more than the amount you paid to remodel your new home. For this purpose, you do not include the value of the inherited part of your property ($62,000) in the cost of your new home.

TaxSaver

In the IRS example above, the $200 of fixing-up expenses did not result in any tax benefit to you. You could have paid less in taxes if you had reduced the price by $200 and let the buyer make the expenditures. This would have reduced your gain to $4,800 (instead of $5,000) and at the same time would have given you an equal amount of cash.

Moving expenses. You cannot increase the basis of your new home by attorneys' fees or similar expenses you deduct as moving expenses. For more information, see Chapter 27, *Moving Expenses.*

Explanation

Attorneys' fees, title fees, escrow fees, state transfer taxes, "points," and loan placement charges that you pay may be deducted as moving expenses or used to reduce your gain on the sale of your home.

Escrow fees, appraisal fees, and title costs may also be deducted as moving expenses or added to the basis of your new home.

TaxPlanner

Generally, it's better to deduct an item as a moving expense than to use it to reduce the gain on the sale of your home or to increase the basis in the home you buy. Moving expenses may be deducted in the current tax year. Basis adjustments result—at best—in tax benefits later on. Therefore, the more you deduct from your ordinary income, the better.

Nevertheless, the deductions you may take for some moving expenses are limited (see Chapter 27, *Moving Expenses*, for more details). Deduct as much as possible in moving expenses, and treat any remaining amount either as an addition to basis or as a reduction in the selling price of your home, whichever is appropriate.

Holding period. If you postpone tax on any part of the gain from the sale of your old home, you will be considered to have owned your new home for the combined period you owned both the old and the new homes. See Chapter 15, *Sale of Property,* for more information on holding periods.

More than one main home bought or sold in a 2-year period. If you buy or build more than one main home during the replacement period, only the last one can be treated as your *new main home* to determine whether you can postpone the gain from the sale of the old home.

If you postponed the gain on the sale of your old home, then sell your new home within 2 years after the sale of your old home, you generally cannot postpone the gain on the sale of the new home.

The following examples illustrate these rules.

Example 1. You sold your first home in March 1992 for $120,000, and you had a $10,000 gain on the sale. You postponed the $10,000 gain because you bought a second home in April 1992 for $135,000. Your basis in the second home, as reported on the Form 2119 filed with your 1992 return, was $125,000 ($135,000 cost less the $10,000 postponed gain).

In June 1993 you sold the second home for $142,000 and you moved into an apartment. You purchased a third home in January 1994 for $146,000.

Your replacement home for the first home you sold (in March 1992) is the last main home you bought in the following 2-year period. This is the third home you bought (in January 1994). Since its $146,000 cost is more than the $120,000 sales price of your first home, your $10,000 gain is postponed. Your basis in your third home is $136,000 ($146,000 cost less the $10,000 postponed gain). You must file a new Form 2119 for 1992 to change the information you gave about your replacement home.

You cannot postpone the gain on the June 1993 sale of your second home. This is because it was within 2 years after the March 1992 sale of your first home on which you postponed the gain. Since you no longer treat your second home as the replacement for your first home, the basis of your second home is its $135,000 cost. You must include the $7,000 gain on its sale ($142,000 sales price less the $135,000 basis) in your 1993 income.

Example 2. Assume the same facts as in Example 1 except you purchased your third home in September 1994 rather than in January. Your second home is the replacement home for your first home (sold in March 1992). This is because it was the only home bought in the following 2-year period.

Although you bought another new main home within 2 years after selling your second home, you cannot postpone the gain on the June 1993 sale of your second home. This is because its sale was within 2 years of the March 1992 sale of your first home. You must report the $17,000 gain on the June 1993 sale of your second home ($142,000 sales price minus $125,000 basis) on your 1993 tax return. Your basis in your third home (that you bought in September 1994) is its cost, $146,000.

TaxPlanner

To defer paying tax on any gain you may make from selling your current principal home, you must own it for at least 2 years after the sale of a previous home for which you deferred the gain.

Exception. The rules for more than one home bought or sold in a 2-year period do not apply if you sell your main home because of a *work-related move.* A "work-related move" is one for which you are allowed a deduction for moving expenses. To qualify for the deduction, the move must be closely related to the start of work, and you must meet the time and distance requirements explained in Chapter 27, *Moving Expenses.*

If the exception applies, treat each sale as though the 2-year rule did not apply.

Explanation

If your move to your newest home is work related, you may postpone gain from the sale of more than one principal home during the replacement period if the following conditions are met:

1. Your new job location is at least 35 miles (50 miles, starting in 1994) farther from your old home than your old job location was.

Table 16-1. **Worksheet for Postponement of Gain**

If you must postpone tax on the gain from the sale of your main home under the rules discussed in this chapter, you can use this worksheet. It will help you figure the gain realized (Form 2119, line 8), gain taxed in the year of sale (Form 2119, line 21), and gain postponed (form 2119, line 22).

A. Gain Realized
1. Enter selling price of old home .... 1. _____
2. Enter selling expenses .... 2. _____
3. Subtract line 2 from line 1. This is the amount realized on sale. Enter here and on line 6 ...... 3. _____
4. Enter adjusted basis of old home .... 4. _____
5. Subtract line 4 from line 3. This is the gain realized. Enter here and on line 12 .... 5. _____

B. Gain Taxed in Year of Sale
6. Enter amount realized on sale from line 3 .... 6. _____
7. Enter fixing-up expenses .... 7. _____
8. Subtract line 7 from line 6. This is the adjusted sales price .... 8. _____
9. Enter cost of new home .... 9. _____
10. Subtract line 9 from line 8. If line 9 is more than line 8, enter zero .... 10. _____
11. Enter the lesser of line 5 or line 10. This is the gain taxed in year of sale .... 11. _____

C. Gain Postponed
12. Enter gain realized from line 5 .... 12. _____
13. Enter gain taxed in year of sale from line 11 .... 13. _____
14. Subtract line 13 from line 12. This is the gain to be postponed. Enter here and on line 16 ... 14. _____

D. Adjusted Basis of New Home
15. Enter cost of new home .... 15. _____
16. Enter gain to be postponed from line 14 .... 16. _____
17. Subtract line 16 from line 15. This is the adjusted basis of new home .... 17. _____

2. You work full time for at least 39 weeks during the 12-month period after you arrive at your new job location (78 weeks during the 24-month period after arrival if you are self-employed).

See below for further explanation.

Example. You sell two homes within 2 years as shown below:

January 1993	You sell your house in **Chicago** at a gain.
February 1993	You buy a more expensive house in **Memphis.**
March 1994	You sell your house in **Memphis** due to a transfer required by your employer.
March 1994	You buy a more expensive house in **New York City.** The move meets the requirements for a moving expense deduction.

When you complete the 1993 Form 2119 for the sale of your house in Chicago, compare the cost of the home bought in Memphis with the adjusted sales price of the house in Chicago, even though you bought another new main home within 2 years (New York City in March 1994).

Explanation

If more than one new home is purchased, only the last one is considered the new residence. If a third home is bought and the second one is sold, you may postpone your gain only on the sale of your first home.

The only exception is that you must sell the second home because of a work-related move and meet the tests for deducting the expenses incurred in that move, as described in Chapter 27, *Moving Expenses*. Also, you

must work full time for at least 39 weeks at the location of the second home.

Your 1994 Form 2119 will compare the adjusted sales price of the house in Memphis (sold March 1994) with the cost of the house in New York City.

Continue to postpone gain. If you bought your present home and postponed tax on gain from a prior sale under the postponement-of-gain rules discussed earlier, you continue to postpone the tax if you replace your present home under those rules.

Example. In 1975 you sold your home, which you had owned since 1965, and bought a new one. The tax on the gain was postponed and the basis of the home you bought in 1975 was reduced by the gain you postponed. This year you sold the home you bought in 1975 and bought a more expensive one. You can postpone tax on the gain from selling the home you bought in 1975.

TaxPlanner

Do not use this worksheet if you are 55 or older and meet all the requirements to exclude $125,000 of your gain discussed later.

How and When to Report

If you sold your home during the year, report the details of the sale as explained in this section. Report the sale even if you have a loss, you postponed the tax on the entire gain, or you have not purchased a new home.

This chapter contains *Table 16-2. How to Report the Sale of Your Home* that highlights the information presented in this section. You may find it helpful when determining how to report the sale of your home.

Table 16-2. How to Report the Sale of Your Home

New Home Purchased and Occupied Within Replacement Period		
	The cost of the new home is—	
	EQUAL to or GREATER than the adjusted sales price of the old home:	LESS than the adjusted sales price of the old home:
If you purchase a new home before you file a return for the year of sale:	Attach a completed Form 2119 to your return for the year of sale.	Attach a completed Form 2119 and Schedule D to your return for the year of sale.
If you purchase a new home after you file a return for the year of sale:	Report the sale by attaching Form 2119 to your return for the year of sale. When you purchase and occupy the new home, file a second Form 2119.	Report the sale by attaching Form 2119 to your return for the year of sale. When you purchase and occupy the new home, file Form 1040X for the year of sale. Attach a second Form 2119 and Schedule D.

New Home NOT Purchased and Occupied Within Replacement Period	
If—	Then—
You do not plan to replace your old home:	Attach a completed Form 2119 and Schedule D to your return for the year of sale.
You originally planned to replace your old home BUT you do not replace it:	Attach Form 2119 to your return for the year of sale. When the replacement period ends or when you decide not to replace your old home, file Form 1040X for the year of sale. Attach a second Form 2119 and Schedule D to Form 1040X.

Form 2119. Use Form 2119, *Sale of Your Home,* to report the sale of your old home and any purchase of a new one. File Form 2119 for the year you sold your old home. You may also have to file a second Form 2119 when you purchase your new home. See Chapter 45, *Sample Form 1040,* for an example of a filled-in Form 2119.

Keep a copy of Form 2119 with your tax records for the year. Form 2119 is also a supporting document that shows an adjustment to your basis in the replacement home. Therefore, you should also keep a copy of Form 2119 with the records for the basis of your new home.

Reporting a loss. You must report the sale of your main home even if you have a loss on the sale. Complete Parts I and II of Form 2119 for the year in which the sale occurred. The loss does not reduce your income.

If you report a loss on the sale, you do not have to file a second Form 2119 if you later purchase a new home. The loss on the sale has no effect on the basis of your new home.

Schedule D (Form 1040). If you report taxable gain on the sale of your main home, you will also have to file a Schedule D (Form 1040), *Capital Gains and Losses,* with your return.

Maximum tax rate on capital gains. Your net capital gain is taxed at a maximum tax rate of 28%, even if you have ordinary income that is taxed at a higher rate. In this case, you figure your tax using the *Schedule D Tax Worksheet* in the Schedule D (Form 1040) instructions.

New home purchased before return filed. If you buy a new home before you file a return for the year of sale of your old home, complete Form 2119 and attach it to your return. Show the price of the new home, the date you first lived in it, how you figured the postponed gain, and the adjusted basis of your new home.

If your new home costs as much as or more than the adjusted sales price of your old home, you postpone the tax on the entire gain. You do not need to report the sale on Schedule D (Form 1040).

If the new home costs less than the adjusted sales price of the old home, the gain is taxed to the extent of the difference. Report the taxable gain on Schedule D (Form 1040) for the year of the sale.

New home not yet purchased. If you plan to replace your home but have not done so by the time your return for the year of sale is due, you must still report the sale. Complete Form 2119, Parts I and II only, and attach it to your return for the year of sale.

New home purchased after return filed. If you buy and live in a new home after you file your return but within the replacement period, you should notify the IRS. File a second Form 2119 giving the date you first lived in the new home and its cost.

New home costs at least as much as adjusted sales price. If your new home costs at least as much as the adjusted sales price of your old home, file this second Form 2119 by itself. Your address, signature, and the date are required on this Form 2119. If you filed a joint return for the year of sale, both you and your spouse must sign the Form 2119. File it with the Director of the Internal Revenue Service Center where you would file your next tax return.

Explanation

If you purchase a replacement residence within the required period and it costs at least as much as the adjusted sales price of your old home, you must postpone the gain on the sale of your old home. Your basis in the new home is then adjusted downward by the amount of the gain that you are entitled to postpone.

New home costs less. If the new home costs less than the adjusted sales price of the old home, you must file an amended return (Form 1040X) for the year of the sale. Attach a second completed Form 2119 and Schedule D (Form 1040) showing the gain you must report. You will have to pay interest on any additional tax due on the amended return. The interest is generally figured from the due date of the return for the year of sale.

Old home not replaced or new home not purchased within replacement period. If you do not plan to replace your old home, you must complete Form 2119 and Schedule D (Form 1040) to report any gain. Attach them to your tax return for the year of the sale. The entire gain is taxable unless you are eligible to exclude all or part of the gain. See *Exclusion of Gain,* later.

You may have postponed gain on the sale of your old home because you planned to replace it. If you do not replace it within the replacement period, you must file a second Form 2119. Attach it to an amended return (Form 1040X) for the year of the sale. Include a Schedule D (Form 1040) to report your gain and any other appropriate schedule. For example, you would have to include Form 6252 to report an installment sale. You will have to pay interest on the additional tax due on your amended return. The interest is generally figured from the due date of the return for the year of sale.

Divorce after sale. If you are divorced after filing a joint return on which you postponed tax on the gain on the sale of your home, but you do not use your share of the proceeds to buy or build a new home (and your former spouse does), you must file an amended joint return to report the tax on your share of the gain. If your former spouse refuses to sign the amended joint return, attach a letter explaining why your former spouse's signature is missing.

Home replaced after tax paid on gain. If you paid tax on the gain from the sale of your old home, and you buy or build and live in a new home within the replacement period, you should file an amended return (Form 1040X) for the year of sale of your old home. Complete a new Form 2119, and include it with your amended return. Report on Schedule D (Form 1040) any gain on which you cannot postpone the tax, and claim a refund of the rest of the tax.

Installment sale. Some sales are made under arrangements that provide for part or all of the selling price to be paid in a later year. These sales are called "installment sales." If you finance the buyer's purchase of your home yourself, instead of having the buyer get a loan or mortgage from a bank, you may have an installment sale. If the sale qualifies, you can report the part of the gain you cannot postpone on the installment basis.

Seller-financed mortgage. If you sell your home and hold a note, mortgage, or other financial agreement, the payments you receive generally consist of both interest and principal. You must report the interest you receive as part of each payment separately as interest income. If the buyer of your home uses the property as a personal residence, you must also report the name, address, and social security number of the buyer on line 1 of either Schedule B (Form 1040) or Schedule 1 (Form 1040A). The buyer must give you his or her social security number and you must give the buyer your social security number. Failure to meet these requirements may result in a $50 penalty for each failure. For more information, see Publication 537, *Installment Sales.*

Statute of limitations. The 3-year limit for assessing tax on the gain from the sale of your home begins when you give the IRS information that shows that:

1) You replaced your old home, and how much the replacement home cost,
2) You do not plan to buy a new home within the replacement period, *or*
3) You did not buy a new home within the replacement period.

This information may be on the Form 2119 attached to your tax return for the year of the sale, or on a second Form 2119 filed later. File the second Form 2119 with the Service Center where you will file your next tax return. If needed, send an amended return for the year of the sale to include in income the gain that you cannot postpone.

Exclusion of Gain

This section discusses how to exclude from gross income all or part of the gain from the sale of your main home if you meet certain age, ownership, and use tests at the time of the sale. This is a one-time exclusion of gain for sales after July 26, 1978.

The decision of when to take the exclusion depends on many factors. You will want to consider your personal tax and financial situation before deciding when to make the choice.

If you change your mind after you file the return for the year of sale, you may be able to make or revoke the choice later. You would have to file an amended return for the year of sale within certain time limits. See *How to Make and Revoke a Choice to Exclude Gain* in Publication 523.

Age, Ownership, and Use

You can choose to exclude from income $125,000 of gain on the sale of your main home ($62,500 if you are married on the date of sale and file separate returns) if you meet *all* the following requirements.

1) You were *55 or older* on the date of the sale.
2) During the *5-year period* ending on the date of the sale, you:
   • *Owned* your main home for at least *3 years,* and
   • *Lived in* your main home for at least *3 years.*
3) Neither you nor your spouse has excluded gain on the sale of a home since July 26, 1978.

For more information and examples, see *Exclusion of Gain* in Publication 523.

Explanation
The following explanation and examples spell out in detail when you may exclude from your gross income some or all of your gain from the sale of your principal home.

Age 55 at time of sale. You must reach age 55 by the date you sell the home to qualify for the $125,000 exclusion. You do not meet the age 55 test if you sell the property during the year in which you will be 55 years old but before you actually become that age. The earliest date on which you may sell your home and still qualify for the exclusion is your 55th birthday.

TAXPLANNER

The IRS generally considers your age for the entire year to be the age you reach by December 31, but this rule is different. Don't make the mistake of selling your residence in the year you become 55 but before your 55th birthday.

TaxSaver 1

You may take advantage of the once-in-a-lifetime $125,000 exclusion available to anyone over age 55 and also defer any remaining gain on the same residence if you purchase a new home that costs at least as much as the difference between the adjusted sales price of the old home and the exclusion claimed.

Example

You sell your home for $240,000. Your adjusted basis in the home is $50,000. The gain on the sale is $190,000. If you elect to apply the $125,000 exclusion, you may reduce your gain to $65,000.

Your new residence costs $200,000. Since the cost of your new home exceeds $115,000 ($240,000 − $125,000), you defer paying tax on the $65,000 gain by reducing your basis in your new residence by that amount. Therefore, your basis in your new home is $135,000 ($200,000 − $65,000). You have deferred your gain as well as used the $125,000 exclusion.

See Chapter 45, *Sample Form 1040*, for an illustration of how to complete Form 2119.

TaxSaver 2

Under certain circumstances, a person may choose *not* to take advantage of the age 55 or older exclusion. If you are purchasing a home that you plan to sell later and if you suspect that this home will appreciate in value and thereby allow you to take a larger exclusion than would be allowed on your original home, you should consider skipping the one-time exclusion this time around. This technique should be considered whenever the gain you realize from the sale of your original residence is less than the full $125,000 that the exclusion allows.

Example 1

Mr. and Mrs. Smith are over 55 years of age and have lived in their home for 3 of the last 5 years. They have decided to sell their house and move into an apartment. They never expect to purchase another home. Rather than pay tax on the gain on the sale of their old home, the Smiths should elect the once-in-a-lifetime exclusion. This is true even if the gain is much less than the $125,000 maximum that may be excluded, since, if they do not now take advantage of the exclusion, they may never have another chance.

Example 2

Alternatively, assume that the Smiths sell their home for $50,000 and buy a new home for $40,000. The Smiths had a $5,000 gain on the sale of their old home. They expect that the new house will appreciate substantially. It may be to the Smiths' advantage to forgo the once-in-a-lifetime exclusion this time, pay tax on the $5,000 gain on the sale of their current home, and hope that when they sell their new house they will have a bigger gain and therefore benefit by taking a bigger slice out of the $125,000 exclusion.

Example 3

Assume that in 1993 the Smiths are in the highest tax bracket (39.6%) and have a $75,000 gain, qualifying them for the $125,000 exclusion. If the Smiths choose not to use the one-time exclusion in 1993, in general, they will pay federal tax of $21,000 ($75,000 × 28%, the maximum tax on capital gains). Therefore, the Smiths should seriously consider utilizing their one-time exclusion in 1993 to save a substantial amount of tax, even if they expect to have another opportunity later.

Explanation

Ownership and use test. The required 3 years of ownership and use during the 5-year period ending on the date of the sale or exchange do not have to be continuous. You meet the test if you can show that you owned and lived in the property as your principal home for either 36 full months or 1,095 days (365 × 3) during the 5-year period. Short temporary absences for vacations or other seasonal absences, even if you rent out the property during the absences, are counted as periods of use.

Examples

A taxpayer who takes 2-month vacations annually may still claim that she was using her home during those vacation periods.

A taxpayer who takes a 1-year sabbatical abroad and leases her house for all or a portion of this period may not claim that she was using the home during this time. The IRS would not view the leave as a short, temporary absence.

TaxSaver

An individual will qualify for the one-time exclusion if, during the 5 years immediately preceding the sale, such individual:

1. Becomes physically or mentally incapable of self-care,
2. Owns and uses the home for at least one year, and
3. Owns the property and resides in a state-licensed facility (including a nursing home) that provides care to the physically or mentally incapacitated.

Explanation

More than one owner. If a husband and wife who meet the age, ownership, and use tests sell their jointly owned home, they are considered one for figuring the gain to be excluded from income. But, if the joint owners of a home are not husband and wife, each owner who meets the age, ownership, and use tests may exclude his or her gain on an individual basis.

Each such owner who chooses to exclude gain from gross income must meet the age, ownership, and use tests. If one owner meets the tests, that does not automatically qualify the other owners to exclude their gain from gross income. A choice by one owner does not prevent the other owners from making a similar choice in the future.

Example 1

Frank Smith and his sister, Mary, each own a half-interest in their jointly owned home. They both meet the age, ownership, and use tests. The adjusted basis of the home is $28,000, or $14,000 each. They sell the home, and the adjusted sales price is $140,000. The adjusted sales price of Frank's interest in the home is $70,000 (½ × $140,000). He may choose to exclude his entire gain of $56,000 ($70,000 − $14,000) from gross income. Mary may also choose to exclude her entire gain from income.

Example 2

John Jones, age 56, jointly owns a house with Betty Murphy, age 54. Jones and Murphy are not related. Both meet the ownership and use tests. If they sell their home, Jones is able to exclude his share of the gain up to the $125,000 limit. Murphy, however, does not qualify, since she does not satisfy the age requirement.

Betty Murphy subsequently purchases another house and uses it as her residence for 3 years. She is then 57 years old and is eligible to exclude $125,000 of gain on the sale of that residence. It is not relevant that a co-owner took the once-in-a-lifetime exclusion on the sale of a residence that she previously jointly owned. Murphy is not bound by the election of any nonspouse owner.

Explanation

Previous home destroyed or condemned. For meeting the ownership and use tests, if you sold or exchanged your principal home, you may add the time you owned and lived in a previous home that was destroyed or condemned to the time you owned and lived in the home on which you wish to exclude gain. This applies if any part of the basis of the home you sold or exchanged depended on the basis of the destroyed or condemned home. Otherwise, you must have owned and lived in the *same* home that was sold or exchanged for 3 out of the 5 years before the sale or exchange to qualify for the exclusion.

Ownership and use tests met at different times. The ownership and use tests may be met during different 3-year periods, as long as both tests are met during the 5-year period ending on the date of the sale or exchange.

Amount excluded. If you meet the age, ownership, and use tests, you may choose to exclude $125,000 of your gain on the sale or exchange of your home. If you are married filing separately, you may choose to exclude only $62,500 of gain on the sale or exchange. Your gain is the amount realized minus the adjusted basis of the home. If there is gain remaining after the exclusion, you may be able to postpone the rest of the gain if, as explained earlier, you buy and live in another home.

Principal home. Principal, or main, home has the same meaning for the exclusion of gain as it has for postponing tax on gain. See *Main Home* earlier in this chapter.

TAXSAVER

The sale of a life estate in a principal residence may qualify for the one-time exclusion of gain from gross income. A life estate interest in a property terminates on the death of the life estate owner.

Example

Bill and Kate (both 60 years of age) sold a life estate in a residence that they had used as a principal residence for 10 years. The life estate represented their entire interest in the residence. Bill and Kate satisfy the age, ownership, and use requirements, and may exclude up to $125,000 of gain on their joint return.

Explanation

When you use only part of the property as your principal home, as explained earlier, the rules discussed in this section of the chapter apply only to the gain on the sale or exchange on the part of the property used as your principal home.

Example

Dr. Martha Russell met the age, ownership, and use tests when she sold her principal home. However, for the whole time she owned the home, she used half of it exclusively as an office for treating her patients. Because Dr. Russell did not use the whole property as her principal home, only the half of the property used as her home qualifies for the choice to exclude gain from gross income. See *Property used partly as your home and partly for business* for an example of how to divide the gain between the part of a property used as your home and the part used for business or other purposes.

Explanation

The fact that a portion of a property has been used for a business or a rental purpose does not necessarily limit the amount of the one-time exclusion that is available.

Example

In the example above, if the amount of the gain allocated to the portion of the property used as Dr. Russell's principal home is $140,000, $125,000 of that gain can be excluded from her gross income.

Explanation

If you trade your old home for a different home, the trade is treated as a sale and a purchase. Gain on the old home may qualify for exclusion from gross income.

Land. If you sell the land on which your principal home is located, but not the house itself, you may not exclude from income any gain you have from the sale of the land.

If your home is condemned for public use, you may treat the transaction as a sale of the home. If you choose to exclude gain on it from gross income, you must first exclude it as explained in this part of the chapter. You may postpone the tax on the rest of the gain as explained earlier, or you may postpone it under the rules for an involuntary conversion. See Publication 549.

If your home is damaged by fire, storm, or other casualty, you may choose to exclude gain from insurance proceeds, or other compensation, as explained in this part of the chapter. However, *unlike a condemnation gain,* you may not postpone the tax on the rest of the gain, as explained earlier in this chapter. The rest may qualify, however, for the tax treatment that applies to involuntary exchanges, explained in Publication 547.

Jointly owned home. Both you and your spouse meet the age, ownership, and use tests if

1. You hold the home either as **joint tenants, tenants by the entirety,** or as **community property** on the date of the sale or exchange
2. You file a joint return for the tax year in which you sell the home
3. Either you or your spouse is 55 or older on the date of sale and has owned and lived in the property as a principal home for the required time before the sale or exchange

Home of spouse who died. You meet the ownership and use tests if on the date you sell your principal home

1. Your spouse is deceased
2. You have not remarried
3. Your deceased spouse had met the ownership and use tests for that principal home, and
4. Your deceased spouse had not previously chosen or joined in choosing to exclude gain on the sale or exchange of another principal home after July 26, 1978

Example

Ellen and Doug Smith were married on January 1, 1991, and afterwards lived in as their principal home property that Doug had owned and lived in continuously as his principal home since January 1, 1978. Doug died on January 1, 1993, never having chosen or joined in choosing to exclude gain on the sale or exchange of any home.

Ellen inherited the property and continued to live in it as her principal home until December 10, 1993, when she sold it. At the date of sale, she was 56 years old, had not remarried, and had never chosen or joined in choosing to exclude gain on the sale or exchange of any home. Because Doug, during the 5-year period ending on the date Ellen sold the property, met the 3-year ownership and use tests for this property, and because Ellen meets the age test, she may choose to exclude from her gross income up to $125,000 of the gain on the sale of her home. See *Making and revoking a choice to exclude gain,* discussed later.

Explanation

Sale by executor. Gain from the sale of a home by the executor of an estate qualifies for this exclusion, if the sale is made under a contract entered into before death by a taxpayer who met the age, ownership, and use tests.

Effect of marital status. You determine your marital status as of the date of sale or exchange of the home. If you are divorced by the date of the sale or exchange, you are not considered married.

If you are married at the time you sell or exchange your home, you may not choose to exclude the gain unless your spouse joins you in making the choice. You must make a joint choice even if

1. You or your spouse owned the home separately
2. You and your spouse filed separate returns, or
3. The spouse not owning an interest in the home had not lived in it for the required period before the sale or exchange

If your spouse died after the sale or exchange but before making the choice to exclude the gain, his or her personal representative (e.g., administrator or executor) must join with you in making the choice. You, as the surviving spouse, are considered the personal representative of your deceased spouse if no one else has been appointed.

If the home is not jointly owned, the spouse who owns the property must meet the age, ownership, and use tests discussed earlier. The other spouse must join in making the choice.

The law requires that both husband and wife join in electing to exclude the gain. This is an important decision, since the election may be made only once. Even if the couple divorces, the spouse who joined in an election to take the exclusion with respect to property owned by the other spouse may not elect to apply the exclusion again. (See immediately below for a further discussion.)

Separate return. If you are married and file a separate return and you meet the tests discussed earlier, you may choose to exclude no more than $62,500 of gain on the sale or exchange of your principal home. Your spouse must show agreement with your choice by writing in the bottom margin of Form 2119 or on an attached statement, "I consent to Part II election" and by signing his or her name.

You or your spouse may exclude gain only once. If you or your spouse chooses to exclude gain from a sale or exchange after July 26, 1978, neither of you may choose to exclude gain again for a sale or exchange after that date. If you and your spouse each owned separate homes before your marriage and sold both homes after your marriage, you may exclude the gain on one of them, but not on both. If, after choosing to exclude gain, you and your spouse divorce, neither of you may exclude gain again. If you remarry, you and your new spouse may not exclude gain on sales or exchanges after your marriage. However, a previous choice may be revoked, as discussed later under *Making and revoking a choice to exclude gain.*

Example 1

Frank and Sheila Brown were married. In January, 1992, they sold their jointly owned home. Frank and Sheila met the age, ownership, and use tests, so they chose to exclude their gain of $70,000 on their joint return for 1992. The Browns divorced in February, 1993.

In July, 1993, Sheila married Mike Jones. Mike had sold his home in March, 1993, when he was single. He met the age, ownership, and use tests at the time of sale. If Mike and Sheila file a joint return for 1993, Mike may choose to exclude up to $125,000 gain, because he was single at the time he sold his home. This is so, even though Sheila joined Frank in choosing to exclude gain.

If Mike files a separate return for 1993, he may exclude only up to $62,500 gain.

Note: The IRS views a married couple as a unit. If a joint return is filed, a $125,000 exclusion is allowed. If separate returns are filed, each partner may exclude up to half that amount, $62,500.

Example 2

Joe Johnson and Betty Smith were single, and each owned a home. In August, 1993, they sold their homes, and each had a gain of $125,000, for a total gain of $250,000. Each met the age, ownership, and use tests at the time of sale.

In October, 1993, Joe and Betty married. Because Joe and Betty were single when they sold their homes, they each may choose to exclude $125,000 of gain ($250,000 total) if they file a joint return.

Example 3

In February, 1993, Bill and Sally White were divorced. At that time, they had their jointly owned home up for sale. Sally married Ken Brown in November, 1993. In December, 1993, Bill and Sally's home was sold. Because Bill and Sally were not married to each other at the time their home was sold and they each met the tests to exclude gain, each may choose to exclude up to $125,000 gain based on the part of the home each owned (See the example under *More than one owner,* earlier.) Sally files a joint return and chooses to exclude up to $125,000 of her part of the gain. Ken joins Sally in her choice. Bill files a single return and chooses to exclude up to $125,000 of his gain.

If Ken Brown later sells a home, he may not choose to exclude gain, because he was required to join Sally in her choice to exclude gain. Ken is considered to have made a lifetime choice.

Example 4

David and Beth Pine sell their jointly owned home. They both meet the ownership and use tests at the time of sale, but David is 62 and Beth is 50. They file separate returns for the year in which their house is sold. Because Beth does not meet the age test, she may not choose to exclude gain on her separate return. David may choose to exclude gain on his separate return only if Beth joins him in making his choice, but he may exclude only up to $62,500 of the gain.

If Beth did join David in making his choice and she later sells a home, she may not choose to exclude gain, because she joined David in his choice to exclude gain.

Explanation

Making and revoking a choice to exclude gain. You may exclude gain on the sale or exchange of your principal home only *once* for sales or exchanges after July 26, 1978.

Time to exclude gain. You may make or revoke a choice to exclude gain from a particular sale or exchange at any time before the latest of three possible dates:

1. Three years from the due date of the return for the year of the sale

2. Three years from the date the return was filed
3. Two years from the date the tax was paid

Making the choice. You make the choice by attaching a filled-in Form 2119 to your income tax return for the year in which you sell or exchange your home. However, if you do not have Form 2119, you can make the choice by attaching a signed statement to your return. The statement must state that you choose to exclude from income the gain from the sale or exchange. It must also include the following:

1. Your name, age, social security number, and marital status on the date of the sale or exchange (if jointly owned, this information is given for each owner)
2. The dates you bought and sold the home
3. The adjusted sales price and the adjusted basis of the property on the date of sale
4. How long you were away from the home during the 5 years before the sale, except for vacation and other seasonal absences, even if you rented out the home during these absences
5. Whether you or a joint owner ever chose to exclude gain on the sale of a home and, if you did, when and where you did so. If you revoked the choice, give the date when it was revoked.

You may, after originally reporting the gain on the sale of your home, choose to exclude the gain from taxable income. You do so by filing an amended return on Form 1040X. You must send a filled-in Form 2119 or a statement with your amended return.

Revoking the choice. The spouse who joined you in making the choice must join you in revoking it. If your spouse is deceased, his or her personal representative must join in revoking any choice previously made by you and your deceased spouse or by you and his or her personal representative. You must revoke your choice in a signed statement, showing your name and social security number. Include in the statement the year in which you made the choice. Send it to the Internal Revenue Service Center where you filed the choice, the Service Center now nearest you, or your local Internal Revenue Service office.

If at the time you revoke your choice less than a year is left in the assessment period (time for determining your correct tax) for the tax year for which the choice was made, you must agree, in writing, that the assessment period will not run out before the end of 1 year after the filing of the statement. You must file this agreement before the end of the assessment period for the tax year in which you made the original choice to exclude gain. The assessment period normally ends on the latest of the dates shown earlier under *Time to exclude gain.*

Example 1

If you are a calendar year taxpayer and you file your 1993 tax return on March 20, 1994, but you do not pay the tax that is due until July 10, 1994, your assessment period expires on April 15, 1997. This date is the latest of (1) April 15, 1997, 3 years after the due date of the

1993 return; (2) March 20, 1997, 3 years after the actual filing of the 1993 return; and (3) July 10, 1996, 2 years after the amount of tax due was paid.

Example 2

Elsie and George Buchanan sold their home on March 10, 1993, for $120,000 and moved into an apartment. The house had been purchased 10 years earlier for $70,000. The Buchanans were both over 55 years old and elected to exclude the $50,000 gain on their home when they filed their 1993 return on April 15, 1994. There was no balance due with their return.

In July, 1994, Elsie Buchanan won the New York State lottery. Due to the change in their financial circumstances, the Buchanans decided to purchase a home for $250,000.

It is to the Buchanans' advantage to roll over the proceeds from the sale of the old residence rather than to use their once-in-a-lifetime exclusion to eliminate the $50,000 gain on that residence's sale. By doing so, they preserve the full $125,000 exclusion, which may then be used to eliminate what may be a considerably greater gain on the subsequent sale of their more expensive new home.

The Buchanans have until April 15, 1997, 3 years after the due date of their 1993 return, to amend their 1993 return and forgo the $125,000 exclusion on the sale of the original house. No tax is due with the amended return. However, filing the amended return is an important formality that must be observed in order to retain the $125,000 exclusion for later years.

Explanation

Filing your return. Even if you exclude the gain on the sale of your home from gross income, you must consider that gain in determining whether you had enough income to require you to file a return.

Your gain is added to all your other income. If that figure falls below a certain amount, you are not required to file a return.

Example

Steve and Joan Johnson are both 60 years old. In 1993, they sold their house, realizing a gain of $100,000. The Johnsons' only other income in 1993 was $5,000 in interest income. They elected to exclude the gain, so their gross income was only $5,000. For 1993, married couples such as the Johnsons with a combined gross income of less than their personal exemptions and standard deductions are not required to file a federal tax return. However, the Johnsons must include the $100,000 excluded gain in their income for purposes of determining whether or not they must file a return. The resulting $105,000 figure means they must file for 1993.

17 | Reporting Gains and Losses

Introduction

For many years, one of the best ways to save tax dollars was to generate long-term capital gains: profits you make from the sale of assets such as stocks, bonds, and real estate. To qualify for long-term capital gains treatment, all you had to do was hold a capital asset for more than 1 year (or, in some years, more than 6 months) and the gain was subject to a lower tax rate.

Under the 1993 Tax Act, the tax benefit of generating long-term capital gains has again become substantial. Under the new law effective January 1, 1993, the top tax rate applicable to long-term capital gains is 28%, while the top rate applicable to ordinary income is 39.6%. Therefore, capital gains are potentially subject to an 11.6% lower tax rate (39.6%-28%). Accordingly, you can achieve substantial tax savings by generating net capital gains in lieu of ordinary income. Your net capital gain equals net long-term capital gain less net short-term capital loss.

These changes will have a profound effect on tax planning and investing. This chapter will provide you with examples of how the rules work. It also provides advice on year-end planning.

Important Changes for 1993

Amount of net capital gain eligible for 28% tax rate. If you include part or all of your net capital gain in investment income when figuring the limit on your investment interest deduction, you must reduce the amount of your net capital gain that is eligible for the 28% maximum capital gains tax rate by the same amount. See *Schedule D Tax Computation,* later in this chapter.

Schedule D–1 eliminated. Schedule D–1, *Continuation Sheet for Schedule D (Form 1040),* has been eliminated for 1993. If you have too many transactions to list on page 1 of Schedule D, *Capital Gains and Losses,* you can now list them on page 2 of Schedule D. Capital loss carryovers and the tax computation using the maximum capital gains rate, which used to be figured on page 2 of Schedule D, are now figured using worksheets in the Schedule D instructions. For more information, see *Capital Losses* and *Schedule D Tax Computation* later in this chapter.

Explanation
For a discussion of the new rules regarding the rollover of gain from the sale of publicly traded securities sold after August 9, 1993 and replaced with the common stock of, or a partnership interest in, a specialized small business investment company see Chapter 15, *Sale of Property.* Also see Chapter 15 for a discussion of the new rules regarding the sale of qualified small business stock issued after August 10, 1993, and held by the taxpayer for more than 5 years. In general, under the new rules, 50% of the gain from such a sale may be excluded from tax.

Important Reminder

Maximum tax rate on capital gains. The maximum tax rate on your net capital gain is still 28% for 1993, even though the maximum tax rate on ordinary income has increased to 39.6%. Your "net capital gain" is your net long-term capital gain minus any net short-term capital loss. See *Schedule D Tax Computation,* later in this chapter, for more information.

This chapter discusses how to report capital gains and losses from sales, exchanges, and other dispositions of investment property on Schedule D of Form 1040. The discussion includes:

- How to report short-term gains and losses,
- How to report long-term gains and losses,
- How to figure capital loss carryovers,
- How to figure your tax using the 28% maximum tax rate on capital gains, if it applies, and
- An illustrated example of how to complete Schedule D.

If you sell or otherwise dispose of property used in a trade or business or for the production of income, see Publication 544, *Sales and Other Dispositions of Assets,* before completing Schedule D.

Useful Items

You may want to see:

Publication

☐ **544** Sales and Other Dispositions of Assets
☐ **550** Investment Income and Expenses

Form (and Instructions)

☐ **Schedule D (Form 1040)** Capital Gains and Losses
☐ **2119** Sale of Your Home
☐ **4797** Sales of Business Property
☐ **8582** Passive Activity Loss Limitations

Schedule D

Report capital gains and losses on Schedule D (Form 1040). If you have too many transactions to list on page 1 of Schedule D, you can list them on page 2 of Schedule D. You can use worksheets in the Schedule D (Form 1040) instructions to figure your capital loss carryover and to figure your tax using the *Schedule D tax computation.*

Explanation

When you sell or dispose of property, you must determine whether your gain or loss is "capital" or "ordinary." Only capital gains and capital losses are reported on Schedule D, while ordinary gains and losses are reported elsewhere. This distinction is significant, because (1) you can use capital losses to offset gains only to the extent of capital gains plus $3,000, and (2) net capital gains may be subject to a lower tax rate than ordinary income. Any unused losses can be carried over to the next year.

Example

Assume that Alan has $12,000 of capital losses and $4,000 of capital gains in 1993. Alan can deduct only $7,000 of his capital losses in 1993, which is equal to his $4,000 of capital gains plus $3,000. Alan's net capital loss for the year is $3,000 ($7,000 of utilizable losses minus $4,000 of capital gains). The remaining $5,000 of losses ($12,000 gross losses minus $7,000 of losses used) may be carried over and used in later years, subject to the $3,000 limitation. If Alan's losses were ordinary, he could have used all of them in 1993, unless subject to other limitations by special provisions of the Internal Revenue Code.

Explanation

Net capital gains are subject to a top marginal rate of 28%. Net capital gains are the excess of (1) net long-term capital gains over (2) net short-term capital losses.

Examples

The taxpayers listed below have the following capital gains and losses for 1993:

	Long-term capital gain	Long-term capital loss	Short-term capital gain	Short-term capital loss
Tom	$800	$(500)	$300	$(100)
Anne	700	0	200	(600)
Neil	600	0	200	(900)

Tom has a net long-term capital gain of $300 ($800 − $500) and a net short-term capital gain of $200 ($300 − $100). Tom's net capital gain subject to the lower tax rate is $300, since Tom has a net long-term capital gain of $300 and no short-term capital loss.

Anne has a net long-term capital gain of $700 and a net short-term capital loss of $(400). Anne's net capital gain subject to the lower tax rate is $300 ($700 − $400).

Neil has a net long-term capital gain of $600 and a short-term capital loss of $(700). Neil has no net capital gain, and his tax return will show a net short-term capital loss of $100, which may be available to offset ordinary income.

Explanation

Taxpayers in the two lowest tax brackets (15% and 28%) need not be concerned with this provision. The special capital gains tax rate only applies to taxpayers whose highest marginal tax rate is greater than 28%.

Example

Linda, an unmarried individual, reported taxable income of $95,000 for 1993. Included in Linda's taxable income is a $20,000 net capital gain from the sale of stock she held for 3 years. Linda computes her tax as follows:

Step 1:

Tax on $95,000 of taxable income	$24,972

Step 2:

Tax on taxable income of $75,000, excluding the net capital gain ($95,000 − $20,000)	$18,772
Tax on capital gain ($20,000 × 28%)	$5,600
Total	$24,372

Linda's tax liability will be the lesser of the amounts computed in Steps 1 or 2. Thus, Linda's 1993 tax liability will be $24,372.

As discussed in Chapter 21, *Limit on Itemized Deductions*, many taxpayers will be subject to phaseouts of itemized deductions and personal exemptions. These phaseouts will also affect tax computations involving net capital gains.

TAXPLANNER

The difference between the new top marginal rate of 39.6% and the top rate on net capital gains of 28% is significant—an 11.6% difference. Accordingly, taxpayers should try to generate long-term capital gains, as opposed to ordinary income, whenever possible. It should be noted, however, that the recently enacted tax legislation recharacterizes gains from certain "conversion transactions" into ordinary income. See later in this chapter for an explanation of "conversion transactions."

Example

Nancy is in the top 39.6% marginal tax bracket for 1993 and 1994, and has the following unrealized capital gains and losses:

Stock A: Unrealized short-term capital gain	$ 10,000
Stock B: Unrealized long-term capital loss	$(13,000)
Stock C: Unrealized long-term capital gain	$ 15,000

Assume that Nancy sells all three stocks in 1993. Nancy will compute her net capital gain for the year as follows:

Net long-term capital gain	$ 2,000
Net short-term capital gain	$10,000
Total gains	$12,000

Nancy has a net capital gain of $2,000. Nancy will pay $560 of tax on her net capital gain ($2,000 × 28%) and $3,960 on her short-term capital gains, which are taxed at her regular 39.6% rate ($10,000 × 39.6%). Thus, Nancy will pay a total tax of $4,520 ($560 + $3,960) on her capital gains.

Assume instead that Nancy sells stocks A and B in 1993, but waits until 1994 to sell stock C.

Nancy will have a net long-term capital loss of $(3,000) for 1993 ($10,000 gain on stock A, less $13,000 loss on stock B). Nancy will be allowed to offset the $3,000 capital loss against her ordinary income, giving her a $1,188 tax saving for 1993.

Nancy will also have a $15,000 net long-term capital gain in 1994 from the sale of stock C. This will represent a net capital gain subject to the maximum 28% rate on net capital gains. Nancy will pay $4,200 of tax in 1994 on her net capital gain ($15,000 × 28%).

By using tax planning, Nancy's total liability on her capital gains would be $3,012 ($4,200 for 1994, less $1,188 of tax savings in 1993). As compared to the $4,520 of tax liability without tax planning, Nancy has saved $1,508. Furthermore, Nancy also delayed the payment of the tax by waiting until 1994 to trigger some of her gains.

The tax savings to Nancy may be small relative to the investment ramifications of holding stock C for a longer period. Nancy must therefore balance the potential tax savings against her overall investment strategy.

Explanation

A capital gain or loss results from (1) the sale or exchange of a capital asset, or (2) net section 1231 gains being treated as a capital gain.

Almost everything you own and use for personal purposes or investment purposes is a capital asset. For example, stocks, bonds, jewelry, and household furnishings generally are all capital assets. Most properties held in a business (i.e., inventory, accounts receivable, machinery) are not capital assets. See Chapter 15, *Sale of Property*, for a further elaboration on what constitutes a capital asset.

A net section 1231 gain is also treated as a capital gain, while a net section 1231 loss is treated as an ordinary loss. A section 1231 gain or loss is any gain or loss from the sale or exchange of real property or depreciable personal property used in your trade or business and held by you for more than 1 year. Any depreciation recapture must be separately computed on the sale of depreciable property and reported as ordinary income. Thus, the portion of the gain that is considered depreciation recapture is ordinary income, rather than a section 1231 gain. The computation of depreciation recapture is discussed in more detail at the end of this chapter.

Section 1231 gains also include recognized gains on the involuntary conversion of (1) property used in a trade or a business and held for more than 1 year, and (2) any capital asset held for more than 1 year and held in connection with a trade or a business or a transaction entered into for profit. Net involuntary conversion losses on these properties are not section 1231 losses but are deductible as ordinary losses. An involuntary conversion is the loss of property resulting from destruction (complete or partial), theft, seizure, requisition, or condemnation. An involuntary conversion also includes the sale or exchange of property under the threat or imminence of seizure, requisition, or condemnation.

For more information, see Publication 544, *Sales and Other Dispositions of Assets*.

Tax treatment of gains and losses. Once the disposition is properly classified, you can determine whether your gains and losses will be considered ordinary, capital, or nondeductible.

Capital losses resulting from the sale of business or investment property are reported on Schedule D. These may be used to offset any other capital gains, including capital gains from business and investment property, which are also reported on Schedule D.

Losses on the sale of personal-use property (e.g., a family car) cannot be used to offset capital gains. These losses are not reported on your income tax return. Capital gains on the sale of personal-use property are taxable, however, and are reported on Schedule D.

You must aggregate all of your section 1231 gains and losses during the year to determine the tax treatment of these items. Net section 1231 gains are treated as capital, while net section 1231 losses are treated as ordinary. Under a special look-back rule, if you have a net section 1231 gain in 1993, the gain will be treated as ordinary income to the extent of any section 1231 losses in the preceding 5 years (which were not previously used to recharacterize gains). Remember, any gain resulting in depreciation recapture is ordinary income and as a result is not considered in these computations. Fill out Form 4797 to report these items. Ordinary gains and losses are generally included in gross income. The capital gain portion is reported on Schedule D.

Capital gains and losses reported on Schedule D are further classified under long-term and short-term. Net section 1231 gains are long-term. For other classifications, see the discussion in Chapter 15, *Sale of Property*.

TAXALERT

The 1993 Tax Act contains a provision that recharacterizes capital gains from certain "conversion transactions" as ordinary income. The purpose of this provision is to prohibit taxpayers from taking advantage of the favorable tax rate on capital gains by entering into transactions which are, in effect, loans but which, because of their form, generate capital gains. In a conversion transaction, the taxpayer is in the economic position of a lender, and substantially all of the taxpayer's return is attributable to the amount of time the investment is held. In order to be a conversion transaction, a transaction must satisfy at least one of the following four criteria: (1) the transaction consists of the acquisition of property by the taxpayer and a substantially contemporaneous agreement to sell the same or substantially identical property in the future; (2) the transaction is a straddle (see Chapter 15, *Sale of Property*); (3) the transaction is one that is marketed or sold to the taxpayer on the basis that it would have the economic characteristics of a loan but the interest-like return would be taxed as capital gain; or (4) the transaction is described in regulations promulgated by the Secretary of the Treasury.

Passive activity gains and losses. If you have gains or losses from a passive activity, you may also have to report them on **Form 8582.** In some cases, the loss may be limited under the passive activity rules. Refer to Form 8582 and its separate instructions for more information about reporting capital gains and losses from a passive activity.

Explanation

For 1993, the gain or loss realized upon the sale or disposition of an interest in a passive activity must be combined with other items of income, expense, gain, or loss from investments in passive activities in order to determine the amount of passive activity losses that will be deductible on Form 1040. See Chapter 13, *Other Income*, for more information.

Form 1099–B transactions. If you sold property, such as stocks, bonds, or certain commodities, through a broker, you should receive Form 1099–B, *Proceeds From Broker and Barter Exchange Transactions*, or an equivalent statement from the broker. Use the Form 1099–B or equivalent statement to complete Schedule D (Form 1040).

Report the gross proceeds shown in box 2 of Form 1099–B as the **gross sales price** in column (d) of either line 1 or line 9 of Schedule D, as applicable. However, if the broker advises you, in box 2 of Form 1099–B, that gross proceeds (gross sales price) less commissions and option premiums were reported to the IRS, enter that **net sales price** in column (d) of either line 1 or line 9 of Schedule D, as applicable. If the net amount is entered in column (d), do not include the commissions and option premiums in column (e).

Be sure to add all sales price entries in column (d) on lines 1 and 2 and lines 9 and 10 and enter the totals on lines 3 and 11. Then add these amounts reported to you for 1993 on Forms 1099–B and Forms 1099–S (or on substitute statements):

1) Proceeds from transactions involving stocks, bonds, and other securities, and
2) Gross proceeds from real estate transactions not reported on another form or schedule.

If this total is more than the total of lines 3 and 11, attach a statement to your return explaining the difference.

If the Form 1099–B you receive includes amounts derived from the sale or exchange of section 1256 contracts or straddles, or from hedging transactions, see Publication 550 for more information about reporting these amounts.

Explanation

Amounts reported to you on Form 1099-B are also reported to the IRS. The IRS matches the amounts reported on Forms 1099-B to your return to make sure you reported all of your security sales. The amounts reported on Forms 1099-B should equal the sum of the amounts on lines 1(c) and 8(c) in column (d). If not, you will probably receive a letter from the IRS asking you to explain the difference. If the amounts are different, you should attach a schedule to your return explaining why.

TAXORGANIZER

Taxpayers who sell stocks, bonds, or other property through a broker should maintain the following documentation in order to facilitate the completion of Schedule D:

- Confirmations received from the broker documenting all sales transactions executed. These can be used to ensure the accuracy of any Forms 1099-B received.
- Confirmations received from the broker documenting all purchase transactions executed. These will be needed to calculate any gains or losses realized upon the sale of the property. The confirmations will also be needed to determine if any gains or losses are long-term or short-term.

Form 1099–S transactions. If you sold or exchanged reportable real estate, you should receive from the real estate reporting person a Form 1099–S, *Proceeds From Real Estate Transactions*, showing the gross proceeds from the sale.

"Reportable real estate" is defined as any present or future ownership interest in any of the following:

1) Improved or unimproved land, including air space,
2) Inherently permanent structures, including any residential, commercial, or industrial building,
3) A condominium unit and its accessory fixtures and common elements, including land, and
4) Stock in a cooperative housing corporation (as defined in section 216 of the Internal Revenue Code).

A "real estate reporting person" could include the buyer's attorney, your attorney, the title or escrow company, a mortgage lender, your broker, the buyer's broker, or the person acquiring the biggest interest in the property.

If you sell your main home that was purchased or improved with federally-subsidized financing from a mortgage credit certificate issued by a state or local government, you may have to increase your tax for the year of sale by all or part of the tax benefit you received in earlier years. For more information, see *Mortgage Interest Credit* in Chapter 35, *Other Credits*.

Your Form 1099–S will show the gross proceeds from the sale or exchange in box 2. Follow the instructions for Schedule D to report these transactions and include them on lines 1 or 9 as appropriate.

Add these amounts reported to you for 1993 on Forms 1099–S and 1099–B (or on substitute statements):

1) Proceeds from transactions involving stocks, bonds, and other securities, and
2) Gross proceeds from real estate transactions not reported on another form or schedule.

If this total is more than the total of lines 3 and 11 of Schedule D, attach a statement to your return explaining the difference.

If the building sold or exchanged was your main home, report the sale on **Form 2119.** Follow the Form 2119 instructions to determine whether you report any gain on Schedule D.

It is unlawful for any real estate reporting person to separately charge you for complying with the requirement to file Form 1099–S.

Other transactions. Enter all sales of stocks, bonds, and real estate transactions (other than the sale of your main home) on line 1 or line 9 of Schedule D as applicable, whether or not you actually received a Form 1099–B or Form 1099–S.

TaxAlert

For transactions occurring after December 31, 1992, the person reporting the real estate transaction is also responsible for including on Form 1099-S the portion of any real property tax that is property allocable to the purchaser. Thus, property tax allocable from the date of sale to year-end is reported on Form 1099-S. Note that if the purchaser agrees to pay the taxes the seller owed on the new home (up to the date of sale), these taxes are not treated as taxes paid by the purchaser, but instead are treated as part of the purchaser's cost. Accordingly, these amounts are not included on Form 1099-S as real property tax allocable to the purchaser. Instead, these amounts are included on Form 1099-S as part of the seller's proceeds.

If you had gains or losses from the disposition of *options,* including puts and calls, see *Options* under *Capital or Ordinary Gain or Loss* in Publication 550.

Property bought at various times. If you sell a block of stock or other property that you bought at various times, report the short-term gain or loss from the sale on one line in Part I of Schedule D and the long-term gain or loss on one line in Part II. Write "Various" in column (b) for the "Date acquired." See the *Comprehensive Example* later in this chapter for an example.

Sale expenses. Add to your cost or basis any expense of sale such as brokers' fees, commissions, state and local transfer taxes, and option premiums. Enter this adjusted amount in column (e) of either Part I or Part II of Schedule D, as applicable, unless you reported the net sales price amount in column (d).

For more information about adjustments to basis, see Chapter 14.

Short-term gains and losses. A capital gain or loss on the sale or trade of investment property held one year or less is a short-term capital gain or loss. Report it in Part I of Schedule D.

You combine your share of short-term capital gains or losses from partnerships, S corporations, and fiduciaries, and any short-term capital loss carryover, with your other short-term capital gains and losses to figure your net short-term capital gain or loss on line 8 of Schedule D.

Property held for personal use. Gain on the sale or exchange of property held for personal use and held for one year or

less is a short-term capital gain. Report it in Part I of Schedule D. Losses on sales or exchanges of property held for personal use are not deductible.

Long-term gains and losses. A capital gain or loss on the sale or trade of investment property held more than one year is a long-term capital gain or loss. Report it in Part II of Schedule D.

Explanation

The shortest length of time that qualifies for long-term status is 1 year plus 1 day. Your holding period begins on the day after you buy the property and includes the day you sell it.

Example

Donald pays $1,000 for Corporation X stock on July 1, 1992. His holding period begins on July 2, 1992. Donald sells the stock on July 1, 1993, for $1,500. His holding period runs from July 2, 1992 (the day after he purchased the stock), through July 1, 1993 (the day he sold the stock). Donald has a short-term capital gain of $500, because he has held the stock for exactly 1 year.

Assume instead that Donald sells the stock on July 2, 1993. His holding period runs from July 2, 1992, through July 2, 1993. His holding period is now in excess of 1 year (1 year and 1 day), so Donald's gain will be long-term.

You also report the following in Part II of Schedule D:

1) All capital gain distributions from regulated investment companies (mutual funds) and real estate investment trusts.
2) Your share of long-term capital gains or losses from partnerships, S corporations, and fiduciaries.
3) Long-term capital loss carryovers.

The result from combining these items with your other long-term capital gains and losses is your net long-term capital gain or loss (line 17 of Schedule D).

Property held for personal use. Gain on the sale or exchange of property held for personal use and held more than one year is a long-term capital gain. Report it in Part II of Schedule D. Loss on the sale or exchange of property held for personal use is not deductible.

Explanation

Most property you own and use for personal purposes or for pleasure, such as your house, furniture, and car, falls under the heading of capital asset. A gain on the sale of this kind of property is treated as a capital gain, but no loss is recognized for income tax purposes unless the property was used for business or investment purposes. If you realize a loss on property used for both business and personal purposes, the portion of the loss that is allocated to the business portion of the property may be deductible.

Capital gain distributions. You report capital gain distributions on line 14, Part II of Schedule D, regardless of how long you have held your investment. If you do not need Schedule D to report any other capital gains or losses and it would not benefit you to compute your tax using the maximum capital gains rate, enter your capital gain distributions for 1993 on line 14 of Form 1040.

Total net gain or loss. To figure your total net gain or loss, combine your net short-term capital gain or loss (line 8) with your net long-term capital gain or loss (line 17). Enter the result on line 18, Part III of Schedule D. If your losses are more than your gains, see *Capital Losses,* next. If both lines 17 and 18 are gains, see *Schedule D Tax Computation,* later.

Explanation

Dividends from mutual funds, which are technically known as **regulated investment companies,** are frequently composed of a combination of long-term capital gains and ordinary income. The nature of the gain is determined by how long the mutual fund has held the underlying property that generates the income, not how long you have held the mutual fund shares. Consequently, you may have a long-term capital gain, although you have held the mutual fund shares for less than the required long-term holding period.

Determination of cost basis and holding period. Mutual fund shares may be acquired on various dates, in various quantities, and at various prices. Some individuals may purchase shares through participation in dividend reinvestment or payroll deduction plans. Shares may also be sold on a periodic basis. As a result, individuals often encounter difficulty in determining their cost basis and hence gain or loss on the sale of their mutual fund shares. Under present law, four methods may be used by mutual fund shareholders to determine the cost basis of shares sold. They are

1. The specific identification method
2. The FIFO (First In–First Out) method
3. The single-category method using the average approach
4. The double-category method using the average approach

The specific identification method. In order to *specifically identify* the shares sold, the following requirements must be met:

1. Specific instructions to the broker or agent must be given by the customer, indicating the particular shares to be sold. These instructions must be given at the time of sale or transfer.
2. Written *confirmation* of this request must be received from the broker or agent within a reasonable time after the sale.

The individual shareholder bears the burden of proof that he or she owned and chose to sell the specific shares at the time of sale.

TaxPlanner

This specific identification method provides an investor with the greatest opportunity to manage his or her reported gain or loss. For example, if a shareholder has other capital losses during the year and wishes to generate capital gains, he or she can specifically identify those shares acquired at the *lowest prices* as the shares being sold. One problem with this method, particularly with mutual funds, is the inability of transfer agents to confirm, in writing, specific shares sold to the shareholder.

Explanation

The FIFO method. Under the FIFO (First In–First Out) method, the basis of shares acquired first represents the cost of the shares sold. In other words, the *oldest shares* held by the taxpayer are considered to be the first sold. The FIFO method is also a *default* method. If specific identification procedures are not or cannot be followed and the average basis approach (discussed below) is not elected, then the FIFO method will apply.

TaxAlert

Trap for the unwary. In a rising market, the FIFO method produces the *greatest gain* (and least loss) and hence, generally, the most tax.

Explanation

The single- and double-category methods using the average approach. The average-basis method must be *elected* by the individual shareholder by attaching a statement to his or her income tax return, for each year the choice applies. The election must indicate whether the single-category method or the double-category method (discussed below) is being used. Once the election is made, it must continue to be used for *all* accounts in the *same* mutual fund. The average method permits the taxpayer to calculate his or her gain or loss based on the average price paid for the shares.

With the single-category method, all shares are included in a single category; that is, the basis of each share is the total adjusted basis of all shares at the time of disposition divided by the total shares. In determining the holding period (long- or short-term), the shares disposed of are considered to be those shares acquired *first* (using a FIFO-type method, discussed earlier).

With the double-category method, all shares in an account are separated into two categories:

1. Short-term—shares held for 1 year or less
2. Long-term—shares held *more* than 1 year

The average cost for each category is calculated; that is, the basis of each share in a category is the total adjusted basis of all shares in that category divided by the total shares in that category. The shareholder can specify from which category shares are sold. The custodian or agent must confirm this to the shareholder in writing. If no selection is made, the shares in the long-term category are deemed to be sold first. After a share has been held for more than 1 year, it must be transferred from the short-term to the long-term category.

Explanation

Mutual fund dividends. If an individual who purchases shares in a mutual fund receives a capital gain dividend and then sells the shares at a loss within 6 months after purchase, the loss is treated as a *long-term* capital loss to the extent of the capital gain dividend received. Just as important, you may have to pay taxes on a capital gain dividend when you have not had a profit on your investment.

Example

You pay $10,000 for ABC Mutual Fund on June 30. On July 1, ABC Mutual Fund pays you a long-term capital gain dividend of $1,000. The same day, the value of your ABC shares drops to $9,000. You haven't made any money on your investment, but you still have to pay a tax on the capital gain dividend.

TAX*SAVER*

If at the end of the year you find that you have only short-term capital gains, you might consider generating capital losses by selling assets that have declined in value. Short-term gains are taxed as ordinary income, but you can avoid paying tax on them by offsetting them against both short-term and long-term losses.

Explanation

Sales or load charges. When a person invests in a mutual fund, he or she may be subject to a "sales or load charge," which is similar to a commission. When shares are sold or redeemed, the sales or load charge is generally taken into account as part of the purchaser's basis for purposes of computing gain or loss on the sale.

If an investor exchanges shares in a mutual fund for shares in the same "family" or complex of funds, an additional sales or load charge may be waived or reduced if the investor acquires a reinvestment right (i.e., the right to acquire stock of one or more mutual funds without the payment of all or part of the standard load charge) on the original purchase. If such an exchange occurs within 90 days of the original purchase of mutual fund shares, the original sales or load charge will not be included as basis in determining the gain or loss on the exchange. This rule only applies to the extent that the additional sales or load charge is waived or reduced on the exchange. To the extent that the sales or load charge is not treated as basis in computing gain or loss, such a charge will be taken into account on shares subsequently sold.

Example

On January 1, 1993, Kurt Norton purchased 100 shares of mutual fund X for $110, which included a $10 sales or load charge. On January 20, 1993, Kurt exchanged these shares for 50 shares of mutual fund X1, worth $115. Mutual fund X1 is in the same family as mutual fund X. The sales or load charge of $10 on Kurt's purchase of mutual fund X1 was waived. Kurt's gain or loss on the exchange is computed as follows:

Sales price of mutual fund X	$115
Cost basis of mutual fund X	100
Gain (loss)	$ 15

The sales or load charge of $10 on the purchase of mutual fund X did not affect the taxable gain or loss on the exchange but will become part of the basis of mutual fund X1.

Capital Losses

If your capital losses are more than your capital gains, you can claim a capital loss deduction. You must figure how much of the loss you can deduct in the year of the loss and how much of it you carry over and use in future tax years.

Example 1

You have capital gains and losses for the year as follows:

	Short-term	Long-term
Gains	$ 700	$ 400
Losses	800	2,000

Your net deductible capital loss is $1,700, which you figure as follows:

Short-term capital losses	$ 800	
Minus: Short-term capital gains	700	
Net short-term capital loss		$ 100
Long-term capital losses	$2,000	
Minus: Long-term capital gains	400	
Net long-term capital loss		$1,600
Net deductible capital loss		$1,700

Your deduction is limited to this $1,700 or your taxable income (adjusted as described later under *Yearly limit*), whichever is smaller.

Example 2

You have a net long-term capital loss of $1,600 and a net short-term capital gain of $450. Your deductible capital loss is $1,150 ($1,600 − $450).

Yearly limit. Your allowable capital loss deduction for any tax year, figured on Schedule D, is limited to the lesser of:

1) $3,000 ($1,500 if you are married and file a separate return), or
2) Your capital loss, as shown on line 18 of Schedule D.

Capital loss carryover. If you have a capital loss on line 18 of Schedule D that is more than the yearly limit on capital loss deductions, you can carry over the unused part to later years until it is completely used up. When you carry over a loss, it remains long term or short term. A short-term capital loss that is carried over to the next tax year is added to short-term losses that occur in that year. A long-term capital loss that is carried over to the next tax year is added to long-term losses that occur in that year.

You can carry over a capital loss that is more than the amount of allowable loss to the next year and treat it as if you had incurred it in that year. When you figure the amount of any capital loss carryover in a later tax year, you must take into account any deductions for capital losses allowed in earlier years.

Use short-term losses first. When figuring how much of your capital loss you can carry over as short term and how much as long term, use your short-term losses first, even if you incurred them after a long-term loss. If you have not reached the limit on the capital loss deduction after using short-term losses, use the long-term losses until you reach the limit.

Explanation

A net loss may be carried forward until it is exhausted or until the taxpayer dies. This carryforward may be used to reduce your tax when you have a capital gain sometime in the future. Even if you do not have future gains, the carryforward loss may be used to offset taxable income up to $3,000 per year.

Figuring your carryover. The amount of your capital loss carryover is the amount of your net capital loss that exceeds the lesser of:

1) Your allowable capital loss deduction for the year, or
2) Your taxable income increased by your allowable capital loss deduction for the year and your deduction for personal exemptions.

If your deductions exceed your gross income for the tax year, use your negative taxable income in computing the amount in item (2). Complete the *Capital Loss Carryover Worksheet* in the Schedule D (Form 1040) instructions to determine the part of your capital loss for 1993 that you can carry over to 1994.

Example. Bob and Gloria sold securities in 1993. The sales resulted in a capital loss of $7,000. They had no other capital transactions. On their joint 1993 return, they can deduct $3,000. The unused part of the loss, $4,000 ($7,000 − $3,000), can be carried over to 1994.

If their capital loss had been $2,000, their capital loss deduction would have been $2,000. They would have no carryover to 1994.

Joint and separate returns. If you are married and filing a separate return, your yearly capital loss deduction is limited to $1,500. Neither you nor your spouse can deduct any part of the other's loss.

If you and your spouse once filed separate returns and are now filing a joint return, you must combine each of your capital loss carryovers. However, if you and your spouse once filed a joint return and are now filing separately, any capital loss carryover can be deducted only on the return of the person who actually had the loss.

A decedent's capital loss. Capital losses cannot be carried over after a taxpayer's death. They are deductible only on the final income tax return filed for the decedent. The capital loss limits discussed earlier still apply in this situation. This loss cannot be deducted by the decedent's estate or carried over to following years.

TAXPLANNER

If the decedent filed a joint return in the year of death, the surviving spouse may offset gains recognized after the decedent's death but before the end of the tax year against the decedent's capital loss carryforward. Therefore, if the surviving spouse has assets that have appreciated in value, he or she should consider selling them in the year of the decedent's death. For a further discussion of this point, see Chapter 4, *Decedents*.

TAXSAVER

If you have an unused capital loss from investing in section 1256 contracts, this loss may be able to be carried back 3 years against prior year "section 1256 contract gains." Section 1256 contracts include certain regulated futures contract, foreign currency contracts, nonequity options, and dealer equity options. You claim your loss by checking box D on Form 6781, *Gains and Losses from section 1256 Contracts and Straddles,* and by filing an amended return for the year of the section 1256 contract gains.

Schedule D Tax Computation

For 1993, your capital gains are taxed at a maximum tax rate of 28% even if you have ordinary income that is taxed at a higher rate. For 1993, the maximum tax rate on ordinary income is 39.6%.

To qualify for the 28% maximum tax rate on capital gains, you must:

1) Have a net long-term capital gain that is more than any net short-term capital loss you may have (this difference is your net capital gain), and
2) Have taxable income that is subject to a tax rate higher than 28%.

If both lines 17 and 18 of Schedule D are net gains and your taxable income, as shown on line 37 of Form 1040, is subject to a tax rate higher than 28%, you can use the *Schedule D Tax Worksheet* in the Schedule D (Form 1040) instructions to figure your tax.

First complete your Form 1040 through line 37. Then complete the *Schedule D Tax Worksheet*. If you use the worksheet to figure your tax, be sure to check box c on line 38 of Form 1040 when you enter your tax on that line.

If you have net capital gains and your taxable income (line 37 of Form 1040) is over the amount shown for your filing status in the following table, you should complete the *Schedule D Tax Worksheet*.

Filing Status	Amount
Single	$53,500
Married filing jointly	$89,150
Married filing separately	$44,575
Head of household	$76,400
Qualifying widow(er)	$89,150

Example. Aretha Johnson, a single taxpayer, had 1993 taxable income of $55,000, including a long-term capital gain of $15,000 on the sale of stock. She had no other capital gains or losses. She enters her $15,000 gain on line 9 of Schedule D, then enters the same amount on lines 16, 17, and 18 of Schedule D and line 13 of Form 1040. Since Aretha's taxable income is more than $53,500, her maximum tax rate will be higher than 28%. To figure her 1993 tax, Aretha completes the *Schedule D Tax Worksheet*. Her filled-in worksheet is shown in *Table 17–1*.

Investment interest deducted. If you claim a deduction for investment interest, you may have to reduce the amount of your net capital gain that is eligible for the 28% maximum capital gains tax rate. Reduce it by the amount of the net capital gain you choose to include in investment income when figuring the limit on your investment interest deduction. For more information about deducting investment interest, see Chapter 3 of Publication 550.

Table 17-1. **Filled-in Schedule D Tax Worksheet**

Use this worksheet to figure your tax **only** if both lines 17 and 18 of Schedule D are gains, and:

Your filing status is: AND	Form 1040, line 37, is over:	Your filing status is: AND	Form 1040, line 37, is over:
Single	$53,500	Married filing separately	$44,575
Married filing jointly or qualifying widow(er)	$89,150	Head of household	$76,400

1. Enter the amount from Form 1040, line 37 .... 1. **55,000**
2. **Net capital gain.** Enter the **smaller** of Schedule D, line 17 or line 18 .... 2. **15,000**
3. If you are filing Form 4952, enter the amount from Form 4952, line 4e .... 3. **-0-**
4. Subtract line 3 from line 2. If zero or less, stop here; you cannot use this worksheet to figure your tax. Instead, use the Tax Table or Tax Rate Schedules 4. **15,000**
5. Subtract line 4 from line 1 .... 5. **40,000**
6. Enter: $22,100 if single; $36,900 if married filing jointly or qualifying widow(er); $18,450 if married filing separately; or $29,600 if head of household 6. **22,100**
7. Enter the **greater** of line 5 or line 6 .... 7. **40,000**
8. Subtract line 7 from line 1 .... 8. **15,000**
9. Figure the tax on the amount on line 7. Use the Tax Table or Tax Rate Schedules, whichever applies 9. **8,334**
10. Multiply line 8 by 28% (.28)... 10. **4,200**
11. Add lines 9 and 10... 11. **12,534**
12. Figure the tax on the amount on line 1. Use the Tax Table or Tax Rate Schedules, whichever applies 12. **12,580**
13. Enter the **smaller** of line 11 or line 12 here and on Form 1040, line 38. Check the box for Schedule D Tax Worksheet........... 13. **12,534**

TAXPLANNER

Effective for tax years ending after December 31, 1993, net capital gains are no longer included in "investment income" for purposes of determining a taxpayer's deduction for investment interest expense. However, you can elect to include capital gains as investment income. If you make such an election, you must reduce the amount of capital gains that are otherwise eligible for the maximum 28% tax rate by the amount included as investment income.

If you are in one of the two lowest tax brackets (15% and 28%), you should generally make this election to the extent that doing so increases your deduction for investment interest expense. Reducing the amount of capital gains that are otherwise eligible for the maximum 28% tax rate will have no impact on you because none of your income is taxed at a rate higher than 28%. This is also the case if you are subject to alternative minimum tax. The highest alternative minimum tax rate is 28%.

If you are in one of the three highest tax brackets (31%, 36%, and 39.6%), the decision whether or not to make the election depends upon whether you have enough non-capital gain investment income to allow you to deduct all of your investment interest expense. (Re-

member that disallowed investment interest expense can be carried forward to future years.) If you can deduct all of your investment interest expense without making the election, you will be better off. All of your capital gains will then be eligible for the maximum 28% rate.

Comprehensive Example

Emily Jones is single and, in addition to her regular employment, she has income from some stocks and other securities. For the 1993 tax year, she had the following capital gains and losses, which she reports on Schedule D. All the Forms 1099 she received showed net sales prices. Her filled-in Schedule D and *Capital Loss Carryover Worksheet* are shown in this chapter.

Capital gains and losses — Schedule D. Emily sold stock in two different companies that she held for less than a year. In June, she sold 100 shares of Bates Trucking Co. common stock that she had purchased in May. She had an adjusted basis of $650 in the Bates stock and sold it for $900, for a gain of $250. In June, she sold 25 shares of Alpha Computing preferred stock that she bought in March. She had an adjusted basis in the Alpha stock of $2,500, and she sold this stock for $2,000, for a loss of $500. Emily enters these short-term transactions on Part I of Schedule D.

During the year, Emily also sold securities in two other corporations. In February, she sold 60 shares of Car Motor Co. for $2,100.

She had inherited the Car stock from her father. Its fair market value at the time of his death was $700, which became her basis. Her gain on the sale, therefore, was $1,400. Because she had inherited the stock, she reports this as a long-term gain, regardless of how long she and her father actually held the stock.

On June 29, 1993, she sold 500 shares of Weeping Willow Furniture Co. nonconvertible preferred stock for $4,100. She bought 100 of those shares on June 25, 1987, for $7,000. She bought 100 more shares on September 10, 1987, for $9,000, and an additional 300 shares on January 30, 1991, for $18,000. Her total basis in the stock is $34,000. She realized a $29,900 ($34,000 − $4,100) loss on this sale.

Emily enters these long-term transactions on Part II of Schedule D.

Capital loss carryover — Schedule D. Emily has a capital loss carryover to 1993 of $800, of which $300 is short-term capital loss, and $500 is long-term capital loss.

She kept a copy of her 1992 Schedule D, so that she could properly report her loss carryover for the 1993 tax year without refiguring it. She completes the *Capital Loss Carryover Worksheet* to figure her capital loss carryover to 1994.

Reconciliation of Forms 1099–B. Emily makes sure that the amounts reported on lines 3 and 11 of Schedule D are not less than the amounts shown on the Forms 1099–B she received from her stockbroker. For 1993, the total of each is $9,100.

Explanation
Computing depreciation recapture. If you sell property at a gain, you must generally compute the portion of your gain that is depreciation recapture. Depreciation recapture is treated as ordinary income. The portion of the gain that is not depreciation recapture is treated as a section 1231 gain. Complete Form 4797 to determine the amount of your gain that is depreciation recapture.

Sale of depreciable personal property. The depreciation recapture rules for depreciable personal property are relatively simple, compared to the rules for real property. Depreciation recapture is the *lesser* of (1) the gain recognized or (2) depreciation taken on the property since 1961. Note that, under these rules, if depreciable personal property is sold at less than its original cost, the full gain will inevitably be depreciation recapture.

Example
In 1988, Alan bought personal property that he used in his trade for $5,000. Alan sold the property for $2,500 in 1993. He had already taken $3,662 in depreciation. Alan computes his gain or loss as follows:

Sales price		$2,500
Purchase price	$5,000	
Less: Depreciation taken	3,662	
Adjusted basis		1,338
Gain on sale		$1,162

Alan's gain on the sale is $1,162, which is less than the $3,662 of depreciation he had taken on the property. Therefore, his depreciation recapture is $1,162. Since this represents the full gain on the sale, no portion of the gain is treated as a section 1231 gain.

Assume instead that the property had appreciated and that Alan sold the property for $6,000:

Sales price	$6,000
Adjusted basis (computed above)	1,338
Gain on sale	$4,662

Since the depreciation Alan took on the property ($3,662) is less than the gain on the sale ($4,662), Alan reports the $3,662 depreciation taken as depreciation recapture. The remaining $1,000 of his gain ($4,662 − $3,662) is treated as a section 1231 gain.

Explanation
Sale of depreciable real estate. The depreciation recapture rules relating to the sale of real estate are quite complex. These rules depend on (1) when you placed the property in service, (2) what method of depreciation was used, and (3) whether the property was residential rental property or held for business use. It should be noted that no depreciation recapture should occur for real property acquired after 1986, because straight-line depreciation is the only method available for such property.

Real property acquired before 1976. If you acquired the real estate before 1976 and used the straight-line method of depreciation, there is no depreciation recapture on sale. If you used an accelerated method, you must go through a number of computations to determine depreciation recapture.

Step 1. Compute the excess depreciation for post-1975 years, which is the difference between the depreciation deductions you took using an accelerated method and the amount you would have taken had you used the straight-line method for the years you depreciated the property after 1975.

Step 2. Compare this amount to your overall gain on the sale. If your overall gain is less than this amount, then the overall gain is the amount of your depreciation recapture and you can stop here. If the overall gain is greater than the post-1975 excess depreciation, go on to Step 3.

Step 3. Subtract the excess depreciation computed in Step 1 from the total overall gain to compute the remaining gain. Then compute the excess depreciation for the years 1970 through 1975, using the same method as in Step 1. Take the smaller of the remaining gain or the excess depreciation for 1970 through 1975, as computed above.

If the property is *not* residential rental property, then the depreciation recapture is the sum of the excess depreciation computed in Step 1, plus the amount computed in Step 3. If the property is residential rental property, you must then compute the "applicable percentage," which depends on how many full months you owned the property. If you held the property less than 100 months, the applicable percentage is 100%. If you held the property for more than 100 full months, the applicable percentage is 100% minus the number of full months you held the property in excess of 100 months.

Multiply this percentage by the amount calculated in Step 3. Add this result to the amount calculated in Step

1 to get the total amount of gain treated as depreciation recapture.

Property acquired after 1975 and before 1981. Generally, all of the excess accelerated depreciation over straight-line depreciation up to the amount of gain has to be recaptured on sale. Certain kinds of property— government-assisted housing, low-income housing, certain rehabilitation expenses, and Title V loan property— are exempt from this rule. In these special cases, 100% of accelerated depreciation has to be recaptured for the first 100 months the property is held. After that, the recapture percentage declines 1% each month, so that after 16⅔ years there is no further recapture.

Nonresidential real property acquired after 1980 and before 1987. If the accelerated rates under the Accelerated Cost Recovery System (ACRS) are used on commercial real property, the entire amount of depreciation is subject to recapture on sale of the property. This means, in essence, that any gain up to the amount of depreciation previously claimed is treated as ordinary income. However, if straight-line ACRS is used, then none of the depreciation has to be recaptured at the time of sale.

Residential real property acquired after 1980 and before 1987. Any gain on the sale of *residential rental property* is ordinary income if the deductions taken under the accelerated ACRS method of depreciation exceed the depreciation allowed under the 15-year straight-line method of depreciation. However, any gain you incur in excess of the amount you have to recapture is treated as a capital gain. For property acquired after March 15, 1984, the ACRS period is 18 years, and, for property acquired after May 8, 1985, the ACRS period is 19 years.

Example

Mary bought an apartment building on January 2, 1985, for $125,000, of which $25,000 was assigned to the building's land and $100,000 to the building. Land may not be depreciated, but the building may. Mary used the accelerated ACRS method of depreciation. She sold the building on January 2, 1993, for $150,000, of which $30,000 was allocated to the land and $120,000 was allocated to the building:

Building cost 1/2/85	$125,000	
Land	(25,000)	
Depreciable basis		$100,000
ACRS depreciation through 1/2/93		(56,000)
Adjusted basis of building		$ 44,000
Selling price of building		$120,000
Adjusted basis of building		(44,000)
Gain on sale		$ 76,000
Total ACRS deduction	$ 56,000	
Straight-line depreciation for 8 years (using a 15-year life)	($ 53,000)	
Excess ACRS depreciation over straight-line method (ordinary income)		($ 3,000)
Portion of proceeds exceeding the adjusted basis and excess depreciation taken (capital gain)		$ 73,000

Mary recognized a gain of $76,000 on the sale of the building, of which $3,000 is characterized as ordinary income and $73,000 is section 1231 gain. The $5,000 gain on the sale of the land is also a section 1231 gain.

Note: By electing accelerated ACRS, Mary gained the advantage of larger depreciation deductions. While Mary had to recapture these on sale, she still reaped their advantage in the years in which they were taken. Assuming that Mary's tax bracket did not increase, this practice clearly worked to her benefit.

SCHEDULE D
(Form 1040)

Department of the Treasury
Internal Revenue Service (T)

Capital Gains and Losses

▶ Attach to Form 1040.　　▶ See Instructions for Schedule D (Form 1040).

▶ Use lines 20 and 22 for more space to list transactions for lines 1 and 9.

OMB No. 1545-0074

1993

Attachment
Sequence No. **12**

Name(s) shown on Form 1040

Emily Jones

Your social security number

458 00 0327

Part I　Short-Term Capital Gains and Losses—Assets Held One Year or Less

(a) Description of property (Example: 100 sh. XYZ Co.)	(b) Date acquired (Mo., day, yr.)	(c) Date sold (Mo., day, yr.)	(d) Sales price (see page D-3)	(e) Cost or other basis (see page D-3)	(f) LOSS If (e) is more than (d), subtract (d) from (e)	(g) GAIN If (d) is more than (e), subtract (e) from (d)
1 100 Shares of Bates Trucking	5-11-93	6-29-93	900	650		250
25 Shares of Alpha Computing	3-16-93	6-29-93	2,000	2,500	500	

2	Enter your short-term totals, if any, from line 21	2		
3	**Total short-term sales price amounts.** Add column (d) of lines 1 and 2 . . .	3	2,900	
4	Short-term gain from Forms 2119 and 6252, and short-term gain or (loss) from Forms 4684, 6781, and 8824	4		
5	Net short-term gain or (loss) from partnerships, S corporations, and fiduciaries from Schedule(s) K-1	5		
6	Short-term capital loss carryover from 1992 Schedule D, line 38	6	300	
7	Add lines 1, 2, and 4 through 6, in columns (f) and (g)	7	(800)	250
8	**Net short-term capital gain or (loss).** Combine columns (f) and (g) of line 7	8	(550)	

Part II　Long-Term Capital Gains and Losses—Assets Held More Than One Year

(a)	(b)	(c)	(d)	(e)	(f)	(g)
9 60 Shares of Car Motor Co.	inherited	2-12-93	2,100	700		1,400
500 Sh. of Weeping Willow Furniture Co.	various	6-29-93	4,100	34,000	29,900	

10	Enter your long-term totals, if any, from line 23	10		
11	**Total long-term sales price amounts.** Add column (d) of lines 9 and 10 . .	11	6,200	
12	Gain from Form 4797; long-term gain from Forms 2119, 2439, and 6252; and long-term gain or (loss) from Forms 4684, 6781, and 8824 . . .	12		
13	Net long-term gain or (loss) from partnerships, S corporations, and fiduciaries from Schedule(s) K-1	13		
14	Capital gain distributions	14		
15	Long-term capital loss carryover from 1992 Schedule D, line 45	15	500	
16	Add lines 9, 10, and 12 through 15, in columns (f) and (g)	16	(30,400)	1,400
17	**Net long-term capital gain or (loss).** Combine columns (f) and (g) of line 16	17	(29,000)	

Part III　Summary of Parts I and II

18	Combine lines 8 and 17. If a loss, go to line 19. If a gain, enter the gain on Form 1040, line 13. **Note:** If both lines 17 and 18 are gains, see the **Schedule D Tax Worksheet** on page D-4 . .	18	(29,550)
19	If line 18 is a (loss), enter here and as a (loss) on Form 1040, line 13, the **smaller** of these losses:		
a	The (loss) on line 18; **or**		
b	($3,000) or, if married filing separately, ($1,500)	19	(3,000)
	Note: See the **Capital Loss Carryover Worksheet** on page D-4 if the loss on line 18 exceeds the loss on line 19 **or** if Form 1040, line 35, is a loss.		

For Paperwork Reduction Act Notice, see Form 1040 instructions.　　Cat. No. 11338H　　Schedule D (Form 1040) 1993

Capital Loss Carryover Worksheet (keep for your records)

Use this worksheet to figure your capital loss carryovers from 1993 to 1994 if Schedule D, line 19, is a loss and **(a)** that loss is a smaller loss than the loss on Schedule D, line 18, **or (b)** Form 1040, line 35, is a loss.

1. Enter the amount from Form 1040, line 35. If a loss, enclose the amount in parentheses 1. 34,580

2. Enter the loss from Schedule D, line 19, as a positive amount   2. 3,000

3. Combine lines 1 and 2. If zero or less, enter -0- 3. 37,580

4. Enter the **smaller** of line 2 or line 3 . . . .   4. 3,000

Note: *If line 8 of Schedule D is a loss, go to line 5; otherwise, skip lines 5 through 9.*

5. Enter the loss from Schedule D, line 8, as a positive amount   5. 550

6. Enter the gain, if any, from Schedule D, line 17 . . . .   6. -0-

7. Enter the amount from line 4 . . . . .   7. 3,000

8. Add lines 6 and 7 . . . .   8. 3,000

9. **Short-term capital loss carryover to 1994.** Subtract line 8 from line 5. If zero or less, enter -0- . . . .   9. -0-

Note: *If line 17 of Schedule D is a loss, go to line 10; otherwise, skip lines 10 through 14.*

10. Enter the loss from Schedule D, line 17, as a positive amount   10. 29,000

11. Enter the gain, if any, from Schedule D, line 8 . . . .   11. -0-

12. Subtract line 5 from line 4. If zero or less, enter -0- 12. 2,450

13. Add lines 11 and 12 . . . .   13. 2,450

14. **Long-term capital loss carryover to 1994.** Subtract line 13 from line 10. If zero or less, enter -0- 14. 26,550

18 | Individual Retirement Arrangements (IRAs)

Introduction

IRAs have two outstanding characteristics. First, an IRA may save you taxes this year and every year you make a contribution. If you are eligible, your annual contribution of up to $2,000 is deductible. Second, you defer paying taxes on the income earned by the funds in your IRA. Your IRA may, as its name implies, provide you with income for your retirement.

IRAs don't benefit everybody equally. If you are working, you may contribute up to $2,000 per year to an IRA. If you work but your spouse does not, the two of you may contribute up to $2,250.

The Tax Reform Act of 1986 imposes tough limits on the deductibility of IRAs if you are an active participant in an employer-provided retirement plan and you have adjusted gross income in excess of $40,000 (joint) or $25,000 (single).

IRAs are a lot more flexible than most people realize. Within limits, funds may be rolled over from one IRA to another. IRAs can also be a home for distributions received from employer-provided plans. Moreover, your IRA can now invest in U.S. gold and silver coins.

Important Change for 1993

Distributions from employer plans. New rules apply to distributions made from qualified employer plans in 1993. The new rules primarily relate to distributions eligible for rollover treatment, withholding requirements, direct rollovers, distributions paid to you, and written explanations to recipients. Get Publication 590 for more information.

Important Reminders

Interest earned. Although interest earned from your IRA(s) is generally not taxed in the year earned, it is **not tax-exempt** interest. **Do not** report this interest on your tax return as tax-exempt interest.

Penalty for failure to file Form 8606. If you make nondeductible IRA contributions and you do not file Form 8606, *Nondeductible IRAs (Contributions, Distributions, and Basis)*, with your tax return, you may have to pay a $50 penalty.

This chapter discusses:

- Who can set up an IRA,
- When and how an IRA can be set up,
- How much you can contribute and deduct,
- How retirement plan assets can be transferred,
- When IRA assets can be withdrawn,
- What acts result in penalties, and
- Simplified Employee Pensions (SEPs).

An individual retirement arrangement (IRA) is a personal savings plan that offers you tax advantages to set aside money for your retirement. That means that you may be able to deduct your contributions to your IRA in whole or in part, depending on your circumstances, and that, generally, amounts in your IRA, including earnings and gains, are not taxed until they are distributed.

If you work for yourself, you may be able to deduct contributions to a Simplified Employee Pension (SEP), which involves the use of IRAs (SEP-IRAs). You may also be able to deduct contributions to other retirement plans for the self-employed (sometimes called Keogh or HR–10 plans). Only self-employed individuals can deduct such contributions. For details, get Publication 560, *Retirement Plans for the Self-Employed*.

TaxPlanner

Self-employed persons and independent contractors often overlook the benefits available to them from establishing an IRA. The only requirement for contributing to an IRA is that you have not reached age 70½ and have earned income, which includes income from your business, provided that your personal efforts create a major portion of the business income. Therefore, a self-employed person could establish both a Keogh plan and an IRA.

TaxSaver

You are a sole proprietor, and you hire your spouse or child to perform bona fide services, such as bookkeeping, as an employee. Assuming that the family member works in a genuine employment relationship, the salary paid is compensation for personal services and should be included in the family member's gross income. The family member's salary is a deductible expense to you. This gross income would entitle that family member to make a contribution to an IRA of up to $2,000.

Your spouse's or child's wages constitute wages subject to social security tax, so this strategy may work to your disadvantage.

Be prepared to defend the genuine employment relationship of your spouse against an IRS attack.

Useful Items

You may want to see:

Publication

☐ **590** Individual Retirement Arrangements (IRAs)

Form (and Instructions)

☐ **5329** Additional Taxes Attributable to Qualified Retirement Plans (Including IRAs), Annuities, and Modified Endowment Contracts

☐ **8606** Nondeductible IRAs (Contributions, Distributions, and Basis)

Explanation

IRS Publication 590 discusses in greater detail some topics that are touched on in this chapter. It also covers some more technical material that is not included here. You may find a further discussion of the following topics in Publication 590:

- How to set up an IRA
- Employer and employee association trust accounts
- Filing requirements for disclosure of information on your IRA
- Withholding on IRA distributions
- Transfer of an IRA due to death or divorce

IRS Publication 560 deals with retirement plans set up by self-employed persons and partners.

TaxSaver

Wealth can be built up much faster in an IRA or other tax-exempt retirement plan than in your own investment program. Since you do not have to pay income tax as your earnings accumulate within the plan, your investments compound in value more quickly. A person in the 31% tax bracket, for example, could end up with 1.8 times more money after tax on a $2,000 deductible IRA contribution held for 20 years than if he or she did not make the contribution. If the person's **marginal tax rate** drops to 15% in retirement, he or she could have 2.2 times more money after tax.

Example

If in 1986 you invested $2,000 in an IRA that earns 10% per year, it will be worth $9,283 in 2006 after all taxes are paid if you are in the 31% bracket. If in 2005 you retire and drop into the 15% tax bracket, your original $2,000 investment will be worth $11,437 after all taxes are paid.

However, if you do not have an IRA, your $2,000 is subject to tax immediately. If you are in the 31% bracket, you are left with only $1,380. Investing that $1,380 in 1986 in a non-IRA investment earning 10%, you will have only $5,241 in 2006 after taxes are paid if you remain in the 31% bracket.

TaxAlert

Note that in 1993 and future years your tax bracket may be as high as 39.6%. Therefore, the savings resulting from an IRA may be even greater than indicated in the example.

Who Can Set Up an IRA?

You can set up and make contributions to an IRA if you received taxable *compensation* during the year and have not reached age 70½ by the end of the year.

Compensation includes wages, salaries, commissions, tips, professional fees, bonuses, and other amounts you receive for providing personal services. The IRS treats as compensation any amount properly shown in box 1 of Form W-2, provided that amount is reduced by any amount properly shown in box 11 (nonqualified plans). Compensation also includes taxable alimony and separate maintenance payments.

If you are self-employed (a sole proprietor or a partner), compensation is your net earnings from your trade or business (provided your personal services are a material income-producing factor), reduced by your deduction for contributions on your behalf to retirement plans and the deduction allowed for one-half of your self-employment taxes.

Compensation includes earnings from self-employment that are not subject to self-employment tax because of your religious beliefs. See Publication 533, *Self-Employment Tax,* for more information.

Compensation does *not* include:

- Earnings and profits from property, such as rental income, interest income, and dividend income,
- Pension or annuity income,
- Deferred compensation received (compensation payments postponed from a past year),

- Foreign earned income and housing cost amounts that are excluded from income, or
- Any other amounts that are excluded from income.

Explanation

For purposes of figuring out your contribution to your IRA, compensation includes sales commissions, the net income from your business, and partnership income that is subject to self-employment tax. Business and partnership income must be reduced by any contributions to a Keogh or SEP plan you make. Compensation does not include nontaxable amounts, deferred compensation, severance pay, or pension distributions. If you have multiple sources of self-employment income and/or partnership income subject to self-employment tax, all gains and losses from these sources must be aggregated for purposes of computing compensation from self-employment. If the result is a gain, it is added to your wages, possibly permitting you to make a larger deductible contribution to your IRA. If the result of your self-employment activities is a loss, however, you need not account for it in determining your IRA contribution. Income earned outside the United States is compensation to the extent that it is taxable in the United States. Your foreign earned income must be adjusted for any foreign income exclusion. For more information, see Chapter 38, *U.S. Citizens Working Abroad*.

IRA for your spouse. You may be eligible to set up and contribute to an IRA for your spouse, whether or not he or she received compensation. This is called a *spousal IRA* and is generally set up for a nonworking spouse. (See *How Much Can I Contribute and Deduct?* later.)

Eligibility requirements. To contribute to a spousal IRA:

- You must be married at the end of the tax year,
- Your spouse must not have reached age 70½ by the end of the tax year,
- You must file a joint return for the tax year,
- You must have taxable compensation for the tax year, and
- Your spouse must either have no compensation or choose to be treated as having no compensation for the tax year.

Example 1

A wife holds a job, and her husband does not. The wife is not covered by her employer's retirement plan, and the two spouses file a joint return. They may contribute a total of $2,250 to their respective IRAs. The contribution can be split between the husband's and wife's accounts in any way they wish, as long as no more than $2,000 is allocated to either account. One year $2,000 could go into the husband's IRA and $250 into the wife's. The next year $2,000 could go into the wife's IRA and $250 into the husband's.

Example 2

The working wife died during the year after earning over $2,250. The nonworking husband is allowed to put $2,000 in his spousal IRA for the year, as long as he files a joint return with his deceased wife. A payment cannot be made to the decedent's IRA for the year of death.

Community property laws should be disregarded when you are determining if you are eligible to make payments to an IRA for your nonworking spouse. Thus, your nonworking spouse is not considered to have earned half your income.

When and How Can an IRA Be Set Up?

You can set up an IRA at any time during a year. However, the time for making contributions for a year is limited. See *When To Contribute,* later.

You can set up different kinds of IRAs with a variety of organizations. You can set up an IRA at a bank or other financial institution, or with a mutual fund or life insurance company. You can also set up an IRA through your stockbroker. Any plan must meet Internal Revenue Code requirements.

Kinds of IRAs. Your IRA can be an individual retirement account or annuity. It can be either a part of a simplified employee pension (SEP) or a part of an employer or employee association trust account.

Explanation

The basic difference between the two types of IRA accounts—Individual Retirement Arrangements and Individual Retirement Annuities—lies in the type of investment and the method of funding it. The Individual Retirement Arrangement is generally a type of trust with varied investments, such as stocks, bonds, savings accounts, certificates of deposit, credit union accounts, common trust funds, and **real estate**, among other things. An Individual Retirement Annuity is an investment in an insurance contract.

Inherited IRAs. If you inherit an IRA from your deceased spouse, you can choose to make it your own. For more information, get Publication 590.

How Much Can I Contribute and Deduct?

Contributions to an IRA must be in the form of money (cash, check, or money order). *You cannot contribute property.*

Explanation

When you receive a property distribution (e.g., shares of stock) from your IRA or a qualified employer plan, you may roll over the property received into an Individual Retirement Arrangement. You are also permitted to sell the property and roll over the sale of the proceeds into an IRA. You may *not* retain the property distribution and roll over the property's cash equivalent.

Contribution Limits

The most that you can contribute for any year to your IRA is *the smaller of* the following:

1) Your compensation (defined earlier) that you must include in income for the year, or
2) $2,000.

This is the most you can contribute regardless of whether your contributions are to one or more IRAs or whether all or part of your contributions are nondeductible. (See *Nondeductible Contributions,* later.)

Example 1. Betty, who is single, earns $24,000 in 1993. Her IRA contributions for 1993 are limited to $2,000.

Example 2. John, a college student working part-time, earns $1,500 in 1993. His IRA contributions for 1993 are limited to $1,500, the amount of his compensation.

Spousal IRA. The total combined contributions you can make each year to your IRA and a spousal IRA (discussed earlier) is *the smaller of:*

1) Your taxable compensation for the year, or
2) $2,250.

You can divide your IRA contributions between your IRA and the spousal IRA any way you choose, but you cannot contribute more than $2,000 to either IRA. (See examples in the next discussion.)

Spouse has compensation during the year. If your spouse also has taxable compensation during the year and each of you is under age 70½ at the end of the year, you each can have regular IRAs. You each can contribute up to the $2,000 limit, unless your taxable compensation (or your spouse's) is less than $2,000.

However, you or your spouse can choose to be treated as having no compensation for the year and use the rules for spousal IRAs. Generally, if one spouse has compensation of less than $250 for the year, a spousal IRA is more advantageous than a regular IRA.

Example

If you and your spouse can both afford to put $2,000 into an IRA, but your spouse has compensation of only $1,500 for the year, his or her IRA contribution is limited to $1,500. The excess $500 that he or she planned to contribute may *not* be applied toward your contribution. You are limited to a combined $3,500 contribution.

Example 1. Bill and Linda file a joint return for 1993. Bill earned $27,000 and Linda earned $190. Linda chose to be treated as having no compensation; therefore, Bill set up a spousal IRA for her. Since he contributed $1,800 to his IRA, the most he can contribute to the spousal IRA is $450 ($2,250 minus $1,800).

Example 2. Assume the same facts as in Example 1 except that Bill's contribution to the spousal IRA is $2,000 (the limit for either IRA). The most he can contribute to his own IRA is $250 ($2,250 minus $2,000).

Spouse under age 70½. You cannot make contributions to your IRA for the year in which you reach age 70½ or any later year. However, for any year you have compensation, you can continue to make contributions of up to $2,000 to a spousal IRA. You can contribute to a spousal IRA until the year your spouse reaches age 70½.

Contributions not required. You are not required to make contributions to your IRA or a spousal IRA for every tax year, even if you can.

If you and your spouse each contribute to an IRA, the contribution limit for each of you is figured separately.

IRA contributions under community property laws. If you work and have an IRA, contributions cannot be made to your IRA based on the earnings of your spouse, unless you have a spousal IRA. The contributions must be based on your own compensation, even in community property states.

Inherited IRAs. You can make contributions to an IRA that you inherited from your spouse. By doing so, you elect to have the IRA treated as your own account.

If you inherited an IRA from someone who died after December 31, 1983, and you were not the decedent's spouse, you will not be allowed to contribute to that IRA.

When To Contribute

You can make contributions to your IRA (or to a spousal IRA) for a year at any time during the year or by the due date of your return for that year, *not* including extensions. For most people, this means that contributions for 1993 must be made by April 15, 1994.

Designating year for which contribution is made. If you contribute an amount to your IRA between January 1, 1994, and April 15, 1994, tell the sponsor (the trustee or issuer) to which year (1993 or 1994) the contribution applies. If you do not tell the sponsor, the sponsor can assume, for reporting to IRS, that the contribution is for 1994, the year the sponsor received it.

Filing before making your contribution. You can file your return claiming an IRA contribution before you actually make the contribution. You must, however, make the contribution by the due date of your return, *not* including extensions.

TAXPLANNER 1

You can make your 1993 IRA contribution as late as April 15, 1994. However, funding your IRA as early as possible maximizes your ending balance. For example, assume you have 20 years until retirement, make the maximum $2,250 contribution, and the account earns 8%. If you make your contributions at year-end, your ending IRA balance will be $102,964. If you make your contributions at the beginning of the year, your ending account balance will be $111,202, an increase of $8,238.

TAXPLANNER 2

If you do not have the cash available to make your 1993 IRA contribution by April 15, 1994, the deadline for 1993 contributions, you could "borrow" money by distributing part or all of an existing IRA account to yourself and use the money to make your 1993 IRA contribution to a different account. You would have to complete the rollover within 60 days of the withdrawal, meaning that you would have to come up with the funds to complete the rollover or be subject to the 10% penalty for early withdrawal. *Note:* You may only roll over an IRA fund to a new IRA once in a 1-year period.

Alternatively, if you want the $2,000-per-year IRA deduction but are not particularly concerned about accumulating income tax-free in your IRA, you can take advantage of the 60-day rollover period so that you have some extra spending money for 2 months.

For more information about rollovers, see the discussion later in this chapter.

Deductible Contributions

Generally, you can take a deduction for the contributions that you are allowed to make to your IRA. However, if you or your spouse is covered by an *employer retirement plan* at any time during the year, your allowable IRA deduction may be less than your contribution. Your deduction may be reduced or eliminated depending on your filing status and the amount of your income, as discussed later under *Deduction Limits*.

Who Is Covered by an Employer Plan?

The **Form W-2,** *Wage and Tax Statement,* you receive from your employer includes a box to indicate whether you are covered for the year. The form should have a mark in the "Pension Plan" box if you are covered.

You are also covered by a plan if you are self-employed and participate in a qualified retirement plan (such as a Keogh plan) or a simplified employee pension (SEP) plan.

If you are not certain whether you are covered by your employer's retirement plan, you should ask your employer. Also see Publication 590 for more information.

TAXPLANNER

We recommend that you check your Form W-2 to ensure that the coverage status is accurate. The rules used to determine if you are covered by an employer's plan will depend on the type of plan maintained by your employer. If you are not sure what type of plan your employer maintains, you should ask your employer. The information may also be found in the Summary Plan Description, which can be obtained from your employer. Generally, you will be considered covered if:

1. Your employer maintains a defined benefit pension plan and you meet the plan's eligibility requirements.
2. Your employer maintains a defined contribution money purchase plan, you meet the plan's eligibility requirements, and your employer is required to make a contribution to your account.
3. Your employer maintains a profit-sharing plan and makes a contribution, a forfeiture is allocated to your account, or you make any contribution with respect to a plan year ending with or within your tax year.

Example

Assume that you first became eligible to participate in your employer's profit-sharing plan on July 1, 1993. Your employer makes a contribution for the plan year ending on June 30, 1994. You will not be considered an active participant until 1994, since that is the first tax year during which an allocation was made to your account.

4. Your employer maintains a 401(k), a SEP, or a 403(b) plan and, if for the year ending with or within your tax year, you elect to defer any compensation.

Employer plans. An employer retirement plan is one that an employer sets up for the benefit of the employees. For purposes of the IRA deduction rules, an employer retirement plan is any of the following:

- A qualified (meets Internal Revenue Code requirements) pension, profit-sharing, stock bonus, money purchase, etc., plan (including Keogh plans),
- A 401(k) plan (generally a profit-sharing or stock bonus plan to which contributions can be made under an arrangement allowing you to choose to take your income in cash or have your employer pay it into the plan),
- A union plan (a qualified stock bonus, pension, or profit-sharing plan created by a collective bargaining agreement between employee representatives and one or more employers),

Table 18-1. Can You Take An IRA Deduction?

This chart sums up whether you can take a full deduction, a partial deduction, or no deduction as discussed in this chapter.

If Your Modified AGI[1] is:		If You Are Covered by a Retirement Plan at Work and Your Filing Status is:			If You Are Not Covered by a Retirement Plan at Work and Your Filing Status is:			
At Least	But Less Than	• Single, • Head of Household	• Married Filing Jointly (even if your spouse *is not* covered by a plan at work) • Qualifying Widow(er)	Married Filing Separately[2]	• Married Filing Jointly (and your spouse *is* covered by a plan at work)	• Single, • Head of Household	• Married Filing Jointly or Separately (and your spouse *is not* covered by a plan at work) • Qualifying Widow(er)	Married Filing Separately (even if your spouse *is* covered by a plan at work)[3]
		You Can Take	You Can Take	You Can Take	You Can Take	You Can Take	You Can Take	You Can Take
$–0–	$10,000	Full deduction	Full deduction	Partial deduction	Full deduction			
$10,000	$25,000	Full deduction	Full deduction	No deduction	Full deduction	Full Deduction	Full Deduction	Full Deduction
$25,000	$35,000	Partial deduction	Full deduction	No deduction	Full deduction			
$35,000	$40,000	No deduction	Full deduction	No deduction	Full deduction			
$40,000	$50,000	No deduction	Partial deduction	No deduction	Partial deduction			
$50,000 or over		No deduction	No deduction	No deduction	No deduction			

[1] **Modified AGI** (adjusted gross income) is: (1) for Form 1040A—the amount on line 14 increased by an excluded series EE bond interest shown on Form 8815, *Exclusion of Interest from Series EE U.S. Savings Bonds Issued after 1989,* or (2) for Form 1040—the amount on line 31, figured without taking into account any IRA deduction or any foreign earned income exclusion and foreign housing exclusion (deduction), or any series EE bond interest exclusion from Form 8815.

[2] If you *did not* live with your spouse *at any time* during the year, your filing status is considered, for this purpose, as Single (therefore your IRA deduction is determined under the "Single" column).

[3] You are entitled to the full deduction *only if* you *did not* live with your spouse *at any time* during the year. If you *did* live with your spouse during the year, you are, for this purpose, treated as though you are covered by a retirement plan at work (therefore, your IRA deduction is determined under the "Married Filing Separately" column in the "If You Are Covered by a Retirement Plan . . ." section of the chart).

- A qualified annuity plan,
- A plan established for employees by a federal, state, or local government, or any of their political subdivisions, agencies, or instrumentalities (other than an eligible state deferred compensation plan),
- A tax-sheltered annuity plan for employees of public schools and certain tax-exempt organizations (403(b) plan),
- A simplified employee pension (SEP) plan, or
- A 501(c)(18) trust (a certain type of tax-exempt trust created before June 25, 1959, that is funded only by employee contributions).

Effects of marital status. Generally, you are considered covered by an employer retirement plan if your spouse is covered by one. To determine whether you are considered covered for the year because of your spouse, you must wait until the last day of the year. This is because your filing status (whether you are considered married or single) for the year depends on your marital status on the last day of the tax year.

If you were married to two different spouses during the same year, for this purpose, you are considered married for the year to the spouse to whom you were married at the end of the year.

If your spouse died during the year, and you file a joint return as the surviving spouse, coverage by an employer retirement plan for that year is determined as if your spouse were still alive.

If you are married filing a joint return, both you and your spouse are considered covered by a plan if either of you is covered by a plan.

If you are married filing a separate return and you are not covered by an employer retirement plan, but your spouse is, you are considered covered if you and your spouse lived together at any time during the year.

Example

Joe and Mary are both employed. During 1993, Mary's compensation was $32,000, and she was not covered by her employer's retirement plan. Joe's compensation was $20,000, and he was covered by his employer's plan. If Joe and Mary file a joint return, they cannot claim a deduction for an IRA contribution. If Joe and Mary didn't live together at all during the year and file separate returns, Joe can deduct an IRA contribution of $2,000 (subject to the adjusted gross income limitation), while Mary can deduct $2,000, since she is not covered by her employer's plan.

If they lived together for part of the year and file separate returns, neither can make a deductible IRA contribution.

Effect of amounts. Even if your employer sets aside only a very small amount for you under a retirement plan, you are considered covered by a plan for that year.

Nonvested employees. If, for a plan year, an amount is allocated to your plan account in a defined contribution plan, or you accrue a benefit in a defined benefit plan, but you have *no vested interest* (legal right) in such account or accrual, you are still an active participant in (covered by) such plan.

Federal judges are considered covered by an employer retirement plan for figuring the IRA deduction.

When Are You Not Covered?

You are not covered by an employer plan if neither you nor your spouse is covered for any part of the year. You are also not covered for this purpose in the following situations.

If you are married filing a separate return and you are not covered by an employer retirement plan, you may not be considered covered by a plan even if your spouse is covered. You would not be considered covered if you and your spouse did not live together at any time during the year.

Coverage under social security or railroad retirement (Tier I and Tier II) does not count as coverage under an employer retirement plan for figuring the IRA deduction.

If you receive retirement benefits from a previous employer's plan, (and you are not covered under your current employer's plan), you are not considered covered for this purpose.

Reservists and volunteer firefighters. Certain members of the reserve units of the Armed Forces (in general, those members who did not serve in excess of 90 days during the year) and certain volunteer firefighters (in general, those members whose accrued retirement benefit at the beginning of the year will not exceed $1,800 per year at retirement) are not considered covered by U.S. or local government retirement plans.

Social Security Recipients

If you receive social security benefits, have taxable compensation, contribute to your IRA, and are covered (or considered covered) by an employer retirement plan, complete the worksheets in Appendix B of Publication 590. Use those worksheets to figure your IRA deduction and the taxable portion, if any, of your social security benefits.

Deduction Limits

As discussed under *Deductible Contributions,* earlier, the deduction you can take for contributions made to your IRA depends on whether you or your spouse is covered for any part of the year by an employer retirement plan. But your deduction is also affected by how much income you have and your filing status, as discussed below under *Adjusted Gross Income Limit.*

Full deduction. If neither you nor your spouse was covered for any part of the year by an employer retirement plan, you can take a deduction for your total contributions to one or more IRAs of up to $2,000, or 100% of your compensation, whichever is less. Your spouse can also take a total deduction of up to $2,000, or 100% of his or her compensation, whichever is less. This amount is reduced by any contributions to a 501(c)(18) plan (generally, a plan created before June 25, 1959, funded entirely by employee contributions).

Reduced or no deduction. If either you or your spouse is covered by an employer retirement plan, your deduction may be reduced or eliminated, depending on your income and your filing status. The deduction begins to decrease *(phase out)* when your income rises above a certain amount and is eliminated altogether when it reaches a higher amount. The amounts vary depending on your filing status.

Adjusted Gross Income Limit

The effect of income on your deduction, as just described, is sometimes called the adjusted gross income limit (AGI limit). To compute your *reduced IRA deduction,* you must first determine your *modified adjusted gross income* and your filing status.

Modified adjusted gross income (modified AGI) is:

- If you file *Form 1040*—the amount on the page 1 "adjusted gross income" line, but modified (changed) by figuring it without taking any:
  a) IRA deduction,
  b) Foreign earned income exclusion,
  c) Foreign housing exclusion or deduction, and
  d) Exclusion of Series EE bond interest shown on Form 8815, *Exclusion of Interest From Series EE U.S. Savings Bonds Issued After 1989.*
- If you file *Form 1040A*—the amount on the page 1 "adjusted gross income" line, but modified by figuring it without any IRA deduction, or any exclusion of series EE bond interest shown on Form 8815.

Note. Do not assume modified AGI is the same as your compensation. You will find that your modified AGI may include income in addition to your taxable compensation (discussed earlier), such as interest, dividends, and taxable IRA distributions.

Filing status. Your filing status depends primarily on your marital status. For this purpose, you need to know if your filing status is single (or head of household), married filing jointly (or qualifying widow(er)), or married filing separately. If you need more information on filing status, see Chapter 2, *Filing Status.*

Married filing separately exception. If you did not live with your spouse at any time during the year and you file a separate return, your filing status is considered, for this purpose, as single.

Deduction phaseout. Your IRA deduction is reduced or eliminated depending on your filing status and modified AGI as follows:

If your *filing status* is:	Your deduction is reduced if your *modified AGI* is within the *phaseout range* of:	Your deduction is eliminated if your *modified AGI* is:
Single, or Head of household	$25,000.01 to $35,000	$35,000 or more
Married—joint return, or Qualifying widow(er)	$40,000.01 to $50,000	$50,000 or more
Married—separate return	$0.01 to $10,000	$10,000 or more

Also, see Table 18–1 earlier.

How To Figure Your Reduced IRA Deduction

You can figure your reduced IRA deduction *for either* Form 1040 or Form 1040A by using the following worksheet. Also, the instructions for these tax forms include similar worksheets.

Note. If you were married and both you and your spouse worked and you both contributed to IRAs, use separate worksheets to figure your deductions.

If you were divorced or legally separated (and did not remarry) before the end of the year, you cannot deduct any contributions you made to your spouse's IRA. You can deduct only the contributions you made to your own IRA, and your deductions are subject to the adjusted gross income limit rules for single individuals.

Deductible (and nondeductible) IRA contributions for an IRA other than a spousal IRA. Complete lines 1 through 8 to figure your deductible and nondeductible contributions for the year.

Worksheet for Reduced IRA Deduction

(Use only if you are covered or considered covered by an employer retirement plan and your modified AGI is within the applicable phaseout range)

If your *filing status* is:	And your *modified AGI* is over:	*Enter* on line 1 below:
Single, or Head of household	$25,000	$35,000
Married—joint return, or Qualifying widow(er)	$40,000	$50,000
Married—separate return	$ –0–	$10,000

1. Enter applicable amount from above..........
2. Enter your *modified AGI* (combined, if married filing jointly) ....

Note: If line 2 is equal to or more than the amount on line 1, **stop here;** your IRA contributions are not deductible. See *Nondeductible Contributions*, later.

3. Subtract line 2 from line 1. (**If line 3 is $10,000 or more, stop here;** you can take a full IRA deduction for contributions of up to $2,000 or 100% of your compensation, whichever is less.)..........
4. Multiply line 3 by .20. If the result is not a multiple of $10, round it to the next highest multiple of $10. (For example, $611.40 is rounded to $620.) However, if the result is less than $200, enter $200 ....
5. Enter your compensation. **Do not** include your spouse's compensation, and, if you file Form 1040, do not reduce your compensation by any losses from self-employment..........
6. Enter contributions you made, or plan to make, to your IRA for 1993, but **do not** enter more than $2,000. (If contributions are more than $2,000, see *Excess Contributions*, later.)..........
7. **IRA deduction.** Compare lines 4, 5, and 6. Enter the smallest amount (or a smaller amount if you choose) here and on the Form 1040 or 1040A line for your IRA, whichever applies. (If line 6 is more than line 7 and you want to make a nondeductible contribution, go to line 8.) ....
8. **Nondeductible contributions.** Subtract line 7 from line 5 or 6, whichever is smaller. Enter the result here and on line 1 of your Form 8606, *Nondeductible IRAs (Contributions, Distributions, and Basis).* ....

Deductible (and nondeductible) IRA contributions for spousal IRA. The deduction phaseout rules that reduce or eliminate your IRA deduction also apply to a spousal IRA. If you have a spousal IRA, are covered by an employer retirement plan, and your modified AGI is within the applicable phaseout range, you can take only a reduced spousal IRA deduction.

Complete lines 9 through 17 to figure deductible and nondeductible contributions (discussed later) for the year to a spousal IRA (see *IRA for your spouse* and *Spousal IRA,* earlier).

9. Enter the smaller of $2,250 or the amount on line 5..........
10. Add lines 7 and 8. Enter the total. **If this amount is equal to or more than line 9, stop here;** you cannot make contributions to a spousal IRA. Also, see *Excess Contributions*, later. ....
11. Subtract line 10 from line 9..........

12. Enter the smallest of:

(a) contributions for 1993 to your spouse's IRA; (b) $2,000; or (c) the amount on line 11. (If contributions are more than $2,000, see *Excess Contributions*, later.) .... _____

13. Multiply line 3 by .225. If the result is not a multiple of $10, round it to the next highest multiple of $10. However, if the result is less than $200, enter $200 .... _____

14. Enter the amount from line 7 .... _____

15. Subtract line 14 from line 13. Enter the result but do not enter more than the amount on line 12 .... _____

16. **Spousal IRA deduction.** Compare lines 4, 5, and 15. Enter the smallest amount (or a smaller amount if you choose) here and on your Form 1040 or 1040A. (If line 12 is more than line 16 and you want to make a nondeductible contribution for your spouse, go to line 17.)................ _____

17. **Spousal IRA nondeductible contributions.** Subtract line 16 from line 12. Enter the result here and on line 1 of your spouse's Form 8606.. _____

Reporting Deductible Contributions

You do not have to itemize deductions to claim your deduction for IRA contributions. If you file *Form 1040,* deduct your IRA contributions for 1993 on line 24a and, if you file a joint return, deduct your spouse's IRA contributions on line 24b.

If you file *Form 1040A,* deduct your contributions on line 15a and, if you file a joint return, deduct contributions to your spouse's IRA on line 15b.

You can use either form in most cases. You cannot use *Form 1040EZ.*

Form 5498. You should receive by May 31, 1994, Form 5498, *Individual Retirement Arrangement Information,* or similar statement, from plan sponsors, showing all the contributions made to your IRA for 1993.

TaxORGANIZER

Keep Form 5498 with your records to substantiate IRA contributions you made during the year.

Trustee's fees. Trustee's administrative fees that are billed separately and paid by you in connection with your IRA are deductible. They *are deductible* (to the extent they are ordinary and necessary) as a miscellaneous deduction on Schedule A (Form 1040). The deduction is subject to the 2% of adjusted gross income limit (see Chapter 30, *Miscellaneous Deductions*). These fees *are not subject to* the IRA contribution limit.

Broker's commissions that you paid in connection with your IRA *are subject to* the IRA contribution limit. They *are not deductible* as a miscellaneous deduction on Schedule A (Form 1040).

Nondeductible Contributions

Although your *deduction* for IRA contributions may be reduced or eliminated because of the adjusted gross income limit (see *Deductible Contributions,* earlier), you can still make **contributions** of up to $2,000 ($2,250 for a regular IRA and a spousal IRA) or 100% of compensation, whichever is less. Often, the difference between your total permitted contributions and your total deductible contributions, if any, is your **nondeductible contribution.**

Example. Sonny Jones is single. In 1993, he is covered by a retirement plan at work. His salary is $52,312. His modified AGI is $55,000. Sonny makes a $2,000 IRA contribution for that year. Because he is covered by a retirement plan and his modified AGI is over $35,000, he cannot deduct his $2,000 IRA contribution. However, he may choose to either:

1) Designate this contribution as a **nondeductible** contribution by reporting it on his tax return, as explained later under *Reporting Nondeductible Contributions,* or
2) Withdraw the contribution as explained later under *Tax-Free Withdrawal of Contributions.*

As long as your contributions are within the contribution limits just discussed, none of the earnings on those contributions (deductible or nondeductible) or gains will be taxed until they are distributed. See *When Can I Withdraw or Use Assets From an IRA?* later.

Cost basis. You will have a cost basis in your IRA to the extent of your nondeductible contributions. Your **basis** is the sum of the nondeductible amounts you have contributed to your IRA less any distributions of those amounts. You can withdraw your basis tax free. See *When Can I Withdraw or Use Assets From an IRA?* later.

TaxPLANNER

The amount designated as a deductible contribution should be limited to the amount that produces a tax benefit. Taxpayers who are required to use the tax tables should take special care, because most of the brackets in the tables are in $50 increments, and, as a result, both a $1 and a $49 contribution can provide a $14 tax reduction.

Example

Jim Single has 1993 taxable income of $41,000 before his IRA deduction. He contributed the maximum of $2,000 to his IRA. Designating $1,951 as a deductible contribution produces the same 1993 tax liability ($8,055) as a $2,000 designation. However, when Jim makes his withdrawals, he will save the tax on $49, since only the deductible contribution ($1,951) will be subject to tax.

Explanation

The chief advantage of nondeductible IRA contributions is that, since the income compounds on a tax-deferred basis, the ending balance will be substantially larger under an IRA. In deciding whether to make nondeductible contributions, you should compare the IRA's rate of return against other investments, such as tax-exempt municipal bonds and annuity contracts, and after-tax rates of return on taxable investments. You must also consider the tax effect when you begin taking distributions. The taxation of IRA distributions is discussed below and in IRS Publication 590, *Individual Retirement Arrangements.*

Reporting Nondeductible Contributions

You must report nondeductible contributions to the IRS, but you do not have to designate a contribution as nondeductible until you file your tax return. When you file, you can also designate otherwise deductible contributions as nondeductible.

To designate contributions as nondeductible, you must file Form 8606, *Nondeductible IRAs (Contributions, Distributions, and Basis).* You must file Form 8606 to report nondeductible contributions even if you do not have to file a tax return for the year.

File Form 8606 if:

- You made nondeductible contributions to your IRA for 1993, or
- You received IRA distributions in 1993 and you have at any time made nondeductible contributions to any of your IRAs.

If you receive a distribution from an IRA in the same year that you make an IRA contribution that may be partly nondeductible, use the worksheet in chapter 6 of Publication 590 to figure the taxable portion of the distribution.

If you do not report nondeductible contributions, all of your IRA contributions will be treated as deductible. Thus, when you make withdrawals from your IRA, they will be taxed unless you can show, with satisfactory evidence, that nondeductible contributions were made.

Penalty for overstatement. If you overstate nondeductible contributions on your Form 8606, you must pay a penalty of $100 for each overstatement, unless it was due to reasonable cause.

Penalty for failure to file Form 8606. You will have to pay a $50 penalty if you do not file a required Form 8606, unless you can prove that the failure was due to reasonable cause.

Explanation

The law subjecting taxpayers to a $50 fine for failure to file Form 8606 has been enacted retroactive to 1987. If you should have filed Form 8606 for a prior tax year but failed to do so, you should consider amending your return. See Chapter 1, *Filing Information,* for additional details regarding amending your return.

Tax-Free Withdrawal of Contributions

If you made IRA contributions in 1993 for either 1992 or 1993, you can withdraw them tax free (except for any earnings on them) by April 15, 1994 (or a later date if you have an extension to file your return). *You can do this if:*

- You did not take a deduction for the contributions you withdraw, *and*
- You also withdraw any interest or other income earned on the contributions. You must report this income on your 1993 return.

IRA trustees must include these amounts in box 1 and, if applicable, in box 2a of Form 1099-R. You must report these amounts on line 16a, Form 1040. If there is an amount in box 2a of Form 1099-R, include it on line 16b of Form 1040.

Premature withdrawal tax. The 10 percent additional tax on withdrawals made before you reach age 59½ does not apply to these withdrawals of your contributions. However, your withdrawal of interest or other income may be subject to this tax.

Excess Contribution tax. If any part of these contributions is an excess contribution for 1992, it is subject to a 6% excise tax, unless you withdrew it from your IRA by April 15, 1993. An excess contribution for 1993 must be withdrawn by April 15, 1994, to avoid the excise tax. See *Excess Contributions* under *What Acts Result in Penalties?,* later.

Examples – Deductible and Nondeductible Contributions

The following examples illustrate the use of the IRA deduction worksheet shown earlier under *How To Figure Your Reduced IRA Deduction.*

Example 1. For 1993, Tom and Betty Smith file a joint return on Form 1040. They both work and Tom is covered by a retirement plan at work. Tom's salary is $40,000 and Betty's is $6,555. They each have an IRA and their combined modified AGI is $46,555. Since they are covered by an employer plan, and their modified AGI is between $40,000 and $50,000, they can only take reduced IRA deductions on a joint return (see *Deduction Limits,* earlier).

For 1993, Tom contributed $2,000 to his IRA and Betty contributed $500 to hers. They must use separate worksheets to figure the reduced IRA deduction for each of them because both had IRAs.

Tom can take a deduction of only $690 (see the worksheet below). Even though he contributed the maximum amount allowable ($2,000), $1,310 ($2,000 minus $690) of his contributions must be treated as nondeductible.

He can choose to treat the $690 as either deductible or nondeductible contributions. He can also either leave the $1,310 of nondeductible contributions in his IRA or withdraw them by April 15, 1994. He decides to treat the $690 as deductible contributions and leave the $1,310 of nondeductible contributions in his IRA.

Betty can treat all or part of her contributions as either deductible or nondeductible. This is because her $500 contribution for 1993 is less than the $690 deduction limit for her IRA contributions that year (see line 4 of her worksheet, later). She decides to treat her $500 IRA contributions as deductible.

Using the *Worksheet for Reduced IRA Deduction,* Tom figures his deductible and nondeductible amounts as follows:

Worksheet for Reduced IRA Deduction

(Use only if you are covered or considered covered by an employer retirement plan and your modified AGI is within the applicable phaseout range)

If your *filing status* is:	And your *modified AGI* is over:	Enter on line 1 below:
Single, or Head of household	$25,000	$35,000
Married—joint return, or Qualifying widow(er)	$40,000	$50,000
Married—separate return	$ –0–	$10,000
1. Enter applicable amount from above		50,000
2. Enter your *modified AGI* (combined, if married filing jointly)		46,555

Note: If line 2 is equal to or more than the amount on line 1, **stop here;** your IRA contributions are not deductible; see *Nondeductible Contributions,* earlier.

3. Subtract line 2 from line 1. (**If line 3 is $10,000 or more, stop here;** you can take a full IRA deduction for contributions of up to $2,000 or 100% of your compensation, whichever is less.) 3,445

4. Multiply line 3 by .20. If the result is not a multiple of $10, round it to the next highest multiple of $10. (For example, $611.40 is rounded to $620). However, if the result is less than $200, enter $200 690

5. Enter your compensation. **Do not** include your spouse's compensation, and, if you file Form 1040, do not reduce your compensation by any losses from self-employment. 40,000

6. Enter contributions you made, or plan to make, to your IRA for 1993, but **do not** enter more than $2,000. (If contributions are more than $2,000, see *Excess Contributions*, later). 2,000

7. **IRA deduction.** Compare lines 4, 5, and 6. Enter the smallest amount (or a smaller amount if you choose) here and on the Form 1040 or 1040A line for your IRA, whichever applies. (If line 6 is more than line 7 and you want to make a nondeductible contribution, go to line 8.) 690

8. **Nondeductible contributions.** Subtract line 7 from line 5 or 6, whichever is smaller. Enter the result here and on line 1 of your Form 8606, *Nondeductible IRAs (Contributions, Distributions, and Basis).* 1,310

Betty figures her IRA deduction as follows:

Worksheet for Reduced IRA Deduction

(Use only if you are covered or considered covered by an employer retirement plan and your modified AGI is within the applicable phaseout range)

If your **filing status** is:	And your **modified AGI** is over:	Enter on line 1 below:
Single, or Head of household	$25,000	$35,000
Married—joint return, or Qualifying widow(er)	$40,000	$50,000
Married—separate return	$ –0–	$10,000

1. Enter applicable amount from above 50,000

2. Enter your **modified AGI** (combined, if married filing jointly) .. 46,555

Note: If line 2 is equal to or more than the amount on line 1, **stop here;** your IRA contributions are not deductible; see *Nondeductible Contributions,* earlier.

3. Subtract line 2 from line 1. (**If line 3 is $10,000 or more, stop here;** you can take a full IRA deduction for contributions of up to $2,000 or 100% of your compensation, whichever is less.)............... 3,445

4. Multiply line 3 by .20. If the result is not a multiple of $10, round it to the next highest multiple of $10. (For example, $611.40 is rounded to $620.) However, if the result is less than $200, enter $200 690

5. Enter your compensation. **Do not** include your spouse's compensation, and, if you file Form 1040, do not reduce your compensation by any losses from self-employment. 6,555

6. Enter contributions you made, or plan to make, to your IRA for 1993, but **do not** enter more than $2,000. (If contributions are more than $2,000, see *Excess Contributions*, later). 500

7. **IRA deduction.** Compare lines 4, 5, and 6. Enter the smallest amount (or a smaller amount if you choose) here and on the Form 1040 or 1040A line for your IRA, whichever applies. (If line 6 is more than line 7 and you want to make a nondeductible contribution, go to line 8.) 500

8. **Nondeductible contributions.** Subtract line 7 from line 5 or 6, whichever is smaller. Enter the result here and on line 1 of your Form 8606, *Nondeductible IRAs (Contributions, Distributions, Basis).* 0

The IRA deductions of $690 and $500 on the joint return for Tom and Betty total $1,190. Betty's unused IRA deduction limit of $190 ($690 − $500) cannot be transferred to Tom to increase his deduction.

Example 2. Assume the facts in Example 1, except that Tom contributed $250 to a spousal IRA because Betty had no compensation for the year and did not contribute to an IRA. Their modified AGI remains at $46,555. Tom uses lines 1 through 8 of his worksheet to complete the spousal IRA portion of the *Worksheet for Reduced IRA Deduction* as follows.

9. Enter the smaller of $2,250 or the amount from line 5 2,250

10. Add lines 7 and 8. Enter the total. **If this amount is equal to or more than line 9, stop here;** you cannot make contributions to a spousal IRA. Also, see *Excess Contributions*, later. 2,000

11. Subtract line 10 from line 9.............. 250

12. Enter the smallest of: (a) contributions for 1993 to your spouse's IRA; (b) $2,000; or (c) the amount on line 11. (If contributions are more than $2,000, see *Excess Contributions*, later.) 250

13. Multiply line 3 by .225. If the result is not a multiple of $10, round it to the next highest multiple of $10. However, if the result is less than $200, enter $200 780

14. Enter the amount from line 7 690

15. Subtract line 14 from line 13. Enter the result but do not enter more than the amount on line 12 90

16. **Spousal IRA deduction.** Compare lines 4, 5, and 15. Enter the smallest amount (or a smaller amount if you choose) here and on your Form 1040 or 1040A. (If line 12 is more than line 16 and you want to make a nondeductible contribution for your spouse, go to line 17.)................... 90

17. **Spousal IRA nondeductible contributions.** Subtract line 16 from line 12. Enter the result here and on line 1 of your spouse's Form 8606.............. 160

Although Tom contributed the maximum amount (a total of $2,250) to his and Betty's IRAs, because of the adjusted gross income limit, their allowable IRA deductions total only $780 ($690 + $90).

Can Retirement Plan Assets Be Transferred?

IRA rules permit you to transfer, tax free, assets (money or property) from other retirement programs (including IRAs) to an IRA. The rules permit the following kinds of transfers:

- Transfers from one trustee to another,
- Rollovers, and
- Transfers incident to a divorce.

Transfer From One Trustee to Another

A transfer of funds in your IRA from one trustee directly to another, either at your request or at the trustee's request, is ***not a rollover.*** It is, however, a tax-free transfer. As such it is not affected by the one-year waiting period that is required between rollovers, discussed next. For information about direct transfers to IRAs from retirement programs other than IRAs, see Publication 590.

Rollovers

Generally, a rollover is a tax-free distribution to you of cash or other assets from one retirement plan that you contribute (roll over) to another retirement plan. The amount you roll over tax free, however, is generally taxable later when the new plan pays that amount to you or your beneficiary.

Kinds of rollovers to an IRA. There are two kinds of rollover contributions to an IRA. In one, you put amounts you receive from one IRA into another. In the other, you put amounts from a qualified (meets certain requirements) employer retirement plan, such as a qualified pension plan, into an IRA.

Distributions from qualified employer plans. New rules apply to distributions made from qualified employer plans that are rolled over or transferred to IRAs. The new rules primarily relate to requirements affecting rollovers, income tax withholding, and notices to recipients. Get Publication 590 for more information.

TaxAlert

New income tax withholding rules apply to distributions made from qualified employer plans *after 1992*. Withholding at a rate of 20% is required on a distribution unless it is transferred directly from your employer to an IRA trustee or another employer plan.

The new withholding rules do *not* apply to distributions from IRAs [or Simplified Employee Pensions (SEPs), discussed later]. However, if you wish to rollover a qualified plan distribution to an IRA, be sure to transfer the amount directly from your employer to an IRA trustee or another employer plan. Otherwise, 20% of the distribution will be withheld while *100%* of the distribution must be rolled over within 60 days. If you don't have the money to cover the 20% shortage, income taxes (and possibly a 10% penalty) will be due on the amount not rolled over.

For further information, see Chapter 11, *Retirement Plans, Pensions and Annuities.*

You cannot deduct a rollover contribution on your tax return.

You must make the rollover contribution by the 60th day after the day you receive the distribution from your IRA or your employer's plan. If the amount distributed to you from an IRA or a qualified employer retirement plan becomes a frozen deposit in a financial institution during the 60-day period allowed for a rollover, a special rule extends the period. For more information, get Publication 590.

Waiting period between rollovers. You can take (receive) a distribution from a particular IRA and make a rollover contribution to another IRA only once in any one-year period. The one-year period begins on the date you receive the IRA distribution, not on the date you roll it over into another IRA.

This rule applies separately to each IRA you own. For example, if you have two IRAs, IRA-1 and IRA-2, and you roll over assets of IRA-1 into a new IRA-3, you may also make a rollover from IRA-2 into IRA-3, or into any other IRA within one year after the rollover distribution from IRA-1. These are both rollovers because you have not received more than one distribution from either IRA within one year. However, you cannot, within the one-year period, again roll over the assets you rolled over into IRA-3 into any other IRA.

Exception. There is an exception to this rule for distributions from certain failed financial institutions. Get Publication 590 for more information.

Partial rollovers. If you withdraw assets from an IRA, you may roll over part of the withdrawal tax free into another IRA and keep the rest of it. The amount you keep is generally taxable (except to the extent it is a return of nondeductible contributions) and may be subject to the 10% additional tax on premature distributions and the 15% tax on excess distributions, discussed later.

Maximum rollover. If you roll over a distribution from your employer's plan into an IRA, the most that you can roll over is the fair market value of the assets that you receive as your share from the plan, minus any nondeductible contributions you made to the plan. *Any later distribution to you from that IRA will not qualify for the special averaging and capital gain treatment applicable to lump-sum pension distributions.*

If you inherited an IRA from your spouse, you can roll it over into an IRA established for you.

If you inherited an IRA from someone (other than your spouse) who died after December 31, 1983, you cannot roll it over or allow it to receive a rollover contribution.

Explanation

You may withdraw the balance in your Individual Retirement Arrangement and reinvest it in another IRA with no tax consequences if the money is reinvested within 60 days after the funds are distributed. This type of rollover may be done only once in a 1-year period. This rule applies to each separate IRA you own.

Example

You have two or more IRAs. You can roll over a single distribution from each or all of them to a new IRA or to another existing IRA within a 1-year period.

TaxPlanner 1

If you transfer funds directly between trustees of your IRA and you never actually control or use the account assets, you may transfer your account as often as you like.

All or part of a **lump-sum distribution** from a qualified employer benefit plan may be transferred to an IRA. You may effect a partial rollover—and be taxed at **ordinary income** rates—only on the portion of the money not reinvested within 60 days. This portion is not eligible for any special tax treatment, which it might have been had the entire amount in your employer benefit plan been reported as current income. As mentioned earlier, withholding at a rate of 20% is required on a post-1992 qualified employer plan distribution unless it is transferred directly from your employer to the trustee of an IRA.

Starting in 1985, however, you can elect to roll over partial distributions received from a qualified retirement plan to an IRA subject to certain requirements, principally, the following:

1. The partial distribution must be at least equal to 50% of the employee's account balance.
2. The partial distribution must not be part of a series of periodic distributions.

TaxAlert

As of January 1, 1993, a partial distribution from a qualified plan is eligible for rollover treatment as long as it is *not*:

1) A required minimum distribution (e.g., for individuals who have attained age 70½); or

2) A distribution which is part of a series of substantially equal payments that are received at least annually over life, life expectancy, or a period of at least 10 years.

For more details, see Chapter 11, *Retirement Plans, Pensions, and Annuities*.

TaxPlanner 2

Not all distributions from qualified employer benefit plans may be rolled over into an IRA. IRAs are specifically prohibited from investing in life insurance contracts. Therefore, if your employer plan distributes to you both cash and a life insurance policy, the value of the life insurance policy (except for your contributions) is currently taxable to you. If this is the case, you should consider rolling over the life insurance contract into another qualified pension, profit-sharing, or stock bonus plan that allows investments in life insurance contracts.

TaxPlanner 3

According to the IRS, it is your responsibility to make sure that the rollover is completed within 60 days. The IRS issued a ruling that a taxpayer flunked the 60-day test when her broker failed to perform her specific and timely instructions. The taxpayer did not discover the problem until after the 60-day period had expired. Nevertheless, the IRS ruled that there is no leeway under the existing law.

The IRS has consistently maintained this position, but the Tax Court has recently ruled that a rollover will not fail the 60-day requirement as a result of a bookkeeping error made by an IRA trustee, as long as the taxpayer established and transferred assets to an IRA within the 60-day period.

A court has held that a tax-free rollover can be made only if the employer's plan and trust are tax-exempt when the distribution is made. In this case, the IRS retroactively revoked the tax-exempt status of the trust. This made the distribution ineligible for a rollover.

Reversing a long-standing position, the IRS now argues that, once you have made a rollover, you cannot change your mind and report the distribution as taxable income.

You may roll over a lump-sum distribution from a former spouse's IRA or employee plan that was transferred to you by a divorce decree or written agreement incident to the divorce.

Reporting Your Rollover

Report a distribution from a qualified plan on line 17a, Form 1040, or line 11a, Form 1040A. If the total distribution was rolled over into an IRA or other qualified plan, enter zero on line 17b, Form 1040, or line 11b, Form 1040A. Otherwise, enter the taxable part of the distribution on line 17b, Form 1040, or line 11b, Form 1040A.

Use lines 16a and 16b, Form 1040, or lines 10a and 10b, Form 1040A, to report distributions from one IRA rolled over into another IRA.

For further information on rollovers, get Publication 590.

Transfers Incident to Divorce

If an interest in an IRA is transferred from your spouse or former spouse to you by a decree of divorce or separate maintenance, or a written document related to such a decree, the interest in the IRA, starting from the date of the transfer, is treated as your IRA. The transfer is tax free. For detailed information, get Publication 590.

When Can I Withdraw or Use Assets From an IRA?

There are rules limiting the withdrawal and use of your IRA assets. Violation of the rules generally results in additional taxes in the year of violation. See *Prohibited Transactions, Premature Distributions (Early Withdrawals), Excess Accumulations (Insufficient Distributions)* and *Excess Distributions,* later.

Explanation

Since 1987, IRA distributions have been taxed in a manner similar to annuities. If you do not make nondeductible contributions, all distributions from an IRA account are taxed as ordinary income. You may not use special 5- or 10-year averaging on a lump-sum distribution from your IRA, even if the account is a rollover from a qualified plan. If you made nondeductible contributions, a portion of the distribution may be excludable from income. The excludable amount is computed as follows:

$$\frac{\text{Undistributed Nondeductible Contributions}}{\text{Total IRA Account Balance}} \times \frac{\text{Distribution}}{\text{Amount}}$$

Example

Assume that Mary has made a $2,000 nondeductible contribution and that the total account balance is $20,000. In 1993, she takes a $5,000 distribution. Her tax-free amount is:

$$\$2,000 \ / \ \$20,000 \ \times \ \$5,000 \ = \ \$500$$

TaxOrganizer

"Undistributed Nondeductible Contributions" are obtained from the last Form 8606 you filed. Therefore, make sure you always keep the most recent copy in your files.

TaxPlanner

Money that you withdraw from your IRA is treated as a distribution to you and may trigger the 10% penalty that is imposed on premature distributions. However, it is possible to "borrow" temporarily from your IRA by terminating the arrangement and rolling over the funds to a new IRA within 60 days. That money and any income you earn on it are not considered premature distributions. However, you may not contribute any money that you do earn to your new IRA account. Instead, you have to keep that money—and pay tax on it.

Age 59½ rule. Generally, until you reach the age of 59½, you cannot withdraw assets (money or other property) from your IRA without having to pay an additional tax. However, there are a number of exceptions to that rule. See *Premature Distributions (Early Withdrawals)*, later.

Required Distributions

You cannot keep funds in your IRA indefinitely. You **must** eventually withdraw them or pay an excise tax on excess accumulations in your IRA. See *Excess Accumulations (Insufficient Distributions)*, later. The requirements for withdrawing IRA funds differ depending on whether you are the IRA owner or the beneficiary of a decedent's IRA.

IRA owners. If you are an IRA owner, you must choose to withdraw the balance in your IRA in one of the following two ways:

1) By withdrawing the entire balance in your IRA by the required beginning date (defined below), or
2) By starting to withdraw **periodic distributions** of the balance in your IRA by the required beginning date.

Required beginning date (age 70½ rule). You must receive the entire balance in your IRA or begin receiving periodic distributions from your IRA by April 1 of the year following the year in which you reach age 70½.

If the distributions are to be made over a period of years, you must receive at least the minimum amount required for each year starting with the year you reach age 70½ (your 70½ year). If you did not receive any distributions (or the full required minimum distribution) in your 70½ year, then you must receive the required minimum distribution by April 1 of the next year. Required distributions for later years must be made by December 31 of each year.

Explanation

The purpose of an IRA is to provide retirement income. Therefore, when you reach age 70½, you are expected to begin withdrawing the proceeds in your IRA rather than continue to let the funds accumulate and use the IRA as a tool to build your estate. If you don't withdraw the minimum amounts yearly, a 50% nondeductible tax is levied on the amount of the minimum payment left in your IRA.

You must start receiving minimum payments from your IRA by April 1 of the year after the year in which you reach age 70½.

It is only your first distribution (the distribution for the year you reach age 70½) that may be delayed until April 1 of the following year. The second distribution must be made by December 31 of the same year. You must determine what effect the doubling of distributions will have on your tax liability.

The minimum distribution is based on either your life expectancy or the joint life expectancies of you and your spouse or other designated beneficiary. If the payments are based on your life expectancy or on the joint life expectancy of you and your spouse, you are entitled to redetermine the life expectancies annually. This may enable you to cut down on the amount of the minimum annual distribution.

It's worth noting that your IRA fund may continue to grow, even if you make the required distributions. For example, if the joint life expectancy of you and your spouse is 20 years, you must withdraw only one-twentieth (5%) of your IRA funds in the first year. If the funds in your IRA are earning income at the rate of 10%, the amount does not begin to diminish until the eleventh year of your distributions.

For more information, including how to figure your required minimum distribution each year and how to figure your required distribution if you are a beneficiary of a decedent's IRA, get Publication 590.

Tax Treatment of Distributions

In general, include IRA distributions in your gross income in the year you receive them. Exceptions to this general rule are rollovers and timely withdrawals of contributions, discussed earlier, and the return of nondeductible contributions, discussed next under *Distributions Fully or Partly Taxable*.

Failed financial institutions. The general rule (you must include IRA distributions in your gross income unless properly rolled over) applies to distributions made (with or without your consent) by the receiver of a savings institution that is placed in receivership. For an exception to the one-year waiting period rule for rollovers of certain distributions from failed financial institutions, see Publication 590.

Ordinary income. IRA distributions that you must include in income are taxed as ordinary income.

No special treatment. In figuring your tax, you cannot use the special averaging or capital gain treatment that applies to lump-sum distributions from qualified employer plans.

Distributions Fully or Partly Taxable

Your IRA distributions may be fully or partly taxable, depending on whether your IRA includes only deductible contributions or any nondeductible contributions.

Fully taxable. If only deductible contributions were made to your IRA (or IRAs, if you have more than one) since it was set up, you have **no basis** in your IRA. Because you have no basis in your IRA, any distributions are fully taxable when received. See *Reporting taxable distributions on your return,* later.

Partly taxable. If you made nondeductible contributions to any of your IRAs, you have a **cost basis** (investment in the contract) to the extent of those contributions. These nondeductible contributions are **not taxed** when they are distributed to you. They are a return of your investment in your IRA.

When IRA distributions are made, special rules apply in figuring the tax on the distributions if:

- Only nondeductible IRA contributions were made and there are any earnings or gains, or
- If both deductible and nondeductible IRA contributions were made.

Only the part of the distribution that represents nondeductible contributions (your cost basis) is tax-free. Once nondeductible contributions have been made, distributions consist partly of nondeductible contributions (basis) and partly of deductible contributions, earnings, or gains. Thus, until you run out of basis, each distribution is partly taxable and partly nontaxable.

Form 8606. You must complete, and attach to your return, Form 8606 if you receive an IRA distribution and, at any time, have made nondeductible IRA contributions. Using the form, you will figure the nontaxable distributions for 1993, and your total IRA basis for 1993 and earlier years.

Distributions reported on Form 1099–R. You will receive Form 1099–R, *Distributions From Pensions, Annuities, Retirement or Profit-Sharing Plans, IRAs, Insurance Contracts, Etc.,* or similar statement, if you receive a distribution from your IRA. IRA distributions are shown in boxes 1 and 2 of Form 1099–R. A number or letter code in box 7 tells you what type of distribution you received from your IRA.

TaxORGANIZER

Keep Form 1099–R with your records to substantiate IRA distributions and federal income tax withholding.

Reporting taxable distributions on your return. Report fully taxable distributions, including taxable premature distributions, on line 16b, Form 1040 (no entry is required on line 16a), or line 10b, Form 1040A. If only part of the distribution is taxable, enter the total amount on line 16a, Form 1040 (or line 10a, Form 1040A), and the taxable part on line 16b, Form 1040 (or line 10b, Form 1040A). You cannot report distributions on Form 1040EZ.

Withholding. Federal income tax is withheld from IRA distributions unless you choose not to have tax withheld. See Chapter 5.

Explanation

You may elect at any time not to have taxes withheld on the distribution. Before electing not to withhold, however, you must review your withholdings from other sources and estimated payments. See Chapter 5, *Tax Withholding and Estimated Tax*, for underpayment penalties.

Distributions paid outside the United States or its possessions. In general, if you are a U.S. citizen or resident alien and your home address is outside the United States or its possessions, you cannot choose exemption from withholding on your IRA payments.

Explanation

A distribution from an IRA is fully taxable, unless it represents a timely withdrawal of an excess contribution, it is rolled over into another IRA within the required 60-day period, or it represents a return of nondeductible contributions.

If you reach age 59½ and are entitled to withdraw the funds in your IRA without penalty but you decide not to, you are not taxed until an actual distribution is made. However, in the following situations, all or part of your IRA is currently taxed:

1. The occurrence of a prohibited transaction causes the entire amount in your individual retirement *account* to be treated as distributed and therefore taxable to you. For instance, if you loan yourself the money in your IRA, the entire amount is then currently taxable to you. However, if you engage in a prohibited transaction with your individual retirement *annuity*, only the amount of the prohibited transaction is sub-

ject to a 5% excise tax (see *Prohibited Transactions,* following.)

2. The pledging of an IRA *account* causes the portion pledged to be treated as distributed. For example, if you have an IRA with a value of $7,500 that you pledge as security for a $5,000 bank loan, you are taxed on the $5,000.

3. The pledging of an IRA *annuity* causes the entire account to be treated as distributed.

If you are under age 59½ and distribute part of your IRA in any of the ways described above, a 10% tax penalty is applied to the distributed portion.

Exception

The nondeductible 10% penalty tax on premature distributions does not apply if you are disabled and the early distribution is made because of your disability. Beginning in 1987, you will not be subject to the 10% penalty if the IRA is distributed as a life annuity.

TaxPLANNER

The life annuity exception may be beneficial if you retire before age 55, your employer's plan does not provide for a life annuity, you don't want to pay the penalty and taxes on the distribution, but you need supplemental income. You will not be subject to the penalty if the plan distribution is rolled over into an IRA and then distributed as part of a series of substantially equal periodic payments over your life expectancy.

If your employer's plan provides for periodic payments but you are not happy with the plan's investment return, the above technique can be used.

What Acts Result in Penalties?

The tax advantages of using IRAs for retirement savings can be offset by additional taxes and penalties if you do not follow the rules. For example, there are additions to the regular tax for using your IRA funds in prohibited transactions. There are also additional taxes for:

- Making excess contributions,
- Making early withdrawals (taking premature distributions),
- Allowing excess amounts to accumulate (failing to make required withdrawals), or
- Receiving excess distributions.

There are penalties for overstating the amount of nondeductible contributions and for failure to file a required Form 8606. See *Reporting Nondeductible Contributions,* earlier.

Prohibited Transactions

Generally, a prohibited transaction is any improper use of your IRA by you or any **disqualified person.**

Some examples of disqualified persons for this purpose are:

Your fiduciary, or
Members of your family (spouse, ancestor, lineal descendent, and any spouse of a lineal descendent).

Some examples of prohibited transactions with an IRA are:

- Borrowing money from it,
- Selling property to it,
- Receiving unreasonable compensation for managing it, or
- Using the IRA as collateral for a loan.

Effect on an IRA account. Generally, if you or your beneficiary engage in a prohibited transaction at any time during the year with your IRA account, it will not be treated as an IRA as of the first day of the year.

Effect on you (or your beneficiary). If you (or your beneficiary) engage in a prohibited transaction with your IRA account at any time during the year, *you (or your beneficiary) must* include the fair market value of all (or part, in certain cases) of the IRA assets in your gross income for that year. The fair market value is the price at which the IRA assets would change hands between a willing buyer and a willing seller, when neither has any need to buy or sell, and both have reasonable knowledge of the relevant facts.

You must use the fair market value of the assets as of the first day of the year you engaged in the prohibited transaction. You may also have to pay the 10% additional tax on premature distributions and the 15% tax on excess distributions, discussed later.

Excise taxes. Those involved in prohibited transactions may be liable for certain other excise taxes. In general, there is a 5% tax on the amount of the prohibited transaction and a 100% additional tax if the transaction is not corrected.

Investment in collectibles. If your IRA invests in collectibles, the amount invested is considered distributed to you in the year invested. You may have to pay the 10% additional tax on premature distributions and the excise taxes discussed above.

Collectibles include art works, rugs, antiques, metals, gems, stamps, coins, alcoholic beverages, and other tangible personal property if specified by the IRS.

Exception. Your IRA can invest in one, one-half, one-quarter, or one-tenth ounce U.S. gold coins, or one ounce silver coins minted by the Treasury Department.

Explanation

The rules relating to prohibited transactions are designed to prevent the manipulation of IRA funds by the person who has set the funds aside for his or her retirement.

A qualified plan run by your employer that engages in a prohibited transaction is subject to a 5% tax on that transaction. Your IRA, which may have been part of your employer's plan, does not lose its tax-exempt status.

Although an investment in tangible property, such as artworks, precious metals or gems, antiques, or alcoholic beverages, is not technically a prohibited transaction, the cost of the item is treated as a distribution from your IRA. The amount is included in your income and subject to the 10% premature distribution penalty tax.

This rule is designed to prevent you from directing your IRA to invest in property that the trustee could conceivably allow you to keep in your home for your personal enjoyment.

In order to help sell U.S.-issued gold and silver coins, Congress removed the penalty for such coins acquired after October 1, 1986.

For more information on prohibited transactions, get Publication 590.

Excess Contributions

Generally, an excess contribution is the amount contributed to your IRA(s) for the year that is more than the smaller of the following amounts:

- Your taxable compensation for the year, or
- $2,000.

Example. You were single and earned $30,000 in 1993. You contributed $2,500 to your IRA for 1993. Your contribution limit is $2,000. Your reduced IRA deduction, figured using the *Worksheet for Reduced IRA Deduction,* is $1,000. You made an excess contribution for 1993 of $500 ($2,500 minus $2,000).

Example

You contribute $2,250 to IRAs you have set up for you and your nonworking spouse. You put $2,050 into your account and $200 into your spouse's account. There is a $50 excess contribution to your account. Only $2,200 ($2,000 + $200) can be contributed and deducted on your joint income tax return. In order to obtain the full $2,250 contribution, you can withdraw the $50 excess contribution from your account and put it into your spouse's account. This must be done no later than April 15, 1994.

Tax on excess contributions. You must pay a 6% tax each year on excess amounts that remain in your IRA at the end of your tax year. The excess is taxed for the year the excess contribution is made and for each year after that until you correct it. The tax cannot be more than 6% of the value of your IRA as of the end of your tax year. The tax does not apply to a rollover contribution.

Excess contributions you withdraw by the date your return is due. You will not have to pay the 6% tax if you withdraw an excess contribution made during a tax year *and* interest or other income earned on it by the date your return for that year is due, including extensions.

You do not have to include in your gross income an excess contribution that you withdraw from your IRA before your tax return is due if:

1) You did not take a deduction for that excess amount on your return, and
2) The interest or other income earned on the excess was also withdrawn.

However, *you must include* in your gross income any interest or other income earned on the excess contribution (whether a deductible or nondeductible contribution). Report it on your return for the year in which the excess contribution was made. Your withdrawal of interest or other income may be subject to an additional 10% tax on early withdrawals, discussed later.

Explanation

Excess payments you withdraw before the due date of the return are not subject to the 6% excise tax, provided that the full amount of income attributable to the excess contribution is also distributed. The income portion of the distribution is then included in your income in the year in which the excess contribution was made. The withdrawn income is subject to the 10% tax on premature distributions (see *Premature Distributions*, following).

Excess contributions you withdraw after your return is due. If the total contributions (other than rollover contributions) for the year were $2,250 or less, and there were no employer contributions, you may withdraw any excess contribution after the due date for filing your return for that year, including extensions. You do not include the withdrawn contribution in your income. This applies only to the part of the excess for which you did not take a deduction. The 6% tax applies to the excess contribution amount that remains in your IRA at the end of a year (this includes the year of the contribution and any later year).

Explanation
Excess payments may also be adjusted by deducting the correct amount in the current year and applying the excess to the following year's contribution.

Example
If you mistakenly contributed $2,000 to your IRA in 1992, when you were entitled to only a $1,500 contribution, you may reduce your 1993 contribution by the excess $500. If you are entitled to a $1,500 contribution in 1993, you should then contribute no more than $1,000 that year. To make this application work, you must deduct only $1,500 for 1992—not the actual $2,000 you contributed. Although you are still subject to the 6% tax on the $500 excess contribution in 1992, if you reduce the following year's contribution to $1,000, there is no excess contribution remaining in your IRA and no tax would be imposed for 1993.

You would receive a $1,500 deduction for 1993 consisting of the $1,000 you actually contributed in 1993 plus the excess contribution from 1992.

Premature Distributions (Early Withdrawals)

You must include premature distributions in your gross income and, because they are premature, there will be an ***additional 10% tax*** on them. Use Form 5329 (discussed later) to figure the tax.

Premature distributions are amounts you withdraw from your IRA before you are 59½.

TaxPlanner 1
Since you may largely determine when you pay tax on money in your IRA by controlling when you distribute the funds, the arrangement provides unusual opportunities for tax planning.

Your best bet is to make your withdrawal during a year in which you have low **taxable income** so that you may recognize your IRA distribution at a lower tax cost than you might otherwise be able to. For example, you might withdraw the funds in your IRA in a year in which you are unemployed or have a loss on your business activities. Or you might distribute them in a year in which you have extraordinarily large deductible expenses, such as medical costs or **casualty losses**.

Another good time to take your IRA funds is when most of your income derives from a lump-sum distribution that qualifies for **5- or 10-year averaging.** Such income is reported on a separate schedule and does not raise your marginal tax rate on other income.

Thus, if your taxable income is low enough, it might be worthwhile to take a premature distribution before you are age 59½ and pay the 10% penalty.

TaxPlanner 2
If you are fortunate enough to have sufficient income without taking any distributions from your IRA, you may wish to postpone withdrawing money from your IRA as long as possible. Distributions do not have to begin until April 1 of the calendar year *following* the year in which you reach age 70½.

TaxAlert
A minimum distribution *must* be made each year based upon the life expectancy of the individual or the joint life expectancy of the individual and his or her designated beneficiary. If the designated beneficiary is someone other than the owner's spouse, it gets more complicated, since there is a new rule called the Minimum Distribution Incidental Benefit Requirement. In general, this additional test will require a higher distribution if the nonspouse beneficiary is more than 10 years younger than the owner.

Example 1
Jack Jones, who became 70½ years old on May 1, 1993, has an IRA with a December 31, 1992, balance of $80,000. By looking at tables published by the IRS, he finds that his life expectancy for purposes of his IRA is 15.3 years. This is the life expectancy for a person who is 71, which he will be during 1993. To figure his minimum distribution, he divides the amount in his IRA by 15.3. He must receive a distribution of $5,229 prior to April 1, 1994, to avoid a penalty.

Example 2
Bill Jones, Jack Jones' twin brother, also has an $80,000 IRA, with his 40-year-old son as a beneficiary. He elects to have his distributions spread over their joint lives. He finds that their joint life expectancy is 42.8. Bill then checks the table for the Minimum Distribution Incidental Benefit Requirement. He finds this factor to be 25.3 years for age 71. Bill must use the smaller of the two factors, or 25.3. He divides $80,000 by 25.3 to determine his minimum distribution of $3,162.

TaxPlanner 3
You are always permitted to take more out of your IRA than the minimum amount you calculated. You are also allowed to recalculate the amount of your IRA distribution based upon your life expectancy in the year in which you are doing the recalculation. This might result in a lower required distribution. If you don't need the money currently, this recalculation will permit you to leave more money in your IRA account to earn income that is not being currently taxed. The recomputation may result in

an increase or a decrease in the required distribution. You can try this computation each year and elect to recompute only in a year in which the required distribution is reduced.

Example

Jack Jones in Example 1 (TaxPlanner 2) will be 73 years old in 1995. Because of prior withdrawals and market fluctuations, his account on December 31, 1994, was $65,000. Since Jack used a 15.3 year factor in 1993 and a 14.3 year factor in 1994, he normally would use a 13.3 year factor in 1995. However, Jack consults the IRS tables and finds that the factor for age 73 is 13.9. Since Jack does not need the funds, he can elect to use the revised life expectancy.

TAXPLANNER 4

If a participant in an IRA dies after distributions have begun, distributions must continue at least as rapidly as before the death. If distributions have not begun, the general rule is that distributions must be completed within 5 years of the death. There are some special rules that provide some exceptions. Consult your tax advisor.

TAXPLANNER 5

Keogh plans. The same withdrawal techniques described in TaxPlanners 1 through 4 may be used with a Keogh plan, a retirement arrangement that self-employed people may set up.

Note: If you have a Keogh plan, you may not receive a distribution before age 59½ unless you become totally disabled.

TAXPLANNER 6

Employee stock bonus plans and company profit-sharing plans. The main attraction of having your employer put some of your compensation into a stock bonus plan or a company profit-sharing plan is that you are not currently taxed on the contributions to or the earnings in the plan. In addition, these plans have certain advantages that IRAs do not:

1. Withdrawals may be made at any age because of retirement, separation from service, or hardship.
2. Borrowing is permitted if the loan is repaid within 5 years.
3. A lump-sum distribution may qualify for 5- or 10-year averaging.

Exceptions. The 10% tax will not apply to the following distributions:

- Portions of any distributions treated as a return of nondeductible contributions.
- Distributions made after the owner's death,
- Distributions made because you become disabled.
- Distributions that are a part of a series of substantially equal payments over your life (or life expectancy), or over the lives of you and your beneficiary (or your life expectancies). For this exception to apply, you must use an IRS-approved distribution method and take at least one distribution annually. Also, the payments must continue for at least 5 years, or until you reach age 59½, whichever is the longer period.

This 5-year rule does not apply if the payment change is because of the death or disability of the IRA owner.
- Distributions that are rolled over, as discussed earlier under *Rollovers.*

For more information on premature distributions, get Publication 590.

Excess Accumulations (Insufficient Distributions)

You cannot keep amounts in your IRA indefinitely. Generally, you must begin receiving distributions by April 1 of the year following the year in which you reach age 70½.

Tax on excess. If distributions from your IRA(s) during the year are less than the required minimum distribution for the year, you may have to pay a *50% excise tax* for that year on the excess amount remaining in your IRA.

Request to excuse the tax. If the excess accumulation is due to reasonable error and you have taken, or are taking, steps to remedy the insufficient distribution, you can request that the tax be excused.

Exemption from tax. IRAs invested in contracts issued by insurance companies may be unable to make required distributions because the insurance company is in state insurer delinquency proceedings. In this case, the 50% excise tax for failure to make required IRA distributions will not apply. However, to qualify for this exemption, the conditions and requirements of Revenue Procedure 92-10 must be satisfied.

TAXALERT

If you cannot receive required distributions from your IRA because your insurance company is in state insurer delinquency proceedings, consult a tax advisor to see if you can avoid the 50% excise tax.

More information. For more information on excess accumulations, see Chapter 7 of Publication 590.

Excess Distributions

If you received *retirement distributions* during the year of more than $150,000, you may have to pay a *15% tax* on the distributions exceeding that amount. The term "retirement distributions" means your distributions from any qualified employer plans, tax-sheltered annuity plans, or IRAs.

This tax is reduced by any tax on premature distributions that applies to the excess distribution. See *Premature Distributions,* discussed earlier.

Excluded distributions. The excess distribution tax does not apply to the following distributions:

- Distributions after the IRA owner's (or employee's) death,
- Distributions that are rolled over,
- Distributions that represent nondeductible contributions,
- Corrective distributions of excess deferrals under a salary reduction arrangement (or a similar qualified plan) discussed in Chapter 8, and
- Corrective distributions of excess aggregate contributions.

For more information on excess distributions, get Publication 590.

Reporting Additional Taxes

Generally you must use **Form 5329,** *Additional Taxes Attributable to Qualified Retirement Plans (Including IRAs), Annuities, and Modified Endowment Contracts,* to report the tax on excess contributions, premature distributions, excess distributions, and excess accumulations. You must file Form 5329 if you receive excess distributions from a qualified retirement plan, whether or not you owe tax on them.

You do not have to use Form 5329 if:

- Distribution code 1 is shown in box 7 of Form 1099-R, *Distributions From Pensions, Annuities, Retirement or Profit-Sharing Plans, IRAs, Insurance Contracts, etc.* Instead, multiply the taxable part of the distribution by 10% and enter the result on line 51 of Form 1040. *However,* if you owe this tax and also owe any other additional tax on a distribution, do not enter this 10% additional tax directly on your Form 1040. You must file Form 5329 to report your additional taxes.
- You qualify for an exception to the tax. You need not report the exception if distribution code 2, 3, or 4 is shown in box 7 of Form 1099-R. *However,* if one of those codes is not shown, or the code shown is incorrect, you must file Form 5329 to report the exception.

If you file Form 1040, complete Form 5329 and attach it to your Form 1040. Enter the total amount of IRA tax due on line 51, Form 1040.

If you do not have to file a Form 1040 but do have to pay one of the IRA taxes mentioned earlier, file the completed Form 5329 with IRS at the time and place you would have filed your Form 1040. Include a check or money order payable to the Internal Revenue Service for the tax you owe, as shown on Form 5329. Write your social security number, tax form number, and tax year on your check or money order.

Simplified Employee Pension (SEP)

A simplified employee pension (SEP) is a written plan that allows an employer to make contributions toward his or her own (if a self-employed individual) and employees' retirement, without becoming involved in more complex retirement plans. The contributions are made to IRAs (SEP-IRAs) of the participants in the plan. By choosing a SEP plan, an employer gives up advantages available to Keogh plans. For example, the special averaging treatment that may apply to Keogh plan lump-sum distributions does not apply to SEP-IRA distributions.

The SEP rules permit an employer to contribute (and deduct) each year to each participating employee's SEP-IRA up to 15% of the employee's compensation or $30,000, whichever is less *(the contribution limit).* The contributions are funded by the employer.

Deduction limit for a self-employed person. If you are self-employed and contribute to your own SEP-IRA, special rules apply when figuring your maximum deduction for these contributions.

For determining the 15% limit, discussed above, your *compensation* is your net earnings from self-employment. See *Net earnings from self-employment,* later. Note that, for this purpose, your net earnings must take into account your deduction for contributions to your own SEP-IRA. Because the deduction amount and the net earnings amount are each dependent on the other, this adjustment presents a problem.

To solve this problem, you make the adjustment to net earnings indirectly by reducing the contribution rate called for in the plan.

Use the following worksheet to find this reduced contribution rate and your maximum deduction. Make no reduction to the contribution rate for any other employees.

1) Contribution rate in plan shown as a decimal .... _____

2) Rate in line (1) plus one .... _____

3) Reduced rate for self-employed person (divide line (1) by line (2)) .... _____

4) Net earnings (if more than $235,840, see Publication 560) not reduced for contributions to your SEP-IRA).................... _____

5) Maximum deduction for contributions to self-employed person's SEP-IRA (multiply line (4) by line (3))................... _____

Example. You are a sole proprietor and have employees. The terms of your SEP provide that you contribute for yourself 15% of your net earnings, and for your employees 15% of their pay. Your net earnings from your business (not taking into account a deduction for contributions to your own SEP-IRA) are $196,000. In figuring this amount, you deducted your employees' pay of $60,000 and contributions for them of $9,000 (15% of $60,000). You also reduced your earnings by the deduction for one-half of your self-employment tax. Using the worksheet, you figure your maximum deduction for contributions to your own SEP-IRA as follows.

1) Contribution rate in plan shown as a decimal .... .15

2) Rate in line (1) plus one 1.15

3) Reduced rate for self-employed person (divide line (1) by line (2))... .130435

4) Net earnings from self-employment (if more than $235,840, see Publication 560) not reduced for contributions to your SEP-IRA $196,000

5) Maximum deduction for contributions to self-employed person's SEP-IRA (multiply line (4) by line (3))................... $25,565

Net earnings from self-employment. For SEP purposes, your net earnings are your gross income from your business minus your allowable deductions for that business. Allowable deductions include contributions to the SEP-IRAs of your employees. You must also reduce your earnings by the deduction for one-half of your self-employment tax. Net earnings do not include tax-free items or deductions related to them. Net earnings include a partner's distributive share of partnership income or loss (other than separately treated items such as capital gains or losses). If paid for services to or for the partnership, net earnings include guaranteed payments to a limited partner. They do not include distributions of income or loss to a limited partner.

The contribution limit (lesser of 15% of compensation or $30,000) discussed earlier *also applies to* any amounts you elect to have taken out of your income and contributed to the plan under a *salary reduction arrangement,* discussed later.

The contribution limit discussed above *does not apply to* contributions up to your IRA contribution limit that you make during the year to your SEP-IRAs or regular IRAs independent of your employer's contributions. See *How Much Can I Contribute and Deduct?* earlier.

Salary reduction arrangement. A SEP may include a salary reduction arrangement. Under it, you can elect to have your employer contribute part of your pay to the SEP-IRA. Only the remaining portion of your pay is currently taxable. The tax on the contribution is deferred. This election is called an elective deferral.

Employer's SEP contributions excluded from your wages on Form W-2. Your employer's contributions to your SEP-IRA are generally excluded from your income rather than deducted from it. Therefore, your employer's contributions should not be included in your Form W–2 wages unless there are contributions in excess of the applicable limit, or unless there are contributions under a salary reduction arrangement. Form W–2 should include contributions under a salary reduction arrangement for social security and Medicare tax purposes only.

Even if your employer makes contributions to your SEP-IRA, *you may be able to* deduct the regular IRA contributions you make to your SEP-IRA or another IRA.

Tax treatment by self-employed individuals. If you are self-employed (a sole proprietor or partner) with a SEP, take your deduction for employer contributions to your own SEP-IRA on line 27, Form 1040. If you also make deductible contributions to your SEP-IRA (or any other IRA you own), independent of your employer contributions, take your deduction on line 24, Form 1040.

Excess contributions. If your employer contributes too much to your SEP-IRA, resulting in an excess contribution, you will not have to pay the 6% tax on it if you withdraw this excess amount (and interest or other income earned on it) from your SEP-IRA before the due date for filing your tax return, plus extensions. However, you must include the excess contribution in your gross income. Your Form W-2 should include the amount.

For more information on a SEP-IRA, get Publication 590.

Explanation

A simplified employee pension plan must meet the following requirements:

1. There must be an individual account or individual annuity for each employee. The use of an IRA bond does not qualify.
2. Contributions must be made for all employees who (a) are at least age 21, (b) have worked for the employer for 3 out of the last 5 years, and (c) have received at least $385 of wages in the calendar year. A contribution must be made for all employees who have met the eligibility requirements even if they are no longer employed.
3. The employer must contribute the same percentage of up to $235,840 in compensation for each individual in the plan.

TaxAlert

The current year compensation cap of $235,840 (referred to in Point 3 above) has been reduced to $150,000 for plan years beginning *after* 1993. The new cap will be indexed annually for inflation.

4. Employees must be able to withdraw the employer's contributions without restriction. If the participant makes a withdrawal after the contribution has been made to the IRA and fails to roll the amount into another IRA within 60 days, the withdrawal must be included in income. Also, if the amount withdrawn is not an excess contribution, made after the participant has attained age 59½, or as a result of disability, the participant will be subject to a 10% excise tax on the amount withdrawn.
5. There must be a written formula for determining allocations to individual employees.

Explanation

Beginning in 1987, certain SEP participants have an option of making a salary reduction contribution. The

requirements that must be met before you can elect to have your employer make a salary reduction contribution to your SEP are as follows:

1. Your employer had 25 or fewer employees in the prior year.
2. The deferral percentage for highly compensated participants cannot exceed 125 % of all other employees.
3. At least 50% of all participants must elect to have contributions made.
4. Your employer's plan permits elective deferrals.

TaxSaver

A self-employed person can claim a deduction to a SEP as long as he or she makes the contribution by the due date of the return, including extensions. Thus, even if you failed to set up a Keogh plan (discussed below) by December 31 of your tax year, as required, you can accomplish much the same thing by establishing a SEP and making a timely payment. Assuming the self-employed person has no employees, the process is easy.

A SEP is basically a profit-sharing plan. The limitation of 15% of your compensation that can be contributed to a SEP is really only 13.043 (see discussion later under Keogh plans.) SEPs don't have all the extra complications that Keogh plans do. For example, for a SEP, there is no requirement to file Form 5500C, 5500R, or 5500EZ each year, as there is for Keogh plans. SEP participants can also have an IRA, subject to the normal rules.

TaxPlanner

Keogh plans. If you are self-employed—that is, you own your own business—and are subject to the self-employment tax, you may set up a Keogh plan. If you have any of the following types of income, you should consider setting up a Keogh plan:

1. Director's fees
2. Executor fees (if they are subject to self-employment tax)
3. Commission income when you are not considered an employee

Keogh plans, like IRAs, must have a trustee. Banks and other financial institutions frequently serve as trustees and often have simple plans available for an individual **proprietor** who does not have any employees. If you do have employees, you should carefully consider the total financial impact of setting up a Keogh plan, since your employees also must be covered.

Like an IRA, a Keogh plan is a valuable vehicle for obtaining current tax deductions and building wealth with pretax dollars. The Keogh rules can be complicated, particularly if you have employees who must be covered. Listed below are a few of the more important rules:

1. A Keogh plan must be established before the end of your tax year.
2. The plan must be written. Prototype plans can frequently be obtained from banks and other financial institutions.
3. A summary description of the plan must be provided

to your employees. There are specific definitions of employees who must be covered. Also, there are specific rules on such items as discrimination and vesting.

4. You should intend for the plan to be permanent.

Generally, a Keogh plan may be classified as either a pension plan or a profit-sharing plan. Pension plans can be further classified into plans in which (1) the retirement benefit is fixed (defined benefit plans) or (2) the contribution is fixed (money purchase plan). Under a defined benefit plan, you, as a self-employed person, determine how much of a retirement benefit you want to provide for yourself and your employees. The required contribution is then actuarially computed. The current maximum benefit that can be provided is limited to the lesser of 100% of income or $115,641 in 1993.

A money purchase plan defines the rate of contribution (usually a percentage of self-employed income or, in the case of employees, wages) that will be made to the plan each year.

Both the defined benefit plan and the money purchase plan are subject to minimum funding requirements. This means that you will be subject to a penalty if you do not properly fund the plan or receive a waiver from the IRS.

Because of its simplicity, a profit-sharing type Keogh plan is the most popular plan. The self-employed person determines the amount of the contribution to the plan on a yearly basis.

Annual contributions to a Keogh plan. In 1984, the limitation on deductible contributions to your Keogh plan was increased to a maximum of $30,000. The distinctions in the tax law between qualified plans of corporations and qualified plans of self-employed individuals have generally been eliminated. The changes also make it more difficult for a self-employed individual to compute the amount he or she may deduct.

Your limitation on the deductible contributions will depend on the type of plan you adopt. Basically, your contribution to a defined benefit pension plan may not exceed the actuarial cost needed to fund the planned future benefit. This type of plan will, as a general rule, provide the greatest deduction for individuals nearing retirement age.

The limitation for a profit-sharing plan is the lesser of 15% of compensation (self-employment income) or $30,000.

Example 1

Marian Campbell is the sole proprietor of an interior decorating business. In 1993, she earned $100,000 before making a contribution to her Keogh profit-sharing plan. Prior to 1984, she could have taken 15% of $100,000 as her deductible Keogh plan contribution. The calculation is no longer that simple. Now the allowable deductible contribution must be subtracted from her self-employment income to determine the base

amount to which the 15% limitation applies. To figure her Keogh contribution, Marian performs the following calculation:

1. 15% × $100,000 = $15,000

2. $15,000 ÷ 1.15 = $13,043

3. Marian checks that the calculation is correct as follows:

Income before Keogh contribution	$100,000
Keogh contribution	(13,043)
	$86,957

Since 15% of $86,957 is $13,043, the calculation is correct.

Note: You need to have $230,000 in self-employment income (before making your Keogh contribution) to reach the maximum $30,000 annual deductible contribution that is allowed.

Self-employed individuals who have only a Keogh profit-sharing plan should investigate establishing a Keogh money purchase pension plan as well. You may contribute up to 20% of your earned income (before making your Keogh contribution) to a Keogh money purchase plan, up to the maximum $30,000 deductible contribution allowed.

Example 2

Assume that Marian Campbell also has a Keogh money purchase pension plan. She could have a combined Keogh deduction of $20,000. If she terminates her Keogh profit-sharing plan, she may make a $20,000 deductible contribution to her Keogh money purchase pension plan.

Example 3

Marian Campbell may also set up both a profit-sharing plan (which is an annual discretionary contribution) and a money purchase plan (an annual fixed obligation). She can then maximize her deduction for the year by making the full 20% aggregate contribution and maintain the flexibility of making or not making an annual discretionary profit-sharing plan contribution.

The contribution could be split between the two plans as follows:

Self-employment earnings	$100,000
Less: Profit-sharing contribution	$ 12,000
Money purchase plan contribution	8,000
Total Keogh contribution	$ 20,000

TaxAlert

Distributions from Keogh plans after 1992 are subject to the 20% withholding rules discussed earlier.

19 | Alimony

Introduction

Designing a divorce decree, a separation agreement, or a support decree is rarely an easy task. Marital settlements are so diverse and so complex that no two situations are the same. One common element, however, is likely to be the payment of **alimony** *—an amount subject to one of these settlement agreements that is not considered* **child support** *or a property settlement and that meets certain specific tests. Alimony is a deduction from gross income for the spouse who pays it; it is included in the income of the spouse who receives it.*

Alimony may take many different forms. The payment by one spouse of the other spouse's share of mortgage costs and interest for jointly owned property may be considered alimony. The payment of life insurance premiums on policies irrevocably assigned to a spouse may also be considered alimony. Alimony may even include the payment of medical and dental expenses. This chapter discusses what should and shouldn't be considered an alimony payment and explains the difference.

While the section of the tax law on alimony occupies only about two pages, there has been an extraordinary amount of litigation on the subject. Alimony is a contentious subject, because there is often continuing animosity between former spouses. Frequently, the IRS is caught in the middle, even though it does not stand to generate more tax revenue, whatever the outcome. Its overriding concern isn't money but consistent enforcement of the laws and regulations.

The Deficit Reduction Act of 1984 completely restructured the alimony rules. The old rules still apply to alimony payments made under pre-1985 divorce and separation agreements—unless those agreements have been specifically modified. For related information refer to dependency exemption (see Chapter 3, Personal Exemptions and Dependents), the child care credit (see Chapter 33, Child and Dependent Care Credit), head of household status (see Chapter 2, Filing Status), and the earned income credit (see Chapter 35, Other Credits).

This chapter discusses the rules that apply to you if you pay or receive alimony and covers the following topics:

- What is alimony
- What payments are not alimony, such as child support
- How to deduct alimony you paid
- How to report alimony income you received
- Whether you must recapture the tax benefits of alimony (Recapture means a deduction was taken in a prior year and part of it had to be added back in your income in 1993.)

Alimony is a payment to or for a spouse or former spouse under a divorce or separation instrument. It does not include voluntary payments that are not required by a divorce or separation instrument.

Explanation
An outline of the old alimony rules that apply to divorce and separation instruments executed before 1985 and not modified after 1984 is shown at the end of this chapter.

Alimony is deductible by the payer and must be included in the spouse's or former spouse's income. Although this chapter is generally written for the payer of the alimony, the recipient can use the information to determine whether an amount received is alimony.

To be alimony, a payment must meet certain requirement

Different requirements apply to payments under instruments executed after 1984 and to payments under instruments executed before 1985. This chapter discusses the rules for payments under instruments executed after 1984. For the rules for payments under pre-1985 instruments, see Publication 504, *Divorced or Separated Individuals.*

Use *Table 19–1* in this chapter as a guide to determine whether certain payments are considered alimony.

Definitions. The following definitions apply throughout this chapter.

Spouse or former spouse. Unless otherwise stated in the following discussions about alimony, the term"spouse" includes "former spouse."

Divorce or separation instrument. The term "divorce or separation instrument" means:

1) A decree of divorce or separate maintenance or a written instrument incident to that decree,
2) A written separation agreement, or
3) A decree or any type of court order requiring a spouse to make payments for the support or maintenance of the other spouse, including a temporary decree, an interlocutory (not final) decree, and a decree of alimony *pendente lite* (while awaiting action on the final decree or agreement).

Useful Items

You may want to see:

Publication

☐ **504**   Divorced or Separated Individuals

General Rules

The following rules apply to alimony regardless of when the divorce or separation instrument was executed.

Payments not alimony. Not all payments under a divorce or separation instrument are alimony. Alimony does not include:

1) Child support,
2) Noncash property settlements,
3) Payments that are your spouse's part of community income (see *Community Property* in Publication 504),
4) Use of property, or
5) Payments to keep up the payer's property.

Explanation: Other Payments Not Deductible as Alimony

Do not deduct as alimony the following:

1. Any payment not required by the decree or agreement
2. Any payment that does not arise out of the marital relationship but that is required by the decree or agreement, such as repayment of a loan to your spouse
3. Any payment you make before the decree or agreement
4. Any payment you agreed to make before the decree or agreement and paid later

5. Any payment you make after your former spouse's remarriage
6. Any payment you make after your divorced spouse's death, even though required by the decree or agreement
7. Any payment you make that is part of a property settlement

Payments to a third party. Payments to a third party on behalf of your spouse under the terms of your divorce or separation instrument may be alimony, if they otherwise qualify. This includes payments for your spouse's medical expenses, housing costs (rent, utilities, etc.), taxes, tuition, etc. The payments are treated as received by your spouse and then paid to the third party.

Life insurance premiums. Premiums you must pay under your divorce or separation instrument for insurance on your life qualify as alimony to the extent your spouse owns the policy.

Explanation

The ownership of a life insurance policy must be assigned to your former spouse before you may deduct the premiums you pay as alimony. In addition, your former spouse must be the irrevocable beneficiary of the policy. Your children may be irrevocable contingent beneficiaries.

If your children are the beneficiaries of a life insurance policy and your former spouse is a contingent beneficiary, you still control the policy. The premiums you pay on it may not be considered alimony.

For the premiums to be considered alimony, your former spouse's benefit from the life insurance policy must be measurable in dollars. If your former spouse would benefit from the policy only under certain contingencies, the economic advantage cannot be measured. Your premiums would not be considered alimony.

Payments for jointly-owned home. If your divorce or separation instrument states that you must pay expenses for a home owned by you and your spouse, some of your payments may be alimony.

Mortgage payments. If you must make all the mortgage payments (principal and interest) on a jointly-owned home, and they otherwise qualify, you can deduct one-half of the total payments as alimony. If you itemize deductions and the home is a qualified residence, you can include the other half of the interest in figuring your deductible interest. Your spouse must report one-half of the payments as alimony received and, if itemizing deductions and the home is a qualified residence, can include one-half of the interest on the mortgage in figuring deductible interest.

Taxes and insurance. If you must pay all the real estate taxes or insurance on a home held as *tenants in common,* you can deduct one-half of these payments as alimony. Your spouse must report one-half of these payments as alimony received. If you and your spouse itemize deductions, you can each deduct one-half of the real estate taxes.

If your home is held as *tenants by the entirety* or *joint tenants* (with the right of survivorship), none of your payments for taxes or insurance are alimony. But if you itemize deductions, you can deduct all of the real estate taxes.

Other payments to a third party. If you made other third-party payments, see Publication 504 to see whether any part of the payments qualify as alimony.

Instruments Executed After 1984

The following rules for alimony apply to payments under divorce or separation instruments executed after 1984. They also apply to payments under earlier instruments that have been modified to:

1) Specify that these rules will apply, or
2) Change the amount or period of payment or add or delete any contingency or condition.

The rules in this section do not apply to divorce or separation instruments executed after 1984 if the terms for alimony are unchanged from an instrument executed before 1985.

Example 1. In November 1984, you and your former spouse executed a written separation agreement. In February 1985, a decree of divorce was substituted for the written separation agreement. The decree of divorce did not change the terms for the alimony you pay your former spouse. The decree of divorce is treated as executed before 1985. Therefore, alimony payments under the decree are not subject to the rules for payments under instruments executed after 1984.

Example 2. Assume the same facts as in Example 1 except that the decree of divorce changed the amount of the alimony. In this example, the decree of divorce is not treated as executed before 1985. Therefore, the alimony payments are subject to the rules for payments under instruments executed after 1984.

Alimony requirements. A payment to or for a spouse under a divorce or separation instrument is alimony if the spouses do not file a joint return with each other and all the following requirements are met.

1) The payment is in cash.
2) The instrument does not designate the payment as not alimony.
3) The spouses are not members of the same household (if separated under a decree of divorce or separate maintenance),
4) There is no liability to make any payment (in cash or property) after the death of the recipient spouse.
5) The payment is not treated as child support.

Each of these requirements is discussed below.

Explanation

For divorce decrees and separation agreements executed or revised after 1984, payments may not be deductible, even if there is a legal obligation to make them. Payments would be deductible only if all the other requirements were fulfilled.

TaxPlanner

Don't overlook the opportunity to use the new rules on an old divorce.

Example

Bob and Mary were divorced in 1975, with Mary agreeing to pay Bob $2,000 per month in qualifying alimony payments. Mary was a stockbroker earning top dollars in 1975. Bob had never had a full-time job. In 1993, Mary's fortunes are not so rosy, whereas Bob is a top Los Angeles real estate broker.

Bob and Mary could agree that, in 1993, Mary will pay less money to Bob but that it won't be considered alimony. If Mary's marginal tax bracket has dropped to 15% and Bob's bracket is 31%, Mary could pay Bob as little as 69% of what her normal payment is ($1,380), and both would win. Mary would be out of pocket $1,700 after tax if she were able to deduct the usual $2,000 payment at her 15% bracket; Bob would receive the $2,000 as taxable income and at his 31% bracket net the $1,380 anyway.

Payment must be in cash. Only cash payments, including checks and money orders, qualify as alimony. Transfers of services or property (including a debt instrument of a third party or an annuity contract), execution of a debt instrument, or the use of property do not qualify as alimony.

TaxPlanner

According to the IRS, an annuity contract given to a spouse is not the same as cash. This would mean that it is a transfer of property. Therefore, the spouse receiving the annuity contract has the same investment cost as the spouse giving it. The only income to the receiving spouse would be for the amounts received in excess of cost. The spouse giving the annuity contract would not be entitled to a deduction for alimony.

If you are the spouse making the payments and you want to make sure that you get a deduction for your costs, you should simply fund the amount of your obligation with an annuity that you purchase and own, rather than transfer the annuity contract to your spouse.

Cash payments to a third party under the terms of your divorce or separation instrument can qualify as a cash payment to your spouse. See *Payments to a third party* under *General Rules,* earlier.

Also, cash payments made to a third party at the written request of your spouse qualify as alimony if all the following requirements are met.

1) The payments are in lieu of payments of alimony directly to your spouse.
2) The written request states that both spouses intend the payments to be treated as alimony.
3) You receive the written request from your spouse before you file your return for the year you made the payments.

Explanation

Medical and dental expenses. If you paid your spouse's medical and dental expenses under a decree or agreement, you may deduct them as alimony. However, a payment of unusually large medical expenses in a given year might trigger the excess front-loading rules. The result could be that you lose the deduction for the payments under the recapture rules, even though they are required as part of the divorce or separation agreement.

Your spouse must report these payments as alimony

received and may include them in medical expenses if he or she is itemizing deductions.

Note: The spouse who pays the medical bills saves tax by claiming the amounts as alimony rather than as medical expenses. Alimony is fully deductible from adjusted gross income, whether or not you itemize your deductions. Medical expenses must exceed 7.5% of adjusted gross income to be deductible.

TAXSAVER

If you pay medical insurance premiums on behalf of a former spouse, you may be entitled to an additional deduction.

Example

A husband who had not been directly ordered by the courts to carry medical insurance for his former wife but who was ordered to pay her reasonable medical expenses was allowed to deduct premiums paid as alimony. (He could not deduct the premiums as a medical expense.) His former wife had to include the amount that her former husband paid for the insurance premiums as income. Both parties treated as alimony the premiums and any actual medical expenses paid that were not reimbursed by insurance payments.

Note: The husband may have created a larger deduction for alimony by taking out an insurance policy on his former wife, since he may deduct the cost of the premiums (his out-of-pocket cost) whether or not his former wife incurs any actual medical expenses. Conversely, the former wife may pay a tax on an amount from which she derives no direct benefit.

Payments designated as not alimony. You and your spouse may designate that otherwise qualifying payments are not alimony by including a provision in your divorce or separation instrument that the payments are not deductible by you and are excludable from your spouse's income. For this purpose, any writing signed by both of you that makes this designation and that refers to a previous written separation agreement is treated as a written separation agreement. If you are subject to temporary support orders, the designation must be made in the original or a subsequent temporary support order.

To exclude the payments from income, your spouse must attach a copy of the instrument designating them as not alimony to his or her return for each year the designation applies.

Spouses cannot be members of the same household. Payments to your spouse while you are members of the same household are not alimony if you are separated under a decree of divorce or separate maintenance. A home you formerly shared is considered one household, even if you physically separate yourselves in the home.

You are not treated as members of the same household if one of you is preparing to leave the household and does leave not more than one month after the date of the payment.

Exception. If you are not legally separated under a decree of divorce or separate maintenance, a payment under a written separation agreement, support decree or other court order may qualify as alimony even if you are members of the same household when the payment is made.

Explanation

Separated and living apart. The courts have traditionally held that spouses living under the same roof are not separated. However, some courts have looked to the facts and circumstances surrounding each case to determine whether or not spouses living in the same house who seldom see each other and who incur duplicate living expenses are, in fact, separated. The Appeals Courts have been reluctant to deal with the highly personalized questions that must be asked to determine whether or not the parties are truly living apart.

Liability for payments after death of recipient spouse. If you must continue to make payments for any period after your spouse's death, none of the payments made before or after the death are alimony.

The divorce or separation instrument does not have to expressly state that the payments cease upon the death of your spouse if, for example, the liability for continued payments would end under state law.

Example. You must pay your former spouse $10,000 in cash each year for 10 years. Your divorce decree states that the payments will end upon your former spouse's death. You must also pay your former spouse or your former spouse's estate $20,000 in cash each year for 10 years. The death of your spouse would not terminate the payments under state law.

The $10,000 annual payments are alimony. But because the $20,000 annual payments will not end upon your former spouse's death, they are not alimony.

Substitute payments. If you must make any payments in cash or property after your spouse's death as a substitute for continuing otherwise qualifying payments, the otherwise qualifying payments are not alimony. Substitute payments, can also include, depending on the facts and circumstances, payments to the extent they increase in amount or begin or accelerate as a result of your spouse's death.

Example 1. Under your divorce decree, you must pay your former spouse $30,000 annually. The payments will stop at the end of 6 years or upon your former spouse's death, if earlier.

Your former spouse has custody of your minor children. The decree provides that if any child is still a minor at your spouse's death, you must pay $10,000 annually to a trust until the youngest child reaches the age of majority. The trust income and corpus (principal) are to be used for your children's benefit.

These facts indicate that the payments to be made after your former spouse's death are a substitute for $10,000 of the $30,000 annual payments. Therefore, $10,000 of each of the $30,000 annual payments is not alimony.

Example 2. Under your divorce decree, you must pay your former spouse $30,000 annually. The payments will stop at the end of 15 years or upon your former spouse's death, if earlier. The decree provides that if your former spouse dies before the end of the 15–year period, you must pay the estate the difference between $450,000 ($30,000 × 15) and the total amount paid up to that time. For example, if your spouse dies at the end of the tenth year, you must pay the estate $150,000 ($450,000 − $300,000).

These facts indicate that the lump-sum payment to be made after your former spouse's death is a substitute for the full amount of the $30,000 annual payments. Therefore, none of the annual payments are alimony. The result would be the same if the payment required at death were to be discounted by an appropriate interest factor to account for the prepayment.

Table 19-1. Alimony Requirements (Instruments executed after 1984)

Payments ARE Alimony if all of the following are true:	Payments ARE NOT Alimony if any of the following are true:
Payments are required by a divorce or separation instrument.	Payment is designated as child support.
Payer and recipient spouse do not file a joint return.	Payment is a noncash property settlement.
Payment is in cash (including checks or money orders).	Payments are spouse's part of community income.
Payment is not designated in the instrument as not alimony.	Payments are to keep up the payer's property.
Spouses separated under a decree of divorce or separate maintenance are not members of the same household.	Payments are not required by a divorce or separation instrument.
Payments are not required after death of the recipient spouse.	
Payment is not designated as child support.	
These payments are deductible by the payer and includible in income by the recipient.	These payments are neither deductible by the payer nor includible in income by the recipient.

Child support. A payment that is specifically designated as child support or treated as specifically designated as child support under your divorce or separation instrument is not alimony. The designated amount or part may vary from time to time. Child support payments are neither deductible by the payer, nor taxable to the payee.

A payment will be treated as specifically designated as child support to the extent that the payment is reduced either:

1) On the happening of a contingency relating to your child, or
2) At a time that can be clearly associated with the contingency.

A payment may be treated as specifically designated as child support even if other separate payments are specifically designated as child support.

TAXPLANNER

Since child support payments are considered fixed, any reductions in child support that are not part of the original decree or a subsequent court-approved modified divorce decree are considered reductions in alimony, not child support. Therefore, be sure to have the court approve any child support reductions so that you can continue to deduct the full alimony payments.

Example

After a taxpayer remarried, his son from his previous marriage began to live with him. The taxpayer and his former wife agreed that, as a result, his child support payments should be eliminated. Even though both for-mer spouses agreed that the payment reductions applied to child support, the courts held that they applied to alimony, because the taxpayer and his former spouse did not obtain a modification of their divorce decree in court.

Contingency relating to your child. A contingency relates to your child if it depends on any event relating to that child. It does not matter whether the event is certain or likely to occur. Events relating to your child include the child's:

Reaching a specified age or income level,
Dying,
Marrying,
Leaving school,
Leaving the household, or
Becoming employed.

Clearly associated with a contingency. Payments are presumed to be reduced at a time clearly associated with the happening of a contingency relating to your child only in the following situations.

1) The payments are to be reduced not more than 6 months before or after the date the child will reach 18, 21, or local age of majority.
2) The payments are to be reduced on two or more occasions that occur not more than one year before or after a different child reaches a certain age from 18 to 24. This certain age must be the same for each child, but need not be a whole number of years.

In all other situations, reductions in payments are not treated as clearly associated with the happening of a contingency relating to your child.

Either you or the IRS may overcome the presumption in the two situations above. This is done by showing that the time at which the payments are to be reduced was determined independently of any contingencies relating to your children. For example, if you can show that the period of alimony payments is customary in the local jurisdiction, such as a period equal to one-half of the duration of the marriage, you can treat the amount as alimony.

Explanation: Child Support in Agreements Executed Before 1985

Child support amounts may not be inferred for payments made under agreements executed before 1985 and not revised. You may not assume that portions of the alimony payments are used by a former spouse for support of a child. The U.S. Supreme Court has held that payments are not treated as child support payments unless they are expressly designated as such in the governing document.

Example

If the agreement that was executed before 1985 and has not been revised says "alimony and child support of $1,000 per month until the child reaches age 18 and then $750 per month," the entire payment is treated as alimony.

Explanation: Child Support in Agreements Executed After 1984

Child support amounts *may* be inferred for payments made under agreements executed or revised after 1984, even if such payments are not specifically earmarked. However, such payments will be reduced upon certain contingencies related to the child. Such contingencies would include the child attaining a certain age or income level, dying, marrying, leaving school, leaving the spouse's household, or getting a job.

Payments that are reduced at a time that can clearly be associated with a contingency will be treated as child support. For example, if a payment was to stop at a certain calendar date that just happened to be the child's nineteenth birthday, that payment would be considered child support.

The parent who has custody of the child is entitled to take the dependency exemption for the child, as long as the parents themselves could have claimed the exemption had they filed a joint return. This will not apply if

1. There is a multiple support agreement in effect specifying who gets the exemption
2. The custodial parent relinquishes the exemption in writing (using language in IRS Form 8332)
3. There is an executed, pre-1985 divorce or separation agreement in effect that provides that the noncustodial parent who also furnishes at least $600 of child support can claim the exemption.

Note: The custodial parent is still entitled to claim the dependent care credit, even if he or she relinquishes the dependency exemption to the noncustodial parent.

A parent can deduct medical expenses that he or she paid directly, even though the dependency exemption for the child is claimed by the other parent. This is the case as long as a multiple-support agreement is not in effect.

TaxPlanner

In 1993, single taxpayers with adjusted gross income over $108,450 and taxpayers filing as head of household with adjusted gross income exceeding $135,600 will not receive full benefit of the deduction for personal exemptions. Taxpayers with adjusted gross income above these thresholds will have the amount of each personal and dependent exemption simultaneously reduced at a rate of 2% for each $2,500 (or fraction thereof) their adjusted gross income exceeds the applicable threshold. As a result, the former spouse with less adjusted gross income may receive a greater tax benefit from claiming the children as dependents than would the spouse with higher income.

How to Deduct Alimony Paid

You can deduct alimony you paid, whether or not you itemize deductions on your return. Enter the alimony on line 29 of Form 1040. You cannot use Form 1040A or Form 1040EZ.

In the space on line 29, enter your spouse's or former spouse's social security number. If you do not, you may have to pay a $50 penalty and your deduction may be disallowed.

If you paid alimony to more than one person, enter the social security number of one of the recipients. Show the social security number and amount paid for each recipient on an attached statement. Enter your total payments on line 29.

Explanation

Even if the validity of a divorce decree is questioned, your spouse must include periodic payments that you make under such a divorce decree in income. You may deduct the payments as alimony. A divorce decree is valid for tax purposes until a court having proper jurisdiction declares it invalid.

The IRS generally recognizes a state court as having proper jurisdiction if that court has personal jurisdiction over the parties involved or if that court has jurisdiction over the subject matter of the action.

Example 1

In the process of separating, a husband and wife entered into a support agreement under a state court. The husband later obtained a Mexican divorce that said nothing about the support agreement. The state considered the divorce to be valid. Even though the Mexican divorce decree made no mention of the support payments, the payments were considered alimony because the original state support agreement had never been invalidated.

Example 2

A husband who obtained a Mexican divorce was later sued by his former wife for support payments and for a legal separation under state law. The state court granted the former wife the support payments. The Mexican divorce was not recognized by the state, but the payments were considered to be alimony.

How to Report Alimony Received

Report alimony you received on line 11 of Form 1040. You cannot use Form 1040A or Form 1040EZ.

You must give the person who paid the alimony your social security number. If you do not, you may have to pay a $50 penalty.

Recapture Rule

If your alimony payments decrease or terminate during the first 3 calendar years, you may be subject to the recapture rule. If you are subject to this rule, you have to include in income in 1993 part of the alimony payments you deducted in 1991 and 1992. Your spouse can deduct in 1993 part of the alimony payments included in income in those previous years.

The 3–year period starts with the first calendar year you make a payment qualifying as alimony under a decree of divorce or separate maintenance, or a written separation agreement. Do not include any time in which payments were being made under temporary support orders. The second and third years are the next 2 calendar years, whether or not payments are made during those years.

The reasons for a reduction or termination of alimony payments can include:

A failure to make timely payments,
A change in your instrument,
A reduction in your spouse's support needs, or
A reduction in your ability to provide support.

Subject to recapture for 1993. You are subject to the recapture rule for 1993, if you answer "Yes" to the following questions.

1) Was 1991 the first year in which you made alimony payments to this spouse under a decree of divorce or separate maintenance, or a written separation agreement?
2) Did your total payments in 1992 or 1993 decrease by more than $15,000 from the prior year?

In answering the above questions, do not include payments required over a period of at least 3 calendar years of a fixed part of your income from a business or property, or from compensation for employment or self-employment. These payments are not subject to the recapture rule.

Exceptions. You are not subject to recapture if your payments were reduced because of the death of either spouse or the remarriage of the spouse receiving the payments.

Including the recapture in income. If you must include a recapture amount in income, show it on Form 1040, line 11 ("Alimony received"). Cross out "received" and write "recapture." On the dotted line next to the amount, enter your spouse's last name and social security number.

Deducting the recapture. If you can deduct a recapture amount, show it on Form 1040, line 29 ("Alimony paid"). Cross out "paid" and write "recapture." In the space provided, enter your spouse's social security number.

Figuring the recapture. Both you and your spouse can use *Table 19–2,* substituting your own figures, to figure recaptured alimony. Publication 504 has a blank worksheet for your use.

Example. Myrna pays Phil the following amounts of alimony under their 1991 divorce decree:

Year	Amount
1991	$60,000
1992	40,000
1993	20,000

The recaptured alimony is $22,500, as shown in *Table 19–2.*

Myrna shows $22,500 as income on line 11 of her 1993 Form 1040. Phil deducts $22,500 on line 29 of his 1993 Form 1040.

TAXSAVER

If the payments are spread out equally over the 3 years, they are all deductible. Also, payments in year 3 are a great deal more beneficial than those in year 2. In the above example, if $5,000 of the alimony paid in 1992 is delayed until 1993, the recapture amount drops from $22,500 to $15,000.

Explanation: Other Alimony Rules

Transfer of property. If property is transferred in settlement of marital rights, the spouse making the transfer does not recognize either gain or loss on the transfer, whether the property has appreciated or declined in value. The transfer is treated like a gift, and the spouse receiving the property takes the basis of the transferring spouse. This is true even if the spouse receiving the property pays cash and the transaction is cast in the form of a sale.

The following are exceptions to the nonrecognition rules:

1. Transfer of an installment note to a trust will cause the deferred gain to be recognized.
2. Transfer of property subject to liabilities in excess of your basis will cause the excess to be recognized.

TAXPLANNER

The transfer between spouses of a note receivable that arose from an installment sale will not be considered a disposition for purposes of accelerating the reporting of previously deferred income. Instead, the recipient of the installment note will have the same tax posture as the spouse who made the transfer.

Explanation

Transfer of business property. The law is silent on the status of unrealized income from normal business accounts receivable that may be transferred. There is no recapture of investment tax credit or depreciation upon the transfer of business property. The spouse making the transfer must provide permanent records of cost basis, accumulated depreciation, holding period, and investment-credit recapture potential to the other spouse. There is no penalty for failure to do so, however.

TAXPLANNER

A spouse who is to receive property with a tax basis substantially less than its current value should carefully evaluate the tax consequences of disposing of it. You

Table 19-2. **Worksheet for Recapture of Alimony** (For instruments executed after 1986)

Note: Do not enter less than zero on any line.

1. Alimony paid in **2nd year** .... $ 40,000

2. Alimony paid in **3rd year** .... $ 20,000

3. Floor $15,000

4. Add lines 2 and 3 35,000

5. Subtract line 4 from line 1 .... $5,000

6. Alimony paid in **1st year** 60,000

7. Adjusted alimony paid in **2nd year** (line 1 less line 5) 35,000

8. Alimony paid in **3rd year** 20,000

9. Add lines 7 and 8 55,000

10. Divide line 9 by 2 27,500

11. Floor $15,000

12. Add lines 10 and 11 42,500

13. Subtract line 12 from line 6 17,500

14. **Recaptured alimony.** Add lines 5 and 13 .... $22,500

*If you deducted alimony paid, report this amount as income on line 11, Form 1040.

If you reported alimony received, deduct this amount on line 29, Form 1040.

Table 19-2. **Worksheet for Recapture of Alimony** (For instruments executed after 1986)

Note: Do not enter less than zero on any line.

1. Alimony paid in **2nd year** .... _____

2. Alimony paid in **3rd year** .... _____

3. Floor $15,000

4. Add lines 2 and 3 .... _____

5. Subtract line 4 from line 1 .... _____

6. Alimony paid in **1st year** .... _____

7. Adjusted alimony paid in **2nd year** (line 1 less line 5) .... _____

8. Alimony paid in **3rd year** .... _____

9. Add lines 7 and 8 .... _____

10. Divide line 9 by 2 .... _____

11. Floor $15,000

12. Add lines 10 and 11 .... _____

13. Subtract line 12 from line 6 .... _____

14. **Recaptured alimony.** Add lines 5 and 13 .... * _____

*If you deducted alimony paid, report this amount as income on line 11, Form 1040.

If you reported alimony received, deduct this amount on line 29, Form 1040.

may be subject to tax from recapture of investment tax credit and depreciation. You should obtain the advice of competent counsel on such matters.

Example

As part of the divorce property settlement, Kyle gives Mary a computer that he used for 4 years in his sole proprietorship business. Kyle paid $5,000 for the computer, claimed investment credit on it, and claimed depreciation of $3,950. Since the computer ceased to be business property when it was given to Mary, she must recapture part of the investment credit claimed by Kyle. Further, Mary must pay ordinary income tax on her profit if she sells the computer for more than $1,050. See Chapter 17, *Reporting Gains and Losses,* and Chapter 35, *Other Credits.*

Explanation

Trust property. If you have placed income-producing property in trust to pay alimony, you do not include the payments in your income, nor do you deduct them. This rule applies whether the alimony payments are made out of the trust income or principal. Trust distributions must be reported by your spouse. If your obligation to pay alimony is stated in a divorce decree, other court order, or written separation agreement, your spouse reports the distributions as alimony on line 11 of Form 1040. If your obligation is not so stated, your spouse reports the income distributions as income received from a trust, on Schedule E (Form 1040).

You may also set up a trust to pay both alimony and child support. If your former spouse remarries and you are no longer required to pay alimony, the trust may continue disbursing monies for child support.

TAXPLANNER

If a trust that is set up to disburse alimony payments holds municipal bonds, the distributions to the former spouse are nontaxable to the extent that they are attributable to the trust's municipal bond income. Also, if the distributions from the trust exceed the trust's income, the excess distribution of trust principal is not taxable.

Explanation

Insurance, endowment, or annuity. If you bought an insurance or endowment policy, or an annuity contract to discharge alimony or support called for in your divorce decree, do not include payments made under the contract in your income and do not deduct them. Your spouse must include the payments in income.

Annulments. Generally, state laws blur the distinction between a divorce and an annulment. The rules on alimony often apply to an annulment decree as well as to a divorce decree. You should examine the law of the state in which you reside to determine if this is the case.

Example

In New York, a marriage was annulled due to the wife's insanity. The husband was required to provide for her care and maintenance. Since under the general rules of law the annulment would be considered a divorce, the husband's payments were treated as alimony.

TAXPLANNER

Expenses of a home. If part of an alimony award is to pay such expenses as real estate taxes, insurance, mortgage interest, and utilities for a home owned by a divorced couple, the facts in each case determine the amount deductible by one spouse and includable by the other spouse. Two facts to consider are the type of ownership and the kinds of expenses that must be paid. However, in each case, the payments must cover a period of more than 10 years or otherwise qualify as periodic payments if made pursuant to a pre-1985 agreement.

Ownership

You should check your state law, your ownership documents, and your divorce decree to determine what type of ownership you have.

1. **Joint tenants or tenants by the entirety.** You and your former spouse own a home jointly as **tenants by the entirety** or **joint tenants** with a right of survivorship. You are each responsible for the mortgage that you owe. If your divorce decree states that your former spouse is to pay the mortgage (principal and interest) on the property from money that he or she receives from you as support, then your former spouse must include one-half of each principal and interest payment as income from alimony and you may deduct one-half of each principal and interest payment as alimony.

   Your former spouse may deduct that half of the interest if your former spouse itemizes deductions on Schedule A (Form 1040). If you itemize your deductions, it is not clear how your share of the interest should be handled. It may be deductible under the home mortgage rules if your children live there and you are not already deducting interest on two personal residences. Or it might be considered investment interest, since, as far as you are concerned, the property is now just an investment. Lastly, it could be personal interest and therefore not deductible.

2. **Tenants in common.** If you and your former spouse own a home as **tenants in common,** your former spouse owns half of the property. Therefore, you may deduct as alimony amounts you pay on your former spouse's half of the property for principal, interest, insurance, and taxes. Your former spouse must include these amounts in income.

   If your former spouse itemizes deductions on Schedule A (Form 1040), he or she may deduct as taxes and interest the part you paid for real estate taxes and interest on your former spouse's half of the property. He or she may not deduct amounts for insurance. Insurance is a nondeductible personal expense.

   Amounts you paid on your half of the property are not deductible as alimony, nor are they includable in income by your former spouse. If you itemize your deductions on Schedule A (Form 1040), you may deduct as taxes and interest the part you pay for real estate taxes and interest on your half of the property. You may not deduct insurance payments on your half of the property.

3. **If your former spouse owns the home** and under a decree or agreement you pay the real estate taxes, mortgage payments, and insurance premiums on it, you may deduct these payments as alimony. Your former spouse must include these payments in income.

   If your former spouse itemizes deductions on Schedule A (Form 1040), he or she may deduct the part of each payment that is for taxes and interest on the mortgage.

4. **If you own the home** lived in rent-free by your former spouse, you may not deduct your mortgage payments or the fair rental value of the home as alimony. However, if you itemize your deductions, you may deduct on Schedule A (Form 1040) any real estate taxes and interest you pay on the property.

Rent. If, under a divorce or separate maintenance decree or written separation agreement, you must pay rent to a third party lessor to provide housing for your spouse or former spouse, you may deduct the rent payments as alimony. Your former spouse must include these payments in income.

Utilities. If your former spouse is the one who has the right to use the home, regardless of the type of ownership, you may deduct as alimony the amount you pay for utilities under a decree or agreement. Your former spouse must include these amounts in income.

There are many consequences of property ownership that must be considered in a divorce settlement. Any payments made by you for the mortgage, property taxes, insurance, and so on, are considered alimony *only* if the house belongs to your former spouse. If you transfer your interest in the property to your children, payments to cover their portion of the mortgage payments would be treated as child support, not alimony.

Example

John and Mary owned a home that cost them $150,000. In their divorce, the court decree holds that Mary can remain in the home until their son, who is 10 years old, reaches 18. Mary must pay rent to John for using his half of the house. In 1995, the house is sold and John and Mary together receive $250,000.

Mary immediately buys another home for more than $250,000. Mary's gain is postponed, because she reinvested more than she received. See Chapter 16, *Selling Your Home*.

John was a landlord during the rental years and probably claimed related expenses and depreciation on his tax return. If the rent charged was reasonable, John could deduct any losses, subject to the restrictions on passive losses.

John is not entitled to postpone his gain by purchasing another home, since the residence sold was not his home at the time of the sale.

TAXPLANNER

Other aspects of obtaining a divorce. IRS Publication 504, *Tax Information for Divorced or Separated*

Individuals, examines more closely some of the tax aspects of obtaining a divorce, including the tax treatment of costs incurred in working out a settlement.

Court costs and legal fees related to the divorce are not deductible. However, the portion of these fees attributable to obtaining alimony is deductible as an itemized deduction, since it is an expense for the production of income. Any additional costs incurred to obtain alimony are also deductible, as are costs for tax advice.

Be sure to have itemized invoices for professional services. Deductible items should be specifically listed on any bill. You may claim only the deductible portion of your own legal expenses. You may not deduct the legal expenses of your spouse. Those expenses also may not be considered alimony payments.

Some part of your legal fees may give you a tax benefit, even though the fees are not spent for obtaining alimony or tax advice. For example, if part of your legal fees may be allocated to obtaining property, the tax basis of the property should be increased by the amount of such fees. If the property is business property, you will have larger **depreciation** deductions and a smaller gain if the property is sold.

There are several additional aspects that you should consider in a year in which you become divorced:

1. **Revising Form W–4.** Form W–4 should be changed if you are no longer able to claim as many withholding allowances due to your change in marital status. This may occur because you no longer file a joint return with your former spouse. It also may occur if you are not entitled to a dependency exemption for one or more of your children. When you revise your Form W–4, your employer adjusts your withheld taxes to reflect the changes in your marital status.

2. **Estimated taxes on alimony.** If you are receiving alimony, you may be required to make estimated tax payments, since alimony is not covered by withholding. (See Chapter 5, *Tax Withholding and Estimated Tax*.)

3. **Allocating joint estimated tax payments between you and your former spouse.** If you and your former spouse are divorced during the year and have been making joint estimated tax payments, the payments you have already made may be applied to either person's separate return or may be divided between you, as the two of you see fit. If no allocation can be agreed on, the estimated payments should be applied between the separate returns in proportion to the taxes due on each.

Example

Your return shows a tax liability of $5,100. Your former spouse's return shows a tax liability of $2,300. You would be entitled to apply 69% [$5,100 ÷ ($5,100 + $2,300)] of your total joint estimated payments against your tax liability.

4. **Retirement plans.** An employed spouse's interest in a qualified retirement plan can be allocated between a current and a former spouse by a Qualified Domestic Relations Order.

Benefits so allocated are taxed to the nonemployed spouse when the payments are actually received. If the benefits are received by anyone other than the employed or the nonemployed spouse, the benefits are taxed to the employed spouse, not the recipient.

5. **Federal income taxes withheld.** Taxes withheld from your income are treated the same way as the income that generates them. If salary is split between you and your spouse because of community property rules, then the income tax withholding is also divided between the two of you.

6. **Alimony and your IRA.** All taxable alimony or separate maintenance payments received by an individual under a decree of divorce or separate maintenance are treated as compensation and are eligible to be contributed to your IRA. See Chapter 18, *Individual Retirement Arrangements (IRAs),* for details.

Explanation: Pre-1985 Rules

Here is an outline of the old alimony rules that apply to divorce or separation instruments executed *before* 1985 and *not* changed after 1984.

Payments you make under a court decree of divorce or separation are included in the income of your spouse or former spouse and may be deducted as alimony by you if they are

1. Required under the decree of divorce or separation, or a written instrument incident to that decree
2. Based on your marital or family relationship
3. Paid after the decree
4. Are periodic instead of a lump sum

Payments made before the divorce decree or separate maintenance agreement issued by the court do not qualify as alimony. The divorce need not be final for the payments to be considered alimony, but the payments must be ordered by the court and, if made under pre-1985 agreements, must satisfy a legal obligation arising from the marriage.

Payments you make under a written separation agreement executed after August 16, 1954, or materially altered or modified after that date, are included in the income of your spouse and may be deducted as alimony by you if they are

1. Based on your marital or family relationship
2. Paid after the agreement is put into effect and while you and your spouse are separated and living apart
3. Paid during a tax year for which you do not file a **joint return** with the spouse who gets these payments
4. Are periodic instead of a lump sum

To be binding, a written agreement must state the amount of the support payments, the length of time over which the payments are to be made, and the items of support covered by the payments. The agreement does not have to mention specifically that the couple is separated.

The written separation agreement must be accepted by both parties. One spouse may not merely designate payments as alimony. The courts have held that a letter from a husband to a wife defining various payments as support do not meet the requirements of a written agreement, even if the payments are accepted by the wife. The agreement takes effect when it has been signed by both parties, no matter what the date is on the agreement.

Example

A wife signed a separation agreement and sent it to her husband. The husband signed it before a notary public but did not return it to the wife for several months. The husband, who had been out of the country, began sending the wife support payments before she received the signed agreement. The court held that the agreement became effective when signed by the husband. All payments were viewed as alimony.

Explanation

Payments you make under a decree for support or any type of court order, including a temporary decree, entered after March 1, 1954, or changed by a court after that date, are included in the income of your spouse and may be deducted as alimony by you if they are

1. Required under the decree or court order
2. Paid while you and your spouse are separated and living apart
3. Paid during a tax year for which you do not file a joint return with the spouse who gets these payments
4. Are periodic instead of a lump sum

Payments you make under a decree for support or any type of court order qualify as alimony, even though the decree is not pursuant to a divorce or **legal separation** agreement. These payments must be specified as being for a spouse, not a child.

Spouses separated under an interlocutory decree retain the relationship of husband and wife, even though payments made pursuant to this type of decree qualify as alimony. However, if payments are being made under an interlocutory decree issued prior to March 1, 1954, and that decree has not yet been revised, the payments are not considered alimony.

Temporary alimony. If you do not file a joint return, you may deduct periodic payments you make under a decree of alimony *pendente lite* (while awaiting action on the final decree or agreement) entered after March 1, 1954. Your spouse must include the payments in income.

Remarriage of former spouse. You may not deduct payments you make under a divorce decree to your former spouse after the spouse remarries, if you have no legal obligation to continue to make the payments. Legal obligation to continue to make the payments would be determined under the law of the state in which your divorce was granted. However, your former spouse must still report the payments as miscellaneous income (not alimony), unless it can be shown that they were gifts, payments on a loan, or were otherwise excludable from income.

Example 1

In 1984, you were divorced from your spouse. The divorce decree calls for you to pay your former spouse

$400 a month as alimony. In April, 1993, your former spouse remarried, but you were not aware of this, and you continued to make the payments.

Under the state law in which you got your divorce, your legal obligation to make the payments ends if your former spouse remarries. Even though you were unaware that your former spouse remarried, you cannot deduct the payments you made after April, 1993. However, your former spouse must include the payments in gross income.

Example 2

Assume the same facts as in Example 1, except that you were aware of your former spouse's remarriage and you continued to make the payments but considered them a gift. In this situation, your former spouse does not have to include the payments made after April, 1993 in gross income, and you may not deduct them.

Explanation

Periodic payments in a community property state to a separated spouse are deductible as alimony only if they are more than that spouse's part of the **community income.**

Example

You live in a community property state. You are separated, and your spouse has no income. Under a written support agreement, you pay your spouse periodic payments of $12,000 of your $20,000 total yearly community income. Under your state law, earnings of a spouse living separate and apart from the other spouse continue as community property. On your separate returns, each of you must report $10,000 gross income (half of the total community income). In addition, your spouse must report $2,000 as alimony received on line 11 of Form 1040. You may deduct $2,000 as alimony paid on line 29 of Form 1040.

Note: If you did *not* make any payments to your spouse or notify him or her of the amount of the community income, the IRS can require that you report the entire $20,000 as your income.

Explanation

A couple's property continues to be considered community property by the IRS until a final divorce is granted. This is true, even though some states—Louisiana, for example—might retroactively recognize the date of separation as the time when property is no longer shared. Consequently, until a final divorce is granted, a spouse should treat as alimony only those payments that are more than his or her share of the community income. Furthermore, alimony paid to a former spouse is generally considered as having been paid from community income when you and your current spouse file separate returns.

Example

A California resident was divorced and remarried. His new wife was a **nonresident alien,** and they filed separate tax returns. The courts held that he could deduct only half of the alimony payments made to his former wife, because he failed to prove that the alimony payments were made from separate income property that he did not share with his new wife. Therefore, his new wife was, in effect, paying half of his alimony payments to his former wife. Her payments were not deductible as alimony.

Explanation

Periodic payments are payments of a fixed amount (e.g., $400 a month) for an indefinite period or payments of an indefinite amount (e.g., 10% of a salary that changes from year to year) for either a fixed or an indefinite period. They need not be made at regular intervals.

Even if a state court describes payments made under a divorce decree as payments for property rights, they may be periodic payments if they are made to fulfill a legal support obligation.

Installment payments that you make to take care of your alimony obligation (the amount you must pay under the decree) generally are not considered periodic payments if the total obligation is stated in the decree or agreement. They may not be deductible at all, or they may be only partly deductible, depending mainly on the period over which you must make the payments.

In general, courts have held that, if an amount specified in the divorce decree can be determined by arithmetical means, it is considered a principal sum. Payments to reach a principal sum are installment payments, not periodic payments, and generally are not deductible as alimony if they are paid over a period of 10 years or less. The following are property settlement payments, not periodic payments:

- Repayment of a debt between husband and wife in equal annual installments
- Repayment on an annual basis of the wife's interest in community property retained by the husband.

Example

A woman purchased a residence in her name. Her former husband had the right to use the residence for his lifetime. The woman was not allowed to deduct the fair rental value of the property as alimony, and the man did not have to include the value in his income as periodic payments. The IRS ruled that, according to state law, the woman was making a one-time transfer of property to her former husband. Such a transfer does not qualify as alimony.

Explanation

If the period stated is 10 years or less, the payments generally are not considered periodic, and, therefore, you may not deduct them. However, if the payments are subject to certain specific contingencies, they are deductible periodic payments, even though under the decree they are for a specified period of 10 years or less. Alimony payments are considered subject to contingencies if they are to end or change in amount on

1. The death of either spouse
2. The remarriage of the spouse receiving them

3. A change in the economic status (amount of money or property owned) of either spouse.

The contingency may be set forth in the terms of the decree or agreement, or may be imposed by local law. The payments must be in the nature of alimony or an allowance for support.

Example

Under the terms of a settlement agreement approved by the divorce decree, you agreed to pay your former spouse $19,000. Of this amount, you paid $14,000 as soon as the decree was entered. You pay the remaining $5,000 for 25 months at $200 a month. The payments will stop if your former spouse dies or remarries. You may not deduct the $14,000 that is a lump-sum payment, and your former spouse does not include it in income. Because the monthly payments of $200 will stop if your former spouse dies or remarries, they are periodic payments. You may deduct them, and your former spouse must include them in income.

Explanation

If the period stated is more than 10 years and the payments are not subject to contingencies, you may deduct a certain amount of each installment payment paid during the year as a periodic payment and your spouse must include it in income. The amount is limited to 10% of the total amount to be paid over the entire time called for by the decree. This 10% limit applies to installment payments made in advance, but not to late installment payments received during your spouse's tax year. If the payments are made for more than 10 years and are subject to contingencies, you may deduct them in full as periodic payments.

Example

Your decree states that you must pay your former spouse $150,000 in installments of $20,000 a year for 5 years and $5,000 a year for the following 10 years. The payments are not subject to any contingencies. You may deduct only 10% of the $150,000, or $15,-000, during each of the first 5 years. During the last 10 years, you may deduct the entire $5,000 you pay each year.

Explanation

The 10% rule is relevant only when the amounts of alimony payments required by the divorce decree are not paid evenly over the specified payment period. The intention of the 10% rule is to prevent property settlements from being disguised as alimony. Alimony is deductible; a property settlement is not. The 10% rule does not apply if the payments would cease on the occurrence of certain contingencies.

TAXPLANNER 1

Although you may deduct only 10% of the total amount of fixed payments in any one year, you may be able to claim a greater deduction than you would normally if you alter the timing of the payments.

Example 1

A husband is obligated to pay $160,000 over a 15-year period by paying $20,000 a year for the first 5 years and $6,000 a year for the last 10 years. Because he may deduct only 10% of the total fixed amount in any 1 year, only $16,000 (10% of $160,000) of the $20,000 paid in each of the first 5 years is deductible. The $4,000-per-year difference ($20,000 paid less $16,000 deductible) is not deductible by the husband or taxable to his former spouse.

In the fifth year, however, the husband makes a payment of only $16,000, instead of the required $20,000. That entire amount is deductible, since it is not more than 10% of the total amount due. If in the sixth year of payments he makes a $10,000 payment (the $6,000 he owes for that year plus the $4,000 from the year before), he may again deduct the entire amount. The $10,000 payment is less than the 10% limitation. Also, back alimony is not subject to the 10% rule. Thus, by shifting the timing of his payments, the husband may take a greater deduction.

Note: The 10% rule does apply to the advance payment of alimony. If in the above example the husband wants to make the $6,000-a-year payments for years 6, 7, and 8 in the sixth year, he may deduct only $16,000 (10% of the total amount due) of the $18,000 paid.

Example 2

Mr. Oldster got behind in his alimony payments. He made a lump-sum settlement of the amounts he owed, as well as future alimony. The amount paid was less than the total amount due and was also less than the amount of delinquent alimony. Since there was no designation of the amounts, he was allowed to deduct the total payment as back alimony.

TAXPLANNER 2

There are certain circumstances in which what appears to be a lump-sum payment may, in fact, be deductible as alimony.

According to an IRS ruling, a lump-sum payment to a former spouse for the remaining portion of alimony payments to which he or she is entitled qualifies as alimony.

Example

A couple divorced, and the divorce decree stipulated that the wife pay $81,000 in alimony, $3,600 per year for 22½ years. After 10 years, the husband could elect to receive the present value of the remaining payments. Since the payments spanned more than 10 years, they were considered periodic. However, because of the 10% limitation rule, the husband had to include only $8,100, 10% of the total payments received over the 22½ years, in his income in the year in which he received the lump-sum payment [(10% × $3,600) × 22.5].

Note: This opinion was given by the IRS before 1985.

TAXPLANNER 3

For installment payments to qualify as periodic payments, the last payment must be made more than 10 years after the decree became effective. There have been numerous errors made in implementing the effective dates of agreements and the ending of the 10-year period.

Example

According to a divorce decree, a husband must make payments at the beginning of each month for 120 months, beginning with the month after the decree becomes final. If the decree became final on December 15, 1984, the first payment was due January 1, 1985. The one-hundred-twentieth and final payment is due December 1, 1994—14 days short of 10 years. Since the payment period falls short of the 10-year-plus requirement, the payments are not deductible as alimony.

Exception. The 10-year rule will not apply to an agreement executed before 1985 if it has been modified after 1984 and expressly provides that the new rules will apply. If a pre-1985 agreement has been modified and there is a change in the term of payment, the new alimony rules enacted in 1984 will apply when expressly indicated.

III Standard Deduction and Itemized Deductions

After you have figured your adjusted gross income, you are ready to subtract the deductions used to figure taxable income. You can subtract either the standard deduction or itemized deductions. For the most part, itemized deductions are deductions for various kinds of personal expenses that are listed on Schedule A (Form 1040). See the following chart for the factors to consider for each type of deduction. The chapters in this part discuss the standard deduction, each itemized deduction and the limit on some of your itemized deductions if your adjusted gross income exceeds certain amounts.

TAKE THE STANDARD DEDUCTION IF:	ITEMIZE YOUR DEDUCTIONS IF:

TAKE THE STANDARD DEDUCTION IF:

- Your standard deduction is more than the total itemized deductions you can claim (Chapters 20, *Standard Deduction*, and 21, *Limit on Itemized Deductions*)

YOUR STANDARD DEDUCTION IS ZERO AND YOU SHOULD ITEMIZE YOUR DEDUCTIONS IF:

- You are filing a tax return with a short tax year,

- You were a nonresident or a dual-status alien during the year (Chapter 20, *Standard Deduction*), or

- You are married filing separately, and your spouse itemizes deductions.

ITEMIZE YOUR DEDUCTIONS IF:

- You cannot take the standard deduction (Chapter 20, *Standard Deduction*).

or

- You had large uninsured medical and dental expenses (Chapter 22, *Medical and Dental Expenses*)

- You paid taxes and interest on your home (Chapters 23, *Taxes You May Deduct* and 24, *Interest Expense*),

- You made large charitable contributions (Chapter 25, *Contributions*),

- You had large uninsured casualty or theft losses (Chapter 26, *Nonbusiness Casualty and Theft Losses*),

- You had certain moving expenses (Chapter 27, *Moving Expenses*),

- You had employee business expenses (Chapter 28, *Car Expenses and Other Employee Business Expenses*),

- You had employee educational expenses (Chapter 29, *Employee Educational Expenses*), or

- You had various miscellaneous expenses (Chapter 30, *Miscellaneous Deductions*),

and

- Your total itemized deductions are more than the standard deduction you can claim (Chapter 20, *Standard Deduction*).

20 | Standard Deduction

Introduction

Taxpayers who do not itemize their deductions are eligible for the standard deduction. However, you must determine whether itemizing deductions or taking the applicable standard deduction produces greater tax savings. In determining the amount of your standard deduction, you must consider many factors, including filing status, age, blindness, unearned income, and whether you are being claimed as an exemption by another. Higher deductions are allowed if you or your spouse are over age 65 or are totally or partially blind. On the other hand, if you can be claimed as a dependent by another taxpayer, your standard deduction may be limited. This chapter, which includes several useful worksheets, will help you to figure out what your standard deduction is.

Important Changes for 1993

Increase in standard deduction. The standard deduction for taxpayers who do not itemize deductions on Schedule A of Form 1040 is higher in 1993 than it was in 1992. The amount depends upon your filing status. See *1993 Standard Deduction Tables,* later.
Itemized deductions. The amount you may deduct for itemized deductions is limited if your adjusted gross income is more than $108,450 ($54,225 if you are married filing separately). See Chapter 21, *Limit on Itemized Deductions* for more information.

This chapter discusses:

- Who can take the standard deduction,
- How to figure the amount of your standard deduction,
- What additional amounts there are for age or blindness,
- How to claim the standard deduction on your return,
- What different rules apply to dependents, and
- Whether to take the standard deduction or to itemize your deductions.

The standard deduction is a dollar amount that reduces the amount of income on which you are taxed.

The standard deduction is a benefit that reduces the need for many taxpayers to itemize actual deductions, such as medical expenses, charitable contributions, or taxes, on Schedule A of Form 1040. If you have a choice, you should use the method that gives you the lower tax.

You benefit from the standard deduction if your standard deduction is more than the total of your allowable itemized deductions.

Figuring the Amount

Most taxpayers have a choice of either taking a standard deduction or itemizing their deductions.
Persons not eligible for the standard deduction. Your standard deduction is *zero* and you should itemize any deductions you have if:

1) You are married and filing a separate return, and your spouse itemizes deductions,
2) You are filing a tax return with a short tax year, or

3) You are a nonresident or dual-status alien during the year. You are considered a dual-status alien if you were both a nonresident and resident alien during the year.

Note. If you are a nonresident alien who is married to a U.S. citizen or resident at the end of 1993, you can choose to be treated as a U.S. resident for 1993. (See Publication 519, *U.S. Tax Guide for Aliens.*) You may take the standard deduction that applies to you.

Explanation
Married persons who file separate returns must be consistent in claiming the standard deduction or itemizing deductions. If one spouse itemizes deductions, the other spouse must also itemize deductions and cannot claim the standard deduction.

A tax return filed for a decedent through the date of death is not considered a short tax year for this rule.

Example
John Thomas dies on June 15, 1993. John's final tax return will cover the period from January 1 through June 15.

The full amount of the standard deduction may be claimed on John's final return.

Dependents may have a limited standard deduction. If you can be claimed as a dependent on another person's return (such as your parents' return), your standard deduction may be limited. See *Standard Deduction for Dependents,* later.

Explanation
The key word is *can.*

You cannot forego an otherwise allowable dependent deduction in order to increase that dependent's standard deduction.

Standard deduction amounts. The standard deduction amounts for most taxpayers are shown in *Table 20-1* in this chapter.

The amount of the standard deduction for a decedent's final return is the same as it would have been had the decedent continued to live. However, if the decedent was not 65 or older at the time of death, the higher standard deduction for age cannot be claimed.

Higher standard deduction for age (65 or older). If you do not itemize deductions, you are entitled to a higher standard deduction if you are age 65 or older at the end of the year. You are considered 65 on the day before your 65th birthday. Therefore, you may take a higher standard deduction for 1993 if your 65th birthday was on or before January 1, 1994.

See *Table 20–2* in this chapter to figure the standard deduction amount you are entitled to.

Higher standard deduction for blindness. If you are blind on the last day of the year and you do not itemize deductions, you are entitled to a higher standard deduction as shown in *Table 20–2.* You qualify for this benefit if you are totally or partly blind.

Totally blind. If you are totally blind, attach a statement to this effect to your return.

Partly blind. If you are partly blind, you must submit with your return each year a certified statement from an eye physician or registered optometrist that:

1) You cannot see better than 20/200 in the better eye with glasses or contact lenses, or
2) Your field of vision is not more than 20 degrees.

If your eye condition will never improve beyond these limits, you can avoid having to get a new certified statement each year by having the examining eye physician include this fact in the certification you attach to your return. In later years just attach a statement referring to the certification. You should keep a copy of the certification in your records.

If your vision can be corrected beyond these limits only by contact lenses that you can wear only briefly because of pain, infection, or ulcers, you may take the higher standard deduction for blindness if you otherwise qualify.

Spouse 65 or older or blind. You may take the higher standard deduction if your spouse is age 65 or older or blind and:

1) You file a joint return, or
2) You file a separate return, and your spouse had no gross income and could not be claimed as a dependent by another taxpayer.

Note. You may not claim the higher standard deduction for an individual, other than your spouse, for whom you can claim an exemption.

TaxSaver

In calculating your taxable income, you should use the larger of your itemized deductions or your standard deduction. By doing some planning, it may be possible to use the standard deduction in some years and to itemize deductions in others.

Example

In December, 1993, Bill and Barbara Chapman add up their itemized deductions for 1993 and find that the total is only $3,500. At that time, they receive an annual real estate tax bill for $1,400, which can be paid anytime before January 31, 1994. A religious organization that the Chapmans are affiliated with is also requesting a $1,300 contribution for its building fund. If the Chapmans make both expenditures in 1993, they will receive

no tax benefit from these tax-deductible expenditures because their itemized deductions would total $6,200, the same as their standard deduction. If they make the expenditures in 1994, they might generate more than $6,200 in deductions for that year. Postponing would be a better strategy.

Example 1. Larry, 46, and Donna, 43, are filing a joint return for 1993. Neither is blind. They decide not to itemize their deductions. They use *Table 20–1.* Their standard deduction is $6,200.

Example 2. Assume the same facts as in Example 1, except that Larry is blind at the end of 1993. Larry and Donna use *Table 20–2.* Their standard deduction is $6,900.

Example 3. Bill and Terry are filing a joint return for 1993. Both are over age 65. Neither is blind. If they do not itemize deductions, they use *Table 20-2.* Their standard deduction is $7,600.

How to report. After you find your standard deduction amount, enter it on line 19 of Form 1040A or line 34 of Form 1040. If you use Form 1040EZ, combine your standard deduction with your personal exemption and check the appropriate box on line 5. If the total of your standard deduction and personal exemption is more than $6,050 ($10,900 if married filing a joint return), you must file Form 1040A or Form 1040.

Standard Deduction for Dependents

The standard deduction for an individual who can be claimed as a dependent on another person's tax return is generally limited to the greater of (a) $600, or (b) the individual's earned income for the year (but not more than the regular standard deduction amount, generally $3,700).

Explanation

Although the reduction in the standard deduction available to your dependent children is well publicized, the reduction for dependent parents is not so well known.

Example

Assume that your 61-year-old widowed mother has $5,500 of interest income. If she is not your dependent, she has no tax liability. Her $3,700 standard deduction plus her $2,350 personal exemption eliminate her taxable income. As your dependent, her standard deduction drops to $600 and she loses her personal exemption entirely. Her taxable income would be $4,900 and her tax would be $735. You might pay less tax because of the additional $2,350 dependent exemption (assuming your exemptions are not phased out because your income is too high), but no one will benefit from the remaining unused standard deduction of $3,100 ($3,700 − $600).

However, if you are a dependent who is 65 or older or blind, your standard deduction may be higher.

If you are a dependent, use *Table 20–3* in this chapter to determine your standard deduction.

Earned income defined. Earned income is salaries, wages,

1993 Standard Deduction Tables

Caution: If you are married filing a separate return and your spouse itemizes deductions, or if you are a dual-status alien, you cannot take the standard deduction even if you were 65 or older or blind.

Table 20-1. Standard Deduction Chart for Most People*

If Your Filing Status is:	Your Standard Deduction Is:
Single	$3,700
Married filing joint return or Qualifying widow(er) with dependent child	6,200
Married filing separate return	3,100
Head of household	5,450

* DO NOT use this chart if you were 65 or older or blind, OR if someone can claim you as a dependent.

Table 20-2. Standard Deduction Chart for People Age 65 or Older or Blind*

Check the correct number of boxes below. Then go to the chart.

You   65 or older ☐   Blind ☐

Your spouse, if claiming spouse's exemption   65 or older ☐   Blind ☐

Total number of boxes you checked ☐

If Your Filing Status is:	And the Number in the Box Above is:	Your Standard Deduction is:
Single	1	$4,600
	2	5,500
Married filing joint return or Qualifying widow(er) with dependent child	1	6,900
	2	7,600
	3	8,300
	4	9,000
Married filing separate return	1	3,800
	2	4,500
	3	5,200
	4	5,900
Head of household	1	6,350
	2	7,250

* If someone can claim you as a dependent, use Table 20-3, instead.

Table 20-3. Standard Deduction Worksheet for Dependents*

If you were 65 or older or blind, check the correct number of boxes below. Then go to the worksheet.

You   65 or older ☐   Blind ☐

Your spouse, if claiming spouse's exemption   65 or older ☐   Blind ☐

Total number of boxes you checked ☐

1. Enter your **earned income** (defined below). If none, go on to line 3	1. _____
2. Minimum amount	2. $600
3. Compare the amounts on lines 1 and 2. Enter the **larger** of the two amounts here.	3. _____
4. Enter on line 4 the amount shown below for your filing status. • Single, enter $3,700 • Married filing separate return, enter $3,100 • Married filing jointly or Qualifying widow(er) with dependent child, enter $6,200 • Head of household, enter $5,450	4. _____
5. Standard deduction. a. Compare the amounts on lines 3 and 4. Enter the **smaller** of the two amounts here. If under 65 and not blind, stop here. This is your standard deduction. Otherwise, go on to line 5b.	5a. _____
b. If 65 or older or blind, multiply $900 ($700 if married or qualifying widow(er) with dependent child) by the number in the box above. Enter the result here.	5b. _____
c. Add lines 5a and 5b. This is your standard deduction for 1993.	5c. _____

Earned income *includes wages, salaries, tips, professional fees, and other compensation received for personal services you performed. It also includes any amount received as a scholarship that you must include in your income.*

* Use this worksheet ONLY if someone can claim you as a dependent.

tips, professional fees, and other amounts received as pay for work you actually perform.

For purposes of the standard deduction, earned income also includes any part of a *scholarship or fellowship grant* that you must include in your gross income. See *Scholarship and Fellowship Grants* in Chapter 13, *Other Income* for more information on what qualifies as a scholarship or fellowship grant.

Where to report your standard deduction. After you find your standard deduction amount, enter it on line 19 of Form 1040A or line 34 of Form 1040. If you use Form 1040EZ, figure your standard deduction on the back of the form and check the appropriate box on line 5. If your standard deduction is more than $3,700 ($6,200 if married filing a joint return), you must file Form 1040A or Form 1040.

Example 1. Michael, who is single, is claimed as a dependent on his parents' 1993 tax return. He has interest income of $700 and wages of $150. He has no itemized deductions. Michael uses *Table 20–3* to find his standard deduction. It is $600 because the greater of $600 or his earned income ($150) is $600.

Example 2. Joe, a 22-year-old full-time college student, is claimed as a dependent on his parents' 1993 tax return. Joe is married and files a separate return. His wife does not itemize deductions on her separate return.

Joe has $1,500 in interest income and wages of $3,200. He has no itemized deductions. Joe finds his standard deduction by using *Table 20–3.* He enters his earned income, $3,200, on line 1. On line 3 he enters $3,200, the larger of his earned income ($3,200) or $600. Since Joe is married filing a separate return, he enters $3,100 on line 4. On line 5a he enters $3,100 as his standard deduction because it is smaller than $3,200, his earned income.

Explanation

The $3,100 limitation applies only to a married dependent who files a separate return.

Example 3. Amy, who is single, is claimed as a dependent on her parents' 1993 tax return. She is 18 years old and blind. She has interest income of $900 and wages of $3,000. She has no itemized deductions. Amy uses *Table 20–3* to find her standard deduction. She enters her wages of $3,000 on line 1. On line 3 she enters $3,000, the larger of her wages on line 1 and the $600 on line 2. Since she is single, Amy enters $3,700 on line 4. She enters $3,000 on line 5a. This is the smaller of the amounts on lines 3 and 4. Because she checked one box in the top part of the worksheet, she enters $900 on line 5b. She then adds the amounts on lines 5a and 5b and enters her standard deduction of $3,900 on line 5c.

Who Should Itemize

Some taxpayers should itemize their deductions because it will save them money. Others should itemize because they do not qualify for the standard deduction, as discussed earlier under *Persons not eligible for the standard deduction.*

Persons who should itemize deductions. If the total of your itemized deductions is more than the standard deduction to which you otherwise would be entitled, you should itemize your deductions. You should first figure your itemized deductions and compare that amount to your standard deduction to make sure you are using the method that gives you the greater benefit.

Caution: You may be subject to a limit on some of your itemized deductions if your adjusted gross income (AGI) is more than $108,450 ($54,225 if you are married filing separately). See Chapter 21, *Limit on Itemized Deductions,* and the instructions for Schedule A (Form 1040), line 26, for more information on figuring the correct amount of your itemized deductions.

TaxAlert

The Revenue Reconciliation Act of 1990 placed an overall limitation on itemized deductions for years beginning *after* December 31, 1990. Allowable itemized deductions (other than medical expenses, casualty and theft losses, and investment interest) are reduced by an amount equal to 3% of a taxpayer's adjusted gross income in excess of $108,450 ($54,225 for married persons filing a separate return). However, allowable itemized deductions other than those listed above are not reduced by more than 80%. You should consider this limitation, if applicable, in determining the benefits from itemizing deductions. See Chapter 21, *Limit on Itemized Deductions*, for more details.

When to itemize. You may benefit from itemizing your deductions on Schedule A of Form 1040 if you:

1) Do not qualify for the standard deduction, or the amount you can claim is limited,
2) Had large uninsured medical and dental expenses during the year,
3) Paid interest and taxes on your home,
4) Had large unreimbursed employee business expenses or other miscellaneous deductions,
5) Had large casualty or theft losses not covered by insurance,
6) Had large moving expenses,
7) Made large contributions to qualified charities, or
8) Have total itemized deductions that are more than the highest standard deduction to which you otherwise are entitled.

These deductions are explained in Chapters 22 – 30.

If you decide to itemize your deductions, complete Schedule A and attach it to your Form 1040. Enter the amount from Schedule A, line 26, on Form 1040, line 34.

Itemizing for state tax or other purposes. If you choose to itemize even though your itemized deductions are less than the amount of your standard deduction, write "IE" (itemized elected) next to line 34 (Form 1040).

Changing your mind. If you do not itemize your deductions and later find that you should have itemized — or if you itemize your deductions and later find you should not have — you can change your return by filing Form 1040X, *Amended U.S. Individual Income Tax Return.* See *Amended Returns and Claims for Refund* in Chapter 1, *Filing Information,* for more information on amended returns.

Married persons who filed separate returns. You can change methods of taking deductions only if you and your spouse both make the same changes. Both of you must file a consent to assessment for any additional tax either one may owe as a result of the change.

You and your spouse can use the method that gives you the lowest total tax, even though one of you may pay more tax than the other. You **both must use the same method** of claiming deductions. If one itemizes deductions, the other should itemize because he or she will not qualify for the standard deduction (see *Persons not eligible for the standard deduction,* earlier).

21 | Limit on Itemized Deductions

Introduction

Ever since the passage of the Tax Reform Act of 1986, Congress has been limiting the amount of itemized deductions that individuals can use to reduce their taxable income. For example, the threshold for deducting medical expenses was increased from 5% to 7.5% of adjusted gross income; miscellaneous deductions were limited to those in excess of 2% of adjusted gross income; the deduction for personal interest expense was phased out; and home mortgage interest expense became subject to various limitations.

Beginning in 1991, Congress placed an additional "overall" limitation on the deductibility of a certain group of itemized deductions. In 1993, this limitation applies only if your adjusted gross income is greater than $108,450 ($54,225 if married filing separately). Itemized deductions that are subject to this limitation include taxes, home mortgage interest, charitable contributions, and miscellaneous itemized deductions. The total of this group of deductions must be reduced by 3% of the amount of your adjusted gross income in excess of $108,450. This limitation is applied after you have used any other limitations that exist in the law, such as the adjusted gross income limitation for charitable contributions and the mortgage interest expense limitations.

Medical expenses, casualty and theft losses, investment interest expense, and gambling losses are not subject to this rule. The threshold amount will be indexed annually for inflation. The "overall" limitation provision was originally scheduled to terminate for years beginning after 1995. However, Congress enacted new legislation that makes the "overall" limitation permanent.

Important Change for 1993

Limit on itemized deductions. You may not be able to deduct all your itemized deductions if your adjusted gross income is more than $108,450 ($54,225 if you are married filing separately).

This chapter discusses an overall limit on itemized deductions. The topics include:

- Who is subject to the limit,
- Which itemized deductions are limited,
- How to figure the limit, and
- How to complete a worksheet on the limit using an illustrated example.

This limit does not apply to you if:

1) Your adjusted gross income (AGI) (line 32 of Form 1040) is $108,450 or less ($54,225 or less if married filing separately), or
2) You are taking the standard deduction.

Useful Items

You may want to see:

Form (and Instructions)

☐ **Schedule A (Form 1040)**   Itemized Deductions

Are You Subject to the Limit?

You are subject to the limit on certain itemized deductions if your AGI is more than $108,450 ($54,225 if you are married filing separately). Your AGI is the amount on line 32 of your Form 1040.

This limit does not apply to estates or trusts.

Which Deductions Are Affected

You are subject to the overall limit on certain itemized deductions if you have any of the following deductions on Schedule A (Form 1040).

- Taxes — line 8
- Home mortgage interest, including points — lines 9a, 9b, and 10
- Charitable contributions — line 16
- Moving expenses — line 18
- Unreimbursed employee expenses and all other miscellaneous deductions that are subject to the 2% of AGI limit — line 24
- Federal estate tax on income in respect of a decedent — line 25
- Amortizable bond premium on bonds acquired before October 23, 1986 — line 25
- Deduction for repayment of certain amounts — line 25
- Certain unrecovered investment in a pension — line 25
- Impairment-related work expenses — line 25

Check the index at the back of this publication to locate discussions of these deductions.

Which Deductions Are Not Affected

The Schedule A (Form 1040) deductions listed next are not subject to the overall limit on itemized deductions. However, they are still subject to other applicable limits.

- Medical and dental expenses — line 4
- Investment interest expense — line 11
- Nonbusiness casualty and theft losses — line 17
- Gambling losses — line 25

Check the index at the back of this publication to locate discussions of these deductions.

Explanation
Whether a particular deduction will be limited or not depends on the character of the deduction.

Example 1
Ed and Sherry Stone file a joint income tax return. They have an adjusted gross income of $308,450. The Stones' only itemized deductions are $20,000 of home mortgage interest and $8,000 of real estate taxes. Since both of these itemized deductions are subject to the limitation, their total deductions of $28,000 must be reduced by 3% of $200,000 (the amount by which AGI exceeds $108,450); or $6,000. They may reduce their taxable income by total itemized deductions of $22,000 ($28,000 − $6,000).

Example 2
Assume the same facts above, except that the Stones live in a downtown apartment, and their only itemized deduction is $20,000 of otherwise allowable investment interest expense. Since investment interest expense is not subject to the 3% limitation, the entire $20,000 will be deductible.

How to Figure the Limit

If your itemized deductions are subject to the limit, they are reduced by the smaller of:

1) 3% of the amount by which your AGI exceeds $108,450 ($54,225 if married filing separately), or
2) 80% of your itemized deductions that are affected by the limit (listed earlier).

Before you figure the overall limit on itemized deductions, you must first complete lines 1 through 25 of Schedule A (Form 1040), including any appropriate forms (such as Form 2106, Form 3903, etc.).

The overall limit on itemized deductions is figured after you have applied all other limits. Other limits figured first include charitable contribution limits (Chapter 25, *Contributions*), limits on moving expenses (Chapter 27, *Moving Expenses*), the limit on certain meals and entertainment (Chapter 28, *Car Expenses and Other Employee Business Expenses*), and the 2% of AGI limit on certain miscellaneous deductions (Chapter 30, *Miscellaneous Deductions*). **Itemized Deductions Worksheet.** After you have completed Schedule A through line 25, you can use the worksheet (*Table 21–1*) in this chapter to figure your limit. Keep the worksheet for your records.

Note: You should compare the amount of your itemized deductions after applying the limit to the amount of your standard deduction. Use the greater amount when completing line 34 of your Form 1040. See Chapter 20, *Standard Deduction*, for information on how to figure your standard deduction.

Example

For tax year 1993, Bill and Terry Willow are filing a joint return and have adjusted gross income of $255,250. Their Schedule A itemized deductions consist of the following.

State income and real estate taxes	$17,900
Home mortgage interest	45,000
Charitable contributions	21,000
Investment interest expense	41,000
Miscellaneous deductions	17,240
Total	**$142,140**

The Willows' investment interest expense is not subject to the overall limit on itemized deductions. Their deduction for miscellaneous deductions is the total after applying the 2% of AGI limit and does not include any gambling losses.

The Willows figure their overall limit as follows:

Itemized Deductions Worksheet
(Keep for your records)

1. Add the amounts on Schedule A, lines 4, 8, 12, 16, 17, 18, 24, and 25. 142,140

2. Add the amounts on Schedule A, lines, 4, 11, and 17, plus any gambling losses included on line 25. 41,000

3. Subtract line 2 from line 1. (If the result is zero, stop here; enter the amount from line 1 above on Schedule A, line 26.) 101,140

4. Multiply the amount on line 3 by 80% (.80). .. 80,912

5. Enter the amount from Form 1040, line 32 255,250

6. Enter $106,450 ($54,225 if married filing
   separately) 106,450

7. Subtract line 6 from line 5. (If the result is
   zero or less, stop here; enter the amount
   from line 1 above on Schedule A, line 26.)...... 146,800

8. Multiply the amount on line 7 by 3% (.03)....... 4,404

9. Enter the smaller of line 4 or line 8. 4,404

10. **Total itemized deductions.** Subtract line 9 from line 1.
    Enter the result here and on Schedule A, line 26...................... 137,736

Of their $142,140 total itemized deductions, the Willows can deduct only $137,736. They enter $137,736 on Schedule A, line 26.

Personal Exemptions	(2,914)
Taxable Income	$199,336

Note: The personal exemptions have been reduced according to the phaseout rules discussed in Chapter 3, *Personal Exemptions and Dependents*.

TAXPLANNER

If your itemized deductions are subject to this 3% limitation, you may want to consider a technique called "bunching." Bunching is effective if you are able to accumulate deductions so that they are high in one year and low in the next.

Example

Assume the same facts as in the previous example. This time, however, the Whites are able to *postpone* payment of their 1993 real estate taxes until January, 1994, and they can also pay $1,500 of their $2,500 charitable contributions in early 1994. Then next year, in December, 1994, they will *accelerate* these payments to make sure that they fall in 1994 and not 1995. The Whites will end up with the following expenses for 1993 and 1994:

	1993	1994
1993 Real estate taxes	—	$5,000
1993 Charitable contributions	$1,000	1,500
1994 Real estate taxes	—	$5,000
1994 Charitable contributions	—	2,500
Total	$1,000	$14,000

By bunching the expenses, the Whites may use the $6,200 standard deduction in 1993 and itemized deductions of $11,000 ($14,000 less the 3% limit of $3,000) in 1994. Total deductions equal $17,200 for the 2 years ($6,200 + $11,000). In 1994, they will have reduced their taxable income by an additional $4,800 ($11,000 − $6,200). Without bunching, the Whites would have been limited to the standard deduction in each year.

TAXSAVER

In certain situations it is possible for the 3% limitation to reduce allowable itemized deductions below the standard deduction amount. You should consider this possibility when you are choosing whether to itemize your deductions or to use the standard deduction.

Example

Tim and Sue White have adjusted gross income of $208,450. They have no mortgage on their home; however, they pay annual real estate taxes of $5,000. Each year they contribute $2,500 to their favorite charity. The Whites would compute their taxable income as follows:

Adjusted gross income		$208,450
Itemized deductions		
Real estate taxes	$5,000	
Charitable contibutions	2,500	
Total	$7,500	
Less 3% of AGI in excess of $108,450	3,000	
Allowable itemized deductions	$4,500	
Standard deduction if married, filing a joint return	$6,200	
Greater of standard deduction or allowable itemized deductions		(6,200)

Table 21-1. Itemized Deductions Worksheet (Keep for your records)

1. Add the amounts on Schedule A, lines 4, 8, 12, 16, 17, 18, 24, and 25 .... 1. _____
2. Add the amounts on Schedule A, lines 4, 11, and 17, plus any gambling losses included on line 25................ 2. _____
   Caution: *Be sure your total gambling losses are clearly identified on the dotted line next to line 25.*
3. Subtract line 2 from line 1. (If the result is zero, stop here; enter the amount from line 1 above on Schedule A, line 26.) .... 3. _____
4. Multiply the amount on line 3 by 80% (.80) .... 4. _____
5. Enter the amount from Form 1040, line 32 .... 5. _____
6. Enter $108,450 ($52,225 if married filing separately) .... 6. _____
7. Subtract line 6 from line 5. (If the result is zero or less, stop here; enter the amount from line 1 above on Schedule A, line 26.).. 7. _____
8. Multiply the amount on line 7 by 3% (.03) .... 8. _____
9. Enter the smaller of line 4 or line 8 .... 9. _____
10. **Total itemized deductions.** Subtract line 9 from line 1. Enter the result here and on Schedule A, line 26 ..... 10. _____

22 | Medical and Dental Expenses

Introduction

Even the IRS has a heart. Tax law is fairly generous in defining medical expenditures that may be deducted from your income.

Deductible medical expenses include payments for the diagnosis, cure, mitigation, treatment, and prevention of disease. Payments for any part or function of the body are allowed, as are payments for the prevention or alleviation of mental illness. You may include even your cab or bus fare to the doctor's office. But you may not include expenditures that are merely beneficial to your general health—like vacation costs, for example—even if they were essential in preventing a complete physical or mental breakdown.

*Unfortunately, while almost any medical expense is deductible, it's difficult to take an actual **deduction** on your tax return, and it's getting more difficult. Your medical expenses must total more than 7.5% of your **adjusted gross income** before you can take any deductions. In other words, someone with an adjusted gross income of $30,000 in 1993 has to have more than $2,250 of medical expenses before he or she may deduct any of them.*

Note: Your 1993 itemized deductions may be subject to certain overall limitations if your adjusted gross income exceeds $108,450. However, deductions for medical expenses are not subject to the overall limitation.

Important Change for 1993

Self-employed health insurance. The special rule that allows self-employed individuals to deduct 25% of health insurance premiums from gross income was extended through December 31, 1993. See *Health Insurance Costs for Self-Employed Persons.*

This chapter discusses how to claim a deduction for your medical and dental expenses. It contains a checklist of items that you can or cannot include in figuring your deduction. It also explains how to treat insurance reimbursements and other reimbursements you may receive for medical care.

It will help you determine:

- Whose expenses you can include,
- What expenses you can include,
- How to claim expenses of a decedent, and
- How to figure your deduction.

To deduct any medical and dental expenses, you must itemize your deductions on **Schedule A** (Form 1040). You must reduce the amount of your medical expenses by any reimbursement you receive for these expenses.

There are limits on the amount you can deduct. You can deduct only the amount of your medical and dental expenses that is ***more than 7.5%*** of your adjusted gross income shown on line 32, Form 1040. See *How to Figure Your Deduction.*

Useful Items

You may want to see:

Publication

☐ 502 Medical and Dental Expenses

Form (and Instructions)

☐ Schedule A (Form 1040) Itemized Deductions

Whose Expenses Can You Include?

You can include medical expenses you pay for yourself and for the individuals discussed in this section.

Spouse. You can include medical expenses you paid for your spouse. To claim these expenses, you must have been married either at the time your spouse received the medical services or at the time you paid the medical expenses.

Example 1. Mary received medical treatment before she married Bill. Bill paid for the treatment after they married. Bill can include these expenses in figuring his medical expense deduction even if Bill and Mary file separate returns.

If Mary had paid the expenses before she and Bill married, Bill could not include Mary's medical expenses on his separate return. Mary would include all the medical expenses she paid during the year on her separate return. If they filed a joint return, the medical expenses both paid during the year would be used to figure their medical expense deduction.

Example 2. During 1993, John paid medical expenses for his wife Louise, who died in 1992. John married Belle in 1993, and they file a joint return. Because John was married to Louise when she incurred the medical expenses, he can include those expenses in figuring his medical deduction for 1993.

Dependents. You can include medical expenses you paid for a person who was your dependent at the time the medical services were provided or at the time you paid the expenses. A person generally qualifies as your dependent for purposes of the medical expense deduction if:

1) That person lived with you for the entire year as a member of your household or is related to you, and
2) That person was a U.S. citizen or resident, or a resident of Canada or Mexico for some part of the calendar year in which your tax year began, and
3) You provided over half of that person's total support for the calendar year.

You can include the medical expenses of any person who is your dependent even if you cannot claim an exemption for him or her on your return only because the dependent received $2,350 or more of gross income or filed a joint return.

Example 1. In 1992, your son was your dependent. In 1993, he no longer qualifies as your dependent. However, you paid $800 in 1993 for medical expenses your son incurred in 1992 when he was your dependent. You can include the $800 in figuring your 1993 medical expense deduction. You cannot include this amount on your 1992 return.

Example 2. You provided more than half of your married daughter's support, including her medical expenses of $1,200. She and her husband file a joint return. Although you may not be able to claim an exemption for your daughter, she is still your dependent and you can include in your medical expenses the $1,200 you paid.

able estate and will not be subject to gift tax or generation-skipping transfer tax. This could result in significant tax savings.

Adopted child. You can include medical expenses that you paid for a child before adoption, if the child qualified as your dependent when the medical expenses were provided or when the expenses were paid. If you pay back an adoption agency or other persons for medical expenses they paid under an agreement with you, you are treated as having paid those expenses. But if you pay back medical expenses incurred and paid before adoption negotiations began, you cannot include them as medical expenses.

Child of divorced or separated parents. If either parent can claim a child as a dependent under the rules for divorced or separated parents, each parent can include the medical expenses he or she pays for the child. See *Support Test for Divorced or Separated Parents* in Chapter 3, *Personal Exemptions and Dependents*.

Support claimed under a multiple support agreement. A multiple support agreement is used when two or more people provide more than half of a person's support, but no one alone provides more than half. If you are considered to have provided more than half under this agreement, you can include medical expenses you pay, even if you cannot claim the person because he or she had gross income of $2,350 or more or filed a joint return.

Any medical expenses paid by others who joined you in the agreement cannot be included as medical expenses by anyone. However, if you and the others shared only the nonmedical support items and you separately paid the medical expenses, you can include the entire amount you paid for medical expenses.

Example. You and your three brothers each provide one-fourth of your mother's total support. Under a multiple support agreement, you claim your mother as a dependent. You paid all of her medical expenses. Your brothers repaid you for three-fourths of these expenses. In figuring your medical expense deduction, you can include only one-fourth of your mother's medical expenses. Your brothers cannot include any part of the expenses.

However, if you and your brothers share the nonmedical support items and you separately pay all of your mother's medical expenses, you can include the amount you paid for her medical expenses in your medical expenses.

TaxPlanner

Although not deductible, medical expenses, paid directly to the provider of the medical service on a nondependent individual's behalf, lend themselves to a means of tax planning. An unlimited gift tax exclusion is available for qualifying medical expenses paid on an individual's behalf. This exclusion is also available for the generation-skipping transfer tax. The generation-skipping transfer tax is a tax on the transfer of assets that is equivalent to the gift or estate tax that would have been paid had the assets been transferred from one generation to the next, instead of skipping a generation. You should consult your tax advisor if you are interested in pursuing this type of tax planning.

Example
A grandparent pays medical expenses directly to the provider of the medical services on a grandchild's behalf. The payments will reduce the grandparent's tax-

TaxSaver

Because you may deduct medical expenses only when they exceed 7.5% of your adjusted gross income, it is often difficult to obtain a tax benefit for medical expenses, including what you pay for the care of an elderly person. Prior to 1986, there was a way to fund the medical costs of an elderly dependent that took advantage of the fact that his or her adjusted gross income was lower than yours. It was a short-term arrangement called a **Clifford trust.**

The key to a Clifford trust was that the income from the property had to be shifted only for a minimum of 10 years and 1 day or until the death of the beneficiary of the trust, whichever came first. The Tax Reform Act of 1986 significantly extends the period that assets have to be shifted to the trust by requiring that the donor retain a residuary interest of less than 5%. According to IRS tables, this means that the assets would have to be shifted for 32 years. Thus, a Clifford trust will not work effectively unless the transfer of income to an elderly dependent is combined with a transfer to someone else after the death of the elderly dependent. The new rules apply to transfers after March 1, 1986.

Medical Expenses

Use *Table 22–1* in this chapter as a guide to determine which medical and dental expenses you can include on Schedule A (Form 1040). See Publication 502, *Medical and Dental Expenses,* for information about other expenses you can include.

TaxOrganizer

In case the IRS challenges your deduction of medical expenses, you should keep the following information in order to support your claim for medical expenses incurred:

- Receipts and canceled checks evidencing payment of medical expenses
- A permanent record of the name and address of the provider of medical care, the amount of the expenses, and the date paid
- Documentation that the expense was to obtain medical treatment, that medicine was prescribed,

Table 22-1. **Medical and Dental Expenses Checklist**

You can include		You cannot include	
• Birth control pills prescribed by your doctor • Capital expenses for equipment or improvements to your home needed for medical care (see Publication 502) • Cost and care of guide dogs or other animals aiding the blind, deaf, and disabled • Cost of lead-based paint removal (see Publication 502) • Expenses of an organ donor • Hospital services fees (lab work, therapy, nursing services, surgery, etc.) • Legal abortion • Legal operation to prevent having children • Meals and lodging provided by a hospital during medical treatment • Medical and hospital insurance premiums (see discussion) • Medical services fees (from doctors, dentists, surgeons, specialists, and other medical practitioners) • Oxygen equipment and oxygen	• Part of life-care fee paid to retirement home designated for medical care • Prescription medicines (those requiring a prescription by a doctor for their use by an individual) and insulin • Psychiatric care at a specially equipped medical center (includes meals and lodging) • Social Security tax for worker providing medical care (see Publication 926) • Special items (artifical limbs, false teeth, eyeglasses, contact lenses, hearing aids, crutches, wheelchair, etc.) • Special school or home for mentally or physically disabled persons (see Publication 502) • Transportation for needed medical care (see discussion) • Treatment at a drug or alcohol center (includes meals and lodging provided by the center) • Wages for nursing services (see Publication 502)	• Diaper service • Expenses for your general health (even if following your doctor's advice) such as— —Health club dues —Household help (even if recommended by a doctor) —Social activities, such as dancing or swimming lessons —Stop smoking program —Trip for general health improvement —Weight loss program • Funeral, burial or cremation expenses • Illegal operation or treatment	• Life insurance or income protection policies, or policies providing payment for loss of life, limb, sight, etc. • Maternity clothes • Medical insurance included in a car insurance policy covering all persons injured in or by your car • Medicine you buy without a prescription • Nursing care for a healthy baby • Surgery for purely cosmetic reasons • Toothpaste, toiletries, cosmetics, etc.

and that the expense was incurred on a doctor's recommendation

Explanation

After reviewing the checklist, you may still be wondering whether a particular expense is deductible or not. The most comprehensive listing of items that you may and may not include when figuring your medical expenses appears in Internal Revenue Publication 502, *Medical and Dental Expenses.*

Examples

Here are some more examples of deductible items:

- A wig, if it is essential to your mental health and not just for enhancing your personal appearance
- Cosmetic surgery that is medically necessary (meaningfully promotes the proper function of the body or prevents or treats illness or disease) and not just for enhancing personal appearance
- Special diet food that is necessary and prescribed by a doctor to the extent that the cost exceeds the amount spent for normal nutritional needs
- Orthopedic shoes in excess of the cost of normal shoes
- Fees paid to someone to accompany and guide a blind person
- Costs attributable to a dog or other animal that assists individuals with physical disabilities
- Fees paid for a note taker for a deaf person
- Legal fees to obtain guardianship over a mental patient who has refused to accept therapy voluntarily
- Fees paid for childbirth preparation classes if instruction relates to obstetrical care
- Costs of a weight loss program for treatment of a specific disease, such as hypertension or obesity
- Costs of a wheelchair lift and its installation in a van
- Reasonable costs for home modifications or improvements to accommodate a handicapped person's condition when incurred for the purpose of medical care or directly related to medical care
- Legal fees necessary to authorize medical treatment for mental illness

Explanation

Drugs that may be obtained without a prescription (aspirin, skin ointments, etc.) are not deductible, even though they may be recommended or prescribed by a physician.

TaxPlanner

Some schools include a fee for medical care in the amount charged for tuition. Since you may deduct only the amount allocated to medical care if it is separately stated, an itemized bill should be requested.

Explanation

Whether or not an expense is deductible is determined by the nature of the services rendered, not by the qualifications and/or experience of the person rendering

them. For example, the services do not necessarily need to be performed by a nurse, as long as the services rendered are generally considered "nursing services". This includes services connected with caring for the patient's condition, such as giving medication or changing bandages, as well as bathing and grooming the patient.

Examples

The courts allowed deductions for payments to a daughter for the care of her arthritic mother to the extent that they were for medical care.

In another instance, the courts allowed a deduction for the compensation paid to a "personal attendant" who was not a registered or a practical nurse. The deduction was permitted because the invalid was recovering from surgery and was in need of constant attendance.

TaxPlanner

An expense may qualify for the child care credit (see Chapter 33, *Child and Dependent Care Credit*), or it may be considered a medical expense. However, the same expense may not be used for both benefits. You should analyze each benefit based on your marginal tax rate and your medical expense deduction limitation (7.5% of adjusted gross income) to determine how best to classify the expense.

Explanation

Payment for psychoanalysis that is required as part of your training to be a psychoanalyst may be a deductible educational expense necessary for professional training. The law specifically permits an itemized deduction for the cost of psychoanalytic training undertaken by psychiatrists as education expenses, since the training maintains or improves skills required in their trade or business and does not qualify them for a new trade or business. (See Chapter 29, *Employees' Educational Expenses.*) The courts have also allowed deductions for expenses incurred by a clinical psychologist in studying to become a psychoanalyst and expenses incurred by a psychiatrist for psychoanalytic training as a condition to accepting the directorship of a child study center.

However, when a psychiatric residency was undertaken to qualify a taxpayer for a new profession, the expenses were not deductible.

TaxSaver

Capital expenses. You may include in medical expenses all or part of the amounts you pay for special equipment installed in your home, or for improvements, if the main reason is for medical care. The amount of your medical expense deduction, however, will depend on the extent to which the equipment or improvement has increased the value of the property.

Example

You have a heart ailment. On your doctor's advice, you install an elevator in your home so that you will not need to climb stairs. The elevator costs $2,000. According to competent appraisals, the elevator increases the value of your home by $1,400. The $600 difference is a medical expense. However, you may include the total cost of $2,000 in medical expenses if the elevator does not increase the value of your home.

Explanation

Operating and upkeep expenses. If a capital expense qualifies as a medical expense, amounts paid for operation or upkeep also qualify as a medical expense, as long as the medical reason for the capital expense still exists. These expenses are medical expenses even if none or only part of the original expense was deductible.

Example

Assume the same facts as in the above example, except that the elevator increased the value of your home by $2,000. In this case, you are not entitled to a medical deduction for the cost of the elevator. However, the costs of electricity to operate the elevator and repairs to maintain it are deductible, as long as the medical reason for the elevator exists.

Exception

An exception to the general rule exists for expenditures incurred to accommodate the condition of a physically handicapped person that generally do not increase the value of a personal residence. These expenses are deductible in full as a medical expense. Examples of expenses made for the primary purpose of accommodating a personal residence to the handicapped condition of a taxpayer, the taxpayer's spouse, or dependents who reside there include:

- Construction of entrance or exit ramps to the residence
- Widening doorways at entrances or exits to the residence
- Widening or otherwise modifying hallways and interior doorways
- Installing railings, support bars, or other modifications to bathrooms
- Lowering or making other modifications to kitchen cabinets and equipment
- Altering the location or otherwise modifying electrical outlets and fixtures
- Installing porch lifts and other forms of lifts (an elevator, however, may also add to the fair market value of the residence, and any deduction would have to be decreased to that extent)
- Modifying fire alarms, smoke detectors, and other warning systems
- Modifying stairs
- Adding handrails or grab bars, whether or not in bathrooms
- Modifying hardware on doors
- Modifying areas in front entrance and exit doorways
- Grading of ground to provide access to the residence

According to the IRS, other similar expenditures may also be incurred in accommodating a personal residence to the handicapped condition of a taxpayer or a

dependent. However, only reasonable costs for accommodating a handicapped person's condition will be considered incurred for the purpose of medical care. Additional costs attributable to personal desires are not deductible.

Example

You are physically handicapped and confined to a wheelchair. You incur expenses to widen doorways and lower kitchen cabinets in your residence to permit access by you. These expenses are deductible, subject to the 7.5% threshold discussed above.

TaxPlanner 1

If you have to make a medically related capital improvement, you should request a written recommendation from your doctor. In addition, obtain a reliable written appraisal from a real estate appraiser or a valuation expert. Be prepared to prove to what extent the value of your property was or was not increased.

TaxPlanner 2

It is often difficult to obtain a medical deduction for the installation of a swimming pool. The IRS has held that swimming pools generally fall within the category of recreational or luxury items and will look at various facts when it is determining the deduction for the cost of a swimming pool, including:

- Whether the primary purpose of the pool is for medical care
- Whether the expenditure is related to medical care
- Whether the pool does more than serve the convenience and/or comfort of the taxpayer

You should contact your tax advisor if you intend to install a swimming pool for medical reasons.

Medical Insurance Premiums

You can include in medical expenses premiums you pay for policies that provide payment for:

- Hospitalization, surgical fees, and other medical and dental expenses,
- Prescription drugs,
- Replacement of lost or damaged contact lenses, or
- Membership in an association that gives cooperative or so-called "free-choice" medical service, or group hospitalization and clinical care.

Explanation

Amounts you pay to receive medical care from a health maintenance organization (HMO) are treated as medical insurance premiums.

TaxAlert

The Revenue Reconciliation Act of 1990 allows a supplemental credit that may be claimed for amounts paid for health insurance coverage that includes one or more qualifying children. See Chapter 35, *Other Credits*, for more information. Your medical expense deduction should be reduced by the amount of any health insurance credit allowed.

TAXSAVER

Employees who pay all or part of their medical insurance premiums via employer plans should ask their employer to investigate a Flexible Spending Arrangement, which is sometimes referred to as a Cafeteria Plan.

Example

You are in the 28% tax bracket, and you pay $2,000 to cover your medical insurance premiums. Since medical expenses are deductible only if they exceed 7.5% of your adjusted gross income, chances are that you are not able to deduct your payments for medical insurance. You must earn $2,775 (before taxes) to be left with the $2,000 (after taxes) needed to pay your medical insurance premiums.

If your company offers medical insurance as part of a cafeteria plan, you may opt to have your wages reduced by $2,000 under a salary reduction plan to cover the cost of the insurance. The cut in wages reduces your income tax, producing a federal tax savings in this case of $560. Additional tax savings may also be enjoyed because of lower state income taxes and reduced FICA taxes.

If you have a policy that provides more than one kind of payment, you can include the premiums for the medical care part of the policy if the charge for the medical part is reasonable. The cost of the medical portion must be separately stated in the insurance contract or given to you in a separate statement.

Cafeteria plans. Do not include in medical and dental expenses (line 1 of Schedule A) insurance premiums paid by an employer-sponsored health insurance plan (cafeteria plan) unless the premiums are included in box 1 of your Form(s) W–2.

Medicare A. If you are covered under social security (or if you are a government employee who paid Medicare tax), you are enrolled in Medicare A. The tax paid for Medicare A is not a medical expense.

If you are not covered under social security (or were not a government employee who paid Medicare tax), you may voluntarily enroll in Medicare A. In this situation the premiums paid in 1993 for Medicare A can be included as a medical expense on your tax return.

Medicare B. Medicare B is supplemental medical insurance. Premiums you pay for Medicare B are a medical expense. If you applied for it at age 65, you can deduct $36.60 for each month in 1993 for which you paid a premium. If you were over age 65 when you first enrolled, check the information you received from the Social Security Administration to find out your premium.

Prepaid insurance. Premiums you pay before you are 65 for insurance covering medical care for yourself, your spouse, or your dependents after you reach 65 are medical care expenses in the year paid if they are:

1) Payable in equal yearly installments, or more often, and
2) Payable for at least 10 years, or until you reach 65 (but not for less than 5 years).

Unused sick leave used to pay premiums. You must include in gross income cash payments you receive at the time of retirement for unused sick leave.

You must also include in gross income the value of unused sick leave that, at your option, your employer applies to the cost of your continuing participation in your employer's health plan after you retire. You can include this cost of continuing participation in the health plan as a medical expense.

If you participate in a health plan where your employer automatically applies the value of unused sick leave to the cost of your continuing participation in the health plan (and you do not have the option to receive cash), you do not include the value of the unused sick leave in gross income. You cannot deduct this cost of continuing participation in that health plan as a medical expense.

Health insurance credit. If you qualify to receive the earned income credit, you may be able to claim a credit based on health insurance premiums you pay. This credit is discussed in Chapter 35, *Other Credits*.

If you claim the health insurance credit, you must subtract the amount of that credit from your total medical expenses to figure your medical expense deduction.

Health Insurance Costs for Self-Employed Persons

If you were self-employed and had a net profit for the year, were a general partner (or a limited partner receiving guaranteed payments) or if you received wages in 1993 from an S corporation in which you were a more than 2% shareholder (who is treated as a partner), you may be able to deduct up to 25% of the amount paid for health insurance on behalf of yourself, your spouse, and dependents. Do this on line 26 of Form 1040. If you itemize your deductions, include the remaining premiums with all other medical care expenses on Schedule A, subject to the 7.5% limit.

You cannot take the deduction for any month in 1993 in which you were eligible to participate in any subsidized health plan maintained by your employer or your spouse's employer.

If you qualify to take the deduction, use the following worksheet to figure the amount you can deduct. But, if either of the following applies, do not use the worksheet. Instead, use the worksheet in Publication 535 to figure your deduction.

- You had more than one source of income subject to self-employment tax.
- You file Form 2555, *Foreign Earned Income,* or Form 2555–EZ.

If you can file Schedule EIC, *Earned Income Credit,* you may also be able to claim the health insurance credit on that schedule. If you do claim that credit, do not use the following worksheet. Instead, use the worksheet in Publication 596, *Earned Income Credit.*

TAXALERT

The 1993 Tax Act retroactively reinstated the 25% deduction for health insurance expenses of the self-employed paid for coverage from July 1, 1992, through December 31, 1993. In addition, under the new law, the determination of whether a self-employed individual or his or her spouse is eligible for employer-paid health insurance benefits is now made on a monthly, rather than on an annual, basis.

TaxSaver

If you filed your 1992 income tax return treating the deduction as having expired on June 30, 1992, you may wish to file an amended return.

Worksheet for Self-Employed Health Insurance Deduction

1. Enter the total amount paid in 1993 for health insurance coverage for 1993 for you, your spouse, and dependents. But do not include amounts for any month you were eligible to participate in an employer-sponsored health plan .... _____

2. Percentage used to figure the deduction .... × .25

3. Multiply line 1 by the percentage on line 2 .... _____

4. Enter your net profit and any other earned income* from the business under which the insurance plan is established, **minus** any deductions you claim on Form 1040, lines 25 and 27 .... _____

5. **Self-employed health insurance deduction.** Enter the **smaller** of line 3 or line 4 here and on Form 1040, line 26. DO NOT include this amount in figuring any medical expense deduction on Schedule A (Form 1040). .... _____

* **Earned income** includes net earnings and gains from the sale, transfer, or licensing of property you created. It does not include capital gain income. If you were a more than 2% shareholder in an S corporation, earned income is your wages from that corporation.

Health insurance costs paid in 1992. For 1992, if you were self-employed, you may have been able to deduct up to 25% of the health insurance premiums paid before July 1. If you paid any amounts between July 1, 1992, and December 31, 1992, you cannot deduct them for 1993. However, if you meet the rules in this section, you may be able to deduct up to 25% of them for 1992. File Form 1040X, *Amended U.S. Individual Income Tax Return,* to claim this deduction. See Publication 553, *Highlights of 1993 Tax Changes.*

Caution. This deduction will not apply in taxable years beginning after 1993.

Meals and Lodging

Payment for meals and lodging provided by a hospital or similar institution as a necessary part of medical care is a medical expense if the main reason for being in the hospital is to receive medical care.

You may be able to include in medical expenses the cost of lodging not provided in a hospital or similar institution. You can include the cost of such lodging while away from home if you meet **all** of the following requirements.

1) The lodging is primarily for and essential to medical care.
2) The medical care is provided by a doctor in a licensed hospital or in a medical care facility related to, or the equivalent of, a licensed hospital.
3) The lodging is not lavish or extravagant under the circumstances.
4) There is no significant element of personal pleasure, recreation, or vacation in the travel away from home.

The amount you include in medical expenses cannot exceed $50 for each night for each person. Lodging is included for a person for

whom transportation expenses are a medical expense because that person is traveling with the person receiving the medical care. For example, if a parent is traveling with a sick child, up to $100 per night for lodging is included as a medical expense. (Meals are not deductible.)

Nursing home. You can include in medical expenses the cost of medical care in a nursing home or home for the aged for yourself, your spouse, or your dependents. This includes the cost of meals and lodging in the home if the main reason for being there is to get medical care.

Do not include the cost of meals and lodging if the reason for being in the home is personal. You can, however, include in medical expenses the part of the cost that is for medical or nursing care.

Medical trip. You cannot include the cost of your meals and lodging while you are away from home for medical treatment if you do not receive the treatment at a medical facility, or if the lodging is not primarily for or essential to the medical care.

Example 1

A businessman who became ill while out of town was allowed to deduct the costs of his meals and hotel room when, due to a shortage of hospital rooms, he was required to move into a hotel. He had not recovered sufficiently to return home. The courts found that the test of deductibility was *not* the nature of the institution (i.e., whether it was a hospital or a similar institution) but the condition of the individual and the nature of the services.

Example 2

The parents of a mentally ill son rented an apartment to be close to the son's clinic. They were not allowed to deduct its costs, because no care was received in the apartment, and the apartment had not been altered in any way to facilitate their son's treatment. Therefore, the court held that the parents had not incurred any expenses for their son's care in the apartment.

Transportation

Amounts paid for transportation primarily for, and essential to, medical care qualify as medical expenses.

Include:

- Bus, taxi, train, and plane fares,
- Ambulance service,
- Car expenses,
- Transportation expenses of a parent who must go with a child who needs medical care,
- Transportation expenses of a nurse or other person who can give injections, medications, or other treatment required by a patient who is traveling to get medical care and is unable to travel alone, and
- Transportation expenses for regular visits to see a mentally ill dependent, if these visits are recommended as part of treatment.

Do not include:

- Transportation expenses to and from work even if your condition requires an unusual means of transportation, or

Explanation

Although the IRS has repeatedly denied *any* deduction for commuting expenses to get to one's place of work— even for disabled individuals—under certain circumstances, a deduction may be permitted for transportation required for medical reasons.

Example

If, at your doctor's advice, you take a job for the purposes of occupational therapy, you may deduct your commuting expenses. Since the employment is prescribed therapy, the expense of going to and from work is incurred in the course of obtaining occupational therapy and thus is deductible as medical transportation.

- Transportation costs if, for nonmedical reasons only, you choose to travel to another city, such as a resort area, for an operation or other medical care prescribed by your doctor.

Explanation

The courts have, however, allowed a deduction for the costs of meals, as well as transportation and lodging between a taxpayer's home and the out-of-state clinic where treatment was obtained when the trip was made for medical reasons. The meals were considered to be part of the transportation costs. In addition, since the taxpayer's husband had to accompany his spouse on the trip, his food costs en route were also deductible.

The expenses of a move to a different climate may be deductible if the principal purpose of the move is to alleviate an illness.

Car expenses. You can include out-of-pocket expenses for your car, such as gas and oil. You cannot include depreciation, insurance, general repair, or maintenance expenses.

If you do not want to figure your actual expenses, you can use a standard rate of *9 cents a mile* for use of your car for medical reasons.

Either way, you can include the cost of parking fees and tolls.

Disabled Dependent Care Expenses

Some disabled dependent care expenses may qualify as medical expenses or as work-related expenses for purposes of taking a credit for dependent care. (See Chapter 33.) You can choose to apply them either way as long as you do not use the same expenses to claim both a credit and a medical expense deduction.

Explanation

Special care for the handicapped. The costs of sending a mentally or physically handicapped person to a special school or home, including certain advance payments for lifetime care, may be included in medical expenses. See Publication 502, *Medical and Dental Expenses*, for more information about medical care expenses for a handicapped person. Enter the amount you paid for special care on line 1b, Schedule A (Form 1040).

The distinguishing characteristic of a special school is the content of its curriculum, which must be designed to enable the student to compensate for or overcome a handicap in order to prepare him or her for future normal education and living. The curriculum of a special school may include some ordinary education, but this must be incidental to the primary purpose of the school.

If a handicapped person attends a school that is not a special school, only those costs that are specifically attributable to medical care are deductible expenses. A school that offers small classes and individual attention does not qualify as a special school.

Example

In addition to the regular tuition for a private school, the parents of a handicapped child paid a special fee for a language development program designed to help students with learning disabilities. Although no deduction was allowed for the regular tuition, the cost of the special course was deductible as a medical expense.

Impairment-Related Work Expenses

Certain unreimbursed expenses may appear to be deductible as either medical or business expenses. Deduct them as business deductions if they are:

- Necessary for you to do your work satisfactorily,
- For goods or services not required or used, other than incidentally, in your personal activities, and
- Not specifically covered under other income tax laws.

Example. You are blind. To do your work, you must use a reader. You use the reader both during your regular working hours at your place of work and outside your regular working hours away from your place of work. The reader's services are only for your work. You can deduct your expenses for the reader as business expenses.

See Publication 907, *Information for Persons with Disabilities,* for more information on expenses that may be impairment-related work expenses.

Example 1

You are confined to a wheelchair. Sometimes you must go out of town on business. Your friend or spouse goes with you to help with such things as carrying your luggage or getting up steps. You do not pay your helper a salary, but you do pay for your helper's travel, meals, and lodging while on such trips. You have learned how to take care of yourself and to do your job in your hometown without a helper. Because the expenses for the transportation, meals, and lodging of your helper are directly related to doing your job, you may deduct them as miscellaneous deductions on Schedule A (Form 1040).

Example 2

Assume the same facts as in the example above, except you are dependent on your friend's help at home as well as while traveling on business. The expenses of the friend are medical expenses, not business expenses.

If, in the above example, your spouse goes with you on

the out-of-town business trips, you may deduct as medical expenses only the out-of-pocket costs for your spouse's transportation. Expenses for your spouse's meals and lodging are not deductible.

Decedents

The survivor or personal representative of a decedent can choose to treat certain expenses paid by the decedent's estate for the decedent's medical care as paid by the decedent at the time the medical services were provided. The expenses must be paid within the one-year period beginning with the day after the date of death. If you are the survivor or personal representative making this choice, you must attach a statement to the decedent's Form 1040 (or the decedent's amended return, Form 1040X), saying that the expenses have not been and will not be claimed on the estate tax return.

Amended returns and claims for refund are discussed in Chapter 1, *Filing Information*.

Example. John filed his 1992 income tax return on April 12, 1993. He died on June 1, 1993. His unpaid medical expenses were $1,500 for 1992 and $2,000 for 1993. His executor paid the $3,500 in medical expenses in January 1994.

The executor can file an amended return for 1992, claiming the $1,500 medical expenses as paid in 1992. The $2,000 for 1993 can be treated as paid in 1993 and included as a medical expense on the return for 1993, which will be the decedent's final return.

Expenses for deceased spouse or dependent. If you paid medical expenses for your deceased spouse or dependent, include them as medical expenses on your Form 1040 in the year paid, whether they are paid before or after the decedent's death.

TaxPlanner

The alternatives presented above offer many options in planning for a decedent's medical expenses. If payment is deferred until after death but paid by the decedent's estate within the 1-year period that begins the day after the date of death, the expenses may be deducted on the decedent's estate tax return or the decedent's final income tax return, whichever is more beneficial. On the other hand, the expenses can be paid and deducted by the surviving spouse, if this is more advantageous. Consult your tax advisor when you are determining which option provides the greatest tax benefit to you.

How to Figure Your Deduction

To figure your medical expense deduction, complete Schedule A (Form 1040). If you need more information on itemized deductions or you are not sure whether you can itemize, see Chapters 20, *Standard Deduction*, and 21, *Limit on Itemized Deductions*.

Write in the amounts you paid for medical and dental care expenses after reducing the amount by payments you received from insurance and other sources. You can deduct only the amount of your medical and dental expenses that is more than 7.5% of your adjusted gross income shown on line 32, Form 1040.

Write the amount of your unreimbursed medical expenses on line 1, Schedule A (Form 1040). For an example, see *Medical and dental expenses (lines 1-4, Schedule A)* under *Itemized Deductions (Schedule A)* in Chapter 45, *Sample Form 1040*.

Separate returns. If you and your spouse live in a noncommunity property state and file separate returns, each of you can include only the medical expenses each actually paid. Any medical expenses paid out of a joint checking account in which you and your spouse have the same interest are considered to have been paid equally by each of you, unless you can show otherwise.

Community property states. If you and your spouse live in a community property state and file separate returns, any medical expenses paid out of community funds are divided equally. Each of you should include half the expenses. If medical expenses are paid out of the separate funds of one spouse, only the spouse who paid the medical expenses can include them. If you live in a community property state, are married, and file a separate return, see Publication 555, *Federal Tax Information on Community Property*.

TaxPlanner

You should consider filing separate returns whenever the medical expenses of either spouse substantially exceed those of the other spouse. Figure your tax filing jointly and filing separately before deciding which alternative to choose.

What expenses can you include in 1993? You can include medical expenses only in the year you paid them. (But see *Decedents*, earlier.) If you pay medical expenses by check, the day you mail or deliver the check generally is the date of payment. If you use a "pay-by-phone" account, the date reported on the statement of the financial institution showing when payment was made is the date of payment. You can include medical expenses you charge to your credit card in the year the charge is made. It does not matter when you actually pay the amount charged.

TaxPlanner

Medical expenses don't usually lend themselves to tax planning. However, since a medical deduction is available *only* in the year of payment, you may be able to maximize your deduction if you can control the timing of your payment.

To determine the most beneficial year of payment, you need to assess your situation prior to the end of the year. If it is clear that your current-year medical expenses will not exceed the nondeductible floor—7.5% of your adjusted gross income—try to defer payment of any medical bills until after year-end. You may be able to salvage a deduction next year.

If you can schedule major or minor surgery in nonemergency cases, you should compare this year's medical deductions with what they are liable to be next year to choose the more beneficial time. It is the date of payment—not the date of surgery—that determines the year in which you may deduct the expense. Remember, putting the charge on a credit card counts as payment at that time.

If you suspect that your adjusted gross income is going to drop substantially next year, defer the payment of medical bills. However, if you think your adjusted gross income is going to skyrocket next year, pay those bills now and try to salvage a deduction.

Figure 22-A. **Is Your Excess Medical Reimbursement Taxable?**

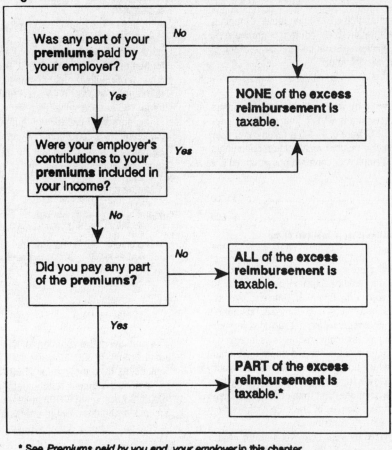

Was any part of your **premiums** paid by your employer?

No → NONE of the excess reimbursement is taxable.

Yes ↓

Were your employer's contributions to your **premiums** included in your income?

Yes → NONE of the excess reimbursement is taxable.

No ↓

Did you pay any part of the premiums?

No → ALL of the excess reimbursement is taxable.

Yes ↓

PART of the excess reimbursement is taxable.*

* See *Premiums paid by you and your employer* in this chapter.

TaxAlert

Prepaid medical expenses generally are not deductible until the year of treatment.

Reimbursements

You must reduce your total medical expenses for the year by all reimbursements for medical expenses that you receive from insurance or other sources during the year. This includes payments from Medicare.

Do not reduce medical expenses by any payment you received for loss of earnings or damages for personal injury or sickness.

Excess reimbursement. If the total reimbursement you received during the year is the same as or more than your total medical expenses for the year, you cannot take a medical deduction. The following discussions explain whether you need to include excess reimbursement in income.

Premiums paid by you. If you pay the entire premium for your medical insurance or all of the cost of a similar plan, do not include an excess reimbursement in your gross income.

Premiums paid by you and your employer. If both you and your employer contribute to your medical insurance plan and your employer's contributions are not included in your gross income, you must include in your gross income the part of an excess reimbursement that is from your employer's contributions.

Explanation

Reimbursements from insurance or other sources received during the year in which the medical expense is paid reduce the medical deduction to the extent of the reimbursement.

If total reimbursements exceed total medical expenses for the year, the excess reimbursement may have to be included in income. The determining factor of whether or not the excess reimbursement has to be included in income depends on who paid the premium for the insurance policy.

If you pay the entire premium for medical insurance, none of the excess reimbursement is includable in income. On the other hand, if you share the cost of the premium with, for example, your employer, the part of the excess reimbursement attributable to the employer's contribution to the premium must be included in income.

Example 1

John's annual medical insurance premium is $3,000. John's employer pays $900 of the premium, and John pays $2,100 of the premium. In 1993, John incurs $5,000 of medical expenses, and his insurance company reimburses him $5,500, an excess reimbursement of $500. The amount of the excess reimbursement that must be included in John's income is $150 ($900/$3,000 × $500).

Example 2

Assume the same fact as in the example above, except John pays for the entire medical insurance premium himself. The $500 excess insurance reimbursement would *not* be included in income.

Example. You are covered by your employer's medical insurance policy. The annual premium is $2,000. Your employer pays $600 of that amount and the balance of $1,400 is taken out of your wages. The part of any excess reimbursement you receive under the policy that is from your employer's contributions is figured like this:

Total annual cost of policy	$2,000
Amount paid by employer	$ 600
Employer's contribution in relation to the annual cost of the policy ($600 ÷ $2,000)	30%

You must include in your gross income 30% of any excess reimbursement you received for medical expenses under the policy.

Premiums paid by your employer. If your employer or your former employer pays the total cost of your medical insurance plan and your employer's contributions are not included in your income, you must report all excess reimbursements as income.

More than one policy. If you are covered under more than one policy, the costs of which are paid by both you and your employer, you must first divide the medical expense among the policies to figure the excess reimbursement from each policy. Then divide the policy costs to figure the part of any excess reimbursement that is from your employer's contribution.

Example. You are covered by your employer's health insurance policy. The annual premium is $1,200. Your employer pays $300, and the balance of $900 is deducted from your wages. You also paid the entire premium of $250 for a personal health insurance policy.

During the year, you paid medical expenses of $3,600. In the same year, you were reimbursed $2,500 under your employer's policy and $1,500 under your personal policy.

You figure the part of any excess reimbursement you receive that is from your employer's contribution like this:

Reimbursement from employer's policy	$2,500
Reimbursement from your policy	1,500
Total reimbursement	$4,000
Amount of medical expenses from your policy [($1,500 ÷ $4,000) × $3,600 total medical expenses]	$1,350
Amount of medical expenses from your employer's policy [($2,500 ÷ $4,000) × $3,600 total medical expenses]	2,250
Total medical expenses	$3,600
Excess reimbursement from your employer's policy ($2,500 − $2,250)	$ 250

Because both you and your employer contribute to the cost of this policy, you must divide the cost to determine the excess reimbursement from your employer's contribution.

Employer's contribution in relation to the annual cost of the policy ($300 ÷ $1,200)	25%
Amount to report as income (25% × $250)	$62.50

Example

John pays $1,800 and his employer pays $600 toward the $2,400 annual premium for health insurance policy no. 1. Additionally, John pays the entire premium, $500, for health insurance policy no. 2. During 1993, John paid $7,200 of medical expenses and in the same year was reimbursed $5,000 under the first policy and $3,000 under the second policy.

The portion of excess reimbursement attributable to the employer's contribution is computed as follows:

Reimbursement from policy no. 1	$5,000
Reimbursement from policy no. 2	3,000
Total reimbursement	$8,000
Amount of reimbursed medical expenses from policy no. 1 ($5,000/$8,000 × $7,200 total medical expenses)	$4,500
Amount of reimbursed medical expenses from policy no. 2 ($3,000/$8,000 × $7,200 total medical expenses)	2,700
Total medical expenses	$7,200
Excess reimbursement from policy no. 1 ($5,000 − $4,500)	$ 500

The employer's contribution to the annual cost of policy no. 1 is 25% ($600/$2,400). Consequently, John must include $125 in income for 1993 ($500 × 25%).

None of the excess reimbursement from policy no. 2, $300 ($3,000 − $2,700), must be included in income, since John paid the entire premium of the policy.

Reimbursement in a later year. If you are reimbursed in a later year for medical expenses you deducted in an earlier year, you must report as income the amount you received from insurance or other sources that is equal to, or less than, the amount you previously deducted as medical expenses. However, you do not have to report the reimbursement you received up to the amount of your medical deductions that did not reduce your tax for the earlier year. For more information about the recovery of an amount that you claimed as an itemized deduction in an earlier year, see *Itemized Deduction Recoveries* in Chapter 13, *Other Income*.

Medical expenses not deducted. If you did not deduct a medical expense in the year you paid it because you did not itemize deductions or because your medical expenses were not more than 7.5% of your adjusted gross income, do not include in income the reimbursement for this expense that you receive in a later year. However, if the reimbursement is more than the expense, see *Excess reimbursement,* earlier.

Example. In 1993, you have medical expenses of $500. You cannot deduct the $500 because it is not more than 7.5% of your adjusted gross income. If, in a later year, you are reimbursed for any of the $500 medical expenses, you do not include that amount in your gross income.

Damages. If you receive an amount in settlement of a personal injury suit, the part that is for medical expenses deducted in an earlier year is included as income in the later year if your medical deduction in the earlier year reduced your income tax in that year. See *Reimbursement in a later year,* earlier.

Future medical expenses. If you receive an amount in settlement of a damage suit for personal injuries that is properly allocable or determined to be for future medical expenses, you must reduce any medical expenses for these injuries until the amount you received has been completely used.

23 | Taxes You May Deduct

Introduction

You have been allowed to deduct taxes you pay—other than your federal income tax—ever since the nation's income tax was first enacted. The underlying theory is that taxes are an involuntary expenditure and therefore should be deducted from an individual's **gross income.** *But there is a practical consideration as well: The payment of state and local taxes makes it more difficult for an individual to meet the federal tax bill.*

Virtually all taxes of any kind used to be deductible, but the list has become shorter and shorter. Fifty years ago, estate, inheritance, and gift taxes were deductible, but they no longer are. Forty years ago, you could deduct any import duties you paid, but that is no longer the case. The last year you could deduct state and local sales taxes was 1986. Today, only a few taxes that Congress has specifically identified are deductible.

The taxes you still may deduct include two of the most significant. They are state and local taxes you pay on property you own and on your income. Taxes you pay to a foreign government may also be deducted. These and other taxes that you may deduct from your federal income tax are described in this chapter.

Note: Your 1993 itemized deductions may be subject to certain limitations if your adjusted gross income exceeds $108,450.

Important Reminder

Limit on itemized deductions. If your adjusted gross income is more than $108,450 ($54,225 if you are married filing separately), the overall amount of your itemized deductions may be limited. See Chapter 21 for more information about this limit.

This chapter discusses which taxes you can deduct if you itemize deductions on Schedule A (Form 1040). It also explains which taxes you can deduct on other schedules or forms, and which taxes you cannot deduct.

The chapter covers the following types of taxes.

- Income taxes (state, local, or foreign)
- Real estate taxes (state, local, or foreign)
- Personal property taxes (state or local)
- Taxes that are expenses of business or producing income
- Taxes you cannot deduct

The end of the chapter explains which form you use to deduct the different types of taxes.

Table. Use *Table 23–1* in this chapter as a guide to determine which taxes you can deduct.

State or local taxes. These are taxes imposed by the 50 states, U.S. possessions, or any of their political subdivisions (such as a county or city), or by the District of Columbia.

Indian tribal government. An Indian tribal government that is recognized by the Secretary of the Treasury as performing substantial government functions will be treated as a state for this purpose. Income taxes, real estate taxes, and personal property taxes imposed by that Indian tribal government (or by any of its subdivisions that are treated as political subdivisions of a state) are deductible.

Foreign taxes. These are taxes imposed by a foreign country or any of its political subdivisions.

Useful Items

You may want to see:

Publication

- ☐ **514** Foreign Tax Credit for Individuals
- ☐ **530** Tax Information for First-Time Homeowners

Form (and Instructions)

- ☐ **Schedule A (Form 1040)** Itemized Deductions
- ☐ **Schedule E (Form 1040)** Supplemental Income and Loss
- ☐ **Form 1116** Foreign Tax Credit
- ☐ **Form 2106** Employee Business Expenses
- ☐ **Form 2119** Sale of Your Home

Table 23-1. **Which Taxes Can You Deduct?**

	You Can Deduct	You Cannot Deduct
Income Taxes	State and local income taxes Foreign income taxes Employee contributions to state disability fund or state unemployment fund	Federal income taxes Employee contributions to private or voluntary disability plan
Real Estate Taxes	State or local real estate taxes Foreign real estate taxes Tenant's share of real estate taxes paid by cooperative housing corporation	Taxes for local benefits Trash and garbage pickup fees Rent increase due to higher real estate taxes Homeowners association charges
Personal Property Taxes	State or local personal property taxes	
Other Taxes	Taxes that are expenses of your trade or business or producing income One-half of self-employment tax paid Taxes on property producing rent or royalty income Occupational taxes	Many taxes, such as state and local sales taxes and federal excise taxes, generally are not deductible. See *Taxes You Cannot Deduct*, later.
Fees and Charges		Fees and charges, such as for driver's licenses or water bills, generally are not deductible. See *Taxes You Cannot Deduct*, later.

Tests to Deduct Any Tax

All the following tests must be met for any tax to be deductible by you.

1) The tax must be imposed on you.
2) The tax must be paid by you.
3) The tax must be paid during your tax year.

The tax must be imposed on you. Generally, you can deduct only taxes that are imposed on you.

Generally, you can deduct property taxes only if you are the property owner. If real estate taxes are paid by your spouse who owns a home, they are deductible on your spouse's separate return or on your joint return.

The tax must be paid by you. You cannot deduct a tax that another person paid for you.

The tax must be paid during your tax year. If you are a cash basis taxpayer, you can deduct only those taxes paid during the calendar year for which you file a return. If you pay your taxes by check, the day you mail or deliver the check is generally the date of payment. If you use a pay-by-phone account, the date reported on the statement of the financial institution showing when payment was made is the date of payment.

If you question a tax liability and use the cash method of accounting, you can deduct the tax only in the year you actually pay it. If you use an accrual method of accounting, you must use special rules for determining when you can deduct the tax liability you are questioning. See *Contested Liabilities* in Publication 538, *Accounting Periods and Methods*, for more information.

Income Taxes

This section discusses the deductibility of state and local income taxes, employee contributions to a state disability or unemployment fund, and foreign income taxes.

State and local income taxes. You can deduct state and local income taxes. However, you cannot deduct state and local income taxes you pay on income that is exempt from federal income tax, unless the exempt income is interest income. For example, you cannot deduct the part of a state's income tax that is on a cost-of-living allowance that is exempt from federal income tax.

Deduct state and local income taxes withheld from your salary in the year they are withheld. For 1993, these taxes will be shown in boxes 18 and 21 of your Form W-2. You may also have state or local income tax withheld on Form 1099-MISC (box 11) or Form 1099-R (boxes 10 and 13). Deduct payments made on taxes for an earlier year in the year they are paid.

Deduct estimated tax payments you make under a pay-as-you-go plan of a state or local government. However, you must have a reasonable basis for making the estimated tax payments. Any estimated state or local tax payments you make that are not reasonably determined in good faith at the time of payment are not deductible. For example, if you made an estimated state income tax payment, but the estimate of your state tax liability for the year shows that you will get a refund of the full amount of your estimated payment, then you had no reasonable basis to believe you had any additional liability to make the payment, and you cannot deduct it.

Also deduct any part of a refund of prior-year state or local income taxes that you chose to have credited to your 1993 estimated state or local income taxes.

Do not reduce your deduction by either of the following:

- Any state or local income tax refund (or credit) you expect to receive for 1993, or
- Any refund of (or credit for) prior year state and local income taxes you actually received in 1993.

Explanation
Generally, all state, county, city, and municipal income taxes are deductible in the year in which you pay them— including the state and local taxes applicable to interest income that is not taxable at the federal level.

Example
You have the following income:

Salary	$18,000
Municipal bond income (exempt from federal tax but taxable by your state)	2,000
Total income	$20,000

If your state income tax is $1,000, then 10%, or $100, is attributable to the federally exempt income. Nevertheless, you may deduct the entire $1,000 on your federal return.

TaxPlanner 1

Municipal bonds issued by your state frequently are not subject to your state's income tax, whereas obligations for another state usually are subject to the state tax.

Be sure to use your effective state rate after the federal tax benefit when you are deciding between investing in a state tax-exempt municipal bond or an obligation that is subject to your state's tax.

TaxPlanner 2

If you deduct an expense when you pay it rather than when the expense is incurred, as most people do, you may deduct the following:

1. State income tax withheld from salary in 1993
2. State **estimated tax** payments made in 1993 for 1993
3. Fourth-quarter state estimated tax payment for 1992 made in January 1993
4. State income tax paid with your 1992 state income tax return filed in 1993
5. Additional state income tax paid in 1993 as a result of an **audit** or an amended return

In most states, the fourth-quarter estimated tax payment is due in January of the following year. A January, 1994 payment for 1993's last quarter is deductible on your 1994 return. If, however, the payment is made by December 31, 1993, it is deductible on your 1993 return. If you can accelerate your payment by a few weeks, you can accelerate your **deduction** for state income taxes by a full year.

TaxAlert

Taxpayers have been denied deductions when state estimated tax payments made on December 31 were substantially in excess of their actual tax liability. To be assured of a deduction, you must be able to prove that the tax payment was based on a reasonable estimate of your actual tax bill.

TaxOrganizer

You should keep canceled checks for payments of state estimated income tax (or any deductible tax) in order to support your claim for deductible taxes.

Refund (or credit). If you receive a refund of (or credit for) state or local (or foreign) income taxes in a year after the year in which you paid them, you may have to include all or part of the refund in income on line 10 of Form 1040, in the year you receive it. This includes refunds resulting from taxes that were overwithheld, applied from a prior year return, not figured correctly, or figured again as a result of an amended return. However, if you did not itemize your deductions in the previous year, you do not have to include the refund in income. For a discussion of how much to include, see *Recoveries* in Chapter 13.

Explanation

If you received a refund of taxes that you paid in an earlier year, such as 1991 or 1992, do not use that refund to reduce your deduction for taxes that you paid during 1993.

However, if you receive a refund of taxes in the same year in which you paid the taxes, you would use the refund to reduce your deduction for taxes.

Example

You paid $4,000 of estimated state income taxes for 1992 in four equal payments. You made your fourth payment in January, 1993. You were not subject to state income tax withholding in 1992. In 1993, you received a $400 tax refund based on your 1992 state income tax return. One hundred dollars (25% of $400) of the refund is attributable to your 1993 payment. Your deduction for state and local income taxes paid in 1993 includes $900 ($1,000 − $100) plus any other payments you made during 1993 and any amount withheld during 1993. The amount of your state tax refund to be reported as income in 1993 would be $300 ($400 − $100).

TaxSaver

Reducing the amount of the reported refund will reduce your adjusted gross income. If your adjusted gross income is lower, you may benefit from greater itemized deductions.

TaxPlanner

If you subtract part of the refund from your other tax payments, the income reported by you will not match the amount reported to the IRS by the state on Form 1099-G. You may then receive a notice proposing an additional assessment of tax.

You may avoid the notice by attaching to your return an explanation of the reduced amount of income reported by you.

Explanation

An overpayment of state income tax that is to be credited against the estimated state tax for the following year is treated as though it were refunded to you. The overpayment may then be deducted as an estimated tax payment.

Example

Your 1992 state return showed an overpayment of $500, which you indicated was to be credited against your 1993 state estimated tax declaration. In addition, you made three quarterly state estimated tax payments of $500 each during 1993. On your 1993 Form 1040, you report a tax refund of $500 on line 10 and a deduction on Schedule A of $2,000.

TaxOrganizer

When you receive your Form 1099-G from your state or local government, keep it as documentation of your refund.

Separate returns. If you and your spouse file separate state and separate federal income tax returns, you each can deduct on your federal return only the amount of your own state income tax.

If you file separate state returns and a joint federal return, you can deduct on your joint federal return the sum of the state income taxes both of you pay.

If you and your spouse file a joint state return and separate federal returns, each of you can deduct on your separate federal return part of the state income taxes. You can deduct only the amount of the total taxes that is proportionate to your gross income compared to the combined gross income of you and your spouse. But you cannot deduct more than the amount you actually paid during the year. If you and your spouse are jointly and individually liable for the full amount of the state income tax, you and your spouse can deduct on your separate federal returns the amount you each actually paid.

TaxPlanner

If you plan on filing a joint state return with your spouse and separate federal returns, and if you are both jointly and individually liable for the full amount of the state tax, the state tax should be paid, to the extent possible, by the person in the higher separate federal income tax bracket. (For advice on filing jointly or separately, see Chapter 2, *Filing Status*.)

Employee contributions to a state disability fund. You can deduct mandatory contributions to state disability benefit funds that provide protection against loss of wages. Payments made to the following disability funds are deductible as state income taxes on Schedule A (Form 1040).

> California Nonoccupational Disability Benefit Fund
> New Jersey Nonoccupational Disability Benefit Fund
> New York Nonoccupational Disability Benefit Fund
> Rhode Island Temporary Disability Benefit Fund
> Washington State Supplemental Workmen's Compensation Fund

Employee contributions to private or voluntary disability plans are not deductible.

Employee contributions to a state unemployment fund that covers you for the loss of wages from unemployment caused by business conditions are deductible as taxes on Schedule A (Form 1040).

Explanation

In addition to the four states listed regarding deductible disability fund payments, amounts withheld for the Alabama Unemployment Compensation Fund, the Washington State Supplemental Workmen's Compensation Fund, and the West Virginia Unemployment Compensation Trust Fund are deductible.

Foreign income taxes. Generally, you can take either a deduction or a credit for income taxes imposed on you by a foreign country or a U.S. possession. However, you cannot take a deduction or credit for foreign income taxes paid on income that is exempt from U.S. tax under the foreign earned income exclusion or the foreign housing exclusion. For information, get Publication 54, *Tax Guide for U.S. Citizens and Resident Aliens Abroad*.

Eligible foreign income taxes are either deducted on Schedule A (Form 1040) under "Other taxes," or taken as a credit on Form 1116, *Foreign Tax Credit*.

Explanation

If you have income from foreign sources, you may be required to pay foreign taxes on that income, or foreign taxes may be withheld on that income before you receive it.

Most foreign income stems from an investment in a foreign company. For example, if you invest in the stock of a Canadian oil company or an Australian mining company, foreign income taxes are withheld from the **dividends** you receive. To avoid having that income taxed twice–once by the foreign country and again by the United States–the IRS allows you either a deduction or a credit for the foreign income tax.

TaxPlanner 1

It is usually better to take a credit for foreign taxes than to deduct them as itemized deductions. Credits reduce your U.S. tax on a dollar-for-dollar basis, whereas a deduction just reduces the amount of income subject to tax. However, if your foreign tax credit is limited and must be carried over to future years, you may want to consider taking a deduction now instead of waiting for a credit. See Chapter 38, *U.S. Citizens Working Abroad*, for more information on foreign tax credit limitations. The following example shows how a credit is usually more advantageous.

Example

You and your spouse had **adjusted gross income** of $60,000 for 1993, $20,000 of which was from foreign sources. You file a joint return and have no **dependents.** You had to pay $2,000 in foreign income taxes on dividend income received from sources within a foreign country. If your itemized deductions are otherwise $6,200, your added deduction for the foreign income tax reduces your U.S. tax by $560. If, however, you choose to claim a credit for the $2,000 foreign tax, your U.S. tax is reduced by the full $2,000. Therefore, you have an additional tax benefit of $1,440 by taking the credit.

TaxPlanner 2

If you have invested in stock of a foreign company and the stock is being held by your stockbroker, ask him or her for the information that permits you to determine your foreign tax credit. In most instances, monthly statements received from brokers show only the *net* amount of foreign dividends received, *after* the foreign income tax has been deducted.

Example

Your brokerage statement shows foreign dividend income of $850. Upon inquiry, you determine that foreign income taxes of $150 have been withheld. Therefore, you should report $1,000 ($850 + $150) of dividend income. You then may be entitled to take a foreign tax credit of $150 or an itemized deduction of $150.

For your files, you should keep your broker's statement showing any amount of foreign taxes paid.

Real Estate Taxes

Deductible real estate taxes are any state, local, or foreign taxes on real property levied for the general public welfare. The taxes must be based on the assessed value of the real property and must be charged uniformly against all property under the jurisdiction of the taxing authority. Deductible real estate taxes generally do not include taxes charged for local benefits and improvements that increase the value of the property. See *Taxes You Cannot Deduct,* later.

An itemized charge for services to specific property or people is not a tax, even if the charge is paid to the taxing authority. You cannot deduct the charge as a real estate tax if it is:

1) A unit fee for the delivery of a service (such as a $5 fee charged for every 1,000 gallons of water you use),
2) A periodic charge for a residential service (such as a $20 per month or $240 annual fee charged to each homeowner for trash collection), or
3) A flat fee charged for a single service provided by your government (such as a $30 charge for mowing your lawn because it was allowed to grow higher than permitted under your local ordinance).

Caution: You must look at your real estate tax bill to determine if any nondeductible itemized charges, such as those just listed, are included in the bill. If your taxing authority (or mortgage lender) does not furnish you a copy of your real estate tax bill, ask for it. **Tenant-shareholders in a cooperative housing corporation.** Generally, you can deduct your share of the real estate taxes the corporation paid or incurred on the property. The corporation should provide you with a statement showing you your share of the taxes. For more information, see *Special Rules for Cooperatives* in Publication 530.

Explanation
Generally, you may deduct only those real estate taxes assessed against property that you own.

Examples
No deduction was allowed for real estate taxes when

- A taxpayer paid, under court order, real estate taxes on his aunt's house, in which he resided.
- A guarantor paid real estate taxes on foreclosed property.
- The executor of an estate paid real estate taxes on a residence belonging to the estate, which she was occupying.
- A tenant–shareholder in a cooperative housing corporation paid his proportionate share of real estate taxes levied on recreational facilities owned and maintained by another corporation.
- A husband paid real estate taxes on property previously transferred to his wife. He had guaranteed payment if his wife defaulted but was not otherwise obligated. He will not be able to claim a deduction unless his wife actually defaults.

You may, however, deduct real estate taxes when you have a beneficial interest in property, if the payment is made to protect that interest.

Examples
Deductions have been allowed in the following instances:

- By a donor of real estate who retained the right to use the property for 5 years
- By a lessee in Hawaii who leased property for 15 years or more and was the "deemed owner" for Hawaiian real estate purposes
- By a lessee who was permitted under local law to have his name entered on the tax assessment roll
- By a U.S. citizen who had a condominium in a foreign country, where he was not permitted to have legal title.

TaxOrganizer

You should keep a copy of your real estate tax bill in order to support your claim for the real estate tax deduction. Also, if you purchased a new house during the year, you should keep the closing statement. Typically, the closing statement will show the amount of taxes you paid to the seller at the time of the purchase.

Purchase or sale of real estate. If you bought or sold real estate during the year, the real estate taxes must be divided between the buyer and the seller.

The buyer and the seller must divide the real estate taxes according to the number of days in the *real property tax year* (the period to which the tax imposed relates) that each owned the property. The seller is treated as paying the taxes up to the date of the sale, and the buyer is treated as paying the taxes beginning with the date of the sale, regardless of the lien dates under local law. Generally, this information is included on the settlement statement provided at closing.

If you (the seller) cannot deduct taxes until they are paid because you use the cash method of accounting, and the buyer of your property is personally liable for the tax, you are considered to have paid your part of the tax at the time of the sale. This lets you deduct the part of the tax to the date of sale even though you did not actually pay it, but you must also include the amount of that tax in the selling price of the property.

You figure your deduction for taxes on each property bought or sold during the real property tax year as follows.

1. Enter the total real estate taxes for the real property tax year ....

2. Enter the number of days in the real property tax year that you owned the property ....

3. Divide line 2 by 365 ....

4. Multiply line 1 by line 3. This is your deduction. Claim it on line 6 of Schedule A (Form 1040) ....

Note. Repeat steps 1 through 4 for each property you bought or sold during the real property tax year.

Example 1. Dennis and Beth White's real property tax year for both their old home and their new home is the calendar year, with payment due August 1. The tax on their old home, sold on May 5, was $620. The tax on their new home, bought on May 4, was $732. Dennis and Beth are considered to have paid a proportionate share of the real estate taxes on the old home even though they did not actually pay them to the taxing authority. On the other hand, they can claim only a proportionate share of the taxes they paid on their new property even though they paid the entire amount.

Dennis and Beth owned their old home during the real property tax year for 124 days (January 1 to May 4, the day before the sale). They figure their deduction for taxes on their old home as follows.

1. Enter the total real estate taxes for the real property tax year $620

2. Enter the number of days in the real property tax year that you owned the property 124

3. Divide line 2 by 365... .34

4. Multiply line 1 by line 3. This is your deduction. Claim it on line 6 of Schedule A (Form 1040)... $211

They owned their new home during the real property tax year for 242 days (May 4 to December 31, including their date of purchase). They figure their deduction for taxes on their new home as follows.

1. Enter the total real estate taxes for the real property tax year $732

2. Enter the number of days in the real property tax year that you owned the property 242

3. Divide line 2 by 365... .66

4. Multiply line 1 by line 3. This is your deduction. Claim it on line 6 of Schedule A (Form 1040)... $483

Dennis and Beth's real estate tax deduction for their old and new homes is the sum of $211 and $483, or $694. They will enter this amount on line 6 of Schedule A (Form 1040).

Example 2. George and Helen Brown bought a home on May 3, 1993. Their real property tax year is the calendar year. Real estate taxes for 1992 were assessed in their state on January 1, 1993, for the prior calendar year. The taxes became due on May 31, 1993, and October 31, 1993. Under state law, the tax became a lien on May 31, 1993.

George and Helen agreed to pay all taxes due after the date of purchase. Real estate taxes for 1992 were $680. George and Helen paid $340 tax on May 31, 1993, and $340 tax on October 31, 1993. These taxes were for the 1992 real property tax year. The Browns cannot deduct them since they did not own the property until 1993. Instead, they must add $680 to the basis (cost) of their home.

In January 1994, George and Helen receive their property tax statement for 1993 taxes of $752, which they will pay in 1994. George and Helen owned their new home during the 1993 real property tax year for 243 days (May 3 to December 31). They will figure their 1994 deduction for taxes as follows.

1. Enter the total real estate taxes for the real property tax year $752

2. Enter the number of days in the real property tax year that you owned the property 243

3. Divide line 2 by 365... .67

4. Multiply line 1 by line 3. This is your deduction. Claim it on line 6 of Schedule A (Form 1040)... $504

The remaining $248 of taxes paid in 1994, along with the $680 paid in 1993, is added to the cost of their home.

Because the taxes up to the date of sale are considered paid by the seller on the date of sale, the person who sold the Browns their home is entitled to a 1993 tax deduction of $928. This is the sum of the $680 for 1992 and the $248 for the 122 days the seller owned the home in 1993. The seller must also include the $928 in the selling price when he or she completes **Form 2119,** *Sale of Your Home,* (which must be attached to the seller's 1993 tax return). The seller should contact the Browns in January 1994 to find out how much real estate tax is due for 1993.

Delinquent taxes. Delinquent taxes are taxes for any real property tax year before the real property tax year in which the property is sold. Even if the buyer agrees to pay the delinquent taxes, the buyer cannot deduct them but must add them to the cost of the property. The seller can deduct these taxes but also must include them in the selling price on the sale of the property.

Form 1099–S. For certain sales or exchanges of real estate, the person responsible for closing the sale (generally the settlement agent) prepares Form 1099–S, *Proceeds From Real Estate Transactions,* to report certain information to the IRS and to the seller of the property. The gross proceeds from the sale appears in box 2 of the form. Generally, gross proceeds includes cash, notes, and liabilities assumed by the buyer, such as any portion of the seller's real estate tax liability that the buyer will pay after the date of sale. The buyer includes this amount in the cost basis of the property, and the seller both deducts this amount as a tax expense and includes it in the sales price of the property.

For a real estate transaction that involves a residence and that occurs after 1992, any real estate tax that the seller paid in advance but that is the liability of the buyer appears in box 5 of Form 1099–S. The buyer deducts this amount as a tax expense, and the seller reduces his or her tax expense by the same amount. See *Refund (or rebate),* later.

Explanation

Frequently, when property is sold, the amount of the real estate taxes for the "real property tax year" is not yet known, so an allocation is made on the closing statement at the time of sale based on the tax bill for the preceding year.

If the actual real estate tax bill for the real property tax year is greater than the amount used in the original allocation, the seller is entitled to a deduction greater than that shown on the real estate closing statement. The difference between the deductible amount and the amount allocated on the closing statement is considered additional proceeds of the sale.

The buyer is entitled to deduct his or her allocable share of the actual bill. The excess of the amount that he or she pays over (1) the deductible amount and (2) the amount paid or received at the closing is added to the cost of the property.

TaxPlanner

If the real estate taxes are actually paid after the year of the sale, the seller may deduct his or her share of the taxes either in the year of the sale or in the year in which the tax is paid, whichever produces the greatest tax advantage.

The situation is slightly different for the buyer. If the buyer is liable for the tax, he or she may deduct his or her allocated share of the tax only in the year in which the payment is made. If the seller is liable for the tax, the buyer may deduct his or her allocated share either in the year of the sale or in the year of payment.

Taxes placed in escrow. If your monthly mortgage payment includes an amount placed in escrow (put in the care of a third party) for real estate taxes, you cannot deduct the total of these amounts included in your payments for the year. You can deduct only the real estate tax that the lender actually paid to the taxing authority. If the lender does not notify you of the amount of real estate tax that was paid for you, contact the lender or the taxing authority to find the proper amount to show on your return.

TaxPlanner

Most lenders arrange for payment of taxes out of escrow accounts on the tax due date. When the due date is shortly after the end of the calendar year, it may be advantageous to accelerate the payment in order to get the deduction for payment a year earlier.

Example

Real estate taxes of $1,200 for the year 1993 became due and payable on February 1, 1994. The taxpayer made monthly escrow payments of $100 each during 1993. If the taxes were paid from the escrow account on the February 1, 1994 due date, the $1,200 is a 1994 deduction. However, if the taxes were paid by December 31, 1993, the $1,200 is a 1993 deduction.

TaxOrganizer

Be sure to keep your yearly escrow statement, which should indicate the amount of real estate taxes paid from the escrow account.

Married filing separate return. If you and your spouse held property as tenants by the entirety and you file separate returns, each of you can deduct only the taxes each of you paid on the property.

Divorced individuals. If your divorce or separation instrument states that you must pay the real estate taxes for a home owned by you and your spouse, part of your payments may be deductible as alimony and part as real estate taxes. See Publication 504, *Divorced or Separated Individuals,* for information.

Minister's and military personnel housing allowances. If you are a minister or a member of the uniformed services and receive a housing allowance that you can exclude from income, you still can deduct all of the real estate taxes you pay on your home.

Items you cannot deduct. The following are not deductible as real estate taxes:

- Taxes for local benefits,
- Trash and garbage pickup fees,
- Rent increases due to higher real estate taxes, and
- Homeowners association charges.

Taxes for local benefits. Deductible real estate taxes generally do not include taxes charged for local benefits and improvements that increase the value of your property. See *Taxes You Cannot Deduct,* later.

Explanation

Real property taxes are deductible if they are levied for the welfare of the general public and are levied at a proportional rate against all property within the taxing jurisdiction.

Real property taxes should be distinguished from assessments paid for local benefits, such as repair of streets, sidewalks, sewers, curbs, gutters, and other improvements that tend to benefit specific properties. Assessments of this type generally are not deductible.

A property owner often has the option of paying a special assessment in one payment or spreading the assessment over a period of years. In either case, the assessment itself is not deductible. However, payment of certain special assessments may increase the tax basis of your home. (See Chapter 14, *Basis of Property,* for a full discussion of this matter.) If an assessment on business or investment property is paid in installments, any interest charged is deductible. If the property is personal rather than business property, the interest would not be deductible. See Chapter 24, *Interest Expense*.

The IRS and the courts have held that the following *are* deductible as real property taxes:

- Assessments for the repair and resurfacing of streets, but not the lengthening or widening of them
- Wheeling, West Virginia, police and fire department charges imposed on owners of buildings and **tangible personal property**

The IRS and some courts have held that the following *are not* deductible as real property taxes:

- Delinquency penalties on California real property taxes
- California utility users tax
- New York State renters tax
- Prince George's County, Maryland, renters tax
- Duluth sprinkling tax
- Vermont land gains tax
- Title registration fees
- Municipal water tax
- Monthly sewer user fees
- Building permit fees
- Sewer assessments

If you pay real estate taxes this year but you are not itemizing your deductions, see Chapter 14, *Basis of Property*.

Different rules apply to real estate taxes paid during the period in which you are making improvements intended for business use. These rules are discussed in Chapter 24, *Interest Expense*.

Trash and garbage pickup fees. Fees charged for trash and garbage pickup services are not taxes. However, real estate taxes are deductible even if used to provide services such as trash collection or fire protection if the taxes are imposed at a like rate against all property in the taxing jurisdiction.

Explanation

If the cost of providing certain services, such as garbage collection or sanitary measures, is paid for out of the general real estate tax fund, the entire amount of your real estate tax bill is deductible. If, however, the amount charged for such services is separately stated or paid into a specific fund, that amount is not deductible.

Rent increase due to higher real estate taxes. If your landlord increases your rent in the form of a tax surcharge because of increased real estate taxes, you cannot deduct the increase as taxes.

Homeowners association charges. These charges are not deductible because they are imposed by the homeowners association, rather than the state or local government.

Refund (or rebate). If you receive a refund or rebate in 1993 of real estate taxes you paid in 1993, you must reduce your deduction by the amount refunded to you. If you receive a refund or rebate in 1993 of real estate taxes you deducted in an earlier year, you generally must include the refund or rebate in income in the year you receive it. However, you only need to include the amount of the deduction that reduced your tax in the earlier year.

For more information, see *Recoveries* in Chapter 13, *Other Income*. If you did not itemize deductions in the year you paid the tax or you filed Form 1040A or Form 1040EZ, do not report the refund as income.

Personal Property Taxes

Personal property tax is deductible if it is a state or local tax that is:

1) Charged on personal property,
2) Based *only* on the value of the personal property, and
3) Charged on a yearly basis, even if it is collected more than once a year, or less than once a year.

A tax can be considered charged on personal property even if it is for the exercise of a privilege. For example, a yearly tax based on value qualifies as a personal property tax even if it is called a registration fee and is for the privilege of registering motor vehicles or using them on the highways.

Example. Your state charges a yearly motor vehicle registration tax of 1% of value plus 50 cents per hundredweight. You paid $32 based on the value ($1,500) and weight (3,400 lbs.) of your car. You can deduct $15 (1% × $1,500) as a personal property tax, since it is based on the value. The remaining $17 ($.50 × 34), based on the weight, is not deductible.

Explanation

Most state automobile license fees are not based on the value of the automobile and, therefore, are not deductible as personal property taxes. Deductions have been allowed for all or part of the automobile license fees or taxes in Arizona, California, Colorado, Georgia, Indiana, Iowa, Maine, Massachusetts, Minnesota, Mississippi, Montana, Nebraska, Nevada, New Hampshire, Oklahoma, Washington, and Wyoming.

In addition, a portion of the Oklahoma annual license registration fees for automobiles, house trailers, mobile homes, travel trailers, and boats is deductible. A portion

of the Colorado specific ownership tax on motor vehicles, trailers, and mobile homes is also deductible.

Taxes That Are Expenses of Business or Producing Income

You can deduct certain taxes not previously listed in this chapter only if they are ordinary and necessary expenses of your trade or business or of producing income. For a discussion of business taxes, see Chapter 9 of Publication 535, *Business Expenses*. In some cases, these taxes are not deducted on Schedule A, but are deducted on other schedules or forms. See *Where to Deduct,* later.

Tax connected with purchase or sale. Generally, any tax paid in connection with the purchase or sale of property must be treated as part of the cost basis of the property or, in the case of a sale, as a reduction in the amount realized. But if the cost of the property is a business expense, such as the cost of supplies, any tax paid is deductible as part of the business expense.

Self-employment tax. If you work for yourself, you can deduct half of the self-employment tax you figured on your 1993 Schedule SE (Form 1040), *Self-Employment Tax.*

Occupational taxes. You can deduct as a business expense an occupational tax charged at a flat rate by a locality for the privilege of working or conducting a business in the locality.

Taxes You Cannot Deduct

Many federal, state, and local government taxes are not deductible.

Nondeductible Federal Taxes

Nondeductible federal taxes include:

Federal income taxes, including those withheld from your pay.

Social security, Medicare, or railroad retirement taxes withheld from your pay.

Federal estate and gift taxes. These taxes are generally not deductible. However, you generally can deduct the estate tax attributable to income in respect of a decedent if you must include that income in gross income. In that case, the estate tax can be deducted as a miscellaneous deduction that is not subject to the 2% of adjusted gross income limit. For more information, see *Estate Tax Deduction* in Publication 559, *Survivors, Executors, and Administrators.*

Social security and other employment taxes for household workers. You generally cannot deduct the social security or other employment taxes you pay on the wages of a household worker. However, you may be able to include them in medical or child care expenses. For more information, see Chapter 22, *Medical and Dental Expenses*, and Chapter 33, *Child and Dependent Care Credit.*

Nondeductible State and Local Taxes and Fees

Nondeductible state and local taxes include:

Inheritance, legacy, succession, or estate taxes.
Gift taxes.
Per capita or poll taxes.
Cigarette, tobacco, liquor, beer, wine, etc., taxes.
Taxes for local benefits. Local benefit taxes that are for improvements to property are not deductible. These include

assessments for streets, sidewalks, water mains, sewer lines, public parking facilities, and similar improvements. You should increase the basis of your property by the amount of the assessment.

Local benefit taxes are deductible only if they are for maintenance, repair, or interest charges related to those benefits. If only a part of the taxes is for maintenance, repair, or interest, you must be able to show the amount of that part to claim the deduction. If you cannot determine what part of the tax is for maintenance, repair, or interest, none of it is deductible.

Taxes for local benefits may be included in your real estate tax bill. If your taxing authority (or mortgage lender) does not furnish you a copy of your real estate tax bill, ask for it. You should use the rules above to determine if the local benefit tax is deductible.

Transfer taxes (or stamp taxes). Transfer taxes and other taxes and charges on the sale of a personal home are not deductible. If they are paid by the seller, they are expenses of the sale and reduce the amount realized on the sale. If paid by the buyer, they are included in the cost basis of the property. If you deduct these taxes and charges as moving expenses as explained in Chapter 27, *Moving Expenses*, you cannot use them either to reduce the amount realized on the sale of your home or to increase the cost basis of your new home.

Nondeductible fees and charges include:

Marriage licenses.
Fines (such as for parking or speeding) and collateral deposits.
Driver's licenses.

Explanation
Other taxes that are *not* deductible include the following:

1. Federal and state excise taxes on telephone service
2. Federal gasoline taxes
3. Federal excise taxes on tobacco products and alcoholic beverages
4. Federal excise taxes on automobiles with low gas mileage (the "gas guzzler" tax)
5. Foreign taxes on income earned by U.S. citizens and U.S. **resident aliens** who qualify for the foreign **earned income** exclusion
6. Passport fees
7. Occupancy taxes
8. Penalties assessed as taxes

Taxes You Can Deduct Only If Business-Connected

Certain taxes are deductible only if connected with your trade or business or income-producing activity.
Federal taxes and charges that are deductible only if connected with your trade or business or income-producing activity include:

Postage.
Federal excise taxes or customs duties. These include the federal taxes on telephone service, air transportation, and gasoline.

TaxAlert
The 1993 Tax Act repeals the non-deductible excise tax assessed on certain luxury items and is retroactively effective to January 1, 1993. The only luxury tax that remains is on automobiles (excluding those used exclusively in the purchaser's trade or business of transporting persons or property, e.g. taxicabs). For automobiles purchased from January 1, 1993 to August 9, 1993, the amount of the tax is 10% of the excess of the purchase price over $30,000. The new law stipulates that this threshold amount will be indexed for inflation. Consequently, the amount of tax for automobiles purchased from August 10, 1993 to December 31, 1993 is 10% of the excess of the purchase price over $32,000. Because the luxury tax on automobiles is an excise tax, it is not deductible on your personal income tax return unless the purchase is connected with your business or an income-producing activity.

If you paid the luxury tax on the purchase of any of the following items in 1993, you may be entitled to a refund. (However, the tax did not apply to wholesale sales or to subsequent sales of used items.) You should request any applicable refund from the seller from whom you purchased the item. Such items may include the following:

1. Furs valued over $10,000, including articles in which fur is a major component.
2. Jewelry valued over $10,000, whether real or imitation, including watches.
3. Boats valued over $100,000, excluding those used exclusively in the purchaser's qualifying trade or business.
4. Aircraft valued over $250,000, if not used at least 80% of the time in a trade or a business. However, this tax did not apply to helicopters used in the oil, gas, and forestry industries.

State and local taxes and charges that are deductible only if connected with your trade or business or income-producing activity include:

Motor vehicle taxes. However, see *Personal Property Taxes*, earlier.
Utility taxes.
Car registration fees, inspection fees, and license plates. However, see *Personal Property Taxes,* earlier.
Dog tags, hunting licenses.
Tolls for bridges and roads, and parking meter deposits.
Water bills, sewer, and other service charges.
Fuel adjustment charges by a municipally-owned electric utility company.
Taxes on gasoline, diesel, and other motor fuels.
Sales taxes. If you buy supplies or other items for your trade or business and can deduct their cost as a business expense, you can deduct the sales tax on the purchase as part of the business expense. Sales tax on the purchase of property whose cost you cannot deduct as a business expense is added to the property's cost. See *Cost Basis* in Chapter 14, *Basis of Property*.

Example 1. You pay sales tax on a purchase of supplies for your business. You can deduct the cost of the supplies, including the sales tax, as a business expense.

Example 2. You pay sales tax on a purchase of a new car that will be used for business. You must add the sales tax to your basis for figuring depreciation on the car. You cannot deduct the sales tax.

Where to Deduct

You deduct taxes on the following schedules:

State and local income taxes. These taxes are deducted only on Schedule A (Form 1040), even if your only source of income is from business, rents, or royalties.

Foreign income taxes. Generally, income taxes you pay to a foreign country or U.S. possession can be claimed as an itemized deduction on Schedule A (Form 1040), or as a credit against your U.S. income tax on Form 1116. For more information, get Publication 514.

Real estate taxes and personal property taxes. These taxes are deducted on Schedule A (Form 1040), unless they are paid on property used in your business or on property that produces rent or royalty income. See *Business taxes,* next, and *Taxes on property producing rent or royalty income,* later.

Business taxes. Taxes that you must pay in operating your business, or on your property used in your business, are generally deducted on Schedule C or C-EZ (Form 1040) or Schedule F (Form 1040).

Taxes that are employee business expenses. Taxes you paid that are deductible as employee business expenses are generally claimed on Schedule A (Form 1040) as a miscellaneous itemized deduction subject to the 2% of adjusted gross income limit. If you also deduct certain other employee business expenses or if you are reimbursed by your employer, you may also have to file Form 2106. The Form 2106 instructions explain who must file that form.

Self-employment tax. Deduct one-half of your self-employment tax on line 25, Form 1040.

Taxes on property producing rent or royalty income. These taxes generally are deducted on Schedule E (Form 1040).

Other taxes. All other deductible taxes are deducted on Schedule A (Form 1040).

24 | Interest Expense

Introduction

Interest expense is the amount of money you pay for the use of borrowed money. Depending upon the use of the borrowed funds certain types of interest expense may be deducted from your income.

To calculate your deduction, you must first segregate your borrowings into five categories: (1) amounts used for investments generating portfolio income (interest, dividends, etc.), (2) amounts used for investment in passive activities (see Chapter 13, Other Income*), (3) amounts used to purchase or improve a personal residence, (4) amounts used in an active trade or business, and (5) amounts used for personal reasons. However, remember that no portion of your personal interest expense is deductible.*

The interest paid on the other four categories of borrowings are subject to different rules regarding deductibility. This chapter will explain those rules and how to account for the use of your borrowings.

Your 1993 itemized deductions may be subject to certain limitations if your adjusted gross income exceeds $108,450. This general limitation does not apply to investment interest expense, but it does apply to home mortgage interest expense.

Important Change for 1993

Refunds of interest shown on Form 1098. New box 3 on Form 1098, *Mortgage Interest Statement,* will show certain interest refunded to you during the current year that you paid in a prior year. See *Refunds of interest* and *Mortgage Interest Statement,* later.

Important Reminders

Personal interest. Personal interest is not deductible. Examples of personal interest include interest charged on credit cards, car loans, and installment plans.

Points shown on Form 1098. The Form 1098, *Mortgage Interest Statement,* you receive will include the amount of points you paid on most mortgage loans during 1993.

Limit on itemized deductions. Certain itemized deductions (including home mortgage interest) are limited if your adjusted gross income is more than $108,450 ($54,225 if you are married filing a separate return). For more information, see Chapter 21, *Limits on Itemized Deductions*.

Seller-financed mortgage interest. If you paid interest to a seller who financed your mortgage, list on line 9b of Schedule A (Form 1040) the seller's social security number (SSN) or employer identification number in addition to the seller's name and address. You are also required to let that person know your SSN. For more information, see *Where to Deduct,* later.

This chapter contains general information on interest expense. It also discusses:

- Limits on the deduction of home mortgage interest,
- How to treat your mortgages,
- The mortgage interest statement,
- Points, and
- Expenses similar to interest that are not deductible.

Use *Table 24–1,* shown later, to see where to deduct various types of interest. This table also shows which publication contains more information on each type of interest listed.

Useful Items

You may want to see:

Publication

- ☐ **225** Farmer's Tax Guide
- ☐ **334** Tax Guide for Small Business
- ☐ **527** Residential Rental Property
- ☐ **535** Business Expenses
- ☐ **550** Investment Income and Expenses
- ☐ **936** Home Mortgage Interest Deduction

Form (and Instructions)

- ☐ **1098** Mortgage Interest Statement
- ☐ **8396** Mortgage Interest Credit

General Rules

Interest is an amount paid for the use of borrowed money. To be deductible, the interest you pay must reflect the true (economic) cost of the indebtedness for the payment period. This chapter, except where noted, assumes that interest paid is the true cost.

Explanation

Loan payments generally are divided between principal and interest. In the absence of any specific division, partial payments are presumed to apply first to interest and then to principal. However, if a single payment is made in full settlement of an outstanding debt, the payment is first applied to the remaining principal balance and then to interest.

Legally liable. To deduct interest on a debt, you must be legally liable for that debt. You cannot deduct payments you make for someone else if you are not legally liable to make them. Both the lender and the borrower must intend that the loan be repaid. In addition, there must be a true debtor-creditor relationship between the lender and the borrower.

Explanation

Interest paid to a related person is deductible, as long as it is paid for a bona fide debt. For example, parents may deduct interest paid on amounts borrowed from their minor children if the interest is otherwise deductible. If the borrower is not legally liable for the debt, or if there is no intent for the loan to be repaid, it is not a bona fide debt and interest payments are not deductible.

To deduct interest that you pay, the interest must be your liability. When two or more persons are jointly liable for the payment of interest, the person actually making the interest payment is entitled to the entire deduction.

It is not necessary to have a fixed percentage interest rate applied to the money that you have borrowed for the interest to be deducted. What is necessary is that the amount of interest paid can be definitely determined. It is usually based on a written agreement between the lender and the borrower.

Low-interest and interest-free loans, which were once popular between family members, now have severe limitations applied to them. See Chapter 8, *Interest Income*.

Interest paid in advance. If you pay interest for a period that goes beyond the end of the tax year, you must spread this interest paid in advance over the tax years to which it applies. You can deduct in each year only the interest for that year. However, see *Points,* later.

Example 1

When Dan borrowed $10,000 on November 1, 1992, he prepaid 16 months of interest ($1,600). Dan should deduct $200 in 1992, $1,200 in 1993, and $200 in 1994.

Example 2

On March 27 Eric signed a note for $1,200 at 8% interest and agreed to repay it in 12 equal installments, beginning on April 28. The interest of $96 ($1,200 ×

8%) was subtracted from the face value of the note, and Eric received $1,104. If Eric uses the cash method of accounting, as most people do, interest is considered to be repaid in 12 installments of $8 each ($96 ÷ 12). Eric may deduct $72 ($8 × 9 months) for the first year. However, if Eric misses 2 payments during the first year, he could deduct only $56.

Refunds of interest. If you receive a refund of interest in the same tax year you pay it, you must reduce your interest expense by the amount refunded to you. If you receive a refund of interest you deducted in an earlier year, you generally must include the refund in income in the year you receive it. But you only need to include the amount of the deduction that reduced your tax in the earlier year.

If you received a refund of interest you overpaid in an earlier year, you generally will receive a Form 1098, *Mortgage Interest Statement,* showing the refund in box 3. For information about Form 1098, see *Mortgage Interest Statement,* later.

For more information on how to treat refunds of interest deducted in earlier years, see *Recoveries* in Chapter 13, *Other Income*.

Example

During 1993, you paid $2,000 in interest on your adjustable rate mortgage. On December 31, 1993, a $200 interest refund was credited to your account. Your net deduction for interest on your loans is $1,800 ($2,000 paid minus $200 refunded).

If you receive the refund in 1994 and did not itemize your deductions in 1993, the refund is not includable in your 1994 income. If you did itemize your deductions in 1993, the refund is includable in your 1994 income.

Home Mortgage Interest

Generally, home mortgage interest is any interest you pay on a loan secured by your home (main home or a second home). These loans include: a mortgage, a second mortgage, a line of credit, and a home equity loan. If the interest is deductible home mortgage interest, you may deduct it on Schedule A (Form 1040).

Limit on the Deduction of Mortgage Interest

In most cases, you will be able to deduct all of your home mortgage interest. Whether it is all deductible depends on the date you took out the mortgage, the amount of the mortgage, and your use of its proceeds.

If all of your mortgages fit into one or more of the following three categories, you can deduct ALL of the interest on those mortgages. If any one mortgage fits into more than one category, add the parts of the mortgage that fit in each category to your other mortgages in the same category. (If one or more of your mortgages is not described below, get Publication 936 to figure the amount of interest you can deduct.)

Explanation

To be fully deductible as home mortgage interest, the interest must be on a debt that is secured by property that is your qualified residence. Your qualified residence is property that is owned by you and used as a principal residence. A principal residence includes, among other things, a house, a cooperative apartment, a condominium, a house trailer, or a houseboat. If your principal residence is a houseboat, it must include basic living accommodations, including sleeping space, a toilet, and cooking facilities.

TaxPlanner

You may treat a home currently under construction as a qualified home for a period of up to 24 months if it becomes a qualifying residence as of the time that it is ready for occupancy. The 24-month period may start on or after the date construction begins.

- Mortgages you took out on or before October 13, 1987 (called grandfathered debt).

Explanation

All mortgage indebtedness existing on October 13, 1987 (grandfathered debt), is treated as acquisition indebtedness, regardless of the amount. The interest on this indebtedness is fully deductible.

Individuals who refinanced and increased their mortgage indebtedness before October 14, 1987, may have greater interest deductions than those individuals who waited until later, because new or refinanced indebtedness is limited in amount, as explained in this chapter.

- Mortgages you took out after October 13, 1987, to buy, build, or improve your home (called home acquisition debt), but only if these mortgages plus any grandfathered debt totaled $1 million or less throughout 1993.

Explanation

This limitation applies only to loans incurred to purchase, construct, or improve a home.

TaxPlanner

When you are purchasing or constructing a home, consider your future financial needs carefully. The original loan can never be refinanced to increase the amount available for this limitation.

If you believe that you will need money for personal uses in the near future, you may want to increase the original mortgage at the time of acquisition or improvement to meet those future needs. Otherwise, if you take out a home equity loan, only the interest on up to $100,000 on the loan is deductible.

- Mortgages you took out after October 13, 1987, other than to buy, build, or improve your home (called home equity debt), but only if these mortgages totaled $100,000 or less throughout 1993.

TaxSaver

Many taxpayers are pursuing home equity loans as a means of paying off their credit card balances, automobile loans, and other types of consumer expenditures. There are two major benefits of home equity borrowing:

1. Interest on home equity loans (up to $100,000) is tax-deductible, whereas personal interest is not.
2. Home equity loans are less expensive than other types of credit. For example, a representative interest rate for home equity loans may be as low as 7%. In comparison, the average interest rates for credit cards, unsecured personal loans, and new automobile loans can be as high as 12% to 18%.

Although home equity loans present several benefits, you should remember that, if you are unable to pay off the loan, your house is in jeopardy—not the item(s) that you purchased with the borrowed funds.

If you are married and file a separate return, the home acquisition debt limit is $500,000 and the home equity debt limit is $50,000.

If the total amount of all mortgages exceeds the fair market value of the home, additional limits may apply. For more information, get Publication 936.

Explanation

According to the IRS, the fair market value of your home, which is real property, cannot be less than the adjusted purchase price at the last day of the taxable year. This does not apply to homes that are personal property, such as boats or motor homes.

Example

John Joyce purchases a home in August, 1993 for $75,000. He makes improvements costing $10,000 to the home during 1993, but these improvements add only $5,000 to the value of the home.

Although the value of the home at the end of 1993 is only $80,000, John is allowed to use $85,000, the cost of the home plus improvements, as the fair market value.

Note. You cannot deduct this interest if you use the proceeds of the mortgage to purchase securities or certificates that produce tax-free income.

TaxSaver

If part of your mortgage is in excess of the qualified mortgage limitation and you have investments that produce taxable income, you could sell some of your investments and use the proceeds to reduce your mortgage principal in order to meet the qualified mortgage limitation. You could then reborrow the funds and trace them to the purchase of new investments. Interest expense on the newly invested loan proceeds remains fully deductible, subject to the investment income limitations dis-

Figure 24-A. Is My Interest Fully Deductible?

(Instructions: Include balances of ALL mortgages secured by your main home and second home. Answer YES only if the answer is true at ALL times during 1993).

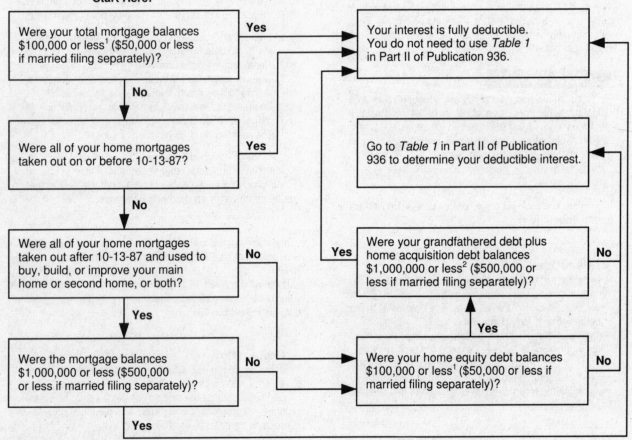

[1] If all mortgages on your first or second home exceed the home's fair market value, a lower limit may apply. See *Fair market value limit* in Publication 936.

[2] Amounts over the $1,000,000 limit ($500,000 if married filing separately) qualify as home equity debt if they are not more than the total home equity debt limit. See Publication 936 for more information about grandfathered debt, home acquisition debt, and home equity debt.

cussed earlier in this chapter. Remember to consider transaction costs of switching investments and the "wash sale" rule discussed in Chapter 15, *Sale of Property*. For additional information, consult your tax advisor.

You can use *Figure 24–A* to check whether your interest is fully deductible.

Determining Mortgages

This section further discusses how to treat your mortgages. Remember that grandfathered mortgages were taken out on or before October 13, 1987, and that home acquisition and home equity mortgages were taken out after October 13, 1987.

Refinanced grandfathered debt. If you refinance grandfathered debt after October 13, 1987, for an amount that is not more than the mortgage principal left on the debt, then you still treat it as grandfathered debt. However, any amount that is more than that mortgage principal is treated as home acquisition or home equity

debt, and the mortgage is a mixed-use mortgage (discussed later). The debt must be secured by the qualified home.

You treat grandfathered debt that was refinanced after October 13, 1987, as grandfathered debt only for the term left on the debt being refinanced. After that, you treat it as home acquisition debt or home equity debt, depending on how you used the proceeds.

Exception. If the principal on the debt being refinanced is not amortized over its term, like a balloon note, then you treat the refinanced debt as grandfathered debt for the term of the first refinancing. This term cannot be more than 30 years.

Explanation

The principal amount of indebtedness incurred when you are refinancing an existing mortgage debt that exceeds the amount owed on the original mortgage debt does not qualify as grandfathered debt. The excess may be treated as home acquisition or home equity indebtedness, but the total qualifying indebtedness cannot exceed the fair market value of the residence. Any refinancing may not extend the term of the preexisting grandfathered debt.

Example
An original mortgage note incurred to purchase a qualified residence had been reduced to $100,000 on June 1, 1993, when the value of the residence was $175,-000. If this mortgage is refinanced, $100,000 of the new mortgage note is treated as grandfathered debt. Up to $75,000 may be treated as home acquisition or home equity indebtedness. If the indebtedness exceeds $175,000, the value of the residence, the excess must be allocated in accordance with the use of the excess amount. Moreover, interest paid on the refinanced mortgage will only be deducted over the number of years remaining on the original mortgage note.

Example. Chester acquired a $200,000 first mortgage on his home in 1985. The mortgage was a five year balloon note and the entire balance on the note was due in 1990. Chester refinanced the debt in 1990 with a new twenty year mortgage. The refinanced debt is treated as grandfathered debt for its entire term (20 years).

Line-of-credit mortgage. If you had a line-of-credit mortgage on October 13, 1987, and borrowed additional amounts against it after that date, then the additional amounts are either home acquisition debt or home equity debt depending on how you used the proceeds. This is also considered a mixed-use mortgage. The balance on the mortgage before you borrowed the additional amounts is grandfathered debt. The newly borrowed amounts are not grandfathered debt because the funds were borrowed after October 13, 1987.

Mixed-use mortgages. If you took out a mortgage after October 13, 1987, and parts of the mortgage are within more than one of the three categories of debt (i.e. home equity debt, grandfathered debt, home acquisition debt), it is a mixed-use mortgage. If the mixed-use mortgage added to your other home mortgages exceed the loan limits discussed earlier under, *Limit on the Deduction of Mortgage Interest,* be sure to get Publication 936.

More than one home. If you had a main home and a second home, the home acquisition and home equity debt dollar limits explained above apply to the total mortgages on both homes. Your main home is the property you live in most of the time. It may be a house, condominium, cooperative, mobile home, boat, or similar property. It must provide basic living accommodations including sleeping space, toilet facilities, and cooking facilities. Your second home is similar property that you select to be your second home.

Explanation
A qualified residence may also be your second home. A second home may be one that you do not occupy, a home that you occupy part of the year, or a home that you rent out. If the home is rented out, it is subject to the use requirements relating to vacation homes. It qualifies as your home only if you used it more than the greater of

1. 14 days, or
2. 10% of the number of days during 1993 that it was rented at a fair rental.

If your home is not rented at any time during the year, it is considered a qualified home, even if it is not used by you. For this purpose, the IRS states that "rented" includes holding the home for rental or for resale.

Example
Mary owns a vacation home in Northern Michigan. Because of business pressures, she is unable to use the home in 1993 or 1994, and lists the home for sale on November 1, 1994.

The house qualifies as a residence in 1993, but in 1994, as Mary did not use it for more than 6 days (10% × 61 days), it is not considered her residence. Since her personal use did not exceed 10% of the number of days the property was held for sale, the home is considered a rental property and not a vacation home.

TaxPlanner 1
If, in the above example, members of Mary's family use the home for a week (7 days) in 1994, she will be considered to have used it for the same period of time and the home will be considered her residence. Members of Mary's family include her brothers or sisters, husband, children and grandchildren, and parents or grandparents.

TaxPlanner 2
If you own more than two homes, you may not deduct interest on more than two of these homes during any one year as home mortgage interest.

You must include your main residence as one of the homes. You may choose any one of your other homes as a qualified residence and may change this choice for each tax year.

However, you cannot choose to treat one home as a second residence for part of a year and another home as a second residence for the remainder of the year if both of these homes were owned by you during the entire year and neither home was your main residence during that year.

Mortgage Interest Statement

If you paid mortgage interest of $600 or more during the year on any one mortgage, you generally will receive a Form 1098, *Mortgage Interest Statement,* or a similar statement. You will receive the statement if you pay interest to a person (including a financial institution or a cooperative housing corporation) in the course of that person's trade or business. A governmental unit is a person for purposes of furnishing the statement.

TaxOrganizer
When you receive Form 1098, keep it with your other important tax documents.

Explanation
An individual who "takes back" a mortgage indebtedness when selling a residence is not required to prepare a Form 1098 or otherwise notify the debtor of the

amount of interest paid. He or she must include the interest income on his or her tax return as seller-financed mortgage interest income and report the payer's name and amount received.

The statement will show the total interest you paid during the year. If you purchase a main home during 1993, it will also show the deductible points you paid during the year. However, it should not show seller payments on a "buy-down" mortgage, or HUD payments under section 235 of the National Housing Act.

If you received a refund of interest you overpaid in an earlier year, you generally will receive a Form 1098 showing the refund in box 3. See *Refunds of interest* , earlier.

Note. Form 1098 will not include points paid for:

1) Home improvement loans on your main home,
2) Purchase or home improvement loans on your second home, vacation property, investment property, or trade or business property,
3) Refinancing, home equity loans, and lines of credit secured by your main home, and
4) Amounts in excess of the points generally charged in your area.

However, certain points not included on Form 1098 may be deductible. See *Points,* later, for more information.

You should receive the statement by January 31, 1994. The mortgage interest information will also be sent to the IRS. If the mortgage interest is fully deductible home mortgage interest, deduct the interest and the points reported to you on Form 1098 on Schedule A (Form 1040).

If you prepaid interest in 1993 that accrued in full by January 15, 1994, this prepaid interest may be included in box 1 of Form 1098. However, even though the prepaid amount may be included in box 1, you cannot deduct the prepaid amount in 1993. You will have to figure the interest that accrued for 1994 and subtract it from the amount in box 1. You will include the interest for 1994 with the interest you pay for 1994. See *Where to Deduct,* later.

If the mortgage interest is not fully deductible home mortgage interest because you used the proceeds of the loan for other purposes, then you may be able to deduct it as investment, business, or passive activity interest, subject to the rules for those deductions.

If your home mortgage interest payments are more than the amount shown on the mortgage interest statement, you can deduct the amount of the interest that you *actually paid.* (However, you must meet the limits discussed earlier.) The interest must be for the tax year you are claiming the deduction.

For example, your mortgage payments are due on the first of the month. Therefore, if you make a January 1 mortgage payment in December of the year before, the interest on the January payment is for December (of the year before) and is deductible in the year paid. You must attach a statement to your tax return explaining this difference.

You can deduct only your share of the mortgage interest you paid. If your mortgage payments were subsidized by a government agency, do not deduct the amount paid for you.

If you and at least one other person (other than your spouse if you file a joint return) were liable for, and paid, interest on a mortgage that was for your home and the other person received a

Form 1098 showing the interest that was paid during 1993, attach a statement to your return explaining this, the interest allocation, and showing the name and address of the person who received the form. In the far left margin, next to line 9b, Schedule A, write "see attached."

If you are the payer of record on a mortgage on which there are other borrowers entitled to a deduction for the interest shown on the Form 1098 you received, you must furnish the other borrowers with information about the proper distribution of the amounts shown on the form you received.

Points

The term "points" is used to describe certain charges paid by a borrower to obtain a home mortgage figured as a percentage of the amount borrowed. They are also called loan origination fees, maximum loan charges, or premium charges. If the payment of any of these charges by a borrower is *only* for the use of money, it is interest.

Explanation

Points that relate to property that is not your principal residence (e.g., second home, investment property, or trade or business property) are not eligible for an immediate deduction.

Usually, for federally regulated mortgage loans, points will be designated on the Uniform Settlement Statement (also known as Form HUD-1) as "loan origination fee," "loan discount," "discount points," or simply "points."

These points are interest paid in advance and you cannot deduct the full amount for points in the year paid. The interest paid as points must be spread over the life (term) of the mortgage. An equal portion is then deducted in each year of the mortgage. See Publication 936.

Explanation

Generally, taxpayers are prohibited from deducting prepaid interest in the year of payment. Rather, they must capitalize the prepaid interest and deduct it ratably over the term of the loan.

However, an exception exists for taxpayers who buy, build, or improve their principal residences and pay "points" in order to obtain a lower interest rate on their loans. The term "points" is a fee paid by the borrower that is like prepaid interest. To be deductible, the charge must represent interest paid for the use of money and must be *paid before* the time for which it represents a charge for the use of the money. Furthermore, the home must be the taxpayer's principal residence.

TaxSaver

To be immediatedly deductible, points paid on home improvement loans must be paid from separate funds at closing—that is they cannot be included in the borrowed amount.

Special rules. You can deduct the amount you pay as points in 1993 if the loan is used to *buy or improve your main home*

and is secured by that home. In addition, all of the following must be satisfied:

1) The payment of points must be an established business practice in the area where the loan was made,
2) The points paid must not exceed the number of points generally charged in this area,
3) The points must be computed as a percentage of the principal amount of the mortgage, and
4) If the loan was used to:
   a) *Improve your main home,* the points must be paid with funds other than those obtained from your lender, or
   b) *Buy your main home,* you must have provided funds at the time of closing other than those obtained from your lender or mortgage broker at least equal to the points charged. For this purpose, funds you provide do not have to be applied as payment of points at closing. They may be applied as down payments, escrow deposits, earnest money applied at the closing, and other funds actually paid over at closing.

Note. The rule above also applies to a loan origination fee charged for services for getting a VA or FHA loan to *buy your main home.*

You can use *Figure 24–B* as a quick check to see if the points you paid in 1993 are fully deductible this year.

You should receive a Form 1098, *Mortgage Interest Statement,* or a similar statement from your lender or mortgage broker by January 31, 1994. It will show not only the interest you paid, but also the deductible points you paid in 1993 to get a loan to buy your main home.

Excess points. If you paid more points than generally paid in this area, your deduction is limited to the points generally charged. Any additional amount of points you paid is interest paid in advance and the deduction must be spread over the life of the mortgage.

Second home. The special rules do not apply to points you pay on loans secured by your second home. You can only deduct these points over the life of the loan.

Mortgage ending early. If you spread points over the life of the mortgage, you can deduct any remaining balance in the year the mortgage ends. A mortgage may end early due to a prepayment, refinancing, foreclosure, or similar event.

Example. Dan refinanced his mortgage in 1989 and paid $3,000 in points that were required to be spread out over the life of the mortgage. He had deducted $800 of these points through 1992.

Dan prepaid his mortgage in full in 1993. He can deduct the remaining $2,200 of points in 1993.

Refinancing. Generally, points you pay to refinance a mortgage are not deductible in full in the year you pay them. This is true even if the new mortgage is secured by your main home. However, if you use part of the refinanced mortgage proceeds to *improve your main home* and you pay the points *out of your private funds* (rather than out of the proceeds of the new loan), you can fully deduct the part of the points related to the improvement in the year paid. You can deduct the remainder of the points over the life of the loan.

TAXPLANNER

Before you refinance your home mortgage, you should consider both tax and financial factors.

For the interest to remain fully deductible, the following tax-related factors should be considered:

- The term of the mortgage should not be extended beyond the original term.

- The total of all mortgage balances should not exceed the lesser of the fair market value of the house or $1 million. However, see previous discussion of *Refinanced Grandfather Debt* if you have a pre-October 13, 1987 mortgage. Other limitations may also apply. See *Limit on the Deduction of Mortgage Interest*, discussed previously in this chapter.

The financial factors you may also want to consider include the following:

- As a rule of thumb, if you intend to keep your home for another 4 to 6 years, and the difference between your current mortgage rate and the new mortgage rate is 2% or more, then refinancing may be worthwhile.

- Since there are refinancing costs, you should determine how many months it would take to recoup these costs. To do so, divide the total amount of estimated refinancing costs (deductible and nondedutible) by the anticipated reduction in your monthly mortgage payment (i.e., the difference between your existing monthly payment of principal and interest and the new monthly payment). If you will recover your refinancing costs before you sell your home, then refinancing may be a smart thing to do.

- You should evaluate whether the current value of the after-tax savings from a lower interest rate exceeds the up-front cost of refinancing. Specifically, consider such factors as taxes, present value, and opportunity costs (lost income on funds used to pay refinancing charges). There is software available that can assist your decision to refinance. Alternatively, you may consult your tax advisor.

For more information on refinancing, see Publication 936.

Explanation

According to the IRS, points paid when you are refinancing an existing mortgage must be written off over the life of the new loan. They are not fully deductible in the year in which they were paid, because they were not paid in connection with the improvement or purchase of a home, even though the original loan met the requirements for deductibility.

However, an Eighth Circuit Court decision allowed a full immediate deduction for points paid by taxpayers in obtaining a permanent mortgage on their home, the proceeds of which were used to pay off a short-term, 3-year mortgage with a balloon payment and a recently obtained home improvement loan secured by a second mortgage. The court indicated that the permanent mortgage obtained was sufficiently "in connection with" the original purchase of the home.

Figure 24-B. Are My Points Fully Deductible This Year?

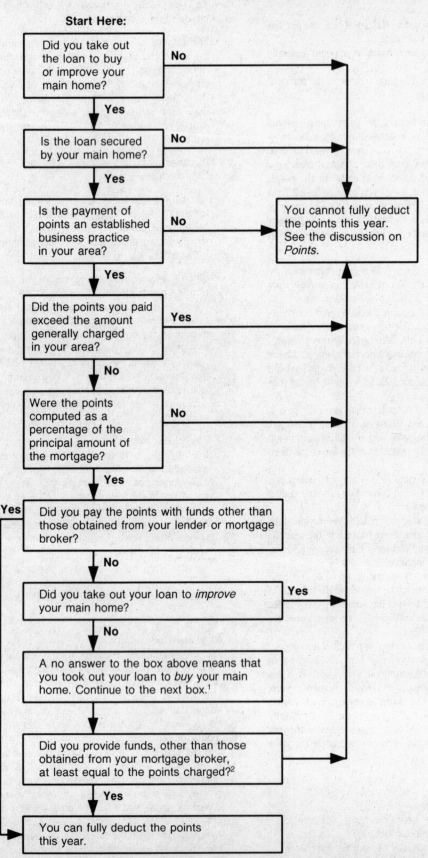

[1]If you have reached this box and satisfy the requirement in the next box, then a loan origination fee charged for services of getting a VA or FHA loan to *buy your main home* is deductible.

[2]The funds you provide do not have to be applied as payment of points at closing. They may be applied as down payments, escrow deposits, earnest money applied at the closing, and funds actually paid at closing.

Points charged for specific services by the lender for the borrower's account are not interest. Examples of fees for services not considered interest are the lender's appraisal fee, preparation costs for the mortgage note or deed of trust, settlement fees, and notary fees.

Expenses that you pay at settlement or closing in connection with buying your home, such as commissions, abstract fees, and recording fees, are capital expenses. You cannot deduct these expenses either as interest or as current business expenses. Add these to the basis of the property.

There are certain settlement fees or closing costs that you cannot deduct or add to the basis of your property. These include:

1) Fire insurance premiums.
2) FHA mortgage insurance premiums.
3) Charges for utilities or other services related to occupancy of the house before closing.
4) Rent for occupancy before closing.
5) The cost of repairs.
6) Any item that you deduct as a moving expense.

Points paid by a seller. The term "points" also is used to describe loan placement fees that the seller may have to pay to the lender to arrange financing for the buyer. The seller ***cannot*** deduct these amounts as interest. But these charges are a selling expense that reduce the amount realized. See Chapter 16 for information on selling your home.

Special Rules

This section contains other information you may need to know about home mortgage interest.

Sale of home. If you sell your home, you can deduct your allowable home mortgage interest paid up to, but not including, the date of sale.

Example. John and Peggy Harris bought a new home on May 4. They sold their old home on May 7. During the year they made home mortgage interest payments of $122 on the old home and $2,864 on the new home. The settlement sheet for the sale of the old home showed $5 interest for the 6–day period in May up to, but not including, the date of sale. Their mortgage interest paid for the year is $2,991 ($122 + $2,864 + $5).

Late payment charge on mortgage payment. You can deduct as home mortgage interest a late payment charge if it was not for a specific service performed by your mortgage holder.

Mortgage interest credit. You may be able to claim a mortgage interest credit if you were issued a qualified mortgage credit certificate that provides financing for the acquisition, qualified rehabilitation, or qualified home improvement of your main home. This credit is figured on Form 8396, *Mortgage Interest Credit*. If you take this credit, you must reduce your mortgage interest deduction by the amount of the credit.

Generally, to figure your credit, multiply the amount of interest paid during the year on the loan amount covered by the certificate by the credit rate (10% to 50%) shown on your certificate. If the credit rate is more than 20%, your credit is limited to $2,000. For information on how to figure the credit, see Chapter 35, *Other Credits*.

Example. The mortgage interest paid on the loan amount shown on your mortgage credit certificate is $3,900. Your certificate credit rate is 30% (.30). You reduce your mortgage interest by $1,170 ($3,900 × .30), your allowable credit, and deduct $2,730 ($3,900 − $1,170) as mortgage interest on line 9a, Schedule A (Form 1040).

Ministers' and military housing allowance. If you are a minister or member of the uniformed services and receive a housing allowance that you can exclude from income, you can still deduct all of the deductible interest on your home mortgage.

Graduated payment mortgages (GPM). GPMs under section 245 of the National Housing Act provide that monthly payments increase every year for a number of years and then stay the same. During the early years, payments are less than the amount of interest owed on the loan. The interest that is not paid becomes part of the principal. Future interest is figured on the increased unpaid mortgage loan balance.

Subject to the applicable limits, you can deduct the interest you actually paid during the year if you are a cash method taxpayer. For example, if the interest owed is $2,551 but your payment for the year is $2,517, you can deduct $2,517. Add $34 to the loan principal.

Mortgage assistance payments. If you qualify for mortgage assistance payments under section 235 of the National Housing Act, part or all of the interest on your mortgage may be paid for you. You cannot deduct any interest that is paid for you. You do not include these payments in your income. These payments do not reduce other deductions, such as taxes.

Redeemable ground rents. If you make annual or periodic rental payments on a redeemable ground rent, you can deduct them as mortgage interest.

Payments made to terminate the lease and to buy the lessor's entire interest in the land are not ground rents. You cannot deduct them. For more information, see Publication 936.

Nonredeemable ground rent. Payments on a nonredeemable ground rent are not interest. You can deduct them as rent if they are a business expense or if they are for rental property held to produce income.

Rental payments. If you live in a house before your final settlement, any payments you make for that period are rent, not interest, even if the settlement papers call them interest. You cannot deduct these payments.

Reverse mortgage loans. A reverse mortgage loan is a loan that is based on the value of your home and is secured by a mortgage on your home. The lending institution pays you the proceeds of the loan in installments over a period of months or years. The loan agreement may provide that interest will be added to the outstanding loan balance monthly as it accrues. If you are a cash method taxpayer, you deduct the interest on a reverse mortgage loan when you actually pay it, not when it is added to the outstanding loan balance.

Mortgage prepayment penalty. If you pay off your qualified home mortgage early, you may have to pay a penalty. You can include that penalty as home mortgage interest. If the proceeds of the loan were used for business or investment purposes, you may be able to deduct it under the rules for those expenses.

Explanation
Shared appreciation mortgages (SAMs). This is one of a number of different financing vehicles that have been developed to help overcome high interest rates.

A typical SAM carries a fixed interest rate below the prevailing rate for conventional home mortgages, but it gives the lender contingent interest in the form of a share of any appreciation in value of the underlying property. On sale of the property or prepayment, you may deduct the contingent interest paid to the lender as interest. If, however, you refinance with a new conventional mortgage that covers the original SAM plus the contingent interest, the contingent interest is not deductible at that time. The deduction is taken as the new mortgage is repaid.

Items You Cannot Deduct

Some interest payments are not deductible. Certain expenses similar to interest also are not deductible. These items include:

* Personal interest
* "Points" if you are a seller
* Nonredeemable ground rent
* Service charges (however, see *List of Other Expenses* in Chapter 30)
* Annual fees for credit cards
* Loan fees
* Credit investigation fees
* Interest relating to tax-exempt income
* Interest to purchase or carry tax-exempt securities
* Interest to purchase or carry certain straddle positions
* Premium on a convertible bond

Explanation
Interest related to the construction of real property (other than home mortgage interest) and certain long-lived personal property is not currently deductible but must be capitalized as part of the cost of the property.

Interest on all indebtedness that was specifically in-

curred for construction must first be capitalized. In addition, if the construction costs exceed that debt, the interest on other indebtedness must be capitalized to the extent that the other indebtedness could have been reduced by the amount of the excess construction costs.

Example
John Hall incurs a $100,000 loan to construct an apartment building. The total cost of the building is $135,000. He owns another apartment building on which there is a mortgage of $125,000.

Interest attributable to the construction period on both the $100,000 loan and $35,000 of the mortgage loan must be capitalized as part of the cost of the new building.

Interest to purchase or carry tax-exempt securities. You cannot deduct interest on money you borrow to buy tax-exempt securities. See Publication 550.

Explanation
While the general rule is that interest paid on a debt incurred to purchase or carry tax-exempt obligations is not deductible, this does not mean that, if you hold tax-exempt obligations, all interest expense deductions are disallowed. The courts have consistently held that there must be a sufficiently direct relationship between the incurring of the debt and the carrying of the tax-exempt obligation before the interest is disallowed. However, if you have significant interest expense and municipal bond income, you may lose your interest deductions.

The IRS has ruled that a direct relationship between debt and the purchase of tax-exempt obligations exists when the debt proceeds are used for, and are directly traceable to, the purchase of tax-exempts. A direct relationship between debt and the carrying of tax-exempt obligations exists when tax-exempts are used as collateral for a loan.

If only part of a debt you have is traceable to the holding of tax-exempt obligations, only that part of the interest paid is not allowed.

Example
The Simpsons borrow $10,000 from a bank and invest $2,500 of the proceeds in tax-exempt obligations. Only 25% ($2,500 ÷ $10,000) of the interest they pay on the loan is not deductible as investment interest.

TaxPlanner
Don't worry about whether or not you use debt to acquire or carry tax-exempt obligations if your investment in tax-exempts is "insubstantial." The IRS defines "insubstantial" as being less than 2% of the average **adjusted basis** of your portfolio investments and business assets.

Amortization of bond premium. There are various ways to treat the premium you pay to buy taxable bonds. See *Bond Premium Amortization* in Publication 550.

TaxSaver

You may deduct amortizable bond premiums directly from interest income. This could be beneficial whether or not you itemize your deductions.

Explanation

Tax-exempt bonds. You must amortize the premium and reduce the basis of tax-exempt bonds. However, you may not deduct the amortized premium. See Publication 535, *Business Expenses.*

Market discounts. You may be able to deduct only some of the interest expense incurred to acquire or carry marketable bonds with market discounts. For debt obligations issued after July 18, 1984, the interest expense deduction will be limited to the sum of:

1. Interest income from marketable bonds
2. The interest expense in excess of interest income in (1) and accrued market discount

The disallowed interest expense is deferred until the bond is sold or matures and is deducted then. The interest limitation does not apply to tax-exempt obligations, U.S. Savings Bonds, obligations with a maturity of 1 year or less, and certain installment obligations.

Example

Sam acquires a $100,000, 9% interest-bearing bond for $90,000 on January 2, 1993. The bond was originally issued at face value in 1989. It matures in 2003, 10 years after Sam purchased it. Sam borrowed money to acquire the bond. In 1993, Sam paid $10,200 in interest on the debt. The allowable interest deduction for the year is figured as follows:

(a)	Interest expense	$10,200
(b)	Interest income ($100,000 × 9%)	(9,000)
(c)	Net interest expense	1,200
(d)	Accrued market discount ($10,000 ÷ 10 yrs.)	(1,000)
(e)	Net interest expense allowable as a deduction	$ 200

Total allowable interest expense is $9,200 [(b) + (e)]. The remaining $1,000 will be allowed as a deduction in the year in which the bond matures or is sold.

Sam may elect to include the accrued market discount in income for the tax years to which it's attributable, thus allowing all interest expense to be deductible. If Sam makes this election, it will apply to all market discount bonds he aquires.

See the discussion earlier in this chapter regarding limitations on the deduction of investment interest.

TaxAlert

For bonds purchased after April 30, 1993, the 1993 Tax Law extends the market discount rules to market discount bonds issued on or before July 18, 1984. The law also extends the rules to tax-exempt obligations requiring that a gain on the sale or other disposition of a market discount bond be treated as ordinary income. Thus, a gain on the disposition of such bonds will be treated as ordinary income to the extent of accrued market discount.

Explanation

Short-term obligations. The rules for short-term obligations, such as Treasury bills, are similar to those for marketable bonds. You may be able to deduct only some of the interest expense incurred to acquire or to carry such obligations. The interest deduction for an amount equal to the daily accrual of the obligation's discount income will be deferred until the short-term obligation is redeemed or sold. If you elect to include the accrued discount in income, you can fully deduct the interest instead of deferring the interest deduction.

Straddles. Generally, you may not deduct interest and carrying charges to purchase or carry a straddle position in personal property, unless the straddle is a hedging transaction. The interest and carrying charges are added to the basis of the straddle property. The amount of interest and carrying charges required to be capitalized may be reduced by income recognized from the straddle property for positions established after July 18, 1984. However, the rules for short sale expenses, deferral of interest deductions with respect to market discount bonds, and deferral of interest deductions with respect to short-term obligations must be applied first. For information, see *Straddles* in Publication 550, *Investment Income and Expenses.*

Penalties. You cannot deduct fines and penalties for violations of law, regardless of their nature.

TaxPlanner 1

To get an interest deduction when you use borrowed funds to pay interest, you need to be careful in structuring the transaction. Generally, the IRS says that meeting an interest obligation by giving a new note or increasing the amount due on an old note does *not* constitute payment. A deduction would be allowed only when the renewed note is paid. If, however, you borrow the money to pay the interest from a *different creditor,* the interest deduction would be allowed.

Nevertheless, the Tax Court allowed an interest deduction when the purpose of the second loan was not limited to the payment of interest on the first loan and the taxpayer showed that he could have paid the interest with other funds. You can't be too cautious in this area. Borrow from a second lender whenever possible.

TaxPlanner 2

Stockbrokers charge you interest on a margin account—an account in which you place the money you have borrowed from your broker to purchase stocks or bonds. For the interest to be deductible, there must be a subsequent payment to your broker in cash. Alternatively, you may specifically allocate proceeds from **dividends,** interest, or stock sales to cover the interest. Merely charging the account does not constitute payment.

Personal Interest

Personal interest is not deductible. Personal interest is any interest that is not home mortgage interest, investment interest, or business interest.

TAXPLANNER

When you are faced with the necessity of purchasing both a house and a large-ticket consumer item (e.g., a car), you should consider the tax nature of the debt, particularly the value of the deductible interest on acquisition debt compared to loans that are repaid with nondeductible interest. Your future plans to purchase consumer items should play an important role in your mortgage and other financing decisions. In addition, if you plan ahead, you can avoid the additional costs of refinancing your mortgage or taking out a home equity loan in order to make your consumer purchase.

Example 1

Suppose you plan to finance the purchase of a car next year. If you take out a longer-term mortgage with lower payments than you might otherwise have done, you can apply the difference to your car payments. This will enable you to reduce the term of your car loan, which most likely will be financed at a higher rate than your mortgage and paid for with nondeductible interest.

Example 2

You are considering purchasing a new house and a new car within a relatively short time period. You may want to decrease your down payment on the house so that there will be extra cash available for a down payment on the car. By paying a larger down payment on the car, your nondeductible interest will be less. Conversely, by decreasing your down payment on the house, you gain a tax benefit in the form of higher mortgage interest deductions.

Personal interest includes such items as:

- Interest on car loans,
- Interest on income tax,
- Installment plan interest,
- Credit card finance charges,
- Retail installment contract finance charges,
- Revolving charge account finance charges,
- Late payment charge by a public utility, and
- Interest on certain gift and demand loans (see Chapter 1 of Publication 550).

Explanation

Interest you pay on student loans or loans acquired to purchase life insurance is also personal interest and is not deductible.

TAXPLANNER

If you have loans outstanding for personal purposes, consider paying off these loans and substituting a different form of indebtedness.

Example

You have a $5,000 indebtedness on your credit card account. The funds were used for various personal purposes, and the interest is not deductible. You also have a $5,000 certificate of deposit (CD) that matures in 1993. Use the $5,000 from the maturity of the CD to pay off the credit card indebtedness. If you wish, you may borrow new funds for investment in a new CD. The interest on the new borrowings will be investment interest. The rules for deducting investment interest expense are more lenient than those for personal interest. Be sure to calculate the amount you would earn after taxes on such a borrowing/investment.

Allocation of Interest

If the proceeds of a loan are applied to mixed uses, an allocation must generally be made to determine the amount of interest for each category. However, you do not have to allocate the home mortgage interest if it is fully deductible regardless of how the funds are used.

You allocate interest (other than fully deductible home mortgage interest) on a loan in the same way as the loan itself is allocated. You do this by tracing disbursements of the debt to specific uses. For details on how to do this, see Chapter 8 of Publication 535.

Explanation

There are five types of interest expense, each of which has different limitations on deductibility:

- Personal interest is not deductible. Examples of personal interest include interest on credit card debts and typical automobile loans. If you have to incur debt, try to make the debt related to either trade or business interest, investment interest, passive activity interest, or qualified residence interest.
- Trade or business interest is fully deductible. Generally, it is interest on debt that relates to your trade or business. However, trade or business interest is *not* deductible if it is in connection with the trade or business of performing services as an employee.
- Investment interest deductions may be limited, because the deduction cannot exceed your net investment income for the taxable year. Any excess investment interest that is not deductible in the taxable year may be deducted in following years.
- Passive activity interest is interest that is used to offset passive activity income. Generally, a passive activity is any interest in real estate or an activity in which you do not materially participate. For tax purposes, you are considered a "material participant" if you are involved in the operations of the activity on a regular, continuous, and substantial basis. For additional discussion, see Chapter 13, *Other Income.*
- Qualified residence interest is interest paid on a debt secured by a first or second mortgage on your home. The debt may have been incurred for any of

the following purposes: personal, investment, or passive activity.

TaxSaver 1

When interest on debt used for investment exceeds investment income, the remaining investment interest may be deducted if it is qualified residence interest.

Example

In 1993, you purchase stock for $200,000, using an 8.5% home equity loan. Your investment income is $5,000.

Interest on your home equity loan	$17,000
Interest on portion of loan up to $100,000	8,500
Balance investment interest expense	8,500
Deductible investment interest equal to investment income	5,000
Investment interest expense carryover to 1994	3,500

TaxSaver 2

Regardless of the rules pertaining to passive income limitations, interest on debt used for a passive activity may be deducted if it is qualified residence interest.

Example 1

Phil borrowed money to purchase a one-fourth interest in a partnership that manages an apartment building. In 1993, Phil paid $16,000 interest on the loan. His share of income and expenses was $60,000 and $40,000, respectively. Phil's passive income is $4,000 ($60,000 − $40,000 − $16,000). If his share of the partnership's expenses had been $50,000 instead of $40,000, Phil's $16,000 in interest expense would have resulted in a passive loss of $6,000 ($60,000 − $50,000 − $16,000). This loss can be carried over to future years in which there is additional passive income.

Example 2

Karen Moore has the following income and expenses in 1993:

Wages	$80,000
Dividends	10,000
Short-term capital gain from sale of stock	2,000
Long-term capital gain taxed at 28%	1,000
Interest	8,000
Investment interest expense	21,000
Investment fees	2,500
Unreimbursed employee expenses	1,000

Karen's total itemized deductions are $3,500 ($2,500 + $1,000). After considering the 2% floor limitation, her allowable deductions are $1,500 [$3,500 − (2% × $100,000 AGI)]. Therefore, Karen's net investment income is $18,500 [($10,000 + $2,000 + $8,000) − $1,500]. Note that, in computing the allowable deductions, the noninvestment expenses were disallowed *before* the investment expenses. A completed Form 4952 appears below.

Explanation

The proceeds of loans, other than qualified mortgage loans, which were used for mixed purposes, must be allocated to each applicable category.

Example

Joan borrows $100,000 on September 1, 1993, at an interest rate of 12% and deposits the funds in one checking account. Joan uses the money to purchase investment securities ($30,000 on September 1), a personal automobile ($30,000 on October 1), and equipment for her business ($40,000 on November 1). Joan pays interest of $1,000 at the end of each month.

Under the allocation rules, the interest on the loan is considered investment interest unless the proceeds are traceable to other purposes. The allocation is made as follows:

	Investment interest		Personal interest		Business interest	
September	100%	$1,000	—		—	
October	70%	700	30%	$300	—	
November	30%	300	30%	300	40%	$400
December	30%	300	30%	300	40%	400
Total		$2,300		$900		$800

When repayments of the debt are made, the repayment amounts are allocated first to nondeductible personal expenditures, then to investment and passive activity expenditures, and then to business expenditures.

TaxOrganizer

The accounting for interest expense on loans used for mixed purposes is extremely complex.

To simplify your tax records, establish separate loan and bank accounts for each category of expenditure.

TaxSaver

Interest on a qualified mortgage loan is not required to be allocated and is fully deductible when paid.

Although borrowing against your residence may ensure deductibility of the interest expense, the residence serves as collateral on the loan and may be foreclosed in the event of default.

Where to Deduct

You must file Form 1040 to deduct any interest expense on your tax return. Where you deduct your interest expense generally depends on how you use the loan proceeds. See *Table 24–1* for a summary of where to deduct your interest expense.

Home mortgage interest and points. Deduct fully deductible home mortgage interest and points reported to you on Form 1098 on line 9a of Schedule A (Form 1040).

Deduct fully deductible home mortgage interest that was ***not*** reported to you on Form 1098 on line 9b of Schedule A (Form 1040). If the interest was paid to an individual, list the person's name and address in the space provided. If the interest was paid to a seller who financed your mortgage, list on line 9b the seller's social security number (SSN) or employer identification number in addition to the name and address. You are also required to let that

OMB No. 1545-0191

Form **4952**

Department of the Treasury
Internal Revenue Service

Investment Interest Expense Deduction

▶ **Attach to your tax return.**

1993

Attachment
Sequence No. **12A**

Name(s) shown on return

Moore, Karen

Identifying number

123-45-6789

Part I   Total Investment Interest Expense

1	Investment interest expense paid or accrued in 1993. See instructions	1	21,000
2	Disallowed investment interest expense from 1992 Form 4952, line 5	2	—
3	Total investment interest expense. Add lines 1 and 2	3	21,000

Part II   Net Investment Income

4a	Gross income from property held for investment (excluding any net gain from the disposition of property held for investment)		4a	18000
b	Net gain from the disposition of property held for investment . . .	4b 3000		
c	Net capital gain from the disposition of property held for investment	4c 1000		
d	Subtract line 4c from line 4b. If zero or less, enter -0-		4d	2000
e	Enter all or part of the amount on line 4c that you elect to include in investment income. Do not enter more than the amount on line 4b. See instructions . . . . ▶		4e	—
f	Investment income. Add lines 4a, 4d, and 4e. See instructions		4f	20,000
5	Investment expenses. See instructions		5	1,500
6	**Net Investment Income.** Subtract line 5 from line 4f. If zero or less, enter -0-		6	18,500

Part III   Investment Interest Expense Deduction

7	Disallowed investment interest expense to be carried forward to 1994. Subtract line 6 from line 3. If zero or less, enter -0-	7	2,500
8	**Investment interest expense deduction.** Enter the smaller of line 3 or 6. See instructions . .	8	18,500

Cat. No. 13177Y

Form **4952** (1993)

Proof as of September 1993 (subject to change)

Table 24-1.   **Where to Deduct Your Interest**

Type of interest	Where to deduct	Where to find information
Deductible home mortgage interest and points reported on Form 1098	Schedule A (Form 1040), line 9a	Publication 936
Deductible home mortgage interest *not* reported on Form 1098	Schedule A (Form 1040), line 9b	Publication 936
Points *not* reported on Form 1098	Schedule A (Form 1040), line 10	Publication 936
Investment interest (other than interest incurred to produce rents or royalties)	Schedule A (Form 1040), line 11	Publication 550
Business interest (non-farm)	Schedule C (Form 1040)	Publications 334 and 535
Farm business interest	Schedule F (Form 1040)	Publications 225 and 535
Interest incurred to produce rents or royalties	Schedule E (Form 1040)	Publications 527 and 535
Personal Interest	Not Deductible	

person know your SSN. Failure to meet either of these requirements may result in a $50 penalty for each failure.

Deduct points paid on a mortgage that were **not** reported to you on Form 1098 on line 10, of Schedule A (Form 1040).
Investment interest. Deduct investment interest, subject to certain limits discussed in Publication 550, on line 11, Schedule A (Form 1040).

Explanation
A deduction is allowed for interest paid on indebtedness incurred to purchase or hold investment property. Investment property includes any property producing interest, dividends, annuities, royalties, or gains.

The amount of investment interest that may be deducted is limited to the amount of investment income less allowable expenses, other than interest, that are directly connected with the production of investment income. The allowable expenses include those expenses that are deducted on your tax return, after the 2% of adjusted gross income limitation on miscellaneous deductions. (For more information, see Chapter 30, *Miscellaneous Deductions*.)

If the investment interest paid exceeds investment income, the excess may be carried forward to offset investment income in future years.

No deduction is allowed for interest paid on indebtedness incurred to hold obligations that are exempt from federal taxation.

Example 1
In 1993, Joyce Montgomery borrows $83,000 to purchase White Company securities. During the same year, she earns $30,000 of net investment income and incurs $10,000 of interest expense on her loan. Joyce can deduct the $10,000 interest expense as investment interest on Schedule A (Form 1040).

Example 2
George and Lisa Johnson, who file a joint return, have the following income and deductions in 1993:

Salary	$30,000
Interest and dividend income	20,000
Short-term capital gain	5,000
Adjusted gross income	$55,000
Investment advisory fees	$2,000
Investment interest expense	31,000

Their deduction for investment interest is figured as follows:

Investment income	$25,000
Direct expense ($2,000 − 2% of $55,000)	900
Net investment income	$24,100
Deduction allowed	$24,100

The $6,900 ($31,000 − $24,100) that is not allowed as a deduction may be carried forward to 1994.

TaxALERT

Effective after December 31, 1992, net long-term capital gains from the disposition of investment property are no longer defined as investment income for purposes of computing the limitation on investment interest deductions. You may however elect to include net long-term capital gain amounts in investment income for this purpose if you also reduce by the same amount the net long-term capital gain that is eligible for the 28% maximum capital gains rate. Short-term capital gains may still be included in the computation of investment income. For an additional discussion of reporting gains and losses, see Chapter 17, *Reporting Gains and Losses*.

Explanation
The 2% limitation on miscellaneous deductions applies first to deductions other than investment expenses.

Example
In the above example, if George and Lisa Johnson also had tax preparation fees of $500, the $1,100 (2% limitation) would reduce this amount first. The remainder, $600, would then reduce the investment expense, leaving $1,400 to be subtracted from investment income.

Explanation
Deduct interest on margin accounts on Schedule A (Form 1040) for the year in which you paid it. Interest on these accounts is considered paid when the broker is paid or when the interest becomes available to the broker through your account. But see *Straddles* under *Items You Cannot Deduct,* earlier.

Deduct interest on money borrowed to buy a money market certificate on Schedule A (Form 1040). You must include the total interest you earn on the certificate in your income.

Example
You deposited $5,000 with a bank and borrowed another $5,000 from the same bank to make up the $10,000 minimum deposit required to buy a 6-month money market certificate. The certificate earned $810 at maturity in 1993, but you received only $380, which represents the $810 you earned minus $430 interest charged on your $5,000 loan. The bank gives you a Form 1099-INT, *Statement of Recipients of Interest Income,* showing the $810 interest you earned. The bank also gives you a statement showing that you paid $430 interest for 1993. You must include the $810 in your income. You may deduct $430 on Schedule A (Form 1040) if you itemize your deductions.

TaxPLANNER

The amount that you forfeit to a bank or a savings institution as a penalty for premature withdrawal of funds from an account is deductible from your **gross income** in figuring your **adjusted gross income.** You need not itemize to get this deduction.

Non-farm business interest. Deduct interest on non-farm business loans on Schedule C (Form 1040).
Farm business interest. Deduct interest on farm business loans on Schedule F (Form 1040).
Income-producing rental or royalty interest. Deduct interest on a loan for income-producing rental or royalty property that is not used in your business in Part I of Schedule E (Form 1040).

TaxPLANNER

Whether interest is a personal or a business expense depends on the use to which the borrowed money is put, not on the nature of the property used to secure the loan. Therefore, if the proceeds of a loan are used in your business, the interest is deductible from business income, even though you might have pledged nonbusiness **assets** as collateral for the loan.

Example. You rent out part of your home and borrow money to make repairs. You can deduct only the interest payment for the rented part in Part I of Schedule E (Form 1040). Deduct the rest of the interest payment on Schedule A (Form 1040) if it is deductible home mortgage interest.

25 | Contributions

Introduction

*Americans give billions of dollars to charity each year. One explanation for that generosity may be that the federal government encourages charitable giving. It has long been the policy of the government to allow individuals tax **deductions** for charitable contributions they make. In effect, Uncle Sam is contributing part of every dollar you give to charity.*

*Even so, there are lots of rules governing charitable contributions, and it's important that you know them. This chapter tells you how to maximize your allowable charitable deductions and minimize your taxes. You'll learn why, for example, you might want to consider giving shares of stock instead of cash to your favorite charity. Just as important, the chapter tells you how to document your contributions—in case you're the subject of an **audit** by the IRS.*

Beware of promoters selling you property with the promise that you will be entitled to a charitable contribution many times the price you pay. Most of these schemes have not withstood IRS scrutiny. You may even be subject to a penalty for overvaluing your property.

Your 1993 itemized deductions may be subject to certain limitations if your adjusted gross income exceeds $108,450.

Important Change for 1993

Alternative minimum tax. If you contributed property to a qualified organization in 1993, any appreciation (increase in its value) is *not* treated as a tax preference item for the alternative minimum tax. Appreciation on property donated before 1993 was a tax preference item in certain cases. If you need more information about alternative minimum tax, see Chapter 31.

Important Reminders

Limit on itemized deductions. Certain itemized deductions (including charitable contributions) are limited if your adjusted gross income is more than $108,450 ($54,225 if you are married filing separately). See Chapter 21.

Flood relief. You can deduct contributions earmarked for "Flood Disaster Relief" to a qualified organization (defined later under *Organizations That Qualify To Receive Deductible Contributions*). However, you cannot deduct contributions earmarked for relief of a particular individual or family.

This chapter discusses:

- What a charitable contribution is,
- Organizations that are qualified to receive charitable contributions,
- The types of contributions you can deduct,
- What records to keep, and
- How to report your charitable contributions.

A charitable contribution is a contribution or gift to, or for the use of, a qualified organization.

To deduct a charitable contribution, you must file Form 1040 and itemize deductions on Schedule A. You report your contri-

butions on lines 13–16 of Schedule A under the heading "Gifts to Charity." The amount of your deduction may be limited if certain rules and limits explained in this chapter apply to you.

Useful Items

You may want to see:

Publication

☐ **526** Charitable Contributions
☐ **561** Determining the Value of Donated Property

Form (and Instructions)

☐ **Schedule A (Form 1040)** Itemized Deductions

Organizations That Qualify To Receive Deductible Contributions

You can deduct your contributions only if you make them to a *qualified organization.* To become a qualified organization, most organizations other than churches must apply to the IRS.

How to find out whether an organization qualifies. You may ask any organization whether it is a qualified organization, and most will be able to tell you. Or you may check IRS Publication 78, *Cumulative List of Organizations,* which lists most qualified organizations. To check Publication 78, go to your local library's reference section or call the IRS toll-free tax help telephone number

Table 25-1. **Examples of Charitable Contributions—A Quick Check**

Use the following lists for a **quick check** of contributions you can or cannot deduct. See the rest of this chapter for more information and additional rules and limits that may apply.

Deductible As Charitable Contributions	Not Deductible As Charitable Contributions
Money or property you give to:	Money or property you give to:
• Churches, synagogues, temples, mosques, and other religious organizations	• Civic leagues, social and sports clubs, labor unions, and chambers of commerce
• Federal, state, and local governments, if your contribution is solely for public purposes	• Foreign organizations
• Nonprofit schools and hospitals	• Groups that are run for personal profit
• Public parks and recreation facilities	• Groups whose purpose is to lobby for law changes
• Salvation Army, Red Cross, CARE, Goodwill Industries, United Way, Boy Scouts, Girl Scouts, Boys and Girls Clubs of America, etc.	• Homeowners' associations
• War veterans' groups	• Individuals
	• Political groups or candidates for public office
Costs you pay for a student living with you, sponsored by a qualified organization	Cost of raffle, bingo, or lottery tickets
Out-of-pocket expenses when you serve a qualified organization as a volunteer	Dues, fees, or bills paid to country clubs, lodges, fraternal orders, or similar groups
	Tuition
	Value of your time or services
	Value of blood given to a blood bank

for your area. These numbers are listed near the back of this publication.

Types of Qualified Organizations

Generally, only the five following types of organizations can be qualified organizations:

1) The United States or any state, the District of Columbia, a U.S. possession (including Puerto Rico), a political subdivision of a state or U.S. possession, or an Indian tribal government or any of its subdivisions that perform substantial government functions.

   Note: To be able to deduct your contribution to this type of organization, you must make it for public purposes only.

Examples
Contributions to the following U.S. and political subdivisions have been allowed:

• Contributions to the National Park Foundation
• Money donated to a state by an individual to defray expenses of hosting a governor's conference
• Contributions to a state for a parade incidental to a presidential inauguration

The IRS has ruled that the following are *not deductible* as contributions:

• Payments made to a state hospital for the purpose of reimbursing the state for the care of a person confined in the hospital do not constitute contributions made to a state for exclusively public purposes.
• The amount spent by a tenant for additions or improvements to government-owned housing is not deductible as a charitable contribution. Such amounts represent a nondeductible personal, living, or family expense.

2) A community chest, corporation, trust, fund, or foundation organized or created in or under the laws of the United States, any state, the District of Columbia, or any possession of the United States (including Puerto Rico). It must be organized and operated only for charitable, religious, educational, scientific, or literary purposes, or for the prevention of cruelty to children or animals. This includes the Red Cross, the United Way, Boy Scouts, and Girl Scouts. Certain organizations that foster national or international amateur sports competition also qualify.

3) War veterans' organizations, including posts, auxiliaries, trusts,

or foundations, organized in the United States or any of its possessions.
4) Domestic fraternal societies, orders, and associations operating under the lodge system.

Note: Your contribution to this type of organization is deductible only if it is to be used only for charitable, religious, scientific, literary, or educational purposes, or for the prevention of cruelty to children or animals.

5) Certain nonprofit cemetery companies or corporations.

Note: Your contribution to this type of organization is not deductible if it can be used for the care of a specific lot or mausoleum crypt.

Examples. Qualified organizations that fit into one of the above categories include:

- Churches, a convention or association of churches, temples, synagogues, mosques, and other religious organizations.
- Civil defense organizations.
- Most nonprofit charitable organizations.
- Most nonprofit educational organizations, including day care centers if substantially all the child care provided is to enable individuals (the parents) to be gainfully employed and the services are available to the general public. However, if your contribution is a substitute for tuition or other enrollment fee, it is not deductible as a charitable contribution, as explained later under *Contributions You Cannot Deduct.*
- Nonprofit hospitals and medical research organizations.
- Nonprofit volunteer fire companies.
- Public parks and recreation facilities.
- Utility company emergency energy programs, if the utility company is an agent for a charitable organization that assists individuals with emergency energy needs.

Explanation
Any organization can tell you if it is a qualified organization.

Generally, charitable contributions must be made to organizations to be deductible. However, the courts have upheld contributions made to certain individuals on the grounds that the contribution was made to him or her as an agent for the organization. Consider the following cases in which deductions were allowed:

- An individual established a scholarship fund consisting of a personal checking account. Recipients were picked by school principals on the basis of need and scholastic merit. Each check was signed by the donor and made payable jointly to the scholar and the school. The donor was not involved in the selection process.
- A host family acting as a caretaker for an individual under a Department of Public Welfare/Medical Assistance Program is entitled to deduct as a charitable contribution any unreimbursed out-of-pocket expenses incurred in supporting a participant.
- A taxpayer directed his bank to send a check to a specifically named missionary. He instructed the bank to inform the missionary that the check was for Presbyterian mission work. The Tax Court held that this was really a contribution to the church through the missionary as an agent for the church.

TaxAlert
The Supreme Court ruled that funds transferred by parents directly to their sons while they served as unpaid missionaries were not charitable contributions "for the use of" the church, even though the funds were requested by the church.

Contributions You Can Deduct

Generally, you can deduct your contributions of money or property that you make to, or for the use of, a qualified organization. A gift or contribution is "for the use of" a qualified organization when it is held in a legally enforceable trust for the qualified organization or in a similar legal arrangement.

If you give property to a qualified organization, you generally can deduct the fair market value of the property at the time of the contribution. See *Contributions of Property,* later in this chapter.

Your deduction for charitable contributions is generally limited to 50% of your adjusted gross income, but in some cases 20% and 30% limits may apply. See *Limit on Deductions,* later.

Table 25–1 lists some examples of contributions you can deduct and some that you cannot deduct.

Explanation
Fair market value generally is the price that property would sell for on the open market. It takes into account many factors that affect the value of property on the date of the contribution.

Example
If you give used clothing to the Salvation Army, the fair market value is the price that typical buyers actually pay for clothing of this age, condition, style, and use. Usually, such items are worth far less than what you paid for them.

TaxPlanner
A valuable tool for determining fair market value is IRS Publication 561, *Determining the Value of Donated Property.* The publication helps donors and appraisers determine the value of property given to qualified organizations and includes the kind of information you must have to support the charitable deduction you claim on your return.

A sale or purchase of similar property reasonably close to the date of your contribution is usually the best indication of fair market value. Replacement cost and opinions of experts are also valid methods for determining value.

IRS Publication 561 discusses pitfalls to be avoided in determining the value of donated property. Some pitfalls and how to avoid them are the following:

1. The best evidence of fair market value depends on actual transactions, not on some artificial estimate.
2. Do not consider unexpected events occurring after your donation of property in making the valuation. Only consider facts known at the time of the gift.
3. Past events are not necessarily reliable in predicting future earnings and fair market value. For example, a

taxpayer contributes all rights in a patent to a charitable organization. The patent has a history of high earnings, but the current trend reflects declining earnings. In this case, more emphasis should be placed on the earnings trend rather than on the earnings history.

The cost of an appraisal is not deductible as a charitable contribution, but it may be claimed as a miscellaneous deduction.

You are required to obtain a qualified appraisal for certain noncash donations. Appraisals are required for the donation of property with a claimed value in excess of $5,000. If you make gifts of two or more items of similar property during the year, the claimed value of all of those items will be added together in determining whether the $5,000 limit is exceeded. Appraisals are not required for the contribution of publicly traded stock and are required only for the contribution of nonpublicly traded securities if their claimed value exceeds $10,000.

The appraisal may not be made by the organization receiving the gift, the party from whom the taxpayer acquired the property, the taxpayer, or certain persons related to any of these persons.

The appraisal fee cannot be based on a percentage of the appraised value of the gift.

Form 8283, containing an acknowledgment of receipt of the property by the receiving organization and a certification by the appraiser, must be filed with the tax return on which the deduction is taken.

TaxAlert

It is very important to get an accurate assessment of donated property, because you may be liable for a special penalty if you overstate its value (or **adjusted basis**). You are liable for the penalty if *both* of the following conditions exist:

1. The value, or adjusted basis, claimed on your return is more than 200% of the correct amount.
2. You underpaid your tax by at least $5,000 because of the overstatement.

The penalty is 20% of the tax underpayment attributable to the overvaluation and may increase to 40% if the value claimed is 400% or more of the correct amount.

Contributions From Which You Benefit

If you receive a benefit as a result of making a contribution to a qualified organization, you can deduct only the amount of your contribution that is more than the value of the benefit you receive.

If you pay more than fair market value to a qualified organization for merchandise, goods, or services, the amount you pay that is more than the value of the item may be a charitable contribution.

Example 1. You pay $75 for a dinner-dance at a church. All of the proceeds of the function go to the church. The dinner, plus any entertainment or other services provided, has a fair market value of $25. Subtract the value of the benefit you received ($25) from your total payment ($75). You can deduct $50 as a contribution to the church.

Example 2. At a fund-raising auction conducted by a charity,

you pay $600 for a week's stay at a beach house. The amount you pay is no more than the fair rental value. You have not made a deductible charitable contribution.

Athletic events. If you make a payment to, or for the benefit of, a college or university and, as a result, you receive the right to buy tickets to an athletic event in the athletic stadium of the college or university, you can deduct 80% of the payment as a charitable contribution.

If any part of your payment is for tickets (rather than the right to buy tickets), that part is not deductible. In that case, subtract the price of the tickets from your payment. 80% of the remaining amount is a charitable contribution.

Example 1. You pay $300 a year for membership in an athletic scholarship program maintained by a university (a qualified organization). The only benefit of membership is that you have the right to buy one season ticket for a seat in a designated area of the stadium at the university's home football games. You can deduct $240 (80% of $300) as a charitable contribution.

Example 2. Assume the same facts as in Example 1 except that your $300 payment included the purchase of one season ticket for the stated ticket price of $120. You must subtract the usual price of a ticket ($120) from your $300 payment. The result is $180. $144 (80% of $180) is a charitable contribution.

Examples

Even though it appears that the taxpayer received a benefit, the following charitable contributions were allowed by the courts and the IRS:

- A tornado destroyed several homes in a town. The local chapter of the American Red Cross provided food and temporary shelter to an individual whose home was destroyed. Motivated by gratitude, the individual made a contribution to the local chapter of the American Red Cross.
- A taxpayer owned a home in an area served by a volunteer fire department. No state or local taxes were used to support the fire department. The taxpayer made a contribution to its annual fund drive.
- A taxpayer's daughter was a member of a local unit of the Girl Scouts of America. The taxpayer made a contribution to that group.
- A taxpayer had a **dependent** parent who was a resident of a home for the elderly that was a member organization of a combined charity fund. The taxpayer made an unrestricted contribution to the combined charity fund, which distributed the contributions to the member organizations according to a formula.
- A taxpayer made a contribution for repairs to a chapel on his land used by the Catholic Church.
- A taxpayer donated fire-damaged buildings to a fire department for use in fire drills. The clearing of the land by the fire drills increased the value of the land. The court approved the deduction, saying that the benefit to the taxpayer was only incidental to the contribution.
- A real estate developer donated a piece of land to the local school board for a school site. The court held that the developer was not required by law to donate the land and did not receive any particular benefit.

A deduction for a charitable contribution was *not* permitted in the following instances:

- A person contributed a computer to a university, and the donor reserved the right to use the computer for 12 weeks per year.
- A person released frontage to a county for widening a road in order to obtain the required approval by the county planning commission of the development plan for certain lots prior to their sale. (However, the cost of the frontage is part of the total cost **basis** of the remaining property for determining the gain or loss on the sale of the property.)
- The amount paid by a taxpayer to purchase building bonds issued by a church was not a gift made to the church. However, if the taxpayer had subsequently given the bonds to the church, he would have been entitled to a charitable deduction for their fair market value at the time of the gift.
- A person made contributions to a nonprofit organization formed by parents of pupils attending a private school. The organization provided school bus transportation for members' children. The contributions served a private rather than a public interest.
- A taxpayer paid a fee to a nonprofit corporation for the privilege of taking up residence in a home operated by the corporation. This fee, along with a required entrance fee, entitled the taxpayer to lifetime care in the home. The fee represented a personal expense.
- A taxpayer paid $7,000 to the Church of Scientology for "auditing" and "training" based on a price list maintained by the Church. According to the Church, the purpose was to erase images that caused irrational behavior and to help the taxpayer gain spiritual competence. The Supreme Court recently decided that the payment was made with the expectation of an identifiable benefit and denied the charitable contribution deduction.

Charity benefit events. If you pay a qualified organization more than fair market value for the right to attend a charity ball, banquet, show, sporting event, or other benefit event, you can deduct only the amount that is more than the value of the privileges or other benefits you receive.

If there is an established charge for the event, that charge is the value of your benefit. If there is no set charge, your contribution is that part of your payment that is more than the reasonable value of the right to attend the event. Whether you use the tickets or other privileges has no effect on the amount you can deduct. However, if you return the ticket to the qualified organization for resale, you can deduct the entire amount you paid for the ticket.

Even if the ticket or other evidence of payment indicates that the payment is a "contribution," this does not necessarily mean you can deduct the entire amount. If the ticket shows the price of admission and the amount of the contribution, you can deduct the contribution amount.

Example. You pay $40 to see a special showing of a movie for the benefit of a qualified organization. Printed on the ticket is "Contribution—$40." If the regular price for the movie is $8, your contribution is $32 ($40 payment − $8 regular price).

Explanation
The IRS requires that charities determine the fair market value of benefits offered in exchange for contributions in advance of the solicitation and state in the solicitation, as well as in the receipt, tickets, or other documents what portion of the contribution is deductible. The charity may advise donors that the full amount of a contribution is deductible if either of the following applies:

- The fair market value of all the benefits received in conjunction with the contribution is not more than the lesser of 2% of the payment or $62.
- The contribution is more than $31 and the only benefits received in connection with the payment are token items, such as bookmarks, calendars, key chains, mugs, posters, tee-shirts, and so forth, bearing the organization's name or logo (i.e., "low-cost articles" with a cost not in excess of $6.20 as adjusted for inflation for the 1993 calendar year).

Example 1
In 1993, a nonprofit broadcast organization sends its patrons a listener's guide for 1 year in return for a contribution of $40. The cost of the production and distribution of the listener's guide is $5 per year per patron, and its fair market value is $7. The listener's guide is not available to nonmembers by paid subscription or through newsstand sales. Since the cost of the listener's guide is $5 and it is received in return for a contribution of $40, the broadcast organization may advise its patrons that the full amount of the payment is a deductible contribution. However, if the value of the publication exceeds the threshold amounts described above, the charitable organization would be required to inform its patrons of the amount by which they should reduce their charitable deductions.

Example 2
Assume the same facts as in Example 1, except that the nonprofit broadcast organization also gives its patrons a coffee mug with the organization's logo. The cost of the mug to the organization is $3. Its fair market value is $5. The aggregate cost of the guide and the mug ($8) exceeds the 1993 limit of $6.20. The organization should inform its patrons that $28 of their contribution is deductible and $12 is not.

Note: The result would be the same even if these benefits were received separately in return for two separate contributions of $40 each.

Token items. You can deduct your entire payment to a qualified organization as a charitable contribution, if:

1) As a result of the payment, you receive low-value or low-cost items such as bookmarks, calendars, mugs, or caps that have on them the organization's name or logo, or
2) You receive a low-cost item that you did not order and can keep even if you do not make a contribution.

Also, the qualified organization must notify you that the value of the item you received is insubstantial and that you can deduct your payment in full.

Membership fees or dues. You may be able to deduct membership fees or dues you pay to a qualified organization. However, you can deduct only the amount that is more than the value of the benefits you receive. You cannot deduct dues, fees, or assessments paid to country clubs and other social organizations. They are not qualified organizations.

Note: If you make a contribution *after 1993* to a qualified organization that is more than $75 and is partly for goods or services, the qualified organization must give you a written statement. The statement must tell you that you can deduct only the amount of your contribution that is more than the value of the goods or services you received. It must also give you a good faith estimate of the value of those goods or services.

An organization will not have to give you this statement if it is:

1) The type of organization described in (1) under *Types of Qualified Organizations,* earlier, or
2) Formed only for religious purposes, and the only benefit you receive is an intangible religious benefit (such as admission to a religious ceremony) that generally is not sold in commercial transactions outside the donative context.

Expenses Paid for Student Living With You

You may be able to deduct some expenses of having a student live with you. You can deduct expenses for a foreign or American student who:

1) Lives in your home under a written agreement between you and a "qualified organization" as part of a program of the organization to provide educational opportunities for the student,
2) Is not your dependent or relative, and
3) Is a full-time student in the twelfth or any lower grade at a school in the United States.

You can deduct up to $50 a month for each full calendar month the student lives with you. Any month when conditions (1) through (3) above are met for 15 days or more counts as a full month.

You cannot deduct the costs of a foreign student living in your home under a mutual exchange program whereby your child will live with a family in a foreign country.

Explanation
The deduction is limited to amounts that you actually spend for the well-being of the student. Amounts you pay for the student's books, tuition, food, clothing, and entertainment qualify for the deduction. Depreciation on your home, the fair market value of lodging at your home, or similar items are not considered an amount spent by you and are not deductible.

If you are compensated or reimbursed for the costs of having a student live with you, you may not take a deduction for any part of these costs.

For additional information, see *Expenses Paid for Student Living With You* in Publication 526, *Charitable Contributions.*

Out-of-Pocket Expenses in Giving Services

You may be able to deduct some amounts you pay in giving services to a qualified organization. The amounts must be:

Unreimbursed,
Directly connected with the services,

Expenses you had only because of the services you gave, and
Not personal, living, or family expenses.

Explanation
Unreimbursed out-of-pocket expenses incurred in rendering services to qualified charities are considered contributions made "to" the charitable entities rather than "for the use of" the charitable entities, and, as such, the deduction may be subject to the 50% limit rather than the 30% limit. See *Limit on Deductions* to see if further limitations apply.

Table 25–2 contains questions and answers that apply to some individuals who volunteer their services.

Conventions. If you are a chosen representative attending a convention of a qualified organization, you can deduct actual unreimbursed expenses for travel and transportation, including a reasonable amount for meals and lodging, while away from home overnight in connection with the convention. However, see *Travel,* later.

You cannot deduct personal expenses for sightseeing, fishing parties, theater tickets, or nightclubs. You also cannot deduct travel, meals and lodging, and other expenses for your spouse or children.

You cannot deduct your expenses in attending a church convention if you go only as a member of your church rather than as a chosen representative. You can deduct unreimbursed expenses that are directly connected with giving services for your church during the convention.

Uniforms. You can deduct the cost and upkeep of uniforms that are not suitable for everyday use and that you must wear while performing donated services for a charitable organization.

Foster parents. You can deduct some of the costs of being a foster parent (foster care provider) if you have no profit motive in providing the foster care and are not, in fact, making a profit.

You can deduct expenses that are:

1) Greater than any nontaxable payments you receive to provide foster care for individuals placed in your home by a charitable organization, and
2) Spent to provide support for those individuals.

For more information, see *Foster-care providers* under *Income Not Taxed* in Chapter 13, *Other Income.*

Explanation
You may deduct reasonable, unreimbursed out-of-pocket expenses you spend for underprivileged children to attend athletic events, movies, or dinners. It must be for a qualifying organization whose goal is to reduce juvenile delinquency. Expenses for yourself are not deductible.

Car expenses. You can deduct unreimbursed out-of-pocket expenses, such as the cost of gas and oil, that are directly related to the use of your car in giving services to a charitable organization. You cannot deduct any part of general repair and maintenance expenses, depreciation, registration fees, or the costs of tires or insurance.

If you do not want to deduct your actual expenses, you can use a standard rate of *12 cents a mile* to figure your contribution.

Table 25-2. **Volunteers' Questions and Answers**

If you do volunteer work for a qualified organization, the following questions and answers may apply to you. All of the rules explained in this chapter also apply. See, in particular, Out-of-Pocket Expenses in Giving Services.

Question	Answer
I do volunteer work 6 hours a week in the office of a qualified organization. The receptionist is paid $6 an hour to do the same work I do. Can I deduct $36 a week for my time?	No, you cannot deduct the value of your time or services.
The office is 30 miles from my home. Can I deduct any of my car expenses for these trips?	Yes, you can deduct the costs of gas and oil that are directly related to getting to the qualified organization where you are a volunteer. If you don't want to figure your actual costs, you can deduct 12 cents for each mile.
I am a Red Cross nurse's aide at a hospital. Can I deduct the cost of uniforms that I must wear?	Yes, you can deduct the cost of buying and cleaning your uniforms if the hospital is a qualified organization, the uniforms are not suitable for everyday use, and you must wear them when volunteering.
I pay a babysitter to watch my children while I do volunteer work for a qualified organization. Can I deduct these costs?	No, you cannot deduct payments for child care expenses as a charitable contribution, even if they are necessary so you can do volunteer work for a qualified organization. (If you have child care expenses so you can work for pay, see Chapter 33.)

You can deduct parking fees and tolls, whether you use your actual expenses or the standard rate.

Travel. You can claim a charitable contribution deduction for travel expenses necessarily incurred while you are away from home performing services for a charitable organization only if there is *no significant element* of personal pleasure, recreation, or vacation in such travel. This applies whether you pay the expenses directly or indirectly. You are paying the expenses indirectly if you make a payment to the charitable organization and the organization pays for your travel expenses.

The deduction will not be denied simply because you enjoy providing services to the charitable organization.

Example 1. You are a troop leader for a tax-exempt youth group and take the group on a camping trip. You can take a charitable contribution deduction for your own travel expenses if you are on duty in a genuine and substantial sense throughout the trip, even though you enjoyed the trip. However, if you have only nominal duties relating to the performance of services for the charity, or for significant portions of the trip you are not required to render services, you cannot deduct your travel expenses.

Example 2. You sail from one island to another and spend 8 hours a day counting whales and other forms of marine life. The project is sponsored by a charitable organization. In most circumstances, you cannot deduct the expenses you incur.

Example 3. You work for several hours each morning on an archaeological excavation sponsored by a charitable organization. The rest of the day is free for recreation and sightseeing. You cannot take a charitable contribution deduction even though you work very hard during those few hours.

Example 4. You spend the entire day attending a charitable organization's regional meeting as a chosen representative. In the evening you go to the theater. You can claim your travel expenses as charitable contributions.

Daily allowance (per diem). If you provide services for a charitable organization and receive a daily allowance to cover reasonable travel expenses, including meals and lodging while away from home overnight, include in income the amount that is more than your actual travel expenses. You can deduct your necessary travel expenses that are more than the allowance.

Deductible travel expenses. These include:

- Air, rail, and bus transportation,
- Out-of-pocket expenses for your car,
- Taxi fares or other costs of transportation between the airport or station and your hotel,
- Lodging costs, and
- The cost of meals.

For additional information, see *Travel Expenses* in Chapter 28, *Car Expenses and Other Employee Business Expenses*.

Contributions You Cannot Deduct

There are some contributions that you cannot deduct. You can deduct only part of other contributions.

Contributions to individuals. You cannot deduct contributions to specific individuals, including:

- **Contributions to fraternal societies** made for the purpose of paying medical or burial expenses of deceased members.
- **Contributions to individuals who are needy or worthy.** This includes contributions to a qualified organization if you indicate that your contribution is for a specific person. But, you can deduct a contribution that you give to a qualified organization that in turn helps needy or worthy individuals if you do not indicate that your contribution is for a specific person.
- **Payments to a member of the clergy** that can be spent as he or she wishes, such as for personal expenses.
- **Expenses you paid for another person** who provided services to a qualified organization.
  Example. Your son does missionary work. You pay his expenses. You cannot claim a deduction for your son's un-reimbursed expenses related to his contribution of services.
- **Payments to a hospital** that are for a specific patient's care or for services for a specific patient. You cannot deduct these payments even if the hospital is operated by a city, a state, or other qualified organization.

TAXPLANNER

Direct contributions to needy or worthy individuals are not deductible. But, if you can show that the economic benefit derived by the specific individual is less than the contribution to the organization in whose care the individual is placed, the excess may be deductible.

Example

An individual made a contribution to a school for crippled children that her son attended. The donor required that a portion of her contribution be used to purchase a wheelchair for the exclusive use of her son. She was allowed a deduction for a charitable contribution for the amount by which the contribution exceeded the cost of the wheelchair. (The cost of the wheelchair qualified as a medical expense.)

Contributions to nonqualified organizations. You cannot deduct contributions to organizations that are not qualified to receive tax-deductible contributions, including:

- **Certain state bar associations,** if:
  a) The state bar is not a political subdivision of a state,
  b) The bar has private, as well as public, purposes, such as promoting the professional interests of members, and
  c) Your contribution is unrestricted and can be used for private purposes.
- **Chambers of commerce** and other business leagues or organizations.
- **Civic leagues and associations.**
- **Communist organizations.**
- **Country clubs** and other social clubs.
- **Foreign organizations.** But you can deduct contributions you make to:
  a) A U.S. organization that transfers funds to a charitable foreign organization if the U.S. organization controls the use of the funds, or if the foreign organization is only an administrative arm of the U.S. organization, or

Example

Unless you indicate that your contribution is to be used exclusively overseas, a contribution to the U.S. Red Cross is deductible, even though some portion of the contribution may be used outside the United States. If you make a contribution to a U.S. organization *directing* that it be used abroad, a deduction is not allowed, because the real recipient is not a domestic organization.

  b) Certain Canadian charitable organizations covered under an income tax treaty with Canada. See Publication 597, *Information on the United States-Canada Income Tax Treaty,* for information on how to figure your deduction.

Explanation

The charitable contributions (other than charitable contributions to a college or a university at which you or a member of your family is or was enrolled) are subject to the U.S. percentage limits on charitable contributions, applied to your Canadian source income.

Canadian organizations must meet the qualifications that U.S. charitable organizations must meet. The organization can tell you if it qualifies for deductible charitable contributions.

- **Homeowners' associations.**
- **Labor unions.** (But, you may be able to deduct union dues as a miscellaneous itemized deduction, subject to the 2% of adjusted gross income limit, on Schedule A (Form 1040). See Chapter 30, *Miscellaneous Deductions*.)
- **Political organizations and candidates.**

Contributions from which you benefit. You cannot deduct contributions that you give to qualified organizations if, as a result, you receive or expect to receive a financial or economic benefit equal to the contribution. These include:

- **Contributions for lobbying.** This includes amounts that you earmark for use in or in connection with influencing specific legislation.

Example

The Lorax Club is a qualified charitable organization that became concerned with proposed legislation. To obtain funds to enable it to influence the legislation, the Lorax Club mailed to its members and the general public literature that described the pending legislation and requested contributions to be used to lobby to defeat the legislation. Contributions to the Lorax Club earmarked for use in, or in connection with, attempting to influence the legislation are not deductible.

- **Contributions to a retirement home** that are clearly for room, board, maintenance, or admittance. Also, if the amount of your contribution depends on the type or size of apartment you will occupy, it is not a charitable contribution.
- **Costs of raffles, bingo, lottery, etc.** You cannot deduct as a charitable contribution amounts you pay to buy raffle or lottery tickets or to play bingo or other games of chance. For more information on how to report gambling winnings and losses, see *Gambling Losses to the Extent of Gambling Winnings* in Chapter 30, *Miscellaneous Deduction*.
- **Dues to fraternal orders** and similar groups.
- **Tuition,** or amounts you pay instead of tuition, even if you pay them for children to attend parochial schools or qualifying nonprofit day care centers. You also cannot deduct any fixed amount you may be required to pay in addition to the tuition fee to enroll in a private school, even if it is designated as a "donation."

Explanation

Tuition-type reimbursement disguised as a charitable contribution is not deductible. Certain rules have been established by the IRS to determine whether an item is a tuition payment or a charitable contribution.

No deduction for a charitable contribution is allowed if *at least one* of the following conditions exists:

1. A contract under which a taxpayer agrees to make a "contribution," and that contract contains provisions ensuring the admission of the taxpayer's child
2. A plan allowing taxpayers either to pay tuition or to make "contributions" in exchange for schooling
3. The designation of a contribution for the direct benefit of a particular child
4. The otherwise unexplained denial of admission or

readmission to a school of children of taxpayers who are financially able but who do not contribute

Other factors that are considered in deciding if a contribution is deductible include the following:

1. The absence of a significant tuition charge
2. Substantial or unusual pressure to contribute applied to parents of students
3. Contribution appeals made as part of the admissions or enrollment process
4. The absence of significant potential sources of revenue for operating the school other than contributions by parents of students

Value of time or services. You cannot deduct the value of your time or services, including:

- **Blood donations** to the Red Cross or to blood banks.
- **The value of income lost** while you work as an unpaid volunteer for a qualified organization.

TaxPlanner

If you contribute *your* services to a charitable organization, you are not permitted to take a charitable deduction for the value of your time or services. However, you are entitled to take a charitable deduction if you acquire the right to services to be performed by another and then gratuitously transfer that right to the charity.

Example

You purchase a series of six golf lessons from a local golf professional. Because you are unable to use the lessons, you donate them to your church for use in their raffle. The cost of the six lessons is deductible as a charitable contribution.

However, if you donate the use of your yacht to the church for use in their raffle, no income tax deduction is allowed for the rental value or other value of the donated use. Direct operating costs, such as fuel, used in connection with the donated use are allowable as a charitable contribution.

Personal expenses. You cannot deduct personal, living, or family expenses, such as:

- **Adoption expenses**, including fees paid to an adoption agency and the costs of keeping a child in your home before adoption is final. However, you may be able to claim an exemption for the child. See *Adoption* in Chapter 3, *Personal Exemptions and Deductions*.
- **The cost of meals** you eat while you perform services for a qualified organization, unless it is necessary for you to be away from home overnight while performing the services.

Appraisal fees. Fees that you pay to find the fair market value of donated property are not deductible as contributions. You can claim them, subject to the 2% of adjusted gross income limit, as miscellaneous deductions on Schedule A (Form 1040). See Chapter 30, *Miscellaneous Deductions*.

Contributions of Property

If you contribute property to a qualified organization, generally the fair market value of the property at the time of the contribution is the amount of your charitable contribution. However, if the property has increased in value, you may have to make some adjustments. See *Giving Property That Has Increased in Value,* later.

For information about the records you must keep and the information you must furnish with your return if you donate property, see *Records To Keep* and *How To Report,* later.

Explanation

If you permit a charitable organization to use your property without charge (or at a minimal rate), no charitable deduction is allowed.

TaxSaver

The IRS, however, will allow charitable deductions for the cost of operation, maintenance, and repair of property directly related to the charitable organization's use of the property.

Partial interest in property. Generally, you cannot deduct a charitable contribution, not made by a transfer in trust, of less than your entire interest in property. A contribution of the right to use property, not made by a transfer in trust, is a contribution of less than your entire interest in that property and is not deductible. For exceptions and more information, see *Partial Interest in Property* in Publication 561.

Explanation

This rule does not apply to a contribution of a partial interest in property if that interest is your entire interest in the property, such as an income interest.

Nevertheless, there are some situations in which you may claim a deduction for a charitable contribution that is less than your entire interest in the property.

1. **Undivided part of your entire interest.** A contribution of an undivided part of your entire interest in property must consist of a part of each and every substantial interest or right you own in the property and must extend over the entire term of your interest in the property.

Examples

You donate 20% of an income interest that you have in a property to a qualified organization. You may deduct the contribution if you have no other interest in the property.

If you own 100 acres of land and give 50 acres to a qualified organization, you may deduct the charitable contribution.

A court recently allowed a taxpayer a deduction when a 10% undivided interest in 44 works of art was donated to an art museum. The art museum did not take physical possession of the works of art at any time within a period that extended for more than a year after the donation. It was held that the art museum clearly had the right to possession for 10% of the days in the year and the fact that the museum did not exercise that right was not relevant.

2. **Remainder interest in a personal home or farm.** You may take a charitable deduction for a gift to a qualified organization of a **remainder interest** in a personal home or a farm if the gift is irrevocable.

Example

If you transfer a remainder interest in your home to your church but keep the right to live there for life, you may take a deduction for the value of the remainder interest transferred.

Valuation of a partial interest in property. The amount of the deduction for a charitable contribution of a partial interest in property is the fair market value of the partial interest at the time of the contribution. If the contribution is a remainder interest in real property, **depreciation** (figured on the **straight-line** method) and **depletion** of the property must be taken into account in determining its value. This future value must be further discounted at 10% per year or at some other rate set by the government.

No deduction is allowed for the value of an interest in property transferred in trust unless the donor's entire interest is contributed to a qualified organization or unless the interest is an income interest or a remainder interest.

TaxPlanner

A charitable contribution of an income interest in property made by a transfer in trust is allowed if the income interest is either a guaranteed **annuity** interest or a **unitrust** interest and if the grantor is treated as the owner of the interest. A unitrust interest is the irrevocable right to receive payment of a fixed percentage of the net fair market value of the trust **assets** determined on a yearly basis.

A charitable contribution of a remainder interest in trust is allowed if the trust is (1) a **pooled income fund,** (2) a charitable remainder annuity trust, or (3) a charitable remainder unitrust.

The use of these trusts may be very beneficial both to the individual and to the individual's favorite charity. Individuals with substantial wealth should consult their tax and legal advisors about using these mechanisms.

Future interests in tangible personal property. You can deduct the value of a charitable contribution of a future interest in tangible personal property only after all intervening interests in and rights to the actual possession or enjoyment of the property have either expired or been turned over to someone other than yourself, a related person, or a related organization.

A future interest is any interest that is to begin at some future time, regardless of whether it is designated as a future interest under state law.

Explanation

The amount of the deduction is the value of the future interest when you and the related person no longer have an interest in the tangible personal property. When these interests end, the deduction is allowed to you, even if there are other outstanding interests that must end before the future interest is realized by the qualified organization.

Example

In 1993 you transferred a painting to your daughter to use and enjoy for life. When your daughter dies, the painting will go to the local art museum. If your daughter irrevocably transfers her life interest to an unrelated person in a later year, you may take a charitable deduction in that year, but not sooner. The amount of your deduction is the value of the future interest in the painting at the time of the transfer to the unrelated person.

Determining Fair Market Value

This section discusses general guidelines for determining the fair market value of various types of donated property. Fair market value is the price at which property would change hands between a willing buyer and a willing seller, neither having to buy or sell, and both having reasonable knowledge of all the relevant facts. Publication 561, *Determining the Value of Donated Property,* contains a more complete discussion.

Used clothing and household goods. Generally, the fair market value of used clothing and household goods is far less than its original cost.

For used clothing, you should claim as the value the price that buyers of used items actually pay in used clothing stores, such as consignment or thrift shops.

See *Household Goods* in Publication 561 for information on the valuation of household goods, such as furniture, appliances, and linens.

Cars, boats, and aircraft. If you contribute a car, boat, or aircraft, you must determine its fair market value.

Certain commercial firms and trade organizations publish guides, commonly called "blue books," containing complete dealer sale prices or dealer average prices for recent model years. The guides may be published monthly or seasonally, and for different regions of the country. These guides also provide estimates for adjusting for unusual equipment, unusual mileage, and physical condition. The prices are not "official" and these publications are not considered an appraisal of any specific donated property. But they do provide clues for making an appraisal and suggest relative prices for comparison with current sales and offerings in your area.

Example. You donate your car to a local high school for use by their students studying automobile repair. Your credit union told you that the "blue book" value of the car is $1,600. However, your car needs extensive repairs and, after some checking, you find that you would not be able to sell it for more than $750. You can deduct $750, the *true* fair market value of the car, as a charitable contribution.

Large quantities. If you contribute a large number of the same item, fair market value is the price at which comparable numbers of the item are being sold.

Giving Property That Has Decreased in Value

If you contribute property with a fair market value that is less than your basis in it, your deduction is limited to fair market value. You cannot claim a deduction for the difference between the property's basis and its fair market value.

If property that you are planning to donate has declined in value, you may consider selling it and giving the proceeds to the charitable organization. By following this strategy, you get the deduction (subject to limitations) for the capital loss, as well as the deduction for the charitable cash gift.

Giving Property That Has Increased in Value

If you contribute property with a fair market value that is more than your basis in it, you may have to reduce the fair market value by the amount of appreciation (increase in value) when you figure your deduction.

Your "basis" in property is generally what you paid for it. See Chapter 14, *Basis of Property*, if you need more information about basis.

Different rules apply to figuring your deduction, depending on whether the property is:

1) Ordinary income property, or
2) Capital gain property.

Ordinary income property. Property is ordinary income property if its sale at fair market value on the date it was contributed would have resulted in ordinary income or in short-term capital gain. Examples of ordinary income property are inventory, works of art created by the donor, manuscripts prepared by the donor, and capital assets held one year or less.

The amount you can deduct for a contribution of ordinary income property is its fair market value less the amount that would be ordinary income or short-term capital gain if you sold the property for its fair market value. Generally, this rule limits the deduction to your basis in the property.

Example. You donate stock that you held for 5 months to your church. The fair market value of the stock on the day you donate it is $1,000, but you paid only $800 (your basis). Because the $200 of appreciation would be short-term capital gain if you sold the stock, your deduction is limited to $800 (fair market value less the appreciation).

Explanation
Ordinary income property. If, on the date it was contributed, the sale of the property would have resulted in ordinary income or a short-term capital gain to the donor, it is ordinary income property. Examples of ordinary income property include inventory, letters, and memoranda given by the person who prepared them (or the person for whom they were prepared), and any property that was acquired and held for 1 year or less.

Example
You contribute inventory to your church with a fair market value of $20,000 and a cost of $8,000. Since the inventory is property that had previously been held for sale in the ordinary course of business, you would have recognized ordinary income of $12,000 had the property been sold. Therefore, your contribution of $20,000

is reduced by $12,000. Your deduction is limited to $8,000.

Capital gain property. Property is capital gain property if its sale at fair market value on the date of the contribution would have resulted in long-term capital gain. It includes capital assets held more than one year, as well as certain real property and depreciable property used in your trade or business and, generally, held more than one year.

When figuring your deduction for a gift of capital gain property, you usually can use the fair market value of the gift. However, in certain situations, you must reduce the fair market value to the property's cost or other basis.

Example
An individual purchased stock in 1981 for $1,000. He contributed it to his church in 1993, at which time it was worth $20,000. His charitable contribution deduction is $20,000, the fair market value at the date of the contribution.

Explanation
You usually may deduct gifts of capital gain property at their fair market value. However, you must reduce the fair market value by 100% of the appreciation in the following instances:

1. If the capital gain property is contributed to certain private foundations. (A private foundation receives only small or no contributions from the general public.)

   Contributions of "qualified appreciated stock" made after July 18, 1984, through 1994 to nonoperating foundations are deductible at full fair market value, subject to the 20% limitation, discussed later. (See *Limit on Deductions*.) If, on the date of contribution, market quotes are readily available and the sale of the corporation's stock would result in a long-term capital gain, it is qualified appreciated stock. An example would be shares of IBM that qualify for long-term capital gain treatment.

2. If you choose the 50% limit instead of the special 30% limit, discussed later. (See *Limit on Deductions*.)
3. If the property contributed is **tangible personal property** that is put to an "unrelated use" by the charity, that is, a use that is unrelated to the purpose or function of the charitable organization for which it was granted its tax-exempt status.

Example
If a painting you contribute to an educational institution is placed in the organization's library for display and study by art students, the use is *not* an unrelated use. But, if the painting is sold and the proceeds are used by the organization for educational purposes, the use is unrelated.

TAXPLANNER

Before you donate a gift of tangible personal property, attempt to determine whether the use will be related to the charitable organization's exempt function. In such circumstances, ask the charitable organization to prepare a statement of intended use and retain it in your tax return file.

TAXSAVER 1

If you donate appreciated securities that you have held for more than the required long-term holding period, not only may you take a deduction based on the fair market value of the securities, but also you will avoid paying tax on the appreciation. Consequently, the cost of your contribution is reduced by the tax deduction you claim and the tax you avoided by not selling the property. In most cases, the charity does not incur any tax when it sells the property.

Example

You own stock worth $1,000. When you bought the stock more than a year ago, it cost you $100. If you sell the stock and donate the $1,000 to your favorite charity, you incur capital gains tax—possibly as much as $252, depending on what tax bracket you're in. If you contribute the stock directly to the charity, the $900 gain is not subject to tax.

TAXSAVER 2

To get the maximum tax benefit from a contribution of appreciated property, be sure that the property qualifies for long-term capital gain treatment if it is sold.

Example

You purchased a stock for $1,000 on January 12, 1992. The stock was donated to your church on January 8, 1993, at which time it was worth $3,000. Because the $2,000 of appreciation would have been a short-term capital gain if you had sold the stock, your deduction is limited to $1,000. If, however, you had waited to make your donation to the church until January 13, 1993, and the stock was still worth $3,000, you would have been able to deduct $3,000.

TAXALERT

The 1993 Tax Act enables you to recognize a charitable contribution for the full fair market value of appreciated property for both regular and alternative minimum tax purpose. Under the old law, if you donated certain appreciated property, the amount of the appreciation was deductible when figuring your regular tax but it was considered a tax preference item for alternative minimum tax purposes.

For contributions of tangible personal property (such as a work of art), the new rules are retroactive to July 1, 1992. For contributions of all other property (such as stock or real estate), the new rules are retroactive to contributions made after December 31, 1992.

If you previously made gifts to a charitable organization that were not fully deductible because of the limits on the percentage of your income you can deduct for charitable gifts in a given year, these amounts may be deducted in future years. However, those amounts will still be considered a tax preference item for AMT purposes in the year in which they are deductible.

TAXSAVER

You may want to consider amending your 1992 tax return if you reported an alternative minimum tax preference item for contributions of tangible personal property made after July 1, 1992 and you actually paid alternative minimum tax in 1992. Consult your tax advisor if you are considering amending your 1992 return.

Bargain sales. A bargain sale of property to a qualified organization (a sale or exchange for less than the property's fair market value) is partly a charitable contribution and partly a sale or exchange. A bargain sale may result in a taxable gain.

For more information on donated appreciated property, see *Giving Property That Has Increased in Value* in Publication 526.

When To Deduct

You can deduct your contributions only in the year you actually make them in cash or other property (or in a later carryover year, as explained later under *Carryovers*). This applies whether you use the cash or an accrual method of accounting.

Usually, you make a contribution at the time of its unconditional delivery. For example, a check that you mail to a charity is considered delivered on the date you mail it. Contributions charged on your bank credit card are deductible in the year you make the charge. If you use a pay-by-phone account, the date you make a contribution is the date the financial institution pays the amount. This date should be shown on the statement the financial institution sends to you.

The gift to a charity of a properly endorsed stock certificate is completed on the date of mailing or other delivery to the charity or to the charity's agent. However, if you give a stock certificate to your agent or to the issuing corporation for transfer to the name of the charity, your gift is not completed until the date the stock is transferred on the books of the corporation.

If you issue and deliver a promissory note to a charitable organization as a contribution, it is not a contribution until you make the note payments. Similarly, if you grant an option to buy real property at a bargain price to a charitable organization, no deduction is allowed until the organization exercises the option.

If you make a contribution with borrowed funds, a deduction is allowed in the year you make the contribution, regardless of when you repay the loan.

Limit on Deductions

If your total contributions for the year are 20% or less of your adjusted gross income (line 32, Form 1040), you do not need to read this section. The limits discussed here do not apply to you.

If your contributions are more than 20% of your adjusted gross income, the amount of your deduction may be limited to either 20%, 30%, or 50% of your adjusted gross income, depending on the type of property you give and the type of organization you give it to.

Your deduction for charitable contributions cannot be more than 50% of your adjusted gross income for the year. For this purpose, do not reduce adjusted gross income by net operating loss carrybacks due to losses you have in later tax years.

If you have contributed amounts that are subject to a 20% or a 30% limit, see *Limits on Deductions* in Publication 526 for more information.

50% limit. This limit applies to gifts *to* organizations listed below under *50% limit organizations.* But it does not apply to such gifts if they are gifts of capital gain property for which you figure your deduction using fair market value without reduction for appreciation. A special 30% limit applies to those gifts (see *Special 30% limit,* later).

50% limit organizations. The following are 50% limit organizations:

1) Churches, and conventions or associations of churches,
2) All public charities,
3) All private operating foundations,
4) Private nonoperating foundations that make qualifying distributions of 100% of contributions within 2½ months following the year they receive the contribution, and
5) Certain private foundations whose contributions are pooled in a common fund, the income and principal of which are paid to public charities.

The organization will be able to tell you if the contributions you make to it qualify for the 50% limit.

30% limit. This limit applies to:

• Gifts *for the use of* any organization, and
• Gifts (other than capital gain property) to all qualified organizations other than 50% limit organizations. This includes gifts to veterans' organizations, fraternal societies, nonprofit cemeteries, and certain private nonoperating foundations.

Special 30% limit. This limit applies to gifts of capital gain property to 50% limit organizations.

There is one exception to this general rule. The special 30% limit does not apply when you choose to reduce the fair market value of the property by the amount that would have been long-term capital gain if you had sold the property. The 50% limit applies instead. For more information, see the rules for electing the 50% limit for capital gain property under *How To Figure Your Deduction When Limits Apply* in Publication 526.

20% limit. This limit applies to gifts of capital gain property to all qualified organizations other than 50% limit organizations.

Explanation

An organization can tell you whether contributions to it qualify for the 50%, 30%, or 20% limit.

Contributions for the use of any charitable organization are limited to 30% of your adjusted gross income. This includes a gift of an income interest in trust to a charitable organization.

How to figure your deduction. To figure your deduction, first, you consider gifts to charitable organizations that qualify for the 50% limit when you figure your deduction. Second, you consider gifts to which the 20% and 30% limits apply. Third, you consider gifts of capital gain property to which the special 30% limit for capital gain property applies.

Example 1

Your adjusted gross income is $50,000 for 1993. On September 1, 1993, you gave your church $2,000 cash plus land, with a fair market value of $30,000 and a basis to you of $10,000. You had held the land for investment for more than 1 year. You also gave $5,000 cash to a private foundation to which the 30% limit applies. Because your allowable contributions— $32,000 ($2,000 + $30,000)—to an organization to which the 50% limit applies are more than $25,000 (50% of $50,000), your deductions subject to the 30% limit are not allowable. The $2,000 cash donated to the church is considered first. The deduction for the gift of land does not have to be reduced by the appreciation in value and is limited to $15,000 (30% × $50,000). The unused part ($15,000) may be carried over for 5 years. Therefore, in 1993, your deduction is limited to $17,000 ($2,000 + $15,000). The $5,000 contribution to the private foundation may also be carried over for 5 years.

Example 2

Your 1993 adjusted gross income was $50,000. During the year, you gave $5,000 cash to a private foundation, to which the 30% limit applies. You made no other charitable contributions. The entire $5,000 is deductible, since 30% of $50,000 is greater than $5,000.

TAXPLANNER 1

Contributions of inventory property that was acquired during the taxable year in which the gift was made are not subject to the percentage limitations rules. The cost of these items is claimed as part of the cost of goods sold.

TAXPLANNER 2

To ease the restrictions on charitable contribution limitations, you may consider making a series of smaller gifts over several years rather than one or two large gifts per year.

Alternatively, you may consider transferring property to a charitable organization in exchange for promissory notes. The value of the gift (i.e., the amount of the charitable deduction) would be the excess of the value of the property over the amount of the notes. You then may make additional gifts by forgiving all or part of the notes as they mature.

Carryovers. You can carry over your contributions that you are not able to deduct in the current year because they exceed your adjusted gross income limit. You can deduct the excess in each of the next 5 years until it is used up, but not beyond that time. For more information, see *Carryovers* in Publication 526.

Explanation

For contributions made to private nonoperating foundations that are in excess of 30% of your adjusted gross income, or 20% for capital gain property, you may deduct the excess in each of the next 5 years until it is used up.

You may not carry over gifts to certain veterans organizations, fraternal societies, and nonprofit cemetery companies on which the 20% limit applies.

For other contributions in excess of the percentage

limitations, you may deduct the amount carried over in the following year to the extent that it is not more than the applicable percentage of your adjusted gross income for that year less the amount donated to qualified organizations during that year.

The carryover amounts retain their respective limitation percentage in the carryover year.

Excess contributions can be carried over only to subsequent returns of the person who made the gift.

Example

You had adjusted gross income of $20,000 in 1992. During the year, you contributed $11,000 to your church. You deducted $10,000 in 1992 (50% of $20,000) and carried over $1,000. In 1993, you had adjusted gross income of $20,000 and contributed $9,000 during the year; you deducted the entire amount that you carried over from 1992. However, if you had contributed $9,500 during 1993, you could have deducted only $500 of the $1,000 you carried over, carrying over to 1994 the balance of $500.

Explanation

If a gift of long-term capital gain property subject to the 30% limitation is made and, for some unforeseen reasons, cannot be utilized entirely in the current year or in carryover years, you may elect to reduce its value by 100% of the gain and deduct the lower net value of the gift under the 50% limitation.

Example

Julia Walsh makes a contribution of long-term capital gain property that cost her $40,000 and now has a fair market value of $50,000. Julia dies during the taxable year. Her adjusted gross income on her final return is $80,000.

Without the election (mentioned above), Julia's deduction would be limited to $24,000 (30% × $80,000). However, if the value of the property is reduced by $10,000, the deduction is increased to $40,000.

Records To Keep

You must keep records to prove the amount of the cash and noncash contributions you make during the year. The kind of records you must keep depends on the amount of your contributions and whether they are cash or noncash contributions.

TaxOrganizer

In case the IRS questions your charitable contribution deductions, you should keep the following information to support your claim for charitable contribution deductions:

- Cancelled checks evidencing payments of charitable contributions;
- Receipts (letter or other written communication) from the charitable organization showing the name of the organization, the date of the contribution, and the amount of the contribution;

- Other reliable written records that include the information described above. Records may be considered reliable if they were made at or near the time of the contribution, were regularly kept by you, or if, in the case of small donations, you have emblems, buttons, or other tokens that are regularly given to persons making small cash contributions; and
- Copies of appraisals (if you are claiming a deduction in excess of $5,000) or other determinations of the market value of the contribution.

TaxAlert

Beginning in 1994, you will be required to obtain a contemporaneous written acknowledgment from any charitable organization to which a contribution of $250 or more is made in order to deduct that contribution. Contemporaneous for this purpose means that you must obtain the written acknowledgment on or before the earlier of 1.) the date on which your 1994 return is actually filed or 2.) the due date for the return, including extensions.

A canceled check will no longer constitute adequate substantiation for a cash contribution. The written acknowledgment will have to state the amount of cash and a description (but not the value) of any property other than cash contributed. It must also state whether the charitable organization provided any goods or services in consideration for the contribution and, if so, a description and good faith estimate of the value of goods or services provided. If the goods or services provided as consideration for the contribution consist solely of intangible religious benefits, a statement to that effect will have to be included in the written acknowledgment.

You will not be required to obtain substantiation for a donation if the charity files a return with the IRS that includes the same information otherwise required from you. Note, however, that the primary responsibility lies with you, not the charitable organization, to request and maintain the required substantiation in your records.

For any contribution over $75 for which the charity provides goods or services, such as a dinner, the charity must provide a statement to the donor that reports the estimated value of the goods or services received by the donor in exchange for the contribution. As under prior law, a payment to a charity is deductible only to the extent that it exceeds the value of any goods or services received in return.

TaxPlanner

In general, separate payments are not combined for purposes of the subtantiation requirement. Therefore, you could deduct separate contributions of less than $250 from each paycheck or make monthly payments to a charity without running afoul of the requirement. However, you could not, for example, simply write multiple checks on the same day in order to avoid substantiation. Similarly, separate payments made at different times with respect to different fund raising events are not totaled in order to determine whether the charity must inform the donor of the value of any benefit received in return for a donation in excess of $75.

Caution: For contributions of $250 or more that you make *after 1993,* you can claim a deduction only if you have an acknowledgement of your contribution from the qualified organization.

In figuring whether your contribution is $250 or more, do not combine separate contributions. However, two checks written on the same date to the same qualified organization may be considered one contribution.

The acknowledgement must meet these tests:

1) It must be written.
2) It must include:
   a) The amount of cash you contributed,
   b) A description (but not the value) of any property you contributed,
   c) Whether the qualified organization gave you any goods or services as a result of your contribution, and
   d) A description and good faith estimate of the value of any goods or services described in (c). If the only benefit you received was an intangible religious benefit (such as admission to a religious ceremony) that generally is not sold in a commercial transaction outside the donative context, the acknowledgement must say so and does not need to describe or estimate the value of the benefit.
3) You must get it on or before the earlier of:
   a) The date you file your return for the year you make the contribution, or
   b) The due date, including extensions, for filing the return.

Cash contributions. Cash contributions include those paid by cash, check, or credit card. They also include your out-of-pocket expenses when donating your services.

If you make a cash contribution, you must keep one of the following for each contribution you make:

1) A canceled check, *or* a legible and readable account statement that shows:
   a) If payment was by check – the check number, amount, date posted, and to whom paid.
   b) If payment was by electronic funds transfer – the amount, date posted, and to whom paid.
   c) If payment was charged to a credit card – the amount, transaction date, and to whom paid.
2) A receipt (or a letter or other written communication) from the charitable organization showing the name of the organization, the date of the contribution, and the amount of the contribution.
3) Other reliable written records that include the information described in (2). Records may be considered reliable if they were made at or near the time of the contribution, were regularly kept by you, or if, in the case of small donations, you have emblems, buttons, or other tokens that are regularly given to persons making small cash contributions.

Noncash contributions. For a contribution not made in cash, the records you must keep depend on whether your deduction for the contribution is:

1) $500 or less,
2) Over $500 but not more than $5,000, or
3) Over $5,000.

Deductions of $500 or less. If you make a noncash contribution, you must get and keep a receipt from the charitable organization showing:

1) The name of the charitable organization,
2) The date and location of the charitable contribution, and
3) A reasonably detailed description of the property.

A letter or other written communication from the charitable organization acknowledging receipt of the contribution and containing the information in (1), (2), and (3) will serve as a receipt. You are not required to have a receipt where it is impractical to get one.

In all cases, you must also keep reliable written records for each item of donated property. Your written records must include the following:

1) The name and address of the organization to which you contributed.
2) The date and location of the contribution.
3) A description of the property in detail reasonable under the circumstances. For a security, keep the name of the issuer, the type of security, and whether it is regularly traded on a stock exchange or in an over-the-counter market.
4) The fair market value of the property at the time of the contribution, and how you figured the fair market value. If it was determined by appraisal, keep a signed copy of the appraisal.
5) The cost or other basis of the property if you must reduce its fair market value by appreciation. Your records should also include the amount of the reduction and how you figured it. If you choose the 50% limit instead of the special 30% limit on certain capital gain property, you must keep a record showing the years for which you made the choice, contributions for the current year to which the choice applies, and carryovers from preceding years to which the choice applies. See *How To Figure Your Deduction When Limits Apply* in Publication 526 for information on how to make the capital gain property election.
6) The amount you claim as a deduction for the tax year as a result of the contribution, if you contribute less than your entire interest in the property during the tax year. Your records must show the amount you claimed as a deduction in any earlier years for contributions of other interests in this property. They must also include the name and address of each organization to which you contributed the other interests, the place where any such tangible property is located or kept, and the name of the person who has possession of the property, if it is someone other than the organization to which you contributed.
7) The terms of any conditions attached to the gift of property.

If the gift was a "qualified conservation contribution," your records must also include the fair market value of the underlying property before and after the gift and the conservation purpose furthered by the gift. See *Qualified conservation contribution* in Publication 561 for more information.

Deductions over $500. You are required to give additional information if you claim a deduction over $500 for noncash charitable contributions. See *Records To Keep* in Publication 526 for more information.

Explanation

A receipt is not required if you deposit property at a charity's unattended drop site. However, you must maintain a written record of the contribution, listing the items contributed and the date and location of the contribution.

Explanation

You are required to file Form 8283, *Noncash Charitable Contributions*, if you claim a deduction of over $500 for a noncash contribution. Additionally, there are special rules for noncash contributions in excess of $5,000, discussed previously in this chapter.

For contributions having a fair market value of more than $500 but less than $5,000, you must provide the following information:

- The name and address of the donee organization

- The description of the donated property

- The date of the contribution

- The date it was acquired by the donor

- How it was acquired by the donor

- The donor's cost or adjusted basis (if available)

- The fair market value of the contribution

- The method used to determine the fair market value (e.g., appraisal, thrift shop value, catalog, market quote, or comparable sales)

Form 8283 must be filed with the tax return on which the deduction is taken.

How To Report

Enter your cash contributions (including out-of-pocket expenses) on line 13, Schedule A (Form 1040).

Enter your noncash contributions on line 14 of Schedule A (Form 1040).

If you claim a deduction over $500 for noncash charitable contributions, you must also file **Form 8283,** *Noncash Charitable Contributions.* See *How To Report* in Publication 526 for more information.

26 | Nonbusiness Casualty and Theft Losses

Introduction

Almost anytime something you own is stolen, damaged, or destroyed in an accident or by an act of nature and you are not compensated by insurance, you are eligible for a tax **deduction.** *The loss need not be connected in any way to your trade or business, and it may include such personal items as jewelry, furs, and antiques. That's small comfort if everything you own has been demolished in a terrible earthquake or a devastating hurricane, but it's something.*

Although it's easy to claim a deduction for **casualty losses** *and theft losses, it's more difficult to get one. You must prove first that the casualty occurred. The more difficult task is substantiating the value of the property you have lost. That gorgeous necklace that your grandmother gave you may be worth a substantial amount, but, unless you can prove it, you're going to have a difficult time claiming a tax deduction if it is stolen. Recordkeeping and documentation are extremely important.*

No matter how good your records are, you must first pass two general limitations on the amount of your casualty and theft loss. First, you may not deduct the first $100 of any loss. Second and more significant, you are able to deduct casualty and theft losses only when the total amount you lost in any year (reduced by $100 per casualty) exceeds 10% of your **adjusted gross income.**

This chapter spells out which casualty losses are deductible. You'll also learn about the intricacies that should be considered in deciding when to take your deduction. Most important, this chapter discusses the records and other evidence you need to support any claim that you make.

Generally, your itemized deductions are limited if your adjusted gross income exceeds $108,450. However, this additional limitation does not apply to casualty or theft losses.

This chapter discusses how you treat casualty and theft losses for tax purposes when the losses are personal and not business related.

You have a casualty loss if you suffer damage to your property as a result of disasters such as hurricanes, fires, car accidents, and similar events. You have a theft loss if someone steals your property. This chapter will cover the following types of losses:

- Loss on deposits,
- Casualty loss, including disasters, and
- Theft loss.

This chapter will also provide information on what you should do once you determine you have a casualty or theft loss. The following information is provided in this chapter:

- How to figure the amount of your loss,
- When to deduct your loss subject to certain limits,

- How to treat insurance and other reimbursements you receive for casualty losses, and
- Which form to use to report your loss.

How to claim a loss. You must file Form 1040 and itemize your deductions on **Schedule A** (Form 1040) to be able to claim a casualty or theft loss of nonbusiness property. You cannot claim these losses if you file Form 1040A or Form 1040EZ.

Publication 584 is available to help you make a list of your damaged goods and figure your loss. That publication can serve as an inventory of your personal goods. It includes schedules to help you figure the loss on your home and its contents, and on your motor vehicles.

Deduction for casualty and theft losses is limited. You must reduce each casualty or theft loss on nonbusiness property by $100. You must further reduce the total of your casualty and theft losses for the year on nonbusiness property by 10% of your adjusted gross income. If these amounts are more than your losses, you do not have a casualty or theft loss deduction.

Disaster area. If you have a casualty loss in a federally declared disaster area, special rules apply. See *Disaster Area Losses* in Publication 547.

Other sources of information. For information on a casualty, theft, or condemnation concerning business or income-producing property, see Chapter 26 in Publication 334, *Tax Guide for Small Business*.

For information on a condemnation of your home, see *Involuntary Conversions* in Publication 544.

Useful Items

You may want to see:

Publication

- ☐ **544** Sales and Other Dispositions of Assets
- ☐ **547** Nonbusiness Disasters, Casualties, and Thefts
- ☐ **550** Investment Income and Expenses
- ☐ **551** Basis of Assets
- ☐ **584** Nonbusiness Disaster, Casualty, and Theft Workbook

Form (and Instructions)

- ☐ **4684** Casualties and Thefts

Loss on Deposits

A loss on deposits can occur when a bank, credit union, or other financial institution becomes insolvent or bankrupt. If you incurred such a loss, you have three choices of how to deduct the loss:

1) As a nonbusiness bad debt,
2) As a casualty loss, or
3) As an ordinary loss.

Note. You cannot choose (2) or (3) if you own at least 1% of the financial institution, are an officer of the financial institution, or are related to that owner or officer.

Choice of loss deduction. If you qualify to choose the kind of deduction as explained above, the following information may help you choose the one best for you.

Nonbusiness bad debt. A nonbusiness bad debt is deducted as a short-term capital loss on Schedule D (Form 1040). The capital loss that can be deducted after offsetting capital gains is limited to $3,000 ($1,500 if married filing separately) for each year. For more details, see *Nonbusiness Bad Debts* in Chapter 4 of Publication 550.

> **Explanation**
> A nonbusiness bad debt is treated as a short-term capital loss. See Chapter 17, *Reporting Gains and Losses*, for an explanation of the limitations regarding the deductibility of capital losses. A nonbusiness bad debt generally arises from loans that are between individuals and not connected with your business.

Casualty loss. A casualty loss deduction has no maximum limit. But in figuring the deduction, reduce the loss by $100 and

your total losses by 10% of adjusted gross income, as explained later. You must itemize deductions on Schedule A (Form 1040).

Ordinary loss. An ordinary loss deduction for a loss on deposits at a particular financial institution is limited to $20,000 ($10,000 if married filing separately) reduced by any expected state insurance proceeds. Further, the deduction is taken as a miscellaneous itemized deduction on Schedule A (Form 1040) and is subject to the 2% of adjusted gross income limit for that year. See Chapter 30 for information on this limit. It may also be affected by the overall limit on itemized deductions that is explained in Chapter 21.

Note. You cannot choose the ordinary loss deduction if any part of the deposits related to the loss is **federally insured** (example — FDIC).

When to choose. You can choose to deduct a loss on deposits as a casualty or an ordinary loss for any year in which you can reasonably estimate how much of your deposits you have lost in an insolvent or bankrupt financial institution. The choice is generally made on the return you file for that year. Once you treat the loss as a casualty or ordinary loss, you cannot treat the same amount of the loss as a nonbusiness bad debt when it actually becomes worthless. Also, the choice applies to all your losses on deposits for the year in the particular financial institution.

If you do not make a choice, you must wait until the actual loss is determined before you can deduct the loss as a nonbusiness bad debt. Once you make this choice, you cannot change it without permission from the Internal Revenue Service.

How to report. The kind of deduction you choose for loss on deposits determines how you report your loss.

- Nonbusiness bad debt — report on Schedule D (Form 1040), Part I, line 1.
- Casualty loss — report on Form 4684 first and then on Schedule A (Form 1040), line 17.
- Ordinary loss — report on Schedule A (Form 1040), line 20.

Get the Form 1040 instructions for more information.

Deducted loss recovered. If you recover an amount you already deducted in an earlier year as a loss, you may have to include the amount recovered in your income for the year of receipt. If any part of the original deduction did not reduce your tax in the earlier year, you do not have to include that part of the recovery in your income. For more information, see *Recoveries* in Chapter 13, *Other Income*.

Casualty

A casualty is the damage, destruction, or loss of property resulting from an identifiable event that is sudden, unexpected, or unusual.

- A *sudden* event is one that is swift, not gradual or progressive.
- An *unexpected* event is one that is ordinarily unanticipated and unintended.
- An *unusual* event is one that is not a day-to-day occurrence and that is not typical of the activity in which you were engaged.

A casualty can also include a government-ordered demolition or relocation of a home unsafe to use because of a disaster. For more information, see *Disaster Area Losses* in Publication 547.

Casualty losses. Deductible casualty losses may result from a number of different causes, including:

Earthquakes
Hurricanes
Tornadoes

Floods
Storms
Volcanic eruptions
Shipwrecks
Mine cave-ins
Sonic boom
Vandalism

Fires. If you set the fire, you cannot deduct the resulting loss.

Car accidents. The loss from an accident to your car is not a casualty loss if your willful negligence or willful act caused the accident. The same is true if the willful act or willful negligence of someone acting for you caused the accident.

Explanation

Damage resulting from faulty but not intentionally reckless driving is a casualty loss. Damage incurred while an automobile was operated by an unauthorized person is also a casualty loss.

The following are examples of casualty losses involving automobiles:

- The loss of an automobile that fell through the ice while the taxpayer was ice fishing
- Damage to an automobile starter caused by a child who pressed the starter button while the automobile's engine was operating

Other accidents. A loss due to the accidental breakage of articles such as glassware or china under normal conditions is not a casualty loss. Neither is a loss due to damage done by a family pet.

Explanation

Losses caused by a person's own negligence are deductible, as are losses that occur, even though they could have been foreseen or prevented. The courts have also *allowed* casualty loss deductions in the following cases:

Animals and insects

- Damage caused by a mass attack of southern pine beetles capable of destroying a tree in 5 to 10 days.
- Death of a horse by swallowing the lining of a hat.

Drought

- Cracking of foundation walls due to soil shrinkage.
- Death of trees and plants within 3 to 4 months as a result of extraordinary drought.

Earthquakes and landslides

- Collapse of a garage wall due to subsoil hydraulic action.
- Damage caused by a mine cave-in. A deduction was allowed even though the landslide was reasonably foreseeable.

Household

- Bursting of hot water boiler caused by air obstruction in water pipes.

- Damage to furniture dropped 16 floors by movers.
- Damage caused by a flood due to faulty construction. However, the cost of repairing the defect was not deductible.

Lightning

- Any damage by lightning is considered a casualty.

Personal belongings

- Damage to a diamond ring inadvertently dropped in a kitchen garbage disposal.
- Damage resulting from the sudden evacuation of the United States from Saigon and that city's subsequent seizure by the North Vietnamese.
- Damage to a ring caused by a husband slamming a car door on his wife's finger.

Progressive deterioration

- The breaking up of a driveway caused by weather conditions over a 4-month period.

Septic tank

- Damage by a tractor plowing the ground.

Storms

- Damage to a beach due to abnormal rains.
- Damage to a home by ice and snow.
- Damage to a beach house that was caused by a hurricane but was not discovered until 2 years later, when the floorboards and porch buckled. The loss was deductible in the year in which the damage was discovered.
- Property damage due to unusually high water levels caused by storms.

Trees, shrubs, and landscaping

- Damage caused by accidental application of chemical weed killer to a lawn.
- Damage to trees caused by blizzards and snowstorms.

Vandalism

- Damage to household appliances caused by vandals who broke into a house under construction.
- Damage and destruction of art objects by vandals or other rough, sudden usage after delivery to a new apartment.

Nondeductible losses. There is no casualty loss deduction if the damage or destruction is caused by:

Termites or moths.

Disease. The damage or destruction of trees, shrubs, or other plants by a fungus, disease, insects, worms, or similar pests is not a deductible casualty loss. But, a sudden, unexpected, or unusual infestation by beetles or other insects may result in a casualty loss. If a storm, flood, or fire damages trees and shrubs, the loss is a casualty.

Explanation

The following are also *not* considered casualty losses: damage to trees and plants caused by moths, damage caused by rat infestation, the death of a horse from colic, and the loss of livestock due to disease.

Progressive deterioration. If a steadily operating cause or a normal process damages your property, it is not considered a casualty. Thus, the steady weakening of a building due to normal wind and weather conditions is not a casualty. The rust and water damage to rugs and drapes caused by the bursting of a water heater qualifies as a casualty. The deterioration and damage to the water heater itself does not qualify.

Explanation

The following also do *not* qualify as casualty losses: damage from faulty construction that caused walls and floors to settle, dry rot to a wooden sloop, and the declining value of a piece of land that got progressively smaller because an entrance road damaged by freezing, thawing, and gradual deterioration had to be repaired and restored.

Drought. When drought causes damage through progressive deterioration, it is not a sudden event.

Explanation

A water well that ran dry because of a drought may not be deducted as a casualty loss. The courts have also *disallowed* deductions for casualty losses in the following cases:

Animals and insects

- Damage to shrubs eaten by a horse.
- Damage to an antique vase by a cat.
- Damage to a fur coat by moths.
- Loss of a valuable dog that strayed off.

Automobiles

- Damage to a fuel pump and muffler caused by high stones in a road. (The taxpayer was unable to prove that it was more than wear and tear.)
- Damage caused by a tire blowout due to overloading.
- Damage caused by exposure to salt water.
- Payments to the owner of a house into which a woman accidentally drove her car.
- The forced sale of an automobile due to divorce.
- Damage caused by potholes in the road.

Earthquakes and landslides

- Any additional loss in value due to buyer resistance. (A deduction is allowed only for physical damage.)

Household items

- Sale of household items by a storage company. (The sale was not an unexpected occurrence.)

Personal belongings

- The loss of a ring from the owner's finger.
- The accidental disposal of tissues in which two rings were wrapped.
- The accidental dropping of eyeglasses and a watch.
- Baggage and contents lost in transit.

Shipwreck

- The snapping of a propellor on a yacht that was not the result of a shipwreck or other casualty.

Trees, shrubs, and landscaping

- Damage to trees from Dutch elm disease. (The disease is progressive and not sudden or unexpected.)
- The gradual suffocation of a root system over a 16-month period.
- Damage to coconut palm trees caused by lethal yellowing.

Theft

A theft is the unlawful taking and removing of money or property with the intent to deprive the owner of it. It includes, but is not limited to, larceny, robbery, and embezzlement.

If money or property is taken as the result of extortion, kidnapping, threats, or blackmail, it may also be a theft. In these instances, you need to show that the taking of your property was illegal under the law of the state where it occurred, and that it was done with criminal intent.

Example

A taxpayer from New York was allowed a deduction for a theft loss for money given to fortune-tellers. Under New York law, fortune-telling is a crime and constitutes a theft offense. The taxpayer's testimony and receipts were sufficient proof of the amounts paid to the fortune-tellers.

Mislaid or lost property. The simple disappearance of money or property is not a theft. However, an accidental loss or disappearance of property may qualify as a casualty, if it results from an identifiable event that is sudden, unexpected, and unusual.

Example. A car door is accidentally slammed on your hand, breaking the setting of your diamond ring. The diamond falls from the ring and is never found. The loss of the diamond is a casualty.

Proof of Loss

To take a deduction for a casualty or theft loss, you must be able to show that there was a casualty or theft. You also must be able to support the amount you take as a deduction.

For a casualty loss, you should be able to show:

- The type of casualty (car accident, fire, storm, etc.) and when it occurred,
- That the loss was a direct result of the casualty, and
- That you were the owner of the property or, if you leased the property from someone else, that you were contractually liable to the owner for the damage.

For a theft loss, you should be able to show:

- When you discovered that your property was missing,
- That your property was stolen, and
- That you were the owner of the property.

TaxOrganizer 1

For a loss from theft to be deductible, you must be able to prove that a theft has taken place. Therefore, if you think a theft may have occurred, you should file a report with the police and attach a copy of the police report to your return. The report should tell of any evidence of breaking and entering and of any witness to the removal of the property. It is not necessary that the police investigate the alleged incident.

TaxOrganizer 2

If you are going to claim a deduction for a casualty or theft loss, it is important that you gather as much supporting evidence as possible. Newspaper clippings about a storm, police reports, and insurance reports may all be helpful in proving the nature of the casualty or theft and when it occurred. You have the burden of proof to establish that a casualty occurred and that your loss was a direct result of the casualty.

Determining the decrease in market value of household items and personal belongings is often difficult. A certain percentage of the original cost of an item has often been used both by the IRS and by the courts to determine the fair market value of a particular item. Therefore, if you can produce evidence of the original cost of the items that were lost or damaged, you help your case.

Losses are deductible only by the owner of the property, unless the property is leased and the lessee is obligated to repair casualty damage to the property.

Examples

If you purchase an automobile for your son or daughter and put the title to the automobile in the child's name, any casualty or theft loss is deductible by the child—not by you.

If you damage another person's property, you may not deduct any payments you make to restore or replace that property.

Members of social clubs may not deduct an assessment to repair hurricane damage to club property.

Amount of Loss

Figure your casualty or theft loss by subtracting any insurance or other reimbursement you receive or expect to receive from the *smaller of* the following two amounts:

1) The *decrease in fair market value* of the property as a result of the casualty or theft, or
2) Your *adjusted basis* in the property before the casualty or theft.

The decrease in fair market value is the difference between the property's value immediately before and immediately after the casualty or theft.

Fair market value (FMV). FMV is the price for which you could sell your property to a willing buyer when neither of you have to sell or buy and both of you know all the relevant facts.

Adjusted basis. Adjusted basis is your basis (usually cost) increased or decreased by various events, such as improvements and casualty losses.

Example 1

A ruby ring valued at $5,000 is stolen from your house. The ring was purchased by your great-grandfather and was handed down through three generations by means of nontaxable gifts. The amount of the loss is limited to the cost of the ring to your great-grandfather.

Example 2

A homeowner was not entitled to a casualty loss deduction resulting from hurricane damage to trees located on his property. A real estate agent's appraisal was not accepted as competent to show any decline in the fair market value of the property. Thus, the decrease in the fair market value of the property as a result of the casualty was zero.

TaxOrganizer

Establishing the amount of your loss may be difficult, but the time you spend documenting the loss may be of great value in reducing your tax. You should make a list of all stolen, lost, damaged, or destroyed items as soon after the theft, disaster, or casualty as possible. IRS Publication 584, *Disaster and Casualty Loss Workbook,* may be useful. It has schedules to help you calculate a loss on your home and its contents and on your automobile, van, truck, or motorcycle.

Theft. The FMV of property immediately after a theft is considered to be zero, since you no longer have the property. Figure your theft loss using the smaller of the stolen property's FMV or adjusted basis.

Example. Several years ago, you purchased silver dollars at face value for $150. This is your adjusted basis in the property. Your silver dollars were stolen this year. The FMV of the coins was $1,000 when stolen, and insurance did not cover them. Your theft loss is $150.

The cost of protection. The cost of protecting your property against a casualty or theft is not part of a casualty or theft loss. For example, you cannot deduct what you spend on insurance or to board up your house against a storm.

If you make permanent improvements to your property to protect it against a casualty or theft, add the cost of these improvements to your basis in the property. An example would be the cost of a dike to prevent flooding.

Explanation

Burglar alarms. The costs of protecting your property against potential casualty are not deductible. This includes such items as burglar alarms and smoke detectors.

Related expenses. The incidental expenses you have due to a casualty or theft, such as expenses for the treatment of personal injuries, for temporary housing, or for a rental car, are not part of your casualty or theft loss.

> ### Explanation
> Money spent for temporary lodging at a hotel or an apartment while your residence is being repaired or rebuilt, the cost of water purchased due to well contamination, the cost of putting up a fence around a fire-damaged residence, and the towing of an automobile to a garage for repairs are all personal expenses that may not be deducted.

Repair and replacement costs. The cost of repairing damaged property or of replacing stolen or destroyed property is not part of a casualty or theft loss. Neither is the cost of cleaning up after a casualty. See *Indication of decrease in FMV,* later.

Example. You bought a new chair 4 years ago for $300. In April, a fire destroyed the chair. You estimated that it would cost $500 to replace it. If you had sold the chair before the fire, you estimate that you could have received only $100 for it because it was 4 years old. The chair was not insured. Your loss is $100, the FMV of the chair before the fire. It is not $500, the replacement value.

> ### Explanation
> Cleanup expenses have been held deductible by courts in the following circumstances:
>
> • Replanting of damaged trees necessary to restore the property to its approximate value before the casualty
> • Removing destroyed or damage trees and shrubs, less any salvage value received
> • The cost of replacing a windstorm-damaged carport
>
> *Note:* Losses must be reduced by the $100 deductible limit and any money paid by insurance company.

Recovered property. If you get your stolen property back, your loss is measured like a casualty loss from vandalism. That is, you must consider the actual FMV of the property when you get it back. Your loss is figured using the smaller of:

• The decrease in the FMV of the property from the time it was stolen until the time it is recovered, or
• Your adjusted basis in the property.

> ### Example
> Your personal automobile is stolen. You paid $7,000 for it, and, on the day it was stolen, it had a fair market value of $5,500. Several days later, your automobile is found damaged and abandoned. The fair market value is reduced to $3,000 because of the damage. Your loss is $2,500. The decrease in market value ($5,500 − $3,000) is less than your cost of $7,000. Therefore, your deduction is limited to $2,500.

Leased property. If you are liable for casualty damage to property you lease, your loss is the amount you must pay to repair the property.

Business or income-producing property. If business or income-producing property is completely destroyed or lost because of a casualty or theft, your loss is:

Your adjusted basis in the property

MINUS

Any salvage value

MINUS

Any insurance or other reimbursement you receive or expect to receive.

The decrease in FMV is not considered. See Chapter 26 in Publication 334.

Separate computations. Generally, if a single casualty or theft involves more than one item of property, you must figure the loss on each item separately. Then combine the losses to determine the total loss from that casualty or theft.

Exception for real property. In figuring a casualty loss on nonbusiness real property, the entire property (including any improvements, such as buildings, trees, and shrubs) is treated as one item. Figure the loss using the smaller of:

• The decrease in FMV of the entire property, or
• The adjusted basis of the entire property.

Decrease in fair market value. To figure the decrease in FMV because of a casualty or theft, you must make a determination of the actual price you could have sold your property for immediately before and immediately after the loss. An appraisal is the best way to make this determination.

> ### Explanation
> Taxpayers have been unable to take deductions for such things as a decline in market value of a house because it is near a newly opened highway or because of the stigma of a previous fire. There must be actual physical damage to the property that is the immediate and direct result of a casualty. However, a court case has held that an owner could deduct as a casualty loss the decrease in fair market value due to permanent buyer resistance resulting from changes made to the neighborhood following a flood.

Items not to be considered. You generally should not consider the following items when attempting to establish the FMV of your property.

Sentimental value. Do not consider sentimental value when determining your loss. If a family portrait, heirloom, or keepsake is damaged, destroyed, or stolen, you must base your loss only on its actual market value.

General decline in market value. A decrease in the value of your property because it is in or near an area that suffered a casualty, or that might again suffer a casualty, is not to be taken into consideration. You have a loss only for actual casualty damage to your property. However, if your home is in a federally declared disaster area, see *Disaster Area Losses* in Publication 547.

Indication of decrease in FMV. You can use the cost of cleaning up or of making repairs after a casualty as a measure of the decrease in FMV if you meet *all* the following conditions.

1) The repairs are necessary to bring the property back to its condition before the casualty.
2) The amount spent for repairs is not excessive.
3) The repairs take care of the damage only.

4) The value of the property after the repairs is not, due to the repairs, more than the value of the property before the casualty.

TaxSaver

If the repairs do not bring the property back to its condition before the casualty, it may be that the decrease in fair market value is greater than the cost of the repairs. The greater loss is deductible.

Example

As a result of a boating accident, the fair market value of your boat drops from $6,000 to $2,500. You originally paid $5,000 for the boat. You spend $2,000 on repairs, which actually increase the market value of the boat to $4,800. Nevertheless, you are entitled to a deduction of $3,500, which is the decrease in market value as a result of the casualty ($6,000 − $2,500).

Restoration of landscaping. The cost of restoring landscaping to its original condition after a casualty may indicate the decrease in FMV. You may be able to measure your loss by what you spend on the following:

1) Removing destroyed or damaged trees and shrubs minus any salvage you receive,
2) Pruning and other measures taken to preserve damaged trees and shrubs, and
3) Replanting necessary to restore the property to its approximate value before the casualty.

Explanation

The IRS takes the position that ornamental trees and shrubbery are an integral part of the **real property** and have no separate value. Therefore, the loss from damage to landscaping is measured by the decline in the fair market value of the entire property, not of an individual tree.

This treatment generally works to your advantage. If you originally planted the trees, your basis in them is probably substantially less than the decline in their fair market value. However, since the trees are regarded as an integral part of the property, your basis for figuring your loss is not just your basis for the trees but your basis for the entire property.

Example

You purchased a lot 10 years ago for $12,000 and spent $2,000 for shrubs and saplings. The entire property is now worth $20,000. A fire destroys all of the now mature shrubs and trees and reduces the market value of the property to $11,000. You are entitled to a deduction of $9,000. Even though you paid only $2,000 for the trees, you paid $14,000 for the entire property. Since the decline in value of $9,000 is less than your basis of $14,000, you may deduct the entire decrease in fair market value.

TaxPlanner

After a storm, damaged or fallen mature trees are often replaced with saplings. You should argue that the re-placements—the saplings—are worth less than the fallen trees and that consequently a loss greater than the cost of the saplings should be allowed. It pays to be aggressive when claiming casualty losses for trees. Even though the IRS does not compute the amount of a loss by assigning values to individual trees or shrubs, that should not stop you from doing so to bolster your claim.

Sources of information. It is often difficult to value your property before and after the casualty or theft. The following sources will be helpful in establishing these values.

Photographs. Photographs taken after a casualty will be helpful in establishing the condition and value of the property after it was damaged.

The costs of photographs obtained for this purpose are not a part of the loss. You can claim this cost as a miscellaneous deduction subject to the 2% of adjusted gross income limit on line 20, Schedule A (Form 1040). The cost of the photographs is an expense of determining your tax liability. See Chapter 30, *Miscellaneous Deductions*.

TaxOrganizer

Photographs or videotapes of your home and its contents may be useful in other ways as well. First, they may provide evidence of value before the casualty. Recent photos or tapes may, for example, be used to prove that the property was in good condition prior to the casualty. Second, they may assist you in determining what items are missing or were destroyed in a fire or theft. People often do not have an accurate inventory of household items. Photos or tapes serve as useful reminders.

The photographs or videotapes should be updated annually and kept outside your house, preferably in your safe-deposit box. They may be even more important in dealing with your insurance claim than they are in helping you with the IRS.

Cars. Books issued by various automobile organizations may be useful in figuring the value of your car if your car is listed in the books. You can use the books' retail values and modify them by such factors as mileage and the condition of your car to figure its value. The prices are not "official," but they may be useful in determining value and suggesting relative prices for comparison with current sales and offerings in your area. If your car is not listed in the books, you determine its value from other sources. A dealer's offer for your car as a trade-in on a new car is not usually a measure of its true value.

Appraisals. The difference between the FMV of the property immediately before a casualty or theft and immediately afterwards should be determined by a competent appraiser. The appraiser must recognize the effects of any general market decline that may occur along with the casualty. This is necessary so that any deduction is limited to the actual loss resulting from damage to the property.

The appraiser should be reliable and experienced. Several factors are important in evaluating the accuracy of an appraisal, including the appraiser's:

- Familiarity with your property before and after the casualty or theft,
- Knowledge of sales of comparable property in the area,

- Knowledge of conditions in the area of the casualty, and
- Method of appraisal.

TAXPLANNER

If a casualty occurs that damages or destroys trees or shrubs on your residential property and you do not plan to repair or replace them, make sure that the appraiser's valuation documenting the decrease in the value of the property considers the estimated cleanup costs.

Appraisal fees. You can deduct your appraisal fees as a miscellaneous deduction subject to the 2% of adjusted gross income limit on line 20, Schedule A (Form 1040). The appraisal fee is an expense of determining your tax liability. It is not a part of the casualty loss. See Chapter 30, *Miscellaneous Deductions*.

TAXPLANNER

If you have property appraised because you have a casualty loss and the loss turns out not to be deductible because it does not exceed 10% of your adjusted gross income (see *10% Rule*), the cost of the appraisal is still deductible as a miscellaneous deduction on Schedule A.

Records. It is important that you have records that will prove your deduction. If you do not have the actual records to support your deduction, you can use other satisfactory evidence that is sufficient to establish your deduction.

Figuring the Loss

Generally, you must figure your loss *separately for each item* stolen, damaged, or destroyed. However, a special rule applies for nonbusiness real property.

Real property. Real property is land, the plants and trees that grow on land, and the buildings and other structures that are placed on land. In figuring a loss to real property you own for personal use, all improvements, such as buildings and ornamental trees, are considered together. The loss is the smaller of the decrease in the fair market value of the entire property or its adjusted basis.

Example. You bought your home a few years ago. You paid $50,000 ($10,000 for the land and $40,000 for the house). You also spent $2,000 for landscaping. This year a fire destroyed your home. The fire also damaged the shrubbery and trees in your yard. The fire was your only casualty or theft loss this year. Competent appraisers valued the property as a whole at $75,000 before the fire, but only $15,000 after the fire. (The loss to your household furnishings is not shown in this example but would be figured separately, as explained later.) You figure your casualty loss deduction as follows:

1) Adjusted basis of the entire property (cost of land, building, and landscaping)	$52,000
2) FMV of entire property before fire	$75,000
3) FMV of entire property after fire	15,000
4) Decrease in FMV of entire property	$60,000
5) Amount of loss (smaller of 1 or 4)	**$52,000**

Personal property. Personal property is generally any property that is not real property. If your personal property is stolen or is damaged or destroyed by a casualty, you must figure your loss separately for each item of property. The loss is the smaller of the decrease in the FMV of the property or its adjusted basis.

Example. A fire in your home destroyed an upholstered chair, an oriental rug, and an antique table. You did not have fire insurance to cover your loss. (This was the only casualty or theft you had during the year.) The chair cost you $750, and you established that it had a FMV of $500 just before the fire. The rug cost you $3,000 and had a FMV of $2,500 just before the fire. You bought the table at an auction for $100, before discovering it was an antique. It had been appraised at $900 before the fire. You figure your loss on each of these items as follows:

	Chair	Rug	Table
1) Basis (cost)	$750	$3,000	$ 100
2) FMV before fire	$500	$2,500	$ 900
3) FMV after fire	–0–	–0–	–0–
4) Decrease in FMV	$500	$2,500	$ 900
5) Loss (smaller of 1 or 4)	$500	$2,500	$ 100
6) Total loss			**$3,100**

Both real and personal properties. When a casualty involves both real and personal properties, you must figure the loss separately for each type of property, as shown in the previous examples. But you apply a single $100 reduction to the total loss. Then you apply the 10% rule. Both are explained later.

Explanation
Business or income-producing property. A loss on business property, property that earns you rent or royalty income, or other income-producing property is not subject to either the $100 rule or the 10% rule. For business or income-producing property, you must figure your loss separately for each item that is stolen, damaged, or destroyed. If casualty damage occurs both to a building and to trees on the same piece of property, the loss is measured separately for each.

Total loss of business or income-producing property. If you have business or income-producing property that is completely lost because of a casualty or theft, your deductible loss is your basis in the property minus any salvage value and minus any insurance or other reimbursement you receive or expect to receive. It does not matter what the decrease in fair market value is.

Example
You owned machinery that you used in your business. The machinery had an adjusted basis of $25,000 when it was completely destroyed by fire. Its fair market value just before the fire was $20,000. Since this was business property, and since it was completely destroyed, your deductible loss is your adjusted basis in the machinery, $25,000, decreased by salvage value and by any insurance or other reimbursement. Fair market value is not considered when you are figuring your loss, even though it is less than your basis in the machinery.

Explanation
Partial loss of business or income-producing property. If business or income-producing property is damaged but not completely destroyed in a casualty, the loss is the decrease in value because of the casualty or your adjusted basis in the property, whichever is less. From this amount (the lesser of your adjusted basis or the decrease in value), you must subtract any insurance or other reimbursement you receive or expect to receive.

Property used partly for business and partly for personal purposes. When property is used partly for personal (nonbusiness) purposes and partly for business or income-producing purposes, the casualty or theft loss deduction must be figured separately for the nonbusiness portion and for the business portion. You must figure each loss separately because the losses attributed to these two uses are figured in two different ways. The $100 rule and the 10% rule (explained later) apply only to the casualty or theft loss on the nonbusiness portion of the property.

TaxSaver

If your automobile is stolen or destroyed, you may be able to deduct more than the value listed in one of the various books issued by automobile organizations. If you use the automobile for business, you must make a separate calculation of the business and personal portions of the loss. This may produce a larger loss.

Example
Blair Hunt's automobile, which cost $8,000, is stolen. The "blue book"—one of the books published by automobile organizations—values his automobile at $5,000. Blair used the automobile for business 40% of the time and has taken $800 depreciation.

	Business portion	Personal portion
Value before theft	$2,000	$3,000
Value after theft	–0–	–0–
Decrease in value	$2,000	$3,000
Adjusted basis:		
Original cost	$3,200	$4,800
Depreciation	(800)	–0–
Adjusted basis	$2,400	$4,800

Blair's casualty loss before the $100 limitation is $5,400, computed as follows:

Business portion—adjusted basis	$2,400
Personal portion—the lower of the decrease in value or the adjusted basis	3,000
Total	$5,400

Insurance and Other Reimbursements

If your property is covered by insurance, you should file a timely insurance claim for reimbursement of a loss. Otherwise, you cannot deduct this loss as a casualty or theft loss. The portion of the loss not covered by insurance (for example, a deductible) is not subject to this rule.

Example. You have a car insurance policy with a $500 deductible. Because your insurance did not cover the first $500 of an auto collision, the $500 would be deductible (subject to the $100 and 10% rules discussed later). This is true even if you do not file an insurance claim since your insurance policy would never have reimbursed you for it.

Reduction of loss. If you receive insurance or another type of reimbursement, you must subtract the reimbursement when you figure your loss. You do not have a casualty or theft loss to the extent you are reimbursed.

If you expect to be reimbursed, but have not yet received payment, you must still subtract the expected reimbursement. See *When to Deduct a Loss,* later.

Gain from reimbursement. If your reimbursement is more than your basis in the property, you have a gain. This is true even if the decrease in the FMV of the property is more than its basis. If you have a gain, you may have to pay tax on it, or you may be able to postpone reporting the gain.

See Publication 547 for more information on how to treat a gain from the reimbursement for a casualty or theft.

Explanation
You do not have to report a gain that results from a reimbursement that exceeds your basis in the lost, damaged, or destroyed property if you use the entire reimbursement to puchase property that is either similar or related in use to the original property. Instead, the recognition of the gain is postponed until the replacement property is sold. Your basis in the replacement property is its cost minus any postponed gain. With a home, the gain may be indefinitely postponed (see the rules discussed in Chapter 16, *Selling Your Home*).

You are allowed a certain amount of time to select and purchase the replacement property. This time period begins on the day of the casualty or theft and ends two years after the close of the tax year in which the reimbursement is received. Thus, if your house was robbed on August 1, 1992, and your insurance company reimbursed you for your loss on May 1, 1993, you would have until December 31, 1995, to repair or replace the damaged goods. If the cost of the replacement property is less than the reimbursement received, the unspent part of the reimbursement must be reconized as a gain.

Example
Your home was destroyed in a tornado in May, 1993. Your basis in the home was $55,000. But the home was worth more than that, and you received $75,000 in insurance proceeds in 1993 to compensate you for your loss. You purchase a new home for $65,000 prior to December 31, 1995. You would be able to postpone a gain of $10,000, but you would also report a $10,000 gain in 1993. Your basis in the new property would be $55,000 (the cost of the new home less the $10,000 postponed gain). The calculation would be as follows:

Proceeds	$75,000	Proceeds	$75,000
Basis	(55,000)	Cost of new home	(65,000)
Gain	$20,000	Taxable gain	$10,000

$20,000 − $10,000 = $10,000 postponed gain.

You must file an amended return for 1993 in order to report the gain.

The gain is reported on Form 4684. As long as the home is strictly for personal use, all of the gain remains a **capital gain.** If the damaged property is held for more than the required long-term holding period, a net gain is a **long-term capital gain**.

Other reimbursements. Insurance is the most common way to be reimbursed for a casualty or theft loss. But you may be reimbursed in some other way. The following items are considered reimbursements:

- The forgiven part (the part you do not have to pay back) of a federal disaster loan under the Disaster Relief and Emergency Assistance Act,
- The repayment and cost of repairs by the person who leases your property,
- The court awards for damages for a casualty or theft loss (the amount you are able to collect) minus lawyers' fees and other necessary expenses,
- The repairs, restoration, or cleanup provided by relief agencies, and
- The payment you receive from a bonding company for a theft loss.

Explanation

If you have use and occupancy insurance for your business and are reimbursed for loss of business income, it does not reduce your casualty or theft loss. However, the reimbursement is considered income and is taxed in the same way as your other business income.

Payments not considered reimbursements. Insurance, grants, gifts, and other payments you receive to help you after a casualty are considered reimbursement *only* if they are specifically designated to repair or replace your property. If the money you receive is designated for other purposes, or if there are no conditions on how you have to use it, the money is not a reimbursement even if you use it to restore your property.

Payments for living costs. If an insurance company pays you for any of your living expenses after you lose the use of your home because of a casualty, the insurance payments are not considered a reimbursement. They do not reduce your casualty loss.

You must report as income insurance payments covering your normal living expenses. However, the part of insurance payments that compensates you for a temporary increase in the living expenses you and your family have during this period does not have to be reported as income. The same rule applies to insurance payments for living expenses if you are denied access to your home by government authorities due to a casualty or the threat of a casualty.

The increase in your living expenses is the excess of your actual living expenses over your normal living expenses. Do not include in income the payment you received for your extra expenses for renting suitable housing and for transportation, food, utilities, and miscellaneous services during the period you are unable to use your home because of the casualty.

Example. As a result of a fire, you vacated your apartment for a month and moved to a motel. You normally pay $525 a month rent. None was charged for the month the apartment was vacated. Your motel rent for this month was $1,200. You received $1,100 reimbursement from your insurance company for rental expenses.

The part of the insurance payment that reimburses you for the temporary increase of your actual rent over your normal rent is $675 ($1,200 − $525). You do not include the $675 in income. But you do include in income the rest of the insurance received, $425 ($1,100 − $675).

Disaster relief. Food, medical supplies, and other forms of assistance you receive do not reduce your casualty loss unless they are replacements for lost or destroyed property. These items are not taxable income to you.

Deduction Limits

After you have figured your casualty or theft loss and subtracted any reimbursements, you must figure how much of the loss you can deduct. If your loss was to property you had for your own or your family's personal use, there are *two limits* on the amount you can deduct for your casualty or theft loss:

1) You must reduce each loss by *$100.*
2) You must further reduce your loss by *10% of your adjusted gross income* (line 32, Form 1040).

$100 rule. A single $100 reduction applies to *each* casualty or theft, no matter how many pieces of property are involved. This rule applies after all reimbursements have been subtracted from your total casualty or theft loss.

Explanation

This rule does not apply if this loss is on business property, property that earns you rent or royalty income, or other income-producing property.

Single event. Generally, events closely related in origin are considered a single casualty or theft. It is a single casualty when the damage is from two or more closely related causes, such as wind and flood damage caused by the same storm. A single casualty may also damage two or more widely separated pieces of property, such as a hail storm that damages both your home and your car parked downtown.

More than one loss. If you have more than one casualty or theft loss during the tax year, you must *reduce each loss by $100.*

Example. Your family car was damaged in an accident in January. Your loss after the insurance reimbursement was $75. In February, your car was damaged in another accident. This time your loss after the insurance reimbursement was $90. Apply the $100 rule to each separate casualty loss. Since neither accident resulted in a loss of over $100, you are not entitled to any deduction for these accidents.

10% rule. You must reduce the total of all your casualty or theft losses by 10% of your adjusted gross income (line 32, Form 1040). Apply this rule after you reduce each loss by any reimbursements and by $100. If you had more than one casualty or theft loss during the year, reduce each loss by any reimbursements and by $100. Then you *reduce the total of all your losses by 10%* of your adjusted gross income. If you have casualty or theft gains, see *Gains and losses,* later in this discussion.

Example 1. In June, you discovered that your house had been burglarized. Your loss after insurance reimbursement was $2,000. Your adjusted gross income is $29,500. You first apply the $100 rule and then the 10% rule. Figure your theft loss as follows:

1. Loss after insurance	$2,000
2. Subtract $100	100

3. Loss after $100 rule	$1,900
4. Subtract 10% of $29,500 AGI	2,950
5. Theft loss deduction	–0–

When you apply the 10% rule, you find you do not have a casualty or theft loss deduction because your loss ($1,900) is less than 10% of your adjusted gross income ($2,950).

Example 2. In March, you had a car accident that totally destroyed your car. You did not have collision insurance on your car, so you did not receive any insurance reimbursement. Your loss on the car was $1,200. In November, you had a fire that damaged your basement and totally destroyed the furniture, washer, dryer, and other items you had stored there. Your loss on the basement items after reimbursement was $1,700. Your adjusted gross income is $25,000. You figure your casualty loss deduction as follows:

	Car	Basement
1. Loss	$1,200	$1,700
2. Subtract $100 per incident	100	100
3. Loss after $100 rule	$1,100	$1,600
4. Total loss		$2,700
5. Subtract 10% of $25,000 AGI		2,500
6. Casualty loss deduction		$ 200

Gains and losses. If you had both gains and losses from casualties or thefts to nonbusiness property, special rules apply. If your total losses are more than your total gains, only the excess losses are subject to the 10% rule.

However, if your total gains are more than your total losses, the difference (gains minus losses) will be treated as capital gain on Schedule D (Form 1040). None of the losses will be subject to the 10% rule.

Table 26–1 gives a brief explanation of how to apply the $100 rule and the 10% rule in various situations. For more detailed explanations and examples, get Publication 547.

Example 1

During 1993, a storm completely destroyed your summer cottage, resulting in a casualty gain of $2,000 after you were reimbursed by your insurance company. Later in the year, your home was broken into on two separate occasions. Jewelry, silverware, and other items of personal property were stolen each time. The loss (after the $100 rule) on the first theft was $900 and on the second theft was $4,000. Your 1993 adjusted gross income is $25,000. Your deductible loss is calculated as follows:

1) Loss on first theft	$ 900
2) Plus: loss on second theft	4,000
3) Total losses	4,900
4) Gain on cottage	2,000
5) Net loss for 1993	2,900
6) Minus: 10% of your adjusted gross income	2,500
7) Casualty and theft loss deduction	$ 400

Example 2

Assume the same facts as in Example 1, except your gain on the summer cottage is $5,000:

1) Loss on first theft	$ 900
2) Plus: loss on second theft	4,000
3) Total losses	4,900
4) Gain on cottage	5,000
5) Net gain for 1993	100

The $100 gain will be reported on Form 4684. See *Insurance and Other Reimbursements*, regarding recognition of gains.

When to Deduct a Loss

A casualty usually is apparent when it happens. A theft may not be discovered until later. This affects the year in which you may deduct a casualty or a theft loss. See *Table 26–2.*

Table 26-1. **Deduction Limit Rules**—These rules apply to a casualty or theft loss to nonbusiness property.

	$100 Rule	**10% Rule**
Definition of Rule	You must reduce each casualty or theft loss by $100 when figuring your deduction. Apply this rule *after* you reduce your loss by any reimbursement	You must reduce your total casualty or theft loss by 10% of your adjusted gross income from line 32 of Form 1040. Apply this rule *after* you reduce each loss by any reimbursement and by $100 (the $100 rule).
Single Event	Apply this rule only once, even if many pieces of property are affected.	Apply the rule only once, even if many pieces of property are affected.
More Than One Loss	Apply this rule to *each* loss.	Apply the rule to the *total* of all your losses.
More Than One Person— With Loss From the Same Event (other than married taxpayers)	Apply the rule *separately* to each person.	Apply the rule *separately* to each person.
Married Taxpayers— With Loss From the Same Event		
Filing jointly	Apply this rule as if you were one person.	Apply this rule as if you were one person.
Filing separately	Apply this rule *separately* to each spouse.	Apply this rule *separately* to each spouse.
More Than One Owner (other than married taxpayers)	Apply the rule separately to each owner of jointly owned property.	Apply the rule separately to each owner of jointly owned property.

Table 26-2. **When to Deduct a Loss**

Type of Loss	Tax Year Deducted	Can You Choose Years?
Casualty losses	Year loss occurred	No
Loss of deposits		
• Casualty loss	Year a reasonable estimate can be made	No
• Bad debt	Year deposits are totally worthless	No
• Ordinary loss	Year a reasonable estimate can be made	No
Federal disasters	Year the disaster occurred or the year immediately before the disaster	Yes
Thefts	Year of discovery of the theft	No

Loss on deposits. When you deduct a loss on deposits in an insolvent or bankrupt financial institution depends on the type of loss you choose to take on your return. See *Loss on Deposits,* earlier.

Casualty losses. Generally, you may deduct casualty losses only in the tax year in which the casualty occurred. This is true even if you do not repair or replace the damaged property until a later year.

Disaster area losses. If you have a casualty loss in a federally declared disaster area, you can choose to deduct the loss on your tax return for the year immediately preceding the year in which the disaster occurred. This may enable you to get an immediate refund of taxes you already paid. For more information, see *Disaster Area Losses* in Publication 547.

Explanation
The following areas were designated disaster areas through June 28, 1993:

Arizona
Flooding
Jan. 5 - Mar. 6

Apache, Cochise, Coconino, Gila, Graham, Greenlee, Maricopa, Navajo, Pima, Pinal, Santa Cruz, Yavapai, and Yuma Counties

California
Severe winter storms, mud and rock slides, flooding and fires
Jan. 5 - Mar. 20

Alpine, Contra Costa, Fresno, Humboldt, Imperial, Lassen, Los Angeles, Madera, Mendocino, Modoc, Monterey, Napa, Orange, Plumas, Riverside, San Bernardino, Santa Barbara, San Diego, Sierra, Siskiyou, Sonoma, Tehama, Tulare, and Trinity Counties, and the cities of Fillmore, Los Angeles, and Culver City

(And as of October 28, 1993: Los Angeles, Orange, Riverside, San Bernardino, San Diego, and Ventura Counties due to wildfires)

Florida
Severe storms, tornadoes, flooding, high tides, high winds, and damage resulting from cold temperatures and frosting conditions
Mar. 12-16

Alachua, Baker, Broward, Calhoun, Charlotte, Citrus, Collier, Columbia, Dade, Dixie, Duval, Franklin, Gilchrist, Glades, Gulf, Hamilton, Hendry, Hernado, Hillsborough, Lafayette, Lake, Levy, Manatee, Marion, Martin, Monroe, Nassau, Pasco, Pinellas, Polk, Putnam, Sarasota, Sumter, Suwannee, Taylor, Volusia, and Walulla Counties

Illinois
Severe storms, Mississippi River flooding, and other riverine floodings
June 7

Adams, Alexander, Boone, Calhoun, Carroll, Greene, Hancock, Henderson, Henry, Jackson, Jersey, Jo Daviess, Lake, Madison, Mercer, McHenry, Monroe, Pike, Randolph, Rock Island, St. Clair, Stephenson, Union, Whiteside, and Winnebago Counties

Iowa
Severe storms and flooding
Mar. 26 - Apr. 12

Benton, Black Hawk, Buchanan, Bulter, Cedar, Des Moines, Floyd, Kossuth, Linn, Louisa, Mitchell, Muscatine, Scott, Tama, and Webster Counties

Severe storms and flooding
Apr. 13

Adair, Adams, Allamakee, Appanoosa, Audubon, Benton, Black Hawk, Boone, Bremer, Buchanan, Buena Vista, Butler, Calhoun, Carroll, Cass, Cedar, Cerro Gordo, Cherokee, Chickasaw, Clarke, Clay, Clayton, Clinton, Crawford, Davis, Decatur, Dallas, Delaware, Des Moines, Dickinson, Dubuque, Emmett, Fayette, Floyd, Franklin, Fremont, Greene, Grundy, Guthrie, Hamilton, Hancock, Hardin, Harrison, Henry, Howard, Humboldt, Ida, Iowa, Jackson, Jasper, Jefferson, Johnson, Jones, Keokuk, Kossuth, Lee, Linn, Louisa, Lucas, Lyon, Madison, Mahaska, Marion, Marshall, Mills, Mitchell, Monona, Monroe, Montgomery, Muscatine, O'Brien, Osceola, Page, Palo Alto, Plymouth, Pocahontas, Polk, Pottawattamie, Poweshiek, Ringgold, Sac, Scott, Shelby, Sioux, Story, Tama, Taylor, Union, Van Buren, Wapello, Warren, Washington, Wayne, Webster, Winnebago, Winneshiek, Woodbury, Worth, and Wright Counties

Louisiana
Severe storms and flooding
Jan. 20-25

Ascension, East Baton Rouge, Iberville, Lafayette, Livingston, St. Martin, St. Tammany, Tangipahoa, and Vermillion Parishes

Maine
Flooding, heavy rain, snowmelt, and ice jams
Apr. 9

Androscoggin, Aroostock, Cumberland, Franklin, Hancock, Kennebec, Lincoln, Oxfford, Penobscot, Piscataquis, Somerset, and Waldo Counties

Minnesota
Severe storms, flooding, and tornadoes
May 6, 1993

Big Stone, Blue Earth, Brown, Carver, Chippewa, Clay, Cottonwood, Dakota, Faribault, Goodhue, Houston, Jackson, LaSueur, Lincoln, Lyon, Martin, McLeod, Murray, Nicollet, Nobles, Pipestone, Ramsey, Redwood, Renville, Rock, Scott, Sibley, Stevens, Swift, Traverse, Washington, Watonwan, and Yellow Medicine Counties

Missouri
Severe storms and flooding
Apr. 15 - May 29, 1993

Jefferson, Lincoln, Marion, Pike, Ralls, St. Charles, St. Genevieve, and St. Louis Counties

Severe storms and flooding
June 28, 1993

Andrew, Atchison, Barry, Bates, Boone, Buchanan, Callaway, Camden, Carroll, Cape Girardeau, Chariton, Clark, Clay, Cole, Cooper, Daviess, Franklin, Gasconade, Gentry, Harrison, Holt, Howard, Jackson, Jefferson, Lafayette, Lewis, Lincoln, Marion McDonald, Miller, Moniteau, Montgomery, Newton, Nodaway, Osage, Perry, Pike, Platte, Pulaski, Ralls, Ray, Saline, Shelby, St. Charles, St. Louis, St. Louis City, St. Genevieve, Stone, Warren, and Worth Counties, and the city of Jefferson City

Nebraska
Ice jams and flooding
Mar. 7-21

Adams, Boyd, Butler, Colfax, Cuming, Dodge, Hall, Merrick, Platte, Sarpy, Saunders, Seward, and Stanton Counties

New York
Explosion
Feb. 26

World Trade Center in New York County

North Dakota
Severe storms and flooding
June 22

Barnes, Burleigh, Cass, Dickey, Emmons, Grant, Hettinger, Kidder, LaMourne, Logan, McIntosh, Morton, Ransom, Richland, Sargent, Sioux, and Stutsman Counties

Oklahoma
Severe storms and tornadoes
Apr. 24

Mayes, Rogers, Tulsa, and Wagoner Counties

Severe storms, tornadoes, and flooding
May 8 - 26, 1993

Adair, Alfalfa, Atoka, Blain, Bryan, Canadian, Carter, Caddo, Cleveland, Cotton, Craig, Creek, Custer, Dewey, Grady, Grant, Haskell, Jefferson, Kay, Kingfisher, Kiowa, Lincoln, Logan, Love, Major, Marshall, McClain, Noble, Nowata, Okfuskee, Oklahoma, Okmulgee, Osage, Pawnee, Payne, Pottawatomie, Pushmataha, Sequoyha, Tulsa, Wagoner, Washington, Washita, Woods, and Woodward Counties

Oregon
Earthquake
Mar. 25

Clackamas, Marion, Washington, and Yamhill Counties

Vermont
Lake and river flooding caused by heavy rain and snowmelt
Apr. 24 - May 26

Addison, Chittenden, Franklin, and Grand Isle Counties

Washington
Severe storms and high winds
Jan. 20-21

King, Lewis, Mason, Pierce, Snohomish, Thurston, and Wahkiakum Counties

Wisconsin
Severe storms, tornadoes, and flooding
June 7

Buffalo, Calumet, Chippewa, Clark, Columbia, Crawford, Dane, Dodge, Dunn, Eau Claire, Fond du Lac, Grant, Green, Green Lake, Iowa, Jackson, Jefferson, Kenosha, LaCrosse, Lafayette, Lincoln, Marathon, Marquette, Milwaukee, Outagamie, Pepin, Pierce, Portage, Price, Racine, Rock, Rusk, Sauk, St. Croix, Trampeauleau, Waupaca, Waushara, Winnebago, Wood, and Vernon Counties

TAX**SAVER**

If you were affected by one of the 1993 disasters, you may get speedier action on your return by writing on the front of the return that a disaster loss is being claimed.

TAX**PLANNER**

If you are not in need of an immediate tax refund, you may want to wait to file until near the April 15th deadline. By waiting, you may be able to determine which tax year provides greater tax savings from the deduction and to choose that year to claim the loss. For more information, consult your tax advisor.

Explanation

A loss in a federally declared disaster area may be deducted on the tax return for the year in which the disaster occurs or in the immediately preceding tax year if certain requirements are met. First, the loss must have been from a disaster in an area that the president says needs federal assistance. Second, the tax return for the preceding year must be amended by the date it is due or, if that date has already passed, by the date the tax return for the year of the disaster is due. In both instances, extensions are allowed. Generally, you would have until April 15, 1994, to amend a 1992 return to report a 1993 disaster loss. An amended return is filed on Form 1040X. A listing of federal disaster areas may be obtained from your newspaper or from local officials.

TAX PLANNER

To determine whether you should claim the disaster loss on your current year's return or on your return for the preceding year, you should calculate the tax effects of claiming the loss in both years. Once you make a choice, it becomes irrevocable 90 days after you file your amended return or on the date on which the return for the year of the loss is due, whichever comes later.

Theft losses. You may generally deduct a theft loss only in the year you discover your property is missing. You must be able to show there was a theft, but you do not have to know when the theft took place. However, you should show when you discovered that your property was missing.

Reimbursement Claims

If there is a reasonable prospect you will be reimbursed for part or all of your loss, you must subtract the expected reimbursement when you figure your loss. You must reduce your loss even if you do not receive payment until a later tax year. You are believed to have a reasonable prospect of reimbursement if you have filed suit for damages.

If you later receive less reimbursement than you expected, you include that difference as a loss with your other losses (if any) on your return for the year in which you can reasonably expect no more reimbursement.

Example. Your personal car had a FMV of $2,000 when it was destroyed in a collision with another car in 1992. The accident was due to the negligence of the other driver. At the end of the year, there was a reasonable prospect that the owner of the other car would reimburse you in full. Therefore, you do not have a deductible loss in 1992.

In January 1993, the court awards you a judgment of $2,000. However, in July it becomes apparent that you will be unable to collect any amount from the other driver. Since this is your only casualty or theft loss, you can deduct the loss in 1993 that is more than $100 and 10% of your 1993 adjusted gross income.

TAX ALERT

Even though there is no formal IRS ruling, many IRS auditors tend to disallow any deduction for the unreimbursed amount if you are fully insured and settle your claim with the insurance carrier for less than the amount of the loss by signing a "proof of loss statement." The proof of loss statement sets the value of the loss between you and the insurance company. Generally, the IRS auditor will only allow a deduction of the unreimbursed loss if he or she is convinced that you have attempted all reasonable remedies against the insurer.

If you later receive more reimbursement than you expected, you may have to report the difference as income. If you have already taken a deduction for a casualty or theft loss in one year, and then in a later year you receive reimbursement, you must include it in your income for the later year to the extent your deduction reduced your tax for the earlier year.

However, if any part of your original deduction for the loss did not actually lower your tax, you do not include that part of the reimbursement in your income. You do not refigure your tax for the year you claimed the deduction. For more information, see *Recoveries* in Chapter 13, *Other Income*.

Publication 525 has a worksheet for you to use when only part of your original deduction reduced your tax in the earlier year.

Note. If the total of all the reimbursements you receive is more than your adjusted basis in the destroyed or stolen property, you will have a *gain* on the casualty or theft. Get Publication 547 for more information on how to treat a gain from the reimbursement of a casualty or theft.

If you receive exactly the reimbursement you expected to receive, you may not have any amount to include in your income or any loss to deduct.

Example. In December 1992, you had a collision while driving your personal car. Repairs to the car cost $950. You had $100 deductible collision insurance. Your insurance company agreed to reimburse you for the rest of the damage. As a result of your expected reimbursement from the insurance company, you do not have a casualty loss deduction in 1992.

Due to the $100 rule, you cannot deduct the $100 you paid as the deductible. When you receive the $850 from the insurance company in 1993, you do not have to report it as income.

Example

A taxpayer suffered a casualty loss from vandalism and filed a claim with her insurance company in the year of the loss. The insurance company denied any liability for the damage. Consequently, the taxpayer filed suit against the insurance company. A court held that the taxpayer could not deduct the loss in the year in which it was incurred, since a reasonable possibility of recovery still existed. No deduction was allowed while the suit against the insurance company was still pending.

Recovered property is your property that was stolen and later returned to you. If you recovered property after you have already taken a theft loss deduction, you must refigure your loss using the smaller of the property's adjusted basis (explained under *Amount of Loss,* earlier) or the decrease in FMV from the time it was stolen until the time it was recovered. Use this amount to refigure your total loss for the year in which the loss was deducted.

This is your refigured loss. If this amount is less than the loss you deducted, you generally have to report the difference as income in the recovery year. But report the difference only up to the amount of the loss that reduced your tax.

How to Report Gains or Losses

If you have a deductible casualty or theft loss from nonbusiness property, you can claim this loss only on Schedule A (Form 1040).

Form 4684. Use Section A of Form 4684 to figure and report your gain or loss. Be sure to attach Form 4684 to your return.

Section A—Personal Use Property. This section is for casualties and thefts of property *not* used in a trade or business or for income producing purposes. You must list each item or article for which you are reporting a casualty or theft on Form 4684. If more than four items of property were stolen or damaged in a single casualty or theft, you will need to complete additional Form(s) 4684. Or, you may want to substitute your own statement for these lines. The statement must include the same information asked on lines 1 through 9. If you have to figure your loss on many different personal and household items, you may want to use the worksheets in Publication 584. Copies of these worksheets can be used in place of additional Forms 4684.

More than one casualty or theft. If you had more than one casualty or theft during the year, you must complete lines 1 through 12 on separate Forms 4684 for each casualty or theft. Use only one Form 4684 for lines 13 through 18.

Losses. If you have only losses from nonbusiness property, transfer the amount from line 18 of Section A, Form 4684, to line 17 of Schedule A (Form 1040). Schedule A is used to itemize deductions. If you do not itemize deductions, you cannot deduct your casualty or theft loss.

Gains. If you have only gains from nonbusiness property, this amount will be shown on line 15 of Section A, Form 4684. You may also have to complete Schedule D (Form 1040). For more information, get Publication 547.

Gains and losses. If you have both gains and losses due to casualties in a single year, get Publication 547.

Example

In 1993, Bob has $100,000 of adjusted gross income, $50,000 of personal casualty gains, and $70,000 of personal casualty losses (after subtracting the required $100 per casualty loss). His losses exceed his casualty gains by $20,000. The $20,000 is subject to the 10% rule. It is reduced by 10% of Bob's adjusted gross income ($10,000). Bob's allowable casualty loss will be $10,000.

TAXPLANNER

When you are applying the 10% rule, do not include your personal casualty gains in your adjusted gross income.

Adjustments to basis. If you have a casualty or theft loss deduction, you must reduce your basis in the property by any deductible loss and any insurance or other reimbursements. The result is your **adjusted basis** in the property. Amounts you spend to restore your property after a casualty increase your adjusted basis. See *Adjusted Basis* in Publication 551 for more information.

Net operating loss. If your casualty or theft losses are more than your income, you may have a net operating loss. You can use a net operating loss to lower your taxes in an earlier year, allowing you to get a refund for taxes that you have already paid. Or, you can use it to lower your taxes in a later year. You do not have to be in business to have a net operating loss from a casualty or theft. For more information, get Publication 536, *Net Operating Losses.*

Explanation

Gain. If you have more than one casualty or theft of personal items, and if you have gains and losses, you have to make the following computation:

The total of all gains and losses (after deducting the required $100 per casualty loss) must be computed. If gains exceed losses, both the gains and the losses will receive capital gain treatment. The 10% of adjusted gross income limitation (see the 10% rule earlier) will not apply. If the losses exceed the gains, the excess loss is deductible, subject to the 10% rule.

TAXPLANNER

If a casualty loss does result in a net operating loss, it must be carried back to your prior 3 years of taxable income before being carried forward to future years, unless you make a written election, included in your return, not to carry the loss back.

You should compare the refund available from a carryback to the expected tax benefits in the future in order to determine whether you should make the election.

27 | Moving Expenses

Introduction

The good news about moving expenses is that you usually may deduct them if you move because you change jobs. The not-so-good news is that, since no two moves are alike, there are several tests you must meet in order to claim the deductions and disagreements with the IRS over moving expenses are frequent.

You must itemize your deductions in order to deduct your moving expenses. Moving expenses, however, are not subject to the 2% rule that applies to many miscellaneous deductions. In other words, moving expenses will be deductible even if your miscellaneous itemized deductions do not exceed 2% of your adjusted gross income.

If you are interested in deducting as much of your move as possible, the first rule you should follow is to keep adequate records of all of your moving-related expenditures. Receipts, plus a log of your activities, generally suffice. The other ins and outs of moving expenses are detailed in this chapter.

Important Reminders

Moving expenses are an itemized deduction. You can deduct moving expenses only if you itemize your deductions on Schedule A (Form 1040). See *How To Report,* later.

Limit on itemized deductions. If your adjusted gross income is more than $108,450 ($54,225 if you are married filing separately), the amount of your itemized deductions may be limited. See Chapter 21, *Limit on Itemized Deductions*, and the instructions for Form 1040.

Change of address. If you change your mailing address, be sure to notify the IRS using Form 8822, *Change of Address.* Mail it to the Internal Revenue Service Center for your old address (addresses for the Service Centers are on the back of the form).

This chapter discusses what expenses you can deduct when you move because of a job. The following topics are covered:

- When moving expenses qualify for a deduction
- Which moving expenses can be claimed
- Dollar limits for certain expenses
- How to report moving expenses on Form 3903, *Moving Expenses*

You may be able to deduct some of your expenses for moving to a new home because you changed job locations or started a new job. You can qualify for the deduction whether you are self-employed or an employee. However, you must meet the *Requirements,* explained later.

This chapter contains three charts that may help you determine whether your move qualifies for a deduction, and if so, how much you can deduct. The charts are:

- Figure 27–A, *Illustration of Distance Test,* which covers the minimum distance you must move before you qualify to deduct moving expenses,
- Figure 27–B, *Qualifying Moves Within the U.S.,* which covers general qualifications, and
- Table 27–1, *Moving Expense Dollar Limits,* which covers how much you can deduct.

Moves to the United States. If you retire while living and working overseas, you may be able to deduct your expenses of moving back to the U.S. If you are the survivor (spouse or dependent) of a person whose main job location at the time of death was outside the U.S., you may be able to deduct your expenses of moving back to the U.S. See *Retirees or Survivors Who Move to the U.S.,* later.

Moves outside the United States. This chapter does not discuss moves outside the U.S. If you are a U.S. citizen or resident alien who moved outside the U.S. or its possessions because of your job or business, see Publication 521, *Moving Expenses,* for special rules that apply to your move.

Caution: If you incur moving expenses after December 31, 1993, you will:

- Not have to itemize deductions to claim moving expenses,
- Have to meet a new distance test, and
- No longer be able to deduct some moving expenses.

See Publication 553, *Highlights of 1993 Tax Changes.*

Useful Items

You may want to see:

Publication

- ☐ **521** Moving Expenses
- ☐ **523** Selling Your Home

Form (and Instructions)

- ☐ **Form 2119** Sale of Your Home
- ☐ **3903** Moving Expenses
- ☐ **3903F** Foreign Moving Expenses
- ☐ **8822** Change of Address

Figure 27-A. Illustration of Distance Test

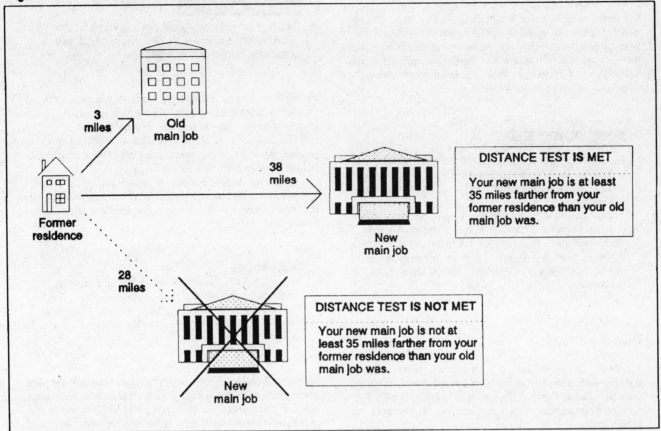

3
miles

Old
main job

Former
residence

38
miles

New
main job

DISTANCE TEST IS MET

Your new main job is at least
35 miles farther from your
former residence than your old
main job was.

28
miles

New
main job

DISTANCE TEST IS NOT MET

Your new main job is not at
least 35 miles farther from your
former residence than your old
main job was.

Requirements

You can deduct your moving expenses, subject to certain dollar limits, if your move is closely related to the start of work and if you meet the distance test and the time test. These two tests are discussed later.

Related to Start of Work

Your move must be closely related, both in time and in place, to the start of work at your new job location.

Closely related in time. In general, moving expenses incurred within one year from the date you first reported to work are considered closely related in time to the start of work at the new location. It is not necessary that you arrange to work before moving to a new location, as long as you actually do go to work.

If you do not move within one year, you ordinarily cannot deduct the expenses unless you can show that circumstances existed that prevented the move within that time.

Example. Your family moved more than a year after you started work at a new location. Their move was delayed because you allowed your child to complete high school. You can deduct your allowable moving expenses.

Explanation

You must make the actual move within a year of starting a new job, unless circumstances prevent you from doing so. Although not moving your family so that your child may complete high school in the same school

is an acceptable reason, not moving because you haven't sold your home is not. Good intentions are not enough.

Closely related in place. A move is generally considered closely related in place to the start of work if the distance from your new home to the new job location is not more than the distance from your former home to the new job location. A move that does not meet this requirement can qualify if you can show that:

A condition of employment requires you to live at your new home, or

You will spend less time or money commuting from your new home to your new job.

Explanation

Assume that your new home is 60 miles from your new job but that your former home was only 55 miles from your new job. If you want to deduct your moving expenses, you must give the IRS an acceptable reason why you now drive farther than you would have if you hadn't moved. An acceptable reason might be that from your new home you are able to use a freeway or a commuter train or bus that saves you time and/or money, whereas before you had to drive across town on local streets all the way to work.

Home defined. Your home means your main home (residence). It may be a house, apartment, or condominium. It also may be a houseboat, house trailer, or similar dwelling. Your home does not include other homes owned or kept up by you or members of your family. It also does not include a seasonal home, such as a summer beach cottage. Your *former home* means your home before you left for your new job location. Your *new home* means your home within the area of your new job location.

TaxSaver

First-time job seekers, such as high school and college graduates, and people reentering the labor force after a substantial period of unemployment may deduct moving expenses.

You must move from a former principal home to a new principal home, which means that you must have a principal home from which to move. According to one court, a college graduate could not deduct his expenses to move to his new job location because his student residence was not his principal home.

Distance Test

Your move will meet the distance test if your new main job location is *at least 35 miles* farther from your former home than your old main job location. For example, if your old job was 3 miles from your former home, your new job must be at least 38 miles from that former home.

The distance between a job location and your home is the shortest of the more commonly traveled routes between them. The distance test considers only the location of your former home. It does not apply to the location of your new home.

Example. You moved to a new home less than 35 miles from your former home because you changed job locations. Your old job was 3 miles from your former home. Your new job is 40 miles from that home. Because your new job is 37 miles farther from your former home than the distance from your former home to your old job, you meet the 35-mile distance test.

Explanation

For 1993, the key is that your new job location must be at least 35 miles farther from your former home than your old job location. The IRS doesn't care how far away you live from your new office in absolute terms. To be able to deduct moving expenses, your new job has to be 35 miles farther from your former home than your old job used to be.

Example

Even though you may now live 55 miles from your office, the fact that your office is only 30 miles more from your old home than it used to be means that you will not be able to deduct your moving expenses.

You can tell whether you meet the distance test simply by subtracting the total miles from your *old* home to the old job from the total miles from the old home to the new job. The difference must be 35 miles or greater.

TaxAlert

The 1993 Tax Act increased the mileage limit for moving expenses from 35 miles to 50 miles for expenses incurred after December 31, 1993.

First job or return to full-time work. If you go to work full time for the first time, your place of work must be at least 35 miles from your former home to meet the distance test.

If you go back to full-time work after a substantial period of part-time work or unemployment, your place of work must also be at least 35 miles from your former home.

Exception for Armed Forces. If you are in the Armed Forces and you moved because of a permanent change of station, you do not have to meet the distance test. See *Members of the Armed Forces,* later.

Explanation

Two months of unemployment is not long enough to qualify as a substantial period of unemployment. If you had only a brief break in employment, you must meet the same distance requirement that you would if you had been working continuously.

Main job location. Your main job location is usually the place where you spend most of your working time. A new job location is a new place where you will work permanently or indefinitely rather than temporarily. If there is no one place where you spend most of your working time, your main job location is the place where your work is centered—for example, where you report for work or are otherwise required to "base" your work.

Union members. If you work for a number of employers on a short-term basis and you get work under a union hall system (such as a construction or building trades worker), your main job location is the union hall.

More than one job. If you have more than one job at any time, your main job location depends on the facts in each case. The more important factors to be considered are:

- The total time you spend at each place,
- The amount of work you do at each place, and
- The money you earn at each place.

Example 1

A consultant working on an assignment in Detroit—a city that was not his main job location—was allowed by the Tax Court to deduct moving expenses when, at the request of his employer, he moved from Canton, Ohio, to Dallas, Texas, even though he continued the consulting assignment in Detroit. The Tax Court's rationale was that Detroit was only a temporary place of work and that the moving expenses arose from a shift from one principal place of work—Canton—to another—Dallas.

Example 2

A government employee moved to Washington, D.C., from Honolulu but took a temporary leave of absence from her job to go to Texas to continue her studies. The Tax Court ruled that she could not deduct her moving expenses to Washington, D.C., since her location during the time of her leave was not in the "general location" of her new work place.

A person on leave is still considered to be a full-time employee and must meet the distance requirements as though he or she were actually working at his or her new business location. In this example, the employee would have had to remain in Washington, D.C., for the required 39 weeks in the year (see below) following her move from Honolulu for her moving expenses to have been deductible.

Time Test

To deduct your moving expenses, you also must meet one of the following time tests.

Time test for employees. If you are an employee, you must work full time for at least *39 weeks during the first 12 months* after you arrive in the general area of your new job location. For this time test, count only your full-time work as an employee; do not count any work you do as a self-employed person. You do not have to work for the same employer for the 39 weeks. You do not have to work 39 weeks in a row. However, you must work full time within the same general commuting area. Full-time employment depends on what is usual for your type of work in your area.

Explanation
The courts have held that the mere enrollment in an employment registry does not by itself constitute full-time employment.

Example
A registered nurse moved to California, where she enrolled with a nursing registry that facilitated the employment of nurses. Even though it may be the customary method to obtain a job in a hospital in California, the mere enrollment in the registry does not establish the taxpayer as a full-time employee.

Temporary absence from work. You are considered to be working full time during any week you are temporarily absent from work because of illness, strikes, lockouts, layoffs, natural disasters, or similar causes. You are also considered to be a full-time employee during any week you are absent from work for leave or vacation that is provided for in your work contract or agreement.

Seasonal work. If your work is seasonal, you are considered to be working full time during the off-season only if your work contract or agreement covers an off-season period and that period is less than 6 months. For example, a school teacher on a 12-month contract who teaches on a full-time basis for more than 6 months is considered a full-time employee for 12 months.

Explanation
According to the IRS, a seasonal employee under contract for less than 39 weeks of work does not meet the 39-week test unless the contract is extended and the employee actually works the required additional time or

is prevented from doing so involuntarily, for example, because of illness, natural disaster, or a similar cause.

Time test for self-employed persons. If you are self-employed, you must work full time for at least *39 weeks during the first 12 months AND* for a total of at least *78 weeks during the first 24 months* after you arrive in the area of your new job location. For this time test, count any full-time work you do as an employee or as a self-employed person. You do not have to work for the same employer or be self-employed in the same trade or business for the 78 weeks.

Self-employment. You are self-employed if you work as the sole owner of an unincorporated business or as a partner in a partnership carrying on a business. You are not considered self-employed if you are semiretired, a part-time student, or work only a few hours each week.

Full-time work. Whether you perform services full time during any week depends on what is usual for your type of work in your area.

If you are an employee and become self-employed before satisfying the 39-week test for employees, you meet the time test if you satisfy the 78-week test for self-employed persons. Under the 78-week test, you still have to work full time for 39 weeks during the first 12 months. However, you can count any full-time work you do as an employee or as a self-employed person.

If you are self-employed and become an employee before satisfying the 78-week test, but you work as an employee for at least 39 weeks during the first 12 months after you arrived at the new job location, you will satisfy the time test for employees. If you cannot satisfy that time test, you can use the time spent as a full-time employee to satisfy the 78-week test. Under the 78-week test, you still have to work full time for 39 weeks during the first 12 months. However, you can count any full-time work you do as an employee or as a self-employed person.

If you are both self-employed and an employee, the amount of time you spend as each determines whether you must meet the 78-week test for self-employed persons or the 39-week test for employees. If you spend most of your working time as a self-employed person, you must meet the 78-week test (which includes a requirement to work 39 weeks during the first 12 months). If you spend most of your working time as an employee, you must meet the 39-week test.

For more information, see *Time test for self-employed persons* in Publication 521.

Joint return. If you are married and file a joint return and both you and your spouse work full time, either of you can satisfy the full-time work test. However, you cannot combine the weeks your spouse worked with the weeks you worked to satisfy that test.

TAXSAVER
If you file separate returns, each person must meet the time test individually and deduct only his or her own expenses.

The time test may be met by either spouse if a joint return is filed. However, weeks worked by both husband and wife cannot be added together to meet the time test.

If you and your spouse are living together, and if both of you have been working full-time but one of you loses your job, you obtain the maximum tax benefits by filing

Figure 27-B. Qualifying Moves Within the U.S. (Non-Military)[1]

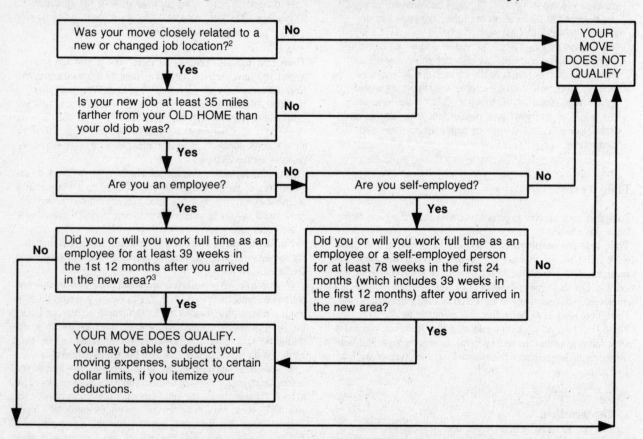

[1]Military persons should see "Members of the Armed Forces," in this chapter, for special rules that apply to them.

[2]Your move must be closely related to the start of work at your new job location. See "Related to Start of Work," earlier.

[3]If you deduct expenses and do not meet this test later, you must either file an amended tax return or report your moving expense deduction as other income. See "Time test not met," later.

a joint return. This is the case even if you reside in a **community property** state. Moving expenses paid by both husband and wife may be aggregated and are deductible in full, subject only to the overall dollar limitation. (See *Dollar Limits* later in this chapter.)

Time test not yet met. You can deduct your moving expenses even if you have not yet met the time test by the date your 1993 return is due. You can do this if you expect to meet the 39-week test in 1994 or the 78-week test in 1995. If you deduct moving expenses but do not meet the time test by then, you must either:

• Amend your 1993 return, or
• Report your moving expense deduction as other income on your Form 1040 for the year you cannot meet the test.

Use Form 1040X, *Amended U.S. Individual Income Tax Return*, to amend your return.

If you do not deduct your moving expenses on your 1993 return and you later meet the time test, you can file an amended return for 1993 to take the deduction.

Home-selling expenses. If your moving expenses become nondeductible because you did not meet the time test, you can use the part of these expenses that is for the sale or exchange of your former home to lower the gain on the sale of your former home. Add the part of these expenses that is for the purchase of your new home to the basis of your new home. For more information, see *Basis* in Chapter 16.

Exceptions to the Time Test

You do not have to meet the time test if one of the following applies:

1) You are in the Armed Forces and you moved because of a permanent change of station—see *Members of the Armed Forces*, in this chapter,
2) You moved to the United States because you retired—see *Retirees or Survivors Who Move to the U.S.*, later,
3) You are the survivor of a person whose main job location at the time of death was outside the United States—see *Retirees or Survivors Who Move to the U.S.*, later,
4) Your job at the new location ends because of death or disability, or
5) You are transferred for your employer's benefit or laid off for a reason other than willful misconduct. For this exception, you must have obtained full-time employment, and you must have expected to meet the test at the time you started the job.

Explanation

The courts have held and the IRS agrees that, if you are fired or laid off, involuntarily lose your job (for other than willful misconduct), or are required to move again by your employer before the 39 weeks are up, you are still able to deduct your moving expenses. Death and disability also exempt a taxpayer from the 39-week requirement. However, if you voluntarily take a leave of absence—even if employment benefits continue—you may not count the leave period toward the 39 weeks.

Example

A taxpayer who terminated his employment voluntarily after working in his new location only 37 weeks (even though he did so in order to start a different job elsewhere) was not allowed the deduction for his original moving costs.

TaxSaver

Since you have 2 years to fulfill the time requirement, you should assume that you will meet it and deduct moving expenses in the year in which you incur them. Even if you expect more moving expenses later, do not wait to deduct those that you already have. Any later expenses that qualify may be deducted in a subsequent year.

If you fail to meet the time test later, you may either file an amended return and repay any tax due along with interest or report as income the amount you previously deducted. In some cases, the 2-year period may be extended.

Example

A woman was allowed to deduct moving expenses incurred 30 months after her transfer because she waited until her child finished school before moving her family. The IRS rule is: You have to demonstrate that there is a good reason for the delay.

Members of the Armed Forces

Members of the Armed Forces

If you are a member of the Armed Forces on active duty and you move because of a permanent change of station, you do not have to meet the *distance and time tests,* discussed earlier. You can deduct your unreimbursed moving expenses, subject to certain dollar limits, which are discussed later.

A permanent change of station includes:

- A move from your home to the area of your first post of duty when you begin active duty,
- A move from one permanent post of duty to another, or
- A move from your last post of duty to your home or to a nearer point in the United States. The move must occur within one year of ending your active duty or within the period allowed under the Joint Travel Regulations.

Spouse and dependents. If a member of the Armed Forces deserts, is imprisoned, or dies, a permanent change of station for the spouse or dependent includes a move to the place of enlistment, or to the member's, spouse's, or dependent's home of record, or to a nearer point in the United States.

If the military moves you and your spouse and dependents to or

from separate locations, the moves are treated as a single move to your new main job location.

Services or reimbursements provided by government. Do not include in income the value of moving and storage services provided by the government in connection with a permanent change of station. If the total reimbursements and allowances you receive from the government in connection with the move are more than your actual moving expenses, include the excess in income. Do not complete Form 3903 or Form 3903F.

If your reimbursements or allowances are less than your actual moving expenses, do not include the reimbursements or allowances in income. You can deduct the expenses, subject to dollar limits, that exceed your reimbursements. See *Deductible Moving Expenses,* later.

How to complete Form 3903 for members of the Armed Forces. Complete Form 3903 if your reimbursements and allowances are less than your actual expenses. Use the following steps:

1) Complete Part I, lines 4 through 15, using your actual expenses. **DO NOT** reduce your expenses by any reimbursements or allowances you received from the government in connection with the move.
2) Complete Part II, lines 16 through 18.
3) Complete line 19. Add the amounts on lines 4, 8, and 18. From that total subtract the total reimbursements and allowances you received from the government in connection with the move. If the result is more than zero, enter the result on line 19, Form 3903, and on Schedule A, line 18.

For information on how to fill out Form 3903F, see the instructions for that form.

Note. You must apply the dollar limits to all expenses other than services provided in kind by the government.

If you are required to relocate and your spouse and dependents move to or from a different location, do not include in income reimbursements, allowances, or the value of moving and storage services provided by the government to move you, your spouse, and your dependents to and from the separate locations.

Do not deduct any expenses for moving services provided by the government. Also, do not deduct any expenses that were reimbursed to you that you did not include in income.

Explanation

If a service member's family can't move to his or her new permanent location, the cost of moving the family to a new location is still deductible (within the normal dollar limitations). For a discussion of the dollar limits on moving expense, see *Dollar Limits.*

A service member's family may deduct expenses for a move to the foreign country to which the service member is transferred, even if the family obtains only 90-day tourist visas. The IRS recognizes the family as being part of the service member's household, residing with him or her before and after the move.

A dislocation allowance received by armed services personnel is included in wages, although no tax need be withheld if it is reasonable to assume that a deduction for moving expenses will be allowed.

Retirees or Survivors Who Move to the U.S.

You may be able to deduct your moving expenses, subject to certain dollar limits, if you move to the U.S. or to a possession of the U.S. You do not have to meet the *time test,* discussed earlier, but you must meet the requirements discussed below.

Retirees. You can deduct moving expenses for a move to a new home in the U.S. when you permanently retire. However, both your former main job location and your former home must have been outside the U.S.

Permanently retired. You are considered permanently retired when you cease gainful full-time employment or self-employment. If at the time you retire, you intend your retirement to be permanent, you will be considered retired even though you later return to work. Your intention to retire permanently will be determined by:

- Your age and health,
- The customary retirement age for people who do similar work,
- Whether you are receiving retirement payments from a pension or retirement fund, and
- The length of time before you will return to full-time work.

Explanation
A retiree may deduct the cost of moving back to a residence in the United States without having to be employed on returning. The dollar limitation is the same as for moves within the United States. Although there is no timetable for the move specified in the law, it must be "in connection with the bona fide retirement of an individual." Moving expenses incurred after a lengthy delay following retirement may not be deductible.

Survivors. You can deduct moving expenses for a move to a home in the U.S. if you are the spouse or the dependent of a person whose main job location at the time of death was outside the U.S. The move must begin within 6 months after the decedent's death. It must be from the decedent's former home outside the U.S. That home must also have been your home.

A move begins when:

- You contract for your household goods and personal effects to be moved to your home in the U.S. However, this applies only if the move is completed within a reasonable time,
- Your household goods and personal effects are packed and on the way to your home in the U.S., or
- You leave your former home to travel to your new home in the U.S.

Deductible Moving Expenses

If you meet the *Requirements* discussed earlier, you can deduct the reasonable expenses of:

Moving your household goods and personal effects (including certain storage expenses),
Traveling to your new home,
Househunting trips before you move,
Living temporarily in the new area,
Selling your former home and buying a new one, and
Settling an old lease and signing a new lease.

Reasonable expenses. You can deduct only those expenses that are reasonable for the circumstances of your move. For example, the cost of traveling from your former home to your new one should be by the shortest, most direct route available by conventional transportation. If, during your trip to your new home, you make side trips for sightseeing, the additional expenses for your side trips are not deductible as moving expenses.

TAXPLANNER
Qualified moving expenses are deductible in 1993 only if you elect to itemize your deductions.

In 1993, your total itemized deductions will be reduced by the lesser of (1) 3% of the excess of your adjusted gross income over $108,450, or (2) 80% of the aggregate of certain itemized deductions. As a result, depending on your adjusted gross income and other itemized deductions in the current year versus those amounts anticipated in the subsequent year, it may be possible to time the payment of moving expenses to maximize your deduction. For a discussion of the limitation on itemized deductions, see Chapter 30, *Miscellaneous Deductions*.

TAXALERT
The 1993 Tax Act changed the method in which moving expenses incurred after December 31, 1993 can be deducted. Moving expenses not paid or reimbursed by your employer will be allowed as a deduction in calculating adjusted gross income instead of being treated as an itemized deduction. Therefore, if you claim the standard deduction, you will be able to deduct your allowable unreimbursed moving expenses in computing your adjusted gross income. In addition, deductible expenses will not be reduced by the 3% limitation on itemized deductions applicable to higher-income taxpayers.

Moving expenses paid for by your employer directly or through reimbursement will be excludable from your gross income and wages for income and employment tax purposes unless you actually deducted the expenses in a prior taxable year.

Travel by car. If you use your car for househunting or to take yourself, members of your household, or your belongings to your new home, you can figure your expenses by deducting either:

1) Your **actual expenses,** such as gas and oil for your car, if you keep an accurate record of each expense, or
2) **9 cents a mile.**

You can deduct parking fees and tolls you paid in moving. You cannot deduct any part of general repairs, general maintenance, insurance, or depreciation for your car.

Explanation
The mileage rate used for moving expenses—9 cents per mile—is less than the rate used for business expenses—28 cents per mile.

The IRS has resisted any attempt to include depreciation of an automobile as a moving expense, maintaining that depreciation does not apply to a personal automobile.

Member of household. You can deduct moving expenses you pay for yourself and members of your household. A member of your household is anyone who has both your former and new home as his or her home. It does not include a tenant or employee, unless you can claim that person as a dependent.

Location of move. There are different rules for moving within or to the U.S. than for moving outside the U.S. This chapter only discusses moves within or to the U.S. The rules for moves outside the U.S. can be found in Publication 521.

Household Goods and Personal Effects

You can deduct the cost of packing, crating, and transporting your household goods and personal effects and those of the members of your household from your former home to your new home. If you use your own car to move your things, see *Travel by car,* earlier. You can include the cost of storing and insuring household goods and personal effects *within any consecutive 30-day period* after the day your things are moved from your former home and before they are delivered to your new home.

You can deduct any costs of connecting or disconnecting utilities to move your household goods, appliances or personal effects.

You can deduct the cost of shipping your car and household pets to your new home.

You can deduct the cost of moving household goods and personal effects from a place other than your former home. Your deduction is limited to the amount it would have cost to move them from your former home.

You cannot deduct the cost of moving furniture you buy on the way to your new home.

Travel Expenses

You can deduct the cost of transportation, meals (see *Meal Expenses,* next), and lodging for yourself and members of your household while traveling from your former home to your new home. This includes expenses for the day you arrive. You can include any meal and lodging expenses you had in the area of your former home within one day after you could not live in your former home because your furniture had been moved. You can deduct expenses for only one trip to your new home for yourself and members of your household. However, all of you do not have to travel together. If you use your own car, see *Travel by car,* earlier.

Meal Expenses

You can deduct only *80% of the cost of meals* you incur during your househunting trip, while traveling to your new residence, and while staying in temporary quarters. Meals include food and beverages. The 80% limit applies to your meal expenses whether or not your employer reimburses you. This limit applies before all other moving expense limits.

If you are self-employed, you are also subject to the 80% limit on meals.

Lavish or extravagant meals. You cannot deduct the cost of meals (for you and your family) that you incur during your move that are lavish or extravagant under the circumstances.

> ### TaxAlert
> Beginning in 1994, the 1993 Tax Act excludes the cost of any meals incurred in connection with a move from the definition of moving expenses. Therefore, no deduction will be allowed.

Pre-Move Househunting Expenses

You must have a job in the new area before you can deduct the cost of trips that you take primarily to look for a new place to live. You can deduct househunting expenses. These include the cost of transportation, meals (see *Meal Expenses,* earlier), and lodging for yourself and members of your household while traveling to and from the area of your new job and while you are there. Your househunting does not have to be successful to qualify for this deduction. You and members of your household can travel separately. There is no limit to the number of trips you or members of your household can take. However, see *Dollar Limits,* later. If you use your own car, see *Travel by car,* earlier.

If you are ***self-employed,*** see *Self-employed* under *Temporary Living Expenses,* next.

> ### Explanation
> Before pre-move house-hunting expenses may be taken, an employee must already have a job at the new location. No particular formalities between you and your employer are required. You do *not* need to have a formal contract in writing.

> ### TaxAlert
> The 1993 Tax Act excludes the cost of premove house hunting trips from the definition of moving expenses. Therefore, no deduction will be allowed for these expenses incurred after December 31, 1993.

Temporary Living Expenses

Temporary living expenses include only the costs of meals (see *Meal Expenses,* earlier) and lodging while occupying temporary quarters in the area of your new job. You can deduct these costs, subject to the *Dollar Limits,* discussed later, for *any consecutive 30-day period* after you get the job but before you move into permanent quarters.

> ### Explanation
> You may not include as deductible temporary living expenses, any expenses for entertainment, laundry, transportation, other personal or family living expenses, or living expenses at your former location.
>
> The IRS has barred a deduction for rent paid by a taxpayer occupying a home he planned to purchase. The IRS's thinking is that rental deductions are included as lodging expenses only if the taxpayer intends to move from the rented quarters. In this case, since he planned to purchase the rented quarters, no deduction for rent payments was allowed.

> ### TaxSaver
> Since you are allowed to deduct temporary living expenses only for any 30 days in a row, try not to interrupt your "temporary stay" with business trips until you've spent 30 days at your new location.

> ### TaxAlert
> The 1993 Tax Act excludes the cost of temporary living expenses from the definition of moving expenses. Therefore, no deduction will be allowed for these expenses incurred after December 31, 1993.

Self-employed. If you are self-employed, do not deduct your expenses for pre-move househunting trips or temporary living expenses unless you have made substantial arrangements to begin work at the new location. See *Self-employed* under *Moves Within or to the United States* in Publication 521 for more information.

> ### Explanation
> Before a self-employed person may take pre-move house-hunting expenses, substantial arrangements to begin work at the new location must be made. Whether or not arrangements are substantial enough is decided on a case-by-case basis, using some of the following criteria: acquisition of a store, office, or other place of business; acquisition of supplies and inventory; and arrangements with employees and customers at the new location.
>
> The IRS maintains that the mere leasing of an office and an apartment at the new location is not substantial enough to be able to deduct pre-move expenses.

Home-Related Expenses

You can deduct the reasonable expenses of selling your former home and getting a new one.

Home sale expenses. When you sell your former home, the following qualify as moving expenses:

Real estate commissions,
Attorneys' fees,
Title fees,
Escrow fees,
"Points" or loan placement charges you are required to pay,
State transfer taxes, and
Similar expenses connected with the sale or exchange of your former home.

You can deduct these sale-related expenses as moving expenses *or* you can use them to reduce the amount you realized from the sale of your former home.

You cannot deduct as a moving expense the cost of physical improvements intended to improve the condition or appearance of your former home.

Home purchase expenses. When you buy your new home, the following qualify as moving expenses:

Attorneys' fees,
Escrow fees,
Appraisal fees,
Title fees,
"Points" or loan placement charges *not* representing payment or prepayment of interest, and
Similar expenses connected with the purchase of your new home.

You can deduct these purchase-related expenses as moving expenses *or* you can add them to the basis of your new home. By adding them to the basis of your new home, you will reduce the amount of gain you realize when you sell it.

No double benefit. If your moving expense deduction includes the expenses of selling your former home, you cannot use the same expenses to reduce the amount realized on the sale of your former home.

If your moving expense deduction includes the expenses of buying your new home, you cannot add the same expenses to the basis of your new home. See Chapter 16, *Selling Your Home*, for information on selling and buying your home.

Explanation
Under no circumstances is a loss on the sale of your personal residence deductible as a moving expense, or as any other kind of expense, even if the move forced you to sell at a loss.

Although you may not deduct property taxes and interest as moving expenses, you may claim them as itemized deductions.

Unexpired lease expenses. When you end an unexpired lease (break a lease) on your former home, you can deduct, subject to the dollar limits, the following expenses:

Payments to the lessor for releasing you from the lease,
Attorneys' fees,
Real estate commissions, and
Expenses, such as the difference between the rent you pay and the rent you receive from an assignee or sublessee.

Expenses of leasing a new home. When you lease a new home, you can deduct, subject to the dollar limits, the following expenses:

Fees, and
Commissions.

These expenses can be for leasing, subleasing, or taking an assignment of a lease. You cannot deduct payments or prepayments of rent. See *Security deposit,* later.

Explanation
Allowing a renter to deduct attorney's fees and commissions is an attempt to afford a renter the same benefits afforded a homeowner. In addition, a renter may deduct

expenses for finding a sublessee. He or she may take a deduction for the difference between the rent paid and the rent received if the rent paid is greater. A renter may not deduct the costs of fixing up a residence for subleasing.

TaxAlert
The 1993 Tax Act excludes the costs of selling your former home (or settling an unexpired lease) and purchasing your new home (or the acquisition of a new lease) from the definition of moving expenses, effective for expenses incurred after December 31, 1993. Therefore, these expenses will no longer be deductible beginning in 1994.

Dollar Limits

The expenses of moving household goods and traveling to your new home are not limited to any amount. However, the combined totals of all your other moving expenses cannot be more than $3,000 per move. Other expenses are:

- Househunting and temporary living expenses,
- Expenses of selling your former home,
- Expenses of buying your new home, and
- Lease expenses.

Despite the overall $3,000 limit, you can deduct no more than $1,500 of it for househunting and temporary living expenses combined. Exceptions are explained later under *Married persons filing separate returns* and *Married persons filing a joint return*.

Exception
For expenses incurred in 1993, if you moved abroad, the overall $3,000 limit is raised to $6,000 and the $1,500 limit for temporary living expenses and pre-move househunting is raised to $4,500. In addition, you are allowed 90 days for temporary living expenses abroad, as opposed to the 30 days allowed for domestic moves. You are also allowed to deduct the cost of storage and handling of household goods and personal effects while in your new job location. The expense must be reasonable, but there is no specific dollar limit. Note: You must use Form 3903F to report the expenses of a foreign move.

TaxAlert
Beginning in 1994, expenses other than those incurred for moving household goods and traveling to your new home will not be deductible. Therefore, the $3,000 limitation on househunting and temporary living expenses, expenses of buying or selling your home, or lease expenses will not be applicable in 1994 because these expenses will not be deductible.

Homeowners. You can choose to deduct any combination of moving expenses that are subject to the dollar limits. You should claim up to $1,500 of househunting and temporary living expenses before you claim the expenses of selling and buying your home.

Any househunting and temporary living expenses that you do not deduct as a moving expense, you cannot deduct any other way. On the other hand, any expenses for selling your home that you cannot deduct because of the $3,000 limit you can use to reduce the amount realized on the sale of your former home. Also, any expenses for buying your home that you cannot deduct because of the limit, you can use to increase the basis of your new home.

TaxSaver

In 1993, you have a choice about how you want to treat all or part of the expenses of selling and/or buying a home. Your decision should be based on, among other things, how close you are to the dollar limits prescribing what you may deduct, your current tax bracket, and future plans for your new house.

Example

If you already have reached the $1,500 maximum in pre-move househunting and temporary living expenses and you also have $1,500 of home sale expenses in addition to the sales commission, treat the sales commission as a selling expense in order to reduce the gain on the sale of your home.

Alternatively, if you have a loss on the sale of your home, which is not deductible, you should treat the sales commission as a moving expense. Include all of the expenditures in buying your new home in the home's cost rather than deduct them as moving expenses.

Married persons filing separate returns. If both of you began work at new job locations and lived together, the overall dollar limit is $1,500 for each of you. Of that limit, each of you can deduct no more than $750 for househunting and temporary living expenses.

If only one of you began work at a new job location, the overall limit for that person is $3,000. Of that limit, the person can deduct no more than $1,500 for househunting and temporary living expenses.

If both of you began work at new job locations, but you have not shared the same new home by the end of the tax year or made plans to do so, the overall limit for each of you is $3,000. Of that limit, each of you can deduct no more than $1,500 for househunting and temporary living expenses.

Example. Tim and Mary Brown are married but separated. Tim moved from New York to Michigan. His moving expenses were $3,600 for househunting trips, temporary living expenses, and selling his home. Mary moved from New York to Washington, DC. Her moving expenses were $3,200 for househunting trips, temporary living expenses, and selling her home. Neither had more than $1,500 in expenses for househunting trips and temporary living expenses. Each can claim $3,000 on a separate return.

Married persons filing a joint return. If both of you began work at new job locations, but at the end of the tax year have not shared the same new home or made plans to do so, your combined overall limit is $6,000 ($3,000 for each of you). Of that limit, you can deduct no more than $3,000 ($1,500 for each of you) for your combined househunting and temporary living expenses.

If you shared the same new home, your combined overall limit is $3,000, of which no more than $1,500 can be deducted for househunting and temporary living expenses.

Explanation

The reasonable costs you incur in transporting your household goods and in traveling to a new home are fully deductible in 1993. The reasonable costs of pre-move travel while searching for a new home, of some temporary lodging in the new location, and of some costs incurred in selling, buying, or leasing a home are deductible within certain dollar limitations. These limitations vary depending on marital status, whether you file jointly or separately, whether one or two homes and jobs are involved, and whether it is a domestic or foreign move.

The basic concept is that, when either or both spouses have jobs and live together, they have one overall $3,000 limitation if they file a joint return ($1,500 each if they file separate returns) for domestic moving expenses other than those arising from transporting household goods and traveling. If both spouses have jobs and do not live together, they each have a separate overall $3,000 limitation, whether they file jointly or separately.

Nondeductible Expenses

You cannot deduct the following items as moving expenses:

Home improvements to help sell your home,
Loss on the sale of your home,
Mortgage penalties,
Losses from disposing of memberships in clubs,
Any part of the purchase price of your new home,
Real estate taxes,
Car tags,
Driver's license,
Refitting carpets and draperies, and
Storage charges except those incurred in transit and for foreign moves.

Security deposit. Do not deduct a security deposit you paid when you signed a new lease. Do not deduct a security deposit that you gave up because the vacated space needed cleaning or redecorating when you ended the lease. However, you can deduct a security deposit that you gave up if you broke the lease as a result of the move.

Explanation

Many moving costs represent real economic losses to you but are not deductible as moving expenses when you are computing your **taxable income.** These nondeductible moving costs are simply considered personal expenses, whether or not you are reimbursed for them. If you itemize your deductions, you might be able to deduct some costs that are not deductible as moving expenses.

Mortgage penalties that are loan prepayment penalties are usually deductible as interest. Real estate taxes are deductible. In many states, automobile tags are deductible as personal property taxes. A portion of your driver's license may be deductible as automobile transportation expenses.

You may not deduct the cost of buying new drapes.

Temporary employment. You cannot take a moving expense deduction and a business expense deduction for the same expenses. You must determine if your expenses are deductible as moving expenses or as business expenses. For example, expenses you have for travel, meals, and lodging while temporarily working at a place away from your regular place of work are deductible as business expenses if you are considered away from home on business. Your work is considered temporary if it does not last more than one year. See *Temporary Assignment or Job* in Chapter 28, *Car Expenses and Other Employee Business Expenses*, for information on deducting your expenses.

How to Report

The following discussions explain how to report your moving expenses and any reimbursements or allowances you received for your move.

Form 3903. Use Form 3903 to report your moving expenses if your move was within or to the United States or its possessions. A filled-in Form 3903 is shown in Chapter 45, *Sample Form 1040*.

Where to deduct. Deduct your moving expenses on Schedule A (Form 1040). You must be able to itemize your deductions to claim the moving expense deduction. The amount of moving expenses you can include in itemized deductions, is shown on line 19, Form 3903. Enter this amount on line 18, Schedule A (Form 1040).

Reimbursements. Include all reimbursements of, or payments for, moving expenses in gross income for the year you receive them. If your employer paid for any part of your move, the employer must include the payment in your wages, as explained later, which you report as income on line 7, Form 1040.

Your employer must give you an itemized list of payments, reimbursements, or allowances that have been paid to you for moving expenses. **Form 4782,** *Employee Moving Expense Information,* may be used for this purpose. See Publication 521 for a filled-in Form 4782.

Your employer must include the amounts shown on Form 4782 in box 1, *Wages, tips, other compensation,* on your Form W–2, *Wage and Tax Statement.* A separate Form W–2 may be provided.

Moving services provided or paid for by your employer. Include in your income the value of moving services provided by your employer to you or to members of your family. For example, if your employer moves your household goods using the employer's truck, you are considered as having received payment equal to the value of the transportation service. You include this amount in income in the year you receive the service.

If your employer pays someone else, such as a moving company, to move your goods, you must include in your income the amount paid to the moving company in the year your employer pays them for their service.

Your employer must include the value of all moving expense reimbursements, services, and payments, in the total income on your Form W–2.

you, although the gain on the sale of the residence is taxed as a **capital gain**, subject to the residence replacement rules, discussed in Chapter 16, *Selling Your Home.*

Any reimbursement by your employer for a loss on the sale of your home must be included in your income. You may not deduct the loss on your home, though you may deduct the amount attributable to the real estate commission, if any, as a selling expense.

If your employer purchases your former home from you at **fair market value** and there is a subsequent decline in its worth, the loss is sustained by your employer. The home's drop in value does not affect you.

If your employer purchases your former home from you at *more* than fair market value, the excess is ordinary taxable income to you. You could not exclude that excess from your income, even if you purchased a new home for more than you got in total for the old one.

Note: The excess is not treated as gain on the sale of a residence that otherwise could be reinvested in a new residence. See Chapter 16, *Selling Your Home.*

Explanation

Some employers use third-party relocation service companies to buy your home from you. If the third party pays any direct home-selling costs that are normally imposed on the seller by local law and/or custom, then you will be treated as having received taxable income.

Example

An employer agreed to pay home-selling costs but required that the employee repay them if he terminated employment within a stipulated period of time. The IRS held that an enforceable debt was created and that the employee had taxable income to report when the debt was cancelled (or not paid). The employer must report the income on Form W-2.

Uniform Relocation Assistance and Real Property Acquisition Policies Act of 1970. Do not include in income any moving expense payments you received under the Uniform Relocation Assistance and Real Property Acquisition Policies Act of 1970. These payments are made to persons displaced from their homes, businesses, or farms by federal projects.

Tax withholding. Your employer is not required to withhold income tax, social security tax, or Medicare tax on allowances or reimbursements for moving expenses if your employer reasonably believes that you will be able to deduct the expenses. This means that at the time your employer pays you the reimbursement or allowance, your employer reasonably believes that you will meet the distance and time tests and that your expenses will be deductible.

For more information on tax withholding, see Publication 521.

Explanation

Your employer may give you a flat amount of money to cover all your moving expenses, some of which may not be deductible. The IRS says that the employer must apply the reimbursement first to the deductible moving expenses that are not subject to withholding and then deduct withholding and social security tax from the remainder.

> ### TaxAlert
> Be sure to take into account reimbursement for nondeductible expenses when you are figuring your **estimated tax** payments.

When to deduct. Deduct your moving expenses in the year you had them or paid them. If you use the cash method of accounting, which is used by most individuals, you can choose to deduct moving expenses in the year your employer reimburses you, if:

You paid the expenses in a year before the year of reimbursement, or

You paid the expenses in the year immediately after the year of reimbursement but by the due date, including extensions, for filing your return for the reimbursement year.

How to make the choice. You can choose to deduct moving expenses in the year that you received reimbursement by taking the deduction on your return, or amended return, for that year.

Example 1. In December 1992, your employer transferred you to another city, where you still work. You are single and were not reimbursed for your moving expenses. In 1992 you paid for a househunting trip, travel to the new city, temporary living expenses, and moving your furniture. You itemized your deductions and deducted these expenses in 1992. In 1993 you paid additional temporary living expenses and certain deductible expenses of selling your home and buying a new home. You deduct these expenses in 1993 if you itemize deductions on Schedule A (Form 1040).

Some of your moving expenses are subject to the *Dollar Limits,* discussed earlier. You apply the 80% limit on your meal expenses before you apply the $1,500 moving expense limit on househunting and temporary quarters.

The dollar limits are not separately applied to the expenses you deduct each year; they apply to the total expenses for that move. You must show on your 1993 Form 3903 the amounts you deducted on your 1992 Form 3903 that were subject to the dollar limits. If you deducted $1,000 in 1992 for househunting and temporary living expenses, you can deduct up to $500 for these expenses in 1993.

In 1992, you deducted $1,000 for househunting and temporary living expenses. In 1993, you incurred $800 for temporary living expenses ($600 for lodging and $200 for meals), $3,500 to sell your old home, and $1,000 to buy a new home. Your deduction for temporary living expenses in 1993 is limited to $500. This is the lesser of $500 ($1,500 limit minus the $1,000 you deducted in 1992) or $760 ($600 lodging plus $160 (80% of your $200 meal expense)).

Your total moving expense deduction for 1993 is $2,000, figured as follows. Add your 1993 househunting and temporary living expenses ($500) to your qualified real estate expenses ($4,500). Compare the $5,000 total to the $3,000 limit and use the smaller amount. The smaller amount ($3,000) could be your moving expense for 1993. However, for the overall move you can deduct only $3,000 for the househunting, temporary living, and qualified real estate expenses. In 1992 you already deducted $1,000 for these expenses. Therefore, you subtract $1,000 from the $3,000, leaving $2,000 as your 1993 moving expense deduction.

You must show your 1992 deduction on your 1993 Form 3903 by writing "$1,000 deducted in 1992" above lines 16 and 18.

Example 2. In December 1992, your employer transferred you to another city. You paid for all of your moving expenses in 1992.

Table 27-1. **Moving Expense Dollar Limits**

Type of Expense	Marital Status		Dollar Limits
Household goods and personal effects (line 4, Form 3903)	Not applicable		No limit
Travel expenses (lines 5–8, Form 3903)*	Not applicable		No limit
Househunting and temporary living expenses (lines 9–13, Form 3903)*	Single		$1,500
	Married filing jointly—		
	1) Spouses shared same new home by end of tax year		$1,500
	2) Both spouses began work at new job locations but lived apart		$3,000 (limited to $1,500 each)
	Married filing separately—		
	1) Both spouses began work at new job locations and lived together		$750 each
	2) One working spouse		$1,500
	3) Both spouses began work at new job locations but lived apart		$1,500 each
Househunting and temporary living expenses; and expense of selling and buying a home, or settling or getting a lease, (lines 13, 14, and 15, Form 3903)*	Single		$3,000
	Married filing jointly—		
	1) Spouses shared same new home by end of tax year		$3,000
	2) Both spouses began work at new job locations but lived apart		$6,000 (limited to $3,000 each)
	Married filing separately—		
	1) Both spouses began work at new job locations and lived together		$1,500 each
	2) One working spouse		$3,000
	3) Both spouses began work at new job locations but lived apart		$3,000 each

*Meals are subject to an 80% limit.

Your employer fully reimbursed you in 1993 for your moving expenses. This reimbursement is included in your 1993 Form W–2. If you itemize deductions, you can deduct your allowable moving expenses in 1992, the year you paid them, *or* you can deduct them in 1993, the year of reimbursement. In either case, your total deduction is the same unless it is subject to the limit on itemized deductions in one or both years.

TaxSaver

You generally deduct your moving expenses in the year in which you pay them. However, if you receive a reimbursement in one year and don't pay the expenses until the next year, you may still deduct the expenses in the earlier year, as long as you pay them before the due date, including extensions, for filing your return for the year of reimbursement.

Example

In 1992, you received $5,000 in reimbursement for moving expenses. You filed your tax return for 1992 on August 15, 1993, after receiving an extension. You paid your moving expenses of $5,000 on July 15, 1993.

The $5,000 reimbursement must be reported in 1992. The $5,000 of expenses may be deducted in 1992 or 1993. If you originally deducted the expenses for 1993, you may amend your 1992 return and claim a refund. You would then have to amend your 1993 return, also.

Once you elect to claim the expenses for 1992, you may not change your mind and claim them for 1993. Therefore, you should not claim them on your original 1992 return if you want to keep your options open.

Furthermore, if you pay the expenses in the year before you receive the reimbursement, you may deduct the expenses in either year. Thus, if you paid the moving expenses in 1992 and were not reimbursed until 1993, you may deduct the expenses in either year. If you originally deducted them in 1992, you may amend your 1992 return and then deduct the expenses in 1993. In summary, you should deduct your expenses in the year in which you will save the most taxes.

You should report your moving expense deduction on Form 3903, unless your move is to a foreign country, in which case you would use Form 3903F.

28 | Car Expenses and Other Employee Business Expenses

Introduction

If you are traveling on business and your employer does not reimburse your expenses, you may deduct many of them on your income tax return.

If you use your automobile partly for business purposes, you may be able to deduct some of your operating expenses. If you entertain a business associate at a restaurant or nightclub, you may probably deduct that expense, too. Within strict limits, business gifts are also deductible. If your employer reimburses you for a business expense but includes the amount of the reimbursement in your income, you still may deduct the expense.

You must be able to prove the business purpose, as well as the amount of the expense, to claim a deduction for employee expenses. All expenses should be substantiated with receipts and records indicating the time, place, and business nature of the expense. Names of the people who attended the particular event should also be noted. To uphold the **deduction** *if it is challenged by the IRS, your records should be clear, complete, and accurate.*

You'll be able to deduct only a portion of the cost of most business meals and entertainment; some costs won't be deductible at all. Substantial limits are placed on the deductibility of tickets to entertainment events, and no deduction will be allowed for travel costs to investment seminars. If you do have any allowable expenses remaining, you can claim them only as an itemized deduction to the extent that the total (along with some other miscellaneous deductions) exceeds 2% of your adjusted gross income. Furthermore, your 1993 deductions may be subject to certain limitations if your adjusted gross income exceeds $108,450.

This chapter explains business-related expenses for travel, transportation, entertainment, and gifts that you may deduct on your income tax return. It also discusses the reporting and recordkeeping requirements for these expenses.

Important Changes for 1993

Travel away from home. Away from home assignments that last for more than one year at a single location are not considered temporary. You cannot deduct any travel expenses paid after 1992 for such assignments. See *Temporary Assignment or Job,* later.

New tax incentives for clean-fuel vehicles. You may be entitled to a tax credit for an electric vehicle or a deduction from gross income for a part of the cost of a clean-fuel vehicle if you place one of these vehicles in service from July 1, 1993, through December 31, 2004. The vehicle must meet certain requirements, and you do not have to use it in your business to qualify for the credit or the deduction. For more information, see *Deductions for Clean-Fuel Vehicles and Refueling Property* in Chapter 15 of Publication 535, *Business Expenses.*

New standard meal allowance rates. For travel on or after March 12, 1993, there are four standard rates for your daily meals and incidental expenses while you are traveling away from home on business. For travel before March 12, 1993, there are only two standard rates. The applicable rate is determined by the location of your travel. See *Table 2* and *Table 3* in Publication 463, *Travel, Entertainment, and Gift Expenses,* for the locations qualifying for the higher rates.

Important Reminders

Standard mileage rate. The standard mileage rate for the cost of operating your car in 1993 remains at 28 cents per mile for all business miles.

Limit on itemized deductions. If you are an employee, you can deduct certain work-related expenses as itemized deductions on Schedule A (Form 1040). The amount you can deduct is limited to the excess over 2% of your adjusted gross income. It may be further limited if your adjusted gross income is more than $108,450 ($54,225 if you are married filing separately). For more information, see chapters 21 and 30 and the instructions for Form 1040.

This chapter discusses rules for deducting business-related expenses connected with:

- Travel away from home,
- Entertainment,
- Business gifts,
- Local business transportation, and
- Business use of a car.

This chapter also discusses:

- What records you must make or keep to prove your expenses,
- How to handle reimbursements of your employee business expenses, and
- How to report your expenses on Form 2106.

Explanation
All employee-related expenses and certain transportation expenses are classified as miscellaneous itemized deductions. Included in this category are expenses incurred by employees that are fully or partially reimbursed or not reimbursed at all by their employer. Also included are any expenses for traveling away from home or for transportation.

The total of all miscellaneous itemized expenses (including those mentioned previously, as well as those discussed in Chapter 30, *Miscellaneous Deductions*) must be reduced by 2% of adjusted gross income. Only the amount over 2% can be claimed as an itemized deduction and generate a tax benefit.

In 1993, your total itemized deductions will be reduced by the lesser of (1) 3% of the excess of your adjusted gross income over $108,450 or (2) 80% of the aggregate of certain itemized deductions. As a result, depending on your adjusted gross income and other itemized deductions in the current year versus those amounts anticipated in the subsequent year, it may be possible to time the payment of employee-related expenses to maximize your deduction.

If you incur expenses as an employee, seek any reimbursement you are entitled to from your employer. The courts have held that transportation expenses, such as taxi fares and automobile-operating expenses, may not be deducted directly by an employee unless the amount of the expenses exceeds the reimbursement. You cannot deduct such expenses on your own tax return, because you simply don't bother to request reimbursement from your employer, even if such reimbursement is not requested based on a belief that it would not be reimbursed.

Example 1
A salesman incurred business expenses but did not submit them to his company for reimbursement because they were incurred due to mistakes he made and therefore were his responsibility. The courts held that these expenses were not deductible by the salesman because they were expenses of another taxpayer. Generally, the payment of an obligation of another is not considered an ordinary and necessary expense.

Example 2
An employee was told that all unessential travel would have to be curtailed. Therefore, he knew he might incur business mileage for which he would not be reimbursed. As a result, he sought and obtained reimbursement for only a portion of the total business use of his automobile. The Tax Court held that, because this employee did not have any of his travel expenses rejected by his employer, he had no reasonable basis to conclude that his unreimbursed business miles would not be reimbursed. Consequently, no tax deduction was allowed for any business mileage.

Exception
When it is company policy to reimburse employees for mileage but employees are verbally instructed by company field representatives not to seek reimbursement, you may rightfully deduct unreimbursed automobile expenses.

TAXPLANNER

You should seek reimbursement for all business mileage incurred on your private automobile. To the extent that reimbursement is denied by your employer, a deduction is available.

Expenses fully reimbursed. You will not need to read this chapter if *all* of the following are true.

1) You fully accounted to your employer for your work-related expenses.
2) You received full reimbursement for your expenses.
3) Your employer required you to return any excess reimbursement and you did so.
4) Box 13 of your Form W–2 shows no amount with a code **L**.

If you meet these four conditions, there is no need to show the expenses or the reimbursement on your return. See *Reimbursements* later in this chapter if you would like more information on reimbursements and accounting to your employer.

If you do not meet all of these conditions, you must complete Form 2106 and itemize your deductions on Schedule A (Form 1040) to claim your expenses. See *Completing Form 2106,* later.

Note: If you meet these conditions and your employer included reimbursements on your Form W–2 in error, ask your employer for a corrected Form W–2.

Explanation
For more information regarding the business use of your home, see Chapter 30, *Miscellaneous Deductions*.

Useful Items

You may want to see:

Publication

☐ **225**   Farmer's Tax Guide
☐ **334**   Tax Guide for Small Business
☐ **463**   Travel, Entertainment, and Gift Expenses
☐ **535**   Business Expenses
☐ **917**   Business Use of a Car

Form (and Instructions)

☐ **Schedule A (Form 1040)**   Itemized Deductions
☐ **Schedule C (Form 1040)**   Profit or Loss From Business
☐ **Schedule C-EZ (Form 1040)**   Net Profit From Business
☐ **Schedule F (Form 1040)**   Profit or Loss From Farming
☐ **Form 2106**   Employee Business Expenses
☐ **Form 4562**   Depreciation and Amortization

Travel Expenses

If you travel away from your tax home, you can use this section to determine if you have deductible travel expenses. This section includes the definition of "tax home" and a discussion of different types of travel expenses. The section then discusses the rules for travel inside and outside the United States and deductible expenses of attending a convention.

Travel expenses defined. For tax purposes, travel expenses are ordinary and necessary expenses that you pay while traveling away from home for your business, profession, or job. An ordinary expense is one that is common and accepted in your field of business, trade, or profession. A necessary expense is one that is helpful and appropriate to your business. An expense does not have to be indispensable to be considered necessary. However, you cannot deduct expenses to the extent they are lavish or extravagant.

Example 1
The courts held that a stockholder of a corporation could not deduct the expense of operating his personal automobile while performing services for the corporation. The stockholder was not an employee or officer of the corporation. He was not reimbursed for his expenses. The courts held that the stockholder's interest in the corporation was too remote for the expense to be an ordinary business expense.

Example 2
A government employee was allowed to deduct unreimbursed expenses incurred in the use of his private airplane for business purposes. He was also allowed to depreciate the business portion of the airplane's use.

TaxPlanner 1
For you to deduct a business expense, a board resolution or a policy statement from the company that employs you should indicate that you may have to incur certain expenses for which you will not be reimbursed in order for you to fulfill your job.

TaxPlanner 2
You are able to deduct only 80% of most business meal and entertainment costs. Other allowable unreimbursed entertainment expenses will be grouped with certain other of your miscellaneous itemized deductions. You will be allowed a tax deduction to the extent that all these deductions exceed 2% of your adjusted gross income.

You will find examples of deductible travel expenses later in this section.

Traveling away from home. You are traveling away from home if:

1) Your duties require you to be away from the general area of your tax home (defined later) substantially longer than an ordinary day's work, and
2) You need to get sleep or rest to meet the demands of your work while away from home.

This rest requirement is not satisfied by merely napping in your car. You do not have to be away from your tax home for a whole day or from dusk to dawn as long as your relief from duty is long enough to get necessary sleep or rest.

Example 1. You are a railroad conductor. You leave your home terminal on a regularly scheduled round-trip run between two cities and return home 16 hours later. During the run, you have 6 hours off at your turnaround point where you eat two meals and rent a hotel room to get necessary sleep before starting the return trip. You are considered to be away from home, and you can deduct travel expenses.

Example 2. You are a truck driver. You leave your terminal and return to it later the same day. You get an hour off at your turnaround point to eat. Because you are not off to get necessary sleep and the brief time off is not an adequate rest period, your trip is not considered as travel away from home. You cannot deduct travel expenses.

Tax Home

To deduct travel expenses, you must first determine the location of your tax home.

Generally, your tax home is your regular place of business or post of duty, regardless of where you maintain your family home. It includes the *entire city or general area* in which your business or work is located. If you have more than one regular place of business, your tax home is your main place of business. If you do not have a regular or a main place of business because of the nature of your work, then your tax home may be the place where you regularly live. See *No main place of business or work,* later.

If you do not fit any of these categories, you are considered a transient (an itinerant) and your tax home is wherever you work. As a transient, you cannot claim a travel expense deduction because you are never considered away from home.

Main place of business or work. If you have more than one place of work, you should use the following factors to determine your main place of business or work:

1) The total time you ordinarily spend working in each area,
2) The degree of your business activity in each area, and
3) The relative amount of your income from each area.

Example. You live in Cincinnati where you have a seasonal job for 8 months and earn $15,000. You work the remaining 4 months in Miami, also at a seasonal job, and earn $4,000. Cincinnati is your main place of work because you spend most of your time there and earn most of your income there.

No main place of business or work. You may have a tax home even if you do not have a regular or main place of work. Your tax home may be the home where you regularly live. If you do not have a regular or main place of business or work, use the following three factors to see if you have a tax home:

1) You have part of your business in the area of your main home and use that home for lodging while doing business there.
2) You have living expenses at your main home that you duplicate because your business requires you to be away from that home.
3) You have not left the area in which both your traditional place of lodging and your main home are located; you have a member or members of your family living at your main home; or you often use that home for lodging.

If you meet all three factors, your tax home is the home where you regularly live, and you may be able to deduct travel expenses. If you meet only two of the factors, you may have a tax home depending on all the facts and circumstances. If you meet only one factor, you are a transient; you do not have a tax home and you cannot deduct travel expenses.

Example

A retired federal district judge was allowed a travel expense deduction for travel from his personal residence, considered his tax home, to the courthouse for recalled active duty.

Example. You are an outside salesperson with a sales territory covering several states. Your employer's main office is in Denver, and you return there for one month each year for business and nonbusiness reasons. Your business work assignments are temporary, and you have no way of knowing where future assignments will be located.

You have lived in Denver for 14 years, first with your spouse in your own house until your divorce, and then with your married sister in her house. You pay your sister $100 a month for a room in her house where you stay when you are in Denver. You also keep in the room your furniture and any clothing that you do not take on your out-of-town business trips.

You have met all three factors listed earlier, including the traditional lodging aspects of factor (3). Therefore, you have a tax home in Denver for travel expense deduction purposes.

Transient workers. If you move from job to job, maintain no fixed home, and are not associated with any particular business locality, each place you work becomes your main place of business and your tax home. You cannot deduct your expenses for meals and lodging.

Explanation

According to the IRS, a home is a "regular place of abode in a real and substantial sense." The criteria are as follows:

1. You work in the same vicinity as your claimed abode and use it while doing business.
2. Your living expenses incurred at your claimed abode are duplicated when you're away on business.
3. You (a) have not abandoned the vicinity in which your place of lodging and claimed abode are both located;

(b) have a family member or members (marital or lineal) currently residing at your claimed abode; or (c) use the claimed abode frequently.

If you maintain no fixed home, the burden of proof is on you to show the business portion of your daily expenses.

Example 1

A traveling salesman could not establish Reno, Nevada, as his tax home, even though he maintained a post office box and a bank account there, had dealings with a local stockbroker, bought an automobile there, stored his personal belongings there, and filed an income tax return from the city. He did not maintain a permanent place in Reno but stayed in hotels while he was there. Since no tax home was established, he could deduct only the business portion of his daily expenses. However, no expenses were allowed, since he did not maintain the necessary records.

Example 2

A traveling saleswoman maintained a room in her sister's home at a nominal rent. She worked for an employer in the same city, who paid her a per diem when she was away from that city. She had established a home for travel expense purposes.

Example 3

A college professor held a tenured position at a university located in Texas. While studying for her Ph.D. degree in Hawaii, she maintained a credit union account, a houseboat on which she paid property taxes, a post office box, and a library card in Texas, and also stored almost all of her possessions there. She returned to the university after receiving her degree. The court ruled that her stay was not for an indefinite period, and she was able to deduct her lodging expenses in Hawaii.

Living away from your tax home. If you (and your family) live in an area outside your tax home (main place of work), you cannot deduct travel expenses between your tax home and your family home. You also cannot deduct the cost of meals and lodging while at your tax home. See *Examples 1 and 2,* below.

If you are working temporarily in the same city where you and your family live, you may be considered as traveling away from home. See *Example 3,* below.

Example 1. You live with your family in Chicago, but work in Milwaukee, where you stay in a hotel and eat in restaurants during the week. You return to Chicago every weekend. You cannot deduct any of your expenses for travel, meals, and lodging in Milwaukee. This is because Milwaukee is your tax home and the travel on weekends is not for a business reason.

Example 2. You are a truck driver and you and your family live in Tucson. You are employed by a trucking firm that has its terminal in Phoenix. At the end of your long runs, you return to your home terminal in Phoenix and spend one night there before returning home. You cannot deduct any of your travel costs in Phoenix because Phoenix is your tax home.

Example 1

Maury Wills, the fleet-footed Los Angeles Dodger short-stop, was not allowed to deduct expenses for meals and lodging in Los Angeles, California, even though he maintained a home in another state. The court found his tax home to be Los Angeles, since it was his principal place of business.

Example 2

A member of the Marine Corps was stationed in Japan. His family remained in California, since they were not allowed to accompany him to his principal place of duty. The marine was not allowed to deduct travel expenses. His tax home was Japan, his principal place of duty. See *Members of the armed forces.*

Example 3. Your family home is in Pittsburgh, where you work 12 weeks a year. The rest of the year you work for the same employer in Baltimore. In Baltimore, you eat in restaurants and sleep in a rooming house. Your salary is the same whether you are in Pittsburgh or Baltimore.

Because you spend most of your working time and earn most of your salary in Baltimore, that city is your tax home. You cannot deduct any expenses you have for meals and lodging there. However, when you return to work in Pittsburgh, you are away from your tax home even though you stay at your family home. Therefore, you can deduct the cost of your round trip between Baltimore and Pittsburgh. You can also deduct your part of your family's living expenses for meals and lodging while you are living and working in Pittsburgh.

Explanation

Where you earn the most money is the principal test for deciding where your tax home is.

Example

The IRS required a taxpayer to claim as his tax home a city away from the home in which his family resided. He earned 75% of his income in the city away from his family and 25% of his income in the city where his family lived. Since his tax home was different from his personal residence, he could deduct travel expenses incurred while living with his family.

Explanation

The distance between your residence and your place of employment is not a factor in determining whether expenses away from home are being incurred.

Example

The courts ruled that a taxpayer's personal decision to live a great distance from the location of his permanent employment did not render his meal and lodging expenses deductible. His place of business was his tax home.

Temporary Assignment or Job

Although you regularly work or carry on your business activities within the city or general area of your tax home, you may have to work or conduct business at another location. It may not be practi-

cal to return home from this other location at the end of each day's work.

If your assignment or job away from your main place of work is *temporary,* your tax home does not change. You are considered to be away from home for the whole period, and your travel expenses are deductible. A temporary assignment is one that is expected to end within a fixed and reasonably short time and does not last more than one year.

However, if your assignment or job is *indefinite,* you are not considered to be away from home, and your travel expenses are not deductible. Your assignment or job is considered indefinite if its end cannot be foreseen within a fixed and reasonably short time.

An assignment or job expected to last for more than one year is considered indefinite and presumed not to be temporary. This is referred to as a *one-year presumption.*

Note. Prior to 1993, you may have been able to overcome this one-year presumption if your assignment lasted between one and two years. However, you cannot deduct any travel expenses paid after 1992 for such assignments. This is true even if the assignment began before 1993.

If you expect employment to last for less than one year, whether your new work assignment is temporary or indefinite depends on all the facts and circumstances. See *Temporary Assignment or Job* in Chapter 1 of Publication 463 for more information.

Explanation

The courts have not always agreed with the IRS position that, if an assignment lasts for more than a year, it is not temporary. Generally, the courts have refused to be bound by a mechanical rule. Instead, they have considered such factors as the nature of the job, the reasonable expectations about the duration of the job, and the financial and personal bonds that remain at the taxpayer's home. However, Congress has settled the IRS' and courts' differences on this matter for expenses paid or incurred after 1992. Because of this new tax legislation, after 1992, your job assignment will not be considered temporary if it lasts for more than one year.

Example 1

A construction worker who had been regularly employed near his home took a job in a city 250 miles away when construction got very slow in his hometown. He lived in his own trailer at the new job location. The job was expected to last 16 months, after which he planned to return home to his family. He frequently visited his hometown and continued to search for work there. The IRS ruled that the worker was temporarily away from his home and could deduct his meals and lodging.

Example 2

A worker sold his residence in his home city, ceased to search for work there, and bought a new home at a new job location. The IRS ruled that the worker's stay was indefinite. He could not deduct the cost of his meals and lodging.

Example 3

Bill Horton, a professional hockey player, was allowed to deduct the cost of meals and lodging while playing hockey in San Diego, California. The Tax Court ruled that his tax home was in Michigan, where he maintained his house. A limited contract and the seasonal nature of the hockey profession caused the court to classify the San Diego job as temporary.

Example 4
A professional gambler spent equal amounts of time each year in Tampa and Gainesville, Florida, engaged in an equal amount of activity in both places, derived equal amounts of income in both places, and rented an apartment in each location. The court ruled that the activities were not temporary because they were "seasonal and recurring" activities. Therefore, the costs of both apartments were not deductible.

TaxAlert

Beginning in 1993, employment away from home in a single location lasting more than one year will not be treated as temporary. However, if employment away from home was initially expected to be for 1 year or less, and then expectations changed for it to be for more than 1 year, the employment will be considered temporary up to the point that the time length expectations changed.

Explanation
The new one-year rule applies to travel expenses paid or incurred after December 31, 1992. For example, if a taxpayer began an employment assignment away from home on March 1, 1992, and remains on assignment at that location until July 31, 1993, only the travel expenses paid or incurred in 1992 would be deductible. The travel expenses paid or incurred in 1993 would not be deductible because the period of employment away from home exceeds one year.

Going home on days off. If you go home on your days off, you are not considered away from home while you are in your hometown. You cannot deduct the cost of your meals and lodging there. However, you can deduct your travel expenses, including meals and lodging, while traveling from the area of your temporary place of work to your hometown and back to work. You can claim these expenses up to the amount it would have cost you for meals and lodging had you stayed at your temporary place of work.

If you keep your hotel room during your visit home, you can deduct the cost of your hotel room. In addition, you can deduct your expenses of returning home up to the amount you would have spent for meals had you stayed at your temporary place of work.

Indefinite Assignment
If your job at the new location is for an indefinite time, that is, if its end cannot be foreseen within a fixed and reasonably short time or it lasts more than one year, that location becomes your new tax home. You cannot deduct your travel, meal, and lodging expenses while there. You must include in your income any amounts you receive from your employer for living expenses, even if they are called travel allowances and you account to your employer for them. You may be able to deduct the cost of relocating to your new tax home as a moving expense. See Chapter 27, *Moving Expenses*, for more information.

You must determine whether your assignment is temporary or indefinite when you start work. A series of assignments to the same location, all for short periods but that together cover a long period, may be considered an indefinite assignment.

Example 1
A steamfitter's work assignment at a nuclear power plant was determined to be indefinite rather than temporary by the Tax Court. The size of the project indicated that the job was of substantial duration.

Example 2
A railroad trainman was regularly based at one terminal. His employment was not considered permanent, because he was required periodically to bid the job. However, the court ruled that his employment there was indefinite, because it was not expected to terminate within a short period of time. He was not permitted to deduct expenses in connection with commuting from his home to the terminal.

Example 3
A construction worker who maintained a residence in Wyoming was employed for three years in Ohio. The court ruled that, although the assignment may have been considered temporary when it began, the duration of the employment resulted in the determination that it was indefinite for tax purposes.

Probationary work period. If you take a job that requires you to move, with the understanding that you will keep the job if your work is satisfactory during a probationary period, the job is indefinite. You cannot deduct any expenses for meals and lodging during the probationary period.

Members of the Armed Forces. If you are a member of the U.S. Armed Forces on a permanent duty assignment overseas, you are not traveling away from home. Therefore, you cannot deduct your expenses for meals and lodging. You cannot deduct these expenses even if you are required to maintain a home in the United States for your family members who are not allowed to accompany you overseas. If you are transferred from one permanent duty station to another, you may have deductible moving expenses, which are explained in Chapter 27, *Moving Expenses*.

A naval officer assigned to permanent duty aboard a ship that has regular eating and living facilities has a tax home aboard ship for travel expense purposes.

What Are Travel Expenses?

Once you have determined that you are traveling away from your tax home, you can determine what travel expenses are deductible on your tax return.

Records. When you travel away from home on business, you should keep records of all the expenses you incur and any advances you receive from your employer. You can use a log, diary, notebook, or any other written record to keep track of your expenses. The types of expenses you need to record, along with supporting documentation, are described later in this chapter under *Recordkeeping*.

Deductible travel expenses include those ordinary and necessary expenses you incur while traveling away from home on business. The type of expense you can deduct depends on the facts and your circumstances. *Table 28–1* summarizes the expenses you may be able to deduct.

You can use the discussion that follows as a general guideline. You may have other deductible travel expenses that are not covered here, depending on the facts and your circumstances.

Explanation

Ordinarily, you can deduct expenses that you incurred to produce or collect income, or to manage, conserve, or maintain property held for producing income only on Schedule A (Form 1040). Therefore, you must itemize your deductions to claim these expenses. See Chapter 30, *Miscellaneous Deductions*.

To be deductible, an expense must be closely associated with an activity that is expected to produce income or must be incurred maintaining property that is held to produce income. Such expenses are deductible only if you itemize.

Travel and other costs of attending investment seminars are specifically disallowed.

Example 1

Transportation expenses to attend a stockholders' meeting are not deductible, unless you can demonstrate that you played a fairly substantial role in the meeting. Otherwise, it is not clear that the expenses were incurred to produce income.

Example 2

The courts held that an individual who spent his lunch hour at brokerage houses could not deduct his travel expenses, because he could not establish the relationship between his visits and his investment activities.

Transportation fares. You can generally deduct travel by airplane, train, or bus between your home and your business destination. Your cost is the amount you paid for your ticket. If you were provided with a ticket or you are riding free as a result of a "frequent flyer" or other similar program, you have no deduction.

If you travel by ship, the amount you can deduct may be limited. See *Luxury Water Travel* and *Cruise ships* (under *Conventions*) in Chapter 1 of Publication 463.

Taxi, commuter bus, and limousine fares. You can generally deduct the fares you pay for taxis, airport limousines, buses, or other types of transportation between the airport or station and your hotel. You can also deduct these fares between your hotel and the work site of your customers or clients, your business meeting place, or your temporary work site. You cannot deduct costs of sightseeing, shopping, or similar nonbusiness expenses.

Baggage and shipping costs. You can deduct the cost of sending baggage and sample or display material between your regular work site and your temporary work site.

Car expenses. You can deduct the cost of operating and maintaining your car when traveling away from home on business. See *Local Transportation Expenses* later in this chapter for information on how to figure this deduction.

Leasing a car. You can deduct the cost of leasing a car for business purposes while you are traveling away from home. However, if you lease a car for 30 days or more, you may have to include an amount called an "inclusion amount" in your income. This inclusion amount is explained in Chapter 3 of Publication 917.

You can also deduct actual operating expenses for a car you lease. Examples are oil, gas, and repairs. However, you cannot claim the standard mileage rate.

Operating expenses. For a car you own, you may have a choice of deducting actual business-related expenses or claiming the standard mileage rate. The 1993 standard mileage rate is 28 cents a mile for all business miles. See *Local Transportation Ex-*

penses later in this chapter for information about using actual expenses or the standard mileage rate.

Lodging. You can deduct the cost of lodging if your business trip is overnight or long enough to require you to stop for sleep or rest to properly perform your duties.

Meals. You can deduct the cost of meals only if your business trip is overnight or long enough to require you to stop for sleep or rest to properly perform your duties. You cannot deduct the cost of meals if it is not necessary for you to rest. If you pay for a business meal when you are not traveling, you can deduct the cost only if you meet the rules for business entertainment. These rules are explained later under *Entertainment Expenses*.

The expense of a meal includes amounts you spend for your food, beverages, taxes, and tips relating to the meal. You can deduct either the actual cost or a standard amount. See *Standard Meal Allowance* later in this section.

80% limit on meals. You can deduct only 80% of the cost of your business-related meals (50% after 1993) unless you are reimbursed for these expenses. This limit applies whether the unreimbursed meal expense is for business travel or business entertainment. The 80% limit is explained later under *Entertainment Expenses*.

Lavish or extravagant. You cannot deduct expenses for meals to the extent they are lavish or extravagant. An expense is not considered lavish or extravagant if it is reasonable based on the facts and circumstances. Expenses will not be disallowed merely because they are more than a fixed dollar amount or take place at deluxe restaurants, hotels, night clubs, or resorts.

Cleaning and laundry expenses. You can deduct reasonable laundry expenses while traveling away from home on business.

Telephone expenses. You can deduct the cost of business calls while you are traveling away from home. This includes the cost of business communication by fax machine or other devices.

Tips. You can deduct tips you pay for any of the expenses in this section.

Other expenses. You can deduct other similar ordinary and necessary expenses that are related to your business travel. Such expenses might include the costs of operating and maintaining a house trailer, public stenographer's fees, and computer rental fees.

Expenses for your spouse. If your spouse goes with you on a business trip or to a business convention, you generally cannot deduct your spouse's expenses for travel, meals, and lodging. However, you can deduct these expenses if you can prove a real business purpose for your spouse's presence. Incidental services, such as typing notes or assisting in entertaining customers, are not enough to warrant a deduction.

Example. You drive to Chicago on business and take your spouse with you. No business purpose is served by your spouse's presence. You pay $115 a day for a double room. A single room costs $90 a day. You can deduct the total cost of driving your car to and from Chicago, but only $90 a day for your hotel room. If you use public transportation, you can deduct only your fare.

Explanation

The IRS and the courts have not been lenient in this area. Acting as a hostess or a receptionist at social functions, taking notes at meetings, and typing are generally considered incidental services, not necessary and bona fide business reasons for a spouse's presence on a trip.

Although the area is not clearly defined, one major

Table 28-1. **Deductible Travel Expenses**

Expense	Description
Transportation	The cost of travel by airplane, train, or bus between your home and your business destination.
Taxi, commuter bus, and limousine	Fares for these and other types of transportation between the airport or station and your hotel, or between the hotel and your work site away from home.
Baggage and shipping	The cost of sending baggage and sample or display material between your regular and temporary work sites.
Car	The costs of operating and maintaining your car when traveling away from home on business. You may deduct actual expenses or the standard mileage rate, including business-related tolls and parking. If you lease a car while away from home on business, you can deduct business-related expenses only.
Lodging	The cost of lodging if your business trip is overnight or long enough to require you to get substantial sleep or rest to properly perform your duties.
Meals	The cost of meals only if your business trip is overnight or long enough to require you to stop to get substantial sleep or rest. Includes amounts spent for food, beverages, taxes, and related tips.
Cleaning	Cleaning and laundry expenses while away from home overnight.
Telephone	The cost of business calls while on your business trip, including business communication by fax machine or other communication devices.
Tips	Tips you pay for any expenses in this chart.
Other	Other similar ordinary and necessary expenses related to your business travel such as public stenographer's fees and computer rental fees.

consideration seems to be whether or not the trip was primarily a vacation for the spouse. If you can show that the trip was not, your argument for deducting your spouse's expenses is considerably stronger. Favorable court decisions have cited some or all of the following factors in allowing deductions for a spouse's expenses:

- The employer requires the spouse's presence (written policy is advisable).
- A business schedule shows that the trip is not a vacation.
- The spouse's time is spent on business activity.
- The spouse's presence helps business prospects.
- Documentation shows the business purpose of the spouse's presence.

If your employer or any other sponsor reimburses you for the personal expenses of a member of your family who accompanies you to a business convention or on a business trip, you must include that amount in your income.

TaxAlert

Beginning in 1994, the new tax law denies a deduction for travel expenses paid or incurred for a spouse, dependent, or other individual accompanying you on a business travel unless certain requirements are met. For the expenses to be deductible, your traveling companion must: (1) be a bona fide employee of the person paying or reimbursing the expenses; (2) be traveling for a bona fide business purpose; and (3) have expenses that are otherwise deductible. The denial of the deduction does not apply to expenses that would otherwise qualify as deductible moving expenses.

Caution: Beginning in 1994, you cannot deduct travel expenses you pay or incur for your spouse, dependent, or other individual who accompanies you on business travel unless the travel satisfies specific requirements. See Publication 553, *Highlights of 1993 Tax Changes,* for more information about this and other tax law changes.

Standard Meal Allowance

You generally can deduct a standard amount for your daily meals and incidental expenses while you are traveling away from home on business. Incidental expenses include costs for laundry, cleaning, and tips for services. In this chapter, the term "standard meal allowance" refers to meals and incidental expenses.

Explanation
Incidental expenses include items such as laundry expenses and fees and tips for waiters and baggage handlers; however, it does not include taxicab fares or the costs of telegrams or telephone calls.

This method is an alternative to the actual cost method and allows you to deduct a set amount, depending on where you travel, instead of keeping records of actual meal expenses. If you use the standard meal allowance, you still must keep records to prove the time, place, and business purpose of your travel. See the record-keeping rules for travel, explained later in this chapter under *Recordkeeping*.

Who can use the standard meal allowance. You can use the standard meal allowance whether you are an employee or self-employed. You cannot use the standard meal allowance, however, if you are related to your employer as defined later.

You can use the standard meal allowance whether or not you are reimbursed for your traveling expenses. However, if you are not reimbursed for meal expenses, you can deduct only 80% of the standard meal allowance (50% after 1993). This 80% limit is figured when you complete Form 2106 or Schedule C. If you file Schedule C-EZ, enter the total amount of your business expenses on line 2. You can only include 80% of the standard meal allowance in that total. If you file Schedule F, enter the total amount of your travel, meals and entertainment expenses on line 34. You can only include 80% of the standard meal allowance in that total.

TaxPlanner
Whether or not you receive meal money from your employer, you may claim the standard meal allowance and therefore minimize your recordkeeping problems. If you are self-employed, you may also claim the standard meal allowance.

Related to employer. You are related to your employer if:

1) Your employer is your brother or sister, half-brother or half-sister, spouse, ancestor, or lineal descendent,
2) Your employer is a corporation in which you own, directly or indirectly, more than 10% in value of the outstanding stock, or
3) Certain fiduciary relationships exist between you and your employer involving grantors, trusts, beneficiaries, etc.

You may be considered to indirectly own stock, for purposes of (2) above, if you have an interest in a corporation, partnership, estate, or trust that owns the stock or if a family member or partner owns the stock.

Amount of standard meal allowance. The standard meal allowance is *$26 a day* for most areas in the United States. Other locations in the United States are designated as high-cost areas, qualifying for higher standard meal allowances.

Table 2 in Publication 463 shows the locations qualifying for a rate of $34 a day for travel before March 12, 1993. *Table 3* in Publication 463 shows the locations qualifying for rates of $30, $34, and $38 a day for travel on or after March 12, 1993.

If you travel to more than one location in one day, use the rate in effect for the area where you stop for sleep or rest. If you work in the transportation industry, however, see *Special rate for transportation workers,* later in this section.

Example. You regularly live and work in Chicago. You sometimes travel overnight to Des Moines for business. Your employer expects you to pay your expenses out of your regular salary and does not separately or specifically reimburse your expenses for business trips. You must keep receipts to prove the amount of your lodging expense. You can claim the standard meal allowance for Des Moines, $26, on your Form 2106. You are subject to the 80% limit on meal and entertainment expenses. You are also subject to the 2% of adjusted gross income limit that applies to most other miscellaneous itemized deductions.

Standard meal allowance for areas outside the continental United States. The previously mentioned standard meal allowance rates do not apply to travel in Alaska, Hawaii, or any other nonforeign locations outside the continental United States. They also do not apply to foreign locations. The federal per diem rates for these locations are published monthly in the *Maximum Travel Per Diem Allowances for Foreign Areas.*

Your employer may have these rates available, or you can purchase the publication from the:

Superintendent of Documents
U.S. Government Printing Office
P.O. Box 371954
Pittsburgh, PA 15250–7954

You can also order it by calling the Government Printing Office at (202)783–3238 (not a toll-free number). To find out the rate for a specific location, you can call the Department of State at (703)875–7910 (not a toll-free number).

Special rate for transportation workers. You may be able to use a special standard meal allowance if you work in the transportation industry. You are in the transportation industry if your work:

1) Directly involves moving people or goods by airplane, barge, bus, ship, train, or truck, and
2) Regularly requires you to travel away from home and, during any single trip, usually involves travel to areas eligible for different standard meal allowance rates.

If this applies to you, you can claim a *$30 a day* standard meal allowance ($34 for travel outside the continental United States) for travel before March 12, 1993. You can claim a *$32 a day* standard meal allowance ($36 for travel outside the continental United States) for travel on or after March 12, 1993.

Using the special rate for transportation workers eliminates the need for you to determine the standard meal allowance for every area where you stop for sleep or rest. If you choose to use the special rate for any trip, however, you must continue to use the special rate (and not use the regular standard meal allowance rates) for all trips you take that year.

Travel for less than 24 hours. If you are not traveling for the entire 24-hour day, you must prorate the standard meal allowance. You can do so by dividing the day into 6-hour quarters. The 6-hour quarters are:

1) Midnight to 6 a.m.,
2) 6 a.m. to noon,
3) Noon to 6 p.m., and
4) 6 p.m. to midnight.

You can claim one-fourth of the full day standard meal allowance for each 6-hour quarter of the day during any part of which you are traveling away from home.

Example 1. You live and work in Los Angeles. Your employer sends you to San Francisco on a temporary assignment. You leave home at 8 a.m. on March 23. Your assignment is completed on March 26. You arrive home at 4 p.m. on that day. You are considered to be traveling for 3½ days (a ¾ day on March 23 + 2 full days + a ¾ day on March 26). Your standard meal allowance is $133 (3½ × $38) while on this assignment.

Example 2. Maria is employed in Milwaukee as a convention planner. In April 1993, she went on a one-week business trip. She left her home in Milwaukee at 7 a.m. on April 5 and flew to Washington, DC, where she spent two nights. She then went to Albany, NY, arriving there at 4 p.m. on April 7. After three nights in Albany, she went to New York City to attend a planning seminar at her employer's request. She arrived at 1 p.m. on April 10. On April 12, she flew back to Milwaukee, arriving at her home at 5:45 p.m.

Maria decides to use the standard meal allowance and arrives at her expense as follows:

City	Number of Days	Allowance Amount	Total
Washington, DC	1¾	$38	$ 66.50
Albany, NY	3	$30	90.00
New York City	2¾	$38	104.50
			$261.00

Maria's total standard meal allowance for the trip is $261.00 ($66.50 + $90.00 + $104.50). If her employer does not reimburse her for her meals, Maria will be able to deduct 80% of her unreimbursed meals as an itemized deduction. She will figure this limit on Form 2106.

Standard meal allowance not allowed. You cannot use the standard meal allowance to prove the amount of your meals if you are traveling for medical, charitable, or moving purposes. However, you can use it if you are traveling for investment reasons. You can also use the standard meal allowance to prove meal expenses you incurred in connection with qualifying educational expenses while traveling away from home. Chapter 29 discusses deductible educational expenses.

Example

An executive traveling to other cities for interviews to obtain a position in another firm in the same business may deduct his or her expenses, as long as the executive is still employed or if there has been no substantial lack of continuity between the time of his or her past employment and the time of seeking new employment.

Travel in the United States

The following discussion applies to travel in the United States. For this purpose, the United States includes the 50 states and the District of Columbia. The treatment of your travel expenses depends on how much of your trip was business related and on how much of your trip occurred within the United States.

Trip Primarily For Business

You can deduct all your travel expenses if your trip was entirely business related. If your trip was primarily for business and, while at your business destination, you extended your stay for a vacation, made a nonbusiness side trip, or had other nonbusiness activities, you can deduct your business-related travel expenses. These expenses include the travel costs of getting to and from your business destination, and you can deduct any business-related expenses at your business destination.

Example. You work in Atlanta and take a business trip to New Orleans. On your way home, you stop in Mobile to visit your parents. You spend $630 for the 9 days you are away from home for travel, meals, lodging, and other travel expenses. If you had not stopped in Mobile, you would have been gone only 6 days, and your total cost would have been $580. You can deduct $580 for your trip, including the round-trip transportation to and from New Orleans. The cost of your meals is subject to the 80% limit discussed earlier.

Trip Primarily For Personal Reasons

If your trip was primarily for personal reasons, such as a vacation, the entire cost of the trip is a nondeductible personal expense. However, you can deduct any expenses you have while at your destination that are directly related to your business.

A trip may be a vacation even if the promoter advertises that a trip to a resort or on a cruise ship is primarily for business. The scheduling of incidental business activities during a trip, such as viewing videotapes or attending lectures dealing with general subjects, will not change what is really a vacation into a business trip.

Explanation

The courts have not allowed expenses to be deducted for trips whose primary purpose is pleasure but whose secondary purpose is the investigation of business rental properties. If the primary purpose of the trip is to search for rental properties, all travel expenses can be deducted.

TaxOrganizer

Careful records should be maintained when family members are along on business trips. If a spouse or other family member on a trip serves a business purpose, care should be taken to document that fact. Otherwise, the incremental travel expenses attributed to the additional person may not be deducted. Receipts and a diary of your activities will be of assistance in documenting the purpose of your trip.

Part of Trip Outside the United States

If part of your trip is outside the United States, use the rules described later under *Travel Outside the United States* for that part of the trip. For the part of your trip that is inside the United States, use the rules in this section. Travel outside the United States does not include travel from one point in the United States to another point in the United States. The following discussion can help you determine whether your trip was entirely within the United States.

Public transportation. If you travel by public transportation, any place in the United States where that vehicle makes a scheduled stop is a point in the United States. Once the transportation mode leaves the last scheduled stop in the United States on its way to a point outside the United States, you apply the rules under *Travel Outside the United States*.

Example 1. You fly from New York to Puerto Rico with a scheduled stop in Miami. You return to New York nonstop. The flight from New York to Miami is in the United States, so only the flight from Miami to Puerto Rico is outside the United States. All of the return trip is outside the United States, as there are no scheduled stops between Puerto Rico and New York.

Example 2. You travel by train from New York to Montreal.

The travel from New York to the last scheduled stop in the United States is travel in the United States.

Private car. Travel by private car in the United States is travel between points in the United States, even when you are on your way to a destination outside the United States.

Example. You travel by car from Denver to Mexico City and return. Your travel from Denver to the border and from the border back to Denver is travel in the United States, and the rules in this section apply. The rules under *Travel Outside the United States* apply to your trip from the border to Mexico City and back to the border.

Private plane. If you travel by private plane, any trip, or part of a trip, for which both your takeoff and landing are in the United States is travel in the United States. This is true even if part of your flight is over a foreign country.

Example. You fly nonstop from Seattle to Juneau. Although the flight passes over Canada, the trip is considered to be travel in the United States.

Travel Outside the United States

If any part of your business travel is outside the United States, some of your travel expense deductions of getting to and from your destination may be limited. For this purpose, the United States includes the 50 states and the District of Columbia.

How much of your travel expenses is deductible depends in part upon how much of your trip outside the United States was business related.

The rules for travel inside the United States were discussed in the previous section.

See Chapter 1 of Publication 463 for information on luxury water travel.

Travel Entirely For Business
If you travel outside the United States and you spend the entire time on business activities, all your expenses of getting to and from your business destination are deductible.

In addition, even if you do not spend your entire time on business activities, your trip is considered entirely for business, and you can deduct all of your business-related travel expenses if you meet *one* of the following four conditions.

1) You did not have substantial control over arranging the trip. You are not considered to have substantial control merely because you control the timing of your trip.

   You are considered not to have substantial control over your trip if you:
   a) Are an employee who was reimbursed or paid a travel expense allowance,
   b) Are not related to your employer, and
   c) Are not a managing executive.

"Related to your employer" was defined earlier in this chapter under *Standard Meal Allowance*. A "managing executive" is an employee who has the authority and responsibility, without being subject to the veto of another, to decide on the need for the business travel.

A self-employed person is generally regarded as having substantial control over arranging business trips.

2) You were outside the United States a week or less, combining business and nonbusiness activities. One week means seven consecutive days. In counting the days, do not count the day you leave the United States, but count the day you return to the United States.

   Example. You traveled to Paris primarily for business. You left Denver on Tuesday and flew to New York. On Wednesday, you flew from New York to Paris, arriving the next morning. On Thursday and Friday, you had business discussions, and from Saturday until Tuesday, you were sightseeing. You flew back to New York, arriving Wednesday afternoon. On Thursday, you flew back to Denver. Although you were away from your home in Denver for more than a week, you were not outside the United States for more than a week. This is because the day of departure does not count as a day outside the United States. You can deduct your cost of the round-trip flight between Denver and Paris. You can also deduct the cost of your stay in Paris for Thursday and Friday while you conducted business. However, you cannot deduct the cost of your stay in Paris from Saturday through Tuesday because those days were spent on nonbusiness activities.

3) You spent less than 25% of the total time you were outside the United States in nonbusiness activities, even if the trip outside the United States was for more than a week. For this purpose, count both the day your trip began and the day it ended.

   Example. You flew from Seattle to Tokyo, where you spent 14 days on business and 5 days on personal matters. You then flew back to Seattle. You spent one day flying in each direction. Because only $5/21$ (less than 25%) of your total time abroad was for nonbusiness activities, you can deduct as travel expenses what it would have cost you to make the trip if you had not engaged in any nonbusiness activity. The amount you can deduct is the cost of the round-trip plane fare and 16 days of meals (subject to the 80% limit), lodging, and other related expenses.

4) You can establish that a personal vacation was not a major consideration, even if you own your business, are related to your employer, are a managing executive, or have substantial control over arranging the trip.

If you do not meet any of these conditions, you may still be able to deduct some of your expenses. See *Travel Primarily For Business,* next.

Travel Primarily For Business
If you traveled outside the United States primarily for business purposes, but spent 25% or more of your time on nonbusiness activities, your travel expense deductions are limited unless you meet one of the four conditions listed earlier under *Travel Entirely For Business*. If your deductions are limited, you must allocate your travel expenses of getting to and from your destination between your business and nonbusiness activities to determine your deductible amount.

Travel allocation rules. If your trip was not entirely for business, you must allocate your travel expenses on a day-to-day basis between days you conducted business and days you did not conduct business.

To figure the deductible amount of your round-trip travel expenses between the United States and your business destination, multiply the total cost by the following fraction. The numerator (top number) is the total number of business days outside the United States. The denominator (bottom number) is the total number of all days outside the United States. The day of your departure from the United States and the day you return to the United States are both counted as days outside the United States.

Counting business days. Your business days include transportation days, days your presence was required, days you spent on business, and certain weekends and holidays.

Transportation day. Count as a business day any day you spend traveling to or from a business destination. However, if because of a nonbusiness activity you do not travel by a direct route, your business days are the days it would have taken you to travel a reasonably direct route to your business destination. Extra days for side trips or nonbusiness activities cannot be counted as business days.

Presence required. Count as a business day any day that your presence is required at a particular place for a specific business purpose, even if you spend most of the day on nonbusiness activities.

Day spent on business. If your principal activity during working hours is in pursuit of your trade or business, the day is counted as a business day. Also, count as a business day any day you are prevented from working because of circumstances beyond your control.

Certain weekends and holidays. Weekends, holidays, and other necessary standby days are counted as business days if they fall between business days. But if they follow your business meetings or activity and you remain at your business destination for nonbusiness or personal reasons, they are not business days.

Example 1. Your tax home is in New York City. You travel to Quebec where you have a business appointment on Friday. You have another appointment on the following Monday. Because you had a business activity on Friday and had another business activity on Monday, the days in between are counted as business days. This is true even though you use that time for sightseeing, personal visiting, or other nonbusiness activities.

Example 2. If, in *Example 1,* you had no other business in Quebec after Friday, but stayed until Monday before starting home, Saturday and Sunday would be nonbusiness days.

Nonbusiness activity on the route to or from your business destination. If you had a vacation or other nonbusiness activity between the United States and your business destination, or between your business destination and the United States, you must allocate your travel expenses between business and nonbusiness days. You can do so as follows:

1) Divide the number of business days by the total number of travel days.
2) Multiply the result in (1) by the cost of round-trip travel between the United States and your nonbusiness destination.
3) Add to the result in (2) the round-trip cost of travel between the United States and your business destination minus the round-trip cost of travel between the United States and your nonbusiness destination. This is the deductible part of your cost of getting to and from your business destination.
4) Add to the result in (3) your business travel expenses while at your business destination. These are your total allowable travel expenses.

Example. You live in New York and flew to Brussels on Thursday, May 27, to attend a conference with a customer that began at noon Friday, May 28. The conference ended at noon Monday, May 31. That evening you flew to Dublin where you visited with friends until the afternoon of June 13, when you flew home to New York. The primary purpose for the trip was to attend the conference.

If you had not stopped in Dublin, you would have arrived home the evening of May 31. You were outside the United States more than a week, and you are unable to show that you had no substantial control over arranging the trip, or that a personal vacation was not a major consideration in making the trip. May 27 through May 31 (5 days) are business days and June 1 through June 13 (13 days) are nonbusiness days. You cannot deduct your expenses while in Dublin. You also cannot deduct $13/18$ of the cost of round-trip airfare and any other expenses from New York to Dublin.

You can deduct the cost of your meals (subject to the 80% limit), lodging, and other business-related travel expenses while

in Brussels. You figure the deductible part of your travel between the United States and Brussels as follows:

1) $5/18$ of the round-trip airfare and other expenses between New York and Dublin, **plus**
2) The cost of the round-trip fare and any other expenses between New York and Brussels minus the cost of the round-trip fare and any other expenses between New York and Dublin.

Assume the round-trip plane fare and other expenses between New York and Brussels are $800 and the expenses between New York and Dublin are $600. Your deductible plane fare and other expenses are $366.67 [($5/18 \times $600) + ($800 - $600)].

Nonbusiness activity at or beyond business destination. If you had a vacation or other nonbusiness activity at or beyond your business destination, you must allocate your travel expenses between your business and nonbusiness days. None of your travel expenses for nonbusiness activities at or beyond your business destination are deductible. You must also allocate your round-trip transportation and other costs between the United States and your business destination as follows.

Multiply the cost of your round-trip travel between the United States and your business destination by a fraction. The numerator (top number) is the number of business days. The denominator (bottom number) is the total number of travel days. Add to this result your other business-related travel expenses at your business destination. The sum is your total deductible travel expenses.

Example. Assume that the dates are the same as in the prior example but that instead of going to Dublin for your vacation, you fly to Venice, Italy, for a vacation. You cannot deduct any part of the cost of your trip from Brussels to Venice and return to Brussels. In addition, you cannot deduct $13/18$ of the airfare and other expenses from New York to Brussels and back to New York. You may deduct $5/18$ of the round-trip plane fare and other expenses from New York to Brussels, plus your meals, lodging, and any other business expenses you had in Brussels. If the round-trip plane fare and other expenses are $800 from New York to Brussels, you can deduct travel costs of $222.22 ($5/18 \times $800). **Other methods.** You can use another method of counting business days if you establish that it more clearly reflects the time spent on nonbusiness activities outside the United States.

Explanation
A business day is established if, during any part of the day, you are required to be present at a business-related event. Weekends falling between business days may be considered business days, but, if they fall at the end of your business meetings and you remain for personal reasons, they are not business days. Transportation days are business days when you travel to your destination on a direct route.

TAXPLANNER

If, in order to take advantage of lower plane fares, your employer reimburses your travel expenses for staying overnight on Saturday at the end of a business trip, the meals and lodging costs for Saturday can be deducted by your employer and excluded from your income to the extent the costs do not exceed the cost savings. The IRS privately ruled that these travel expenses relating to the Saturday night away are deductible even though the day is spent sightseeing.

Travel Primarily For Vacation

If your travel was primarily for vacation, or for **investment** purposes, and you spent some time attending brief professional seminars or a continuing education program, the entire cost of the trip is a nondeductible personal expense. You may, however, deduct your registration fees and any other expenses incurred that were directly related to your business.

Example. You are a doctor practicing medicine and are a member of a professional association. The association sponsored a 2-week trip to two foreign countries with three professional seminars in each country. Each seminar was 2 hours long and was held in a different city. You also made an optional side trip to a well-known tourist attraction in each of the countries visited. At the end of the trip you received a Certificate of Continuing Education in Medicine.

You paid the cost of airfare, hotel accommodations, meals, a special escort, transportation to and from hotels, and tips. No part of the cost was specifically stated for the seminars, which were arranged for you by the sponsoring professional association.

Your participation in the professional seminars did not change what was essentially a vacation into a business trip. Your travel expenses were not related primarily to your business. You had no other expenses that were directly for your business. Therefore, you cannot deduct the cost of your trip as an ordinary and necessary business expense.

Conventions

You can deduct your travel expenses when you attend a convention if you can show that your attendance benefits your trade or business. You cannot deduct the travel expenses for your family. If the convention is for **investment,** political, social, or other purposes unrelated to your trade or business, you cannot deduct the expenses. Nonbusiness expenses, such as social or sightseeing expenses, are personal expenses and are not deductible.

Your appointment or election as a delegate does not, in itself, entitle you to or deprive you of a deduction. Your attendance must be connected to your own trade or business.

Convention agenda. The agenda of the convention does not have to deal specifically with your official duties or the responsibilities of your position or business. It is enough if the agenda is so related to your active trade or business and your responsibilities that attendance for a business purpose is justified.

Explanation
To determine whether a trip is primarily for business, the courts have used the following guidelines:

1. The amount of time spent on personal activity compared with the amount of time spent on business activity.
2. The location of the convention. The setting of a convention at a resort does not mean that the expense is disallowed, but a more businesslike setting increases the strength of your case.
3. The attitude of your sponsor toward the purpose of the meeting.

The courts must also be satisfied that the primary purpose of the convention is business related.

Expenses paid by others. You cannot deduct expenses paid by others or personal expenses you paid for your family members.

You must reduce the expenses you pay by reimbursements or allowances you received from others.

Foreign conventions. See Chapter 1 of Publication 463 for information on conventions held outside the North American area.

Explanation
The amount of expenses you incur when you travel on an ocean liner or cruise ship may not be fully deductible. Generally, the amount of the deduction is limited to twice the per diem rate of an employee of the executive branch of the U.S. goverment multiplied by the number of days you travel on the ship. For travel between January 1, 1993 and March 11, 1993, the executive per diem rate is $174. For travel on or after March 12, 1993, the executive per diem rate is $178. However, if you attend a convention while aboard the cruise ship, you may still deduct up to $2,000 per individual per calendar year if the following requirements are met.

1. The meeting must be directly related to the active conduct of a business.
2. The cruise ship must be registered in the United States and may travel only to ports in the United States or its possessions.
3. You must include in your tax return a written statement containing a breakdown by hours and by days of the business meetings on the trip and a note signed by the cruise's sponsor attesting to your attendance at specific business meetings.

Example
You have a business meeting in Puerto Rico and choose to travel by ship. You spend 6 days on the cruise ship from the time you depart until the time you return. The total cost of the 6-day cruise package is $3,000. You may deduct only $2,000 of the $3,000 costs.

Entertainment Expenses

You may be able to deduct business-related entertainment expenses you have for entertaining a client, customer, or employee.

To be deductible, the expense must be both ordinary and necessary. An ordinary expense is one that is common and accepted in your field of business, trade, or profession. A necessary expense is one that is helpful and appropriate for your business. An expense does not have to be indispensable to be considered necessary.

In addition, the entertainment expense must meet one of two tests:

1) Directly-related test, or
2) Associated test.

You must also meet the requirements discussed later in this chapter under *Recordkeeping*.

Even if you meet all the requirements for claiming a deduction for entertainment expenses, the amount you can deduct may be limited. Generally, you can deduct only 80% of your unreimbursed entertainment expenses (50% after 1993). This limit is discussed later in this section under *80% Limit*.

Entertainment. Entertainment includes any activity generally considered to provide entertainment, amusement, or recreation. Examples include entertaining guests at night clubs; at social, athletic, and sporting clubs; at theaters; at sporting events; on yachts; or on hunting, fishing, vacation, and similar trips. If you buy a ticket to an entertainment event for a client, you generally cannot deduct more than the face value of the ticket.

A meal as a form of entertainment. Entertainment includes the cost of a meal you provide to a customer, or client, whether the meal is a part of other entertainment or by itself. A meal sold as a normal course of your business is not entertainment. Generally, to deduct an entertainment-related meal, you or your employee must be present when the food or beverages are provided.

A meal expense includes the cost of food, beverages, taxes, and tips for the meal.

No double deduction allowed for meals. You cannot claim the cost of your meal as an entertainment expense if you are also claiming the cost of your meal as a travel expense.

Taking turns paying for meals or entertainment. Expenses are *not* deductible when a group of business acquaintances take turns picking up each other's meal or entertainment checks without regard to whether any business purposes are served.

Trade association meetings. You can deduct expenses that are directly related to and necessary for attending business meetings or conventions of certain exempt organizations. These organizations include business leagues, chambers of commerce, real estate boards, trade associations, and professional associations. The expenses of your attendance must be related to your active trade or business. These expenses are subject to the 80% limit on entertainment expenses.

Explanation
The courts have held that costs of entertaining fellow employees are not deductible, even though the entertaining may have contributed to high morale and increased productivity.

Additional information. For more information on entertainment expenses, including discussions of the directly-related and associated tests and entertainment facilities, see Chapter 2 of Publication 463.

80% Limit

In general, you can deduct only 80% of your business-related meal and entertainment expenses. This limit applies to employees or their employers, and to self-employed persons (including independent contractors) or their clients, depending on whether the expenses are reimbursed.

TaxAlert
Beginning in 1994, the 1993 Tax Act amended this provision to limit the deductible portion of meal and entertainment expenses to 50%.

Caution: Beginning in 1994, the limit on business meals and entertainment expenses is reduced from 80% to 50%.

The 80% limit applies to meals or entertainment expenses incurred while:

1) Traveling away from home (whether eating alone or with others) on business,

2) Entertaining business customers at your place of business, a restaurant, or other location, or

3) Attending a business convention or reception, business meeting, or business luncheon at a club.

TaxAlert
Beginning in 1994, the new tax law denies a deduction for amounts paid or incurred for membership in any club organized for business, pleasure, recreation, or other social purpose.

Taxes and tips relating to a business meal or entertainment activity are included in the amount that is subject to the 80% limit. Expenses such as cover charges for admission to a night club, rent paid for a room in which you hold a dinner or cocktail party, or the amount paid for parking at a sports arena are also subject to the 80% limit. However, the cost of transportation to and from a business meal or a business-related entertainment activity is not subject to the 80% limit.

If you pay or incur an expense for goods and services consisting of meals, entertainment, and other services (such as lodging or transportation), you must allocate that expense between the cost of meals and entertainment and the cost of the other services. You must have a reasonable basis for making this allocation. For example, you must allocate your expenses if a hotel includes one or more meals in its room charge, or if you are provided with one per diem amount to cover both your lodging and meal expenses.

Application of 80% limit. The 80% limit on meal and entertainment expenses applies if the expense is otherwise deductible and is not covered by the exception discussed later in this section.

The 80% limit also applies to other activities that are not a trade or business. It applies to meal and entertainment expenses incurred for the production of income including rental or royalty income. In 1993, it also applies to deductible moving and educational expenses.

When to apply the 80% limit. You apply the 80% limit after determining the amount that would otherwise qualify for a deduction. You first determine the amount of meal and entertainment expenses that would be deductible under the rules discussed in this chapter.

You then apply the 80% limit. If you are an employee, use Form 2106 to figure the limit. If you are self-employed, figure the limit on Schedule C. If you file Schedule C-EZ, enter the total amount of your business expenses on line 2. You can only include 80% of your meal and entertainment expenses in that total. If you file Schedule F, enter 80% of your meal and entertainment expenses on line 34.

Finally, to determine the actual amount you can deduct if you are an employee, you must apply the 2% of adjusted gross income limit on Schedule A (Form 1040).

Example 1. You spend $100 for a business-related meal. If $40 of that amount is not allowable because it is considered lavish and extravagant, the remaining $60 is subject to the 80% limit. Your deduction cannot be more than $48 (.80 × $60).

Example 2. You purchase two tickets to a concert and give them to a client. You purchased the tickets through a ticket agent. You paid $150 for the two tickets, which had a face value of $60 each ($120 total). Your deduction cannot be more than $96 (.80 × $120).

Explanation

Although entertaining a client or a business associate often makes sound business sense, entertainment deductions have sometimes been abused. For this reason, Congress has imposed limitations on the deductibility of entertainment expenses. Generally, only 80% of otherwise allowable entertainment expenses will be deductible. The 20% disallowance generally applies to all taxpayers, regardless of the nature of the business. Even before the 20% disallowance, entertainment expenses are subject to stringent recordkeeping requirements and must pass one of two tests:

1. **"Directly related" test.** The expenditure is directly related to the active conduct of your business.
2. **"Associated with" test.** The expenditure is associated with the active conduct of your business, and the entertainment directly precedes or follows a substantial, bona fide business discussion.

Business meals—those that have a business purpose as opposed to a social and personal one—are not subject to these entertainment rules if they occur in surroundings conducive to business discussion, the taxpayer or an employee of the taxpayer is present when the food or beverages are served, and the expenses are properly substantiated.

Deductions for entertainment or business meals may not be taken if such expenses are considered lavish or extravagant.

Example

State police officers who are required to eat meals while on duty in public places were permitted to deduct expenses for these meals. The court found that the officers were significantly restricted by their employment regarding the time and place they were permitted to eat and that the meals were often subject to business-related interruptions.

Explanation

Entertainment directly related to business. The "directly related" test is satisfied if all of the following are true:

- You expect to derive income or some other specific business benefit (other than mere goodwill) at some indefinite future time. However, it is not necessary to demonstrate that you actually receive the benefit.
- You actively engage in a business meeting, discussion, or other bona fide business transaction with the person being entertained.
- Your principal purpose of the combined business-entertainment activity is the *active conduct* of your business. It is not necessary to devote more time to business than to the entertainment to meet this requirement.

Certain entertainment activities generally do not meet the "directly related" test unless proven otherwise. If you are not present for the entertainment, if the group entertained includes persons other than business associates (such as spouses), or if there are substantial distractions (as may occur in nightclubs, theaters, sport-

ing events, and vacation resorts), your activity may fail the "directly related" test.

The IRS gives taxpayers some relief from these strict rules when the activity is clearly in a business setting. For example, expenditures made to further your business by providing a hospitality room at a convention are treated as entertainment expenses directly related to business. Additionally, situations in which no meaningful personal or social relationship exists between you and the persons entertained are often considered to have occurred in a business setting. For example, entertaining business and civic leaders at the opening of a new hotel or theatrical production—for the purpose of obtaining business publicity rather than creating or maintaining goodwill—is a deductible entertainment expense directly related to business.

Example

An attorney paid for the costs of an annual fishing trip with three business associates who were sources of referrals to his law practice. He also used his cabin 75% of the time for entertaining business clients. The attorney could not prove that substantial and bona fide business discussions occurred during the fishing trip or on any of the occasions when business clients used the cabin. He showed that, at most, he had just a generalized expectation of deriving income or other business benefits at some indefinite future time from those entertained. As a result, he was denied deductions for these expenses, because they did not meet the "directly related" test.

Explanation

Entertainment associated with business. If an entertainment expenditure does not meet the "directly related" requirements, it may still be deductible if it passes the "associated with" test. An entertainment activity passes the "associated with" test only if it satisfies two conditions:

- The activity has a clear business purpose.
- The entertainment directly precedes or follows a substantial, bona fide business discussion.

The desire to obtain new business and the intent to maintain an existing business relationship—goodwill—are objectives that have a clear business purpose. A substantial, bona fide business discussion occurs when you actively engage in a business transaction to obtain some business benefit and the business meeting, negotiation, or discussion is substantial in relation to the entertainment. However, it is not necessary to spend more time on business than on entertainment.

Example

Bonnie McDonald, an independent consultant, spends 4 hours delivering a new management program to a group of executives in her client's New Orleans office. After the meeting, Bonnie takes the group to the French Quarter for dinner and a show. Dixieland jazz is played throughout dinner.

The entertainment passes the "associated with" test and is therefore deductible (subject to the 80% limitation), because Bonnie is maintaining a business relationship and the entertainment follows a substantial business meeting. The expense would not pass the "directly related" test, because (1) goodwill generally does not qualify and (2) substantial distractions exist.

Explanation

Entertainment directly precedes or follows a substantial business discussion if it occurs on the same day. If the entertainment and business discussion do not occur on the same day, the facts and circumstances of each case determine whether or not the entertainment and the business discussion occur close enough in time so that the expenses can be deducted.

Example

A group of business associates come to Denver and hold substantial discussions with a taxpayer. Entertainment for the business guests on the evening prior to or after the day of the business discussions is generally regarded as directly preceding or following the business discussion. Therefore, 80% of the entertainment expenses are deductible.

Explanation

Deducting goodwill entertainment. Generally, entertaining for goodwill alone is not deductible. However, you may deduct goodwill expenditures when

- The goodwill occurs during a quiet business lunch or dinner
- The goodwill precedes or follows a substantial business discussion (i.e., passes the "associated with" test)

Example 1

Liz Brown, a partner of a management consulting firm, plans a dinner party in a New York City hotel. She invites a number of current and prospective clients. Business is only casually discussed; her main goal is to cultivate goodwill. The expense for the dinner party is not deductible. The goodwill is a clear business purpose, but the dinner is not preceded or followed by a substantial business discussion.

Example 2

After considering the tax cost of the nondeductible goodwill expenses, Liz Brown holds a second dinner party, but she adds a formal presentation, which is substantial in relation to the time spent cultivating goodwill. The costs of the refreshments and dinner qualify as goodwill entertainment, since the entertainment is associated with business and the goodwill (the business purpose) is preceded by a substantial business discussion (the presentation). As a result, 80% of the qualifying expenses are deductible.

Explanation

Out-of-pocket entertaining costs at clubs and lodges. Congress has made it clear that out-of-pocket entertainment costs—that otherwise qualify as directly related or associated with business expenses—may still be partially deducted, even if they are incurred at an entertainment facility. Again, 20% of such costs may not be deducted.

An entertainment facility is usually **real property,** such as a fishing camp, a ski lodge, an apartment, or a hotel suite, that may also include personal property, such as a yacht, an airplane, or an automobile. You may own or rent the facility or just be a member of a club or organization, such as a country club or a sporting group, that provides use of a facility.

Example

Mike Franklin, a sports equipment manufacturer, takes a customer to a hunting lodge on an overnight trip. Immediately after the trip, the customer discusses products and market projections. The discussion ends with the customer placing his semiannual order.

In this instance, 80% of the costs of the meals, hunting rights, drinks in the nightclub, and transportation to and from the lodge are deductible. These costs qualify as entertainment associated with business and followed by a substantial business discussion (i.e., the expenses pass the "associated with" test). Because 80% of the entertainment costs would have been deductible if not incurred at an entertainment facility, they are also deductible even though the hunting lodge is an entertainment facility. These costs are not directly associated with the operation and maintenance of the place. However, the cost of the lodging is associated with the operation and maintenance of the facility. Therefore, the lodging expense, though partially deductible if incurred at a nonentertainment facility (e.g., a hotel instead of the hunting lodge), is not deductible.

TaxAlert

Starting in 1994, you cannot take a deduction for amounts paid or incurred for membership in any club organized for business, pleasure, recreation, or other social purpose. Specific business expenses, such as meals and entertainment that my occur at a club would be deductible if they otherwise satisfy the standard for deductibility as discussed in this chapter.

Explanation

Deducting club dues and fees. Dues and fees paid to social, athletic, and sporting clubs are 80% deductible

- Only if the club is used primarily to further your business
- Only to the extent that the club use is directly related to the active conduct of your business

A club's use is primarily to further business when more than 50% of your utilization of it is business related. This business use may be directly related to a business activity, or it may be merely associated with business. Therefore, goodwill entertainment that is provided at a club and that precedes or follows a substantial business discussion also counts toward the "primarily for business" test (i.e., the "more than 50%" test).

Although the "associated with" goodwill entertainment counts for the "primarily for business" test, it is not directly related to business. Therefore, the portion of the dues or fees attributable to the "associated with" entertainment is not deductible. Remember, the use of a club's restaurant for a quiet business meal counts as use that is directly related to business.

Example

Use of a country club

Business meals	25%
Other "directly related" entertainment	20%
Total "directly related" use	45%
"Associated with" entertainment	20%
Total "primarily for business" use	65%
Personal use	35%
Total use	100%

Club use in this example is primarily for business, since the total business use (65%) exceeds 50%. However, only 45% of the club dues may be deducted. This percentage test applies only to the dues or fees. The costs of business meals are subject to the 80% limit, as are all the other qualifying entertainment expenses (out-of-pocket costs) incurred at the club.

Explanation

Deductions for the costs of tickets to cultural, theatrical, or sporting events are severely limited. In addition to meeting the "directly related" or "associated with" tests, the allowable portion of the ticket cost is limited to the face value of the ticket. The allowable portion of the ticket cost must be further reduced, because only 80% of the allowable expense may be deducted.

Example

You pay a scalper $150 for three tickets to a sporting event. The face value of each ticket is $20. Your deduc-tion is limited to $48 ($20 face value × three tickets × 80%). A similar rule also applies to the cost of luxury sky boxes at sports arenas. Costs for the business use of a suite, an apartment, an automobile, or an airplane are generally deductible. Personal use of an entertainment facility may be considered compensation, and the individual may be subject to tax.

Exception to the 80% Limit

The 80% limit on meal and entertainment expenses applies if the expense is otherwise deductible based on the tests and rules explained in this chapter.

You can use *Figure 28–A* to help you determine if the 80% limit applies to you. Your meal or entertainment expense is **not** subject to the 80% limit if the expense meets the following exception.

Employee's reimbursed expenses. As an employee, you are not subject to the 80% limit if your employer reimburses you under an accountable plan and does not treat your reimbursement as wages. Accountable plans are discussed later in this chapter under *Reimbursements*.

This exception does not apply to the cost of meals you are claiming as moving expenses in 1993. You are subject to the 80% limit on the cost of these meals even if your employer reimburses you for the expense. For more information, see Chapter 27, *Moving Expenses*.

Exceptions

Entertainment test exceptions. Expenses incurred in the following situations generally are not subject to the "directly related" and "associated with" tests:

- Business meals in surroundings normally considered conducive to a business discussion
- Recreational and social activities primarily benefiting employees (e.g., company picnics, office Christmas parties, and golf outings)

Figure 28-A. Does the 80% Limit Apply to Your Expenses?

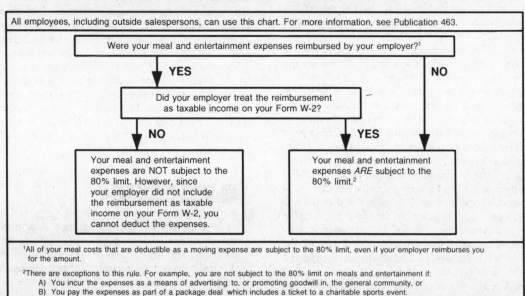

All employees, including outside salespersons, can use this chart. For more information, see Publication 463.

Were your meal and entertainment expenses reimbursed by your employer?[1]

YES / **NO**

Did your employer treat the reimbursement as taxable income on your Form W-2?

NO: Your meal and entertainment expenses are NOT subject to the 80% limit. However, since your employer did not include the reimbursement as taxable income on your Form W-2, you cannot deduct the expenses.

YES: Your meal and entertainment expenses *ARE* subject to the 80% limit.[2]

[1]All of your meal costs that are deductible as a moving expense are subject to the 80% limit, even if your employer reimburses you for the amount.

[2]There are exceptions to this rule. For example, you are not subject to the 80% limit on meals and entertainment if:
  A) You incur the expenses as a means of advertising to, or promoting goodwill in, the general community, or
  B) You pay the expenses as part of a package deal which includes a ticket to a charitable sports event.

- Business meetings of employees, stockholders, agents, or directors
- Attendance at a business meeting of a tax-exempt business league (e.g., a chamber of commerce, a board of trade, or a professional organization)
- Employee entertainment or recreation that is treated as compensation on the employee's income tax return and as wages for withholding purposes
- Nonemployee entertainment or recreation that is treated as income on the nonemployee's tax return and reported to him or her on an informational return (Form 1099)

Exceptions to the 80% Limit. Expenses incurred in the following situations are not subject to the 20% disallowance provision:

- Reimbursed meal or entertainment expenses
- Employer-paid recreational expenses for employees (e.g, a holiday party)
- Entertainment taxable to the recipient
- Entertainment expenses made available to the general public
- Entertainment expenses related to charitable fund-raising sports events

Business Gift Expenses

If you give business gifts in the course of your trade or business, you can deduct the cost subject to the limits and rules in this section.

Limit on business gifts. You can deduct no more than $25 for business gifts you give directly or indirectly to any one person during your tax year. A gift to a company that is intended for the eventual personal use or benefit of a particular person or a limited class of people will be considered an indirect gift to that particular person or to the individuals within that class of people who receive the gift.

A gift to the spouse of a business customer or client is an indirect gift to the customer or client. However, if you have an independent bona fide business connection with the spouse, the gift generally will not be considered an indirect gift to the other spouse. It will, however, be considered an indirect gift to the other spouse if it is intended for that spouse's eventual use or benefit. These rules also apply to gifts to any other family member.

If you and your spouse both give gifts, both of you are treated as one taxpayer. It does not matter whether you have separate businesses, are separately employed, or whether each of you has an independent connection with the recipient. If a partnership gives gifts, the partnership and the partners are treated as one taxpayer.

Incidental costs. Incidental costs, such as engraving on jewelry, or packaging, insuring, and mailing, are generally not included in determining the cost of a gift for purposes of the $25 rule.

A related cost is considered incidental only if it does not add substantial value to the gift. For example, the cost of gift wrapping is considered an incidental cost. However, the purchase of an ornamental basket for packaging fruit is not considered an incidental cost of packaging if the basket has a substantial value compared to the value of the fruit.

Exceptions. The following items are not subject to the $25 limit for business gifts.

1) An item that costs $4 or less and:
   a) Has your name clearly and permanently imprinted on the gift, and
   b) Is one of a number of identical items you widely distribute. Examples include pens, desk sets, and plastic bags and cases.
2) Signs, display racks, or other promotional material to be used on the business premises of the recipient.

Explanation

Business gifts are subject to close scrutiny. The IRS views this area as one of potential abuse. Business gifts are subject to strict substantiation requirements. The date of the gift and the name of the recipient must be noted in your records to uphold the deduction.

The business gift limitations do not apply to the following types of donations:

- Fellowship grants or scholarships
- Achievement prizes and awards
- Death benefits to an employer's survivors

Examples

The cost of beer offered by a service station owner to entice customers into his service station was allowed as a business gift deduction. The courts held that the expenses were directly related to the active conduct of his business and were incurred to sell additional goods and services.

Wine samples distributed in connection with a public offering of stock were allowed as a business gift subject to the $25 per recipient limitation.

Employee achievement awards. Employee achievement awards are not treated as gifts. For information on the requirements you must meet in order to deduct the cost of these awards, see *Bonuses and Awards* in Chapter 2 of Publication 535.

Gift or entertainment. Any item that might be considered either a gift or an entertainment expense generally will be considered an entertainment expense. However, if you give a customer packaged food or beverages that you intend the customer to use at a later date, treat it as a gift expense.

If you give tickets to a theater performance or sporting event to a business customer and you do not go with the customer to the performance or event, you can choose to treat the tickets as either a gift or entertainment expense, whichever is to your advantage.

You can change your treatment of the tickets at a later date, but not after the time allowed for the assessment of income tax. In most instances, this assessment period ends 3 years after the due date of your income tax return. But if you go with the customer to the event, you must treat the cost of the tickets as an entertainment expense. You cannot choose, in this case, to treat the tickets as a gift expense.

TaxPlanner

It is usually to your advantage to define a particular item as an entertainment expense rather than as a gift. Although entertainment expenses are subject to the 80% limitation, there is no fixed dollar limitation on the deduction, though the expenses must be considered ordinary and necessary.

Local Transportation Expenses

This section discusses expenses you can deduct for local business transportation. It also discusses deductions you can take for business use of your car, whether you use it for business-related local transportation or for traveling away from home overnight on business.

Local transportation expenses include the ordinary and necessary expenses of getting from one workplace to another in the course of your business or profession when you are traveling within your tax home area. Tax home is defined earlier.

Local transportation expenses also include the cost of getting from your home to a temporary workplace when you have one or more regular places of work. These temporary workplaces can be either within the area of your tax home or outside that area.

Local business transportation does *not* include expenses you have while traveling away from home overnight. Transportation expenses you can deduct while traveling away from home overnight and the definition of tax home are discussed earlier in this chapter under *Travel Expenses.*

Local business transportation expenses include the cost of transportation by air, rail, bus, taxi, etc., and the cost of driving and maintaining your car.

You can deduct your expenses for local business transportation, including the business use of your car, if the expenses are ordinary and necessary. An ordinary expense is one that is common and accepted in your field of trade, business, or profession. A necessary expense is one that is helpful and appropriate for your business. An expense does not have to be indispensable to be considered necessary.

Commuting expenses. You cannot deduct the costs of taking a bus, trolley, subway, taxi, or driving a car between *your home* and your main or regular place of work. These costs are personal commuting expenses. You cannot deduct commuting expenses no matter how far your home is from your regular place of work. You cannot deduct commuting expenses even if you work during the commuting trip.

Example. You had a telephone installed in your car. You sometimes use that telephone to make business calls while commuting to and from work. Sometimes business associates ride with you to and from work, and you have a business discussion in the car. These activities do not change the trip's expenses from commuting to business. Your commuting expenses are not deductible.

Parking fees. Fees you pay to park your car at your place of business are nondeductible commuting expenses. You can, however, deduct business-related parking fees when visiting a customer or client.

Advertising display on car. The use of your car to display material that advertises your business does not change the use of your car from personal use to business use. If you use this car for commuting or other personal uses, your commuting or personal expenses are not deductible.

Union members' trips from a union hall. If you get your work assignments at a union hall and then go to your place of work, these costs are nondeductible commuting expenses.

Deductible local transportation. The following examples illustrate when you can deduct local transportation expenses based on the location of your work and your residence.

Example 1. Your office is in the same city as your home. You cannot deduct the cost of transportation between your home and your office. This is a personal commuting expense. You can deduct the cost of round-trip transportation between your office and a client or customer's place of business.

Example 2. You regularly work in an office in the city where you live. Your employer requires that you attend a one-week training session at a different office in the same city. You travel directly from your home to the training site and return each day. You can deduct the cost of your daily round-trip transportation between your home and the training site.

Example 3. Your only office is in your home. (The rules for "office in the home" are discussed in Chapter 30, *Miscellaneous Deductions.*) You can deduct the round-trip business-related local transportation expenses between your qualifying home office and your client's or customer's place of business. You must, however, distinguish between business and personal transportation.

Example 4. You have no regular office, and you do not have an office in your home. In this case, the location of your first business contact is considered your office. Transportation expenses between your home and this first contact are nondeductible commuting expenses. In addition, transportation expenses between your last business contact and your home are also nondeductible commuting expenses. Although you cannot deduct the costs of these first and last trips, you can deduct the costs of going from one client or customer to another.

Illustration of local transportation. *Figure 28–B* illustrates the rules for deducting local transportation expenses. You may want to refer to it when deciding whether you can deduct your local business transportation expenses.

Temporary work location. If you have one or more regular places of business and commute to a temporary work location, you can deduct the expenses of the daily round-trip transportation between your residence and the temporary location. The temporary work must be irregular or short term (generally a matter of days or weeks).

If the temporary work location is beyond the general area of your regular place of work, and you stay overnight, you are traveling away from home and may have deductible travel expenses as discussed earlier in this chapter.

If you do not have a regular place of work, but you ordinarily work at different locations in the metropolitan area where you live, you can deduct daily transportation costs between your home and a temporary work site *outside* your metropolitan area. Generally, a metropolitan area includes the area within the city limits and the suburbs that are considered part of that metropolitan area. You cannot deduct daily transportation costs between your home and temporary work sites *within* your metropolitan area. These are nondeductible commuting costs.

TAXPLANNER

In a recent Internal Revenue ruling, the IRS changed its position regarding commuting expenses between an employee's residence and temporary work site. A taxpayer may now deduct the expenses of daily transportation between his or her residence and any temporary work site as long as he or she has a regular work site. Previously, the IRS had allowed a deduction for temporary-site transportation expenses only if the temporary work site was located outside the metropolitan area in which the taxpayer ordinarily worked. The IRS's change in position applies retroactively. Therefore, temporary-site transportation expenses may be claimed for any open tax year by filing an amended return.

Two places of work. If you work at two places in a day, whether or not for the same employer, you can deduct the expense of getting from one workplace to the other. However, if for some

Figure 28-B. When Are Local Transportation Expenses Deductible?

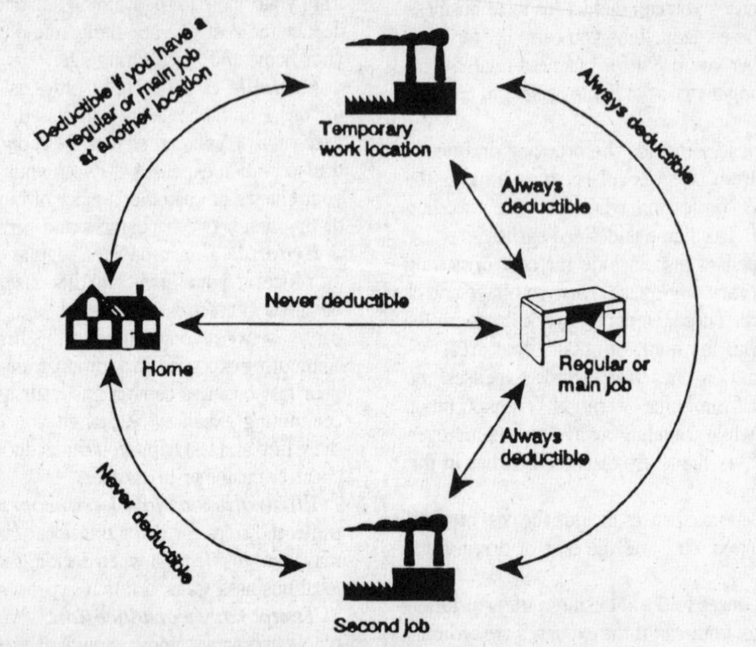

Home: The place where you reside. Transportation expenses between your home and your main or regular place of work are personal commuting expenses.

Regular or main job: Your principal place of business. If you have more than one job, you must determine which one is your regular or main job. Consider the time you spend at each, the activity you have at each, and the income you earn at each.

Temporary work location: A place where your work assignment is irregular or short-term, generally a matter of days or weeks. Unless you have a regular place of business, you can only deduct your transportation expenses to a temporary location outside your metropolitan area.

Second job: If you regularly work at two or more places in one day, whether or not for the same employer, you can deduct your transportation expenses of getting from one workplace to another. You cannot deduct your transportation costs between your home and a second job on a day off from your main job.

personal reason you do not go directly from one location to the other, you can deduct only the amount it would have cost you to go directly from the first location to the second. Transportation expenses you have in going between home and a part-time job on a day off from your main job are commuting expenses. You cannot deduct them.

Example 1
A doctor who practiced at a private clinic could not deduct the automobile expenses incurred on his regular and emergency trips between his home and the hospital. Under the hospital rules, the doctor was required to visit the hospital daily, as well as to spend a day "on call" each month. The court ruled that, since the hospital was an integral and regular place of business for the doctor, his travel was a nondeductible commuting expense.

Example 2
A doctor could not deduct the cost of traveling between his office at home and the clinic where he practiced. Although he kept his medical and business records in his office in the home, he didn't see patients there. The

court ruled that it was neither a principal business office nor a focal point for his medical practice and disallowed the deduction.

Example 3
A doctor who maintained two separate offices was denied a deduction for the costs of commuting between his residence and the places where he conducted his medical practices. He was, however, permitted to deduct commuting costs between his offices and to the hospital where he made his rounds.

Example 4
A college professor who maintained a home office was not allowed to deduct transportation expenses from his home to the college. The court determined that the focal point of his activities was the college at which he taught.

Exception
A police officer was recently allowed to claim a deduction for automobile expenses traveling to and from work,

because he was under orders to consider himself at work from the moment he left home until he returned.

Armed Forces reservists. A meeting of an Armed Forces reserve unit is considered a second place of business if the meeting is held on the same day as your regular job. You can deduct the expense of getting to or from one workplace to the other as just discussed under *Two places of work.* You usually cannot deduct the expense if the meeting is held on a nonworkday for your regular job. In this case, your transportation is generally considered a nondeductible commuting cost.

For reserve meetings held on nonworkdays, you can deduct your daily round-trip transportation expenses only if the location of the meeting is temporary and you have one or more regular placesof work.

If you ordinarily work in a particular metropolitan area but not at any specific location and the reserve meeting is held at a temporary location outside that metropolitan area, you can deduct your daily transportation expenses.

If you travel away from home overnight to attend a guard or reserve meeting, you can deduct your travel expenses. These include the costs of your meals, lodging, and your round-trip transportation between your home and the meeting site. For more information, see *Travel Expenses* earlier in this chapter.

Explanation
If you are on temporary active duty and maintain an active business elsewhere, you may deduct expenses for meals and lodging.

Car Expenses

If you use your car for business purposes, you may be able to deduct car expenses. You generally can use one of two methods to figure your expenses: actual expenses or the standard mileage rate.

Explanation
Fixed and variable rate. Under certain circumstances, employees' business expenses for car expenses will be deemed substantiated when their employer reimburses such expenses with a mileage allowance different from the 28-cents-per-mile standard mileage rate.

You may be entitled to a tax credit for an electric vehicle or a deduction from gross income for a part of the cost of a clean-fuel vehicle if you place one of these vehicles in service from July 1, 1993, through December 31, 2004. The vehicle must meet certain requirements, and you do not have to use it in your business to qualify for the credit or the deduction. For more information, see *Deductions for Clean-Fuel Vehicles and Refueling Property* in Chapter 15 of Publication 535.

Car expense records. Whether you use actual expenses or the standard mileage rate, you must keep records to show when you started using your car for business and the cost or other basis of the car. Your records must also show the business miles and the total miles you drove your car during the year.

Explanation
A court held that it was sufficient for a salesman to maintain records of personal miles driven only. The difference between his total mileage and his personal mileage represented his business mileage.

The courts have allowed a taxpayer a deduction for depreciation of a car used in business, even though his travel records were not very accurate or complete. Depreciation of a business asset is not subject to the strict recordkeeping requirements that other types of travel expenses are. A deduction for depreciation is allowed if you can simply show that the car was used for business.

Actual expenses. If you deduct actual expenses, you must keep records of the costs of operating the car, such as car insurance, interest, taxes, licenses, maintenance, repairs, depreciation, gas, and oil. If you lease a car, you must also keep records of this cost.

Actual Expenses
If you choose to deduct actual expenses, you can deduct the cost of the following items:

Depreciation	Lease fees	Rental fees
Garage rent	Licenses	Repairs
Gas	Oil	Tires
Insurance	Parking fees	Tolls

Interest on car loans. Beginning after 1990, if you are an employee, you cannot deduct any interest paid on a car loan. This interest is treated as personal interest and is not deductible. However, if you are self-employed and use your car in that business, see Chapter 8 of Publication 535.

Personal property taxes on your car. If you are an employee, you can deduct personal property taxes you paid on your car only if you itemize deductions on Schedule A (Form 1040). (See Chapter 23 for more information on taxes.) You cannot deduct luxury or sales taxes, even if you use your car 100% for business as an employee. Luxury and sales taxes are part of your car's basis and may be recovered through depreciation. If you are not an employee, see Chapter 9 of Publication 535 for information on taxes.

Explanation
Interest paid on loans to purchase automobiles used in performing services as an employee is considered personal interest. Before 1987, personal interest was deductible as an itemized deduction. Personal interest is no longer deductible as an itemized deduction.

TAXPLANNER
If an employee who owns a home finances the purchase of an automobile through a loan secured by the home, the interest would be fully deductible as home mortgage interest if the employee is within the $100,000 home equity indebtedness rules.

Explanation
Sales taxes on business automobiles were deductible prior to 1987. These amounts must now be added to the basis of the automobile and must be depreciated.

Business and personal use. If you use your car for both business and personal purposes, you must divide your expenses between business and personal use.

Example. You are a contractor and drive your car 20,000 miles during the year: 12,000 miles for business use and 8,000 miles for personal use. You can claim only 60% (12,000 ÷ 20,000) of the cost of operating your car as a business expense.

Explanation
To claim a deduction for car expenses properly, you must establish that you are entitled to the deduction because the car was used at least partially for business. The deduction will be allowed only to the extent of business use. If you can establish that you are entitled to the deduction but are unable to establish the precise amount of the deduction, the court will apply its own best judgment to make an approximation of the business portion of the expenses.

Example 1
A doctor who is constantly on emergency call may not deduct all of his automobile expenses and depreciation. He must calculate how much of the automobile's use is business and how much is personal. The business portion is deductible.

Example 2
A construction worker who kept a log book of miles driven but failed to distinguish between business and personal mileage was not allowed to take any deduction.

Example 3
A salesman was able to prove that he used his automobile exclusively for business except for his round trip to and from work of 16 miles. However, he was unable to establish how many miles were dedicated to business use. The court concluded that his business use was 75% and his personal use was 25%.

Hauling tools or instruments. If you haul tools or instruments in your car while commuting to and from work, this does not make your commuting costs deductible. However, you can deduct additional costs, such as renting a trailer that you tow with your vehicle, for carrying equipment to and from your job.

Example
A teacher could not deduct the expenses for an automobile she used to carry books and teaching materials to her classes, even though she could not store them at the school. She also used her automobile on days on which she came to school just to attend meetings. It took an hour to drive to school. Getting there by alternative means of transportation took 1½ hours and was very inconvenient. The court concluded that she would have driven even if she didn't have to transport books and that her expenses were merely commuting costs and not deductible.

Car pools. You cannot deduct the cost of using your car in a nonprofit car pool. Do not include payments you receive from the passengers in your income. These payments are considered reimbursements of your expenses. However, if you operate a car pool for a profit, you must include these payments from passengers in your income, and you can deduct your car expenses (using the rules in this chapter).

Fines and collateral. Fines and collateral for traffic violations are not deductible.

Fringe benefits. If your employer provided you with the use or availability of a vehicle, you received a fringe benefit. Generally, you must include the value of such use or availability in your income as compensation. However, there are exceptions if the use of the vehicle qualifies as a working condition fringe benefit or the vehicle is a qualified nonpersonal use vehicle. Employers should see Chapter 4 of Publication 535 for information on fringe benefits.

Leasing a car. If you lease a car that you use in your business, you can deduct the part of each lease payment that is for the use of the car in your business. You cannot deduct any part of a lease payment that is for commuting to your regular job or for any other personal use of the car.

You must spread any advance payments over the entire lease period. You cannot deduct any payments you make to buy a car even if the payments are called lease payments.

If you lease a car that you use in your business for 30 days or more, you may have to include in income an amount called an "inclusion amount." For more information, see Chapter 3 of Publication 917.

TAXPLANNER
If you buy an automobile and finance it, you cannot deduct any of the interest charges. If you finance the car by taking out a home equity loan, the interest will be deductible as home mortgage interest. See Chapter 8, *Interest Income.* However, if you are **self-employed** and use your car in your trade or business, you may deduct 100% of the business portion of the interest charges. If you simply use your car as an **employee,** you may pay less tax by leasing a car rather than buying it, because you can deduct your lease payments subject to the business use rules discussed elsewhere in this chapter.

Leasing an automobile. Deducting employee business expenses for the cost of a leased automobile is similar to doing so for an automobile you own. You may deduct the portion of the total lease payments that is attributable to business use, using the ratio of business miles to total miles to make the calculation. This deduction represents the depreciation and financing costs. Normal operating costs and maintenance (if not included in the lease) and business parking may also be deducted.

The luxury automobile rules are intended to impose the same unfavorable treatment for leased automobiles as for purchased automobiles. If you lease an automobile for business use, you can deduct the lease payments and operating expenses for that business use. If you leased the automobile between June 18, 1984, and April 3, 1985, and it had a value of over $16,500, you are deemed to have received additional income in each of the first 3 taxable years of the lease. This additional income must be reported on your tax return. The amount is 7.5% of the excess of the value of the automobile over $16,500, multiplied by your business use percentage. If you lease the automobile for more than 3 years *and* it was worth more than $22,500 when originally leased, you also have to report additional income in those later lease years, per IRS tables.

For automobiles leased after April 2, 1985, and before January 1, 1987, you are deemed to have received additional income if the value of the automobile exceeds only $11,250.

For automobiles leased after 1986 and before January 1, 1991, with a fair market value of more than $12,800, you must include additional income on your tax return each year during which you lease the automobile. In 1991, the fair market value was $13,400. In 1992, the fair market value increased to $13,700. In 1993, the fair market value is $14,300.

Note: You must recapture a portion of your lease payment deductions and report them as income if your business use of the automobile falls below 50%.

See Publications 534, *Depreciation,* and 917, *Business Use of a Car,* for further details and the tables for computing the lease adjustments.

Depreciation and section 179 deductions. If you use your car for business purposes as an employee or as a sole proprietor, you may be able to recover its cost by claiming a depreciation or section 179 deduction. The amount you may claim depends on the year you placed the car in service and the amount of your business use.

Explanation
For more information on the section 179 deduction, see Chapter 36, *If You Are Self-Employed*.

Explanation
For more information on depreciation, see Chapter 10, *Rental Income and Expenses*.

For more information, see the instructions for Form 2106 (if you are an employee) or Form 4562 (if you are self-employed). Also see Chapter 2 of Publication 917 for a detailed discussion of these deductions.

Explanation
Severe limitations on deductions apply after June 18, 1984, on "luxury" automobiles and automobiles used for both business and personal purposes. These limitations are adjusted for inflation for automobiles placed in service after 1988. The inflation adjustment is based on the automobile component of the Consumer Price Index, and any increase is rounded to the nearest $100. For automobiles placed in service in 1993, the maximum depreciation allowance is

$2,860   for the first taxable year in its recovery period

$4,600   for the second taxable year in its recovery period

$2,750   for the third taxable year in its recovery period

$1,675   for each later taxable year in its recovery period, limited to the remaining undepreciated cost

These limitations are proportionately reduced for business usage less than 100%.

Example
You buy an automobile on March 1, 1993, and use it 80% for business. Your maximum deduction in 1993 is $2,288 ($2,860 × 80%). Your maximum deduction in 1994 will be $3,680 ($4,600 × 80%) unless your business use percentage changes.

Explanation
If qualified business use of a vehicle purchased after 1986 is over 50%, then you can claim 200% declining balance depreciation over a 5-year period. Declining balance depreciation is described in Chapter 10, *Rental Income and Expenses.* Qualified business use means direct use in your trade or business, including your job. It does not include looking after your investments. However, if you use your automobile more than 50% in your trade or business, you can then use accelerated 5-year depreciation for the part used for looking after your investments.

If qualified business use is 50% or less, depreciation must be calculated on a straight-line basis over 5 years, with a proration of the maximum deduction. Although a 5-year life rate is used, only a half-year's depreciation is deductible in the first year. The other half-year is not deductible until the sixth year. Again, depreciation in excess of the allowed amounts is carried over to future years to depreciate fully the business portion of the asset.

Example
You buy an automobile in 1993 and use it 60% for business, 10% for looking after your investments, and 30% for personal use. You can deduct 70% of your depreciation, calculated using accelerated depreciation. If you use your automobile only 45% for business and 25% for looking after your investments, you can still deduct 70%, but it must be computed on a straight-line basis.

Standard Mileage Rate
Instead of figuring actual expenses, you may be able to use the standard mileage rate. You can only use the standard mileage rate for a car that you own. For 1993, the standard mileage rate is **28 cents** a mile for all business miles. However, if you are a U.S. Postal Service employee who collects and delivers mail on a rural route, your standard mileage rate for 1993 is 42 cents a mile. These rates are adjusted periodically for inflation.

If you choose to take the standard mileage rate, you **cannot** deduct actual operating expenses, such as:

Depreciation,
Maintenance and repairs,
Gasoline (including gasoline taxes),
Oil,
Insurance, and
Vehicle registration fees.

You generally can use the standard mileage rate regardless of whether you are reimbursed and whether any reimbursement is more or less than the amount figured using the standard mileage rate. See *Reimbursements* later in this chapter.

Choosing the standard mileage rate. If you want to use the standard mileage rate for a car (including a van, pickup truck, or panel truck), you must choose to use it in the first year you place the car in service in business. Then in later years, you can choose to use the standard mileage rate or actual expenses.

If you choose to use the standard mileage rate, you are considered to have made an election not to use the modified accelerated cost recovery system (MACRS). This is because the standard mileage rate allows for depreciation. You also cannot claim the section 179 deduction. If you change to the actual expenses method in a later year, but before your car is considered fully depreciated, you have to estimate the useful life of the car and use straight line depreciation. For information on how to figure that depreciation, see the exception in *Methods of depreciation* under *Depreciation Deduction* in Publication 917.

Explanation

If you select the actual cost method (operating expenses and ACRS or MACRS), the standard mileage rate may never be used for that automobile. However, if you use the standard mileage rate for the first year, you may switch to the actual cost method, but you then must use a straight-line depreciation rate for the remaining estimated life of the automobile. Generally, actual expenses exceed the monies you may claim by using the standard mileage rate. As long as you keep adequate records, you will probably be better off claiming actual expenses.

Standard mileage rate not allowed. You cannot use the standard mileage rate if you:

1) Do not own the car,
2) Use the car for hire (such as a taxi),
3) Operate two or more cars at the same time (as in fleet operations), or
4) Claimed a deduction for the car in an earlier year using:
   a) ACRS or MACRS depreciation, or
   b) A section 179 deduction.

Example

A newspaper deliveryman contracted to distribute newspapers on two delivery routes. Although the deliveryman's wife never contracted with the newspaper, she operated one route. He and his wife each used a separate car to deliver the newspapers. The courts held that the deliveryman and his wife were precluded from using standard mileage rates rather than actual automobile expenses, because the two delivery routes constituted one single business operation.

Two or more cars. If you own two or more cars that are used for business at the same time, you cannot take the standard mileage rate for the business use of any car. However, you may be able to deduct a part of the actual expenses for operating each of the cars. See *Actual Car Expenses* in Chapter 2 of Publication 917 for information on how to figure your deduction.

You are *not* using two or more cars for business at the same time if you alternate using (use at different times) the cars for business.

The following examples illustrate the rules for when you can and cannot use the standard mileage rate for two or more cars.

Example 1. Marcia, a salesperson, owns a car and a van that she alternates using for calling on her customers. She can take the standard mileage rate for the business mileage of the car and the van.

Example 2. Tony uses his own pickup truck in his landscaping business. During 1993, he traded in his old truck for a newer one. Tony can take the standard mileage rate for the business mileage of both the old and the new trucks.

Example 3. Chris owns a repair shop and an insurance business. He uses his pickup truck for the repair shop and his car for the insurance business. No one else uses either the pickup truck or the car for business purposes. Chris can take the standard mileage rate for the business use of the truck and the car.

Example 4. Maureen owns a car and a van that are both used in her housecleaning business. Her employees use the car and she uses the van to travel to the various customers. Maureen cannot take the standard mileage rate for the car or the van. This is because both vehicles are used in Maureen's business at the same time. She must use actual expenses for both vehicles.

Parking fees and tolls. In addition to using the standard mileage rate, you can deduct any business-related parking fees and tolls. (Parking fees that you pay to park your car at your place of work are nondeductible commuting expenses.)

Basis of car. To figure gain or loss on a car you used for business, you must figure its adjusted basis by subtracting from the basis any depreciation (including any section 179 or clean-fuel vehicle deduction) that you claimed. If you used the standard mileage rate for the business use of your car, depreciation was included in that rate. The rate of depreciation that was allowed in the standard mileage rate is shown in the chart that follows. This depreciation reduces the basis of your car (but not below zero) in figuring its adjusted basis when you dispose of it.

Note. These rates do not apply for any year in which the actual cost method was used.

Year	Rate per Mile
1992 – 1993	11½ cents
1989 – 1991	11 cents
1988	10½ cents
1987	10 cents
1986	9 cents
1983 – 1985	8 cents
1982	7½ cents
1980 – 1981	7 cents

For tax years before 1990, the rates applied to the first 15,000 miles. For tax years after 1989, the depreciation rate applies to all business miles.

Example. In 1989, you bought a car for exclusive use in your business. The car cost $14,000. From 1989 through 1993, you used the standard mileage rate to figure your car expense deduction. You drove your car at least 15,000 business miles in 1989. You drove your car 20,000 miles in 1990, 18,750 miles in 1991, 19,200 miles in 1992, and 18,100 miles in 1993. The depreciation allowed is figured as follows:

Year	Miles × Rate	Amount
1989	15,000 × .11	$ 1,650
1990	20,000 × .11	$ 2,200
1991	18,750 × .11	$ 2,063
1992	19,200 × .115	$ 2,208
1993	18,100 × .115	$ 2,082
Total		$10,203

At the end of 1993, your adjusted basis in the car is $3,797 ($14,000 − $10,203).

Reimbursements not included in income. If you adequately account to your employer for reimbursements or allowances for the use of your car and your employer does not include the reimbursed amounts in your income, you can deduct only the cost that is more than your reimbursement or allowance. See *Reimbursements,* later in this chapter.

Explanation

Unreimbursed automobile expenses are deductible only as miscellaneous itemized deductions. Employees formerly classified as "outside sales representatives" are also subject to this provision.

As a result, these expenses will be deductible only to the extent that, when aggregated with your other miscellaneous itemized deductions, they exceed 2% of your adjusted gross income.

Example. You drive your car 14,000 miles in your work. You get $900 worth of gas from your employer, who has a gas pump for the business. You adequately account to your employer for the gas. The $900 is not included on your Form W–2. You decide to use the standard mileage rate to figure your car expenses for 1993. You can deduct $3,020 figured as follows.

Business miles driven	14,000
Standard mileage rate	× .28
Total expense	$3,920
Less employer-paid expense	− 900
Deductible Expense	$3,020

Explanation

In some cases, you may be able to deduct a greater mileage rate than the IRS customarily permits. For example, the courts have allowed truck drivers who were reimbursed at a greater rate than the standard rate to deduct the greater rate. The truck drivers had kept detailed weekly records of their trucks' operating costs.

TaxSaver

If you own an expensive business automobile, the standard mileage rate is probably inadequate to cover your operating costs. You should keep detailed records of your total expenses so that you may claim a larger deduction than you would be able to by using the standard mileage rate.

Recordkeeping

This section discusses the written records you need to keep if you plan to deduct an expense discussed in this chapter. By keeping timely and accurate records, you will have support to show the IRS if your tax return is ever examined. Or, your employer may require proof of expenses for which you are reimbursed under an accountable plan, as discussed later under *Adequate Accounting.*

Proof required. You must be able to prove (substantiate) your deductions for travel, entertainment, business gift, and local transportation expenses. You should keep adequate records or have sufficient evidence that will support your own statement. Estimates or approximations do not qualify as proof of an expense.

TaxPlanner

Good recordkeeping is a good business practice and a must for tax purposes. A clear and consistent set of records is the first step in justifying your expense deduction. Reasonable estimates of expenses are no longer acceptable, even if the estimate is moderate in relation to the income generated.

Form 4562, which is used to show your automobile depreciation, specifically asks whether you have evidence to support your business use percentage.

You must maintain adequate records or sufficient evidence, either written or oral, that will corroborate your own statement. Sufficient evidence includes account books, trip sheets, expense reports, appointment calendars, statements of witnesses, and certain accountings to an employer. Contemporaneous logs are no longer required, but a report made at the event would be more credible than records prepared at a later date.

If you are required to turn in the original copies of your receipts and logbooks to your employer, you should make copies for yourself. If the confidentiality of names is a consideration, special arrangements might have to be made with your employer to make necessary information available if and when it is needed.

When records are lost in circumstances beyond your control, such as destruction by fire, flood, earthquake, or other casualty, the IRS is more lenient in accepting reconstructed records and secondary evidence than it is when records are not available because of carelessness or mysterious disappearance.

Example

Travel expense records were lost during a change of residence resulting from marital problems. The court ruled that marital difficulties did not constitute a casualty warranting the use of reconstructed records.

Chart that shows proof required. *Table 28-2* summarizes the factors needed to prove the elements of your expenses for travel, entertainment, gifts, and local business transportation. These factors are discussed in more detail in Chapter 5 of Publication 463.

To deduct these expenses, you must be able to prove the items listed in column 1 of the chart. You prove these items by having the information and receipts (where required) for the expenses listed in columns 2, 3, 4, or 5, whichever apply.

Adequate records. You should keep the proof you need for these items in an account book, diary, statement of expense, or similar record, and keep adequate documentary evidence (such as receipts, canceled checks, or bills), that together will support each element of an expense. Documentary evidence is explained in more detail later in this discussion. Written evidence has considerably more value than oral evidence alone.

Timely recordkeeping. You do not need to write down the elements of every expense at the time of the expense. However, a record of the elements of an expense or of a business use made at or near the time of the expense or use, supported by sufficient documentary evidence, has more value than a statement prepared later when generally there is a lack of accurate recall. A log maintained on a

Table 28-2. **Elements to Prove Certain Business Expenses**

Elements to be proved (1)	Expense			
	Travel (2)	Entertainment (3)	Gift (4)	Transportation (car) (5)
Amount	Amount of each separate expense for travel, lodging, and meals. Incidental expenses may be totaled in reasonable categories, such as taxis, daily meals for traveler, etc.	Amount of each separate expense. Incidental expenses such as taxis, telephones, etc., may be totaled on a daily basis.	Cost of gift.	1) Amount of each separate expense including cost of the car, 2) Mileage for each business use of the car, and 3) Total miles for the tax year.
Time	Date you left and returned for each trip, and number of days for business.	Date of entertainment or use of a facility for entertainment. For meals or entertainment directly before or after a business discussion, the date and duration of the business discussion.	Date of gift.	Date of the expense or use.
Place	Name of city or other designation.	Name and address or location of place of entertainment, or place of use of a facility for entertainment. Type of entertainment if not otherwise apparent. Place where business discussion was held if entertainment is directly before or after a business discussion.	Not applicable.	Name of city or other designation if applicable.
Description	Not applicable.	Not applicable.	Description of gift.	Not applicable.
Business purpose	Business reason for travel or the business benefit gained or expected to be gained.	Business reason or the business benefit gained or expected to be gained. Nature of business discussion or activity.	Business reason for giving the gift or the business benefit gained or expected to be gained.	Business reason for the expense or use of the car.
Business relationship	Not applicable.	Occupations or other information—such as names or other designations—about persons entertained that shows their business relationship to you. If all people entertained did not take part in business discussion, identify those who did. You must also prove that you or your employee was present if entertainment was a business meal.	Occupation or other information—such as name or other designation—about recipient that shows his or her business relationship to you.	Not applicable.

weekly basis, which accounts for use during the week, is considered a record made at or near the time of the expense or use.

Duplicate information. You do not have to record information in your account book or other record that duplicates information shown on a receipt as long as your records and receipts complement each other in an orderly manner. You do not have to record amounts your employer pays directly for any ticket or other travel item. However, if you charge these items to your employer, through a credit card or otherwise, you must make a record of the amounts you spend.

Expense accounts. An expense account statement you give your employer, client, or customer is considered to have been made at or near the time of the expense or use. The statement must be copied from your account book, diary, statement of expense, or similar record.

Separating expenses. Each separate payment usually is considered a separate expense. If you entertain a customer or client at dinner and then go to the theater, the dinner expense and the cost

of the theater tickets are two separate expenses. You must record them separately in your records.

Totaling items. You may make one daily entry for reasonable categories of expenses such as taxi fares, telephone calls, gas and oil, or other incidental travel costs. Meals should be in a separate category. You should include tips with the costs of the services you received.

Expenses of a similar nature occurring during the course of a single event are considered a single expense. For example, if during entertainment at a cocktail lounge, you pay separately for each serving of refreshments, the total expense for the refreshments is treated as a single expense.

Documentary evidence. You generally must have documentary evidence, such as receipts, canceled checks, or bills, to support your expenses. However, this evidence is not required if:

1) You have meals or lodging expenses while traveling away from home for which you account to your employer under an account-

able plan and you use a per diem allowance method that includes meals and/or lodging,

2) You are reimbursed under a mileage allowance,
3) Your expense, other than lodging, is less than $25, *or*
4) You have a transportation expense for which a receipt is not readily available.

Accountable plans and per diem and mileage allowances are discussed later in this chapter under *Reimbursements*.

Adequate evidence. Documentary evidence ordinarily will be considered adequate if it shows the amount, date, place, and essential character of the expense.

For example, a hotel receipt is enough to support expenses for business travel if it has:

1) The name and location of the hotel,
2) The dates you stayed there, and
3) Separate amounts for charges such as lodging, meals, and telephone calls.

A restaurant receipt is enough to prove an expense for a business meal if it has:

1) The name and location of the restaurant,
2) The number of people served, and
3) The date and amount of the expense.

If a charge is made for items other than food and beverages, the receipt must show that this is the case.

Canceled check. A canceled check, together with a bill from the payee, ordinarily establishes the cost. However, a canceled check by itself does not prove a business expense without other evidence to show that it was for a business purpose.

TAXPLANNER

You must maintain detailed records and report the required information on your tax return if you wish to claim a deduction for expenses that exceed reimbursements. You must keep these records, even though you do not have to give the completely detailed information to your employer because reimbursements by your employer meet the IRS per diem standards.

Business purpose. A written statement of the business purpose of an expense is generally required. However, the degree of proof varies according to the circumstances in each case. If the business purpose of an expense is clear from the surrounding circumstances, a written explanation is not required.

Example. A sales representative who calls on customers on an established sales route does not have to submit a written explanation of the business purpose for traveling that route.

Confidential information. Confidential information relating to an element of a deductible expense, such as the place, business purpose, or business relationship, need not be put in your account book, diary, or other record. However, the information has to be recorded elsewhere at or near the time of the expense and be available to fully prove that element of the expense.

Inadequate records. If you do not have adequate records to prove an element of an expense, then you must prove the element by:

1) Your own statement, whether written or oral, that contains specific information about the element, and
2) Other supporting evidence that is sufficient to establish the element.

Additional information for the IRS. The IRS may require additional information to clarify or to establish the accuracy or reliability of information contained in your records, statements, testimony, or documentary evidence before a deduction is allowed.

How long to keep records and receipts. You must keep proof to support your claim to a deduction as long as your income tax return can be examined. Generally, it will be necessary for you to keep your records for 3 years from the date you file the income tax return on which the deduction is claimed. A return filed early is considered as filed on the due date.

Explanation

If you use your automobile less than 50% for business and claim actual expenses, you must keep those records for at least 6 years (the straight-line, useful life depreciation period).

Employees who give their records and documentation to their employers and are reimbursed for their expenses generally do not have to keep duplicate copies of this information. However, you may be required to prove your expenses if:

1) You claim deductions for expenses that are more than reimbursements,
2) Your expenses are reimbursed under a nonaccountable plan,
3) Your employer does not use adequate accounting procedures to verify expense accounts, or
4) You are related to your employer, as defined earlier under *Standard Meal Allowance*.

See the next section, *How to Report,* for a discussion of reimbursements, adequate accounting, and nonaccountable plans.

Explanation

If you have expenses greater than your reimbursement and want to deduct them, you are required to put a statement in your tax return showing the total of all expenses you incurred and all reimbursements you received for that year. This information may be given in broad categories, such as transportation, meals and lodging while **away from home overnight,** entertainment expenses, and other business expenses. The statement must show the total of any charges paid or borne directly by your employer through credit cards or any other means. See *Records* for more details.

Self-employed persons and independent contractors must be able to show that the expenses were directly related to, or associated with, their business.

Example

An accountant was not allowed to deduct expenses incurred at a country club, because she failed to indicate the business purpose of the activities that generated the expenses and she did not maintain a detailed record of the persons entertained on each occasion. Lacking any documentation to the contrary, a court concluded that there was a likelihood that the expenses were at least partially personal.

Additional information. See Chapter 5 of Publication 463 for more information on recordkeeping, including a discussion on how to prove each type of expense discussed in this chapter.

How to Report

This section explains how to report on your tax return the expenses that are discussed in this chapter. It discusses reimbursements, including treatment of accountable and nonaccountable plans, adequate accounting, and per diem allowances. This section ends by showing you how to complete Form 2106.

Explanation

Employees receiving the standard meal allowance under a nonaccountable plan (discussed below) may claim 80% of the standard meal allowance as a miscellaneous itemized deduction, subject to the 2% limitation. Reimbursements under accountable plans are not included in the employee's taxable compensation. Therefore, such employees receive no deduction, and the 80% limitation applies to the employer's deduction.

Self-employed. If you are self-employed, you must report your income and expenses on Schedule C or C-EZ (Form 1040) if you are a sole proprietor, or on Schedule F (Form 1040) if you are a farmer. You do not use Form 2106. See Publication 535 or Publication 225 and your form instructions for information on how to complete your tax return.

Both self-employed and an employee. If you are both self-employed and an employee, you must keep separate records for each business activity. Report your business expenses for self-employment on Schedule C, Schedule C-EZ, or on Schedule F, as discussed earlier. Report your business expenses for your work as an employee on Form 2106, as discussed next.

Employees. If you are an employee, you must complete Form 2106 to deduct any employee business expenses that exceed reimbursements. If you received no reimbursement, you generally must complete Form 2106 to deduct the expenses discussed in this chapter. See *Completing Form 2106* later in this chapter.

Statutory employees. If you received a Form W–2 and the "Statutory employee" box in box 15 was checked, you report your income and expenses related to that income on Schedule C or C-EZ (Form 1040). Do not complete Form 2106. See your Form 1040 instructions for more information.

Statutory employees include full-time life insurance salespersons, certain agent or commission drivers, traveling salespersons, and certain homeworkers.

Example 1

John Smith, a salesman working on behalf of a principal, solicits orders from wholesalers and restaurants for merchandise intended for resale. John reports his income and expenses on Schedule C as a statutory employee.

Example 2

An agent–driver engaged in distributing meat, vegetables, bakery goods, beverages (other than milk), or dry cleaning services is classified as a statutory employee.

Unclaimed reimbursement. If you are entitled to a reimbursement from your employer but you do not claim it, you cannot claim a deduction for the expenses to which that reimbursement applies.

Explanation

While you may not claim a deduction for an expense that your employer would reimburse, you may be entitled to a deduction for a work-related expense that you feel was necessary to do your job but that your employer does not reimburse.

Example

You are a technician who works in a laboratory in which your employer requires you to wear a certain type of uniform while on the job. The uniform is unsuitable for street wear. Your employer refuses to reimburse you for the cost of the uniform. You are entitled to deduct the expense on your own income tax return.

Reimbursement for personal expenses. If your employer reimburses you for nondeductible personal expenses, such as for vacation trips, you must report the reimbursement as wage income on your tax return. You cannot deduct personal expenses.

Reimbursements

This section explains what to do when you receive an advance or are reimbursed for any of the employee business expenses discussed in this chapter.

If you received an advance, allowance, or reimbursement for your expenses, how you report this amount and your expenses depends on whether the reimbursement was paid to you under an accountable plan or a nonaccountable plan.

This section explains the two types of plans, how per diem allowances simplify proving the amount of your expenses, and the tax treatment of your reimbursements and expenses.

TaxSaver

If the various requirements discussed below are met, reimbursements are excluded from the employee's gross income for income tax as well as employment tax purposes. Amounts considered paid under a nonaccountable plan are subject to income tax as well as to employment taxes. A tax deduction is allowable as a miscellaneous itemized deduction, subject to applicable limitations, for employee business expenses reimbursed under a nonaccountable plan.

A *reimbursement or other expense allowance arrangement* is a system or plan that an employer uses to pay, substantiate, and recover the expenses, advances, reimbursements, and amounts charged to the employer for employee business expenses. It can also be a system used to keep track of amounts you receive from your employer's agent or a third party. Arrangements include per diem and mileage allowances. If a single payment includes both wages and an expense reimbursement, the amount of the reimbursement must be specifically identified.

Your employer has different options for reimbursing you for business-related travel expenses:

1) Reimbursing you for your actual expenses, as discussed throughout this chapter,
2) Reimbursing you for business use of your car:
   a) Based on your actual operating expenses, or

b) Using a car or mileage allowance as discussed in Chapter 5 of Publication 917,

3) Using the meals only allowance (discussed later in this chapter) to reimburse your meals and incidental expenses and reimbursing you for your actual lodging expenses,

4) Using the regular federal per diem rate (discussed later in this section),

5) Using the high-low method (discussed later in this chapter), or

6) Reimbursing you under any other method that is acceptable to the IRS.

Your employer should tell you what method of reimbursement is used and what records your employer requires.

No reimbursement. If you are paid a salary or commission with the understanding that you will pay your own expenses, you are not reimbursed or given an allowance for your expenses. In this situation, you have no reimbursement or allowance arrangement, and you deduct your expenses using either Form 2106 and Schedule A (Form 1040), or only Schedule A (Form 1040) if you are not required to file Form 2106. You do not have to read this section on reimbursements. Instead, see *Completing Form 2106,* later in this chapter, for information on completing your tax return.

TAXSAVER

You may claim a deduction for business expenses even if you don't receive specific reimbursements from your employer. You should have your employer supply you with a written document explaining that your compensation plan is based on the expectation that you will incur various travel, transportation, automobile, entertainment, and business gift expenses.

Travel, transportation, automobile expenses, entertainment, business gifts, and other expenses should be reported as miscellaneous deductions on Schedule A of Form 1040.

If you are repeatedly spending money for business expenses, it is probably advantageous for you to make an arrangement with your employer to adjust your salary and/or commission downward and to give you an expense allowance. This could help you justify your deductions if you are subject to an IRS examination.

Accountable Plans

To be an accountable plan, your employer's reimbursement or allowance arrangement must require you to meet all three of the following rules:

1) Your expenses must have a business connection — that is, you must have paid or incurred deductible expenses while performing services as an employee of your employer,

2) You must adequately account to your employer for these expenses within a reasonable period of time, and

3) You must return any excess reimbursement or allowance within a reasonable period of time.

"Adequate accounting" and "reasonable period of time" are discussed later in this chapter.

Explanation

For a reimbursement or other expense allowance arrangement to be an accountable plan, it must satisfy the substantiation requirement. Generally, for each expense item and for each business use, the employee must report the amount, time, place, and business purpose.

Example 1

An employer proposed to reimburse its district manager's business expenses in lieu of paying additional salary. This would result in a portion of the district manager's salary being recharacterized as paid under a reimbursement or other expense allowance arrangement and, thus, it would fail the reimbursement requirement. Therefore, the reimbursements would be subject to employment taxes since they would not be paid under an arrangement that is an accountable plan.

Example 2

Where a taxpayer did not substantiate expenses or return excess allowance amounts, such amounts were paid under a nonaccountable plan and, thus, were includible in gross income.

Exception 1

The substantiation requirement for expense amounts related to business meals and lodging can be satisfied by using a per diem allowance. Per diem reimbursements of such expenses are not included in taxable income to the extent of the government rate.

Exception 2

The substantiation requirement for expenses relating to the business use of an employee's private automobile can be satisfied by using the standard mileage rate (28 cents per business mile) or the fixed-and-variable-rate allowance. Under the fixed-and-variable-rate allowance method, an employer reimburses an employee's business mileage expenses using a flat rate or a stated schedule of fixed and variable rate payments that incorporates specific rules to approximate the employee's actual automobile expenses.

An *excess reimbursement or allowance* is any amount you are paid that is more than the business-related expenses that you adequately accounted for to your employer. See *Returning Excess Reimbursements* later in this chapter for information on how to handle these excess amounts.

Employee meets accountable plan rules. If you meet the three rules for accountable plans, your employer should not include any reimbursements in your income in box 1 of your Form W–2. If your expenses equal your reimbursement, you do not complete Form 2106. You have no deduction since your expenses and reimbursement are equal.

Note: If your employer included reimbursements in box 1 of your Form W–2 and you meet all three rules for accountable plans, ask your employer for a corrected Form W–2.

Employee does not meet accountable plan rules. You may be reimbursed under your employer's accountable plan but only part of your expenses may meet all three rules.

If your expenses are reimbursed under an otherwise accountable plan but you do not return, within a reasonable period of time, any reimbursement of expenses for which you did not adequately account, then only the amount for which you did adequately account is considered as paid under an accountable plan. The remaining

Table 28-3. **Reporting Employee Business Expenses and Reimbursements**

Type of Reimbursement (or Other Expense Allowance) Arrangement	Employer Reports on Form W–2	Employee Shows on Form 2106
Accountable		
Actual expense reimbursement Adequate accounting and excess returned	Not reported	Not shown if expenses do not exceed reimbursement
Actual expense reimbursement Adequate accounting and return of excess both required but excess not returned	Excess reported as wages in box 1.[1] Amount adequately accounted for is reported only in box 13—it is *not* reported in box 1.	All expenses (and reimbursements reported on Form W–2, box 13), *only* if some or all of the excess expenses are claimed.[2] Otherwise, form is not filed.
Per diem or mileage allowance (up to federal rate) Adequate accounting and excess returned	Not reported	All expenses and reimbursements *only* if excess expenses are claimed.[2] Otherwise, form is not filed.
Per diem or mileage allowance (exceeds federal rate) Adequate accounting up to the federal rate only and excess not returned	Excess reported as wages in box 1.[1] Amount up to the federal rate is reported only in box 13—it is *not* reported in box 1.	All expenses (and reimbursements equal to the federal rate) *only* if expenses in excess of the federal rate are claimed.[2] Otherwise, form is not filed.
Nonaccountable		
Either adequate accounting or return of excess, or both, not required by plan	Entire amount is reported as wages in box 1.[1]	All expenses[2]
No reimbursement	Normal reporting of wages, etc.	All expenses[2]

[1] Excess is also reported in boxes 3 and 5, if applicable.

[2] Any allowable business expense is carried to line 19 of Schedule A (Form 1040) and deducted as a miscellaneous itemized deduction.

expenses are treated as having been reimbursed under a nonaccountable plan (discussed later in this chapter).

If you received an allowance or advance that was higher than the federal rate, see *Returning Excess Reimbursements,* later.

TAXPLANNER

A plan providing per diem allowances or mileage allowances that are reasonably calculated not to exceed the employee's expenses will satisfy the requirement for the return of excess reimbursement, even though the employee is not required to return the excess allowance. However, the employee must return the portion of the allowance attributable to unsubstantiated days or miles of travel.

Example

An employee receives a monthly mileage allowance of $120, based on anticipated business miles of 400 per month, reimbursed at the rate of 30-cents-per-mile. The 30-cent-per-mile rate is reasonably calculated not to exceed the employee's expenses. The employee travels and substantiates only 300 business miles. The requirement to return the excess is satisfied if the employee is required to return the $30 (100 miles × 30 cents) advance allowance that is attributable to the 100 unsubstantiated business miles. The employee is not required to return the $6 (300 miles × 2 cents) reimbursement amount in excess of the 28-cent standard mileage rate for substantiated business miles.

Reasonable period of time. The definition of "reasonable period of time" depends on the facts of your situation. The IRS will consider it reasonable for you to:

1) Receive an advance within 30 days of the time you have an expense,
2) Adequately account for your expenses within 60 days after they were paid or incurred, and
3) Return any excess reimbursement within 120 days after the expense was paid or incurred.

If you are given a periodic statement (at least quarterly) that asks you to either return or adequately account for outstanding reimbursements and you comply within 120 days of the statement, the IRS will consider the amount adequately accounted for or returned within a reasonable period of time.

TaxAlert

It is imperative that the substantiation be done and that excess amounts be returned within a reasonable period of time. If the reasonable time requirement is not met, the unsubstantiated or excess amounts are treated as reimbursements under a nonaccountable plan.

Reimbursement of nondeductible expenses. You may be reimbursed under your employer's accountable plan for expenses related to that employer's business, some of which are deductible as employee business expenses and some of which are not deductible. The reimbursements you receive for the nondeductible expenses are treated as paid under a nonaccountable plan.

Example. Your employer's plan may reimburse you for travel expenses you incurred while away from home on business, and for meal expenses you paid when you work late at the office, even though you are not away from home. The part of the arrangement that reimburses you for the nondeductible meals while you work late at the office is treated as a second arrangement. The payments under this arrangement are treated as paid under a nonaccountable plan.

Per diem allowances. If you are reimbursed by a per diem allowance (daily amount) that you received under an accountable plan, two facts affect your reporting:

1) The federal rate for the area where you traveled, and
2) Whether the allowance or your actual expenses were more than the federal rate.

For this purpose, the *federal rate* can be figured by using any one of three methods:

1) The regular federal per diem rate (discussed later in this chapter),
2) The high-low method (discussed later in this chapter), or
3) The standard meal allowance (discussed earlier under *What Are Travel Expenses?*).

The following discussions explain where to report your expenses depending upon how the amount of your per diem allowance compares to the federal rate.

Per diem allowance LESS than or EQUAL to the federal rate. If your per diem allowance is less than or equal to the federal rate, the allowance will not be included in boxes 1, 3, and 5 of your Form W–2. You do not need to report the related expenses or the per diem allowance on your return if your expenses are equal to or less than the allowance.

However, if your actual expenses are more than the per diem allowance, you can complete Form 2106 and deduct your excess expenses on Schedule A (Form 1040). In this case, you must be prepared to prove to the IRS the total amount of your expenses and reimbursements for the entire year.

Example 1. In April 1993, Jeremy takes a 2-day business trip to Atlantic City. The federal rate in Atlantic City is $145 per day. As required by his employer's accountable plan, he accounts for the time (dates), place, and business purpose of the trip. His employer reimburses him $145 a day ($290 total) for living expenses. Jeremy's living expenses in Atlantic City are not more than $145 a day.

Jeremy's employer does not include any of the reimbursement on his Form W–2. Jeremy does not deduct the expenses on his return.

Example 2. The facts in Matt's case are the same as those in *Example 1* above. However, Matt's employer uses the high-low method (discussed later in this chapter) to reimburse employees. Since Atlantic City is a high-cost area, Matt is given an advance of $150 a day ($300 total) for his lodging, meals, and incidental expenses. Matt's actual expenses totaled $360.

Matt is reimbursed under an accountable plan. However, since his $360 of expenses exceed his $300 advance, Matt itemizes his deductions on Schedule A (Form 1040) in order to claim the excess expenses. Matt completes Form 2106 (showing *all* of his expenses and reimbursements) and enters $60 [$360 − ($150 a day × 2)] on line 19 of Schedule A.

Per diem allowance MORE than the federal rate. If your per diem allowance is more than the federal rate, your employer is required to include the allowance amount up to the federal rate in box 13 (code **L**) of your Form W–2. This amount is not taxable. However, the per diem allowance in excess of the federal rate will be included in box 1 (and in boxes 3 and 5 if applicable) of your Form W–2. You must report this part of your reimbursement as if it were wage income. The IRS does not require you to return it to your employer. However, see *Returning Excess Reimbursements,* later.

If your actual expenses are less than or equal to the federal rate, you do not complete Form 2106 or claim any of your expenses on your return.

However, if your actual expenses are more than the federal rate, you can complete Form 2106 and deduct those expenses that are more than the federal rate on Schedule A (Form 1040). You must report on Form 2106 your reimbursements up to the federal rate (as shown in box 13 of your Form W–2) and all your expenses. You should be able to prove these amounts to the IRS.

Example 1. Laura lives and works in Austin. Her employer sent her to Dallas for 2 days on business. Laura's employer paid the hotel directly for her lodging and reimbursed Laura $40 a day ($80 total) for meals and incidental expenses. Laura's actual meal expenses did not exceed the federal rate for Dallas, which is $34 per day.

Her employer included the $12 excess over the federal rate [($40 − $34) × 2] in boxes 1, 3, and 5 of Laura's Form W–2. Her employer shows $68 ($34 a day × 2) in box 13 of her Form W–2. This amount is not included in Laura's income. Laura does not have to complete Form 2106; however, she must include the $12 excess in her gross income as wages (by reporting the total amount shown in box 1 of her Form W–2). The IRS does not require Laura to return the $12 to her employer.

Example 2. Joe also lives in Austin and works for the same employer as Laura. In May 1993, the employer sent Joe to Washington, DC, and paid the hotel directly for his hotel bill. The employer reimbursed Joe $45 a day for his meals and incidental expenses. The federal rate for Washington, DC, is $38 a day.

Joe can prove that his actual meal expenses totaled $120. His employer's accountable plan will not pay more than $45 a day for travel to Washington, DC, so Joe does not give his employer the records that prove that he actually spent $120. However, he does account for the time, place, and business purpose of the trip. This is Joe's only business trip in 1993.

Joe was reimbursed $90 ($45 × 2 days), which is $14 more than the federal rate of $76 ($38 × 2 days). The employer includes the $14 as income on Joe's Form W–2 in boxes 1, 3, and 5. The employer also enters $76 in box 13 of Joe's Form W–2, along with a code **L**.

Joe completes Form 2106 to figure his deductible expenses. He enters the total of his actual expenses for the year ($120) on Form

2106. He also enters the reimbursements that were not included in his income ($76). His total deductible expense, before the 80% limit, is $44. After he figures the 80% limit on his unreimbursed meals and entertainment, he will enter the balance, $35, on line 19 of Schedule A (Form 1040).

Car or mileage allowances. How you report a car or mileage allowance that you received under an accountable plan depends on whether the reimbursement or your actual expenses were more than the standard mileage rate of 28 cents a mile for 1993. The standard mileage rate is considered to be the federal rate. If your allowance was equal to or less than 28 cents a mile, see *Per diem allowance LESS than or EQUAL to the federal rate,* earlier. If your allowance was more than 28 cents a mile, see *Per diem allowance MORE than the federal rate,* earlier.

Example 1. Nicole drives 10,000 miles a year for business. As required by her employer's accountable plan, she accounts for the time (dates), place, and business purpose of each trip. Her employer pays her a mileage allowance of 28 cents a mile. Nicole's expenses of operating her car do not exceed 28 cents a mile.

Nicole's employer does not include any of the reimbursement on her Form W–2. Nicole does not deduct the expenses on her return because her expenses are not more than the allowance she received.

Example 2. The facts are the same as in *Example 1,* except Nicole gets reimbursed 35 cents a mile, which is 7 cents a mile more than the standard mileage rate. Her employer must include the reimbursement amount up to the standard mileage rate, $2,800 (10,000 miles × 28 cents) in box 13 (code **L**) of her Form W–2. That amount is not taxable.

Nicole's employer must also include $700 (10,000 miles × 7 cents) in box 1 (and boxes 3 and 5, if applicable) of her Form W–2. This is the reimbursement in excess of the standard mileage rate. Nicole must include the $700 in her wage income. Because her reimbursement is equal to or more than her expenses, Nicole does not complete Form 2106.

Employer's plan. The employer makes the decision whether to reimburse employees under an accountable plan or a nonaccountable plan. If you are an employee who receives payments under a nonaccountable plan, you cannot convert these amounts to payments under an accountable plan by voluntarily accounting to your employer for the expenses and voluntarily returning excess reimbursements to the employer.

Adequate Accounting

One of the three rules listed earlier, under *Accountable Plans,* for a reimbursement or other expense allowance arrangement to qualify as an accountable plan was that you adequately account to your employer for your expenses. You adequately account by giving your employer documentary evidence of your mileage, travel, and other employee business expenses, along with a statement of expense, an account book, a diary, or a similar record in which you entered each expense at or near the time you had it. Documentary evidence includes receipts, canceled checks, and bills. See *Recordkeeping,* earlier, for a discussion of the aspects or elements of each expense that you must prove.

You must account for *all* amounts received from your employer during the year as advances, reimbursements, or allowances for business use of your car, travel, entertainment, gifts, or any other expenses. This includes amounts that were charged to your employer by credit card or other method. You must give your employer the same type of records and supporting information that you would be required to give to the IRS if the IRS questioned a deduction on your return. You must pay back the amount of any reimbursement or other expense allowance for which you do not adequately account or that exceeds the amount for which you accounted.

Per diem allowance or reimbursement. You may be able to prove the amount of your travel expenses by using a per diem allowance amount. If your employer reimburses you for your lodging, meal, and incidental expenses at a fixed amount per day of business travel, that amount is called a per diem allowance.

The term "incidental expenses" includes, but is not limited to, laundry expenses, cleaning and pressing expenses, and fees and tips for persons who provide services, such as food servers and luggage handlers. Incidental expenses do not include taxicab fares or the costs of telegrams or telephone calls.

A per diem allowance satisfies the adequate accounting requirements for the amount in question if:

1) Your employer reasonably limits payments of the travel expenses to those that are ordinary and necessary in the conduct of the trade or business,
2) The allowance is similar in form to and not more than the federal per diem (that is, your allowance varies based on where and how long you were traveling),
3) You are not related to your employer (as defined earlier under *Standard Meal Allowance*), and
4) The time, place, and business purpose of the travel are proved, as explained earlier under *Recordkeeping.*

If the IRS finds that an employer's travel allowance practices are not based on reasonably accurate estimates of travel costs, including recognition of cost differences in different areas, you will not be considered to have accounted to your employer. In this case, you may be required to prove your expenses to the IRS.

Allowance for meals. These rules also apply if you are reimbursed only for your meal expenses or get a separate per diem allowance for meals and incidental expenses. Your reimbursement or allowance must not be more than the standard meal allowance. A per diem allowance is paid separately for meals and incidental expenses if your employer furnishes lodging in kind, pays you a meal allowance plus the actual cost of your lodging, or pays the hotel, motel, etc. directly for your lodging. A per diem allowance is also paid separately for meals and incidental expenses if your employer does not have a reasonable belief that you incurred lodging expenses, such as when you stay with friends or relatives or sleep in the cab of your truck.

Proving your expenses with a per diem allowance. If your employer pays for your expenses using a per diem allowance, including a meals only allowance, you can generally use the allowance as proof for the amount of your expenses. However, the amount of expense that can be proven this way cannot be more than the regular federal per diem rate or the high-low method, both discussed later.

The per diem allowance can only be used as proof of the cost of meals and/or lodging under the adequate accounting requirements. You must still provide other proof of the time, place, and business purpose for each expense.

Example
Jean Smith receives a $100 per diem travel advance totaling $1,000 from ABC Industries. The $100 per diem is reasonably calculated not to exceed Jean's business travel expenses. Jean substantiates to ABC Industries 6 days of business travel. The requirement to return excess amounts is considered satisfied, as long as Jean returns $400 to ABC Industries within 120 days. This is true, regardless of the amount of Jean's actual travel expenses.

Regular federal per diem rate. The regular federal per diem rate is the highest amount that the federal government will pay to its employees for lodging, meal, and incidental expenses (or meal and incidental expenses only) while they are traveling away from home in a particular area. The rates are different for different locations. You must use the rate in effect for the area where you stop for sleep or rest. Your employer should have these rates available. (Employers can get Publication 1542, *Per Diem Rates,* which gives the rates in the continental United States for the current year.)

The federal rates for meals and incidental expenses are the same as those rates discussed earlier under *Standard Meal Allowance.*

High-low method. This is a simplified method of computing the federal per diem rate for travel within the continental United States. Called the "high-low method," it eliminates the need to keep a current list of the per diem rate in effect for each city in the continental United States.

Before March 12, 1993. Under the high-low method, the per diem amount for travel from January 1, 1993 through March 11, 1993, is $147 for certain locations. All other areas have a per diem amount of $93. The areas eligible for the $147 per diem amount under the high-low method are listed in *Table 28–4.*

On or After March 12, 1993. Under the high-low method, the per diem amount for travel on or after March 12, 1993, is $150 for certain locations. All other areas have a per diem amount of $94. The areas eligible for the $150 per diem amount under the high-low method are listed in *Table 28–5.*

Allocation of per diem on partial days of travel. The federal per diem rate or the federal meal and incidental expenses (also known as "M&IE") rate is for a full 24-hour day of travel. If you travel for part of a day, the full day rate must be allocated. You can use either of the following methods to figure the federal per diem rate for that day.

1) Count one-fourth of the federal rate for each 6-hour quarter of the day during any portion of which you are traveling away from home for business. The 6-hour quarters are mid-night to 6 a.m.; 6 a.m. to noon; noon to 6 p.m.; and 6 p.m. to midnight.
2) Prorate the federal rate using any method that is consistently applied and is in accordance with reasonable business practice. For example, an employer can treat 2 full days of per diem paid for travel away from home from 9 a.m. of one day to 5 p.m. of the next day as being no more than the federal rate. This is true even though a federal employee would be limited to a reimbursement for only 1½ days.

These rules apply whether your employer uses the regular federal per diem rate or the high-low method.

Car or mileage allowance. A car or mileage allowance satisfies the adequate accounting requirements for the amount if:

1) Your employer reasonably limits payments of the transportation expenses to those that are ordinary and necessary in the conduct of the trade or business,
2) The allowance is paid at the standard mileage rate, at another rate per mile, or other acceptable method, and
3) You prove the time (dates), place, and business purpose of the travel to your employer within a reasonable period of time.

If your employer pays for your expenses using a car or mileage allowance, you can generally use the allowance as proof for the amount of your expenses. However, the amount of expense that can be proven this way cannot be more than the standard mileage rate or the amount of the fixed and variable rate allowance that your employer does *not* include in boxes 1, 3, and 5 of your Form W–2.

Only the amount can be proven under the adequate accounting requirements. You must still prove the time (dates), place, and business purpose for each expense.

Returning Excess Reimbursements

Under an accountable plan, you must be required to return any excess reimbursement for your travel expenses to the person paying the reimbursement or allowance. *Excess reimbursement* means any amount for which you did not adequately account

Table 28-4. Locations Eligible for $147 Per Diem Amount — For Travel Before March 12, 1993

City	County*	City	County*
California		**Massachusetts**	
Death Valley	Inyo	Boston	Suffolk
Los Angeles	Los Angeles, Kern, Orange, Ventura; Edwards AFB, China Lake Naval Center	Martha's Vineyard/ Nantucket	Nantucket, Dukes
San Francisco	San Francisco	**New Jersey**	
		Atlantic City	Atlantic
Colorado		Newark	Bergen, Essex, Hudson, Passaic, Union
Aspen	Pitkin		
Keystone/ Silverthorne	Summit	Ocean City/Cape May	Cape May
Vail	Eagle	**New York**	
		New York City	Bronx, Brooklyn, Manhattan, Staten Island, Queens; Nassau, Suffolk
District of Columbia			
Washington, DC	Virginia counties of Arlington, Loudoun, and Fairfax and cities of Alexandria, Falls Church, and Fairfax. Maryland counties of Montgomery and Prince George's	White Plains	Westchester
		Pennsylvania	
		Philadelphia	Philadelphia; city of Bala Cynwyd
		Rhode Island	
		Newport	Newport
Florida		**South Carolina**	
Key West	Monroe	Hilton Head	Beaufort
Illinois		**Virginia**	See District of Columbia
Chicago	Cook, Lake, Du Page		
Maryland (see also District of Columbia)			
Columbia	Howard		
Ocean City	Worcester		

*Includes parishes, boroughs, military installations, etc.

within a reasonable period of time. For example, if you received a travel advance and you did not spend all the money on business-related expenses, or if you do not have proof of all your expenses, you have an excess reimbursement.

"Adequate accounting" and "reasonable period of time" were discussed earlier in this chapter.

Travel advance. If your employer provides you with an expense allowance before you actually have the expense, and the allowance is reasonably calculated not to exceed your expected expenses, you have received a travel advance. Under an accountable plan, you must be required to adequately account to your employer for this advance and be required to return any excess within a reasonable period of time. See *Reasonable period of time,* earlier in this chapter. If you do not adequately account or do not return any excess advance within a reasonable period of time, the amount you do not account for or return will be treated as having been paid under a nonaccountable plan (discussed later).

Unproven amounts. If you do not prove that you actually traveled on each day for which you received a per diem or mileage allowance (proving the elements described earlier under *Recordkeeping*), you must return this unproven amount of the travel advance within a reasonable period of time. If you fail to do this, your employer will include as income in boxes 1, 3, and 5 of your Form W-2 the unproven amount of per diem allowance as excess reimbursement. This unproven amount is considered paid under a nonaccountable plan (discussed later in this section).

Per diem MORE than federal rate. If your employer's accountable plan pays you a per diem or similar allowance that is higher than the federal rate for the area you traveled to, you do not have to return the difference between the two rates for the period you can prove business-related travel expenses. However, the difference will be reported as wages on your Form W-2. This excess amount is considered paid under a nonaccountable plan (discussed later in this section).

Example. Your employer sends you on a 5-day business trip to Miami and gives you a $200 advance to cover your meals and incidental expenses. The federal per diem for meals and incidental expenses in Miami is $34. Your trip lasts only 3 days. You must

return the $80 ($40 × 2 days) advance for the 2 days you did not travel. You do not have to return the $18 difference [($40 − $34) × 3 days]. However, the $18 will be reported on your Form W-2 as wages.

Nonaccountable Plans

A *nonaccountable plan* is a reimbursement or expense allowance arrangement that does not meet the three rules listed earlier under *Accountable Plans.*

In addition, the following payments made under an accountable plan will be treated as being paid under a nonaccountable plan:

1) Excess reimbursements you fail to return to your employer, and
2) Reimbursements of nondeductible expenses related to your employer's business. See *Reimbursement of nondeductible expenses* earlier under *Accountable Plans.*

If you are not sure if the reimbursement or expense allowance arrangement is an accountable or nonaccountable plan, see your employer.

Your employer will combine the amount of any reimbursement or other expense allowance paid to you under a nonaccountable plan with your wages, salary, or other compensation. Your employer will report the total in box 1 (and boxes 3 and 5 if applicable) of your Form W-2.

You must complete Form 2106 and itemize your deductions on Schedule A (Form 1040) to deduct your expenses for travel, transportation, meals, or entertainment. Your meal and entertainment expenses will be subject to the 80% limit discussed earlier under *Entertainment Expenses.* Also, your total expenses will be subject to the 2% of adjusted gross income limit that applies to most miscellaneous itemized deductions. This 2% limit is figured on Schedule A (Form 1040). You should be able to prove these amounts to the IRS.

Example. Kim's employer gives her $500 a month, $6,000 total this year, for her business expenses. Her employer does not require Kim to provide any proof of her expenses, and Kim can keep any funds that she does not spend.

Kim is being reimbursed under a nonaccountable plan. Her em-

Table 28-5. Locations Eligible for $150 Per Diem Amount — For Travel On or After March 12, 1993

City	County*	City	County*
California		**Massachusetts**	
Death Valley	Inyo	Boston	Suffolk
Los Angeles	Los Angeles, Kern, Orange, Ventura; Edwards AFB, China Lake Naval Center	Cambridge/Lowell	Middlesex
		Martha's Vineyard/ Nantucket	Nantucket, Dukes
San Francisco	San Francisco	**New Jersey**	
Colorado		Atlantic City	Atlantic
Aspen	Pitkin	Newark	Bergen, Essex, Hudson, Passaic, Union
Keystone/ Silverthorne	Summit	Ocean City/Cape May	Cape May
Vail	Eagle	**New York**	
District of Columbia		New York City	Bronx, Brooklyn, Manhattan, Staten Island, Queens; Nassau, Suffolk
Washington, DC	Virginia counties of Arlington, Loudoun, and Fairfax and cities of Alexandria, Falls Church, and Fairfax. Maryland counties of Montgomery and Prince George's	White Plains	Westchester
		Pennsylvania	
		Philadelphia	Philadelphia; city of Bala Cynwyd
		Rhode Island	
Florida		Newport	Newport
Key West	Monroe	**Virginia**	See District of Columbia
Illinois			
Chicago	Cook, Lake, Du Page		
Maryland (see also District of Columbia)			
Ocean City	Worcester		

*Includes parishes, boroughs, military installations, etc.

ployer will include the $6,000 on Kim's Form W–2 as if it were wages. If Kim wants to deduct her business expenses, she must complete Form 2106 and itemize her deductions on Schedule A (Form 1040). The 80% limit applies to her meal and entertainment expenses, and the 2% of adjusted gross income limit applies to her total employee business expenses.

Part of reimbursement paid under accountable plan. If your expenses are reimbursed under an otherwise accountable plan but you do not return, within a reasonable period of time, any reimbursement for which you do not adequately account, only the amount for which you do not adequately account is considered as paid under a nonaccountable plan. The remainder is treated as having been paid under an accountable plan (as discussed earlier in this chapter).

Completing Form 2106

This section briefly describes how employees complete Form 2106. *Table 28–3* explains what the employer reports on Form W–2 and what the employee reports on Form 2106. The *Instructions for Form 2106* have more information on completing the form.

Car expenses. If you used a car or other vehicle to perform your job as an employee, you may be able to deduct certain vehicle expenses. Vehicle expenses are generally figured in Part II of Form 2106, and then claimed on line 1, Column A, of Part I of Form 2106.

Local transportation expenses. Show your local business transportation expenses that did not involve overnight travel on line 2, Column A, of Form 2106. Also include on this line business expenses you have for parking fees and tolls. Do not include expenses of operating your car or expenses of commuting between your home and work.

Employee business expenses other than meals and entertainment. Show your other employee business expenses on lines 3 and 4, Column A, of Form 2106. Do not include expenses for meals and entertainment on those lines. Line 4 is for expenses such as business gifts, educational expenses (tuition and books), office-in-the-home expenses, and trade and professional publications. For information on educational expenses that you may be able to deduct, see Chapter 29, *Employee's Educational Expenses*.

Meal and entertainment expenses. Show the full amount of your expenses for business-related meals and entertainment on line 5, Column B, of Form 2106. Include meals you paid for while away from your tax home overnight and other business meals and entertainment. Figure your meal and entertainment expenses that are subject to the 80% limit on lines 9 and 10 in Column B of Form 2106.

Reimbursements. Enter on line 7 of Form 2106 the amounts your employer (or third party) reimbursed you for employee business expenses that were *not* included in box 1 of your Form W–2. This includes any reimbursement reported under code **L** in box 13 of Form W–2.

Allocating your reimbursement. If you were reimbursed under an accountable plan and want to deduct excess expenses that were not reimbursed, you may have to allocate your reimbursement. If your employer paid you a single amount that covers meals or entertainment, as well as other business expenses, you must allocate the reimbursement so that you know how much to enter in Column A and Column B of line 7 of Form 2106.

Use the following worksheet to allocate your reimbursement.

1. Enter the total amount of the reimbursements your employer gave you that were not reported to you in box 1 of your Form W–2 .... _____

2. Enter the total amount of your expenses for the periods covered by this reimbursement .... _____

3. Of the amount on line 2, enter the part of your total expense for meals and entertainment .... _____

4. Divide line 3 by line 2. Enter the result as a decimal (to at least two places) .... _____

5. Multiply line 1 by line 4. Enter the result here and in Column B, line 7 .... _____

6. Subtract line 5 from line 1. Enter the result here and in Column A, line 7 .... _____

Example. Assume your employer paid you an expense allowance of $5,000 during 1993 under an accountable plan. It is not clear how much of the allowance is for the cost of deductible meals. You actually spent $6,500 during the year ($2,000 for meals and $4,500 for automobile expenses). First, divide your meal expenses by your total expenses ($2,000 ÷ $6,500). The result is .31. Multiply your reimbursement by this decimal ($5,000 × .31). The result is $1,550 (the amount of reimbursement attributable to your meals). Enter this amount on line 7, Column B, of Form 2106. Enter the remainder of the reimbursement, $3,450 ($5,000 − $1,550), on line 7, Column A of Form 2106.

Schedule A (Form 1040). After you have completed your Form 2106, follow the directions on that form to deduct your expenses on the appropriate line of your tax return. For most taxpayers this is on line 19 of Schedule A (Form 1040). However, if you are a performing artist or a disabled employee with impairment-related work expenses, see *Special Rules*, later.

Limits on employee business expenses. Your employee business expenses may be subject to any of the three limits described below. These limits are figured in the following order on the form specified.

1. Limit on meals and entertainment. Certain meal and entertainment expenses are subject to an 80% limit. Employees figure this limit on line 9 of Form 2106. See *80% Limit* under *Entertainment Expenses*, earlier in this chapter.

2. Limit on employee business expenses. Employees deduct employee business expenses (as figured on Form 2106) on line 19 of Schedule A (Form 1040). Most miscellaneous itemized deductions, including employee business expenses, are subject to a 2% of adjusted gross income limit. This limit is figured on line 23 of Schedule A.

3. Limit on total itemized deductions. If your adjusted gross income (line 32 of Form 1040) is more than $108,450 ($54,225 if you are married filing separately), the amount of your overall itemized deductions, including employee business expenses, may be limited. See Chapter 21, *Limit on Itemized Deductions*, for more information on this limit.

Special Rules

This section discusses special rules that apply only to performing artists and disabled employees with impairment-related work expenses.

Expenses of certain performing artists. If you are a performing artist, you may qualify to deduct your employee business expenses as an adjustment to gross income rather than as a miscellaneous itemized deduction. To qualify, you must meet *all* of the following requirements.

1) During the tax year, you perform services in the performing arts for at least two employers.
2) You receive at least $200 each from any two of these employers.
3) Your related performing-arts business expenses are more than 10% of your gross income from the performance of such services.

4) Your adjusted gross income is not more than $16,000 before deducting these business expenses.

Special rules for married persons. If you are married, you must file a joint return unless you lived apart from your spouse at all times during the tax year.

If you file a joint return, you must figure requirements (1), (2), and (3) separately for both you and your spouse. However, requirement (4) applies to your and your spouse's combined adjusted gross income.

Where to report. If you meet all of the above requirements, you should first complete Form 2106. Then you include your performing-arts related expenses from line 11 of Form 2106 in the total on line 30 of Form 1040. Write "QPA" and the amount of your performing-arts related expenses in the space to the left of line 30 of Form 1040.

If you do not meet all of the above requirements, you do not qualify to deduct your expenses as an adjustment to gross income. Instead, you must complete Form 2106 and deduct your employee business expenses on line 19 of Schedule A (Form 1040).

Expenses of disabled employees. If you are an employee with a physical or mental disability, your impairment-related work expenses are not subject to the 2% of adjusted gross income limit that applies to most other employee business expenses. After you complete Form 2106, enter your impairment-related work expenses from line 11 of Form 2106 on line 25 of Schedule A (Form 1040). Enter your employee business expenses that are **unrelated** to your disability from line 11 of Form 2106 on line 19 of Schedule A.

Impairment-related work expenses are your allowable expenses for attendant care at your workplace and other expenses you have in connection with your workplace that you incur to allow you to work. For more information, see Publication 907, *Information for Persons with Disabilities.*

Illustrated Example

Bill Wilson is an employee of Fashion Clothing Co. in Manhattan, NY. In a typical week, Bill leaves his home on Long Island on Monday morning and drives to Albany to exhibit the Fashion line for 3 days to prospective customers. Then he drives to Troy to show X Department Store, an old customer, Fashion's new line of merchandise. While in Troy, he talks with Tom Brown, purchasing agent for X Department Store, to discuss the new line. He later takes John Smith of Y Co., Troy, out to dinner to discuss Y Co.'s buying Fashion's new line of clothing.

Bill uses the standard mileage rate for car expense purposes. He records his total mileage, business mileage, parking fees, and tolls for the year. Bill timely records his expenses and other pertinent information in a travel expense log (not shown). He obtains receipts for his expenses for lodging and for any other expenses of $25 or more.

During the year, Bill drove a total of 25,000 miles of which 20,000 miles were for business. Following the instructions for Part II of Form 2106, he answers all the questions and figures his vehicle expense to be $5,600 (20,000 business miles × 28 cents standard mileage rate).

His total employee business expenses are shown in the following table. He received no expense allowance or reimbursement.

Type of Expense	Amount
Parking fees and tolls	$ 400
Vehicle expenses	$ 5,600
Meals	$ 2,632
Lodging, laundry, cleaning	$10,000
Entertainment	$ 1,870
Gifts, education, etc.	$ 400
Total	**$20,902**

Bill files Form 2106 with his tax return. His filled-in form is shown at the end of this chapter.

Form 2106 (1993)

Part II   Vehicle Expenses (See instructions to find out which sections to complete.)

Section A.—General Information

		(a) Vehicle 1	(b) Vehicle 2
12	Enter the date vehicle was placed in service	12	1/2/91	
13	Total miles vehicle was driven during 1993	13	25,000 miles	miles
14	Business miles included on line 13	14	20,000 miles	miles
15	Percent of business use. Divide line 14 by line 13	15	80 %	%
16	Average daily round trip commuting distance	16	10 miles	miles
17	Commuting miles included on line 13	17	2,600 miles	miles
18	Other personal miles. Add lines 14 and 17 and subtract the total from line 13.	18	2,400 miles	miles

19 Do you (or your spouse) have another vehicle available for personal purposes? . . . . ☑ Yes ☐ No

20 If your employer provided you with a vehicle, is personal use during off duty hours permitted? ☐ Yes ☐ No ☑ Not applicable

21a Do you have evidence to support your deduction? . . . . ☑ Yes ☐ No

21b If "Yes," is the evidence written? . . . . ☑ Yes ☐ No

Section B.—Standard Mileage Rate (Use this section only if you own the vehicle.)

22 Multiply line 14 by 28¢ (.28). Enter the result here and on line 1. (Rural mail carriers, see instructions.) | 22 | 5,600

Section C.—Actual Expenses

		(a) Vehicle 1	(b) Vehicle 2
23	Gasoline, oil, repairs, vehicle insurance, etc.	23		
24a	Vehicle rentals	24a		
b	Inclusion amount (see instructions)	24b		
c	Subtract line 24b from line 24a	24c		
25	Value of employer-provided vehicle (applies only if 100% of annual lease value was included on Form W-2—see instructions)	25		
26	Add lines 23, 24c, and 25	26		
27	Multiply line 26 by the percentage on line 15	27		
28	Depreciation. Enter amount from line 38 below	28		
29	Add lines 27 and 28. Enter total here and on line 1.	29		

Section D.—Depreciation of Vehicles (Use this section only if you own the vehicle.)

		(a) Vehicle 1	(b) Vehicle 2
30	Enter cost or other basis (see instructions)	30		
31	Enter amount of section 179 deduction (see instructions)	31		
32	Multiply line 30 by line 15 (see instructions if you elected the section 179 deduction)	32		
33	Enter depreciation method and percentage (see instructions)	33		
34	Multiply line 32 by the percentage on line 33 (see instructions)	34		
35	Add lines 31 and 34	35		
36	Enter the limitation amount from the table in the line 36 instructions	36		
37	Multiply line 36 by the percentage on line 15	37		
38	Enter the smaller of line 35 or line 37. Also, enter this amount on line 28 above	38		

Form **2106**

Department of the Treasury
Internal Revenue Service (T)

Employee Business Expenses

▶ See separate instructions.
▶ Attach to Form 1040.

OMB No. 1545-0139
1993
Attachment Sequence No. 54

Your name Bill Wilson

Social security number 555 00 5555

Occupation in which expenses were incurred Sales

Part I   Employee Business Expenses and Reimbursements

STEP 1   Enter Your Expenses

		Column A Other Than Meals and Entertainment	Column B Meals and Entertainment
1	Vehicle expense from line 22 or line 29	1	5,600	
2	Parking fees, tolls, and transportation, including train, bus, etc., that did not involve overnight travel	2	400	
3	Travel expense while away from home overnight, including lodging, airplane, car rental, etc. Do not include meals and entertainment	3	10,000	
4	Business expenses not included on lines 1 through 3. Do not include meals and entertainment	4	400	
5	Meals and entertainment expenses (see instructions)	5		4,502
6	Total expenses. In Column A, add lines 1 through 4 and enter the result. In Column B, enter the amount from line 5	6	16,400	4,502

Note: If you were not reimbursed for any expenses in Step 1, skip line 7 and enter the amount from line 6 on line 8.

STEP 2   Enter Amounts Your Employer Gave You for Expenses Listed in STEP 1

7	Enter amounts your employer gave you that were not reported to you in box 1 of Form W-2. Include any amount reported under code "L" in box 13 of your Form W-2 (see instructions)	7		

STEP 3   Figure Expenses To Deduct on Schedule A (Form 1040)

8	Subtract line 7 from line 6	8	16,400	4,502

Note: If both columns of line 8 are zero, stop here. If Column A is less than zero, report the amount as income on Form 1040, line 7, and enter -0- on line 10, Column A.

9	Enter 20% (.20) of line 8, Column B	9		900
10	In Column A, enter the amount from line 8. In Column B, subtract line 9 from line 8	10	16,400	3,602
11	Add the amounts on line 10 of both columns and enter the total here. Also, enter the total on Schedule A (Form 1040), line 19. (Qualified performing artists and individuals with disabilities, see the instructions for special rules on where to enter the total.) ▶	11	20,002	

For Paperwork Reduction Act Notice, see instructions.

Cat. No. 11700N

Form **2106** (1993)

443

29 | Employees' Educational Expenses

Introduction

Educational expenses are generally considered to be personal in nature and nondeductible. The law, however, does recognize that certain educational expenses are necessary for you as an **employee. Deductions** *may be allowed for these expenses, as well as for reasonable expenses incurred in acquiring the education.*

It's often difficult to determine if educational expenses are deductible. You do not necessarily have to earn a new degree for such expenses to be claimed. And earning a degree doesn't necessarily make the expenses deductible either. The expenses do have to meet certain tests. For example, they are deductible if the education either maintains or improves skills required in your trade or business or if the courses are required for you to retain your current job. The expenses are not deductible if they are spent on education that is required for you to meet the minimum educational requirements of your position. Also, you may not deduct expenses for law school, medical school, or any other course of study that helps you qualify for a new trade or business, even if you do not plan on entering the new trade or business. In addition, travel as a form of education is not deductible.

This chapter teaches you about deductible educational expenses. You'll learn that you may deduct not only your fees for educational instruction but also a number of other expenses that you incur because you are simultaneously working and in school.

Educational expenses and other miscellaneous itemized deductions are deductible only to the extent that they exceed 2% of your adjusted gross income.

It is also important to note that your 1993 itemized deductions may be subject to certain other limitations if your adjusted gross income exceeds $108,450.

Important Changes for 1993

Employer-provided educational assistance. The exclusion from income of up to $5,250 of educational assistance provided to you by your employer under a qualified plan had expired for amounts paid after June 30, 1992. The exclusion has been reinstated and applies to payments made after that date.

For tax years beginning after December 31, 1988, amounts paid or incurred by your employer for your education or training that do not qualify as educational assistance may still be excludable from your income. You may exclude these amounts if (and only if) the expense would have been a deductible employee business expense had you paid it.

These changes may entitle you to a refund of income, social security, and Medicare taxes. For more information, see the discussion beginning with *Refund procedure for employees* under *Expenses Relating to Tax-Exempt Income*, later.

TaxAlert

Congress retroactively reinstated the exclusion for employer-provided educational assistance benefits through December 31, 1994. The exclusion is one of a number of tax incentives that originally expired on July 1, 1992. The exclusion applies for both undergraduate and graduate-level classes, whether or not you are seeking a degree. The ceiling of $5,250 for educational assistance benefits provided during any calendar year remains the same.

TaxSaver

If your employer provided you with educational benefits during the second half of 1992 and you paid tax on this benefit because it was included on your 1992 W-2, you should be entitled to a refund. Employees seeking refunds of income taxes should obtain Form W-2c (Statement of Corrected Income and Tax Amounts) from their employer and file Form 1040X (Amended U.S. Individual Income Tax Return). Employees should also request reimbursement of Social Security and Medicare taxes from their employers. For further detail, see *Refund Procedure For Employees* later in this chapter, or contact your tax advisor.

Important Reminder

Limit on itemized deductions. If your adjusted gross income is more than $108,450 ($54,225 if you are married filing separately), the overall amount of your itemized deductions may be limited. See Chapter 21 if you need more information about this limit.

This chapter discusses how employees deduct their costs of work-related education. To figure the deduction, you must know:

- Whether the courses qualify,
- What expenses are deductible, and
- How to report the expenses.

First, you must determine whether the courses you are taking are qualifying courses. Not all courses are qualifying education. Courses must meet certain requirements before the related expenses can be deducted. This is explained in the first section.

If your courses qualify, you can then determine which expenses qualify to be deducted. Only certain expenses of education are deductible. This is explained in the second section.

If you know which expenses qualify, you can then determine how to report those educational expenses. You may not be able to fully deduct all of your expenses. This is explained in the third section.

Useful Items

You may want to see:

Publication

☐ **508** Educational Expenses

Form (and Instructions)

☐ **2106** Employee Business Expenses

Qualifying Education

Education must meet certain requirements before the expenses of that education can be deducted. If these requirements are met, the education is qualifying education. You may be able to deduct the costs of qualifying education even though the education may lead to a degree.

Requirements. The education must:

1) Be required by your employer or the law to keep your present salary, status, or job (and serve a business purpose of your employer), or
2) Maintain or improve skills needed in your present work.

Exception. Even if your education meets one of the requirements above, it is not qualifying education if it:

1) Is needed to meet the minimum educational requirements of your present trade or business, or
2) Is part of a program of study that can qualify you for a new trade or business, even if you have no plans to enter that trade or business.

See *Nonqualifying Education,* later.

Present work. Your education must relate to your present work. Education that will relate to work you may enter in the future is not qualifying education. Education that prepares you for a future occupation includes any education that keeps you up-to-date for a return to work or that qualifies you to reenter a job you had in the past.

Explanation
Only expenses for education relating to your present work are deductible.

Examples
A college student obtaining employment through his or her college cooperative program or work/study program is not engaged in a trade or a business. His or her college fees are not deductible, since they are incurred in preparation for an occupation.

A full-time student does not have a trade or a business and may not deduct the cost of courses toward a college degree, even though the student may be employed full-time during the summer months.

A fully retired individual is not considered to have a trade or a business and is not entitled to a deduction for educational expenses.

TaxPlanner

The IRS does not explicitly allow or disallow educational expenses for a semi-retired person. Therefore, it appears that education expenses to maintain skills are deductible, even though the individual has reduced the scope of his or her trade or business.

An individual who abandons a former profession for a period of years and acquires a new profession may not deduct courses related to resuming his or her original profession.

Temporary absence. If you stop work for a year or less and then go back to the same kind of work, your absence is ordinarily considered temporary. Education during a vacation, temporary leave, or other temporary absence from your job is considered related to your present job. However, after your temporary absence you must return to the same kind of work.

Example. You quit your biology research job to become a full-time biology graduate student for one year. If you return to work in biology research after completing the courses, the education is related to your present work. You may even choose to take a similar job with another employer.

Explanation

While the IRS defines a temporary leave of absence as a period of 1 year or less, the courts have been more lenient, approving deductions for educational expenses for a leave of more than 1 year. The cases turn on whether or not the taxpayer expects to reenter the same trade or business, regardless of whether or not it is with a new employer.

Examples

A manager who quit his job to pursue a 2-year masters of business administration course but who expected to reenter the same trade or business was allowed to deduct the cost of his courses.

A parochial school teacher ended her employment to raise a family. Over the next 23 years, she attended several different colleges, until she was awarded a Bachelor's degree in Education. The following fall, she began employment again as a full-time teacher. The court determined that, when she left the parochial school, there was no indication that she was on a leave of absence or that she planned to resume teaching in the future. Consequently, the court denied the deduction for the educational expenses.

Education Required by Employer or by Law

Once you have met the minimum educational requirements for your job, your employer or a law may require you to get more education. This additional education must be required for you to keep your present salary, status, or job. It must serve a business purpose of your employer and not be part of a program that will qualify you for a new trade or business.

Example 1

As a result of a corporate downsizing policy, you are taking courses to be retrained in another trade or business. If this education qualifies you to enter a new trade or business, even with the same employer, the costs are non-deductible.

Example 2

Your employer is restructuring its workforce. The company has said that additional education is required for you to retain your current job. Since the education serves a business purpose of your employer, the additional education expenses are deductible.

When you take more education than your employer or the law requires, the additional education is qualifying only if it maintains or improves skills required in your present work. See *Education to Maintain or Improve Skills,* later.

Example. You are a teacher who has satisfied the minimum requirements for teaching. Your employer requires you to take an additional college course each year to keep your teaching job. You take a course and pay for it yourself. This is qualifying education even if you eventually receive a master's degree and an increase in salary because of this extra education.

Explanation

Educational expenses are deductible if the failure to satisfy certain educational requirements results in losing any of the advantages of your present position.

Example

A teacher incurred educational expenses that would enable her to receive annual salary increases. The education was not required to maintain her teaching position. A court held that the expenses were deductible because without the education she would lose one of the benefits of her teaching position.

Explanation

Educational expenses that lead to a new position, to substantial advancement, or to an advanced degree may still be deductible if they are required to retain salary status or employment. However, the expenses are not deductible if they qualify you for a new trade or business.

Example

To be reappointed as a college tutor, you are required to pursue a course of graduate study. The expense is deductible, even though the course qualifies you for a full-time teaching position.

Education to Maintain or Improve Skills

If your education is not required by your employer or a law, it must maintain or improve skills needed in your job to be qualifying education. This includes refresher courses, courses on current developments, and academic or vocational courses. However, courses you take that are needed to meet the minimum educational requirements of your job or to qualify you for a new trade or business are not qualifying education. See *Education to Qualify for a New Trade or Business,* later.

Explanation

Since most jobs, trades, or businesses do not have continuing educational requirements, general educational expenses are disallowed.

Example. You repair televisions, radios, and stereo sets for XYZ Store. To keep up with the latest changes, you take special courses in radio and stereo service. These courses maintain and improve skills required in your work.

Explanation

If, as a result of technological changes, new skills are required to maintain your present salary, status, and employment, the learning costs are deductible.

Example

An airline converts to jets from piston planes. Courses required by employees to operate jet planes qualify as deductible educational expenses.

Figure 29-A. Are Your Educational Expenses Deductible?

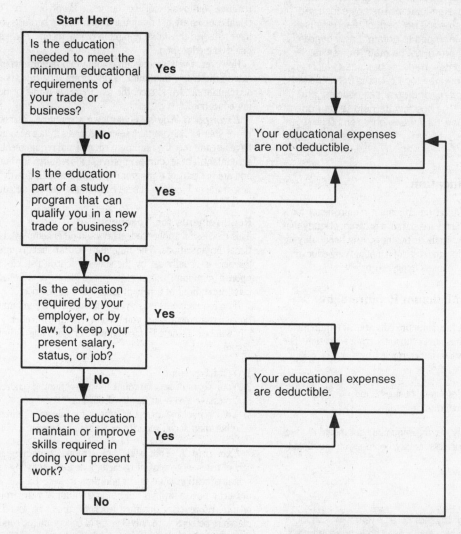

Explanation

For expenses to be deductible, they do not have to be spent on courses closely related to your duties, as long as the courses improve required skills.

Examples

The following are examples of educational expenses that were *deductible* because the courses maintained or improved skills:

- A tax attorney attended an out-of-town tax forum. The course was valuable for him in maintaining current knowledge of the tax laws.
- An engineering aide took night courses that improved his skills but were not required by his employer.
- A concert harpist took music lessons. The costs were deductible as maintaining or improving her skills.
- A doctor, engaged in the private practice of psychiatry, undertook a program of study and training at an accredited psychoanalytic institute that enabled him to qualify to practice psychoanalysis. The expenditures were deductible, because the study and training maintained or improved skills required in the doctor's trade or business and didn't qualify the doctor for a new trade or a business.
- A farmer could deduct the cost of a welding course that improved his welding skills. Welding skills were necessary in the farming operation to keep the machinery repaired.
- An ordained minister could deduct the cost of undergraduate courses in psychology, education, and business. The court determined that the courses maintained and improved the skills that he needed to lead a congregation competently: counseling, teaching, and managing the financial affairs of the church.

The following are examples of educational expenses that were *not deductible,* because the courses qualified the taxpayer for a new trade or a business:

- A bookkeeper and tax return preparer returned to school and earned a bachelor's degree in accounting. The degree qualifies her to sit for the certified public accounting examination. The costs incurred in earning the degree are not deductible, because the courses were intended to obtain a new degree rather than to improve or maintain her skills; it qualified her for a new trade or business.

- A quality control foreman took courses in business law, corporate strategy and business policies, and business finance. The costs were held to be non-deductible because they were only remotely related to his duties.

Nonqualifying Education

If you need education to meet the minimum requirements for a trade or business or the education is part of a program of study that will qualify you for a new trade or business, it is nonqualifying education. You cannot deduct the costs of nonqualifying education. Education that is nonqualifying is explained below.

Education to Meet Minimum Requirements

Education needed to meet the minimum educational requirements for your present trade or business is nonqualifying education. The minimum education necessary is determined by:

1) Laws and regulations,
2) Standards of your profession or business, and
3) Your employer's requirements.

You have not necessarily met the minimum educational requirements of your trade or business simply because you are already doing the work.

Example

You have completed 2 years of a 3-year law school course and are hired by a law firm to do legal research and to perform other functions on a full-time basis. As a condition of employment, you are required to obtain a law degree and to pass the state bar examination. You complete the law school education by attending night classes and take a bar review course in order to prepare for the bar examination. The law courses and the bar review course are considered the minimum educational requirements needed to qualify for your trade or business, and, thus, the costs of such courses are not deductible.

Once you have met the minimum educational requirements that were in effect when you were hired, you do not have to satisfy this rule again. This means that if the minimum requirements change, any education you need to meet the new requirements is qualifying education.

Example 1. You are a full-time engineering student. You work part time as an engineer for a firm that will employ you full time as an engineer after you finish college. Although your college engineering courses improve your skills in your present job, you have not met the minimum job requirements for a full-time engineer. The education is nonqualifying education.

Example 2. You are an accountant and you have met the minimum educational requirements of your employer. Your employer later changes the minimum educational requirements and requires you to take college courses to keep your job. These additional courses are not minimum requirements because you already have satisfied the initial minimum requirements. The education is qualifying education.

However, a new accountant coming into the firm would have to satisfy these new minimum requirements. The education the new accountant needed to meet the requirements would be nonqualifying education.

Example 3. You have your own accounting business. To improve your skills, you take several courses in tax accounting. You have already met the minimum educational requirements to be an accountant. These courses improve skills required in your business and are not part of a program of study that will qualify you for a new trade or business. These courses are qualifying education.

Requirements for Teachers

This discussion applies to teachers and others employed by educational organizations. The minimum educational requirement for teachers is usually set by the state or school district. It is based upon a minimum number of college hours or a college degree usually required of a person hired for that position.

If no requirements exist, you will have met the minimum educational requirement when you become a faculty member. You generally will be considered a faculty member when one of the following occurs.

1) You have tenure.
2) Your years of service count toward obtaining tenure.
3) You have a vote in faculty decisions.
4) Your school makes contributions for you to a retirement plan other than social security or a similar program.

Example 1. Your state law requires beginning secondary school teachers to have a bachelor's degree, including ten professional education courses. In addition, to keep the job, a teacher must complete a fifth year of training within 10 years from the date of hire. However, if qualified teachers cannot be found, a school may hire persons with only 3 years of college on the condition that they get the bachelor's degree and the required professional education courses within 3 years.

Under these facts, the bachelor's degree, whether it includes the ten professional education courses or not, is considered the minimum educational requirement for qualification as a teacher in your state.

If you have all of the required education except the fifth year, you have met the minimum educational requirements. However, if the fifth year will qualify you for a new trade or business, it is nonqualifying education. See *Education to Qualify for a New Trade or Business,* later.

Example 2. Assume the same facts as in Example 1. If you have a bachelor's degree and only six professional education courses, the additional four education courses would be qualifying education. Because a bachelor's degree is the minimum requirement for qualification as a teacher, you have already met the minimum requirements, even though you do not have all of the required courses.

Example 3. Assume the same facts as in Example 1. If you are hired with only 3 years of college, the courses you take that lead to a bachelor's degree (including those in education) are nonqualifying education. They are required to meet the minimum education for employment as a teacher.

Example 4. You have a bachelor's degree and you work as a temporary instructor at a university. At the same time, you take graduate courses toward an advanced degree. The rules of the university state that you may become a faculty member only if you get a graduate degree. Also, you may keep your job as an instructor only as long as you show satisfactory progress toward getting this degree. You have not met the minimum educational requirements to qualify you as a faculty member. The graduate courses are nonqualifying education.

Certification in a new state. Once you have met the minimum educational requirements for your state, you are considered to have met the minimum educational requirements in a new state, even if you must take additional education to be certified in the new state. Any additional education you need is qualifying education.

Example. You hold a permanent teaching certificate in State A and are employed as a teacher in that state for several years. You move to State B and are promptly hired as a school teacher. You are required, however, to complete certain prescribed courses to get a permanent teaching certificate in State B. These additional courses are qualifying education because the teaching position in State B involves the same general kind of work for which you were qualified in State A. You have already met the minimum requirements for teaching and have not entered a new trade or business.

TAXSAVER

It's possible to maximize an education deduction by carefully limiting preemployment education to minimum job requirements. Courses taken after employment is secured may then be deductible as maintaining or improving skills.

Example 1
Denise Thomas is starting her final semester of education courses that will enable her to be a registered nurse. She needs 6 credit hours of nursing courses to reach the required level of education. In addition to the 6 credit hours, Denise also wants to take an advanced nursing course. To reduce her taxes, Denise should complete the minimum job requirements for nursing. If she takes the advanced nursing course after she has qualified to be a nurse, the cost is deductible.

Example 2
Robert Taylor is a recent law school graduate and is considering the pursuit of a full-time graduate law (LL.M) program in international law. To qualify for a deduction, Robert should secure employment as a lawyer and complete the minimum requirements for practicing law (i.e., bar admission) before starting any graduate program. After meeting these minimum requirements for practicing law, Robert may begin a graduate law program in international law and deduct the related educational expenses.

Education to Qualify for a New Trade or Business

Education that is part of a program of study that can qualify you for a new trade or business is nonqualifying education. This is true even if you are not seeking a new job.

If you are an employee, a change of duties is not a new trade or business if the new duties involve the same general work you did in your old job.

Example 1. You are an accountant. Your employer requires you to get a law degree at your own expense. You register at a law school for the regular curriculum that leads to a law degree. Even if you do not intend to become a lawyer, the education is nonqualifying because the law degree will qualify you for a new trade or business.

Example 2. You are a general practitioner of medicine. You take a 2-week course to review new developments in several specialized fields of medicine. The course does not qualify you for a new profession. It is qualifying education because it maintains or improves skills required in your present profession.

Example 3. While working in the private practice of psychiatry, you enter a program to study and train at an accredited psychoanalytic institute. The program will lead to qualifying you to practice psychoanalysis. The psychoanalytic training does not qualify you for a new profession. It is qualifying education because it maintains or improves skills required in your present profession.

Explanation
A change of duties is limited to employees. It does not pertain to the **self-employed.**

The IRS defines the phrase "the same general type of work" very narrowly. The onus is on the taxpayer to prove that he or she has not qualified for a new trade or a business. Generally, however, teachers are given more latitude (see below).

No deduction has been allowed for law school educational expenses, even if they are required by an employer for employees in the following trades or businesses: accountant, insurance claims adjuster, industrial arts teacher, engineer, probation officer, patent examiner, mathematics teacher, IRS agent, hospital administrator, doctor, philosophy professor, and computer systems analyst.

Examples
The following are other examples of areas in which the courts have found educational expenses to be nondeductible because they qualify the taxpayer for a new trade or a business:

- A licensed nurse's expenses to qualify as either a physician's assistant or a registered nurse
- A commercial pilot's expenses for helicopter flight lessons
- A computer operator's course fees to become a programmer

Nevertheless, the courts have *allowed deductions* in some special cases:

- A night manager of a supermarket took food management courses at a local university. The courses elevated his rank within the management structure and also qualified him for a day manager position. The court held that the general management progression did not represent a change in business and allowed the deductions.
- An engineer whose duties were changing to include more management and administrative skills took courses and received a degree in business management and administration. The courses were deductible, because the education did not qualify him for a new trade or a business but were directly related to his current position. The courses

also allowed him to maintain and improve skills required by his employer.
• Costs incurred in becoming a specialist within your trade or business are deductible.

TaxSaver

You may be able to deduct expenses incurred in gaining a specialty within a trade or a business if the expenses are delayed until after you have established yourself in the trade or business.

Examples

A dentist engaged in general practice returned full-time to dental school for postgraduate study in orthodontics while continuing her practice on a part-time basis. On completing her postgraduate training, she limited her practice to orthodontic patients. The expenditures incurred by the dentist in her studies were deductible, because they improved her skills as a dentist and did not qualify her for a new trade or a business.

A certified clinical social worker participated in a course in psychoanalysis in order to improve the diagnostic and therapy skills required in assisting her patients. Since clinical social workers are qualified to practice psychotherapy, the course improved her skills as a clinical social worker and did not qualify her for a new trade or a business. The costs were deductible as educational expenses.

Bar or CPA Review Course

Review courses to prepare for the bar examination or the certified public accountant (CPA) examination are nonqualifying education. These are personal expenses that qualify you for a new profession.

Explanation

Bar review courses are not deductible, even if you are currently practicing in one state and are seeking admission to the bar in another state.

Qualifications for Teachers

All teaching and related duties are considered the same general kind of work. If you change duties in any of the following ways, it is not considered a change to a new business.

1) Elementary school teacher to secondary school teacher.
2) Teacher of one subject, such as biology, to teacher of another subject, such as art.
3) Classroom teacher to guidance counselor.
4) Classroom teacher to school administrator.

Explanation

If you are an employed teacher who meets the minimum education requirements of one state, you may deduct the cost of required courses to qualify as a teacher in another state. Changing employers and locations is not a significant change of duties and does not create a new trade or a business. Likewise, deductions have been allowed for a Canadian teacher taking courses to qualify to teach in the United States.

What Educational Expenses Are Deductible

If your education meets the requirements described earlier under *Qualifying Education,* you can deduct your educational expenses if you itemize your deductions or if you are self-employed.
Deductible expenses. The following educational expenses can be deducted:

1) Tuition, books, supplies, lab fees, and similar items.
2) Certain transportation and travel costs.
3) Other educational expenses, such as costs of research and typing when writing a paper as part of an educational program.

TaxOrganizer

In case the IRS challenges your deduction of educational expenses, you should keep the following information in order to support your claim for educational expenses incurred:

• Tuition statements and cancelled checks;
• Receipts for books, supplies, lab fees, etc.;
• Records of travel and transportation expenses, including miles driven and parking receipts; and
• Receipts for meal expenses.

Nondeductible expenses. Educational expenses do not include personal or capital expenses. For example, you cannot deduct the dollar value of vacation time or annual leave you take to attend classes. This amount is a personal expense.

Unclaimed reimbursement. If you do not claim reimbursement that you are entitled to receive from your employer, you cannot deduct the expenses to which that reimbursement applies. For example, your employer agrees to pay your educational expenses if you file a voucher showing your expenses. You do not file a voucher, and you do not get reimbursed. Because you did not file a voucher, you cannot deduct the expenses.

Transportation Expenses

If your education qualifies, you can deduct local transportation costs of going directly from work to school. If you are regularly employed and go to school on a strictly *temporary basis,* you can also deduct the costs of returning from school to home. A temporary basis is irregular or short-term attendance, generally a matter of days or weeks.

If you go directly from home to school on a temporary basis, you can deduct the round-trip costs of transportation in going from your home to school to home. This is true regardless of the location of the school, the distance traveled, or whether you attend school on non-work days.

Transportation expenses include the actual costs of bus, subway, cab, or other fares, as well as the costs of using your own car. Transportation expenses do not include amounts spent for travel, meals, or lodging while you are away from home overnight.

Using Your Car

If you use your car for transportation to school, you can deduct your actual expenses or use the standard mileage rate to figure the amount you can deduct. The standard mileage rate for 1993 is 28 cents per mile. If you use either method, you may also deduct parking fees and tolls. See *Car Expenses* in Chapter 28 for information on deducting your actual expenses of using a car.

Example 1. You regularly work in Camden, New Jersey, and also attend school every night for 3 weeks to take a course that improves your job skills. Since you are attending school on a temporary basis, you can deduct your daily round-trip transportation expenses in going between home and school. This is true regardless of the distance traveled.

Example 2. Assume the same facts as in Example 1 except that on certain nights you go directly from work to school and then home. You can deduct your transportation expenses from your regular work site to school and then home.

Example 3. Assume the same facts as in Example 1 except that you attend the school for 6 consecutive Saturdays, non-work days. Since you are attending school on a temporary basis, you can deduct your round-trip transportation expenses in going between home and school.

Example 4. Assume the same facts as in Example 1 except that you attend classes twice a week for one year. Since your attendance in school is not considered temporary, you cannot deduct your transportation expenses in going between home and school. However, if you go directly to school from work, you can deduct the transportation expenses of going from work to school.

Travel Expenses

You can deduct expenses for travel, meals, and lodging if you travel overnight to obtain qualified education and the main purpose of the trip is to attend a work-related course or seminar. However, you cannot deduct expenses for personal activities, such as sightseeing, visiting, or entertaining.

If your travel away from home is mainly personal, you cannot deduct all of your expenses for travel, meals, and lodging. However, during the time you attend the qualified educational activities, you can deduct your expenses for meals and lodging.

Whether a trip's purpose is mainly personal or mainly educational depends upon the facts and circumstances. An important factor is the comparison of the amount of time spent on personal activities with the amount of time spent on educational activities. If you spend more time on personal activities, the trip is considered mainly educational only if you can show a substantial nonpersonal reason for traveling to a particular location.

Example 1. John works in Newark, New Jersey. He traveled to Chicago to take a deductible one-week course at the request of his employer. While there, he took a sightseeing trip, entertained some personal friends, and took a side trip to Pleasantville for a day. Since the trip was mainly for business, he can deduct his round-trip airfare to Chicago, but he cannot deduct his transportation expenses of going to Pleasantville. Only the meals and lodging connected with his educational activities can be claimed as educational expenses.

Example 2. Dave works in Nashville and recently traveled to California to take a deductible 2-week seminar. While there, he spent an additional 8 weeks on personal activities. The facts, including the extra 8-week stay, indicate that his main purpose was to take a vacation. He cannot deduct his round-trip airfare or his meals and lodging for the 8 weeks. He can deduct only his expenses for meals and lodging for the 2 weeks he attended the seminar.

TaxSaver

Through careful planning and documentation, as well as recognition of the stringent tests applied by the courts, it's possible to mix business with pleasure and deduct some or all of your travel expenses. If you travel away from home primarily to obtain education, your expenditures for the education, as well as for travel, meals, and lodging while away from home, are deductible. It is helpful to be able to prove that the location you are visiting is unique and that, if education is involved, the education cannot be obtained elsewhere.

However, if you engage in some personal activity while on the trip, such as sightseeing, social visiting, entertaining, or other recreation, your expenses attributable to those personal activities are nondeductible personal expenses.

If your travel away from home is primarily personal, your expenditures for travel, meals, and lodging (other than meals and lodging during the time spent participating in deductible educational pursuits) are not deductible.

Whether a particular trip is primarily personal or primarily educational depends on all the facts and circumstances of each case, including the time devoted to personal activity as compared with the time devoted to educational pursuits.

Example

David, a self-employed tax practitioner, decides to take a 1-week course in new developments in taxation that is offered in Baltimore, Maryland, 500 miles from his home. His primary purpose in going to Baltimore is to take the course, but he also takes a side trip to Washington, D.C. (about 50 miles from Baltimore) for 1 day, takes a sightseeing trip while in Baltimore, and entertains some personal friends. David's transportation expenses to Baltimore are deductible, but his transportation expenses to Washington, D.C., are not. His expenses for meals and lodging while away from home are allocated between his educational pursuits and his personal activities. Those expenses that are entirely personal, such as sightseeing and entertaining friends, are not deductible.

The cost of deductible meals must be reduced by 20%.

TaxAlert

Beginning January 1, 1994, the cost of deductible meals and entertainment must be reduced by 50%.

Cruises and conventions. Certain cruises and conventions offer seminars or courses as part of their itinerary. Even if these are work-related, your deduction for travel may be limited. This applies to:

1) Travel by ocean liner, cruise ship, or other form of luxury water transportation, and
2) Conventions outside the North American area.

The limits are the same that apply to cruises and conventions for other business purposes. These are discussed under *Luxury Water Travel* and *Conventions* in Publication 463, *Travel, Entertainment, and Gift Expenses.*

Meal Expenses

If your educational expenses qualify for deduction, you can deduct the cost of meals that qualify as travel expenses.

80% limit. You can deduct only 80% of your business-related meals that were not reimbursed by your employer and that qualify for deduction. This includes meals while traveling away from home to obtain your education. Employees must use Form 2106 to apply the 80% limit.

Note. For tax years beginning after 1993, the limit will be reduced to 50%.

If your educational expenses include expenses for travel, see *Travel Expenses* in Chapter 28, *Car Expenses and Other Employee Business Expenses*.

Travel as Education

You cannot deduct the cost of travel that in itself is a form of education even though the travel may be directly related to your duties in your work or business.

Example. You are a French language teacher. While on sabbatical leave granted for travel, you traveled through France to improve your knowledge of the French language. You chose your itinerary and most of your activities to improve your French language skills. You cannot deduct your travel expenses as educational expenses, even though you spent most of your time visiting French schools and families, attending movies or plays, and learning French in similar activities.

Expenses Relating to Tax-Exempt Income

Some qualified educational assistance you receive may be tax-exempt income. This is income you receive that you are not required to report on your tax return. The rules for determining whether any item is taxable or nontaxable are not discussed here. See Chapter 13, *Other Income*, for information on the rules on tax-exempt income.

Since you do not pay tax on this income, you may not be able to deduct the related expenses. Examples of tax-exempt income include scholarships, veterans' educational assistance, and employer-provided education. If you received assistance from any of these sources, see *Expenses Relating to Tax-Exempt Income* in Publication 508.

TaxALERT

You may be eligible to exclude from income the interest you receive from qualified U.S. Savings Bonds if you pay qualified higher education expenses. These are expenses for tuition and required fees at an eligible educational institution for you, your spouse, or your dependent. A "qualified U.S. Savings Bond" is a Series EE Savings Bond that is issued after December 31, 1989, to an individual who is 24 years of age or older. If your educational expenses qualify for deduction, you must reduce the expenses by the amount of interest excluded from income. For more information on the interest exclusion, see Chapter 8, *Interest Income*.

Refund procedure for employees. Because the annual exclusion of income of up to $5,250 of employer-provided educational assistance was extended retroactively from July 1, 1992, you may be entitled to refunds of federal income, social security, and Medicare taxes paid on excludable educational assistance benefits provided in the second half of 1992 and social security and Medicare taxes paid on excludable benefits provided in 1993.

Those not entitled to refunds. If your employer continued to exclude these benefits from your income after June 30, 1992, you have not overpaid taxes on educational benefits and, are not entitled to a refund.

Employee income tax refunds. If you are entitled to an income tax refund for 1992, you can claim it by filing a Form 1040X, *Amended U.S. Individual Income Tax Return*. To do this, you need a Form W–2c *Statement of Corrected Income and Tax Amounts* from your employer showing the corrected wages.

The IRS has developed special procedures to make it easier for affected employees to get income tax refunds faster. Under these special procedures, you need only include your name, address, social security number and "1992 tax year" on the Form 1040X, sign the form, and attach your Form W–2c. To speed up the processing of these amended returns, you should write "IRC 127" in the top margin of your Form 1040X.

Earned income credit. If your Form W–2c shows corrected wages of $22,370 or less for 1992, and you qualify for the earned income credit, you should file a 1992 Schedule EIC with Form 1040X. If you received the earned income credit in 1992, you do not need to complete another Schedule EIC. The IRS will automatically recalculate the earned income credit and make the appropriate adjustments.

Employee social security and Medicare tax refunds. If you are entitled to a refund because of the change in taxation of educational assistance benefits, you may also request reimbursement of social security and Medicare taxes from your employer for 1992 and 1993. In the unusual case in which you are not able to get a refund of 1992 and 1993 social security and Medicare taxes from your employer, you can file a Form 843, *Claim for Refund and Request for Abatement* with the IRS. If you claim a refund on Form 843, you should write "IRC 127" in the top margin to speed up processing of your claim.

Other refunds due to retroactive legislation. If employer-provided educational assistance was included in your income for tax years beginning after 1988, and this assistance did not qualify for the employer-provided educational assistance exclusion, but it could have been excludable as a working condition fringe benefit, you may be entitled to an income tax refund for any open year (generally, 1990 or later year for which the statute of limitations has not expired).

If you are affected by this provision, you can file an amended income tax return (Form 1040X) for the open year or years. To do this, you need a corrected Form W–2 from your employer (Form W–2c) showing your corrected wages for the year or years. Complete the Form 1040X and attach the Form W–2c to it.

You may also be entitled to the earned income credit and refunds of social security and Medicare taxes for those years. See *Earned income credit,* and *Employee social security and Medicare tax refunds,* earlier, for the procedures for claiming the credit and the refund of the taxes (except do not write "IRC 127" at the top of any claim (Form 1040X or Form 843) you file).

How to Report Educational Expenses

Self-employed persons and employees report their educational expenses differently.

This section explains how to deduct your expenses of qualified education. If you are an employee, you must take into account any reimbursement you receive. How you treat the reimbursement depends on the type of reimbursement arrangement and the amount of the reimbursement. For information on how to report your reimbursement, see Chapter 28, *Car Expenses and Other Employee Business Expenses*.

Self-Employed Persons

Self-employed persons must report their educational expenses on the appropriate form used to report their business income and expenses.

For example, if you are a sole proprietor or an independent contractor, use Schedule C or Schedule C–EZ. If you use Schedule C, list and total your educational expenses for tuition, books, laboratory fees, and similar items on line 46 and enter them on line 27. List your transportation and travel expenses for education on lines 10 and 24 of Schedule C. See the instructions for the form that you file for more information.

Employees

To deduct expenses of work-related education, you must take into account all of the following.

1) Your expenses must be for qualified education.
2) You must file Form 1040.
3) You generally must itemize your deductions on Schedule A (Form 1040). Your educational expenses are deducted on line 19 as a miscellaneous deduction. You can deduct only your expenses over 2% of adjusted gross income from line 32 of Form 1040.
4) You may need to complete Form 2106 if your expenses for education include meal and transportation expenses or if you receive reimbursement from your employer.

Note. If your adjusted gross income is more than $108,450 ($54,225 if you are married filing separately), your deduction for itemized deductions may be limited. See Chapter 21, *Limit on Itemized Deductions*.

If you are a *qualified performing artist,* you may deduct work-related educational expenses even if you do not itemize your deductions. See *Performing Artists* in Publication 529, *Miscellaneous Deductions,* for more information.

Form 2106. Whether you must report your educational expenses on Form 2106 depends primarily on the type of expense, the type of reimbursement or allowance arrangement, and the amount of reimbursement. Reimbursement arrangements are explained in Chapter 28, *Car Expenses and Other Employee Business Expenses*.

Employee business expenses, including educational expenses, are reported on Form 2106. Use this form to figure your allowable travel, transportation, meal, and other work-related expenses of education. To deduct these expenses, complete Part I of Form 2106 and enter the result on Schedule A (Form 1040) as a miscellaneous itemized deduction. (Use Part II only if you have personal vehicle expenses.) Part I of Form 2106 has three steps:

- Step 1 shows your total business expenses. Lines 1 through 3 are for travel and transportation expenses that are related to your qualifying education. Line 4 is for educational expenses such as tuition and books. Line 5 is for meals while traveling away from home to obtain education.
- Step 2 shows amounts your employer gave you (your reimbursement) for the expenses listed in Step 1. These are amounts your employer did not include as wages in box 1 of your Form W–2.
- Step 3 figures the expenses to deduct on Schedule A (Form 1040). If your employer did not reimburse you, or reimbursed you under a nonaccountable plan, for work-related meals, your deduction is limited to 80% of your expenses. This allowable amount is figured on lines 8 through 10. The allowable meal expenses are added to your other unreimbursed expenses and the total is entered on line 19 of Schedule A (Form 1040).

Exception. You do not have to complete Form 2106 if either of the following applies:

1) Your reimbursements not included in box 1 of Form W–2 are at least as much as your deductible expenses. (Do not deduct the expenses or report the reimbursement as income.)
2) You are not deducting any expenses for travel, transportation, meals, or entertainment, and you were not reimbursed for any expenses. (Unreimbursed expenses for tuition, books, and lab fees can be listed directly on line 19 of Schedule A of Form 1040.)

Even if you were not reimbursed, you must file Form 2106 if you are a *qualified performing artist* or an *individual with a disability claiming impairment-related work expenses.* See Publication 529, *Miscellaneous Deductions.*

Schedule A (Form 1040). Unreimbursed educational expenses, or expenses that are more than the amount reimbursed by your employer, are entered on line 19 of Schedule A (Form 1040). Generally, you must first use Form 2106 to compute the amount to enter on line 19. To claim these educational expenses, you must be able to itemize your deductions on Schedule A (Form 1040). (If you're not sure whether you can itemize, see Chapter 20, *Standard Deduction*.)

You can deduct only the amount of job expenses and most other miscellaneous deductions that is more than 2% of your adjusted gross income. This 2% limit is applied after all other deduction limits have been applied (such as the 80% limit on meal expenses, discussed earlier).

Recordkeeping

You must keep proof to support your claim to a deduction as long as your income tax return can be examined. Generally, you should keep your records for 3 years from the date of filing the return and claiming the deduction. For specific information about keeping records of business expenses, see *Recordkeeping* in Chapter 28.

30 | Miscellaneous Deductions

Introduction

This chapter covers a variety of expenses that you are allowed to deduct. These expenses can be broadly broken down into three categories: deductible employee expenses, deductible expenses of producing income, and other deductible expenses. Just as important, this chapter tells you what type of items you may not deduct.

The general rule is that you may deduct any expense that is related to your trade or business, that is connected with producing other income, or that is paid to determine your tax. Expenses other than these are generally considered personal and probably may not be deducted. But, as is often the case, with careful and proper planning, you may be able to deduct more than you think.

It is more difficult to deduct the majority of miscellaneous expenses in 1993. Only the amount of those expenses that, as a group, exceed 2% of your adjusted gross income is deductible. Also bear in mind that, if your miscellaneous expenses include meals and entertainment, only 80% of those expenses are deductible before arriving at the amount subject to the 2% floor. Further, your 1993 miscellaneous itemized deductions may also be subject to an additional limitation if your adjusted gross income exceeds $108,450.

Important Reminder

Limit on itemized deductions. For 1993, if your adjusted gross income is more than $108,450 ($54,225 if you are married filing separately), the overall amount of your itemized deductions may be limited. See Chapter 21, *Limit on Itemized Deductions*, if you need more information about this limit.

This chapter explains what expenses you can claim as miscellaneous itemized deductions on **Schedule A** (Form 1040). You must reduce the total of most miscellaneous itemized deductions by 2% of your adjusted gross income. This chapter identifies:

- Deductions subject to the 2% limit,
- Deductions not subject to the 2% limit, and
- Expenses you cannot deduct.

It also describes how to report your deductions.

Expenses in each category are first presented in a convenient list. Following each list is information about those items that need more explanation.

Useful Items

You may want to see:

Publication

- ☐ **463** Travel, Entertainment, and Gift Expenses
- ☐ **525** Taxable and Nontaxable Income
- ☐ **529** Miscellaneous Deductions
- ☐ **534** Depreciation
- ☐ **535** Business Expenses
- ☐ **587** Business Use of Your Home
- ☐ **917** Business Use of a Car
- ☐ **946** How To Begin Depreciating Your Property

Form (and Instructions)

- ☐ **2106** Employee Business Expenses

Deductions Subject to the 2% Limit

You can deduct the following expenses only as miscellaneous itemized deductions on Schedule A (Form 1040). You can claim them only to the extent that the total you claim is more than 2% of your adjusted gross income. This means you figure your deduction by subtracting 2% of your adjusted gross income from the total amount of these expenses. You can find your adjusted gross income on line 32, Form 1040.

Generally, you apply the 2% limit after you apply any other deduction limit (such as the 80% limit on business-related meals and entertainment).

Deductions subject to the 2% limit are discussed in the two general categories that are shown on Schedule A (Form 1040): unreimbursed employee expenses and other expenses. But see Chapter 28 if you have unreimbursed employee business expenses for travel, transportation, entertainment, or gifts.

Explanation
Business travel and entertainment. Generally, only 80% of the amount spent for business meals (including meals away from home on overnight business) and entertainment will be deductible. This limit must be applied before arriving at the amount subject to the 2% floor.

TaxAlert
Beginning after 1993, the deductible portion of business meals and entertainment expenses is limited to 50%.

Business gifts. You can deduct no more than $25 for business gifts to any one person per year. See Chapter 28, *Car Expenses and Other Employee Business Expenses,* for more information.

Exception for performing artists. If you are a qualifying performing artist, you may be able to deduct your employee business expenses as an adjustment to gross income rather than as a miscellaneous itemized deduction. See *Special Rules* in Chapter 28 if you need more information about this exception. This exception only applies to performing artists with adjusted gross incomes of not more than $16,000 before deducting these expenses.

List of Unreimbursed Employee Business Expenses

To be deductible, an unreimbursed employee business expense must be:

1) Paid or incurred by you during the taxable year,
2) For carrying on your trade or business of being an employee, and
3) An ordinary and necessary expense.

An expense is *ordinary* if it is common and accepted in that type of trade or business. An expense is *necessary* if it is appropriate and helpful to your trade or business.

Explanation
Unreimbursed employee business expenses. If you are an employee and have business expenses that are not reimbursed or that are more than the amount reimbursed by your employer, you can generally deduct them only as a miscellaneous deduction (subject to the 2% limit) on Schedule A (Form 1040).

The following common expenses that meet these requirements are deductible.

- Business bad debt of employee
- Business liability insurance premiums
- Damages paid to former employer for breach of employment contract
- Depreciation on a home computer or cellular telephone your employer requires you to use in your work
- Dues to chamber of commerce if membership helps you do your job
- Dues to professional societies
- Education that is employment related (see Chapter 29)
- Home office or part of home used regularly and exclusively in work
- Job search expenses in your present occupation
- Laboratory breakage fees
- Malpractice insurance premiums
- Medical examinations required by employer
- Occupational taxes you paid
- Passport for business trip
- Repayment of income aid payment
- Research expenses of a college professor
- Subscriptions to professional journals and trade magazines related to your work
- Tools and supplies used in your work
- Travel, transportation, entertainment, and gift expenses that are unreimbursed and related to your work (see Chapter 28)
- Union dues and expenses
- Work clothes and uniforms if required and not suitable for everyday use

Examples
A corporate executive could deduct the cost of insurance against the hazard of sudden dismissal from her job for reasons other than her own actions or disability.

An elected official was allowed a deduction for expenses incurred in fighting against attempts to hold a special election to vote him out of office.

TaxPlanner
If you can get your employer to reimburse you for what would otherwise be unreimbursed business expenses in lieu of an equal amount of salary, you should do so. You gain at no additional cost to your employer. Reimbursed employee business expenses for which you have adequately accounted to your employer are not subject to the 2% floor that might otherwise limit their deductibility. The reimbursement for those expenses is also not included on your Form W-2.

Business Liability Insurance
You can deduct insurance premiums you paid for protection against personal liability for wrongful acts on the job.

Damages for Breach of Employment Contract
If you break an employment contract, you can deduct damages you pay your former employer if the damages are attributable to the pay you received from that employer.

Depreciation on Home Computers or Cellular Telephones

If you purchased a home computer or cellular telephone, you can claim a depreciation deduction if you use these items in your work as an employee and you meet the following tests. Your use of these items must be:

1) For the convenience of your employer, and
2) Required as a condition of your employment.

If you use your computer to produce income other than from a business, such as from investments, see *Depreciation on Home Computer,* under *List of Other Expenses,* later.

For more information about the rules and exceptions to the rules affecting the allowable deductions for a home computer or cellular telephone, see *Depreciation on Home Computers or Cellular Telephones* in Publication 529.

TaxOrganizer

In case the IRS challenges your deductions for depreciation on home computers or cellular telephones, you should keep the following information to support your claim for home computer and cellular telephone depreciation deductions:

- Documentation from your employer that use of the home computer or cellular telephone is required by the employer; and
- A log of time spent using the computer or cellular phone and whether such time was for personal or business use.

Reporting and recordkeeping. To claim the depreciation deduction for these items, you must complete Part V of **Form 4562,** *Depreciation and Amortization,* and attach the form to your tax return. Also, you must maintain records to prove your percentage of business use.

For more information about depreciation (including the section 179 deduction) and recordkeeping requirements, get Publication 946, *How To Begin Depreciating Your Property.*

TaxPlanner

Personal computers. Home computers are frequently used for both business and personal purposes. Video games, children's homework, holiday card lists, and personal finances are considered personal uses. Although many families have business cars and personal cars, it is unlikely—at least for now—that a family has a business computer and a personal computer. Therefore, some type of allocation should be made between business use and personal use.

Adequate records must be maintained to support your business use of the property in order to claim a depreciation expense deduction. For details, see Chapter 10, *Rental Income and Expenses*. The section 179 deduction is explained in Chapter 36, *If You Are Self-Employed*.

The point to remember is this: It's difficult to claim tax breaks on your home computer.

The IRS position is that no deduction will be allowed for a personal computer unless it is a condition of employment and is exclusively used at the employee's place of business.

Dues to Chamber of Commerce

You can deduct dues paid to a chamber of commerce or similar organization if membership helps you carry out the duties of your job.

TaxAlert

Effective after 1993, no deduction is allowed for club dues. The intent of this law appears to be a denial of dues paid to a club that is organized for a social purpose but used for a business purpose by the taxpayer. Examples of such clubs include luncheon, athletic, sporting, hotel, airport, and country clubs. Specific business expenses, such as meals and entertainment that occur at a club would be deductible to the extent that they otherwise satisfy the standard for deductibility. For details, see Chapter 28, *Car Expenses and Other Employee Business Expenses.*

TaxPlanner

You may want to consider prepaying certain club dues by December 31, 1993, assuming the club has billed you in advance for club dues not in excess of 12 months. There are limitations on the extent to which a prepaid expense can be deducted. For example, in the past, the IRS limited deductions for an individual's prepaid miscellaneous business and investment expenses. If you make a payment in the current year as a prepayment for several years of expense, the IRS may only allow a deduction for the portion of the payment that relates to the year immediately following the tax year in which the payment is made.

Home Office

If you use a part of your home regularly and exclusively for business purposes, you may be able to deduct a part of the operating and depreciation expenses on your home. You cannot deduct any part of your personal expenses that are for family household purposes.

TaxAlert

Individuals claiming home office deductions on Schedule C are required to figure those deductions on Form 8829, *Expenses for Business Use of Your Home.* However, if you are an employee claiming unreimbursed job-related expenses, use Form 2106, if applicable, or include the amount directly on Schedule A. See *How to Report,* later in this chapter.

Requirements for claiming the deduction. You may deduct certain expenses for operating a part of your home only if that part of your home is used *regularly* and *exclusively* as:

1) Your principal place of business for any trade or business in which you engage, or

2) A place to meet or deal with your patients, clients, or customers in the normal course of your trade or business.

You may also deduct certain expenses of operating a separate structure not attached to your home, if you use it regularly and exclusively for your trade or business.

In addition, if the regular and exclusive business use is for your work as an employee, the use must be *for the convenience of your employer* and not just appropriate and helpful in your job.

If you claim a home office deduction based on meeting with patients, clients, or customers, you must physically meet with them on your premises, and your meetings with them must be substantial and integral to the conduct of your business. Occasional meetings and telephone calls are insufficient.

You can have a principal place of business for each trade or business in which you engage. For example, as a teacher, your principal place of business for teaching is the school. If you also engage in a retail sales business and use part of your home as your principal place of business for retail selling, expenses for this business use of your home may be deductible.

Explanation
A deduction for the business use of a home is allowed whether you are an employee or a self-employed person. A home may be a house, an apartment, a condominium, a mobile home, or even a boat. It may also be other structures on the same property as the house you live in, such as a studio, a barn, a greenhouse, or an unattached garage.

The office at home must be maintained for the convenience of your employer. It is not sufficient that the home office is helpful to your job; it must be a requirement of your employer and justified by the nature of your job.

Generally, teachers are not allowed to deduct home office expenses.

Oddly enough, the courts have held that the principal place of business of an employer need not be the principal place of business for his or her employees. Thus, a musician who was required to practice many hours to maintain and perfect his skills was allowed an office as a home deduction because his employer did not have any private practice rooms.

TaxAlert
The Supreme Court recently reached a decision which makes it more difficult for most employees to qualify for a home office deduction. While the law states that the home must be used as a "principal place of business," the Court's interpretation of that phrase is very restrictive. The two primary factors in determining whether a deduction is allowed are 1) the relative importance of the activities performed at home and at the employer's office, and 2) the amount of time spent at each location. The necessity of the activities performed at home is now much less significant than it used to be. Futhermore, the fact that an employer may not provide adequate office space is not relevant in determining the "principal place of business." As a result of this decision, you should exercise caution if you plan to deduct any home office expenses.

TaxPlanner
If you cannot substantiate that your home activities are more important than those at your other work locations and that you spend more time working at home than at the office, there may still be two ways to qualify for the deduction. One is to use your home to meet with clients, patients, or customers on a regular basis. The other is to have a separate structure (e.g., an unattached garage) which is used exclusively for business.

Examples
A college professor could not deduct the expenses of maintaining one room in his home as an office, even though the college did not provide him with an office.

A taxpayer who claimed a deduction for a home office because he dealt with clients and customers by phone from his home was denied the deduction by a court.

A deduction was denied to a taxpayer's wife who used an office at home to maintain the records of an electronics repair business, pay bills pertaining to the business, and prepare the employee payroll. All the repair work was done and all customers delivered and picked up their merchandise at the business's main location.

Exceptions

- A recent court case held that a college professor should have been allowed to deduct home office expenses because his principal place of business was not the college where he taught but his home office, where he did the research and writing required to retain his position.
- The owner of a laundromat was allowed a deduction for an office in her home when the court determined that she spent most of her time in the home office, performed her most important managerial functions there, and had a valid business reason for not establishing an office at the laundromat.

TaxPlanner
A home office may be used for *any* trade or business you are engaged in—it does not have to be your *principal* trade or business.

Example
You are a lawyer who maintains offices outside your home. You also maintain an office at home from which you actively manage rental properties that you own. The expenses of your home office are deductible in calculating the net income from your rental activities.

You cannot deduct any operating or depreciation expenses for the use of your home if the use is not in a trade or business. For example, you cannot deduct these expenses if you use a part of your home, even though regularly and exclusively, to read financial periodicals and reports, clip bond coupons, and perform similar investment activities on your own behalf, because these activities are not a trade or business.

Explanation

See *Other Expenses* for a discussion of expenses that are deductible by investors.

The use of a part of your home for both personal and business purposes does not meet the exclusive use test, and you cannot deduct expenses for business use. If, for example, you use the den of your home to write legal briefs, prepare tax returns, or perform similar activities, as well as for personal purposes, you cannot deduct any expenses for the business use of that part of your home.

For more information on requirements for claiming the deduction, see Publication 587, *Business Use of Your Home.*

Explanation

The exclusive-use rule does not apply to people who use their home to provide day care for children, persons age 65 or older, or individuals who are physically or mentally incapable of caring for themselves. The day care provider must be licensed or certified under applicable state law, or exempt from licensing, for this exception to apply.

How to figure the deduction. To figure the percentage of your home used for business, you may compare the square feet of space used for business to the total square feet in your home. Or, if the rooms in your home are approximately the same size, you may compare the number of rooms used for business to the total number of rooms in your home. You may also use any other reasonable method. Generally, you figure the business part of your expenses by applying the percentage to the total of each expense.

Example

The room in your home that you use for business measures 120 square feet. Your home measures 1,200 square feet. Therefore, you are using one-tenth, or 10%, of the total area for business.

If you use one room for business in a five-room house and the rooms in your home are about the same size, you are using one-fifth, or 20%, of the total area for business.

TaxSaver

Day-care providers who operate businesses in their homes may benefit from a recent IRS ruling. The square footage of a room that is regularly used for day care and is available throughout the business day will be considered used for day care for the entire business day. Previously, taxpayers had to take partial days based on the hours of actual business use. The deduction for day-care providers is equal to the total costs of maintaining the home (i.e. electricity, gas, water, trash collection, general maintenance, etc.) to provide day care, multiplied by the following two fractions:

$$\frac{\text{Total square feet available and used regularly each day}}{\text{Total square feet of home}}$$

$$\frac{\text{Total hours each year home used for day care business}}{\text{Total hours each year (8,760 hours)}}$$

The resulting deduction is subject to the income limitation, discussed below. IRS Form 8829 will help you work through this calculation

Example

A day-care provider uses a bedroom (available for child care throughout the business day) for the children's morning and afternoon naps every day. Although the bedroom is not used during every hour of the business day, the total square footage of that room is considered as day-care usage for the entire business day when the total area for business is calculated.

Limit on the deduction. The deduction for the business use of your home is limited to the gross income from that business use minus the sum of:

1) The business percentage of the otherwise deductible mortgage interest, real estate taxes, and casualty and theft losses, and
2) The expenses for your business that are not attributable to the use of your home (for example, salaries or supplies).

Repairs. You can deduct the cost of painting and repairing rooms that are used only for business purposes, subject to the limit. You cannot deduct the costs of painting and repairing rooms used for other purposes.

You can deduct part of the cost of painting the outside of your home or repairing the roof based on the percentage of your home used for business. However, you cannot deduct expenses for lawn care and landscaping.

Explanation

The general rule is that the expenses you have for maintaining and running your entire home may be taken in part as deductions, since they benefit both the business and the personal parts of your home.

TaxOrganizer

To support your claim for the "business use of home" deduction, you should keep the following information:

- Receipts, cancelled checks, credit card slips, etc., evidencing payment of repair and maintenance expenses; and
- A notation indicating whether the repair and maintenance expenses benefit only the business part of the home or the entire home. An expense benefitting the entire home may qualify for a partial deduction since it benefits both the business and the personal parts of the home.

If you have purchased your home, you may deduct part of the interest you pay on your home mortgage as a business expense. To figure the business part of your mortgage interest, multiply the mortgage interest by the part of your home used for business. If you rent a home, you may deduct part of the rent you pay using a similar calculation.

If you have a casualty loss (see Chapter 26, *Nonbusiness Casualty and Theft Losses*) on your home or other property that you use in business, you may deduct the business part of the loss as a business expense. The amount of the loss that qualifies for a deduction depends on what property is affected. If the loss is sustained on property that you use only in your business, the entire loss is treated as a business deduction. If the loss affects property used for both business and personal purposes, only the business part is a business deduction.

If you use part of your home for business, you may also deduct part of the expenses for utilities and services, such as electricity, gas, trash removal, and cleaning services. Expenses that are related only to your business, such as business long-distance telephone calls and depreciation of office furniture and equipment, are fully deductible.

Likewise, if you use part of your home for business, you may deduct part of your insurance on your home. However, if your insurance premium gives you coverage for a period that extends past the end of your tax year, you may deduct for business only the part of the premium that covers you for the tax year.

Example

If you paid a 2-year premium of $240 on September 1, 1993, only 4 months of the policy are included in your 1993 tax year. Therefore, only four-twenty-fourths (1/6) of the premium is deductible in 1993. In 1994, you may deduct twelve-twenty-fourths (1/2), and in 1995 eight-twenty-fourths (1/3) would be deductible.

Explanation

When it comes to repairs, you may deduct the cost of labor and supplies for the business part of your home. Your own labor, however, is not a deductible expense.

Example

A repair to your furnace benefits the entire home. If 10% of the area of your home is used for business, 10% of the cost of the furnace repair is deductible.

Depreciation. You can deduct depreciation on the part of your home used for business subject to the *limit on the deduction* discussed above. For more information on depreciation of your home, see Publication 587.

Home leased to employer. If you lease any part of your home to your employer, you cannot claim a home office deduction for that part for any period you use that part of your home to perform services for your employer.

TaxPlanner

Storage use. You can deduct certain business expenses for the part of your home that you regularly use to store goods you sell at retail or wholesale in your trade or business. Your home must be the only fixed location of that business. This storage space can have other uses, but the space must be a specific area.

Example

Your home is the sole fixed location of your business of selling mechanics' tools at retail. You regularly use half of your basement for inventory storage and occasionally use the same space for personal purposes. The expenses for the storage space are deductible, even though this part of your basement is not used exclusively for business.

TaxPlanner

Many home sales operations require a great deal of personal time and attention but produce a minimum of deductible expenses. The storage use concept may produce valuable deductions for otherwise underutilized spaces, such as attics and basements. Remember, the storage space must be a specific area that is used as a part of your principal place of business.

Example

A recent court decision held that a home sale distributor who used his storage room and den, but not his living room, exclusively for business activities was entitled to a home office deduction for his use of the storage room and den.

How to report. If you are an employee, you generally report your expenses for the business use of your home (insurance, maintenance, utilities, depreciation) on **Form 2106,** if you are required to file that form. You then carry over the amount on line 11 of Form 2106 to line 19 of Schedule A (Form 1040). If you are not required to file Form 2106, enter the amount directly on line 19 of Schedule A.

Include the home office expenses for mortgage interest, real estate taxes, and casualty and theft losses on the appropriate lines of Schedule A, along with your deductible nonbusiness expenses in those categories.

Records. You should keep records that will give the information needed to figure the deduction according to these rules. Also keep canceled checks or account statements, and receipts of the expenses paid, to prove the deductions you claim.

TaxOrganizer

If you intend to deduct home office expenses, it is extremely important that you keep adequate records. You should keep records of: clients who come to your house, hours worked at home, and office equipment purchases. Additionally, you should keep track of repairs that can be allocated to your home office. See the *Records You Should Keep* section at the front of this book for other items that you should keep.

Examples

The courts have denied deductions in the following cases:

- An attorney had a computer consulting business at home but collected income from his consulting business through his legal practice. He did not bill clients separately for legal and consulting work. Consequently, the court concluded that he received no income from his consulting business and denied his home office deduction.

- A salesman in the movie industry testified that, in his opinion, 25% of his house (including pool and watchdog) was devoted to business use. However he offered no specific evidence (written or otherwise) of what business purpose that space served or which business activities took place.
- An attorney lost $3,800 in deductions over 2 years because he could not produce substantiating evidence; the records had been destroyed by a flood in his basement.

For more information on using your home in your work and how to compute your allowable deduction, get Publication 587.

Explanation

Your business deductions for the business use of your home are deducted in the following order:

1. The business percentage of the expenses that would otherwise be allowable as deductions, that is, mortgage interest, real estate taxes, and deductible casualty losses.
2. The direct expenses for your business in your home, such as expenses for supplies and compensation, but not the other expenses of the office in your home (such as those listed in item 3, below).
3. The other expenses for the business use of your home, such as maintenance, utilities, insurance, and depreciation. Deductions that adjust the basis in your home are taken last.

Deductions for the business use of your home may not create or add to a business loss. However, the excess of your home office expenses over the income from your business may be carried over to your next tax year and deducted in that year, assuming that you have income from the business in the next tax year. If you do not have income from the business in the next tax year, the deductions may be carried to any later year in which you have gross income from the business.

Example

Peggy Green is an employee who works in her home for the convenience of her employer. She uses 20% of her home regularly and exclusively for this business purpose. In 1993, her gross income, expenses for the business, and computation of the deduction for the business use of her home are as follows:

Gross income from business use of home		$7,500
Minus:		
Business percentage (20% of home use) of mortgage interest and real estate taxes	$2,000	
Other business expenses (supplies, transportation, etc.)	5,000	7,000
Modified net income		$ 500

Business use of home expenses		
Maintenance, insurance, utilities (20%)........		$ 800
Depreciation (20%)		700
Total		$1,500
Deduction limited to modified net income		500
Carryover expenses to 1994 (subject to income limitation in 1994).............................		$1,000

The deduction of $500 is considered to be maintenance, insurance, and utilities. Peggy will not reduce the basis in her home for the $700 of depreciation until that amount is deducted in a future year.

Job Search Expenses

You may be able to deduct certain expenses you have in looking for a new job in your present occupation, even if you do not get a new job. You cannot deduct these expenses if you are looking for a job in a new occupation, even if you get the job.

If you are unemployed, the kind of work you did for your past employer is your occupation. If there is a substantial break between the time of your past job and your looking for a new one, you cannot deduct your expenses.

You cannot deduct your expenses if you are seeking employment for the first time, even if you get the job.

Examples

- A certified public accountant employed by a national accounting firm was permitted to deduct expenses incurred in investigating whether or not he could practice his profession as a **self-employed** person.
- A corporate executive could deduct expenses involved in seeking a position as a corporate executive with another corporation.
- An attorney for a state agency could deduct the costs of taking an examination for a position as an attorney in another city because the new position would be in the same trade or business.
- An unemployed electrician was allowed to deduct transportation costs for going to the union hall to check on potential job opportunities. He was considered to be in the electrical trade, even though he was unemployed at the time.

Employment and outplacement agency fees. You can deduct employment and outplacement agency fees you pay in looking for a new job in your present occupation.

If, in a later year, your employer pays you back for employment agency fees, you must include the amount you receive in your gross income to the extent of your tax benefit in the earlier year (which is explained under *Recoveries* in Chapter 13, *Other Income*). If your employer pays the fees directly to the employment agency and you were not responsible for them, you do not include them in your gross income.

Job search expenses and fees are deductible, even if the agency does not find you a suitable job.

Expenses for career counseling are deductible if they are incurred in your effort to find other employment in the same trade or business.

TaxOrganizer

In case the IRS challenges your deduction for job search expenses, you should keep the following information to support your claim for job search expense deductions:

- Evidence of your current occupation at the time the job search expenses were incurred;
- Written records, such as a letter from a prospective employer or an employment agency contract, evidencing a search for employment and the nature of the job;
- Receipts, cancelled checks, credit card slips, plane tickets, etc., evidencing the amount and payment of job search expenses;
- Detailed records and evidence of costs, such as automobile mileage, for which a direct payment is not made; and
- A log allocating the time spent while traveling on personal activities compared to the time spent looking for a job.

Résumé. You can deduct amounts you spend for typing, printing, and mailing copies of a résumé to prospective employers if you spent the amounts in looking for a new job in your present occupation.

Travel and transportation expenses. If you travel to an area and, while there, you look for a new job in your present occupation, you may be able to deduct travel expenses to and from the area. To be deductible, the trip must be primarily to look for a new job. The amount of time you spend on personal activity compared to the amount of time you spend in looking for work is important in determining whether the trip is primarily personal and not deductible.

Even if the travel expenses to and from an area are not deductible, you can deduct the expenses of looking for a new job in your present occupation, while in the area.

If you use the standard mileage rate to figure your car expenses, use 28 cents per mile. See Chapter 28 for more information. If your job search expenses include travel and transportation expenses, you must file Form 2106, as discussed later under *How to Report.*

Repayment of Income Aid Payment
If you repay a lump-sum income aid payment that you received and included in income in an earlier year, you can deduct the repayment. An "income aid payment" is one that is received under an employer's plan to aid employees who lose their jobs due to lack of work.

Research Expenses of a College Professor
If you are a college professor, you can deduct research expenses, including travel expenses, for teaching, lecturing, or writing and publishing on subjects that relate directly to the field of your teaching duties. The research must be undertaken as a means of carrying out the duties expected of a professor and without expec-

tation of profit apart from salary. However, no deduction is allowed for travel as a form of education.

Tools Used in Your Work
Generally, amounts you spend for tools used in your work are deductible expenses if the tools wear out and are thrown away within one year from the date of purchase. The cost of tools expected to last more than a year can be depreciated. For more information about depreciation, get Publication 946.

Union Dues and Expenses
You can deduct dues and initiation fees you pay for union membership.

You can also deduct assessments for benefit payments to unemployed union members. However, you cannot deduct the part of the assessments or contributions that provides funds for the payment of sick, accident, or death benefits. Also, you cannot deduct contributions to a pension fund even if the union requires you to make such contributions.

A fine paid by a union member is deductible if by not paying the fine the member would be dropped from the union.

If a union contract provides that all employees, regardless of whether or not they are union members, must pay union dues, the nonmembers may also deduct the union dues.

Work Clothes and Uniforms
You can deduct the cost and upkeep of work clothes only if you must wear them as a condition of your employment and they are not suitable for everyday wear. To qualify for the deduction, both conditions must be met. It is not enough that you wear distinctive clothing; the clothing must be specifically required by your employer. Nor is it enough that you do not in fact wear your work clothes away from work; the clothing must not be suitable for taking the place of your regular clothing.

Examples of workers who may be required to wear uniforms which qualify are: delivery workers, firefighters, health care workers, law enforcement officers, letter carriers, professional athletes, and transportation workers (air, rail, bus, etc.).

Musicians and entertainers can deduct the cost of theatrical clothing and accessories if they are not suitable for everyday wear.

However, work clothing consisting of white cap, white shirt or white jacket, white bib overalls, and standard work shoes, which a painter is required by his union to wear on the job, is not distinctive in character or in the nature of a uniform. Similarly, the costs of buying and maintaining blue work clothes worn by a welder at the request of a foreman are not deductible.

Protective clothing. You can deduct the cost of protective clothing required in your work, such as safety shoes or boots, safety glasses, hard hats, and work gloves.

Examples of workers who may be required to wear safety items are: carpenters, cement workers, chemical workers, electricians, fishing boat crew members, machinists, oil field workers, pipe fitters, steamfitters, and truck drivers.

Military uniforms. You generally cannot deduct the cost of your uniforms if you are on full-time active duty in the armed forces. However, if you are an armed forces reservist, you can deduct the unreimbursed cost of your uniform if military regulations restrict you from wearing it except while on duty as a reservist. In figuring the deduction, you must reduce the cost by any nontaxable allowance you receive for these expenses.

If local military rules do not allow you to wear fatigue uniforms when you are off duty, you can deduct the amount by which the cost of buying and keeping up these uniforms is more than the uniform allowance you receive.

If you are a student at an armed forces academy, you cannot deduct the cost of your uniforms if they replace regular clothing. However, you can deduct the cost of insignia, shoulder boards, and related items.

You can deduct the cost of your uniforms if you are a civilian faculty or staff member of a military school.

Explanation

The initial expense and the costs of maintaining work clothes and business uniforms are deductible, not only if they must be worn as a condition of employment and they are not suitable for general or personal use, but also if they are not in fact used for personal purposes. Taxpayers have been allowed to deduct costs relating to uniforms in the following cases:

- An art teacher deducted the costs of protective smocks.
- An airline clerk deducted the cost of "unfeminine, businesslike" shoes that she was required to wear and, in fact, wore only at work.
- A hospital worker deducted work clothes he kept in a locker at the hospital. He was in frequent contact with contagious persons and never brought the clothing home.
- A private-duty nurse deducted a uniform that served as a mark of her profession and was necessary for patient care.
- A member of the National Ski Patrol was allowed to deduct the cost of the parkas and ski trousers patrol members are required to wear.
- Scoutmasters, Red Cross volunteers, and others who wear uniforms while performing charitable activities may deduct the cost of the uniforms as charitable donations.

List of Other Expenses

You can deduct certain other expenses as miscellaneous itemized deductions subject to the 2% of adjusted gross income limit. You claim them on line 20 of Schedule A (Form 1040). These are expenses you pay:

1) To produce or collect income,
2) To manage, conserve, or maintain property held for producing income, or
3) To determine, contest, pay, or claim a refund of any tax.

The expenses for (1) and (2) above must be directly related to the income or income-producing property, and the income must be taxable to you.

These other expenses include:

- Appraisal fees for a casualty loss or charitable contribution
- Clerical help and office rent in caring for investments
- Depreciation on home computers to the extent used for investments
- Excess deductions (including administrative expenses) allowed a beneficiary on termination of an estate or trust

- Fees to collect interest and dividends
- Hobby expenses, but generally not more than hobby income
- Indirect miscellaneous deductions of pass-through entities
- Investment fees and expenses
- Legal fees related to producing or collecting taxable income, doing or keeping your job, or getting tax advice
- Loss on deposits in an insolvent or bankrupt financial institution
- Repayments of income
- Repayments of social security benefits
- Safe deposit box rental
- Service charges on dividend reinvestment plans
- Tax advice and preparation fees, including fees for electronic filing
- Trustee's fees for your IRA, if separately billed and paid

If the income is only partially taxable, see *Tax-Exempt Income Expenses,* later, under *Nondeductible Expenses.*

Explanation

Deductions have also been allowed for the following:

Monthly service charges paid to a bank to participate in an automatic investment service plan.

Service charges subtracted from cash dividends before the dividends are reinvested.

Premiums on indemnity bonds posted to secure replacement of lost taxable securities.

Trustee's commission for administering a revocable trust.

Expenses incurred by an official of the National Association of Investment Clubs in attending conventions.

Transportation and parking costs on trips to the taxpayer's stockbroker.

Packing, moving, and storage expenses of condominium furniture when the only tenant the taxpayer could find wanted the unit unfurnished.

Depreciation on a safe used to store securities and other financial certificates.

Expenses incurred in moving the office in which a taxpayer carries on his or her investment activities to a new location.

Postage related to investment activities.

A fee paid to a broker engaged to find another company that could be merged with the taxpayer's closely-held company, even though no company was found.

Safe-deposit box rental when the box was used to store Series EE Treasury Bonds, even though no income is reportable in the tax year because the taxpayer elected to report the appreciation when the bonds matured.(See Chapter 8, *Interest Income,* for details.)

Entertainment expenses in connection with taxable investments.

Investor's payment to a stockholders' committee that sought changes in corporate management.

Travel expenses to a director's meeting of a director who was also a substantial minority shareholder (The taxpayer feared that the policies of the majority would endanger his investment. Because the expense was incurred to protect his investment, it was deductible.)

Costs incurred in a proxy fight opposing management.

Explanation
You may deduct a reward paid for the return of business property you have lost.

Example
A man left his briefcase on the train. A deduction was allowed for the reward given and the cost of the ad offering the reward.

Appraisal Fees
You can deduct appraisal fees if you pay them to figure a casualty loss or the fair market value of donated property.

Clerical Help and Office Rent
You can deduct office expenses, such as rent and clerical help, that you have in connection with your investments and collecting the taxable income on them.

Depreciation on Home Computer
You can deduct depreciation on your home computer to the extent you use it to produce income (for example, managing your investments that produce taxable income). If you work as an employee and use the computer in that work, see *Depreciation on Home Computers or Cellular Telephones* under *List of Unreimbursed Employee Business Expenses,* earlier. For more information on depreciation, see Publication 946.

Excess Deductions of an Estate
If the deductions in the estate's last tax year (other than deductions for personal exemptions and charitable contributions) are more than gross income for that year, the beneficiaries succeeding to the estate's property can claim such excess as a deduction in figuring taxable income. The beneficiaries can claim the deduction only for the tax year in which or with which the estate terminates, whether the year of termination is a normal year or a short tax year. For more information, see Publication 559, *Survivors, Executors, and Administrators.*

Fees to Collect Interest and Dividends
You can deduct fees you pay to a broker, bank, trustee, or similar agent to collect your taxable bond interest or dividends on shares of stock. But you cannot deduct a fee you pay to a broker to buy investment property, such as stocks or bonds. You must add the fee to the cost of the property.

You cannot deduct the fee you pay to a broker to sell securities unless you are a dealer in securities. You must offset the fee against the selling price.

Hobby Expenses
You can generally deduct hobby expenses, but only up to the amount of hobby income. A hobby is not a business, because it is not carried on to make a profit. See *Activity not for profit* in Chapter 13 under *Miscellaneous Taxable Income.*

Indirect Deductions of Pass-Through Entities
Pass-through entities include partnerships, S corporations, and mutual funds. Deductions of pass-through entities are passed through to the partners or shareholders. If the deductions are miscellaneous itemized deductions, they are generally subject to the 2% limit.

Information returns. You should receive information returns from these entities. Partnerships and S corporations issue **Schedule K–1,** which lists the items and amounts you must report, and identifies the tax return schedules and lines to use.

Example. You are a member of an investment club that is formed solely to invest in securities. The club is treated as a partnership. The partnership's income is solely from taxable dividends, interest, and gains from sales of securities. In this case, you can deduct your share of the partnership's operating expenses as miscellaneous itemized deductions subject to the 2% limit. However, if the investment club partnership has investments that also produce nontaxable income, you cannot deduct your share of the partnership's expenses that produce the nontaxable income. You should receive a copy of **Schedule K–1** (Form 1065), *Partner's Share of Income, Credits, Deductions, Etc.*

Allocated expenses of mutual funds. The allocable investment expenses of nonpublicly-offered mutual funds are subject to the 2% limit. Those of publicly-offered mutual funds are not subject to the 2% limit.

Nonpublicly-offered mutual funds. These funds will send you a Form 1099–DIV, *Dividends and Distributions,* or substitute form, showing your share of gross income and investment expenses. You can claim the expenses only as a miscellaneous itemized deduction subject to the 2% limit.

Publicly-offered mutual funds. These funds will send you a Form 1099–DIV, or substitute form, showing the net amount of dividend income (gross dividends minus investment expenses). This net figure is the amount you report on your return. A "publicly-offered" mutual fund is one that is:

1) Continuously offered pursuant to a public offering,
2) Regularly traded on an established securities market, or
3) Held by or for at least 500 persons at all times during the tax year.

Contact your mutual fund if you are not sure if your fund is publicly-offered.

Investment Fees and Expenses
You can deduct investment fees, custodial fees, trust administration fees, and other expenses you paid for managing your investments that produce taxable income.

Legal Expenses
You can usually deduct legal expenses that you incur in attempting to produce or collect taxable income or that you pay in connection with the determination, collection, or refund of any tax.

TAXPLANNER

Legal, accounting, and professional fees often have deductible and nondeductible elements. Whether professional fees should be deducted, capitalized, or considered personal expenses depends on the reasons the fees were incurred. To be deductible as a miscellaneous expense on Schedule A, the expense must either be connected to producing income (advising you on your employment, collecting alimony, and the like) or be incurred for a tax-related matter.

You can also deduct legal expenses that are:

1) Related to either doing or keeping your job, such as those you paid to defend yourself against criminal charges arising out of your trade or business.
2) For tax advice related to a divorce if the bill specifies how much is for tax advice and it is determined in a reasonable way.
3) To collect taxable alimony.

Expenses allocated to resolving tax issues relating to profit or loss from business (Schedule C), rentals or royalties (Schedule E), or farm income and expenses (Schedule F), are deductible on the appropriate schedule. The expenses allocated to resolving nonbusiness tax issues are deductible on Schedule A. See *Tax Preparation Fees,* later.

Loss on Deposits in an Insolvent or Bankrupt Financial Institution

For information on whether, and if so how, you may deduct a loss on your deposit in a qualified financial institution, see *Loss on deposits in an insolvent or bankrupt financial institution* in Chapter 15.

Repayments of Income

If you had to repay an amount that you included in income in an earlier year, you may be able to deduct the amount you repaid. If the amount you had to repay was ordinary income of $3,000 or less, the deduction is subject to the 2% limit. If it is more than $3,000, see *Repayments Under Claim of Right* under *Deductions Not Subject to the 2% Limit,* later.

Repayments of Social Security Benefits

For information on how to deduct your repayments of certain social security benefits, see *Repayments More Than Gross Benefits* in Chapter 12.

Safe Deposit Box Rent

You can deduct safe deposit box rent if you use the box to store taxable income-producing stocks, bonds, or investment-related papers and documents. You cannot deduct the rent if you use the box only for jewelry or other personal items or for tax-exempt securities.

Service Charges on Dividend Reinvestment Plans

You can deduct service charges you pay as a subscriber in a dividend reinvestment plan. These service charges include payments for:

1) Holding shares acquired through a plan,
2) Collecting and reinvesting cash dividends, and
3) Keeping individual records and providing detailed statements of accounts.

Tax Preparation Fees

You can usually deduct tax preparation fees in the year you pay them. Thus, on your 1993 return, you can deduct fees paid in 1993 for preparing your 1992 return.

These fees include the cost of tax preparation software programs and tax publications. It also includes any fee you paid for electronic filing of your return.

Expenses allocated to preparing tax schedules relating to profit or loss from business (Schedule C), rentals or royalties (Schedule E), or farm income and expenses (Schedule F), are deductible on the appropriate schedule. The expenses allocated to preparing the remainder of the return are deductible on Schedule A.

Trustee's Administrative Fees for IRA

You can deduct an IRA trustee's administrative fees that are billed separately and that you paid in connection with your individual retirement arrangement (IRA), if they are ordinary and necessary. These fees do not include capital expenditures such as brokers' commissions that you must add to the cost of securities you buy through brokers. These fees also do not include disguised IRA contributions. These trustee's fees are not subject to the annual dollar limit on contributions you can make to an IRA. Deduct them on line 20, Schedule A (Form 1040), not with your IRA deduction. For more information about IRAs, see Chapter 18, *Individual Retirement Arrangements (IRAs)*.

TAX**SAVER**

Administrative fees paid to **IRA** trustees are deductible if the fees are billed to, and paid by, the account owner separate from any IRA contribution. If the trustee takes the fee out of your $2,000 contribution, your total deduction is less than what it could be (only $2,000 instead of $2,000 plus the trustee's fee); also, you then have less money remaining in the IRA account for investment. Since the income in the IRA account accumulates tax-free, the difference in these two amounts—the full $2,000 and the remainder of that sum after fees—compounded annually, becomes significant over the years.

Deductions Not Subject to the 2% Limit

The following expenses are deductible as miscellaneous itemized deductions. However, they are not subject to the 2% limit. Report these expenses on line 25, Schedule A (Form 1040).

List of Deductions Not Subject to the 2% Limit

- Amortizable premium on taxable bonds
- Federal estate tax on income in respect of a decedent
- Gambling losses to the extent of gambling winnings
- Impairment-related work expenses of persons with disabilities
- Repayments under a claim of right
- Unrecovered investment in a pension

Amortizable Premium on Taxable Bonds

Bond premium is the amount you pay for bonds that is greater than the face value of the bonds. You can choose to amortize the premium on taxable bonds.

For a bond purchased before October 23, 1986, the amortization of the premium is a miscellaneous itemized deduction not subject to the 2% limit.

For a bond acquired after October 22, 1986, and before January 1, 1988, the amortization of the premium is investment interest expense subject to the investment interest limit, unless you choose to treat it as an offset to interest income on the bond.

For a bond acquired after December 31, 1987, the amortization of the premium is an offset to interest income on the bond rather than a separate interest deduction item.

TAX**ORGANIZER**

You should keep documentation that shows the date of purchase, face value, and the purchase price of the bond. The types of documents you may want to keep include your broker's confirmation or monthy account statement.

For more information, see *Bond Premium Amortization* in Publication 550, *Investment Income and Expenses*.

Federal Estate Tax on Income in Respect of a Decedent

You can deduct the federal estate tax attributable to income in respect of a decedent that you as a beneficiary include in your gross income. Income in respect of the decedent is gross income that the decedent would have received had death not occurred and that was not properly includible in the decedent's final income tax return. See Chapter 4, *Decedents*, for more information.

Gambling Losses to the Extent of Gambling Winnings

You cannot deduct gambling losses that are more than the gambling winnings you report on line 22, Form 1040. You must keep an accurate diary or similar record of your losses and winnings, and you must be able to prove the amounts of your winnings and losses by receipts, tickets, or statements. For more information about gambling winnings and losses, and information on record-keeping to substantiate gambling losses, see Publication 529.

Impairment-Related Work Expenses

If you have a physical or mental disability that limits your being employed, or substantially limits one or more of your major life activities, such as performing manual tasks, walking, speaking, breathing, learning, and working, your impairment-related work expenses are deductible.

Impairment-related work expenses are allowable business expenses for attendant care services at your place of work and other expenses in connection with your place of work that are necessary for you to be able to work. See Publication 907, *Information for Persons with Disabilities,* for more information.

If you are an employee, you enter impairment-related work expenses on Form 2106. From the amount on line 11 of Form 2106, you enter the amount that is related to your impairment on line 25, Schedule A (Form 1040), and the amount that is unrelated to your impairment on line 19, Schedule A (Form 1040).

Repayments Under Claim of Right

If you had to repay more than $3,000 that you included in your income in an earlier year because at the time you thought you had an unrestricted right to it, you may be able to deduct the amount you repaid, or take a credit against your tax. See *Repayments* in Chapter 13 for more information.

Unrecovered Investment in Pension

If a retiree had contributed to the cost of a pension or annuity, a part of each payment received can be excluded from income as a tax-free return of the retiree's investment. If the retiree dies before the entire investment is returned, any unrecovered investment is allowed as a deduction on the retiree's final return. See Chapter 11 for more information about the tax treatment of pensions and annuities.

Nondeductible Expenses

You cannot deduct the following expenses.

List of Nondeductible Expenses

- Adoption expenses
- Burial or funeral expenses, including the cost of a cemetery lot
- Campaign expenses

- Capital expenses
- Check-writing fees
- Commuting expenses
- Expenses to influence general public on legislation or elections
- Fees and licenses, such as car licenses, marriage licenses, and dog tags
- Fines and penalties, such as parking tickets
- Health spa expenses
- Hobby losses
- Home repairs, insurance, and rent
- Illegal bribes and kickbacks—See *Bribes and kickbacks* in Chapter 16 of Publication 535
- Investment-related seminars
- Life insurance premiums
- Losses from the sale of your home, furniture, personal car, etc.
- Lost or misplaced cash or property—but see *Mislaid or lost property* under *Theft* in Chapter 26
- Lunches with co-workers
- Meals while working late
- Personal disability insurance premiums
- Personal legal expenses
- Personal, living, or family expenses
- Political contributions
- Professional accreditation fees
- Professional reputation, expenses to improve
- Relief fund contributions
- Residential telephone line
- Stockholders' meeting, expenses of attending
- Tax-exempt income expenses
- Voluntary unemployment benefit fund contributions
- Wristwatches

Explanation

In certain instances, the courts have allowed a **deduction** for expenses to attend a stockholders' meeting.

While funeral and burial expenses may not be deducted on your personal return, they may be deducted on your federal estate tax return.

Adoption Expenses

You cannot deduct the expenses you paid to adopt a child.

Campaign Expenses

Campaign expenses of a candidate for any office, even if the candidate is running for reelection to the office, are not deductible. These include qualification and registration fees for primary elections. **Legal fees.** You cannot deduct legal fees paid to defend charges that arise from participation in a political campaign.

Check-Writing Fees

If you have a personal checking account, you cannot deduct fees charged by the bank for the privilege of writing checks, even if the account pays interest.

Commuting Expenses

You cannot deduct commuting expenses (the cost of transportation between your home and your main or regular place of work). If you haul tools, instruments, etc., in your car to and from work, you can deduct only additional costs, such as renting a trailer you towed with your vehicle.

Expenses to Influence Legislation

You cannot deduct gifts or amounts spent to influence the general public on legislative matters, elections, or referenda.

Fines or Penalties

You cannot deduct fines or penalties you pay to a governmental unit for violating a law. This includes an amount paid in settlement of your actual or potential liability for a fine or penalty (civil or criminal). Fines or penalties include parking tickets, tax penalties, and penalties deducted from teachers' paychecks after an illegal strike.

Health Spa Expenses

You cannot deduct health spa expenses, even if there is a job requirement to stay in excellent physical condition, such as might be required of a law enforcement officer.

Homeowners' Insurance Premiums

You cannot deduct insurance premiums that you pay or that are placed in escrow for your home, such as fire and liability or mortgage insurance.

Investment-Related Seminars

You cannot deduct any expenses for attending a convention, seminar, or similar meeting for investment purposes.

Life Insurance Premiums

You cannot deduct premiums you pay on your life insurance. Premiums you pay on life insurance policies assigned to your ex-spouse may be deductible as alimony. See Chapter 19, *Alimony*, for information on alimony.

Lunches with Co-Workers

You cannot deduct the expenses of lunches with co-workers, except while traveling away from home on business. See Chapter 28, *Car Expenses and Other Employee Business Expenses*, for information on these deductible expenses.

Meals While Working Late

You cannot deduct the cost of meals while working late. However, you may be able to claim a deduction if it is a deductible entertainment expense or you are traveling away from home. See Chapter 28, *Car Expenses and Other Employee Business Expenses,* for information on these deductible expenses.

Personal Legal Expenses

You cannot deduct personal legal expenses such as those for the following:

1) Custody of children,
2) Breach of promise (to marry) suit,
3) Civil or criminal charges resulting from a personal relationship,
4) Damages for personal injury,
5) Preparation of a title (or to defend or perfect title),
6) Preparation of a will, and
7) Property claims or property settlement in a divorce.

You cannot deduct these expenses even if a result of the legal proceeding is the loss of income-producing property.

Political Contributions

You cannot deduct contributions made to a political candidate, a campaign committee, or a newsletter fund.

Professional Accreditation Fees

You cannot deduct professional accreditation fees such as the following:

1) Accounting certificate fees paid for the initial right to practice accounting,
2) Bar exam fees and incidental expenses in securing admission to the bar, and
3) Medical and dental license fees paid to get initial licensing.

Professional Reputation

You cannot deduct expenses of radio and TV appearances to increase your personal prestige or establish your professional reputation.

Relief Fund Contributions

You cannot deduct contributions paid to a private plan that pays benefits to any covered employee who cannot work because of any injury or illness not related to the job.

Residential Telephone Service

You cannot deduct any charge (including taxes) for basic local telephone service for the first telephone line to your residence, even if it is used in a trade or business.

Stockholders' Meetings

You cannot deduct transportation and other expenses you pay to attend stockholders' meetings of companies in which you own stock but have no other interest. You cannot deduct these expenses even if you are attending the meeting to get information that would be useful in making further investments.

Explanation

The courts have allowed deductions for stockholders' meetings when the shareholders' interests are more extensive. Consider the following:

- A shareholder who went to a meeting to present a resolution that management stop diluting shareholder equity was entitled to deduct his travel expenses. (See Chapter 28, *Car Expenses and Other Employee Business Expenses*.)
- A court held that an investor's travel expenses to an investment convention were deductible because (1) the trip was part of a rationally planned, systematic investigation of business operations; (2) the costs were reasonable in relation to the size of the investment and the value of the information expected; (3) there was no disguised personal motive for the trip; and (4) there was evidence of practical application of the information obtained on the trip.

  Nevertheless, if a person owns only a very small interest in a large corporation and cannot reasonably expect that his or her attendance at a stockholders' meeting would affect his or her income or investment, the deduction of travel expenses probably would not be allowed.

Tax-Exempt Income Expenses

You cannot deduct expenses to produce tax-exempt income. You cannot deduct interest on a debt incurred or continued to buy or carry tax-exempt securities.

If you have expenses to produce both taxable and tax-exempt income, but you cannot identify the expenses that produce each type of income, you must allocate the expenses to determine the amount that you can deduct.

Example. During the year, you received taxable interest of $4,800 and tax-exempt interest of $1,200. In earning this income, you had expenses of $500 during the year. If you cannot identify the amount of each expense item that is for each income item, you must allocate 80% ($4,800/$6,000) of the expense to taxable interest and 20% ($1,200/$6,000) to tax-exempt interest. You can deduct, subject to the 2% limit, expenses of $400 (80% of $500).

Voluntary Unemployment Benefit Fund Contributions

You cannot deduct voluntary unemployment benefit fund contributions you make to a union fund or a private fund. However, contributions are deductible as taxes if state law requires you to make them to a state unemployment fund that covers you for the loss of wages from unemployment caused by business conditions.

Wristwatches

You cannot deduct the cost of a wristwatch, even if there is a job requirement that you know the correct time to properly perform your duties.

Explanation

The courts have found the following to be nondeductible expenses:

- Amounts paid to guard a personal residence against burglary attempts.
- The cost of a home security system installed to protect a collector's stamps and coins. (The IRS reasoned that the activity was an investment activity and not a regular trade or business. Consequently, the expense did not meet the home office rules, discussed earlier in this chapter.)
- Payments for general advice pertaining to a family trust.
- Legal fees for defending a libel suit arising out of the purchase of the taxpayer's personal residence.

TaxAlert

The cost of specific legal advice on the disposition of a stock is not deductible as a miscellaneous expense on Schedule A but must be treated as a selling expense and used to increase your basis in the stock.

How to Report

You must itemize deductions on Schedule A (Form 1040) to be able to claim miscellaneous deductions.

If you have unreimbursed employee business expenses, generally you must first complete **Form 2106.** See Publication 529 for a more detailed explanation of whether you must file Form 2106.

Carry over the amount of unreimbursed employee business expenses from line 11 of Form 2106 to line 19 of Schedule A (Form 1040). Attach the completed Form 2106 to Form 1040.

If you don't have to fill out Form 2106, just list the type and amount of your unreimbursed employee business expenses on the dotted line for line 19 of Schedule A (Form 1040). Enter one total on line 19.

Claim any other miscellaneous deductions subject to the 2% limit on line 20 of Schedule A (Form 1040).

If you have miscellaneous deductions not subject to the 2% limit, claim these amounts on line 25 of Schedule A (Form 1040).

IV | Figuring Your Taxes and Credits

The five chapters in this part explain how to figure your tax and how to figure the tax of certain children who have more than $1,200 of investment income. They also discuss tax credits. Credits, unlike deductions, are subtracted directly from your tax and therefore reduce your tax dollar for dollar. There are tax credits for the elderly or for the permanently and totally disabled, for the expense of having your child or disabled dependent cared for so that you can work, for the purchase of a qualified electric vehicle, and for other kinds of expenses. Chapter 35 discusses the earned income credit and how you might be able to get the credit paid to you in advance (from your employer) throughout the year rather than wait until you file your tax return.

31 | How to Figure Your Tax

Introduction

This chapter explains how to calculate your tax liability under all three available tax forms—Form 1040EZ, Form 1040A, and Form 1040. It also will help you decide which of the forms to file.

In particular, you should review the section of this chapter on the alternative minimum tax to determine if that tax may apply to you.

Important Changes for 1993

Expanded Form 1040EZ. If your filing status is married filing a joint return and you do not claim any dependents, you may be able to file Form 1040EZ for 1993. See *Which Form Should I Use?* in Chapter 1, *Filing Information*.

Increase in top marginal tax rates. For tax years beginning after 1992, the top marginal tax rate was raised to 36%, and a 10% surtax was imposed on high-income taxpayers.

Election to pay additional 1993 taxes in installments. If you have to pay additional 1993 taxes because of the increase in income tax rates, you may be able to elect to pay them in three equal installments. For information on this election, see *Deferral of Additional 1993 Taxes* later , and Form 8841, *Deferral of Additional 1993 Taxes*.

Expanded Form 1040A. Beginning with 1993 tax returns, you can report alternative minimum tax on Form 1040A. For more information, see *Total tax* under *Form 1040A* later, and the *Alternative minimum tax worksheet* in the Form 1040A instructions.

Important Reminders

Maximum tax rate on capital gains. The tax rates for individuals that are higher than 28% do not apply to net capital gains. The maximum income tax rate on net capital gain income is 28%. Net capital gain is the excess of net long-term capital gain for the year over the net short-term capital loss for the year.

Limit on exemption amount. If your adjusted gross income is more than a specified amount based on your filing status, the amount of your deduction for exemptions is reduced. These amounts are explained later in this chapter under *Exemptions*.

Amount you owe. If you did not pay enough tax through either withholding or estimated tax payments, you may be charged a penalty for underpayment of estimated tax. If you determine that you owe tax, see *Underpayment Penalty* in Chapter 5, *Tax Withholding and Estimated Tax*.

This chapter discusses the steps you need to take to figure your tax on:

- Form 1040EZ,
- Form 1040A, and
- Form 1040.

Also, this chapter discusses the requirements you must meet to have the IRS figure your tax.

Form 1040EZ

If you file Form 1040EZ, you must figure your adjusted gross income and taxable income before you can find your tax.

Adjusted gross income (line 4, Form 1040EZ). This is the total of your wages, salaries, tips, taxable scholarships or fellowship grants, and taxable interest income.

Taxable income (line 6, Form 1040EZ). Your taxable income is your adjusted gross income (line 4), minus the total of your standard deduction and the deduction for your personal exemption(s) (line 5). The amount of these deductions depends on whether you (or your spouse if married) can be claimed as a dependent on someone else's return, such as your parents'. The rules for determining whether you are a dependent are in Chapter 3.

Not a dependent. If you (and your spouse if married) are not dependents, the total of your standard deduction and your personal exemption(s) is $6,050 if single or $10,900 if married. Check the *No* box and enter the appropriate amount on line 5.

> **Explanation**
> It doesn't matter whether you, in fact, are claimed as a dependent on someone else's return; your personal exemption is zero if you could have been claimed on another's return.

Dependent. If you (or your spouse if married) can be claimed as a dependent by another taxpayer, check the *Yes* box on line 5 and complete the worksheet on the back of Form 1040EZ. Enter the result from line G of the worksheet on line 5. You cannot claim a personal exemption for a person who can be claimed as a dependent by another taxpayer.

Tax withheld. After you have figured your taxable income, enter the total of your federal income tax withheld on line 7. This amount is shown in box 2 of your Form(s) W–2. Copy B of Form(s) W–2 must be attached to the return.

See the instructions for Form 1040EZ if withholding tax is shown in box 4 of any 1099–INT you receive, or you paid any tax with a **Form 4868**, *Automatic Extension of Time to File U.S. Individual Income Tax Return*.

Tax. To find your tax, use the Tax Table at the back of this publication or in the instructions for Form 1040EZ. Find the income line that includes your taxable income shown on line 6 of your Form 1040EZ. Next, find the column heading for your filing status (single or married filing jointly) and read down the column. The amount shown where the income line and filing status column meet is your tax. Enter it on line 8.

Refund or amount you owe. If line 7 is larger than line 8, subtract line 8 from line 7 and enter the result on line 9. This is the amount of your refund. For information on refunds, see *Refunds* in Chapter 1, *Filing Information*.

If line 8 is larger than line 7, subtract line 7 from line 8 and enter the result on line 10. This is the amount you owe. For information on how to pay, see *Amount You Owe* in Chapter 1, *Filing Information*.

Filled-in form. A filled-in Form 1040EZ is shown in Chapter 43, *Sample Form 1040EZ*.

Form 1040A

If you file Form 1040A, you must find your adjusted gross income and your taxable income before you can figure your tax.

Adjusted gross income (lines 16 and 17, Form 1040A). This is your total income (line 14) minus your IRA deduction, and your spouse's IRA deduction if you file a joint return. You can figure your IRA deduction by completing the worksheet in the instructions for Form 1040A. Also see Chapter 18, *Individual Retirement Arrangements (IRA)*.

Taxable income (line 22 Form 1040A). This is your adjusted gross income (line 17) minus your standard deduction (line 19) and the deduction for your exemptions (line 21).

Standard deduction. Your standard deduction is based on your filing status, whether you are 65 or older or blind, and whether you can be claimed as a dependent on another person's return. For information, see *Standard Deduction,* later, and Chapter 20, *Standard Deduction*.

Exemptions. To figure the deduction for your exemptions, multiply $2,350 by the number of exemptions claimed on line 6e. If you or your spouse can be claimed as a dependent on someone else's return, check the box on line 18b. You cannot claim an exemption for a person who can be claimed as a dependent by another taxpayer.

Tax, credits, and payments. Next, you must figure your tax. Subtract from your tax any credits or payments to determine whether you owe additional tax or are due a refund.

Note. If this is the return of a child under age 14 on January 1, 1994, with more than $1,200 of investment income, you cannot use the Tax Table. Instead, you must check the box marked "Form 8615" on line 23. Use **Form 8615**, *Tax for Children Under Age 14 Who Have Investment Income of More Than $1,200*, to compute your tax. Form 8615 should not be filed if neither parent is alive at the end of the year. For more information, see Chapter 32, *Tax on Investment Income of Certain Minor Children*.

Tax. To find your tax, use the Tax Table at the back of this publication or in the instructions for Form 1040A. In the Tax Table, find the income line that includes your taxable income shown on line 22. Next, find the column heading that describes your filing status and read down the column. The amount shown where the income line and filing status column meet is your tax. Enter it on line 23 and check the box marked "Tax Table."

Credits. There are three credits that can be claimed on Form 1040A. Credits, unlike deductions, are subtracted after you find your tax from the tax table and, therefore, reduce your tax dollar for dollar. These credits are:

1) Credit for child and dependent care expenses,
2) Credit for the elderly or the disabled, and
3) Earned income credit.

The earned income credit is explained later under *Payments*.

If you claim the credit for child and dependent care expenses (line 24a), you must complete all applicable parts of Schedule 2 (Form 1040A) and attach it to your return. For information on the credit for child and dependent care expenses, see Chapter 33, *Child and Dependent Care Credit*.

If you claim the credit for the elderly or the disabled (line 24b), you must complete Schedule 3 (Form 1040A) and attach it to your return. For information on the credit for the elderly or the disabled, see Chapter 34, *Credit for the Elderly or the Disabled*.

Add lines 24a and 24b and enter the result on line 24c. Subtract your total credits (line 24c) from your tax (line 23) and enter the result on line 25.

Total tax. If you received advance earned income credit payments, the amount will be shown on your Form(s) W–2, box 9. Enter the amount of these payments on line 26. For more information, see *Advance Earned Income Credit Payments* in Chapter 35, *Other Credits*.

Add the amounts on lines 25 and 26. Enter the total on line 27. Also, if you owe the alternative minimum tax, include that tax in the total on line 27. This sum is your total tax.

If the amount on line 17, plus any tax-exempt interest on line 8b is more than $45,000 if your filing status is married filing jointly or qualifying widow(er); more than $33,750 if your filing status is single or head of household; or more than $22,500 if your filing status is married filing separately, and the amount on line 21 is more than $9,400, complete the *Alternative minimum tax worksheet* in the Form 1040A instructions to see if you owe this tax and, if you do, the amount to include on line 27.

Caution. If filing for a child under age 14 and the amount on Form 1040A, line 17, plus the child's tax-exempt interest from private activity bonds issued after August 7, 1986 is more than the total of $1,000 plus the amount on Form 1040A, line 7, do not file Form 1040A. Instead, file Form 1040 for the child and use Form 6251 to see if the child owes the alternative minimum tax.

Payments. The next step is to figure your total payments. On line 28a, enter the total federal income tax withheld from your pay. This amount is shown in box 2 of your Form(s) W–2. If you have more than one employer, carefully add the amounts from these boxes and enter the total on line 28a.

If you received a Form 1099 showing income tax withheld on dividends, interest, IRA distributions, or pensions, check the box on line 28a and include the amount withheld in the total on line 28a. It is important to check all of your Form 1099 statements to see whether any income tax was withheld. A table showing the proper boxes that record withholding is included later. See *Payments* under *Form 1040*.

On line 28b, enter your 1993 estimated tax payments and any overpayment applied from your 1992 federal income tax return.

On line 28c, enter your **earned income credit.** You may be able to take this credit if you earned less than $23,050 and a child who meets certain age and other requirements lived with you. Figure the amount of your earned income credit by completing Schedule EIC. Attach Schedule EIC to your return. For information on the earned income credit, see Chapter 35, *Other Credits*.

Add the amounts on lines 28a, 28b, and 28c and enter this total on line 28d. This sum is your total payments.

Include on line 28d any excess social security or railroad retirement tax withheld. Write "Excess SST" and the amount in the space to the left of line 28d. See Chapter 36 for a discussion on this, *Other Credits*.

Also include on line 28d any tax you paid if you filed Form 4868 to get an automatic extension of time to file your Form 1040A. Write "Form 4868" and the amount in the space to the left of line 28d. Also include any amount paid with Form 2688.

Refund or Amount You Owe

After you have your total tax (line 27) and your total payments (line 28d), you can determine if you are due a tax refund or if you owe additional tax.

Refund

If line 28d is more than line 27, subtract line 27 from line 28d and enter the result on line 29. This is the amount of your overpayment. If you want the entire amount on line 29 refunded, enter that amount on line 30. Enter on line 30 the exact amount you want refunded. For information on refunds, see *Refunds* in Chapter 1, *Filing Information*.

If you want all or part of your refund applied to your 1994 estimated tax, you must enter the appropriate amount on line 31. The amount on line 31 will be credited to your 1994 estimated taxes unless you request us to apply it to your spouse's account. This request should include your spouse's social security number. The amount on line 31 generally cannot be refunded to you until you file a tax return for 1994.

Amount You Owe

If line 27 is more than line 28d, subtract line 28d from line 27 and enter the result on line 32. This is the amount you owe. For information on how to pay, see *Amount You Owe* in Chapter 1, *Filing Information*.

Filled-in form. A filled-in Form 1040A is shown in Chapter 44, *Sample Form 1040A*.

Form 1040

If you file Form 1040, you must compute your adjusted gross income and taxable income before you can figure your tax.

Adjusted Gross Income (line 31, Form 1040)

Adjusted gross income (line 31, Form 1040) is your total income (line 23) minus any adjustments for the following:

1) IRA deduction for you (line 24a), and for your spouse (line 24b). See Chapter 18, *Individual Retirement Arrangements (IRA)*.
2) Deduction for one-half of your self-employment tax (line 25). See Publication 533, *Self-Employment Tax*.
3) Self-employed health insurance deduction (line 26). See Chapter 22, *Medical and Dental Expenses*.
4) Keogh retirement plan and self-employed SEP deduction (line 27). See Publication 560, *Retirement Plans for the Self-Employed*.
5) Penalty on early withdrawal of savings (line 28). See Chapter 8, *Interest Income*.
6) Alimony paid. You must show the recipient's social security number in the space provided on line 29. See Chapter 19, *Alimony*.
7) Other adjustments. Write in the following adjustments in the space to the left of line 30 and include them in the total on line 30.
   a) Certain expenses of qualified performing artists. See Chapter 30, *Miscellaneous Deductions*.

b) Jury duty pay given to your employer. See Chapter 13, *Other Income*.
c) Amortization of the costs of forestation or reforestation if you do not have to file Schedule C, C–EZ, or Schedule F. See Publication 535, *Business Expenses*.
d) Certain required repayments of supplemental unemployment benefits. See Chapter 6, *Wages, Salaries, and Other Earnings*.
e) Contributions to a Section 501(c)(18) pension plan.
f) Deduction for nonbusiness clean-fuel vehicle property. See Publication 535.
g) Expenses from the rental of personal property.

Taxable Income (line 37, Form 1040)

There are two ways to figure the amount of your taxable income (line 37, Form 1040). You can choose to itemize your deductions on Schedule A (Form 1040) or take the standard deduction, whichever is greater.

Itemizing Your Deductions

You can itemize your deductions (such as medical expenses, taxes, mortgage interest, and casualty losses) on Schedule A (Form 1040). **Benefits of itemizing.** You may benefit from itemizing your deductions on Schedule A if you:

1) Do not qualify for the standard deduction, or the amount you can claim is limited,
2) Had large uninsured medical and dental expenses during the year,
3) Paid interest and taxes on your home,
4) Had large unreimbursed employee business expenses or other miscellaneous deductions,
5) Had large casualty or theft losses not covered by insurance,
6) Had large unreimbursed moving expenses,
7) Made large contributions to qualified charities, or
8) Have total itemized deductions that are more than the highest standard deduction amount to which you otherwise are entitled.

Some taxpayers itemize deductions because they do not qualify for the standard deduction or the amount they qualify for is limited (see Chapter 20).

If you decide to itemize your deductions, complete and attach Schedule A to your return. Enter the amount from line 26 of Schedule A on line 34 of Form 1040.

Separate returns. If you and your spouse file separate returns, you can use the method that gives you the lowest total tax, even though one of you may pay more than the other. However, if one of you itemizes deductions, the other should also itemize because the standard deduction of a married individual filing a separate return where either spouse itemizes deductions is zero.

TAXPLANNER

If you claimed the standard deduction in a prior year and later discover that you could have itemized your deductions, you should consider filing an amended return to obtain a refund. The statute of limitations for filing an amended return is generally three years.

Changing your mind. If you do not itemize your deductions and later find you should have itemized—or if you itemize and later find you should not have—you can change your return by filing Form 1040X, *Amended U.S. Individual Income Tax Return.*

Separate returns. If you and your spouse filed separate returns, you can change methods of taking deductions only if you and your spouse make the same changes. Both of you must consent in writing to the assessment for any additional tax either one may owe as a result of the change.

Taxable income. If you itemize your deductions, your taxable income (line 37) is your adjusted gross income (line 32) minus your itemized deductions (line 34) and your exemptions (line 36).

Standard Deduction

The standard deduction is based on your filing status and whether you are 65 or older or blind.

65 or older or blind. If you were 65 or older or blind in 1993, you are entitled to a higher standard deduction than taxpayers under 65 and not blind. For information on who qualifies for the higher standard deduction for age and blindness, see Chapter 20, *Standard Deduction.* The standard deduction amounts are given in the standard deduction charts and worksheet in Chapter 20.

Special rules. Your standard deduction is *zero* if:

1) Your spouse itemizes deductions on a separate return,
2) You are a dual-status or nonresident alien, or
3) You have a short tax year on account of a change in your annual accounting period.

Dependent. If you can be claimed as a dependent on another person's return, your standard deduction may be limited. See *Standard Deduction for Dependents* in Chapter 20, *Standard Deduction.*

Amount of the standard deduction. If you decide to take the standard deduction, show the amount on line 34 of Form 1040.

The amount of the standard deduction for most people is shown on Form 1040 to the left of line 34. Others must use the standard deduction charts and worksheet in Chapter 20, *Standard Deduction* or in the Form 1040 instructions to find their standard deduction.

Taxable income. If you take the standard deduction, your taxable income (line 37) is your adjusted gross income (line 32) minus your standard deduction (line 34) and your exemptions (line 36).

Exemptions

Whether you itemize your deductions or use the standard deduction, you can generally deduct $2,350 for each exemption you can claim. However, if your adjusted gross income (AGI) is more than the dollar amount for your filing status as shown in the following table, the amount of your deduction is less.

Filing Status	AGI more than:
Single	$106,450
Married filing jointly	162,700
Married filing separately	81,350
Head of household	135,800
Qualifying widow(er)	162,700

See Chapter 3, *Personal Exemptions and Dependents,* for an explanation of this reduction and a worksheet to figure the amount of your deduction.

Enter the amount you figure for your exemptions on line 36.

Tax, Credits, and Payments

After finding your taxable income, the next step is to figure your tax liability. This tax amount is then reduced by any credits you may have. Finally, you apply any payments or other credits against your liability to determine whether you owe additional tax or are entitled to a refund.

Tax

Most people use the Tax Table to figure their tax. However, you must use the Tax Rate Schedules to figure your tax if your taxable income is $100,000 or more.

If you have a net capital gain, your tax may be less if you figure it using the worksheet in the instructions for Schedule D. Form 8615 may have to be used to figure the tax for a child under age 14 at the end of the year with more than $1,200 of investment income.

Tax Table. The Tax Table is shown in the back of this publication and in the instructions for Form 1040.

To find your tax, read down the income column to the line that includes your taxable income as shown on line 37. Then read across the line to the column heading that describes your filing status. The amount shown where the income line and filing status column meet is your tax. Enter it on line 38 and check the box marked *Tax Table.*

Tax Rate Schedules. If your taxable income (line 37) is $100,000 or more, you must figure your tax by using Tax Rate Schedules X, Y–1, Y–2, or Z unless you can use the Schedule D Tax Worksheet or are required to use Form 8615.

The Tax Rate Schedules are shown at the back of this publication and in the Form 1040 instructions. Enter your tax on line 38, and check the box marked *Tax Rate Schedules.*

Maximum tax rate on capital gains (Schedule D). The highest tax rate on taxable income is 39.6%. However, the highest tax rate on a net capital gain is 28%. A net capital gain is the excess of your net long-term capital gains over your net short-term capital losses. Therefore, the maximum 28% rate applies if you have a long-term capital gain shown on line 17, Schedule D (Form 1040), and a net gain shown on line 18, Schedule D (Form 1040).

You should complete the worksheet in the instructions for Schedule D (Form 1040) to figure your tax only if your taxable income (line 37, Form 1040) is more than the amount shown for your filing status in the following table.

Filing Status	Amount
Married filing jointly	$89,150
Qualifying widow(er)	89,150
Head of household	76,400
Single	53,500
Married filing separately	44,575

If you use the worksheet in the instructions for Schedule D, enter your tax from line 13 of the worksheet on line 38, Form 1040, and check the box marked *Schedule D Tax Worksheet.*

Investment income of certain minor children. If a child under age 14 at the end of the year has more than $1,200 of interest, dividends, and other investment income, part of that income may be taxed at the parent's rate. The tax is figured using **Form 8615,** *Tax for Children Under Age 14 Who Have Investment Income of More Than $1,200.*

Form 8615 should not be filed if neither parent is alive at the end of the year or if a parent chooses to include the child's interest and dividend income on his or her return. For more information, see Chapter 32, *Tax on Investment Income of Certain Minor Children.*

Additional taxes. If you owe either of the taxes shown on line 39 (Form 1040), attach **Form 4970,** *Tax on Accumulation Distribution of Trusts,* or **Form 4972,** *Tax on Lump-Sum Distributions.* On line 39, check the box that applies to you and enter the amount of additional taxes.

Credits

After you have figured your tax and entered the total of lines 38 and 39 on line 40, figure your credits and enter them on lines 41 through 45. Enter the total credits on line 45. Subtract line 45 from line 40. Enter the result on line 46.

This chapter does not explain whether you are eligible for these credits. The following table is a summary of the credits and where to report them on Form 1040. Additional information is provided in the paragraphs that follow the table.

Credit	Line
Child Care	41
Elderly or Disabled	42
Foreign Tax	43
General Business	44
Mortgage Interest	44
Prior Year Minimum Tax	44
Qualified Electric Vehicle	44
Nonconventional Fuel Source	45

Credit for child and dependent care expenses. Enter on line 41 (Form 1040) the amount of this credit, which you figure on **Form 2441**, *Child and Dependent Care Expenses.* See Chapter 33, *Child and Dependent Care Credit,* for information on this credit.

Credit for the elderly or the disabled. Enter on line 42 (Form 1040) the amount of this credit, which you figure on Schedule R. See Chapter 34, *Credit for the Elderly or the Disabled,* for more information.

Foreign tax credit. Enter on line 43 (Form 1040) the amount of foreign tax credit, which you figure on Form 1116. Foreign tax credit is discussed in Publication 514, *Foreign Tax Credit for Individuals.*

Other credits. Enter other credits on line 44 and check the appropriate box or enter the form number to identify which form you are attaching.

General business credit. The general business credit is made up of a number of separate business-related credits. If you have 2 or more of the separate credits, use **Form 3800,** *General Business Credit,* and check box *a* on line 44. If you have only one of these credits, check box *d* and enter the form number for that credit. See Form 3800 for more information.

Mortgage interest credit. Use **Form 8396,** *Mortgage Interest Credit,* to figure the amount of this credit and check box *b* on line 44. See *Mortgage Interest Credit* in Publication 530, *Tax Information for First-Time Homeowners.*

Credit for prior year minimum tax. Complete **Form 8801,** *Credit For Prior Year Minimum Tax—Individuals and Fiduciaries,* if you paid alternative minimum tax in 1992 on deferred preference items or have a carryforward of the minimum tax credit. Attach this form to your tax return and check box *c* on line 44. For information on this credit, see Publication 909, *Alternative Minimum Tax for Individuals.*

Qualified electric vehicle credit. If you bought a qualified electric vehicle after June 30, 1993, use **Form 8834,** *Qualified Electric Vehicle Credit* to figure the amount of your credit. See Chapter 35, *Other Credits,* for information on this credit.

Credit for fuel from a nonconventional source. Include this credit in the total for line 45. Write the amount and "FNS" on the dotted line next to line 45. Also attach a separate schedule showing how you figured the credit. See *Internal Revenue Code section 29* for further information.

Total credits. Add lines 41 through 44. Put the total on line 45. Line 45 is your total credits.

Other Taxes

If you owe any other taxes or if you received advance earned income credit payments, complete any of lines 47 through 52 that apply to you and enter the total on line 53.

This chapter does not explain these taxes. The following table is a summary of the taxes and where to report them on Form 1040. Additional information is provided in the paragraphs that follow the table.

Other Taxes	Line
Self-Employment Tax	47
Alternative Minimum Tax	48
Recapture Taxes	49
Social Security and Medicare Tax on Tips	50
IRA or Qualified Retirement Plan Penalty Tax	51
Advance Earned Income Credit Payments	52
Section 72(m)(5) Excess Benefits Tax	53
Uncollected Tax on Tips or Life Insurance Premiums	53
Tax on excess Golden Parachute Payments	53

Self-employment tax. You must file Schedule SE (Form 1040) if both of the following apply to you (or your spouse if you file a joint return):

1) You were self-employed, and your net earnings from self-employment were $400 or more (or you had church employee income of $108.28 or more), and
2) You did not have wages (and tips) of $135,000 or more that were subject to social security and Medicare tax (or railroad retirement tax).

Complete Schedule SE (Form 1040) and show any tax you owe on line 47 (Form 1040). See Publication 533, *Self-Employment Tax,* for more information.

Alternative minimum tax. Use Form 6251 to see if you owe any alternative minimum tax. Enter the result on line 48 (Form 1040). This tax is briefly discussed later in this chapter and in depth in Publication 909.

Recapture taxes. If you are required to recapture investment tax credit on Form 4255, low-income housing credit on Form 8611, or federal mortgage subsidy on Form 8828, enter the amount on line 49 (Form 1040) and check the appropriate box.

Social security and Medicare tax on tip income not reported to employer. Attach **Form 4137,** *Social Security and Medicare Tax on Unreported Tip Income,* and show on line 50 (Form 1040) the tax due on tip income you did not report to your employer. See Chapter 7, *Income for Tips,* for more information.

Tax on qualified retirement plans, including IRAs. You may owe additional taxes on your IRA or other qualified retirement plan if you:

1) Received any early distributions from a qualified retirement plan (including your IRA), annuity, or modified endowment contract (entered into after June 20, 1988),
2) Received any excess distributions from a qualified retirement plan,
3) Made excess contributions to your IRA, or
4) Had excess accumulations in a qualified retirement plan.

If any of the above apply, get **Form 5329,** *Return for Additional Taxes Attributable to Qualified Retirement Plans (Including IRAs), Annuities, and Modified Endowment Contracts,* to see if you owe this tax and if you must file this form. Enter the tax from Form 5329 on line 51. See Chapter 18, *Individual Retirement Arrangements (IRAs),* for more information.

Advance earned income credit payments. Include on line 52 any advance earned income credit payments you received in 1993. Your W–2 form(s) will show these payments in box 9.

Section 72(m)(5) excess benefits. If you are or were a 5% owner of a business and you received a distribution of excess benefits from a qualified pension or annuity plan, you may have to pay a penalty tax of 10% of the excess benefits distribution. Include the amount of the penalty in your total for line 53. Also write the amount and "Section 72(m)(5)" on the dotted line next to line 53. See Publication 560, *Retirement Plans for the Self-Employed,* for more information.

Uncollected employee social security and Medicare or RRTA tax on tips (or group-term life insurance). If you did not have enough wages to cover the social security tax and Medicare tax or railroad retirement (RRTA) tax due on tips you reported to your employer (or on group-term life insurance), include the tax due in the total for line 53. The amount of tax due will be shown on your Form W–2. Also write the amount and "Uncollected Tax" on the dotted line next to line 53. See Chapter 7, *Income from Tips,* for more information.

Golden parachute payments. If you received an excess parachute payment (EPP), you must pay a tax equal to 20% of this excess payment. Include the amount of this tax in your total for line 53. Also write the amount and "EPP" on the dotted line next to line 53. See *Form 1040 Instructions for Line 53* for more information.

Total tax. Add lines 46 through 52. Put the total on line 53. Line 53 is your total tax.

Payments

Once you have figured your total tax on line 53, figure your total payments. Enter the payments that apply to you on lines 54 through 59.

This chapter does not discuss all of these payments. The following table is a summary of the payments (and credits that are considered payments) and where to report them on Form 1040. Additional information is provided in the paragraphs that follow the table.

Payments	Line
Income Tax Withheld	54
Estimated Tax Paid	55
Earned Income Credit	56
Paid with Extension	57
Excess Tax Withheld	58a
Deferral of Additional 1993 Taxes	58b
Regulated Investment Company Credit	59
Fuel Tax Credit	59

Federal income tax withheld. On line 54, enter your federal income tax withheld. This includes amounts from Forms W–2, W–2G, 1099–R, and any other Form 1099. It is important to check all of your statements to see whether any tax was withheld and to carefully add the amounts before making an entry on line 54. The following table shows the proper boxes that record income tax withholding.

FORM NUMBER	LOCATION
W–2	Box 2
W–2G	Box 2
1099–B	Box 4
1099–DIV	Box 2
1099–G	Box 4
1099–INT	Box 4
1099–MISC	Box 4
1099–OID	Box 4
1099–PATR	Box 4
1099–R	Box 4

Estimated tax payments. If you made estimated tax payments for 1993, enter the total of these payments on line 55. Also enter on line 55 any overpayment from your 1992 return that you applied to your 1993 estimated tax.

If you paid joint estimated tax but are now filing separate income tax returns, or if you divorced or changed your name in 1993, see *Estimated Tax* in Chapter 5, *Tax Withholding and Estimated Tax,* for further directions.

Earned income credit. Enter your earned income credit on line 56. You may be able to take this credit if you earned less than $23,050 and a child who meets certain age and other requirements lived with you. Figure the amount of your earned income credit on Schedule EIC and attach it to your return. The earned income credit is explained in Chapter 35, *Other Credits.*

Tax paid with extension. If you paid any tax with Forms 4868, 2688, or 2350 (extensions of time to file), enter this amount on line 57.

Excess tax withheld. If you worked for more than one employer and had too much social security tax, Medicare tax, or railroad retirement tax withheld, enter the excess amount on line 58a. This is explained in Chapter 35, *Other Credits.*

Deferral of additional 1993 taxes. If you are liable for additional 1993 taxes due solely to the tax rate increases, and you do not owe alternative minimum tax for 1993, you may be eligible to elect to pay the additional 1993 taxes in three equal annual installments. To find out if you can make this election, see *Deferral of Additional 1993 Taxes* in Chapter 1, *Filing Information,* and **Form 8841,** *Deferral of Additional 1993 Taxes.* The amount of the additional 1993 taxes deferred is entered on line 58b.

Regulated investment company credit. If you can take a regulated investment company credit, attach Copy B of **Form 2439,** *Notice to Shareholder of Undistributed Long-Term Capital Gains.* Include the amount of the credit on line 59 and check box **a.**

Fuel tax credit. If you can take a credit for tax on gasoline, diesel fuel, and other fuels used in your business, or for certain diesel-powered cars, vans, and light trucks, attach Form 4136. Include the amount of the credit on line 59 and check box **b.**

Total payments. Add lines 54 through 59 and enter this total on line 60. This sum is your total payments.

Refund or Amount You Owe

After you have your total tax (line 53) and your total payments (line 60), you must determine if you are due a tax refund or if you owe additional tax.

Refund

If the amount on line 60 is more than the amount on line 53 subtract line 53 from line 60 and enter the result on line 61. This is the amount of tax you have overpaid. If you want the entire amount refunded to you, enter the amount on line 62. If you want all of your overpayment applied to your 1994 estimated tax, enter the amount on line 63. If you want part of your overpayment applied to your 1994 estimated tax, you must complete both lines 62 and 63. The amount on line 63 will be credited to your 1994 estimated taxes unless you request us to apply it to your spouse's account. This request should include your spouse's social security number. For information on refunds, see *Refunds* in Chapter 1, *Filing Information*.

Amount You Owe

If the amount on line 53 is more than the amount on line 60, subtract line 60 from line 53 and enter the result on line 64. This is the amount you owe. For information on how to pay, see *Amount You Owe* in Chapter 1, *Filing Information*.

Explanation

For information on how to elect to pay your 1993 tax in installments, see Chapter 1, *Filing Information* under the section entitled *Amount You Owe*.

Filled-in form. A filled-in Form 1040 with certain forms and schedules is shown in Chapter 45, *Sample Form 1040*.

Alternative Minimum Tax

The tax laws give special treatment to some kinds of income and allow special deductions and credits for some kinds of expenses. Taxpayers who benefit from these laws may have to pay at least a minimum amount of tax through an additional tax. This additional tax is called the *alternative minimum tax (AMT)*.

You may have to pay the alternative minimum tax if your taxable income for regular tax purposes, combined with any of the adjustments and preference items that apply to you, is more than:

$45,000 if your filing status is married filing a joint return (or a qualifying widow(er) with dependent child),
$33,750 if your filing status is single or head of household, or
$22,500 if your filing status is married filing a separate return.

Explanation

Individuals, trusts, and estates must pay the alternative minimum tax (AMT) if it exceeds their regular tax liability for the year. The amount subject to the AMT will be determined by adding a number of preference items to your taxable income and making various adjustments to your regular taxable income. This amount is reduced by the exemption amounts, and the balance is subject to the following AMT rates:

Rate	Married Filing Separately	All Other Filers
26%	Up to $87,500 over exemption amount	Up to $175,000 over exemption amount
28%	Greater than $87,500 over exemption amount	Greater than $175,000 over exemption amount

Exemption Amount

Filing status	Base amount	Less 25% of the amount by which AMTI* exceeds
Single	$33,750	$112,500
Married filing jointly, surviving spouses	45,000	150,000
Married filing separately, estates and trusts	22,500	75,000

*Alternative Minimum Taxable Income

TAXALERT

Under the new AMT rules, it appears that joint filers with regular taxable income of $72,846 or less will be better off because of the higher exemption available ($45,000 versus $40,000 under the old law). Joint filers with higher income levels, such as $150,000 or $200,000, appear to fall more easily into AMT. However, when the regular taxable income levels of the joint filers exceeds $327,800, it becomes less likely that they will be subject to the AMT since they are paying much more in regular tax due to the higher regular marginal tax rates.

Adjustments. Adjustments to taxable income include:

- Addition of *personal exemptions,*
- Addition of the *standard deduction* (if claimed),
- Addition of *itemized deductions* claimed for state and local taxes, certain interest, most miscellaneous deductions, and part of medical expenses,
- Subtraction of any *refund of state and local taxes* included in gross income,
- Change in amount of *depreciation* claimed on certain property,
- Change in method of determining income from *long-term contracts* entered into on or after March 1, 1986,
- Difference between *gain or loss* on the sale of property reported for regular tax purposes and AMT purposes,
- For stock acquired during the year through the exercise of an *incentive stock option,* add any excess fair market value of the stock over the amount you paid for it,
- Change in method of determining income from *certain installment sales,* and
- Change in method of determining *passive activity loss* deduction.

TAXALERT

If your deduction for state taxes is unusually high—for example, perhaps you made a large payment with your 1992 state tax return when you filed in April of 1993, or perhaps you have substantial state tax withholding during 1993 on your regular income—you should take a closer look at the possibility of being subject to the AMT.

Explanation

Besides accounting for tax preference items, certain adjustments (increases or decreases) must be made to taxable income to arrive at alternative minimum taxable income. The adjustments are as follows:

1. An alternative depreciation deduction (using less accelerated methods and longer depreciable lives) is substituted for the regular tax depreciation deduction for real and personal property and certified pollution control facilities placed in service after 1986. Recomputations are done in the aggregate; that is, the amount of the adjustment is not determined on a property-by-property basis. *Note:* This adjustment does not apply if you have elected to apply the alternative depreciation system (ADS) for regular tax purposes.
2. Mining exploration and development costs must be amortized over 10 years using the straight-line method.
3. The percentage-of-completion method of accounting must be used for long-term contracts entered into on or after March 1, 1986. Certain small construction contracts entered into on or after June 21, 1988, must use new, simplified procedures for cost allocations in the percentage-of-completion calculation.
4. An alternative tax net operating loss deduction replaces the regular net operating loss deduction.
5. The installment method of accounting is disallowed for certain installment sales occurring after March 1, 1986.
6. The treatment of itemized deductions is modified as follows:

   - Medical expenses are deductible only to the extent that they exceed 10% of the taxpayer's adjusted gross income.
   - State, local, and foreign real property and income taxes, and state and local personal property taxes are deductible for AMT purposes only if they are deductible for regular tax purposes in computing adjusted gross income. *Note:* These are taxes related to business, rental property, and farming that are deducted on Schedule C, E, or F.
   - Investment interest is deductible to the extent of net investment income that is adjusted for amounts relating to tax-exempt interest earned on certain private-activity bonds.
   - Home mortgage interest is allowed as a deduction for AMT purposes. However, the definition of such interest is narrower than that of "qualified residence interest" for regular tax purposes. Refinanced home mortgage interest that is applicable to any mortgage in excess of the outstanding mortgage before refinancing is not deductible.
   - No deduction is allowed for miscellaneous itemized deductions subject to the 2% of adjusted gross income limit.

7. No deduction is allowed for the standard deduction.
8. Circulation expenditures and research/experimental costs must be amortized over 3- and 10-year periods, respectively.
9. Deductions for passive farm losses are denied, except to the extent that the taxpayer is insolvent or the activity is disposed of during the year.
10. Rules limiting passive loss deductions also apply to the AMT, except that (a) otherwise disallowed losses are reduced by the amount by which the taxpayer is insolvent, and (b) all AMT adjustments and preferences are taken into consideration in computing income and/or losses from passive activities.
11. For beneficiaries of estates and trusts, the difference between a distribution included in income for regular tax and the AMT income shown on Schedule K-1 must be taken into account.
12. For property disposed of during the year, the gain or loss is refigured to take into consideration the impact that AMT adjustments, such as depreciation, have on the taxpayer's basis in the property.
13. For partners in partnerships and shareholders in S corporations, the income or loss is refigured to take into account AMT adjustments.
14. In exercising an Incentive Stock Option (ISO), the taxpayer needs to adjust for the difference between the option price and the fair market value at the time the option is exercised. In calculating the AMT gain or loss on the subsequent sale of the ISO stock, the AMT basis in the stock is the sum of the option price paid and the AMT adjustment included in alternative minimum taxable income when the stock becomes substantially vested.

TAX ALERT

If you plan to exercise incentive stock options that have been granted to you by your employer, you should always evaluate the potential AMT impact prior to doing so. Although you will not report any income for regular tax purposes when you exercise the incentive options, you will be required to report income (which is measured as the difference between what you paid to exercise the option and the fair market value of the stock on the day of exercise) for AMT purposes. See Chapter 42, *Planning Ahead for 1994 and Beyond,* for an additional discussion about AMT planning.

Tax preference items. Tax preference items include:

- That part of a deduction for certain **depletion** that is more than the adjusted basis of the property,
- Part of a deduction for certain **intangible drilling costs** if the deduction (minus the amount that could have been deducted if the cost were amortized over 120 months) is more than 65% of the net income from oil, gas, and geothermal properties,

TAX SAVER

To avoid treating excess intangible drilling costs as a tax preference item, you may elect to capitalize and amortize these expenses over a 10-year period in your regular tax calculation.

- **Tax-exempt interest** on certain private activity bonds, and

- Accelerated *depreciation* on certain property placed in service before 1987.

Explanation

You will only pay the AMT if it is higher than your regular tax. You may, however, offset your AMT liability by using any foreign tax credit, as computed under the AMT rules, that you are allowed to claim. Other nonrefundable credits cannot, under any circumstances, reduce your AMT liability. To the extent that no tax benefit is obtained for these nonrefundable credits for the year in which the AMT applies, such credits are generally carried back or forward.

The law provides a credit against the regular tax for all or a portion of the AMT you paid in previous years. The credit is the AMT attributable to deferral, rather than exclusion, items. Deferral items such as accelerated depreciation are those that have the effect of reducing your regular taxable income relative to alternative minimum taxable income in early years, but the situation reverses over time. Thus, the same total of deductions is eventually allowed under both tax systems. When you pay AMT as a result of deferral preferences, the law gives you a credit that can be used to reduce your regular tax liability in the future. This avoids double taxation on the same income. Exclusion preferences, such as certain tax-exempt interest income, reduce your regular taxable income permanently. Since these preferences never reverse in the future, you are not given a credit for AMT paid. The credit is carried forward indefinitely from the year of payment and cannot be carried back.

Example

The following example demonstrates how you would calculate your regular tax and your AMT for calendar year 1993:

	Regular tax	Alternative minimum tax
Salary	$150,000	$150,000
Dividends	11,000	11,000
Long-term capital gains	80,000	80,000
Net passive losses	(25,000)	(25,000)
Passive losses disallowed by Tax Reform Act of 1986	25,000	25,000
Adjusted gross income	241,000	241,000
State taxes	(30,000)	n/a*
Charitable contributions	(40,000)	(40,000)
Interest expense—principal residence	(27,000)	(27,000)
Interest expense—investments	(10,000)	(10,000)
Reduction in itemized deductions for adjusted gross income over $108,450	3,977	n/a
Exemptions (4)	(3,512)	n/a
Tax preference items: Incentive stock options	n/a	25,000
Alternative taxable income before exemption	n/a	189,000
Exemption ($45,000 less 25% of alternative taxable income in excess of $150,000)	n/a	(35,250)
Taxable income	$134,465	$153,750
Tax due	$34,213	$39,975

*n/a means "not applicable."

Since your regular tax is less than your AMT, you must pay the AMT of $39,975.

Note: The $30,000 you paid in state income tax did not reduce the alternative minimum taxable income. Good planning would require minimizing your state income taxes and your miscellaneous deductions to the extent that you are able in a year when it is possible you will be subject to the AMT.

More information. For more information about the alternative minimum tax and how to figure it, see Publication 909, *Alternative Minimum Tax for Individuals,* and the instructions for **Form 6251,** *Alternative Minimum Tax—Individuals.*

Tax Figured by IRS

The IRS will figure your tax on Form 1040EZ, Form 1040A, or Form 1040.

If the IRS figures your tax and you paid too much, you will receive a refund. If you did not pay enough, you will receive a bill for the balance. You may avoid interest or the penalty for late payment if you pay the bill within 30 days of the date of the bill or by the due date for your return, whichever is later.

TAXPLANNER

If you make a preliminary calculation and see that you owe money to the IRS, you might consider waiting until April 15 to file your return and letting the IRS figure your tax. It will take the IRS some time to process your return and compute your tax. You will not have to come up with the money you owe until 30 days after the IRS sends you a bill. You will not have to pay any interest if you pay within 30 days of receiving your bill.

Changing your mind. If you choose to have the IRS figure your tax, you may later change your mind by filing an amended return (Form 1040X).

Form 1040EZ

If you file Form 1040EZ by April 15, 1994, you may choose to have the IRS figure your tax. Put your name and address label on your return. If you do not have a label, print (do not type) your name, address, and social security number in the spaces provided.

What to complete. Read lines 1 through 7 and fill in the lines that apply to you. If you are filing a joint return, use the space under the "Note" to the left of line 6 to separately show your taxable income and your spouse's taxable income. Sign and date your return (both spouses must sign a joint return). Attach Copy B or the first copy of your Form W–2 to your return. Mail the return to the Internal Revenue Service Center for the area where you live.

Form 1040A

If you file Form 1040A by April 15, 1994, you may choose to have the IRS figure your tax. Place your name and address label on your return. If you do not have a label, fill in (print or type) your name, address, and social security number. If you are married, give the social security numbers of both spouses even if you file separately.

If you are required to use **Form 8615,** *Tax for Children Under Age 14 Who Have Investment Income of More Than $1,200,* or if you want any of your refund applied to your 1994 estimated tax, IRS cannot figure your tax for you.

What to complete. Read lines 1 through 22 and fill in the lines that apply to you. If you file a joint return, use the space to the left of line 22 to separately show your own and your spouse's taxable income.

Credit for child and dependent care expenses. If you can take this credit, complete Schedule 2 and attach it to your return. You must show on Schedule 2 the name, address, and identifying number of the person or organization who provided the care. Enter the amount of the credit on line 24a (Form 1040A). The IRS will not figure this credit.

Credit for the elderly or the disabled. If you can take this credit, attach Schedule 3 to your return and write "CFE" in the space to the left of line 24b (Form 1040A). The IRS will figure this credit for you. Check the box on Schedule 3 for your filing status and age, and fill in lines 11 and 13 of Part III if applicable. Also complete Part II if applicable.

Advance earned income credit payment. If you received any advance earned income credit payment during 1993, enter the amount on line 26. Your Form(s) W–2 will show these payments in box 9.

Payments. Place any income tax withheld that is shown in box 2 of Form W–2, or the appropriate box of Form 1099, on line 28a. Place any estimated tax payments you made on line 28b.

Earned income credit. If you can take the earned income credit, as discussed in Chapter 35, *Other Credits,* the IRS will figure the credit for you. Write "EIC" in the space to the left of line 28c. Fill in page 1 of Schedule EIC and attach it to your Form 1040A. **Form W–2.** Attach Copy B or the first copy of your Form W–2 to your return. Also attach any Form 1099–R you received that has withholding tax in box 4.

Filing the return. Sign and date your return. Also fill in your occupation. If you are filing a joint return, both you and your spouse must sign it. Show both of your occupations on a joint return. Mail the return to the Internal Revenue Service Center for the area where you live.

Form 1040

If you file Form 1040 by April 15, 1994, you may choose to have the IRS figure your tax if you meet all of the conditions described below:

1) All of your income for 1993 was from wages, salaries, tips, interest, dividends, taxable social security benefits, unemployment compensation, IRA distributions, pensions, or annuities.
2) Your taxable income on line 37 is less than than $100,000.
3) You do not itemize deductions.
4) You do not file any of the following forms:
   a) **Schedule D,** *Capital Gains and Losses.*
   b) **Form 2555,** *Foreign Earned Income.*
   c) **Form 2555-EZ,** *Foreign Earned Income Exclusion.*
   d) **Form 4137,** *Social Security and Medicare Tax on Unreported Tip Income.*
   e) **Form 4970,** *Tax on Accumulation Distribution of Trusts.*
   f) **Form 4972,** *Tax on Lump-Sum Distributions.*
   g) **Form 6198,** *At-Risk Limitations.*
   h) **Form 6251,** *Alternative Minimum Tax—Individuals.*
   i) **Form 8615,** *Tax for Children Under Age 14 Who Have Investment Income of More Than $1,200.*
   j) **Form 8814,** *Parent's Election To Report Child's Interest and Dividends.*
5) You do not want any of your refund applied to your 1994 estimated tax.

Name, address, and social security number. Put your name and address label on your return. If you do not have a label, fill in (print or type) your name, address, and social security number. If you are married, give the social security numbers of both spouses even if you file separately.

What to complete. Read lines 1 through 37 and fill in the lines that apply to you.

If you are filing a joint return, use the space under the words *Adjustments to Income* on the front of your return to show your taxable income and your spouse's taxable income separately.

Read lines 39 through 59. Fill in the lines that apply to you, but do not fill in the *Total* lines. Please be sure to fill in line 54 for federal income tax withheld.

Fill in any forms or schedules asked for on the lines you completed, and attach them to your return when you file it.

Credit for the elderly or the disabled. If you can take the credit for the elderly or the disabled, as discussed in Chapter 34,

Credit for the Elderly or the Disabled, attach Schedule R. Write"CFE" on the dotted line next to line 42 of Form 1040. The IRS will figure the credit for you. On Schedule R, check the box for your filing status and age, and fill in lines 11 and 13 of Part III if applicable. Also complete Part II of Schedule R if applicable.

Earned income credit. If you can take the earned income credit, as discussed in Chapter 35, *Other Credits,* fill in page 1 of Schedule EIC and attach it to your return. Write "EIC" on the dotted line next to line 56 of Form 1040. The IRS will figure the credit for you.

Payments. Place any income tax withheld that is shown in box 2 of Form W–2, or the appropriate box of Form 1099, on line 54. Attach Copy B or the first copy of your Form(s) W–2 to your return. Also attach any Form 1099–R you received that has withholding tax in box 4.

Place any estimated tax payments you made on line 55.

Filing the return. Be sure to sign and date your return and show your occupation(s). If you are filing a joint return, both you and your spouse must sign it. Mail your return to the Internal Revenue Service Center for the area where you live.

32 | Tax on Investment Income of Certain Minor Children

Introduction

There's nothing easy about bringing up children these days, and that applies to their tax returns as well. It is enormously complicated to determine the correct tax and fill out a proper tax return for children under age 14 who have unearned income.

Unearned income of children under 14 is taxed at the marginal rate of their parents, as if the parents had received the income, rather than at the child's lower rate. Generally, this isn't going to give your child a break. Since most parents have a higher marginal tax rate, these rules generally eliminate the benefits of transferring income-producing assets, such as stocks or bonds, to your minor children in order for the income to be taxed at the children's lower marginal rate. These changes made many children into first-time taxpayers.

The following are additional complications:

1. *A child may not claim a personal exemption for himself or herself if he or she is eligible to be claimed on your return.*
2. *A child's unearned income falls under special rules. The child can use $600 of his or her standard deduction to offset unearned income. The next $600 of unearned income is taxed at the child's tax bracket. The balance of a child's unearned income will be taxed as if it were included in your return. Note that Form 8615 is required for this purpose. A copy of the form is included in Chapter 49, 1993 Federal Tax Forms and Schedules You Can Use.*
3. *If a child also has earned income, his or her tax return gets more complicated still. The earned income can increase his or her allowable standard deduction.*

This chapter will help you sort through all the complications. Here's hoping that, while you're muddling through it, your children will be out having fun.

This chapter discusses two special tax rules that apply to certain investment income of a child under age 14:

- When can a parent choose to include the child's interest and dividend income on the parent's return so the child does not have to file a return, (see *Parent's Election to Report Child's Unearned Income,* later), and
- When is a child's interest, dividends, and other investment income that is more than $1,200 taxed at the parent's tax rate instead of the child's tax rate. See *Child's Return Filed (Parent's Election Not Made),* later.

For this purpose, the term "child" includes a legally adopted child and a stepchild. These rules apply whether or not the child is a dependent.

These rules do **not** apply if:

- The child is not required to file a tax return, or
- Neither of the child's parents were living at the end of the tax year.

own tax bracket (which will probably be lower than yours). Third, if the property appreciates in value while your child is a minor, the appreciation will not complicate your tax situation.

Useful Items

You may want to see:

Publication

☐ **929** Tax Rules for Children and Dependents

Form (and Instructions)

☐ **8615** Tax for Children Under Age 14 Who Have Investment Income of More Than $1,200
☐ **Form 8814** Parents' Election To Report Child's Interest and Dividends

Which Parent's Return To Use

For parents who do not file a joint return, the following discussions explain which parent's tax return must be used when applying the special tax rules for the investment income of a child under 14. Only that parent can make the election described later under *Parent's Election to Report Child's Unearned Income,* and only that parent's tax rate and other return information is used in the computations explained later under *Child's Return Filed (Parent's Election Not Made).*

Child's parents married. If the child's parents are married to each other and file separate returns, use the return of the parent with the greater taxable income. If they file a joint return, use the joint return.

Parents treated as not married. If a child's parents are married but not living together, and the parent with whom the child lives (the custodial parent) is considered unmarried, use the return of the custodial parent. If the custodial parent is not considered unmarried, use the return of the parent with the greater taxable income.

For an explanation of how a married person is considered unmarried, see *Head of Household* in Chapter 2, *Filing Status.*

Child's parents divorced. If a child's parents are divorced or legally separated, and the parent who had custody of the child for the greater part of the year (the custodial parent) has not remarried, use the return of the custodial parent.

Custodial parent remarried. If the custodial parent has remarried, the stepparent (rather than the noncustodial parent) is treated as the child's other parent. Therefore, the earlier discussion under *Child's parents married* applies.

Explanation
When both parents have custody of a child with unearned income, the custodial parent is the parent with custody for the greater portion of the calendar year.

Child's parents never married. If a child's parents did not marry each other, but lived together all year, use the return of the parent with the greater taxable income. If the parents did not live together all year, the rules explained earlier under *Child's parents divorced* apply.

Widows and widowers. Widows and widowers must use the rules explained earlier under *Child's parents divorced.*

Parent's Election to Report Child's Unearned Income

If you elect to include your child's interest and dividend income on your tax return, the child does not have to file a return.

You can make this election for 1993 only if *all* the following conditions are met.

1) Your child was under age 14 on January 1, 1994.
2) Your child was required to file a return for 1993.
3) Your child had income only from interest and dividends (including Alaska Permanent Fund dividends).
4) The dividend and interest income was more than $500 and less than $5,000.
5) No estimated tax payment was made for 1993 and no 1992 overpayment was applied to 1993 under your child's name and social security number.
6) No federal income tax was withheld from your child's income under the backup withholding rules.
7) You are the parent whose return must be used when applying the special tax rules for children under 14. (See *Which Parent's Return To Use,* earlier.)

How to elect. Make the election by attaching **Form 8814,** to your Form 1040 or Form 1040NR. Attach a separate Form 8814 for each child for whom you make the election. If you file Form 8814, you cannot file Form 1040A or Form 1040EZ.

Tax effect of election. The federal income tax on your child's income may be more if you make the Form 8814 election rather than file a return for the child. The Form 8814 Step 1 base amount ($1,000 not taxed at your higher rate) and the Step 2 nontaxable amount ($500) are not increased for inflation, as are the comparable tax benefits on the child's return. Also, by making the Form 8814 election, you cannot take certain deductions the child would be entitled to on his or her return, as explained next.

Deductions you cannot take. If you use Form 8814, you cannot take any of the following deductions that could have been taken on your child's return:

1) Standard deduction of $600 ($1,500 if your child was blind),
2) Deduction for penalty on early withdrawal of your child's savings, and
3) Itemized deductions (such as your child's investment expenses or charitable contributions).

Deductible investment interest. If you use Form 8814, your child's investment income will be considered your investment income. Thus, for purposes of figuring your deductible investment interest, increase your investment income by that amount. However, if your child received Alaska Permanent Fund dividends, these dividends are not considered investment income. See Publication 550, *Investment Income and Expenses,* for further details.

TaxAlert
Most individuals will not want to elect to file Form 8814, since, as the IRS notes, in some cases, it could result in more total tax.

Figure 32-A. Can You Include Your Child's Income On Your Tax Return?

Start Here

Was your child under age 14 on January 1, 1994? — No →

↓ Yes

Was your child required to file a tax return for 1993? — No →

↓ Yes

Was the child's only income interest and dividends? — No →

↓ Yes

Was the child's income more than $500 and less than $5,000? — No →

↓ Yes

Did the child make any estimated tax payments for 1993? — Yes →

↓ No

Did the child have an overpayment of tax on his or her 1992 return applied to the 1993 estimated tax? — Yes →

↓ No

Was any federal income tax withheld from the child's income (backup withholding)? — Yes →

↓ No

Are you the parent whose return must be used*? — No →

↓ Yes

You can include your child's income on your tax return by completing Form 8814 and attaching it to your return. If you do, your child is not required to file a return.

You cannot include your child's income on your return.

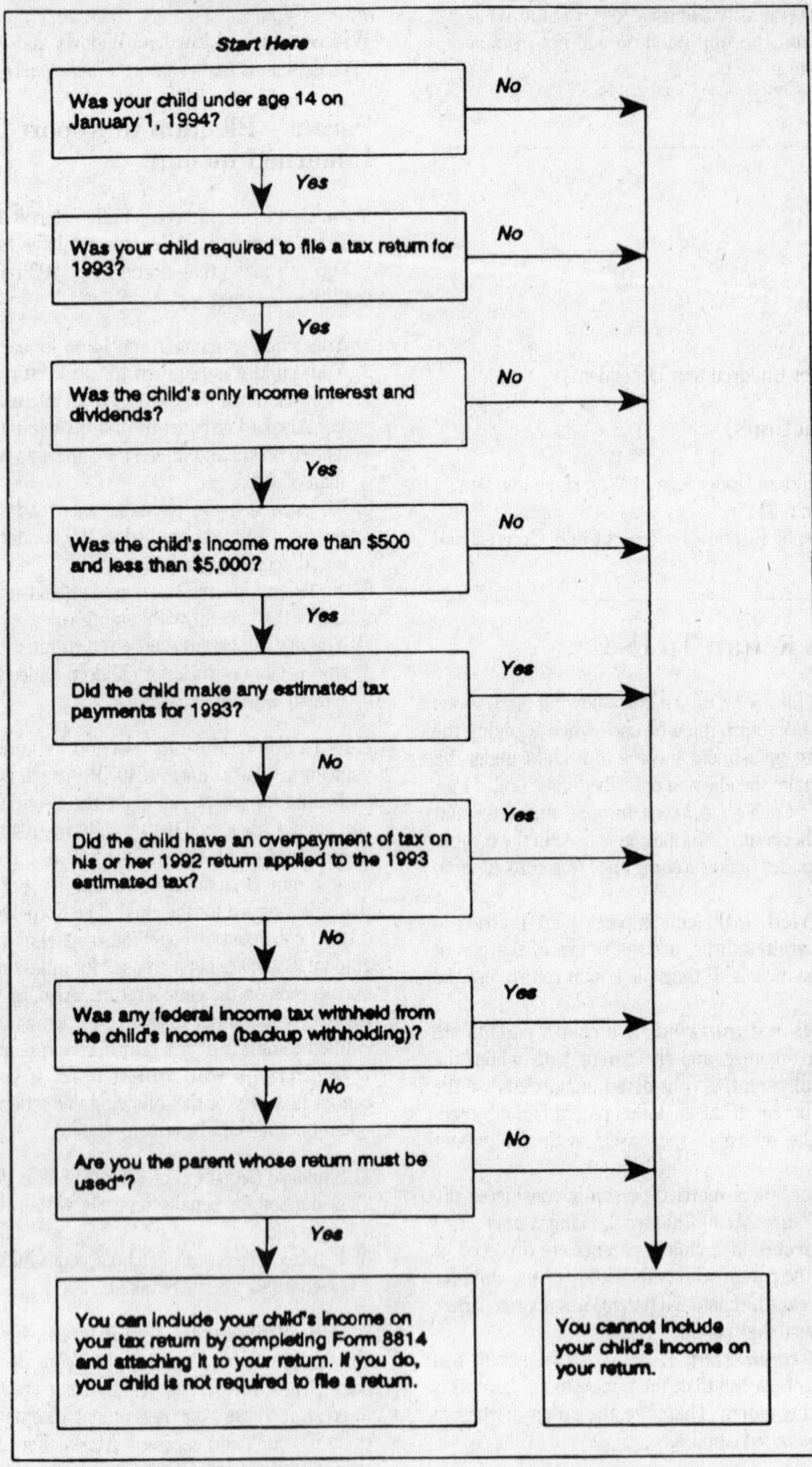

* See *Which Parent's Return to Use*

Increased adjusted gross income. If you use Form 8814 to add your child's income to yours, your increased adjusted gross income may reduce certain items on your return, including the following:

1) Deduction for contributions to an individual retirement arrangement (IRA),
2) Itemized deductions for medical expenses, casualty and theft losses, and certain miscellaneous expenses,
3) Total itemized deductions,
4) Credit for child and dependent care expenses,
5) Personal exemptions, and
6) Earned income credit.

Penalty for underpayment of estimated tax. If you make this election for 1993 and did not have enough tax withheld or pay enough estimated tax to cover the tax you owe, you may be subject to a penalty. If you plan to make this election for 1994, you may need to increase your federal income tax withholding or your estimated tax payments to avoid the penalty. See Chapter 5, *Tax Withholding and Estimated Tax*, for information.

Figuring Amount of Child's Income To Report

Step 1 of Form 8814 is used to figure the amount of your child's income to report on your return. Only the amount in excess of $1,000 is added to your income. Include the amount from line 5, of all your Forms 8814, in the total on line 22, Form 1040 or Form 1040NR. In the space next to line 22, write "Form 8814" and the total from line 5 of all your Forms 8814.

Alternative minimum tax. If your child received any interest from private activity bonds that is a tax preference item, include it as a tax preference item when figuring your alternative minimum tax. Get Publication 909, *Alternative Minimum Tax for Individuals,* for information.

Capital gain distributions. Include in the total on line 2a of Form 8814 any capital gain distributions your child received. Treat these capital gain distributions in the same way as ordinary dividends, unless you file Schedule D (Form 1040) to report capital gains and losses.

If you file Schedule D, part or all of these capital gain distributions should be reported on that schedule (where they may be offset by your capital losses). Get Publication 929 and use the worksheet under *Capital gain distributions* to figure the amount to report on Schedule D and the amount to report on line 5, Form 8814.

Figuring Additional Tax

Step 2 of Form 8814 is used to figure the tax on the amount of your child's interest and dividends that you do not include in your income ($1,000 or less), minus $500. This tax is added to the tax figured on your taxable income.

This additional tax is figured at the lowest tax rate (15%) on the *smaller* of:

1) Your child's gross income minus $500, or
2) $500 ($1,000 minus $500).

The tax cannot be more than $75 (15% × $500).

Include the amount from line 8 of all your Forms 8814 in the total on line 38, Form 1040, or line 37, Form 1040NR. On Form 1040, enter the total from line 8 of all your Forms 8814 in the space provided next to line 38. On Form 1040NR, enter the total of the line 8 amounts in the space provided next to line 37.

Illustrated Example

The facts in this example are illustrated on the filled-in Form 8814 in this chapter.

David and Linda Parks are married and will file separate tax returns for 1993. Their only child, Philip, is 8. For 1993, Philip received a Form 1099-INT showing $3,200 taxable interest income and a Form 1099-DIV showing $300 ordinary dividends. His parents decide to include that income on one of their returns so that they will not have to file a return for Philip.

First, David and Linda each figure their taxable income (Form 1040, line 37) without regard to Philip's income. David's taxable income is $41,700 and Linda's is $59,300. Because her taxable income is greater, Linda can elect to include Philip's income on her return.

On Form 8814, Linda enters her name and social security number, then Philip's name and social security number. She enters Philip's taxable interest income, $3,200, on line 1a. Philip had no tax-exempt interest income, so she leaves line 1b blank. Linda enters Philip's ordinary dividends, $300, on line 2a. Philip did not have any nontaxable distributions, so she leaves line 2b blank and enters $300 on line 2c.

Linda adds the amounts on lines 1a and 2c and enters the result, $3,500, on line 3. From that amount she subtracts the $1,000 base amount shown on line 4 and enters the result, $2,500, on line 5. This is the portion of Philip's income that Linda must add to her income.

Linda includes the $2,500 in the total on line 22 of her Form 1040 and, on the dotted line next to that line writes "Form 8814—$2,500." Adding that amount to her income increases each of the amounts on lines 23, 31, 32, 35, and 37 of her Form 1040 by $2,500. Therefore, her revised taxable income on line 37 is $61,800 ($59,300 + $2,500).

On Form 8814, Linda subtracts the $500 shown on line 6 from the $3,500 on line 3 and enters the result, $3,000, on line 7. Because that amount is $500 or more, she enters $75 on line 8. This is the tax on the $1,000 of Philip's income that Linda did not add to her income. She must add this additional tax to the tax figured on her revised taxable income.

Linda enters $75 in the space provided next to line 38 of her Form 1040. She figures the tax on her $61,800 revised taxable income is $15,430, then adds $75, and enters the $15,505 total on line 38.

Linda attaches Form 8814 to her Form 1040.

Child's Return Filed (Parent's Election Not Made)

Part of a child's 1993 investment income may be subject to tax at the parent's tax rate if:

1) The child was under age 14 on January 1, 1994,
2) The child's investment income was more than $1,200, and
3) The child was required to file a return for 1993.

If the child's parent does not or cannot choose to include the child's income on his or her return, figure the child's tax on **Form 8615.** Attach the form to the child's Form 1040, Form 1040A, or Form 1040NR.

On Form 8615, enter the names and social security numbers of the child and the parent in the spaces provided. (If the parents filed a joint return, enter the name and social security number of the parent who is listed first on the joint return.) Check the box for the parent's filing status. Then figure the child's tax on Form 8615 in these three steps:

Form **8814**	**Parents' Election To Report Child's Interest and Dividends** ▶ See instructions below and on back. ▶ Attach to parents' Form 1040 or Form 1040NR.	OMB No. 1545-1128

Department of the Treasury
Internal Revenue Service

1993

Attachment Sequence No. **40**

Name(s) shown on your return: **Linda Parks**

Your social security number: **123 00 1234**

A Child's name (first, initial, and last): **Philip Parks**

B Child's social security number: **000 00 5678**

C If more than one Form 8814 is attached, check here . . . . ▶ ☐

Step 1 — **Figure amount of child's interest and dividend income to report on your return**

1a Enter your child's **taxable** interest income. If this amount is different from the amounts shown on the child's Forms 1099-INT and 1099-OID, see the instructions . . . . | **1a** | 3,200 |

b Enter your child's **tax-exempt** interest income. **DO NOT** include this amount on line 1a . . . . | **1b** |

2a Enter your child's gross dividends, including any Alaska Permanent Fund dividends. If none, enter -0- on line 2c and go to line 3. If your child received any capital gain distributions or dividends as a nominee, see the instructions . . . . | **2a** | 300 |

b Enter your child's nontaxable distributions that are included on line 2a. These should be shown in box 1d of Form 1099-DIV . . . . | **2b** |

c Subtract line 2b from line 2a . . . . | **2c** | 300 |

3 Add lines 1a and 2c. If the total is $1,000 or less, skip lines 4 and 5 and go to line 6. If the total is $5,000 or more, **do not** file this form. Your child **must** file his or her own return to report the income . . . . | **3** | 3,500 |

4 Base amount . . . . | **4** | 1,000 00 |

5 Subtract line 4 from line 3. If you checked the box on line C above or if line 2a includes any capital gain distributions, see the instructions. Also, include this amount in the total on Form 1040, line 22, or Form 1040NR, line 22. In the space next to line 22, enter "Form 8814" and show the amount. Go to line 6 below . . . . ▶ | **5** | 2,500 |

Step 2 — **Figure your tax on the first $1,000 of child's interest and dividend income**

6 Amount not taxed . . . . | **6** | 500 00 |

7 Subtract line 6 from line 3. If the result is zero or less, enter -0- . . . . | **7** | 3,000 |

8 **Tax.** Is the amount on line 7 less than $500?
- **NO.** Enter $75 here and see the **Note** below.
- **YES.** Multiply line 7 by 15% (.15). Enter the result here and see the **Note** below.
| **8** | 75 |

Note: *If you checked the box on line C above, see the instructions. Otherwise, include the amount from line 8 in the tax you enter on Form 1040, line 38, or Form 1040NR, line 37. Also, enter the amount from line 8 in the space provided next to line 38 on Form 1040, or next to line 37 on Form 1040NR.*

General Instructions

Purpose of Form.—Use this form if you elect to report your child's income on your return. If you do, your child will not have to file a return. You can make this election if your child meets **all** of the following conditions:

- Was under age 14 on January 1, 1994.
- Is required to file a 1993 return.
- Had income only from interest and dividends, including Alaska Permanent Fund dividends.
- Had gross income for 1993 that was less than $5,000.

- Had no estimated tax payments for 1993.
- Did not have any overpayment of tax shown on his or her 1992 return applied to the 1993 return.
- Had no Federal income tax withheld from his or her income (backup withholding).

You must also qualify as explained on page 2 of these instructions.

Step 1 of the form is used to figure the amount of your child's income to report on your return. **Step 2** is used to figure an additional tax that must be added to your tax.

How To Make the Election.—To make the election, complete and attach Form 8814 to your tax return and file your return by the due date (including extensions). A separate Form 8814 must be filed for **each** child whose income you choose to report.

Caution: *The Federal income tax on your child's income may be less if you file a tax return for the child instead of making this election. This is because you cannot take certain deductions that your child would be entitled to on his or her own return. For details, see **Deductions You May Not Take** on page 2.*

For Paperwork Reduction Act Notice, see back of form.

Cat. No. 10750J

Form **8814** (1993)

Figure 32-B. Do You have to Use Form 8615 to Figure Your Child's Tax?

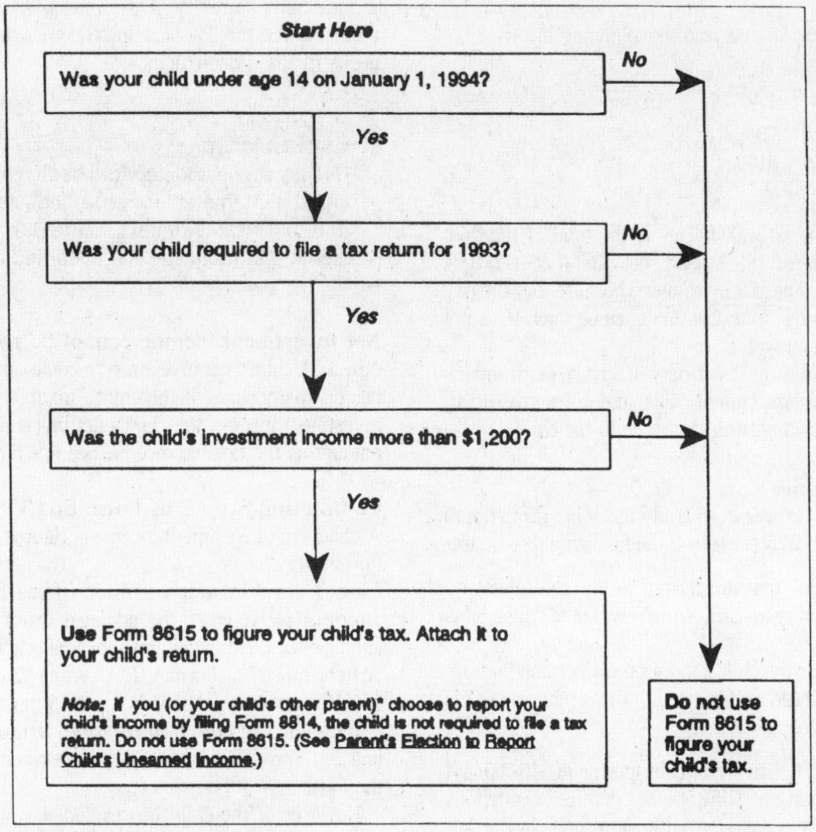

Start Here

Was your child under age 14 on January 1, 1994? — No →

Yes

Was your child required to file a tax return for 1993? — No →

Yes

Was the child's investment income more than $1,200? — No →

Yes

Use Form 8615 to figure your child's tax. Attach it to your child's return.

Note: If you (or your child's other parent)* choose to report your child's income by filing Form 8814, the child is not required to file a tax return. Do not use Form 8615. (See Parent's Election to Report Child's Unearned Income.)

Do not use Form 8615 to figure your child's tax.

* See *Which Parent's Return to Use*

Step 1. Figure the child's net investment income.

Step 2. Figure a tentative tax on the net investment income based on the parent's tax rate.

Step 3. Figure the child's tax.

Alternative minimum tax. A child may be subject to alternative minimum tax (AMT) if he or she has certain items given preferential treatment under the tax laws or certain adjustments to taxable income that totals more than an exemption amount. See *Alternative Minimum Tax* in Chapter 31, *How to Figure Your Tax*.

For information on special limits that apply to a child who files Form 6251, see *Limit on AMT* under *Alternative Minimum Tax* in Publication 929.

Parent's return information. See *Which Parent's Return To Use,* at the beginning of this chapter, for information on which parent's return information must be used on Form 8615.

Different tax years. If the parent and the child do not have the same tax year, complete the form using the information on the parent's return for the tax year that ends in the child's taxable year.

Using estimates. If the information needed from the parent's return is not known by the time the child's return is due (usually April 15), you can file the return using estimates.

Any reasonable estimate can be used. This includes using information from last year's return. If you use an estimated amount on Form 8615 write "Estimated" on the line next to the amount.

When you get the correct information, file an amended return on Form 1040X, *Amended U.S. Individual Income Tax Return.* See *Parent's return information not available* under *Child's Return*

Filed (Parent's Election Not Made) in Publication 929 for more information.

Step 1. Figuring Net Investment Income

The first step in figuring a child's tax using Form 8615 is to figure the child's net investment income. To do that, first figure the child's gross (total) investment income.

Investment Income

Investment income generally includes all income other than salaries, wages, and other amounts received as pay for work actually done. It includes taxable interest, dividends, capital gains, the taxable part of social security payments, and pension payments and certain distributions from trusts.

Nontaxable income. For this purpose, investment income includes only amounts that the child must include in total income. Nontaxable investment income, such as tax-exempt interest and the nontaxable part of social security and pension payments, is not included.

Sources of income. A child's investment income includes all income produced by property belonging to the child, regardless of whether the property was transferred to the child or purchased by the child, and regardless of when the property was transferred or purchased or who transferred it. Investment income includes amounts produced by assets the child obtained with earned income (such as interest on a savings account into which the child deposited wages).

A child's investment income includes income produced by property given as a gift to the child under the Uniform Gift to Minors Act.

Example. Phil Black, 13, received the following income:

Dividends — $600
Wages — $2,100
Taxable interest — $1,200
Tax-exempt interest — $100
Net capital gains — $100.

Phil's investment income is $1,900. This is the total of the dividends ($600), taxable interest ($1,200), and net capital gains ($100). His wages are earned income (not investment) because they are pay received for work actually done. His tax-exempt interest is not included because it is nontaxable.

Trust income. If a child is the beneficiary of a trust, distributions of taxable interest, dividends, capital gains, and other investment income from the trust are investment income to the child.

Net Investment Income

A child's net investment income is generally his or her gross (total) investment income reduced by the sum of the following three items:

1) Adjustments to income that are related to the investment income (such as the penalty on early withdrawal of savings), plus
2) $600, plus
3) The greater of $600 or the child's itemized deductions that are **directly connected** (defined later) with the production of his or her investment income.

Example 1. Eleanor, 8, has investment income of $16,000 and an early withdrawal penalty of $100. She has itemized deductions of $1,100 that are directly connected with the production of her investment income. Her net investment income is $14,200. This is her total investment income of $16,000, reduced by $1,800. The $1,800 is the sum of the early withdrawal penalty ($100), plus $600, plus the directly-connected itemized deductions ($1,100).

Example 2. Roger, 12, has investment income of $8,000, no adjustments to income, and itemized deductions of $300 that are directly connected with his investment income. His net investment income is $6,800. This is his total investment income of $8,000, reduced by $1,200 ($600 + $600).

His investment income is reduced by $1,200 because he has no adjustments to income and his directly-connected itemized deductions ($300) are not more than $600.

TaxSaver

If your child is under 14 years of age and has investment income and you are in the top income bracket, you may want to consider altering his or her investment strategy. Since a child with over $1,200 in unearned income will be taxed at his or her parent's rate, it might be advisable to seek out deferred or tax-exempt income. Tax-exempt municipal bonds or U.S. Government EE Bonds could be appropriate choices.

Directly-connected itemized deductions. Itemized deductions are directly connected with the production of investment income if they are for expenses paid to produce or collect taxable income or to manage, conserve, or maintain property held for producing income. These expenses include custodian fees and service charges, service fees to collect taxable interest and dividends, and certain investment counsel fees. They are deducted on Schedule A (Form 1040) to the extent that they, plus certain other miscellaneous itemized deductions, are more than 2% of adjusted gross income. See Chapter 30, *Miscellaneous Deductions*, for more information about the 2% of adjusted gross income limit on miscellaneous itemized deductions.

Explanation

Directly connected itemized deductions also include any investment interest expense deducted in the child's return that relates to debt incurred to finance the investments that produced the unearned income.

Net investment income cannot be more than taxable income. A child's net investment income cannot be more than his or her taxable income. If the child's taxable income is less than net investment income, the child's net investment income is the same amount as the taxable income. See line 5 of Form 8615.

Completing Step 1 of Form 8615

A child's net investment income is figured on lines 1 through 5 of Form 8615.

Line 1 (investment income). If the child had *investment income only,* enter the adjusted gross income shown on the child's return. Adjusted gross income is shown on line 32 of Form 1040 or line 17 of Form 1040A or line 32 of Form 1040NR. Form 1040EZ cannot be used if Form 8615 must be filed.

If the child had *earned income,* figure the amount to enter on line 1 of Form 8615 by using the worksheet in the instructions for the form.

However, if the child has excluded any *foreign earned income* or deducted either a *loss from self-employment* or a *net operating loss* from another year, use the worksheet in Publication 929 to figure the amount to enter on line 1.

Step 2. Figuring Tentative Tax at Parent's Tax Rate

The tentative tax is the difference in the tax on the parent's taxable income figured with and without the child's net investment income. Figure it as follows:

1) Figure the tax on the total of the parent's taxable income plus the child's net investment income at the parent's tax rate.
2) Figure the tax on the parent's taxable income without including the child's net investment income.
3) Subtract the tax in (2) from the tax in (1). This is the tentative tax.

Caution. When making these computations, do not take into account the child's net investment income in figuring any exclusion, deduction, or credit on the parent's return.

Special rule. See *Trusts* under *Figuring Tentative Tax at Parent's Tax Rate* in Publication 929 for information about a special rule that may apply if the parent is the grantor of a trust.

More Than One Child

If the tax return information of the child's parent is used on Forms 8615 for other children (including adopted children and stepchildren), the net investment income of all these children is used in figuring the tentative tax. The tentative tax is then allocated to each child according to the child's share of the total net investment income.

If the net investment income of the other children is not available when the return is due, either file the return using estimates or use an extension of time to file. Extensions are discussed under *Extensions of Time to File* in Chapter 1, *Filing Information*.

Allocation of tentative tax. The tentative tax is allocated to each child by multiplying the total tentative tax by a fraction. The numerator (top number) of the fraction is the child's net investment income. The denominator (bottom number) is the total of the net investment income of all the children. The result of each multiplication is that child's share of the tentative tax.

Example. The Oaks' two children, Bill and Patty, ages 11 and 12, have $2,000 and $3,000 of net investment income. Tax on their incomes must be figured at their parents' rate. On Form 8615, Bill's and Patty's net investment incomes are combined and the total ($5,000) is added to their parents' taxable income shown on their joint tax return. The difference between (1) the tax figured on the total of their parents' taxable income plus the children's net investment income and (2) the actual tax on their parents' return is $1,750. This difference (the tentative tax) must be allocated between Bill and Patty.

The amount allocated to Bill is $700.

$$\frac{\$2,000}{\$5,000} \times \$1,750 = \$700$$

The amount allocated to Patty is $1,050.

$$\frac{\$3,000}{\$5,000} \times \$1,750 = \$1,050$$

Completing Step 2 of Form 8615

The tentative tax based on the parent's tax rate is figured on lines 6 through 13 of Form 8615.

Line 9 (tax figured on parent's taxable income plus children's net investment income). How you figure the tax to enter on line 9 depends on whether there is any net capital gain included in the total on line 8.

Net capital gain is the excess of net long-term capital gain over net short-term capital loss.

The maximum tax rate on net capital gain is 28%.

No net capital gain on line 8. If there is no net capital gain included in the amounts on lines 5, 6, or 7, use the Tax Table or Tax Rate Schedules to figure the tax to enter on line 9.

If the amount on line 8 is less than $100,000, you must use the Form 1040 Tax Table to figure the tax to enter on line 9. If the amount on line 8 is $100,000 or more, you must use the Tax Rate Schedules.

Net capital gain on line 8. If there is net capital gain included in the amounts on lines 5, 6, or 7, the tax on line 9 may be less if you can use the *Schedule D Tax Worksheet* in the Schedule D instructions. You can use the Schedule D Tax Worksheet to figure the tax if:

The parent's filing status is:	AND	The amount on Form 8615, line 8, is over:
• Single		• $53,500
• Married filing joint return or Qualifying widow(er) with dependent child		• $89,150
• Married filing separate return		• $44,575
• Head of household		• $76,400

See Publication 929 for information on how to complete the *Schedule D Tax Worksheet*. If you cannot use the *Schedule D Tax Worksheet* to figure the tax, you must use the Tax Table or Tax Rate Schedule, whichever applies.

Step 3. Figuring the Child's Tax

The final step in figuring a child's tax using Form 8615 is to determine the *larger* of:

1) The total of:
   a) The child's share of the tentative tax based on the parent's tax rate, plus
   b) The tax on the child's taxable income in excess of net investment income, figured at the child's tax rate, or
2) The tax on the child's taxable income, figured at the child's tax rate.

Completing Step 3 of Form 8615

The child's tax is figured on lines 14 through 18 of Form 8615.

Line 15 (tax on excess of child's taxable income over child's net investment income). Generally, you must use the Tax Table (use the single column) or Tax Rate Schedule X to figure the tax to enter on line 15. However, if the amount on line 14 is more than $53,500 and includes net capital gain, the tax on line 14 may be less if the *Schedule D Tax Worksheet* is used.

Net capital gain on line 14. If net capital gain is included on line 1 (Form 8615) and the *Schedule D Tax Worksheet* can be used, the net capital gain included on line 14 must be figured before the *Schedule D Tax Worksheet* can be completed. See Publication 929.

Illustrated Example

The following example includes a completed Form 8615.

John and Laura Brown have one child, Sara. She is 13 and has $2,400 taxable interest and dividend income and $1,500 earned income. She does not itemize deductions. John and Laura file a joint return with John's name and social security number listed first. They claim three exemptions, including an exemption for Sara, on their return.

Because Sara has both earned and unearned income and her gross income is more than $600, she must file a tax return. Because she is under age 14 and has more than $1,200 investment income, part of her income may be subject to tax at her parents' rate. A completed Form 8615 must be attached to her return.

Sara's father, John, fills out Sara's return for her.

John enters his name and social security number on Sara's Form 8615 because his name and number are listed first on the joint return he and Laura are filing. He checks the box for married filing jointly.

He enters Sara's investment income, $2,400, on line 1. Sara does not itemize deductions, so John enters $1,200 on line 2. He enters $1,200 on line 3 ($2,400 − $1,200).

Sara's taxable income, as shown on line 22 of her Form 1040A, is $2,400. This is her total income ($3,900) minus her standard deduction ($1,500). Her standard deduction is limited to the amount of her earned income. John enters $2,400 on line 4.

John compares the amounts on lines 3 and 4 and enters the smaller amount, $1,200, on line 5.

John enters $48,000 on line 6. This is the taxable income from line 37 of John and Laura's joint Form 1040 return. Sara is an only child, so line 7 is blank. He adds the amounts on line 5 ($1,200), line 6 ($48,000), and line 7 and enters the $49,200 total on line 8.

Using the column for married filing jointly in the Tax Table, John finds the tax on $49,200. He enters the tax, $8,986, on line 9. He enters $8,650 on line 10. This is the tax from line 38 of John and Laura's Form 1040. He enters $336 on line 11 ($8,986 − $8,650).

John skips lines 12a and 12b and enters $336 on line 13.

John subtracts the amount on line 5 ($1,200) from the amount on line 4 ($2,400) and enters the result, $1,200, on line 14. Using the column for single filing status in the Tax Table, John finds the tax on $1,200. He enters this tax, $182, on line 15. He adds the amounts on lines 13 ($336) and 15 ($182) and enters the total, $518, on line 16.

Using the column for single filing status in the Tax Table, John finds the tax on $2,400 (the amount on line 4). He enters this tax, $362, on line 17.

John compares the amounts on lines 16 and 17 and enters the larger amount, $518, on line 18 of Sara's Form 8615. He also enters that amount on line 23 of Sara's Form 1040A and checks the box on that line for "Form 8615." John also completes Schedule 1 (Form 1040A) for Sara.

Form **8615**

Department of the Treasury
Internal Revenue Service

Tax for Children Under Age 14
Who Have Investment Income of More Than $1,200

▶ See instructions below and on back.
▶ Attach ONLY to the child's Form 1040, Form 1040A, or Form 1040NR.

OMB No. 1545-0998

1993

Attachment
Sequence No. **33**

Child's name shown on return	Child's social security number
Sara L. Brown	989 00 4351

A Parent's name (first, initial, and last). **Caution:** See instructions on back before completing.

John J. Brown

B Parent's social security number

459 00 9962

C Parent's filing status (check one):

☐ Single ☑ Married filing jointly ☐ Married filing separately ☐ Head of household ☐ Qualifying widow(er)

Step 1	Figure child's net investment income		
1	Enter child's investment income, such as taxable interest and dividend income. See instructions. If this amount is $1,200 or less, **stop here;** do not file this form	**1**	2,400
2	If the child DID NOT itemize deductions on Schedule A (Form 1040 or Form 1040NR), enter $1,200. If the child ITEMIZED deductions, see instructions	**2**	1,200
3	Subtract line 2 from line 1. If the result is zero or less, **stop here;** do not complete the rest of this form but ATTACH it to the child's return	**3**	1,200
4	Enter child's **taxable** income from Form 1040, line 37; Form 1040A, line 22; or Form 1040NR, line 36	**4**	2,400
5	Enter the **smaller** of line 3 or line 4 here . . . . ▶	**5**	1,200

Step 2	Figure tentative tax based on the tax rate of the parent listed on line A		
6	Enter parent's **taxable** income from Form 1040, line 37; Form 1040A, line 22; Form 1040EZ, line 6; or Form 1040NR, line 36. If the parent transferred property to a trust, see instructions . .	**6**	48,000
7	Enter the total net investment income, if any, from Forms 8615, line 5, of ALL OTHER children of the parent identified above. **Do not** include the amount from line 5 above	**7**	
8	Add lines 5, 6, and 7	**8**	49,200
9	Tax on line 8 based on the **parent's** filing status. See instructions. If from Schedule D Tax Worksheet, enter amount from line 4 of that worksheet here ▶ _____	**9**	8,986
10	Enter parent's tax from Form 1040, line 38; Form 1040A, line 23; Form 1040EZ, line 8; or Form 1040NR, line 37. If from Schedule D Tax Worksheet, enter amount from line 4 of that worksheet here ▶ _____	**10**	8,650
11	Subtract line 10 from line 9. If line 7 is blank, enter on line 13 the amount from line 11; skip lines 12a and 12b	**11**	336
12a	Add lines 5 and 7	**12a**	
b	Divide line 5 by line 12a. Enter the result as a decimal (rounded to two places)	**12b**	× .
13	Multiply line 11 by line 12b . . . . ▶	**13**	336

Step 3	Figure child's tax—If lines 4 and 5 above are the same, go to line 16 now.		
14	Subtract line 5 from line 4	**14**	1,200
15	Tax on line 14 based on the **child's** filing status. See instructions. If from Schedule D Tax Worksheet, enter amount from line 4 of that worksheet here ▶ _____	**15**	182
16	Add lines 13 and 15	**16**	518
17	Tax on line 4 based on the **child's** filing status. See instructions. If from Schedule D Tax Worksheet, check here . . . . ▶ ☐	**17**	362
18	Enter the **larger** of line 16 or line 17 here and on Form 1040, line 38; Form 1040A, line 23; or Form 1040NR, line 37. Be sure to check the box for "Form 8615" even if line 17 is more than line 16 . ▶	**18**	518

General Instructions

A Change To Note.—If line 8 of Form 8615 is over $70,000 (over $140,000 if the parent's filing status is married filing jointly or qualifying widow(er)), the election to defer additional 1993 taxes may apply to the child. Get **Form 8841,** Deferral of Additional 1993 Taxes, for details. If the election is made, Form 1040A **cannot** be filed for the child.

Purpose of Form.—For children under age 14, investment income over $1,200 is taxed at the parent's rate if the parent's rate is higher than the child's rate. If the child's investment income is more than $1,200, use this form to figure the child's tax.

Investment Income.—As used on this form, "investment income" includes all taxable income other than earned income as defined on page 2. It includes income such as taxable interest, dividends, capital gains, rents, royalties, etc. It also includes pension and annuity income and income (other than earned income) received as the beneficiary of a trust.

Who Must File.—Generally, Form 8615 must be filed for any child who was under age 14 on January 1, 1994, had more than $1,200 of investment income, and is required to file a tax return. If neither parent was alive on December 31, 1993, do not use Form 8615.

Instead, figure the child's tax in the normal manner.

Note: The parent may be able to elect to report the child's interest and dividends on his or her return. If the parent makes this election, the child will not have to file a return or Form 8615. For more details, see the instructions for Form 1040 or Form 1040A, or get **Form 8814,** Parents' Election To Report Child's Interest and Dividends.

Additional Information.—For more details, get **Pub. 929,** Tax Rules for Children and Dependents.

Incomplete Information for Parent.—If the parent's taxable income or filing status or the net investment income of

For Paperwork Reduction Act Notice, see back of form.

Cat. No. 64113U

Form **8615** (1993)

33 | Child and Dependent Care Credit

Introduction

*A credit that directly reduces your taxes is available for certain child and **dependent** care expenses that enable you to work. The credit may be as much as $720 if you have one qualifying individual or $1,440 if you have more than one qualifying individual. The credit is designed to help ease the tax burden of persons who must work and who also have the responsibility for the care of children or disabled dependents and spouses.*

*In general, to claim this credit, you must pay someone to care for a qualifying individual so that you can work or look for work. You must also have **earned income** from your work during the year and must have maintained a home for yourself and the qualifying individual. This chapter spells out all the details.*

Important Reminders

Child born in 1993. If you claim the part of the earned income credit that is an extra credit for a child born in 1993, you cannot claim the credit for child and dependent care expenses for care of that child. You also cannot exclude from income any dependent care benefits for that child.

If you are eligible to claim both credits for the same child, you must choose only one. If you need more information about the extra credit for a child born in 1993, see Chapter 35, *Other Credits*.

Caution. Beginning in 1994, new law changes the earned income credit. The extra credit for a child born during the year will no longer be available. See Publication 553, *Highlights of 1993 Tax Changes*, for information on changes to the earned income credit.

You may have to pay employment taxes. If you pay someone to come to your home and care for your dependent or spouse, you may be a household employer who has to pay employment taxes. Usually, you are *not* a household employer if the person who cares for your child or dependent does so at his or her home or place of business. See Publication 926, *Employment Taxes for Household Employers*, for a discussion of employment taxes and what forms you must file if you are a household employer.

Provider identification. You must provide certain information on all persons or organizations that care for your child or dependent. For information on this identification, see *Provider Identification Test*, later.

This chapter discusses the credit for child and dependent care expenses and covers the following topics:

- Tests you must meet to claim the credit
- How to figure the credit
- How to claim the credit
- Employment taxes you may have to pay as a household employer

To qualify for the credit, you must pay someone to care for your dependent under age 13 or your disabled spouse or dependent. You must pay these expenses so you can work or look for work. You must also meet certain other tests, which are explained in this chapter.

Useful Items

You may want to see:

Publication

- ☐ **503** Child and Dependent Care Expenses
- ☐ **596** Earned Income Credit
- ☐ **926** Employment Taxes for Household Employers

Form (and Instructions)

- ☐ **W-10** Dependent Care Provider's Identification and Certification
- ☐ **940** Employer's Annual Federal Unemployment (FUTA) Tax Return
- ☐ **940-EZ** Employer's Annual Federal Unemployment (FUTA) Tax Return
- ☐ **942** Employer's Quarterly Tax Return for Household Employees
- ☐ **Schedule 2 (Form 1040A)** Child and Dependent Care Expenses for Form 1040A Filers
- ☐ **2441** Child and Dependent Care Expenses
- ☐ **6251** Alternative Minimum Tax—Individuals

Tests to Claim the Credit

To be able to claim the credit for child and dependent care expenses, you must meet **all** the following tests. These tests are presented in *Figure 33–A* and are also explained in detail in this chapter. You must file Form 1040 or Form 1040A, not Form 1040EZ.

1) The care must be for one or more qualifying persons. For information about who is a qualifying person, see *Qualifying Person Test,* later.
2) You (and your spouse if you are married) must keep up a home that you live in with the qualifying person or persons. (See *Keeping Up a Home Test,* later.)
3) You (and your spouse if you are married) must have earned income during the year. (However, under *Earned Income Test,* later, see *Rule for a student-spouse or spouse not capable of self-care.*)
4) You must pay child and dependent care expenses so you (and your spouse if you are married) can work or look for work. (See *Work-Related Expense Test,* later, for more information.)
5) Your filing status is Single, Head of household, Qualifying widow(er) with dependent child, or Married filing jointly. You must file a joint return if you are married, unless an exception discussed later under *Joint Return Test* applies to you.
6) You must identify the care provider on your tax return. (See *Provider Identification Test,* later.)
7) You must make payments for child and dependent care to someone you (or your spouse) cannot claim as a dependent. If you make payments to your child, he or she cannot be your dependent and must be age 19 or older by the end of the year. (See *Payments to Relatives,* later.)
8) You exclude less than $2,400 (less than $4,800 if two or more qualifying persons were cared for) of dependent care assistance benefits. See *Reduced Dollar Limit,* under *Dollar Limit,* later.

Qualifying Person Test

Your child and dependent care expenses must be for the care of one or more members of your home who are qualifying persons. A qualifying person is:

1) Your dependent who was under age 13 when the care was provided and for whom you can claim an exemption (for exceptions, see *Child born in 1993* and *Child of Divorced or Separated Parents,* later),
2) Your spouse who was physically or mentally unable to care for himself or herself, or
3) Your dependent who was physically or mentally unable to care for himself or herself and for whom you can claim an exemption (or could claim an exemption except the person had $2,350 or more of gross income).

Physically or mentally unable to care for oneself. Persons who are not able to dress, clean, or feed themselves because of physical or mental problems are considered not capable of self-care. Also, persons who require constant attention to prevent them from injuring themselves or others are considered not capable of self-care.

Person qualifying for part of year. You determine a person's qualifying status each day. For example, if the person you pay child and dependent care expenses for no longer qualifies on September 16, count only those expenses through September 15. Also see *Dollar Limit,* later.

Child born in 1993. If you claim the part of the earned income credit that is an extra credit for a child born in 1993, you cannot claim the credit for child and dependent care expenses for care of that child. That child is not a qualifying person for purposes of the child and dependent care credit.

If you claim the extra credit for a child born in 1993, you can still claim the child and dependent care credit for another qualifying person. If you need more information about the extra credit for a child born in 1993, see Chapter 35, *Other Credits*.

Child of Divorced or Separated Parents

To be a qualifying person, your child usually must be your dependent for whom you can claim an exemption. But an exception may apply if you are divorced or separated. Under the exception, if you are the custodial parent, you can treat your child as a qualifying person even if you cannot claim the child's exemption. If you are the noncustodial parent, you cannot treat your child as a qualifying person even if you can claim the child's exemption.

This exception applies if:

1) One or both parents had custody of the child for more than half of the year,
2) One or both parents provided more than half of the child's support for the year, and
3) Either—
   a) The custodial parent signed Form 8332, *Release of Claim to Exemption for Child of Divorced or Separated Parents,* or a similar statement, agreeing not to claim the child's exemption for the year, or
   b) The noncustodial parent provided at least $600 for the child's support and can claim the child's exemption under a pre-1985 decree of divorce or separate maintenance, or written agreement.

You can use *Figure 33–B* to see whether this exception applies to you. If it applies, only the custodial parent can treat the child as a qualifying person. If the exception does not apply, follow the regular rules for a qualifying person under *Qualifying Person Test,* earlier.

If you can take the credit because of this exception, write your child's name in the space to the left of line 3, Form 2441 or Schedule 2 (Form 1040A).

Example. You are divorced and have custody of your 8-year-old child. You sign Form 8332 to allow your ex-spouse to take the exemption. You pay child care expenses so you can work. Your child is a qualifying person and you, the custodial parent, can claim the credit for those expenses, even though your ex-spouse claims an exemption for the child.

Custodial parent. You are the custodial parent if, during the year, you have custody of your child longer than your child's other parent has custody.

Figure 33-A. Can You Claim the Credit?

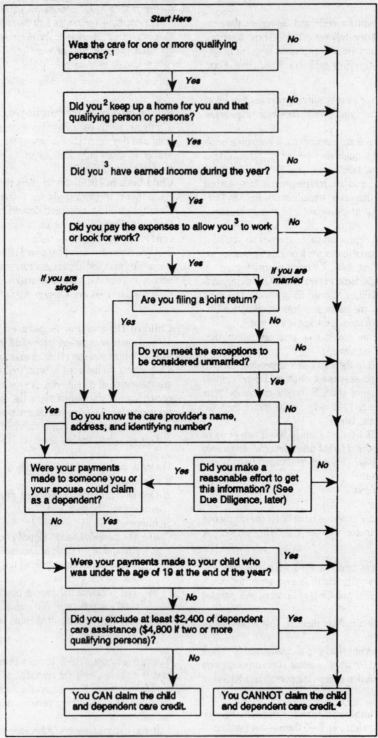

1. If you claim the extra credit for a child born in 1993 (part of the earned income credit) for your child, that child is not a qualifying person.

2. You and your spouse if you were married.

3. This also applies to your spouse, unless your spouse was disabled or a full-time student.

4. If you had expenses that met the requirements for 1992, except that you did not pay them until 1993, you may be able to claim those expenses in 1993. See *Expenses not paid until the following year,* later.

Figure 33-B. **Is a Child of Divorced or Separated Parents a Qualifying Person?**

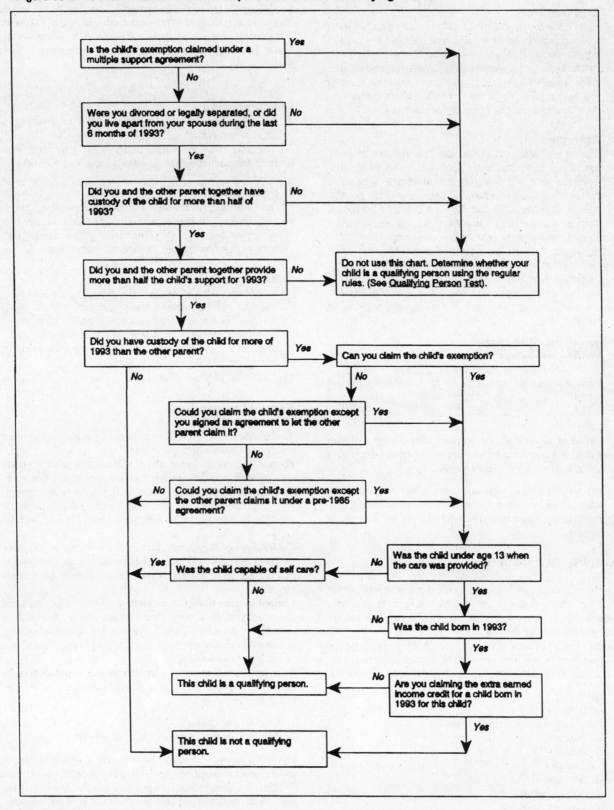

Explanation

To take the credit, you do not have to claim the child as a dependent. If you have custody of the child but have signed a statement that entitles another person to the child's dependency exemption, you may still claim the credit. To receive the credit, however, you must attach to your tax return a copy of the signed statement authorizing the release of your dependency claim.

Example

Charles and Margaret Collins are divorced and share custody of their 3-year-old son, Alan. Alan lives 10 months a year with Margaret and attends a day-care center while his mother works. Charles and Margaret provide all of Alan's support. Alan is a qualifying person, since he is under age 13, is in the custody of his parents for more than half the year, and receives more than half his support from his parents. He is a qualifying person for Margaret and not Charles, because Margaret has custody of him for a longer period than does Charles. Alan is a qualifying person for Margaret, even if she has released her right to claim him as a dependent to Charles.

TaxAlert

In no case may two taxpayers filing separate returns claim separate tax credits for the same qualifying individual.

Divorced or separated. For purposes of determining whether your child is a qualifying person, you are considered divorced or separated if either of the following apply.

1) You are divorced or separated under a decree of divorce or separate maintenance or a written separation agreement, or
2) You lived apart from your spouse for all of the last 6 months of the year.

Keeping Up a Home Test

To claim the credit, you (and your spouse if you are married) must keep up a home that you live in with one or more qualifying persons. You are keeping up a home if you pay more than half the cost of running it for the year.

Home. The term "home" means the main home for both you and the qualifying person. Your home can be the main home even if the qualifying person does not live there all year because of his or her:

   Birth,
   Death, or
   Temporary absence due to:
1) Sickness,
2) School,
3) Business,
4) Vacation,
5) Military service, or
6) Custody agreement.

Costs of keeping up home. The costs of keeping up a home normally include property taxes, mortgage interest, rent, utility charges, home repairs, insurance on the home, and food eaten at home.

The costs of keeping up a home do not include payments for

clothing, education, medical treatment, vacations, life insurance, transportation, and mortgage principal. They also do not include the purchase, permanent improvement, or replacement of property. For example, you cannot include the cost of replacing a water heater. However, you can include the cost of repairing a water heater.

Explanation

It is not sufficient that you maintain a household without also living there.

If more than one family occupies living quarters in common, each family constitutes a separate household.

Example 1

Ann Bailey and her children and Monica Stewart and her children share a house. Both Ann and Monica provide more than half the costs of maintaining their respective families. Each is treated as maintaining a household.

Example 2

Ruth Martin is the 10-year-old daughter of Lynne Martin. She lives with her mother, who provides more than half the costs of running their home. During the summer, Ruth spends three months with her father. Her absence does not prevent Lynne's home from being Ruth's residence.

Earned Income Test

To claim the credit, you (and your spouse if you are married) must have earned income during the year.

Earned income includes wages, salaries, tips, other employee compensation, and net earnings from self-employment. Earned income also includes strike benefits and any disability pay you report as wages. Earned income is reduced by any net loss from self-employment. See Chapter 11, *Retirement Plans, Pensions, and Annuities*.

   Members of the clergy. Certain income earned by ministers, members of religious orders, and Christian Science practitioners may not be considered earned income for this purpose. See Publication 503.

Earned income does not include pensions or annuities, social security payments, workers' compensation, interest, dividends, or unemployment compensation. It also does not include scholarship or fellowship grants, except for amounts paid to you for teaching, research, or other services.

Rule for a student-spouse or spouse not capable of self-care. Your spouse is treated as having earned income for any month that he or she is:

1) A full-time student, or
2) Physically or mentally not capable of self-care.

Figure the earned income of the nonworking spouse as shown under *Earned Income Limit,* under *How to Figure the Credit,* later.

   This rule applies to only one spouse for any one month. If, in the same month, both you and your spouse do not work and are either full-time students or physically or mentally not capable of self-care, only one of you can be treated as having earned income in that month.

   Full-time student. You are a full-time student if you are enrolled at and attend a school for the number of hours or classes that the school considers full time. You must have been a student for some part of each of 5 calendar months during the year. (The months need not be consecutive.) If you attend school only at night, you are not a full-time student. However, as part of your full-time course of study, you may attend some night classes.

The term "school" includes elementary schools, junior and senior high schools, colleges, universities, and technical, trade, and mechanical schools. It does not include on-the-job training courses, correspondence schools, and night schools.

Example

James and Janet are married and file a joint return. Janet works full-time. James was a full-time student from January through May and from September through December. Their 4-year-old son attends a day-care center while James is in school. Since James was a full-time student during at least 5 months of the year, the minimum required by the IRS, he is considered to have worked each of the 9 months he was a full-time student.

Assume the same facts, except that both James and Janet were full-time students for 9 months during the year. Only one of them may be considered as having worked during the months they were students. They would not be able to claim a credit for child care expenses.

Assume instead that, while James and Janet were full-time students, James also held a part-time job. Both may now be considered as having worked during the 9 months they were students—James because he was working and Janet because she was a full-time student. They may claim a credit for child care expenses.

Work-Related Expense Test

Child and dependent care expenses must be work-related to qualify for the credit. Expenses are considered work-related only if:

- They allow you (and your spouse if you are married) to work or look for work, and
- They are for a qualifying person's care.

Working or Looking for Work

To be work related, your expenses must be to allow you to work or look for work. If you are married, generally both you and your spouse must work or look for work. Your spouse is treated as working during any month he or she is a full-time student or is physically or mentally not capable of self-care. See *Rule for a student-spouse or spouse not capable of self-care* under *Earned Income Test,* earlier.

Whether your expenses allow you to work or look for work depends on the facts. For example, the cost of a baby sitter while you and your spouse go out to eat is not normally a work-related expense. Also, expenses are not considered work related merely because you had them while you were working.

Your work can be for others or in your own business or partnership. It can be either full time or part time. Work also includes actively looking for work. However, if you do not find a job and have no earned income for the year, you cannot take this credit. See *Earned Income Limit,* later. Unpaid volunteer work or volunteer work for a nominal salary does not qualify.

Example 1

Susan Green is single. She began looking for a job in November, 1993. Prior to this time, she had not worked. While looking for a job, she paid a sitter to watch her 4-year-old daughter. She finally found a job in February, 1994. Her child care expenses during November and December, 1993 were $125. Since Susan did not have income from work in 1993, she may not claim a credit for her child care expenses for that year.

Assume the same facts, except that Susan had worked until October, 1993, when she was laid off and began looking for a new job. In this instance, she did have income from work during the year, so she may claim a credit for her child care expenses incurred while looking for work.

Example 2

Mary Smith works 12 hours per week as an unpaid volunteer in the library of the local elementary school. She pays a sitter to watch her 3-year-old twins while she is working. Since she is not compensated for her work, she may not claim a credit for her child care expenses.

If Mary were paid $15 per week for her services in the library, she still could not claim a credit for her child care expenses because her work is for a nominal salary. What is considered a nominal salary is determined by the facts and circumstances of each situation. As a general rule, however, if you are working for less than the minimum wage, you are probably working for a nominal salary.

Work test met for part of year. If you work or actively look for work during only part of the period covered by the expenses, then you must figure your expenses for each day. For example, if you work all year and pay care expenses of $120 a month ($1,440 for the year), all the expenses are work related. However, if you work or look for work for only 2 months and 15 days during the year and pay expenses of $120 a month, your work-related expenses are limited to $300 (2½ months × $120).

Payments while you are out sick. Do not count as work-related expenses amounts you pay for child and dependent care while you are off work because of illness. These amounts are not paid to allow you to work. This applies even if you get sick pay and are still considered an employee.

Example

Samantha Street has a housekeeper during the day to watch her 9-year-old daughter while Samantha works. She pays the housekeeper $1,000 a month. As a result of illness, Samantha was home 20 days during September. Her illness was not mentally or physically disabling. Samantha's work-related expenses for the month are $333 [(10 work days ÷ 30) × $1,000].

If you know that your total work-related expenses for the year will exceed the limits, it is not necessary to perform this calculation.

Care of a Qualifying Person

To be work related, your expenses must be to provide care for a qualifying person. You do not have to choose the least expensive way of providing the care.

Expenses for household services qualify if part of the services is for the care of qualifying persons. For details, see *Household services,* later.

Expenses are for the care of a qualifying person only if their main purpose is the person's well-being and protection. Expenses for care do not include amounts you pay for food, clothing, and entertainment. However, if these amounts are incident to and cannot be separated from the cost of caring for the qualifying person, you can count the total cost.

Schooling. You can count the total cost of sending your child to school if:

1) Your child is not in the first grade or any higher grade, *and*
2) The amount you pay for schooling is incident to and cannot be separated from the cost of care.

Therefore, you can use the total cost of schooling below first grade only if the cost of schooling cannot be separated from the cost of the child's care. If your child is in the first grade or higher, or if the cost of schooling can be separated, you must divide the total cost between the cost of care and the cost of schooling. You can count only the cost of care in figuring your credit.

Example 1. You take your 3-year-old child to a nursery school that provides lunch and educational activities as a part of its pre-school child care service. You can count the total cost in figuring the credit.

Example 2. Your 5-year-old child goes to kindergarten in the morning. In the afternoon, she attends an after-school day care program at the same school. Your total cost for sending her to the school is $3,000, of which $1,800 is for the after-school program. Only the $1,800 qualifies for figuring the credit.

Example 3. You place your 10-year-old child in a boarding school so you can work full time. Only the part of the boarding school expense that is for the care of your child is a work-related expense. You cannot count any part of the amount you pay the school for your child's education.

Care outside your home. You can count the cost of care provided outside your home if the care is for your dependent under age 13, or any other qualifying person who regularly spends at least 8 hours each day in your household.

Dependent care center. You can count care provided outside your home by a dependent care center if the center complies with all applicable state and local regulations. A dependent care center is a place that provides care for more than six persons (other than persons who live there) and receives a fee, payment, or grant for providing services for any of those persons, even if the center is not run for profit.

Explanation

If a care center has six or fewer individuals enrolled on the day on which you enroll a qualified person, you may presume that it is not a dependent care center for the tax year. You may also presume that, if a center was not a dependent care center in the prior year and has six or fewer individuals enrolled on January 1, it will not be considered a dependent care center during the current year.

As the IRS text notes, if care is provided by a dependent care center, the center must meet local and state regulations for your expenses to qualify for the credit. For example, most states stipulate the maximum permissible ratio of children to adult workers in a day-care center. You may wish to inquire at a center if it meets all state and local regulations. Ask to see a copy of the center's most recent certification from the proper authorities. However, if care is provided by a center that is not a dependent care center, the center need not meet local and state regulations for your expenses to qualify for the credit.

Example

Sam Anderson attends a child care center during the week while his mother works. The center regularly cares for 15 children and does not meet local and state regulations. The center is a dependent care center, but, since the center does not meet the appropriate government regulations, expenses for Sam's care do not qualify for the tax credit.

Assume the same facts, except that the center regularly cares for five children. Now the center is not a dependent care center. Expenses for Sam's care qualify for the tax credit, although the center does not meet government regulations.

Camp. The cost of sending your child to an overnight camp is *not* considered a work-related expense.

Transportation. The cost of getting a qualifying person from your home to the care location and back, or from the care location to school and back, is *not* considered a work-related expense. This includes the costs of bus, subway, taxi, or private car. Also, if you pay the transportation cost for the care provider to come to your home, you cannot count this cost as a work-related expense.

Household services. Expenses you pay for household services meet the work-related expense test if they are at least *partly* for the well-being and protection of a qualifying person.

Household services are ordinary and usual services done in and around your home that are necessary to run your home. They include the services of a housekeeper, maid, or cook. However, they do not include the services of a chauffeur, bartender, or gardener. See *Household Services* in Publication 503, for more information.

TaxPlanner

There are no hard-and-fast rules that govern when an allocation is reasonable or when the expense for other services is small in relation to the total expense. The facts and circumstances of each case are the determining factors. Use your best judgment. If you must make an allocation, you should document how the allocation is made. If you decide that an allocation is not necessary, you should also document the basis for your decision. A note in your personal records should be sufficient.

Taxes paid on wages. If you pay wages for household help, you may have to pay the employer's portion and withhold the employee's portion of the social security and Medicare taxes. You may also have to pay federal unemployment (FUTA) tax and similar state taxes. The taxes you pay on wages for qualifying child and dependent care services are work-related expenses. See Chapter 37, *What to Do If You Employ Domestic Help.*

Payments to Relatives

You can count work-related payments you pay to relatives who are not your dependents, even if they live in your home. However, do not count any amounts you pay to:

1) A dependent for whom you (or your spouse if you are married) can claim an exemption, or

2) Your child who was under age 19 at the end of the year, even if he or she is not your dependent.

Example

Georgia Stephens lives with her daughter Sara and cares for her granddaughter Marie after school while Sara is at work. Sara pays her mother $300 per month and does not claim her as a dependent. These payments qualify as work-related expenses for Sara.

Assume, instead, that Sara pays her other daughter, Frances, $150 per month to look after Marie, Frances's sister. Frances turns 19 during the year but is claimed as a dependent by Sara. Sara's payments to Frances are not qualified work-related expenses.

Joint Return Test

Generally, married couples must file a joint return to take the credit. However, if you are legally separated or living apart from your spouse, you may be able to file a separate return and still take the credit.

Married couple. If you are married at the end of your tax year, you must file a joint return with your spouse to take the credit. If your spouse died during the year and you do not remarry before the end of the year, you must file a joint return to take the credit. If you do remarry before the end of the year, the credit can be claimed on your deceased spouse's separate return.

Legally separated. You are not considered married if you are legally separated from your spouse under a decree of divorce or separate maintenance. You are eligible to take the credit on a separate return.

Married and living apart. You are not considered married and are eligible to take the credit if **all** the following apply:

1) You file a separate return.
2) Your home is the home of a qualifying person for more than half the year.
3) You pay more than half the cost of keeping up your home for the year.
4) Your spouse does not live in your home for the last 6 months of the year.

Example

Mark and Katherine Bristol separated in April. They are not **legally separated** at the end of the year and plan to file separate returns. Their two children lived with Katherine for the entire year, and she provided more than half the costs of maintaining her household for the year. Katherine may claim a credit on her separate return.

Assume, instead, that Mark and Katherine were separated in August. Since Mark lived in Katherine's home during part of the last 6 months of the year, a joint return must be filed to claim the credit.

Provider Identification Test

You must identify all persons or organizations that provide care for your child or dependent. Do this on the same form you use to claim the credit. If you file Form 1040, use Part I of Form 2441 to report the required information. If you file Form 1040A, use Part I of Schedule 2.

Information required. To identify the care provider, you must give the provider's:

1) Name,
2) Address, and
3) Taxpayer identification number.

If the care provider is an individual, the taxpayer identification number is his or her social security number. If the care provider is an organization, then it is the employer identification number (EIN).

The taxpayer identification number is not required if the care provider is one of certain tax-exempt organizations (such as a church or school). In this case, write "Tax-Exempt" in the space where the tax form calls for the number.

If you cannot provide all of the information required, or the information is incorrect, you must be able to show that you used due diligence (discussed later) in trying to furnish the required information.

Getting the information. You can use **Form W–10** to request the required information from the care provider. If you do not use Form W–10, you can get the required information from:

1) A copy of the provider's social security card,
2) A copy of the provider's driver's license (in a state where the license includes the social security number),
3) A copy of the provider's completed Form W–4 if he or she is your household employee,
4) A copy of the statement furnished by your employer if the provider is your employer's dependent care assistance program, or
5) A letter or invoice from the provider if it shows the required information.

You should keep the required information about the care provider with your tax records. Do not send Form W–10 (or other document containing this information) to the Internal Revenue Service.

TAXORGANIZER

Keep Form W-10 with your tax records to substantiate the name, address, and taxpayer identification number(s) of your day-care provider(s). If Form W-10 is not used, keep any other documents that substantiate the required information.

Due diligence. If the care provider information you give is incorrect or incomplete, your credit may not be allowed. However, if you can show that you used due diligence in trying to supply the required information, you can still claim the credit.

You can show due diligence by getting and keeping the provider's completed Form W–10 or one of the other sources of information listed above. Care providers can be penalized if they do not provide this information to you or if they provide incorrect information.

Provider refusal. If the provider refuses to give you the required information, you should report whatever information you have (such as the name and address) on the form you use to claim the credit. Write "See page 2" in the columns calling for the information you do not have. On the bottom of page 2, explain that you requested the information from the care provider, but the provider did not give you the information. This statement will show that you used due diligence in trying to furnish the required information.

How to Figure the Credit

Your credit is a percentage of your work-related expenses. Your expenses are subject to the earned income limit and the dollar limit. The percentage is based on your adjusted gross income.

Figuring Total Work-Related Expenses

To figure the credit for 1993 work-related expenses, count only those you paid by December 31, 1993.

Expenses prepaid in an earlier year. If you pay for services before they are provided, you can count the prepaid expenses only in the year the care is received. Fill out your Form 2441 or Schedule 2 (Form 1040A) for the later year as if the prepaid expense was actually paid in the later year.

Example
Martha Winters paid $1,800 in November, 1993 to the day-care center her son attends. The payment was for the 6-month period from November, 1993 through April, 1994. She may use $600 (2/6 × $1,800) of this payment in calculating her credit for 1993. This amount represents payment for services rendered in November and December, 1993. She may use $1,200 (4/6 × $1,800) of this payment in 1994. This amount represents payment for services rendered in January through April, 1994.

Expenses not paid until the following year. Do *not* count 1992 expenses that you paid in 1993 as work-related expenses for 1993. You may be able to claim an additional credit for them on your 1993 return, but you must figure it separately. See *Payments for previous year's expenses* under *Amount of Credit,* later.

If you had expenses in 1993 that you did not pay until 1994, you cannot count them when figuring your 1993 credit. You may be able to claim a credit for them on your 1994 return.

TAXPLANNER

The general rule is that expenses used in computing your child care credit are included in figuring your tax for the year in which the expenses are paid or for the year in which the services are provided, whichever is later. However, regardless of when they are paid, expenses are subject to the dollar limitation for the year in which the services are provided. You may not reap an additional tax advantage by paying your expenses in a year that is different from the one in which the services are provided.

Example
Jennifer Reid, who is divorced and files a separate return, paid $300 in January, 1993 for care provided for her daughter in November and December, 1992. Her adjusted gross income and earned income in 1992 were $25,000, and she paid $1,200 for work-related ex-

penses in 1992. Jennifer may increase her 1993 child care credit by $66 (as calculated in Column A below).

		Column A	Column B
1)	1992 expenses paid in 1992	$ 1,200	$ 2,500
2)	1992 expenses paid in 1993	300	300
3)	Total 1992 expenses	$ 1,500	$ 2,800
4)	Limitation for one qualifying person	$ 2,400	$ 2,400
5)	Earned income limitation	25,000	25,000
6)	Smallest of lines 3, 4, and 5	1,500	2,400
7)	Child care expenses used in calculating 1992 credit	(1,200)	(2,400)
8)	1992 expenses carried over to 1993	$ 300	$ —0—
9)	Credit percentage applicable for 1992 adjusted gross income	22%	22%
10)	Increase in 1993 credit (line 8 × line 9)	$ 66	$ —0—

Jennifer should attach a statement to her 1993 return, showing the above calculation in Column A as support for her inclusion of $66 on line 10, Form 2441.

Assume, instead, that Jennifer paid $2,500 in work-related expenses during 1992. No increase in her 1993 credit is available (see Column B above), since the maximum amount of expenses for 1992 is already used in calculating the credit. She receives no benefit for the $300 paid in 1993, as she would have received no benefit if it had been paid in 1992.

Expenses reimbursed. If a state social services agency pays you a nontaxable amount to reimburse you for some of your child and dependent care expenses, you cannot count the expenses that are reimbursed as work-related expenses.

Example. You paid work-related expenses of $3,000. You are reimbursed $2,000 by a state social services agency. You can use only $1,000 to figure your credit.

Employer's dependent care assistance plan. Do *not* count as work-related expenses any child and dependent care benefits provided by your employer that you do not include in your income. You can exclude benefits from your income only if they are paid under a qualified plan. Your employer can tell you whether your benefit plan qualifies. If it does, you must complete Part III of either Form 2441 or Schedule 2 (Form 1040A) to claim the exclusion.

The amount you can exclude cannot be more than the smallest of:

1) Your earned income,
2) Your spouse's earned income, or
3) $5,000 ($2,500 if married filing separately).

Statement for employee. Your employer must give you a Form W–2, *Wage and Tax Statement* (or similar statement), showing in box 10 the total amount of dependent care assistance benefits provided to you during the year.

Forfeitures. Forfeitures are amounts credited to your dependent care assistance account and included in the amount shown in box 10 of your Form W–2, but which you did not receive because you did not incur the expense. You must subtract any forfeitures from the total dependent care benefits reported by your employer.

To do this, enter the forfeited amount on line 12 of Form 2441 or Schedule 2 (Form 1040A). Forfeitures do not include amounts that you expect to receive in the future.

Medical expenses. Some expenses for the care of a qualifying person who is not capable of self-care may qualify as work-related expenses and also as medical expenses. You can use them either way, but you cannot use the same expenses to claim both a credit and a medical expense deduction.

If you use these expenses to figure the credit and they are more than the earned income limit or the dollar limit, discussed later, you can add the excess to your medical expenses. However, if you use your total expenses to figure your medical expense deduction, you cannot use any part of them to figure your credit.

> ### Example
> During the year, you pay $2,750 to a private-duty nurse for the care of your physically handicapped dependent daughter, who is not able to care for herself. These expenses are for work done in your home and qualify as medical expenses. Your earned income for the year is $25,000. Because your work-related expenses are for one qualifying person, you may take a maximum of $2,400 of these expenses into account in figuring your tax credit. You may treat the remaining $350 as a medical expense.

Note. Amounts excluded from your income under your employer's dependent care assistance plan *cannot* be used to claim a medical expense deduction.

> ### TaxOrganizer
> Keep copies of receipts and cancelled checks to document the amount of dependent care expenses that you paid for the year. The fact that you may have provided these to your employer's plan may not be sufficient without such records.

Earned Income Limit

The amount of work-related expenses you use to figure your credit cannot be more than:

1) Your earned income for the year, if you are *single* at the end of the year, or
2) The smaller of your earned income or your spouse's earned income for the year, if you are *married* at the end of the year.

For purposes of item (2), use your spouse's earned income for the entire year, even if you were married for only part of the year.

Separated spouse. If you are legally separated or married and living apart from your spouse (as described under *Joint Return Test,* earlier), you are not considered married for purposes of the earned income limit. Use only your income when figuring the earned income limit.

Surviving spouse. If your spouse died during 1993 and you file a joint return as a surviving spouse, you are not considered married for purposes of the earned income limit. Use only your income in figuring the earned income limit.

Earned income. Earned income is defined under *Earned Income Test,* earlier.

Community property laws. You should disregard community property laws when you figure your earned income for this credit.

> ### Example
> Harry and Elizabeth Jones are married and live in a community property state. Harry earns $52,000 as an engineer, while Elizabeth earns $15,000 as a nurse. Under community property laws, each is considered to have earned half the other's compensation. Hence, each is considered to bring in $33,500 [(50% × $52,000) + (50% × $15,000)]. For the purpose of calculating this tax credit, however, Harry has $52,000 of earned income and Elizabeth has $15,000.

Self-employment. If you are self-employed, include your net earnings in earned income. For purposes of the child and dependent care credit, net earnings from self-employment generally means the amount from line 3 of Schedule SE (either Section A or Section B) *minus* any deduction for self-employment tax on line 25 of Form 1040. Include your self-employment earnings in earned income, even if they are less than $400 and you did not file Schedule SE. If you filed Schedule C or C–EZ to report income as a statutory employee, also include as earned income the amount from line 1 of that Schedule C or C–EZ.

You must reduce your earned income by any net loss from self-employment.

Optional method. If your net earnings from self-employment are low or you have a net loss, you may be able to figure your net earnings by the optional method, instead of the regular method. Get Publication 533, *Self-Employment Tax,* for details. If you can use either optional method to figure net earnings for self-employment tax purposes, include those net earnings in your earned income for this credit. In this case, subtract any deduction you claimed on Form 1040, line 25, from the total of the amounts on Schedule SE, Section B, lines 3 and 4b, to figure your net earnings.

> ### TaxPlanner
> At year end, if you are self-employed you should review your income and expenses for the year. To the extent it is possible, income and expenses for the remaining part of the year should be timed to take maximum advantage of the dependent care credit.

Student-spouse or spouse not capable of self-care. As discussed earlier under *Earned Income Test,* your spouse who is either a full-time student or not capable of self-care is treated as having earned income. His or her earned income for each month is considered to be at least $200 if there is one qualifying person in your home, or at least $400 if there are two or more. If your spouse works during that month, use the higher of $200 (or $400) or his or her actual earned income for that month. If your spouse is a full-time student or not capable of self-care for only part of a month, the full $200 (or $400) still applies.

If, in the same month, both you and your spouse are either full-time students or not capable of self-care, only one spouse can be considered to have this earned income of $200, or $400, for that month.

Example

Mary Smith works full-time as a real estate broker and earns $25,000. John Smith is a full-time medical student for 11 months during the year and has no earned income. They have a 5-year-old son whose day-care expenses for the year are $5,000. John is treated as earning $2,200 for the year ($200 per month for the 11 months he is a student). Their work-related expenses for the year may therefore not exceed $2,200.

Dollar Limit

There is a dollar limit on the amount of your work-related expenses you can use to figure the credit. This limit is $2,400 for one qualifying person, or $4,800 for two or more qualifying persons.

Yearly limit. The dollar limit is a yearly limit. The amount of the limit remains the same no matter how long you have a qualifying person in your household. Use the $2,400 limit if you paid work-related expenses for the care of one qualifying person at any time during the year. Use $4,800 if you paid work-related expenses for the care of more than one qualifying person at any time during the year.

Example

Patricia Ellis employs a full-time housekeeper to care for her two children while she works. Her older child turned 13 years old during the year. The dollar limit on her work-related expenses is $4,800, since at some time during the year she had two qualifying persons.

Assume the same facts, except that Patricia has only one child, who turned 13 years old on August 31. The dollar limit on her work-related expenses is $2,400. Only her expenses through August 31 may be used. The limit is the maximum amount that may be used in calculating the credit. If her actual expenses through August are less than $2,400, she must use that amount in calculating her tax credit.

Reduced Dollar Limit

If you received child and dependent care benefits from your employer that you do not include in your income, you must subtract the excluded amount from the dollar limit that applies to you. See *Employer's dependent care assistance plan,* earlier, for information on excluding these benefits.

Example. You are a widower with one child and earn $20,000 a year. You pay work-related expenses of $1,600 for your 4-year-old child and qualify to claim the credit for child and dependent care expenses. Your employer pays an additional $1,000 under a dependent care assistance plan. This $1,000 is excluded from your income. The dollar limit for your work-related expenses is $2,400 (one qualifying person). However, your credit is figured on only $1,400 of the $1,600 work-related expenses you paid because the dollar limit is reduced to $1,400 by the excludable benefits as follows:

Dollar limit: Maximum allowable expenses for one qualifying person	$2,400
Minus: dependent care benefits you can exclude from income	1,000
Reduced limit on expenses you can use for the credit	$1,400

Amount of Credit

To determine the amount of your credit, multiply your work-related expenses (after applying the earned income and dollar limits) by the applicable percentage. The applicable percentage depends on your adjusted gross income shown on line 32 of Form 1040 or line 17 of Form 1040A. The following table shows the applicable percentage based on adjusted gross income.

Adjusted Gross Income		Applicable Percentage
Over	But not over	
$ 0 —	$10,000	30%
10,000 —	12,000	29%
12,000 —	14,000	28%
14,000 —	16,000	27%
16,000 —	18,000	26%
18,000 —	20,000	25%
20,000 —	22,000	24%
22,000 —	24,000	23%
24,000 —	26,000	22%
26,000 —	28,000	21%
28,000 —	No Limit	20%

Example

Mary Smith is single, has adjusted gross income of $23,500, and has $1,800 in qualified expenses for 1993. The credit available to her is $414 (23% × $1,800).

Assume, instead, that Mary has adjusted gross income of $28,500. Now her available tax credit is $360 (20% × $1,800).

Alternative minimum tax limit. If you file Form 1040, your credit may be limited because of the alternative minimum tax. If you file Schedules C, C–EZ, D, E, or F (Form 1040), you should complete Form 6251 to figure whether your credit will be limited. If you did not file any of those schedules, you should complete the worksheet that comes with the instructions for Form 2441, to see if you still need to complete Form 6251.

You may have to figure alternative minimum tax if you file Form 1040A. See the Form 1040A instructions for line 27 for more information.

Payments for previous year's expenses. If you had work-related expenses in 1992 that you paid in 1993, you may be able to increase the credit on your 1993 return. There is a worksheet in Publication 503 to figure this amount.

How to Claim the Credit

To claim the credit, you can file Form 1040 or Form 1040A. You cannot claim the credit on Form 1040EZ. You must file a joint return if you are married, unless the exceptions discussed earlier under *Joint Return Test* apply to you.

Form 1040. You must complete **Form 2441,** and attach it to your Form 1040. Enter the credit on line 41 of your Form 1040.

Form 1040A. You must complete **Schedule 2** and attach it to your Form 1040A. Enter the credit on line 24a of your Form 1040A. See Chapter 44, *Sample Form 1040A*, for an example and a filled-in Schedule 2.

Tax credit not refundable. Your credit for child and dependent care expenses cannot be more than the amount of your tax liability. Therefore, you cannot get a refund for any part of the credit that is more than your tax.

> ### Example
> Sharon White has a tax liability of $400 before credits and a potential child care credit of $720. She may use $400 of the child care credit to bring her tax liability to zero. The excess credit of $320 is effectively lost. It may not be refunded, carried forward to a future year, or carried back to a prior year.

Records. You should keep records of your work-related expenses. Also, if your dependent or spouse is not capable of self-care, your records should show both the nature and the length of the disability. Other records you should keep to support your claim for the credit are described earlier under *Provider Identification Test*.

> ### TAXORGANIZER
> Your records of work-related expenses may be either cancelled checks or cash receipt tickets. A note in your files recording the nature and length of a person's disability should be sufficient documentation in most cases.
>
> ### Explanation
> If you have a household employee, such as a housekeeper, a baby-sitter, or a companion, see Chapter 37, *What to Do If You Employ Domestic Help*.

Examples

The following examples show how to figure the credit. Example 2 is illustrated by the filled-in Form 2441 at the end of this chapter.

Example 1: Child Care—Two Children. Ann and Jerry Jones are married and keep up a home for their two preschool children, ages 2 and 4. They claim their children as dependents and file a joint return using Form 1040A. Their adjusted gross income (line 17) is $22,500 and the entire amount is earned income. Ann earned $12,500 and Jerry earned $10,000.

During the year, they pay work-related expenses of $3,000 for child care at a neighbor's home and $2,200 for child care at Pine Street Nursery School.

They figure the credit on Schedule 2 as follows:

Child care by neighbor	$3,000
Child care by nursery school	2,200
Total work-related expenses	$5,200
Dollar limit	$4,800
Amount of credit (23% of $4,800)	$1,104

Because their earned income is more than $4,800, the earned income limit, discussed earlier, does not apply.

Example 2: Dependent Care Assistance Benefits. Joan Thomas is divorced and has two children, ages 3 and 9. She works at ACME Computers. Her adjusted gross income is $29,000, and the entire amount is earned income.

Joan's younger child stays at her employer's on-site child care center while she works. The benefits from this child care center qualify to be excluded from her income. Her employer reports the value of this service as $3,000 for the year. This $3,000 is shown in box 10 of her Form W–2, but is not included in taxable wages in box 1.

A neighbor cares for Joan's older child after school, on holidays, and during the summer. She pays her neighbor $2,400 for this care.

Joan figures her credit on Form 2441 as follows:

Work-related expenses Joan paid	$2,400
Dollar limit	$4,800
Minus: Dependent care benefits excluded from income	3,000
Reduced dollar limit	$1,800
Amount of credit (20% of $1,800)	$ 360

Note. The dollar limit for two or more qualifying persons ($4,800), is reduced by the amount of excluded benefits, as discussed earlier under *Reduced Dollar Limit*.

This example, using Form 2441 (Form 1040), is illustrated at the end of this chapter. The illustration shows how to claim the child and dependent care credit, how to exclude the dependent care benefits, and how to report the identification of the care provider.

> ### Example 1
> Janice Johnson is single and works to keep up a home for herself and her dependent father. Her adjusted gross income of $25,000 is entirely earned income.
>
> Her father was disabled and incapable of self-care for 6 months. To keep working, she paid a housekeeper $500 per month to care for her father, prepare lunch and dinner, and do housework.
>
> Her credit is as follows:
>
> | | |
> |---|---:|
> | Total work-related expenses (6 × $500) | $3,000 |
> | Maximum allowable expenses | $2,400 |
> | Amount of credit (22% of $2,400) | $ 528 |
>
> ### TAXALERT
> As stated earlier under *Qualifying Person Test,* if the dependent for whom you have work-related expenses is disabled for only part of a month, the total work-related expenses are limited to that part of the month.
>
> ### Example 2
> Diane and Richard are married and file a joint return. Because of an accident, Richard is incapable of self-care for the entire tax year. To keep working, Diane pays a neighbor $2,000 to take care of him. Diane's adjusted

gross income is $29,000. The entire amount is earned income.

They figure their credit on the smallest of the following amounts:

1) Total work-related expenses	$ 2,000
2) Diane's earned income	$29,000
3) Income considered earned by Richard (12 × $200)	$ 2,400
Allowable credit (20% of $2,000)	$ 400

Example 3

John Harris works and keeps up a home for himself, his wife Peggy, and their two children (both under age 13).

John has adjusted gross income of $35,000. The entire amount is earned income.

Peggy is a full-time student at State University from January 4 through June 10. She does not return to school after June 10.

They paid a neighbor $500 per month from January 4 to June 10 (total $3,000) to care for their two children in her home while they are not in school.

They figure the credit on the smallest of the following amounts:

1) Total work-related expenses	$ 3,000
2) John's earned income	$35,000
3) Income considered earned by Peggy (6 × $400)	$ 2,400
Allowable credit (20% of $2,400)	$ 480

Form 2441 (1993)

Part III **Dependent Care Benefits**—Complete this part **only** if you received these benefits.

11 Enter the total amount of **dependent care benefits** you received for 1993. This amount should be shown in box 10 of your W-2 form(s). DO NOT include amounts that were reported to you as wages in box 1 of Form(s) W-2 .... | 11 | 3,000

12 Enter the amount forfeited, if any. See the instructions .... | 12 |

13 Subtract line 12 from line 11 .... | 13 | 3,000

14 Enter the total amount of **qualified expenses** incurred in 1993 for the care of the qualifying person(s) ..... | 14 | 5,400

15 Enter the **smaller** of line 13 or 14 ...... | 15 | 3,000

16 Enter YOUR **earned income** .... | 16 | 29,000

17 If married filing a joint return, enter YOUR SPOUSE'S earned income (if student or disabled, see the line 6 instructions); if married filing a separate return, see the instructions for the amount to enter; **all others,** enter the amount from line 16 | 17 | 29,000

18 Enter the **smallest** of line 15, 16, or 17 .... | 18 | 3,000

19 **Excluded benefits.** Enter here the **smaller** of the following:
 • The amount from line 18, or
 • $5,000 ($2,500 if married filing a separate return and you were required to enter your spouse's earned income on line 17). | 19 | 3,000

20 **Taxable benefits.** Subtract line 19 from line 13. Also, include this amount on Form 1040, line 7. On the dotted line next to line 7, write "DCB" | 20 | -0-

To claim the child and dependent care credit, complete lines 21–25 below, and lines 4–10 on the front of this form.

21 Enter the amount of qualified expenses you incurred and paid in 1993. DO NOT include on this line any excluded benefits shown on line 19 | 21 | 2,400

22 Enter $2,400 ($4,800 if two or more qualifying persons) | 22 | 4,800

23 Enter the amount from line 19 .... | 23 | 3,000

24 Subtract line 23 from line 22. If zero or less, **STOP.** You cannot take the credit. **Exception.** If you paid 1992 expenses in 1993, see the line 10 instructions. | 24 | 1,800

25 Enter the **smaller** of line 21 or 24 here **and** on line 4 on the front of this form | 25 | 1,800

Form **2441** (1993)

Form **2441**

Department of the Treasury
Internal Revenue Service (T)

Child and Dependent Care Expenses

▶ Attach to Form 1040.
▶ See separate instructions.

OMB No. 1545-0068

1993

Attachment Sequence No. **21**

Name(s) shown on Form 1040   Joan Thomas

Your social security number   569 00 3436

You need to understand the following terms to complete this form: **Dependent Care Benefits, Earned Income, Qualified Expenses,** and **Qualifying Person(s).** See **Important Terms** on page 1 of the Form 2441 instructions. Also, if you had a child born in 1993 and line 32 of Form 1040 is less than $23,050, see **A Change To Note** on page 2 of the instructions.

Part I **Persons or Organizations Who Provided the Care**—You **must** complete this part.
(If you need more space, use the bottom of page 2.)

1	(a) Care provider's name	(b) Address (number, street, apt. no., city, state, and ZIP code)	(c) Identifying number (SSN or EIN)	(d) Amount paid (see instructions)
	Pat Green	12 Ash Avenue Hometown, TX 75240	240-00-3911	2,400
	Acme Computers	See W-2		

2 Add the amounts in column (d) of line 1 .... | 2 | 2,400

3 Enter the number of qualifying persons cared for in 1993. ▶ | 2

Did you receive dependent care benefits?
 NO ——▶ Complete only Part II below.
 YES ——▶ Complete Part III on the back now.

Part II **Credit for Child and Dependent Care Expenses**

4 Enter the amount of **qualified expenses** you incurred and paid in 1993. DO NOT enter more than $2,400 for one qualifying person or $4,800 for two or more persons. If you completed Part III, enter the amount from line 25 .... | 4 | 1,800

5 Enter YOUR **earned income** .... | 5 | 29,000

6 If married filing a joint return, enter YOUR SPOUSE'S earned income (if student or disabled, see instructions); **all others,** enter the amount from line 5 .... | 6 | 29,000

7 Enter the **smallest** of line 4, 5, or 6 .... | 7 | 1,800

8 Enter the amount from Form 1040, line 32 ...... | 8 | 29,000

9 Enter on line 9 the decimal amount shown below that applies to the amount on line 8 | 9 | × .20

If line 8 is—		Decimal amount is	If line 8 is—		Decimal amount is
Over	But not over		Over	But not over	
$0—10,000		.30	$20,000—22,000		.24
10,000—12,000		.29	22,000—24,000		.23
12,000—14,000		.28	24,000—26,000		.22
14,000—16,000		.27	26,000—28,000		.21
16,000—18,000		.26	28,000—No limit		.20
18,000—20,000		.25			

10 Multiply **line 7** by the decimal amount on line 9. Enter the result. Then, see the instructions for the amount of credit to enter on Form 1040, line 41
Caution: If you paid $50 or more in a calendar quarter to a person who worked in your home, you must file an employment tax return. Get **Form 942** for details. | 10 | 360

For Paperwork Reduction Act Notice, see separate instructions.   Cat. No. 11862M   Form **2441** (1993)

34 | Credit for the Elderly or the Disabled

Introduction

When Congress passed legislation giving the elderly a tax credit, the idea was to provide a measure of tax relief for older citizens who were not receiving adequate amounts of social security or other nontaxable **pensions.** *Consequently, if you or your spouse is 65 years old or older, you may be entitled to a credit of as much as $1,125 against your tax.*

Taxpayers under 65 years of age who are permanently and totally disabled may also be eligible for the credit.

In general, if you file as a **single** *individual, you do* **not** *qualify for the tax credit if you are 65 years old or over and (1) you receive nontaxable social security or other nontaxable pensions of $5,000 or more, (2) your* **adjusted gross income** *is $17,500 or more, or (3) your tax is zero. This chapter tells you specifically if you are eligible for the credit for the elderly and, if so, how you may claim it.*

This chapter discusses:

- Who qualifies for the credit for the elderly or the disabled, and
- How to figure this credit.

The maximum credit available is $1,125. You may be able to claim this credit if you:

- Are age 65 or older, or
- Are retired on permanent and total disability.

You also must:

- File either Form 1040 or Form 1040A, and
- Fill out either Schedule R (Form 1040) or Schedule 3 (Form 1040A).

Explanation
See Chapter 12, *Social Security and Equivalent Railroad Retirement Benefits,* for a discussion of how social security and equivalent railroad retirement benefits are taxed.

Internal Revenue Service (IRS) will figure your credit. If you choose to have the IRS figure your tax on Form 1040 or Form 1040A, and you qualify for the credit for the elderly or the disabled, the IRS will also figure the credit for you. See *Credit Figured for You,* later.

TaxAlert

With the aid of this book, you should not have to rely on the IRS to calculate your credit. Although the IRS routinely checks the mathematics on a return, it, too, can make computational errors. Also, as noted in Chapter 31, *How To Figure Your Tax,* you must still provide certain information to enable the IRS to calculate the credit. Therefore, our advice is to give the calculation of your credit a try.

Useful Items

You may want to see:

Publication

- ☐ **524** Credit for the Elderly or the Disabled
- ☐ **554** Tax Information for Older Americans

Forms (and Instructions)

- ☐ **Schedule 3 (Form 1040A)** Credit for the Elderly or the Disabled for Form 1040A Filers
- ☐ **Schedule R (Form 1040)** Credit for the Elderly or the Disabled

Can You Take the Credit?

You can take the credit for the elderly or the disabled if you are a qualified individual and if your income is not more than certain limits. *Figure 34–A and Figure 34–B* can be used as guides to see if you qualify.

Read Figure 34–A first to see if you are a qualified individual. If you are, go to Figure 34–B to make sure your income is not too high. If your income is too high, you cannot take the credit. If it is not too high, you will qualify for the credit and this chapter will help you figure the correct amount.

If you want, the IRS will figure the credit for you. See *Credit Figured for You,* later.

Qualified Individual

You are a qualified individual for this credit if you are a U.S. citizen or resident and:

1) You are age 65 or older by the end of the tax year, or
2) You are under age 65 at the end of the tax year, and
    a) You are retired on permanent and total disability,
    b) You did not reach mandatory retirement age before 1993, and
    c) You received taxable disability benefits in 1993.

Explanation
To qualify for the credit, you cannot have reached your employer's mandatory retirement age before the beginning of the year. The reason for the requirement is that any amount received from your employer *after* you have reached mandatory retirement age is *not* disability income.

Age 65. You are considered 65 on the day before your 65th birthday. Therefore, you are 65 by the end of 1993 if your 65th birthday is on January 1, 1994.

U.S. citizen or resident. You must be a U.S. citizen or resident to claim the credit. Generally, you may not claim the credit if you were a nonresident alien at any time during the tax year. However, if you are a nonresident alien who is married to a U.S. citizen or resident at the end of the tax year and you both choose to be treated as U.S. residents and be taxed on your worldwide income, you may be able to claim the credit.

Also, if you were a nonresident alien at the beginning of the year and a resident at the end of the year, and you were married to a U.S. citizen or resident at the end of the year, you may both choose to be treated as U.S. residents for the entire year and thus be allowed to claim the credit. For information on these choices, see Publication 519, *U.S. Tax Guide for Aliens.*

Explanation
For more information about nonresident aliens, see Chapter 39, *Foreign Citizens Living in the United States.*

Married Persons

Generally, if you are married at the end of the tax year, you and your spouse must file a joint return to claim the credit. If you and your spouse did not live in the same household at any time during the tax year, you may file either joint or separate returns and still take the credit.

If you are married, living with your child and apart from your spouse, you may be considered unmarried. See *Head of Household* in Chapter 2, *Filing Status,* for the tests you must meet.

Example 1
Tom and Betsy Fitch are both past the age of 65 and are married at year's end, but they have been living apart since May. They must file a joint return to claim the credit. Next year, if they remain married and live apart for the entire year, they may file separate returns and claim the credit.

Example 2
George and Sylvia Thompson are married at year's end and have lived apart for the entire year. Sylvia is 63 years old and receives a disability pension from her former employer. George is 69 years old. They may file separate returns, and each may claim a credit, since both meet the basic tests for eligibility.

Community property. Married persons living apart and not filing a joint return may be able to disregard certain community property laws when figuring the credit. If either you or your spouse or both are domiciled in a community property state, see *Spouses Living Apart* in Publication 555, *Federal Tax Information on Community Property,* for more information. In applying the rules discussed in Publication 555, treat as earned income your retirement and disability pay, other than social security and the social security equivalent portion of tier 1 railroad retirement benefits. These social security and equivalent railroad retirement benefits are not community income for purposes of this credit.

Qualified Individual Under Age 65

If you are under age 65, you may qualify for the credit only if you are retired on permanent and total disability.

You are considered retired, even if you do not retire formally, when you have stopped working because of your disability. You are retired on permanent and total disability if:

1) You were permanently and totally disabled when you retired, and
2) You retired on disability before the close of the tax year.

If you retired on disability before 1977, and were not permanently and totally disabled at that time, you can qualify for the credit if you were permanently and totally disabled on January 1, 1976, or January 1, 1977.

Example 1
Bill Russell is 62 years old and receives a disability pension from his former employer. He is eligible for the disability credit if he meets the other tests.

Figure 34-A. Are You a Qualified Individual?

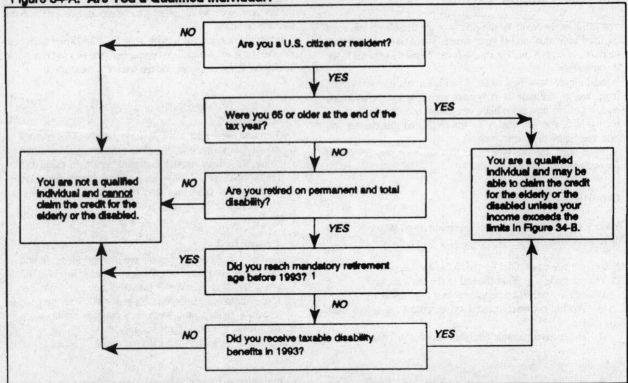

1 Mandatory retirement is the age set by your employer at which you would have been required to retire, had you not become disabled.

Figure 34-B. Income Limits

If your income is more than the limits in this Figure, you cannot claim the credit.

If you are:	You cannot take the credit if the amount from Form 1040A, line 17 or Form 1040, line 32 is:
Single, Head of household, or Qualifying widow(er) with dependent child	$17,500 or more, or you received $5,000 or more of nontaxable social security or other nontaxable pensions
Married filing a joint return and only one spouse qualifies in Figure 34-A	$20,000 or more, or you received $5,000 or more of nontaxable social security or other nontaxable pensions
Married filing a joint return and both spouses qualify in Figure 34-A	$25,000 or more, or you received $7,500 or more of nontaxable social security or other nontaxable pensions
Married filing a separate return and you did not live with your spouse all year	$12,500 or more, or you received $3,750 or more of nontaxable social security or other nontaxable pensions

Example 2

Harry Carter retired at age 60 and is receiving a pension from his former employer. Harry was not disabled when he retired. In 1993, when Harry was 62 years old, he was in an accident that left him permanently and totally disabled. Harry is not eligible for the disability credit in 1993, because, when he retired, he was not permanently and totally disabled.

Example 3

Marian Sloan retired in 1976 at age 47 on disability, even though she was not at the time permanently and totally disabled. However, by January 1, 1977, she was permanently and totally disabled. In 1993, she is still receiving disability payments from her former employer and has not yet reached her employer's mandatory retirement age. Marian is eligible for the credit in 1993.

Permanent and total disability. You are permanently and totally disabled if you cannot engage in any substantial gainful activity because of your physical or mental condition. A physician must certify that the condition has lasted or can be expected to last continuously for 12 months or more, or that the condition can be expected to result in death. See *Physician's statement,* later.

Substantial gainful activity. Substantial gainful activity is the performance of significant duties over a reasonable period of time while working for pay or profit, or in work generally done for pay or profit.

Full-time work (or part-time work done at your employer's convenience) in a competitive work situation for at least the minimum wage conclusively shows that you are able to engage in substantial gainful activity. The minimum wage is $4.25 an hour.

Substantial gainful activity is not work you do to take care of yourself or your home. It is not unpaid work on hobbies, institutional therapy or training, school attendance, clubs, social programs, and similar activities. However, the kind of work you do may show that you are able to engage in substantial gainful activity. The fact that you have not worked for some time is not, in itself, conclusive evidence that you cannot engage in substantial gainful activity. The following examples illustrate the tests of substantial gainful activity.

Explanation

The test of whether you are able to engage in substantial gainful activity is dependent upon the facts and circumstances of your particular situation. No strict rule governs every case. The most important guideline to keep in mind is whether you hold a job that pays at least the minimum wage. This means any job, not just the job you held before your disability.

Example 1. Trisha, a sales clerk, retired on disability. She is 53 years old and now works as a full-time babysitter for the minimum wage. Even though Trisha is doing different work, she is able to do the duties of her new job in a full-time competitive work situation for the minimum wage. She is able to engage in substantial gainful activity and, therefore, cannot take the credit.

Example 2. Tom, a bookkeeper, retired on disability. He is 59 years old and now drives a truck for a charitable organization. He sets his own hours and is not paid. Duties of this nature generally are performed for pay or profit. Some weeks he works 10 hours, and some weeks he works 40 hours. Over the year he averages 20 hours a week. The kind of work and his average hours a week conclusively show that Tom is able to engage in substantial gainful activity. This is true even though Tom is not paid and he sets his own hours. He cannot take the credit.

Example 3. John, who retired on disability, took a job with a former employer on a trial basis. The purpose of the job was to see if John could do the work. The trial period lasted for 6 months during which John was paid the minimum wage. Because of John's disability, he was assigned only light duties of a nonproductive "make-work" nature. The activity was gainful because John was paid at least the minimum wage. But the activity was not substantial because his duties were nonproductive. These facts do not, by themselves, show that John is able to engage in substantial gainful activity.

Example 4. Joan, who retired on disability from employment as a bookkeeper, lives with her sister who manages several motel units. Joan assisted her sister for one or two hours a day by performing duties such as washing dishes, answering phones, registering guests, and bookkeeping. Joan can select the time of day when she feels most fit to perform the tasks undertaken. Work of this nature, performed off and on during the day at Joan's convenience, is not activity of a "substantial and gainful" nature even if she is paid for the work. The performance of these duties does not, of itself, show that Joan is able to engage in substantial gainful activity.

Sheltered employment. Certain work offered at qualified locations to physically or mentally impaired persons is considered sheltered employment. These locations are in sheltered workshops, hospitals and similar institutions, homebound programs, and Department of Veterans Affairs (VA) sponsored homes. Compared to commercial employment, pay is lower for sheltered employment. Therefore, one usually does not look for sheltered employment if he or she can get other employment. The fact that one has accepted sheltered employment is not proof of that person's ability to engage in substantial gainful activity.

Physician's statement. If you are under 65, a doctor must certify that you are permanently and totally disabled. You must complete Part II of either Schedule R (Form 1040) or Schedule 3 (Form 1040A). However, check the box on line 2 and do not complete the physician's statement if:

1) You filed a physician's statement for this disability for 1983 or an earlier year, or you filed a statement for tax years after 1983 and your physician signed line B on the statement, and
2) Due to your continued disabled condition, you were unable to engage in any substantial gainful activity in 1993.

If you have not filed a physician's statement in a previous year, or if the statement you filed did not meet these conditions, your doctor must complete the statement.

Veterans. If the Department of Veterans Affairs (VA) certifies that you are permanently and totally disabled, you can file VA Form 21–0172, *Certification of Permanent Total Disability,* instead of the physician's statement. VA Form 21–0172 must be signed by a person authorized by the VA to do so. You can get this form from the VA.

Disability income. Disability income must meet the following two requirements:

1) The income must be paid under your employer's accident or health plan or pension plan.
2) The income must be includible in your income as wages or payments in lieu of wages for the time you are absent from work because of permanent and total disability.

Any payment you receive from a plan that does not provide for disability retirement is not disability income. Any lump-sum payment for accrued annual leave that you receive when you retire on disability is a salary payment and is not disability income.

For purposes of the credit for the elderly or the disabled, disability income does **not** include amounts you receive after you reach mandatory retirement age. Mandatory retirement age is the age set by your employer at which you would have been required to retire, had you not become disabled.

For purposes of reporting your disability income, disability payments are taxable as wages only until you reach minimum retirement age. After you reach the minimum retirement age set by your employer, disability income is taxable as a pension. Minimum retirement age is generally the earliest age at which you may receive a pension whether or not you are disabled. Minimum retirement age does not affect the credit for the elderly or the disabled. For more information, see Publication 525, *Taxable and Nontaxable Income*.

Example 1

Marie Carter retired in June at age 55 with a total and permanent disability. At retirement, she received a $5,000 payment for accrued vacation and sick leave days. The amount is not disability income, since it is not paid to her as wages or in lieu of wages because of her permanent and total disability.

Example 2

George Martin turned 62 years old on September 9, 1993. He had retired several years earlier as a result of a total and permanent disability. He has received disability payments from his employer since retirement. His former employer's mandatory retirement age is 62. As a result, any amount George receives after he reaches the age of 62 will *not* be disability income.

Figuring the Credit

You can figure the credit yourself (see the explanation that follows), or the IRS will figure it for you. See *Credit Figured for You*, later.
Figuring the credit yourself. If you figure the credit yourself, fill out the front of either Schedule R (if you are filing Form 1040) or Schedule 3 (if you are filing Form 1040A). Next, fill out Part III of either Schedule R or Schedule 3. There are three steps to follow:

1) Determine your *base amount* (lines 10–12, of either Schedule R or Schedule 3).
2) Subtract from your base amount any *nontaxable social security or railroad retirement benefits* and other nontaxable pensions and disability benefits you received (Part III, lines 13a, 13b, and 13c of either Schedule R or Schedule 3).
3) Then subtract from your base amount part of your *adjusted gross income*, depending on the level of your income (Part III, lines 14–17, of either Schedule R or Schedule 3).

These three steps are discussed later.
Amount of credit. If (1) is more than (2) and (3), multiply the difference by 15% to get the amount of your credit. If (2) and (3) are more than (1), you cannot claim the credit. This computation is found in Part III, lines 18–21, of either Schedule R or Schedule 3. In certain cases the amount of your credit may be limited. See *Limits on Credit*, later.

Step 1. Base Amount

To figure the credit, you must first determine your base amount. See *Table 34–1* for the base amount figures.
Base amounts for persons under age 65. If you are a qualified individual under age 65 and you have disability income (defined earlier) of less than $5,000, your base amount is limited to the amount of your taxable disability income. If you are married filing a joint return and both you and your spouse are qualified individuals under age 65 with a combined taxable disability income of less than $7,500, your base amount is limited to your combined taxable disability income. If you are married filing a joint return and one of you is age 65 or older and the other is a qualified individual under age 65, your base amount is $5,000 plus the taxable disability income of the spouse under age 65. The total cannot be more than $7,500.

Example 1

Thomas Washington, who is 59 years old and single, retired during the year because of a total and permanent physical disability. He received $4,300 in income during the year from his prior employer because of his disability. He received no other income. The base amount Thomas uses in calculating his credit is $4,300.

If Thomas had received $6,900 in disability income, his base amount would be $5,000.

Example 2

Henry Jefferson is 72 years old and files a joint return with his wife, Abigail. Abigail is 63 years old and is permanently and totally disabled. She received $3,000 from her previous employer because of her disability. The initial base amount they use in calculating their credit is $7,500, which is the lesser of (1) the $7,500 initial base amount for married couples filing joint returns or (2) $5,000 plus the $3,000 disability income received by the person under the age of 65.

Step 2. Subtract Certain Nontaxable Income

Once you have determined your base amount, you must reduce it by the total amount of nontaxable social security and certain other nontaxable payments (covered later) you receive during the year.

Enter these nontaxable payments on lines 13a and 13b of either Schedule R or Schedule 3. If you are married filing a joint return, you must reduce your base amount by the total amount of nontaxable payments both you and your spouse receive.

Use the worksheet in the Form 1040 or Form 1040A instructions to determine if any part of your social security benefits (or equivalent railroad retirement benefits, if applicable) is taxable. The nontaxable portions are used to reduce your base amount.
Subtract the total of the following payments from your base amount.

- Nontaxable social security payments. This includes the gross amount of nontaxable social security benefits (Form 1099-SSA), which includes disability benefits, any amounts that are withheld to pay premiums on supplementary Medicare insurance, and any reduction because of receipt of a benefit under worker's compensation.

  Do not include in the gross amount of nontaxable social security benefits a lump-sum death benefit payment you may receive as a surviving spouse, or a surviving child's

Table 34.1 **Base Amounts for Schedule R and Schedule 3**

If Your Filing Status Is:	Your Base Amount to enter on line 10 of Schedule R or Schedule 3 Is:
Single, an unmarried head of household, or a qualifying widow or widower and	
• 65 or older	$5,000
• under 65 and retired on permanent and total disability[1]	$5,000
Married filing a joint return and	
• both of you are 65 or older	$7,500
• both of you are under 65 and one of you retired on permanent and total disability[1]	$5,000
• both of you are under 65 and both of you retired on permanent and total disability[1]	$7,500
• one of you is 65 or older, and the other is under 65 and retired on permanent and total disability[2]	$7,500
• one of you is 65 or older, and the other is under 65 and **not** retired on permanent and total disability	$5,000
Married filing a separate return and did not live with your spouse at any time during the year and	
• 65 or older	$3,750
• under 65 and retired on permanent and total disability[1]	$3,750

[1] Your base amount cannot be more than your total taxable disability income for 1993.
[2] Your base amount is $5,000 plus the taxable disability income of the spouse under age 65, but not more than $7,500.

insurance benefit payments you may receive as a guardian. If you are married filing a separate return and either you or your spouse or both of you live in a community property state, your social security benefits will be your separate property.

In order to avoid mistakes in figuring the credit which could result in additional tax to you later, it is important to correctly report all these nontaxable amounts. These amounts are verified by the IRS through information supplied by other government agencies.

Example 1

Jim and Jeanette are married and file a joint return. He is 69 years old and she is 64, and each receives $1,000 in social security. The base amount used to figure their credit is $5,000, since only Jim is 65 years of age or older. This base amount must be reduced by the $2,000 in social security that they received during the year. Next year, when Jeanette becomes 65 years old, their base amount will rise to $7,500.

Example 2

Jean Blair retired in January, 1993 at age 62 because of a permanent disability and collected $4,600 from her former employer as a disability pension. She also received $3,600 in social security benefits in 1993. Jean is single, and her adjusted gross income is less than $5,000. Jean must subtract the social security income from her disability income in computing the amount eligible for the disability credit. Her credit is $150 [15% × ($4,600 − $3,600)].

Explanation

Do not reduce the base amount used to figure your credit by any of the following:

Amounts that are treated as a return of your cost of an annuity or a pension
Veterans Administration service-connected disability compensation
Payments from accident or health insurance policies
Basic or supplementary Medicare benefits
Amounts paid by or for an employer to the estate or to the beneficiaries of an **employee**
Amounts received by beneficiaries of an employee's **trust**
Death compensation paid by the Veterans Administration to the surviving spouse of a veteran who died from sickness or injury incurred in active service
Life insurance payments received when the insured person dies

- Social security equivalent part of tier 1 railroad retirement pension payments that are not taxed (Form 1099-RRB).
- Nontaxable pension or annuity payments or disability benefits that are paid under a law administered by the Department of Veterans Affairs (VA). Do not include amounts received as a pension, annuity, or similar allowance for personal injuries or sickness resulting from active service in the armed forces of any country or in the Coast and Geodetic Survey or the Public Health Service, or as a disability annuity under Section 808 of the Foreign Service Act of 1980.
- Pension or annuity payments or disability benefits that are excluded from income under any provision of federal law other than the Internal Revenue Code. Amounts that are a return of your cost of a pension or annuity do not reduce your base amount.

Step 3. Subtract Excess Adjusted Gross Income

You also have to subtract the amount of your excess adjusted gross income from the base amount used to figure your credit.

You figure your **excess adjusted gross income** as follows:

1) Subtract from your adjusted gross income the amount shown for your filing status in the following list:
   a) **$7,500** if you are single, a head of household, or a qualifying widow(er) with a dependent child,
   b) **$10,000** if you are married filing a joint return, or
   c) **$5,000** if you are married filing a separate return and you and your spouse did not live in the same household at any time during the tax year.
2) Divide the result of (1) by 2.

Example 1

Henry is over age 65 and single, with $8,900 in adjusted gross income, which is in excess of the $7,500 allowed for his single filing status. He must reduce his base amount by $700 (½ of the $1,400 difference between $8,900 and $7,500). Henry also receives $1,000 in nontaxable social security payments. The adjusted base amount he uses to compute his credit is $3,300, calculated as follows:

Base amount	$5,000
Less:	
Nontaxable social security	1,000
Excess adjusted gross income	700
Adjusted base amount	$3,300
Tentative credit (15% of $3,300)	$ 495

Note: 15% times the adjusted base amount is the method you use in calculating your tentative credit.

Example 2

Dennis and Constance are married, both are over age 65, and they file a joint return. Their adjusted gross income for the year is $12,000. They receive $1,750 in nontaxable social security. Their adjusted base amount used to figure their credit is $4,750, calculated as follows:

Base amount	$7,500
Less:	
Nontaxable social security	1,750
Excess adjusted gross income [½ ($12,000 − $10,000)]	1,000
Adjusted base amount	$4,750
Tentative credit (15% of $4,750)	$ 713

Figure your excess adjusted gross income on lines 14 through 17 of either Schedule R or Schedule 3.

Income Limits

If your income is more than certain limits, you cannot claim the credit. You can use *Figure 34–B,* earlier, to see if you qualify for the credit based on your income.

If your income for your filing status is less than the amount shown in Figure 34–B, you may be able to take the credit. If your income equals or exceeds the amount in Figure 34–B, you cannot take the credit.

If the total of your nontaxable social security or other nontaxable pensions or disability benefits (line 13c of either Schedule R or Schedule 3) plus your excess adjusted gross income (line 17 of either Schedule R or Schedule 3) equals or is more than your base amount, you will not be able to take the credit.

Explanation

To summarize the situations outlined above, based on your filing status, you may not claim the credit for the elderly and disabled if (1) your nontaxable social security and other nontaxable pensions, or (2) 50% of your excess adjusted gross income, or (3) the sum of (1) and (2) equals or exceeds your base amount.

A simple way to compute your credit is as follows:

1. Subtract from your base amount the sum of your nontaxable social security income, other nontaxable pensions, and your excess adjusted gross income.
2. Multiply the amount from Step 1 by 15%. This is your credit for the year.

Example. You are 66 years old and your spouse is 64. Your spouse is not disabled. You file a joint return on Form 1040. Your adjusted gross income is $14,630. Together you received $3,200 from social security, which was nontaxable. You figure the credit as follows:

1) Base amount			$5,000
2) Subtract the total of:			
a) Social security and other nontaxable pensions		$3,200	
b) Excess adjusted gross income [($14,630 − $10,000) ÷ 2]		2,315	5,515
3) Balance (Not less than —0—)			—0—
4) **Credit**			—0—

You may not take the credit since your nontaxable social security (line 2a) plus your excess adjusted gross income (line 2b) is more than your base amount (line 1).

Limits on Credit

Your credit is limited to the amount of your tax liability (line 40, Form 1040, or line 23, Form 1040A). This means the amount of your credit cannot be more than your tax liability. For example, if you have a credit of $100 and a zero tax liability, your credit would be zero.

The amount of your credit may also be limited if:

1) You file Schedule C, C-EZ, D, E, or F (Form 1040), and
2) The amount on Form 1040, line 23, is more than:
   $33,750 if single or head of household,
   $45,000 if married filing jointly or qualifying widow(er) with a dependent child, or
   $22,500 if married filing separately.

For purposes of (2), any tax-exempt interest from private activity bonds issued after August 7, 1986, and any net operating loss deduction must be added to the amount from Form 1040, line 23.

If both (1) and (2) do not apply, your credit is not subject to this limit. Enter the amount of the credit from Schedule R, line 21, on Form 1040, line 42.

If you meet both (1) and (2), get Form 6251, *Alternative Minimum Tax—Individuals,* and complete it through line 24. The limit on your credit will be the smaller of:

1) Your credit as computed, or
2) Your regular tax minus—
   a) Any credit for child and dependent care expenses, and
   b) Any amount shown on line 24, Form 6251.

Enter the smaller of (1) or (2) on Form 1040, line 42. If (2) is the smaller amount, also write "AMT" on the dotted line next to line 42, Form 1040, and replace the amount on Schedule R, line 21, with that amount.

Example

John and Betty Jeffries, both 68 years old, are married and file a joint return. Their total income on line 23 of Form 1040 is $8,500. They have tax-exempt interest from private activity bonds issued after August 7, 1986, of $42,000. Since the total of these two amounts ($50,500) is greater than $45,000, they must complete Form 6251, *Alternative Minimum Tax—Individuals*. The amount of their credit can not be greater than the difference between their regular tax on Form 1040 and their alternative minimum tax, if any, on Form 6251. (See Chapter 31, *How to Figure Your Tax,* and Chapter 42, *Planning Ahead for 1994 and Beyond*, for further discussion of how tax-exempt interest is treated for alternative minimum tax purposes.)

Credit Figured for You

If you claim the credit, complete either Schedule R (Form 1040) or Schedule 3 (Form 1040A), and attach it to your return when you file. There are separate instructions available for each schedule, which you should use to help you complete it.

If you file Form 1040 and you want the IRS to figure your credit, see *Form 1040* under *Tax Figured by IRS* in Chapter 31, *How to Figure Your Tax.*

If you file Form 1040A and you want the IRS to figure your credit, see *Form 1040A* under *Tax Figured by IRS* in Chapter 31, *How to Figure Your Tax.*

Examples

The following examples illustrate the credit for the elderly or the disabled. Assume that none of the taxpayers in these examples had to file a Form 6251. The base amounts are taken from *Table 34–1*, shown earlier.

Example 1. Jerry Ash is 68 years old, single, and files Form 1040A. He received the following income for the year:

Nontaxable social security received	$3,120
Interest (taxable)	215
Pension (all taxable)	3,600
Wages from a part-time job	4,245

Jerry's adjusted gross income is $8,060 ($4,245 + $3,600 + $215). Jerry figures the credit as follows:

1) Base amount		$5,000
2) Subtract the total of:		
a) Social security and other nontaxable pensions	$3,120	
b) Excess adjusted gross income [($8,060 − $7,500) ÷ 2]	280	3,400
3) Balance		$1,600
4) **Credit** (15% of $1,600)		$ 240

Jerry's credit is $240. He files Schedule 3 (Form 1040A) and shows this amount on line 24b of Form 1040A.

Example 2. James Davis is 58 years old, single, and files Form 1040. Two years ago he retired on permanent and total disability, and he is still permanently and totally disabled. He filed the required physician's statement with his return for the year he retired on disability, so this year he checks the box in Part II of Schedule R.

He received the following income for the year:

Nontaxable social security received	$3,000
Interest (taxable)	100
Taxable disability pension	8,400

James' adjusted gross income is $8,500 ($8,400 + $100). He figures the credit as follows:

1) Base amount		$5,000
2) Taxable disability pension		$8,400
3) Smaller of (1) or (2)		$5,000
4) Subtract the total of:		
a) Nontaxable disability benefits (social security)	$3,000	
b) Excess adjusted gross income [($8,500 − $7,500) ÷ 2]	500	3,500
5) Balance (Not less than 0)		$1,500
6) **Credit** (15% of $1,500)		$ 225

His credit is $225. He enters $225 on line 42 of Form 1040.

Example 3. William White is 53. His wife Helen is 49. William had a stroke in 1986 and retired on permanent and total disability. He is still permanently and totally disabled because of the stroke. In November of 1993, Helen was injured in an accident at work and retired on permanent and total disability.

William received nontaxable social security disability benefits of $3,000 this year and a taxable disability pension of $6,000. Helen earned $9,200 from her job and received a taxable disability pension of $1,000. Their joint return on Form 1040 shows adjusted gross income of $16,200 ($6,000 + 9,200 + 1,000).

Helen got her doctor to complete Part II of Schedule R. William had filed a physician's statement with their return for the year he had the stroke. His doctor had signed on line B to certify that William was permanently and totally disabled. William does not have to file another physician's statement this year. He must fill out Part II of a separate Schedule R (not shown) and attach it to the joint return. He checks the box in Part II and writes his first name in the space above line 2.

William and Helen use Schedule R to figure their $135 credit for the elderly or the disabled. They enter this amount on line 42 of Form 1040. See their filled-in Schedule R on the next page.

Schedule R (Form 1040)

Schedule R (Form 1040) 1993

Part III Figure Your Credit

10 If you checked (in Part I):   Enter:
- Box 1, 2, 4, or 7 .... $5,000
- Box 3, 5, or 6 .... $7,500
- Box 8 or 9 .... $3,750

Caution: *If you checked box 2, 4, 5, 6, or 9 in Part I, you MUST complete line 11 below. All others, skip line 11 and enter the amount from line 10 on line 12.* | **10** | 7,500

11 If you checked:
- Box 6 in Part I, add $5,000 to the taxable disability income of the spouse who was under age 65. Enter the total.
- Box 2, 4, or 9 in Part I, enter your taxable disability income.
- Box 5 in Part I, add your taxable disability income to your spouse's taxable disability income. Enter the total.

TIP: For more details on what to include on line 11, see the instructions. | **11** | 7,000

12 • If you completed line 11, look at lines 10 and 11. Enter the **smaller** of the two amounts.
• All others, enter the amount from line 10. | **12** | 7,000

13 Enter the following pensions, annuities, or disability income that you (and your spouse if filing a joint return) received in 1993:

a Nontaxable part of social security benefits, **and**
Nontaxable part of railroad retirement benefits treated as social security. See instructions. | **13a** | 3,000

b Nontaxable veterans' pensions, **and**
Any other pension, annuity, or disability benefit that is excluded from income under any other provision of law. See instructions. | **13b** |

c Add lines 13a and 13b. (Even though these income items are not taxable, they **must** be included here to figure your credit.) If you did not receive any of the types of nontaxable income listed on line 13a or 13b, enter -0- on line 13c. | **13c** | 3,000

14 Enter the amount from Form 1040, line 32 | **14** | 16,200

15 If you checked (in Part I):   Enter:
- Box 1 or 2 .... $7,500
- Box 3, 4, 5, 6, or 7 .... $10,000
- Box 8 or 9 .... $5,000 | **15** | 10,000

16 Subtract line 15 from line 14. If line 15 is more than line 14, enter -0- | **16** | 6,200

17 Divide line 16 above by 2 | **17** | 3,100

18 Add lines 13c and 17 | **18** | 6,100

19 Subtract line 18 from line 12. If line 18 is more than line 12, stop here; you **cannot** take the credit. Otherwise, go to line 21 | **19** | 900

20 Decimal amount used to figure the credit | **20** | × .15

21 Multiply line 19 above by the decimal amount (.15) on line 20. Enter the result here and on Form 1040, line 42. **Caution:** *If you file Schedule C, C-EZ, D, E, or F (Form 1040), your credit may be limited. See the instructions for line 21 for the amount of credit you can claim.* | **21** | 135

Instructions for Physician's Statement

Taxpayer
If you retired after December 31, 1976, enter the date you retired in the space provided in Part II.

Physician
A person is permanently and totally disabled if **both** of the following apply:

1. He or she cannot engage in any substantial gainful activity because of a physical or mental condition, and

2. A physician determines that the disability has lasted or can be expected to last continuously for at least a year or can lead to death.

Schedule R
(Form 1040)

Department of the Treasury
Internal Revenue Service (T)

Credit for the Elderly or the Disabled

▶ Attach to Form 1040.   ▶ See separate instructions for Schedule R.

OMB No. 1545-0074

1993

Attachment
Sequence No. **16**

Name(s) shown on Form 1040   **William M. and Helen A. White**   Your social security number   **222 00 3333**

You may be able to use Schedule R to reduce your tax if by the end of 1993:

- You were age 65 or older, **OR** • You were under age 65, you retired on **permanent and total disability**, and you received taxable disability income.

But you must also meet other tests. See the separate instructions for Schedule R.
Note: *In most cases, the IRS can figure the credit for you. See page 25 of the Form 1040 instructions.*

Part I Check the Box for Your Filing Status and Age

If your filing status is:	And by the end of 1993:	Check only one box:
Single, Head of household, or Qualifying widow(er) with dependent child	**1** You were 65 or older	☐
	2 You were under 65 and you retired on permanent and total disability	☐
Married filing a joint return	**3** Both spouses were 65 or older	☐
	4 Both spouses were under 65, but only one spouse retired on permanent and total disability	☐
	5 Both spouses were under 65, and both retired on permanent and total disability	☑
	6 One spouse was 65 or older, and the other spouse was under 65 and retired on permanent and total disability	☐
	7 One spouse was 65 or older, and the other spouse was under 65 and **NOT** retired on permanent and total disability	☐
Married filing a separate return	**8** You were 65 or older and you lived apart from your spouse for all of 1993	☐
	9 You were under 65, you retired on permanent and total disability, and you lived apart from your spouse for all of 1993	☐

If you checked box 1, 3, 7, or 8, skip Part II and complete Part III on the back. All others, complete Parts II and III.

Part II Statement of Permanent and Total Disability (Complete only if you checked box 2, 4, 5, 6, or 9 above.)

IF: 1 You filed a physician's statement for this disability for 1983 or an earlier year, or you filed a statement for tax years after 1983 and your physician signed line B on the statement, **AND**

2 Due to your continued disabled condition, you were unable to engage in any substantial gainful activity in 1993, check this box .... ▲ ☐

- If you checked this box, you do not have to file another statement for 1993.
- If you **did not** check this box, have your physician complete the following statement.

Physician's Statement (See instructions at bottom of page 2.)

I certify that   **Helen A. White**
                              Name of disabled person

was permanently and totally disabled on January 1, 1976, or January 1, 1977, **OR** was permanently and totally disabled on the date he or she retired. If retired after December 31, 1976, enter the date retired. ▶ **November 2, 1993**

Physician: Sign your name on **either** line A or B below.

A The disability has lasted or can be expected to last continuously for at least a year

B There is no reasonable probability that the disabled condition will ever improve

A Physician's signature *John A. Doctor*	Date
B Physician's signature	Date **2/7/94**

Physician's name   **John A. Doctor**   Physician's address   **101 Green St. Hometown, Md. 20000**

For Paperwork Reduction Act Notice, see Form 1040 instructions.   Cat. No. 11359K   Schedule R (Form 1040) 1993

35 Other Credits

Introduction

This chapter discusses eight credits you may use to reduce your tax liability. Four of these credits are nonrefundable; that is, although they may be used to bring your tax liability to zero, any credit in excess of your liability is not refunded to you. The other three credits are refundable. Any excess credit is refunded to you.

The four nonrefundable credits are:

1. *The minimum tax credit*
2. *The mortgage interest credit*
3. *The electric vehicle credit*
4. *The foreign tax credit*

Any portion of a nonrefundable credit that is not utilized in the current year may be carried over and utilized in another year.

The four refundable credits are:

1. *The excess social security, Medicare tax, or railroad retirement tax credit*
2. *The regulated investment company credit*
3. *The diesel-fuel vehicles credit*
4. *The earned income credit*

Note: *The investment tax credit, which was available for most tangible property used in a trade or a business, was generally repealed by the Tax Reform Act of 1986, effective for property placed in service after December 31, 1985. A brief discussion of this credit appears at the end of the section on nonrefundable credits.*

Important Changes for 1993

Credit for electric vehicles. You may be allowed a tax credit if you placed an electric vehicle in service after June 30, 1993. The credit is limited to $4,000 for each vehicle. For more information, see *Credit for Electric Vehicles.*

Excess withholding of social security tax, railroad retirement tax tier 1, and Medicare tax. Social security and railroad retirement tax (RRTA) were both withheld at a rate of 6.2% on the first $57,600 of wages in 1993. Medicare tax was withheld at a rate of 1.45% on the first $135,000 of wages. If you had two or more employers and they withheld too much social security, RRTA, or Medicare tax during 1993, you may be entitled to a credit of the excess withholding. For more information about the credit and how to get it, see *Credit for Excess Social Security Tax, Medicare Tax, or Railroad Retirement Tax Withheld.*

In addition to the child and dependent care credit (Chapter 33, *Child and Dependent Care Credit*), the credit for the elderly or the disabled (Chapter 34, *Credit for the Elderly or the Disabled*), and the earned income credit (discussed later in this chapter) you may be able to claim other tax credits. This chapter is divided into two parts and discusses eight credits in the following order.

- Part 1, Nonrefundable Credits:
   Credit for prior year minimum tax,
   Mortgage interest credit,
   Credit for electric vehicles, and
   Foreign tax credit.

- Part 2, Refundable Credits:
   Credit for excess social security tax, Medicare tax, or railroad retirement tax withheld,
   Credit from a regulated investment company,
   Credit on diesel-powered highway vehicles, and
   Earned income credit.

Nonrefundable credits. The first part of the chapter, *Nonrefundable Credits,* covers four credits that you subtract directly from your tax. These credits may reduce your tax to zero. If these credits are more than your tax, the excess is not refunded to you.

Refundable credits. The second part of this chapter, *Refundable Credits,* covers four credits that are refundable to you and treated as payments. These credits are added to the federal income tax withheld and any estimated tax payments you made. If these credits are more than your total tax, the excess will be refunded to you.

Useful Items

You may want to see:

Publication

- ☐ **378** Fuel Tax Credits and Refunds
- ☐ **514** Foreign Tax Credit for Individuals
- ☐ **564** Mutual Fund Distributions

☐ **909** Alternative Minimum Tax for Individuals
☐ **936** Home Mortgage Interest Deduction

Form (and Instructions)

☐ **1040** U.S. Individual Income Tax Return
☐ **1116** Foreign Tax Credit
☐ **2439** Notice to Shareholder of Undistributed Long-Term Capital Gains
☐ **4136** Credit for Federal Tax Paid on Fuels
☐ **8396** Mortgage Interest Credit
☐ **8801** Credit For Prior Year Minimum Tax—Individuals and Fiduciaries
☐ **8828** Recapture of Federal Mortgage Subsidy
☐ **8834** Qualified Electric Vehicle Credit

Nonrefundable Credits

The following credits are discussed in this part:

• Credit for prior year minimum tax
• Mortgage interest credit
• Credit for electric vehicles
• Foreign tax credit.

Credit for Prior Year Minimum Tax

The tax laws give special treatment to some kinds of income and allow special deductions and credits for some kinds of expenses. If you benefit from these laws, you may have to pay at least a minimum amount of tax. This is called the alternative minimum tax.

The special treatment of some items of income and expenses only allows you to postpone paying tax until a later year. It does not allow you to completely avoid the tax. In these situations, you may be able to claim a credit for prior year minimum tax against your current year's tax. The amount of the credit cannot reduce your current year's tax below your current year's tentative alternative minimum tax.

Also, you may be able to take a credit this year for last year's unused credit for fuel produced from a nonconventional source and last year's unused orphan drug credit.

You may be able to take a credit against your regular tax if you:

1) Paid alternative minimum tax in 1992,
2) Had an unused minimum tax credit that you are carrying forward from 1992 to 1993, or
3) Had certain unallowed nonconventional-source fuel or orphan drug credits in 1992.

Credit amount. The credit is generally the amount of alternative minimum tax you actually paid in 1992 reduced by the part of it generated by exclusion items. Add to this any credit carried forward, certain unallowed nonconventional-source fuel and orphan drug credits.

Exclusion items. These are adjustments and preference items that result in the permanent exclusion of income for regular tax purposes. The exclusion items are:

The standard deduction,
Medical and dental expenses,
Miscellaneous itemized deductions,
Taxes,
Interest expense,
The charitable deduction for certain appreciated property,
Tax-exempt interest from certain private activity bonds, and
Depletion.

How to claim the credit. Figure your 1993 credit and any carryforward to 1994 on **Form 8801**, and attach it to your Form 1040. Include the credit in your total for line 44, Form 1040, and check box c. You can carry forward any unused credit for prior year minimum tax to later years until it is completely used.

For additional information about the credit and an illustrated example, get Publication 909, *Alternative Minimum Tax for Individuals.*

TaxPlanner 1

Taxpayers reporting varying income from year to year may find themselves in a regular tax position in one year and in an AMT position the next. By accelerating income into an AMT year and deferring expenses until a regular tax year, you may take advantage of the different tax rates between the regular tax and the AMT. The effect of such a strategy is reduced due to the AMT credit, which is designed to even out the effect of AMT over time. However, the AMT credit will be of no benefit for AMT arising from itemized deductions, certain tax-exempt interest, and depletion. This should be considered if you undertake any plans to defer or accelerate income or expenses.

TaxPlanner 2

Where possible, you should arrange income and deductions so that any AMT incurred will result in an AMT credit that is quickly usable.

Mortgage Interest Credit

Mortgage credit certificates issued by state and local governments may entitle a certificate holder to a mortgage interest credit. The certificate must be used in connection with the purchase, qualified rehabilitation, or qualified home improvement of the certificate holder's main home.

Who qualifies. You may be able to claim a mortgage interest credit if you were issued a mortgage credit certificate (MCC) under a qualified MCC program. The MCC must relate to your main home.

Amount of credit. You figure the credit by multiplying the certificate credit rate by the lesser of the interest you paid during the year on your actual loan amount (mortgage) or the interest you paid on the loan amount shown on your MCC. The certificate credit rate and the maximum loan amount are shown on the MCC.

Limit. If the certificate credit rate is more than 20%, the credit cannot be more than $2,000.

Dividing the credit. If two or more persons (other than a married couple filing a joint return) hold an interest in the home to which the MCC relates, the credit must be divided based on the interest held by each person.

Example. John and his brother, George, were issued a MCC. They used the certificate to obtain a mortgage on a home that is their main home. John has a 60% interest and George has a 40% interest. John paid $5,400 mortgage interest and George paid $3,600.

The MCC shows a credit rate of 25% and a maximum loan amount of $65,000. Their actual mortgage loan is $60,000, which is less than the $65,000 maximum. However, their combined credit is limited to $2,000 because the credit rate is more than 20%.

John's credit is limited to $1,200 ($2,000 × 60%). He figures the credit by multiplying the interest he paid ($5,400) by the certificate credit rate (25%) for a total of $1,350. However, his credit is limited to the $1,200 above.

George's credit is limited to $800 ($2,000 × 40%). He figures the credit by multiplying the interest he paid ($3,600) by the certificate credit rate (25%) for a total of $900. His credit is limited to the $800 above.

Carryforward. If your allowable credit is more than your tax liability reduced by certain credits, you can carry forward the unused portion of the credit to your next 3 tax years or until used, whichever comes first.

If you are subject to the $2,000 limit because your certificate credit rate is more than 20%, no amount over the $2,000 (or your prorated share of the $2,000 if you must allocate the credit) may be carried forward.

Reduced home mortgage interest deduction. If you itemize your deductions on Schedule A (Form 1040), reduce your home mortgage interest deduction by the amount of mortgage interest credit figured before you add in any credit carryforwards from previous years. For more information about the home mortgage interest deduction, see Chapter 24, *Interest Expense.*

How to claim the credit. Figure the credit and any carryforward to next year on **Form 8396,** and attach it to your Form 1040. Be sure to include any carryforward from 1990, 1991, and 1992. You cannot use a carryforward from 1990 on your tax return for any year after 1993.

Include the credit in your total for line 44 (Form 1040), and check box b.

Recapture of Federal mortgage subsidy. If you closed on a mortgage from a qualified mortgage bond program and received a mortgage credit certificate after December 31, 1990, you may be subject to a recapture rule. The recapture would generally occur if you sold or disposed of your home during the first 9 years following the date of closing. See Publication 523, *Selling Your Home,* for more information.

Credit for Electric Vehicles

You may be allowed a 10% tax credit if you placed a qualified electric vehicle in service after June 30, 1993.

Qualified electric vehicle. This is a motor vehicle that:

1) Has at least four wheels and is manufactured for use on public streets, roads, and highways.
2) Is powered *primarily* by an electric motor that draws its power from rechargeable batteries, fuel cells, or other portable sources of electrical current.
3) Is originally used by you.
4) Is acquired for your own use, not for resale.

Amount of credit. The credit is equal to 10% of the cost of the vehicle. However, if the vehicle is a depreciable business asset, you must reduce the cost by any section 179 deduction before figuring the credit. Get Publication 917, *Business Use of a Car,* for information on the section 179 deduction.

The credit is limited to $4,000 for each vehicle.

Special rules. You cannot take the credit if you use the vehicle predominately outside the United States.

The credit will be subject to recapture if, within 3 years after the date you place the vehicle in service, the vehicle is modified so that it is no longer eligible for the credit.

How to claim the credit. Figure the credit on **Form 8834,** and attach it to your Form 1040. Include the credit in your total for line 44 and check box d.

Foreign Tax Credit

You generally can choose to claim income taxes you paid or accrued during the year to a foreign country or U.S. possession as a credit against your U.S. income tax. Or, you can deduct them as an itemized deduction.

To take the foreign tax credit, complete **Form 1116** and attach it to your Form 1040. Enter the credit on line 43, Form 1040. For more information, get Publication 514.

Explanation

To take the foreign tax credit, the foreign taxes must have been imposed on you, and you must have paid or accrued the tax during your tax year. Furthermore, if you work overseas and elect to claim the foreign earned income exclusion or the foreign housing exclusion, the amount of foreign taxes eligible for credit is reduced. The foreign earned income exclusion allows U.S. citizens or residents who meet the residency test for living abroad to exclude up to $70,000 of foreign earned income from their **taxable income.** The foreign housing exclusion allows U.S. citizens to exclude excess foreign housing costs from their taxable income. See Chapter 38, *U.S. Citizens Working Abroad,* for a more complete discussion of these subjects.

The amount you may claim as a foreign tax credit is limited. You can figure your maximum credit by performing the following calculation.

$$\frac{\text{Taxable income from sources outside the U.S.}}{\text{Taxable income from all sources}} \times \frac{\text{U.S. income}}{\text{tax}} = \frac{\text{Maximum}}{\text{credit}}$$

Separate foreign tax credit limitations must be calculated for earned income, passive income, and several other categories.

However, while you are limited in the amount of credit for foreign taxes you may claim in any 1 year, you are able to carry back the credit for 2 years and also carry forward the credit for 5 years. See Chapter 38, *U.S. Citizens Working Abroad,* for a further discussion of how to calculate your foreign tax credit.

TAXPLANNER

It is usually better to claim a credit for foreign taxes than to deduct them as itemized deductions. Credits reduce your U.S. tax on a dollar-for-dollar basis, whereas a deduction just reduces the amount of income subject to tax. (For an example of this point, see Chapter 23, *Taxes You May Deduct.*)

Explanation

Investment Tax Credit. The investment tax credit, which was available for qualified tangible personal property used in your trade or business, was repealed by the Tax Reform Act of 1986, effective for property placed in service after December 31, 1985. You cannot claim a credit for qualifying property placed in service after 1985, subject to various transition rules. However, if the property was placed in service prior to January 1, 1986, and you were unable to utilize all of the credit on your prior years' returns, you may have a carryover of unused investment tax credit. The amount of credit available as a carryover in future years is reduced by 35% for tax years beginning after June 30, 1987. For more information, see Publication 572, *Investment Credit*.

Refundable Credits

The following credits are refundable and are treated as payments of tax:

- Credit for excess social security tax, Medicare tax, or railroad retirement tax withheld,
- Credit from a regulated investment company, and
- Credit on diesel-powered highway vehicles.

Credit for Excess Social Security Tax, Medicare Tax, or Railroad Retirement Tax Withheld

There are limits on the amount of wages subject to social security, Medicare, and railroad retirement tax (RRTA). If you worked for two or more employers in 1993, and together they paid you wages that exceeded these limits, you may be entitled to a credit for any excess amount of tax withheld on those wages. This is a credit against your income tax. The limits are:

1) **$57,600** in wages subject to social security and tier 1 RRTA withholding tax of not more than $3,571.20,
2) **$135,000** in wages subject to Medicare withholding tax of not more than $1,957.50 (this applies to both social security and tier 1 RRTA wages), or
3) **$42,900** in wages subject to tier 2 RRTA withholding tax of not more than $2,102.10.

One employer. If any one employer withheld social security, Medicare, or RRTA tax that exceeded the limits in the preceding list, you cannot claim the extra amount withheld by that employer as a credit against your income tax. Your employer must adjust this for you.

Joint return. If you are filing a joint return, you cannot add the social security, Medicare, or RRTA tax withheld from your spouse's wages to the amount withheld from your wages. Figure the credit separately for both you and your spouse to determine if either of you has excess withholding.

Where to report the credit. If you file Form 1040, enter the credit on line 58a. If you file Form 1040A, include the credit in the total on line 28d. Write "Excess SST" and show the amount of the credit in the space to the left of the line.

Example 1

Marie Gibson earned $59,000 during 1993. Her sole employer for the year inadvertently withheld $4,466.70 in social security and Medicare taxes from her salary. The amount that should have been withheld was $4,426.70 (6.2% × $57,600 plus 1.45% × $59,000). She may not claim the $40 overwithholding as a credit on her return. Instead, her employer should adjust her next check for this amount.

Example 2

Assume instead that Marie worked for two firms during the year and that her total withholding for social security and Medicare taxes was $4,466.70. Each firm withheld less than $4,426.70. She should now claim the $40 overwithholding as a credit.

Note. You cannot claim the credit for excess social security, Medicare tax, or railroad retirement tax on Form 1040EZ.

How to figure the credit if you did not work for a railroad. If you did not work for a railroad during 1993, figure the credit as follows:

1. Add all social security tax withheld (but not more than $3,571.20 for each employer). Enter the total here .... _____

2. Enter any uncollected social security tax on tips or group-term life insurance included in the total on Form 1040, line 53 .... _____

3. Add lines 1 and 2. If $3,571.20 or less, enter –0– on line 5 and go to line 6 .... _____

4. Social security tax limit 3,571.20

5. Subtract line 4 from line 3. .... _____

6. Add all Medicare tax withheld (but not more than $1,957.50 for each employer) .... _____

7. Enter any uncollected Medicare tax on tips or group-term life insurance included in the total on Form 1040, line 53 ...... _____

8. Add lines 6 and 7. If $1,957.50 or less, enter –0– on line 10 and go to line 11 .... _____

9. Medicare tax limit 1,957.50

10. Subtract line 9 from line 8. .... _____

11. Credit. Add lines 5 and 10. Enter the result here and on Form 1040, line 58a (or Form 1040A, line 28d) .... _____

Example. You are married and file a joint return with your spouse who had no gross income in 1993. During 1993 you worked for the Brown Shoe Company and earned $35,000 in wages. Social security tax of $2,170 and Medicare tax of $507.50 was withheld. You also worked for another employer in 1993 and earned $25,000 in wages. $1,550 of social security tax and $362.50 of Medicare tax was withheld from these wages. Because you worked for more than one employer and your total wages were more than $57,600, you can claim a credit of $148.80 for the excess social security tax withheld. There is no tax credit for the Medicare tax withheld since your total wages did not exceed $135,000. A filled-in worksheet follows.

1. Add all social security tax withheld (but not more than $3,571.20 for each employer). Enter the total here $3,720.00

2. Enter any uncollected social security tax on tips or group-term life insurance included in the total on Form 1040, line 53 .... –0–

3. Add lines 1 and 2. If $3,571.20 or less, enter –0– on line 5 and go to line 6 .... 3,720.00

4. Social security tax limit 3,571.20

5. Subtract line 4 from line 3. .... 148.80

6. Add all Medicare tax withheld (but not more than $1,957.50 for each employer) 870.00

7. Enter any uncollected Medicare tax on tips or group-term life insurance included in the total on Form 1040, line 53...... —0—

8. Add lines 6 and 7. If $1,957.50 or less, enter —0— on line 10 and go to line 11.. 870.00

9. Medicare tax limit.. 1,957.50

10. Subtract line 9 from line 8.. —0—

11. Credit. Add lines 5 and 10. Enter the result here and on Form 1040, line 58a (or Form 1040A, line 28d) 148.80

How to figure the credit if you worked for a railroad. If you were a railroad employee during 1993, figure the credit as follows:

1. Add all security tax or tier 1 RRTA tax withheld (but not more than $3,571.20 for each employer). Enter the total here ....

2. Enter any uncollected social security and tier 1 RRTA tax on tips or group-term life insurance included in the total on Form 1040, line 53 ....

3. Add lines 1 and 2. If $3,571.20 or less, enter —0— on line 5 and go to line 6 ....

4. Social security and tier 1 RRTA tax limit.......................... 3,571.20

5. Subtract line 4 from line 3. ....

6. Add all Medicare tax withheld (but not more than $1,957.50 for each employer)..

7. Enter any uncollected Medicare tax on tips or group-term life insurance included in the total on Form 1040, line 53......

8. Add lines 6 and 7. If $1,957.50 or less, enter —0— on line 10 and go to line 11..

9. Medicare tax limit.. 1,957.50

10. Subtract line 9 from line 8..

11. Add all tier 2 RRTA tax withheld (but not more than $2,102.10 for each employee). Enter the total here ....

12. Enter any uncollected tier 2 railroad retirement tax on tips or group-term life insurance included in the total on Form 1040, line 53 ....

13. Add lines 11 and 12. If $2,102.10 or less, enter —0— on line 15 and go to line 16 ....

14. RRTA tier 2 limit 2,102.10

15. Subtract line 14 from line 13. ....

16. Credit. Add lines 5, 10, and 15. Enter the result here and on Form 1040, line 58a (or Form 1040A, line 28d) ....

Example
In 1993, Maurice Evans worked for a railroad for 7 months and had $1,953.00 in tier 1 railroad retirement tax, $456.75 in Medicare tax, and $1,102.50 in tier 2 railroad retirement tax withheld. He worked the remain-

ing 5 months for a nonrailroad employer and had $1,705 in social security tax and $398.75 in Medicare tax withheld. He had no income from tips or group-term life insurance on either job. His credit is calculated as follows:

1. Total social security and tier 1 RRTA tax withheld (do not include more than $3,571.20 for each employer	$3,658.00
2. Total social security and tier 1 RRTA tax on tips or group-term life insurance shown on any 1993 Form(s) W–2	0
3. Total: Add lines 1 and 2	3,658.00
4. Limit	$3,571.20
5. Subtract line 4 from line 3	86.80
6. Total Medicare tax withheld (do not include more than $1,957.50 for each employer)	855.50
7. Total Medicare tax on tips or group-term life insurance shown on any 1993 Form(s) W–2	0
8. Add lines 6 and 7	855.50
9. Limit	1,957.50
10. Subtract line 9 from line 8	0
11. Total tier 2 RRTA tax withheld	1.102.50
12. Total tier 2 RRTA on tips	0
13. Add lines 11 and 12	1,102.50
14. Limit	2,102.10
15. Subtract line 14 from line 13	0
16. Credit. Add lines 5, 10, and 15	$ 86.80

Credit from a Regulated Investment Company

You must include in your income any amounts that an investment company allocated to you as capital gain distributions, even if you did not actually receive them. If the investment company paid a tax on the capital gain, you are allowed a credit for the tax since it is considered paid by you. The company will send you **Form 2439** showing the undistributed capital gains amount and the tax paid, if any. Claim the credit by entering the amount on line 59, Form 1040, and checking box a. Also attach Copy B of Form 2439 to your return. See *Capital Gain Distributions* in Chapter 9, *Dividends and Other Corporate Distributions,* for more information on undistributed capital gains.

Credit on Diesel-Powered Highway Vehicles

If you purchased a diesel-powered highway vehicle, you may be entitled to a *one-time* credit if:

1) You are the first owner of the vehicle, and
2) You did not purchase the vehicle for the purpose of reselling it.

Amount of credit. The credit is $102 if you purchased a diesel-powered automobile or $198 if you purchased a diesel-powered light van or truck.

How to claim the credit or refund. To claim the credit or refund, complete **Form 4136** and attach it to Form 1040. Enter the credit on line 59, Form 1040, and check box b.

For more information, see the discussion of *Diesel-Powered Highway Vehicles* in Publication 378.

Earned Income Credit

This section discusses the earned income credit. The earned income credit is a special credit for certain workers who have a child or children living with them. The credit reduces the amount of tax you owe (if any) and is intended to offset some of the increases in living expenses and social security taxes. The earned income credit is made up of three different credits. Generally, you may qualify for the credit even if you do not claim the child as a dependent. The three credits are:

1) The basic credit,
2) The health insurance credit, and
3) The extra credit for a child born in 1993.

Useful Items

You may want to see:

Publication

☐ **503** Child and Dependent Care Expenses
☐ **504** Divorced or Separated Individuals
☐ **533** Self-Employment Tax
☐ **535** Business Expenses
☐ **596** Earned Income Credit

Form (and Instructions)

☐ **Schedule EIC** Earned Income Credit
☐ **2441** Child and Dependent Care Expenses

To get the credit:

1) File a tax return—even if:
• You do not owe any tax, or
• You did not earn enough money to file a return.
2) Fill out Schedule EIC and attach it to either Form 1040 or Form 1040A.
3) Meet certain rules. These rules are explained under *Who May Take the Credit?*
4) *An easier way* — Let the Internal Revenue Service figure the credit for you. Fill out page 1 of Schedule EIC and attach it to your return.

Now, read the rest of this section to learn more about the earned income credit.

Basic Credit

This credit is part of the earned income credit. It is based on how many qualifying children live with you. If you have one qualifying child, your credit may be as much as $1,434. If you have two or more qualifying children, your credit may be as much as $1,511. The $1,511 is the maximum amount of the basic credit even if you have more than two qualifying children.

Explanation
The first earned income credit is the basic credit. The amount of the credit depends on your income and whether you have one or two qualifying children. The maximum number of children that are considered is two, regardless of how many children you have. The maximum credit is $1,511.

Health Insurance Credit

This credit is another part of the earned income credit. You may be able to take this credit in addition to the basic credit and the extra credit for a child born in 1993. You can take the health insurance credit if you paid health insurance premiums that include coverage for one or more qualifying children. If the health insurance credit is more than what you paid during the year for health insurance premiums, you can claim only the amount you paid. If you claim this part of the earned income credit, your health insurance credit could be as much as $465.

Extra Credit for a Child Born in 1993

This credit is another part of the earned income credit. You may be able to take this credit in addition to the basic credit and the health insurance credit. This **extra credit** is limited to one qualifying child who is under age 1 on December 31, 1993. Your extra credit could be as much as $388.

Child and dependent care credit. This credit is not part of the earned income credit. But, if you have a child under age 1, you may have a choice to make. You may take the extra credit **OR** the child and dependent care credit (if eligible) for the same child. You can choose only one of these credits. *You cannot take both for the same child.* If you choose the extra credit instead of the child and dependent care credit, you can still take the child and dependent care credit for your other qualifying children. To figure the child and dependent care expenses, use Form 2441 if you file Form 1040. Use Schedule 2, *Child and Dependent Care Expenses for Form 1040A Filers,* if you file Form 1040A).

Which credit is better for you? If you qualify for both the child and dependent care credit (or the exclusion of dependent care benefits) and the extra credit, you should claim the credit that is better for you.

Who May Take the Credit?

There are certain rules you must meet to claim any of the three credits that are part of the earned income credit. To take any of these credits you must meet **all** the following rules:

1) You and a qualifying child must live in the same main home in the United States for more than one-half of the year (the whole year for an eligible foster child).
2) You must have earned income during the year.
3) Your earned income and adjusted gross income must each be less than $23,050.
4) Your return must cover a 12–month period. This does not apply if you file a short period return because of an individual's death.
5) Your filing status can be any filing status *except* married filing a separate return.
6) You cannot be a qualifying child of another person.

7) Your qualifying child cannot be the qualifying child of another person whose adjusted gross income is more than yours.

8) You usually must claim as a dependent a qualifying child who is married.

9) You did not file Form 2555, *Foreign Earned Income,* (or Form 2555–EZ, *Foreign Earned Income Exclusion*) to exclude from your gross income any income earned in foreign countries, or deduct or exclude a foreign housing amount. U.S. possessions are not foreign countries. See Publication 54, *Tax Guide for U.S. Citizens and Resident Aliens Abroad,* for more information.

Important Note. If you meet ***all*** these rules, fill in the parts of Schedule EIC that apply to you. If you ***do not*** meet ***all*** these rules, enter "NO" on the dotted line to the left of line 56, Form 1040 (or on the line to the left of line 28c, Form 1040A).

How To Figure the Credit

Once you know that you qualify for the earned income credit, you need to know how to figure the amount of the credit. You have two choices of how to figure the credit.

1) Have the IRS figure the credit for you.

2) If you want to figure the credit yourself, fill out Schedule EIC and attach it to your filled-in Form 1040 or 1040A.

Form 1040 and Schedule EIC

Figure your credit on Schedule EIC if your total earned income (line 7, Schedule EIC) and your adjusted gross income (line 9, Schedule EIC) are each less than $23,050 and you meet all the rules (shown earlier).

If you ***do not*** meet all the rules, then you do not qualify for the earned income credit. If you do not qualify, enter "No" on the dotted line to the left of Form 1040, line 56.

If You Do Not Have To File a Return

If you did not earn enough money in 1993 to file a return, you may still be able to get the earned income credit. To do this, you must meet all the rules under *Who May Take the Credit?* earlier is this chapter.

> ### TaxAlert
>
> You *must* file a tax return to receive the earned income credit. If the tax you owe is less than the amount of the earned income credit, you will receive a refund from the government. Therefore, even if you are not required to file a tax return because your income is less than the income required to file, you still must do so in order to receive the credit.

Advance Earned Income Credit Payments

Would you like to get your earned income credit now instead of waiting until after the end of the year? If you work for someone and expect to qualify for the earned income credit in 1994, you can choose to get part of the credit in advance. Give your employer a 1994 Form W–5 and he or she will include part of the credit regularly in your pay.

Important Note. Only part of the credit for one qualifying child is payable in advance. You cannot get advance payments of the credit for a second child or if you do not have a qualifying child. **Caution.** Beginning in 1994, the advance earned income credit payment could be as much as 60% of the maximum credit for one qualifying child.

> ### TaxPlanner 1
>
> If you believe that you will qualify for the basic earned income credit for 1994, you do not have to wait until 1995 when you file your tax return to get it. Instead, you may file Form W-5 in 1994 with your employer and receive a portion of the credit throughout the year as part of your paycheck. Available advance payments are limited. A separate Form W-5 must be submitted each year.

> ### TaxPlanner 2
>
> Beginning in 1994, the health insurance credit and the credit for a child under the age of one have been repealed. However, the basic credit has been increased and will also be available to low-income workers who do not have children, are between the ages of 25 and 65, and are not claimed as a dependent by another taxpayer. For 1994, a taxpayer without any qualifying children may be eligible for a maximum credit of $306. A taxpayer with one child may be eligible for a maximum credit of $2,038 while a taxpayer with two or more qualifying children may be eligible for a maximum credit of $2,527.

Advance earned income credit payments received in 1993. If you received advance payments of the earned income credit in 1993, you must file a tax return to report the payments. Report the amount on line 52, Form 1040, or line 26, Form 1040A. Your Form W–2, box 9 will show the amount you received.

Earned Income Credit (EIC) Eligibility Checklist

CAN YOU REALLY CLAIM THE EARNED INCOME CREDIT?

You may claim the earned income credit if all the following statements are TRUE. If any statement is FALSE, you cannot claim the earned income credit.

	TRUE	FALSE
1. You and a qualifying child live in the same main home in the United States for more than one-half of the year (the whole year if a foster child).	☐	☐
2. The total of your taxable and nontaxable earned income is at least $1 but less than $23,050. (See "What Is Earned Income", earlier.)	☐	☐
3. Your adjusted gross income (Form 1040, line 31 or Form 1040A, line 16) is less than $23,050.	☐	☐
4. Your filing status is married filing a joint return, head of household, qualifying widow(er) with dependent child, or single.	☐	☐
5. You are not a qualifying child of another person.	☐	☐
6. Your qualifying child is NOT the qualifying child of another person whose adjusted gross income is more than yours.	☐	☐
7. If your qualifying child is married, you did claim the child as a dependent. If your qualifying child is not married, answer "True".	☐	☐
8. You did not exclude from your gross income any income earned in foreign countries or deduct or exclude a foreign housing amount, by filing Form 2555 or Form 2555-EZ.	☐	☐
9. Your return covers a 12-month period. (This does not apply if a short period return is filed because of an individual's death.)	☐	☐

If you answered TRUE to all statements, you can claim the EIC. Remember to fill out Schedule EIC and attach it to your return to get the credit.

If you answered FALSE to any statement, you are not eligible to claim the EIC. Enter "No" on Form 1040, line 56 or Form 1040A, line 28c.

V | Special Situations and Tax Planning

The first four chapters in this part discuss some special situations. Chapter 36 is essential reading for anybody who is self-employed—freelancers, artists, and small business owners. Chapter 37 will be of interest to taxpayers who employ domestic help, whether it be to care for their children or a disabled or elderly dependent. Chapter 38 discusses how U.S. citizens working abroad should handle their taxes. Among other matters, it explains how you can get a credit against your U.S. taxes for taxes you have paid to a foreign government. Chapter 39 is for foreign aliens living in the United States. Chapter 40 tells you how to prepare for your accountant. Ernst & Young prepares tax returns for thousands of individuals, so you won't be surprised to learn this is a matter that we've considered quite carefully. The next chapters offer a further helping hand. With luck, you won't need to refer to Chapter 41, but, in case your tax return is examined, you will find it useful. Chapter 42 can help you save money on your taxes next year. It discusses new provisions of the tax law that will take effect for the first time in 1994. In addition, the chapter includes a discussion of estate planning. Even though you can pass on a significant amount of money to your heirs tax-free, it is essential that you give some thought to estate planning while you're still healthy and vigorous.

36 If You Are Self-Employed: How to File Schedule C

Introduction

Many people work for themselves. And with tougher economic times, more and more individuals are striking out on their own. Whether such a business—already existing or new—is your sole source of income or whether it supplements other income, you will face a number of perplexing tax questions that ordinary wage earners do not. What income do you report? What expenses can you deduct? What forms do you need to file?

Unlike a partnership or a regular corporation, a sole proprietorship is not a separate entity. In a sole proprietorship, you and your business are one and the same. You report net profit or loss for the year from a sole proprietorship on Form 1040, Schedule C, and it becomes part of your adjusted gross income. In addition to owing income tax on such income, you, as the sole proprietor, usually will be liable for self-employment tax and will also be required to make payments of estimated taxes. A net loss from the business generally can be deducted when you compute your adjusted gross income.

This chapter concentrates on how a sole proprietorship recognizes business profit and losses on federal Form 1040, Schedule C and Schedule SE.

Who Must File Schedule C

If you are a sole proprietor, a statutory employee, or a statutory independent contractor, you may be required to report business income and expenses on Schedule C.

Sole proprietor. If you operate a business as a sole proprietor, you must file Schedule C to report your income and expenses from your business. If you operate more than one business, or if you and your spouse had separate businesses, you must prepare a separate Schedule C for each business.

Statutory employee. If you are a statutory employee, you are permitted to file Schedule C. A statutory employee includes the following occupations:

1. Certain agent and commission drivers
2. Full-time life insurance sales representatives
3. Certain home workers performing work, according to specifications furnished by the person for whom the services are performed
4. Certain traveling or city salespeople who work full-time (except for sidelines sales activities) for one firm or person, soliciting orders from customers

For further explanation of who qualifies as a statutory employee, refer to IRS Publication 937, *Employment Taxes and Information Returns.*

If you meet the definition of a statutory employee, your employer must indicate this classification by checking box 15 on your Form W-2. This indicates to the IRS that you have the right to report your income and expenses on Schedule C.

As a statutory employee, you are considered an employee for Social Security and Medicare purposes. However, if you and your employer agree, federal income tax withholding is optional rather than mandatory.

A statutory employee reports his or her wages from box 1 of Form W-2 on line 1 of Schedule C. He or she then deducts allowable expenses on Part II of Schedule C to arrive at reportable income.

Statutory independent contractor. If you are a statutory independent contractor, you must file Schedule C to report your income and expenses.

There are two categories of statutory independent contractors. If you are either a direct seller of consumer products or a qualified real estate agent, you must file Schedule C.

For a further explanation of who qualifies as a statutory independent contractor, see IRS Publication 937, *Employment Taxes and Information Returns.*

TaxAlert

Unlike a statutory employee, a statutory independent contractor is not subject to social security and Medicare withholding. Therefore, he or she is required to pay self-employment tax on net earnings. Additionally, federal income tax withholding is not required; therefore, estimated taxes must be made.

What's Included on Schedule C

Schedule C is used to report income and related expenses applicable to the above activities. Income includes cash, property, and services received from all sources, unless specifically excluded under the tax code. Expenses include all necessary and ordinary expenses incurred in connection with the activity.

For sole proprietorships in the business of selling goods or inventory, the primary expense will be the cost of goods sold. The cost of goods sold represents the cost of materials, labor, and overhead included in the inventory sold during the year. Other expenses that you deduct on Schedule C include salaries and wages, interest on loans used in the activity, rent, depreciation, bad debts, travel and entertainment, insurance, real estate taxes, state and local taxes, and an allocable portion of your tax return preparation fee.

TAXPLANNER

Schedule C-EZ. You may use Schedule C-EZ instead of Schedule C if you operated a business or practiced a profession as a sole proprietorship and you have met all of the requirements listed below:

- Had gross receipts from your business of $25,000 or less
- Had business expenses of $2,000 or less
- Use the cash method of accounting
- Did not have an inventory at any time during the year
- Did not have a net loss from your business
- Had only one business as a sole proprietor

  and you

- Had no employees during the year
- Are not required to file Form 4562, *Depreciation and Amortization*
- Do not deduct expenses for business use of your home
- Do not have prior-year, unallowed passive activity losses from this business

Where to Report on Your Return

Adjusted gross income (AGI). The net income or net loss arrived at on Schedule C should be reported on page 1 of Form 1040. The net income or net loss (subject to certain limitations) generated on your Schedule C will cause either an increase or a decrease in your AGI.

TAXALERT

It is important to note that, if you are filing Schedule C, you must use Form 1040, not Form 1040A or Form 1040EZ.

Losses. If Schedule C expenses exceed Schedule C income, a loss will result. There is a possibility that the amount of Schedule C loss that can be deducted on your current year's income tax return may be limited. The amount of the loss that can be deducted on your return depends on whether or not you materially participate in the operation of the business or whether or not you have enough investment at risk to cover the loss.

For more information, see Chapter 13, *Other Income* and IRS Publication 925, *Passive Activity and At-Risk Rules.*

Carrybacks and Carryforwards. If you have incurred a Schedule C loss, it is possible that the loss may be large enough to offset all taxable income reported on your Form

1040. If this is the case, you may have generated a net operating loss (NOL).

If you have incurred an NOL you can carry back or carry forward the loss and utilize it to offset income in other years. Generally, you must carry back an NOL to the 3 tax years before the NOL year and then carry over any NOL remaining for up to 15 years after the NOL year. The NOL year is the year in which the NOL occurred. You cannot deduct any part of the NOL that remains after the 15-year carryover period.

You may elect not to carry back your NOL. If you make this election, you may use your NOL only during the 15-year carryforward period. To make this election, attach a statement to your tax return for the NOL year. This statement must show that you are electing to forgo the carryback period under section 172(b) (3) of the Internal Revenue Code.

TAXSAVER

If your income was subject to tax at a lower tax bracket during the carryback period and you expect your future income to be subject to tax at a higher tax bracket, you may wish to elect to forgo the carryback of the NOL.

Example

In 1993, you incur an NOL of $20,000. You have been profitable in all 3 previous years, and the profits have been taxed at a 15% tax rate. You expect to generate large income in future years, and you expect to be taxed at a 39% tax rate. By electing to forgo the carryback of the NOL, you can save $4,800 in taxes [$20,000 × (39% − 15%)].

For more information on net operating losses, see Form 1045 and Publication 536, *Net Operating Losses.*

Self-Employment Income and Social Security Tax

Income reported on Schedule C is classified as self-employment income for both the sole proprietor and the statutory independent contractor. It is not classified as self-employment income for a statutory employee and is therefore not subject to self-employment tax.

Self-employment tax is calculated on Schedule 1040SE. Self-employment tax is composed of a social security tax of 12.4% and a Medicare tax of 2.9%. For 1993, the maximum amount of wages and/or self-employment income subject to the social security part of the self-employment tax is $57,600, while the maximum amount subject to the Medicare part of the self-employment tax is $135,000. The maximum amount of self-employment tax that you can pay for 1993 is $11,057. One-half of your self-employment tax can be deducted on line 25 of Form 1040. No self-employment tax is due on your self-employment income if the total amount you received in 1993 as an employee was $135,000 or more and was subject to social security and Medicare tax.

TAXALERT

Estimated income taxes. You may be required to pay estimated tax on your self-employment income. This depends on how much income and self-employment tax you expect for the year and how much of your income will be subject to withholding tax. For years beginning after 1993, the ceiling on the maximum amount of wages and self-employment income subject to the Medicare tax is repealed and the amount of income subject to the social security tax has been increased to $60,600. These changes should be considered when calculating your estimated tax for 1994. For more information, see Chapter 5, *Tax Withholding and Estimated Tax.*

TaxPlanner

If you are a salaried employee as well, you may cover your estimated self-employment tax payments by having your employer increase the amount of income tax withheld from your pay.

TaxSaver

If you have more than one trade or business, you must combine the net earnings from each business to determine your net self-employment income. A loss that you incur in one business will offset your income in another business.

When an individual's self-employment earnings are less than $400, he or she is not required to file Schedule 1040SE or to pay self-employment tax.

How to Determine Items of Income and Expenses

Start-up and preoperating expenses

Start-up expenditures are the costs of getting started in business before you actually begin business operations. Start-up costs may include expenses for such things as advertising, travel, utilities, repairs, or employees' wages. These are often the same kinds of costs that can be deducted when they occur after you open for business.

Start-up costs include what you pay for both investigating a prospective business and getting the business started. For example, they may include costs for the following items:

- A survey of potential markets
- An analysis of available facilities, labor, supplies, and so forth
- Advertisements for the opening of the business
- Salaries and wages for employees who are being trained, and their instructors
- Travel and other necessary costs for securing prospective distributors, suppliers, or customers
- Salaries and fees for executives and consultants, or for other professional services

Start-up costs do not include deductible interest, taxes, and research and experimental costs. Therefore, subject to other limitations, these items are currently deductible.

Whether or not you can deduct your start-up expenditures depends on whether you actually begin the active trade or business.

If you go into business. When your business actually begins, all of the costs you incurred to start it up are not currently deductible and must be capitalized. However, an election can be made to amortize these start-up costs ratably over a minimum of 60 months. To amortize your start-up costs, the costs must meet the following tests:

1. They must be costs that would be deductible if they were paid or incurred to operate an existing trade or business (i.e., wages, advertising) but not to purchase machinery.
2. They must be paid or incurred by you before you actually begin business operations.

Electing to amortize expenses. An election to amortize expenses must be made by the due date of the return (including extensions) for the year in which active business begins.

The election must include a description of the expenditures, the amounts, the dates they were incurred, the month in which the business began, and the number of months in the amortization period. The amount of amortization is reported on Form 4562, Part VI.

Example

John's repair shop started business on June 1, 1993. Prior to starting business, John incurred various expenses totaling $6,000 to set up shop. John makes an election on his 1993 income tax return to amortize these expenses over a 60-month period. John is permitted a tax deduction for amortization of start-up expenses of $700 in 1993 [$6,000 ÷ 60 months) × 7 months in 1993].

TaxAlert

Though the IRS has been instructed to do so, it has not issued any guidance as to when a trade or a business begins. When it does, the IRS is likely to take a conservative stance. In the meantime, there has been substantial litigation about this issue. The generally accepted rule seems to be that, even though a taxpayer has made a firm decision to enter into a business and over a considerable period of time has spent money in preparation for entering that business, he or she still has not engaged in carrying on any trade or business until such time as the business has begun to function as a going concern and has performed those activities for which it was organized.

If you fail to go into business. If your attempt to go into business is not successful, whether or not you can deduct the expenses you incurred in trying to establish yourself in business depends on the type of expenses you incurred.

Investigatory expenses. The costs you incurred before making a decision to acquire or to begin a specific business are classified as personal and therefore are not deductible. Investigatory expenses include costs incurred in the course of a general search for, or preliminary investigation of, a business prior to reaching a decision to acquire or enter any business. Examples include expenses incurred for the analysis or survey of potential markets, products, labor supply, transportation facilities, and so on.

Start-up expenses. The costs that you incur after you've made a decision to acquire or to establish a particular business and prior to its actual operation are classified as capital expenditures and may be deductible in the year in which your attempt to go into business fails.

Business sold. If you completely dispose of a trade or a business before the end of the amortization period you have selected, any deferred start-up costs for the trade or business that have not yet been deducted may be deducted to the extent that they qualify as a loss from a trade or a business.

Tax Year

Every taxpayer must determine taxable income and file a tax return on the basis of an annual accounting period. The term "tax year" is the annual accounting period you use for keeping your records and for reporting your income and expenses. The accounting periods you can use are as follows:

1. A calendar year
2. A fiscal year

You adopt a tax year when you file your first income tax return. It cannot be longer than 12 months.

Calendar tax year. If you adopt the calendar year for your annual accounting period, you must maintain your books and records, and report your income and expenses for the period from January 1 through December 31 of each year.

If you filed your first return using the calendar tax year, and you later begin business as a sole proprietor, you must continue to use the calendar tax year, unless you get permission from the IRS to change. You must report your income from all sources, including your sole proprietorship, using the same tax year.

Fiscal tax year. A regular fiscal tax year is 12 consecutive months, ending on the last day of any month except December.

If you adopt a fiscal tax year, you must maintain your books and records, and report your income and expenses using the same tax year.

Accounting Methods

Accounting methods are described in Chapter 1, *Filing Information*. The discussion that follows relates mainly to self-employed entrepreneurs, sole proprietors, and others who file Schedule C. No single accounting method is required for all taxpayers. Generally, you may figure your taxable income under any of the following accounting methods:

1. Cash method
2. Accrual method
3. Special methods of accounting for certain items of income and expenses
4. Combination (hybrid) method using elements of (1), (2), or (3)

Cash method. The cash method of accounting is used by most individuals and many small businesses with no inventories. However, if inventories are necessary in accounting for your income, you must use the accrual method for your sales and purchases. If you are not required to maintain inventories, it is often advisable to use the cash method, since it allows you more flexibility and control over your income.

Income. Under the cash method, your gross income includes all items of income you actually receive during the year. You must include in your income property and services you recieve at their fair market value.

Expenses. Usually, you must deduct expenses in the tax year in which you actually pay them. However, you may be required to postpone the deduction for expenses you pay in advance. In addition, you may have to capitalize certain costs.

Accrual method. Under an accrual method of accounting, income generally is reported in the year in which it is earned, regardless of when the income is actually collected, and expenses generally are deducted in the year in which they are incurred, regardless of when the expenses are paid. The purpose of an accrual method of accounting is to match your income and your expenses. If inventories are necessary in your business, only the accrual method of accounting can be used for purchases and sales.

Income. All items of income are generally included in your gross income when you earn them, even though you may receive payment in another tax year. All events that fix your right to receive the income must have happened, and you must be able to determine the amount with reasonable accuracy.

Example

You are a calendar year taxpayer. You sold a radio on November 28, 1993. You billed the customer 3 days later but did not receive payment until February, 1994. You must include the amount of the sale in your income for 1993, because you earned the income in 1993.

Income received in advance. Prepaid income is generally included in gross income in the year you receive it. Your method of accounting does not matter as long as the income is available to you. Prepaid income includes rents or interest received in advance and compensation for services to be performed later.

If, under an agreement, you receive advance payment for services to be performed by the end of the next tax year, you can defer the inclusion in income of the payments received until you earn them by performing the service. You **must** be an accrual method taxpayer to defer recognition of income on advance payments for services. You cannot defer the income beyond the year after the year you receive the payment.

Example

You are in the television repair business. In 1992 you received payment for one-year contracts under which you agree to repair or replace certain parts that fail to function properly in television sets that were sold by an unrelated party. You include the payments in gross income as you earn them by performing the services as specified under the accrual method of including advance payments.

If for any reason you do not perform part of the services by the end of the following tax year, 1993, you must include in gross income for 1993 the amount of the advance payments that are for the unperformed services.

Example

You own a dance studio. On November 4, 1992, you received payment for a 1-year contract, beginning on that date and providing for 48 one-hour lessons. You gave 8 lessons in 1992. If you recognize income under the accrual method of including advance payments, you must include one-sixth ($8/48$) of the payment in income for 1992 and five-sixths ($40/48$) of the payment in 1993.

Expenses. You deduct expenses when you become liable for them, whether or not you pay them in the same year. Before you can deduct expenses, all events that set the amount of the liability must have happened, you must be able to determine the amount of the liability with reasonable accuracy, and economic performance (see below) must occur.

Economic performance rule. Even if all of the events that determine the amount of your expenses have occurred, you still cannot deduct business expenses until economic performance occurs. If your expense is for property or services provided to you, or for use of property by you, economic performance occurs as the property or services are provided or as the property is used. If your expense is for property or services that you provide to others, economic performance occurs as the property or services are provided or as the property is used.

Special rules for related persons. An accrual basis taxpayer cannot deduct business expenses and interest owed to a related cash basis taxpayer until the amount is paid.

For purposes of applying this rule, related persons include, but are not limited to:

1. Members of the immediate family, including only brothers and sisters, husband and wife, ancestors, and lineal descendants

2. An individual and a corporation, if more than 50% in value of the outstanding stock is owned, directly or indirectly, by or for such individual

3. An S corporation, and any individual who owns any of the stock of such S corporation

4. A partnership, and any person who owns any capital interest or profits interest of such partnership.

Special methods. In addition to the cash or accrual methods, certain items of income or expenses are accounted under special methods. They include

- Depreciation
- Amortization and depletion
- Bad debts
- Installment sales

The method of accounting for depreciation and bad debts is discussed later in this chapter. Methods for deducting amortization and depletion are discussed in IRS Publication 535, *Business Expenses*. Methods for reporting installment sales are discussed in IRS Publication 537, *Installment Sales*.

Combination (hybrid) method. Any combination of cash, accrual, and special methods of accounting can be used if the combination clearly reflects income and is consistently used. As an example, if you maintain inventory, the accrual method of accounting for purchases and sales must be used; however, you may use the cash method for all other items of income and expenses.

Two or more businesses. If you operate more than one business, you generally may use a different accounting method for each separate and distinct business if the method you use for each clearly reflects your income. For example, if you operate a personal-service business and a manufacturing business, you may use the cash method for the personal-service business, but you must use the accrual method for the manufacturing business.

How to Complete Schedule C

Schedule C is divided into five parts:

Part I: Income
Part II: Expenses
Part III: Cost of Goods Sold
Part IV: Information on Your Vehicle
Part V: Other Expenses

In addition, Schedule C requires that you complete a number of general questions about the activity.

General Information

Line A asks for the principal business or profession, including the product or service that provided your principal source of income.

Line B asks for the four-digit code that identifies your principal business or professional activity. The instructions to Schedule C contains a list of the principal business or professional activity codes that you should use.

Line C asks for your business name. If none, leave this line blank.

Line D asks for your employer identification number (EIN). An EIN is needed only if you had a Keogh plan [discussed later in this chapter and in Chapter 18, *Individual Retirement Arrangements (IRAs)*] or if you were required to file an employment or excise tax return. If you do not have an EIN, do not enter your social security number. To apply for an EIN, you must file Form SS-4 with the IRS where you file your individual tax return.

Line E requests your business address. If you conducted business out of your home, you do not have to complete this line.

Line F asks for your accounting method, as discussed earlier in this chapter and in Chapter 1, *Filing Information*.

Line G asks for the method used to value closing inventory, if your business maintains inventory. The inventory can be valued under any one of the following three methods: (1) cost, (2) lower of cost or market, or (3) any other method approved by the IRS. Methods of valuing inventory will be discussed later in this chapter.

Line H does not need to be answered if your business does not have inventory. If the business does maintain inventory, and there was a change in determining quantities, costs, or valuations between opening and closing inventories, answer the question "yes" and attach an explanation for the change.

Line I asks whether or not you "materially participated" in the business. If you did not, your losses from the business that you can deduct currently may be limited. See Chapter 13, *Other Income*.

Line J must be checked if this is the initial Schedule C filed for this particular business.

Income

Part I of Schedule C is used to report the gross income from the business. You should include on line 1 gross receipts or sales from your business. Do not combine receipts from two separate businesses on this line. Remember that you must file a separate Schedule C for each business. Statutory employees enter the amount from box 1 of Form W-2 and check the box on line 1.

On line 2, report such items as sales returns, rebates, and allowances. For example, if an item you previously sold is returned for a cash refund, the cash refund should be reported here and not included as a reduction of the gross receipts or sales reported on line 1.

Subtract line 2 from line 1, and enter the difference on line 3. From this amount, deduct the cost of goods sold. After deducting the cost of goods sold, you arrive at the gross profit from the business.

Costs of Goods Sold

Part III of Schedule C is used to determine your cost of goods sold. If you make or buy goods to sell, you are entitled to deduct the cost of the goods sold on your tax return. However, to determine these costs, you must maintain inventories.

Inventories are required to be determined at the beginning and end of each tax year for manufacturers, wholesalers, retailers, and every other business that makes, buys, or sells goods to produce income. Inventories include goods held for sale in the normal course of business, work in process, and raw materials and supplies that will physically become a part of merchandise intended for sale.

Add to your beginning inventory the cost of inventory items purchased during the year, including all other items entering into the cost of obtaining or producing the inventory. From this total, subtract your inventory at the end of the year. The remainder represents the cost of goods sold during the tax period. It should not include selling expenses or any other expenses that are not directly related to obtaining or producing the goods sold.

Inventory methods. To determine the value of your inventory, you need a method for identifying the items in your inventory and a method for valuing these items. In general, there are three methods of identifying items in inventory: (1) specific identification, (2) First In-First Out (FIFO), and (3) Last In-First Out (LIFO).

The specific identification method is used to identify the cost of each inventoried item by matching the item with its cost of acquisition in addition to other allocable costs, such as labor and transportation. This method is most often used by retailers of bulk items.

If there is no specific identification of items with their costs, you must make an assumption to decide which items were sold and which remain in inventory. You make this identification by either the FIFO or the LIFO method.

The FIFO method assumes that the items you purchased or produced first are the first items you sold, consumed, or otherwise disposed of.

The LIFO method assumes that the items of inventory that you purchased or produced last are sold or removed from inventory first.

The FIFO method and the LIFO method produce different results in income, depending on the trend of price levels of the goods included in those inventories. In times of inflation, when prices are rising, LIFO will produce a larger cost of goods sold and a lower closing inventory. Under FIFO, the cost of goods sold will be lower and the closing inventory will be higher. However, in times of falling prices, LIFO will produce a smaller cost of goods sold and a higher closing inventory. Under FIFO, the reverse will be true.

Valuing inventory. Valuing the items in your inventory is a major factor in figuring your taxable income. The two common ways to value your inventory if you use the FIFO method are the specific-cost identification method and the lower-of-cost-or-market method.

Adopting LIFO method. To adopt the LIFO method, you are required to file Form 970 *Application To Use LIFO Inventory Method,* or a statement that has all the information required in Form 970. You must file the form (or the statement) with your timely-filed tax return for the year in which you first use LIFO.

Once a method is selected you may not change to another method without the permission of the IRS. For a further discussion of inventory, see Publication 334, *Tax Guide for Small Business.*

Expenses

Part II of Schedule C is used to report expenses associated with your business. To be deductible, a business expense must be both ordinary and necessary. An ordinary expense is one that is common and accepted in your field of business, trade, or profession. A necessary expense is one that is helpful and appropriate for your trade, business, or profession. An expense does not have to be indispensable to be considered necessary. Examples of deductible business expenses include (1) reasonable allowance for salaries and other compensation, (2) traveling expenses while away from home, and (3) rentals or other payments for property used in a trade or a business.

You must keep business expenses separate from personal expenses. If you have any expense that is partly business and partly personal, a reasonable allocation should be made to separate the personal part from the business part.

Capital expenditures. A capital expenditure is defined as an expense that must be capitalized rather than deducted. These costs are considered a part of your investment in your business. There are, in general, three types of costs that must be capitalized: (1) costs of going into business, (2) costs to purchase business assets, and (3) cost of improvements.

Although you generally cannot directly deduct a capital expenditure, you may be able to take deductions for the amount you spend through a method of depreciation, amortization, or depletion.

A discussion of some of the more common expenses you will encounter in your business follows.

Bad Debts

If someone owes you money that you cannot collect, you have a bad debt. You may be able to deduct the amount owed to you when you figure your business income in the year in which the debt becomes worthless. There are two kinds of bad debts: business bad debts and nonbusiness bad debts. A business bad debt generally is one that comes from your trade or business. All other bad debts are nonbusiness bad debts. For a discussion of nonbusiness bad debts and when a debt becomes worthless, see Chapter 15, *Sale of Property.*

Business bad debts usually occur because of credit sales to customers. They can also be loans to suppliers, employees, and others associated with your trade or business. These debts are usually shown on your books as either accounts receivable or notes receivable. If you are unable to collect any part of these accounts or notes receivable, the uncollectible part is a business bad debt.

You may take a bad debt deduction on your accounts and notes receivable only if you have basis in the debt; that is, you already included the amount you are owed in your current or earlier gross income, or you actually loaned the money. Only individuals filing a Schedule C using either the accrual or hybrid (cash accrual) accounting method will be able to deduct bad debts relating to accounts receivable. Cash method taxpayers do not report income that is due them until they actually receive payment. Therefore, they cannot take a bad-debt deduction on payments they cannot collect.

Example 1

Paul, who uses the accrual method on his Schedule C, reported income in 1992 of $1,000 related to an account receivable from a customer. In 1993 that account receivable became worthless. Because Paul is on the accrual method and has already included the $1,000 in income, he is permitted to recognize a bad-debt deduction in 1993.

Example 2

Assume the same facts as in Example 1, except that Paul is on the cash method. Since Paul has not recognized the $1,000 sale in income in 1992, he cannot take a bad-debt deduction when the debt becomes worthless in 1993.

The net effect on Paul's income in either situation is the same.

	Accrual	Cash
Income recognized in 1992	$1,000	-0-
Less bad-debt deduction in 1993	1,000	-0-
Net effect	-0-	-0-

Methods of treating bad debts. The method of accounting for bad debts is referred to as the "specific charge-off method," because it requires the specific identification of the debt that has become worthless. Using the specific charge-off method, you can deduct specific business bad debts that become either partly or totally worthless during the tax year.

Partially worthless debts. You may deduct specific bad debts that are partially uncollectible. To take the deduction, however, the amount must be written off on your books; that is, you must eliminate the worthless portion of the debt from your books as an asset. You do not have to write off and deduct your partially worthless debts annually. Instead, you may delay the write-off until a later year. Also, you may wait until more of the debt has become worthless or until you have collected all you can on the debt and it is totally worthless. You may not, however, deduct any part of the bad debt in a year after the year in which the debt becomes totally worthless. This rule permits you the opportunity to select the year in which to claim the partial bad debt deduction.

Totally worthless debts. A totally worthless debt is deducted only in the tax year in which it becomes totally worthless. The deduction for the debt must not include any amount deducted in an earlier tax year when the debt was only partially worthless. You are not required to make an actual write-off on your books to claim a bad-debt deduction for a totally worthless debt. However, you may want to do so. If a debt you claim to be totally worthless is not written off on your books and the IRS later rules that the debt is only partially worthless, you will not be allowed any deduction unless you had written off the amount on your books.

Recovery of bad debt. If you deducted a bad debt and in a later tax year recover (collect) all or part of it, you may have to include the amount you recover in your gross income. However, you may exclude from gross income the amount recovered, up to the amount of the deduction that did not reduce your tax in the year in which it was deducted.

Example

In 1989, John had a $25,000 bad-debt loss relating to his Schedule C. He also had $25,000 of income from the activity and other deductions totaling $2,480. John had no taxable income for 1989.

In 1993, John recovered the entire $25,000 debt. To figure how much he should include in his 1993 income, see the calculation below.

	1989 With bad debt	1989 Without bad debt
Income:		
Schedule C	$25,000	$25,000
Bad-debt loss	(25,000)	-0-
Adjusted gross income	-0-	$25,000
Less:		
Standard deductions	-0-	$3,000
Personal exemption	-0-	$1,950
Taxable income	-0-	$20,050

The calculations show that John's 1989 taxable income was reduced by $20,050 by including the bad debt. Therefore, $20,050 is included in John's taxable income for 1993, the year in which he collected the $25,000 debt.

Automobile and Truck Expenses

If you use your automobile for business purposes, you may be able to deduct expenses associated with the business use of the automobile. You generally can use one of two methods to figure your expense: actual expenses or the standard mileage rate. Refer to Chapter 28, *Car Expenses and Other Employee Business Expenses,* for more information on expenses for business use of your automobile.

TaxAlert

The 1993 Schedule C has been changed to simplify the reporting of business vehicle information. You can use Part IV of Schedule C instead of Form 4562 if you are claiming the standard mileage rate, you lease your vehicle, or your vehicle is fully depreciated. However, if you wish to deduct actual automobile expenses or if you must file Form 4562 for any other reason, you must continue to use Part V of Form 4562 to report the vehicle information.

Depreciation and Expensing Certain Assets

When you use property in your business, you are permitted to recover your investment in the property through tax deductions. You do this by "depreciating" the property, by deducting some of your cost on your income tax return each year. You can depreciate "tangible" property, such as a car, a building, or machinery, and amortize "intangible" property, such as a copyright or a patent. Depreciation is reported on Part II or Part III of Form 4562, whereas amortization is reported on Part VI of Form 4562. You cannot depreciate land, property you rent, or inventory.

TaxAlert

Recently enacted changes to the tax law permit an amortization deduction for the capitalized cost of certain intangible property that is acquired and is held in connection with the conduct of a trade or business or an activity engaged in for the production of income. The amount of the deduction is determined by amortizing the adjusted basis (generally the cost) of the intangible property ratably over a 15-year period. The amortization period begins with the month that the intangible property is acquired.

In general, the change applies to section 197 intangible property acquired by a taxpayer after August 10, 1993. The term "section 197 intangible" is defined as any property that is included in any one or more of the following categories:

1. Goodwill and going conern value;
2. Certain specified types of intangible property that generally relate to work force, information base, know-how, customers, suppliers, or other similar items;
3. Any license, permit, or other right granted by a governmental unit or an agency or instrumentality thereof;
4. Any covenant not to compete (or other arrangement to the extent that the arrangement has substantially the same effect as a covenant not to compete) entered into in connection with the direct or indirect acquisition of an interest in a trade or business (or substantial portion thereof); and
5. Any franchise, trademark, or trade name.

Special rules apply if a taxpayer disposes of some, but not all, of section 197 intangible property that was acquired in a transaction. No loss is to be recognized by reason of such a disposition. Instead, the adjusted bases of the retained section 197 intangible properties that were acquired in connection with such transaction are increased by the amount of any loss that is not recognized.

The change is generally effective for property acquired after August 10, 1993. However, you may elect to apply the new law retroactively to all property acquired after July 25, 1991.

Property is depreciable if it meets the following requirements:

1. It must be used in business or held for the production of income.

2. It must have a determinable life, and that life must be longer than 1 year.
3. It must be something that wears out, decays, gets used up, becomes obsolete, or loses value from natural causes.

In general, if property does not meet all three of these conditions, it is not depreciable.

The amount of depreciation you can deduct depends on (1) how much the property costs, (2) when you began using it, (3) how long it will take to recover your cost, and (4) which of several depreciation methods you use.

You begin to claim depreciation on property when you place it in service in your trade or business or for the production of income. You continue to depreciate the property until you recover your basis (generally the cost) in it, dispose of it, or stop using it for business or investment purposes.

Form 4562, *Depreciation and Amortization,* is used to report your depreciation. For a further discussion of depreciation, see Chapter 10, *Rental Income and Expenses.* Additional information can be found in Publication 534, *Depreciation.*

Expensing certain assets (Section 179 deduction). You can elect to treat all or part of the cost, not to exceed $17,500, of certain qualifying property as an expense in the year in which the property is purchased, rather than capitalize the cost and depreciate it over its life. This means that you can deduct all or part of the cost in 1 year rather than take depreciation deductions spread out over several years. You must decide for each item of qualifying property whether to deduct, subject to the yearly limit, or capitalize and depreciate its cost.

Qualifying property is property purchased for use in your trade or business and property that would have qualified for the investment tax credit.

Basis of qualifying property. The amount you elect to deduct is subtracted from the basis of the qualifying property. If you elect the section 179 deduction, the amount of your allowable ACRS or MACRS deduction for this property will be reduced. If you and your spouse file separate returns, you can each deduct only $8,750, unless you and your spouse agree on a different split of the $17,500.

Other restrictions. The amount of the section 179 deduction cannot be greater than the income from the trade or business (computed without regard to the property to be expensed). Any section 179 deductions disallowed under this income limitation are carried forward to the succeeding taxable year and added to the allowable amount for such year. Therefore, in the following year, you are eligible to receive the $17,500 deduction plus the carryover from the preceding year, limited to the amount of income. Also, the $17,500 amount is reduced dollar for dollar for property investments in excess of $200,000.

Cost. The cost of property for the section 179 deduction does not include any part of the basis of the property that is determined by reference to the basis of other property held at any time by the person acquiring this property. For example, if you buy a new truck to use in your business, your cost for purposes of the section 179 deduction does not include the adjusted basis of the truck you trade in on the new vehicle.

Example

You buy a new piece of equipment, paying $2,500 cash and trading in your old equipment, which had an undepreciated cost to you of $4,000. Even though the new equipment has a tax cost to you of $6,500, you may claim only the section 179 deduction on the $2,500 you paid out.

When to elect. You must make an election to take the section 179 deduction. You make this election only in the first tax year in which the property is placed in service.

If you elect to deduct the cost of qualifying property, you must specify the items to which the election applies and the part of the cost of each you elect to deduct. If in 1993, you purchase and place in service two items of qualifying property costing $8,700 and $15,300, and you want to elect the $17,500 deduction, you must specify what part of the $8,700 property or the $15,300 property you want to deduct. You may arbitrarily allocate the maximum $17,500 between the two properties.

Use Form 4562 to make your election and report your section 179 deduction. You make the election by taking the deduction on Form 4562, filed with your original tax return. The election cannot be made on an amended tax return filed after the due date (including extensions), and once made can be revoked only with the consent of the Internal Revenue Service.

You should consult your tax advisor regarding the section 179 rules, particularly when you acquire or dispose of assets.

Computers. If you use a computer for both business and personal use, there are special rules that may limit the amount of depreciation that can be deducted.

The amount of depreciation you are allowed to deduct depends on what percentage of use was business and what percentage was personal. The allocation is made on the basis of the most appropriate unit of time. For example, determine the percentage of use in a trade or a business for a tax year by dividing the number of hours the computer is used for business purposes by the total number of hours the computer is used for any purpose for that tax year.

Luxury automobiles. See Chapter 28, *Car Expenses and Other Employee Business Expenses,* for a discussion of luxury cars and depreciation.

Leasing Business Assets

Many sole proprietors decide to lease a business asset, rather than purchase it. This is ideal if the asset is only needed for a limited period of time. For example, a tax practitioner may only need a computer for the months of February through April. Instead of incurring the large capital outlay required to purchase the asset, he or she can free up cash by leasing a computer.

Generally, the entire expense for leasing a business asset is deductible. This assumes that the asset is used 100% of the time for business purposes. If, however, the asset is used for both business and personal use, only the portion attributable to business use is allowed as a deduction. The most common business asset that is leased by a sole proprietor and a statutory employee is an automobile.

If you lease an automobile, you can deduct the part of each lease payment that is for the use of the automobile in your business or work. You cannot deduct any part of a lease payment that is for commuting to your regular job or other personal use of the automobile. You must amortize any advance payments made on the lease over the entire lease period.

If you leased an automobile after December 31, 1986, that you use in your business, for a lease term of 30 days or more, you may have to include in your income for each tax year in which you lease the car an "inclusion amount." If the fair market value of the automobile when the lease began was more than $12,800 ($13,400 for leases beginning in 1991, $13,700 for leases beginning in 1992 and $14,300 for leases beginning in 1993), you must include in your gross income an inclusion amount each tax year during which you lease the automobile. Refer to Publication 917, *Business Use of a Car,* for a more in-depth discussion of the calculation of the inclusion amount.

Health Insurance

As a result of recently enacted tax law changes, self-employed individuals, including those filing Schedule C, may again be able to deduct part of the amount paid for health insurance on behalf of themselves, their spouses, and dependents. This deduction is only available if you had net profits from self-employment for the year and were not eligible to participate in a subsidized health plan maintained by you or your spouse's employer. The determination of whether a self-employed individual or his spouse may be eligible for employer-paid health benefits is made on a monthly basis.

The allowable deduction is limited to the lesser of (1) 25% of the amount paid for health insurance during the year for the self-employed individual, spouse, and dependents, or (2) the net profit from the trade or business less the amount claimed for a Keogh plan or a SEP deduction on Form 1040, line 27.

The deduction is not claimed on Schedule C and is not allowed as a deduction for self-employment tax purposes. The deduction is claimed on Form 1040, line 26 as an adjustment to income. Any medical insurance expenses in excess of the allowable deduction may be claimed as an itemized deduction on Schedule A (Form 1040), subject to the 7.5% of AGI floor for medical expenses.

TaxAlert

The tax provision that permitted self-employed individuals to deduct part of the amount paid for health insurance expired as of July 1, 1992. The recently passed Tax Act has retroactively extended this provision from July 1, 1992, through December 31, 1993. If your 1992 federal income tax return was filed before the enactment of the Tax Act, and you incurred health insurance costs subsequent to July 1, 1992, you may find it beneficial to amend your 1992 income tax return to take advantage of this retroactive change.

Employees

Who are employees? Before you can know how to treat payments that you make for services rendered to you, you must first know the business relationship that exists between you and the person performing those services. The person performing the services may be: (1) an independent contractor, (2) a common-law employee, (3) a statutory employee, or (4) a statutory independent contractor.

The determination of a worker's classification can have significant tax consequences on an employer. When workers are not treated as employees, the employer can avoid employment tax and wage withholding responsibilities, as well as costs related to pension plans, health insurance, and other fringe benefits.

Independent contractors. People such as lawyers, contractors, subcontractors, public stenographers, auctioneers, and so on, who follow an independent trade, business, or profession in which they offer their services to the general public, are generally not employees. However, whether such people are employees or independent contractors depends on the facts in each case. The general rule is that an individual is an independent contractor if you, the employer, have the right to control or direct only the result of the work and not the means and methods of accomplishing the result.

You do not have to withhold or pay taxes on payments that you make to independent contractors.

Common-law employees. Under common-law rules, every individual who performs services subject to the will and control of an employer, as to both what must be done and how it must be done, is an employee. It does not matter that the employer allows the employee discretion and freedom of action, so long as the employer has the legal right to control both the method and the result of the services.

Two usual characteristics of an employer–employee relationship are that the employer has the right to discharge the employee and that the employer supplies the employee with tools and a place to work.

No distinction is made between classes of employees. Superintendents, managers, and other supervisory personnel are all employees. An officer of a corporation is generally an employee, but a director is not. An officer who performs no services or only minor services, and neither receives nor is entitled to receive any pay, is not considered an employee.

You generally must withhold and pay federal, social security, and Medicare taxes on wages you pay to common-law employees.

Statutory employees and statutory independent contractors are discussed at the beginning of this chapter.

Salaries, wages, and other forms of pay that you make to employees are generally deductible business expenses. However, a deduction for salaries and wages must be reduced by any jobs credit determined for the tax year. This will be discussed later in this chapter.

Tests for Deductibility

To be deductible, employees' pay must meet all of the following four tests:

Test 1—Ordinary and necessary. You must be able to show that salaries, wages, and other payments for employees' services are ordinary and necessary expenses directly connected with your trade or business.

Test 2—Reasonable. What is reasonable pay is determined by the facts. Generally, it is the amount that would ordinarily be paid for these services by like enterprises under similar circumstances.

Test 3—For services performed. You must be able to prove that the payments were made for services actually performed.

Test 4—Paid or incurred. You must have actually made the payments or incurred the expense during the tax year.

If you use the cash method of accounting, the expense for salaries and wages can be deducted only in the year in which the salaries and wages were paid. If you use the accrual method of accounting, the expense for salaries and wages is deducted when your obligation to make the payments is established and economic performance occurs (generally, when an employee performs his or her services for you). In addition, the expense must be paid within $2\frac{1}{2}$ months after the end of the tax year. However, the deduction of an accrual of salary to an owner may be limited. (See the previous discussion on the deduction of an accrual to a related party.)

Payroll Taxes

General Rules for Withholding

As an employer, you must generally withhold income taxes, social security, and Medicare taxes from wages that you pay employees. In addition, the amounts withheld with respect to social security and Medicare taxes will have to be matched by you, the employer. Also, unemployment tax payments may be required.

For information about the payroll tax deposit rules, see IRS Circular E, *Employer's Tax Guide.*

TaxSaver

You may find it helpful to remember the following general rules for withholding:

1. *Independent contractors.* You do not withhold income tax or social security and Medicare taxes from amounts you pay an independent contractor.
2. *Common-law employees.* You generally have to withhold income tax, social security tax, and Medicare tax from the wages you pay common-law employees. You also have to pay federal unemployment tax and your share of social security and Medicare taxes on these wages.
3. *Statutory employees.* You are not required to withhold income tax from the wages of statutory employees. You must withhold and pay social security and Medicare taxes. Unless they are full-time life insurance sales agents or work at home, you must also pay federal unemployment tax on their wages.
4. *Statutory independent contractors.* You do not withhold or pay taxes on payments to statutory independent contractors.

Reporting payments to independent contractors and statutory independent contractors. If you pay an independent contractor $600 or more during the year in the course of your trade or business, you must file with the IRS and provide the independent contractor a Form 1099-MISC, *Miscellaneous Income.*

Reporting payments to common-law employees. To report wages paid to a common-law employee, you must complete a Form W-2. The Form W-2 must show the total wages and other compensation paid, total wages subject to social security taxes, total wages subject to Medicare taxes, the amounts deducted for income, social security, and Medicare taxes, and any other information required on the statement. For information on preparing Form W-2, see the Instructions that come with Form W-2.

Reporting payments to statutory employees. To report wages paid to a statutory employee, you must complete a Form W-2. You must report the same information that you reported for common-law employees. If the statutory employee and employer have elected not to withhold income tax, this information does not have to be furnished. Also, the employer must check box 15, "statutory employee," on Form W-2.

When hiring new employees, you are required to have the employee complete a Form W-4, *Employee's Withholding Allowance Certificate,* and a Form I-9, *Employment Eligibility Verification Form.* In addition, the employee is required to file various payroll forms to the government. For more information on which payroll forms the employee must file, see IRS Circular E, *Employer's Tax Guide.*

Office in the Home and Form 8829

It is not unusual for a person filing a Schedule C to use part of his or her home for business. If you use part of your home regularly and exclusively for business, you may be able to deduct certain operating and depreciation expenses on your home.

Requirements for claiming the deduction. You may deduct certain expenses for operating out of a part of your home only if that part of your home is used regularly and exclusively as

1. Your principal place of business for any trade or business in which you engage, or
2. A place to meet or deal with your patients, clients, or customers in the normal course of your trade or business

TaxAlert

The U.S. Supreme Court has recently clarified the factors to be used in determining whether a taxpayer's home office is his principal place of business. The Court noted that the ultimate determination of the principal place of business is dependent upon the particular facts of each case. There are, however, two primary considerations in deciding whether a home office is a taxpayer's principal place of business: 1) the relative importance of the activities performed at each business location and 2) the time spent at each place. A comparison of the relative importance of the activities performed at each business location depends on the characteristics of each business. If the nature of the business requires that you meet or confer with clients or patients, or that you deliver goods or services to a customer, the place where that contact occurs must be given great weight in determining where the most important activities are performed. Performance of necessary or essential activities in your home office (such as planning for services or the delivery of goods, or the accounting or billing for those activities or goods) does not, in and of itself, allow you to claim a home office deduction.

You may also deduct certain expenses for operating out of a separate structure that is not attached to your home, if you use it regularly and exclusively for your trade or business. (See Chapter 30, *Miscellaneous Deductions,* for more about deducting these expenses.)

TaxSaver

Even if you do *not* qualify for a business use of the home deduction, you may be allowed to take a depreciation deduction or elect a section 179 deduction for furniture and equipment you use in your home for business or work as an employee. For more information, see Publication 587, *Business Use of Your Home.*

If you use part of your home for business and meet the requirements discussed earlier, you must divide the expenses of operating out of your home between personal and business use. Some expenses are divided on an area basis. Some of these are further divided on a time–usage basis. If neither of these methods is appropriate, you can choose any other reasonable method to figure the business part of the expense.

What to deduct. Some expenses you pay to maintain your home are directly related to its business use; others are indirectly related; some are unrelated. You can deduct direct expenses and part of your indirect expenses, both subject to certain limitations. If you are a cash basis taxpayer, you can deduct only the expenses you pay during the tax year.

Unrelated expenses benefit only the parts of your home that you do not use for business. These include repairs to personal areas of your home, lawn care, and landscaping. You cannot deduct unrelated expenses. For more information, also see Chapter 30, *Miscellaneous Deductions.*

Form 8829. Report on the appropriate lines of Form 8829

Can You Deduct Business Use of the Home Expenses?

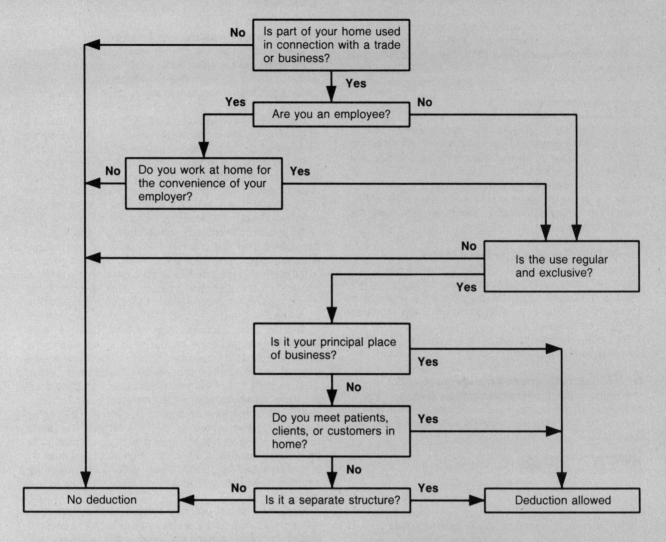

the home expenses that would not be allowable if you did not use your home for business (insurance, maintenance, utilities, depreciation, etc.). If you rent rather than own your home, include the rent you paid on line 20. If any of these expenses exceed the deduction limit, carry them over to next year. They will be subject to the gross income limit from the business use of your home next year.

Where to Deduct

Figuring deduction limit and carryover. If you file Schedule C (Form 1040), figure your deduction limit on Form 8829, *Expenses for Business Use of Your Home.* Enter the amount from line 34 of Form 8829 on Schedule C, line 30.

Recordkeeping. You do not have to use a particular method of recordkeeping, but you must keep records that provide the information needed to figure your deductions for the business use of your home. Your records must show the following:

1. The part of your home you use for business
2. That you use this part of your home exclusively and regularly for business as either your principal place of business or as the place where you meet or deal with clients or customers in the normal course of your business

3. The depreciation and expenses for the business part of your home

For more information on recordkeeping, see Publication 583, *Taxpayers Starting a Business.*

Retirement Plans

If you are self-employed, you can take an income tax deduction for certain contributions that you make for yourself to a retirement plan. You can also deduct a trustee's fees if contributions to the plan do not cover them. Deductible contributions plus the plan's earnings on them are tax-free until you receive distributions from the plan in later years. If you are a sole proprietor, you can deduct contributions you make for your common-law employees, as well as contributions you make for yourself. A common-law employee cannot take a deduction for your contributions.

There are two types of plans that a self-employed person may set up: a Keogh plan or a Simplified Employee Pension (SEP) plan.

Keogh Plans

A Keogh (HR 10) plan is a retirement plan that can be established by a sole proprietor. The plan must be for the exclusive benefit of employees or their beneficiaries. As an employer, you can usually deduct, subject to limits, contributions you make to a Keogh plan, including those made for your own retirement.

For further information about Keogh plans, see Chapter 18, *Individual Retirement Arrangements (IRAs)*.

Where to deduct on Form 1040. Take the deduction for contributions for yourself on line 27 of Form 1040. Deduct the contributions for your common-law employees on Schedule C.

TAXPLANNER

Because the deduction for your contribution to a Keogh plan for your benefit is reported on Form 1040, line 27, not on Schedule C, the contribution does not reduce your self-employment income that is subject to tax.

Reporting requirements. As the Keogh plan administrator or the employer, you may have to file an annual return/report form by the last day of the seventh month following the end of the plan year.

Simplified Employee Pension (SEP)

A simplified employee pension (SEP) is a written plan that allows an employer to make contributions toward an employee's retirement, and his or her own, if the employer is self-employed, without becoming involved in a more complex Keogh retirement plan.

For further information about SEPs, see Chapter 18, *Individual Retirement Arrangements (IRAs)*.

Individual Retirement Arrangements (IRA)

In addition to the retirement plans already discussed, a self-employed person may also make a contribution, which may or may not be deductible, to an Individual Retirement Arrangement (IRA).

TAXALERT

The earnings on your contributions generated by the plan are generally not subject to tax. The distributions of your contributions and the earnings from the plan, which are subject to certain limitations, are taxable to you upon withdrawal.

For further information about IRAs, see Chapter 18, *Individual Retirement Arrangements (IRAs)*.

Travel and Entertainment

Business travel and meals and entertainment expenses are deductible, subject to certain limits, assuming that these amounts are both ordinary and necessary, as defined earlier in the chapter.

For a self-employed person, the meals and entertainment expenses to be deducted are subject to the 80% limit (50% limit for years beginning after December 31, 1993) and certain documentation requirements as discussed in Chapter 28, *Car Expenses and Other Employee Business Expenses*. (Also see Chapter 28 for a more complete discussion of the deductibility of both travel and meals and entertainment expenses.)

Other Schedule C Deductions

Various other expenses not previously mentioned are allowed as a deduction on Schedule C. Examples of these expenses are advertising, commissions and fees, insurance (other than health), interest, legal and professional services, office expenses, including supplies and other items used in the office, general rent, repairs and maintenance, taxes, utilities, and any other business expense that can be classified as ordinary and necessary.

Sales of Business Property Used in Your Business

How Different Assets are Treated

A sole proprietorship usually has many assets. When sold, these assets must be classified as either depreciable personal property used in the business, real property used in the business, or property held for sale to customers, such as inventory or stock in trade or capital assets.

The gain or loss on each asset is figured separately. The sale of inventory results in ordinary income or loss and is reported on Schedule C. The sale of a capital asset results in a capital gain or loss and is reported on Schedule D. The sale of depreciable personal property and real property used in the business results in section 1231 gains or losses and is reported on Form 4797. (For further information about section 1231 transactions, see Chapter 17, *Reporting Gains and Losses*).

Any gain realized on sales and certain other dispositions of depreciable personal property and, under certain circumstances depreciable real property is treated as ordinary income to the extent of depreciation deductions taken prior to the sale. The amount of depreciation recapture is the lesser of (1) the gain recognized or (2) depreciation taken on the property. For more see Chapters 14, 15 and 17.

Section 1231 business gain or loss. Once you have determined your gain or loss on your personal and real property that is not subject to depreciation recapture, you must combine all gains and losses from the sale and disposition of section 1231 property for the tax year including section 1231 gains and losses reported to you through partnerships and S corporations in which you have an interest. In general, if all of your section 1231 transactions resulted in a net gain, the gain is treated as a long-term capital gain. If all of your section 1231 transactions resulted in a net loss, the loss is treated as an ordinary loss. See Chapter 17, *Reporting Gains and Losses,* for a further discussion of how to treat section 1231 gains and losses.

Recapture of net ordinary losses. A net section 1231 gain is treated as ordinary income to the extent that it does not exceed your nonrecaptured net section 1231 losses taken in prior years. Nonrecaptured losses are net section 1231 losses deducted for your 5 most recent tax years that have not yet been applied (recaptured) against any net section 1231 gains in a tax year beginning after 1984. Your losses are recaptured, beginning with the earliest year that is subject to recapture.

Sale of the Entire Business

Because a sole proprietorship is not a separate entity, a sale of the business will be treated as if each asset in the business had been sold separately. The gain or loss on such a sale is the total of the gains or losses as separately computed for each individual asset.

Both the buyer and the seller of a group of assets constituting a trade or a business must report to the IRS on Form 8594 various information about the acquisition of assets, including the following:

1. The name of the buyer and seller of the assets
2. The fair market value of the assets transferred
3. The allocation of the sales price to the assets transferred
4. Whether the buyer purchased a license, covenant not to compete or enter into a lease agreement, employment contract, management contract, or similar arrangement with the seller.

Business Tax Credit

Tax credits are distinguished from deductions in that a deduction reduces taxable income and a credit reduces tax liability. Consequently, $1 in tax credit is more valuable than $1 in tax deduction.

Form 3800. The general business tax credit consists of the following:

1. The investment credit (Form 3486)
2. The jobs credit (Form 5884)
3. The credit for alcohol used as fuel (Form 6478)
4. The credit for increasing research activities (Form 6765)
5. The low-income housing credit (Form 8586)
6. The enhanced oil recovery credit (Form 8830)
7. The disabled access credit (Form 8826)

If you have more than one of these credits, if you have a carryback or carryforward of any of these credits, or if any of these credits is from a passive activity, you must attach the appropriate credit forms and summarize them on Form 3800. If you have only one of these credits and that credit is not from a passive activity, you do not have to file Form 3800. Instead, use the applicable form to claim the credit. For example, if you have only a 1993 jobs credit, you may use Form 5884, *Jobs Credit*. You do not have to file Form 3800.

Targeted jobs credit. If you employ someone you may be eligible for the targeted jobs credit. The jobs credit provides an incentive to hire persons from targeted groups that have a particularly high unemployment rate or other special employment needs. If you hire members of the targeted group, you may elect to take a credit of 40% of the first $6,000 of qualified wages paid to the individual within the first year of employment. To claim the credit, you must complete Form 5884.

TaxAlert

The tax provision that permitted a tax credit for targeted jobs expired as of July 1, 1992. The 1993 Tax Act has retroactively extended this provision from July 1, 1992 through December 31, 1994. If your 1992 Federal tax return was filed before the enactment of the tax bill, and you hired individuals belonging to any of the targeted groups after June 30, 1992, you may file an amended 1992 tax return in order to claim the credit and obtain a refund.

Any unused credit can be carried back 3 tax years or forward 15 tax years as part of the general business credit.

Special Situations

Hobby Losses

Frequently, individuals carry on an activity that has no profit motive. The IRS will not classify this as a business. Instead, it will be classified as a hobby, and it will be subject to the hobby loss rules.

If your activity or the activity you invest in is not carried on to make a profit, the deductions you can take are limited to the income of the hobby, if any, and no loss is allowed to offset other income.

To determine whether an activity is carried on for profit, all of the facts with regard to the activity are taken into account. No one factor alone is decisive. For a discussion of Hobby Losses see the discussion of them in Chapter 13, *Other Income*.

Artists and Authors

The proper way for artists and authors to account for their expenses has been the topic of much debate in recent years. A special exception excludes authors and artists from the uniform capitalization rules for certain qualified creative expenses that they incur in their trade or business. As a result, these expenses can be currently deducted and not capitalized. A "qualified creative expense" is defined as any expense that is paid or incurred by an individual in the trade or business of being a writer or an artist and that would be allowable as a deduction for the taxable year.

Although you are allowed currently to deduct those expenses that are classified as qualified creative expenses, there are some expenses that need to be capitalized. Examples of such expenses include any expense related to printing, photographic plates, motion pictures, videotapes, and similar items.

There is an alternative way for an artist or an author to treat his or her qualified creative expenses. If the artist or author so chooses, he or she can capitalize all qualified creative costs. In the current year he or she is able to deduct 50% of the eligible costs and then deduct the remaining 50% ratably over the next 2 years. The reason one may choose this method over deducting all qualified creative expenses currently is that the meaning of a qualified creative cost is broader in this instance. It includes the costs of films, sound recordings, videotapes, and books. These expenses would normally need to be capitalized and amortized over their estimated useful lives.

How to Complete Schedule SE

Line by Line Briefly

Self-employed individuals filing Schedule C may be required to pay self-employment tax if they did not earn FICA wages in excess of $135,000 in 1993. Self-employment income and the related tax are discussed earlier in this chapter.

When completing Form 1040, Schedule SE, you must first determine whether you need to file the short Schedule SE form or the long Schedule SE form. You must use the long Schedule SE form if any of the following apply:

- You received wages or tips and the total of all of your wages (and tips) subject to social security, Medicare, or railroad retirement tax plus your net earnings from self-employment is more than $57,600.
- You use either "optional method" to figure your net earnings from self-employment.
- You are a minister, a member of a religious order, or a Christian Science practitioner and you received IRS approval (by filing Form 4361) not to be taxed on your earnings from these sources, but you owe self-employment tax on other earnings.
- You had church employee income of $108.28 or more that was reported to you on Form W-2.
- You received tips subject to Social Security, Medicare, or railroad retirement tax, but you did not report those tips to your employer.

If none of these conditions exist, you are able to use the short Schedule SE form.

As a Schedule C filer, you would report your Schedule C income on line 2 of Section A for the short form Schedule SE or Section B for the long form Schedule SE (remember do not include the income reported on Schedule C as a statutory employee).

Example

Pete Thirsty owns a refreshment stand on the beach. His net income from self employment on Schedule C in 1993 is $54,000. He had no other earned income for that year. Pete is eligible to use the short Schedule SE form. Pete's self-employment tax liability for 1993 is calculated as follows:

Net earnings from	
self-employment $54,000 × .9325)	$49,869
SE tax rate	15.3%
SE tax	$ 7,630

One half of your self-employment tax can be deducted. The deduction is taken on Line 25 of Form 1040. In this example, you would be able to take a deduction of $3,815.

Comprehensive Schedule C/ Self-Employment Example

John Paul Jones is a self-employed comic book salesman. He does business as JPJ Comics. The majority of his business consists of retail sales of comic books. John Paul works out of his home, located at 64-09 79th Street, Queens, New York 11379, where he has been running the business for the past 3 years. One-fourth of his home is used solely for the purpose of running his business. John accounts for his purchases and sales on the accrual method. All other income and expense items are accounted for by use of the cash method. He is also a professor and has $54,000 of W-2 wages in 1993.

John Paul had the following income and expenses during 1993:

Gross receipts from sales of comic books—accrual basis	$30,000
Beginning inventory	2,200
Purchases	13,000
Ending inventory	2,700
Business subscriptions	350
Advertising	1,700
Bad debts	200
Supplies	1,200
Meals and entertainment	600
Travel	900
Telephone	600
Annual home insurance	2,000
Annual mortgage interest	6,000
Annual real estate taxes	4,000
Annual utilities	1,200
Basis of home purchased on 6/1/88	220,000
Amount attributable to land	40,000
Amount attributable to house	180,000

John Paul has established a money purchase pension plan, providing for a maximum contribution of 25% of compensation. For 1993, John Paul has made the maximum contribution before filing his tax return.

Schedule C (Form 1040) 1993

Part III Cost of Goods Sold (see page C-5)

33	Inventory at beginning of year. If different from last year's closing inventory, attach explanation	33	2,200
34	Purchases less cost of items withdrawn for personal use	34	13,000
35	Cost of labor. Do not include salary paid to yourself	35	
36	Materials and supplies	36	
37	Other costs	37	
38	Add lines 33 through 37	38	15,200
39	Inventory at end of year	39	2,700
40	Cost of goods sold. Subtract line 39 from line 38. Enter the result here and on page 1, line 4	40	12,500

Part IV Information on Your Vehicle. Complete this part ONLY if you are claiming car or truck expenses on line 10 and are not required to file Form 4562 for this business.

41 When did you place your vehicle in service for business purposes? (month, day, year) ▶ / /

42 Of the total number of miles you drove your vehicle during 1993, enter the number of miles you used your vehicle for:

a Business _____ b Commuting _____ c Other _____

43	Do you (or your spouse) have another vehicle available for personal use?	☐ Yes	☐ No
44	Was your vehicle available for use during off-duty hours?	☐ Yes	☐ No
45a	Do you have evidence to support your deduction?	☐ Yes	☐ No
b	If "Yes," is the evidence written?	☐ Yes	☐ No

Part V Other Expenses. List below business expenses not included on lines 8–26 or line 30.

Subscriptions 350

46 Total other expenses. Enter here and on page 1, line 27	46	350

♻ Printed on recycled paper

SCHEDULE C (Form 1040)

Department of the Treasury
Internal Revenue Service (T)

Profit or Loss From Business
(Sole Proprietorship)

▶ Partnerships, joint ventures, etc., must file Form 1065.
▶ Attach to Form 1040 or Form 1041. ▶ See Instructions for Schedule C (Form 1040).

OMB No. 1545-0074

1993

Attachment Sequence No. 09

Name of proprietor: John Paul Jones

Social security number (SSN): 111 22 3344

A Principal business or profession, including product or service (see page C-1): Retail Sales of Comic Books

B Enter principal business code (see page C-6) ▶ 5 0 1 2

C Business name. If no separate business name, leave blank.: JPJ Comics

D Employer ID number (EIN), if any: 13 9999909

E Business address (including suite or room no.) ▶ 64-09 79th Street
City, town or post office, state, and ZIP code ▶ Queens, New York 11379

F Accounting method: (1) ☐ Cash (2) ☒ Accrual (3) ☐ Other (specify) ▶ Hybrid

G Method(s) used to value closing inventory: (1) ☒ Cost (2) ☐ Lower of cost or market (3) ☐ Other (attach explanation) (4) ☐ Does not apply (if checked, skip line H) [Yes/No]

H Was there any change in determining quantities, costs, or valuations between opening and closing inventory? If "Yes," attach explanation .... ☐ Yes ☒ No

I Did you "materially participate" in the operation of this business during 1993? If "No," see page C-2 for limit on losses. ☒ Yes ☐ No

J If you started or acquired this business during 1993, check here .... ▶ ☐

Part I Income

1	Gross receipts or sales. Caution: If this income was reported to you on Form W-2 and the "Statutory employee" box on that form was checked, see page C-2 and check here ▶ ☐	1	30,000
2	Returns and allowances	2	
3	Subtract line 2 from line 1	3	30,000
4	Cost of goods sold (from line 40 on page 2)	4	12,500
5	Gross profit. Subtract line 4 from line 3	5	17,500
6	Other income, including Federal and state gasoline or fuel tax credit or refund (see page C-2)	6	
7	Gross income. Add lines 5 and 6 ▶	7	17,500

Part II Expenses. Caution: Do not enter expenses for business use of your home on lines 8–27. Instead, see line 30.

8	Advertising	8	1,700	19 Pension and profit-sharing plans	19	
9	Bad debts from sales or services (see page C-3)	9	200	20 Rent or lease (see page C-4):		
10	Car and truck expenses (see page C-3)	10		a Vehicles, machinery, and equipment	20a	
11	Commissions and fees	11		b Other business property	20b	
12	Depletion	12		21 Repairs and maintenance	21	1,200
13	Depreciation and section 179 expense deduction (not included in Part III) (see page C-3)	13		22 Supplies (not included in Part III)	22	
14	Employee benefit programs (other than on line 19)	14		23 Taxes and licenses	23	
15	Insurance (other than health)	15		24 Travel, meals, and entertainment:		
16	Interest:			a Travel	24a	900
a	Mortgage (paid to banks, etc.)	16a		b Meals and entertainment	600	
b	Other	16b		c Enter 20% of line 24b subject to limitations (see page C-4)	120	
17	Legal and professional services	17		d Subtract line 24c from line 24b	24d	480
18	Office expense	18		25 Utilities	25	600
				26 Wages (less jobs credit)	26	
				27 Other expenses (from line 46 on page 2)	27	350

28	Total expenses before expenses for business use of home. Add lines 8 through 27 in columns. ▶	28	5,930
29	Tentative profit (loss). Subtract line 28 from line 7	29	12,070...
30	Expenses for business use of your home. Attach Form 8829	30	4,729
31	Net profit or (loss). Subtract line 30 from line 29.	31	7,341

• If a profit, enter on Form 1040, line 12, and ALSO on Schedule SE, line 2 (statutory employees, see page C-5). Fiduciaries, enter on Form 1041, line 3.

• If a loss, you MUST go on to line 32.

32 If you have a loss, check the box that describes your investment in this activity (see page C-5).

• If you checked 32a, enter the loss on Form 1040, line 12, and ALSO on Schedule SE, line 2 (statutory employees, see page C-5). Fiduciaries, enter on Form 1041, line 3.

• If you checked 32b, you MUST attach Form 6198.

32a ☐ All investment is at risk.
32b ☐ Some investment is not at risk.

For Paperwork Reduction Act Notice, see Form 1040 instructions.   Cat. No. 11334P   Schedule C (Form 1040) 1993

SCHEDULE SE
(Form 1040)

Department of the Treasury
Internal Revenue Service (T)

Self-Employment Tax

▶ See Instructions for Schedule SE (Form 1040).
▶ Attach to Form 1040.

OMB No. 1545-0074

1993

Attachment Sequence No. 17

Name of person with self-employment income (as shown on Form 1040) **John Paul Jones**

Social security number of person with self-employment income ▶ **111 : 22 : 3344**

Who Must File Schedule SE

You must file Schedule SE if:

• Your wages (and tips) subject to social security AND Medicare tax (or railroad retirement tax) were less than $135,000; **AND**

• Your net earnings from self-employment from other than church employee income (line 4 of Short Schedule SE or line 4c of Long Schedule SE) were $400 or more; **OR**

• You had church employee income of $108.28 or more. Income from services you performed as a minister or a member of a religious order is **not** church employee income. See page SE-1.

Note: Even if you have a loss or a small amount of income from self-employment, it may be to your benefit to file Schedule SE and use either "optional method" in Part II of Long Schedule SE. See page SE-3.

Exception: If your only self-employment income was from earnings as a minister, member of a religious order, or Christian Science practitioner, **AND** you filed Form 4361 and received IRS approval not to be taxed on those earnings, **DO NOT** file Schedule SE. Instead, write "Exempt-Form 4361" on Form 1040, line 47.

May I Use Short Schedule SE or MUST I Use Long Schedule SE?

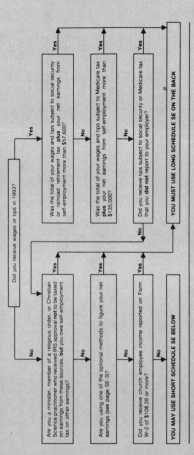

Did you receive wages or tips in 1993?
- **No** → Are you a minister, member of a religious order, or Christian Science practitioner who received IRS approval **not** to be taxed on earnings from these sources, **but** you owe self-employment tax on other earnings?
  - **No** → Are you using one of the optional methods to figure your net earnings (see page SE-3)?
    - **No** → Did you receive church employee income reported on Form W-2 of $108.28 or more?
      - **No** → YOU MAY USE SHORT SCHEDULE SE BELOW
      - **Yes** → YOU MUST USE LONG SCHEDULE SE ON THE BACK
    - **Yes** → YOU MUST USE LONG SCHEDULE SE ON THE BACK
  - **Yes** → YOU MUST USE LONG SCHEDULE SE ON THE BACK
- **Yes** → Was the total of your wages and tips subject to social security or railroad retirement tax **plus** your net earnings from self-employment more than $57,600?
  - **Yes** → YOU MUST USE LONG SCHEDULE SE ON THE BACK
  - **No** → Was the total of your wages and tips subject to social security tax **plus** your net earnings from self-employment more than $135,000?
    - **Yes** → YOU MUST USE LONG SCHEDULE SE ON THE BACK
    - **No** → Did you receive tips subject to social security or Medicare tax that you **did not** report to your employer?
      - **Yes** → YOU MUST USE LONG SCHEDULE SE ON THE BACK
      - **No** → YOU MAY USE SHORT SCHEDULE SE BELOW

Section A—Short Schedule SE. Caution: Read above to see if you can use Short Schedule SE.

1	Net farm profit or (loss) from Schedule F, line 36, and farm partnerships, Schedule K-1 (Form 1065), line 15a	1
2	Net profit or (loss) from Schedule C, line 31; Schedule C-EZ, line 3; and Schedule K-1 (Form 1065), line 15a (other than farming). Ministers and members of religious orders see page SE-1 for amounts to report on this line. See page SE-2 for other income to report.	2
3	Combine lines 1 and 2	3
4	**Net earnings from self-employment.** Multiply line 3 by 92.35% (.9235). If less than $400, **do not file this schedule; you do not owe self-employment tax** ▲	4
5	**Self-employment tax.** If the amount on line 4 is: • $57,600 or less, multiply line 4 by 15.3% (.153) and enter the result. • More than $57,600 but less than $135,000, multiply the amount in excess of $57,600 by 2.9% (.029). Then, add $8,812.80 to the result and enter the total. • $135,000 or more, enter $11,057.40. Also enter on **Form 1040, line 47.** (**Important:** You are allowed a deduction for **one-half** of this amount. Multiply line 5 by 50% (.5) and enter the result on **Form 1040, line 25.**)	5

For Paperwork Reduction Act Notice, see Form 1040 instructions.   Cat. No. 11358Z   **Schedule SE (Form 1040) 1993**

Schedule SE (Form 1040) 1993   Attachment Sequence No. **17**   Page **2**

Name of person with self-employment income (as shown on Form 1040)   Social security number of person with self-employment income ▶ **111 : 22 : 3344**

Section B—Long Schedule SE

Part I   Self-Employment Tax

Note: If your only income subject to self-employment tax is church employee income, skip lines 1 through 4b. Enter -0- on line 4c and go to line 5a. Income from services you performed as a minister or a member of a religious order is not church employee income. See page SE-1.

A If you are a minister, member of a religious order, or Christian Science practitioner **AND** you filed Form 4361, but you had $400 or more of **other** net earnings from self-employment, check here and continue with Part I. ▶ ☐

1	Net farm profit or (loss) from Schedule F, line 36, and farm partnerships, Schedule K-1 (Form 1065), line 15a. **Note:** Skip this line if you use the farm optional method. See page SE-3	1
2	Net profit or (loss) from Schedule C, line 31; Schedule C-EZ, line 3; and Schedule K-1 (Form 1065), line 15a (other than farming). Ministers and members of religious orders see page SE-1 for amounts to report on this line. See page SE-2 for other income to report. **Note:** Skip this line if you use the nonfarm optional method. See page SE-3	2 7,341
3	Combine lines 1 and 2	3 7,341
4a	If line 3 is more than zero, multiply line 3 by 92.35% (.9235). Otherwise, enter amount from line 3	4a 6,779
b	If you elected one or both of the optional methods, enter the total amount from line 3 and 19 here	4b
c	Combine lines 4a and 4b. If less than $400, **do not file this schedule; you do not owe self-employment tax. Exception.** If less than $400 and you had church employee income, enter -0- and continue ▶	4c 6,779
5a	Enter your church employee income from Form W-2. **Caution:** See page SE-1 for definition of church employee income	5a
b	Multiply line 5a by 92.35% (.9235). If less than $100, enter -0-	5b
6	**Net earnings from self-employment.** Add lines 4c and 5b	6 6,779
7	Maximum amount of combined wages and self-employment earnings subject to social security tax or the 6.2% portion of the 7.65% railroad retirement (tier 1) tax for 1993	7 57,600 00
8a	Total social security wages and tips (from Form(s) W-2) and railroad retirement (tier 1) compensation **8a 54,000**	
b	Unreported tips subject to social security tax (from Form 4137, line 9) **8b**	
c	Add lines 8a and 8b	8c 54,000
9	Subtract line 8c from line 7. If zero or less, enter -0- here and on line 10 and go to line 12a ▶	9 3,600
10	Multiply the **smaller** of line 6 or line 9 by 12.4% (.124)	10 446
11	Maximum amount of combined wages and self-employment earnings subject to Medicare tax or the 1.45% portion of the 7.65% railroad retirement (tier 1) tax for 1993	11 135,000 00
12a	Total Medicare wages and tips (from Form(s) W-2) and railroad retirement (tier 1) compensation **12a 54,000**	
b	Unreported tips subject to Medicare tax (from Form 4137, line 14) **12b**	
c	Add lines 12a and 12b	12c 54,000
13	Subtract line 12c from line 11. If zero or less, enter -0- here and on line 14 and go to line 15	13 81,000
14	Multiply the **smaller** of line 6 or line 13 by 2.9% (.029)	14 197
15	**Self-employment tax.** Add lines 10 and 14. Enter here and on **Form 1040, line 47.** (**Important:** You are allowed a deduction for **one-half** of this amount. Multiply line 15 by 50% (.5) and enter the result on **Form 1040, line 25.**)	15 643

Part II   Optional Methods To Figure Net Earnings (See page SE-3)

Farm Optional Method. You may use this method **only** if **(a)** Your gross farm income[1] was not more than $2,400 **or (b)** Your gross farm income[1] was more than $2,400 and your net farm profits[2] were less than $1,733.

16	Maximum income for optional methods	16 1,600 00
17	Enter the **smaller** of: two-thirds (⅔) of gross farm income[1] (not less than zero) **or** $1,600. Also, include this amount on line 4b above	17

Nonfarm Optional Method. You may use this method **only** if **(a)** Your net nonfarm profits[3] were less than $1,733 and also less than 72.189% of your gross nonfarm income,[4] **and (b)** You had net earnings from self-employment of at least $400 in 2 of the prior 3 years. **Caution:** You may use this method no more than five times.

18	Subtract line 17 from line 16	18
19	Enter the **smaller** of: two-thirds (⅔) of gross nonfarm income[1] (not less than zero) **or** the amount on line 18. Also, include this amount on line 4b above	19

[1]From Schedule F, line 11, and Schedule K-1 (Form 1065), line 15b.   [3]From Schedule C, line 31; Schedule C-EZ, line 3; and Schedule K-1 (Form 1065), line 15a.
[2]From Schedule F, line 36, and Schedule K-1 (Form 1065), line 15a.   [4]From Schedule C, line 7; Schedule C-EZ, line 1; and Schedule K-1 (Form 1065), line 15c.

Schedule SE (Form 1040) 1993

Form **8829**	**Expenses for Business Use of Your Home**	OMB No. 545-1266
	► File only with Schedule C (Form 1040). Use a separate Form 8829 for each home you used for business during the year.	**1993**
Department of the Treasury Internal Revenue Service (T)	► See separate instructions.	Attachment Sequence No. **66**

Name(s) of proprietor(s) **John Paul Jones**   Your social security number **111 22 3344**

Part I — Part of Your Home Used for Business

1	Area used regularly and exclusively for business, regularly for day care, or for inventory storage. See instructions	1	200 SQ. FT.
2	Total area of home	2	800 SQ. FT.
3	Divide line 1 by line 2. Enter the result as a percentage	3	25 %

- For day-care facilities not used exclusively for business, also complete lines 4–6.
- All others, skip lines 4–6 and enter the amount from line 3 on line 7.

4	Multiply days used for day care during year by hours used per day	4		hr.
5	Total hours available for use during the year (365 days × 24 hours). See instructions	5	8,760 hr.	
6	Divide line 4 by line 5. Enter the result as a decimal amount	6	.	
7	Business percentage. For day-care facilities not used exclusively for business, multiply line 6 by line 3 (enter the result as a percentage). All others, enter the amount from line 3 ►	7	25 %	

Part II — Figure Your Allowable Deduction

		(a) Direct expenses	(b) Indirect expenses		
8	Enter the amount from Schedule C, line 29, **plus** any net gain or (loss) derived from the business use of your home and shown on Schedule D or Form 4797. If more than one place of business, see instructions			8	12,070
	See instructions for columns (a) and (b) before completing lines 9–20.				
9	Casualty losses. See instructions	9			
10	Deductible mortgage interest. See instructions	10	6,000		
11	Real estate taxes. See instructions	11	4,000		
12	Add lines 9, 10, and 11	12	10,000		
13	Multiply line 12, column (b) by line 7		13	2,500	
14	Add line 12, column (a) and line 13			14	2,500
15	Subtract line 14 from line 8. If zero or less, enter -0-			15	9,570
16	Excess mortgage interest. See instructions	16			
17	Insurance	17	2,000		
18	Repairs and maintenance	18			
19	Utilities	19	1,200		
20	Other expenses. See instructions	20			
21	Add lines 16 through 20	21	3,200		
22	Multiply line 21, column (b) by line 7	22	800		
23	Carryover of operating expenses from 1992 Form 8829, line 41	23			
24	Add line 21 in column (a), line 22, and line 23			24	800
25	Allowable operating expenses. Enter the **smaller** of line 15 or line 24			25	800
26	Limit on excess casualty losses and depreciation. Subtract line 25 from line 15			26	8,770
27	Excess casualty losses. See instructions	27			
28	Depreciation of your home from Part III below	28	1,429		
29	Carryover of excess casualty losses and depreciation from 1992 Form 8829, line 42	29			
30	Add lines 27 through 29			30	1,429
31	Allowable excess casualty losses and depreciation. Enter the **smaller** of line 26 or line 30			31	1,429
32	Add lines 14, 25, and 31			32	4,729
33	Casualty loss portion, if any, from lines 14 and 31. Carry amount to **Form 4684**, Section B			33	
34	Allowable expenses for business use of your home. Subtract line 33 from line 32. Enter here and on Schedule C, line 30. If your home was used for more than one business, see instructions ►			34	4,729

Part III — Depreciation of Your Home

35	Enter the **smaller** of your home's adjusted basis or its fair market value. See instructions	35	220,000
36	Value of land included on line 35	36	40,000
37	Basis of building. Subtract line 36 from line 35	37	180,000
38	Business basis of building. Multiply line 37 by line 7	38	45,000
39	Depreciation percentage. See instructions	39	3.175 %
40	Depreciation allowable. Multiply line 38 by line 39. Enter here and on line 28 above. See instructions	40	1,429

Part IV — Carryover of Unallowed Expenses to 1994

41	Operating expenses. Subtract line 25 from line 24. If less than zero, enter -0-	41	
42	Excess casualty losses and depreciation. Subtract line 31 from line 30. If less than zero, enter -0-	42	

For Paperwork Reduction Act Notice, see page 1 of separate instructions.   Cat. No. 13232M   Form **8829** (1993)

37 | What to Do If You Employ Domestic Help

Introduction

*If you have a domestic helper who qualifies as your **employee,** you may have to pay social security and Medicare taxes, as well as federal and state unemployment taxes. You may also have to withhold federal income tax and make **earned income credit** advance payments. In general, a person who works in or around your house qualifies as your employee if you control his or her working conditions—pay, work schedule, conduct, and appearance. This chapter spells out what rules govern domestic help and advises you on how to comply with them.*

Both you and your employee are subject to social security and Medicare taxes if you pay your employee $50 or more during any calendar quarter during the year. If you have paid any employee $1,000 or more in any calendar quarter during the current or preceding year, you are subject to federal unemployment taxes on every employee during the current year. You should contact the appropriate state authorities for information about state unemployment tax.

Your employee may ask you to withhold federal income tax from compensation. If you decide to do so, you must withhold the proper amount from each paycheck. Income tax withheld from your employee's wages must be remitted quarterly to the IRS.

Employment Taxes for Household Employers

Generally, if you pay someone to work in your home, such as a baby sitter, that person is your household employee. If the individuals who work in your home are self-employed, you are not liable for any of the taxes discussed in this section. Self-employed persons who are in business for themselves are not household employees.

TaxAlert

Even if your domestic employee does not have legal authorization to work in the U.S., you are still liable for the payroll taxes discussed in this chapter.

If you use a placement agency to get a baby sitter or companion who works in your home, that person is not your employee if the agency sets the fee and exercises control over the sitter. This control could include providing rules of conduct and appearance and requiring regular reports. In this case, you do not have to pay employment taxes. But, if an association merely gives you a list of sitters and you hire one from that list, the sitter may be your employee.

If you have a household employee you may be subject to:

1) Social security and Medicare taxes,
2) Federal unemployment tax, and
3) Federal income tax withholding.

Social security and Medicare taxes are withheld from the employee's pay and matched by the employer. Federal unemployment tax (FUTA tax) is paid by the employer only and is for the employee's unemployment insurance. Federal income tax is withheld from the employee's total pay if the employee asks you to do so and you agree.

Get Publication 926 for more specific information.

You may also be subject to state withholding tax and state unemployment tax. You should contact your state unemployment tax office for information on how to file the state tax returns and for a state reporting number.

Explanation

Whether or not a person who provides services in and around your house is your employee depends on the facts and circumstances of the situation. In general, a person is your employee if you control his or her working

542

conditions and compensation. A person does not have to work for you full-time to qualify as your employee.

Generally, workers are classified based on how they perform their work and their accountability for it. By definition, independent contractors are responsible for *results*, not how their tasks are accomplished. On the other hand, individuals who are instructed as to when, where, and how to complete their jobs would probably be considered employees. If you determine that your domestic helpers are employees, you must withhold and match social security payments and may be subject to paying federal and state unemployment taxes as well.

To gain a better understanding of the distinction between an independent contractor and an employee, consider the person who mows your lawn. If the person works for an independent lawn service and is supervised by the lawn company, that also provides its own equipment—all you provide is the grass—there's little question that the provider is an independent contractor. However, if a teenager from down the street cuts your lawn using your mower, and you give specific instructions as to how and when to do the job, he or she will be considered your employee.

To enable you to determine whether a person is indeed an independent contractor, there are certain common indicators that can help. An independent contractor:

- works for several homeowners;
- provides his or her own tools and supplies to perform the job;
- can bring in additional help if he or she deems necessary;
- determines how the results will be accomplished;
- is paid by the job, not by the hour;
- advertises his or her services;
- may be fired at will; and
- can set his or her own hours and leave when the job is completed.

If you have reason to believe that a person is an independent contractor and not your employee, you should not withhold social security tax (FICA) from his or her compensation. You may want to get a signed letter from this person indicating that he or she is an independent contractor and is responsible for his or her own employment taxes.

TaxPlanner

When you hire a household employee, make a record of that person's name and social security number exactly as it appears on his or her social security card. You will need this information when you remit social security, Medicare, federal unemployment, and withholding of federal income taxes.

An employee who does not have a social security number should apply for one on Form SS–5, *Application for a Social Security Card.* This form is available in Chapter 46, *1993 Federal Tax Forms and Schedules You Can Use,* and at all Social Security Administration offices as well as at most IRS offices, and post offices.

Social Security and Medicare Taxes

If you pay a household employee cash wages of $50 or more during a calendar quarter, those wages are subject to social security and Medicare taxes. Payments in kind (meals, transportation, etc.) are not used to figure the $50 amount or to figure the taxes. The taxes are figured on all cash wage payments in the quarter, regardless of when they were earned.

Family members. Social security and Medicare taxes do not apply to household services performed by your spouse or by your child under 21. Social security and Medicare taxes **apply** to wages you pay your parents for household services if:

1) Your child lives with you and is under age 18 or requires adult supervision for at least 4 continuous weeks in a calendar quarter due to a mental or physical condition, and

2) You are divorced and have not remarried, widowed, or married to a person who cannot care for your child because of a mental or physical condition.

TaxAlert

If a person is an employee whom you pay a total of $50 or more per quarter, you have tax filing and payment responsibilities.

The earnings limit here certainly isn't very liberal. It would only require paying the same baby sitter for a few hours every other month before you would have paid $50 to that person in one quarter. (Congress is already considering an increase in the threshold, perhaps to $300 or $400 annually.) The key exception for many households is whether or not the service provider qualifies as an independent contractor. Independent contractors are responsible for filing and paying their own taxes.

TaxPlanner

If the baby sitter watches your children in your house at the time your specify, IRS rulings conclude that the person is an employee. It's not enough to stop giving the sitter a ride home in an attempt to make him or her appear more independent. You would need to use sitters who watch children in *their* homes or other facilities during set business hours. Or you can rotate sitters to avoid paying any one more than $50 per quarter.

Paying the tax. Both you and the employee pay a share of the social security and Medicare taxes on the employee's wages. For 1993, the tax rate for social security is 6.2% for both you and the employee (a total of 12.4%). The tax rate for Medicare is 1.45% for both you and the employee (a total of 2.9%). The 6.2% social security tax applies only to the first $57,600 you paid each employee during calendar year 1993. The 1.45% Medicare tax applies to the first $135,000.

TaxAlert

For 1994, the social security and Medicare tax rates will not change. The wage bases upon which the social security tax is calculated will, however, increase to $60,600. The Medicare tax will apply to all wages, without limit.

You must pay the total of these taxes yourself if you do not deduct the employee's share from his or her wages. Any of the employee's share you pay is added income to the employee. This income must be included in box 1, *Wages, tips, other compensation,* on Form W–2, *Wage and Tax Statement,* but do not count it as cash wages for social security and Medicare purposes. You must also include the employee social security and Medicare taxes you pay in boxes 4 and 6 of the employee's Form W–2, even though the taxes were not actually withheld.

TAXPLANNER

If you would rather pay your employee's share of social security and Medicare taxes without deducting it from wages, you may do so. Any portion you do pay, however, is added to the compensation to your employee, even though it does not constitute cash wages for social security purposes. Although it may be easier if you pay your employee's share of social security and Medicare taxes, it does raise *your* cost. You should come to an agreement with your employee on this issue before he or she begins work.

Example

Meredith Cabot pays her full-time housekeeper a $15,000 salary. She also pays both the employer's share of the social security and Medicare taxes (7.65% of $15,000, or $1,147.50) and the employee's share (7.65% of $15,000, or $1,147.50). The housekeeper's total compensation for the year is $16,147.50 ($15,000 plus $1,147.50), even though only $15,000 is subject to social security and Medicare taxes.

You report and pay the social security and Medicare taxes quarterly on Form 942, *Employer's Quarterly Tax Return for Household Employees.* See Filing Form 942, later.

Federal Income Tax Withholding

If your household employee requests income tax withholding, and you agree, you must withhold an amount from each payment based on the information shown on the **Form W–4**, *Employee's Withholding Allowance Certificate,* given to you by the employee. Publication 15 (*Circular E*), Employer's Tax Guide, explains how to figure the amount to withhold.

TAXPLANNER

It is your decision whether or not to withhold income tax from your employee's compensation, even if withholding is requested by your employee. However, if you do withhold for an employee, everything that you pay your employee—whether cash or noncash—is income subject to withholding. Some of the more common forms of compensation for household employees are (1) salaries, (2) bonuses, (3) meals, unless provided in your home and for your convenience, and (4) lodging, unless provided in your home, for your convenience, and as a condition of employment. As a general rule, if you have live-in domestic help, any meals and lodging you provide are *not* considered compensation.

Since you already should be withholding or paying your employee's share of social security and Medicare taxes, withholding of income tax should be little additional burden. If your employee asks you to withhold

income tax, there is generally no reason why you should not honor the request.

Any income tax withholding you pay for an employee without deducting it from the employee's wages is added income to the employee and subject to both income, social security, and Medicare taxes. There is no reason why you should pay your employee's income taxes.

Copies of Form W–4 and Publication 15 are available from the IRS Center where you file your income tax return.

Earned income credit advance payment. You must make advance payments of the earned income credit to any employee who is eligible to claim the earned income credit and requests advance payment of it. Who is eligible to claim the credit is explained in Chapter 35, *Other Credits.*

The employee makes the request by giving you a completed **Form W–5**, *Earned Income Credit Advance Payment Certificate.* Each payday, you make the payments to your employee from the social security, Medicare, and withheld income taxes that you would otherwise pay to the Internal Revenue Service. For more information, see Publication 15.

You must notify any employees not having federal income tax withheld that they may be eligible for an income tax refund because of the earned income credit. For more information, see the instructions for Form 942.

Filing Form 942. You must report on Form 942 the taxes withheld each quarter if:

1) You are liable for social security and Medicare taxes, or

2) Your employee asked you to withhold federal income tax and you agreed.

If you own a business as a sole proprietor, you can include your household employee on Form 941, *Employer's Quarterly Federal Tax Return.* Do **not** include your household employees on a Form 941 filed for a partnership or corporation.

When to file. File starting with the first quarter in which you:

1) Pay wages subject to social security and Medicare taxes, or

2) Withhold any federal income tax.

Due Dates for Returns

Quarter	Ending	Due Date
Jan.-Feb.-Mar.	Mar. 31	Apr. 30
Apr.-May-June	June 30	July 31
July-Aug.-Sept.	Sept. 30	Oct. 31
Oct.-Nov.-Dec.	Dec. 31	Jan. 31

If the due date for filing a return falls on a Saturday, Sunday, or a legal holiday, you can file the return on the first business day after that day.

You may request copies of Form 942 from the IRS Center where you file your income tax return. When you are completing your initial Form 942, if you do not have an employer identification number, you must obtain one from the IRS. This can be done by telephone by calling the IRS "Tele-TIN" number for your IRS center listed in the instructions to Form SS-4. You must still submit a completed Form SS-4 to the IRS. Alternatively, allowing five weeks' response time, you can submit the Form SS-4 to the IRS by mail. When you have an employer identification number, the IRS will send you Form 942 each quarter, pre-printed with your name, address, and employer identification number. If you receive Form 942 for a quarter when you did not pay any taxable wages, write "none" on line 8 and return the form to the IRS.

For more information about employment, see Publication 926, *Employment Taxes for Household Employers,* and the instructions for Form 942.

Federal Unemployment Tax (FUTA Tax)

Federal unemployment tax (FUTA) is for your employee's unemployment insurance. If you paid cash wages of $1,000 or more to household employees in any calendar quarter this year or last year, you are liable for FUTA tax for any employees you have this year. However, the tax does not apply to wages paid to your spouse, to your parents, or your children under 21 years old.

Rate. The rate for 1993 and 1994 is 6.2% on the first $7,000 of cash wages paid to each employee during the calendar year.

The tax is imposed on you as the employer. Unlike social security and federal income tax, federal unemployment tax is *solely* an employer's responsibility. It is an additional cost to you of having domestic help. You must not collect or deduct it from the wages of your employees.

When you file Form 940, you may claim a credit against your federal unemployment tax for the state unemployment tax you paid on time during the year. Your liability for state unemployment tax is based on your experience rate, which, in turn, is based on the number of your former employees who have filed for unemployment benefits. The fewer former employees there are who have filed, the lower is your experience rate. However, until you develop a history, your rate will probably be the maximum 6.2%. In the end, however, you come out even. What you do not pay to the state, you end up paying the federal government. Form 940 leads you through the mechanics of actually claiming the credit. Your net federal tax may be as low as 0.8% if you pay the state tax on time.

When you hire a household employee, you should contact your state employment tax office to get information on how to file the state return and to get a state reporting number. The state will give you your experience rate, which you use to figure the amount of tax you will pay the state.

Reporting and paying FUTA tax. You may be required to make deposits of FUTA tax before filing a return. Federal tax deposits are explained in Publication 926.

You must file an annual return on Form 940–EZ or Form 940, *Employer's Annual Federal Unemployment (FUTA) Tax Return,* by January 31 following the close of the calendar year for which the tax is due. Form 940–EZ is a less complicated version of Form 940 and can be used if:

1) You paid state unemployment tax to only one state,

2) You paid all your state unemployment tax by the due date of Form 940–EZ, and

3) Your Federal unemployment (FUTA) wages were also taxable for your state's unemployment tax.

4) You pay wages in a state that is not a credit reduction state. The Department of Labor determines these states.

If you do not meet these requirements, you must use Form 940 to report your federal unemployment taxes. Any tax still due must be paid with the return.

After you have filed your first return, the IRS will mail Form 940–EZ or Form 940 to you. However, if you do not receive it, get one in time to file.

For more information, see Publication 926 and the instructions to Form 940–EZ or Form 940.

Example 1

George Darby paid his housekeeper $3,000 in cash during the first quarter of 1993. He must pay federal unemployment tax (FUTA) for any employees he has during any part of 1993. Since he was liable for FUTA in 1993, any cash wages he pays to his employees in 1994 will also be subject to FUTA.

Example 2

George Darby paid his housekeeper and sole employee $12,000 for all of 1993. Since FUTA is assessed only on the first $7,000 of cash compensation paid to each employee during the calendar year, George's FUTA liability (before any credit for state unemployment taxes) was $434 ($7,000 × 6.2%).

TAXPLANNER

Even though Form 940 is filed annually, you may have to make quarterly deposits of your taxes. If your liability for unemployment taxes for any quarter (plus your liability for any earlier quarter that you have not yet deposited) is in excess of $100, you must deposit these taxes with your local bank within 1 month after the close of the quarter. Each deposit should be accompanied by Form 8109, *Federal Tax Deposit Coupon.*

38 | U.S. Citizens Working Abroad: Tax Treatment of Foreign Earned Income

Introduction

*U.S. citizens and **resident aliens** are taxed on their worldwide income regardless of where it is earned, paid, or received. But U.S. citizens living abroad get certain tax benefits that are not available back home. **Employees** and **self-employed** individuals living abroad may annually exclude up to $70,000 of their foreign-earned income from taxation in 1993 and later years. In addition, employees and self-employed individuals may also exclude or deduct part of their housing costs from **taxable** income. This chapter tells you about all the tax benefits you get from living abroad and what you have to do to qualify for them.*

How to qualify for the foreign earned income exclusion. You qualify for the foreign **earned income exclusion** if you are a U.S. citizen, you have a **tax home** in a foreign country, and you meet either the foreign residence test or the physical presence test, described below.

Generally, if you are a resident alien of the United States, you may qualify for the foreign **earned income exclusion** if you satisfy the physical presence test. This assumes that you have not permanently left the United States and that you plan to continue your resident alien status.

Tax home. Your tax home generally is the location of your principal place of employment, which may or may not coincide with the location of your family's residence. Among the factors that are important in determining whether or not your tax home is outside the United States are the anticipated duration of your overseas assignment and whether or not you will return to the same employment location in the United States. Under IRS guidelines, an anticipated short-term (less than 1-year) assignment overseas, followed by a return to the same place of employment in the United States, would indicate that you do not have a tax home outside the United States.

If you meet either the foreign residence test or the physical presence test, you are eligible for two exclusions—the foreign earned income exclusion and the foreign housing exclusion. Self-employed individuals are eligible for a housing **deduction** rather than the housing exclusion. (See the discussion later in this chapter.)

Foreign residence test. The foreign residence test re-quires that you be a "bona fide resident" of a foreign country (or several foreign countries) for an uninterrupted period that includes an entire tax year. Whether or not you are a bona fide resident is a subjective question of your intent, the answer to which is determined by the facts and circumstances of each situation, including the purpose of your trip and the nature and length of your term abroad.

The following types of factors are considered by the IRS in determining your intent to reside in a specific place:

1. The type of quarters you occupy (hotel or rooming house, rented quarters, purchased quarters, or quarters furnished by your employer)
2. How long your family resided with you during the tax year
3. The length of the uninterrupted period during which you have been living outside the United States
4. The nature of any conditions or limitations concerning your employment agreement and the type and term of your visa
5. Whether you maintain a home in the United States and, if so, its rental status and the relationship of any tenants to you

If you make a statement to the authorities of a foreign country that you are not a resident of that country, and if you are not taxed as a resident of that country, you do not qualify as a bona fide resident of that country.

Once you have met the foreign residence test for an entire tax year, your qualification is retroactive to the first day you established your bona fide residence. Occasional trips to the

United States for business or vacation do not affect your qualification.

Example 1

You moved from the United States to a foreign country, arriving on September 15, 1993. You entered the country under a resident visa with your family for a 3-year assignment. You did not declare to the foreign authorities that you were not a resident. You qualify as a bona fide resident of the foreign country if these facts remain the same through December 31, 1994. You may file your 1993 U.S. income tax return (or amend your original 1993 tax return) to claim the benefits of a bona fide resident of a foreign country for the period September 15, 1993, through December 31, 1993.

Example 2

George has been a resident of the United Kingdom for 5 consecutive years. If he moves to France this year, he continues to be a bona fide resident of a foreign country. An uninterrupted period of bona fide residence may include residence in more than one foreign country.

Example 3

Amy moved to France with her family on June 15, 1992, for a job assignment of indefinite length. On December 3, 1993, she was transferred back to the United States. She did not satisfy the bona fide residence test, since she did not maintain a bona fide residence in a foreign country for a period that includes a complete tax year. However, she may qualify under the physical presence test.

Physical presence test. This test simply requires that you be physically present in a foreign country (or countries) for 330 full days during any consecutive 12-month period. This is a purely objective test. There is no reference to your intentions or to any other factors that determine bona fide residence abroad.

Two important rules regarding this test are the following:

1. A full day is a 24-hour period commencing at midnight. Thus, a day in which you travel to or from the United States is not a full day in a foreign country.
2. When you travel *between foreign countries,* the travel days will qualify as full days in a foreign country, provided that the time spent outside of either foreign country during the journey (i.e., is, time spent over international waters and/or time spent in the United States) is less than 24 hours.

TAXORGANIZER

Keep a copy of your calendar of days in and out of the U.S. The calendar can be supported by airline tickets or stamped passports documenting arrival and departure dates.

Explanation: The Foreign Earned Income Exclusion

If you qualify, you may elect to exclude a maximum of $70,000 per year in foreign earned income from your U.S. taxable income in 1993 and later years.

The amount of income you may exclude depends on (1) the number of days during the year in which you were a bona fide resident or (2) the number of days you were physically present in the country during a 12-month period. If you are out of the country for the entire year, you may exclude all of your earned income up to the $70,000 limit. However, if you are out of the country for only part of the year, you generally must prorate the exclusion based on your number of qualifying days during the taxable year.

Example

You were a bona fide resident of a foreign country for 300 days during 1993. The maximum amount of income you may exclude from U.S. taxes is 300/365 × $70,000, or $57,534. Your exclusion is, of course, limited by the amount of foreign income you earn. If you earn less than the maximum allowed, you may exclude only that amount.

Only foreign earned income is eligible for the exclusion. Earned income is income received for the performance of personal services. It does *not* include **dividends, interest, capital gains,** and **rental property income.** For example, interest earned on a bank account in the United Kingdom by a U.S. expatriate on assignment in London is not eligible for the exclusion, since it is not foreign *earned* income.

Earned income may be received in cash or benefits in kind, including the following:

- Salaries, wages, bonuses, commissions, overseas incentive premiums, and so on.
- A housing allowance. This may take the form of a cash payment or of housing provided by your employer. When a cash payment is received, you must report the full amount as income. When housing is provided, your employer should furnish you with an estimate of its **fair market value.**
- An automobile allowance. A cash allowance for an automobile should be included in your income. When an automobile is provided by your employer, an amount representing the value of its personal use to you should be included in your income.
- A cost of living allowance.
- An education allowance.
- Home leave. The value of home leave benefits provided to you and your family is included in your income. However, if you spend a significant portion of your home leave on business, you may be justified in characterizing the trip as a business trip and thereby exclude your travel expenses from income.
- Rest and relaxation airfare.
- A moving expense reimbursement or allowance.
- A tax reimbursement or allowance.

Source of earned income. The source of earned income depends on the place where the services are rendered. If the services are performed in the United States, the income is considered U.S. source income. If the services are performed in a foreign country, the income is foreign source. For the income to be excluded from your U.S. income, the earned income must be from sources within a foreign country (or countries).

How to compute your foreign source income. To compute your foreign source income for purposes of the foreign earned income exclusion, you must determine your earned income from sources outside the United States.

Foreign source earned income includes *all* income received for personal services performed outside the United States. The place of payment is irrelevant. A payment made in the United States by a U.S.-based employer for services performed outside the United States is foreign source income. If you have performed services both within and without the United States during the tax year, you must determine what portion of your income was from U.S. sources and what portion was from foreign sources.

Example

You received $50,000 for services performed in 1993. You worked a total of 240 days during the year, 235 days in the United Kingdom on foreign assignment and 5 days in the United States for a technical meeting. The source of your earned income is as follows:

$$\frac{5 \text{ days worked in the United States}}{240 \text{ days worked worldwide}} \times \$50,000 = \$1,042$$

$$\frac{235 \text{ days worked outside the United States}}{240 \text{ days worked worldwide}} \times \$50,000 = \$48,958$$

Your U.S. source income is $1,042. Your foreign source income is $48,958.

There are several other considerations to keep in mind when you are figuring out the source of your income:

1. If there has been a significant change in your rate of compensation during the year, it may be appropriate to allocate your compensation separately for the days worked and income earned in the respective periods.
2. If payment is received during the year for services performed in a prior year, it may be appropriate to report that payment based on the days worked in the prior year. Such income cannot be excluded under the current year's foreign earned income exclusion, but it can be excluded on your current year's tax return to the extent that your prior year's exclusion was not fully utilized.
3. Do not figure travel to the United States for a vacation as part of your calculation.

Example

In 1992, you were eligible for the full $70,000 foreign earned income exclusion but only had $64,000 of foreign source earned income that was excluded on your 1992 tax return. In 1993, your compensation includes $10,000 of foreign source income earned in 1992. You can exclude $6,000 of the $10,000 on your 1993 tax return. The $6,000 exclusion is in addition to any exclusion you might have for compensation earned and paid in 1993.

Explanation: Foreign Housing Exclusion

If you qualify as a U.S. citizen living abroad, you may elect to exclude from your U.S. taxable income the excess of reasonable housing expenses over a "base housing amount." The base housing amount is 16% of the salary for a U.S. government employee at the GS–14, step 1 level—$8,737 for 1993. The base amount is prorated by the ratio of the number of qualifying days to the total days in the year.

Example

You had $16,000 of qualified housing expenses in 1993. Based on an allocation of your earned income, you determine that you had $98,000 of foreign source income. Furthermore, you had a qualifying period of 330 days in the tax year. Assume that the base housing amount is $8,737. Your housing exclusion is computed a follows:

1) Housing expenses	$16,000
2) Number of qualifying days	330
3) Total days in the tax year	365
4) Assumed base housing amount	$8,737

5) 330/365 × $8,737	$7,899
6) Housing exclusion (line 1 − line 5)	$8,101

Assuming the same facts, you calculate your foreign earned income exclusion as follows:

1) Maximum foreign earned income exclusion	$70,000
2) Number of qualifying days	330
3) Total days in tax year	365
4) 330/365 × $70,000	$63,288
5) Total foreign source income	$98,000
6) Less: Housing exclusion	$8,101
7) Total foreign source income available for exclusion	$89,899
8) Smaller of lines 4 or 7	$63,288

Your foreign earned income exclusion is $63,288. In addition, your foreign housing exclusion is $8,101. Your total exclusion is: $71,389.

Foreign housing deduction for self-employed individuals. If you are a self-employed individual and you do not have an employer to provide housing, you may *deduct* the cost of foreign housing in computing your **adjusted gross income.** Your housing deduction is limited to the amount of foreign earned income that exceeds your foreign earned income exclusion for that year.

If you are both an employee and a self-employed individual during the same tax year, see Publication 54, *Tax Guide for U.S. Citizens and Resident Aliens Abroad.*

When to elect the foreign earned income exclusion and the foreign housing exclusion. You elect the foreign earned income exclusion and the foreign housing exclusion separately. The elections can be made on a tax return that you file on time, on an amended tax return, or on a late-filed tax return that is filed within 1 year of the original due date. A recent change in the rules allows the elections to be made later under certain circumstances. When you are deciding whether or not to use the exclusions, you should take into account a number of factors, including the level of taxation in the foreign country in which you are living, the type of foreign assignment you are on, and your employer's expatriate policy.

When you elect the foreign income exclusion, you are required to reduce your deductible expenses associated with the excluded income. Similarly, foreign taxes available for the foreign tax credit must also be reduced (see *Explanation: Foreign Tax Credit,* later).

If you are living in a foreign country with a high tax rate, you may be better off forgoing the exclusions and claiming a larger foreign tax credit. In this case, forgoing the exclusions may result in a higher current tax liability but may also create large foreign tax credits that may be carried forward and used to offset the tax in years after you return to the United States and receive a bonus or tax reimbursement that is foreign source income.

In countries with moderate or low tax rates, it is usually to your advantage to claim the exclusions. You should calculate your taxes with and without the exclusions to see which is more beneficial.

You may revoke your election of the foreign earned income exclusion or the foreign housing exclusion for any tax year by attaching a statement to your return or your amended return saying that you do not wish to claim the exclusion. Once revoked, you may not claim the exclusions again for the next 5 years without obtaining IRS approval.

Explanation: Employer-Provided Meals and Lodging

Meals and lodging provided in kind by, or on behalf of, an employer to an employee or to his or her spouse or **dependents** are excluded from taxable income if certain requirements are met:

1. The meals are provided by the employer on his or her business premises and for his or her convenience.
2. Lodging is provided by the employer on his or her premises and for his or her convenience, and the employee is required to accept such lodging as a condition of employment.

The IRS has taken a narrow view of the lodging exclusion. As a result, most employer-provided lodging is not excludable from your income. However, the exclusion applies if the employee resides in a camp that is provided by the employer because the employee's work site is in a remote area where satisfactory housing is not available on the open market. The camp has to be located as near as is practicable to the work site and should be furnished with a common area or enclave that is not available to the general public and normally accommodates 10 or more employees.

TaxAlert

You do not have to be living abroad to take advantage of this exclusion for employer-provided meals and lodging. All taxpayers are entitled to exclude the value of meals and lodging from taxable income when they are provided on the employer's premises for the employer's convenience and when the lodging must be accepted as a condition of employment.

Explanation: Foreign Tax Credit

You may elect to claim a credit for foreign income taxes paid or accrued during the tax year, or you may claim the taxes paid as an itemized deduction. Generally, claiming a credit is more beneficial. The foreign tax credit on your U.S. return is limited to the lesser of (1) the actual foreign income taxes paid or accrued during the year (including carrybacks or carryforwards) or (2) the amount of U.S. tax attributable to foreign source taxable income for the year. The foreign tax credit is elected and calculated on Form 1116.

If you elect to take either the foreign earned income exclusion or the foreign housing exclusion, the amount of foreign taxes that you may receive credit for is reduced.

TaxOrganizer

Keep a copy of your foreign tax return supporting the tax credit calculations. This may be needed if your return is audited.

Example 1

You had $98,000 of foreign source income and $16,000 of qualified housing expenses in 1993. The total amount you may exclude from your income is $71,389. (See the foreign housing exclusion example above to learn how this number is calculated.) You paid $4,000 in foreign taxes for the year. You figure the amount that you may claim as a foreign tax credit as follows:

$$\frac{\$71,389}{\$98,000} \times \$4,000 = \$2,914$$

A maximum of $1,086 ($4,000 − $2,914) may be claimed as a foreign tax credit.

Example 2

You are a U.S. citizen currently residing in the United Kingdom. Your total **gross income** for the year is $120,000, all of which is compensation. You qualify for a foreign earned income exclusion of $70,000 and a housing exclusion of $5,000, a total of $75,000. You spent 10% of your working days in the United States. You have $6,200 of **itemized deductions.** The amount you may claim as a foreign tax credit is computed as follows:

Compensation from foreign sources (90% of $120,000)	$108,000
Deductions allocated to foreign source compensation: $\frac{\$108,000}{\$120,000} \times \$6,200$	5,580
	$102,420
Less: Foreign earned income and housing exclusions	75,000
Foreign source taxable income	$27,420
U.S. source compensation (10% of $120,000)	12,000
Balance of itemized deductions ($6,200 minus $5,580)	(620)
U.S. taxable income before personal exemptions	$ 38,800

The foreign tax credit limitation is calculated by determining the ratio of foreign source taxable income to U.S. taxable income (as shown above). The ratio in the above example would be

$$\frac{\$27,420}{\$38,800} = .7067$$

This ratio is then multiplied by the U.S. tax liability for the year to determine the maximum amount of credit usable for the year. If the U.S. tax were, say, $4,500, the maximum credit would be $3,180 (.7067 × $4,500).

Carryback and carryforward of foreign tax credit. Example 1 (above) shows how to determine the amount of foreign taxes that may be used as a credit. Example 2 shows how to determine the maximum amount of foreign tax credit that may be currently used as a credit against your U.S. taxes. If the amount of the foreign tax credit that is generated exceeds the amount that can be used currently, you may carry back the excess 2 years. The remainder, if any, may be carried forward 5 years.

TaxPlanners

Here is a list of items you should consider in planning and preparing your tax return:

1. **Rental of your personal residence.** The vacation home rules disallowing certain deductions in excess of rental income (see Chapter 10, *Rental Income and Expenses*) do not apply when you rent your principal residence during a qualified rental period, which consists of 12 or more months during which your residence is rented or available to be

rented. A period of less than 12 months qualifies if the period ends because your residence was sold or exchanged.

2. **Sale of your principal residence.** The replacement period described in Chapter 16, *Selling Your Home*, is suspended during the time in which you have a tax home outside the United States. The period may not exceed 4 years beyond the date of sale of your home.

3. **Individual Retirement Arrangements (IRAs).** An expatriate who contributes to an **IRA** [see Chapter 18, Individual Retirement Arrangements (IRAs)] must have earned income in excess of the total of his or her foreign earned income and foreign housing exclusions if he or she elects to use the exclusions.

If you are covered by a company pension plan, your **adjusted gross income** must be below a certain level for your IRA contribution to be tax-deductible. If the foreign-earned income exclusion reduces an expatriate's adjusted gross income below the required ceiling, he or she will be eligible to make a tax-deductible IRA contribution.

4. **Alternative minimum tax (AMT).** For taxable years beginning after December 31, 1986, the maximum amount of AMT (see Chapter 31, *How To Figure Your Tax*) that can be offset with foreign tax credits is 90%. Prior to this effective date, the entire amount of AMT may be offset by foreign tax credits to the extent that such credits are available.

39 | Foreign Citizens Living in the United States

Introduction

Almost everybody living in the United States—whether a U.S. citizen or not—is subject to U.S. income tax laws.

*Foreign nationals working in the United States are either **resident aliens** or **nonresident aliens**. Resident aliens, like U.S. citizens, are subject to U.S. tax on their worldwide income. Nonresident aliens are subject to U.S. tax only on their U.S. source income. Some foreign citizens living in the United States are not taxed at all—at least not by the U.S. government. A foreign citizen resident in the United States who works for a foreign government doing normal diplomatic work is exempt from the U.S. tax laws, provided that U.S. government employees working in that foreign country are exempt from its tax laws. Tax treaties between the United States and some foreign governments contain numerous other exceptions.*

This chapter tells you how to determine if you are a resident or nonresident alien and how you should calculate your tax.

Determining Your Status

Whether you are a resident alien or nonresident alien is of critical importance when you determine how much U.S. income tax you will pay. Your residency status will determine your filing status, the tax rate schedule applicable to your income, and the amount of your income that will be subject to U.S. income tax. Under rules that became effective in 1985, an alien must meet *either* of two tests in order to be considered a resident of the United States for tax purposes. The tests are as follows:

1. **The green card test.** Have you been lawfully admitted to the United States for permanent residency? In other words, do you have a green card?
2. **The substantial presence test.** Have you been present in the United States for a substantial period of time? If you have been present in the United States for at least 31 days in the current year and if the total days you are present in the United States during the calendar year, plus one-third of the days present in the preceding calendar year, plus one-sixth of the days present in the second preceding calendar year are equal to at least 183 days, you will meet the substantial presence test and will be considered a resident alien.

If you are considered a U.S. resident under the substantial presence test (and you were not a U.S. resident in the prior year), your *residency* period generally begins on the first day on which you were present in the United States that year. However, if you visit the United States, and the total days you spend in the United States during the visit amount to 10 days or less, you may, under certain circumstances, ignore those days for purposes of determining when your residency period began.

Example

You move to the United States on June 1, 1993, and spend a sufficient number of days in this country in 1993 to meet the substantial presence test. Prior to your actual arrival on June 1, you spent 10 days in the United States from February 2 through February 11 to house hunt and to meet with your U.S. employer while you maintained your tax home in a foreign country. Your U.S. residency period begins on June 1. If you had stayed in the United States until February 12 (11 days), your U.S. residency period would have begun on February 2.

A similar rule applies in the year in which your U.S. residency terminates. Your residency period generally ends on the last day of the year. However, if you can show that you have closer connections to a foreign country for the remainder of the year, your U.S. residency generally ends on the last day on which you are present in the United States. Visits to the United States totaling 10 days or less following your departure may be disregarded in determining the last day of your U.S. residency.

Example

In 1993 you lived in the United States continuously from January 1 through October 31, when you moved to a foreign country. Under the substantial presence test, you are considered to be a resident of the United States through October 31. If you return to the United States on business trips or on vacation during November and December and spend 10 days or less in total in the United States, your residency period terminates on October 31. If you spend more than 10 days in total in the United States in November and December, your U.S. residency period will be extended beyond October 31. The actual termination date will depend on the specific dates of your visits.

TaxOrganizer

To substantiate your arrival and departure dates to and from the U.S., copies of travel tickets (airline, boat, etc.) or stamped passports should be retained in your tax files.

TaxAlert

Even if you meet the substantial presence test, you can avoid being considered a resident alien if you are present in the United States for less than 183 days in the current year *and* you can show closer ties to a tax home in a foreign country (or in the case of a move, no more than two foreign countries) than to the United States for the entire year. Whether you have closer ties to the United States or to a foreign country depends on the facts and circumstances. Consult a tax advisor for details. You may be required to furnish a statement to the IRS to this effect.

Election to be treated as a resident. The Tax Reform Act of 1986 contains a provision that allows an alien to elect to be treated as a resident of the United States for tax purposes, even though he or she does not meet the green card or substantial presence tests. The provision allows an alien with significant U.S. presence toward the end of one year and who meets the substantial presence test in the following year to elect to be treated as a U.S. resident alien in the earlier year. The alien can only make this election after he or she has met the substantial presence test in the next year. This may necessitate the filing of an extension. This election will be advantageous to some aliens, such as those who incur significant expenses when they first arrive in the United States (interest, deductible mortgage points, and real estate taxes incurred in connection with a new U.S. residence, for example), which would be deductible for a resident but not for a nonresident. The election could also benefit married aliens who would be required to file using married filing separate rates as nonresidents. As U.S. residents under this election, they would be permitted to make a further election to be treated as residents for the entire year (see the following Example), thus permitting the filing of a joint return and the use of the more favorable joint return rates. An alien who meets the following criteria may make the election:

1. Doesn't meet the green card or substantial presence tests for the current year.
2. Was not a resident alien in the prior year.
3. Meets the substantial presence test in the following year.
4. Is present in the United States for at least 31 consecutive days in the current year.
5. Spends at least 75% of the days between the first of the 31 consecutive days and year-end in the United States (*Note:* Up to 5 non-U.S. days will be counted as U.S. days for the purposes of this test.)

Under 1992 final IRS regulations, an alien who makes the election to be treated as a resident may also make a similar election on his or her tax return on behalf of dependent children if the children are not required to file tax returns on their own, assuming, of course, that the children also meet the requirements of the eletion. The filing of the election will enable an alien to take dependency exemptions for the children.

Example

Assume that an alien is present in the United States for the following periods:

7/4–8/15	43 days
9/16–11/25	71 days
12/16–12/31	16 days

During the testing period of July 4 through December 31, the individual is in the United States 130 days out of 181 days total. Including the 5 additional non-U.S. days, which can be counted as U.S. days, the individual is present in the United States on less than 75% of the days and cannot make the election for this period.

$$\frac{130 \text{ plus } 5}{181} = 74.6\%$$

However, if, during the testing period of September 16 through December 31, the individual will be in the United States 87 days out of 107, which exceeds 75%, the individual could elect to be treated as a resident for the period of September 16 through December 31 (assuming that the other tests regarding the prior and subsequent years are also met).

TaxPlanner 1

If you have a green card, you should be aware that you are considered a resident alien and are subject to tax on all of your income. If you have substantial U.S. or foreign investment income, you may want to transfer the income-producing assets to somebody else, for example, a spouse or other close relative who is still living abroad.

TaxPlanner 2

If you meet the substantial presence test described above, but you are present in the United States less than 183 days each year, you should examine your ties to another country. You might qualify for the exception to the substantial presence test if you can demonstrate that your ties to another country are stronger than your ties to the United States. You must file a statement with your tax return supporting your claim, or, if no return is required, a statement alone must be filed with the IRS.

If your ties are weak and you want to try to strengthen them, consider

1. Maintaining a home in that country
2. Obtaining a driver's license issued by that country
3. Joining a religious, political, or cultural organization in that country
4. Maintaining or establishing a membership in a social organization in that country
5. Having a bank account in that country
6. Having personal property in the country such as cars, clothing, jewelry, and so on
7. Continuing to vote in that country

If you spend a significant amount of time in the United States each year, you should carefully monitor the days to keep them below the 183-day threshold during the 3-year period considered under the substantial presence test.

Note: Do not assume that nonresident alien filing status necessarily results in greater savings than resident alien status. Resident alien status may result in a lower U.S. tax if you can use the lower joint return rates (for married resident aliens), are eligible for greater itemized deductions, and/or benefit from the foreign tax credit.

Some existing or proposed income tax treaties may have the effect of overriding the provisions of the law. Consult a tax advisor for details.

Generally, tax treaties are consulted when an individual is a dual resident, that is, a resident of both the United States and a foreign country. When a treaty is used to claim that an individual is a nonresident of the United States, the individual must file Form 1040NR and attach a statement to the return presenting facts to support the claim of U.S. nonresidence.

An election to be treated as a nonresident of the United States under a treaty will apply for *all* purposes in computing the alien's income tax liability for the dual residency period.

TaxAlert

Filing Form 1040NR may affect the determination by the Immigration and Naturalization Service as to whether you qualify as a U.S. resident for immigration purposes (i.e., green card). Consult with immigration counsel to evaluate the impact of this rule on your personal situation

Dual-status aliens. A dual-status alien is a person who is considered a resident alien and a nonresident alien during the same tax year.

You are most likely to have dual status in the year of your arrival or departure from the United States. You could, for example, be a resident alien until your departure from the United States. At that time, you would become a nonresident alien.

For purposes of computing your tax liability, different rules apply to the time when you are a resident alien and the time when you are a nonresident alien. However, it is necessary to fill out only one tax return. You may make a special election that may decrease your taxes for some years in which you have dual status. This election is discussed in the following section.

TaxPlanner

An alien's residency status may not be the same for all purposes. The definition discussed above applies for federal income tax laws. Different rules apply in determining residency for state income tax and federal estate tax purposes.

Explanation: How Resident Aliens Are Taxed

Like U.S. citizens, resident aliens are subject to tax on the worldwide income they receive, regardless of its source. Resident aliens compute their **taxable income** and file their income tax in the same way in which U.S. citizens do. They include the same items in income and are entitled to take the same **deductions** as U.S. citizens.

Dual-status aliens. Dual-status aliens who are resident aliens for part of the tax year are taxed somewhat differently from U.S. citizens.

If you file an individual return, you are taxed on your worldwide income for the part of the year in which you are a resident alien. For the part of the year in which you are a nonresident alien, only your U.S. source income is taxed.

Dual-status aliens who are married may not file a **joint return** or claim the standard deduction. Married taxpayers are taxed on their worldwide income for the part of the year in which they are resident aliens and only on their U.S. source income for the part of the year in which they are nonresidents. They are not, however, able to file jointly and take advantage of the lower joint rates.

Exceptions

Dual-status aliens have two other alternatives in the year in which they arrive in the United States:

1. **The Section 6013 (h) election.** This election is available only in cases in which both spouses are resident aliens at year-end. An alien choosing this alternative is treated as a resident of the United States for the *entire tax year*. The most significant consequences of making this choice are:
   a) All income, both U.S. and foreign source, is subject to tax, including any income you had during the period in which you were not a resident of the United States. This income would have been exempt from U.S. taxes or taxed at a reduced rate if you had not made the Section 6013 (h) election.
   b) You may claim **itemized deductions** for the period in which you were not a resident of the United States, if such items would otherwise qualify for deduction. Some examples are foreign real property taxes, mortgage interest, and medical expenses.
   c) You may deduct, or elect to claim as a credit, foreign income taxes attributable to the period during which you were not a U.S. resident, which may substantially eliminate U.S. income tax. Other benefits, however, like being able to file a joint return and thus be taxed at accordingly lower rates, are left intact. The result is that your net U.S. tax liability may be reduced.
2. **The Section 6013 (g) election.** This choice is available only to an arriving alien who is a resident alien at year-end but whose spouse is not. Under the Section 6013 (g) election, a married couple may file a joint return as full-year residents of the United States if at the end of the tax year one spouse is a nonresident alien and the other is a citizen or resident of the United States.

The effects of making this election are the same as choosing the Section 6013 (h) election, with one very significant and beneficial distinction. The Section 6013 (g) election is valid for all subsequent years in which you and your spouse qualify, including the year in which the resident alien leaves the United States. The fact that you may qualify for this status in the year of your departure may eventually give you a big tax break. Once made, these elections can be revoked. However, if you revoke the election, you cannot make another such election in the future.

Example

You and your spouse became U.S. residents on April 1, 1993. Prior to your arrival in the United States, you earned $5,000 in wages and your spouse earned $1,000 in wages. Both of you also had $500 in joint interest income for the first 3 months of the year. Once in the United States, you earned $75,000 from April through December. Your spouse did not work in the United States. You had an additional $700 in joint interest income. Your itemized deductions equal the standard deduction. Your tax liabilities are computed as follows:

Alternative 1: Dual-status return, married filing separately (for period while a U.S. resident)

Salary	$75,000
Interest	350
Itemized deductions	(3,100)
Exemptions	(2,350)

Taxable income	$69,900
Tax	$17,933

You would not be taxed on your non-U.S. source income.
Alternative 2: Full-year election, joint return

Salary	$81,000
Interest	1,200
Itemized deductions	(6,200)
Exemptions	(4,700)
Taxable Income	$71,300
Tax	$15,167

By electing to be treated as a resident alien for the entire tax year, you save $2,766 in income taxes. Note that your spouse could not be claimed as a dependent under Alternative 1, since your spouse had income during the U.S. residency period. Your spouse does not need to file a return under Alternative 1, since your spouse's income did not exceed the amount that requires you to file. (See Chapter 1, *Filing Information*).

The $6,500 in income that you and your spouse earned in your home country would probably be subject to tax there. If so, you would be eligible for the foreign tax credit if you filed under Alternative 2. The tax credit would further lower your taxes. See Chapter 35, *Other Credits*, for a discussion of the foreign tax credit.

Explanation: How Nonresident Aliens Are Taxed

A nonresident alien is taxed as follows:

Compensation for services rendered in the United States or other income that is effectively connected with a U.S. trade or business is generally taxed on a net basis at graduated rates. A nonresident alien may deduct certain expenses incurred in producing that income, such as business expenses and state and local taxes. In addition, he or she may deduct casualty losses and qualifying charitable contributions. However, a nonresident alien may not benefit from the standard deduction.

For taxable years beginning after 1986, income that is effectively connected with a U.S. trade or business at the time it is earned will be considered "effectively connected" at the time it is received, even if receipt occurs in a different tax year.

A nonresident alien is able to claim a personal exemption for himself or herself. However, a nonresident alien who is a resident of Mexico or Canada or a national of the United States is also entitled to claim personal exemptions for

1. A spouse, if the spouse had no gross income for U.S. tax purposes and was not the dependent of another taxpayer
2. Other dependents, if they meet the same requirements as a U.S. citizen

A married nonresident alien is taxed under the "married filing separately" Tax Rate Schedule, which is the highest Tax Rate Schedule applicable to individuals. You may not claim **head of household** status if you are a nonresident alien. A nonresident alien who is **single** would use the "unmarried" Tax Rate Schedule.

Dividends, interest, royalties, pensions, annuities, and U.S. source income that are not effectively connected with a U.S. trade or business are usually subject to a 30% tax rate unless a lesser rate has been established by a tax treaty. No deduc-

tions or exemptions are allowed against this income. Interest earned on bank accounts, as well as certain other investments (known as "portfolio" debt instruments), is exempt from U.S. taxes.

Gains and losses from the sale of **capital assets,** other than real property from U.S. sources, may be taxed in either of two ways. If the gains and losses are not connected with a trade or business in the United States, any gain (after deducting losses) is taxed at a 30% rate if the nonresident alien is in the United States for 183 days or more during the tax year. If a gain is derived from the sale of capital assets effectively connected with a trade or a business in the United States, it is taxed as though a U.S. citizen had incurred the gain. Capital gains from the sale of real property located in the United States are considered to be connected with a U.S. trade or business and are subject to special U.S. tax laws. (For a more detailed discussion of the tax treatment of gains and losses, see IRS Publication 519, *U.S. Tax Guide for Aliens.*)

Foreign students. Foreign students who enter the U.S. under an "F" visa (academic or language student) or a "J" visa (educational and cultural exchange visitor) are nonresidents for U.S. tax purposes, as long as they substantially comply with the terms of their visa.

TAXPLANNER

Foreign nationals who become U.S. residents are taxed on their worldwide income from the day on which they become residents. You may, however, take several steps before you become a U.S. resident that limit your U.S. tax liability. Consider the following:

1. If you anticipate receiving a payment of compensation for past services, such as a bonus, arrange to receive this payment before becoming a resident of the United States. If this payment is received after you become a U.S. resident alien, it will be taxable in full by the United States, even though the related services were rendered prior to coming to the United States.
2. If you anticipate incurring expenses that will be deductible for U.S. income tax purposes, such as mortgage points, interest, or certain charitable contributions, consider deferring these payments until after you are a resident of the United States.
3. If you sell a stock for a gain prior to your arrival in the United States, the entire gain is not subject to U.S. tax. However, if you sell a stock at a profit after you become a U.S. resident, the entire gain is subject to U.S. tax, even if the entire appreciation of the stock occurred before you became a U.S. resident. Our advice is to sell stocks in which you have a profit before you become a U.S. resident.

   If you have a loss and the entire loss was generated before you became a U.S. resident, but you did not realize the loss until after you took up residency, you may deduct the loss.

4. If you receive a **lump-sum distribution** from a government or private retirement plan after you have become a U.S. resident, the entire amount may be subject to U.S. tax. Our advice is, if at all possible, arrange to receive the payment before you become a U.S. resident, when it is not subject to U.S. tax.
5. If you sell your principal residence before becoming a U.S. resident, the proceeds are not normally subject to any U.S. tax. However, if you become a U.S. resident and elect to be taxed as a resident alien for the entire year to take advan-

tage of lower joint filing rates (see *Exceptions,* earlier), you may end up paying tax on the sale of your principal residence. Be sure to consider this fact before you elect to be taxed as a resident alien for the entire year.

If you acquire a personal residence in the United States and subsequently sell it while you are a U.S. resident, you are taxed on any gain you incur unless you buy a new principal residence within 2 years. (See Chapter 16, *Selling Your Home,* for details.) Your new home may be in the United States or any other country, including your home country.

6. You may be able to take advantage of a "window," a situation in which certain income is never taxed. This requires analyzing the tax laws of your home country and the United States. A window may be created if you come from a country that does not tax income of its nonresident citizens.

Example
Humphrey Benson is a citizen of the United Kingdom who decides to move to the United States. He owns securities that have appreciated by $100,000. On his move to the United States, Humphrey goes to Bermuda for 2 weeks. While there, he sells all his securities. The result is that he does not have to pay any tax in the United Kingdom, in the United States, or in Bermuda.

TaxPlanner

The main point to remember is that the best time for you to minimize your U.S. tax burden is *before* you make an investment in the United States and *before* you become a U.S. resident.

Departing from the United States
Before you depart from the United States, you must obtain a certificate of compliance, indicating that you have satisfied your federal tax liability. This certificate, frequently referred to as a "sailing permit" or an "exit permit," is obtained by filing Form 1040C or Form 2063. To get the permit, you must either pay all of the U.S. income tax due prior to departure or demonstrate that your departure from the United States will not impair the collection of the tax. The forms may be obtained from your nearest IRS office. An exit permit is valid only for the 30 days prior to your anticipated departure date. If you postpone your departure, you probably have to apply for a new exit permit. See IRS Publication 519, *U.S. Tax Guide for Aliens,* for more details.

TaxOrganizer
The IRS representative must see actual departure tickets in order to issue your "sailing permit." Make sure you bring these along to the IRS.

A certificate of compliance is not a substitute for an annual income tax return. A federal tax return still must be filed in accordance with regular filing procedures. Any payment in conjunction with the filing of Form 1040C is treated as a payment on your annual tax return.

TaxPlanner 1
You cannot defer the gain on the sale of your principal residence if you sell your home after your departure from the United States. If you intend to reinvest the proceeds in another residence in your home country (or anywhere else) and want to defer paying taxes on any gain you might have from the sale, you should sell *prior* to departing from the United States. If this cannot be done, consider returning to the United States for a sufficient number of days after the sale in order to extend your residency period under the substantial presence rules discussed earlier. Note that the rules for tax deferral discussed in Chapter 16, *Selling Your Home,* do not apply to nonresident aliens.

TaxPlanner 2
For tax years beginning after 1986, "effectively connected" salary income that is paid in a tax year after the alien's year of departure will be considered "effectively connected" and taxed at the regular graduated rates. If the alien was in the highest tax bracket in the year in which the income was earned, the receipt of the income in a subsequent year will cause it to be taxed at the lowest marginal tax rate first, for example, 15% in 1993.

40 | How to Prepare for Your Accountant

Introduction
Millions of Americans prepare their own tax returns every year, while others rely on accountants to do the work for them. In fact, over half of those filing individual tax returns seek some kind of professional assistance. Which path you should take depends primarily on how complicated your financial affairs are and, of course, your willingness to puzzle through IRS forms. This chapter will help you organize your financial affairs, whether or not you have an accountant.

Who Needs an Accountant?
You will probably benefit from the advice and expertise of an accountant if you find yourself in one or more of the following conditions:

1. You have more than one source of income.
2. You think you are eligible for a lot of deductions.
3. You want to take advantage of a tax credit.

You probably do *not* need an accountant if your return appears to be relatively simple. *If you are planning to file using Form 1040EZ, there is probably no reason for you to seek professional help.*

Choosing an Accountant
Finding an accountant. Choosing an accountant is not something that should be done casually. There are over 300,000 certified public accountants in the United States. Most of them are single practitioners or in business with a few other people. The bread and butter of their work is preparing tax returns for individuals. The rest of the nation's accountants work mostly for larger accounting firms or for individual companies.

Questions to ask your tax return preparer. Before choosing your tax preparer, you may want to get satisfactory answers to the following questions:

1. Are you a certified public accountant? What are your professional qualifications? Are you affiliated with any financial institution or investment company?
2. Do you have experience in preparing returns for others in my occupation and in handling tax issues similar to mine?
3. How much will it cost to prepare my tax return?
4. Is there anything I can do to reduce the cost of return preparation?
5. What type of information do you need to prepare my return? In what format would you like it submitted and by what date?
6. If I am owed a refund, when can I expect to receive it?
7. Will you inform me if any items on my return are likely to be challenged by the IRS or state authorities?

8. Will you inform me if I am passing up any opportunities to reduce my tax liability?
9. What should I do if I receive a notice from the IRS or state authorities concerning my return?
10. Will you represent me before the IRS or state authorities if I am audited?
11. Who in your office would work on my return? Do you use outside computer service firms to help prepare tax returns?
12. Can you give me the names of clients who would be references for your work?

What an accountant should do for you. You should be able to rely on your accountant for more than preparing your annual tax return. As your accountant becomes increasingly familiar with your personal and financial affairs, he or she should become a valuable and trusted financial advisor.

Anytime you are entering into a major financial transaction, it is a good idea to give your accountant a call and review the alternatives available. Your accountant should advise you of any possibilities that will minimize your taxes. If you're buying or selling a house, for example, your accountant should be consulted regarding certain procedures that may have significant tax consequences. While an accountant certainly cannot take the place of your broker, he or she can remind you of the tax consequences of buying or selling stocks and bonds.

The cost of an accountant. The cost of having your tax return prepared by an accountant can vary widely. Although some charge a fixed fee for the preparation of a return, the cost usually depends on the time your accountant spends on your return. You can help reduce this time by gathering, organizing, and summarizing your information yourself.

While you do not need to furnish your accountant with supporting cancelled checks or other documents, you should provide those documents about which you have questions. Considerable time may have to be spent on your return if the law governing some of your transactions is particularly difficult or unclear.

The hourly rates charged by national accounting firms are

ordinarily higher than those charged by local firms. However, the fees charged by some of the larger local firms approximate those of the national firms. *The fee structure should be discussed and agreed on before your accountant begins work.*

Getting good service. You should expect good service from your accountant. Your telephone calls should be returned promptly. Your questions should be answered willingly and in understandable language. Your return should be completed and available to you with adequate time for you to review it before it must be filed.

A key factor in choosing your accountant is whether he or she is "independent." For example, you should know the relationship, if any, that your accountant has to any investment he or she recommends to you. Does your accountant have a significant financial interest in the investment that he or she recommends? Is your accountant an officer, director, or otherwise related to the investment? In addition, you should know the nature and amount of compensation, if any, that your accountant receives from any other person for his or her recommendations.

Switching accountants. If you are dissatisfied with your present accountant, you may wish to consider switching to another. As a matter of professional courtesy, most accountants will cooperate with a new accountant to make the transition as smooth as possible.

You may want your new accountant to have copies of your prior accountant's work papers. Although these work papers are the property of the prior accountant, most will make them available to you or your new accountant. If your files with your prior accountant are extensive, you should discuss an acceptable billing arrangement to cover the cost of providing them to your new accountant.

Preparing for Your Accountant

When to see your accountant. You probably do not need to see your accountant more than once a year, especially if he or she has prepared your return in prior years. If you have a new accountant, however, you might want to get together to go over your situation before your return is prepared. Otherwise, you can easily send your accountant whatever documentation is necessary to prepare your return and talk on the telephone if need be.

A good time to see your accountant is after he or she has prepared your return so that you can go over it together. It is usually wise to do this as soon as possible so that, if any mistakes have been made, they can be easily corrected before the filing deadline.

Tax*Organizer*

The remainder of this chapter discusses the documentation you should keep to support the information contained in your tax return.

What to bring to your accountant. Whether you prepare your own tax return or let an accountant do the work, the task of gathering your tax information together is unavoidable. The better prepared you are to discuss your affairs with your accountant, the more efficient the entire process of preparing your return will be. In general, you should have documentation that supports all income, deductions, and credits that will appear on your return.

Supporting documentation comes in many forms. The most common types of documentation and the items they substantiate are outlined in the following table.

Item	Documentation
1) Wages and salaries	W–2 forms; usually provided by your employer
2) Dividends and interest	Form 1099-Div and Form 1099-Int; usually provided by the bank or company paying the dividend or interest
3) Capital gains and losses	Broker's statements for purchase and sale of assets disposed of during the year and Form 1099-B; usually provided by the broker who sold the assets
4) Business income from sole proprietorships, rents, and royalties	Books and records (Form 1099-MISC *may* also be provided by the payor of the income)
5) Business income from partnerships, estates, trusts, and S corporations	Form K–1; usually provided by the partnership, etc.
6) Unemployment compensation	Form 1099-G; usually provided by the governmental agency paying the unemployment compensation
7) Social security benefits	Form SSA-1099; usually provided by the federal government
8) State and local income tax refunds	Form 1099-G; usually provided by the state or city that refunded the taxes
9) Original issue discount	Form 1099-OID; usually provided by the issuer of the long-term debt obligation
10) All distributions, both total and partial, from pensions, annuities, insurance contracts, retirement or profit-sharing plans, and Individual Retirement Arrangements (IRAs)	Form 1099-R; usually provided by the trustee for the plan making the distribution
11) Barter income	Form 1099-B; usually provided by the barter exchange through which property or services were exchanged
12) Sale of your home	Form 1099-S; provided by the person responsible for closing a real estate transaction
13) IRA contributions	Form 5498; provided by the trustee or custodian of the IRA
14) Moving and employee business expenses	Receipts and cancelled checks and Form 4782, if moving expenses are paid or reimbursed by your employer
15) Medical expenses	Receipts and cancelled checks
16) Mortgage Interest and points paid on the purchase of a principal residence	Form 1098 or mortgage company statement; usually provided by mortgage company
17) Business and investment interest	Cancelled checks and brokers' statements

Check Analysis

Date	Check #	Payee	Amount	Medical	Taxes	Interest	Contributions	Other	Description
2/17	1459	Dr. Broline	$ 55.00	$ 55.00					
3/04	1502	Cancer Society	25.00				$ 25.00		
3/26	1542	State Comptroller	494.00		$494.00				
4/20	1590	First National Bank	350.00			$350.00			
5/16	1630	Church	75.00				75.00		
6/12	1665	Acme Moving	783.00					$783.00	Moving
7/18	1721	Dr. Broline	40.00	40.00					
7/18	1722	Ace Pharmacy	27.00	27.00					
10/22	1853	Church	75.00				75.00		
11/15	1902	First National Bank	300.00			300.00			
Totals			$2,224.00	$122.00	$494.00	$650.00	$175.00	$783.00	

18) Real estate taxes	Receipts, cancelled checks, and mortgage company statements (if applicable)	
19) Other taxes	Receipts and cancelled checks	
20) Contributions	Receipts and cancelled checks	

What *not* to bring to your accountant. You need not bring all of your documentation to your accountant. For example, if you prepare a summary of your dividends or charitable contributions, just provide your accountant with the summary. If you do give your accountant all of your documentation, he or she will probably feel obligated to verify the accuracy of your summaries, which, as you well know, can be a time-consuming process. Your fee increases accordingly. However, you should be able to provide full documentation on request.

Collecting Your Tax Information

1. **Study last year's tax return.** A good place to start when you are gathering information is your prior year's tax return. This return is a record of your taxable transactions during the previous year. If your economic activities have not significantly changed during the current year, then your prior year's return will give you a good indication of the kinds of documentation you should gather for your accountant. The old return may also serve as a powerful reminder of a little-used bank account that paid you interest or some other source of income, great or small, that you otherwise might

forget. You should retain copies of prior years' returns for future reference.

2. **Review all checks.** At some point, you should be sure to review all the checks you have written during the year to search for possible tax deductions. To simplify your task, it's wise, if possible, to pay all of your checks from a single account. If, for example, you have a money market account and a checking account at your bank, it might be easier for recordkeeping purposes to transfer money into your checking account as necessary rather than to write checks on both accounts. If you want to be absolutely certain not to miss anything, prepare a worksheet like the one that follows. Do so each month throughout the year as you reconcile your bank statement. Various computer software programs are also available to help simplify the task of recordkeeping.

3. **Fill out a tax questionnaire.** To make sure that you don't miss anything, many accountants use questionnaires or checklists to obtain information about all of your taxable transactions during the year. Even if you're not planning to use an accountant, it might be a good idea to fill out an accountant's questionnaire. For a sample questionnaire, refer to the Individual Tax Organizer in the front of this book.

A final reminder: The common goal that you share with your accountant is the preparation of a complete and accurate return. The closer you work together, the more likely it is that your return will be satisfactory. Just as important, the closer you work together, the better your chances will be of saving money on your taxes.

41 | If Your Return Is Examined

Introduction

This chapter is probably not for you. Overall, the IRS examines only a small fraction of all tax returns that are filed. However, if you are contacted by the IRS about your tax return, this material may be very important to you. Just how important will depend on how carefully your return was prepared and the sources and amount of your income.

An IRS examination is nothing to be feared, if you have kept accurate records to support your deductions and all of your income has been reported. In most cases, IRS audits are rather routine. In fact, in about 25% of the cases, the IRS makes no changes or issues a refund. Whatever the result, you won't do yourself much good by making things difficult for the IRS. An IRS examiner has the legal power to force a taxpayer to produce books and records to complete the examination. The best strategy is almost invariably one of concluding the examination as quickly as possible by providing the facts needed and by meeting deadlines.

On the other hand, an IRS examination is nothing to take lightly. You should be prepared, and that preparation starts with keeping receipts and records, followed by careful preparation of your return. The IRS examiner must follow certain rules in conducting the examination. Since you'd be well advised to know what they are, this chapter tells you about them.

In 1988, the Congress for the first time codified a "taxpayer bill of rights." The statutory language is part of the Technical and Miscellaneous Revenue Act of 1988. Most of the provisions either restate the law as found elsewhere or make into law some of the IRS's administrative practices. You should read the IRS Publication 1, Your Rights as a Taxpayer. *It may be especially helpful in cases that involve the delinquent payment of assessed taxes. This chapter tells you about your rights when your return is examined. You should know these rights, since they affect you and your pocketbook.*

The Examination and Appeals Process

The IRS examines returns for correctness of income, exemptions, credits, and deductions.

TAXPLANNER

Who gets audited? The odds that your return will be examined by the IRS are, in fact, quite low. Recently, the IRS has examined approximately 1% (0.8% in 1990) of all individual returns files, down from about 5% in the mid-1960s. The odds shift substantially, depending on your income level. For taxpayers reporting less than $25,000 of income on their returns, the audit rate in many districts is not more than about 0.5%. For taxpayers reporting $50,000 and over in income (not including Schedule C or Schedule F), the audit rate in many districts is not more than about 1.75%. Slightly over 3% of self-employed individuals reporting total gross receipts of $100,000 or more have their returns audited.

Here is a list of some items or circumstances that can frequently draw the IRS's attention:

• Total Schedule C (business income) gross receipts of $100,000 or more. According to one recent study, the IRS has concluded that individuals filing Schedule C are most likely not to report income.
• Large business expenses in relation to your income. (e.g., tips received by waiters or taxi drivers).
• A return submitted by an accountant or a tax preparer who is on an IRS list of "problem preparers" because they have repeatedly violated the law.

- Complex investment or business transactions without clear explanations.

Fairness if Your Return is Examined

Most taxpayers' returns are accepted as filed. But if your return is selected for examination, it does not suggest that you are dishonest. The examination may or may not result in more tax. Your case may be closed without change. Or, you may receive a refund.
Courtesy and consideration. You are entitled to courteous and considerate treatment from IRS employees at all times. If you ever feel that you are not being treated with fairness, courtesy, and consideration by an IRS employee, you should tell the employee's supervisor. Publication 1, *Your Rights as a Taxpayer,* explains the many rights you have as a taxpayer. You can get free publications by calling our toll-free number.

TaxPlanner

While the "taxpayer bill of rights" did not break new legal ground, it did create a single document that informs you of your rights. It is useful to review it to be aware of the rights you have. Here is a summary of the most important points:

Pay only the required tax. You have the right to plan your business and personal finances in such a way that you will pay the least tax that is due under the law. You are liable only for the correct amount of tax. Our purpose is to apply the law consistently and fairly to all taxpayers.
Privacy and confidentiality. You have the right to have your tax case kept confidential. Under the law, the IRS must protect the privacy of your tax information. However, if a lien or a lawsuit is filed, certain aspects of your tax case will become public record. People who prepare your return or represent you must also keep your information confidential.

You also have the right to know why we are asking you for the information, exactly how we will use it, and what might happen if you do not give it.

Examination of Returns

An examination usually begins when we notify you that your return has been selected. We will tell you which records you will need. If you gather your records before the examination, it can be completed with the least amount of effort.
How returns are selected. We select returns for examination by several methods. A computer program called the Discriminant Function System (DIF) is used to select most returns. In this method, the computer uses historical data to give parts of the return a score. IRS personnel then screen the return.

Some returns are selected at random. We also select returns by examining claims for credit or refund and by matching information documents, such as Forms W–2 and 1099, with returns.

Explanation

The IRS uses five general methods to attempt to verify that the proper amount of tax is being paid by taxpayers:

1. **Document perfection.** Every return is checked for mathematical, tax calculation, and clerical errors immediately on receipt. If a mistake is discovered, a recalculation of the tax due and a notice of explanation are sent to the taxpayer. This procedure is not an **audit**—an important distinction.

   The IRS determines whether the return is in "processible form." The law lets the IRS avoid payment of interest on any refund until the return contains the taxpayer's name, address, identifying number, and required signature. Furthermore, the return must be on the permitted form and contain sufficient information to permit the mathematical verification of the tax liability shown on the return. The IRS has carried this to extremes by sending tax returns back to taxpayers for failing to check a box, not attaching all required forms, and not making alternative minimum tax computations when it is obvious no such action is due. While the IRS concentrates on refund returns with small errors that permit them to avoid large refunds, it has also sent balance-due returns back after depositing any checks attached. If the return is not perfected and returned before the due date, the IRS says the return is delinquent. The IRS has lost this issue in the Tax Court but persists in its position.

2. **Discriminant Function System (DIF).** Basically, DIF assigns a numerical value to certain items on your return. If the total of all the values equals or exceeds a minimum set by the IRS, the computer will single out the return for a possible audit. IRS agents will then check the return to see if it is worth the IRS's time to conduct an audit. This will depend on, among other things, staffing in your IRS district office. Even if your return is selected for an audit, it is likely that only specific items, such as charitable contributions or employee business expenses, would be examined, not your entire return.

   It's a closely guarded secret what weight DIF assigns to which items. Some things this computer program is on the lookout for include:

   - Large amounts of income not subject to withholding
   - More deductions than seem to be reasonable for your income level
   - Claims for an unusual number of dependency deductions as compared to withholding and other items on the return
   - Discrepancies such as a change of address combined with deductions claimed for owning a residence when you have not reported that you sold your old residence.

   The DIF system is being used less as a selection source in recent years, especially in the case of Schedule C filers. The Audit Specialization Program is taking its place (see below).

3. **Taxpayer Compliance Measurement Program (TCMP).** The type of examination triggered by TCMP is more intensive than that generated by DIF. Typically, every item on your tax return is questioned, and you must substantiate everything. You will be advised

by the IRS that your return is being examined under the TCMP.

The bad news about a TCMP examination is that almost every item on your return can be examined. If you are married, you may be required to produce your marriage certificate. If you claim exemptions for your children, the IRS may ask to see their birth certificates. The IRS uses TCMP examinations to construct a computer model and to keep its taxpayer profile up to date.

The good news about a TCMP examination is twofold. Since the IRS randomly chooses about 50,000 returns to examine each year, the chances of you being selected are slim—the odds are about 2,000 to 1. In addition, unlike other IRS audits, a majority of TCMP examinations do not result in additional tax.

4. **Document-Matching Program.** The IRS matches the information supplied by your bank, your employer, and others on Forms W–2 and 1099 and other information documents with the information supplied on your return. If an item is omitted from your return or conflicts with what is reported to the IRS, the IRS computer will generate a notice that recalculates your tax with corrections for the omitted income or overstated deduction. The Revenue Reconciliation Act of 1989 repealed the section of the tax law that gave the IRS the presumption of being correct in asserting a negligence penalty if you fail to report correctly relevant amounts reflected on information returns. The change applies to returns filed after December 31, 1989. It is probable that the IRS will continue to assert not only the negligence penalty but also the substantial understatement penalty. This procedure does not technically constitute a formal examination.

5. **The Audit Specialization Program (ASP) and other special projects.** The ASP process begins when IRS agents examine several returns for a specific industry or trade group, to become well versed in their business practices and accounting procedures. Once sufficient returns have been examined, procedures and techniques to identify specific tax issues are incorporated into a written examination guide. Additional examiners are then trained to examine returns. Tax returns are screened by IRS service centers to select returns which will be reviewed by specialized examiners. ASP procedures, for example, are being used in the Western Region to select and examine returns of attorneys, bail bondsmen, insurance agents/brokers, auto repair shops, and others. The process will be expanded nationwide in 1994.

In addition, the IRS initiates "Compliance 2000" projects on a district-by-district basis to identify areas of noncompliance. For example, one district examined all the drywall contractors in a major metro area and claims to have found widespread underreporting of gross receipts as well as nonfilers. Another district selected returns of individuals who had renegotiated loans and examined them to determine if they were subject to tax because an indebtedness had been forgiven.

IRS service centers conduct other projects. Several service centers screened returns to determine if taxpayers who requested extensions of time to file were understating the tax that would be due. The IRS then treated extensions as invalid when the difference between the tax shown on the return and the extension exceeded certain tolerances. Other IRS service centers screened tax returns to detect failure to report gain on residences which were not replaced.

Arranging the examination. Many examinations are handled by mail. For information get the free Publication 1383, *The Correspondence Process (Income Tax Accounts)*. If we notify you that your examination is to be conducted through a personal interview, or if you request an interview, you have the right to ask that the examination take place at a reasonable time and place that is convenient for both you and the IRS. If the time or place we suggest is not convenient, the examiner will try to work out something more suitable. However, we will make the final determination on how, when, and where an examination takes place.

Explanation

Correspondence audit. After a tax return is initially selected for examination, the IRS may first conduct a "correspondence audit," requesting that documentation of a specific item on your tax return be submitted by mail. If it is more convenient, you may request that the audit be held at the IRS's local district office. However, by law, the IRS has the right to make the final decision on where and how an examination will be conducted, as long as it is not unreasonable in exercising its discretion. The taxpayer bill of rights directed the IRS to publish regulations defining reasonable time and place. These regulations were published in temporary form, effective June 4, 1990.

Office audit. If the examination is conducted at an IRS office, its scope may be expanded to cover all questionable items. Although correspondence audits may be resolved more quickly than examinations conducted at an IRS office, there is no rule of thumb for which type of audit would be more beneficial to you. However, it is generally to your disadvantage to request that a correspondence audit be changed to an office audit or a field audit. Correspondence audits are limited in scope. You open the opportunity for the examiner to question other items if you request an interview audit at an IRS office or an audit at your place of business.

The easier you make the IRS's job, the less the amount of time will be required to conclude the audit and the greater the likelihood will be that you will avoid any arbitrary adjustments.

An examination verifies the accuracy of your tax liability on a specific item as reported on a tax return, claim, or other filing. An examination is generally limited to the study of those matters bearing directly on the tax question at hand. The IRS has the authority to examine information that may not appear to be directly related to your tax liability. For example, the IRS may study your living expenses to determine if your reported income can support your life-style or whether you may have unreported income.

Transfers to another district. Generally, your individual return is examined in the IRS district office nearest your home. However, not all offices have examination facilities. Your business return is examined where your books and records are maintained. If the place of examination is not convenient, you may ask to have the examination done in another office or transferred to a different district.

Representation. Throughout the examination, you may represent yourself, have someone else accompany you, or, with proper written authorization, have someone represent you in your absence. If you want to consult an attorney, an enrolled agent, or any other person permitted to represent a taxpayer during an examination, we will stop and reschedule the interview. We cannot suspend the interview if you are there because of an administrative summons.

Explanation
In recent years, some districts and some examiners have been very aggressive in demanding that the taxpayer, even though represented by a qualified practitioner with a power of attorney, appear personally to answer questions. This practice was admittedly to probe for unreported income and to establish if the taxpayer's life-style might suggest other problems in compliance with tax laws. The taxpayer bill of rights now specifies that the IRS "may not require a taxpayer to accompany the representative in the absence of an administrative summons," and a properly qualified practitioner with a power of attorney is authorized to represent a client in any interview without the taxpayer's presence, except for criminal cases or matters involving the integrity of an IRS employee. Furthermore, the law specifies that, "if a taxpayer clearly states at any time during an interview," except where an administrative summons has been enforced or accepted, "that the taxpayer wishes to consult with an attorney, certified public accountant, enrolled agent, enrolled actuary, or any other person permitted to represent the taxpayer," the IRS "shall suspend such interview, regardless of whether the taxpayer may have answered one or more questions."

TAXPLANNER
Do you need professional help? The answer is: It depends on the issues involved and your ability to represent yourself. If the amounts involved are small, it may not be worth it to pay for an advisor's time. If your return was prepared by a certified public accountant or a lawyer, you will want to inquire whether his or her fee included representing you at an audit. If it didn't and you *want him or her to represent you, you should agree on a fee* at the beginning of the process. You will certainly want an accountant or a lawyer to represent you if (1) the law involved in the audit is unclear *or complicated*, (2) highly technical supporting information may be required, (3) you *think other issues may come up,* or (4) you are too nervous or emotionally involved to handle the matter yourself.

Recordings. You can generally make an audio recording of an interview with an IRS Examination officer. Your request to record the interview should be made in writing. You must notify us 10 days before the meeting and bring your own recording equipment. We also can record an interview. If we initiate the recording, we will notify you 10 days before the meeting, and you can get a copy of the recording at your expense.

TAXPLANNER
Upon advance request, you have the statutory right to tape record all audit meetings for whatever purpose you deem necessary. Be advised, however, that, if you tape the meeting, the IRS will probably also want to tape it, and you will be setting up an adversarial relationship.

Repeat examinations. We try to avoid repeat examinations of the same items, but sometimes this happens. If we examined your tax return for the same items in either of the 2 previous years and proposed no change to your tax liability, please contact us as soon as possible so that we can see if we should discontinue the examination.

Explanation
Generally, in connection with auditing your return for a particular year, the IRS may inspect your books only once. But there may be a second examination if you request it or if the IRS notifies you in writing that an additional audit is necessary. A further investigation could be considered necessary simply if the IRS suspects that additional tax is owed.

You may refuse the IRS's request to make a second examination. In fact, if you do not object, you have, in effect, given your consent for the examination to take place. If you refuse to produce records, the IRS must issue a summons. If you still resist, the IRS will be forced to obtain court assistance to enforce the summons.

The ban on second examinations does not apply when (1) the original audit, although prolonged and characterized by IRS staffing changes, is still going on; (2) the examination is not considered an examination as such (e.g., when the IRS contacts you to verify the amount of dividends or interest on your return because that figure does not match what was otherwise reported); (3) the second examination is for a different kind of tax (e.g., employment or excise tax, instead of income tax) than was dealt with in the first examination; or (4) a mere visual inspection of the return has taken place, not an examination of your books and records.

In sum, it is difficult for the IRS to justify a second examination of your books and records for the same year, but, if there is a legitimate reason to do so, the IRS is usually within its rights.

Explanation of changes. If we propose any changes to your return, we will explain the reasons for the changes. It is important that you understand the reasons for any proposed change. You should not hesitate to ask about anything that is unclear to you.

Agreement with changes. If you agree with the proposed changes, you may sign an agreement form and pay any additional tax you may owe. You must pay interest on any additional tax. If you pay when you sign the agreement, the interest is generally figured from the due date of your return to the date you paid.

Explanation
The IRS uses misleading language when it describes this consent form as an "agreement form." When you sign a Form 870 or Form 4549, you are simply permitting the IRS to make its assessment of tax without waiting 90 days, as required by law, and you are forfeiting your right to go to the Tax Court. You are not bound to follow the IRS position in subsequent years and may even file a claim for a refund for the years covered by the Form 870 after the tax has been paid.

If you do not pay the additional tax when you sign the agreement, you will receive a bill. The interest on the additional tax is generally figured from the due date of your return to the billing date. However, you will not be billed for more than 30 days additional interest, even if the bill is delayed.

If you are due a refund, we can refund your money more quickly if you sign the agreement form. You will be paid interest on the refund.

TaxPlanner
An IRS examiner has virtually unlimited authority to determine the "facts." Since most examination issues concern factual matters, the examiner has considerable discretion in accepting secondary evidence and in deciding what constitutes acceptable proof. On technical legal issues, though, he or she must adhere to established IRS policy. Therefore, even if certain court cases support your argument, the examiner must disallow it if the IRS has decided not to follow the precedents established by these cases.

In theory, IRS examiners are also not permitted to trade off items, letting you take one deduction in return for disallowing another. In practice, negotiations with the IRS are commonplace.

An important reminder. IRS examiners are under considerable pressure to close cases by reaching an agreement at the initial examination. An agent is given high marks for explaining the IRS position in a convincing manner. Contrary to popular belief, examiners are not rated by the amount of money they bring in or by the number of cases they close.

While all examination reports have a chance of being reviewed, except for cases that fall into a mandatory review category, the review is on a sample basis, so only a small percentage of cases are actually reviewed. The mandatory categories include cases involving refunds in excess of $1 million, tax shelters, TCMP, and fraud. All unagreed cases are subject to a limited review upon receipt of a protest asking for an appeal's hearing. This review is primarily focused on perfecting the IRS case based on your arguments in the protest. *One important point:* If you and the IRS auditor reach an agreement on the issue under examination, the auditor will be on your side if his or her report is reviewed by his or her boss.

Appealing the Examination Findings

If you do not agree with the examiner's report, you may meet with the examiner's supervisor to discuss your case further. If you still do not agree with the examiner's findings, you have the right to appeal them. The examiner will explain your appeal rights and give you a copy of Publication 5, *Appeal Rights and Preparation of Protests for Unagreed Cases.* This free publication explains your appeal rights in detail and tells you exactly what to do if you want to appeal.

TaxPlanner
If you and the IRS examiner disagree over the proper interpretation of a point of law, either you or the examiner may request technical advice from the IRS national office. Technical advice will be given only if the issue is unusual or complex, or if there is a lack of uniformity within the IRS about its treatment. If you ask for technical advice and the examiner denies the request, you may appeal to the Chief of the Examination Division. If he or she also denies the request and you disagree with the denial, all data will be forwarded to the Assistant Commissioner (Examination) in the national office for review. Action on the disputed issue generally will be suspended until it is decided whether or not technical advice will be issued.

Technical disagreements may be resolved by taking them to the agent's supervisor. However, this course of action is not recommended unless you are absolutely certain you are correct. The supervisor could point out an alternative position that might be more favorable to the examining agent.

Appeals Office. You can appeal the findings of an examination within the IRS through our Appeals Office. The Appeals Office is independent of your examiner and IRS District Director or Service Center Director. Most differences can be settled through this appeals system without expensive and time-consuming court trials. If the matter cannot be settled to your satisfaction in Appeals, you can take your case to court.

Explanation
Appeal within the IRS. There is a single level of appeal within the IRS. You make your appeal about the findings of the examiner to the Appeals Office in your region. Appeals conferences are conducted as informally as possible.

If you want an appeals conference, address your request to your District Director, according to the instructions in the IRS letter to you. Your District Director will forward your request to the Appeals Office, which will arrange for a conference at a convenient time and place. You or your representative should be prepared to discuss all disputed issues and to present your views at this meeting in order to save the time and expense of additional conferences. Most differences are resolved at this level.

If agreement is not reached at your appeals conference, you may, at any stage of the procedures, take your case to court. See *Appeals to the Courts,* later.

Written protests. Along with your request for a conference, you may need to file a written protest with your District Director.

You do not have to file a written protest if

1. The proposed increase or decrease in tax, or claimed refund, is not more than $2,500 for any of the tax periods involved
2. Your examination was conducted by correspondence or in an IRS office by a tax auditor

If a written protest is required, you should send it within the period granted in the letter that you received with the examination report. Your protest should contain the following:

1. A statement that you want to appeal the findings of the examiner to the Appeals Office
2. Your name and address
3. The date and symbols from the letter, showing the adjustments and findings you are protesting
4. The tax periods or years involved
5. An itemized schedule of the adjustments with which you do not agree
6. A statement of facts supporting your position in any issue with which you do not agree
7. A statement outlining the law or other authority on which you rely

If the additional tax exceeds $2,500 but does not exceed $10,000, items 6 and 7 above are not required.

The statement of facts under item 6 must be declared true under penalties of perjury. This may be done by adding to the protest the following signed declaration: "Under the penalties of perjury, I declare that I have examined the statement of facts presented in this protest and in any accompanying schedules and, to the best of my knowledge and belief, it is true, correct, and complete."

If your representative submits the protest for you, he or she may substitute a declaration stating the following:

1. That he or she prepared the protest and accompanying documents
2. Whether he or she knows personally that the statement of facts contained in the protest and accompanying documents is true and correct

Representation. You may represent yourself at your appeals conference, or you may be represented by an attorney, a certified public accountant, or a person enrolled to practice before the IRS.

If your representative attends a conference without you, he or she may receive or inspect confidential information only if a power of attorney or a tax information authorization has been filed. Form 2848, *Power of Attorney and Declaration of Representative,* or Form 8821, *Tax Information Authorization,* or any other properly written power of attorney or authorization may be used for this purpose.

You may also bring witnesses to support your position. You should consider consulting an attorney specializing in tax law before you do this.

TaxPlanner

Whereas an IRS examiner must follow established IRS policy on statutory and procedural points, the appeals officer may bargain with you. He or she may consider whether litigation is worthwhile, given the strength of the views at odds with the IRS's position. If you make an unsuitable good-faith settlement offer, the appeals officer may reject it but indicate a settlement he or she would recommend be accepted. In arriving at a figure, the appeals officer may calculate the chances of the IRS prevailing in court. Generally, however, the IRS will not settle a case just because it is a nuisance to continue to pursue it.

Appeals officers do not have final settlement authority in all cases and for all issues. Accordingly, it is good practice in negotiating a settlement to ask the appeals officer if any part of a settlement proposed is subject to a supervisory review.

If no agreement can be reached at the appeals conference, you have two options:

1. Pay the additional tax generated by the disputed issue and sue for the refund of this payment in your District Court or the U.S. Court of Federal Claims (formerly the U.S. Claims Court) (see *Appeals to the Courts,* below).
2. Wait for the arrival of your closing letter, and select a course of action at that point. If you do not pay the disputed amount, you will also receive from the IRS a notice of deficiency, which is also known as a 90-day letter. A Tax Court suit may not be filed before receipt of the 90-day letter.

Some words of caution: Special procedures apply to certain partnerships and S corporations. The amount of any adjustment is determined at the partnership or S corporation level. The procedures are complex, regular statutory notices are not issued, and you should consult a professional if you want to contest a partnership or S corporation issue raised in the examination of your return.

Appeals to the courts. Depending on whether you first pay the disputed tax, you can take your case to the U.S. Tax Court, the U.S. Court of Federal Claims, or your U.S. District Court. These courts are entirely independent of the IRS. However, a U.S. Tax Court case is generally reviewed by our Appeals Office before it is heard by the Tax Court. As always, you can represent yourself or have someone admitted to practice before the court represent you.

If you did not yet pay the additional tax and you disagree about whether you owe it, you generally have the right to take your case to the Tax Court. Ordinarily you have 90 days from the time we mail you a formal notice (called a "notice of deficiency") telling you that you owe additional tax to file a petition with the Tax Court.

If you have already paid the disputed tax in full and filed a claim for refund (discussed later) for it that we disallowed (or on which we did not take action within 6 months), then you may take your case to the U.S. District Court or U.S. Court of Federal Claims.

Court decisions. We follow Supreme Court decisions. However, we can lose cases in other courts involving taxpayers with the same issue and still apply our interpretation of the law to your situation. You have the right to appeal our decision to do so.

Explanation

Appeals to the courts. If you and the IRS still disagree after your conference, or if you skipped the IRS appeals system, you may take your case to the U.S. Tax Court, the U.S. Court of Federal Claims, or your U.S. District Court. These courts are independent judicial bodies and have no connection with the IRS.

Tax Court. If your case involves a disagreement over whether you owe additional income tax, estate tax, gift tax, windfall profit tax on domestic crude oil, or certain excise taxes of private foundations, public charities, qualified pension and other retirement plans, or real estate investment trusts, you may take it to the U.S. Tax Court. For you to appeal your case to the Tax Court, the IRS must first issue a formal letter, called a *notice of deficiency*. You have 90 days from the date this notice is mailed to you to file a petition with the Tax Court (150 days if it is addressed to you outside the United States). If you do not file your petition within the 90 or 150 days, you lose your opportunity to appeal to the Tax Court.

Generally, the Tax Court hears cases only if the tax has not been assessed and paid; however, you may pay the tax after the notice of deficiency has been issued and still petition the Tax Court for review. Therefore, you must be sure that your petition to the Tax Court is filed on time. If it is not, the proposed liability will be automatically assessed against you. Once the tax is assessed, a notice of tax due (a bill) will be sent to you, and you may no longer take your case to the Tax Court. Once the assessment has been made, collection of the full amount due may proceed, even if you believe that the assessment was excessive. Publication 586A, *The Collection Process (Income Tax Accounts),* explains IRS collection procedures.

If you filed your petition on time, the Tax Court will schedule your case for trial at a location that is convenient to you. You may represent yourself before the Tax Court, or you may be represented by anyone admitted to practice before that Tax Court.

If your case involves a dispute of not more than $10,000 for any 1 tax year, the Tax Court provides a simple alternative for resolving disputes. At your request, and with the approval of the Tax Court, your case may be handled under the *Small Tax Case* procedures, whereby you can present your own case to the Tax Court for a binding decision. If your case is handled under this procedure, the decision of the Tax Court is final and cannot be appealed. You can get more information about the small tax case procedures and other Tax Court matters from the U.S. Tax Court, 400 Second Street, N.W., Washington, D.C. 20217.

A note of caution: Since many taxpayers represent themselves in small cases, the IRS has a very high win record. Filing your own petition may not be a good idea, especially if the amount is substantial to you. In any event, be careful in following the instructions *to the letter,* especially regarding the date for filing, the required fee, and the address of the Tax Court.

District Court and U.S. Court of Federal Claims. Generally, the District Court and the U.S. Court of Federal Claims hear tax cases only after you have paid the tax and have filed a claim for a credit or a refund. As explained later under *Claims for Refund,* you may file a claim for a credit or a refund if, after you pay your tax, you believe that the tax is incorrect or too high. If your claim is rejected, you will receive a notice of disallowance of the claim, unless you signed a Form 2297, *Waiver of Statutory Notification of Claim Disallowance.* If the IRS has not acted on your claim within 6 months from the date on which you filed it, you may then file suit for refund. You must file suit for a credit or a refund no later than 2 years after the IRS disallows your claim or a Form 2297 is issued.

You may file your credit or refund suit in your U.S. District Court or in the U.S. Court of Federal Claims. However, the U.S. Court of Federal Claims does not have jurisdiction if your claim was filed after July 18, 1984, and is for credit or refund of a penalty that relates to promoting an abusive tax shelter or to aiding and abetting the understatement of tax liability on someone else's return.

For information about procedures for filing suit in either court, contact the Clerk of your District Court or the Clerk of the U.S. Court of Federal Claims. The addresses of the District Courts and the U.S. Court of Federal Claims are in Publication 556, *Examination of Returns, Appeal Rights, and Claims for Refund.*

TAXPLANNER

Here are some of the factors that you might want to consider before you decide to file your suit in Tax Court, District Court, or U.S. Court of Federal Claims.

1. Which court has most recently arrived at favorable rulings on similar disputed issues.
2. The amount of tax involved. You may file a suit in Tax Court without paying the IRS the amount it claims you owe. If the tax has already been paid and you wish to file suit to obtain a refund, the District Court and the U.S. Court of Federal Claims are your only choices. However, to stop the accumulation of interest, you can at any time make a deposit of the tax that an examiner says you owe. *Caution:* Such a payment must be clearly labeled as a deposit. If you are successful in an appeal, you will draw no interest on the deposits returned. A deposit does not prevent you from going to the Tax Court. Once you file a suit in Tax Court, you may then pay the alleged tax deficiency and your suit will not be thrown out of court. If you do make the payment at this point in the process, you will not be liable for interest charges past the payment date. If you win, the government will then owe you interest from the date on which you made the payment. A deposit will be converted to a payment of the tax after you file a petition with the Tax Court. It is important to distinguish between payments of tax and deposits to stop the accumulation of interest.
3. Jury trials are available only in the District Courts. If your case rests on a question of equity, rather than on a finer point of tax law, a jury might be more responsive to your arguments. Remember, however, that both parties may appeal a District Court or a Tax Court decision.

4. A person who is not an attorney may appear before the Tax Court.
5. Filing a suit before the Tax Court suspends the statute of limitation on the tax return that you are contesting. Consequently, if the IRS chooses, it could raise new issues and assess additional tax while your case is pending in court.
6. You're more likely to avoid embarrassing publicity before the Claims Court. The U.S. Court of Federal Claims is located in Washington, D.C. There is a District Court near your hometown. The Tax Court tries cases on a circuit-riding basis in most major cities.
7. You may file suit in Tax Court only within 90 days (150 days if outside the United States) after the IRS issues a statutory notice of deficiency. You have more time to file before the District Court and the U.S. Court of Federal Claims.
8. In Tax Court, settlement negotiations are conducted with the IRS. In District Court and U.S. Court of Federal Claims, lawyers from the Tax Division of the Department of Justice will oppose your case.
9. Tax Court and District Court cases are appealed to the Court of Appeals and then to the Supreme Court. U.S. Court of Federal Claims decisions may be appealed to the Court of Appeals for the Federal Circuit and then to the Supreme Court.
10. Any court of the United States may now award attorney's fees and other costs for cases initiated after December 31, 1985, including certain costs incurred in an administrative appeal if the IRS's position was not substantially justified.

Recovering litigation expenses. If the court agrees with you on most of the issues in your case, and finds the IRS's position to be largely unjustified, you may be able to recover some of your litigation expenses from us. But to do this, you must have used up all the administrative remedies available to you within the IRS, including going through our Appeals system. You may also be able to recover administrative expenses from the IRS. Free Publication 556, *Examination of Returns, Appeal Rights, and Claims for Refund,* explains your appeal rights.

Explanation
The taxpayer bill of rights corrects an inequity in prior law by permitting the courts to award costs, not only for litigating, but also for administrative proceedings once a taxpayer's administrative appeal rights have been exhausted and a "notice of decision" by the IRS or a statutory notice of deficiency has been issued, whichever occurs earlier. The prior law had been interpreted to permit recovery only after the IRS's attorneys had taken a position before the courts. To recover, a taxpayer must substantially prevail through a determination in an administrative proceeding, after the point specified above, or in a court of law and must establish that the position of the United States in the proceeding was not substantially justified. In collection matters, when neither notice is issued, only litigation costs are recoverable.

Reasonable administrative costs include the following:

- Fees or charges imposed by the IRS
- Reasonable expert witness fees
- Reasonable costs of studies and analyses
- Costs associated with engineering or test reports
- Reasonable fees (generally not in excess of $75 per hour) for a qualified representative of the taxpayer in connection with the administrative action

Other remedies. If you believe that tax, penalty, or interest was unjustly charged, you have rights that can remedy the situation.

Claims for refund. Once you have paid your tax, you have the right to file a claim for a credit or refund if you believe the tax is too much. The procedure for filing a claim is explained in Chapter 1, *Filing Information.*

Explanation
Some courts have held that an informal claim for a refund will, under certain circumstances, prevent the statutory period from expiring before you can accumulate and submit all your data. An informal claim should be in writing, should notify the IRS that a right to a refund is being asserted, and should tell as fully as possible the reasons why you feel the refund would be valid. A formal claim for the refund filed on official IRS forms should be made as soon as practical thereafter.

Note: Informal claims that mention vague and general future possibilities to justify a refund will not be considered valid.

TAXPLANNER

If you file an amended return with the wrong IRS Service Center, it is under no obligation to forward that return to the correct Service Center. If you do not hear from the IRS within 6 months of filing Form 1040X, you should make a point of contacting it to determine the source of the delay.

Claims (Form 1040X) should always specifically ask "for such greater amount as is legally refundable" to ensure refund of interest and interest on interest where appropriate.

Cancellation of penalties. You have the right to ask that certain penalties (but not interest, as discussed later) be canceled (abated) if you can show reasonable cause for the failure that led to the penalty (or can show that you exercised due diligence, if that is the applicable standard for the penalty).

If you relied on wrong advice given to you by IRS employees on the toll-free telephone system, we will cancel certain penalties that may result. But you have to show that your reliance on the advice was reasonable.

Reduction of interest. If our error caused a delay in your case, and this is grossly unfair, you may be entitled to a reduction of the interest that would otherwise be due. Only delays caused by procedural or mechanical acts that do not involve exercising judgment or discretion qualify. If you think we caused such a delay, please discuss it with the examiner and file a claim.

TaxSaver

If the IRS made an error, sent you a refund check, and then made you pay interest when you repaid it, you now can strike back. According to the Tax Reform Act of 1986, the IRS may not charge you interest from the date of the erroneous refund to the date they demanded you repay it. The law has also given the IRS the discretion to refund or abate excessive interest that you may have paid on an underpayment of your tax if an IRS employee was dilatory or made an error in processing it. To qualify, you must not have caused the error in any way. The erroneous refund must have been less than $50,000. Use Form 843 to file your claim.

TaxPlanner

The taxpayer bill of rights recognized that taxpayers occasionally may have problems paying taxes due on their returns because of unanticipated changes upon examination or other unexpected difficulties. To ensure fair treatment, the taxpayer bill of rights made some changes in how notices are issued, how much time is allowed for payment, how taxpayers can get help, and so on. The key provisions relating to past-due taxes are as follows:

1. The period from when the IRS provides written notice to a taxpayer to the first permissible date on which the IRS can levy on bank accounts, wages, and so on, is increased from 10 days to 30 days. The IRS also cannot levy on property on any day on which the person appears before the IRS in response to a summons, unless the IRS determines the collection of the tax is in jeopardy. In addition, financial institutions are required to hold accounts garnished by the IRS for 21 days after receipt of the notice of levy.

2. The IRS was required to establish a formal system for the appeal of liens similar to that existing in the income tax deficiency area. The appeals procedures are printed on the notice of lien.

3. The IRS now has the legal right to enter into installment agreements with taxpayers so that they can more easily pay delinquent taxes. The agreement will remain in effect unless the taxpayer has provided inaccurate information, does not pay an installment when it is due, fails to respond to a reasonable request for updated financial information, or the collection of the balance is in jeopardy. In addition, the IRS may only modify or terminate an agreement if the taxpayer's financial condition has significantly changed. Notification of the reason for the action has to be given at least 30 days prior to any action.

4. The Taxpayer Ombudsman is authorized to issue a taxpayer assistance order (TAO) in any situation in which the taxpayer is suffering or about to suffer a significant hardship as a result of the manner in which the IRS laws are being administered. During the period in which the order is in effect, the statute of limitations is suspended and any further IRS action is halted. Only an IRS executive (District Director, etc.) can modify or rescind the order. The Taxpayer Ombudsman administers the IRS Problem Resolution Program, which was created to resolve problems not remedied through normal operating channels.

The IRS has designed a form (Form 911) to assist taxpayers in applying for a TAO.

The taxpayer bill of rights has many other provisions that may be helpful to you. If you have further problems with the IRS and believe that you are being treated unfairly, you should contact the district Problem Resolution Officer or a knowledgeable professional.

42 | Planning Ahead for 1994 and Beyond

Introduction

Tax planning is never easy and has been made even more difficult by the almost annual changes in the law. And 1993 was not an exception. The 1993 Tax Act made some significant changes in the law. Some of the changes, most notably higher tax rates on high-income Americans, will affect your 1993 taxes. But, others, such as new rules regarding moving expenses, will kick in for the first time in 1994. This chapter spells out many of the changes that will take effect for the first time in 1994. (These new changes are also noted—usually as TaxAlerts—in the appropriate chapters of this book.)

Although certain tax strategies are best left to later in the year when you have a more complete picture of your tax situation, it is not too early to start thinking about how to lower your 1994 taxes now. The ideas presented in this chapter will get you started. We have also included some estate planning strategies that you may find useful. Because the impact of tax laws can vary according to the facts involved, we recommend that you consult with your advisor before taking any action.

The tax strategies explained in this chapter are all based on the tax laws that were in effect when we went to press in December. The laws may well change; nevertheless, starting early allows you to take maximum advantage of strategies that may not be available later in the year either because the law may change or because it takes several months to realize the maximum tax benefits.

The following material discusses certain tax planning techniques concerning various types of income and deductions. The first steps in beginning such tax planning should be to prepare a projection of your taxable income for 1994 and 1995.

I. Individual Tax Rates, Personal Exemptions, and Standard Deductions

We expect that there will continue to be five tax brackets in 1994, just as there were in 1993. Although the 1993 Tax Act wasn't passed until the middle of summer, the new tax brackets are retroactive to January 1, 1993. The three lowest brackets that cover most Americans are 15%, 28% and 31%. A fourth tax bracket of 36% applies to taxable income (in 1993) exceeding the following amounts based on filing status:

- $115,000 (single)
- $127,500 (head of household)
- $140,000 (married filing jointly
- $70,000 (married filing separately)

A 39.6% bracket is applicable to income in excess of $250,000 (for all individuals, except married filing separately for whom the threshold is $125,000). Long-term capital gains continue to be subject to a maximum tax rate of 28%. (The 1994 Tax Rate Tables were not yet available as we went to press in December, 1993.) Since the income amounts at which the

15%, 28%, and 31% tax rates take effect will be adjusted each year for inflation, the dollar amounts for 1994 will be slightly higher.

The increasing number of tax brackets and the widening gap between the highest tax bracket and the top capital gains rate makes tax planning increasingly important—and complicated. If you find that you may be subject to a higher tax bracket, you will want to consider ways to shift income from one year to another if you have reason to believe that you will be in a lower bracket (because you have less income) in one of those years.

In addition, since the gap between the rate at which ordinary income and long-term capital gains income is taxed is now 11.6%—while before the passage of the 1993 Tax Act, there was only a 3% difference—you would be wise to look for ways to have income taxed at the lower long-term capital gains rate, if such an opportunity presents itself. Individuals with several different sources of income—say, salary as well as investment income—would be well advised to pay careful attention and to consult closely with a tax advisor or financial planner. If you are on the verge of retirement, you also need to plan carefully.

Starting in 1993, the individual alternative minimum tax has been increased. This, too, will make your tax planning more difficult. For more information, see Alternative Minimum Tax later in this chapter.

Personal Exemption Phaseout

The benefits of the personal and dependent exemptions phase out for higher-income individuals and families. For 1994 returns, the phaseout will be calculated before arriving at your taxable income. The phaseout is equal to 2% per $2,500 of *adjusted gross income* (or fraction thereof) above new threshold amounts, depending on your filing status. The 1994 threshold amounts for the phaseout of personal and dependent exemptions will be the 1993 amounts after they have been adjusted for inflation. See Chapter 3, *Personal Exemptions and Dependents,* for further information.

TAXPLANNER 1

Because of the phaseouts of personal and dependent exemptions and deductions limitations being imposed by the tax law, you should carefully examine how various increments of your income are taxed. If you can control when you receive certain income, you may, in some instances, save on your taxes.

Example

In doing their tax planning, Ralph and Nancy know that the effective tax rate on their income in excess of the phaseout threshold increases as their exemptions are being phased out. They could save on their taxes if they have income that can be

moved to another year when they expect their exemptions will be completely phased out due to anticipated high adjusted gross income (AGI) or to a year when they anticipate that total AGI will fall below the phaseout threshold.

TAXPLANNER 2

If you are divorced, it will require planning to determine whether you or your former spouse should claim the dependent exemptions for the children of your marriage. For example, one spouse could have such high income that the exemption is of no benefit at all. The other could be at an income level where claiming the exemption could reduce his or her taxes by 31% of the exemption amount. The advantage to one spouse claiming the exemption for a child over the other spouse could be considerable each year. Generally, the custodial spouse is entitled to the deduction; however, the parties may contract otherwise. Exemptions for children of divorced parents are discussed in Chapter 3, *Personal Exemptions and Dependents.*

Standard Deduction

The standard deduction is a flat allowance that may be taken in lieu of itemized deductions. The amount of the standard deduction depends upon your filing status, age, and whether or not the taxpayer is blind. The base standard deduction is increased for taxpayers who are 65 or older and for taxpayers who are legally blind. You should only claim the standard deduction if your deductions for charitable contributions, certain local taxes, interest, allowable casualty losses, miscellaneous expenses, and medical expenses are less than the standard deduction.

II. New Provisions of the Tax Law for 1994

Estimated taxes for individuals. You are required to pay your anticipated tax liability as it accrues during the year through withholding and/or the payment of estimated taxes in quarterly installments. You can be penalized for not paying enough tax for a particular installment period. The penalty for underpayment of estimated taxes can be avoided if the total of taxes withheld and estimated tax payments are at least equal to:

1. 90% of the current year's actual tax liability, or
2. 100% of the tax reported on your tax return for the prior tax year, if your previous year's adjusted gross income was $150,000 or less ($75,000 or less if married filing separately). If your previous year's adjusted gross income exceeded $150,000, you must pay 110% of last year's liability in order to avoid underpayment penalties.

In either case, the amount arrived at is divided equally among the four installment periods for purposes of determining the amount of each actual quarterly payment of estimated tax.

Example

Joy Brown's 1994 income tax liability is $55,000. Her adjusted gross income in 1993 was $175,000, while her 1993 tax liability was $40,000. Brown will avoid an underpayment penalty in 1994 if the total amount of tax withheld and estimated tax payments exceeds 110% of her 1993 tax liability, or

$44,000, because her 1993 adjusted gross income exceeded $150,000.

Alternative Minimum Tax (AMT)

Starting in 1993, the individual alternative minimum tax (AMT) has been increased and made somewhat more complicated. You are required to pay an AMT if it exceeds your regular tax liability. The income amount subject to the AMT is determined by adding back to your regular taxable income a number of so-called preference items and by making other adjustments. These preferences and adjustments typically reduce your regular taxable income and include, for example, itemized deductions such as state and local income taxes, real property taxes, and accelerated depreciation claimed on buildings and equipment. The amount arrived at is called alternative minimum taxable income (AMTI). Your AMTI is then reduced by certain so-called "exemption amounts." These exemption amounts vary depending on your filing status and the amount of your AMTI. The balance is subject to the AMT rate, which, according to the new tax law, also varies depending on the amount to be taxed. (A more complete explanation of the AMT can be found in Chapter 31, *How to Figure Your Tax.*)

Under the old tax law, the AMT rate was a flat 24%. The 1993 Tax Act raised the AMT rate to 26% on AMTI of up to $175,000 in excess of the exemption amount, and 28% on AMTI of more than $175,000 above the exemption amount. For married taxpayers filing separately, the 28% AMT rate applies to the extent that your AMTI is more than $87,500 above the exemption amount.

While the new tax law hiked that AMT rate, meaning that if you are subject to the AMT you will pay more in tax, it also hiked the exemption amount, theoretically meaning that less income will be subject to the AMT. Starting in 1993, the exemption amounts were increased to $45,000 (married filing jointly), $33,750 (single and heads of household) and $22,500 (married filing separately and estates and trusts).

The following table summarizes the rates for 1993:

Rate	Married Filing Separately	All Other Filers
26%	Up to $87,500 over exemption amount	Up to $175,000 over exemption amount
28%	Greater than $87,500 over exemption amount	Greater than $175,000 over exemption amount

TAXPLANNER1

The new AMT rates and exemption amounts will affect different taxpayers differently and in some curious ways. Consider the following table comparing how the AMT works under the prior and new tax laws:

	Minimum Dollar Amount of Preference/Adjustments to Trigger AMT	
Regular Taxable Income	Prior Law	New Law
$50,000	$28,346	$30,396
$72,846	32,154	32,154
150,000	42,097	37,628
200,000	43,763	40,369
327,800	64,477	64,477
500,000	114,704	135,818

Taxpayers filing jointly with regular taxable income of up to $72,846 will be better off under the new law because of the higher exemption amount ($45,000) available. In other words, such taxpayers can absorb more AMT adjustments before the AMT would apply. However, at somewhat higher income—for example, $150,000 or $200,000 of regular taxable income—it is easier to be subject to AMT under the new law. But, there's another twist further up the income scale. Joint filers with regular taxable income in excess of $327,800 will be less likely to be subject to the AMT. The bad news: the reason these high income taxpayers are less likely to face the AMT is essentially because they will be paying more in regular tax because of the new higher regular marginal tax rates.

TAXPLANNER2

A number of strategies may be used to help minimize the impact of the AMT:

- If you will be subject to the AMT in one year and the regular tax in the next year, you should generally consider deferring deductions and accelerating income into the AMT year only if the AMT is attributable to what are known as exclusion preferences (e.g., depletion and tax-exempt interest). Those itemized deductions that are not allowed at all in determining the AMT are also exclusion preferences. These deductions include state and local income taxes, property taxes, medical expenses between 7.5% and 10% of AGI, and miscellaneous itemized deductions. If possible, these deductions should be shifted into a non-AMT year. Such shifting will result in a tax savings equal to the amount of the deduction claimed

multiplied by the marginal tax rate (excluding consideration of the phaseouts for certain high-income taxpayers).

However, even when the AMT is attributable to deferral preferences (e.g., accelerated depreciation), advantages may be obtained in some cases by deferring deductions and accelerating income into the AMT year if your regular tax rate in the AMT year is less than the regular tax rate in the following year.

- Net passive losses may not be deducted in arriving at alternative minimum taxable income (AMTI); therefore, it is important for you (if subject to the AMT) to move into income-producing investments in passive activities in order to salvage some of your losses in the current tax year. (See Chapter 31, *How to Figure Your Tax.*)
- Certain interest from home equity loans may not be deductible for AMT purposes. If you are subject to AMT and have home equity interest, you should determine whether you are subject to this limitation.

Taxation of Social Security Benefits

Starting in 1994, a higher percentage of social security benefits will be subject to income tax for certain higher-income recipients of social security benefits. In general, recipients of social security benefits whose income exceeds $44,000 for married individuals ($34,000 for unmarried individuals) will be liable for tax on up to 85% of their social security benefits. Under the prior law, only up to 50% of social security benefits were subject to tax. For more information, see Chapter 31, *How to Figure Your Tax.*

Medicare Tax

The dollar limit on wages and self-employment income subject to the 1.45% Medicare tax (2.9% for self-employed individuals) will be eliminated for wages and other earned income starting in 1994. For 1993, the Medicare tax did not apply to wages and other earned income above $135,000.

Business Meals and Entertainment

The deductible portion of business meals and entertainment expenses is 50% starting in 1994. The deductible limit in 1993 was 80%. For more information, see Chapter 28, *Car Expenses and Other Employee Business Expenses.*

Charitable Contributions

If you make a contribution of $250 or more in 1994, you generally must have a written acknowledgement from the organization in order to deduct the contribution. Your cancelled check will not be sufficient. See Chapter 25, *Contributions.*

Moving Expense Deduction

Tougher rules for deducting moving expenses take effect in 1994. If you are contemplating a move for business reasons, see Chapter 27, *Moving Expenses.*

Passive Activity Losses

Beginning in 1994, active real estate professionals (defined as working more than half of their time in real estate with a minimum of 750 hours and at least a 5% ownership in their employer if they are an employee) are able to offset passive losses against all of their income. See Chapter 13, *Other Income,* for further information.

III. More Tax Strategies for 1994 and Beyond

A traditional strategy is to try to defer income from one year to the next whenever possible. However, in some cases, if you expect to be in a higher tax bracket next year or are subject to the AMT this year, you may benefit from an opposite strategy. With certain exceptions, the switching of income between years is somewhat more difficult for the average taxpayer than the switching of deductions. This is because, under the tax law, income must generally be recognized in the year in which you acquire an unrestricted right to its use. Here's a list of some options that you may want to consider.

Automobiles. If you are an employee who must use your automobile for business purposes, consider leasing the automobile. In this way, the interest element of your lease payments may be deductible.

Capital Gains and Losses. With appropriate tax planning, you can realize significant tax benefits when recognizing capital gains and losses. You should keep in mind that transactions other than sales of stock or securities may also generate capital gains or losses. For example, a capital gain (but not a deductible loss) may result from the sale of a personal residence or from the sale of other personal assets such as valuable antiques or paintings.

Tax savings may frequently be achieved by taking year-end losses to offset gains previously realized or by realizing year-end gains to take advantage of previously incurred losses. The following points should be kept in mind in deciding both whether to enter into additional transactions and in deciding what to sell.

1. Since long-term gains are taxed at preferential rates, both long- and short-term capital losses will generally provide greater tax benefits when they are used to offset short-term gains.
2. A loss on the sale of stock or securities is not deductible if the seller has acquired substantially identical stock or securities within a period beginning 30 days before the date of sale and ending 30 days after the date of sale. A sale on such a loss which is disallowed under this rule is referred to as a "wash sale."
3. If a taxpayer owns two or more lots of the same stock or security which have different cost bases, different tax results may be achieved by proper identification of the lot sold.
4. Capital gains can be deferred from 1994 to 1995 by the use of short sales against the box or puts. See Chapter 15, *Sale of Property,* for further details.

Itemized Deductions

If your AGI exceeds a threshold amount ($108,450 for married filing jointly for 1993—the 1994 rate has not been set yet), the benefit of certain itemized deductions is phased out at the rate of 3% of your AGI in excess of the threshold. Medical expenses, casualty and theft losses, and investment interest expense are not subject to these rules, and in no case can the reduction be more than 80% of your otherwise allowable deductions. (Also, this limitation does not apply if you are subject to the alternative minimum tax.) This threshold is adjusted annually for inflation.

This limitation can represent more bad news to you if you have a significant amount of miscellaneous itemized deductions subject to the 2% of adjusted gross income floor. These miscellaneous itemized deductions are subject first to the 2% floor and then to the 3% limitation.

TAXPLANNER

If your tax bracket will be higher in 1994 than it will be in 1995, you need to consider whether or not you should accelerate your itemized deductions subject to the phaseout into 1994. As a general rule, you should try to move itemized deductions to years when your AGI will fall below the threshold amount. Note, however, that your itemized deductions could be limited even in years in which you show no *taxable* income, because the limitation is based on your AGI. Furthermore, you need to consider whether or not you will be subject to the AMT.

2% floor for other deductions. If your other miscellaneous deductions are close to the 2% floor, you should attempt to bunch these expenses in one year so that you can claim the maximum deduction. For example, you might have paid your 1993 tax return fee in 1994, but you also might want to pay for any 1994 tax advice that might not normally be billed until 1995 before December 31. By bunching deductions in this way, you might more easily reach the 2% floor and thus be able to deduct some of the cost of these expenses.

Interest Expense

In order to consider planning opportunities in this area, you must first divide your nonbusiness interest expense into four categories: (1) consumer interest, (2) mortgage interest, (3) investment interest, and (4) passive activity interest. The rules for the deductibility of interest expense vary among these four categories.

Consumer interest. Consumer interest includes interest on your personal automobile loan, tax deficiencies, student loans, insurance policies, and other loans used for personal purposes; it is not deductible.

It is generally more beneficial to eliminate any expense in the consumer interest expense category by:

• Paying off your consumer debt, if possible.
• Replacing consumer debt with debt that would fall into either the mortgage interest category or the investment interest category. For example, it may be possible to refinance your home to obtain additional funds to pay off consumer debt.

Before doing so, you should analyze the economics of the transaction. Refinancing to obtain a home equity loan will involve appraisal fees, financing fees, and other miscellaneous fees. Also, the interest expense may not be deductible for AMT purposes. You should consider obtaining a home equity loan under a line of credit arrangement if you believe that you may need additional funds in the future. This may allow you to incur all of the refinancing costs at one time instead of paying additional costs later, should you need to borrow additional money.

To obtain the full tax benefit from replacing consumer debt with a margin loan, you would have to sell the investment, pay off the consumer loan, and then repurchase the investment with a margin loan. In addition to weighing the tax consequences of the sale and the fees involved, you must remember that the investment interest expense category also has some limitations. Be sure to evaluate the interest rate, fees, and repayment terms of the margin loan.

If you have borrowed against your life insurance policy, the interest generally would be considered personal or consumer interest. If you can't pay off the loan, think about using a home equity loan to replace the life insurance policy loan or possibly exchanging the policy for another type in which smaller loans or no loans are involved. The economics of the transaction need to be carefully reviewed, since the interest rate on the policy loan may be lower than the after-tax rate of the replacement loan.

Mortgage interest. Generally, you can deduct interest attributed to a home equity loan on your principal or second residence of up to $100,000. The loan proceeds could be used for any personal purpose, and the interest expense would all be deductible as mortgage interest.

Investment interest. Generally, investment interest expense that exceeds the amount of your net investment income is not deductible. If you are not able to deduct all of your investment interest expense because of the net investment income limitation, make sure you maintain records that reflect that you have unused investment interest. Investment interest that is limited because of insufficient investment income can be carried forward and deducted in a year in which you have investment income.

Interest related to passive activity investments. The passive activity rules place limitations on the deductibility of passive activity interest. Passive activity interest expense is treated as a passive deduction, since it is related to a passive activity. For a detailed discussion of passive activity losses, see Chapter 13, *Other Income.*

Interest allocations. If you have borrowed money and have used the debt proceeds for various purposes, such as for both passive activities and personal expenditures, it is difficult to identify the type of interest expense. For this reason, you should avoid commingling borrowed funds with unborrowed funds. Separate bank accounts should be maintained for each activity when loans are involved. See Chapter 24, *Interest Expense,* for more information.

Tax-exempt securities. Consider whether tax-exempt income makes sense given your tax bracket and investment plan. Generally, the interest rates paid on tax-exempt state and local obligations are lower than those paid on taxable bonds. However, you may find these lower rates attractive when you compare them with the after-tax yield from taxable instruments. If you are in the 31% bracket, a 7% yield on a tax-exempt investment provides you with the same after-tax return of a taxable investment yielding 10.14%. If you are in a 40% bracket, a 7% yield is equivalent to a taxable investment yielding 11.67%.

U.S. Treasury securities. U.S. Treasuries have several beneficial characteristics. Though subject to federal income tax, the interest earned is exempt from state and local taxes. The interest on Treasury bills, short-term (up to one year) debt obligations of the U.S. Treasury, is taxable when the Treasury bill matures. If you buy a Treasury bill that matures next year, you can defer reporting interest from the date of purchase until the following year. Series EE bonds offer an attractive "tax-sheltered investment." If you do not elect to pay taxes on interest each year, the interest on the bonds is deferred and taxed when the bonds are either redeemed or reach final maturity. This allows you to select the most desirable taxable year to recognize the income.

Gifts. Making gifts to your children may not save as much income tax as it used to. However, giving gifts can still save some taxes. Giving gifts under a long-term plan is still one of the best ways to lower your estate tax.

IRAs. If you are eligible to make an IRA contribution, do so as early in the year as you can. The extra interest earned compounds rapidly.

Deferring interest income. Start planning now so that income from investments comes in 1995 and not in 1994. For example, you might purchase Treasury bills that are due in January or purchase bonds that pay interest in July and January.

Present value of money. Whenever you accelerate expenditures to save taxes, you should be aware of the potential earning power you lose by making an early payment.

Salary deferral. A salary deferral can be accomplished through an agreement with your employer prior to the time you perform the services, provided that your employer is willing to enter into such an arrangement. Also, consider maximizing contributions to your employer's 401(k) plan.

Worthless securities. Make sure that you examine your portfolio for any securities that might have become worthless and that you obtain appropriate documentation to support a worthless securities loss deduction.

Review your personal financial plan. Include in this review your estate and gift-giving plan, your insurance program, and your investment strategies. These matters should be reviewed periodically. It's never too late and certainly never too early. If your estate planning includes giving gifts to children who are in lower tax brackets, you should make your gifts early, so you can shift more income to them.

IV. Planning Your Estate

Chapter 4, *Decedents,* discusses what must be done when a person dies. This section, however, is very much for the living. It tells you how your estate tax will be calculated and gives you some ideas about estate planning. Most importantly, it clearly spells out the things that you should be aware of in planning your estate so that the least possible amount of tax will be paid.

Transfers of money or property during life or at death are subject to federal tax under the unified estate and gift tax system. A single, unified tax rate schedule assesses tax at progressively higher rates on the total of your lifetime gifts and transfers at death. Yet, you may never have to concern yourself with this unified tax on transfers. The law provides a "unified credit" to offset both gift and estate taxes. The unified credit effectively allows each individual to make up to $600,000 in gifts and bequests tax-free.

The federal estate tax is the tax the government levies on the transfer of property at death. It is paid by the estate of the decedent, not by the beneficiary or heir who may be receiving the property.

Certain key terms are necessary to understanding this tax:

Gross estate. Your gross estate is everything you own. It includes real estate (including your home), bank deposits, securities, and other personal property (car, jewelry, furniture, etc.). It may also include insurance, jointly held property, your interest in trusts, and the proceeds from your pension and profit-sharing plans.

Adjusted gross estate. Certain amounts may be deducted from your gross estate, including your outstanding debts at the time of your death, funeral costs, and expenses paid to administer your estate. The gross estate minus these deductions is called the adjusted gross estate.

Marital deduction. Your estate is entitled to an *unlimited* deduction for the value of property passing to your spouse. In effect, the marital deduction enables a couple to postpone estate taxes until the surviving spouse dies. Property will be deductible if it is left outright or passes through certain types of trusts to your spouse (see TaxPlanner 1, below).

The marital deduction is not allowed if the surviving spouse is not a U.S. citizen, unless the property passes to a special trust called a Qualified Domestic Trust. See your tax advisor if either you or your spouse is not a U.S. citizen.

Tax-free gifts. You may give away $10,000 per year tax-free—$20,000 if you are married and your spouse consents—to as many people as you want. If you exceed the annual per person limit, you owe gift tax. Gift tax liability may, however, be reduced or eliminated by the unified credit mentioned above and discussed in more detail below.

Exception. There are several instances when a gift of $10,000—$20,000 if you are married and your spouse consents—may not be completely tax-free. The most common exception is, if you make a gift of life insurance and die within 3 years of making the gift, your estate is subject to tax on the death benefit paid out by the policy.

Tax rates and credits. The federal estate and gift tax rate is progressive in nature and ranges from a marginal rate of 18% to 55% on total lifetime and estate transfers over $3 million. Usually, the lowest rate at which an estate or a gift may be taxed is 37%. The unified credit (discussed below) has the effect of eliminating all estate and gift tax on amounts that would be taxed below the 37% bracket.

A considerable chunk of your estate is exempt from taxation. Everyone is allowed a unified credit against the combined gift and estate taxes. The effect of the credit is to exempt $600,000 of property in an estate from taxation. These tax-free amounts are in addition to the unlimited number of $10,000 ($20,000 if you are married) gifts that you may give away tax-free every year.

The graduated rates and the unified credit are phased out for estates consisting of property valued between $10,000,000 and $21,040,000.

In most circumstances, if your estate or the combined estate of you and your spouse is less than $600,000, you do not have to worry about estate tax planning. Your estate will not pay any tax at all. Many people do not think they have enough wealth to worry about estate planning. But you may be richer than you think. Your gross estate will include everything that you own, including death benefits paid out by life insurance you own and employee benefits. It would be wise to compile a complete inventory of all your assets. If your estate or the combined estate of you and your spouse is likely to exceed $600,000, you should consult your tax advisor.

Do You Need a Will?

Whether or not your estate will be more than $600,000, it is vital that you have a will. Without it, you are powerless to ensure that your estate will pass in desired amounts to those you intend to benefit. If you die without a will, that is, intestate,

your assets will be distributed according to state law, regardless of what you would have wished.

For example, state laws typically divide an intestate husband's property among his widow and children, even though he might have preferred that his wife have use of the entire estate during her life. And those children may receive their inheritance before they are mature enough to manage it wisely.

If you have adopted children, a will is particularly important to avoid protracted and expensive legal proceedings concerning your estate.

If you have minor children, a will gives you the ability to designate a guardian for your children. If there is no designated guardian, a state agency will be responsible for choosing the person who will raise your children.

Handling property unaffected by a will. Certain types of property you hold will pass by law outside of your will and are unaffected by it. For example, life insurance proceeds are paid to the beneficiaries named in the policy. Similarly, pension benefits are paid to the beneficiaries whose names are specified by you. And your share of property owned jointly with the right of survivorship will pass automatically to the surviving joint owner. If changed circumstances outdate these arrangements, making a will is not the remedy. Other changes, such as redesignating beneficiaries, will typically be needed.

Is your will current? An outdated will—one that no longer reflects your wishes or the current law—is little better than no will at all and may even be worse. Since you executed your will, have you married, divorced, or been widowed? Have you become a grandparent or settled on a favorite charity? Has the applicable law changed? (It frequently does.) See your tax advisor and attorney if any of these apply.

Estate planning tips

If it is likely your estate will exceed $600,000, the following estate planning tips should be considered.

TaxPlanner 1

Leaving property to your spouse. You can select from a variety of techniques to transfer property to your surviving spouse that will qualify for the unlimited marital deduction. These methods allow you to choose the degree of control you want your spouse to have over property inherited from your estate.

Outright transfer. You can leave property outright to your spouse in your will. He or she will also automatically inherit full ownership of any property that the two of you hold jointly with the right of survivorship. In either case, your spouse will have absolute ownership of the assets received and may do with them as he or she wishes. An outright transfer gives your spouse the greatest flexibility to react to changing circumstances after your death. On the other hand, outright transfers leave the deceased spouse with the least amount of control over his or her property.

Marital deduction trust. The marital deduction trust can be used to give you more control over assets while still qualifying for the marital deduction. The trust must pay all of its income to the surviving spouse at least once a year. The spouse must have the power to determine who ultimately will receive the property, including his or her own estate.

Why use a marital deduction trust? The major reason is that a decedent can appoint a trustee to control and manage property transferred during the surviving spouse's lifetime.

Qualified Terminable Interest Property Trust (QTIP trust). The QTIP trust offers you the greatest amount of control over property transferred to your spouse, while still qualifying for the marital deduction. By using this trust, you can limit or even eliminate your spouse's access to trust principal, and you hold the sole right to designate the ultimate recipients of your assets. However, the trust is obligated to pay out all of its income (at least annually) *exclusively* to your surviving spouse *for life*. No exceptions are permitted.

The QTIP trust can be particularly appropriate when stock of a family business is involved and a family member other than the surviving spouse is active in the company. A QTIP trust is also a convenient way to assure your spouse adequate income during his or her life, while at the same time ensuring that your assets ultimately go to your children. Thus, if your spouse remarries after your death, your children could be assured that they will eventually be the beneficiaries of your estate.

For many, bequeathing property directly to a surviving spouse can effectively accomplish your objectives. An outright bequest is less cumbersome and saves administrative costs over transferring property through a trust. However, marital and QTIP trusts enable the decedent to control the management of property after his or her death and/or its ultimate distribution. Consult your tax advisor to see which method best meets your needs.

TaxPlanner 2

Be sure both spouses use up their own $600,000 exemptions. Many married couples have prepared "mirror" wills; that is, if the husband dies first, everything goes to the wife, and vice versa. Property transferred under this arrangement will qualify for the unlimited marital deduction. As a result, the estate tax on the estate of the first spouse to die is reduced to zero.

At first glance, this looks like effective tax planning. But for couples with assets totalling over $600,000, just using the marital deduction to eliminate the estate tax on the death of the first spouse may ultimately result in substantially higher estate taxes owed—up to nearly $200,000 more—when the surviving spouse dies.

This occurs because the first spouse has not taken advantage of the ability to pass up to $600,000 tax-free to beneficiaries other than the surviving spouse. Using the marital deduction does not permanently wipe out estate tax due on the assets owned by the first spouse to die. Instead, it merely *postpones* the payment of the tax until the death of the surviving spouse.

The solution is to be sure that each spouse fully utilizes his or her own $600,000 unified credit equivalent before using the marital deduction; that is, you should leave property worth $600,000 to those beneficiaries you intend to receive the property after your spouse's death. No estate tax will be due on these assets at your death because of the unified credit, and no tax will be due at your spouse's death, since the property will not be included in his or her estate.

If you want your spouse to be able to live off these assets, you can arrange for the property to be transferred to a trust that can pay out income to your surviving spouse for as long as you wish. You can even permit your spouse limited access to the trust's principal. This often-used device is called a "bypass" trust, because the property it holds, along with any appreciation and accumulated income, will bypass taxation in the surviving spouse's estate.

With proper planning, each spouse's unified credit can be used to transfer a total of $1.2 million of property, with no estate tax being paid at either spouse's death.

TaxPlanner 3

Shrinking your estate by making lifetime gifts. Most people have a difficult time parting with money, but the way in which the tax laws work, you're better off giving money away while you're still alive than letting the government take some of it after you die.

Since you may give away $10,000 a year—$20,000 if you're married and your spouse consents—to any person and not pay gift tax, you may, over a number of years, remove substantial amounts of property from your estate without paying taxes on it.

In addition to the $10,000 ($20,000 if you and your spouse agree) annual exclusion, you can make *unlimited* payments for another person's education or medical expenses free from gift tax. A wealthy grandparent, for example, could significantly reduce the size of his or her estate tax-free by paying the tuition bills for all of the grandchildren. Be careful, though—to qualify for this unlimited gift tax exclusion, the donor must pay the school or health care provider directly. Also, eligible educational expenses include tuition only; room, board, and other fees do not qualify. Other income tax complications may apply if the payments satisfy a parental support obligation.

Transferring appreciated property by gift before death may not always be a good idea. If you make a gift of property that has appreciated in value to your children, their cost basis in the property will be the same as your cost basis in the property plus any gift tax you pay on the appreciation. If they sell the property, they will have to report a capital gain and, in all likelihood, pay a tax on that gain. However, if the property were transferred to your children upon your death, their cost basis in the property would be the property's fair market value at the time of death. The capital gains tax would never have to be paid.

On the other hand, it may be wise to make a gift of property that is likely to appreciate substantially in the future, even if you have to pay some gift tax. If the property increases in value after you have made the gift and before your death, you will have succeeded in removing all of the post-gift appreciation from your taxable estate.

TaxPlanner 4

How to deal with your life insurance policy. There is a widespread and mistaken belief that the proceeds of life insurance paid on account of death are not subject to estate tax. Ordinarily, these proceeds are included in your estate. If they are paid to your spouse, the marital deduction is available and so there will be no tax.

If the proceeds are to be paid to someone else, estate tax may be avoided by making a gift of the ownership of the policy, either to the beneficiary or to an irrevocable trust while you are still alive. By making a gift of your life insurance policy, you can avoid the estate taxes applicable to the proceeds, which, at a minimum, would be taxed at a 37% rate.

It's better to act sooner than later. If you die within 3 years of transferring the life insurance policy, the proceeds of the insurance are taxable to your estate.

If you make a gift of your life insurance policy, the value of the policy (not the face amount but the value of the policy as determined by the insurance company) qualifies for the annual gift tax exclusion of up to $10,000 (or $20,000 if you're married), explained earlier in this chapter. It's possible to give the policy away in trust and still qualify for the gift exclusion. Consult your tax advisor for details.

If you continue to pay the premiums on a policy that you have given as a gift, you will be making a gift each time you make a payment, since the obligation to pay the premium is on the owner of the policy. Under certain circumstances, these annual payments of the premium can qualify for the $10,000 gift tax exclusion ($20,000 if you're married). Consult your tax advisor.

TAXPLANNER 5

Joint tenancy—a tax trap? Holding title to property as joint tenants with the right of survivorship is a popular form of property ownership. If a husband and wife own property as joint tenants, one-half of the property is included in the estate of the first to die. There is no estate tax, since the property qualifies for the marital deduction. But there might be some unfavorable income and estate tax consequences.

Example 1

John and Mary are married. They own stock in joint tenancy. The stock cost $1,000 and is now worth $101,000.

John dies. On his death, Mary becomes the sole owner of the stock, since it was held in joint tenancy. Mary's basis in the stock is $51,000 [one-half of the fair market value ($50,500) plus one-half of the original cost ($500)]. If she sells the stock for $101,000, she has a gain of $50,000.

The tax situation would have been quite different if John had owned the stock in his name only. The basis in the stock would then have been $101,000, its fair market value at the time of his death. If Mary sold the stock at that price, there would be no gain to report and thus no tax to pay.

Of course, if John owned the stock in his name only and *Mary* died first, his basis would remain at $1,000. If the stock had been held in joint tenancy, John's basis in the stock would be $51,000.

Example 2

John and Mary have $1.2 million in assets, all of which are held in joint tenancy.

John dies. On his death, Mary becomes the sole owner of all the assets. Mary subsequently dies. Upon her death, her estate will pay tax on the amount in excess of the $600,000 unified credit equivalent. Mary and John and their heirs might have been better off if they had set up a unified credit shelter (bypass) trust. (See TaxPlanner 2 for details.)

TAXPLANNER 6

Use of the Uniform Gift to Minors Act. Gifts to minors are often made by using a state's Uniform Gifts to Minors Act. A custodian is appointed to deal with the property until the child reaches the age of majority—usually 18 or 21, depending on state law.

Many individuals making such gifts have appointed themselves as custodian. This is not always a good idea. If the donor/custodian dies before the child reaches the age of majority, the entire value of the property at the date of death is included in the decedent's estate. If, however, the custodian is not the donor, the property is not included in the donor's estate. Consider appointing a spouse, a relative, or a trusted friend as custodian.

TAXPLANNER 7

Using a revocable living trust. Setting up a revocable living trust can add flexibility to your financial plan and cut the costs of administering your estate. A living trust is created during your lifetime, and all of the assets placed into it remain fully subject to your control. You keep the right to take the property as you wish.

Since you control the entire trust, the property held in it will be included in your gross estate. Also, you are taxed on all income earned in the trust. In essence, there are no tax advantages gained by establishing revocable trusts. But there can be some financial and administrative benefits, including the following:

Avoiding probate. Living trust assets pass to the beneficiaries you name in the trust document and are not controlled by your will. This cuts out the costs and delays arising from the probate process. And, unlike probate, the identity and instructions for distributing estate property are not part of the public record. Your privacy is maintained.

Relief from financial responsibility. If you desire, you can use an independent trustee to relieve you of the details of managing your property and investments, recordkeeping chores, and preparation and filing of income tax returns. An "agency account," for example, managed by a bank trust department can do these things, too, but it does not provide the other benefits of using a revocable trust.

Avoiding legal guardianship. If you become incapacitated, the assets kept in your living trust can be managed automatically by a trustee you named in the trust document. Otherwise, the determination of whether, and to what extent, you are disabled or incompetent and who is going to handle your affairs could be left to public, and potentially costly, guardianship proceedings. (Note that a durable power of attorney can also be an effective tool for prearranging the management of your affairs in the event you become incapacitated. See the checklist at the end of this chapter.)

Other considerations. Living trusts come with some drawbacks and are not suited to everyone. For one thing, expect to pay legal fees and other expenses, such as recording fees and possibly transfer taxes, to set the trust up and transfer property to it. You will also owe recurring trustee and administrative charges if you use a corporate trustee in lieu of managing the trust yourself.

Probate cost savings may not be dramatic. With the adoption of streamlined probate procedures in many states, probate for a variety of estates can be completed more easily and less expensively than in the past, often without an attorney, and with little or no court supervision.

Moreover, using a living trust will not necessarily save on other legal, accounting, and executor's fees paid to handle your estate. After all, whether your assets are held in a living trust or pass through probate, the same sort of work will generally be needed to value your assets, prepare federal and state tax returns, settle creditors' claims, and resolve disputes among beneficiaries.

Consult your tax advisor to see if a living trust makes sense for you.

TAXPLANNER 8

A charitable bequest that reduces your taxes while you are alive. Your estate will receive an unlimited estate tax deduction for any money or property you bequeath to charity. If you are planning to make a bequest to charity, here is a way in which you can cut future estate taxes *and* get an immediate income tax break while you are still alive. It is called a "charitable remainder trust."

Suppose you plan to leave $50,000 to your college in your will. Instead, consider setting up a $50,000 trust fund today. The trust provides a yearly payment to you of a percentage of the value of the trust property. After you die, whatever property is in the trust goes to your college.

Even though the college won't get the money until after you die, you are entitled to a *current* income tax deduction for part of the value of the property that you placed in the trust. The amount of your current deduction is based on tables published by the government.

Example
You are 65 years old. You put $50,000 into a charitable remainder trust. The trust makes an annual $4,000 payment to you for the rest of your life. After your death, the proceeds of the trust are turned over to your community hospital. Based on currently applicable IRS tables, you are able to deduct approximately $12,300 on your income tax return in the year in which you fund the trust.

Once you create the trust, you may not change it. You receive the payment you specified whether the trust earns more or less than that amount.

A note of caution: This is a very technical and complex area. Consult your tax advisor, and be sure you have a complete understanding of the pros and cons of this type of arrangement.

TaxPlanner 9

Where should you be domiciled? Your estate can be taxed by the state in which you are domiciled. Your rights in property and the rules that govern the transfer of your property at death are largely determined by the state in which you are domiciled. Domicile is a legal concept used to identify where you live and the place where you intend to come back to if you are temporarily absent. Indications of where you are domiciled include where you are registered to vote, where you have your driver's license, and where you have a permanent home.

Some states have community property laws that apply to property acquired during a marriage. Generally, in community property states, each spouse has a vested interest in one-half of the family property. Community property laws are different for each state in which they are in effect. If you live in a community property state, you should consult your lawyer.

Different states have different types of inheritance taxes. Some states, like California, Illinois, and Florida, have "pick-up" taxes: The state tax on your estate is figured by picking up the so-called state death tax credit, the credit that the federal government allows against your federal estate tax. There is no *extra* cost to your estate, since payment of the state tax produces a credit against the federal tax.

Other states, like New York, compute state death taxes separately. These state taxes are often more but never less than a pick-up tax.

People with two homes may be able to establish their domicile in a state with only a pick-up tax. You should consult your attorney and/or tax advisor.

TaxPlanner 10

Other taxes. In addition to the regular estate and gift taxes discussed above, additional taxes may be imposed on excess accumulations in your qualified retirement plan and on transfers you make to individuals two generations or more younger than you. You should consult your tax advisor if you think that you might be subject to one or both of these taxes.

A Checklist of Actions to Consider

- Compile a schedule listing the location of all important financial and legal documents, and inform your spouse and other appropriate persons of its location.
- Have a will prepared for you and your spouse or have your current wills reviewed to see if they still reflect your wishes and current law.
- Be sure information about the location of your safe-deposit box and other important keys is up to date in your list of important documents. Keep the *original* of your will in your safe-deposit box and a copy with your other documents.
- Be sure your spouse, or whomever you designate as the executor of your estate, knows your attorney, accountant, trust officer, broker, insurance advisor, and other appropriate advisors.
- Review whom you have chosen to be the beneficiary of your retirement plans (including IRAs) and life insurance.
- Compile and keep up-to-date information on the cost and approximate purchase date of all your assets, including your residence.
- Execute a durable power of attorney, authorizing your spouse or other appropriate person to act on your behalf when necessary because of your illness, incapacity, or absence.
- Execute a letter apart from your will that states how you would like to dispose of your personal effects that have sentimental value. Using a letter allows you to update your plans or change your mind *without going to the expense of changing your will.* It can also assist your executor in the administering of your estate.
- If you don't want your life to be prolonged by artificial means in the event of a terminal illness, an attorney can draft a "living will" for you. These documents, however, are not legally binding in every state.
- If you wish to make a donation of your body or certain organs for transplantation or medical research, consider completing a Uniform Donor Card. Make sure that your family knows your wishes and where to locate the card.

Personal Records and Advisors

An integral aspect of personal financial planning is to document the location of important personal records and to identify who your advisors are. By condensing this information into one readily available list, you will be providing necessary and important data for your family or personal representative. After you have completed the following, you should retain a copy in a safe location at your home and office. In addition, it would be advisable to disclose the location of these lists to a family member or advisor. Include the name of the contact person, addresses, and telephone numbers for each category.

1) Location of your safe-deposit box and keys.

_____

_____

2) Location of your will, codicils, and trust agreements.

_____

_____

3) Location of the will, codicils, and trust agreements of your spouse.

_____

_____

4) Location of insurance policies.

_____

_____

5) Location of stock certificates and bonds.

_____

_____

6) Location of IRA and Keogh documents.

_____

_____

7) Location of real estate records: deed, mortgage, title insurance, closing statements, building costs, leases.

_____

_____

8) Location of automobile titles.

_____

_____

9) Location of income tax returns for the last 4 years.

_____

_____

10) Location of gift tax returns filed.

_____

_____

11) Attorney

Name _____

Address _____

_____

Telephone (   ) _____

12) Accountant

Name _____

Address _____

_____

Telephone (   ) _____

13) Insurance advisor

Name _____

Address _____

_____

Telephone (   ) _____

14) Investment advisor

Name _____

Address _____

_____

_____

Name _____

Address _____

_____

Telephone (   ) _____

VI | Sample Returns and Federal Tax Forms

The chapters in this part give examples of filled-in tax returns and provide you with forms, schedules, and tables you can use. Chapter 43 illustrates Form 1040EZ. Chapter 44 illustrates Form 1040A with the schedules that you may need to fill out and file with it. Chapter 45 illustrates Form 1040 with many of the schedules and forms that may need to be filled out and filed with it. Chapter 46 provides 1993 tax forms that you can fill out in preparing your tax return. The final chapter includes the tax tables and tax rate schedules that you need to complete your tax return.

43 | Sample Form 1040EZ

Introduction

Form 1040EZ is the simplest tax form available, but only single and joint filers with no dependents and who are not blind or over 65 can even consider using it. To use Form 1040EZ your taxable income needs to be less than $50,000 and only from wages, salaries, and tips, and from interest of $400 or less; you cannot claim any itemized deductions, adjustments to income, or tax credits. See Chapter 1, Filing Information, for more information.

The sample return that follows illustrates how the form can be used. Note, however, that even though it may be easier to file Form 1040EZ, it may not necessarily be your best course of action—especially if you may be entitled to claim some additional deductions.

Even if your situation is covered in this sample return, you may profit from reading the relevant sections in this book indicated by the circled page references. The examples presented by the IRS ordinarily use facts that are either very straightforward or favorable to the IRS interpretation of the law. They do little to reveal the real ambiguity that pervades much of our tax laws.

Pat Brown is single and has no dependents. She is 22 years old and a full-time student at State University where she has a scholarship which covers her tuition and $500 of her room and board. Her parents are able to claim her as a dependent. In January of this year, she received her Form W–2 which shows she earned $1,850 in wages and had $250 in Federal tax withheld during 1993. She also received a Form 1099–INT showing she had $277 in interest income for 1993. Pat filed Form 1040EZ in 1992, so the IRS sent her the Form 1040EZ tax package. Since she meets all the requirements for using Form 1040EZ (see *Which Form Should I Use?* in Chapter 1, *Filing Information*), she decides to use it again for 1993.

To make processing her return quicker and to speed her refund, Pat prints (does not type) her numbers and keeps them inside the boxes on her Form 1040EZ. She does not use dollar signs.

Name, Address, and Social Security Number

Pat uses the mailing label that came with her forms package. The label has her name, address, and social security number. She checks the label to make sure it is correct. However, she does not put the label on her tax return until the return is completed and she is sure it is accurate.

Pat would use the label even if some of the information on it was incorrect. She would make the necessary changes directly on the label and then place it on her completed return.

Presidential Election Campaign Fund. Pat wants $3 of her taxes to go to this fund, so she checks the first "Yes" box. Checking "Yes" will not change her tax or reduce her refund.

Filing Status

Pat is single so she checks the "Single" box on line 1.

Report Your Income

Pat has two items of income which must be combined and entered on line 2 of Form 1040EZ. The part of her scholarship that is for room and board ($500) is taxable. She adds this amount to her wages ($1,850), which are shown in Box 1 of her Form W–2. Pat enters the total ($2,350) on line 2. On line 3, she enters her interest income of $277. Pat has no tax-exempt interest, so she does not have to write "TEI" and show any amount to the left of line 3. She adds her wages, taxable scholarship, and interest together to figure her adjusted gross income of $2,627. She enters $2,627 on line 4.

Standard deduction and personal exemption. If Pat could not be claimed as a dependent by her parents or someone else, she would have a standard deduction amount of $3,700 and a personal exemption of $2,350. She would check the "No" box and enter $6,050 on line 5.

However, since she can be claimed as a dependent by her parents, Pat checks the "Yes" box on line 5. She uses the worksheet on the back of her Form 1040EZ to figure her standard deduction. Her completed worksheet is shown next. She enters the result ($2,350) on line 5.

| A. Enter the amount from line 2 on front. | A. | 2,350 |
| B. Minimum standard deduction. | B. | 600 |

C. Enter the LARGER of line A or line B here.   C.   2,350

D. Maximum standard deduction. If single, enter $3,700; if married, enter $6,200.   D.   3,700

E. Enter the SMALLER of the line C or line D here. This is your standard deduction.   E.   2,350

F. Exemption amount.

- If single, enter 0.

- If married and both you and your spouse can be claimed as dependents, enter 0.

- If married and only one of you can be claimed as a dependent, enter $2,350.   F.   0

G. Add lines E and F. Enter the total here and on line 5 on the front.   G.   2,350

Note. Because Pat checked the "Yes" box on line 5, and because her parents can claim her as a dependent on their own tax return, she cannot claim an exemption for herself.

Pat subtracts line 5 ($2,350) from line 4 ($2,627) and enters the result of $277 on line 6. This amount is Pat's taxable income. She will figure her income tax on this amount.

Figure Your Tax

Pat had $250 of Federal income tax withheld from her wages by her employer. She found this amount in Box 2 of her 1993 Form W–2. She enters this amount on line 7 of Form 1040EZ.

Note. If Pat wanted the IRS to compute her tax for her, she would stop at this point. She would make sure lines 1 through 7 were accurately completed. Then she would enter her occupation, sign and date the return.

Pat decides to figure the tax herself. She takes the amount on line 6, her taxable income of $277, and goes to the Tax Table. She reads down the income column of the Tax Table until she finds the line that includes her taxable income shown on line 6 of her Form 1040EZ.

She reads across the line to find the Single column. The amount shown at the point where the income line and the filing status column meet is her tax ($43).

She enters this amount on line 8 of her Form 1040EZ.

Refund or Amount You Owe

Pat compares line 7 and line 8. Since line 7 is larger, she subtracts line 8 ($43) from line 7 ($250) to arrive at her refund of $207. She enters this amount on line 9. Pat will receive a tax refund of $207.

If her employer had not withheld any Federal income tax from her wages, Pat would have owed $43 in income tax. She would have been instructed to enter that amount on line 10. She would then attach a check or money order for the full amount of $43, payable to "Internal Revenue Service." She would write on the front of her check or money order:

Her name,
Her address,
Her social security number,
Her daytime telephone number, and
"1993 Form 1040EZ."

Sign Your Return

Pat goes back over her return to make sure that she entered the numbers clearly and correctly and that she did the math correctly.

Pat enters her occupation, and signs and dates her return in the spaces provided at the bottom of the form. Now that she has filled in her Form 1040EZ, she takes her pre-printed mailing label from the front of her forms package and places it in the address portion at the top of her return. She attaches Copy B of her Form W–2 to the location indicated on the front of Form 1040EZ.

She makes a copy of her filled-in tax return for her records. Then she mails her return to the Service Center in the envelope that came with her forms package.

A filled-in copy of Pat's return follows.

Form **1040EZ**

Department of the Treasury—Internal Revenue Service

Income Tax Return for Single and Joint Filers With No Dependents (T) **1993**

(16)

OMB No. 1545-0675

Use the IRS label (See page 10.) Otherwise, please print.

LABEL HERE

CAR-RT SORT**CR01
PB 571-00-4684 S29 21
PAT A BROWN
3408 UNION ST
HOMETOWN MD 21214

(16) **Your social security number**

Spouse's social security number (16)

(17) **See instructions on back and in Form 1040EZ booklet.**

Presidential Election Campaign (See page 11.)

Note: Checking "Yes" will not change your tax or reduce your refund.

	Yes	No
Do you want $3 to go to this fund? ▶	✓	
If a joint return, does your spouse want $3 to go to this fund? ▶		

(16)

Filing status (28) 1 ☑ Single (29) ☐ Married filing joint return (even if only one had income)

	Line	Dollars	Cents
Report your income — **2** Total wages, salaries, and tips. This should be shown in box 1 of your W-2 form(s). Attach your W-2 form(s). (102) (89) (81)	2	2,350	00
3 Taxable interest income of $400 or less. If the total is over $400, you cannot use Form 1040EZ. (108)	3	277	00
4 Add lines 2 and 3. This is your **adjusted gross income.** (471)	4	2,627	00
5 Can your parents (or someone else) claim you on their return? ☑ **Yes.** Do worksheet on back; enter amount from line G here. ☐ **No.** If **single,** enter 6,050.00. If **married,** enter 10,900.00. For an explanation of these amounts, see back of form. (317)	5	2,350	00
6 Subtract line 5 from line 4. If line 5 is larger than line 4, enter 0. This is your **taxable income.** (471)	6	277	00
Figure your tax — (65) **7** Enter your Federal income tax withheld from box 2 of your W-2 form(s).	7	250	00
8 **Tax.** Look at line 6 above. Use the amount on **line 6** to find your tax in the tax table on pages 24–28 of the booklet. Then, enter the tax from the table on this line.	8	43	00
Refund or amount you owe — (18) **9** If line 7 is larger than line 8, subtract line 8 from line 7. This is your **refund.**	9	207	00
(19) **10** If line 8 is larger than line 7, subtract line 7 from line 8. This is the **amount you owe.** For details on how to pay, including what to write on your payment, see page 16.	10		

Attach Copy B of Form(s) W-2 here. Attach any tax payment on top of Form(s) W-2.

Note: *You **must** check Yes or No.*

Sign your return (18) Keep a copy of this form for your records.

I have read this return. Under penalties of perjury, I declare that to the best of my knowledge and belief, the return is true, correct, and accurately lists all amounts and sources of income I received during the tax year.

Your signature		Spouse's signature if joint return	
Pat A. Brown			
Date	**Your occupation**	**Date**	**Spouse's occupation**
2-15-94	Student		

For IRS Use Only — Please do not write in boxes below.

For Privacy Act and Paperwork Reduction Act Notice, see page 4. Cat. No. 11329W Form 1040EZ (1993)

44 | Sample Form 1040A

Form 1040A has been expanded.

The expanded 1040A now lets you report pension and annuity payments, taxable social security and railroad retirement benefits, and payments from your IRA. It also allows you to claim a deduction for contributions to an IRA and lets you claim the credit for the elderly or the disabled, take credit for your estimated tax payments, and make an election to apply all or part of your 1993 refund to your 1994 estimated tax.

Even if your situation is covered in this sample return, you may profit from reading the relevent sections in this book indicated by the circled page references. The examples presented by the IRS ordinarily use facts that are either very straightforward or favorable to the IRS interpretation of the law. They do little to reveal the real ambiguity that pervades much of our tax laws.

Don and Jean Smith are a married couple with two young children. Don worked full time as a carpenter during 1993. Jean worked full time as a secretary until September when she was laid off. She received a distribution from her company's profit-sharing plan and also received unemployment compensation. Their 10-month-old son, Todd, went to a day-care center while both were working. Their 7-year-old daughter, Lynn, stayed with a neighbor before and after school.

The Smiths filed Form 1040A for 1992 so the IRS sent them the Form 1040A tax package this year. Since they meet all the requirements for using Form 1040A (see *Which Form Should I Use?* in Chapter 1, *Filing Information*), they decide to use it again for 1993.

Their filled-in Form 1040A is shown at the end of this chapter.

Name, Address, and Social Security Number

Don and Jean use the label that came with their forms package. The label has their names, address, and social security numbers. They check the label to make sure it is correct, but they do not put it on the return until they have completed and checked the return to make sure it is accurate. Because they use the label, their tax return can be processed faster.

The Smiths should use the label even if some of the information on it is incorrect. They would make any necessary changes directly on the label.

Presidential Election Campaign Fund. Don and Jean each want $3 of their tax to go to this fund. They check both *Yes* boxes. Checking *Yes* does not increase their tax or reduce their refund.

Filing Status

Don and Jean must choose their filing status before they figure their tax liability.

Filing status (lines 1–5). Don and Jean check the box on line 2 to file a joint return. Because they are married and living together, they must file a joint return in order to claim the child care credit.

Exemptions

Don and Jean must indicate the number of exemptions they can claim.

Exemptions (lines 6a–e). Don and Jean can take two personal exemptions, one for each of them. They check these exemptions in the boxes on lines 6a and 6b and enter the total,"2", on the line at the right. On line 6c, column 1, they write their children's names and enter"2" on the line "lived with you" at the right.

They have to enter the social security number for any dependent who is at least 1 year old. They write Lynn's social security number in column 3. Because Todd was not yet 1 at the end of 1993, they put a checkmark in column 2 by his name. They write their children's relationship to them (daughter and son) in column 4. They enter "12" in column 5 for each child since their daughter lived with them all year and their son was born during the year. They do not have any other dependents, so in the box on line 6e they enter "4" as the total number of exemptions.

Total Income

Don and Jean report their income on **lines 7–13b** and total it on **line 14.**

Wages (line 7). Don's Form W–2, *Wage and Tax Statement,* shows he earned $22,250 in 1993. Jean's Form W–2 shows she earned $12,155. They find these amounts in box 1 of their Forms W–2 (shown later). They add the amounts and put the total, $34,405, on line 7.

Interest income (lines 8a–b and Part I of Schedule 1). Don and Jean received a statement (Form 1099–INT) from their bank showing they earned $410 of taxable interest income last year. Because their interest income is over $400, they must list the name of the bank and the amount received in Part I of Schedule 1. They also enter this amount on line 8a of Form 1040A. They also received $35 of tax-exempt interest from a municipal bond. They enter $35 on line 8b. This amount does not increase their taxable income.

Dividends (line 9). Don and Jean opened an account in a mutual fund last year. They received a statement (Form 1099–DIV) from the fund showing they earned dividends of $20. They also received a Form 1099–DIV from the XYZ Corporation showing they earned dividends of $80 last year. Because the total amount of their dividends is not over $400, they do not have to list them in Part II of Schedule 1. They enter the total amount of their dividends, $100, on line 9 of Form 1040A.

Pensions (lines 11a–b). Jean received Form 1099–R, *Distributions From Pensions, Annuities, Retirement or Profit-Sharing Plans, IRAs, Insurance Contracts, etc.* from her employer's profit-sharing plan showing a distribution of $2,250 in box 1. Box 2a shows -0- and box 7 shows Code **G.** Her Form 1099–R is shown later.

Before the distribution was made, Jean received an explanation from the plan administrator that advised her that the distribution would be tax free with no withholding if she elected a direct rollover into an IRA. Jean, age 40, made the election, and the plan administrator directly transferred the entire amount of the distribution into her IRA account. This transfer qualifies as a tax-free rollover under the rules described in Chapter 11, *Retirement Plans, Pensions and Annuities*.

Jean reports $2,250 on line 11a and $0 on line 11b. Because she rolled over the entire distribution into her IRA, Jean does not have to file Form 5329 or pay the 10% tax on early distributions.

Unemployment compensation (line 12). Jean received Form 1099–G, *Certain Government Payments,* from her state, showing $1,010 in unemployment compensation. She enters this amount on line 12.

Nontaxable income. Don and Jean also received a Form 1099–G showing a 1992 state tax refund they received in 1993. Because they did not itemize deductions on their 1992 federal return, they do not report the refund as income in 1993. If they had itemized, part or all of the refund may have had to be included in income.

Total (line 14). Their total income is the sum of the amounts shown on lines 7, 8a, 9, and 12. Don and Jean add these lines and enter the total, $35,925, on line 14.

Adjusted Gross Income

Don and Jean figure their **adjusted gross income** on **lines 15 and 16.**

IRA deduction (lines 15a–c). In 1993, Don contributed $750 to his IRA and Jean contributed $650 to hers. Jean also contributed an additional $100 to her IRA in January 1994 and asked that it be counted for 1993. They complete lines 1–3 of *IRA worksheet 1* (as shown later) in their forms instruction package to figure how much of their contributions they can deduct. The entire amount of their contributions to both IRAs is deductible. They enter $750 for Don

on line 15a and $750 for Jean on line 15b. The sum of their IRA contributions to both IRAs, $1,500, is entered on line 15c.

Adjusted gross income (line 16). Don and Jean subtract their total IRA deduction on line 15c from their total income on line 14. They enter the result, $34,425, on line 16 and on line 17. This amount is their adjusted gross income. Since it is not less than $23,050, they do not qualify for the earned income credit.

Taxable Income

Don and Jean figure their **taxable income** on **lines 17–22. Standard deduction (lines 18a–c and 19).** Lines 18a–c do not apply to either Don or Jean. They enter their standard deduction amount of $6,200 (see Chapter 20, *Standard Deduction*) on line 19. They subtract their standard deduction on line 19 from their adjusted gross income on line 17 and enter the result, $28,225, on line 20.

Exemptions (line 21). Then, Don and Jean deduct $2,350 for each exemption shown on line 6e. They multiply $2,350 by 4 (the number of exemptions shown on line 6e) and enter the result, $9,400, on line 21. They subtract the amount on line 21 ($9,400) from the amount on line 20 ($28,225) and put the difference, $18,825 on line 22. This amount is their taxable income.

Tax, Credits, and Payments

Next, Don and Jean figure their tax liability.

Tax (line 23). Don and Jean use the Tax Table in the 1040A instructions to find their tax. The Smiths' taxable income from line 22 is $18,825. Don and Jean first look for the large print" **18,000** " in the table. Under this, they look down to the line for taxable income of at least 18,800, but less than 18,850. Their taxable income is between these two amounts. They then find their tax, $2,824, in the column for married filing jointly. They put this amount on line 23 and check the box for "Tax Table."

Credit for child and dependent care expenses (line 24a and Schedule 2). Don and Jean paid $3,325 of qualified expenses for the time both of them worked in 1993. Their son, Todd, went full time to a day-care center. The cost for his care was $2,325. Their daughter, Lynn, was cared for by a neighbor before and after school. The neighbor also cared for the children when school and the day care center were not in session. They paid the neighbor $1,000. Their employers did not provide any dependent care benefits.

Don and Jean prepare Parts I and II of Schedule 2. They enter the names, addresses, and taxpayer identification numbers (employer identification number and social security number) of the day-care

IRA worksheet 1—Lines 15a and 15b (keep for your records)

		(a) Your IRA	(b) Your working spouse's IRA
1.	Enter IRA contributions you made, or will make by April 15, 1994, for 1993. But **do not** enter more than $2,000 in either column. 1.	750	750
2.	Enter wages, salaries, and tips for each person from Form 1040A, line 7. 2.	22,250	12,155
3.	Enter the **smaller** of line 1 or line 2. Enter on Form 1040A, line 15a, the amount from line 3, column (a). Enter on Form 1040A, line 15b, the amount, if any, from line 3, column (b). If filing a joint return and contributions were made to your nonworking spouse's IRA, go to line 4. 3.	750	750

center and the neighbor who provided the care on line 1, columns a, b, and c.

The Smiths enter the amounts they paid to the child-care providers on line 1, column d, and enter the total of these amounts, $3,325, on line 2. Because they had qualified expenses for two children, they enter "2" in the box for line 3. On line 4 they enter the amount of qualified expenses, $3,325, they paid when both parents were working. On line 5, Don enters his earned income; on line 6, Jean enters her earned income. Because their child-care expenses were less than Jean's earned income and less than Don's earned income, all the expenses can be used to figure the credit. So they enter $3,325 on line 7. They enter their adjusted gross income from Form 1040A, line 17 ($34,425) on line 8. Then they check the table for line 9 to see what percentage of their child care expenses they can take as a credit.

Since the Smiths' adjusted gross income on line 17 of Form 1040A is $34,425, they can take 20% of $3,325, or $665, as their credit. They put .20 on line 9 and $665 on line 10. They have no tax-exempt interest from private activity bonds, so their credit is not limited and they do not complete the credit limit worksheet. They enter $665 on line 24a of Form 1040A. Because their credit is less than their tax, they can use all of it to reduce their income tax liability.

Total tax (line 27). Don and Jean leave line 24b blank because they do not claim a credit for the elderly or the disabled. They subtract their total credits on line 24c ($665) from the tax on line 23 ($2,824) and enter the difference, $2,159, on lines 25 and 27. The amount on line 27 is their total tax liability.

The Smiths do not complete the alternative minimum tax worksheet because:

1) Their adjusted gross income plus their tax-exempt interest income is not more than $45,000, and
2) They do not claim more than four exemptions.

Total payments (lines 28a–d). Don and Jean then check box 2 of their Forms W–2 and box 4 of Form 1099–R for the amount of federal income tax withheld from their income. Don's Form W–2 shows $1,756 tax withheld and Jean's Form W–2 shows $998 tax withheld. Jean's Form 1099–R shows no withholding. She elected not to have taxes withheld since the entire amount was rolled into her IRA account tax free. Tax was not withheld from Jean's unemployment compensation. The Smiths did not make any estimated tax payments for 1993. They are not entitled to the earned income credit on line 28c. Their total payments are $2,754. They enter this amount on lines 28a and 28d.

Refund or Amount You Owe

The tax withheld from the Smiths' wages is more than their total tax. They subtract their tax on line 27, $2,159, from their total payments shown on line 28d, $2,754, and enter the difference, $595, on lines 29 and 30. This is the amount that will be refunded to them.

If Don and Jean had not had at least $2,159 withheld for federal income tax, they would have owed tax. They would have entered the difference between their tax (line 27) and their payments (line 28d) on line 32. They would then attach a check or money order for the full amount owed (line 32), payable to "Internal Revenue Service." They would also make sure the following information is on the check:

Their names,
Their address,
Don's social security number (since his name and social security number are listed on the return first),
A daytime telephone number, and
"1993 Form 1040A."

Sign Your Return

Don and Jean sign and date their return and list their occupations. Then they check their return to make sure it is accurate and complete. They remove the mailing label from the forms package and put it in the address portion on the top of the form. Then they attach Copy B of their Forms W–2 to the location indicated on the front of their return.

They use the envelope that came with their forms package to mail their return to the service center. Don and Jean save a copy of the return for their records.

a Control number	Void ☐		
b Employer's identification number 10-1111111		1 Wages, tips, other compensation 22,250.00	2 Federal income tax withheld 1,756.00
c Employer's name, address, and ZIP code Woodworks Inc. 817 Highland Blvd. Hometown, MI 48001		3 Social security wages 22,250.00	4 Social security tax withheld 1,379.50
		5 Medicare wages and tips 22,250.00	6 Medicare tax withheld 322.63
		7 Social security tips	8 Allocated tips
d Employee's social security number 329-00-1000		9 Advance EIC payment	10 Dependent care benefits
e Employee's name, address, and ZIP code Don J. Smith 90 Beaver Court Hometown, MI 48001		11 Nonqualified plans	12 Benefits included in Box 1
		13 See Instrs. for Box 13	14 Other

15 Statutory employee ☐ Deceased ☐ Pension plan ☐ Legal rep ☐ 942 emp ☐ Subtotal ☐ Deferred compensation ☐

16 State Employer's state I.D. No MI 10-1111111	17 State wages, tips, etc 22,250.00	18 State income tax 882.00	19 Locality name	20 Local wages, tips, etc	21 Local income tax

Department of the Treasury—Internal Revenue Service

Form **W-2** Wage and Tax Statement **1993**

This information is being furnished to the Internal Revenue Service.

Copy B To Be Filed With Employee's FEDERAL Tax Return

OMB No 1545-0008

---

a Control number	Void ☐		
b Employer's identification number 10-0000000		1 Wages, tips, other compensation 12,155.00	2 Federal income tax withheld 998.00
c Employer's name, address, and ZIP code Mountain Lumber Co. 190 Midland Road Hometown, MI 48001		3 Social security wages 12,155.00	4 Social security tax withheld 753.61
		5 Medicare wages and tips 12,155.00	6 Medicare tax withheld 176.25
		7 Social security tips	8 Allocated tips
d Employee's social security number 410-00-1111		9 Advance EIC payment	10 Dependent care benefits
e Employee's name, address, and ZIP code Jean P. Smith 90 Beaver Court Hometown, MI 48001		11 Nonqualified plans	12 Benefits included in Box 1
		13 See Instrs. for Box 13	14 Other

15 Statutory employee ☐ Deceased ☐ Pension plan ☐ Legal rep ☐ 942 emp ☐ Subtotal ☐ Deferred compensation ☐

16 State Employer's state I.D. No. MI 10-0000000	17 State wages, tips, etc 12,155.00	18 State income tax 449.00	19 Locality name	20 Local wages, tips, etc	21 Local income tax

Department of the Treasury—Internal Revenue Service

Form **W-2** Wage and Tax Statement **1993**

This information is being furnished to the Internal Revenue Service

Copy B To Be Filed With Employee's FEDERAL Tax Return

OMB No 1545-0008

☐ CORRECTED (if checked)

PAYER'S name, street address, city, state, and ZIP code MLC Retirement Fund 190 Midland Road Hometown, MI 48001	1 Gross distribution $2,250.00	OMB No 1545-0119 **1993**	**Distributions From Pensions, Annuities, Retirement or Profit-Sharing Plans, IRAs, Insurance Contracts, etc.**
	2a Taxable amount $ 0		
	2b Taxable amount not determined ☐	Total distribution ☐	**Copy B** Report this income on your Federal tax return. If this form shows Federal income tax withheld in box 4, attach this copy to your return.
PAYER'S Federal identification number	RECIPIENT'S identification number	3 Capital gain (included in box 2a) $	4 Federal income tax withheld $ 0
10-9111119	410-00-1111		
RECIPIENT'S name Jean P. Smith		5 Employee contributions or insurance premiums $	6 Net unrealized appreciation in employer's securities $
Street address (including apt. no.) 90 Beaver Court		7 Distribution code G	IRA/SEP ☐	8 Other $ %	This information is being furnished to the Internal Revenue Service.
City, state, and ZIP code Hometown, MI 48001		9 Your percentage of total distribution %	
Account number (optional)		10 State income tax withheld $ 0	11 State/Payer's state number 10-9111119	12 State distribution $
		13 Local income tax withheld $	14 Name of locality	15 Local distribution $

Form **1099-R**

Department of the Treasury - Internal Revenue Service

Form **1040A** Department of the Treasury—Internal Revenue Service
U.S. Individual Income Tax Return (T) **1993** (16) IRS Use Only—Do not write or staple in this space.

OMB No. 1545-0085

Label (See page 15.)

Use the IRS label. Otherwise, please print or type.

LABEL HERE

```
                                  CAR-RT SORT**CR01
BN 329-00-1000                    410-00-1111  S29  30
DON J. & JEAN P. SMITH
90 BEAVER COURT                                 203
HOMETOWN      MI       48001
```

Your social security number (16)

Spouse's social security number

For Privacy Act and Paperwork Reduction Act Notice, see page 4.

(17) **Presidential Election Campaign Fund** (See page 16.)

	Yes	No
Do you want $3 to go to this fund?	✓	
If a joint return, does your spouse want $3 to go to this fund?	✓	

Note: *Checking "Yes" will not change your tax or reduce your refund.*

Check the box for your filing status (See page 16.) Check only one box.

(28) 1 ☐ Single
(29) 2 ☑ Married filing joint return (even if only one had income)
(31) 3 ☐ Married filing separate return. Enter spouse's social security number above and full name here. ▶
(33) 4 ☐ Head of household (with qualifying person). (See page 17.) If the qualifying person is a child but not your dependent, enter this child's name here. ▶
(35) 5 ☐ Qualifying widow(er) with dependent child (year spouse died ▶ 19). (See page 18.)

Figure your exemptions (See page 19.)

(37) 6a ☑ **Yourself.** If your parent (or someone else) can claim you as a dependent on his or her tax return, **do not** check box 6a. But be sure to check the box on line 18b on page 2.

(37) b ☑ **Spouse**

No. of boxes checked on 6a and 6b: 2

(38) c **Dependents:**

(1) Name (first, initial, and last name)	(2) Check if under age 1	(3) If age 1 or older, dependent's social security number	(4) Dependent's relationship to you	(5) No. of months lived in your home in 1993
Lynn R. Smith		410-00-7070	daughter	12
Todd B. Smith	✓	(17)	son	12

If more than seven dependents, see page 22.

No. of your children on 6c who:
• lived with you: 2
• didn't live with you due to divorce or separation (see page 22) (48)
Dependents on 6c not entered above
Add numbers entered on lines above: 4

(48) d If your child didn't live with you but is claimed as your dependent under a pre-1985 agreement, check here ▶ ☐

e Total number of exemptions claimed.

Figure your total income

Attach Copy B of your Forms W-2 and 1099-R here.

If you didn't get a W-2, see page 24.

If you are attaching a check or money order, put it on top of any Forms W-2 or 1099-R.

Line	Description		Amount
(89) 7	Wages, salaries, tips, etc. This should be shown in box 1 of your W-2 form(s). Attach Form(s) W-2. (81) (102)	7	34,405
(108) 8a	**Taxable** interest income (see page 25). If over $400, also complete and attach Schedule 1, Part I.	8a	410
(126) b	**Tax-exempt** interest. DO NOT include on line 8a. 8b 35		
(128) 9	Dividends. If over $400, also complete and attach Schedule 1, Part II.	9	100
10a	Total IRA distributions. 10a (292) — 10b Taxable amount (see page 26). (292)	10b	
11a	Total pensions and annuities. 11a 2,250 (157) — 11b Taxable amount (see page 26).	11b	-0-
(93) 12	Unemployment compensation (see page 30).	12	1,010
13a	Social security benefits. (172) 13a — (173) 13b Taxable amount (see page 30).	13b	
14	Add lines 7 through 13b (far right column). This is your **total income.** ▶	14	35,925

Figure your adjusted gross income

Line	Description		Amount
(282) 15a	Your IRA deduction (see page 32). 15a 750		
(283) b	Spouse's IRA deduction (see page 32). 15b 750		
c	Add lines 15a and 15b. These are your **total adjustments.**	15c	1,500
16	Subtract line 15c from line 14. This is your **adjusted gross income.** (471) If less than $23,050 and a child lived with you, see page 63 to find out if you can claim the "Earned income credit" on line 28c. ▶	16	34,425

Cat. No. 11327A **1993 Form 1040A page 1**

Name(s) shown on page 1	Your social security number
Don J. & Jean P. Smith	329 : 00 : 1000

Figure your standard deduction, exemption amount, and taxable income

(318)

17 Enter the amount from line 16. ⓘ318 **17** 34,425

(318) **18a** Check if: ☐ **You** were 65 or older ☐ **Blind** ⎫ Enter number of
☐ **Spouse** was 65 or older ☐ **Blind** ⎭ boxes checked ▶ 18a ☐

(318) **b** If your parent (or someone else) can claim you as a dependent, check here . . . . ▶ 18b ☐

(320) **c** If you are married filing separately and your spouse files Form 1040 and itemizes deductions, see page 36 and check here ▶ 18c ☐

(319) **19** Enter the **standard deduction** shown below for your filing status. **But if you checked any box on line 18a or b,** go to page 36 to find your standard deduction. **If you checked box 18c, enter -0-.**

- Single—$3,700 ● Head of household—$5,450
- Married filing jointly or Qualifying widow(er)—$6,200
- Married filing separately—$3,100 **19** 6,200

20 Subtract line 19 from line 17. If line 19 is more than line 17, enter -0-. **20** 28,225

21 Multiply $2,350 by the total number of exemptions claimed on line 6e. **21** 9,400

(472) **22** Subtract line 21 from line 20. If line 21 is more than line 20, enter -0-. This is your **taxable income.** ▶ **22** 18,825

Figure your tax, credits, and payments

If you want the IRS to figure your tax, see the instructions for line 22 on page 37.

(691) **23** Find the tax on the amount on line 22. Check if from:
☐ Tax Table (pages 50–55) or ☐ Form 8615 (see page 38). **23** 2,824

(492) **24a** Credit for child and dependent care expenses.
Complete and attach Schedule 2. **24a** 665

(506) **b** Credit for the elderly or the disabled.
Complete and attach Schedule 3. **24b**

c Add lines 24a and 24b. These are your **total credits.** **24c** 665

25 Subtract line 24c from line 23. If line 24c is more than line 23, enter -0-. **25** 2,159

26 Advance earned income credit payments from Form W-2. **26**

(521) **27** Add lines 25 and 26. This is your **total tax.** ▶ **27** 2,159

(65) **28a** Total Federal income tax withheld. If any tax is from Form(s) 1099, check here. ▶ ☐ **28a** 2,754

(75) **b** 1993 estimated tax payments and amount applied from 1992 return. **28b**

(520) **c** **Earned income credit.** Complete and attach Schedule EIC. **28c**

d Add lines 28a, 28b, and 28c. These are your **total payments.** ▶ **28d** 2,754

Figure your refund or amount you owe

(18) **29** If line 28d is more than line 27, subtract line 27 from line 28d. This is the amount you **overpaid.** **29** 595

30 Amount of line 29 you want **refunded to you.** **30** 595

(80) **31** Amount of line 29 you want **applied to your 1994 estimated tax.** **31**

(19) **32** If line 27 is more than line 28d, subtract line 28d from line 27. This is the **amount you owe.** For details on how to pay, including what to write on your payment, see page 42. **32**

(83) **33** Estimated tax penalty (see page 43).
Also, include on line 32. **33**

Sign your return

(18)

Keep a copy of this return for your records.

Under penalties of perjury, I declare that I have examined this return and accompanying schedules and statements, and to the best of my knowledge and belief, they are true, correct, and accurately list all amounts and sources of income I received during the tax year. Declaration of preparer (other than the taxpayer) is based on all information of which the preparer has any knowledge.

Your signature	Date	Your occupation
Don J. Smith	4/8/94	Carpenter
Spouse's signature. If joint return, BOTH must sign.	Date	Spouse's occupation
Jean P. Smith	4/8/94	Secretary

Paid preparer's use only

Preparer's signature ▶	Date	Check if self-employed ☐	Preparer's social security no.
Firm's name (or yours if self-employed) and address ▶		E.I. No.	
		ZIP code	

Schedule 2 (Form 1040A) — Child and Dependent Care Expenses for Form 1040A Filers (m)

Department of the Treasury—Internal Revenue Service

1993

OMB No. 1545-0085

Name(s) shown on Form 1040A: **Don J. and Jean P. Smith**

Your social security number: **329 00 1000**

(497) You need to understand the following terms to complete this schedule: **Dependent care benefits, Earned income, Qualified expenses,** and **Qualifying person(s).** See important terms on page 58. Also, if you had a child born in 1993 and line 17 of Form 1040A is less than $23,050, see **A change to note** on page 59.

Part I — Persons or organizations who provided the care

(499) You MUST complete this part.

	(a) Care provider's name	(b) Address (number, street, apt. no., city, state, and ZIP code)	(c) Identifying number (SSN or EIN)	(d) Amount paid (see page 61)
1	Anytime Childcare Center	612 Castle Street Hometown, MI 48001	10-0077000	2,325
	Marie Thomas	38 Minton Lane Hometown, MI 48001	326-00-4000	1,000

(If you need more space, use the bottom of page 2.)

2 Add the amounts in column (d) of line 1 . . . . . . ▶ 2 | 3,325

3 Enter the number of qualifying persons cared for in 1993 . . . . . [2] (520)

Did you receive dependent care benefits?
- NO ──▶ Complete only Part II below.
- YES ──▶ Complete Part III on the back now.

Part II — Credit for child and dependent care expenses

4 (497) Enter the amount of qualified expenses you incurred and paid in 1993. DO NOT enter more than $2,400 for one qualifying person or $4,800 for two or more persons. If you completed Part III, enter the amount from line 25. | 4 | 3,325

5 (496) Enter YOUR earned income. | 5 | 22,250

6 (496) If married filing a joint return, enter YOUR SPOUSE'S earned income (if student or disabled, see page 61); all others, enter the amount from line 5. | 6 | 12,155

7 Enter the **smallest** of line 4, 5, or 6. | 7 | 3,325

8 Enter the amount from Form 1040A, line 17. | 8 | 34,425

9 Enter on line 9 the decimal amount shown below that applies to the amount on line 8.

If line 8 is—		Decimal amount is	If line 8 is—		Decimal amount is
Over	But not over		Over	But not over	
$0	10,000	.30	$20,000	22,000	.24
10,000	12,000	.29	22,000	24,000	.23
12,000	14,000	.28	24,000	26,000	.22
14,000	16,000	.27	26,000	28,000	.21
16,000	18,000	.26	28,000	No limit	.20
18,000	20,000	.25			

9 | × .20

10 Multiply line 7 by the decimal amount on line 9. Enter the result. Then, see page 61 for the amount of credit to enter on Form 1040A, line 24a. | 10 = | 665

Caution: If you paid $50 or more in a calendar quarter to a person who worked in your home, you must file an employment tax return. Get **Form 942** for details.

For Paperwork Reduction Act Notice, see Form 1040A Instructions.   Cat. No. 10749I   1993 Schedule 2 (Form 1040A) page 1

Schedule 1 (Form 1040A) — Interest and Dividend Income for Form 1040A Filers (m)

Department of the Treasury—Internal Revenue Service

1993

OMB No. 1545-0085

Name(s) shown on Form 1040A: **Don J. and Jean P. Smith**

Your social security number: **329 00 1000**

Part I — Interest Income

(See pages 25 and 56.)

(124)

Note: If you received a Form 1099-INT, Form 1099-OID, or substitute statement from a brokerage firm, enter the firm's name and the total interest shown on that form.

1 List name of payer. If any interest is from a seller-financed mortgage and the buyer used the property as a personal residence, see page 56 and list this interest first. Also, show that buyer's social security number and address.

	Amount
Hometown Savings Bank	1	410

2 Add the amounts on line 1. | 2 | 410

3 Excludable interest on series EE U.S. savings bonds issued after 1989 from Form 8815, line 14. You MUST attach Form 8815 to Form 1040A. | 3 |

4 Subtract line 3 from line 2. Enter the result here and on Form 1040A, line 8a. | 4 | 410

Part II — Dividend Income

(See pages 25 and 57.)

(134)

Note: If you received a Form 1099-DIV or substitute statement from a brokerage firm, enter the firm's name and the total dividends shown on that form.

5 List name of payer

	Amount
	5	

6 Add the amounts on line 5. Enter the total here and on Form 1040A, line 9. | 6 |

For Paperwork Reduction Act Notice, see Form 1040A Instructions.   Cat. No. 12075R   1993 Schedule 1 (Form 1040A) page 1

45 | Sample Form 1040

Introduction

Form 1040 is designed to handle every taxpayer's situation regardless of the size and complexity of his or her economic activity.

The sample return that follows addresses some of the more common situations. It is by no means an exhaustive treatment of all tax-related possibilities. If you have to cope with a situation that is not covered in this sample return, you should turn to the appropriate chapter in the book. To make your task easier, many of the sample tax forms in this chapter contain circles directing you to the page where more information can be found.

Even if your situation is covered in this sample return, you may profit from reading the relevant sections in this book indicated by the circled page references. The examples presented by the IRS ordinarily use facts that are either very straightforward or favorable to the IRS interpretation of the law. They do little to reveal the real ambiguity that pervades much of our tax laws.

Frank and Evelyn Jones are a married couple with two children. The sample tax return at the end of this chapter is based on their situation. It shows the proper reporting of items on the tax forms.

Frank works full time as an electrician. He is also a partner in the Jones Brothers Partnership. Evelyn, a retired state government employee, is a partner in the Gateway Travel Agency. Frank and Evelyn own some stocks and bonds, and Frank owns rental property. He is also a beneficiary of a trust set up by his father.

In May 1993, Frank and Evelyn sold their home and moved to a new home in a nearby city. Soon after their move, they called the IRS and asked for Form 8822, *Change of Address*. They completed the form and mailed it to the Internal Revenue Service Center where they filed their last return.

Because the IRS received Frank and Evelyn's Form 8822 before the address labels for the 1993 tax packages were prepared, their new address appears on the address label that came on their Form 1040 package for 1993. They do not put the label on their return until they have completed and checked the return to make sure it is accurate.

The forms they received in their tax package were based on the return and schedules they filed for 1992. They used the order blank in their tax package to order any other forms they needed.

Presidential Election Campaign Fund. Frank and Evelyn each want $3 of their tax to go to the Presidential Election Campaign Fund. They check both *Yes* boxes. Checking "Yes" will not increase their tax or reduce their refund.

Filing Status and Exemptions

Frank and Evelyn show their filing status and personal exemptions on lines 1–6e.

Filing status (lines 1–5). Because Frank and Evelyn decide to file a joint return, they check the filing status box on line 2, *Married filing joint return*.

Exemptions (lines 6a–6e). Frank and Evelyn show the exemption for Frank on line 6a and the exemption for Evelyn on line 6b. They enter "2" on the line to the right of lines 6a and b.

Their daughter, Marie, who is 18, earned $2,500 last year. Frank and Evelyn provided more than half her support. The gross income test does not apply because she is under 19 and the other dependency tests were met. They claim Marie as a dependent on line 6c. (See *Exemptions for Dependents* in Chapter 3, *Personal Exemptions and Dependents.*)

Their son, James, who is 22, goes to a local college full time. During the summer, James earned $2,600, which he spent for his support. The gross income test does not apply because he is a full-time student under age 24. Frank and Evelyn provided more than $2,600 toward their son's support and the other dependency tests were met. On line 6c of the return, they claim James as a dependent. Frank and Evelyn write the information asked about Marie and James on line 6c, columns (1), (3), (4), and (5). They do not check column (2) because neither Marie nor James is under age 1. They enter "2" on the first line to the right of line 6c because both Marie and James lived at home.

Grace Smith, Evelyn's mother, lives with Frank and Evelyn and their two children. Grace gets a pension of $2,100 a year and social security of $2,900 a year. She spent this money for clothing and other personal things. Only $1,500 of her pension is gross income for her and taxable. The rest of the pension is not taxable because it is a return of her cost.

Frank and Evelyn must figure Grace's total support to know if they can claim her exemption. Because five persons live in the household, Grace's total support includes one-fifth of the family's food costs and one-fifth of the rental value of the house. Frank and Evelyn paid a total of $8,000 for food for the family. The fair rental value of their house was $13,000 for the year. They also bought Grace a $200 television set for her bedroom, paid $700 for a trip she took, and paid her unreimbursed medical and drug expenses of $300. Grace's total support is:

Expenses paid by Grace		$ 5,000
Expenses paid by Frank and Evelyn:		
TV set	$ 200	
Trip	700	
Medical	300	
Food—Grace's share (⅕ of $8,000)	1,600	
Lodging—Grace's share (⅕ of $13,000)	2,600	
Total		$ 5,400
Total support		$10,400

The support Frank and Evelyn provided is more than half of Grace's total support, so they meet the support test to claim her as a dependent. Since Grace had less than $2,350 gross income, Frank and Evelyn also meet the gross income test to claim her as a dependent. The other dependency tests are also met, so Frank and Evelyn can claim Grace as a dependent. They write the information asked about Grace on line 6c of their return.

Frank Jones and his two brothers provided $3,500 for the total support of their sister, Clara Jones. Frank provided 35%, one brother provided 35%, and the other brother provided the remaining 30%. Any one of them may claim the exemption for Clara if a written statement from each of the others is attached to the income tax return of the brother claiming the exemption. The brothers agree to let Frank claim Clara as his dependent this year. They each give Frank a signed Form 2120, *Multiple Support Declaration*, for Frank to attach to his return. (Forms 2120 are not shown here.) Frank and Evelyn write the information asked about Clara on line 6c. They enter "2" on the third line to the right of line 6c for Grace and Clara.

They then enter "6" in the box to the right of line 6e to show the total exemptions they claim.

Income

Frank and Evelyn report the kinds of income they received for the year on lines 7–22.

Wages (line 7). Frank's Form W–2, *Wage and Tax Statement*, shows he earned $20,940. (Form W–2 is not shown here.) Frank and Evelyn enter $20,940 on line 7.

Interest income (lines 8a and 8b and Part I of Schedule B). Frank and Evelyn have a statement savings account, a certificate of deposit (CD) in which Frank's brother, Chuck Jones, also has a one-third investment, and a tax-exempt municipal bond. The Forms 1099–INT that they received show that they had interest income of $330 on their statement savings account with National Bank and $150 on their CD with First Savings and Loan. They must report their interest income on Schedule B because they received part of the interest as nominees for Chuck. (Even if they did not receive interest as nominees, they would still have to report their interest on Schedule B because it is more than $400.) In addition, they received $500 interest from a municipal bond. They did not receive a Form 1099–INT for this tax-exempt interest and do not report it on Schedule B.

On line 1, Part 1 of Schedule B, they enter the names of the financial institutions and the interest received from each, including the interest they received as nominees for Chuck. They show Chuck's share of the interest, $50 ($150 × one-third), separately below a $480 subtotal of all interest income listed. They identify the $50 as "Nominee Distribution" and subtract it from the $480 subtotal. They report the remainder, $430, on line 2. They file a Form 1099–INT and Form 1096, *Annual Summary and Transmittal of*

U.S. Information Returns, with their Internal Revenue Service Center showing the $50 distribution to Chuck. They give Chuck Copy B of the Form 1099–INT. (Form 1099–INT and Form 1096 are not shown here.)

They did not have excludable savings bond interest (explained in *Education Savings Bond Program* in Chapter 8), so they leave line 3 blank and enter $430 on line 4, Schedule B, and on line 8a, Form 1040. They show the $500 tax-exempt interest on line 8b, Form 1040. The tax-exempt interest will not be included in their total income on line 23.

Dividends (line 9 and Part II of Schedule B). During 1993, Frank and Evelyn received or had credited to their accounts the following dividends and other corporate distributions:

Forms 1099–DIV

Acme Publishing Company	
Gross dividends, etc. (Box 1a)	$210
Ordinary dividends (Box 1b)	210
Zepco, Inc.	
Gross dividends, etc. (Box 1a)	$310
Ordinary dividends (Box 1b)	300
Nontaxable distributions (Box 1d)	10
Equity Mutual Fund	
Gross dividends, etc. (Box 1a)	$ 50
Ordinary dividends (Box 1b)	50
Tiger Mutual Fund	
Gross dividends, etc. (Box 1a)	$ 60
Capital gain distributions (Box 1c)	60
Equity Brokers	
Gross dividends, etc. (Box 1a)	$ 40
Ordinary dividends (Box 1b)	40

Schedule K–1 (Form 1065)

Frank's share of dividends on stock owned by his partnership	$ 80

Frank and Evelyn received more than $400 in dividends, so they must report them on Schedule B.

They list all payers and the total amount received from each payer on line 5, Part II of Schedule B. This includes capital gain distributions and nontaxable distributions. They show the total on line 6. Frank and Evelyn put their capital gain distributions of $60 from the Tiger Mutual Fund on line 7. They also enter this amount on line 14, Part II of Schedule D. The $10 nontaxable distribution from Zepco, Inc., is entered on line 8. They reduce their basis in the stock by this amount.

Frank and Evelyn add the amounts on lines 7 and 8 and enter the total, $70, on line 9. They subtract this amount from the $750 on line 6 and enter the result, $680, on line 10, Part II of Schedule B, and on line 9, Form 1040.

Foreign accounts and foreign trusts (Part III of Schedule B). Evelyn has a foreign checking account that she uses for her travel agency. Because she had less than $10,000 in the account during 1993, she answers *No* to the question on line 11a in Part III of Schedule B. Neither Frank nor Evelyn was a grantor of, or transferor to, a foreign trust, so they answer *No* to the question on line 12 in Part III of Schedule B.

State and local income tax refunds (line 10). Frank and Evelyn received a 1992 state tax refund of $110 in 1993. This amount is shown on the Form 1099–G, *Certain Government Payments*, sent to them by their state. Because they itemized their deductions on Schedule A for 1992, they must use the worksheet in their forms instructions package to figure the taxable part of their refund. They use their copy of their 1992 tax return to fill out lines 2, 3, and 4 of the worksheet. Their filled-in worksheet is shown here.

State and Local Income Tax Refund Worksheet — Line 10

1. Enter the income tax refund from Form(s) 1099–G (or similar statement).. $ 110

2. Enter the amount from your 1992 Schedule A, line 26 .... $6,261

3. Enter on line 3 the amount shown below for the filing status claimed on your 1992 Form 1040:
   Single, enter $3,600
   Married filing jointly or Qualifying
   widow(er), enter $6,000
   Married filing separately, enter $3,000
   Head of household, enter $5,250.................................... $6,000

4. If you didn't complete line 33a on your 1992 Form 1040, enter -0-.. -0-

5. Add lines 3 and 4.. $6,000

6. Subtract line 5 from line 2. If zero or less, enter -0-.............. $ 261

7. Taxable part of your refund. Enter the smaller of line 1 or line 6 here and on Form 1040, line 10 .... $ 110

They report $110 as income on line 10 of their Form 1040.

Capital gain or loss (line 13 and Schedule D). On line 13, Frank and Evelyn show their income from the sale or exchange of capital assets from Schedule D.

Short-term capital gains and losses (Part I of Schedule D). In Part I of Schedule D, they show their short-term capital gains and losses from assets they held one year or less. This year they had a short-term loss of $300 on the sale of stock they bought in 1992 and held for 5 months, and a short-term gain of $100 on the sale of stock they bought in January 1993 and held for 2 months. They list these transactions on line 1.

In 1986, Frank lent $200 to a former co-worker. The debt became worthless in May 1993. Because it is a nonbusiness bad debt, he reports it as a short-term capital loss on line 1.

Frank and Evelyn also had a short-term capital loss carryover of $500 from 1992. They show this on line 6.

They add the amounts in column (f) of lines 1 through 6 and enter ($1,000), the total short-term loss, on line 7, column (f). They add the amounts in column (g) of lines 1 through 5 and enter $100, the total short-term gain, on line 7, column (g). They combine the amounts in columns (f) and (g), line 7, and enter their $900 net short-term loss on line 8.

Long-term capital gains and losses (Part II of Schedule D). In Part II of Schedule D, Frank and Evelyn show their long-term capital gains and losses from assets they held more than one year. On line 9, they show a $3,000 gain from the sale of stock and a $560 loss from a worthless bond. They also enter $300, Frank's share of long-term capital gain from his partnership, on line 13 and their $60 capital gain distributions on line 14. They do not report the sale of their home on Schedule D. (See *Sale of Home,* later.)

They add the amounts in column (f) of lines 9 through 15 and enter ($560) on line 16, column (f). They add the amounts in column (g) of lines 9 through 14 and enter $3,360 on line 16, column (g). They combine the amounts in columns (f) and (g), line 16, and enter their $2,800 net long-term gain on line 17.

Summary (Part III of Schedule D). In Part III of Schedule D they must summarize Parts I and II. They combine their $900 net short-term capital loss with their $2,800 net long-term capital gain

and enter the result, $1,900, on line 18, Schedule D, and on line 13, Form 1040. Their taxable income is not over $89,150, so they will not use the *Schedule D Tax Worksheet.*

Pensions (lines 17a and 17b). Evelyn retired in 1992 on her 63rd birthday. She received pension income of $850 in 1992 and $2,550 in 1993. $150 of her $9,000 pension cost was recovered tax free in 1992. Evelyn uses the worksheet in her forms instructions package to figure the taxable part of her pension for 1993. Her filled-in worksheet is shown here.

Worksheet for Simplified General Rule

1. Enter the total pension or annuity payments received this year. Also enter this amount on Form 1040, line 17a $2,550

2. Enter your cost in the plan at the annuity starting date plus any death benefit exclusion.. $9,000

3. Age at annuity starting date: Enter:

55 and under	300
56 – 60	260
61 – 65	240
66 – 70	170
71 and older	120 .... $240

4. Divide line 2 by the number on line 3. .... $37.50

5. Multiply line 4 above by the number of months for which this year's payments were made. If your annuity starting date was **before** 1987, also enter this amount on line 8; skip lines 6 and 7. Otherwise, go to line 6................................ $450

6. Enter the amount, if any, recovered tax free in years after 1986 .... $150

7. Subtract line 6 from line 2. .... $8,850

8. Enter the smaller of line 5 or line 7... $450

9. **Taxable amount.** Subtract line 8 from line 1. Enter the result, but not less than zero. Also enter this amount on Form 1040, line 17b. If your Form 1099–R shows a larger amount, use the amount on this line instead of the amount from Form 1099–R.. $2,100

Evelyn shows the total amount of her pension on line 17a, Form 1040. She shows the taxable amount, $2,100, on line 17b.

Rental, partnership, and trust income (line 18 and Schedule E). Frank and Evelyn show their total income from these sources on Schedule E and on line 18, Form 1040.

Rental income (Part I of Schedule E). Frank received rental income from two properties he owns, a store building and an unimproved piece of land. On line 1, Schedule E, he lists the building and its location in the space marked "A," and the land and its location in the space marked "B." On line 2, he checks the *No* box for both properties because neither was used for personal purposes.

On line 3, Frank enters his $8,400 rental income from the building in column A, his $720 rental income from the land in column B, and the total, $9,120, in the "Totals" column. Then he lists expenses, such as insurance, interest, general repairs, and real estate taxes, on the appropriate lines in each column. On line 6, column A, he shows his auto expenses connected with the rental of the building, figured at 28 cents a mile. Because he is claiming auto expenses, he completes Part V of Form 4562, *Depreciation and Amortization.*

In Part I of Schedule E, he adds the expenses for each property and on line 19 enters $5,420 in column A, $100 in column B, and the total, $5,520, in the "Totals" column.

Frank's records show that he purchased the store building in

1976. His basis for the building is $40,000, and he is using the straight line method of depreciation with a 40–year life. Frank shows depreciation of $1,000 for 1993 on line 20 in column A and the "Totals" column. Because the building was placed in service before 1981, he can figure the depreciation on the building on a separate worksheet and enter it on line 20 of Schedule E. He does not need to enter it on Form 4562 or attach his worksheet.

Frank enters the total expenses for each property on line 21, columns A and B. In each column he subtracts the amount on line 21 from the amount on line 3 and enters the result on line 22. He adds the amounts on line 22 and enters his total rental income, $2,600, on lines 24 and 26.

Partnership income (Part II of Schedule E). Frank is an active partner in the Jones Brothers Partnership. The following amounts are shown as his share of income and deductions on the Schedule K–1 (Form 1065) given to him by the partnership.

Ordinary income from trade or business	**$4,600**
Net long-term capital gain	300
Dividends	80
Charitable contributions	50
Net earnings from self-employment	4,600

Evelyn is an active partner in the Gateway Travel Agency. The following amounts are shown as her share of items on Schedule K–1 (Form 1065).

Ordinary income from trade or business	**$1,900**
Net earnings from self-employment	1,900

Frank and Evelyn list their partnerships in column (a) of line 27, in the spaces marked "A" and "B," and complete columns (b) and (d) for each. Because they are at risk for the amounts invested in each of their partnerships, they check column (e) and do not complete Form 6198, *At-Risk Limitations.*

Because Frank and Evelyn actively participate in their partnerships' business activities, they report the ordinary business income from both of the partnerships as nonpassive income in column (k), line 27. They enter the total partnership nonpassive income of $6,500 on line 28a in column (k), and also on lines 29 and 31.

Frank and Evelyn report their other partnership items as follows:

> Dividends— line 5 of Schedule B. Also, see *Dividends (line 9 and Part II of Schedule B),* earlier.
>
> Net long-term capital gain— line 13, column (g) of Schedule D. Also, see *Capital gain or loss (line 13 and Schedule D),* earlier.
>
> Contributions— line 13 of Schedule A. Also, see *Itemized Deductions (Schedule A),* later.
>
> Net earnings from self-employment— line 2, Section A of Schedule SE. Also, see *Other Taxes,* later. Frank and Evelyn report their net earnings on separate Schedules SE.

Trust income (Part III of Schedule E). Frank had taxable income of $1,400 from a trust set up by his father. He shows the trust's name and employer identification number in columns (a) and (b) of line 32. He shows the $1,400 income as passive income in column (d) of line 32. He also enters $1,400 in column (d) of line 33a, and on lines 34 and 36.

Summary (Part V of Schedule E). In Part V of Schedule E, Frank and Evelyn combine the amounts on lines 26, 31, and 36. They enter the total, $10,500, on line 40, Schedule E, and on line 18, Form 1040.

Other income (line 22). Frank won a $50 prize in a photogra-

phy contest. Frank and Evelyn show this income on line 22, Form 1040.

Total income (line 23). Frank and Evelyn add the amounts on lines 7 through 22 to figure their total income, $36,710. They enter this amount on line 23.

Sale of Home (Form 2119)

Frank and Evelyn do not have a taxable gain on the sale of their home. However, they must report the sale on Form 2119, *Sale of Your Home.* Some of the expenses of the sale of the old home and the purchase of the new home qualify as a moving expense deduction.

Frank and Evelyn bought and moved into their new home May 5, 1993, and sold their old home May 6, 1993. They are over 55 and meet all of the tests for the once-in-a-lifetime exclusion of up to $125,000 of the gain on the sale. They choose to take the exclusion.

They received a Form 1099–S, *Proceeds From Real Estate Transactions,* showing gross proceeds of $160,000 from the sale of their old home. The Form 1099–S will also show the part of the real estate tax that is treated as tax imposed on the buyer. Their records also show the following items.

Old home

Original basis (purchased 1968)		$18,000
Improvements..		7,000
Adjusted basis		$25,000
Fixing-up expenses for sale..		$1,000
Selling price		$160,000

Settlement charges at closing (old home):

Realtor's commission	$8,000	
Balance of mortgage..	4,500	
Penalty for prepayment of mortgage...........................	50	
Mortgage interest (4/1/93–5/5/93)	20	
Points—paid by seller for buyer (loan origination fee, 1% of loan amount)..	1,000	
Real estate taxes (1/1/93–5/5/93)	630	14,200
Net received		$145,800

New home

Purchase price..		$90,000

Settlement charges at closing (new home):

Title search, attorney fees, other settlement fees ..	$1,300	
Points charged to buyer (1% of loan amount).........	400	
Mortgage assumed	(40,000)	
Down payment..	(5,000)	
Real estate taxes (1/1/93–5/4/93—Paid by buyer for seller)	(300)	(43,600)
Balance due		**$46,400**

Frank and Evelyn qualify to deduct moving expenses. They have to fill out Form 3903, *Moving Expenses,* before filling out Form 2119. This is because they must decide which of the expenses of the sale of their old home and the purchase of their new home to claim as part of their moving expense deduction. Qualifying moving expenses include only the $8,000 realtor's commission and

$1,000 points paid on the sale of their old home, and the $1,300 of settlement fees paid on the purchase of their new home. Because of the $3,000 limit on certain moving expenses, however, they decide to claim only $2,340 of the selling expenses of their old home as moving expenses. (See *Moving expenses* under *Itemized Deductions,* later.) They use the remaining $6,660 of selling expenses ($9,000 − $2,340) to reduce the amount they realized from the sale.

They deduct certain of the amounts paid at settlement when they sold their old home and purchased their new home as itemized deductions on Schedule A. Their itemized deduction for interest includes the $50 penalty for prepayment of the mortgage on their old home, the $20 interest on the old house from April 1, 1993, through May 5, 1993, and the $400 points paid for the mortgage on their new home. See *Interest you paid (lines 9a–12, Schedule A)* under *Itemized Deductions,* later.

Frank and Evelyn figure the amount realized and the gain realized on the sale of their old home as follows:

Selling price	$160,000
Less: Selling expenses	6,660
Amount realized	$153,340
Less: Adjusted basis of home sold	25,000
Gain realized	$128,340

They use these figures to fill out Parts I, II, and III of Form 2119. They then complete Part IV of Form 2119 to figure the new home's adjusted basis of $87,960.

Frank and Evelyn put all this information on the appropriate lines of Form 2119. They do not have to sign Form 2119 since they are attaching it to their tax return.

Adjustments to Income

Frank and Evelyn report their adjustments to income on lines 24a–30.

IRA deduction (lines 24a and 24b). Frank and Evelyn each made contributions to an individual retirement arrangement (IRA). Frank contributed $2,000 to his 1993 IRA. In February 1994, Evelyn contributed $900 to her IRA for 1993.

Because neither Frank nor Evelyn was covered by an employer retirement plan during 1993, they each figure their deduction using lines 1 through 3 of *IRA Worksheet 1* in their forms instructions package. Before completing their worksheets, they must each figure their earned income by completing a Schedule SE (see *Other Taxes,* later) and figuring their deductions for self-employment tax on line 25 (explained next). Frank's earned income is $25,215. This is his $20,940 wages plus $4,600 (the amount on his Schedule SE, Section A, line 3) minus $325 (his deduction for self-employment tax on line 25). Evelyn's earned income is $1,765. This is $1,900 (the amount on her Schedule SE, Section A, line 3) minus $135 (her deduction for self-employment tax on line 25).

Only Frank's column of the worksheet is shown here.

IRA Worksheet 1

1. Enter IRA contributions you made, or will make by April 15, 1994, for 1993. But **do not** enter more than $2,000	$2,000
2. Enter wages and other earned income from Form 1040, minus any deductions on Form 1040, lines 25 and 27. Do not reduce wages by any loss from self-employment.	25,215
3. Enter the **smaller** of line 1 or line 2. Enter on Form 1040, line 24a the amount from line 3 you choose to deduct	$2,000

Both Frank and Evelyn can deduct their total contribution. They show Frank's $2,000 contribution on line 24a and Evelyn's $900 contribution on line 24b.

Deduction for self-employment tax (line 25). Both Frank and Evelyn owe self-employment tax for 1993. Before they figure the amount they can deduct, they each complete a Schedule SE and enter their combined self-employment tax, $919, on line 47. (See *Other Taxes,* later.) Then they enter one-half of that amount, $460, on line 25.

Adjusted gross income (line 31). Frank and Evelyn add the amounts from lines 24a, 24b, and 25, and enter $3,360 on line 30. Then they subtract line 30 from line 23. This amount, $33,350, is their adjusted gross income. They enter it on lines 31 and 32. This is the amount they use to figure the limit on their medical deduction and the limit on their miscellaneous deductions. They will also use this amount to figure whether their total itemized deductions and deduction for exemptions are limited.

Standard Deduction

Frank and Evelyn must decide whether to take the standard deduction or itemize their actual deductions. They find the standard deduction for their filing status next to line 34. Their standard deduction is $6,200. They will use this amount to compare with their itemized deductions when they complete Schedule A.

Itemized Deductions (Schedule A)

Frank and Evelyn figure their total itemized deductions by completing Schedule A.

Medical and dental expenses (lines 1–4, Schedule A). Frank and Evelyn paid $2,564 for medical and dental expenses that were not reimbursed by insurance. This includes $300 for Grace Smith (Evelyn's dependent mother) and $700 for Clara Jones (Frank's dependent sister). It also includes $800 for health insurance premiums that Frank paid. They cannot claim the 25% deduction for health insurance of a self-employed person (line 26, Form 1040) because Frank participated all year in his employer's subsidized health plan.

They enter $2,564 on line 1 and their adjusted gross income, $33,350, on line 2. On line 3, they enter $2,501, which is 7.5% of their adjusted gross income. They subtract line 3 from line 1 and enter the result, $63, on line 4.

Taxes you paid (lines 5–8, Schedule A). Frank and Evelyn next itemize the deductible taxes they paid during the year.

Frank had $751 state income tax withheld from his salary during 1993. He and Evelyn also made estimated state income tax payments of $550 for 1993 during 1993. They enter the total, $1,301, on line 5.

Frank and Evelyn's tax year for real estate taxes on both their old and new homes is the calendar year, with payment due August 1. Their share of the tax on their old home, sold on May 6, was $630. Frank and Evelyn are considered to have paid their share of the real estate taxes on their old home even though they did not actually pay them to the tax authority.

They can claim only their share of the real estate taxes paid on their new home even though they paid the entire amount of $910. Their share of the taxes on the new home is $610.

Frank and Evelyn also paid $200 real estate taxes on a lakeside cottage they own.

Frank and Evelyn's real estate tax deduction is $1,440 ($630 + $610 + $200). They write this amount on line 6.

Frank and Evelyn show their total taxes paid, $2,741, on line 8.

Interest you paid (lines 9a–12, Schedule A). Frank and

Evelyn made mortgage interest payments on both their old and new homes in 1993.

They received a Form 1098, *Mortgage Interest Statement,* from the financial institution that holds the mortgage on their new home. Box 1 shows they paid $2,300 interest in 1993. Box 2 shows they paid $400 deductible points at closing. They add these amounts and enter the total, $2,700, on line 9a of Schedule A.

They did not receive a Form 1098 from the financial institution that held the mortgage on their old home. From January to April they paid $140 interest on the mortgage on their old home. The settlement sheet for the sale of their old home showed a $50 penalty for prepayment of the mortgage and $20 interest for the period April 1 through May 5. They enter the total of these amounts, $210, on line 9b.

They add the amounts on lines 9a and 9b and show their total deductible interest, $2,910, on line 12. Frank and Evelyn also paid $260 interest expense on their credit card and revolving charge accounts. They cannot deduct this interest expense.

Gifts to charity (lines 13–16, Schedule A). Frank and Evelyn made cash charitable contributions of $778. They have receipts for all their contributions. Frank's share of the charitable contributions made by the Jones Brothers Partnership, as shown on his Schedule K–1 (Form 1065), is $50. Frank and Evelyn enter the total, $828, on line 13. They also enter this amount on line 16.

Casualty and theft losses (line 17, Schedule A). Frank and Evelyn did not have any casualty or theft losses, so they enter –0– on line 17.

Moving expenses (line 18, Schedule A, and Form 3903). Frank was transferred by his employer to a new job in another city. Frank and Evelyn decided to sell their home and buy a townhouse closer to Frank's new job. They kept their partnership interests at the old location because they can still carry out their duties by mail and telephone from their new home and do not have to commute. Frank's employer did not reimburse him for any of the moving expenses.

Frank and Evelyn make sure that the move meets the distance and time tests explained under *Requirements* in Chapter 27. The distance from their old home to Frank's new job is 91 miles farther than the distance from their old home to Frank's old job. Therefore, they meet the 35-mile distance test. Also, Frank expects to meet the 39-week full-time work test.

Their records show the following expenses for the move.

Paid to van company for moving furniture and household goods	$ 530
Car mileage to drive from old to new home—100 miles at 9¢ a mile	9
Motel room rent for one night on the day of arrival	61
Meals on the day of arrival	50
Pre-move mileage and motel expenses while looking for new home	500
Pre-move meals while looking for new home	200
Expenses of selling old home (realtor's commission and points) ..	9,000
Expenses of buying new home (settlement fees)	1,300

They figure their moving expense deduction on Form 3903, *Moving Expenses,* which they attach to their return.

Transportation of household goods (Section A, Part I of Form 3903). They show the total cost to move furniture and other household goods, $530, on line 4, Form 3903.

Expenses of moving from old to new home (Section B, Part I of Form 3903). The amount they show on line 5 is $70. This is the total of the car mileage and the motel room rent. They show the $50 they spent for meals on the day of their arrival on line

6. They enter $40 ($50 × .80) on line 7. They add the amounts on lines 5 and 7 and enter the total, $110, on line 8.

Pre-move househunting expenses (Section C, Part I of Form 3903). On line 9, Frank and Evelyn show their pre-move mileage and motel expenses of $500. Since they did not have any temporary quarters expenses, they leave line 10 blank. They enter their $200 of pre-move meal expenses on line 11. They show $160 ($200 × .80) on line 12. Frank and Evelyn add the amounts on lines 9 and 12 and enter the total, $660, on line 13.

Qualified real estate expenses (Section D, Part I of Form 3903). They enter the expenses of selling the old home, $9,000, on line 14, and check box *a.* They enter the expense of buying the new home, $1,300, on line 15, and check box *a.*

Dollar limits and moving expense deduction (Part II of Form 3903). The amount on line 13, $660, is less than the $1,500 limit, so Frank and Evelyn enter $660 on line 16. They add lines 14, 15, and 16, and enter the total, $10,960, on line 17. This total is more than the $3,000 limit, so they enter $3,000 on line 18. Because the $660 pre-move expenses are not deductible on any other schedule or form, they decide to use them and $2,340 of the selling expenses to make up the $3,000 limit. They use the remaining $6,660 of selling expenses and the $1,300 of expenses of buying the new home on Form 2119. (See *Sale of Home,* earlier.)

Frank and Evelyn add lines 4, 8, and 18, and enter the result, $3,640, on line 19 of Form 3903 and on line 18, Schedule A.

Job expenses and miscellaneous deductions (lines 19–24, Schedule A). Frank and Evelyn list union dues of $350, subscriptions to trade magazines of $75, and small tools needed for Frank's job costing $335, and enter the total of these deductions, $760, on line 19. They do not have any expenses on line 20, so they also enter $760 on line 21.

They enter their adjusted gross income, $33,350, on line 22 and $667 ($33,350 × .02) on line 23. They subtract line 23 from line 21 and enter the result, $93, on line 24.

Other miscellaneous deductions (line 25). Frank and Evelyn do not have any miscellaneous deductions not subject to the 2% of adjusted gross income limit, so they enter –0– on line 25.

Total itemized deductions (line 26, Schedule A). Because the amount Frank and Evelyn entered on line 32 was not more than $108,450, they now add lines 4, 8, 12, 16, 18, and 24, and write the total of their itemized deductions, $10,275, on line 26. Since this total is larger than their standard deduction ($6,200), they enter $10,275 on line 34, Form 1040.

Tax Computation

Frank and Evelyn are now ready to figure their tax on lines 32–40. None of the situations described on lines 33a, 33b, or 33c apply to them, so they leave the boxes on those lines blank. They subtract their itemized deductions on line 34 from their adjusted gross income on line 32 and enter $23,075 on line 35. They multiply $2,350 by the six exemptions they claimed on line 6e, and they enter the result, $14,100, on line 36. They subtract this from line 35. The result, $8,975, is their taxable income. They enter it on line 37.

Frank and Evelyn must use the Tax Table to figure their tax because their taxable income is less than $100,000. They read down the income column until they find the line that includes their $8,975 taxable income. Next, they find the column heading that describes their filing status—married filing jointly—and read down the column. The amount shown where the income line and filing status column meet, $1,346, is their tax. They write it on line 38 and check the box marked *Tax Table.* Because Frank and Evelyn do not owe any additional taxes (line 39), they also write $1,346 on line 40.

Credits

On July 7, 1993, Evelyn bought a small electric car for personal use. She paid $12,000 for the car. Following the instructions for Form 8834, *Qualified Electric Vehicle Credit,* she found that she qualified for a credit of $1,200. She completes Form 8834 and attaches it to her return. She checks box d on line 44 of Form 1040 and writes "8834" in the space that follows. Frank and Evelyn enter $1,200 on line 44 and, because they have no other credits, on line 45. They subtract that amount from the amount of their tax, $1,346, on line 40 and enter the result, $146, on line 46.

Other Taxes

Frank and Evelyn each have self-employment income over $400 and their total self-employment tax is the only "Other" tax they show on lines 47–52.

Self-employment tax (line 47 and Schedules SE). Frank and Evelyn each figure their self-employment tax on a separate Schedule SE. They can each use the short Schedule SE (Section A).

Evelyn enters her self-employment income of $1,900 on line 2 of Section A. She also enters $1,900 on line 3 and multiplies that amount by .9235. She enters the result, $1,755, on line 4. She multiplies the amount on line 4 by .153 to figure her self-employment tax of $269, which she enters on line 5.

On a separate Schedule SE, Frank enters his self-employment income, $4,600, on lines 2 and 3 of Section A. He multiplies that amount by .9235 and enters the result, $4,248, on line 4. Frank's self-employment tax is $650 ($4,248 × .153), which he enters on line 5.

They add Frank's self-employment tax and Evelyn's self-employment tax and enter the total, $919, on line 47, Form 1040. They also enter one-half of this amount on line 25. (See *Deduction for self-employment tax,* under *Adjustments to Income,* earlier.) They attach both Schedules SE to their Form 1040.

Because they are not liable for any other taxes, they add the amount on line 47 to the amount on line 46. This total, $1,065, is Frank and Evelyn's total tax. They enter it on line 53.

Payments

Frank and Evelyn enter $1,655 on line 54. This is the amount of federal income tax withheld from Frank's salary, as shown on his Form W–2. On line 55, they write $250—the amount of estimated tax payments they made for 1993.

Frank and Evelyn enter on line 60, Form 1040, the total of these payments, $1,905.

Refund or Amount Owed

Because line 60 is more than line 53, Frank and Evelyn have overpaid their taxes. They write the amount of the overpayment, $840, on line 61. Because they do not want the amount credited to their 1994 estimated tax, they also enter $840 on line 62. This is the amount of their refund.

They check their return to make sure they have completed all the items and the schedules called for and that the schedules and forms are attached in attachment sequence number order. The attachment sequence number is just below the year in the upper right corner of each schedule or form. They remove the mailing label from the forms instructions package and put it in the address portion on the top of Form 1040. Both Frank and Evelyn sign the return and date it, because it is a joint return. Also, they enter their occupations in the space provided next to the signature lines.

Frank and Evelyn make a copy of the return to keep for their records. Then they use the envelope that came with their forms package to mail the return to the Service Center for their area.

Form 1040

Department of the Treasury—Internal Revenue Service

U.S. Individual Income Tax Return (T) 1993

For the year Jan. 1–Dec. 31, 1993, or other tax year beginning ____ 1993, ending ____, 19___   OMB No. 1545-0074

IRS Use Only—Do not write or staple in this space.

Label (See instructions on page 12.)
Use the IRS label. Otherwise, please print or type.

LABEL HERE

```
                    CAR-RT  SORT**CR01
JT 516-00-1492      575-00-1776    S29  30
FRANK R & EVELYN D JONES
3807 MILLWAY                          203
LAKECITY        NY        14010
```

Your social security number

Spouse's social security number

For Privacy Act and Paperwork Reduction Act Notice, see page 4.

Presidential Election Campaign (See page 12.)

	Yes	No	Note: Checking "Yes" will not change your tax or reduce your refund.
Do you want $3 to go to this fund?	✓		
If a joint return, does your spouse want $3 to go to this fund?	✓		

Filing Status
(See page 12.) Check only one box.

1 ☐ Single
2 ✓ Married filing joint return (even if only one had income)
3 ☐ Married filing separate return. Enter spouse's social security no. above and full name here. ▶ _____
4 ☐ Head of household (with qualifying person). (See page 13.) If the qualifying person is a child but not your dependent, enter this child's name here. ▶ _____
5 ☐ Qualifying widow(er) with dependent child (year spouse died ▶ 19___). (See page 13.)

Exemptions
(See page 13.)

6a ✓ **Yourself.** If your parent (or someone else) can claim you as a dependent on his or her tax return, **do not** check box 6a. But be sure to check the box on line 33b on page 2

b ✓ **Spouse**

c **Dependents:**

(1) Name (first, initial, and last name)	(2) Check if under age 1	(3) If age 1 or older, dependent's social security number	(4) Dependent's relationship to you	(5) No. of months lived in your home in 1993
Marie Jones		123 00 4567	Daughter	12
James R. Jones		234 00 5678	Son	12
Grace L. Smith		345 00 6789	Mother	12
Clara D. Jones		456 00 7890	Sister	0 *

If more than six dependents, see page 14.

d If your child didn't live with you but is claimed as your dependent under a pre-1985 agreement, check here ▶ ☐
e Total number of exemptions claimed

No. of boxes checked on 6a and 6b: **2**
No. of your children on 6c who:
• lived with you **2**
• didn't live with you due to divorce or separation (see page 15) ____
Dependents on 6c not entered above **2**
Add numbers entered on lines above ▶ **6**

Income

Attach Copy B of your Forms W-2, W-2G, and 1099-R here.

If you did not get a W-2, see page 10.

If you are attaching a check or money order, put it on top of any Forms W-2, W-2G, or 1099-R.

7 Wages, salaries, tips, etc. Attach Form(s) W-2	7	20,940
8a **Taxable** interest income (see page 16). Attach Schedule B if over $400	8a	430
b **Tax-exempt** interest (see page 17). DON'T include on line 8a 8b 500		
9 Dividend income. Attach Schedule B if over $400	9	680
10 Taxable refunds, credits, or offsets of state and local income taxes (see page 17)	10	110
11 Alimony received	11	
12 Business income or (loss). Attach Schedule C or C-EZ	12	
13 Capital gain or (loss). Attach Schedule D	13	1,900
14 Capital gain distributions not reported on line 13 (see page 17)	14	
15 Other gains or (losses). Attach Form 4797	15	
16a Total IRA distributions 16a b Taxable amount (see page 18)	16b	
17a Total pensions and annuities 17a 2,550 b Taxable amount (see page 18)	17b	2,100
18 Rental real estate, royalties, partnerships, S corporations, trusts, etc. Attach Schedule E	18	10,500
19 Farm income or (loss). Attach Schedule F	19	
20 Unemployment compensation (see page 19)	20	
21a Social security benefits 21a b Taxable amount (see page 19)	21b	
22 Other income. List type and amount—see page 20 Photo contest prize	22	50
23 Add the amounts in the far right column for lines 7 through 22. This is your **total income** ▶	23	36,710

Adjustments to Income
(See page 20.)

24a Your IRA deduction (see page 20)	24a	2,000	
b Spouse's IRA deduction (see page 20)	24b	900	
25 One-half of self-employment tax (see page 21)	25	460	
26 Self-employed health insurance deduction (see page 22)	26		
27 Keogh retirement plan and self-employed SEP deduction	27		
28 Penalty on early withdrawal of savings	28		
29 Alimony paid. Recipient's SSN ▶	29		
30 Add lines 24a through 29. These are your **total adjustments** ▶		30	3,360

Adjusted Gross Income

31 Subtract line 30 from line 23. This is your **adjusted gross income.** *If this amount is less than $23,050 and a child lived with you, see page EIC-1 to find out if you can claim the "Earned Income Credit" on line 56*

31	33,350

* Form 2120 Attached (not shown)

Cat. No. 11320B

Form **1040** (1993)

598

Tax Compu-tation	32	Amount from line 31 (adjusted gross income)	32	33,350

33a Check if: ☐ **You** were 65 or older, ☐ Blind; ☐ **Spouse** was 65 or older, ☐ Blind.
Add the number of boxes checked above and enter the total here . . . . ▶ **33a** ☐

(See page 23.)

b If your parent (or someone else) can claim you as a dependent, check here ▶ **33b** ☐

c If you are married filing separately and your spouse itemizes deductions or you are a dual-status alien, see page 24 and check here . . . . . . ▶ **33c** ☐

34 Enter the larger of your:

- **Itemized deductions** from Schedule A, line 26, **OR**
- **Standard deduction** shown below for your filing status. **But if** you checked any box on line 33a or b, go to page 24 to find your standard deduction. If you checked **box 33c**, your standard deduction is zero.
  - Single—$3,700　　● Head of household—$5,450
  - Married filing jointly or Qualifying widow(er)—$6,200
  - Married filing separately—$3,100

34	10,275

35	Subtract line 34 from line 32	35	23,075
36	If line 32 is $81,350 or less, multiply $2,350 by the total number of exemptions claimed on line 6e. If line 32 is over $81,350, see the worksheet on page 25 for the amount to enter .	36	14,100
37	**Taxable income.** Subtract line 36 from line 35. If line 36 is more than line 35, enter -0-	37	8,975

38 Tax. Check if from **a** ☑ Tax Table, **b** ☐ Tax Rate Schedules, **c** ☐ Schedule D Tax Worksheet, or **d** ☐ Form 8615 (see page 25). Amount from Form(s) 8814 ▶ **e** _____

38	1,346

If you want the IRS to figure your tax, see page 24.

39	Additional taxes (see page 25). Check if from **a** ☐ Form 4970 **b** ☐ Form 4972	39	
40	Add lines 38 and 39 . . . . ▶	40	1,346

Credits (See page 25.)					
	41	Credit for child and dependent care expenses. Attach Form 2441	41		
	42	Credit for the elderly or the disabled. Attach Schedule R . .	42		
	43	Foreign tax credit. Attach Form 1116	43		
	44	Other credits (see page 26). Check if from **a** ☐ Form 3800 **b** ☐ Form 8396 **c** ☐ Form 8801 **d** ☑ Form (specify) 8834	44	1,200	
	45	Add lines 41 through 44	45		1,200
	46	Subtract line 45 from line 40. If line 45 is more than line 40, enter -0- . ▶	46		146

Other Taxes				
	47	Self-employment tax. Attach Schedule SE. Also, see line 25 . . .	47	919
	48	Alternative minimum tax. Attach Form 6251	48	
	49	Recapture taxes (see page 26). Check if from **a** ☐ Form 4255 **b** ☐ Form 8611 **c** ☐ Form 8828	49	
	50	Social security and Medicare tax on tip income not reported to employer. Attach Form 4137	50	
	51	Tax on qualified retirement plans, including IRAs. If required, attach Form 5329	51	
	52	Advance earned income credit payments from Form W-2 . . .	52	
	53	Add lines 46 through 52. This is your **total tax** . . . . . ▶	53	1,065

Payments Attach Forms W-2, W-2G, and 1099-R on the front.					
	54	Federal income tax withheld. If any is from Form(s) 1099, check ▶ ☐	54	1,655	
	55	1993 estimated tax payments and amount applied from 1992 return .	55	250	
	56	**Earned income credit.** Attach Schedule EIC	56		
	57	Amount paid with Form 4868 (extension request)	57		
	58a	Excess social security, Medicare, and RRTA tax withheld (see page 28) .	58a		
	b	Deferral of additional 1993 taxes. Attach Form 8841 . . .	58b		
	59	Other payments (see page 28). Check if from **a** ☐ Form 2439 **b** ☐ Form 4136	59		
	60	Add lines 54 through 59. These are your **total payments** . . . ▶	60		1,905

Refund or Amount You Owe				
	61	If line 60 is more than line 53, subtract line 53 from line 60. This is the amount you **OVERPAID**. ▶	61	840
	62	Amount of line 61 you want **REFUNDED TO YOU**. . . . . ▶	62	840
	63	Amount of line 61 you want **APPLIED TO YOUR 1994 ESTIMATED TAX** ▶	63	
	64	If line 53 is more than line 60, subtract line 60 from line 53. This is the **AMOUNT YOU OWE**. For details on how to pay, including what to write on your payment, see page 29	64	
	65	Estimated tax penalty (see page 29). Also include on line 64	65	

Sign Here Keep a copy of this return for your records.				
Under penalties of perjury, I declare that I have examined this return and accompanying schedules and statements, and to the best of my knowledge and belief, they are true, correct, and complete. Declaration of preparer (other than taxpayer) is based on all information of which preparer has any knowledge.				
Your signature ▶ *Frank R. Jones*	Date 4-4-94	Your occupation Electrician		
Spouse's signature. If a joint return, BOTH must sign. ▶ *Evelyn D. Jones*	Date 4-4-94	Spouse's occupation Travel Agent		

Paid Preparer's Use Only				
Preparer's signature ▶	Date	Check if self-employed ☐	Preparer's social security no.	
Firm's name (or yours if self-employed) and address ▶		E.I. No.		
		ZIP code		

Schedule A — Itemized Deductions (Form 1040) 1993

SCHEDULES A&B (Form 1040)
Department of the Treasury — Internal Revenue Service

Schedule A—Itemized Deductions
(Schedule B is on back)
▶ Attach to Form 1040. ▶ See Instructions for Schedules A and B (Form 1040).

OMB No. 1545-0074 1993 Attachment Sequence No. 07

Name(s) shown on Form 1040: **Frank R. & Evelyn D. Jones**
Your social security number: **516 00 1492**

Medical and Dental Expenses (324)
Caution: Do not include expenses reimbursed or paid by others.
1 Medical and dental expenses (see page A-1) ... 1 2,564
2 Enter amount from Form 1040, line 32. | 2 | 33,350 |
3 Multiply line 2 above by 7.5% (.075) ... 3 2,501
4 Subtract line 3 from line 1. If zero or less, enter -0- ... 4 63

Taxes You Paid (335) (See page A-2.)
5 State and local income taxes ... 5 1,301
6 Real estate taxes (see page A-2) ... 6 1,440
7 Other taxes. List—include personal property taxes ▶ ... 7
8 Add lines 5 through 7 ... 8 2,741

Interest You Paid (346) (See page A-2.)
9a Home mortgage interest and points reported to you on Form 1098 ... 9a 2,700
b Home mortgage interest not reported to you on Form 1098. If paid to the person from whom you bought the home, see page A-3 and show that person's name, identifying no., and address ▶ ... 9b 210
10 Points not reported to you on Form 1098. See page A-3 for special rules. ... 10
11 Investment interest. If required, attach Form 4952. (See page A-3.) ... 11
12 Add lines 9a through 11 ... 12 2,910

Gifts to Charity (361) (See page A-3.)
Caution: If you made a charitable contribution and received a benefit in return, see page A-3.
13 Contributions by cash or check ... 13 828
14 Other than by cash or check. If over $500, you MUST attach Form 8283 ... 14
15 Carryover from prior year ... 15
16 Add lines 13 through 15 ... 16 828

Casualty and Theft Losses (377)
17 Casualty or theft loss(es). Attach Form 4684. (See page A-4.) ... 17 -0-

Moving Expenses (392)
18 Moving expenses. Attach Form 3903 or 3903-F. (See page A-4.) ... 18 3,640

Job Expenses and Most Other Miscellaneous Deductions (407)
19 Unreimbursed employee expenses—job travel, union dues, job education, etc. If required, you MUST attach Form 2106. (See page A-4.) ▶ Union dues-550, subscriptions-15, tools-335 ... 19 760
20 Other expenses—investment, tax preparation, safe deposit box, etc. List type and amount ▶ ... 20 760
21 Add lines 19 and 20 ... 21 760
22 Enter amount from Form 1040, line 32. | 22 | 33,350 |
23 Multiply line 22 above by 2% (.02) ... 23 667
24 Subtract line 23 from line 21. If zero or less, enter -0- ... 24 93

Other Miscellaneous Deductions (454)
25 Other—from list on page A-5. List type and amount ▶ ... 25 -0-

Total Itemized Deductions (454)
26 Is the amount on Form 1040, line 32, more than $108,450 (more than $54,225 if married filing separately)?
• NO. Your deduction is not limited. Add lines 4, 8, 12, 16, 17, 18, 24, and 25 and enter the total here. Also enter on Form 1040, line 34, the larger of this amount or your standard deduction.
• YES. Your deduction may be limited. See page A-5 for the amount to enter. ... 26 10,275

For Paperwork Reduction Act Notice, see Form 1040 instructions. Cat. No. 11330X Schedule A (Form 1040) 1993 (321)

Schedule B — Interest and Dividend Income (Form 1040) 1993

Schedules A&B (Form 1040) 1993
Name(s) shown on Form 1040. Do not enter name and social security number if shown on other side.
Frank R. & Evelyn D. Jones
OMB No. 1545-0074 Page 2
Your social security number: **516 00 1492**

Schedule B—Interest and Dividend Income
Attachment Sequence No. 08

Part I Interest Income (See pages 16 and B-1.)
Note: If you had over $400 in taxable interest income, you must also complete Part III.

	Interest Income	Amount
1	List name of payer. If any interest is from a seller-financed mortgage and the buyer used the property as a personal residence, see page B-1 and list this interest first. Also show that buyer's social security number and address ▶	
(108)	National Bank	330
	First Savings & Loan	150
	Subtotal	480
	Nominee Distribution	(50)
		1 430
2	Add the amounts on line 1	2 430
3	Excludable interest on series EE U.S. savings bonds issued after 1989 from Form 8815, line 14. You MUST attach Form 8815 to Form 1040	3
4	Subtract line 3 from line 2. Enter the result here and on Form 1040, line 8a ▶	4 430

Note: If you had over $400 in gross dividends and/or other distributions on stock, you must also complete Part III.

Part II Dividend Income (See pages 17 and B-1.)

	Dividend Income	Amount
5	List name of payer. Include gross dividends and/or other distributions on stock here. Any capital gain distributions and nontaxable distributions will be deducted on lines 7 and 8 ▶	
(128)	Acme Publishing Company	210
	Zepco Inc.	310
	Equity Mutual Fund	50
	Tiger Mutual Fund	40
	Equity Brokers	80
	Jones Brothers Partnership	
		5 750
6	Add the amounts on line 5	6 750
7	Capital gain distributions. Enter here and on Schedule D*	7 60
8	Nontaxable distributions. (See the inst. for Form 1040, line 9.)	8 10
9	Add lines 7 and 8	9 70
10	Subtract line 9 from line 6. Enter the result here and on Form 1040, line 9 ▶	10 680

*If you received capital gain distributions but do not need Schedule D to report any other gains or losses, see the instructions for Form 1040, lines 13 and 14.

Part III Foreign Accounts and Trusts (See page B-2.) (18)
If you had over $400 of interest or dividends OR had a foreign account or were a grantor of, or a transferor to, a foreign trust, you must complete this part.

		Yes	No
11a	At any time during 1993, did you have an interest in or a signature or other authority over a financial account in a foreign country, such as a bank account, securities account, or other financial account? See page B-2 for exceptions and filing requirements for Form TD F 90-22.1		✓
b	If "Yes," enter the name of the foreign country ▶		
12	Were you the grantor of, or transferor to, a foreign trust that existed during 1993, whether or not you have any beneficial interest in it? If "Yes," you may have to file Form 3520, 3520-A, or 926.		✓

For Paperwork Reduction Act Notice, see Form 1040 instructions. Schedule B (Form 1040) 1993

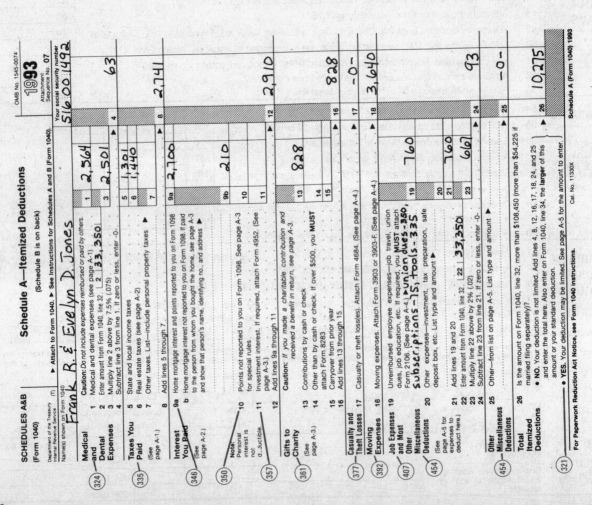

SCHEDULE D
(Form 1040)

Department of the Treasury
Internal Revenue Service (T)

Capital Gains and Losses

▶ Attach to Form 1040.   ▶ See Instructions for Schedule D (Form 1040).

▶ Use lines 20 and 22 for more space to list transactions for lines 1 and 9.

OMB No. 1545-0074

1993

Attachment
Sequence No. **12**

Name(s) shown on Form 1040

Frank R. & Evelyn D. Jones

Your social security number

516 00 1492

Part I — Short-Term Capital Gains and Losses—Assets Held One Year or Less

(271)

(a) Description of property (Example: 100 sh. XYZ Co.)	(b) Date acquired (Mo., day, yr.)	(c) Date sold (Mo., day, yr.)	(d) Sales price (see page D-3)	(e) Cost or other basis (see page D-3)	(f) LOSS If (e) is more than (d), subtract (d) from (e)	(g) GAIN If (d) is more than (e), subtract (e) from (d)
1 100 Sh. A Co.	12-7-92	5-3-93	800	1,100	300	
50 sh. B Co.	1-4-93	3-1-93	600	500		100
Bad Debt - John Green	Statement attached *				200	

2 Enter your short-term totals, if any, from line 21 . . . . | **2** | | | | |

3 **Total short-term sales price amounts.** Add column (d) of lines 1 and 2 . . . | **3** | 1,400 | | | |

4 Short-term gain from Forms 2119 and 6252, and short-term gain or (loss) from Forms 4684, 6781, and 8824 | **4** | | |

5 Net short-term gain or (loss) from partnerships, S corporations, and fiduciaries from Schedule(s) K-1 | **5** | | |

(273) **6** Short-term capital loss carryover from 1992 Schedule D, line 38 . . . . | **6** | 500 | |

7 Add lines 1, 2, and 4 through 6, in columns (f) and (g) . . . . | **7** | (1,000) | 100 |

8 **Net short-term capital gain or (loss).** Combine columns (f) and (g) of line 7 . . . . | **8** | (900) |

Part II — Long-Term Capital Gains and Losses—Assets Held More Than One Year

(271)

9 300 sh. XYZ Co.	2-11-85	5-3-93	6,000	3,000		3,000
Bond-D Co.	1-30-89	Worthless		560	560	

10 Enter your long-term totals, if any, from line 23 . . . . | **10** | | | | |

11 **Total long-term sales price amounts.** Add column (d) of lines 9 and 10 . . . | **11** | 6,000 | | | |

12 Gain from Form 4797; long-term gain from Forms 2119, 2439, and 6252; and long-term gain or (loss) from Forms 4684, 6781, and 8824 . . . . | **12** | | |

13 Net long-term gain or (loss) from partnerships, S corporations, and fiduciaries from Schedule(s) K-1 . . . . | **13** | | 300 |

(271) **14** Capital gain distributions | **14** | | 60 |

(273) **15** Long-term capital loss carryover from 1992 Schedule D, line 45 . . . . | **15** | | |

16 Add lines 9, 10, and 12 through 15, in columns (f) and (g) . . . . | **16** | (560) | 3,360 |

17 **Net long-term capital gain or (loss).** Combine columns (f) and (g) of line 16 . . . . | **17** | 2,800 |

Part III — Summary of Parts I and II

18 Combine lines 8 and 17. If a loss, go to line 19. If a gain, enter the gain on Form 1040, line 13.
Note: If both lines 17 and 18 are gains, see the **Schedule D Tax Worksheet** on page D-4 . . | **18** | 1,900 |

19 If line 18 is a (loss), enter here and as a (loss) on Form 1040, line 13, the **smaller** of these losses:

a The (loss) on line 18; **or**

b ($3,000) or, if married filing separately, ($1,500) . . . . | **19** | ( ) |

Note: See the **Capital Loss Carryover Worksheet** on page D-4 if the loss on line 18 exceeds the loss on line 19 or if Form 1040, line 35, is a loss.

(279)

For Paperwork Reduction Act Notice, see Form 1040 instructions.   Cat. No. 11338H   Schedule D (Form 1040) 1993

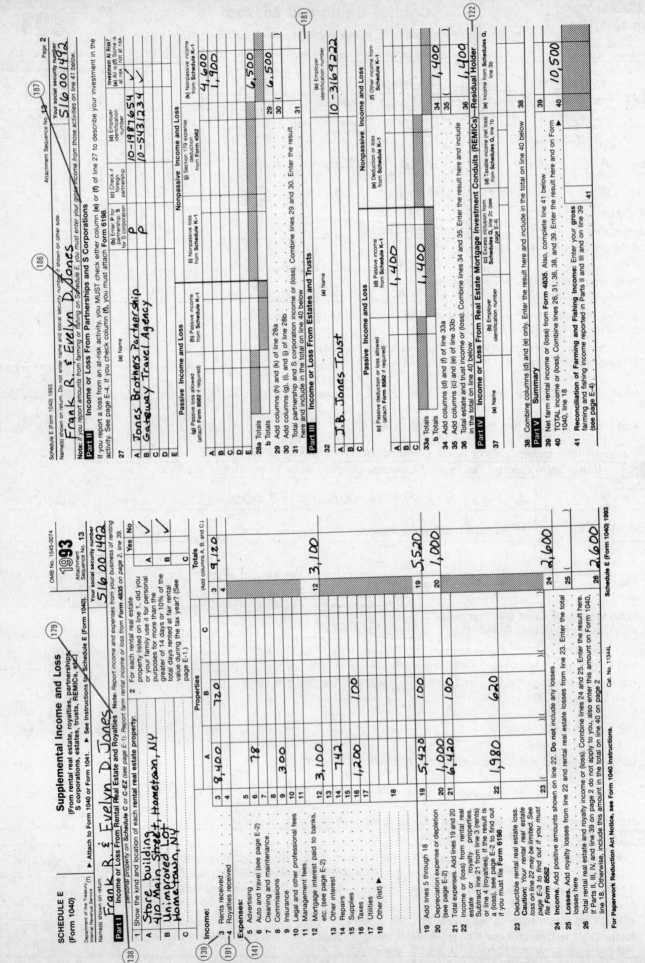

SCHEDULE E (Form 1040)
Department of the Treasury — Internal Revenue Service

Supplemental Income and Loss
(From rental real estate, royalties, partnerships, S corporations, estates, trusts, REMICs, etc.)
▶ Attach to Form 1040 or Form 1041. ▶ See Instructions for Schedule E (Form 1040).

OMB No. 1545-0074
1993
Attachment Sequence No. 13

Name(s) shown on return: **Frank R. & Evelyn D. Jones**
Your social security number: **516:00:1492**

Part I Income or Loss From Rental Real Estate and Royalties

Note: Report income and expenses from your business of renting personal property on Schedule C or C-EZ (see page E-1). Report farm rental income or loss from Form 4835 on page 2, line 39.

1 Show the kind and location of each rental real estate property:
A **Store building, 410 Main Street, Hometown, NY**
B **Unimproved Lot, Hometown, NY**
C

2 For each rental real estate property listed on line 1, did you or your family use it for personal purposes for more than the greater of 14 days or 10% of the total days rented at fair rental value during the tax year? (See page E-1.)

	Yes	No
A		✓
B		✓
C		

Income:		Properties A	Properties B	Properties C	Totals (Add columns A, B, and C)
3 Rents received	3	9,400	720		3 9,120
4 Royalties received	4				4
Expenses:					
5 Advertising	5				
6 Auto and travel (see page E-2)	6	78			
7 Cleaning and maintenance	7				
8 Insurance	8	300			
9 Commissions	9				
10 Legal and other professional fees	10				
11 Management fees	11				
12 Mortgage interest paid to banks, etc. (see page E-2)	12	3,100			12 3,100
13 Other interest	13	742			
14 Repairs	14				
15 Supplies	15		100		
16 Taxes	16	1,200			
17 Utilities	17				
18 Other (list) ▶	18				
19 Add lines 5 through 18	19	5,420	100		19 5,520
20 Depreciation expense or depletion (see page E-2)	20	1,000			20 1,000
21 Total expenses. Add lines 19 and 20	21	6,420	100		
22 Income or (loss) from rental real estate or royalty properties. Subtract line 21 from line 3 (rents) or line 4 (royalties). If the result is a (loss), see page E-2 to find out if you must file Form 6198	22	1,980	620		
23 Deductible rental real estate loss. Caution: Your rental real estate loss on line 22 may be limited. See page E-3 to find out if you must file Form 8582	23				

24 Income. Add positive amounts shown on line 22. Do not include any losses ... 24 **2,600**
25 Losses. Add royalty losses from line 22 and rental real estate losses from line 23. Enter the total losses here ... 25 (   )
26 Total rental real estate and royalty income or (loss). Combine lines 24 and 25. Enter the result here. If Parts II, III, IV, and line 39 on page 2 do not apply to you, also enter this amount on Form 1040, line 18. Otherwise, include this amount in the total on line 40 on page 2 ... 26 **2,600**

For Paperwork Reduction Act Notice, see Form 1040 instructions.   Cat. No. 11344L   Schedule E (Form 1040) 1993

Schedule E (Form 1040) 1993   Page 2

Name(s) shown on return. Do not enter name and social security number if shown on other side.
Frank R. & Evelyn D. Jones
Your social security number **516:00:1492**
Attachment Sequence No. 13

Part II Income or Loss From Partnerships and S Corporations

If you report a loss from an at-risk activity, you MUST check either column (e) or (f) of line 27 to describe your investment in the activity. See page E-4. If you check column (f), you must attach Form 6198.

27 (a) Name	(b) Enter P for partnership; S for S corporation	(c) Check if foreign partnership	(d) Employer identification number	(e) All is at risk	(f) Some is not at risk
A Jones Brothers Partnership	P		10-1981654	✓	
B Gateway Travel Agency			10-5431234		
C					
D					
E					

	Passive Income and Loss		Nonpassive Income and Loss		
	(g) Passive loss allowed (attach Form 8582 if required)	(h) Passive income from Schedule K-1	(i) Nonpassive loss from Schedule K-1	(j) Section 179 expense deduction from Form 4562	(k) Nonpassive income from Schedule K-1
A					4,600
B					1,900
C					
D					
E					
28a Totals					6,500
b Totals					6,500

29 Add columns (h) and (k) of line 28a ... 29
30 Add columns (g), (i), and (j) of line 28b ... 30 (   )
31 Total partnership and S corporation income or (loss). Combine lines 29 and 30. Enter the result here and include in the total on line 40 below ... 31

Part III Income or Loss From Estates and Trusts

32 (a) Name
A J.B. Jones Trust
B
C

	(b) Employer identification number	Passive Income and Loss		Nonpassive Income and Loss	
		(c) Passive deduction or loss allowed (attach Form 8582 if required)	(d) Passive income from Schedule K-1	(e) Deduction or loss from Schedule K-1	(f) Other income from Schedule K-1
A	10-3169222		1,400		
B					
C					
33a Totals			1,400		
b Totals					

34 Add columns (d) and (f) of line 33a ... 34 **1,400**
35 Add columns (c) and (e) of line 33b ... 35 (   )
36 Total estate and trust income or (loss). Combine lines 34 and 35. Enter the result here and include in the total on line 40 below ... 36 **1,400**

Part IV Income or Loss From Real Estate Mortgage Investment Conduits (REMICs)—Residual Holder

37 (a) Name	(b) Employer identification number	(c) Excess inclusion from Schedules Q, line 2c (see page E-4)	(d) Taxable income (net loss) from Schedules Q, line 1b	(e) Income from Schedules Q, line 3b
A				
B				

38 Combine columns (d) and (e) only. Enter the result here and include in the total on line 40 below ... 38

Part V Summary

39 Net farm rental income or (loss) from Form 4835. Also, complete line 41 below ... 39
40 TOTAL income or (loss). Combine lines 26, 31, 36, 38, and 39. Enter the result here and on Form 1040, line 18 ... 40 **10,500**
41 Reconciliation of Farming and Fishing Income: Enter your gross farming and fishing income reported in Parts II, III, IV, and line 39 (see page E-4) ... 41

Schedule E (Form 1040) 1993

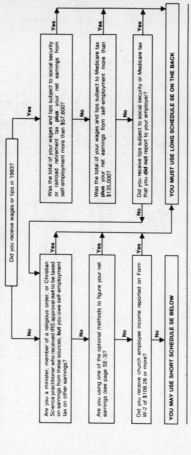
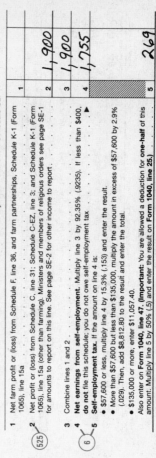

SCHEDULE SE (Form 1040)

Department of the Treasury
Internal Revenue Service (T)

Self-Employment Tax

► See Instructions for Schedule SE (Form 1040).
► Attach to Form 1040.

OMB No. 1545-0074
1993
Attachment Sequence No. 17

Name of person with **self-employment** income (as shown on Form 1040) Evelyn D. Jones

Social security number of person with **self-employment income** ► 525 00 1776   (5)

Who Must File Schedule SE

You must file Schedule SE if:
- Your **wages** (and tips) subject to social security AND Medicare tax (or railroad retirement tax) were less than $135,000; **AND**
- Your net earnings from self-employment from other than church employee income (line 4 of Short Schedule SE or line 4c of Long Schedule SE) were $400 or more; **OR**
- You had church employee income of $108.28 or more. Income from services you performed as a minister or a member of a religious order is **not** church employee income. See page SE-1.

Note: Even if you have a loss or a small amount of income from self-employment, it may be to your benefit to file Schedule SE and use either "optional method" in Part II of Long Schedule SE. See page SE-3.

Exception. If your only self-employment income was from earnings as a minister, member of a religious order, or Christian Science practitioner, **AND** you filed Form 4361 and received IRS approval not to be taxed on those earnings, **DO NOT** file Schedule SE. Instead, write "Exempt–Form 4361" on Form 1040, line 47.

May I Use Short Schedule SE or MUST I Use Long Schedule SE?

Did you receive wages or tips in 1993?

Are you a minister, member of a religious order, or Christian Science practitioner who received IRS approval **not** to be taxed on earnings from these sources, **but** you owe self-employment tax on other earnings?

Are you using one of the optional methods to figure your net earnings (see page SE-3)?

Did you receive church employee income reported on Form W-2 of $108.28 or more?

Was the total of your **wages** (and tips) subject to social security **or** railroad retirement tax **plus** your net earnings from self-employment more than $57,600?

Was the total of your wages and tips subject to Medicare tax **plus** your net earnings from self-employment more than $135,000?

Did you receive tips subject to social security or Medicare tax that you **did not** report to your employer?

YOU MAY USE SHORT SCHEDULE SE BELOW

YOU MUST USE LONG SCHEDULE SE ON THE BACK

Section A—Short Schedule SE. Caution: *Read above to see if you can use Short Schedule SE.*

1 Net farm profit or (loss) from Schedule F, line 36, and farm partnerships, Schedule K-1 (Form 1065), line 15a	1	
2 Net profit or (loss) from Schedule C, line 31; Schedule C-EZ, line 3; and Schedule K-1 (Form 1065), line 15a (other than farming). Ministers and members of religious orders see page SE-1 for amounts to report on this line. See page SE-2 for other income to report.	2	1,900
3 Combine lines 1 and 2	3	1,900
4 Net earnings from self-employment. Multiply line 3 by 92.35% (.9235). If less than $400, **do not** file this schedule; you do not owe self-employment tax	4	1,755
5 Self-employment tax. If the amount on line 4 is: • $57,600 or less, multiply line 4 by 15.3% (.153) and enter the result. • More than $57,600 but less than $135,000, multiply the amount in excess of $57,600 by 2.9% (.029). Then, add $8,812.80 to the result and enter the total. • $135,000 or more, enter $11,057.40. Also enter on **Form 1040, line 47. (Important:** You are allowed a deduction for **one-half** of this amount. Multiply line 5 by 50% (.5) and enter the result on **Form 1040, line 25.)**	5	269

For Paperwork Reduction Act Notice, see Form 1040 instructions.   Cat. No. 11358Z   Schedule SE (Form 1040) 1993

SCHEDULE SE (Form 1040)

Department of the Treasury
Internal Revenue Service (T)

Self-Employment Tax

► See Instructions for Schedule SE (Form 1040).
► Attach to Form 1040.

OMB No. 1545-0074
1993
Attachment Sequence No. 17

Name of person with **self-employment** income (as shown on Form 1040) Frank R. Jones

Social security number of person with **self-employment income** ► 516 00 1492   (5)

Who Must File Schedule SE

You must file Schedule SE if:
- Your **wages** (and tips) subject to social security AND Medicare tax (or railroad retirement tax) were less than $135,000; **AND**
- Your net earnings from self-employment from other than church employee income (line 4 of Short Schedule SE or line 4c of Long Schedule SE) were $400 or more; **OR**
- You had church employee income of $108.28 or more. Income from services you performed as a minister or a member of a religious order is **not** church employee income. See page SE-1.

Note: Even if you have a loss or a small amount of income from self-employment, it may be to your benefit to file Schedule SE and use either "optional method" in Part II of Long Schedule SE. See page SE-3.

Exception. If your only self-employment income was from earnings as a minister, member of a religious order, or Christian Science practitioner, **AND** you filed Form 4361 and received IRS approval not to be taxed on those earnings, **DO NOT** file Schedule SE. Instead, write "Exempt–Form 4361" on Form 1040, line 47.

May I Use Short Schedule SE or MUST I Use Long Schedule SE?

Did you receive wages or tips in 1993?

Are you a minister, member of a religious order, or Christian Science practitioner who received IRS approval **not** to be taxed on earnings from these sources, **but** you owe self-employment tax on other earnings?

Are you using one of the optional methods to figure your net earnings (see page SE-3)?

Did you receive church employee income reported on Form W-2 of $108.28 or more?

Was the total of your **wages** (and tips) subject to social security **or** railroad retirement tax **plus** your net earnings from self-employment more than $57,600?

Was the total of your wages and tips subject to Medicare tax **plus** your net earnings from self-employment more than $135,000?

Did you receive tips subject to social security or Medicare tax that you **did not** report to your employer?

YOU MAY USE SHORT SCHEDULE SE BELOW

YOU MUST USE LONG SCHEDULE SE ON THE BACK

Section A—Short Schedule SE. Caution: *Read above to see if you can use Short Schedule SE.*

1 Net farm profit or (loss) from Schedule F, line 36, and farm partnerships, Schedule K-1 (Form 1065), line 15a	1	
2 Net profit or (loss) from Schedule C, line 31; Schedule C-EZ, line 3; and Schedule K-1 (Form 1065), line 15a (other than farming). Ministers and members of religious orders see page SE-1 for amounts to report on this line. See page SE-2 for other income to report.	2	4,600
3 Combine lines 1 and 2	3	4,600
4 Net earnings from self-employment. Multiply line 3 by 92.35% (.9235). If less than $400, **do not** file this schedule; you do not owe self-employment tax	4	4,248
5 Self-employment tax. If the amount on line 4 is: • $57,600 or less, multiply line 4 by 15.3% (.153) and enter the result. • More than $57,600 but less than $135,000, multiply the amount in excess of $57,600 by 2.9% (.029). Then, add $8,812.80 to the result and enter the total. • $135,000 or more, enter $11,057.40. Also enter on **Form 1040, line 47. (Important:** You are allowed a deduction for **one-half** of this amount. Multiply line 5 by 50% (.5) and enter the result on **Form 1040, line 25.)**	5	650

For Paperwork Reduction Act Notice, see Form 1040 instructions.   Cat. No. 11358Z   Schedule SE (Form 1040) 1993

Form 2119 — Sale of Your Home

Form 2119

Department of the Treasury
Internal Revenue Service

Sale of Your Home

▶ Attach to Form 1040 for year of sale.
▶ See separate instructions.

OMB No. 1545-0072

1993

Attachment Sequence No. 20

Your first name and initial. If a joint return, also give spouse's name and initial. | Last name

Frank R. & Evelyn D. Jones

Your social security number | Spouse's social security number

516:00:1492 | 575:00:1776

Fill in Your Address Only If You Are Filing This Form by Itself and Not With Your Tax Return

Present address (no., street, and apt. no., rural route, or P.O. box no. if mail is not delivered to street address)

City, town or post office, state, and ZIP code

Part I — General Information

1	Date your former main home was sold (month, day, year) ▶	1	5 / 6 / 93	
2	Have you bought or built a new main home?	2	☑Yes ☐No	
3	Is or was any part of either main home rented out or used for business? If "Yes," see instructions	3	☐Yes ☑No	

Part II — Gain on Sale—Do not include amounts you deduct as moving expenses.

4	Selling price of home. Do not include personal property items you sold with your home	4	160,000
5	Expense of sale (see instructions)	5	6,660
6	Amount realized. Subtract line 5 from line 4	6	153,340
7	Adjusted basis of home sold (see instructions)	7	25,000
8	Gain on sale. Subtract line 7 from line 6	8	128,340

Is line 8 more than zero?

☐ Yes → If line 2 is "Yes," you **must** go to Part III or Part IV, whichever applies. If line 2 is "No," go to line 9.

☐ No → **Stop** and attach this form to your return.

9 If you haven't replaced your home, do you plan to do so within the **replacement period** (see instructions)? ☐ Yes ☐ No
• If line 9 is "Yes," stop here, attach this form to your return, and see **Additional Filing Requirements** in the instructions.
• If line 9 is "No," you **must** go to Part III or Part IV, whichever applies.

Part III — One-Time Exclusion of Gain for People Age 55 or Older—By completing this part, you are electing to take the one-time exclusion (see instructions). If you are not electing to take the exclusion, go to Part IV now.

10	Who was age 55 or older on the date of sale?	☐ You ☐ Your spouse	☑ Both of you
11	Did the person who was age 55 or older own and use the property as his or her main home for a total of at least 3 years (except for short absences) of the 5-year period before the sale? If "No," go to Part IV now.	☑ Yes ☐ No	
12	At the time of sale, who owned the home?	☐ You ☐ Your spouse	☑ Both of you
13	Social security number of spouse at the time of sale if you had a different spouse from the one above. If you were not married at the time of sale, enter "None" ▶	13	
14	**Exclusion.** Enter the **smaller** of line 8 or $125,000 ($62,500 if married filing separate return). Then, go to line 15	14	125,000

Part IV — Adjusted Sales Price, Taxable Gain, and Adjusted Basis of New Home

15	If line 14 is blank, enter the amount from line 8. Otherwise, subtract line 14 from line 8	15	3,340
	• If line 15 is zero, stop and attach this form to your return.		
	• If line 15 is more than zero and line 2 is "Yes," go to line 16 now.		
	• If you are reporting this sale on the installment method, stop and see the instructions.		
	• All others, stop and **enter the amount** from line 15 on Schedule D, col. (g), line 4 or line 12.		
16	Fixing-up expenses (see instructions for time limits)	16	124,000
17	Adjusted sales price. Subtract line 16 from line 15	17	27,340
18	Date you moved into new home ▶ 5/5/93	19b Cost of new home (see instructions)	19b	91,300
19a	Date you moved into new home ▶ 5/5/93			
20	Subtract line 19b from line 18. If zero or less, enter -0-	20	-0-
21	**Taxable gain.** Enter the **smaller** of line 15 or line 20	21	-0-
	• If line 21 is zero, go to line 22 and attach this form to your return.		
	• If you are reporting this sale on the installment method, see the line 15 instructions and go to line 22.		
	• All others, **enter the amount** from line 21 on Schedule D, col. (g), line 4 or line 12, and go to line 22.		
22	Postponed gain. Subtract line 21 from line 15	22	3,340
23	**Adjusted basis of new home.** Subtract line 22 from line 19b	23	87,960

Sign Here Only If You Are Filing This Form by Itself and Not With Your Tax Return

Under penalties of perjury, I declare that I have examined this form, including attachments, and to the best of my knowledge and belief, it is true, correct, and complete.

Your signature | Date | Spouse's signature | Date

▶ If a joint return, both must sign.

For Paperwork Reduction Act Notice, see separate instructions. ♻ Printed on recycled paper

Cat. No. 11710J | Form **2119** (1993)

Form 3903 — Moving Expenses

Form 3903

Department of the Treasury
Internal Revenue Service

Moving Expenses

▶ Attach to Form 1040.
▶ See separate instructions.

OMB No. 1545-0062

1993

Attachment Sequence No. 62

Name(s) shown on Form 1040

Frank R. & Evelyn D. Jones

Your social security number

516:00:1492

Caution: If you are a member of the armed forces, see the instructions before completing this form.

1	Enter the number of miles from your old home to your **new workplace**	1	96
2	Enter the number of miles from your old home to your **old workplace**	2	5
3	Subtract line 2 from line 1. Enter the result but not less than zero	3	91

If line 3 is 35 or more miles, complete the rest of this form. Also, see **Time Test** in the instructions. If line 3 is less than 35 miles, you may not deduct your moving expenses.

Part I — Moving Expenses

Note: Any payments your employer made for any part of your move (including the value of any services furnished in kind) should be included on your W-2 form. Report that amount on **Form 1040, line 7.** See **Reimbursements** in the instructions.

Section A—Transportation of Household Goods

4	Transportation and storage for household goods and personal effects	4	530

Section B—Expenses of Moving From Old To New Home

5	Travel and lodging not including meals	5	70
6	Total meals	6	50
7	Multiply line 6 by 80% (.80)	7	40
8	Add lines 5 and 7	8	110

Section C—Pre-move Househunting Expenses and Temporary Quarters (for any 30 days in a row after getting your job)

9	Pre-move travel and lodging **not** including meals	9	500
10	Temporary quarters expenses **not** including meals	10	
11	Total meal expenses for both pre-move househunting and temporary quarters	11	200
12	Multiply line 11 by 80% (.80)	12	160
13	Add lines 9, 10, and 12	13	660

Section D—Qualified Real Estate Expenses

14 Expenses of (check one) a ☑ selling or exchanging your old home, or
b ☐ if renting, settling an unexpired lease.

14		9,000

15 Expenses of (check one) a ☐ buying your new home, or
b ☐ if renting, getting a new lease.

15		1,300

Part II — Dollar Limits and Moving Expense Deduction

Note: If you and your spouse moved to separate homes, see the instructions.

16 Enter the **smaller** of:
• The amount on line 13, or
• $1,500 ($750 if married filing a separate return and at the end of 1993 you lived with your spouse who also started work in 1993).

16		660

17 Add lines 14, 15, and 16

17		10,960

18 Enter the **smaller** of:
• The amount on line 17, or
• $3,000 ($1,500 if married filing a separate return and at the end of 1993 you lived with your spouse who also started work in 1993).

18		3,000

19 Add lines 4, 8, and 18. Enter the total here and on Schedule A, line 18. This is your moving expense deduction ▶

19		3,640

For Paperwork Reduction Act Notice, see separate instructions. Cat. No. 12490K ♻ Printed on recycled paper | Form **3903** (1993)

(Margin reference numbers: 243, 244, 261, 251, 249, 392, 399, 400, 398, 401, 110)

Form 4562 — Depreciation and Amortization (Including Information on Listed Property)

OMB No. 1545-0172

1993

Department of the Treasury, Internal Revenue Service

▶ See separate instructions.   ▶ Attach this form to your return.

Attachment Sequence No. 67

Name(s) shown on return: Frank R. & Evelyn D. Jones

Identifying number: 516-00-1492

Business or activity to which this form relates: Rental of Store building

Part I — Election To Expense Certain Tangible Property (Section 179) (Note: If you have any "Listed Property," complete Part V before you complete Part I.)

1	Maximum dollar limitation (If an enterprise zone business, see instructions.)	1	$17,500
2	Total cost of section 179 property placed in service during the tax year (see instructions)	2	
3	Threshold cost of section 179 property before reduction in limitation	3	$200,000
4	Reduction in limitation. Subtract line 3 from line 2, but do not enter less than -0-	4	
5	Dollar limitation for tax year. Subtract line 4 from line 1, but do not enter less than -0-. (If married filing separately, see instructions.)	5	

6 (a) Description of property	(b) Cost	(c) Elected cost

7	Listed property. Enter amount from line 26.	7	
8	Total elected cost of section 179 property. Add amounts in column (c), lines 6 and 7	8	
9	Tentative deduction. Enter the smaller of line 5 or line 8	9	
10	Carryover of disallowed deduction from 1992 (see instructions)	10	
11	Taxable income limitation. Enter the smaller of taxable income or line 5 (see instructions)	11	
12	Section 179 expense deduction. Add lines 9 and 10, but do not enter more than line 11	12	
13	Carryover of disallowed deduction to 1994. Add lines 9 and 10, less line 12 ▶ 13		

Note: Do not use Part II or Part III below for listed property (automobiles, certain other vehicles, cellular telephones, certain computers, or property used for entertainment, recreation, or amusement). Instead, use Part V for listed property.

Part II — MACRS Depreciation For Assets Placed in Service ONLY During Your 1993 Tax Year (Do Not Include Listed Property)

(a) Classification of property	(b) Month and year placed in service	(c) Basis for depreciation (business/investment use only—see instructions)	(d) Recovery period	(e) Convention	(f) Method	(g) Depreciation deduction
14 General Depreciation System (GDS) (see instructions):						
a 3-year property						
b 5-year property						
c 7-year property						
d 10-year property						
e 15-year property						
f 20-year property						
g Residential rental property			27.5 yrs.	MM	S/L	
			27.5 yrs.	MM	S/L	
h Nonresidential real property				MM	S/L	
				MM	S/L	
15 Alternative Depreciation System (ADS) (see instructions):						
a Class life					S/L	
b 12-year			12 yrs.		S/L	
c 40-year			40 yrs.	MM	S/L	

Part III — Other Depreciation (Do Not Include Listed Property)

16	GDS and ADS deductions for assets placed in service in tax years beginning before 1993 (see instructions)	16	
17	Property subject to section 168(f)(1) election (see instructions)	17	
18	ACRS and other depreciation (see instructions)	18	

Part IV — Summary

19	Listed property. Enter amount from line 25.	19	
20	**Total.** Add deductions on line 12, lines 14 and 15 in column (g), and lines 16 through 19. Enter here and on the appropriate lines of your return. (Partnerships and S corporations—see instructions)	20	
21	For assets shown above and placed in service during the current year, enter the portion of the basis attributable to section 263A costs (see instructions)	21	

For Paperwork Reduction Act Notice, see page 1 of the separate instructions.   Cat. No. 12906N   Form **4562** (1993)

Form 4562 (1993)   Page **2**

Part V — Listed Property—Automobiles, Certain Other Vehicles, Cellular Telephones, Certain Computers, and Property Used for Entertainment, Recreation, or Amusement

For any vehicle for which you are using the standard mileage rate or deducting lease expense, complete only 22a, 22b, columns (a) through (c) of Section A, all of Section B, and Section C if applicable.

Section A—Depreciation and Other Information (Caution: See instructions for limitations for automobiles.)

22a Do you have evidence to support the business/investment use claimed? ☐ Yes ☐ No   22b If "Yes," is the evidence written? ☐ Yes ☐ No

(a) Type of property (list vehicles first)	(b) Date placed in service	(c) Business/investment use percentage	(d) Cost or other basis	(e) Basis for depreciation (business/investment use only)	(f) Recovery period	(g) Method/Convention	(h) Depreciation deduction	(i) Elected section 179 cost
23 Property used more than 50% in a qualified business use (see instructions):								
		%						
		%						
		%						
24 Property used 50% or less in a qualified business use (see instructions):								
USA coupe	9-3-91	3 %				S/L –		
		%				S/L –		
		%				S/L –		

25	Add amounts in column (h). Enter the total here and on line 19, page 1	25	
26	Add amounts in column (i). Enter the total here and on line 7, page 1	26	

Section B—Information Regarding Use of Vehicles—If you deduct expenses for vehicles:

- Always complete this section for vehicles used by a sole proprietor, partner, or other "more than 5% owner," or related person.
- If you provided vehicles to your employees, first answer the questions in Section C to see if you meet an exception to completing this section for those vehicles.

	(a) Vehicle 1	(b) Vehicle 2	(c) Vehicle 3	(d) Vehicle 4	(e) Vehicle 5	(f) Vehicle 6
27 Total business/investment miles driven during the year (DO NOT include commuting miles)	280					
28 Total commuting miles driven during the year	2,200					
29 Total other personal (noncommuting) miles driven	7,820					
30 Total miles driven during the year. Add lines 27 through 29.	10,300					
	Yes	No	Yes	No	Yes	No	Yes	No	Yes	No	Yes	No
31 Was the vehicle available for personal use during off-duty hours?	✓					
32 Was the vehicle used primarily by a more than 5% owner or related person?		✓				
33 Is another vehicle available for personal use?		✓				

Section C—Questions for Employers Who Provide Vehicles for Use by Their Employees

Answer these questions to determine if you meet an exception to completing Section B. Note: Section B must always be completed for vehicles used by sole proprietors, partners, or other more than 5% owners or related persons.

	Yes	No
34 Do you maintain a written policy statement that prohibits all personal use of vehicles, including commuting, by your employees?		
35 Do you maintain a written policy statement that prohibits personal use of vehicles, except commuting, by your employees? (See instructions for vehicles used by corporate officers, directors, or 1% or more owners.)		
36 Do you treat all use of vehicles by employees as personal use?		
37 Do you provide more than five vehicles to your employees and retain the information received from your employees concerning the use of the vehicles?		
38 Do you meet the requirements concerning qualified automobile demonstration use (see instructions)?		
Note: If your answer to 34, 35, 36, 37, or 38 is "Yes," you need not complete Section B for the covered vehicles.		

Part VI — Amortization

(a) Description of costs	(b) Date amortization begins	(c) Amortizable amount	(d) Code section	(e) Amortization period or percentage	(f) Amortization for this year
39 Amortization of costs that begins during your 1993 tax year:					

40	Amortization of costs that began before 1993	40	
41	**Total.** Enter here and on "Other Deductions" or "Other Expenses" line of your return	41	

Form **4562** (1993)

605

Form **8834**

Department of the Treasury
Internal Revenue Service

Qualified Electric Vehicle Credit

▶ Attach to your tax return.

OMB No. 1545-1374

1993

Attachment
Sequence No. **96**

Name(s) shown on return

Frank R. & Evelyn D. Jones

Identifying number

575-00-1776

Part I — Tentative Credit

			(a)	(b)	(c)
1	Cost of vehicle	1	12,000		
2	Section 179 expense deduction. See instructions	2	-0-		
3	Subtract line 2 from line 1	3	12,000		
4	Multiply line 3 by 10% (.10)	4	1,200		
5	Limitation per vehicle	5	4,000	4,000	4,000
6	Enter the **smaller** of line 4 or line 5	6	1,200		

7	**Current year qualified electric vehicle credit.** Add line 6, columns (a) through (c)	7	1,200
8	Passive activity credits included on line 7. See instructions	8	-0-
9	Subtract line 8 from line 7	9	1,200
10	Passive activity credits allowed for 1993. See instructions	10	-0-
11	**Tentative qualified electric vehicle credit.** Add lines 9 and 10	11	1,200

Part II — Tax Liability Limitation

12	Enter the amount of your regular tax:		
a	Individuals. Enter the amount from Form 1040, line 40		
b	Corporations. Enter the amount from Form 1120, Schedule J, line 3	12	1,346
c	Other filers. Enter your regular tax before credits from your return		
13	Credits that reduce regular tax before the qualified electric vehicle credit:		
a	Credit for child and dependent care expenses (Form 2441, line 10)	13a	
b	Credit for the elderly or the disabled (Schedule R (Form 1040), line 21)	13b	
c	Mortgage interest credit (Form 8396, line 11)	13c	
d	Foreign tax credit (Form 1116, line 32, or Form 1118, Sch. B, Part III, line 12)	13d	
e	Possessions tax credit (Form 5735, line 14)	13e	
f	Orphan drug credit (Form 6765, line 10)	13f	
g	Credit for fuel from a nonconventional source	13g	
h	Add lines 13a through 13g	13h	-0-
14	Net regular tax. Subtract line 13h from line 12. If zero or less, do not complete the rest of this form	14	1,346
15	Tentative minimum tax (see instructions):		
a	Individuals. Enter the amount from Form 6251, line 26		
b	Corporations. Enter the amount from Form 4626, line 14	15	-0-
c	Estates and trusts. Enter the amount from Form 1041, Schedule H, line 37		
16	Excess of net regular tax over tentative minimum tax. Subtract line 15 from line 14. If zero or less, do not file this form; you cannot claim this credit	16	1,346
17	**Qualified electric vehicle credit allowed.** Enter the **smaller** of line 11 or line 16. Also, enter on Form 1040, line 44; Form 1120, Schedule J, line 4d; Form 1041, Schedule G, line 2b; or the appropriate line of other income tax returns	17	1,200

46 | 1993 Federal Tax Forms and Schedules You Can Use

Introduction

This chapter contains many, if not all, of the official IRS tax forms that you need to complete your income tax return. The forms can be easily torn out and used. It is perfectly acceptable to use these forms in filling out your return.

A listing of all the tax forms included in this book—some of which are samples and others of which are provided for your use—can be found in the Table of Contents.

Here are the forms that are included in this chapter:

Form SS-5: Application For a Social Security Number Card

Form 1040EZ: Income Tax Return for Single and Joint Filers with No Dependents

Form 1040A: U.S. Individual Income Tax Return

  Schedule 1: Interest and Dividend Income for Form 1040A Filers

  Schedule 2: Child and Dependent Care Expenses for Form 1040A Filers

  Schedule 3: Credit for the Elderly or the Disabled for Form 1040A Filers

Form 1040: U.S. Individual Income Tax Return

  Schedule A: Itemized Deductions

  Schedule B: Interest and Dividend Income

  Schedule C: Profit or Loss from Business (Sole Proprietorship)

  Schedule D: Capital Gains and Losses

  Schedule E: Supplemental Income and Loss

  Schedule EIC: Earned Income Credit

  Schedule F: Profit or Loss From Farming

  Schedule R: Credit for the Elderly or the Disabled

  Schedule SE: Self-Employment Tax

Form 1040X: Amended U.S. Individual Income Tax Return

Form 1116: Foreign Tax Credit

Form 2106: Employee Business Expenses

Form 2119: Sale of Your Home

Form 2120: Multiple Support Declaration

Form 2441: Child and Dependent Care Expenses

Form 2688: Application for Additional Extension of Time to File U.S. Individual Income Tax Return

Form 3903: Moving Expenses

Form 4562: Depreciation and Amortization

Form 4684: Casualties and Thefts

Form 4797: Sales of Business Property

Form 4868: Application for Automatic Extension of Time To File U.S. Individual Income Tax Return

Form 4972: Tax on Lump-Sum Distributions

Form 6251: Alternative Minimum Tax—Individuals

Form 6252: Installment Sale Income

Form 8271: Investor Reporting of Tax Shelter Registration Number

Form 8283: Noncash Charitable Contributions

Form 8582: Passive Activity Loss Limitations

Form 8606: Nondeductible IRAs

*Form 8615: Tax for Children Under Age 14
Who Have Investment Income of More Than $1,200.*

Form 8801: Credit For Prior Year Minimum Tax—Individuals and Fiduciaries

Form 8814: Parent's Election to Report Child's Interest and Dividends

*Form 8815: Exclusion of Interest From Series EE U.S. Savings Bonds Issued
After 1989*

Form 8822: Change of Address

Form 8829: Expenses for Business Use of Your Home

Draft Form 8841: Deferral of Additional 1993 Taxes

SOCIAL SECURITY ADMINISTRATION
Application for a Social Security Card

Form Approved
OMB No. 0960-0066

INSTRUCTIONS

- Please read "How To Complete This Form" on page 2.
- Print or type using black or blue ink. DO NOT USE PENCIL.
- After you complete this form, take or mail it along with the required documents to your nearest Social Security office.
- If you are completing this form for someone else, answer the questions as they apply to that person. Then, sign your name in question 16.

1 NAME
To Be Shown On Card

▶ FIRST — FULL MIDDLE NAME — LAST

FULL NAME AT BIRTH
IF OTHER THAN ABOVE

FIRST — FULL MIDDLE NAME — LAST

OTHER NAMES USED

2 MAILING ADDRESS
Do Not Abbreviate

▶ STREET ADDRESS, APT. NO., PO BOX, RURAL ROUTE NO.

CITY — STATE — ZIP CODE

3 CITIZENSHIP
(Check One)

☐ U.S. Citizen ☐ Legal Alien Allowed To Work ☐ Legal Alien Not Allowed To Work ☐ Foreign Student Allowed Restricted Employment ☐ Conditionally Legalized Alien Allowed To Work ☐ Other (See Instructions On Page 2)

4 SEX ☐ Male ☐ Female

5 RACE/ETHNIC DESCRIPTION
(Check One Only—Voluntary)

☐ Asian, Asian-American Or Pacific Islander ☐ Hispanic ☐ Black (Not Hispanic) ☐ North American Indian Or Alaskan Native ☐ White (Not Hispanic)

6 DATE OF BIRTH
MONTH DAY YEAR

7 PLACE OF BIRTH
(Do Not Abbreviate)
CITY — STATE OR FOREIGN COUNTRY — FCI

☐ Office Use Only

8 MOTHER'S MAIDEN NAME
FIRST — FULL MIDDLE NAME — LAST NAME AT HER BIRTH

9 FATHER'S NAME
FIRST — FULL MIDDLE NAME — LAST

10 Has the person in item 1 ever received a Social Security number before?

☐ Yes (If "yes", answer questions 11-13.) ☐ No (If "no", go on to question 14.) ☐ Don't Know (If "don't know", go on to question 14.)

11 Enter the Social Security number previously assigned to the person listed in item 1.

☐☐☐ - ☐☐ - ☐☐☐☐

12 Enter the name shown on the most recent Social Security card issued for the person listed in item 1.

FIRST — MIDDLE — LAST

13 Enter any different date of birth if used on an earlier application for a card.
MONTH DAY YEAR

14 TODAY'S DATE ▶ MONTH DAY YEAR

15 DAYTIME PHONE NUMBER ▶ ( ) AREA CODE

DELIBERATELY FURNISHING (OR CAUSING TO BE FURNISHED) FALSE INFORMATION ON THIS APPLICATION IS A CRIME PUNISHABLE BY FINE OR IMPRISONMENT, OR BOTH.

16 YOUR SIGNATURE
▶

17 YOUR RELATIONSHIP TO THE PERSON IN ITEM 1 IS:

☐ Self ☐ Natural Or Adoptive Parent ☐ Legal Guardian ☐ Other (Specify)

DO NOT WRITE BELOW THIS LINE (FOR SSA USE ONLY)				
NPN	DOC	NTI	CAN	ITV
PBC	EVI	EVA	EVC	PRA	NWR	DNR	UNIT

EVIDENCE SUBMITTED

SIGNATURE AND TITLE OF EMPLOYEE(S) REVIEWING EVIDENCE AND/OR CONDUCTING INTERVIEW

DATE

DCL

DATE

Form SS-5 (9/89) 5/88 edition may be used until supply is exhausted

609

Department of the Treasury—Internal Revenue Service

Form
1040EZ

Income Tax Return for Single and Joint Filers With No Dependents (T) 1993

OMB No. 1545-0675

Use the IRS label
(See page 10.)
Otherwise, please print.

L A B E L / H E R E

Print your name (first, initial, last)

If a joint return, print spouse's name (first, initial, last)

Home address (number and street). If you have a P.O. box, see page 11. | Apt. no.

City, town or post office, state and ZIP code. If you have a foreign address, see page 11.

Your social security number

Spouse's social security number

See instructions on back and in Form 1040EZ booklet.

Presidential Election Campaign
(See page 11.)

Note: *Checking "Yes" will not change your tax or reduce your refund.*

Do you want $3 to go to this fund? ▶

If a joint return, does your spouse want $3 to go to this fund? ▶

Yes   No

Filing status

1 ☐ Single   ☐ Married filing joint return (even if only one had income)

Dollars   Cents

Report your income

Attach Copy B of Form(s) W-2 here. Attach any tax payment on top of Form(s) W-2.

Note: *You must check Yes or No.*

2 Total wages, salaries, and tips. This should be shown in box 1 of your W-2 form(s). Attach your W-2 form(s). 2

3 Taxable interest income of $400 or less. If the total is over $400, you cannot use Form 1040EZ. 3

4 Add lines 2 and 3. This is your **adjusted gross income.** 4

5 Can your parents (or someone else) claim you on their return?
☐ **Yes.** Do worksheet on back; enter amount from line G here.
☐ **No.** If **single,** enter 6,050.00. If **married,** enter 10,900.00. For an explanation of these amounts, see back of form. 5

6 Subtract line 5 from line 4. If line 5 is larger than line 4, enter 0. This is your **taxable income.** 6

Figure your tax

7 Enter your Federal income tax withheld from box 2 of your W-2 form(s). 7

8 **Tax.** Look at line 6 above. Use the amount on **line 6** to find your tax in the tax table on pages 24–28 of the booklet. Then, enter the tax from the table on this line. 8

Refund or amount you owe

9 If line 7 is larger than line 8, subtract line 8 from line 7. This is your **refund.** 9

10 If line 8 is larger than line 7, subtract line 7 from line 8. This is the **amount you owe.** For details on how to pay, including what to write on your payment, see page 16. 10

Sign your return

Keep a copy of this form for your records.

I have read this return. Under penalties of perjury, I declare that to the best of my knowledge and belief, the return is true, correct, and accurately lists all amounts and sources of income I received during the tax year.

Your signature | Spouse's signature if joint return

Date | Your occupation | Date | Spouse's occupation

For IRS Use Only — Please do not write in boxes below.

1993   Instructions for Form 1040EZ

Use this form if

- Your filing status is single or married filing jointly.
- You do not claim any dependents.
- You had **only** wages, salaries, tips, and taxable scholarship or fellowship grants, and your taxable interest income was $400 or less. **But** if you earned tips, including allocated tips, that are not included in box 5 and box 7 of your W-2, you may not be able to use Form 1040EZ. See page 13.
- You did not receive any advance earned income credit payments.
- You (and your spouse if married) were under 65 on January 1, 1994, and not blind at the end of 1993.
- Your taxable income (line 6) is less than $50,000.

Caution: *If married and either you or your spouse had total wages of over $57,600, you may not be able to use this form. See page 6.*

If you are not sure about your filing status, see page 12. If you have questions about dependents, call Tele-Tax (see page 22) and listen to topic 354. If you **can't use this form,** call Tele-Tax (see page 22) and listen to topic 352.

Filling in your return

Because this form is read by a machine, please print your numbers inside the boxes like this:

9 8 7 6 5 4 3 2 1 0   Do not type your numbers. Do not use dollar signs.

Most people can fill in the form by following the instructions on the front. But you will have to use the booklet if you received a scholarship or fellowship grant or tax-exempt interest income, such as on municipal bonds. Also, use the booklet if you received a Form 1099-INT showing income tax withheld (backup withholding).

Remember, you must report all wages, salaries, and tips even if you don't get a W-2 form from your employer. You must also report all your taxable interest income, including interest from banks, savings and loans, credit unions, etc., even if you don't get a Form 1099-INT.

If you paid someone to prepare your return, see page 17.

Worksheet for dependents who checked "Yes" on line 5

Use this worksheet to figure the amount to enter on line 5 if someone can claim you (or your spouse if married) as a dependent, even if that person chooses not to do so. To find out if someone can claim you as a dependent, call Tele-Tax (see page 22) and listen to topic 354.

A. Enter the amount from line 2 on the front.   A. _____
B. Minimum standard deduction.   B. _____ 600.00
C. Enter the LARGER of line A or line B here.   C. _____
D. Maximum standard deduction. If single, enter 3,700.00; if married, enter 6,200.00.   D. _____
E. Enter the SMALLER of line C or line D here. This is your standard deduction.   E. _____
F. Exemption amount.
   - If single, enter 0.
   - If married and both you and your spouse can be claimed as dependents, enter 0.
   - If married and only one of you can be claimed as a dependent, enter 2,350.00.   F. _____
G. Add lines E and F. Enter the total here and on line 5 on the front.   G. _____

If you checked "No" on line 5 because no one can claim you (or your spouse if married) as a dependent, enter on line 5 the amount shown below that applies to you.

- Single, enter 6,050.00. This is the total of your standard deduction (3,700.00) and personal exemption (2,350.00).
- Married, enter 10,900.00. This is the total of your standard deduction (6,200.00), exemption for yourself (2,350.00), and exemption for your spouse (2,350.00).

Avoid mistakes

Please see page 17 of the Form 1040EZ booklet for a list of common mistakes to avoid that will help you make sure your form is filled in correctly.

Mailing your return

Mail your return by **April 15, 1994.** Use the envelope that came with your booklet. If you don't have that envelope, see page 29 for the address to use.

Form
1040A

Department of the Treasury—Internal Revenue Service

U.S. Individual Income Tax Return (T)   **1993**

IRS Use Only—Do not write or staple in this space.

OMB No. 1545-0085

Label

(See page 15.)

Use the IRS label. Otherwise, please print or type.

L A B E L · H E R E

Your first name and initial	Last name
If a joint return, spouse's first name and initial	Last name
Home address (number and street). If you have a P.O. box, see page 16.	Apt. no.
City, town or post office, state, and ZIP code. If you have a foreign address, see page 16.	

Your social security number

Spouse's social security number

For Privacy Act and Paperwork Reduction Act Notice, see page 4.

Presidential Election Campaign Fund (See page 16.)

Do you want $3 to go to this fund? . . . .
If a joint return, does your spouse want $3 to go to this fund?

Yes	No

Note: *Checking "Yes" will not change your tax or reduce your refund.*

Check the box for your filing status

(See page 16.)

Check only one box.

1 ☐ Single
2 ☐ Married filing joint return (even if only one had income)
3 ☐ Married filing separate return. Enter spouse's social security number above and full name here. ▶
4 ☐ Head of household (with qualifying person). (See page 17.) If the qualifying person is a child but not your dependent, enter this child's name here. ▶
5 ☐ Qualifying widow(er) with dependent child (year spouse died ▶ 19___). (See page 18.)

Figure your exemptions

(See page 19.)

If more than seven dependents, see page 22.

6a ☐ **Yourself.** If your parent (or someone else) can claim you as a dependent on his or her tax return, **do not** check box 6a. But be sure to check the box on line 18b on page 2.

b ☐ **Spouse**

c Dependents:

(1) Name (first, initial, and last name)	(2) Check if under age 1	(3) If age 1 or older, dependent's social security number	(4) Dependent's relationship to you	(5) No. of months lived in your home in 1993

d If your child didn't live with you but is claimed as your dependent under a pre-1985 agreement, check here . . . . ▶ ☐

e Total number of exemptions claimed.

No. of boxes checked on 6a and 6b ___

No. of your children on 6c who:
• lived with you ___
• didn't live with you due to divorce or separation (see page 22) ___

Dependents on 6c not entered above ___

Add numbers entered on lines above ___

Figure your total income

Attach Copy B of your Forms W-2 and 1099-R here.

If you didn't get a W-2, see page 24.

If you are attaching a check or money order, put it on top of any Forms W-2 or 1099-R.

7 Wages, salaries, tips, etc. This should be shown in box 1 of your W-2 form(s). Attach Form(s) W-2. — **7**

8a **Taxable** interest income (see page 25). If over $400, also complete and attach Schedule 1, Part I. — **8a**

b Tax-exempt interest. DO NOT include on line 8a.   **8b**

9 Dividends. If over $400, also complete and attach Schedule 1, Part II. — **9**

10a Total IRA distributions.   10a | **10b** Taxable amount (see page 26). — **10b**

11a Total pensions and annuities.   11a | **11b** Taxable amount (see page 26). — **11b**

12 Unemployment compensation (see page 30). — **12**

13a Social security benefits.   13a | **13b** Taxable amount (see page 30). — **13b**

14 Add lines 7 through 13b (far right column). This is your **total income.** ▶ **14**

Figure your adjusted gross income

15a Your IRA deduction (see page 32).   15a

b Spouse's IRA deduction (see page 32).   15b

c Add lines 15a and 15b. These are your **total adjustments.** — **15c**

16 Subtract line 15c from line 14. This is your **adjusted gross income.** If less than $23,050 and a child lived with you, see page 63 to find out if you can claim the "Earned income credit" on line 28c. ▶ **16**

Cat. No. 11327A

1993 Form 1040A page 1

Name(s) shown on page 1	Your social security number

Figure your standard deduction, exemption amount, and taxable income

17 Enter the amount from line 16.   **17**

18a Check if: ☐ **You** were 65 or older ☐ Blind   ☐ **Spouse** was 65 or older ☐ Blind   **Enter number of boxes checked ▶ 18a**

b If your parent (or someone else) can claim you as a dependent, check here . . . . ▶ **18b** ☐

c If you are married filing separately and your spouse files Form 1040 and itemizes deductions, see page 36 and check here ▶ **18c** ☐

19 Enter the **standard deduction** shown below for your filing status. **But if you checked any box on line 18a or b,** go to page 36 to find your standard deduction. **If you checked box 18c,** enter -0-.
- Single—$3,700   • Head of household—$5,450
- Married filing jointly or Qualifying widow(er)—$6,200
- Married filing separately—$3,100   **19**

20 Subtract line 19 from line 17. If line 19 is more than line 17, enter -0-.   **20**

21 Multiply $2,350 by the total number of exemptions claimed on line 6e.   **21**

22 Subtract line 21 from line 20. If line 21 is more than line 20, enter -0-. This is your **taxable income.**   ▶ **22**

Figure your tax, credits, and payments

If you want the IRS to figure your tax, see the instructions for line 22 on page 37.

23 Find the tax on the amount on line 22. Check if from: ☐ Tax Table (pages 50–55) or ☐ Form 8615 (see page 38).   **23**

24a Credit for child and dependent care expenses. Complete and attach Schedule 2.   **24a**

b Credit for the elderly or the disabled. Complete and attach Schedule 3.   **24b**

c Add lines 24a and 24b. These are your **total credits.**   **24c**

25 Subtract line 24c from line 23. If line 24c is more than line 23, enter -0-.   **25**

26 Advance earned income credit payments from Form W-2.   **26**

27 Add lines 25 and 26. This is your **total tax.**   ▶ **27**

28a Total Federal income tax withheld. If any tax is from Form(s) 1099, check here. ▶ ☐   **28a**

b 1993 estimated tax payments and amount applied from 1992 return.   **28b**

c **Earned income credit.** Complete and attach Schedule EIC.   **28c**

d Add lines 28a, 28b, and 28c. These are your **total payments.**   ▶ **28d**

Figure your refund or amount you owe

29 If line 28d is more than line 27, subtract line 27 from line 28d. This is the amount you **overpaid.**   **29**

30 Amount of line 29 you want **refunded to you.**   **30**

31 Amount of line 29 you want **applied to your 1994 estimated tax.**   **31**

32 If line 27 is more than line 28d, subtract line 28d from line 27. This is the **amount you owe.** For details on how to pay, including what to write on your payment, see page 42.   **32**

33 Estimated tax penalty (see page 43). Also, include on line 32.   **33**

Sign your return

Keep a copy of this return for your records.

Under penalties of perjury, I declare that I have examined this return and accompanying schedules and statements, and to the best of my knowledge and belief, they are true, correct, and accurately list all amounts and sources of income I received during the tax year. Declaration of preparer (other than the taxpayer) is based on all information of which the preparer has any knowledge.

Your signature	Date	Your occupation
Spouse's signature. If joint return, BOTH must sign.	Date	Spouse's occupation

Paid preparer's use only

Preparer's signature	Date	Check if self-employed ☐	Preparer's social security no.
Firm's name (or yours if self-employed) and address		E.I. No.	
		ZIP code	

Schedule 1
(Form 1040A)

Department of the Treasury—Internal Revenue Service

**Interest and Dividend Income
for Form 1040A Filers** (T)

1993

OMB No. 1545-0085

Name(s) shown on Form 1040A	Your social security number

Part I

Interest income

(See pages 25 and 56.)

Note: *If you received a Form 1099–INT, Form 1099–OID, or substitute statement from a brokerage firm, enter the firm's name and the total interest shown on that form.*

	1	List name of payer. If any interest is from a seller-financed mortgage and the buyer used the property as a personal residence, see page 56 and list this interest first. Also, show that buyer's social security number and address.		Amount	
			1		
	2	Add the amounts on line 1.	2		
	3	Excludable interest on series EE U.S. savings bonds issued after 1989 from Form 8815, line 14. You MUST attach Form 8815 to Form 1040A.	3		
	4	Subtract line 3 from line 2. Enter the result here and on Form 1040A, line 8a.	4		

Part II

Dividend income

(See pages 25 and 57.)

Note: *If you received a Form 1099–DIV or substitute statement from a brokerage firm, enter the firm's name and the total dividends shown on that form.*

	5	List name of payer		Amount	
			5		
	6	Add the amounts on line 5. Enter the total here and on Form 1040A, line 9.	6		

For Paperwork Reduction Act Notice, see Form 1040A instructions.   Cat. No. 12075R   **1993 Schedule 1 (Form 1040A) page 1**

615

Schedule 2
(Form 1040A)

Department of the Treasury—Internal Revenue Service

Child and Dependent Care Expenses for Form 1040A Filers (T)   1993

OMB No. 1545-0085

Name(s) shown on Form 1040A | Your social security number

You need to understand the following terms to complete this schedule: **Dependent care benefits, Earned income, Qualified expenses,** and **Qualifying person(s).** See **Important terms** on page 58. Also, if you had a child born in 1993 and line 17 of Form 1040A is less than $23,050, see **A change to note** on page 59.

Part I

Persons or organizations who provided the care

You MUST complete this part.

1

(a) Care provider's name	(b) Address (number, street, apt. no., city, state, and ZIP code)	(c) Identifying number (SSN or EIN)	(d) Amount paid (see page 61)

(If you need more space, use the bottom of page 2.)

2 Add the amounts in column (d) of line 1.   **2**

3 Enter the number of **qualifying persons** cared for in 1993 . . . ▶ ☐

Did you receive dependent care benefits? → **NO** ──→ Complete only Part II below.

→ **YES** ──→ Complete Part III on the back now.

Part II

Credit for child and dependent care expenses

4 Enter the amount of **qualified expenses** you incurred and paid in 1993. DO NOT enter more than $2,400 for one qualifying person or $4,800 for two or more persons. If you completed Part III, enter the amount from line 25.   **4**

5 Enter YOUR **earned income.**   **5**

6 If married filing a joint return, enter YOUR SPOUSE'S earned income (if student or disabled, see page 61); **all others,** enter the amount from line 5.   **6**

7 Enter the **smallest** of line 4, 5, or 6.   **7**

8 Enter the amount from Form 1040A, line 17.   **8**

9 Enter on line 9 the decimal amount shown below that applies to the amount on line 8.

If line 8 is—		Decimal amount is	If line 8 is—		Decimal amount is
Over	But not over		Over	But not over	
$0—10,000		.30	$20,000—22,000		.24
10,000—12,000		.29	22,000—24,000		.23
12,000—14,000		.28	24,000—26,000		.22
14,000—16,000		.27	26,000—28,000		.21
16,000—18,000		.26	28,000—No limit		.20
18,000—20,000		.25			

9   × .

10 Multiply **line 7** by the decimal amount on line 9. Enter the result. Then, see page 61 for the amount of credit to enter on Form 1040A, line 24a.   **10**   =

Caution: *If you paid $50 or more in a calendar quarter to a person who worked in your home, you must file an employment tax return. Get **Form 942** for details.*

For Paperwork Reduction Act Notice, see Form 1040A instructions.   Cat. No. 107491   **1993 Schedule 2 (Form 1040A) page 1**

Name(s) shown on page 1	Your social security number

Part III

Dependent care benefits

Complete this part **only** if you received these benefits.

11 Enter the total amount of **dependent care benefits** you received for 1993. This amount should be shown in box 10 of your W-2 form(s). DO NOT include amounts that were reported to you as wages in box 1 of Form(s) W-2. ... **11**

12 Enter the amount forfeited, if any. See page 62. ... **12**

13 Subtract line 12 from line 11. ... **13**

14 Enter the total amount of **qualified expenses** incurred in 1993 for the care of the qualifying person(s). ... **14**

15 Enter the **smaller** of line 13 or 14. ... **15**

16 Enter YOUR **earned income.** ... **16**

17 If married filing a joint return, enter YOUR SPOUSE'S earned income (if student or disabled, see the line 6 instructions); if married filing a separate return, see the instructions for the amount to enter; **all others,** enter the amount from line 16. ... **17**

18 Enter the **smallest** of line 15, 16, or 17. ... **18**

19 **Excluded benefits.** Enter here the **smaller** of the following:
  • The amount from line 18, or
  • $5,000 ($2,500 if married filing a separate return **and** you were required to enter your spouse's earned income on line 17). ... **19**

20 **Taxable benefits.** Subtract line 19 from line 13. Also, include this amount on Form 1040A, line 7. In the space to the left of line 7, write "DCB." ... **20**

To claim the child and dependent care credit, complete lines 21–25 below, and lines 4–10 on the front of this schedule.

21 Enter the amount of qualified expenses you incurred and paid in 1993. DO NOT include on this line any excluded benefits shown on line 19. ... **21**

22 Enter $2,400 ($4,800 if two or more qualifying persons). ... **22**

23 Enter the amount from line 19. ... **23**

24 Subtract line 23 from line 22. If zero or less, **STOP.** You cannot take the credit. **Exception.** If you paid 1992 expenses in 1993, see the line 10 instructions. ... **24**

25 Enter the **smaller** of line 21 or 24 here **and** on line 4 on the front of this schedule. ... **25**

Schedule 3 (Form 1040A)	Department of the Treasury—Internal Revenue Service **Credit for the Elderly or the Disabled** **for Form 1040A Filers** (T)	**1993**	OMB No. 1545-0085

Name(s) shown on Form 1040A	Your social security number

You may be able to use Schedule 3 to reduce your tax if by the end of 1993:

- You were age 65 or older, **OR**
- You were under age 65, you retired on **permanent and total** disability, and you received taxable disability income.

But you must also meet other tests. See the separate instructions for Schedule 3.

Note: *In most cases, the IRS can figure the credit for you. See page 38 of the Form 1040A instructions.*

Part I

Check the box for your filing status and age

If your filing status is:	And by the end of 1993:	Check only one box:
Single, Head of household, or Qualifying widow(er) with dependent child	1 You were 65 or older.	1 ☐
	2 You were under 65 and you retired on permanent and total disability	2 ☐
Married filing a joint return	3 Both spouses were 65 or older	3 ☐
	4 Both spouses were under 65, but only one spouse retired on permanent and total disability	4 ☐
	5 Both spouses were under 65, and both retired on permanent and total disability	5 ☐
	6 One spouse was 65 or older, and the other spouse was under 65 and retired on permanent and total disability .	6 ☐
	7 One spouse was 65 or older, and the other spouse was under 65 and **NOT** retired on permanent and total disability	7 ☐
Married filing a separate return	8 You were 65 or older and you lived apart from your spouse for all of 1993	8 ☐
	9 You were under 65, you retired on permanent and total disability, and you lived apart from your spouse for all of 1993	9 ☐

If you checked box 1, 3, 7, or 8, skip Part II and complete Part III on the back. All others, complete Parts II and III.

Part II

Statement of permanent and total disability

Complete this part **only** if you checked box 2, 4, 5, 6, or 9 above.

IF: 1 You filed a physician's statement for this disability for 1983 or an earlier year, or you filed a statement for tax years after 1983 and your physician signed line B on the statement, **AND**

2 Due to your continued disabled condition, you were unable to engage in any substantial gainful activity in 1993, check this box . . . . ▶ ☐

- If you checked this box, you do not have to file another statement for 1993.
- If you **did not** check this box, have your physician complete the following statement:

Physician's statement (See instructions at bottom of page 2.)

I certify that _____
Name of disabled person

was permanently and totally disabled on January 1, 1976, or January 1, 1977, **OR** was permanently and totally disabled on the date he or she retired. If retired after December 31, 1976, enter the date retired ▶ _____

Physician: Sign your name on **either** line A or B below.

A The disability has lasted or can be expected to last continuously for at least a year . . . .

	Physician's signature	Date

B There is no reasonable probability that the disabled condition will ever improve . . . .

	Physician's signature	Date

Physician's name	Physician's address

For Paperwork Reduction Act Notice, see Form 1040A instructions.   Cat. No. 12064K   **1993 Schedule 3 (Form 1040A) page 1**

Name(s) shown on page 1	Your social security number

Part III
Figure your credit

10 If you checked (in Part I):   **Enter:**
Box 1, 2, 4, or 7 . . . . $5,000
Box 3, 5, or 6 . . . . $7,500
Box 8 or 9 . . . . $3,750   **10**

Caution: If you checked box 2, 4, 5, 6, or 9 in Part I, you **MUST** complete line 11 below. All others, skip line 11 and enter the amount from line 10 on line 12.

11
- If you checked box 6 in Part I, add $5,000 to the taxable disability income of the spouse who was under age 65. Enter the total.
- If you checked box 2, 4, or 9 in Part I, enter your taxable disability income.
- If you checked box 5 in Part I, add your taxable disability income to your spouse's taxable disability income. Enter the total.

TIP: For more details on what to include on line 11, see the instructions.   **11**

12
- If you completed line 11, look at lines 10 and 11. Enter the **smaller** of the two amounts.
- All others, enter the amount from line 10.   **12**

13 Enter the following pensions, annuities, or disability income that you (and your spouse if filing a joint return) received in 1993:

a Nontaxable part of social security benefits, and
Nontaxable part of railroad retirement benefits treated as social security. See instructions.   **13a**

b Nontaxable veterans' pensions and any other pension, annuity, or disability benefit that is excluded from income under any other provision of law. See instructions.   **13b**

c Add lines 13a and 13b. (Even though these income items are not taxable, they **must** be included here to figure your credit.) If you did not receive any of the types of nontaxable income listed on line 13a or 13b, enter -0- on line 13c.   **13c**

14 Enter the amount from Form 1040A, line 17.   **14**

15 If you checked (in Part I):   **Enter:**
Box 1 or 2 . . . . $7,500
Box 3, 4, 5, 6, or 7 . . . . $10,000
Box 8 or 9 . . . . $5,000   **15**

16 Subtract line 15 from line 14. If line 15 is more than line 14, enter -0-.   **16**

17 Divide line 16 above by 2.   **17**

18 Add lines 13c and 17.   **18**

19 Subtract line 18 from line 12. If line 18 is more than line 12, stop here; you **cannot** take the credit. Otherwise, go to line 21.   **19**

20 Decimal amount used to figure the credit.   **20**   × .15

21 Multiply line 19 above by the decimal amount (.15) on line 20. Enter the result here and on Form 1040A, line 24b.   **21**

Instructions for physician's statement

Taxpayer.—If you retired after December 31, 1976, enter the date you retired in the space provided in Part II.
Physician.—A person is permanently and totally disabled if **both** of the following apply:
1. He or she cannot engage in any substantial gainful activity because of a physical or mental condition, and
2. A physician determines that the disability has lasted or can be expected to last continuously for at least a year or can lead to death.

Form **1040**

Department of the Treasury—Internal Revenue Service

U.S. Individual Income Tax Return (T) 1993

For the year Jan. 1–Dec. 31, 1993, or other tax year beginning _____, 1993, ending _____, 19___   OMB No. 1545-0074

IRS Use Only—Do not write or staple in this space.

Label

(See instructions on page 12.)

Use the IRS label. Otherwise, please print or type.

L A B E L   H E R E

Your first name and initial Last name	Your social security number
If a joint return, spouse's first name and initial Last name	Spouse's social security number
Home address (number and street). If you have a P.O. box, see page 12. Apt. no.	**For Privacy Act and Paperwork Reduction Act Notice, see page 4.**
City, town or post office, state, and ZIP code. If you have a foreign address, see page 12.	

Presidential Election Campaign
(See page 12.)

Do you want $3 to go to this fund? . . . .

If a joint return, does your spouse want $3 to go to this fund? . . . .

	Yes	No

Note: Checking "Yes" will not change your tax or reduce your refund.

Filing Status

(See page 12.)

Check only one box.

1 ☐ Single

2 ☐ Married filing joint return (even if only one had income)

3 ☐ Married filing separate return. Enter spouse's social security no. above and full name here. ▶

4 ☐ Head of household (with qualifying person). (See page 13.) If the qualifying person is a child but not your dependent, enter this child's name here. ▶

5 ☐ Qualifying widow(er) with dependent child (year spouse died ▶ 19___). (See page 13.)

Exemptions

(See page 13.)

If more than six dependents, see page 14.

6a ☐ **Yourself.** If your parent (or someone else) can claim you as a dependent on his or her tax return, **do not** check box 6a. But be sure to check the box on line 33b on page 2

b ☐ **Spouse**

c **Dependents:**

(1) Name (first, initial, and last name)	(2) Check if under age 1	(3) If age 1 or older, dependent's social security number	(4) Dependent's relationship to you	(5) No. of months lived in your home in 1993

d If your child didn't live with you but is claimed as your dependent under a pre-1985 agreement, check here ▶ ☐

e Total number of exemptions claimed . . . .

No. of boxes checked on 6a and 6b ___

No. of your children on 6c who:
- lived with you ___
- didn't live with you due to divorce or separation (see page 15) ___

Dependents on 6c not entered above ___

Add numbers entered on lines above ▶ ___

Income

Attach Copy B of your Forms W-2, W-2G, and 1099-R here.

If you did not get a W-2, see page 10.

If you are attaching a check or money order, put it on top of any Forms W-2, W-2G, or 1099-R.

7	Wages, salaries, tips, etc. Attach Form(s) W-2	**7**
8a	**Taxable** interest income (see page 16). Attach Schedule B if over $400	**8a**
b	**Tax-exempt** interest (see page 17). DON'T include on line 8a **8b**	
9	Dividend income. Attach Schedule B if over $400	**9**
10	Taxable refunds, credits, or offsets of state and local income taxes (see page 17) . .	**10**
11	Alimony received	**11**
12	Business income or (loss). Attach Schedule C or C-EZ	**12**
13	Capital gain or (loss). Attach Schedule D	**13**
14	Capital gain distributions not reported on line 13 (see page 17) . . .	**14**
15	Other gains or (losses). Attach Form 4797	**15**
16a	Total IRA distributions . **16a** ___ b Taxable amount (see page 18)	**16b**
17a	Total pensions and annuities **17a** ___ b Taxable amount (see page 18)	**17b**
18	Rental real estate, royalties, partnerships, S corporations, trusts, etc. Attach Schedule E	**18**
19	Farm income or (loss). Attach Schedule F	**19**
20	Unemployment compensation (see page 19)	**20**
21a	Social security benefits **21a** ___ b Taxable amount (see page 19)	**21b**
22	Other income. List type and amount—see page 20 _____	**22**
23	Add the amounts in the far right column for lines 7 through 22. This is your **total income** ▶	**23**

Adjustments to Income

(See page 20.)

24a	Your IRA deduction (see page 20) **24a**
b	Spouse's IRA deduction (see page 20) **24b**
25	One-half of self-employment tax (see page 21) . . . **25**
26	Self-employed health insurance deduction (see page 22) **26**
27	Keogh retirement plan and self-employed SEP deduction **27**
28	Penalty on early withdrawal of savings **28**
29	Alimony paid. Recipient's SSN ▶ _____ **29**
30	Add lines 24a through 29. These are your **total adjustments** . . . . ▶	**30**

Adjusted Gross Income

31 Subtract line 30 from line 23. This is your **adjusted gross income.** If this amount is less than $23,050 and a child lived with you, see page EIC-1 to find out if you can claim the "Earned Income Credit" on line 56 . . . . ▶ | **31** |

Cat. No. 11320B   Form **1040** (1993)

621

Tax Computation (See page 23.)	**32**	Amount from line 31 (adjusted gross income)		**32**	
	33a	Check if: ☐ **You** were 65 or older, ☐ Blind; ☐ **Spouse** was 65 or older, ☐ Blind.			
		Add the number of boxes checked above and enter the total here . . . . ▶ **33a**			
	b	If your parent (or someone else) can claim you as a dependent, check here . ▶ **33b** ☐			
	c	If you are married filing separately and your spouse itemizes deductions or you are a dual-status alien, see page 24 and check here . . . . ▶ **33c** ☐			
	34	Enter the **larger** of your:	**Itemized deductions** from Schedule A, line 26, **OR** **Standard deduction** shown below for your filing status. **But if you checked any box on line 33a or b,** go to page 24 to find your standard deduction. If you checked **box 33c,** your standard deduction is zero. • Single—$3,700 • Head of household—$5,450 • Married filing jointly or Qualifying widow(er)—$6,200 • Married filing separately—$3,100	**34**	
If you want the IRS to figure your tax, see page 24.	**35**	Subtract line 34 from line 32		**35**	
	36	If line 32 is $81,350 or less, multiply $2,350 by the total number of exemptions claimed on line 6e. If line 32 is over $81,350, see the worksheet on page 25 for the amount to enter .		**36**	
	37	**Taxable income.** Subtract line 36 from line 35. If line 36 is more than line 35, enter -0-		**37**	
	38	Tax. Check if from **a** ☐ Tax Table, **b** ☐ Tax Rate Schedules, **c** ☐ Schedule D Tax Worksheet, or **d** ☐ Form 8615 (see page 25). Amount from Form(s) 8814 ▶ **e** [ ]		**38**	
	39	Additional taxes (see page 25). Check if from **a** ☐ Form 4970 **b** ☐ Form 4972 . .		**39**	
	40	Add lines 38 and 39 . . . . ▶		**40**	
Credits (See page 25.)	**41**	Credit for child and dependent care expenses. Attach Form 2441	**41**		
	42	Credit for the elderly or the disabled. Attach Schedule R . .	**42**		
	43	Foreign tax credit. Attach Form 1116	**43**		
	44	Other credits (see page 26). Check if from **a** ☐ Form 3800 **b** ☐ Form 8396 **c** ☐ Form 8801 **d** ☐ Form (specify) [ ]	**44**		
	45	Add lines 41 through 44		**45**	
	46	Subtract line 45 from line 40. If line 45 is more than line 40, enter -0- . . . . . ▶		**46**	
Other Taxes	**47**	Self-employment tax. Attach Schedule SE. Also, see line 25 .		**47**	
	48	Alternative minimum tax. Attach Form 6251		**48**	
	49	Recapture taxes (see page 26). Check if from **a** ☐ Form 4255 **b** ☐ Form 8611 **c** ☐ Form 8828		**49**	
	50	Social security and Medicare tax on tip income not reported to employer. Attach Form 4137 .		**50**	
	51	Tax on qualified retirement plans, including IRAs. If required, attach Form 5329 . .		**51**	
	52	Advance earned income credit payments from Form W-2		**52**	
	53	Add lines 46 through 52. This is your **total tax** . . . . ▶		**53**	
Payments Attach Forms W-2, W-2G, and 1099-R on the front.	**54**	Federal income tax withheld. If any is from Form(s) 1099, check ▶ ☐	**54**		
	55	1993 estimated tax payments and amount applied from 1992 return .	**55**		
	56	**Earned income credit.** Attach Schedule EIC	**56**		
	57	Amount paid with Form 4868 (extension request)	**57**		
	58a	Excess social security, Medicare, and RRTA tax withheld (see page 28) .	**58a**		
	b	Deferral of additional 1993 taxes. Attach Form 8841	**58b**		
	59	Other payments (see page 28). Check if from **a** ☐ Form 2439 **b** ☐ Form 4136	**59**		
	60	Add lines 54 through 59. These are your **total payments** . . . . ▶		**60**	
Refund or Amount You Owe	**61**	If line 60 is more than line 53, subtract line 53 from line 60. This is the amount you **OVERPAID.** ▶		**61**	
	62	Amount of line 61 you want **REFUNDED TO YOU.** . . . . ▶		**62**	
	63	Amount of line 61 you want **APPLIED TO YOUR 1994 ESTIMATED TAX** ▶	**63**		
	64	If line 53 is more than line 60, subtract line 60 from line 53. This is the **AMOUNT YOU OWE.** For details on how to pay, including what to write on your payment, see page 29 . .		**64**	
	65	Estimated tax penalty (see page 29). Also include on line 64	**65**		

Sign Here Keep a copy of this return for your records.	Under penalties of perjury, I declare that I have examined this return and accompanying schedules and statements, and to the best of my knowledge and belief, they are true, correct, and complete. Declaration of preparer (other than taxpayer) is based on all information of which preparer has any knowledge.		
	Your signature	Date	Your occupation
	Spouse's signature. If a joint return, BOTH must sign.	Date	Spouse's occupation

Paid Preparer's Use Only	Preparer's signature ▶	Date	Check if self-employed ☐	Preparer's social security no.
	Firm's name (or yours if self-employed) and address ▶		E.I. No.	
			ZIP code	

SCHEDULES A&B
(Form 1040)

Department of the Treasury
Internal Revenue Service (T)

Schedule A—Itemized Deductions

(Schedule B is on back)

► Attach to Form 1040. ► See Instructions for Schedules A and B (Form 1040).

OMB No. 1545-0074

1993

Attachment
Sequence No. **07**

Name(s) shown on Form 1040

Your social security number

Medical and Dental Expenses

Caution: *Do not include expenses reimbursed or paid by others.*

1	Medical and dental expenses (see page A-1)	1
2	Enter amount from Form 1040, line 32. |_**2**_|	
3	Multiply line 2 above by 7.5% (.075)	3
4	Subtract line 3 from line 1. If zero or less, enter -0- . . . ►	4

Taxes You Paid

(See page A-1.)

5	State and local income taxes	5
6	Real estate taxes (see page A-2)	6
7	Other taxes. List—include personal property taxes ►	7
8	Add lines 5 through 7 . . . . ►	8

Interest You Paid

(See page A-2.)

Note: Personal interest is not deductible.

9a	Home mortgage interest and points reported to you on Form 1098	9a
b	Home mortgage interest not reported to you on Form 1098. If paid to the person from whom you bought the home, see page A-3 and show that person's name, identifying no., and address ►	9b
10	Points not reported to you on Form 1098. See page A-3 for special rules	10
11	Investment interest. If required, attach Form 4952. (See page A-3.)	11
12	Add lines 9a through 11 . . . . ►	12

Gifts to Charity

(See page A-3.)

Caution: *If you made a charitable contribution and received a benefit in return, see page A-3.*

13	Contributions by cash or check	13
14	Other than by cash or check. If over $500, you **MUST** attach Form 8283	14
15	Carryover from prior year	15
16	Add lines 13 through 15 . . . . ►	16

Casualty and Theft Losses

17	Casualty or theft loss(es). Attach Form 4684. (See page A-4.) . . . . . . ►	17

Moving Expenses

18	Moving expenses. Attach Form 3903 or 3903-F. (See page A-4.) . . . . ►	18

Job Expenses and Most Other Miscellaneous Deductions

(See page A-5 for expenses to deduct here.)

19	Unreimbursed employee expenses—job travel, union dues, job education, etc. If required, you **MUST** attach Form 2106. (See page A-4.) ►	19
20	Other expenses—investment, tax preparation, safe deposit box, etc. List type and amount ►	20
21	Add lines 19 and 20	21
22	Enter amount from Form 1040, line 32. |_**22**_|	
23	Multiply line 22 above by 2% (.02)	23
24	Subtract line 23 from line 21. If zero or less, enter -0- . . . ►	24

Other Miscellaneous Deductions

25	Other—from list on page A-5. List type and amount ►	
	►	25

Total Itemized Deductions

26 Is the amount on Form 1040, line 32, more than $108,450 (more than $54,225 if married filing separately)?

- **NO.** Your deduction is not limited. Add lines 4, 8, 12, 16, 17, 18, 24, and 25 and enter the total here. Also enter on Form 1040, line 34, the **larger** of this amount or your standard deduction. ► | 26 |
- **YES.** Your deduction may be limited. See page A-5 for the amount to enter.

For Paperwork Reduction Act Notice, see Form 1040 instructions.   Cat. No. 11330X   **Schedule A (Form 1040) 1993**

Name(s) shown on Form 1040. Do not enter name and social security number if shown on other side.

Schedule B—Interest and Dividend Income

Attachment
Sequence No. **08**

**Part I
Interest
Income**

(See
pages 16
and B-1.)

Note: If you
received a Form
1099-INT, Form
1099-OID, or
substitute
statement from
a brokerage firm,
list the firm's
name as the
payer and enter
the total interest
shown on that
form.

Note: *If you had over $400 in taxable interest income, you must also complete Part III.*

Interest Income		Amount	
1 List name of payer. If any interest is from a seller-financed mortgage and the buyer used the property as a personal residence, see page B-1 and list this interest first. Also show that buyer's social security number and address ▶		**1**	
2 Add the amounts on line 1		**2**	
3 Excludable interest on series EE U.S. savings bonds issued after 1989 from Form 8815, line 14. You MUST attach Form 8815 to Form 1040		**3**	
4 Subtract line 3 from line 2. Enter the result here and on Form 1040, line 8a ▶		**4**	

**Part II
Dividend
Income**

(See
pages 17
and B-1.)

Note: If you
received a Form
1099-DIV or
substitute
statement from
a brokerage
firm, list the
firm's name as
the payer and
enter the total
dividends
shown on that
form.

Note: *If you had over $400 in gross dividends and/or other distributions on stock, you must also complete Part III.*

Dividend Income		Amount	
5 List name of payer. Include gross dividends and/or other distributions on stock here. Any capital gain distributions and nontaxable distributions will be deducted on lines 7 and 8 ▶		**5**	
6 Add the amounts on line 5		**6**	
7 Capital gain distributions. Enter here and on Schedule D* .	**7**		
8 Nontaxable distributions. (See the inst. for Form 1040, line 9.)	**8**		
9 Add lines 7 and 8		**9**	
10 Subtract line 9 from line 6. Enter the result here and on Form 1040, line 9 . ▶		**10**	

*If you received capital gain distributions but do not need Schedule D to report
any other gains or losses, see the instructions for Form 1040, lines 13 and 14.*

**Part III
Foreign
Accounts
and
Trusts**

(See
page B-2.)

If you had over $400 of interest or dividends OR had a foreign account or were a grantor of, or a transferor to, a foreign trust, you must complete this part.

	Yes	No
11a At any time during 1993, did you have an interest in or a signature or other authority over a financial account in a foreign country, such as a bank account, securities account, or other financial account? See page B-2 for exceptions and filing requirements for Form TD F 90-22.1		
b If "Yes," enter the name of the foreign country ▶		
12 Were you the grantor of, or transferor to, a foreign trust that existed during 1993, whether or not you have any beneficial interest in it? If "Yes," you may have to file Form 3520, 3520-A, or 926 .		

For Paperwork Reduction Act Notice, see Form 1040 instructions.

Schedule B (Form 1040) 1993

SCHEDULE C (Form 1040)	Profit or Loss From Business	OMB No. 1545-0074

SCHEDULE C (Form 1040)

Department of the Treasury
Internal Revenue Service (T)

Profit or Loss From Business
(Sole Proprietorship)
▶ Partnerships, joint ventures, etc., must file Form 1065.
▶ **Attach to Form 1040 or Form 1041.** ▶ **See Instructions for Schedule C (Form 1040).**

OMB No. 1545-0074

1993

Attachment Sequence No. **09**

Name of proprietor

Social security number (SSN)

A Principal business or profession, including product or service (see page C-1)

B Enter principal business code (see page C-6) ▶

C Business name. If no separate business name, leave blank.

D Employer ID number (EIN), if any

E Business address (including suite or room no.) ▶ ....
City, town or post office, state, and ZIP code

F Accounting method: **(1)** ☐ Cash **(2)** ☐ Accrual **(3)** ☐ Other (specify) ▶ ....

G Method(s) used to value closing inventory: **(1)** ☐ Cost **(2)** ☐ Lower of cost or market **(3)** ☐ Other (attach explanation) **(4)** ☐ Does not apply (if checked, skip line H)

	Yes	No
H Was there any change in determining quantities, costs, or valuations between opening and closing inventory? If "Yes," attach explanation		
I Did you "materially participate" in the operation of this business during 1993? If "No," see page C-2 for limit on losses. . . .		

J If you started or acquired this business during 1993, check here . . . . ▶ ☐

Part I Income

1	Gross receipts or sales. **Caution:** *If this income was reported to you on Form W-2 and the "Statutory employee" box on that form was checked, see page C-2 and check here* . . . . ▶ ☐	**1**
2	Returns and allowances	**2**
3	Subtract line 2 from line 1	**3**
4	Cost of goods sold (from line 40 on page 2)	**4**
5	**Gross profit.** Subtract line 4 from line 3	**5**
6	Other income, including Federal and state gasoline or fuel tax credit or refund (see page C-2) . .	**6**
7	**Gross income.** Add lines 5 and 6 . . . . ▶	**7**

Part II Expenses. Caution: *Do not enter expenses for business use of your home on lines 8–27. Instead, see line 30.*

8	Advertising	**8**	**19** Pension and profit-sharing plans	**19**	
9	Bad debts from sales or services (see page C-3) . .	**9**	**20** Rent or lease (see page C-4):		
			a Vehicles, machinery, and equipment .	**20a**	
10	Car and truck expenses (see page C-3) . .	**10**	b Other business property . .	**20b**	
11	Commissions and fees. . .	**11**	**21** Repairs and maintenance . .	**21**	
12	Depletion	**12**	**22** Supplies (not included in Part III) .	**22**	
13	Depreciation and section 179 expense deduction (not included in Part III) (see page C-3) . .	**13**	**23** Taxes and licenses . . .	**23**	
			24 Travel, meals, and entertainment:		
			a Travel	**24a**	
14	Employee benefit programs (other than on line 19) . . .	**14**	b Meals and entertainment		
15	Insurance (other than health) .	**15**	c Enter 20% of line 24b subject to limitations (see page C-4) .		
16	Interest:				
a	Mortgage (paid to banks, etc.) .	**16a**	d Subtract line 24c from line 24b .	**24d**	
b	Other	**16b**	**25** Utilities	**25**	
17	Legal and professional services	**17**	**26** Wages (less jobs credit) . .	**26**	
18	Office expense . . .	**18**	**27** Other expenses (from line 46 on page 2)	**27**	

28	**Total expenses** before expenses for business use of home. Add lines 8 through 27 in columns . ▶	**28**
29	Tentative profit (loss). Subtract line 28 from line 7	**29**
30	Expenses for business use of your home. Attach **Form 8829**	**30**
31	**Net profit or (loss).** Subtract line 30 from line 29. • If a profit, enter on **Form 1040, line 12,** and ALSO on **Schedule SE, line 2** (statutory employees, see page C-5). Fiduciaries, enter on Form 1041, line 3. • If a loss, you MUST go on to line 32.	**31**

32 If you have a loss, check the box that describes your investment in this activity (see page C-5).
• If you checked 32a, enter the loss on **Form 1040, line 12,** and ALSO on **Schedule SE, line 2** (statutory employees, see page C-5). Fiduciaries, enter on Form 1041, line 3.
• If you checked 32b, you MUST attach **Form 6198.**

32a ☐ All investment is at risk.
32b ☐ Some investment is not at risk.

For Paperwork Reduction Act Notice, see Form 1040 instructions. Cat. No. 11334P Schedule C (Form 1040) 1993

Part III   **Cost of Goods Sold** (see page C-5)

33	Inventory at beginning of year. If different from last year's closing inventory, attach explanation . .	33	
34	Purchases less cost of items withdrawn for personal use	34	
35	Cost of labor. Do not include salary paid to yourself	35	
36	Materials and supplies	36	
37	Other costs	37	
38	Add lines 33 through 37	38	
39	Inventory at end of year	39	
40	**Cost of goods sold.** Subtract line 39 from line 38. Enter the result here and on page 1, line 4 . .	40	

Part IV   **Information on Your Vehicle. Complete this part ONLY if you are claiming car or truck expenses on line 10 and are not required to file Form 4562 for this business.**

41   When did you place your vehicle in service for business purposes? (month, day, year) ▶ ..../.............../........ .

42   Of the total number of miles you drove your vehicle during 1993, enter the number of miles you used your vehicle for:

  a Business .... **b** Commuting .... **c** Other ....

43   Do you (or your spouse) have another vehicle available for personal use? . . . . ☐ **Yes**   ☐ **No**

44   Was your vehicle available for use during off-duty hours? . . . . ☐ **Yes**   ☐ **No**

45a   Do you have evidence to support your deduction? . . . . ☐ **Yes**   ☐ **No**
  b If "Yes," is the evidence written? . . . . ☐ **Yes**   ☐ **No**

Part V   **Other Expenses.** List below business expenses not included on lines 8–26 or line 30.

....		
....		
....		
....		
....		
....		
....		
....		
....		
46	**Total other expenses.** Enter here and on page 1, line 27	46	

Capital Gains and Losses

► Attach to Form 1040.   ► See Instructions for Schedule D (Form 1040).

► Use lines 20 and 22 for more space to list transactions for lines 1 and 9.

OMB No. 1545-0074

1993

Attachment
Sequence No. **12**

Name(s) shown on Form 1040

Your social security number

Part I   Short-Term Capital Gains and Losses—Assets Held One Year or Less

(a) Description of property (Example: 100 sh. XYZ Co.)	(b) Date acquired (Mo., day, yr.)	(c) Date sold (Mo., day, yr.)	(d) Sales price (see page D-3)	(e) Cost or other basis (see page D-3)	(f) LOSS If (e) is more than (d), subtract (d) from (e)	(g) GAIN If (d) is more than (e), subtract (e) from (d)
1						

2 Enter your short-term totals, if any, from line 21 . . . . | **2** | | | | |

3 **Total short-term sales price amounts.** Add column (d) of lines 1 and 2 . . . | **3** | | | |

4 Short-term gain from Forms 2119 and 6252, and short-term gain or (loss) from Forms 4684, 6781, and 8824 . . . . | **4** |

5 Net short-term gain or (loss) from partnerships, S corporations, and fiduciaries from Schedule(s) K-1 . . . . | **5** |

6 Short-term capital loss carryover from 1992 Schedule D, line 38 . . . . | **6** |

7 Add lines 1, 2, and 4 through 6, in columns (f) and (g). . . . . | **7** ( ) |

8 **Net short-term capital gain or (loss).** Combine columns (f) and (g) of line 7 . . . . | **8** |

Part II   Long-Term Capital Gains and Losses—Assets Held More Than One Year

9						

10 Enter your long-term totals, if any, from line 23 . . . . | **10** | | | | |

11 **Total long-term sales price amounts.** Add column (d) of lines 9 and 10 . . . | **11** | | | |

12 Gain from Form 4797; long-term gain from Forms 2119, 2439, and 6252; and long-term gain or (loss) from Forms 4684, 6781, and 8824 . . . . | **12** |

13 Net long-term gain or (loss) from partnerships, S corporations, and fiduciaries from Schedule(s) K-1 . . . . | **13** |

14 Capital gain distributions | **14** |

15 Long-term capital loss carryover from 1992 Schedule D, line 45 . . . . | **15** |

16 Add lines 9, 10, and 12 through 15, in columns (f) and (g) . . . . . . | **16** ( ) |

17 **Net long-term capital gain or (loss).** Combine columns (f) and (g) of line 16 . . . . | **17** |

Part III   Summary of Parts I and II

18 Combine lines 8 and 17. If a loss, go to line 19. If a gain, enter the gain on Form 1040, line 13.
Note: *If both lines 17 and 18 are gains, see the* **Schedule D Tax Worksheet** *on page D-4* . . | **18** |

19 If line 18 is a (loss), enter here and as a (loss) on Form 1040, line 13, the **smaller** of these losses:

a The (loss) on line 18; **or**

b ($3,000) or, if married filing separately, ($1,500) . . . . | **19** ( ) |

Note: *See the* **Capital Loss Carryover Worksheet** *on page D-4 if the loss on line 18 exceeds the loss on line 19* **or** *if Form 1040, line 35, is a loss.*

For Paperwork Reduction Act Notice, see Form 1040 instructions.   Cat. No. 11338H   Schedule D (Form 1040) 1993

Name(s) shown on Form 1040. Do not enter name and social security number if shown on other side. | **Your social security number**

Part IV   Short-Term Capital Gains and Losses—Assets Held One Year or Less *(Continuation of Part I)*

(a) Description of property (Example: 100 sh. XYZ Co.)	(b) Date acquired (Mo., day, yr.)	(c) Date sold (Mo., day, yr.)	(d) Sales price (see page D-3)	(e) Cost or other basis (see page D-3)	(f) LOSS If (e) is more than (d), subtract (d) from (e)	(g) GAIN If (d) is more than (e), subtract (e) from (d)
20						
21 Short-term totals. Add columns (d), (f), and (g) of line 20. Enter here and on line 2	**21**					

Part V   Long-Term Capital Gains and Losses—Assets Held More Than One Year *(Continuation of Part II)*

22						
23 Long-term totals. Add columns (d), (f), and (g) of line 22. Enter here and on line 10	**23**					

SCHEDULE E
(Form 1040)

Department of the Treasury
Internal Revenue Service (T)

Supplemental Income and Loss

(From rental real estate, royalties, partnerships,
S corporations, estates, trusts, REMICs, etc.)

▶ **Attach to Form 1040 or Form 1041.** ▶ **See Instructions for Schedule E (Form 1040).**

OMB No. 1545-0074

1993

Attachment
Sequence No. **13**

Name(s) shown on return

Your social security number

Part I Income or Loss From Rental Real Estate and Royalties **Note:** *Report income and expenses from your business of renting personal property on **Schedule C** or **C-EZ** (see page E-1). Report farm rental income or loss from **Form 4835** on page 2, line 39.*

	1 Show the kind and location of each **rental real estate property:**	2 For each rental real estate property listed on line 1, did you or your family use it for personal purposes for more than the greater of 14 days or 10% of the total days rented at fair rental value during the tax year? (See page E-1.)	Yes	No
A		A		
B		B		
C		C		

Income:		Properties			Totals (Add columns A, B, and C.)	
		A	B	C		
3 Rents received	3				3	
4 Royalties received	4				4	
Expenses:						
5 Advertising	5					
6 Auto and travel (see page E-2) .	6					
7 Cleaning and maintenance . . .	7					
8 Commissions	8					
9 Insurance	9					
10 Legal and other professional fees	10					
11 Management fees	11					
12 Mortgage interest paid to banks, etc. (see page E-2)	12				12	
13 Other interest	13					
14 Repairs	14					
15 Supplies	15					
16 Taxes	16					
17 Utilities	17					
18 Other (list) ▶	18					
19 Add lines 5 through 18	19				19	
20 Depreciation expense or depletion (see page E-2)	20				20	
21 Total expenses. Add lines 19 and 20	21					
22 Income or (loss) from rental real estate or royalty properties. Subtract line 21 from line 3 (rents) or line 4 (royalties). If the result is a (loss), see page E-2 to find out if you must file **Form 6198** . .	22					
23 Deductible rental real estate loss. **Caution:** *Your rental real estate loss on line 22 may be limited. See page E-3 to find out if you must file **Form 8582***	23	( )	( )	( )		

24	**Income.** Add positive amounts shown on line 22. **Do not** include any losses	24	
25	**Losses.** Add royalty losses from line 22 and rental real estate losses from line 23. Enter the total losses here	25	( )
26	**Total rental real estate and royalty income or (loss). Combine lines 24 and 25. Enter the result here. If Parts II, III, IV, and line 39 on page 2 do not apply to you, also enter this amount on Form 1040, line 18. Otherwise, include this amount in the total on line 40 on page 2	26	

For Paperwork Reduction Act Notice, see Form 1040 instructions. Cat. No. 11344L **Schedule E (Form 1040) 1993**

Name(s) shown on return. Do not enter name and social security number if shown on other side.	**Your social security number**

Note: *If you report amounts from farming or fishing on Schedule E, you must enter your gross income from those activities on line 41 below.*

Part II   Income or Loss From Partnerships and S Corporations

If you report a loss from an at-risk activity, you MUST check either column **(e)** or **(f)** of line 27 to describe your investment in the activity. See page E-4. If you check column **(f)**, you must attach **Form 6198**.

27	(a) Name	(b) Enter P for partnership; S for S corporation	(c) Check if foreign partnership	(d) Employer identification number	Investment At Risk? (e) All is at risk	(f) Some is not at risk
A						
B						
C						
D						
E						

	Passive Income and Loss		Nonpassive Income and Loss		
	(g) Passive loss allowed (attach **Form 8582** if required)	(h) Passive income from **Schedule K–1**	(i) Nonpassive loss from **Schedule K–1**	(j) Section 179 expense deduction from **Form 4562**	(k) Nonpassive income from **Schedule K–1**
A					
B					
C					
D					
E					
28a Totals					
b Totals					

29	Add columns (h) and (k) of line 28a	29	
30	Add columns (g), (i), and (j) of line 28b	30 (	)
31	Total partnership and S corporation income or (loss). Combine lines 29 and 30. Enter the result here and include in the total on line 40 below	31	

Part III   Income or Loss From Estates and Trusts

32	(a) Name	(b) Employer identification number
A		
B		
C		

	Passive Income and Loss		Nonpassive Income and Loss	
	(c) Passive deduction or loss allowed (attach **Form 8582** if required)	(d) Passive income from **Schedule K–1**	(e) Deduction or loss from **Schedule K–1**	(f) Other income from **Schedule K–1**
A				
B				
C				
33a Totals				
b Totals				

34	Add columns (d) and (f) of line 33a	34	
35	Add columns (c) and (e) of line 33b	35 (	)
36	Total estate and trust income or (loss). Combine lines 34 and 35. Enter the result here and include in the total on line 40 below	36	

Part IV   Income or Loss From Real Estate Mortgage Investment Conduits (REMICs)—Residual Holder

37	(a) Name	(b) Employer identification number	(c) Excess inclusion from **Schedules Q**, line 2c (see page E-4)	(d) Taxable income (net loss) from **Schedules Q**, line 1b	(e) Income from **Schedules Q**, line 3b

38	Combine columns (d) and (e) only. Enter the result here and include in the total on line 40 below	38	

Part V   Summary

39	Net farm rental income or (loss) from **Form 4835**. Also, complete line 41 below	39	
40	TOTAL income or (loss). Combine lines 26, 31, 36, 38, and 39. Enter the result here and on Form 1040, line 18 . . . . ▶	40	
41	**Reconciliation of Farming and Fishing Income:** Enter your **gross** farming and fishing income reported in Parts II and III and on line 39 (see page E-4)	41	

SCHEDULE EIC
(Form 1040A or 1040)

Department of the Treasury
Internal Revenue Service \(T)

Earned Income Credit

▶ Attach to Form 1040A or 1040.

▶ See Instructions for Schedule EIC.

OMB No. 1545-0074

1993

Attachment
Sequence No. **43**

Name(s) shown on return

Your social security number

Want the IRS to figure the credit for you? Just fill in this page. We'll do the rest.

General Information

To take this credit ⟶
- You **must** have worked and earned **less** than $23,050, **and**
- Your adjusted gross income (Form 1040A, line 16, or Form 1040, line 31) **must** be **less** than $23,050, **and**
- Your filing status can be any status **except** married filing a separate return, **and**
- You **must** have at least one qualifying child (see boxes below), **and**
- You **cannot** be a qualifying child yourself.

A **qualifying child** is a child who: ⟶

is your:		**was (at the end of 1993):**		**who:**
son daughter adopted child grandchild stepchild or foster child	**A N D**	under age 19 or under age 24 and a full-time student or any age and permanently and totally disabled	**A N D**	lived with you in the U.S. for more than half of 1993* (or all of 1993 if a foster child*)

*If the child didn't live with you for the required time (for example, was born in 1993), see the **Exception** on page 64 (1040A) or page EIC-2 (1040).

Do you have at least one qualifying child?	No ▶	You **cannot** take the credit. Enter "NO" next to line 28c of Form 1040A (or line 56 of Form 1040).
	Yes ▶	Go to line 1. But if the child was married or is also a qualifying child of another person (other than your spouse if filing a joint return), first see page 64 (1040A) or page EIC-2 (1040).

Information About Your Qualifying Child or Children

1(a) Child's name (first, initial, and last name) *(If more than two qualifying children, see page 65 (1040A) or page EIC-2 (1040).)*	(b) Child's year of birth	For a child born **before 1975**, check if child was—		(e) If child was born **before 1993**, enter the child's social security number	(f) Child's relationship to you (for example, son, grandchild, etc.)	(g) Number of months child lived with you in the U.S. in 1993
		(c) a student under age 24 at end of 1993	(d) disabled (see booklet)			
	19					
	19					

Caution: *If a child you listed above was born in 1993 **and** you chose to claim the credit or exclusion for child care expenses for this child on **Schedule 2** (Form 1040A) or **Form 2441** (Form 1040), check here* ▶ ☐

Do you want the IRS to figure the credit for you?	Yes ▶	Fill in lines 2 and 3; **and** enter the amount from Form 1040A, line 16, or Form 1040, line 31, here. ▶	$
	No ▶	Go to page 2 on the back now.	

Other Information

2	Enter any **nontaxable earned income** (see page 65 (1040A) or page EIC-2 (1040)) such as military housing and subsistence or contributions to a 401(k) plan. Also, list type and amount here. ▶ _____	**2**	
3	Enter the total amount you paid in 1993 for health insurance that covered at least one qualifying child. See instructions	**3**	

If you want the IRS to figure the credit for you:	**S T O P** ▶	**Attach this schedule to your return.** • If filing Form 1040A, print "EIC" on the line next to line 28c. • If filing Form 1040, print "EIC" on the dotted line next to line 56.

For Paperwork Reduction Act Notice, see Form 1040A or 1040 instructions.   Cat. No. 13339M   **Schedule EIC (Form 1040A or 1040) 1993**

631

Figure Your Basic Credit

4   Enter the amount from line 7 of Form 1040A or Form 1040. If you received a taxable scholarship or fellowship grant, see instructions **4**

5   Enter any **nontaxable earned income** (see page 65 (1040A) or page EIC-2 (1040)) such as military housing and subsistence or contributions to a 401(k) plan. Also, list type and amount here. ▶ **5**

6   **Form 1040 Filers Only:** If you were self-employed **or** used Sch. C or C-EZ as a statutory employee, enter the amount from the worksheet on page EIC-3 . . . .   **6**

7   **Earned income.** Add lines 4, 5, and 6. If $23,050 or more, you **cannot** take the credit. Enter "NO" next to line 28c of Form 1040A (or line 56 of Form 1040) . . . . . ▶   **7**

8   Use **line 7** above to find your credit in **TABLE A** on pages **69 and 70** (1040A) or pages **EIC-4 and 5** (1040). Enter here **8**

9   **Adjusted gross income.** Enter the amount from Form 1040A, line 16, or Form 1040, line 31 ▶   **9**

10   **Is line 9 $12,200 or more?**

     YES. Use **line 9** to find your credit in **TABLE A** on pages **69 and 70** (1040A) or pages **EIC-4 and 5** (1040). Enter here **10**

     NO. Go to line 11.

11   **Basic credit:**
- If you answered "YES" to line 10, enter the **smaller** of line 8 or line 10.
- If you answered "NO" to line 10, enter the amount from line 8.   . . . .   **11**

     Next: To take the health insurance credit, fill in lines 12–16. To take the extra credit for a child born in 1993, fill in lines 17–19. Otherwise, go to line 20 now.

Figure Your Health Insurance Credit

12   Use **line 7** above to find your credit in **TABLE B** on page **71** (1040A) or page **EIC-6** (1040). Enter here **12**

13   **Is line 9 above $12,200 or more?**

     YES. Use **line 9** to find your credit in **TABLE B** on page **71** (1040A) or page **EIC-6** (1040). Enter here. **13**

     NO. Go to line 14.

14
- If you answered "YES" to line 13, enter the **smaller** of line 12 or line 13.
- If you answered "NO" to line 13, enter the amount from line 12.   **14**

15   Enter the total amount you paid in 1993 for health insurance that covered at least one qualifying child. See instructions **15**

16   **Health insurance credit.** Enter the **smaller** of line 14 or line 15 . . . .   **16**

Figure Your Extra Credit for Child Born in 1993

     Take this credit **only** if you did not take the credit or exclusion for child care expenses on **Schedule 2** or **Form 2441** for the same child.

     TIP: You can take **both** the **basic credit** and the **extra credit** for your child born in 1993.

17   Use **line 7** above to find your credit in **TABLE C** on page 72 (1040A) or page **EIC-7** (1040). Enter here **17**

18   **Is line 9 above $12,200 or more?**

     YES. Use **line 9** to find your credit in **TABLE C** on page 72 (1040A) or page **EIC-7** (1040). Enter here **18**

     NO. Go to line 19.

19   **Extra credit for child born in 1993:**
- If you answered "YES" to line 18, enter the **smaller** of line 17 or line 18.
- If you answered "NO" to line 18, enter the amount from line 17.   . . . .   **19**

Figure Your Total Earned Income Credit

20   Add lines 11, 16, and 19. Enter the total here and on Form 1040A, line 28c (or on Form 1040, line 56). This is your **total earned income credit** . . . . ▶   **20**

     TIP: Do you want the earned income credit added to your take-home pay in 1994? To see if you qualify, get **Form W-5** from your employer or by calling the IRS at 1-800-829-3676.

Profit or Loss From Farming

▶ Attach to Form 1040, Form 1041, or Form 1065.

▶ See Instructions for Schedule F (Form 1040).

OMB No. 1545-0074

1993

Attachment
Sequence No. **14**

Name of proprietor

Social security number (SSN)

A Principal product. Describe in one or two words your principal crop or activity for the current tax year.

B Enter principal agricultural activity code (from page 2) ▶

D Employer ID number (EIN), if any

C Accounting method: **(1)** ☐ Cash   **(2)** ☐ Accrual

E Did you "materially participate" in the operation of this business during 1993? If "No," see page F-2 for limit on losses.   ☐ Yes ☐ No

Part I Farm Income—Cash Method. Complete Parts I and II (Accrual method taxpayers complete Parts II and III, and line 11 of Part I.)
Do not include sales of livestock held for draft, breeding, sport, or dairy purposes; report these sales on Form 4797.

1	Sales of livestock and other items you bought for resale	**1**	
2	Cost or other basis of livestock and other items reported on line 1 . . .	**2**	
3	Subtract line 2 from line 1		**3**
4	Sales of livestock, produce, grains, and other products you raised		**4**
5a	Total cooperative distributions (Form(s) 1099-PATR) **5a**	**5b** Taxable amount	**5b**
6a	Agricultural program payments (see page F-2) **6a**	**6b** Taxable amount	**6b**
7	Commodity Credit Corporation (CCC) loans (see page F-2):		
a	CCC loans reported under election		**7a**
b	CCC loans forfeited or repaid with certificates **7b**	**7c** Taxable amount	**7c**
8	Crop insurance proceeds and certain disaster payments (see page F-2):		
a	Amount received in 1993 . . . . **8a**	**8b** Taxable amount	**8b**
c	If election to defer to 1994 is attached, check here ▶ ☐	**8d** Amount deferred from 1992 . .	**8d**
9	Custom hire (machine work) income		**9**
10	Other income, including Federal and state gasoline or fuel tax credit or refund (see page F-3)		**10**
11	**Gross income.** Add amounts in the right column for lines 3 through 10. If accrual method taxpayer, enter the amount from page 2, line 51. . . . . ▶		**11**

Part II Farm Expenses—Cash and Accrual Method. Do not include personal or living expenses such as taxes, insurance, repairs, etc., on your home.

12	Car and truck expenses (see page F-3—also attach **Form 4562**) . .	**12**	**25**	Pension and profit-sharing plans	**25**	
13	Chemicals	**13**	**26**	Rent or lease (see page F-4):		
14	Conservation expenses. Attach **Form 8645**.	**14**	**a**	Vehicles, machinery, and equipment	**26a**	
15	Custom hire (machine work). .	**15**	**b**	Other (land, animals, etc.) . .	**26b**	
16	Depreciation and section 179 expense deduction not claimed elsewhere (see page F-4) . .	**16**	**27**	Repairs and maintenance . .	**27**	
			28	Seeds and plants purchased .	**28**	
			29	Storage and warehousing . .	**29**	
17	Employee benefit programs other than on line 25. . . .	**17**	**30**	Supplies purchased	**30**	
18	Feed purchased	**18**	**31**	Taxes	**31**	
19	Fertilizers and lime	**19**	**32**	Utilities	**32**	
20	Freight and trucking	**20**	**33**	Veterinary, breeding, and medicine .	**33**	
21	Gasoline, fuel, and oil . . .	**21**	**34**	Other expenses (specify):		
22	Insurance (other than health) .	**22**	**a**	....	**34a**	
23	Interest:		**b**	....	**34b**	
a	Mortgage (paid to banks, etc.) .	**23a**	**c**	....	**34c**	
b	Other	**23b**	**d**	....	**34d**	
24	Labor hired (less jobs credit) .	**24**	**e**	....	**34e**	
			f	....	**34f**	

35	**Total expenses.** Add lines 12 through 34f . . . . ▶	**35**
36	**Net farm profit or (loss).** Subtract line 35 from line 11. If a profit, enter on **Form 1040, line 19,** and ALSO on **Schedule SE, line 1.** If a loss, you MUST go on to line 37 (fiduciaries and partnerships, see page F-5) . . .	**36**

37 If you have a loss, you MUST check the box that describes your investment in this activity (see page F-5).
If you checked 37a, enter the loss on **Form 1040, line 19,** and ALSO on **Schedule SE, line 1.**
If you checked 37b, you MUST attach **Form 6198.**

37a ☐ All investment is at risk.
37b ☐ Some investment is not at risk.

For Paperwork Reduction Act Notice, see Form 1040 instructions.   Cat. No. 11346H   **Schedule F (Form 1040) 1993**

Part III   **Farm Income—Accrual Method** (see page F-5)

Do not include sales of livestock held for draft, breeding, sport, or dairy purposes; report these sales on Form 4797 and do not include this livestock on line 46 below.

38	Sales of livestock, produce, grains, and other products during the year	38	
39a	Total cooperative distributions (Form(s) 1099-PATR) **39a** **39b** Taxable amount	39b	
40a	Agricultural program payments **40a** **40b** Taxable amount	40b	
41	Commodity Credit Corporation (CCC) loans:		
a	CCC loans reported under election	41a	
b	CCC loans forfeited or repaid with certificates **41b** **41c** Taxable amount	41c	
42	Crop insurance proceeds	42	
43	Custom hire (machine work) income	43	
44	Other income, including Federal and state gasoline or fuel tax credit or refund	44	
45	Add amounts in the right column for lines 38 through 44	45	
46	Inventory of livestock, produce, grains, and other products at beginning of the year	46	
47	Cost of livestock, produce, grains, and other products purchased during the year	47	
48	Add lines 46 and 47	48	
49	Inventory of livestock, produce, grains, and other products at end of year	49	
50	Cost of livestock, produce, grains, and other products sold. Subtract line 49 from line 48*	50	
51	**Gross income.** Subtract line 50 from line 45. Enter the result here and on page 1, line 11 ▶	51	

*If you use the unit-livestock-price method or the farm-price method of valuing inventory and the amount on line 49 is larger than the amount on line 48, subtract line 48 from line 49. Enter the result on line 50. Add lines 45 and 50. Enter the total on line 51.

Part IV   **Principal Agricultural Activity Codes**

Caution: *File **Schedule C** (Form 1040), Profit or Loss From Business, or **Schedule C-EZ** (Form 1040), Net Profit From Business, instead of Schedule F if:*

- *Your principal source of income is from providing agricultural services such as soil preparation, veterinary, farm labor, horticultural, or management for a fee or on a contract basis, or*
- *You are engaged in the business of breeding, raising, and caring for dogs, cats, or other pet animals.*

Select one of the following codes and write the 3-digit number on page 1, line B:

120 **Field crop,** including grains and nongrains such as cotton, peanuts, feed corn, wheat, tobacco, Irish potatoes, etc.

160 **Vegetables and melons,** garden-type vegetables and melons, such as sweet corn, tomatoes, squash, etc.

170 **Fruit and tree nuts,** including grapes, berries, olives, etc.

180 **Ornamental floriculture and nursery products**

185 **Food crops grown under cover,** including hydroponic crops

211 **Beefcattle feedlots**

212 **Beefcattle,** except feedlots

215 **Hogs, sheep, and goats**

240 **Dairy**

250 **Poultry and eggs,** including chickens, ducks, pigeons, quail, etc.

260 **General livestock,** not specializing in any one livestock category

270 **Animal specialty,** including bees, fur-bearing animals, horses, snakes, etc.

280 **Animal aquaculture,** including fish, shellfish, mollusks, frogs, etc., produced within confined space

290 **Forest products,** including forest nurseries and seed gathering, extraction of pine gum, and gathering of forest products

300 **Agricultural production,** not specified

Schedule R (Form 1040)	Credit for the Elderly or the Disabled	OMB No. 1545-0074
Department of the Treasury Internal Revenue Service (T)	▶ Attach to Form 1040. ▶ See separate instructions for Schedule R.	1993 Attachment Sequence No. 16

Name(s) shown on Form 1040	Your social security number

You may be able to use Schedule R to reduce your tax if by the end of 1993:

- You were age 65 or older, **OR** ● You were under age 65, you retired on **permanent and total** disability, and you received taxable disability income.

But you must also meet other tests. See the separate instructions for Schedule R.

Note: *In most cases, the IRS can figure the credit for you. See page 25 of the Form 1040 instructions.*

Part I Check the Box for Your Filing Status and Age

If your filing status is:	And by the end of 1993:	Check only one box:
Single, Head of household, or Qualifying widow(er) with dependent child	**1** You were 65 or older **1**	☐
	2 You were under 65 and you retired on permanent and total disability . . . **2**	☐
Married filing a joint return	**3** Both spouses were 65 or older **3**	☐
	4 Both spouses were under 65, but only one spouse retired on permanent and total disability **4**	☐
	5 Both spouses were under 65, and both retired on permanent and total disability **5**	☐
	6 One spouse was 65 or older, and the other spouse was under 65 and retired on permanent and total disability **6**	☐
	7 One spouse was 65 or older, and the other spouse was under 65 and **NOT** retired on permanent and total disability **7**	☐
Married filing a separate return	**8** You were 65 or older and you lived apart from your spouse for all of 1993 . . **8**	☐
	9 You were under 65, you retired on permanent and total disability, and you lived apart from your spouse for all of 1993 . . . . **9**	☐

If you checked box 1, 3, 7, or 8, skip Part II and complete Part III on the back. All others, complete Parts II and III.

Part II Statement of Permanent and Total Disability (Complete **only** if you checked box 2, 4, 5, 6, or 9 above.)

IF: 1 You filed a physician's statement for this disability for 1983 or an earlier year, or you filed a statement for tax years after 1983 and your physician signed line B on the statement, **AND**

2 Due to your continued disabled condition, you were unable to engage in any substantial gainful activity in 1993, check this box . . . . ▶ ☐

- If you checked this box, you do not have to file another statement for 1993.
- If you **did not** check this box, have your physician complete the following statement.

Physician's Statement (See instructions at bottom of page 2.)

I certify that _____
Name of disabled person

was permanently and totally disabled on January 1, 1976, or January 1, 1977, **OR** was permanently and totally disabled on the date he or she retired. If retired after December 31, 1976, enter the date retired. ▶ _____

Physician: Sign your name on **either** line A or B below.

A The disability has lasted or can be expected to last continuously for at least a year . . . . _____

Physician's signature	Date

B There is no reasonable probability that the disabled condition will ever improve . . . . _____

Physician's signature	Date

Physician's name	Physician's address

Cat. No. 11359K **Schedule R (Form 1040) 1993**

Part III　　**Figure Your Credit**

10　If you checked (in Part I):　　　　　　　　**Enter:**

Box 1, 2, 4, or 7 . . . . $5,000 ⎫

Box 3, 5, or 6 . . . . $7,500 ⎬ **10**

Box 8 or 9 . . . . $3,750 ⎭

Caution: *If you checked box 2, 4, 5, 6, or 9 in Part I, you **MUST** complete line 11 below. All others, skip line 11 and enter the amount from line 10 on line 12.*

11　If you checked:

- Box 6 in Part I, add $5,000 to the taxable disability income of the spouse who was under age 65. Enter the total.

- Box 2, 4, or 9 in Part I, enter your taxable disability income. ⎬ **11**

- Box 5 in Part I, add your taxable disability income to your spouse's taxable disability income. Enter the total.

TIP: For more details on what to include on line 11, see the instructions.

12　• If you completed line 11, look at lines 10 and 11. Enter the

　　　　smaller of the two amounts. ⎬ **12**

　　• All others, enter the amount from line 10.

13　Enter the following pensions, annuities, or disability income that you (and your spouse if filing a joint return) received in 1993:

a　Nontaxable part of social security benefits, and

　Nontaxable part of railroad retirement benefits treated as ⎬ . . . **13a**

　social security. See instructions.

b　Nontaxable veterans' pensions, and

　Any other pension, annuity, or disability benefit that is ⎬ . . . **13b**

　excluded from income under any other provision of law.

　See instructions.

c　Add lines 13a and 13b. (Even though these income items are not taxable, they **must** be included here to figure your credit.) If you did not receive any of the types of nontaxable income listed on line 13a or 13b, enter -0- on line 13c **13c**

14　Enter the amount from Form 1040, line 32　　**14**

15　If you checked (in Part I):　　　**Enter:**

Box 1 or 2 . . . . $7,500 ⎫

Box 3, 4, 5, 6, or 7 . . . . $10,000 ⎬　**15**

Box 8 or 9 . . . . $5,000 ⎭

16　Subtract line 15 from line 14. If line 15 is

more than line 14, enter -0- . . . . . 　**16**

17　Divide line 16 above by 2 . . . . **17**

18　Add lines 13c and 17 . . . . **18**

19　Subtract line 18 from line 12. If line 18 is more than line 12, stop here; you **cannot** take the credit. Otherwise, go to line 21 . . . . **19**

20　Decimal amount used to figure the credit . . . . **20**　　× .15

21　Multiply line 19 above by the decimal amount (.15) on line 20. Enter the result here and on Form 1040, line 42. **Caution:** *If you file Schedule C, C-EZ, D, E, or F (Form 1040), your credit may be limited. See the instructions for line 21 for the amount of credit you can claim* **21**

Instructions for Physician's Statement

Taxpayer

If you retired after December 31, 1976, enter the date you retired in the space provided in Part II.

Physician

A person is permanently and totally disabled if **both** of the following apply:

　1. He or she cannot engage in any substantial gainful activity because of a physical or mental condition, and

2. A physician determines that the disability has lasted or can be expected to last continuously for at least a year or can lead to death.

SCHEDULE SE **(Form 1040)** Department of the Treasury Internal Revenue Service (T)	**Self-Employment Tax** ► See Instructions for Schedule SE (Form 1040). ► **Attach to Form 1040.**	OMB No. 1545-0074 **1993** Attachment Sequence No. **17**

Name of person with **self-employment** income (as shown on Form 1040)	Social security number of person with **self-employment** income ►

Who Must File Schedule SE

You must file Schedule SE if:

- Your wages (and tips) subject to social security AND Medicare tax (or railroad retirement tax) were less than $135,000; **AND**

- Your net earnings from self-employment from other than church employee income (line 4 of Short Schedule SE or line 4c of Long Schedule SE) were $400 or more; **OR**

- You had church employee income of $108.28 or more. Income from services you performed as a minister or a member of a religious order **is not** church employee income. See page SE-1.

Note: *Even if you have a loss or a small amount of income from self-employment, it may be to your benefit to file Schedule SE and use either "optional method" in Part II of Long Schedule SE. See page SE-3.*

Exception. If your only self-employment income was from earnings as a minister, member of a religious order, or Christian Science practitioner, **AND** you filed Form 4361 and received IRS approval not to be taxed on those earnings, **DO NOT** file Schedule SE. Instead, write "Exempt–Form 4361" on Form 1040, line 47.

May I Use Short Schedule SE or MUST I Use Long Schedule SE?

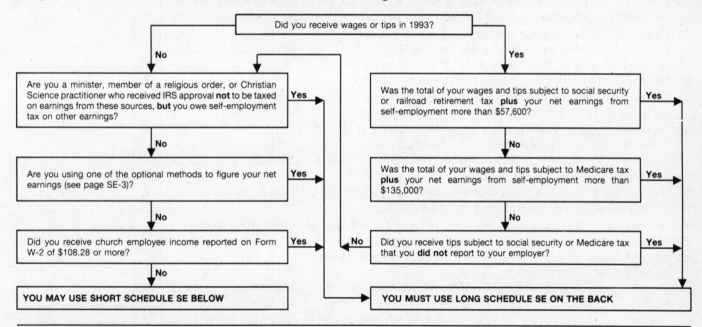

YOU MAY USE SHORT SCHEDULE SE BELOW	**YOU MUST USE LONG SCHEDULE SE ON THE BACK**

Section A—Short Schedule SE. Caution: *Read above to see if you can use Short Schedule SE.*

1	Net farm profit or (loss) from Schedule F, line 36, and farm partnerships, Schedule K-1 (Form 1065), line 15a	**1**
2	Net profit or (loss) from Schedule C, line 31; Schedule C-EZ, line 3; and Schedule K-1 (Form 1065), line 15a (other than farming). Ministers and members of religious orders see page SE-1 for amounts to report on this line. See page SE-2 for other income to report	**2**
3	Combine lines 1 and 2	**3**
4	**Net earnings from self-employment.** Multiply line 3 by 92.35% (.9235). If less than $400, **do not** file this schedule; you do not owe self-employment tax . . . . ►	**4**

5	**Self-employment tax.** If the amount on line 4 is:
	    • $57,600 or less, multiply line 4 by 15.3% (.153) and enter the result.
	    • More than $57,600 but less than $135,000, multiply the amount in excess of $57,600 by 2.9% (.029). Then, add $8,812.80 to the result and enter the total.
	    • $135,000 or more, enter $11,057.40.
	    Also enter on **Form 1040, line 47. (Important:** You are allowed a deduction for **one-half** of this amount. Multiply line 5 by 50% (.5) and enter the result on **Form 1040, line 25.)** . . . .
		5

For Paperwork Reduction Act Notice, see Form 1040 instructions.   Cat. No. 11358Z   **Schedule SE (Form 1040) 1993**

Name of person with **self-employment** income (as shown on Form 1040)	Social security number of person with **self-employment** income ▶	:	:

Section B—Long Schedule SE

Part I   Self-Employment Tax

Note: *If your only income subject to self-employment tax is church employee income, skip lines 1 through 4b. Enter -0- on line 4c and go to line 5a. Income from services you performed as a minister or a member of a religious order **is not** church employee income. See page SE-1.*

A   If you are a minister, member of a religious order, or Christian Science practitioner **AND** you filed Form 4361, but you had $400 or more of **other** net earnings from self-employment, check here and continue with Part I . . . . . . ▶ ☐

1	Net farm profit or (loss) from Schedule F, line 36, and farm partnerships, Schedule K-1 (Form 1065), line 15a. **Note:** *Skip this line if you use the farm optional method. See page SE-3* . .	**1**	
2	Net profit or (loss) from Schedule C, line 31; Schedule C-EZ, line 3; and Schedule K-1 (Form 1065), line 15a (other than farming). Ministers and members of religious orders see page SE-1 for amounts to report on this line. See page SE-2 for other income to report. **Note:** *Skip this line if you use the nonfarm optional method. See page SE-3*	**2**	
3	Combine lines 1 and 2	**3**	
4a	If line 3 is more than zero, multiply line 3 by 92.35% (.9235). Otherwise, enter amount from line 3	**4a**	
b	If you elected one or both of the optional methods, enter the total of lines 17 and 19 here . .	**4b**	
c	Combine lines 4a and 4b. If less than $400, **do not** file this schedule; you do not owe self-employment tax. **Exception.** If less than $400 and you had church employee income, enter -0- and continue . ▶	**4c**	
5a	Enter your church employee income from Form W-2. **Caution:** *See page SE-1 for definition of church employee income* **5a**		
b	Multiply line 5a by 92.35% (.9235). If less than $100, enter -0-	**5b**	
6	**Net earnings from self-employment.** Add lines 4c and 5b	**6**	
7	Maximum amount of combined wages and self-employment earnings subject to social security tax or the 6.2% portion of the 7.65% railroad retirement (tier 1) tax for 1993	**7**	57,600 00
8a	Total social security wages and tips (from Form(s) W-2) and railroad retirement (tier 1) compensation **8a**		
b	Unreported tips subject to social security tax (from Form 4137, line 9) **8b**		
c	Add lines 8a and 8b	**8c**	
9	Subtract line 8c from line 7. If zero or less, enter -0- here and on line 10 and go to line 12a ▶	**9**	
10	Multiply the **smaller** of line 6 or line 9 by 12.4% (.124)	**10**	
11	Maximum amount of combined wages and self-employment earnings subject to Medicare tax or the 1.45% portion of the 7.65% railroad retirement (tier 1) tax for 1993	**11**	135,000 00
12a	Total Medicare wages and tips (from Form(s) W-2) and railroad retirement (tier 1) compensation **12a**		
b	Unreported tips subject to Medicare tax (from Form 4137, line 14) . **12b**		
c	Add lines 12a and 12b	**12c**	
13	Subtract line 12c from line 11. If zero or less, enter -0- here and on line 14 and go to line 15 .	**13**	
14	Multiply the **smaller** of line 6 or line 13 by 2.9% (.029)	**14**	
15	**Self-employment tax.** Add lines 10 and 14. Enter here and on **Form 1040, line 47. (Important:** You are allowed a deduction for **one-half** of this amount. Multiply line 15 by 50% (.5) and enter the result on **Form 1040, line 25.)**	**15**	

Part II   Optional Methods To Figure Net Earnings (See page SE-3.)

Farm Optional Method. You may use this method **only** if **(a)** Your gross farm income[1] was not more than $2,400 **or (b)** Your gross farm income[1] was more than $2,400 and your net farm profits[2] were less than $1,733.

16	Maximum income for optional methods	**16**	1,600 00
17	Enter the **smaller** of: two-thirds (⅔) of gross farm income[1] (not less than zero) **or** $1,600. Also, include this amount on line 4b above	**17**	

Nonfarm Optional Method. You may use this method **only** if **(a)** Your net nonfarm profits[3] were less than $1,733 and also less than 72.189% of your gross nonfarm income,[4] **and (b)** You had net earnings from self-employment of at least $400 in 2 of the prior 3 years. **Caution:** *You may use this method no more than five times.*

18	Subtract line 17 from line 16	**18**	
19	Enter the **smaller** of: two-thirds (⅔) of gross nonfarm income[4] (not less than zero) **or** the amount on line 18. Also, include this amount on line 4b above	**19**	

[1]From Schedule F, line 11, and Schedule K-1 (Form 1065), line 15b.   [3]From Schedule C, line 31; Schedule C-EZ, line 3; and Schedule K-1 (Form 1065), line 15a.
[2]From Schedule F, line 36, and Schedule K-1 (Form 1065), line 15a.   [4]From Schedule C, line 7; Schedule C-EZ, line 1; and Schedule K-1 (Form 1065), line 15c.

638

Form **1040X** (Rev. October 1993)	Department of the Treasury—Internal Revenue Service **Amended U.S. Individual Income Tax Return** ▶ See separate instructions.	OMB No. 1545-0091 Expires 10-31-96

This return is for calendar year ▶ 19_____ , OR fiscal year ended ▶ _____ , 19____

Please print or type

Your first name and initial	Last name	Your social security number
If a joint return, spouse's first name and initial	Last name	Spouse's social security number
Home address (number and street). If you have a P.O. box, see instructions.	Apt. no.	Telephone number (optional) ( )
City, town or post office, state, and ZIP code. If you have a foreign address, see instructions.		**For Paperwork Reduction Act Notice, see page 1 of separate instructions.**

Enter name and address as shown on original return. If same as above, write "Same." If changing from separate to joint return, enter names and addresses from original returns.

A Service center where original return was filed _____

B Has original return been changed or audited by the IRS? ☐ Yes ☐ No
If "No," have you been notified that it will be? . . . . . ☐ Yes ☐ No
If "Yes," identify the IRS office ▶

C Are you amending your return to include any item (loss, credit, deduction, other tax benefit, or income) relating to a tax shelter required to be registered? . . . . ☐ Yes ☐ No
If "Yes," you must attach **Form 8271,** Investor Reporting of Tax Shelter Registration Number.

D Filing status claimed. **Note:** *You cannot change from joint to separate returns after the due date has passed.*

On original return ▶ ☐ Single ☐ Married filing joint return ☐ Married filing separate return ☐ Head of household ☐ Qualifying widow(er)
On this return ▶ ☐ Single ☐ Married filing joint return ☐ Married filing separate return ☐ Head of household ☐ Qualifying widow(er)

Income and Deductions (see instructions)

Caution: *Be sure to complete Part II on page 2.*

			A. As originally reported or as previously adjusted (see instructions)	**B.** Net change— Increase or (Decrease)—explain on page 2	**C.** Correct amount
1	Total income	1			
2	Total adjustments (such as IRA deduction, alimony paid, etc.)	2			
3	Adjusted gross income. Subtract line 2 from line 1 . . .	3			
4	Itemized deductions or standard deduction . . .	4			
5	Subtract line 4 from line 3	5			
6	Exemptions. If changing, fill in Parts I and II on page 2 .	6			
7	Taxable income. Subtract line 6 from line 5	7			

Tax Liability

8	Tax (see instructions). Method used in col. C _____	8			
9	Credits (see instructions)	9			
10	Subtract line 9 from line 8. Enter the result but not less than zero	10			
11	Other taxes (such as self-employment tax, alternative minimum tax, etc.)	11			
12	Total tax. Add lines 10 and 11	12			

Payments

13	Federal income tax withheld and excess social security, Medicare, and RRTA taxes withheld. If changing, see instructions	13			
14	Estimated tax payments	14			
15	Earned income credit	15			
16	Credits for Federal tax paid on fuels, regulated investment company, etc.	16			
17	Amount paid with Form 4868, Form 2688, or Form 2350 (application for extension of time to file) .		17		
18	Amount paid with original return plus additional tax paid after it was filed		18		
19	Total payments. Add lines 13 through 18 in column C		19		

Refund or Amount You Owe

20	Overpayment, if any, as shown on original return or as previously adjusted by the IRS . . .	20	
21	Subtract line 20 from line 19 (see instructions)	21	
22	**AMOUNT YOU OWE.** If line 12, column C, is more than line 21, enter the difference and see instructions .	22	
23	**REFUND** to be received. If line 12, column C, is less than line 21, enter the difference . . .	23	

Sign Here
Keep a copy of this return for your records.

Under penalties of perjury, I declare that I have filed an original return and that I have examined this amended return, including accompanying schedules and statements, and to the best of my knowledge and belief, this amended return is true, correct, and complete. Declaration of preparer (other than taxpayer) is based on all information of which the preparer has any knowledge.

▶ _____ Your signature ____ Date _____   ▶ _____ Spouse's signature. If a joint return, BOTH must sign. ____ Date

Paid Preparer's Use Only

Preparer's signature ▶	Date	Check if self-employed ☐	Preparer's social security no.
Firm's name (or yours if self-employed) and address ▶		E.I. No.	
		ZIP code	

Cat. No. 11360L   Form **1040X** (Rev. 10-93)

Part I **Exemptions.** See Form 1040 or Form 1040A instructions.		**A.** Number originally reported	**B.** Net change	**C.** Correct number
If you are not changing your exemptions, do not complete this part. If claiming more exemptions, complete lines 24–30 and, if applicable, line 31. If claiming fewer exemptions, complete lines 24–29.				

		A	B	C
24	Yourself and spouse **24**			
	Caution: *If your parents (or someone else) can claim you as a dependent (even if they chose not to), you cannot claim an exemption for yourself.*			
25	Your dependent children who lived with you **25**			
26	Your dependent children who did not live with you due to divorce or separation **26**			
27	Other dependents **27**			
28	Total number of exemptions. Add lines 24 through 27 . . . . . **28**			
29	Multiply the number of exemptions claimed on line 28 by the amount listed below for the tax year you are amending. Enter the result here and on line 6.			

Tax Year	Exemption Amount	But see the instructions if the amount on line 3 is over:
1993	$2,350	$81,350
1992	2,300	78,950
1991	2,150	75,000
1990	2,050	Not applicable for tax year 1990.

30 Dependents (children and other) not claimed on original return:

(a) Dependent's name (first, initial, and last name)	**(b)** Check if under age 1 (under age 2 if a 1990 return)	**(c)** If age 1 or older (age 2 or older if a 1990 return), enter dependent's social security number	**(d)** Dependent's relationship to you	**(e)** No. of months lived in your home

No. of your children on line 30 who lived with you . . ▶ ☐

No. of your children on line 30 who **didn't** live with you due to divorce or separation (see instructions) ▶ ☐

No. of dependents on line 30 not entered above . ▶ ☐

31 If your child listed on line 30 didn't live with you but is claimed as your dependent under a pre-1985 agreement, check here ▶ ☐

Part II Explanation of Changes to Income, Deductions, and Credits

Enter the line number from page 1 for each item you are changing and give the reason for each change. Attach all supporting forms and schedules for items changed. If you don't, your Form 1040X may be returned. Be sure to include your name and social security number on any attachments.

If the change pertains to a net operating loss carryback or a general business credit carryback, attach the schedule or form that shows the year in which the loss or credit occurred. See instructions. Also, check here . . . . ▶ ☐

_____

_____

_____

_____

_____

_____

_____

Part III **Presidential Election Campaign Fund.** Checking below will not increase your tax or reduce your refund.

If you did not previously want to have $3 (or $1 if a 1992 return) go to the fund but now want to, check here . . . . ▶ ☐ $3 for 1993   ☐ $1 for 1992

If a joint return and your spouse did not previously want to have $3 (or $1 if a 1992 return) go to the fund but now wants to, check here . . . . ▶ ☐ $3 for 1993   ☐ $1 for 1992

Form **1116**

Department of the Treasury
Internal Revenue Service

Foreign Tax Credit

(Individual, Fiduciary, or Nonresident Alien Individual)

▶ Attach to Form 1040, 1040NR, 1041, or 990-T.

▶ See separate instructions.

OMB No. 1545-0121

1993

Attachment
Sequence No. **19**

Name

Identifying number as shown on page 1 of your tax return

*Report all amounts in U.S. dollars except where specified in Part II. Use a separate Form 1116 for each category of income listed below. Check only **one** box. Before you check a box, read **Categories of Income** on page 3 of the instructions. Complete this form for credit for taxes on:*

a ☐ Passive income

b ☐ High withholding tax interest

c ☐ Financial services income

d ☐ Shipping income

e ☐ Dividends from a DISC or former DISC

f ☐ Certain distributions from a foreign sales corporation (FSC) or former FSC

g ☐ Lump-sum distributions (see instructions before completing form)

h ☐ General limitation income—all other income from sources outside the United States (including income from sources within U.S. possessions)

i Resident of (name of country) ▶

Note: *If you paid taxes to one foreign country or U.S. possession, use column A in Part I and line A in Part II. If you paid taxes to **more than one** foreign country or U.S. possession, use a separate column and line for each country or possession. However, see the exception under **A Change To Note** on page 1 of the Instructions.*

Part I — Taxable Income or Loss From Sources Outside the United States for Separate Category Checked Above

	Foreign Country or U.S. Possession			Total
	A	**B**	**C**	(Add cols. A, B, and C.)
j Enter the name of the foreign country or U.S. possession . . . . ▶				
1 Gross income from sources within country shown above and of the type checked above. See instructions:				**1**
Applicable deductions and losses. (See instructions.):				
2 Expenses directly allocable to the income on line 1 (attach schedule)				
3 Pro rata share of other deductions not directly allocable:				
a Certain itemized deductions or standard deduction. See instructions				
b Other deductions (attach schedule)				
c Add lines 3a and 3b				
d Gross foreign source income. See instructions .				
e Gross income from all sources. See instructions				
f Divide line 3d by line 3e				
g Multiply line 3c by line 3f				
4 Pro rata share of interest expense. See instructions:				
a Home mortgage interest from line 5 of the worksheet on page 6 of the instructions . . .				
b Other interest expense				
5 Losses from foreign sources				
6 Add lines 2, 3g, 4a, 4b, and 5				**6**
7 Subtract line 6 from line 1. Enter the result here and on line 14 . . . . ▶				**7**

Part II — Foreign Taxes Paid or Accrued (See instructions.)

Country	Credit is claimed for taxes (you must check one)		Foreign taxes paid or accrued								
			In foreign currency				In U.S. dollars				
	(k) ☐ Paid		Taxes withheld at source on:			**(q)** Other foreign taxes paid or accrued	Taxes withheld at source on:			**(u)** Other foreign taxes paid or accrued	**(v)** Total foreign taxes paid or accrued (add cols. (r) through (u))
	(l) ☐ Accrued										
	(m) Date paid or accrued	**(n)** Dividends	**(o)** Rents and royalties	**(p)** Interest		**(r)** Dividends	**(s)** Rents and royalties	**(t)** Interest			
A											
B											
C											

8 Add lines A through C, column (v). Enter the total here and on line 9 . . . . ▶ **8**

For Paperwork Reduction Act Notice, see page 1 of separate instructions.   Cat. No. 11440U   Form **1116** (1993)

Part III   **Figuring the Credit**

9	Enter amount from line 8. This is the total foreign taxes paid or accrued for the category of income checked above Part I	**9**	
10	Carryback or carryover (attach detailed computation)	**10**	
11	Add lines 9 and 10	**11**	
12	Reduction in foreign taxes. See instructions	**12**	

13	Subtract line 12 from line 11. This is the total amount of foreign taxes available for credit	**13**	
14	Enter amount from line 7. This is your taxable income or (loss) from sources outside the United States (before adjustments) for the category of income checked above Part I. See instructions . . .	**14**	
15	Adjustments to line 14. See instructions	**15**	
16	Combine the amounts on lines 14 and 15. This is your net foreign source taxable income. (If the result is zero or less, you have no foreign tax credit for the category of income you checked above Part I. Skip lines 17 through 21.)	**16**	
17	**Individuals:** Enter amount from Form 1040, line 35. If you are a nonresident alien, enter amount from Form 1040NR, line 34. **Estates and trusts:** Enter your taxable income without the deduction for your exemption	**17**	

Caution: If you figured your tax using the maximum tax rate on capital gains, see instructions.

18	Divide line 16 by line 17. If line 16 is more than line 17, enter the figure "1"	**18**	
19	**Individuals:** Enter amount from Form 1040, line 40, **less** any amounts on Form 1040, lines 41, 42, and any mortgage interest credit (from Form 8396) on line 44. If you are a nonresident alien, enter amount from Form 1040NR, line 39, less any amount on Form 1040NR, line 40 and any mortgage interest credit (from Form 8396) on line 42.		
	Estates and trusts: Enter amount from Form 1041, Schedule G, line 1c, or Form 990-T, line 37. .	**19**	
20	Multiply line 19 by line 18 (maximum amount of credit)	**20**	
21	Enter the amount from line 13 or line 20, whichever is smaller. (If this is the only Form 1116 you are completing, skip lines 22 through 29 and enter this amount on line 30. Otherwise, complete the appropriate lines in Part IV.) . . . . ▶	**21**	

Part IV   **Summary of Credits From Separate Parts III** (See instructions.)

22	Credit for taxes on passive income	**22**	
23	Credit for taxes on high withholding tax interest	**23**	
24	Credit for taxes on financial services income	**24**	
25	Credit for taxes on shipping income	**25**	
26	Credit for taxes on dividends from a DISC or former DISC	**26**	
27	Credit for taxes on certain distributions from a FSC or former FSC	**27**	
28	Credit for taxes on lump-sum distributions	**28**	
29	Credit for taxes on general limitation income (all other income from sources outside the United States)	**29**	

30	Add lines 22 through 29	**30**	
31	Reduction of credit for international boycott operations. See instructions for line 12	**31**	
32	Subtract line 31 from line 30. This is your foreign tax credit. Enter here and on Form 1040, line 43; Form 1040NR, line 41; Form 1041, Schedule G, line 2a; or Form 990-T, line 38a . . . . ▶	**32**	

Form **2106**	**Employee Business Expenses**	OMB No. 1545-0139

Department of the Treasury
Internal Revenue Service (T)

► See separate instructions.

► Attach to Form 1040.

1993

Attachment
Sequence No. **54**

Your name	Social security number	Occupation in which expenses were incurred

Part I Employee Business Expenses and Reimbursements

STEP 1 Enter Your Expenses

		Column A Other Than Meals and Entertainment	Column B Meals and Entertainment
1	Vehicle expense from line 22 or line 29	1	
2	Parking fees, tolls, and transportation, including train, bus, etc., that **did not** involve overnight travel	2	
3	Travel expense while away from home overnight, including lodging, airplane, car rental, etc. **Do not** include meals and entertainment	3	
4	Business expenses not included on lines 1 through 3. **Do not** include meals and entertainment	4	
5	Meals and entertainment expenses (see instructions)	5	
6	**Total expenses.** In Column A, add lines 1 through 4 and enter the result. In Column B, enter the amount from line 5	6	

Note: *If you were not reimbursed for any expenses in Step 1, skip line 7 and enter the amount from line 6 on line 8.*

STEP 2 Enter Amounts Your Employer Gave You for Expenses Listed in STEP 1

7	Enter amounts your employer gave you that were **not** reported to you in box 1 of Form W-2. Include any amount reported under code "L" in box 13 of your Form W-2 (see instructions)	7	

STEP 3 Figure Expenses To Deduct on Schedule A (Form 1040)

8	Subtract line 7 from line 6	8	
	Note: *If **both columns** of line 8 are zero, **stop here.** If Column A is less than zero, report the amount as income on Form 1040, line 7, and enter -0- on line 10, Column A.*		
9	Enter 20% (.20) of line 8, Column B	9	
10	In Column A, enter the amount from line 8. In Column B, subtract line 9 from line 8	10	

11 Add the amounts on line 10 of both columns and enter the total here. **Also, enter the total on Schedule A (Form 1040), line 19.** (Qualified performing artists and individuals with disabilities, see the instructions for special rules on where to enter the total.) ► | 11 |

For Paperwork Reduction Act Notice, see instructions.   Cat. No. 11700N   Form **2106** (1993)

Part II	**Vehicle Expenses** (See instructions to find out which sections to complete.)				

Section A.—General Information

			(a) Vehicle 1	**(b)** Vehicle 2
12	Enter the date vehicle was placed in service	12	/ /	/ /
13	Total miles vehicle was driven during 1993	13	miles	miles
14	Business miles included on line 13	14	miles	miles
15	Percent of business use. Divide line 14 by line 13	15	%	%
16	Average daily round trip commuting distance	16	miles	miles
17	Commuting miles included on line 13	17	miles	miles
18	Other personal miles. Add lines 14 and 17 and subtract the total from line 13	18	miles	miles

19 Do you (or your spouse) have another vehicle available for personal purposes? . . . . ☐ Yes ☐ No

20 If your employer provided you with a vehicle, is personal use during off duty hours permitted? ☐ Yes ☐ No ☐ Not applicable

21a Do you have evidence to support your deduction? . . . . ☐ Yes ☐ No

21b If "Yes," is the evidence written? . . . . ☐ Yes ☐ No

Section B.—Standard Mileage Rate (Use this section only if you own the vehicle.)

22	Multiply line 14 by 28¢ (.28). Enter the result here and on line 1. (Rural mail carriers, see instructions.)	22		

Section C.—Actual Expenses

			(a) Vehicle 1		**(b)** Vehicle 2	
23	Gasoline, oil, repairs, vehicle insurance, etc.	23				
24a	Vehicle rentals	24a				
b	Inclusion amount (see instructions)	24b				
c	Subtract line 24b from line 24a	24c				
25	Value of employer-provided vehicle (applies only if 100% of annual lease value was included on Form W-2—see instructions)	25				
26	Add lines 23, 24c, and 25 . .	26				
27	Multiply line 26 by the percentage on line 15 . . .	27				
28	Depreciation. Enter amount from line 38 below	28				
29	Add lines 27 and 28. Enter total here and on line 1	29				

Section D.—Depreciation of Vehicles (Use this section only if you own the vehicle.)

			(a) Vehicle 1		**(b)** Vehicle 2	
30	Enter cost or other basis (see instructions)	30				
31	Enter amount of section 179 deduction (see instructions) .	31				
32	Multiply line 30 by line 15 (see instructions if you elected the section 179 deduction) . . .	32				
33	Enter depreciation method and percentage (see instructions) .	33				
34	Multiply line 32 by the percentage on line 33 (see instructions) . .	34				
35	Add lines 31 and 34 . . .	35				
36	Enter the limitation amount from the table in the line 36 instructions	36				
37	Multiply line 36 by the percentage on line 15 . . .	37				
38	Enter the **smaller** of line 35 or line 37. Also, enter this amount on line 28 above	38				

Form **2119**	**Sale of Your Home**	OMB No. 1545-0072

Department of the Treasury
Internal Revenue Service

► **Attach to Form 1040 for year of sale.**

► **See separate instructions.** ► **Please print or type.**

1993

Attachment
Sequence No. **20**

Your first name and initial. If a joint return, also give spouse's name and initial.　　Last name

Your social security number

Fill in Your Address Only If You Are Filing This Form by Itself and Not With Your Tax Return

Present address (no., street, and apt. no., rural route, or P.O. box no. if mail is not delivered to street address)

Spouse's social security number

City, town or post office, state, and ZIP code

Part I General Information

1 Date your former main home was sold (month, day, year) . . . . ► | **1** | / /

2 Have you bought or built a new main home? . . . . ☐ Yes ☐ No

3 Is or was any part of either main home rented out or used for business? If "Yes," see instructions . . ☐ Yes ☐ No

Part II Gain on Sale—Do not include amounts you deduct as moving expenses.

4	Selling price of home. Do not include personal property items you sold with your home . .	**4**	
5	Expense of sale (see instructions)	**5**	
6	Amount realized. Subtract line 5 from line 4	**6**	
7	Adjusted basis of home sold (see instructions)	**7**	
8	**Gain on sale.** Subtract line 7 from line 6	**8**	

Is line 8 more than zero?

Yes ──────► If line 2 is "Yes," you **must** go to Part III or Part IV, whichever applies. If line 2 is "No," go to line 9.

No ──────► **Stop** and attach this form to your return.

9 If you haven't replaced your home, do you plan to do so within the **replacement period** (see instructions)? ☐ Yes ☐ No

● If line 9 is "Yes," stop here, attach this form to your return, and see **Additional Filing Requirements** in the instructions.

● If line 9 is "No," you **must** go to Part III or Part IV, whichever applies.

Part III One-Time Exclusion of Gain for People Age 55 or Older—By completing this part, you are electing to take the one-time exclusion (see instructions). If you are not electing to take the exclusion, go to Part IV now.

10 Who was age 55 or older on the date of sale? . . . . ☐ You ☐ Your spouse ☐ Both of you

11 Did the person who was age 55 or older own and use the property as his or her main home for a total of at least 3 years (except for short absences) of the 5-year period before the sale? If "No," go to Part IV now . . ☐ Yes ☐ No

12 At the time of sale, who owned the home? . . . . ☐ You ☐ Your spouse ☐ Both of you

13 Social security number of spouse at the time of sale if you had a different spouse from the one above. If you were not married at the time of sale, enter "None" . . . . ► | **13** |

14 **Exclusion.** Enter the **smaller** of line 8 or $125,000 ($62,500 if married filing separate return). Then, go to line 15 . . . . | **14** |

Part IV Adjusted Sales Price, Taxable Gain, and Adjusted Basis of New Home

15 If line 14 is blank, enter the amount from line 8. Otherwise, subtract line 14 from line 8 . . | **15** |

● If line 15 is zero, stop and attach this form to your return.

● If line 15 is more than zero and line 2 is "Yes," go to line 16 now.

● If you are reporting this sale on the installment method, stop and see the instructions.

● All others, stop and **enter the amount from line 15 on Schedule D, col. (g), line 4 or 12.**

16	Fixing-up expenses (see instructions for time limits)	**16**	
17	If line 14 is blank, enter amount from line 16. Otherwise, add lines 14 and 16	**17**	
18	**Adjusted sales price.** Subtract line 17 from line 6	**18**	
19a	Date you moved into new home ► ⌊ / / ⌋ **b** Cost of new home (see instructions)	**19b**	
20	Subtract line 19b from line 18. If zero or less, enter -0-	**20**	
21	**Taxable gain.** Enter the **smaller** of line 15 or line 20	**21**	

● If line 21 is zero, go to line 22 and attach this form to your return.

● If you are reporting this sale on the installment method, see the line 15 instructions and go to line 22.

● All others, **enter the amount from line 21 on Schedule D, col. (g), line 4 or 12,** and go to line 22.

22	Postponed gain. Subtract line 21 from line 15	**22**	
23	**Adjusted basis of new home.** Subtract line 22 from line 19b	**23**	

Sign Here Only If You Are Filing This Form by Itself and Not With Your Tax Return

Under penalties of perjury, I declare that I have examined this form, including attachments, and to the best of my knowledge and belief, it is true, correct, and complete.

► Your signature　　Date　　Spouse's signature　　Date

If a joint return, both must sign.

For Paperwork Reduction Act Notice, see separate instructions.　　Cat. No. 11710J　　Form **2119** (1993)

♻ *Printed on recycled paper*

Form **2120**

(Rev. May 1991)

Department of the Treasury
Internal Revenue Service

Multiple Support Declaration

▶ **Attach to Form 1040 or Form 1040A.**

OMB No. 1545-0071
Expires 5-31-94

Attachment
Sequence No. **50**

Name of taxpayer claiming person as a dependent

Social security number

During the calendar year 19 .... , I paid over 10% of the support of

----
(Name of person)

I could have claimed this person as a dependent except that I did not pay over 50% of his or her support. I understand that this person is being claimed as a dependent on the income tax return of

----
(Name)

(Address)

I agree not to claim this person as a dependent on my Federal income tax return for any tax year that began in this calendar year.

(Your signature)

(Your social security number)

(Date)

(Address)

Instructions

Paperwork Reduction Act Notice

We ask for the information on this form to carry out the Internal Revenue laws of the United States. You are required to give us the information. We need it to ensure that you are complying with these laws and to allow us to figure and collect the right amount of tax.

The time needed to complete and file this form will vary depending on individual circumstances. The estimated average time is: **Recordkeeping,** 7 minutes; **Learning about the law or the form,** 2 minutes; **Preparing the form,** 7 minutes; **Copying, assembling, and sending the form to the IRS,** 10 minutes.

If you have comments concerning the accuracy of these time estimates or suggestions for making this form more simple, we would be happy to hear from you. You can write to both the IRS and the Office of Management and Budget at the addresses listed in the instructions of the tax return with which this form is filed.

Purpose

When two or more individuals together pay over 50% of another person's support, Form 2120 is used to allow one of them to claim the person as a dependent for tax purposes.

General Information

To claim someone as a dependent, you must pay over 50% of that person's living expenses (support). However, sometimes no one individual pays over 50%; but two or more together provide over 50% of the support. If each individual could have claimed the person as a dependent except for the 50% support rule, then one individual, but only one, can still claim the dependent.

All of those who paid over 10% of the support should decide who will claim the person as a dependent. If you are chosen, you can claim the dependent only if

● You paid over 10% of the support, AND
● All others who paid over 10% agree not to claim the person as a dependent.

How To File

The individuals who agree not to claim the person as a dependent do so by each signing a Form 2120. They give the signed forms to the one who does claim the person as a dependent.

If you are the one who claims the person as a dependent, you must attach all Forms 2120 from the others to YOUR return. Be sure to enter your name and social security number at the top of each Form 2120. In addition, you must meet all of the other rules for claiming dependents. See **Pub. 501,** Exemptions, Standard Deduction, and Filing Information.

Cat. No. 11712F

Form **2120** (Rev. 5-91)

Department of the Treasury
Internal Revenue Service (T)

Child and Dependent Care Expenses

▶ Attach to Form 1040.

▶ See separate instructions.

OMB No. 1545-0068

1993

Attachment
Sequence No. **21**

Name(s) shown on Form 1040 | Your social security number

You need to understand the following terms to complete this form: **Dependent Care Benefits, Earned Income, Qualified Expenses,** and **Qualifying Person(s).** See **Important Terms** on page 1 of the Form 2441 instructions. Also, if you had a child born in 1993 and line 32 of Form 1040 is less than $23,050, see **A Change To Note** on page 2 of the instructions.

Part I — Persons or Organizations Who Provided the Care—You **must** complete this part.
(If you need more space, use the bottom of page 2.)

1	(a) Care provider's name	(b) Address (number, street, apt. no., city, state, and ZIP code)	(c) Identifying number (SSN or EIN)	(d) Amount paid (see instructions)

2   Add the amounts in column (d) of line 1 . . . . **2**

3   Enter the number of **qualifying persons** cared for in 1993 . . . . ▶ ☐

| Did you receive **dependent care benefits?** | **NO** ──────▶ Complete only Part II below. |
| | **YES** ──────▶ Complete Part III on the back now. |

Part II — Credit for Child and Dependent Care Expenses

4   Enter the amount of **qualified expenses** you incurred and paid in 1993. DO NOT enter more than $2,400 for one qualifying person or $4,800 for two or more persons. If you completed Part III, enter the amount from line 25 . . . . | **4** |

5   Enter YOUR **earned income** . . . . | **5** |

6   If married filing a joint return, enter YOUR SPOUSE'S earned income (if student or disabled, see instructions); **all others,** enter the amount from line 5 . . . . | **6** |

7   Enter the **smallest** of line 4, 5, or 6 . . . . | **7** |

8   Enter the amount from Form 1040, line 32 . . . . . . | **8** |

9   Enter on line 9 the decimal amount shown below that applies to the amount on line 8

If line 8 is—		Decimal amount is	If line 8 is—		Decimal amount is
Over	But not over		Over	But not over	
$0—10,000		.30	$20,000—22,000		.24
10,000—12,000		.29	22,000—24,000		.23
12,000—14,000		.28	24,000—26,000		.22
14,000—16,000		.27	26,000—28,000		.21
16,000—18,000		.26	28,000—No limit		.20
18,000—20,000		.25			

| **9** | X . |

10   Multiply **line 7** by the decimal amount on line 9. Enter the result. Then, see the instructions for the amount of credit to enter on Form 1040, line 41 . . . . | **10** |

Caution: *If you paid $50 or more in a calendar quarter to a person who worked in your home, you must file an employment tax return. Get* **Form 942** *for details.*

For Paperwork Reduction Act Notice, see separate instructions.   Cat. No. 11862M   Form **2441** (1993)

Part III **Dependent Care Benefits**—Complete this part **only** if you received these benefits.

11 Enter the total amount of **dependent care benefits** you received for 1993. This amount should
be shown in box 10 of your W-2 form(s). DO NOT include amounts that were reported to you
as wages in box 1 of Form(s) W-2 . . . . **11**

12 Enter the amount forfeited, if any. See the instructions **12**

13 Subtract line 12 from line 11 . . . . **13**

14 Enter the total amount of **qualified expenses** incurred in 1993
for the care of the qualifying person(s) **14**

15 Enter the **smaller** of line 13 or 14 . . . . **15**

16 Enter YOUR **earned income** **16**

17 If married filing a joint return, enter YOUR SPOUSE'S earned
income (if student or disabled, see the line 6 instructions); if
married filing a separate return, see the instructions for the
amount to enter; **all others,** enter the amount from line 16 . . **17**

18 Enter the **smallest** of line 15, 16, or 17. . . . . **18**

19 **Excluded benefits.** Enter here the **smaller** of the following:

• The amount from line 18, or
• $5,000 ($2,500 if married filing a separate return
and you were required to enter your spouse's
earned income on line 17). **19**

20 **Taxable benefits.** Subtract line 19 from line 13. Also, include this amount on Form 1040,
line 7. On the dotted line next to line 7, write "DCB" **20**

To claim the child and dependent care credit, complete
lines 21–25 below, and lines 4–10 on the front of this form.

21 Enter the amount of qualified expenses you incurred and paid in 1993. DO NOT include on
this line any excluded benefits shown on line 19 . . . . **21**

22 Enter $2,400 ($4,800 if two or more qualifying persons) . . . **22**

23 Enter the amount from line 19 . . . . **23**

24 Subtract line 23 from line 22. If zero or less, **STOP**. You cannot take the credit. **Exception.** If
you paid 1992 expenses in 1993, see the line 10 instructions **24**

25 Enter the **smaller** of line 21 or 24 here **and** on line 4 on the front of this form **25**

Department of the Treasury
Internal Revenue Service

Application for Additional Extension of Time To File
U.S. Individual Income Tax Return

▶ See instructions on back.
▶ You MUST complete all items that apply to you.

OMB No. 1545-0066

1993

Attachment
Sequence No. **59**

Please type or print.

File the original and one copy by the due date for filing your return.

Your first name and initial	Last name	Your social security number
If a joint return, spouse's first name and initial	Last name	Spouse's social security number
Home address (number, street, and apt. no. or rural route). If you have a P.O. box, see the instructions.		
City, town or post office, state, and ZIP code		

1 I request an extension of time until ...., 19......., to file Form 1040EZ, Form 1040A, or Form 1040 for the calendar year 1993, or other tax year ending ...., 19....... .

2 Have you filed Form 4868 to request an extension of time to file for this tax year? . . . . ☐ **Yes** ☐ **No**

If you checked "No," we will grant your extension only for undue hardship. Fully explain the hardship on line 3.

3 Explain why you need an extension ▶ ....

....

....

....

If you expect to owe gift or generation-skipping transfer (GST) tax, complete line 4.

4 If you or your spouse plan to file a gift tax return (Form 709 or 709-A) for 1993, generally due by April 15, 1994, see the instructions and check here . . . . } **Yourself** . ▶ ☐ **Spouse** . ▶ ☐

Signature and Verification

Under penalties of perjury, I declare that I have examined this form, including accompanying schedules and statements, and to the best of my knowledge and belief, it is true, correct, and complete; and, if prepared by someone other than the taxpayer, that I am authorized to prepare this form.

Signature of taxpayer ▶ _____ Date ▶ _____

Signature of spouse ▶ _____ Date ▶ _____
(If filing jointly, BOTH must sign even if only one had income)

Signature of preparer
other than taxpayer ▶ _____ Date ▶ _____

File original and one copy. The IRS will show below whether or not your application is approved and will return the copy.

Notice to Applicant—To Be Completed by the IRS

☐ We **HAVE** approved your application. Please attach this form to your return.

☐ We **HAVE NOT** approved your application. Please attach this form to your return. However, because of your reasons stated above, we have granted a 10-day grace period from the date shown below or due date of your return, whichever is later. This grace period is considered to be a valid extension of time for elections otherwise required to be made on returns filed on time.

☐ We **HAVE NOT** approved your application. After considering your reasons stated above, we cannot grant your request for an extension of time to file. We are not granting the 10-day grace period.

☐ We cannot consider your application because it was filed after the due date of your return.

☐ We **HAVE NOT** approved your application. The maximum extension of time allowed by law is 6 months.

☐ Other ....

_____

Director

By _____

_____
Date

Please type or print

Name	
Number and street (include suite, room, or apt. no.) or P.O. box number if mail is not delivered to street address	If you want the copy of this form returned to you at an address other than that shown above or to an agent acting for you, enter the name of the agent and/or the address where the copy should be sent.
City, town or post office, state, and ZIP code	

For Paperwork Reduction Act Notice, see back of form.   Cat. No. 11958F   Form **2688** (1993)

General Instructions

Paperwork Reduction Act Notice.—We ask for the information on this form to carry out the Internal Revenue laws of the United States. You are required to give us the information. We need it to ensure that you are complying with these laws and to allow us to figure and collect the right amount of tax.

The time needed to complete and file this form will vary depending on individual circumstances. The estimated average time is: **Learning about the law or the form,** 7 min.; **Preparing the form,** 10 min.; and **Copying, assembling, and sending the form to the IRS,** 20 min.

If you have comments concerning the accuracy of these time estimates or suggestions for making this form more simple, we would be happy to hear from you. You can write to both the **Internal Revenue Service,** Attention: Reports Clearance Officer, PC:FP, Washington, DC 20224; and the **Office of Management and Budget,** Paperwork Reduction Project (1545-0066), Washington, DC 20503. **DO NOT** send this form to either of these offices. Instead, see **Where To File** later.

Purpose of Form

Caution: *If the new tax rates for high-income taxpayers apply to you, you may be able to defer part of your 1993 tax liability. But to do so, you **must** pay by the regular due date of your return, at least 90% of your 1993 tax liability, minus the tax you would be eligible to defer. For details, get **Form 8841,** Deferral of Additional 1993 Taxes.*

Use Form 2688 to ask for more time to file **Form 1040EZ, Form 1040A,** or **Form 1040.** Generally, use it only if you already asked for more time on **Form 4868** (the "automatic" extension form) and that time was not enough. We will make an exception to this rule only for undue hardship.

To get the extra time you **MUST:**
● Complete and file Form 2688 on time, **AND**

● Have a good reason why the first 4 months were not enough. Explain the reason on line 3.

Generally, we will not give you more time to file just for the convenience of your tax return preparer. But if the reasons for being late are beyond his or her control or, despite a good effort, you cannot get professional help in time to file, we will usually give you the extra time.

You cannot have the IRS figure your tax if you file after the regular due date of your return. An extension of time to file a 1993 calendar year income tax return also extends the time to file a gift tax return for 1993.

Caution: *If we give you more time to file and later find that the statements made on this form are false or misleading, the extension is null and void. You will owe the late filing penalty explained on this page.*

If You Live Abroad.—U.S. citizens or resident aliens living abroad may qualify for special tax treatment if they meet the required residence or presence tests. If you do not expect to meet either of those tests by the due date of your return,

request an extension to a date after you expect to qualify. Ask for it on **Form 2350,** Application for Extension of Time To File U.S. Income Tax Return. Get **Pub. 54,** Tax Guide for U.S. Citizens and Resident Aliens Abroad.

Total Time Allowed

We cannot extend the due date of your return for more than 6 months. This includes the 4 extra months allowed by Form 4868. There may be an exception if you live abroad. See previous discussion.

When To File

If you filed Form 4868, file Form 2688 by the extended due date of your return. For most people, this is August 15, 1994. If you didn't file Form 4868 first because of undue hardship, file Form 2688 by the due date of your return, April 15, 1994, for a calendar year return. Be sure to fully explain why you are filing Form 2688 first. Also, file Form 2688 early so that if your request is not approved you can still file your return on time.

Out of the Country.—You may have been allowed 2 extra months to file if you were a U.S. citizen or resident out of the country on the due date of your return. "Out of the country" means either (1) you live outside the United States and Puerto Rico **and** your main place of work is outside the United States and Puerto Rico, **or** (2) you are in military or naval service outside the United States and Puerto Rico.

Where To File

Mail Form 2688 AND a copy to the Internal Revenue Service Center where you send your return.

Filing Your Tax Return

You may file Form 1040EZ, 1040A, or Form 1040 any time before your extension of time is up. But remember, Form 2688 does not extend the time to pay taxes. If you do not pay the amount due by the regular due date, you will owe interest. You may also be charged penalties.

Interest.—You will owe interest on any tax not paid by the regular due date of your return. The interest runs until you pay the tax. Even if you had a good reason for not paying on time, you will still owe interest.

Late Payment Penalty.—The penalty is usually ½ of 1% of any tax (other than estimated tax) not paid by the regular due date. It is charged for each month or part of a month the tax is unpaid. The maximum penalty is 25%. You might not owe this penalty if you have a good reason for not paying on time. Attach a statement to your return, not Form 2688, explaining the reason.

Late Filing Penalty.—A penalty is usually charged if your return is filed after the due date (including extensions). It is usually 5% of the tax not paid by the regular due date for each month or part of a month your return is late. Generally, the maximum penalty is 25%. If your return is more than 60 days late, the minimum penalty is $100 or the balance of tax due on your return, whichever is smaller. You might not owe the penalty if you have a good reason for filing late. Attach a full explanation to your return, not Form 2688, if you file late.

How To Claim Credit for Payment Made With This Form.—Include any payment you sent with Form 2688 on the appropriate line of your tax return. If you file Form 1040EZ, the instructions for line 7 will tell you how to report the payment. If you file Form 1040A, see the instructions for line 28d. If you file Form 1040, enter the payment on line 57.

If you and your spouse each filed a separate Form 2688 but later file a joint return for 1993, enter the total paid with both Forms 2688 on the appropriate line of your joint return.

If you and your spouse jointly filed Form 2688 but later file separate returns for 1993, you may enter the total amount paid with Form 2688 on either of your separate returns. Or you and your spouse may divide the payment in any agreed amounts. Be sure each separate return has the social security numbers of both spouses.

Specific Instructions

Name, Address, and Social Security Number (SSN).—Enter your name, address, and SSN. If you plan to file a joint return, also enter your spouse's name and SSN. If the post office does not bring mail to your street address and you have a P.O. box, enter the box number instead.

Note: *If you changed your mailing address after you filed your last return, you should use **Form 8822,** Change of Address, to notify the IRS of the change. A new address shown on Form 2688 will not update your record. You can get Form 8822 by calling 1-800-829-3676.*

Line 3.—Clearly describe the reasons that will delay your return. We cannot accept incomplete reasons, such as "illness" or "practitioner too busy," without adequate explanations. If it is clear that you have no important reason but only want more time, we will deny your request. The 10-day grace period will also be denied.

If because of undue hardship you are filing Form 2688 without filing Form 4868 first, clearly explain why on line 3. Attach any information you have that helps explain the hardship.

Line 4.—If you or your spouse plan to file Form 709 or 709-A for 1993, check whichever box applies. But if your spouse files a separate Form 2688, do not check the box for your spouse.

Your Signature.—This form must be signed. If you plan to file a joint return, both of you should sign. If there is a good reason why one of you cannot, the other spouse may sign for both. Attach a statement explaining why the other spouse cannot sign.

Others Who Can Sign for You.—Anyone with a power of attorney can sign. But the following can sign for you without a power of attorney:

● Attorneys, CPAs, and enrolled agents.

● A person in close personal or business relationship to you who is signing because you cannot. There must be a good reason why you cannot sign, such as illness or absence. Attach an explanation to this form.

Form **3903**	**Moving Expenses**	OMB No. 1545-0062
Department of the Treasury Internal Revenue Service	► **Attach to Form 1040.** ► **See separate instructions.**	**19**93 Attachment Sequence No. **62**

Name(s) shown on Form 1040	Your social security number

Caution: *If you are a member of the armed forces, see the instructions before completing this form.*

1	Enter the number of miles from your **old home** to your **new workplace**	1	
2	Enter the number of miles from your **old home** to your **old workplace**	2	
3	Subtract line 2 from line 1. Enter the result but not less than zero . . . . ►	3	

If line 3 is 35 or more miles, complete the rest of this form. Also, see **Time Test** in the instructions. If line 3 is less than 35 miles, you may not deduct your moving expenses.

Part I — Moving Expenses

Note: *Any payments your employer made for any part of your move (including the value of any services furnished in kind) should be included on your W-2 form. Report that amount on **Form 1040, line 7**. See **Reimbursements** in the instructions.*

Section A—Transportation of Household Goods

4	Transportation and storage for household goods and personal effects	4	

Section B—Expenses of Moving From Old To New Home

5	Travel and lodging **not** including meals	5	
6	Total meals	6	
7	Multiply line 6 by 80% (.80)	7	
8	Add lines 5 and 7	8	

Section C—Pre-move Househunting Expenses and Temporary Quarters
(for any 30 days in a row after getting your job)

9	Pre-move travel and lodging **not** including meals	9	
10	Temporary quarters expenses **not** including meals	10	
11	Total meal expenses for both pre-move househunting and temporary quarters	11	
12	Multiply line 11 by 80% (.80)	12	
13	Add lines 9, 10, and 12	13	

Section D—Qualified Real Estate Expenses

14	Expenses of (check one) **a** ☐ selling or exchanging your old home, or **b** ☐ if renting, settling an unexpired lease. } .	14	
15	Expenses of (check one) **a** ☐ buying your new home, or **b** ☐ if renting, getting a new lease. }	15	

Part II — Dollar Limits and Moving Expense Deduction

Note: *If you and your spouse moved to separate homes, see the instructions.*

16	Enter the **smaller** of: • The amount on line 13, or • $1,500 ($750 if married filing a separate return and at the end of 1993 you lived with your spouse who also started work in 1993). } . .	16	
17	Add lines 14, 15, and 16	17	
18	Enter the **smaller** of: • The amount on line 17, or • $3,000 ($1,500 if married filing a separate return and at the end of 1993 you lived with your spouse who also started work in 1993). }	18	
19	Add lines 4, 8, and 18. Enter the total here and on Schedule A, line 18. This is your **moving expense deduction** ►	19	

Cat. No. 12490K   Form **3903** (1993)

Form **4562**

Department of the Treasury
Internal Revenue Service   (T)

Depreciation and Amortization

(Including Information on Listed Property)

▶ See separate instructions.   ▶ Attach this form to your return.

OMB No. 1545-0172

1993

Attachment
Sequence No. **67**

Name(s) shown on return

Identifying number

Business or activity to which this form relates

Part I   **Election To Expense Certain Tangible Property (Section 179)** (**Note:** *If you have any "Listed Property,"* *complete Part V before you complete Part I.*)

1	Maximum dollar limitation (If an enterprise zone business, see instructions.)	**1** $17,500
2	Total cost of section 179 property placed in service during the tax year (see instructions) . .	**2**
3	Threshold cost of section 179 property before reduction in limitation	**3** $200,000
4	Reduction in limitation. Subtract line 3 from line 2, but do not enter less than -0-	**4**
5	Dollar limitation for tax year. Subtract line 4 from line 1, but do not enter less than -0-. (If married filing separately, see instructions.)	**5**

(a) Description of property	(b) Cost	(c) Elected cost
6		

7	Listed property. Enter amount from line 26.	**7**
8	Total elected cost of section 179 property. Add amounts in column (c), lines 6 and 7	**8**
9	Tentative deduction. Enter the smaller of line 5 or line 8	**9**
10	Carryover of disallowed deduction from 1992 (see instructions).	**10**
11	Taxable income limitation. Enter the smaller of taxable income or line 5 (see instructions) . .	**11**
12	Section 179 expense deduction. Add lines 9 and 10, but do not enter more than line 11 . .	**12**
13	Carryover of disallowed deduction to 1994. Add lines 9 and 10, less line 12 ▶ **13**	

Note: *Do not use Part II or Part III below for listed property (automobiles, certain other vehicles, cellular telephones, certain computers, or property used for entertainment, recreation, or amusement). Instead, use Part V for listed property.*

Part II   **MACRS Depreciation For Assets Placed in Service ONLY During Your 1993 Tax Year (Do Not Include Listed Property)**

(a) Classification of property	(b) Month and year placed in service	(c) Basis for depreciation (business/investment use only—see instructions)	(d) Recovery period	(e) Convention	(f) Method	(g) Depreciation deduction
14 General Depreciation System (GDS) (see instructions):						
a 3-year property						
b 5-year property						
c 7-year property						
d 10-year property						
e 15-year property						
f 20-year property						
g Residential rental property			27.5 yrs.	MM	S/L	
			27.5 yrs.	MM	S/L	
h Nonresidential real property				MM	S/L	
				MM	S/L	
15 Alternative Depreciation System (ADS) (see instructions):						
a Class life					S/L	
b 12-year			12 yrs.		S/L	
c 40-year			40 yrs.	MM	S/L	

Part III   **Other Depreciation (Do Not Include Listed Property)**

16	GDS and ADS deductions for assets placed in service in tax years beginning before 1993 (see instructions)	**16**
17	Property subject to section 168(f)(1) election (see instructions)	**17**
18	ACRS and other depreciation (see instructions)	**18**

Part IV   **Summary**

19	Listed property. Enter amount from line 25.	**19**
20	**Total.** Add deductions on line 12, lines 14 and 15 in column (g), and lines 16 through 19. Enter here and on the appropriate lines of your return. (Partnerships and S corporations—see instructions)	**20**
21	For assets shown above and placed in service during the current year, enter the portion of the basis attributable to section 263A costs (see instructions) **21**	

For Paperwork Reduction Act Notice, see page 1 of the separate instructions.   Cat. No. 12906N   Form **4562** (1993)

Part V	Listed Property—Automobiles, Certain Other Vehicles, Cellular Telephones, Certain Computers, and Property Used for Entertainment, Recreation, or Amusement

*For any vehicle for which you are using the standard mileage rate or deducting lease expense, complete **only** 22a, 22b, columns (a) through (c) of Section A, all of Section B, and Section C if applicable.*

Section A—Depreciation and Other Information (Caution: *See instructions for limitations for automobiles.*)

22a Do you have evidence to support the business/investment use claimed? ☐ **Yes** ☐ **No**   **22b** If "Yes," is the evidence written? ☐ **Yes** ☐ **No**

(a) Type of property (list vehicles first)	(b) Date placed in service	(c) Business/ investment use percentage	(d) Cost or other basis	(e) Basis for depreciation (business/investment use only)	(f) Recovery period	(g) Method/ Convention	(h) Depreciation deduction	(i) Elected section 179 cost
23 Property used more than 50% in a qualified business use (see instructions):								
		%						
		%						
		%						
24 Property used 50% or less in a qualified business use (see instructions):								
		%			S/L –			
		%			S/L –			
		%			S/L –			

25 Add amounts in column (h). Enter the total here and on line 19, page 1 . . . . . . | **25** |

26 Add amounts in column (i). Enter the total here and on line 7, page 1 . . . . | **26** |

Section B—Information Regarding Use of Vehicles—*If you deduct expenses for vehicles:*
- *Always complete this section for vehicles used by a sole proprietor, partner, or other "more than 5% owner," or related person.*
- *If you provided vehicles to your employees, first answer the questions in Section C to see if you meet an exception to completing this section for those vehicles.*

	(a) Vehicle 1	(b) Vehicle 2	(c) Vehicle 3	(d) Vehicle 4	(e) Vehicle 5	(f) Vehicle 6
27 Total business/investment miles driven during the year (DO NOT include commuting miles)						
28 Total commuting miles driven during the year						
29 Total other personal (noncommuting) miles driven						
30 Total miles driven during the year. Add lines 27 through 29						

	Yes	No	Yes	No	Yes	No	Yes	No	Yes	No	Yes	No
31 Was the vehicle available for personal use during off-duty hours?												
32 Was the vehicle used primarily by a more than 5% owner or related person?												
33 Is another vehicle available for personal use?												

Section C—Questions for Employers Who Provide Vehicles for Use by Their Employees
Answer these questions to determine if you meet an exception to completing Section B. **Note:** *Section B must always be completed for vehicles used by sole proprietors, partners, or other more than 5% owners or related persons.*

	Yes	No
34 Do you maintain a written policy statement that prohibits all personal use of vehicles, including commuting, by your employees?		
35 Do you maintain a written policy statement that prohibits personal use of vehicles, except commuting, by your employees? (See instructions for vehicles used by corporate officers, directors, or 1% or more owners.)		
36 Do you treat all use of vehicles by employees as personal use?		
37 Do you provide more than five vehicles to your employees and retain the information received from your employees concerning the use of the vehicles?		
38 Do you meet the requirements concerning qualified automobile demonstration use (see instructions)? . .		
Note: *If your answer to 34, 35, 36, 37, or 38 is "Yes," you need not complete Section B for the covered vehicles.*		

Part VI	**Amortization**

(a) Description of costs	(b) Date amortization begins	(c) Amortizable amount	(d) Code section	(e) Amortization period or percentage	(f) Amortization for this year
39 Amortization of costs that begins during your 1993 tax year:					

40 Amortization of costs that began before 1993 . . . . | **40** |

41 **Total.** Enter here and on "Other Deductions" or "Other Expenses" line of your return . . . | **41** |

Form 4684

Department of the Treasury
Internal Revenue Service

Casualties and Thefts

▶ See separate instructions.
▶ Attach to your tax return.
▶ Use a separate Form 4684 for each different casualty or theft.

OMB No. 1545-0177

1993

Attachment
Sequence No. **26**

Name(s) shown on tax return

Identifying number

SECTION A—Personal Use Property (Use this section to report casualties and thefts of property **not** used in a trade or business or for income-producing purposes.)

1 Description of properties (show type, location, and date acquired for each):

Property **A** ....

Property **B** ....

Property **C** ....

Property **D** ....

Properties (Use a separate column for each property lost or damaged from one casualty or theft.)

		A	B	C	D
2	Cost or other basis of each property				
3	Insurance or other reimbursement (whether or not you filed a claim). See instructions . . . . . **Note:** *If line 2 is more than line 3, skip line 4.*				
4	Gain from casualty or theft. If line 3 is **more than** line 2, enter the difference here and skip lines 5 through 9 for that column. See instructions if line 3 includes insurance or other reimbursement you did not claim, or you received payment for your loss in a later tax year				
5	Fair market value **before** casualty or theft . . .				
6	Fair market value **after** casualty or theft				
7	Subtract line 6 from line 5				
8	Enter the **smaller** of line 2 or line 7				
9	Subtract line 3 from line 8. If zero or less, enter -0-				

10	Casualty or theft loss. Add the amounts on line 9. Enter the total	**10**
11	Enter the amount from line 10 or $100, whichever is **smaller**	**11**
12	Subtract line 11 from line 10 . . . . **Caution:** *Use only one Form 4684 for lines 13 through 18.*	**12**
13	Add the amounts on line 12 of all Forms 4684	**13**
14	Combine the amounts from line 4 of all Forms 4684	**14**
15	• If line 14 is **more than** line 13, enter the difference here and on Schedule D. Do not complete the rest of this section (see instructions). • If line 14 is **less than** line 13, enter -0- here and continue with the form. • If line 14 is **equal to** line 13, enter -0- here. Do not complete the rest of this section.	**15**
16	If line 14 is **less than** line 13, enter the difference	**16**
17	Enter 10% of your adjusted gross income (Form 1040, line 32). Estates and trusts, see instructions	**17**
18	Subtract line 17 from line 16. If zero or less, enter -0-. Also enter result on Schedule A (Form 1040), line 17. Estates and trusts, enter on the "Other deductions" line of your tax return	**18**

For Paperwork Reduction Act Notice, see page 1 of separate instructions.

Cat. No. 12997O

Form **4684** (1993)

Name(s) shown on tax return. Do not enter name and identifying number if shown on other side.	Identifying number

SECTION B—Business and Income-Producing Property (Use this section to report casualties and thefts of property used in a trade or business or for income-producing purposes.)

Part I   Casualty or Theft Gain or Loss (Use a separate Part I for each casualty or theft.)

19   Description of properties (show type, location, and date acquired for each):

Property **A** ....

Property **B** ....

Property **C** ....

Property **D** ....

		Properties (Use a separate column for each property lost or damaged from one casualty or theft.)			
		A	**B**	**C**	**D**
20 Cost or adjusted basis of each property	**20**				
21 Insurance or other reimbursement (whether or not you filed a claim). See the instructions for line 3. **Note:** *If line 20 is more than line 21, skip line 22.*	**21**				
22 Gain from casualty or theft. If line 21 is **more than** line 20, enter the difference here and on line 29 or line 34, column (**c**), except as provided in the instructions for line 33. Also, skip lines 23 through 27 for that column. See the instructions for line 4 if line 21 includes insurance or other reimbursement you did not claim, or you received payment for your loss in a later tax year	**22**				
23 Fair market value **before** casualty or theft	**23**				
24 Fair market value **after** casualty or theft	**24**				
25 Subtract line 24 from line 23	**25**				
26 Enter the **smaller** of line 20 or line 25	**26**				
Note: *If the property was totally destroyed by casualty or lost from theft, enter on line 26 the amount from line 20.*					
27 Subtract line 21 from line 26. If zero or less, enter -0-	**27**				
28 Casualty or theft loss. Add the amounts on line 27. Enter the total here and on line 29 **or** line 34 (see instructions).	**28**				

Part II   Summary of Gains and Losses (from separate Parts I)

(a) Identify casualty or theft		(b) Losses from casualties or thefts		(c) Gains from casualties or thefts includible in income
		(i) Trade, business, rental or royalty property	(ii) Income-producing property	

Casualty or Theft of Property Held One Year or Less

29		(	) (	)
		(	) (	)
30 Totals. Add the amounts on line 29	**30**	(	) (	)

31 Combine line 30, columns (b)(i) and (c). Enter the net gain or (loss) here and on Form 4797, line 15. If Form 4797 is not otherwise required, see instructions   **31**

32 Enter the amount from line 30, column (b)(ii) here and on Schedule A (Form 1040), line 20. Partnerships, S corporations, estates and trusts, see instructions   **32**

Casualty or Theft of Property Held More Than One Year

33 Casualty or theft gains from Form 4797, line 34   **33**

34		(	) (	)
		(	) (	)
35 Total losses. Add amounts on line 34, columns (b)(i) and (b)(ii)	**35**	(	) (	)

36 Total gains. Add lines 33 and 34, column (c)   **36**

37 Add amounts on line 35, columns (b)(i) and (b)(ii)   **37**

38 If the loss on line 37 is **more than** the gain on line 36:

a Combine line 35, column (b)(i) and line 36, and enter the net gain or (loss) here. Partnerships and S corporations see the note below. All others enter this amount on Form 4797, line 15. If Form 4797 is not otherwise required, see instructions   **38a**

b Enter the amount from line 35, column (b)(ii) here. Partnerships and S corporations see the note below. Individuals enter this amount on Schedule A (Form 1040), line 20. Estates and trusts, enter on the "Other deductions" line of your tax return   **38b**

39 If the loss on line 37 is **equal to** or **less than** the gain on line 36, combine these lines and enter here. Partnerships, see the note below. All others, enter this amount on Form 4797, line 3   **39**

Note: *Partnerships, enter the amount from line 38a, 38b, or line 39 on Form 1065, Schedule K, line 7. S corporations, enter the amount from line 38a or 38b on Form 1120S, Schedule K, line 6.*

Form **4797**

Department of the Treasury
Internal Revenue Service (T)

Sales of Business Property

(Also Involuntary Conversions and Recapture Amounts
Under Sections 179 and 280F(b)(2))

▶ Attach to your tax return.   ▶ See separate instructions.

OMB No. 1545-0184

1993

Attachment
Sequence No. **27**

Name(s) shown on return

Identifying number

1   Enter here the gross proceeds from the sale or exchange of real estate reported to you for 1993 on Form(s) 1099-S (or a substitute statement) that you will be including on line 2, 11, or 22 . . . . | 1 |

Part I   Sales or Exchanges of Property Used in a Trade or Business and Involuntary Conversions From Other Than Casualty or Theft—Property Held More Than 1 Year

(a) Description of property	(b) Date acquired (mo., day, yr.)	(c) Date sold (mo., day, yr.)	(d) Gross sales price	(e) Depreciation allowed or allowable since acquisition	(f) Cost or other basis, plus improvements and expense of sale	(g) LOSS ((f) minus the sum of (d) and (e))	(h) GAIN ((d) plus (e) minus (f))
2							

3   Gain, if any, from Form 4684, line 39 . . . . | 3 |
4   Section 1231 gain from installment sales from Form 6252, line 26 or 37 . . . . | 4 |
5   Section 1231 gain or (loss) from like-kind exchanges from Form 8824 . . . . | 5 |
6   Gain, if any, from line 34, from other than casualty or theft . . . . | 6 |
7   Add lines 2 through 6 in columns (g) and (h) . . . . | 7 ( ) |
8   Combine columns (g) and (h) of line 7. Enter gain or (loss) here, and on the appropriate line as follows: . . . . | 8 |

Partnerships—Enter the gain or (loss) on Form 1065, Schedule K, line 6. Skip lines 9, 10, 12, and 13 below.

S corporations—Report the gain or (loss) following the instructions for Form 1120S, Schedule K, lines 5 and 6. Skip lines 9, 10, 12, and 13 below, unless line 8 is a gain and the S corporation is subject to the capital gains tax.

All others—If line 8 is zero or a loss, enter the amount on line 12 below and skip lines 9 and 10. If line 8 is a gain and you did not have any prior year section 1231 losses, or they were recaptured in an earlier year, enter the gain as a long-term capital gain on Schedule D and skip lines 9, 10, and 13 below.

9   Nonrecaptured net section 1231 losses from prior years (see instructions) . . . . | 9 |
10   Subtract line 9 from line 8. If zero or less, enter -0-. Also enter on the appropriate line as follows (see instructions): | 10 |

S corporations—Enter this amount (if more than zero) on Schedule D (Form 1120S), line 13, and skip lines 12 and 13 below.

All others—If line 10 is zero, enter the amount from line 8 on line 13 below. If line 10 is more than zero, enter the amount from line 9 on line 13 below, and enter the amount from line 10 as a long-term capital gain on Schedule D.

Part II   Ordinary Gains and Losses

11   Ordinary gains and losses not included on lines 12 through 18 (include property held 1 year or less):

12   Loss, if any, from line 8 . . . . | 12 |
13   Gain, if any, from line 8, or amount from line 9 if applicable . . . . | 13 |
14   Gain, if any, from line 33 . . . . | 14 |
15   Net gain or (loss) from Form 4684, lines 31 and 38a . . . . | 15 |
16   Ordinary gain from installment sales from Form 6252, line 25 or 36 . . . . | 16 |
17   Ordinary gain or (loss) from like-kind exchanges from Form 8824 . . . . | 17 |
18   Recapture of section 179 expense deduction for partners and S corporation shareholders from property dispositions by partnerships and S corporations (see instructions) . . . . | 18 |
19   Add lines 11 through 18 in columns (g) and (h) . . . . | 19 ( ) |
20   Combine columns (g) and (h) of line 19. Enter gain or (loss) here, and on the appropriate line as follows: . . . . | 20 |
 a   For all except individual returns: Enter the gain or (loss) from line 20 on the return being filed.
 b   For individual returns:
   (1) If the loss on line 12 includes a loss from Form 4684, line 35, column (b)(ii), enter that part of the loss here and on line 20 of Schedule A (Form 1040). Identify as from "Form 4797, line 20b(1)." See instructions . . . | 20b(1) |
   (2) Redetermine the gain or (loss) on line 20, excluding the loss, if any, on line 20b(1). Enter here and on Form 1040, line 15 . | 20b(2) |

For Paperwork Reduction Act Notice, see page 1 of separate instructions.   Cat. No. 13086I   Form **4797** (1993)

659

Part III Gain From Disposition of Property Under Sections 1245, 1250, 1252, 1254, and 1255

21	(a) Description of section 1245, 1250, 1252, 1254, or 1255 property:		(b) Date acquired (mo., day, yr.)	(c) Date sold (mo., day, yr.)
A				
B				
C				
D				

	Relate lines 21A through 21D to these columns ▶		Property A	Property B	Property C	Property D
22	Gross sales price (**Note:** *See line 1 before completing.*)	22				
23	Cost or other basis plus expense of sale	23				
24	Depreciation (or depletion) allowed or allowable	24				
25	Adjusted basis. Subtract line 24 from line 23	25				
26	Total gain. Subtract line 25 from line 22	26				
27	**If section 1245 property:**					
a	Depreciation allowed or allowable from line 24	27a				
b	Enter the **smaller** of line 26 or 27a	27b				
28	**If section 1250 property:** If straight line depreciation was used, enter -0- on line 28g, except for a corporation subject to section 291.					
a	Additional depreciation after 1975 (see instructions)	28a				
b	Applicable percentage multiplied by the **smaller** of line 26 or line 28a (see instructions)	28b				
c	Subtract line 28a from line 26. If residential rental property or line 26 is not more than line 28a, skip lines 28d and 28e	28c				
d	Additional depreciation after 1969 and before 1976	28d				
e	Enter the **smaller** of line 28c or 28d	28e				
f	Section 291 amount (corporations only)	28f				
g	Add lines 28b, 28e, and 28f	28g				
29	**If section 1252 property:** Skip this section if you did not dispose of farmland or if this form is being completed for a partnership.					
a	Soil, water, and land clearing expenses	29a				
b	Line 29a multiplied by applicable percentage (see instructions)	29b				
c	Enter the **smaller** of line 26 or 29b	29c				
30	**If section 1254 property:**					
a	Intangible drilling and development costs, expenditures for development of mines and other natural deposits, and mining exploration costs (see instructions)	30a				
b	Enter the **smaller** of line 26 or 30a	30b				
31	**If section 1255 property:**					
a	Applicable percentage of payments excluded from income under section 126 (see instructions)	31a				
b	Enter the **smaller** of line 26 or 31a	31b				

Summary of Part III Gains. Complete property columns A through D, through line 31b before going to line 32.

32	Total gains for all properties. Add columns A through D, line 26	32	
33	Add columns A through D, lines 27b, 28g, 29c, 30b, and 31b. Enter here and on line 14	33	
34	Subtract line 33 from line 32. Enter the portion from casualty or theft on Form 4684, line 33. Enter the portion from other than casualty or theft on Form 4797, line 6	34	

Part IV Recapture Amounts Under Sections 179 and 280F(b)(2) When Business Use Drops to 50% or Less See instructions for Part IV.

			(a) Section 179	(b) Section 280F(b)(2)
35	Section 179 expense deduction or depreciation allowable in prior years	35		
36	Recomputed depreciation (see instructions)	36		
37	Recapture amount. Subtract line 36 from line 35. See instructions for where to report	37		

Form 4868

Department of the Treasury
Internal Revenue Service

Application for Automatic Extension of Time To File U.S. Individual Income Tax Return

▶ This is not an extension of time to pay your tax.
▶ See separate instructions.

OMB No. 1545-0188

1993

Please Type or Print

Your first name and initial	Last name	Your social security number
If a joint return, spouse's first name and initial	Last name	Spouse's social security number
Home address (number, street, and apt. no. or rural route). If you have a P.O. box, see the instructions.		
City, town or post office, state, and ZIP code		

I request an automatic 4-month extension of time to August 15, 1994, to file Form 1040EZ, Form 1040A, or Form 1040 for the calendar year 1993 or to _____ , 19 _____ , for the fiscal tax year ending _____ , 19 _____ .

Part I   Individual Income Tax—You must complete this part.

1 Total tax liability for 1993. This is the amount you expect to enter on Form 1040EZ, line 8; Form 1040A, line 27; or Form 1040, line 53. If you expect this amount to be zero, enter -0-.

  Caution: *You MUST enter an amount on line 1 or your extension will be denied. You can estimate this amount, but be as exact as you can with the information you have. If we later find that your estimate was not reasonable, the extension will be null and void.*

1	

2 Total payments for 1993. This is the amount you expect to enter on Form 1040EZ, line 7; Form 1040A, line 28d; or Form 1040, line 60   . . . .

2	

3 BALANCE DUE. Subtract line 2 from line 1. If line 2 is more than line 1, enter -0-. For details on how to pay, including what to write on your payment, see the instructions   . . . . . ▶

3	

Part II   Gift or Generation-Skipping Transfer (GST) Tax—Complete this part if you expect to owe either tax.

Caution: *Do not include income tax on lines 5a and 5b. See the instructions.*

4 If you or your spouse plan to file a gift tax return (Form 709 or 709-A) for 1993, generally due by April 15, 1994, see the instructions and check here   . . .   Yourself ▶ ☐   Spouse ▶ ☐

5a Enter the amount of gift or GST tax **you** are paying with this form   . . . .

5a	

  b Enter the amount of gift or GST tax **your spouse** is paying with this form   . . . .

5b	

Signature and Verification

Under penalties of perjury, I declare that I have examined this form, including accompanying schedules and statements, and to the best of my knowledge and belief, it is true, correct, and complete; and, if prepared by someone other than the taxpayer, that I am authorized to prepare this form.

▶ _____   _____   ▶ _____   _____
Your signature   Date   Spouse's signature, if filing jointly   Date

▶ _____   _____
Preparer's signature (other than taxpayer)   Date

If you want correspondence regarding this extension to be sent to you at an address other than that shown above or to an agent acting for you, please enter the name of the agent and/or the address where it should be sent.

Please Type or Print

Name	
Number and street (include suite, room, or apt. no.) or P.O. box number if mail is not delivered to street address	
City, town or post office, state, and ZIP code	

For Paperwork Reduction Act Notice, see separate instructions.   Cat. No. 13141W   Form **4868** (1993)

Form **4972**

Department of the Treasury
Internal Revenue Service

Tax on Lump-Sum Distributions

(Use This Form Only for Lump-Sum Distributions From
Qualified Retirement Plans)

▶ Attach to Form 1040 or Form 1041.   ▶ See separate instructions.

OMB No. 1545-0193

1993

Attachment
Sequence No. **28**

Name of recipient of distribution

Identifying number

Part I Complete this part to see if you qualify to use Form 4972.

			Yes	No
1	Did you roll over any part of the distribution? If "Yes," do not complete the rest of this form	**1**		
2	Was the retirement plan participant born before 1936? If "No," do not complete the rest of this form	**2**		
3	Was this a lump-sum distribution from a qualified pension, profit-sharing, or stock bonus plan? (See **Distributions That Qualify for the 20% Capital Gain Election or for 5- or 10-Year Averaging** in the instructions.) If "No," do not complete the rest of this form	**3**		
4	Was the participant in the plan for at least 5 years before the year of the distribution?	**4**		
5	Was this distribution paid to you as a beneficiary of a plan participant who died?	**5**		
	If you answered "No" to both questions 4 **and** 5, do not complete the rest of this form.			
6	Was the plan participant:			
a	An employee who received the distribution because he or she quit, retired, was laid off, or was fired?	**6a**		
b	Self-employed or an owner-employee who became permanently and totally disabled before the distribution?	**6b**		
c	Age 59½ or older at the time of the distribution?	**6c**		
	If you answered "No" to question 5 and **all** parts of question 6, do not complete the rest of this form.			
7	Did you use Form 4972 in a prior year for any distribution received after 1986 for the same plan participant, including yourself, for whom the 1993 distribution was made? If "Yes," do not complete the rest of this form	**7**		

If you qualify to use this form, you may choose to use Part II, Part III, or Part IV; **or** Part II and Part III; **or** Part II and Part IV.

Part II Complete this part to choose the 20% capital gain election. (See instructions.)

8	Capital gain part from box 3 of Form 1099-R. (See instructions.)	**8**		
9	Multiply line 8 by 20% (.20) and enter here. If you do not choose to use Part III or Part IV, also enter the amount on Form 1040, line 39, or Form 1041, Schedule G, line 1b	**9**		

Part III Complete this part to choose the 5-year averaging method. (See instructions.)

10	Ordinary income from Form 1099-R, box 2a minus box 3. If you did not complete Part II, enter the taxable amount from box 2a of Form 1099-R. (See instructions.)	**10**		
11	Death benefit exclusion. (See instructions.)	**11**		
12	Total taxable amount—Subtract line 11 from line 10	**12**		
13	Current actuarial value of annuity, if applicable (from Form 1099-R, box 8)	**13**		
14	Adjusted total taxable amount—Add lines 12 and 13. If this amount is $70,000 or more, skip lines 15 through 18, and enter this amount on line 19	**14**		
15	Multiply line 14 by 50% (.50), but **do not** enter more than $10,000 .	**15**		
16	Subtract $20,000 from line 14. If line 14 is $20,000 or less, enter -0-	**16**		
17	Multiply line 16 by 20% (.20) .	**17**		
18	Minimum distribution allowance—Subtract line 17 from line 15	**18**		
19	Subtract line 18 from line 14	**19**		
20	Federal estate tax attributable to lump-sum distribution. Do not deduct on Form 1040 or Form 1041 the amount attributable to the ordinary income entered on line 10. (See instructions.) .	**20**		
21	Subtract line 20 from line 19	**21**		
22	Multiply line 21 by 20% (.20)	**22**		
23	Tax on amount on line 22. See the Tax Rate Schedule for the 5-Year Method in the instructions	**23**		
24	Multiply line 23 by five (5). If line 13 is blank, skip lines 25 through 30, and enter this amount on line 31	**24**		
25	Divide line 13 by line 14 and enter the result as a decimal. (See instructions.)	**25**	×	.
26	Multiply line 18 by the decimal amount on line 25	**26**		
27	Subtract line 26 from line 13	**27**		
28	Multiply line 27 by 20% (.20)	**28**		
29	Tax on amount on line 28. See the Tax Rate Schedule for the 5-Year Method in the instructions	**29**		
30	Multiply line 29 by five (5)	**30**		
31	Subtract line 30 from line 24. (Multiple recipients, see instructions.)	**31**		
32	Tax on lump-sum distribution—Add Part II, line 9, and Part III, line 31. Enter on Form 1040, line 39, or Form 1041, Schedule G, line 1b ▶	**32**		

For Paperwork Reduction Act Notice, see separate instructions.   Cat. No. 13187U   Form **4972** (1993)

Part IV   **Complete this part to choose the 10-year averaging method.** (See instructions.)

33 Ordinary income part from Form 1099-R, box 2a minus box 3. If you did not complete Part II, enter the taxable amount from box 2a of Form 1099-R. (See instructions.) . . . . | **33** |

34 Death benefit exclusion. (See instructions.) . . . . | **34** |

35 Total taxable amount—Subtract line 34 from line 33 . . . . . | **35** |

36 Current actuarial value of annuity, if applicable (from Form 1099-R, box 8) . . . . | **36** |

37 Adjusted total taxable amount—Add lines 35 and 36. If this amount is $70,000 or more, skip lines 38 through 41, and enter this amount on line 42 . . . . . . | **37** |

38 Multiply line 37 by 50% (.50), but **do not** enter more than $10,000 . | **38** |

39 Subtract $20,000 from line 37. If line 37 is $20,000 or less, enter -0- . . . . . . | **39** |

40 Multiply line 39 by 20% (.20) . . . . | **40** |

41 Minimum distribution allowance—Subtract line 40 from line 38 . . . . | **41** |

42 Subtract line 41 from line 37 . . . . | **42** |

43 Federal estate tax attributable to lump-sum distribution. Do not deduct on Form 1040 or Form 1041 the amount attributable to the ordinary income entered on line 33. (See instructions.) . . | **43** |

44 Subtract line 43 from line 42 . . . . | **44** |

45 Multiply line 44 by 10% (.10) . . . . | **45** |

46 Tax on amount on line 45. See the Tax Rate Schedule for the 10-Year Method in the instructions | **46** |

47 Multiply line 46 by ten (10). If line 36 is blank, skip lines 48 through 53, and enter this amount on line 54 . . . . | **47** |

48 Divide line 36 by line 37 and enter the result as a decimal. (See instructions.) . . . . . . | **48** |

49 Multiply line 41 by the decimal amount on line 48 . . . . . . | **49** |

50 Subtract line 49 from line 36 . . . . | **50** |

51 Multiply line 50 by 10% (.10) . . . . | **51** |

52 Tax on amount on line 51. See the Tax Rate Schedule for the 10-Year Method in the instructions | **52** |

53 Multiply line 52 by ten (10) . . . . | **53** |

54 Subtract line 53 from line 47. (Multiple recipients, see instructions.) . . . . . . | **54** |

55 Tax on lump-sum distribution—Add Part II, line 9, and Part IV, line 54. Enter on Form 1040, line 39, or Form 1041, Schedule G, line 1b . . . . . . ▶ | **55** |

Form **6251**	**Alternative Minimum Tax—Individuals**	OMB No. 1545-0227
Department of the Treasury Internal Revenue Service (T)	▶ See separate instructions. ▶ Attach to Form 1040 or Form 1040NR.	**1993** Attachment Sequence No. **32**

Name(s) shown on Form 1040 | Your social security number

Part I Adjustments and Preferences

1	If you itemized deductions on Schedule A (Form 1040), go to line 2. If you did not itemize deductions, enter your standard deduction from Form 1040, line 34, and skip to line 6 . .	**1**
2	Medical and dental expenses. See instructions	**2**
3	Taxes. Enter the amount from Schedule A, line 8	**3**
4	Certain interest on a home mortgage not used to buy, build, or improve your home . . .	**4**
5	Miscellaneous itemized deductions. Enter the amount from Schedule A, line 24 . .	**5**
6	Refund of taxes. Enter any tax refund from Form 1040, line 10 or 22	**6** ( )
7	Investment interest. Enter difference between regular tax and AMT deduction . . .	**7**
8	Post-1986 depreciation. Enter difference between regular tax and AMT depreciation . .	**8**
9	Adjusted gain or loss. Enter difference between AMT and regular tax gain or loss . . .	**9**
10	Incentive stock options. Enter excess of AMT income over regular tax income . . .	**10**
11	Passive activities. Enter difference between AMT and regular tax income or loss	**11**
12	Beneficiaries of estates and trusts. Enter the amount from Schedule K-1 (Form 1041), line 8	**12**
13	Tax-exempt interest from private activity bonds issued after 8/7/86	**13**
14	Other. Enter the amount, if any, for each item and enter the total on line 14.	

a Charitable contributions .		**g** Long-term contracts . .	
b Circulation expenditures .		**h** Loss limitations . . .	
c Depletion		**i** Mining costs	
d Depreciation (pre-1987) .		**j** Pollution control facilities .	
e Installment sales . . .		**k** Research and experimental	
f Intangible drilling costs .		**l** Tax shelter farm activities .	
		m Related adjustments . .	**14**

15	**Total Adjustments and Preferences.** Combine lines 1 through 14 . . . . . ▶	**15**

Part II Alternative Minimum Taxable Income

16	Enter the amount from **Form 1040, line 35.** If less than zero, enter as a (loss) . . . . ▶	**16**
17	Net operating loss deduction, if any, from Form 1040, line 22. Enter as a positive amount .	**17**
18	If Form 1040, line 32, is over $108,450 (over $54,225 if married filing separately), enter your itemized deductions limitation, if any, from line 9 of the worksheet for Schedule A, line 26	**18** ( )
19	Combine lines 15 through 18 . . . . ▶	**19**
20	Alternative tax net operating loss deduction. See instructions	**20**
21	**Alternative Minimum Taxable Income.** Subtract line 20 from line 19. (If married filing separately and line 21 is more than $165,000, see instructions.) . . . . ▶	**21**

Part III Exemption Amount and Alternative Minimum Tax

22 **Exemption Amount.** (If this form is for a child under age 14, see instructions.)

If your filing status is:	And line 21 is not over:	Enter on line 22:	
Single or head of household	$112,500	$33,750	
Married filing jointly or qualifying widow(er)	150,000	45,000	**22**
Married filing separately	75,000	22,500	

If line 21 is **over** the amount shown above for your filing status, see instructions.

23	Subtract line 22 from line 21. If zero or less, enter -0- here and on lines 26 and 28 . . ▶	**23**
24	If line 23 is $175,000 or less ($87,500 or less if married filing separately), multiply line 23 by 26% (.26). Otherwise, see instructions	**24**
25	Alternative minimum tax foreign tax credit. See instructions	**25**
26	Tentative minimum tax. Subtract line 25 from line 24 . . . . ▶	**26**
27	Enter your tax from Form 1040, line 38 (plus any amount from Form 4970 included on Form 1040, line 39), minus any foreign tax credit from Form 1040, line 43	**27**
28	**Alternative Minimum Tax.** (If this form is for a child under age 14, see instructions.) Subtract line 27 from line 26. If zero or less, enter -0-. Enter here and on Form 1040, line 48 . . ▶	**28**

For Paperwork Reduction Act Notice, see separate instructions. | Cat. No. 13600G | Form **6251** (1993)

665

Form **6252**	**Installment Sale Income**	OMB No. 1545-0228
Department of the Treasury Internal Revenue Service	▶ See separate instructions. ▶ Attach to your tax return. ▶ Use a separate form for each sale or other disposition of property on the installment method.	**1993** Attachment Sequence No. **79**

Name(s) shown on return	Identifying number

1 Description of property ▶ ....

2a Date acquired (month, day, and year) ▶ _____/_____/_____   **b** Date sold (month, day, and year) ▶ _____/_____/_____

3 Was the property sold to a related party after May 14, 1980? See instructions . . . . ☐ Yes ☐ No

4 If the answer to question 3 is "Yes," was the property a marketable security? If "Yes," complete Part III. If "No," complete Part III for the year of sale and for 2 years after the year of sale. . . . . ☐ Yes ☐ No

Part I Gross Profit and Contract Price. Complete this part for the year of sale only.

5	Selling price including mortgages and other debts. Do not include interest whether stated or unstated	**5**	
6	Mortgages and other debts the buyer assumed or took the property subject to, but not new mortgages the buyer got from a bank or other source .	**6**	
7	Subtract line 6 from line 5	**7**	
8	Cost or other basis of property sold	**8**	
9	Depreciation allowed or allowable	**9**	
10	Adjusted basis. Subtract line 9 from line 8	**10**	
11	Commissions and other expenses of sale.	**11**	
12	Income recapture from Form 4797, Part III. See instructions	**12**	
13	Add lines 10, 11, and 12	**13**	
14	Subtract line 13 from line 5. If zero or less, **stop here.** Do not complete the rest of this form .	**14**	
15	If the property described on line 1 above was your main home, enter the total of lines 14 and 22 from Form 2119. Otherwise, enter -0-	**15**	
16	**Gross profit.** Subtract line 15 from line 14	**16**	
17	Subtract line 13 from line 6. If zero or less, enter -0-	**17**	
18	**Contract price.** Add line 7 and line 17	**18**	

Part II Installment Sale Income. Complete this part for the year of sale and any year you receive a payment or have certain debts you must treat as a payment on installment obligations.

19	Gross profit percentage. Divide line 16 by line 18. For years after the year of sale, see instructions	**19**	
20	**For year of sale only**—Enter amount from line 17 above; otherwise, enter -0-	**20**	
21	Payments received during year. See instructions. Do not include interest whether stated or unstated	**21**	
22	Add lines 20 and 21	**22**	
23	Payments received in prior years. See instructions. Do not include interest whether stated or unstated	**23**	
24	**Installment sale income.** Multiply line 22 by line 19	**24**	
25	Part of line 24 that is ordinary income under recapture rules. See instructions	**25**	
26	Subtract line 25 from line 24. Enter here and on Schedule D or Form 4797. See instructions .	**26**	

Part III Related Party Installment Sale Income. Do not complete if you received the final payment this tax year.

27 Name, address, and taxpayer identifying number of related party ....

28 Did the related party, during this tax year, resell or dispose of the property ("second disposition")? . . . ☐ Yes ☐ No

29 **If the answer to question 28 is "Yes," complete lines 30 through 37 below unless one of the following conditions is met. Check only the box that applies.**

a ☐ The second disposition was more than 2 years after the first disposition (other than dispositions of marketable securities). If this box is checked, enter the date of disposition (month, day, year) ▶ _____/_____/_____

b ☐ The first disposition was a sale or exchange of stock to the issuing corporation.

c ☐ The second disposition was an involuntary conversion where the threat of conversion occurred after the first disposition.

d ☐ The second disposition occurred after the death of the original seller or buyer.

e ☐ It can be established to the satisfaction of the Internal Revenue Service that tax avoidance was not a principal purpose for either of the dispositions. If this box is checked, attach an explanation. See instructions.

30	Selling price of property sold by related party	**30**	
31	Enter contract price from line 18 for year of first sale	**31**	
32	Enter the **smaller** of line 30 or line 31	**32**	
33	Total payments received by the end of your 1993 tax year. Add lines 22 and 23	**33**	
34	Subtract line 33 from line 32. If zero or less, enter -0-	**34**	
35	Multiply line 34 by the gross profit percentage on line 19 for year of first sale	**35**	
36	Part of line 35 that is ordinary income under recapture rules. See instructions	**36**	
37	Subtract line 36 from line 35. Enter here and on Schedule D or Form 4797. See instructions	**37**	

For Paperwork Reduction Act Notice, see separate instructions.   Cat. No. 13601R   Form **6252** (1993)

Form **8271**	Investor Reporting of Tax Shelter Registration Number	OMB No. 1545-0881

Form **8271**
(Rev. March 1993)
Department of the Treasury
Internal Revenue Service

Investor Reporting of Tax Shelter Registration Number

▶ Attach to your tax return.

▶ If you received this form from a partnership, S corporation, or trust, see the instructions.

OMB No. 1545-0881
Expires 3-31-96

Attachment
Sequence No. **71**

Investor's name(s) shown on return | Investor's identifying number | Investor's tax year ended

	(a) Tax Shelter Name	(b) Tax Shelter Registration Number (11-digit number)	(c) Tax Shelter Identifying Number
1			
2			
3			
4			
5			
6			
7			
8			
9			
10			

General Instructions

Paperwork Reduction Act Notice

We ask for the information on this form to carry out the Internal Revenue laws of the United States. We are required to give us the information. We need it to ensure that you are complying with these laws and to allow us to figure and collect the right amount of tax.

The time needed to complete and file this form will vary depending on individual circumstances. The estimated average time is:

Recordkeeping . . . . . . 7 min.

**Learning about
the law or the form** . . . . 15 min.

Preparing the form . . . . 17 min.

**Copying, assembling,
and sending the form
to the IRS** . . . . 14 min.

If you have comments concerning the accuracy of these time estimates or suggestions for making this form more simple, we would be happy to hear from you. You can write to both the IRS and the Office of Management and Budget at the addresses listed in the instructions for the tax return with which this form is filed.

Purpose of Form

Use Form 8271 to report the tax shelter registration number the IRS assigns to certain tax shelters required to be registered under section 6111 of the Internal Revenue Code ("registration-required tax shelters") and to report the name and identifying number of the tax shelter. This information must be reported even if the particular interest is producing net income for the filer of Form 8271. Use additional forms to report more than 10 tax shelter registration numbers.

Note: *A tax shelter registration number does not indicate that the tax shelter or its claimed tax benefits have been reviewed, examined, or approved by the IRS.*

Who Must File

Any person claiming or reporting any deduction, loss, credit, or other tax benefit, or reporting any income on any tax return from an interest purchased or otherwise acquired in a registration-required tax shelter must file Form 8271. If you are an investor in a partnership or an S corporation, look at item G, Schedule K-1 (Form 1065), or item C, Schedule K-1 (Form 1120S). If a tax shelter registration number or the words "Applied for" appear there, then the entity is a registration-required tax shelter. If the interest is purchased or otherwise acquired by a pass-through entity, both the pass-through entity and its partners, shareholders, or beneficiaries must file Form 8271.

A pass-through entity that is the registration-required tax shelter does not have to prepare Form 8271 and give copies to its partners, shareholders, or beneficiaries unless the pass-through entity itself has invested in a registration-required tax shelter.

In certain cases, a tax shelter that does not expect to reduce the cumulative tax liability of any investor during the 5-year period ending after the date the investment is first offered for sale may be considered a "projected income investment." Such a tax shelter will not have to register, and thus not have to furnish a tax shelter registration number to investors, unless and until it ceases to be a projected income investment. It is possible, therefore, that you may not be furnished a tax shelter registration number, and not have to report it, for several years after you

purchase or otherwise acquire your interest in the tax shelter. If you are later furnished a tax shelter registration number because the tax shelter ceased to be a projected income investment, follow these instructions. However, you must file Form 8271 only for tax years ending on or after the date the tax shelter ceases to be a projected income investment.

Note: *Even if you have an interest in a registration-required tax shelter, you do not have to file Form 8271 if you did not claim or report any deduction, loss, credit, or other tax benefit, or report any income on your tax return from an interest in the registration-required tax shelter. This could occur, for example, if for a particular year you are unable to claim any portion of a loss because of the passive activity loss limitations, and that loss is the only tax item reported to you from the shelter.*

Filing Form 8271

Attach Form 8271 to any return on which a deduction, loss, credit, or other tax benefit is claimed or reported, or any income reported, from an interest in a registration-required tax shelter. These returns include applications for tentative refunds (Forms 1045 and 1139) and amended returns (Forms 1040X and 1120X).

Furnishing Copies of Form 8271 to Investors

A pass-through entity that has invested in a registration-required tax shelter must furnish copies of its Form 8271 to its partners, shareholders, or beneficiaries.

However, in the case where (a) the pass-through entity acquired at least a 50% interest in one tax year in a registered tax shelter (and in which it had not held an interest in a prior year), and **(b)** the investment would not meet the definition of a tax shelter immediately following the acquisition if it had been offered for sale at that time, the pass-through entity need not distribute copies of Form 8271 to its investors. The pass-through entity alone is required to prepare Form 8271 and include it with the entity tax return.

Penalty For Not Including Registration Number on Return

A $250 penalty will be charged for each failure to include a tax shelter registration number on a return on which it is required to be included unless the failure is due to reasonable cause.

Specific Instructions

Investor's Identifying Number

Enter the social security number or employer identification number shown on the return to which this Form 8271 is attached.

Investor's Tax Year Ended

Enter the date the tax year ended for the return to which this Form 8271 is attached.

Columns (a) Through (c)

Enter the name, the 11-digit tax shelter registration number, and the identifying number of the tax shelter in the columns provided.

You must be given the tax shelter registration number at the time of your purchase or acquisition of an interest in a registration-required tax shelter or (if later) within 20 days after the seller or transferor receives the registration number. The seller or transferor of the interest in the tax shelter must give you the tax shelter registration number in a written statement that also provides the other information needed to complete columns (a) and (c) of Form 8271.

If you acquired your interest in the tax shelter from a pass-through entity that has invested in a tax shelter, the entity must give you a copy of its Form 8271. The copy of the entity's Form 8271 contains the information needed to complete columns (a) through (c) of your Form 8271.

If the person from whom you purchased or otherwise acquired an interest in the tax shelter notifies you that a registration number has been applied for, but has not yet been received, enter "Applied for" in column (b). Also enter in column (b) the name of the person who has applied for registration of the tax shelter, and complete columns (a) and (c). This notification must be in a written statement that includes the information you need to complete columns (a) through (c). If you have not received any notification, enter "No notification" in column (b) and complete columns (a) and (c) if you have this information.

Form **8283**

(Rev. November 1992)

Department of the Treasury
Internal Revenue Service

Noncash Charitable Contributions

▶ **Attach to your tax return if the total deduction claimed
for all property contributed exceeds $500.**

▶ **See separate instructions.**

OMB No. 1545-0908
Expires 11-30-95

Attachment
Sequence No. **55**

Name(s) shown on your income tax return	Identifying number

Note: *Figure the amount of your contribution deduction before completing this form. See your tax return instructions.*

Section A—Include in this section **only** items (or groups of similar items) for which you claimed a deduction of $5,000 or less per item or group, and certain publicly traded securities (see instructions).

Part I   **Information on Donated Property**—If you need more space, attach a statement.

1	(a) Name and address of the donee organization	(b) Description of donated property
A		
B		
C		
D		
E		

Note: *If the amount you claimed as a deduction for an item is $500 or less, you do not have to complete columns (d), (e), and (f).*

	(c) Date of the contribution	(d) Date acquired by donor (mo., yr.)	(e) How acquired by donor	(f) Donor's cost or adjusted basis	(g) Fair market value	(h) Method used to determine the fair market value
A						
B						
C						
D						
E						

Part II   **Other Information**—If you gave less than an entire interest in property listed in Part I, complete lines 2a–2e. If restrictions were attached to a contribution listed in Part I, complete lines 3a–3c.

2   If less than the entire interest in the property is contributed during the year, complete the following:

   a   Enter letter from Part I that identifies the property _____. If Part II applies to more than one property, attach a separate statement.

   b   Total amount claimed as a deduction for the property listed in Part I: **(1)** For this tax year _____
     (2) For any prior tax years _____.

   c   Name and address of each organization to which any such contribution was made in a prior year (complete only if different than the donee organization above).

     Name of charitable organization (donee)

     Address (number, street, and room or suite no.)

     City or town, state, and ZIP code

   d   For tangible property, enter the place where the property is located or kept _____

   e   Name of any person, other than the donee organization, having actual possession of the property _____

3   If conditions were attached to any contribution listed in Part I, answer the following questions and attach the required statement (see instructions):

		Yes	No
a	Is there a restriction, either temporary or permanent, on the donee's right to use or dispose of the donated property?		
b	Did you give to anyone (other than the donee organization or another organization participating with the donee organization in cooperative fundraising) the right to the income from the donated property or to the possession of the property, including the right to vote donated securities, to acquire the property by purchase or otherwise, or to designate the person having such income, possession, or right to acquire?		
c	Is there a restriction limiting the donated property for a particular use?		

For Paperwork Reduction Act Notice, see separate instructions.   Cat. No. 62299J   Form **8283** (Rev. 11-92)

Name(s) shown on your income tax return | Identifying number

Section B—Appraisal Summary—Include in this section only items (or groups of similar items) for which you claimed a deduction of more than $5,000 per item or group. Report contributions of certain publicly traded securities only in Section A.

If you donated art, you may have to attach the complete appraisal. See the **Note** in Part I below.

Part I — Information on Donated Property—To be completed by the taxpayer and/or appraiser.

4 Check type of property:

☐ Art* (contribution of $20,000 or more)   ☐ Real Estate   ☐ Gems/Jewelry   ☐ Stamp Collections
☐ Art* (contribution of less than $20,000) ☐ Coin Collections ☐ Books ☐ Other

*Art includes paintings, sculptures, watercolors, prints, drawings, ceramics, antique furniture, decorative arts, textiles, carpets, silver, rare manuscripts, historical memorabilia, and other similar objects.

Note: *If your total art contribution deduction was $20,000 or more, you must attach a complete copy of the signed appraisal. See instructions.*

5	(a) Description of donated property (if you need more space, attach a separate statement)	(b) If tangible property was donated, give a brief summary of the overall physical condition at the time of the gift	(c) Appraised fair market value
A			
B			
C			
D			

	(d) Date acquired by donor (mo., yr.)	(e) How acquired by donor	(f) Donor's cost or adjusted basis	(g) For bargain sales, enter amount received	(h) Amount claimed as a deduction	(i) Average trading price of securities
A						
B						
C						
D						

Part II — Taxpayer (Donor) Statement—List each item included in Part I above that is separately identified in the appraisal as having a value of $500 or less. See instructions.

I declare that the following item(s) included in Part I above has to the best of my knowledge and belief an appraised value of not more than $500 (per item). Enter identifying letter from Part I and describe the specific item: _____

Signature of taxpayer (donor) ▶   Date ▶

Part III — Certification of Appraiser

I declare that I am not the donor, the donee, a party to the transaction in which the donor acquired the property, employed by, married to, or related to any of the foregoing persons, or an appraiser regularly used by any of the foregoing persons and who does not perform a majority of appraisals during the taxable year for other persons.

Also, I declare that I hold myself out to the public as an appraiser or perform appraisals on a regular basis; and that because of my qualifications as described in the appraisal, I am qualified to make appraisals of the type of property being valued. I certify that the appraisal fees were not based upon a percentage of the appraised property value. Furthermore, I understand that a false or fraudulent overstatement of the property value as described in the qualified appraisal or this appraisal summary may subject me to the civil penalty under section 6701(a) (aiding and abetting the understatement of tax liability). I affirm that I have not been barred from presenting evidence or testimony by the Director of Practice.

Sign Here   Signature ▶   Title ▶   Date of appraisal ▶

Business address (including room or suite no.) | Identifying number

City or town, state, and ZIP code

Part IV — Donee Acknowledgment—To be completed by the charitable organization.

This charitable organization acknowledges that it is a qualified organization under section 170(c) and that it received the donated property as described in Section B, Part I, above on _____
(Date)

Furthermore, this organization affirms that in the event it sells, exchanges, or otherwise disposes of the property (or any portion thereof) within 2 years after the date of receipt, it will file an information return (**Form 8282,** Donee Information Return) with the IRS and furnish the donor a copy of that return. This acknowledgment does not represent concurrence in the claimed fair market value.

Name of charitable organization (donee) | Employer identification number

Address (number, street, and room or suite no.) | City or town, state, and ZIP code

Authorized signature | Title | Date

<table>
<tr><td>Form **8582**</td><td>**Passive Activity Loss Limitations**</td><td>OMB No. 1545-1008</td></tr>
</table>

Form **8582**

Department of the Treasury
Internal Revenue Service

Passive Activity Loss Limitations

▶ See separate instructions.
▶ Attach to Form 1040 or Form 1041.

OMB No. 1545-1008

1993

Attachment
Sequence No. **88**

Name(s) shown on return

Identifying number

Part I   **1993 Passive Activity Loss**

Caution: *See the instructions for Worksheets 1 and 2 on page 7 before completing Part I.*

Rental Real Estate Activities With Active Participation (For the definition of active participation see **Active Participation in a Rental Real Estate Activity** on page 3 of the instructions.)

1a Activities with net income (from Worksheet 1, column (a)) . . .   **1a**

 b Activities with net loss (from Worksheet 1, column (b)) . . . .   **1b** ( )

 c Prior year unallowed losses (from Worksheet 1, column (c)) . .   **1c** ( )

 d Combine lines 1a, 1b, and 1c **1d**

All Other Passive Activities

2a Activities with net income (from Worksheet 2, column (a)) . . .   **2a**

 b Activities with net loss (from Worksheet 2, column (b)) . . . .   **2b** ( )

 c Prior year unallowed losses (from Worksheet 2, column (c)) . .   **2c** ( )

 d Combine lines 2a, 2b, and 2c **2d**

3 Combine lines 1d and 2d. If the result is net income or zero, see the instructions for line 3. If this line and line 1d are losses, go to line 4. Otherwise, enter -0- on line 9 and go to line 10 .   **3**

Part II   **Special Allowance for Rental Real Estate With Active Participation**

Note: *Enter all numbers in Part II as positive amounts. (See instructions on page 7 for examples.)*

4 Enter the **smaller** of the loss on line 1d or the loss on line 3 . . . .   **4**

5 Enter $150,000. If married filing separately, see the instructions .   **5**

6 Enter modified adjusted gross income, but not less than zero (see instructions) **6**

  Note: *If line 6 is equal to or greater than line 5, skip lines 7 and 8, enter -0- on line 9, and then go to line 10. Otherwise, go to line 7.*

7 Subtract line 6 from line 5 . . . .   **7**

8 Multiply line 7 by 50% (.5). **Do not** enter more than $25,000. If married filing separately, see instructions   **8**

9 Enter the **smaller** of line 4 or line 8 . . . .   **9**

Part III   **Total Losses Allowed**

10 Add the income, if any, on lines 1a and 2a and enter the total **10**

11 **Total losses allowed from all passive activities for 1993.** Add lines 9 and 10. See the instructions to find out how to report the losses on your tax return **11**

For Paperwork Reduction Act Notice, see separate instructions.   Cat. No. 63704F   Form **8582** (1993)

Caution: *The worksheets are not required to be filed with your tax return and may be detached before filing Form 8582. Keep a copy of the worksheets for your records.*

Worksheet 1—For Form 8582, Lines 1a, 1b, and 1c (See instructions on page 7.)

Name of activity	Current year		Prior year	Overall gain or loss	
	(a) Net income (line 1a)	**(b) Net loss (line 1b)**	**(c) Unallowed loss (line 1c)**	**(d) Gain**	**(e) Loss**
Total. Enter on Form 8582, lines 1a, 1b, and 1c. . . . . ▶				/////////	/////////

Worksheet 2—For Form 8582, Lines 2a, 2b, and 2c (See instructions on page 7.)

Name of activity	Current year		Prior year	Overall gain or loss	
	(a) Net income (line 2a)	**(b) Net loss (line 2b)**	**(c) Unallowed loss (line 2c)**	**(d) Gain**	**(e) Loss**
Total. Enter on Form 8582, lines 2a, 2b, and 2c. . . . . ▶				/////////	/////////

Worksheet 3—Use this worksheet if an amount is shown on Form 8582, line 9 (See instructions on page 8.)

Name of activity	Form or schedule to be reported on	**(a) Loss** (See instructions.)	**(b) Ratio** (See instructions.)	**(c) Special allowance** (See instructions.)	**(d) Subtract column (c) from column (a)** (See instructions.)
Total . . . . ▶			1.00		

Worksheet 4—Allocation of Unallowed Losses (See instructions on page 8.)

Name of activity	Form or schedule to be reported on	**(a) Loss** (See instructions.)	**(b) Ratio** (See instructions.)	**(c) Unallowed loss** (See instructions.)
Total . . . . ▶			1.00	

Worksheet 5—Allowed Losses (See instructions on page 8.)

Name of activity	Form or schedule to be reported on	**(a) Loss** (See instructions.)	**(b) Unallowed loss** (See instructions.)	**(c) Allowed loss** (See instructions.)
Total . . . . ▶				

Worksheet 6—Activities With Losses Reported on Two or More Different Forms or Schedules (See instructions on page 8.)

Name of Activity:	(a) (See instr.)	(b) (See instr.)	(c) Ratio (See instr.)	(d) Unallowed loss (See instr.)	(e) Allowed loss (See instr.)
Form or Schedule To Be Reported on:					
1a Net loss plus prior year unallowed loss from form or schedule ▶					
b Net income from form or schedule . . . . ▶					
c Subtract line 1b from line 1a. If zero or less, enter -0- . . . . ▶					
Form or Schedule To Be Reported on:					
1a Net loss plus prior year unallowed loss from form or schedule ▶					
b Net income from form or schedule . . . . ▶					
c Subtract line 1b from line 1a. If zero or less, enter -0- . . . . ▶					
Form or Schedule To Be Reported on:					
1a Net loss plus prior year unallowed loss from form or schedule ▶					
b Net income from form or schedule . . . . ▶					
c Subtract line 1b from line 1a. If zero or less, enter -0- . . . . ▶					
Total . . . . ▶			1.00		

676

Form **8606**	Nondeductible IRAs (Contributions, Distributions, and Basis) ▶ **Please see What Records Must I Keep? below.** ▶ **Attach to Form 1040, Form 1040A, or Form 1040NR.**	OMB No. 1545-1007
Department of the Treasury Internal Revenue Service		**1993** Attachment Sequence No. **47**

Name. If married, file a separate Form 8606 for each spouse. See instructions.	**Your social security number**

Fill in Your Address Only If You Are Filing This Form by Itself and Not With Your Tax Return ▷	Home address (number and street, or P.O. box if mail is not delivered to your home)	Apt. no.
	City, town or post office, state, and ZIP code	

Contributions, Nontaxable Distributions, and Basis

1	Enter your IRA contributions for 1993 that you choose to be nondeductible. Include those made during 1/1/94–4/15/94 that were for 1993. See instructions	**1**
2	Enter your total IRA basis for 1992 and earlier years. See instructions	**2**
3	Add lines 1 and 2	**3**

> **Did you receive any IRA distributions (withdrawals) in 1993?**
> — No —▶ Enter the amount from line 3 on line 12. Then, **stop** and read **When and Where To File** on page 2.
> — Yes —▶ Go to line 4.

4	Enter only those contributions included on line 1 that were made during 1/1/94–4/15/94. This amount will be the same as line 1 if all of your nondeductible contributions for 1993 were made in 1994 by 4/15/94. See instructions	**4**
5	Subtract line 4 from line 3	**5**
6	Enter the total value of **ALL** your IRAs as of 12/31/93 plus any outstanding rollovers. See instructions	**6**	
7	Enter the total IRA distributions received during 1993. Do not include amounts rolled over before 1/1/94. See instructions	**7**	
8	Add lines 6 and 7	**8**	
9	Divide line 5 by line 8 and enter the result as a decimal (to at least two places). Do not enter more than "1.00"	**9**	$\times$.
10	Multiply line 7 by line 9. This is the amount of your **nontaxable distributions for 1993**	**10**
11	Subtract line 10 from line 5. This is the **basis in your IRA(s) as of 12/31/93**	**11**
12	Add lines 4 and 11. This is your **total IRA basis for 1993 and earlier years**	**12**

Taxable Distributions for 1993

13	Subtract line 10 from line 7. Enter the result here and on Form 1040, line 16b; Form 1040A, line 10b; or Form 1040NR, line 17b, whichever applies	**13**

Sign Here Only If You Are Filing This Form by Itself and Not With Your Tax Return	Under penalties of perjury, I declare that I have examined this form, including accompanying attachments, and to the best of my knowledge and belief, it is true, correct, and complete.
	▶ Your signature _____ ▶ Date _____

Cat.No. 63966F

Form **8606** (1993)

- Page 1 of Forms 1040 (or Forms 1040A or Forms 1040NR) filed for each year you make a nondeductible contribution.
- Forms 5498 or similar statements received each year showing contributions you made.
- Forms 5498 or similar statements you received showing the value of your IRA(s) for each year you received a distribution.
- Forms 1099-R and W-2P received for each year you received a distribution.

When and Where To File

Attach Form 8606 to your 1993 Form 1040, Form 1040A, or Form 1040NR.

If you are required to file Form 8606 but do not have to file an income tax return because you do not meet the requirements for filing a return, you still **must** file Form 8606 with the Internal Revenue Service at the same time and place you would be required to file Form 1040, Form 1040A, or Form 1040NR.

Penalty for Not Filing

If you are required to file Form 8606 but do not do so, you will have to pay a $50 penalty for each failure to file this form unless you can show reasonable cause.

Penalty for Overstatement

If you overstate your nondeductible contributions for any tax year, you must pay a $100 penalty for each overstatement unless it was due to reasonable cause.

Additional Information

For more details on nondeductible contributions, IRA basis, and distributions, get **Pub. 590,** Individual Retirement Arrangements (IRAs).

Amending Form 8606

After you file your return, you may change a nondeductible contribution made on a prior year's return to a deductible contribution or vice versa. To do this, complete a new Form 8606 showing the revised information and attach it to **Form 1040X,** Amended U.S. Individual Income Tax Return. Send both of these forms to the Internal Revenue Service Center shown in the Form 1040X instructions for your area.

Specific Instructions

Section references are to the Internal Revenue Code.

Note: *If you received an IRA distribution in 1993 and you also made IRA contributions for 1993 that may not be fully deductible because of the income limits, you need to make a special computation before completing this form. For details, including how to complete Form 8606, see* **Tax Treatment of Distributions** *in Chapter 6 of Pub. 590.*

Name and Social Security Number

If you file a joint return on Form 1040 or Form 1040A, enter the name and social security number of the spouse whose IRA information is shown.

Line 1

If you used IRA Worksheet 2 in the Form 1040 or Form 1040A instructions, include the following on line 1 of Form 8606:

- The amount shown on line 10 of IRA Worksheet 2 (Form 1040) or line 8 of IRA Worksheet 2 (Form 1040A) that you choose to make nondeductible.
- The part, if any, of the amount shown on line 9 of IRA Worksheet 2 (Form 1040) or line 7 of IRA Worksheet 2 (Form 1040A) that you choose to make nondeductible. You cannot take a deduction for the part included on line 1.

Note: *Enter any nondeductible contributions for your* **nonworking spouse** *from the appropriate lines of IRA Worksheet 2 on line 1 of your spouse's* **separate** *Form 8606.*

If none of your contributions are deductible, you may choose to make up to $2,000 (but not more than your earned income) of your contributions nondeductible. Enter on line 1 of Form 8606 your contributions that you choose to make nondeductible.

If contributions were also made to your nonworking spouse's IRA, you may choose to make nondeductible contributions up to $2,250 (but not more than your earned income). Enter on line 1 of your Form 8606 the total nondeductible contributions you are making to your IRA. Enter the balance on line 1 of your nonworking spouse's Form 8606. Do not enter more than $2,000 on either your or your spouse's Form 8606. Also, the total of the two amounts cannot be more than $2,250.

If you used IRA Worksheet 1 in the Form 1040 or Form 1040A instructions but choose not to deduct the full amount shown on line 3 of that worksheet, subtract the amount you are deducting from the amount on line 3. Enter the result on line 1 of your Form 8606.

If contributions were made to your nonworking spouse's IRA but you choose not to deduct the full amount shown on line 8 of IRA Worksheet 1, subtract the amount you are deducting for your nonworking spouse from the amount on line 8. Enter the result on line 1 of your nonworking spouse's Form 8606.

Line 2

If this is the first year you are required to file Form 8606, enter zero. If you filed a Form 8606 for any year **after 1988,** enter the amount from line 14 of the **last** Form 8606 you filed. Otherwise, enter the total of the amounts from lines 7 and 16 of your **1988** Form 8606. Or, if you didn't file a 1988 Form 8606, enter the total of the amounts from lines 4 and 13 of your **1987** Form 8606.

Line 4

If you made contributions in 1993 and 1994 that are for 1993, you may choose to

apply the contributions made in 1993 first to nondeductible contributions and then to deductible contributions, or vice versa. But the amount on line 1 minus the amount on line 4 cannot be more than the IRA contributions you actually made in 1993.

Example. You made contributions of $1,000 in 1993, and $1,000 in 1994. $1,500 of your contributions are deductible and $500 are nondeductible. You choose $500 of your contribution in 1993 to be nondeductible. In this case, the $500 would be entered on line 1, but not on line 4, and would become part of your basis for 1993.

Line 5

Although the 1993 IRA contributions you made during 1/1/94–4/15/94 (line 4) can be treated as nondeductible for purposes of line 1, they are not included in your basis for purposes of figuring the nontaxable part of any distributions you received in 1993. This is why you subtract line 4 from line 3.

Line 6

Enter the total value of **ALL** your IRAs as of 12/31/93 **plus** any outstanding rollovers. You should receive a statement by 1/31/94 for each IRA account showing the value on 12/31/93. A **rollover** is a tax-free distribution from one IRA that is contributed to another IRA. The rollover must be completed within 60 days of receiving the distribution from the first IRA. An **outstanding rollover** is any amount distributed to you from one IRA within 60 days of the end of 1993 (between Nov. 2 and Dec. 31) that you did not roll over to another IRA by 12/31/93, but that you roll over to another IRA in 1994 within the normal 60-day rollover period.

Line 7

Do not include on line 7:

- Distributions received in 1993 and rolled over to another IRA by 12/31/93,
- Outstanding rollovers included on line 6,
- Contributions under section 408(d)(4) returned to you on or before the due date of the return, or
- Excess contributions under section 408(d)(5) returned to you after the due date of the return.

Line 11

This is the total of your nondeductible IRA contributions made in 1993 and earlier years minus the total of any nontaxable IRA distributions received in those years.

Line 12

This is the total of your IRA basis as of 12/31/93 and any nondeductible IRA contributions for 1993 that you made in 1994 by 4/15/94.

This amount will be used on Form 8606 in future years if you make nondeductible IRA contributions or receive distributions.

Form **8615**	**Tax for Children Under Age 14** **Who Have Investment Income of More Than $1,200** ▶ See instructions below and on back. ▶ Attach ONLY to the child's Form 1040, Form 1040A, or Form 1040NR.	OMB No. 1545-0998
Department of the Treasury Internal Revenue Service		**19****93** Attachment Sequence No. **33**

Child's name shown on return	Child's social security number

A Parent's name (first, initial, and last). **Caution:** See instructions on back before completing.	**B** Parent's social security number

C Parent's filing status (check one):

☐ Single ☐ Married filing jointly ☐ Married filing separately ☐ Head of household ☐ Qualifying widow(er)

Step 1 — Figure child's net investment income

1	Enter child's investment income, such as taxable interest and dividend income. See instructions. If this amount is $1,200 or less, **stop here;** do not file this form	1	
2	If the child DID NOT itemize deductions on Schedule A (Form 1040 or Form 1040NR), enter $1,200. If the child ITEMIZED deductions, see instructions	2	
3	Subtract line 2 from line 1. If the result is zero or less, **stop here;** do not complete the rest of this form but ATTACH it to the child's return	3	
4	Enter child's **taxable** income from Form 1040, line 37; Form 1040A, line 22; or Form 1040NR, line 36	4	
5	Enter the **smaller** of line 3 or line 4 here ▶	5	

Step 2 — Figure tentative tax based on the tax rate of the parent listed on line A

6	Enter parent's **taxable** income from Form 1040, line 37; Form 1040A, line 22; Form 1040EZ, line 6; or Form 1040NR, line 36. If the parent transferred property to a trust, see instructions	6	
7	Enter the total net investment income, if any, from Forms 8615, line 5, of ALL OTHER children of the parent identified above. **Do not** include the amount from line 5 above	7	
8	Add lines 5, 6, and 7	8	
9	Tax on line 8 based on the **parent's** filing status. See instructions. If from Schedule D Tax Worksheet, enter amount from line 4 of that worksheet here ▶ _____	9	
10	Enter parent's tax from Form 1040, line 38; Form 1040A, line 23; Form 1040EZ, line 8; or Form 1040NR, line 37. If from Schedule D Tax Worksheet, enter amount from line 4 of that worksheet here ▶ _____	10	
11	Subtract line 10 from line 9. If line 7 is blank, enter on line 13 the amount from line 11; skip lines 12a and 12b	11	
12a	Add lines 5 and 7 . . . . . **12a** _____		
b	Divide line 5 by line 12a. Enter the result as a decimal (rounded to two places)	12b	× .
13	Multiply line 11 by line 12b ▶	13	

Step 3 — Figure child's tax—If lines 4 and 5 above are the same, go to line 16 now.

14	Subtract line 5 from line 4 . . . . **14** _____		
15	Tax on line 14 based on the **child's** filing status. See instructions. If from Schedule D Tax Worksheet, enter amount from line 4 of that worksheet here ▶ _____	15	
16	Add lines 13 and 15	16	
17	Tax on line 4 based on the **child's** filing status. See instructions. If from Schedule D Tax Worksheet, check here . . . . ▶ ☐	17	
18	Enter the **larger** of line 16 or line 17 here and on Form 1040, line 38; Form 1040A, line 23; or Form 1040NR, line 37. Be sure to check the box for "Form 8615" even if line 17 is more than line 16 . ▶	18	

General Instructions

A Change To Note.—If line 8 of Form 8615 is over $70,000 (over $140,000 if the parent's filing status is married filing jointly or qualifying widow(er)), the election to defer additional 1993 taxes may apply to the child. Get **Form 8841,** Deferral of Additional 1993 Taxes, for details. If the election is made, Form 1040A **cannot** be filed for the child.

Purpose of Form.—For children under age 14, investment income over $1,200 is taxed at the parent's rate if the parent's rate is higher than the child's rate. If the child's investment income is more than $1,200, use this form to figure the child's tax.

Investment Income.—As used on this form, "investment income" includes all taxable income other than earned income as defined on page 2. It includes income such as taxable interest, dividends, capital gains, rents, royalties, etc. It also includes pension and annuity income and income (other than earned income) received as the beneficiary of a trust.

Who Must File.—Generally, Form 8615 must be filed for any child who was under age 14 on January 1, 1994, had more than $1,200 of investment income, and is required to file a tax return. If neither parent was alive on December 31, 1993, do not use Form 8615.

Instead, figure the child's tax in the normal manner.

Note: The parent may be able to elect to report the child's interest and dividends on his or her return. If the parent makes this election, the child will not have to file a return or Form 8615. For more details, see the instructions for Form 1040 or Form 1040A, or get **Form 8814,** Parents' Election To Report Child's Interest and Dividends.

Additional Information.—For more details, get **Pub. 929,** Tax Rules for Children and Dependents.

Incomplete Information for Parent.—If the parent's taxable income or filing status or the net investment income of

---

For Paperwork Reduction Act Notice, see back of form. Cat. No. 64113U Form **8615** (1993)

the parent's other children is not known by the due date of the child's return, reasonable estimates may be used. Write "Estimated" on the appropriate line(s) of Form 8615. For more details, see Pub. 929.

Amended Return.—If after the child's return is filed, the parent's taxable income is changed or the net investment income of any of the parent's other children is changed, the child's tax must be refigured using the adjusted amounts. If the child's tax is changed as a result of the adjustment(s), file **Form 1040X,** Amended U.S. Individual Income Tax Return, to correct the child's tax.

Alternative Minimum Tax.—A child whose tax is figured on Form 8615 may owe the alternative minimum tax. For details, get **Form 6251,** Alternative Minimum Tax—Individuals, and its instructions.

Line Instructions

Section references are to the Internal Revenue Code.

Lines A and B.—If the child's parents were married to each other and filed a joint return, enter the name and social security number (SSN) of the parent who is listed first on the joint return. For example, if the father's name is listed first on the return and his SSN is entered in the block labeled "Your social security number," enter his name on line A and his SSN on line B.

If the parents were married but filed separate returns, enter the name and SSN of the parent who had the **higher** taxable income. If you do not know which parent had the higher taxable income, see Pub. 929.

If the parents were unmarried, treated as unmarried for Federal income tax purposes, or separated either by a divorce or separate maintenance decree, enter the name and SSN of the parent who had custody of the child for most of the year (the custodial parent).

Exception. If the custodial parent remarried and filed a joint return with his or her new spouse, enter the name and SSN of the person listed first on the joint return, even if that person is not the child's parent. If the custodial parent and his or her new spouse filed separate returns, enter the name and SSN of the person with the **higher** taxable income, even if that person is not the child's parent.

Note: *If the parents were unmarried but lived together during the year with the child, enter the name and SSN of the parent who had the **higher** taxable income.*

Line 1.—If the child had no earned income (defined later), enter the child's adjusted gross income from Form 1040, line 32; Form 1040A, line 17; or Form 1040NR, line 32.

If the child had earned income, use the following worksheet to figure the amount to enter on line 1. But if the child files **Form 2555,** Foreign Earned Income, or **Form 2555-EZ,** Foreign Earned Income Exclusion, has a net loss from self-employment, or claims a net operating loss deduction, **do not** use the worksheet below. Instead, use the worksheet in Pub. 929 to figure the amount to enter on line 1.

Worksheet (keep a copy for your records)

1. Enter the amount from the child's Form 1040, line 23; Form 1040A, line 14; or Form 1040NR, line 24, whichever applies . . .   _____

2. Enter the child's **earned income** (defined below) plus any deduction the child claims on Form 1040, line 28, or Form 1040NR, line 28, whichever applies   _____

3. Subtract line 2 from line 1. Enter the result here and on Form 8615, line 1 . . .   _____

Earned income includes wages, tips, and other payments received for personal services performed. Generally, earned income is the total of the amounts reported on Form 1040, lines 7, 12, and 19; Form 1040A, line 7; or Form 1040NR, lines 8, 13, and 20.

Line 2.—If the child itemized deductions, enter on line 2 the **greater** of:

● $600 plus the portion of the amount on Schedule A (Form 1040), line 26, or Schedule A (Form 1040NR), line 17, that is directly connected with the production of the investment income on Form 8615, line 1; **OR**

● $1,200.

Line 6.—If the parent's taxable income is less than zero, enter zero on line 6. If the parent filed a joint return, enter the taxable income shown on that return even if the parent's spouse is not the child's parent. If the parent transferred property to a trust which sold or exchanged the property during the year at a gain, include any gain that was taxed to the trust under section 644 in the amount entered on line 6. Enter "Section 644" and the amount to the right of the line 6 entry. Also, see the instructions for line 10.

Line 9.—Figure the tax using the Tax Table, Tax Rate Schedules, or the Schedule D Tax Worksheet, whichever applies. If any net capital gain is included on lines 5, 6, and/or 7, the tax on the amount on line 8 may be less if the Schedule D Tax Worksheet can be used to figure the tax. See Pub. 929 for details on how to figure the net capital gain included on line 8 and how to complete the worksheet. The Schedule D Tax Worksheet should be used to figure the tax if:

the parent's filing status is:	AND	the amount on Form 8615, line 8, is over:
● Single		$53,500
● Married filing jointly or Qualifying widow(er)		$89,150
● Married filing separately		$44,575
● Head of household		$76,400

If the Schedule D Tax Worksheet is used to figure the tax, enter on Form 8615, line 9, the amount from line 13 of that worksheet. Also, enter the amount from line 4 of that worksheet in the space next to line 9 of Form 8615.

Line 10.—If the parent filed a joint return, enter the tax shown on that return even if the parent's spouse is not the child's parent. If the parent filed Form 8814, enter "Form 8814" and the total tax from line 8 of Form(s) 8814 in the space next to line 10 of Form 8615.

If line 6 includes any gain taxed to a trust under section 644, add the tax imposed under section 644(a)(2)(A) to the tax shown on the parent's return. Enter the total on line 10 instead of the tax from the parent's return. Also, enter "Section 644" next to line 10.

Line 15.—Figure the tax using the Tax Table, Tax Rate Schedule X, or the Schedule D Tax Worksheet, whichever applies. If line 14 is more than $53,500 and includes any net capital gain, the tax may be less if the Schedule D Tax Worksheet is used to figure the tax. See Pub. 929 for details on how to figure the net capital gain included on line 14 and how to complete the worksheet.

Line 17.—Figure the tax as if these rules did not apply. For example, if the child files Schedule D and can use the Schedule D Tax Worksheet to figure his or her tax, complete that worksheet.

Paperwork Reduction Act Notice.—We ask for the information on this form to carry out the Internal Revenue laws of the United States. You are required to give us the information. We need it to ensure that you are complying with these laws and to allow us to figure and collect the right amount of tax.

The time needed to complete and file this form will vary depending on individual circumstances. The estimated average time is: **Recordkeeping,** 13 min.; **Learning about the law or the form,** 12 min.; **Preparing the form,** 45 min.; and **Copying, assembling, and sending the form to the IRS,** 17 min.

If you have comments concerning the accuracy of these time estimates or suggestions for making this form more simple, we would be happy to hear from you. You can write to both the IRS and the Office of Management and Budget at the addresses listed in the instructions of the tax return with which this form is filed.

Form **8801**	Credit For Prior Year Minimum Tax—	OMB No. 1545-1073
Department of the Treasury Internal Revenue Service	Individuals and Fiduciaries	**1993**
	▶ Attach to your tax return.	Attachment Sequence No. **74**

Name(s) shown on return | Identifying number

Part I Net Minimum Tax on Exclusion Items

1	Enter the amount from line 4 of your 1992 Form 6251. Form 1041 filers, see instructions . .	**1**	
2	Enter adjustments and preferences treated as exclusion items. See instructions	**2**	
3	**Minimum tax credit net operating loss deduction.** See instructions	**3**	( )
4	Combine lines 1, 2, and 3. If zero or less, enter -0- here and on line 15 and go to Part II. If more than $155,000 and you were married filing separately for 1992, see instructions	**4**	
5	Enter the amount from line 12 of your 1992 Form 6251. Form 1041 filers, enter $20,000 . .	**5**	
6	Enter the amount from line 13 of your 1992 Form 6251. Form 1041 filers, enter $75,000 . .	**6**	
7	Subtract line 6 from line 4. If zero or less, enter -0- here and on line 8 and go to line 9 . .	**7**	
8	Multiply line 7 by 25% (.25)	**8**	
9	Subtract line 8 from line 5. If zero or less, enter -0-. If completing for a child under 14, see instructions	**9**	
10	Subtract line 9 from line 4. If zero or less, enter -0- here and on line 15, and go to Part II . .	**10**	
11	Multiply line 10 by 24% (.24). Form 1040NR filers, see instructions	**11**	
12	**Minimum tax foreign tax credit on exclusion items.** See instructions	**12**	
13	**Tentative minimum tax on exclusion items.** Subtract line 12 from line 11	**13**	
14	Enter the amount from line 21 of your 1992 Form 6251, or line 38c of 1992 Form 1041, Schedule H	**14**	
15	**Net minimum tax on exclusion items.** Subtract line 14 from line 13. If zero or less, enter -0-	**15**	

Part II Minimum Tax Credit and Carryforward to 1994

16	Enter the amount from line 22 your of 1992 Form 6251, or line 39 of your 1992 Form 1041, Schedule H	**16**	
17	Enter the amount from line 15 above	**17**	
18	Subtract line 17 from line 16. If less than zero, enter as a negative amount	**18**	
19	**1992 minimum tax credit carryforward.** Enter the amount from line 26 of your 1992 Form 8801	**19**	
20	Enter your 1992 unallowed credit for fuel produced from a nonconventional source, plus your 1992 unallowed orphan drug credit. See instructions	**20**	
21	Combine lines 18, 19, and 20. If zero or less, **stop here** and see instructions	**21**	
22	Enter your 1993 regular income tax liability minus allowable credits. See instructions	**22**	
23	Enter the amount from line 26 of your 1993 Form 6251, or line 37 of your 1993 Form 1041, Schedule H	**23**	
24	Subtract line 23 from line 22. If zero or less, enter -0-	**24**	
25	**Minimum tax credit.** Enter the **smaller** of line 21 or line 24. Also enter this amount on the appropriate line of your 1993 tax return. See instructions	**25**	
26	**Minimum tax credit carryforward to 1994.** Subtract line 25 from line 21. See instructions . .	**26**	

General Instructions

Section references are to the Internal Revenue Code.

Purpose of Form

Form 8801 is used by individuals, trusts, and estates to compute the minimum tax credit, if any, for alternative minimum tax (AMT) incurred in prior tax years after 1986. The form is also used to figure any minimum tax credit carryforward that may be used in future years.

Who Should File

Form 8801 should be completed by individuals, trusts, and estates that had:

● An AMT liability in 1992 and adjustments or preferences (other than exclusion items) in 1992;

● A minimum tax credit carryforward from 1992 to 1993; or

● A 1992 unallowed nonconventional source fuel credit or unallowed orphan drug credit (see the instructions for line 20).

Recordkeeping.—Use Form 8801 each year to see if you have a minimum tax credit and to keep track of any credit carryforward (see line 26 of your 1992 Form 8801).

Specific Instructions

The AMT is attributable to two types of adjustments and preferences— "deferral items" and "exclusion items." The minimum tax credit is allowed only on the AMT attributable to deferral items.

Deferral items are generally adjustments and preferences that do not cause a permanent difference in taxable income over a number of years (e.g., depreciation). **Exclusion items,** on the other hand, cause a permanent difference in taxable income (e.g., the standard deduction).

Cat. No. 10002S | Form **8801** (1993)

Form **8814**	**Parents' Election To Report Child's Interest and Dividends**	OMB No. 1545-1128

Department of the Treasury
Internal Revenue Service

► See instructions below and on back.
► Attach to parents' Form 1040 or Form 1040NR.

1993

Attachment Sequence No. **40**

Name(s) shown on your return | Your social security number

A Child's name (first, initial, and last) | **B** Child's social security number

C If more than one Form 8814 is attached, check here . . . . ►

Step 1   **Figure amount of child's interest and dividend income to report on your return**

1a Enter your child's **taxable** interest income. If this amount is different from the amounts shown on the child's Forms 1099-INT and 1099-OID, see the instructions **1a**

b Enter your child's **tax-exempt** interest income. **DO NOT** include this amount on line 1a **1b**

2a Enter your child's gross dividends, including any Alaska Permanent Fund dividends. If none, enter -0- on line 2c and go to line 3. If your child received any capital gain distributions or dividends as a nominee, see the instructions **2a**

b Enter your child's nontaxable distributions that are included on line 2a. These should be shown in box 1d of Form 1099-DIV . . .   **2b**

c Subtract line 2b from line 2a   **2c**

3 Add lines 1a and 2c. If the total is $1,000 or less, skip lines 4 and 5 and go to line 6. If the total is $5,000 or more, **do not** file this form. Your child **must** file his or her own return to report the income **3**

4 Base amount . . . .   **4**   1,000 | 00

5 Subtract line 4 from line 3. If you checked the box on line C above or if line 2a includes any capital gain distributions, see the instructions. Also, include this amount in the total on Form 1040, line 22, or Form 1040NR, line 22. In the space next to line 22, enter "Form 8814" and show the amount. Go to line 6 below . . . . ►   **5**

Step 2   **Figure your tax on the first $1,000 of child's interest and dividend income**

6 Amount not taxed . . . .   **6**   500 | 00

7 Subtract line 6 from line 3. If the result is zero or less, enter -0- **7**

8 **Tax.** Is the amount on line 7 less than $500?
- **NO.** Enter $75 here and see the **Note** below.
- **YES.** Multiply line 7 by 15% (.15). Enter the result here and see the **Note** below.

   8

Note: *If you checked the box on line C above, see the instructions. Otherwise, include the amount from line 8 in the tax you enter on Form 1040, line 38, or Form 1040NR, line 37. Also, enter the amount from line 8 in the space provided next to line 38 on Form 1040, or next to line 37 on Form 1040NR.*

General Instructions

Purpose of Form.—Use this form if you elect to report your child's income on your return. If you do, your child will not have to file a return. You can make this election if your child meets **all** of the following conditions:

- Was under age 14 on January 1, 1994.
- Is required to file a 1993 return.
- Had income only from interest and dividends, including Alaska Permanent Fund dividends.
- Had gross income for 1993 that was less than $5,000.

- Had no estimated tax payments for 1993.
- Did not have any overpayment of tax shown on his or her 1992 return applied to the 1993 return.
- Had no Federal income tax withheld from his or her income (backup withholding).

You must also qualify as explained on page 2 of these instructions.

Step 1 of the form is used to figure the amount of your child's income to report on your return. **Step 2** is used to figure an additional tax that must be added to your tax.

How To Make the Election.—To make the election, complete and attach Form 8814 to your tax return and file your return by the due date (including extensions). A separate Form 8814 must be filed for **each** child whose income you choose to report.

Caution: *The Federal income tax on your child's income may be less if you file a tax return for the child instead of making this election. This is because you cannot take certain deductions that your child would be entitled to on his or her own return. For details, see **Deductions You May Not Take** on page 2.*

For Paperwork Reduction Act Notice, see back of form.   Cat. No. 10750J   Form **8814** (1993)

Parents Who Qualify To Make the Election.—You qualify to make this election if you file Form 1040 or Form 1040NR and any of the following apply:

• You are filing a joint return for 1993 with the child's other parent.

• You and the child's other parent were married to each other but file separate returns for 1993 AND you had the **higher** taxable income. If you do not know if you had the higher taxable income, get **Pub. 929,** Tax Rules for Children and Dependents.

• You were unmarried, treated as unmarried for Federal income tax purposes, or separated from the child's other parent by a divorce or separate maintenance decree. You must have had custody of your child for most of the year (you were the custodial parent). If you were the custodial parent and you remarried, you may make the election on a joint return with your new spouse. But if you and your new spouse do not file a joint return, you qualify to make the election only if you had **higher** taxable income than your new spouse.

Note: *If you and the child's other parent were not married but lived together during the year with the child, you qualify to make the election only if you are the parent with the **higher** taxable income.*

Deductions You May Not Take.—If you elect to report your child's income on your return, you may not take any of the following deductions that your child would be entitled to on his or her own return.

• Standard deduction of $600 ($1,500 for a blind child).

• Penalty on early withdrawal of child's savings.

• Itemized deductions such as child's investment expenses or charitable contributions.

If any of the above apply to your child, first figure the tax on your child's income as if he or she is filing a return. Next, figure the tax as if you are electing to report your child's income on **your** return. Then, compare the methods to determine which results in the lower tax.

Alternative Minimum Tax.—If your child received any tax-exempt interest (or exempt-interest dividends paid by a regulated investment company) from certain private activity bonds, you must take this into account in determining if you owe the alternative minimum tax. Get **Form 6251,** Alternative Minimum Tax— Individuals, and its instructions for details.

Investment Interest Expense.—Your child's income (excluding Alaska Permanent Fund dividends and capital gain distributions) that you report on your return is considered to be **your** investment income for purposes of figuring your investment interest expense deduction. If your child received Alaska Permanent Fund dividends or capital gain distributions, get **Pub. 550,** Investment Income and Expenses, to figure the amount you may treat as your investment income.

Foreign Accounts and Trusts.—If your child had a foreign financial account or was the grantor of, or transferor to, a foreign trust, complete Part III of **Schedule B** (Form 1040) for the child. If you answered "Yes" to either of the questions, you must file this Schedule B with **your** return. Also, complete line 11b if applicable. Write "Form 8814" next to line 11a or line 12, whichever applies.

Change of Address.—If your child filed a return for a year before 1993 and the address shown on the last return filed is not your child's current address, be sure to notify the IRS, in writing, of the new address. To do this, you may use **Form 8822,** Change of Address, or you may write to the Internal Revenue Service Center where your child's last return was filed, or to the Chief, Taxpayer Service Division, in your local IRS district office.

Additional Information.—For more details, see Pub. 929.

Line Instructions

Name and Social Security Number.— Enter your name as shown on your return. If filing a joint return, include your spouse's name but enter the social security number of the person whose name is shown first on the return.

Line 1a.—Enter **ALL** taxable interest income received by your child in 1993. If your child received a **Form 1099-INT** for tax-exempt interest, such as from municipal bonds, write the amount and "Tax-exempt interest" on the dotted line next to line 1a. Be sure to include this interest on line 1b but **do not** include it in the total for line 1a.

If your child received, as a **nominee,** interest that actually belongs to another person, write the amount and "ND" (for nominee distribution) on the dotted line next to line 1a. **Do not** include amounts received as a nominee in the total for line 1a.

If your child had accrued interest that was paid to the seller of a bond, amortizable bond premium (ABP) allowed as a reduction to interest income, or if any original issue discount (OID) included on line 1a is less than the amount shown on your child's **Form 1099-OID,** follow the instructions above for nominee interest to see how to report the nontaxable amounts. But on the dotted line next to line 1a, write the nontaxable amount and "Accrued interest," "ABP adjustment," or "OID adjustment," whichever applies. **Do not** include any nontaxable amounts in the total for line 1a.

Line 1b.—If your child received any tax-exempt interest income, such as interest on certain state and municipal bonds, enter the total tax-exempt interest on line 1b. Also, include any exempt-interest dividends your child received as a shareholder in a mutual fund or other regulated investment company. **Do not** include this interest on lines 1a or 3.

Note: *If line 1b includes tax-exempt interest or exempt-interest dividends paid by a regulated investment company from private activity bonds, see **Alternative Minimum Tax** on this page.*

Line 2a.—Enter gross dividends received by your child in 1993, including capital gain distributions and nontaxable distributions. Gross dividends should be shown in box 1a of **Form 1099-DIV.** Also, include dividends your child received through a partnership, an S corporation, or an estate or trust.

If line 2a includes any **capital gain distributions** see the line 5 instuctions below. These should be shown in box 1c of Form 1099-DIV.

If your child received, as a **nominee,** dividends that actually belong to another person, write the amount and "ND" on the dotted line next to line 2a. **Do not** include amounts received as a nominee in the total for line 2a.

Line 5.—If you checked the box on line C, add the amounts from line 5 of **all** your Forms 8814. Include the total on line 22 of Form 1040 or Form 1040NR, whichever applies. Be sure to write "Form 8814" and show the total of the line 5 amounts in the space next to line 22.

If line 2a includes any **capital gain distributions** and you are filing **Schedule D** (Form 1040), part or all of your child's capital gain distributions should be reported on your Schedule D instead of on Form 8814, line 5. Before you enter an amount on line 5, see Pub. 929 for details on how to figure the amount to report on your Schedule D.

Line 8.—If you checked the box on line C, add the amounts from line 8 of **all** your Forms 8814. Include the total on Form 1040, line 38, or Form 1040NR, line 37. Be sure to enter the total of the line 8 amounts in the space provided next to line 38 on Form 1040 or next to line 37 on Form 1040NR.

Paperwork Reduction Act Notice.—We ask for the information on this form to carry out the Internal Revenue laws of the United States. You are required to give us the information. We need it to ensure that you are complying with these laws and to allow us to figure and collect the right amount of tax.

The time needed to complete and file this form will vary depending on individual circumstances. The estimated average time is: **Recordkeeping,** 20 min.; **Learning about the law or the form,** 8 min.; **Preparing the form,** 16 min.; and **Copying, assembling, and sending the form to the IRS,** 35 min.

If you have comments concerning the accuracy of these time estimates or suggestions for making this form more simple, we would be happy to hear from you. You can write to both the IRS and the Office of Management and Budget at the addresses listed in the instructions of the tax return with which this form is filed.

Form **8815**

Department of the Treasury
Internal Revenue Service

Exclusion of Interest From Series EE
U.S. Savings Bonds Issued After 1989
(For Filers With Qualified Higher Education Expenses)

▶ Attach to Form 1040 or Form 1040A.

▶ See instructions on back.

OMB No. 1545-1173

1993

Attachment
Sequence No. **57**

Caution: *If your filing status is married filing a separate return, **do not** file this form. You **cannot** take the exclusion even if you paid qualified higher education expenses in 1993.*

Name(s) shown on return	Your social security number

1

(a)
Name of person (you, your spouse, or your dependent) who was enrolled at or attended an eligible educational institution

(b)
Name and address of eligible educational institution

If you need more space, attach a statement.

2	Enter the total qualified higher education expenses you paid in 1993 for the persons listed in column (a) of line 1. See the instructions to find out which expenses qualify	**2**
3	Enter the total of any nontaxable educational benefits (such as nontaxable scholarship or fellowship grants) received for 1993 for the persons listed in column (a) of line 1. See instructions	**3**
4	Subtract line 3 from line 2. If zero or less, **STOP;** you **cannot** take the exclusion	**4**
5	Enter the total proceeds (principal and interest) from all series EE U.S. savings bonds **issued after 1989** that you **cashed during 1993**	**5**
6	Enter the interest included on line 5. See instructions	**6**
7	Is line 4 **less than** line 5? ● **No.** Enter "1.00." ● **Yes.** Divide line 4 by line 5. Enter the result as a decimal (to at least two places).	**7** × .
8	Multiply line 6 by line 7	**8**
9	Enter your modified adjusted gross income. See instructions . . . **Note:** *If line 9 is $60,500 or more ($98,250 or more if married filing a joint return), **STOP;** you **cannot** take the exclusion.*	**9**
10	Enter $45,500 ($68,250 if married filing a joint return)	**10**
11	Subtract line 10 from line 9. If zero or less, skip line 12, enter -0- on line 13, and go to line 14	**11**
12	Divide line 11 by $15,000 (by $30,000 if married filing a joint return). Enter the result as a decimal (to at least two places)	**12** × .
13	Multiply line 8 by line 12	**13**
14	**Excludable savings bond interest.** Subtract line 13 from line 8. Enter the result here and on Schedule B (Form 1040), line 3, or Schedule 1 (Form 1040A), line 3, whichever applies . . ▶	**14**

Paperwork Reduction Act Notice

We ask for the information on this form to carry out the Internal Revenue laws of the United States. You are required to give us the information. We need it to ensure that you are complying with these laws and to allow us to figure and collect the right amount of tax.

The time needed to complete and file this form will vary depending on individual circumstances. The estimated average time is: **Recordkeeping,** 53 min.; **Learning about the law or the form,** 11 min.; **Preparing the form,** 35 min.; and **Copying, assembling, and sending the form to the IRS,** 34 min.

If you have comments concerning the accuracy of these time estimates or suggestions for making this form more simple, we would be happy to hear from you. You can write to both the IRS and the Office of Management and Budget at the addresses listed in the instructions of the tax return with which this form is filed.

Cat. No. 10822S

Form **8815** (1993)

General Instructions

Purpose of Form

If you cashed series EE U.S. savings bonds in 1993 that were issued after 1989, you may be able to exclude from your income part or all of the interest on those bonds. Use Form 8815 to figure the amount of any interest you may exclude.

Who May Take the Exclusion

You may take the exclusion if **all four** of the following apply:

1. You cashed qualified U.S. savings bonds in 1993 that were issued after 1989.

2. You paid qualified higher education expenses in 1993 for yourself, your spouse, or your dependents.

3. Your filing status is single, married filing a joint return, head of household, or qualifying widow(er) with dependent child.

4. Your modified adjusted gross income is less than $60,500 (less than $98,250 if married filing a joint return). Use the line 9 worksheet on this page to figure your modified adjusted gross income.

Note: *If your filing status is married filing a separate return, you* **cannot** *take the exclusion.*

U.S. Savings Bonds That Qualify for Exclusion

To qualify for the exclusion, the bonds must be series EE U.S. savings bonds issued after 1989 in your name, or, if you are married, they may be issued in your name and your spouse's name. Also, you must have been age 24 or older before the bonds were issued. **Bond information will be verified with Department of the Treasury records.**

Note: *A bond bought by a parent and issued in the name of his or her child who is under age 24 will not qualify for the exclusion by the parent or child.*

Recordkeeping Requirements

To verify the amount of interest you exclude, you should keep the following records:

● A written record of each post-1989 series EE U.S. savings bond that you cash. Your written record must include the serial number, issue date, face value, and total redemption proceeds (principal and interest) of each bond. For this purpose, you may use **Form 8818,** Optional Form To Record Redemption of Series EE U.S. Savings Bonds Issued After 1989.

● Bills, receipts, canceled checks, or other documentation showing that you paid qualified higher education expenses during the year.

Specific Instructions

To figure the amount of interest you may exclude, you must complete the following lines on your tax return if they apply to you.

Form 1040 filers, complete lines 7, 8b, 9 through 22, and 24a through 30. Also, complete Schedule B (Form 1040) through line 2.

Form 1040A filers, complete lines 7, 8b, 9 through 13b, and 15a through 15c. Also,

complete Schedule 1 (Form 1040A) through line 2.

But if you received social security benefits, use the worksheet in **Pub. 915,** Social Security Benefits and Equivalent Railroad Retirement Benefits, to figure the taxable amount, if any, of your benefits. **Do not** use the social security worksheet in the instructions for Form 1040 or Form 1040A. **Also,** if you made contributions to your IRA for 1993 and you were covered by a retirement plan at work or through self-employment, use the chart and worksheets in **Pub. 590,** Individual Retirement Arrangements (IRAs), to figure your IRA deduction. **Do not** use the chart or IRA worksheet in the instructions for Form 1040 or Form 1040A.

Line 1

Column (a).—Enter the name of the person who was enrolled at or attended an eligible educational institution. This person must be you, your spouse, or your dependent(s) whom you claim on line 6c of Form 1040 or Form 1040A.

Column (b).—Enter the name and address of the eligible educational institution. If the person was enrolled at or attended more than one institution, list the names and addresses of all institutions. An **eligible educational institution** is a college, university, or vocational education school.

Line 2

Enter the total **qualified higher education expenses** you paid in 1993. These include only tuition and fees required for the enrollment or attendance of the person(s) listed on line 1, column (a), at the eligible educational institution(s) listed on line 1, column (b). They **do not** include expenses for the following:

● Room and board.

● Courses involving sports, games, or hobbies that are not part of a degree or certificate granting program.

Do not include on line 2 expenses that were covered by nontaxable educational benefits paid directly to, or by, the educational institution.

Line 3

Enter on this line the total qualified higher education expenses included on line 2 that were covered by nontaxable educational benefits.

Example. You paid $10,000 of qualified higher education expenses in 1993 to the eligible educational institution your son attended. You claim your son as a dependent on line 6c of your 1993 tax return. Your son received a $2,000 nontaxable scholarship grant for 1993, which was paid directly to him. You would enter $10,000 on line 2 and $2,000 on line 3.

Nontaxable educational benefits include:

● Scholarship or fellowship grants excludable from income under Internal Revenue Code section 117.

● Veterans' educational assistance benefits.

● Employer-provided educational assistance benefits.

● Any other payments (but not gifts, bequests, or inheritances) for educational expenses that are exempt from income tax by any U.S. law.

Do not include on line 3 nontaxable educational benefits paid directly to, or by, the educational institution.

Line 6

If you used Form 8818 to record the bonds you cashed in 1993, enter on line 6 the amount from Form 8818, line 5. If you did not use Form 8818, use the worksheet below to figure the amount to enter on line 6.

Worksheet—Line 6 (keep for your records)

1. Enter the face value of all post-1989 bonds cashed in 1993 . . . . _____

2. Enter the amount from Form 8815, line 5 . . . . . . _____

3. Multiply line 1 above by 50% (.50) . . . . _____

4. Subtract line 3 from line 2. This is the interest on the bonds. Enter the result here and on Form 8815, line 6 . . . . _____

Line 9

Use the worksheet below to figure your modified adjusted gross income. But if any of the following apply, see **Pub. 550,** Investment Income and Expenses, before using the worksheet.

● You are filing **Form 2555,** Foreign Earned Income, **Form 2555-EZ,** Foreign Earned Income Exclusion, or **Form 4563,** Exclusion of Income for Bona Fide Residents of American Samoa.

● You are excluding income from Puerto Rico.

● You have investment interest expense attributable to royalty income.

Worksheet—Line 9 (keep for your records)

1. Form 1040 filers, enter the amount from Schedule B, line 2.

Form 1040A filers, enter the amount from Schedule 1, line 2. _____

2. Form 1040 filers, add the amounts on lines 7, 9 through 15, 16b, 17b, 18 through 20, 21b, and 22. Enter the total.

Form 1040A filers, add the amounts on lines 7, 9, 10b, 11b, 12, and 13b. Enter the total. _____

3. Add lines 1 and 2 . . . _____

4. Form 1040 filers, enter the amount from line 30.

Form 1040A filers, enter the amount from line 15c. _____

5. Subtract line 4 from line 3. Enter the result here and on Form 8815, line 9 . . . _____

Form 8822
(Rev. May 1992)

Department of the Treasury
Internal Revenue Service

Change of Address

▶ Please type or print.

▶ See instructions on back.　　▶ Do not attach this form to your return.

OMB No. 1545-1163

Expires 5-31-95

Part I	Complete This Part To Change Your Home Mailing Address

Check **ALL** boxes this change affects:

1 ☐ Individual income tax returns (Forms 1040, 1040A, 1040EZ, 1040NR, etc.)

　▶ If your last return was a joint return and you are now establishing a residence separate
　　from the spouse with whom you filed that return, check here . . . . ▶ ☐

2 ☐ Employment tax returns for household employers (Forms 942, 940, and 940-EZ)

　▶ Enter your employer identification number here . . . . ▶ _____

3 ☐ Gift, estate, or generation-skipping transfer tax returns (Forms 706, 709, etc.)

　▶ For Forms 706 and 706NA, enter the decedent's name and social security number below.

　▶ Name　　　　　　　　　　　　　　　　　▶ Social security number

4a Your name (first name, initial, and last name)	4b Your social security number
5a Spouse's name (first name, initial, and last name)	5b Spouse's social security number

6 Prior name(s). See instructions.

7a Your old address (no., street, city or town, state, and ZIP code). If a P.O. box or foreign address, see instructions	Apt. no.
7b Spouse's old address, if different from line 7a (no., street, city or town, state, and ZIP code). If a P.O. box or foreign address, see instructions	Apt. no.
8 New address (no., street, city or town, state, and ZIP code). If a P.O. box or foreign address, see instructions	Apt. no.

Part II	Complete This Part To Change Your Business Mailing Address or Business Location

Check **ALL** boxes this change affects:

9 ☐ Employment, excise, and other business returns (Forms 720, 941, 990, 1041, 1065, 1120, etc.)

10 ☐ Employee plan returns (Forms 5500, 5500 C/R, and 5500EZ)

11 ☐ Business location

12a Business name	12b Employer identification number
13 Old address (no., street, city or town, state, and ZIP code). If a P.O. box or foreign address, see instructions	Room or suite no.
14 New address (no., street, city or town, state, and ZIP code). If a P.O. box or foreign address, see instructions	Room or suite no.
15 New business location (no., street, city or town, state, and ZIP code). If a foreign address, see instructions	Room or suite no.

Part III	Signature

Daytime telephone no. of person to contact (optional) ▶ ( )

Please Sign Here

▶ _____ _____ ▶ _____ _____
　Your signature　　　　　　　　　Date　　　　　Spouse's signature. If joint return, both should sign　Date

▶ _____ _____ _____
　If Part II completed, signature of owner, officer, or representative　Date　　Title

For Privacy Act and Paperwork Reduction Act Notice, see back of form.　　　Cat. No. 12081V　　　Form **8822** (Rev. 5-92)

Privacy Act and Paperwork Reduction Act Notice

We ask for this information to carry out the Internal Revenue laws of the United States. We may give the information to the Department of Justice and to other Federal agencies, as provided by law. We may also give it to cities, states, the District of Columbia, and U.S. commonwealths or possessions to carry out their tax laws. And we may give it to foreign governments because of tax treaties they have with the United States.

If you fail to provide the Internal Revenue Service with your current mailing address, you may not receive a notice of deficiency or a notice and demand for tax. Despite the failure to receive such notices, penalties and interest will continue to accrue on the tax deficiencies.

The time needed to complete and file this form will vary depending on individual circumstances. The estimated average time is 16 minutes.

If you have comments concerning the accuracy of this time estimate or suggestions for making this form more simple, we would be happy to hear from you. You can write to both the **Internal Revenue Service**, Washington, DC 20224, Attention: IRS Reports Clearance Officer, T:FP; and the **Office of Management and Budget**, Paperwork Reduction Project (1545-1163), Washington, DC 20503. **DO NOT** send this form to either of these offices. Instead, see **Where To File** on this page.

Purpose of Form

You may use Form 8822 to notify the Internal Revenue Service if you changed your home or business mailing address or your business location. If this change also affects the mailing address for your children who filed income tax returns, complete and file a separate Form 8822 for each child.

Note: *If you moved after you filed your return and you are expecting a refund, also notify the post office serving your old address. This will help forward your check to your new address.*

Prior Name(s)

If you or your spouse changed your name due to marriage, divorce, etc., complete line 6. Also, be sure to notify the **Social Security Administration** of your new name so that it has the same name in its records that you have on your tax return. This prevents delays in processing your return and safeguards your future social security benefits.

P.O. Box

If your post office does not deliver mail to your street address and you have a P.O. box, show your P.O. box number instead of your street address.

Foreign Address

If your address is outside of the United States or its possessions or territories, enter the information in the following order: number, street, city, province or state, postal code, and country. **Do not** abbreviate the country name. Be sure to include any apartment, room, or suite number in the space provided.

Employee Plan Returns

A change in the mailing address for employee plan returns must be shown on a separate Form 8822 unless the **Exception** below applies.

Exception. If the employee plan returns were filed with the same service center as your other returns (individual, business, employment, gift, estate, etc.), you do not have to use a separate Form 8822. See **Where To File** below.

Where To File

Send this form to the **Internal Revenue Service Center** shown below for your old address. But if you checked the box on line 10 (employee plan returns), send it to the address shown in the far right column.

If your old address was in:	Use this address:
Florida, Georgia, South Carolina	Atlanta, GA 39901
New Jersey, New York (New York City and counties of Nassau, Rockland, Suffolk, and Westchester)	Holtsville, NY 00501
New York (all other counties), Connecticut, Maine, Massachusetts, New Hampshire, Rhode Island, Vermont	Andover, MA 05501
Alaska, Arizona, California (counties of Alpine, Amador, Butte, Calaveras, Colusa, Contra Costa, Del Norte, El Dorado, Glenn, Humboldt, Lake, Lassen, Marin, Mendocino, Modoc, Napa, Nevada, Placer, Plumas, Sacramento, San Joaquin, Shasta, Sierra, Siskiyou, Solano, Sonoma, Sutter, Tehama, Trinity, Yolo, and Yuba), Colorado, Idaho, Montana, Nebraska, Nevada, North Dakota, Oregon, South Dakota, Utah, Washington, Wyoming	Ogden, UT 84201
California (all other counties), Hawaii	Fresno, CA 93888

Indiana, Kentucky, Michigan, Ohio, West Virginia	Cincinnati, OH 45999
Kansas, New Mexico, Oklahoma, Texas	Austin, TX 73301
Delaware, District of Columbia, Maryland, Pennsylvania, Virginia	Philadelphia, PA 19255
Alabama, Arkansas, Louisiana, Mississippi, North Carolina, Tennessee	Memphis, TN 37501
Illinois, Iowa, Minnesota, Missouri, Wisconsin	Kansas City, MO 64999
American Samoa	Philadelphia, PA 19255
Guam	Commissioner of Revenue and Taxation 855 West Marine Dr. Agana, GU 96910
Puerto Rico (or if excluding income under section 933) Virgin Islands: Nonpermanent residents	Philadelphia, PA 19255
Virgin Islands: Permanent residents	V. I. Bureau of Internal Revenue Lockharts Garden No. 1A Charlotte Amalie, St. Thomas, VI 00802
Foreign country: U.S. citizens and those filing Form 2555 or Form 4563	Philadelphia, PA 19255
All A.P.O. and F.P.O. addresses	Philadelphia, PA 19255

Employee Plan Returns ONLY (Form 5500 series)

If the principal office of the plan sponsor or the plan administrator was in:	Use this address:
Connecticut, Delaware, District of Columbia, Foreign Address, Maine, Maryland, Massachusetts, New Hampshire, New Jersey, New York, Pennsylvania, Puerto Rico, Rhode Island, Vermont, Virginia	Holtsville, NY 00501
Alabama, Alaska, Arkansas, California, Florida, Georgia, Hawaii, Idaho, Louisiana, Mississippi, Nevada, North Carolina, Oregon, South Carolina, Tennessee, Washington	Atlanta, GA 39901
Arizona, Colorado, Illinois, Indiana, Iowa, Kansas, Kentucky, Michigan, Minnesota, Missouri, Montana, Nebraska, New Mexico, North Dakota, Ohio, Oklahoma, South Dakota, Texas, Utah, West Virginia, Wisconsin, Wyoming	Memphis, TN 37501
All Form 5500EZ filers	Andover, MA 05501

Form 8829

Department of the Treasury Internal Revenue Service (T)

Expenses for Business Use of Your Home

▶ File only with Schedule C (Form 1040). Use a separate Form 8829 for each home you used for business during the year.

▶ See separate instructions.

OMB No. 1545-1266

1993

Attachment Sequence No. **66**

Name(s) of proprietor(s)

Your social security number

Part I — Part of Your Home Used for Business

1	Area used regularly and exclusively for business, regularly for day care, or for inventory storage. See instructions	1	
2	Total area of home	2	
3	Divide line 1 by line 2. Enter the result as a percentage	3	%

• **For day-care facilities not used exclusively for business, also complete lines 4–6.**

• **All others, skip lines 4–6 and enter the amount from line 3 on line 7.**

4	Multiply days used for day care during year by hours used per day	4	hr.
5	Total hours available for use during the year (365 days × 24 hours). See instructions	5	8,760 hr.
6	Divide line 4 by line 5. Enter the result as a decimal amount	6	.
7	Business percentage. For day-care facilities not used exclusively for business, multiply line 6 by line 3 (enter the result as a percentage). All others, enter the amount from line 3 ▶	7	%

Part II — Figure Your Allowable Deduction

		(a) Direct expenses	(b) Indirect expenses	
8	Enter the amount from Schedule C, line 29, **plus** any net gain or (loss) derived from the business use of your home and shown on Schedule D or Form 4797. If more than one place of business, see instructions			8
	See instructions for columns (a) and (b) before completing lines 9–20.			
9	Casualty losses. See instructions	9		
10	Deductible mortgage interest. See instructions	10		
11	Real estate taxes. See instructions	11		
12	Add lines 9, 10, and 11	12		
13	Multiply line 12, column (b) by line 7		13	
14	Add line 12, column (a) and line 13			14
15	Subtract line 14 from line 8. If zero or less, enter -0-			15
16	Excess mortgage interest. See instructions	16		
17	Insurance	17		
18	Repairs and maintenance	18		
19	Utilities	19		
20	Other expenses. See instructions	20		
21	Add lines 16 through 20	21		
22	Multiply line 21, column (b) by line 7		22	
23	Carryover of operating expenses from 1992 Form 8829, line 41		23	
24	Add line 21 in column (a), line 22, and line 23			24
25	Allowable operating expenses. Enter the **smaller** of line 15 or line 24			25
26	Limit on excess casualty losses and depreciation. Subtract line 25 from line 15			26
27	Excess casualty losses. See instructions		27	
28	Depreciation of your home from Part III below		28	
29	Carryover of excess casualty losses and depreciation from 1992 Form 8829, line 42		29	
30	Add lines 27 through 29			30
31	Allowable excess casualty losses and depreciation. Enter the **smaller** of line 26 or line 30			31
32	Add lines 14, 25, and 31			32
33	Casualty loss portion, if any, from lines 14 and 31. Carry amount to **Form 4684,** Section B			33
34	Allowable expenses for business use of your home. Subtract line 33 from line 32. Enter here and on Schedule C, line 30. If your home was used for more than one business, see instructions ▶			34

Part III — Depreciation of Your Home

35	Enter the **smaller** of your home's adjusted basis or its fair market value. See instructions	35	
36	Value of land included on line 35	36	
37	Basis of building. Subtract line 36 from line 35	37	
38	Business basis of building. Multiply line 37 by line 7	38	
39	Depreciation percentage. See instructions	39	%
40	Depreciation allowable. Multiply line 38 by line 39. Enter here and on line 28 above. See instructions	40	

Part IV — Carryover of Unallowed Expenses to 1994

41	Operating expenses. Subtract line 25 from line 24. If less than zero, enter -0-	41	
42	Excess casualty losses and depreciation. Subtract line 31 from line 30. If less than zero, enter -0-	42	

For Paperwork Reduction Act Notice, see page 1 of separate instructions.

Cat. No. 13232M

Form **8829** (1993)

ATTENTION: The final Form 8841 was not available when this book went to press. You cannot file this draft form with the IRS, but you can use it to calculate the amount of tax you can defer.

Form **8841**	**Deferral of Additional 1993 Taxes**	OMB. No. 1545-XXXX
Department of the Treasury Internal Revenue Service	▶ See instructions on back. ▶ Attach to Form 1040 or Form 1040NR	**1993** Attachment Sequence No. 99

Name(s) shown on Form 1040   Social security number

Part I — Modified Regular Tax

1	Enter your taxable income from Form 1040, line 37	**1**
2	Figure the tax on the amount on line 1 using a top marginal rate of 31%. See instructions	**2**
3	Enter any amount from Form 4970 included on Form 1040, line 39	**3**
4	If you completed Part III of Form 4972, refigure that part using the tax computation in instructions for line 4 and enter the refigured amount from that part here. If you completed Part II or IV, also include the amount from that part here	**4**
5	Add lines 2 through 4 above and enter the result	**5**

Part II — Modified Credits. Skip this part if Form 1040, line 45, is zero.

6	Enter the amount from Form 6251, line 24. You must complete Form 6251 through line 24 to figure the amount to enter on this line	**6**
7	Subtract line 6 from line 5. If zero or less, enter -0-	**7**
8	Add line 10 of Form 2441 before the credit limit and line 7 of Form 8396	**8**
9	Enter the smaller of line 7 or line 8	**9**
10	Recompute your foreign tax credit on Form 1116 by substituting the excess of line 5 over line 9 for the amount on Form 1116, line 19	**10**
11	Enter the amount from Form 3800, line 7. If you had a general business credit but did not file Form 3800, enter the amount of the current year credit before the tax liability limitation	**11**
12	Add line 21 of Form 8801, line 11 of Form 8834, line 4 of Form 6765, and any nonconventional source fuel credit before the tax liability limitation, and enter the result	**12**
13	Add lines 11 and 12	**13**
14	Subtract the sum of lines 9 and 10 from line 7. If zero or less, enter -0-	**14**
15	Enter the smaller of line 13 or line 14	**15**
16	Add lines 9, 10, and 15	**16**

Part III — Modified Other Taxes

17	Subtract the amount on line 16, if any, from line 5	**17**
18	Add Form 1040, lines 47, 49 through 52, and any write-in entries included on line 53	**18**
19	Enter the amount from Form 6251, line 24. You must complete Form 6251 through line 24 to figure the amount to enter on this line	**19**
20	Subtract line 10 from the sum of lines 2 and 3	**20**
21	Subtract line 20 from line 19. If zero or less, enter -0- (If this form is for a child under age 14, see instructions)	**21**
22	Add lines 17, 18, and 21	**22**

Part IV — Deferral of Additional 1993 Taxes

23	Enter the amount from Form 1040, line 53	**23**
24	Enter the amount from line 22	**24**
25	Subtract line 24 from line 23. If zero or less, stop here; you do not have any additional 1993 taxes to defer	**25**
26	Deferral of additional 1993 taxes. Enter ⅓ of line 25 here and on Form 1040, line 59a. See instructions	**26**

Cat. No. 15994L   Form **8841** (1993)

ATTENTION: The final Form 8841 was not available when this book went to press. You cannot file this draft form with the IRS, but you can use it to calculate the amount of tax you can defer.

Form ~~8294~~ 8841 (1993)

Page **2**

General Instructions

Paperwork Reduction Act Notice

We ask for the information on this form to carry out the Internal Revenue laws of the United States. You are required to give us the information. We need it to ensure that you are complying with these laws and to allow us to figure and collect the right amount of tax.

The time needed to complete and file this form will vary depending on individual circumstances. The estimated average time is:

Recordkeeping . . . . min.

Learning about the law
or the form . . . . min.

Preparing the form. . . . . . . hr.

Copying, assembling, and
sending the form to the IRS . min.

If you have comments concerning the accuracy of these time estimates, we would be happy to hear from you. You can write to both the IRS and the Office of Management and Budget at the addresses listed in the instructions for Form 1040.

Purpose of Form

Use Form 8841 if you elect to pay the additional 1993 taxes solely due to the rate increases reflected in the 1993 tax rate schedules in three equal annual installments. These installments are due by April 15, 1994; April 17, 1995; and April 15, 1996. The April 15, 1994 installment is part of the tax you pay with your 1993 return.

Who Can File

You can file Form 8841 only if you do not owe alternative minimum tax for 1993 and your taxable income on Form 1040, line 37, exceeds the amount shown below for your filing status:

- Single $115,000
- Married filing jointly or
  qualifying widow(er) 140,000
- Head of household . . .127,500
- Married filing separately . . 70,000

In addition, your total payments made by April 15 from Form 1040, lines 54 through 58 and 59b, plus any amount you pay with your return by April 15, must be at least as much as one-half of the amount you enter on Form 8841, line 26.

Exception. Children under age 14 who file Form 8615, Tax for Children Under Age 14 Who Have Investment Income of More Than $1,200, may also file Form 8841 if the amount on Form 8615, line 8, exceeds the amount shown above for the parent's filing status.

Specific Instructions

Line 2

- If you checked box a or b on Form 1040, line 38, figure your tax as follows based on your filing status.

Single.—Enter $12,107 plus 31% of the amount on line 1 that exceeds $53,500.

Married filing jointly or qualifying widow(er).—Enter $20,165 plus 31% of the amount on line 1 that exceeds $89,150.

Married filing separately.—Enter $10,082.50 plus 31% of the amount on line 1 that exceeds $44,575.

Head of household.—Enter $17,544 plus 31% of the amount on line 1 that exceeds $76,400.

- If you checked box c on Form 1040, line 38, refigure your tax on the Schedule D Tax Worksheet by using the above computation for your filing status to figure the tax on lines 9 and 12 of the worksheet.

- If you checked box d on Form 1040, line 38, refigure your tax on Form 8615 by using the above computation, if applicable, for the parent's filing status to figure the tax on lines 9 and 10 of that form, and for the child's filing status to figure the tax on lines 15 and 17 of that form.

- If you entered an amount on Form 1040, line 38e, also include the same amount in the total for line 2.

Line 4

If Form 4972, line 22 or 28 is:	Enter on Form 4972, line 23 or 29:
$0–$22,100	15% of that amount
$22,100–$53,500	$3,315 + 28% of the amount over $22,100
Over $53,500	$12,107 + 31% of the amount over $53,500

Line 26

The amount on this line is your deferred additional 1993 tax. You must pay one-half of this amount by April 17, 1995. You must pay the other half by April 15, 1996. The IRS will send you a bill for these installments. Do not include these installments when figuring your withholding or estimated tax payments for 1994 or 1995.

No interest is due on the deferred tax if paid on time. If you fail to pay the installments on time, the entire unpaid tax must be paid immediately upon notice and demand from the IRS.

DRAFT

SUBJECT TO CHANGE Do not file

47 | Tax Table and Tax Rate Schedules

Introduction

This chapter includes the official 1993 Tax Table and the 1993 Tax Rate Schedules.

The Tax Table is used to determine the tax on **taxable income** *of less than $50,000 for Form 1040EZ (line 6), and Form 1040A (line 22), and less than $100,000 for Form 1040 (line 37). The Tax Rate Schedules are generally used by individuals with $100,000 or more in taxable income to determine their tax.*

1993 Tax Table

Use if your taxable income is less than $100,000. If $100,000 or more, use the Tax Rate Schedules.

Example. Mr. and Mrs. Brown are filing a joint return. Their taxable income on line 37 of Form 1040 is $25,300. First, they find the $25,300–25,350 income line. Next, they find the column for married filing jointly and read down the column. The amount shown where the income line and filing status column meet is $3,799. This is the tax amount they must enter on line 38 of their Form 1040.

Sample Table

At least	But less than	Single	Married filing jointly	Married filing separately	Head of a household
			Your tax is—		
25,200	25,250	4,190	3,784	4,665	3,784
25,250	25,300	4,204	3,791	4,679	3,791
25,300	25,350	4,218	(3,799)	4,693	3,799
25,350	25,400	4,232	3,806	4,707	3,806

At least	But less than	Single	Married filing jointly *	Married filing separately	Head of a household
			Your tax is—		
0	5	0	0	0	0
5	15	2	2	2	2
15	25	3	3	3	3
25	50	6	6	6	6
50	75	9	9	9	9
75	100	13	13	13	13
100	125	17	17	17	17
125	150	21	21	21	21
150	175	24	24	24	24
175	200	28	28	28	28
200	225	32	32	32	32
225	250	36	36	36	36
250	275	39	39	39	39
275	300	43	43	43	43
300	325	47	47	47	47
325	350	51	51	51	51
350	375	54	54	54	54
375	400	58	58	58	58
400	425	62	62	62	62
425	450	66	66	66	66
450	475	69	69	69	69
475	500	73	73	73	73
500	525	77	77	77	77
525	550	81	81	81	81
550	575	84	84	84	84
575	600	88	88	88	88
600	625	92	92	92	92
625	650	96	96	96	96
650	675	99	99	99	99
675	700	103	103	103	103
700	725	107	107	107	107
725	750	111	111	111	111
750	775	114	114	114	114
775	800	118	118	118	118
800	825	122	122	122	122
825	850	126	126	126	126
850	875	129	129	129	129
875	900	133	133	133	133
900	925	137	137	137	137
925	950	141	141	141	141
950	975	144	144	144	144
975	1,000	148	148	148	148

1,000

At least	But less than	Single	Married filing jointly *	Married filing separately	Head of a household
1,000	1,025	152	152	152	152
1,025	1,050	156	156	156	156
1,050	1,075	159	159	159	159
1,075	1,100	163	163	163	163
1,100	1,125	167	167	167	167
1,125	1,150	171	171	171	171
1,150	1,175	174	174	174	174
1,175	1,200	178	178	178	178
1,200	1,225	182	182	182	182
1,225	1,250	186	186	186	186
1,250	1,275	189	189	189	189
1,275	1,300	193	193	193	193

At least	But less than	Single	Married filing jointly *	Married filing separately	Head of a household
1,300	1,325	197	197	197	197
1,325	1,350	201	201	201	201
1,350	1,375	204	204	204	204
1,375	1,400	208	208	208	208
1,400	1,425	212	212	212	212
1,425	1,450	216	216	216	216
1,450	1,475	219	219	219	219
1,475	1,500	223	223	223	223
1,500	1,525	227	227	227	227
1,525	1,550	231	231	231	231
1,550	1,575	234	234	234	234
1,575	1,600	238	238	238	238
1,600	1,625	242	242	242	242
1,625	1,650	246	246	246	246
1,650	1,675	249	249	249	249
1,675	1,700	253	253	253	253
1,700	1,725	257	257	257	257
1,725	1,750	261	261	261	261
1,750	1,775	264	264	264	264
1,775	1,800	268	268	268	268
1,800	1,825	272	272	272	272
1,825	1,850	276	276	276	276
1,850	1,875	279	279	279	279
1,875	1,900	283	283	283	283
1,900	1,925	287	287	287	287
1,925	1,950	291	291	291	291
1,950	1,975	294	294	294	294
1,975	2,000	298	298	298	298

2,000

At least	But less than	Single	Married filing jointly *	Married filing separately	Head of a household
2,000	2,025	302	302	302	302
2,025	2,050	306	306	306	306
2,050	2,075	309	309	309	309
2,075	2,100	313	313	313	313
2,100	2,125	317	317	317	317
2,125	2,150	321	321	321	321
2,150	2,175	324	324	324	324
2,175	2,200	328	328	328	328
2,200	2,225	332	332	332	332
2,225	2,250	336	336	336	336
2,250	2,275	339	339	339	339
2,275	2,300	343	343	343	343
2,300	2,325	347	347	347	347
2,325	2,350	351	351	351	351
2,350	2,375	354	354	354	354
2,375	2,400	358	358	358	358
2,400	2,425	362	362	362	362
2,425	2,450	366	366	366	366
2,450	2,475	369	369	369	369
2,475	2,500	373	373	373	373
2,500	2,525	377	377	377	377
2,525	2,550	381	381	381	381
2,550	2,575	384	384	384	384
2,575	2,600	388	388	388	388
2,600	2,625	392	392	392	392
2,625	2,650	396	396	396	396
2,650	2,675	399	399	399	399
2,675	2,700	403	403	403	403

At least	But less than	Single	Married filing jointly *	Married filing separately	Head of a household
2,700	2,725	407	407	407	407
2,725	2,750	411	411	411	411
2,750	2,775	414	414	414	414
2,775	2,800	418	418	418	418
2,800	2,825	422	422	422	422
2,825	2,850	426	426	426	426
2,850	2,875	429	429	429	429
2,875	2,900	433	433	433	433
2,900	2,925	437	437	437	437
2,925	2,950	441	441	441	441
2,950	2,975	444	444	444	444
2,975	3,000	448	448	448	448

3,000

At least	But less than	Single	Married filing jointly *	Married filing separately	Head of a household
3,000	3,050	454	454	454	454
3,050	3,100	461	461	461	461
3,100	3,150	469	469	469	469
3,150	3,200	476	476	476	476
3,200	3,250	484	484	484	484
3,250	3,300	491	491	491	491
3,300	3,350	499	499	499	499
3,350	3,400	506	506	506	506
3,400	3,450	514	514	514	514
3,450	3,500	521	521	521	521
3,500	3,550	529	529	529	529
3,550	3,600	536	536	536	536
3,600	3,650	544	544	544	544
3,650	3,700	551	551	551	551
3,700	3,750	559	559	559	559
3,750	3,800	566	566	566	566
3,800	3,850	574	574	574	574
3,850	3,900	581	581	581	581
3,900	3,950	589	589	589	589
3,950	4,000	596	596	596	596

4,000

At least	But less than	Single	Married filing jointly *	Married filing separately	Head of a household
4,000	4,050	604	604	604	604
4,050	4,100	611	611	611	611
4,100	4,150	619	619	619	619
4,150	4,200	626	626	626	626
4,200	4,250	634	634	634	634
4,250	4,300	641	641	641	641
4,300	4,350	649	649	649	649
4,350	4,400	656	656	656	656
4,400	4,450	664	664	664	664
4,450	4,500	671	671	671	671
4,500	4,550	679	679	679	679
4,550	4,600	686	686	686	686
4,600	4,650	694	694	694	694
4,650	4,700	701	701	701	701
4,700	4,750	709	709	709	709
4,750	4,800	716	716	716	716
4,800	4,850	724	724	724	724
4,850	4,900	731	731	731	731
4,900	4,950	739	739	739	739
4,950	5,000	746	746	746	746

Continued on next page

* This column must also be used by a qualifying widow(er).

If line 6 (Form 1040EZ), line 22 (Form 1040A), or line 37 (Form 1040) is—		And you are—				If line 6 (Form 1040EZ), line 22 (Form 1040A), or line 37 (Form 1040) is—		And you are—				If line 6 (Form 1040EZ), line 22 (Form 1040A), or line 37 (Form 1040) is—		And you are—			
At least	But less than	Single	Married filing jointly *	Married filing sepa-rately	Head of a house-hold	At least	But less than	Single	Married filing jointly *	Married filing sepa-rately	Head of a house-hold	At least	But less than	Single	Married filing jointly *	Married filing sepa-rately	Head of a house-hold
		Your tax is—						Your tax is—						Your tax is—			
5,000						**8,000**						**11,000**					
5,000	5,050	754	754	754	754	8,000	8,050	1,204	1,204	1,204	1,204	11,000	11,050	1,654	1,654	1,654	1,654
5,050	5,100	761	761	761	761	8,050	8,100	1,211	1,211	1,211	1,211	11,050	11,100	1,661	1,661	1,661	1,661
5,100	5,150	769	769	769	769	8,100	8,150	1,219	1,219	1,219	1,219	11,100	11,150	1,669	1,669	1,669	1,669
5,150	5,200	776	776	776	776	8,150	8,200	1,226	1,226	1,226	1,226	11,150	11,200	1,676	1,676	1,676	1,676
5,200	5,250	784	784	784	784	8,200	8,250	1,234	1,234	1,234	1,234	11,200	11,250	1,684	1,684	1,684	1,684
5,250	5,300	791	791	791	791	8,250	8,300	1,241	1,241	1,241	1,241	11,250	11,300	1,691	1,691	1,691	1,691
5,300	5,350	799	799	799	799	8,300	8,350	1,249	1,249	1,249	1,249	11,300	11,350	1,699	1,699	1,699	1,699
5,350	5,400	806	806	806	806	8,350	8,400	1,256	1,256	1,256	1,256	11,350	11,400	1,706	1,706	1,706	1,706
5,400	5,450	814	814	814	814	8,400	8,450	1,264	1,264	1,264	1,264	11,400	11,450	1,714	1,714	1,714	1,714
5,450	5,500	821	821	821	821	8,450	8,500	1,271	1,271	1,271	1,271	11,450	11,500	1,721	1,721	1,721	1,721
5,500	5,550	829	829	829	829	8,500	8,550	1,279	1,279	1,279	1,279	11,500	11,550	1,729	1,729	1,729	1,729
5,550	5,600	836	836	836	836	8,550	8,600	1,286	1,286	1,286	1,286	11,550	11,600	1,736	1,736	1,736	1,736
5,600	5,650	844	844	844	844	8,600	8,650	1,294	1,294	1,294	1,294	11,600	11,650	1,744	1,744	1,744	1,744
5,650	5,700	851	851	851	851	8,650	8,700	1,301	1,301	1,301	1,301	11,650	11,700	1,751	1,751	1,751	1,751
5,700	5,750	859	859	859	859	8,700	8,750	1,309	1,309	1,309	1,309	11,700	11,750	1,759	1,759	1,759	1,759
5,750	5,800	866	866	866	866	8,750	8,800	1,316	1,316	1,316	1,316	11,750	11,800	1,766	1,766	1,766	1,766
5,800	5,850	874	874	874	874	8,800	8,850	1,324	1,324	1,324	1,324	11,800	11,850	1,774	1,774	1,774	1,774
5,850	5,900	881	881	881	881	8,850	8,900	1,331	1,331	1,331	1,331	11,850	11,900	1,781	1,781	1,781	1,781
5,900	5,950	889	889	889	889	8,900	8,950	1,339	1,339	1,339	1,339	11,900	11,950	1,789	1,789	1,789	1,789
5,950	6,000	896	896	896	896	8,950	9,000	1,346	1,346	1,346	1,346	11,950	12,000	1,796	1,796	1,796	1,796
6,000						**9,000**						**12,000**					
6,000	6,050	904	904	904	904	9,000	9,050	1,354	1,354	1,354	1,354	12,000	12,050	1,804	1,804	1,804	1,804
6,050	6,100	911	911	911	911	9,050	9,100	1,361	1,361	1,361	1,361	12,050	12,100	1,811	1,811	1,811	1,811
6,100	6,150	919	919	919	919	9,100	9,150	1,369	1,369	1,369	1,369	12,100	12,150	1,819	1,819	1,819	1,819
6,150	6,200	926	926	926	926	9,150	9,200	1,376	1,376	1,376	1,376	12,150	12,200	1,826	1,826	1,826	1,826
6,200	6,250	934	934	934	934	9,200	9,250	1,384	1,384	1,384	1,384	12,200	12,250	1,834	1,834	1,834	1,834
6,250	6,300	941	941	941	941	9,250	9,300	1,391	1,391	1,391	1,391	12,250	12,300	1,841	1,841	1,841	1,841
6,300	6,350	949	949	949	949	9,300	9,350	1,399	1,399	1,399	1,399	12,300	12,350	1,849	1,849	1,849	1,849
6,350	6,400	956	956	956	956	9,350	9,400	1,406	1,406	1,406	1,406	12,350	12,400	1,856	1,856	1,856	1,856
6,400	6,450	964	964	964	964	9,400	9,450	1,414	1,414	1,414	1,414	12,400	12,450	1,864	1,864	1,864	1,864
6,450	6,500	971	971	971	971	9,450	9,500	1,421	1,421	1,421	1,421	12,450	12,500	1,871	1,871	1,871	1,871
6,500	6,550	979	979	979	979	9,500	9,550	1,429	1,429	1,429	1,429	12,500	12,550	1,879	1,879	1,879	1,879
6,550	6,600	986	986	986	986	9,550	9,600	1,436	1,436	1,436	1,436	12,550	12,600	1,886	1,886	1,886	1,886
6,600	6,650	994	994	994	994	9,600	9,650	1,444	1,444	1,444	1,444	12,600	12,650	1,894	1,894	1,894	1,894
6,650	6,700	1,001	1,001	1,001	1,001	9,650	9,700	1,451	1,451	1,451	1,451	12,650	12,700	1,901	1,901	1,901	1,901
6,700	6,750	1,009	1,009	1,009	1,009	9,700	9,750	1,459	1,459	1,459	1,459	12,700	12,750	1,909	1,909	1,909	1,909
6,750	6,800	1,016	1,016	1,016	1,016	9,750	9,800	1,466	1,466	1,466	1,466	12,750	12,800	1,916	1,916	1,916	1,916
6,800	6,850	1,024	1,024	1,024	1,024	9,800	9,850	1,474	1,474	1,474	1,474	12,800	12,850	1,924	1,924	1,924	1,924
6,850	6,900	1,031	1,031	1,031	1,031	9,850	9,900	1,481	1,481	1,481	1,481	12,850	12,900	1,931	1,931	1,931	1,931
6,900	6,950	1,039	1,039	1,039	1,039	9,900	9,950	1,489	1,489	1,489	1,489	12,900	12,950	1,939	1,939	1,939	1,939
6,950	7,000	1,046	1,046	1,046	1,046	9,950	10,000	1,496	1,496	1,496	1,496	12,950	13,000	1,946	1,946	1,946	1,946
7,000						**10,000**						**13,000**					
7,000	7,050	1,054	1,054	1,054	1,054	10,000	10,050	1,504	1,504	1,504	1,504	13,000	13,050	1,954	1,954	1,954	1,954
7,050	7,100	1,061	1,061	1,061	1,061	10,050	10,100	1,511	1,511	1,511	1,511	13,050	13,100	1,961	1,961	1,961	1,961
7,100	7,150	1,069	1,069	1,069	1,069	10,100	10,150	1,519	1,519	1,519	1,519	13,100	13,150	1,969	1,969	1,969	1,969
7,150	7,200	1,076	1,076	1,076	1,076	10,150	10,200	1,526	1,526	1,526	1,526	13,150	13,200	1,976	1,976	1,976	1,976
7,200	7,250	1,084	1,084	1,084	1,084	10,200	10,250	1,534	1,534	1,534	1,534	13,200	13,250	1,984	1,984	1,984	1,984
7,250	7,300	1,091	1,091	1,091	1,091	10,250	10,300	1,541	1,541	1,541	1,541	13,250	13,300	1,991	1,991	1,991	1,991
7,300	7,350	1,099	1,099	1,099	1,099	10,300	10,350	1,549	1,549	1,549	1,549	13,300	13,350	1,999	1,999	1,999	1,999
7,350	7,400	1,106	1,106	1,106	1,106	10,350	10,400	1,556	1,556	1,556	1,556	13,350	13,400	2,006	2,006	2,006	2,006
7,400	7,450	1,114	1,114	1,114	1,114	10,400	10,450	1,564	1,564	1,564	1,564	13,400	13,450	2,014	2,014	2,014	2,014
7,450	7,500	1,121	1,121	1,121	1,121	10,450	10,500	1,571	1,571	1,571	1,571	13,450	13,500	2,021	2,021	2,021	2,021
7,500	7,550	1,129	1,129	1,129	1,129	10,500	10,550	1,579	1,579	1,579	1,579	13,500	13,550	2,029	2,029	2,029	2,029
7,550	7,600	1,136	1,136	1,136	1,136	10,550	10,600	1,586	1,586	1,586	1,586	13,550	13,600	2,036	2,036	2,036	2,036
7,600	7,650	1,144	1,144	1,144	1,144	10,600	10,650	1,594	1,594	1,594	1,594	13,600	13,650	2,044	2,044	2,044	2,044
7,650	7,700	1,151	1,151	1,151	1,151	10,650	10,700	1,601	1,601	1,601	1,601	13,650	13,700	2,051	2,051	2,051	2,051
7,700	7,750	1,159	1,159	1,159	1,159	10,700	10,750	1,609	1,609	1,609	1,609	13,700	13,750	2,059	2,059	2,059	2,059
7,750	7,800	1,166	1,166	1,166	1,166	10,750	10,800	1,616	1,616	1,616	1,616	13,750	13,800	2,066	2,066	2,066	2,066
7,800	7,850	1,174	1,174	1,174	1,174	10,800	10,850	1,624	1,624	1,624	1,624	13,800	13,850	2,074	2,074	2,074	2,074
7,850	7,900	1,181	1,181	1,181	1,181	10,850	10,900	1,631	1,631	1,631	1,631	13,850	13,900	2,081	2,081	2,081	2,081
7,900	7,950	1,189	1,189	1,189	1,189	10,900	10,950	1,639	1,639	1,639	1,639	13,900	13,950	2,089	2,089	2,089	2,089
7,950	8,000	1,196	1,196	1,196	1,196	10,950	11,000	1,646	1,646	1,646	1,646	13,950	14,000	2,096	2,096	2,096	2,096

* This column must also be used by a qualifying widow(er).

Continued on next page

If line 6 (Form 1040EZ), line 22 (Form 1040A), or line 37 (Form 1040) is—		And you are—			
At least	But less than	Single	Married filing jointly *	Married filing separately	Head of a household
		Your tax is—			

14,000

At least	But less than	Single	Married filing jointly	Married filing separately	Head of a household
14,000	14,050	2,104	2,104	2,104	2,104
14,050	14,100	2,111	2,111	2,111	2,111
14,100	14,150	2,119	2,119	2,119	2,119
14,150	14,200	2,126	2,126	2,126	2,126
14,200	14,250	2,134	2,134	2,134	2,134
14,250	14,300	2,141	2,141	2,141	2,141
14,300	14,350	2,149	2,149	2,149	2,149
14,350	14,400	2,156	2,156	2,156	2,156
14,400	14,450	2,164	2,164	2,164	2,164
14,450	14,500	2,171	2,171	2,171	2,171
14,500	14,550	2,179	2,179	2,179	2,179
14,550	14,600	2,186	2,186	2,186	2,186
14,600	14,650	2,194	2,194	2,194	2,194
14,650	14,700	2,201	2,201	2,201	2,201
14,700	14,750	2,209	2,209	2,209	2,209
14,750	14,800	2,216	2,216	2,216	2,216
14,800	14,850	2,224	2,224	2,224	2,224
14,850	14,900	2,231	2,231	2,231	2,231
14,900	14,950	2,239	2,239	2,239	2,239
14,950	15,000	2,246	2,246	2,246	2,246

15,000

At least	But less than	Single	Married filing jointly	Married filing separately	Head of a household
15,000	15,050	2,254	2,254	2,254	2,254
15,050	15,100	2,261	2,261	2,261	2,261
15,100	15,150	2,269	2,269	2,269	2,269
15,150	15,200	2,276	2,276	2,276	2,276
15,200	15,250	2,284	2,284	2,284	2,284
15,250	15,300	2,291	2,291	2,291	2,291
15,300	15,350	2,299	2,299	2,299	2,299
15,350	15,400	2,306	2,306	2,306	2,306
15,400	15,450	2,314	2,314	2,314	2,314
15,450	15,500	2,321	2,321	2,321	2,321
15,500	15,550	2,329	2,329	2,329	2,329
15,550	15,600	2,336	2,336	2,336	2,336
15,600	15,650	2,344	2,344	2,344	2,344
15,650	15,700	2,351	2,351	2,351	2,351
15,700	15,750	2,359	2,359	2,359	2,359
15,750	15,800	2,366	2,366	2,366	2,366
15,800	15,850	2,374	2,374	2,374	2,374
15,850	15,900	2,381	2,381	2,381	2,381
15,900	15,950	2,389	2,389	2,389	2,389
15,950	16,000	2,396	2,396	2,396	2,396

16,000

At least	But less than	Single	Married filing jointly	Married filing separately	Head of a household
16,000	16,050	2,404	2,404	2,404	2,404
16,050	16,100	2,411	2,411	2,411	2,411
16,100	16,150	2,419	2,419	2,419	2,419
16,150	16,200	2,426	2,426	2,426	2,426
16,200	16,250	2,434	2,434	2,434	2,434
16,250	16,300	2,441	2,441	2,441	2,441
16,300	16,350	2,449	2,449	2,449	2,449
16,350	16,400	2,456	2,456	2,456	2,456
16,400	16,450	2,464	2,464	2,464	2,464
16,450	16,500	2,471	2,471	2,471	2,471
16,500	16,550	2,479	2,479	2,479	2,479
16,550	16,600	2,486	2,486	2,486	2,486
16,600	16,650	2,494	2,494	2,494	2,494
16,650	16,700	2,501	2,501	2,501	2,501
16,700	16,750	2,509	2,509	2,509	2,509
16,750	16,800	2,516	2,516	2,516	2,516
16,800	16,850	2,524	2,524	2,524	2,524
16,850	16,900	2,531	2,531	2,531	2,531
16,900	16,950	2,539	2,539	2,539	2,539
16,950	17,000	2,546	2,546	2,546	2,546

17,000

At least	But less than	Single	Married filing jointly	Married filing separately	Head of a household
17,000	17,050	2,554	2,554	2,554	2,554
17,050	17,100	2,561	2,561	2,561	2,561
17,100	17,150	2,569	2,569	2,569	2,569
17,150	17,200	2,576	2,576	2,576	2,576
17,200	17,250	2,584	2,584	2,584	2,584
17,250	17,300	2,591	2,591	2,591	2,591
17,300	17,350	2,599	2,599	2,599	2,599
17,350	17,400	2,606	2,606	2,606	2,606
17,400	17,450	2,614	2,614	2,614	2,614
17,450	17,500	2,621	2,621	2,621	2,621
17,500	17,550	2,629	2,629	2,629	2,629
17,550	17,600	2,636	2,636	2,636	2,636
17,600	17,650	2,644	2,644	2,644	2,644
17,650	17,700	2,651	2,651	2,651	2,651
17,700	17,750	2,659	2,659	2,659	2,659
17,750	17,800	2,666	2,666	2,666	2,666
17,800	17,850	2,674	2,674	2,674	2,674
17,850	17,900	2,681	2,681	2,681	2,681
17,900	17,950	2,689	2,689	2,689	2,689
17,950	18,000	2,696	2,696	2,696	2,696

18,000

At least	But less than	Single	Married filing jointly	Married filing separately	Head of a household
18,000	18,050	2,704	2,704	2,704	2,704
18,050	18,100	2,711	2,711	2,711	2,711
18,100	18,150	2,719	2,719	2,719	2,719
18,150	18,200	2,726	2,726	2,726	2,726
18,200	18,250	2,734	2,734	2,734	2,734
18,250	18,300	2,741	2,741	2,741	2,741
18,300	18,350	2,749	2,749	2,749	2,749
18,350	18,400	2,756	2,756	2,756	2,756
18,400	18,450	2,764	2,764	2,764	2,764
18,450	18,500	2,771	2,771	2,775	2,771
18,500	18,550	2,779	2,779	2,789	2,779
18,550	18,600	2,786	2,786	2,803	2,786
18,600	18,650	2,794	2,794	2,817	2,794
18,650	18,700	2,801	2,801	2,831	2,801
18,700	18,750	2,809	2,809	2,845	2,809
18,750	18,800	2,816	2,816	2,859	2,816
18,800	18,850	2,824	2,824	2,873	2,824
18,850	18,900	2,831	2,831	2,887	2,831
18,900	18,950	2,839	2,839	2,901	2,839
18,950	19,000	2,846	2,846	2,915	2,846

19,000

At least	But less than	Single	Married filing jointly	Married filing separately	Head of a household
19,000	19,050	2,854	2,854	2,929	2,854
19,050	19,100	2,861	2,861	2,943	2,861
19,100	19,150	2,869	2,869	2,957	2,869
19,150	19,200	2,876	2,876	2,971	2,876
19,200	19,250	2,884	2,884	2,985	2,884
19,250	19,300	2,891	2,891	2,999	2,891
19,300	19,350	2,899	2,899	3,013	2,899
19,350	19,400	2,906	2,906	3,027	2,906
19,400	19,450	2,914	2,914	3,041	2,914
19,450	19,500	2,921	2,921	3,055	2,921
19,500	19,550	2,929	2,929	3,069	2,929
19,550	19,600	2,936	2,936	3,083	2,936
19,600	19,650	2,944	2,944	3,097	2,944
19,650	19,700	2,951	2,951	3,111	2,951
19,700	19,750	2,959	2,959	3,125	2,959
19,750	19,800	2,966	2,966	3,139	2,966
19,800	19,850	2,974	2,974	3,153	2,974
19,850	19,900	2,981	2,981	3,167	2,981
19,900	19,950	2,989	2,989	3,181	2,989
19,950	20,000	2,996	2,996	3,195	2,996

20,000

At least	But less than	Single	Married filing jointly	Married filing separately	Head of a household
20,000	20,050	3,004	3,004	3,209	3,004
20,050	20,100	3,011	3,011	3,223	3,011
20,100	20,150	3,019	3,019	3,237	3,019
20,150	20,200	3,026	3,026	3,251	3,026
20,200	20,250	3,034	3,034	3,265	3,034
20,250	20,300	3,041	3,041	3,279	3,041
20,300	20,350	3,049	3,049	3,293	3,049
20,350	20,400	3,056	3,056	3,307	3,056
20,400	20,450	3,064	3,064	3,321	3,064
20,450	20,500	3,071	3,071	3,335	3,071
20,500	20,550	3,079	3,079	3,349	3,079
20,550	20,600	3,086	3,086	3,363	3,086
20,600	20,650	3,094	3,094	3,377	3,094
20,650	20,700	3,101	3,101	3,391	3,101
20,700	20,750	3,109	3,109	3,405	3,109
20,750	20,800	3,116	3,116	3,419	3,116
20,800	20,850	3,124	3,124	3,433	3,124
20,850	20,900	3,131	3,131	3,447	3,131
20,900	20,950	3,139	3,139	3,461	3,139
20,950	21,000	3,146	3,146	3,475	3,146

21,000

At least	But less than	Single	Married filing jointly	Married filing separately	Head of a household
21,000	21,050	3,154	3,154	3,489	3,154
21,050	21,100	3,161	3,161	3,503	3,161
21,100	21,150	3,169	3,169	3,517	3,169
21,150	21,200	3,176	3,176	3,531	3,176
21,200	21,250	3,184	3,184	3,545	3,184
21,250	21,300	3,191	3,191	3,559	3,191
21,300	21,350	3,199	3,199	3,573	3,199
21,350	21,400	3,206	3,206	3,587	3,206
21,400	21,450	3,214	3,214	3,601	3,214
21,450	21,500	3,221	3,221	3,615	3,221
21,500	21,550	3,229	3,229	3,629	3,229
21,550	21,600	3,236	3,236	3,643	3,236
21,600	21,650	3,244	3,244	3,657	3,244
21,650	21,700	3,251	3,251	3,671	3,251
21,700	21,750	3,259	3,259	3,685	3,259
21,750	21,800	3,266	3,266	3,699	3,266
21,800	21,850	3,274	3,274	3,713	3,274
21,850	21,900	3,281	3,281	3,727	3,281
21,900	21,950	3,289	3,289	3,741	3,289
21,950	22,000	3,296	3,296	3,755	3,296

22,000

At least	But less than	Single	Married filing jointly	Married filing separately	Head of a household
22,000	22,050	3,304	3,304	3,769	3,304
22,050	22,100	3,311	3,311	3,783	3,311
22,100	22,150	3,322	3,319	3,797	3,319
22,150	22,200	3,336	3,326	3,811	3,326
22,200	22,250	3,350	3,334	3,825	3,334
22,250	22,300	3,364	3,341	3,839	3,341
22,300	22,350	3,378	3,349	3,853	3,349
22,350	22,400	3,392	3,356	3,867	3,356
22,400	22,450	3,406	3,364	3,881	3,364
22,450	22,500	3,420	3,371	3,895	3,371
22,500	22,550	3,434	3,379	3,909	3,379
22,550	22,600	3,448	3,386	3,923	3,386
22,600	22,650	3,462	3,394	3,937	3,394
22,650	22,700	3,476	3,401	3,951	3,401
22,700	22,750	3,490	3,409	3,965	3,409
22,750	22,800	3,504	3,416	3,979	3,416
22,800	22,850	3,518	3,424	3,993	3,424
22,850	22,900	3,532	3,431	4,007	3,431
22,900	22,950	3,546	3,439	4,021	3,439
22,950	23,000	3,560	3,446	4,035	3,446

* This column must also be used by a qualifying widow(er).

Continued on next page

If line 6 (Form 1040EZ), line 22 (Form 1040A), or line 37 (Form 1040) is—		And you are—			
At least	But less than	Single	Married filing jointly *	Married filing separately	Head of a household
		Your tax is—			

23,000

At least	But less than	Single	Married filing jointly	Married filing separately	Head of a household
23,000	23,050	3,574	3,454	4,049	3,454
23,050	23,100	3,588	3,461	4,063	3,461
23,100	23,150	3,602	3,469	4,077	3,469
23,150	23,200	3,616	3,476	4,091	3,476
23,200	23,250	3,630	3,484	4,105	3,484
23,250	23,300	3,644	3,491	4,119	3,491
23,300	23,350	3,658	3,499	4,133	3,499
23,350	23,400	3,672	3,506	4,147	3,506
23,400	23,450	3,686	3,514	4,161	3,514
23,450	23,500	3,700	3,521	4,175	3,521
23,500	23,550	3,714	3,529	4,189	3,529
23,550	23,600	3,728	3,536	4,203	3,536
23,600	23,650	3,742	3,544	4,217	3,544
23,650	23,700	3,756	3,551	4,231	3,551
23,700	23,750	3,770	3,559	4,245	3,559
23,750	23,800	3,784	3,566	4,259	3,566
23,800	23,850	3,798	3,574	4,273	3,574
23,850	23,900	3,812	3,581	4,287	3,581
23,900	23,950	3,826	3,589	4,301	3,589
23,950	24,000	3,840	3,596	4,315	3,596

24,000

At least	But less than	Single	Married filing jointly	Married filing separately	Head of a household
24,000	24,050	3,854	3,604	4,329	3,604
24,050	24,100	3,868	3,611	4,343	3,611
24,100	24,150	3,882	3,619	4,357	3,619
24,150	24,200	3,896	3,626	4,371	3,626
24,200	24,250	3,910	3,634	4,385	3,634
24,250	24,300	3,924	3,641	4,399	3,641
24,300	24,350	3,938	3,649	4,413	3,649
24,350	24,400	3,952	3,656	4,427	3,656
24,400	24,450	3,966	3,664	4,441	3,664
24,450	24,500	3,980	3,671	4,455	3,671
24,500	24,550	3,994	3,679	4,469	3,679
24,550	24,600	4,008	3,686	4,483	3,686
24,600	24,650	4,022	3,694	4,497	3,694
24,650	24,700	4,036	3,701	4,511	3,701
24,700	24,750	4,050	3,709	4,525	3,709
24,750	24,800	4,064	3,716	4,539	3,716
24,800	24,850	4,078	3,724	4,553	3,724
24,850	24,900	4,092	3,731	4,567	3,731
24,900	24,950	4,106	3,739	4,581	3,739
24,950	25,000	4,120	3,746	4,595	3,746

25,000

At least	But less than	Single	Married filing jointly	Married filing separately	Head of a household
25,000	25,050	4,134	3,754	4,609	3,754
25,050	25,100	4,148	3,761	4,623	3,761
25,100	25,150	4,162	3,769	4,637	3,769
25,150	25,200	4,176	3,776	4,651	3,776
25,200	25,250	4,190	3,784	4,665	3,784
25,250	25,300	4,204	3,791	4,679	3,791
25,300	25,350	4,218	3,799	4,693	3,799
25,350	25,400	4,232	3,806	4,707	3,806
25,400	25,450	4,246	3,814	4,721	3,814
25,450	25,500	4,260	3,821	4,735	3,821
25,500	25,550	4,274	3,829	4,749	3,829
25,550	25,600	4,288	3,836	4,763	3,836
25,600	25,650	4,302	3,844	4,777	3,844
25,650	25,700	4,316	3,851	4,791	3,851
25,700	25,750	4,330	3,859	4,805	3,859
25,750	25,800	4,344	3,866	4,819	3,866
25,800	25,850	4,358	3,874	4,833	3,874
25,850	25,900	4,372	3,881	4,847	3,881
25,900	25,950	4,386	3,889	4,861	3,889
25,950	26,000	4,400	3,896	4,875	3,896

26,000

At least	But less than	Single	Married filing jointly	Married filing separately	Head of a household
26,000	26,050	4,414	3,904	4,889	3,904
26,050	26,100	4,428	3,911	4,903	3,911
26,100	26,150	4,442	3,919	4,917	3,919
26,150	26,200	4,456	3,926	4,931	3,926
26,200	26,250	4,470	3,934	4,945	3,934
26,250	26,300	4,484	3,941	4,959	3,941
26,300	26,350	4,498	3,949	4,973	3,949
26,350	26,400	4,512	3,956	4,987	3,956
26,400	26,450	4,526	3,964	5,001	3,964
26,450	26,500	4,540	3,971	5,015	3,971
26,500	26,550	4,554	3,979	5,029	3,979
26,550	26,600	4,568	3,986	5,043	3,986
26,600	26,650	4,582	3,994	5,057	3,994
26,650	26,700	4,596	4,001	5,071	4,001
26,700	26,750	4,610	4,009	5,085	4,009
26,750	26,800	4,624	4,016	5,099	4,016
26,800	26,850	4,638	4,024	5,113	4,024
26,850	26,900	4,652	4,031	5,127	4,031
26,900	26,950	4,666	4,039	5,141	4,039
26,950	27,000	4,680	4,046	5,155	4,046

27,000

At least	But less than	Single	Married filing jointly	Married filing separately	Head of a household
27,000	27,050	4,694	4,054	5,169	4,054
27,050	27,100	4,708	4,061	5,183	4,061
27,100	27,150	4,722	4,069	5,197	4,069
27,150	27,200	4,736	4,076	5,211	4,076
27,200	27,250	4,750	4,084	5,225	4,084
27,250	27,300	4,764	4,091	5,239	4,091
27,300	27,350	4,778	4,099	5,253	4,099
27,350	27,400	4,792	4,106	5,267	4,106
27,400	27,450	4,806	4,114	5,281	4,114
27,450	27,500	4,820	4,121	5,295	4,121
27,500	27,550	4,834	4,129	5,309	4,129
27,550	27,600	4,848	4,136	5,323	4,136
27,600	27,650	4,862	4,144	5,337	4,144
27,650	27,700	4,876	4,151	5,351	4,151
27,700	27,750	4,890	4,159	5,365	4,159
27,750	27,800	4,904	4,166	5,379	4,166
27,800	27,850	4,918	4,174	5,393	4,174
27,850	27,900	4,932	4,181	5,407	4,181
27,900	27,950	4,946	4,189	5,421	4,189
27,950	28,000	4,960	4,196	5,435	4,196

28,000

At least	But less than	Single	Married filing jointly	Married filing separately	Head of a household
28,000	28,050	4,974	4,204	5,449	4,204
28,050	28,100	4,988	4,211	5,463	4,211
28,100	28,150	5,002	4,219	5,477	4,219
28,150	28,200	5,016	4,226	5,491	4,226
28,200	28,250	5,030	4,234	5,505	4,234
28,250	28,300	5,044	4,241	5,519	4,241
28,300	28,350	5,058	4,249	5,533	4,249
28,350	28,400	5,072	4,256	5,547	4,256
28,400	28,450	5,086	4,264	5,561	4,264
28,450	28,500	5,100	4,271	5,575	4,271
28,500	28,550	5,114	4,279	5,589	4,279
28,550	28,600	5,128	4,286	5,603	4,286
28,600	28,650	5,142	4,294	5,617	4,294
28,650	28,700	5,156	4,301	5,631	4,301
28,700	28,750	5,170	4,309	5,645	4,309
28,750	28,800	5,184	4,316	5,659	4,316
28,800	28,850	5,198	4,324	5,673	4,324
28,850	28,900	5,212	4,331	5,687	4,331
28,900	28,950	5,226	4,339	5,701	4,339
28,950	29,000	5,240	4,346	5,715	4,346

29,000

At least	But less than	Single	Married filing jointly	Married filing separately	Head of a household
29,000	29,050	5,254	4,354	5,729	4,354
29,050	29,100	5,268	4,361	5,743	4,361
29,100	29,150	5,282	4,369	5,757	4,369
29,150	29,200	5,296	4,376	5,771	4,376
29,200	29,250	5,310	4,384	5,785	4,384
29,250	29,300	5,324	4,391	5,799	4,391
29,300	29,350	5,338	4,399	5,813	4,399
29,350	29,400	5,352	4,406	5,827	4,406
29,400	29,450	5,366	4,414	5,841	4,414
29,450	29,500	5,380	4,421	5,855	4,421
29,500	29,550	5,394	4,429	5,869	4,429
29,550	29,600	5,408	4,436	5,883	4,436
29,600	29,650	5,422	4,444	5,897	4,447
29,650	29,700	5,436	4,451	5,911	4,461
29,700	29,750	5,450	4,459	5,925	4,475
29,750	29,800	5,464	4,466	5,939	4,489
29,800	29,850	5,478	4,474	5,953	4,503
29,850	29,900	5,492	4,481	5,967	4,517
29,900	29,950	5,506	4,489	5,981	4,531
29,950	30,000	5,520	4,496	5,995	4,545

30,000

At least	But less than	Single	Married filing jointly	Married filing separately	Head of a household
30,000	30,050	5,534	4,504	6,009	4,559
30,050	30,100	5,548	4,511	6,023	4,573
30,100	30,150	5,562	4,519	6,037	4,587
30,150	30,200	5,576	4,526	6,051	4,601
30,200	30,250	5,590	4,534	6,065	4,615
30,250	30,300	5,604	4,541	6,079	4,629
30,300	30,350	5,618	4,549	6,093	4,643
30,350	30,400	5,632	4,556	6,107	4,657
30,400	30,450	5,646	4,564	6,121	4,671
30,450	30,500	5,660	4,571	6,135	4,685
30,500	30,550	5,674	4,579	6,149	4,699
30,550	30,600	5,688	4,586	6,163	4,713
30,600	30,650	5,702	4,594	6,177	4,727
30,650	30,700	5,716	4,601	6,191	4,741
30,700	30,750	5,730	4,609	6,205	4,755
30,750	30,800	5,744	4,616	6,219	4,769
30,800	30,850	5,758	4,624	6,233	4,783
30,850	30,900	5,772	4,631	6,247	4,797
30,900	30,950	5,786	4,639	6,261	4,811
30,950	31,000	5,800	4,646	6,275	4,825

31,000

At least	But less than	Single	Married filing jointly	Married filing separately	Head of a household
31,000	31,050	5,814	4,654	6,289	4,839
31,050	31,100	5,828	4,661	6,303	4,853
31,100	31,150	5,842	4,669	6,317	4,867
31,150	31,200	5,856	4,676	6,331	4,881
31,200	31,250	5,870	4,684	6,345	4,895
31,250	31,300	5,884	4,691	6,359	4,909
31,300	31,350	5,898	4,699	6,373	4,923
31,350	31,400	5,912	4,706	6,387	4,937
31,400	31,450	5,926	4,714	6,401	4,951
31,450	31,500	5,940	4,721	6,415	4,965
31,500	31,550	5,954	4,729	6,429	4,979
31,550	31,600	5,968	4,736	6,443	4,993
31,600	31,650	5,982	4,744	6,457	5,007
31,650	31,700	5,996	4,751	6,471	5,021
31,700	31,750	6,010	4,759	6,485	5,035
31,750	31,800	6,024	4,766	6,499	5,049
31,800	31,850	6,038	4,774	6,513	5,063
31,850	31,900	6,052	4,781	6,527	5,077
31,900	31,950	6,066	4,789	6,541	5,091
31,950	32,000	6,080	4,796	6,555	5,105

* This column must also be used by a qualifying widow(er).

Continued on next page

32,000

At least	But less than	Single	Married filing jointly *	Married filing separately	Head of a household
32,000	32,050	6,094	4,804	6,569	5,119
32,050	32,100	6,108	4,811	6,583	5,133
32,100	32,150	6,122	4,819	6,597	5,147
32,150	32,200	6,136	4,826	6,611	5,161
32,200	32,250	6,150	4,834	6,625	5,175
32,250	32,300	6,164	4,841	6,639	5,189
32,300	32,350	6,178	4,849	6,653	5,203
32,350	32,400	6,192	4,856	6,667	5,217
32,400	32,450	6,206	4,864	6,681	5,231
32,450	32,500	6,220	4,871	6,695	5,245
32,500	32,550	6,234	4,879	6,709	5,259
32,550	32,600	6,248	4,886	6,723	5,273
32,600	32,650	6,262	4,894	6,737	5,287
32,650	32,700	6,276	4,901	6,751	5,301
32,700	32,750	6,290	4,909	6,765	5,315
32,750	32,800	6,304	4,916	6,779	5,329
32,800	32,850	6,318	4,924	6,793	5,343
32,850	32,900	6,332	4,931	6,807	5,357
32,900	32,950	6,346	4,939	6,821	5,371
32,950	33,000	6,360	4,946	6,835	5,385

33,000

At least	But less than	Single	Married filing jointly *	Married filing separately	Head of a household
33,000	33,050	6,374	4,954	6,849	5,399
33,050	33,100	6,388	4,961	6,863	5,413
33,100	33,150	6,402	4,969	6,877	5,427
33,150	33,200	6,416	4,976	6,891	5,441
33,200	33,250	6,430	4,984	6,905	5,455
33,250	33,300	6,444	4,991	6,919	5,469
33,300	33,350	6,458	4,999	6,933	5,483
33,350	33,400	6,472	5,006	6,947	5,497
33,400	33,450	6,486	5,014	6,961	5,511
33,450	33,500	6,500	5,021	6,975	5,525
33,500	33,550	6,514	5,029	6,989	5,539
33,550	33,600	6,528	5,036	7,003	5,553
33,600	33,650	6,542	5,044	7,017	5,567
33,650	33,700	6,556	5,051	7,031	5,581
33,700	33,750	6,570	5,059	7,045	5,595
33,750	33,800	6,584	5,066	7,059	5,609
33,800	33,850	6,598	5,074	7,073	5,623
33,850	33,900	6,612	5,081	7,087	5,637
33,900	33,950	6,626	5,089	7,101	5,651
33,950	34,000	6,640	5,096	7,115	5,665

34,000

At least	But less than	Single	Married filing jointly *	Married filing separately	Head of a household
34,000	34,050	6,654	5,104	7,129	5,679
34,050	34,100	6,668	5,111	7,143	5,693
34,100	34,150	6,682	5,119	7,157	5,707
34,150	34,200	6,696	5,126	7,171	5,721
34,200	34,250	6,710	5,134	7,185	5,735
34,250	34,300	6,724	5,141	7,199	5,749
34,300	34,350	6,738	5,149	7,213	5,763
34,350	34,400	6,752	5,156	7,227	5,777
34,400	34,450	6,766	5,164	7,241	5,791
34,450	34,500	6,780	5,171	7,255	5,805
34,500	34,550	6,794	5,179	7,269	5,819
34,550	34,600	6,808	5,186	7,283	5,833
34,600	34,650	6,822	5,194	7,297	5,847
34,650	34,700	6,836	5,201	7,311	5,861
34,700	34,750	6,850	5,209	7,325	5,875
34,750	34,800	6,864	5,216	7,339	5,889
34,800	34,850	6,878	5,224	7,353	5,903
34,850	34,900	6,892	5,231	7,367	5,917
34,900	34,950	6,906	5,239	7,381	5,931
34,950	35,000	6,920	5,246	7,395	5,945

35,000

At least	But less than	Single	Married filing jointly *	Married filing separately	Head of a household
35,000	35,050	6,934	5,254	7,409	5,959
35,050	35,100	6,948	5,261	7,423	5,973
35,100	35,150	6,962	5,269	7,437	5,987
35,150	35,200	6,976	5,276	7,451	6,001
35,200	35,250	6,990	5,284	7,465	6,015
35,250	35,300	7,004	5,291	7,479	6,029
35,300	35,350	7,018	5,299	7,493	6,043
35,350	35,400	7,032	5,306	7,507	6,057
35,400	35,450	7,046	5,314	7,521	6,071
35,450	35,500	7,060	5,321	7,535	6,085
35,500	35,550	7,074	5,329	7,549	6,099
35,550	35,600	7,088	5,336	7,563	6,113
35,600	35,650	7,102	5,344	7,577	6,127
35,650	35,700	7,116	5,351	7,591	6,141
35,700	35,750	7,130	5,359	7,605	6,155
35,750	35,800	7,144	5,366	7,619	6,169
35,800	35,850	7,158	5,374	7,633	6,183
35,850	35,900	7,172	5,381	7,647	6,197
35,900	35,950	7,186	5,389	7,661	6,211
35,950	36,000	7,200	5,396	7,675	6,225

36,000

At least	But less than	Single	Married filing jointly *	Married filing separately	Head of a household
36,000	36,050	7,214	5,404	7,689	6,239
36,050	36,100	7,228	5,411	7,703	6,253
36,100	36,150	7,242	5,419	7,717	6,267
36,150	36,200	7,256	5,426	7,731	6,281
36,200	36,250	7,270	5,434	7,745	6,295
36,250	36,300	7,284	5,441	7,759	6,309
36,300	36,350	7,298	5,449	7,773	6,323
36,350	36,400	7,312	5,456	7,787	6,337
36,400	36,450	7,326	5,464	7,801	6,351
36,450	36,500	7,340	5,471	7,815	6,365
36,500	36,550	7,354	5,479	7,829	6,379
36,550	36,600	7,368	5,486	7,843	6,393
36,600	36,650	7,382	5,494	7,857	6,407
36,650	36,700	7,396	5,501	7,871	6,421
36,700	36,750	7,410	5,509	7,885	6,435
36,750	36,800	7,424	5,516	7,899	6,449
36,800	36,850	7,438	5,524	7,913	6,463
36,850	36,900	7,452	5,531	7,927	6,477
36,900	36,950	7,466	5,542	7,941	6,491
36,950	37,000	7,480	5,556	7,955	6,505

37,000

At least	But less than	Single	Married filing jointly *	Married filing separately	Head of a household
37,000	37,050	7,494	5,570	7,969	6,519
37,050	37,100	7,508	5,584	7,983	6,533
37,100	37,150	7,522	5,598	7,997	6,547
37,150	37,200	7,536	5,612	8,011	6,561
37,200	37,250	7,550	5,626	8,025	6,575
37,250	37,300	7,564	5,640	8,039	6,589
37,300	37,350	7,578	5,654	8,053	6,603
37,350	37,400	7,592	5,668	8,067	6,617
37,400	37,450	7,606	5,682	8,081	6,631
37,450	37,500	7,620	5,696	8,095	6,645
37,500	37,550	7,634	5,710	8,109	6,659
37,550	37,600	7,648	5,724	8,123	6,673
37,600	37,650	7,662	5,738	8,137	6,687
37,650	37,700	7,676	5,752	8,151	6,701
37,700	37,750	7,690	5,766	8,165	6,715
37,750	37,800	7,704	5,780	8,179	6,729
37,800	37,850	7,718	5,794	8,193	6,743
37,850	37,900	7,732	5,808	8,207	6,757
37,900	37,950	7,746	5,822	8,221	6,771
37,950	38,000	7,760	5,836	8,235	6,785

38,000

At least	But less than	Single	Married filing jointly *	Married filing separately	Head of a household
38,000	38,050	7,774	5,850	8,249	6,799
38,050	38,100	7,788	5,864	8,263	6,813
38,100	38,150	7,802	5,878	8,277	6,827
38,150	38,200	7,816	5,892	8,291	6,841
38,200	38,250	7,830	5,906	8,305	6,855
38,250	38,300	7,844	5,920	8,319	6,869
38,300	38,350	7,858	5,934	8,333	6,883
38,350	38,400	7,872	5,948	8,347	6,897
38,400	38,450	7,886	5,962	8,361	6,911
38,450	38,500	7,900	5,976	8,375	6,925
38,500	38,550	7,914	5,990	8,389	6,939
38,550	38,600	7,928	6,004	8,403	6,953
38,600	38,650	7,942	6,018	8,417	6,967
38,650	38,700	7,956	6,032	8,431	6,981
38,700	38,750	7,970	6,046	8,445	6,995
38,750	38,800	7,984	6,060	8,459	7,009
38,800	38,850	7,998	6,074	8,473	7,023
38,850	38,900	8,012	6,088	8,487	7,037
38,900	38,950	8,026	6,102	8,501	7,051
38,950	39,000	8,040	6,116	8,515	7,065

39,000

At least	But less than	Single	Married filing jointly *	Married filing separately	Head of a household
39,000	39,050	8,054	6,130	8,529	7,079
39,050	39,100	8,068	6,144	8,543	7,093
39,100	39,150	8,082	6,158	8,557	7,107
39,150	39,200	8,096	6,172	8,571	7,121
39,200	39,250	8,110	6,186	8,585	7,135
39,250	39,300	8,124	6,200	8,599	7,149
39,300	39,350	8,138	6,214	8,613	7,163
39,350	39,400	8,152	6,228	8,627	7,177
39,400	39,450	8,166	6,242	8,641	7,191
39,450	39,500	8,180	6,256	8,655	7,205
39,500	39,550	8,194	6,270	8,669	7,219
39,550	39,600	8,208	6,284	8,683	7,233
39,600	39,650	8,222	6,298	8,697	7,247
39,650	39,700	8,236	6,312	8,711	7,261
39,700	39,750	8,250	6,326	8,725	7,275
39,750	39,800	8,264	6,340	8,739	7,289
39,800	39,850	8,278	6,354	8,753	7,303
39,850	39,900	8,292	6,368	8,767	7,317
39,900	39,950	8,306	6,382	8,781	7,331
39,950	40,000	8,320	6,396	8,795	7,345

40,000

At least	But less than	Single	Married filing jointly *	Married filing separately	Head of a household
40,000	40,050	8,334	6,410	8,809	7,359
40,050	40,100	8,348	6,424	8,823	7,373
40,100	40,150	8,362	6,438	8,837	7,387
40,150	40,200	8,376	6,452	8,851	7,401
40,200	40,250	8,390	6,466	8,865	7,415
40,250	40,300	8,404	6,480	8,879	7,429
40,300	40,350	8,418	6,494	8,893	7,443
40,350	40,400	8,432	6,508	8,907	7,457
40,400	40,450	8,446	6,522	8,921	7,471
40,450	40,500	8,460	6,536	8,935	7,485
40,500	40,550	8,474	6,550	8,949	7,499
40,550	40,600	8,488	6,564	8,963	7,513
40,600	40,650	8,502	6,578	8,977	7,527
40,650	40,700	8,516	6,592	8,991	7,541
40,700	40,750	8,530	6,606	9,005	7,555
40,750	40,800	8,544	6,620	9,019	7,569
40,800	40,850	8,558	6,634	9,033	7,583
40,850	40,900	8,572	6,648	9,047	7,597
40,900	40,950	8,586	6,662	9,061	7,611
40,950	41,000	8,600	6,676	9,075	7,625

* This column must also be used by a qualifying widow(er).

Continued on next page

If line 6 (Form 1040EZ), line 22 (Form 1040A), or line 37 (Form 1040) is—		And you are—			
At least	But less than	Single	Married filing jointly *	Married filing sepa-rately	Head of a house-hold
		Your tax is—			
41,000					
41,000	**41,050**	8,614	6,690	9,089	7,639
41,050	**41,100**	8,628	6,704	9,103	7,653
41,100	**41,150**	8,642	6,718	9,117	7,667
41,150	**41,200**	8,656	6,732	9,131	7,681
41,200	**41,250**	8,670	6,746	9,145	7,695
41,250	**41,300**	8,684	6,760	9,159	7,709
41,300	**41,350**	8,698	6,774	9,173	7,723
41,350	**41,400**	8,712	6,788	9,187	7,737
41,400	**41,450**	8,726	6,802	9,201	7,751
41,450	**41,500**	8,740	6,816	9,215	7,765
41,500	**41,550**	8,754	6,830	9,229	7,779
41,550	**41,600**	8,768	6,844	9,243	7,793
41,600	**41,650**	8,782	6,858	9,257	7,807
41,650	**41,700**	8,796	6,872	9,271	7,821
41,700	**41,750**	8,810	6,886	9,285	7,835
41,750	**41,800**	8,824	6,900	9,299	7,849
41,800	**41,850**	8,838	6,914	9,313	7,863
41,850	**41,900**	8,852	6,928	9,327	7,877
41,900	**41,950**	8,866	6,942	9,341	7,891
41,950	**42,000**	8,880	6,956	9,355	7,905
42,000					
42,000	**42,050**	8,894	6,970	9,369	7,919
42,050	**42,100**	8,908	6,984	9,383	7,933
42,100	**42,150**	8,922	6,998	9,397	7,947
42,150	**42,200**	8,936	7,012	9,411	7,961
42,200	**42,250**	8,950	7,026	9,425	7,975
42,250	**42,300**	8,964	7,040	9,439	7,989
42,300	**42,350**	8,978	7,054	9,453	8,003
42,350	**42,400**	8,992	7,068	9,467	8,017
42,400	**42,450**	9,006	7,082	9,481	8,031
42,450	**42,500**	9,020	7,096	9,495	8,045
42,500	**42,550**	9,034	7,110	9,509	8,059
42,550	**42,600**	9,048	7,124	9,523	8,073
42,600	**42,650**	9,062	7,138	9,537	8,087
42,650	**42,700**	9,076	7,152	9,551	8,101
42,700	**42,750**	9,090	7,166	9,565	8,115
42,750	**42,800**	9,104	7,180	9,579	8,129
42,800	**42,850**	9,118	7,194	9,593	8,143
42,850	**42,900**	9,132	7,208	9,607	8,157
42,900	**42,950**	9,146	7,222	9,621	8,171
42,950	**43,000**	9,160	7,236	9,635	8,185
43,000					
43,000	**43,050**	9,174	7,250	9,649	8,199
43,050	**43,100**	9,188	7,264	9,663	8,213
43,100	**43,150**	9,202	7,278	9,677	8,227
43,150	**43,200**	9,216	7,292	9,691	8,241
43,200	**43,250**	9,230	7,306	9,705	8,255
43,250	**43,300**	9,244	7,320	9,719	8,269
43,300	**43,350**	9,258	7,334	9,733	8,283
43,350	**43,400**	9,272	7,348	9,747	8,297
43,400	**43,450**	9,286	7,362	9,761	8,311
43,450	**43,500**	9,300	7,376	9,775	8,325
43,500	**43,550**	9,314	7,390	9,789	8,339
43,550	**43,600**	9,328	7,404	9,803	8,353
43,600	**43,650**	9,342	7,418	9,817	8,367
43,650	**43,700**	9,356	7,432	9,831	8,381
43,700	**43,750**	9,370	7,446	9,845	8,395
43,750	**43,800**	9,384	7,460	9,859	8,409
43,800	**43,850**	9,398	7,474	9,873	8,423
43,850	**43,900**	9,412	7,488	9,887	8,437
43,900	**43,950**	9,426	7,502	9,901	8,451
43,950	**44,000**	9,440	7,516	9,915	8,465

If line 6 (Form 1040EZ), line 22 (Form 1040A), or line 37 (Form 1040) is—		And you are—			
At least	But less than	Single	Married filing jointly *	Married filing sepa-rately	Head of a house-hold
		Your tax is—			
44,000					
44,000	**44,050**	9,454	7,530	9,929	8,479
44,050	**44,100**	9,468	7,544	9,943	8,493
44,100	**44,150**	9,482	7,558	9,957	8,507
44,150	**44,200**	9,496	7,572	9,971	8,521
44,200	**44,250**	9,510	7,586	9,985	8,535
44,250	**44,300**	9,524	7,600	9,999	8,549
44,300	**44,350**	9,538	7,614	10,013	8,563
44,350	**44,400**	9,552	7,628	10,027	8,577
44,400	**44,450**	9,566	7,642	10,041	8,591
44,450	**44,500**	9,580	7,656	10,055	8,605
44,500	**44,550**	9,594	7,670	10,069	8,619
44,550	**44,600**	9,608	7,684	10,083	8,633
44,600	**44,650**	9,622	7,698	10,098	8,647
44,650	**44,700**	9,636	7,712	10,114	8,661
44,700	**44,750**	9,650	7,726	10,129	8,675
44,750	**44,800**	9,664	7,740	10,145	8,689
44,800	**44,850**	9,678	7,754	10,160	8,703
44,850	**44,900**	9,692	7,768	10,176	8,717
44,900	**44,950**	9,706	7,782	10,191	8,731
44,950	**45,000**	9,720	7,796	10,207	8,745
45,000					
45,000	**45,050**	9,734	7,810	10,222	8,759
45,050	**45,100**	9,748	7,824	10,238	8,773
45,100	**45,150**	9,762	7,838	10,253	8,787
45,150	**45,200**	9,776	7,852	10,269	8,801
45,200	**45,250**	9,790	7,866	10,284	8,815
45,250	**45,300**	9,804	7,880	10,300	8,829
45,300	**45,350**	9,818	7,894	10,315	8,843
45,350	**45,400**	9,832	7,908	10,331	8,857
45,400	**45,450**	9,846	7,922	10,346	8,871
45,450	**45,500**	9,860	7,936	10,362	8,885
45,500	**45,550**	9,874	7,950	10,377	8,899
45,550	**45,600**	9,888	7,964	10,393	8,913
45,600	**45,650**	9,902	7,978	10,408	8,927
45,650	**45,700**	9,916	7,992	10,424	8,941
45,700	**45,750**	9,930	8,006	10,439	8,955
45,750	**45,800**	9,944	8,020	10,455	8,969
45,800	**45,850**	9,958	8,034	10,470	8,983
45,850	**45,900**	9,972	8,048	10,486	8,997
45,900	**45,950**	9,986	8,062	10,501	9,011
45,950	**46,000**	10,000	8,076	10,517	9,025
46,000					
46,000	**46,050**	10,014	8,090	10,532	9,039
46,050	**46,100**	10,028	8,104	10,548	9,053
46,100	**46,150**	10,042	8,118	10,563	9,067
46,150	**46,200**	10,056	8,132	10,579	9,081
46,200	**46,250**	10,070	8,146	10,594	9,095
46,250	**46,300**	10,084	8,160	10,610	9,109
46,300	**46,350**	10,098	8,174	10,625	9,123
46,350	**46,400**	10,112	8,188	10,641	9,137
46,400	**46,450**	10,126	8,202	10,656	9,151
46,450	**46,500**	10,140	8,216	10,672	9,165
46,500	**46,550**	10,154	8,230	10,687	9,179
46,550	**46,600**	10,168	8,244	10,703	9,193
46,600	**46,650**	10,182	8,258	10,718	9,207
46,650	**46,700**	10,196	8,272	10,734	9,221
46,700	**46,750**	10,210	8,286	10,749	9,235
46,750	**46,800**	10,224	8,300	10,765	9,249
46,800	**46,850**	10,238	8,314	10,780	9,263
46,850	**46,900**	10,252	8,328	10,796	9,277
46,900	**46,950**	10,266	8,342	10,811	9,291
46,950	**47,000**	10,280	8,356	10,827	9,305

If line 6 (Form 1040EZ), line 22 (Form 1040A), or line 37 (Form 1040) is—		And you are—			
At least	But less than	Single	Married filing jointly *	Married filing sepa-rately	Head of a house-hold
		Your tax is—			
47,000					
47,000	**47,050**	10,294	8,370	10,842	9,319
47,050	**47,100**	10,308	8,384	10,858	9,333
47,100	**47,150**	10,322	8,398	10,873	9,347
47,150	**47,200**	10,336	8,412	10,889	9,361
47,200	**47,250**	10,350	8,426	10,904	9,375
47,250	**47,300**	10,364	8,440	10,920	9,389
47,300	**47,350**	10,378	8,454	10,935	9,403
47,350	**47,400**	10,392	8,468	10,951	9,417
47,400	**47,450**	10,406	8,482	10,966	9,431
47,450	**47,500**	10,420	8,496	10,982	9,445
47,500	**47,550**	10,434	8,510	10,997	9,459
47,550	**47,600**	10,448	8,524	11,013	9,473
47,600	**47,650**	10,462	8,538	11,028	9,487
47,650	**47,700**	10,476	8,552	11,044	9,501
47,700	**47,750**	10,490	8,566	11,059	9,515
47,750	**47,800**	10,504	8,580	11,075	9,529
47,800	**47,850**	10,518	8,594	11,090	9,543
47,850	**47,900**	10,532	8,608	11,106	9,557
47,900	**47,950**	10,546	8,622	11,121	9,571
47,950	**48,000**	10,560	8,636	11,137	9,585
48,000					
48,000	**48,050**	10,574	8,650	11,152	9,599
48,050	**48,100**	10,588	8,664	11,168	9,613
48,100	**48,150**	10,602	8,678	11,183	9,627
48,150	**48,200**	10,616	8,692	11,199	9,641
48,200	**48,250**	10,630	8,706	11,214	9,655
48,250	**48,300**	10,644	8,720	11,230	9,669
48,300	**48,350**	10,658	8,734	11,245	9,683
48,350	**48,400**	10,672	8,748	11,261	9,697
48,400	**48,450**	10,686	8,762	11,276	9,711
48,450	**48,500**	10,700	8,776	11,292	9,725
48,500	**48,550**	10,714	8,790	11,307	9,739
48,550	**48,600**	10,728	8,804	11,323	9,753
48,600	**48,650**	10,742	8,818	11,338	9,767
48,650	**48,700**	10,756	8,832	11,354	9,781
48,700	**48,750**	10,770	8,846	11,369	9,795
48,750	**48,800**	10,784	8,860	11,385	9,809
48,800	**48,850**	10,798	8,874	11,400	9,823
48,850	**48,900**	10,812	8,888	11,416	9,837
48,900	**48,950**	10,826	8,902	11,431	9,851
48,950	**49,000**	10,840	8,916	11,447	9,865
49,000					
49,000	**49,050**	10,854	8,930	11,462	9,879
49,050	**49,100**	10,868	8,944	11,478	9,893
49,100	**49,150**	10,882	8,958	11,493	9,907
49,150	**49,200**	10,896	8,972	11,509	9,921
49,200	**49,250**	10,910	8,986	11,524	9,935
49,250	**49,300**	10,924	9,000	11,540	9,949
49,300	**49,350**	10,938	9,014	11,555	9,963
49,350	**49,400**	10,952	9,028	11,571	9,977
49,400	**49,450**	10,966	9,042	11,586	9,991
49,450	**49,500**	10,980	9,056	11,602	10,005
49,500	**49,550**	10,994	9,070	11,617	10,019
49,550	**49,600**	11,008	9,084	11,633	10,033
49,600	**49,650**	11,022	9,098	11,648	10,047
49,650	**49,700**	11,036	9,112	11,664	10,061
49,700	**49,750**	11,050	9,126	11,679	10,075
49,750	**49,800**	11,064	9,140	11,695	10,089
49,800	**49,850**	11,078	9,154	11,710	10,103
49,850	**49,900**	11,092	9,168	11,726	10,117
49,900	**49,950**	11,106	9,182	11,741	10,131
49,950	**50,000**	11,120	9,196	11,757	10,145

* This column must also be used by a qualifying widow(er).

Continued on next page

If line 37 (Form 1040) is—		And you are—			
At least	But less than	Single	Married filing jointly *	Married filing separately	Head of a household
		Your tax is—			

50,000

At least	But less than	Single	Married filing jointly *	Married filing separately	Head of a household
50,000	50,050	11,134	9,210	11,772	10,159
50,050	50,100	11,148	9,224	11,788	10,173
50,100	50,150	11,162	9,238	11,803	10,187
50,150	50,200	11,176	9,252	11,819	10,201
50,200	50,250	11,190	9,266	11,834	10,215
50,250	50,300	11,204	9,280	11,850	10,229
50,300	50,350	11,218	9,294	11,865	10,243
50,350	50,400	11,232	9,308	11,881	10,257
50,400	50,450	11,246	9,322	11,896	10,271
50,450	50,500	11,260	9,336	11,912	10,285
50,500	50,550	11,274	9,350	11,927	10,299
50,550	50,600	11,288	9,364	11,943	10,313
50,600	50,650	11,302	9,378	11,958	10,327
50,650	50,700	11,316	9,392	11,974	10,341
50,700	50,750	11,330	9,406	11,989	10,355
50,750	50,800	11,344	9,420	12,005	10,369
50,800	50,850	11,358	9,434	12,020	10,383
50,850	50,900	11,372	9,448	12,036	10,397
50,900	50,950	11,386	9,462	12,051	10,411
50,950	51,000	11,400	9,476	12,067	10,425

51,000

At least	But less than	Single	Married filing jointly *	Married filing separately	Head of a household
51,000	51,050	11,414	9,490	12,082	10,439
51,050	51,100	11,428	9,504	12,098	10,453
51,100	51,150	11,442	9,518	12,113	10,467
51,150	51,200	11,456	9,532	12,129	10,481
51,200	51,250	11,470	9,546	12,144	10,495
51,250	51,300	11,484	9,560	12,160	10,509
51,300	51,350	11,498	9,574	12,175	10,523
51,350	51,400	11,512	9,588	12,191	10,537
51,400	51,450	11,526	9,602	12,206	10,551
51,450	51,500	11,540	9,616	12,222	10,565
51,500	51,550	11,554	9,630	12,237	10,579
51,550	51,600	11,568	9,644	12,253	10,593
51,600	51,650	11,582	9,658	12,268	10,607
51,650	51,700	11,596	9,672	12,284	10,621
51,700	51,750	11,610	9,686	12,299	10,635
51,750	51,800	11,624	9,700	12,315	10,649
51,800	51,850	11,638	9,714	12,330	10,663
51,850	51,900	11,652	9,728	12,346	10,677
51,900	51,950	11,666	9,742	12,361	10,691
51,950	52,000	11,680	9,756	12,377	10,705

52,000

At least	But less than	Single	Married filing jointly *	Married filing separately	Head of a household
52,000	52,050	11,694	9,770	12,392	10,719
52,050	52,100	11,708	9,784	12,408	10,733
52,100	52,150	11,722	9,798	12,423	10,747
52,150	52,200	11,736	9,812	12,439	10,761
52,200	52,250	11,750	9,826	12,454	10,775
52,250	52,300	11,764	9,840	12,470	10,789
52,300	52,350	11,778	9,854	12,485	10,803
52,350	52,400	11,792	9,868	12,501	10,817
52,400	52,450	11,806	9,882	12,516	10,831
52,450	52,500	11,820	9,896	12,532	10,845
52,500	52,550	11,834	9,910	12,547	10,859
52,550	52,600	11,848	9,924	12,563	10,873
52,600	52,650	11,862	9,938	12,578	10,887
52,650	52,700	11,876	9,952	12,594	10,901
52,700	52,750	11,890	9,966	12,609	10,915
52,750	52,800	11,904	9,980	12,625	10,929
52,800	52,850	11,918	9,994	12,640	10,943
52,850	52,900	11,932	10,008	12,656	10,957
52,900	52,950	11,946	10,022	12,671	10,971
52,950	53,000	11,960	10,036	12,687	10,985

53,000

At least	But less than	Single	Married filing jointly *	Married filing separately	Head of a household
53,000	53,050	11,974	10,050	12,702	10,999
53,050	53,100	11,988	10,064	12,718	11,013
53,100	53,150	12,002	10,078	12,733	11,027
53,150	53,200	12,016	10,092	12,749	11,041
53,200	53,250	12,030	10,106	12,764	11,055
53,250	53,300	12,044	10,120	12,780	11,069
53,300	53,350	12,058	10,134	12,795	11,083
53,350	53,400	12,072	10,148	12,811	11,097
53,400	53,450	12,086	10,162	12,826	11,111
53,450	53,500	12,100	10,176	12,842	11,125
53,500	53,550	12,115	10,190	12,857	11,139
53,550	53,600	12,130	10,204	12,873	11,153
53,600	53,650	12,146	10,218	12,888	11,167
53,650	53,700	12,161	10,232	12,904	11,181
53,700	53,750	12,177	10,246	12,919	11,195
53,750	53,800	12,192	10,260	12,935	11,209
53,800	53,850	12,208	10,274	12,950	11,223
53,850	53,900	12,223	10,288	12,966	11,237
53,900	53,950	12,239	10,302	12,981	11,251
53,950	54,000	12,254	10,316	12,997	11,265

54,000

At least	But less than	Single	Married filing jointly *	Married filing separately	Head of a household
54,000	54,050	12,270	10,330	13,012	11,279
54,050	54,100	12,285	10,344	13,028	11,293
54,100	54,150	12,301	10,358	13,043	11,307
54,150	54,200	12,316	10,372	13,059	11,321
54,200	54,250	12,332	10,386	13,074	11,335
54,250	54,300	12,347	10,400	13,090	11,349
54,300	54,350	12,363	10,414	13,105	11,363
54,350	54,400	12,378	10,428	13,121	11,377
54,400	54,450	12,394	10,442	13,136	11,391
54,450	54,500	12,409	10,456	13,152	11,405
54,500	54,550	12,425	10,470	13,167	11,419
54,550	54,600	12,440	10,484	13,183	11,433
54,600	54,650	12,456	10,498	13,198	11,447
54,650	54,700	12,471	10,512	13,214	11,461
54,700	54,750	12,487	10,526	13,229	11,475
54,750	54,800	12,502	10,540	13,245	11,489
54,800	54,850	12,518	10,554	13,260	11,503
54,850	54,900	12,533	10,568	13,276	11,517
54,900	54,950	12,549	10,582	13,291	11,531
54,950	55,000	12,564	10,596	13,307	11,545

55,000

At least	But less than	Single	Married filing jointly *	Married filing separately	Head of a household
55,000	55,050	12,580	10,610	13,322	11,559
55,050	55,100	12,595	10,624	13,338	11,573
55,100	55,150	12,611	10,638	13,353	11,587
55,150	55,200	12,626	10,652	13,369	11,601
55,200	55,250	12,642	10,666	13,384	11,615
55,250	55,300	12,657	10,680	13,400	11,629
55,300	55,350	12,673	10,694	13,415	11,643
55,350	55,400	12,688	10,708	13,431	11,657
55,400	55,450	12,704	10,722	13,446	11,671
55,450	55,500	12,719	10,736	13,462	11,685
55,500	55,550	12,735	10,750	13,477	11,699
55,550	55,600	12,750	10,764	13,493	11,713
55,600	55,650	12,766	10,778	13,508	11,727
55,650	55,700	12,781	10,792	13,524	11,741
55,700	55,750	12,797	10,806	13,539	11,755
55,750	55,800	12,812	10,820	13,555	11,769
55,800	55,850	12,828	10,834	13,570	11,783
55,850	55,900	12,843	10,848	13,586	11,797
55,900	55,950	12,859	10,862	13,601	11,811
55,950	56,000	12,874	10,876	13,617	11,825

56,000

At least	But less than	Single	Married filing jointly *	Married filing separately	Head of a household
56,000	56,050	12,890	10,890	13,632	11,839
56,050	56,100	12,905	10,904	13,648	11,853
56,100	56,150	12,921	10,918	13,663	11,867
56,150	56,200	12,936	10,932	13,679	11,881
56,200	56,250	12,952	10,946	13,694	11,895
56,250	56,300	12,967	10,960	13,710	11,909
56,300	56,350	12,983	10,974	13,725	11,923
56,350	56,400	12,998	10,988	13,741	11,937
56,400	56,450	13,014	11,002	13,756	11,951
56,450	56,500	13,029	11,016	13,772	11,965
56,500	56,550	13,045	11,030	13,787	11,979
56,550	56,600	13,060	11,044	13,803	11,993
56,600	56,650	13,076	11,058	13,818	12,007
56,650	56,700	13,091	11,072	13,834	12,021
56,700	56,750	13,107	11,086	13,849	12,035
56,750	56,800	13,122	11,100	13,865	12,049
56,800	56,850	13,138	11,114	13,880	12,063
56,850	56,900	13,153	11,128	13,896	12,077
56,900	56,950	13,169	11,142	13,911	12,091
56,950	57,000	13,184	11,156	13,927	12,105

57,000

At least	But less than	Single	Married filing jointly *	Married filing separately	Head of a household
57,000	57,050	13,200	11,170	13,942	12,119
57,050	57,100	13,215	11,184	13,958	12,133
57,100	57,150	13,231	11,198	13,973	12,147
57,150	57,200	13,246	11,212	13,989	12,161
57,200	57,250	13,262	11,226	14,004	12,175
57,250	57,300	13,277	11,240	14,020	12,189
57,300	57,350	13,293	11,254	14,035	12,203
57,350	57,400	13,308	11,268	14,051	12,217
57,400	57,450	13,324	11,282	14,066	12,231
57,450	57,500	13,339	11,296	14,082	12,245
57,500	57,550	13,355	11,310	14,097	12,259
57,550	57,600	13,370	11,324	14,113	12,273
57,600	57,650	13,386	11,338	14,128	12,287
57,650	57,700	13,401	11,352	14,144	12,301
57,700	57,750	13,417	11,366	14,159	12,315
57,750	57,800	13,432	11,380	14,175	12,329
57,800	57,850	13,448	11,394	14,190	12,343
57,850	57,900	13,463	11,408	14,206	12,357
57,900	57,950	13,479	11,422	14,221	12,371
57,950	58,000	13,494	11,436	14,237	12,385

58,000

At least	But less than	Single	Married filing jointly *	Married filing separately	Head of a household
58,000	58,050	13,510	11,450	14,252	12,399
58,050	58,100	13,525	11,464	14,268	12,413
58,100	58,150	13,541	11,478	14,283	12,427
58,150	58,200	13,556	11,492	14,299	12,441
58,200	58,250	13,572	11,506	14,314	12,455
58,250	58,300	13,587	11,520	14,330	12,469
58,300	58,350	13,603	11,534	14,345	12,483
58,350	58,400	13,618	11,548	14,361	12,497
58,400	58,450	13,634	11,562	14,376	12,511
58,450	58,500	13,649	11,576	14,392	12,525
58,500	58,550	13,665	11,590	14,407	12,539
58,550	58,600	13,680	11,604	14,423	12,553
58,600	58,650	13,696	11,618	14,438	12,567
58,650	58,700	13,711	11,632	14,454	12,581
58,700	58,750	13,727	11,646	14,469	12,595
58,750	58,800	13,742	11,660	14,485	12,609
58,800	58,850	13,758	11,674	14,500	12,623
58,850	58,900	13,773	11,688	14,516	12,637
58,900	58,950	13,789	11,702	14,531	12,651
58,950	59,000	13,804	11,716	14,547	12,665

* This column must also be used by a qualifying widow(er).

Continued on next page

59,000

If line 37 (Form 1040) is— At least	But less than	Single	Married filing jointly *	Married filing separately	Head of a household
59,000	59,050	13,820	11,730	14,562	12,679
59,050	59,100	13,835	11,744	14,578	12,693
59,100	59,150	13,851	11,758	14,593	12,707
59,150	59,200	13,866	11,772	14,609	12,721
59,200	59,250	13,882	11,786	14,624	12,735
59,250	59,300	13,897	11,800	14,640	12,749
59,300	59,350	13,913	11,814	14,655	12,763
59,350	59,400	13,928	11,828	14,671	12,777
59,400	59,450	13,944	11,842	14,686	12,791
59,450	59,500	13,959	11,856	14,702	12,805
59,500	59,550	13,975	11,870	14,717	12,819
59,550	59,600	13,990	11,884	14,733	12,833
59,600	59,650	14,006	11,898	14,748	12,847
59,650	59,700	14,021	11,912	14,764	12,861
59,700	59,750	14,037	11,926	14,779	12,875
59,750	59,800	14,052	11,940	14,795	12,889
59,800	59,850	14,068	11,954	14,810	12,903
59,850	59,900	14,083	11,968	14,826	12,917
59,900	59,950	14,099	11,982	14,841	12,931
59,950	60,000	14,114	11,996	14,857	12,945

60,000

At least	But less than	Single	Married filing jointly *	Married filing separately	Head of a household
60,000	60,050	14,130	12,010	14,872	12,959
60,050	60,100	14,145	12,024	14,888	12,973
60,100	60,150	14,161	12,038	14,903	12,987
60,150	60,200	14,176	12,052	14,919	13,001
60,200	60,250	14,192	12,066	14,934	13,015
60,250	60,300	14,207	12,080	14,950	13,029
60,300	60,350	14,223	12,094	14,965	13,043
60,350	60,400	14,238	12,108	14,981	13,057
60,400	60,450	14,254	12,122	14,996	13,071
60,450	60,500	14,269	12,136	15,012	13,085
60,500	60,550	14,285	12,150	15,027	13,099
60,550	60,600	14,300	12,164	15,043	13,113
60,600	60,650	14,316	12,178	15,058	13,127
60,650	60,700	14,331	12,192	15,074	13,141
60,700	60,750	14,347	12,206	15,089	13,155
60,750	60,800	14,362	12,220	15,105	13,169
60,800	60,850	14,378	12,234	15,120	13,183
60,850	60,900	14,393	12,248	15,136	13,197
60,900	60,950	14,409	12,262	15,151	13,211
60,950	61,000	14,424	12,276	15,167	13,225

61,000

At least	But less than	Single	Married filing jointly *	Married filing separately	Head of a household
61,000	61,050	14,440	12,290	15,182	13,239
61,050	61,100	14,455	12,304	15,198	13,253
61,100	61,150	14,471	12,318	15,213	13,267
61,150	61,200	14,486	12,332	15,229	13,281
61,200	61,250	14,502	12,346	15,244	13,295
61,250	61,300	14,517	12,360	15,260	13,309
61,300	61,350	14,533	12,374	15,275	13,323
61,350	61,400	14,548	12,388	15,291	13,337
61,400	61,450	14,564	12,402	15,306	13,351
61,450	61,500	14,579	12,416	15,322	13,365
61,500	61,550	14,595	12,430	15,337	13,379
61,550	61,600	14,610	12,444	15,353	13,393
61,600	61,650	14,626	12,458	15,368	13,407
61,650	61,700	14,641	12,472	15,384	13,421
61,700	61,750	14,657	12,486	15,399	13,435
61,750	61,800	14,672	12,500	15,415	13,449
61,800	61,850	14,688	12,514	15,430	13,463
61,850	61,900	14,703	12,528	15,446	13,477
61,900	61,950	14,719	12,542	15,461	13,491
61,950	62,000	14,734	12,556	15,477	13,505

62,000

At least	But less than	Single	Married filing jointly *	Married filing separately	Head of a household
62,000	62,050	14,750	12,570	15,492	13,519
62,050	62,100	14,765	12,584	15,508	13,533
62,100	62,150	14,781	12,598	15,523	13,547
62,150	62,200	14,796	12,612	15,539	13,561
62,200	62,250	14,812	12,626	15,554	13,575
62,250	62,300	14,827	12,640	15,570	13,589
62,300	62,350	14,843	12,654	15,585	13,603
62,350	62,400	14,858	12,668	15,601	13,617
62,400	62,450	14,874	12,682	15,616	13,631
62,450	62,500	14,889	12,696	15,632	13,645
62,500	62,550	14,905	12,710	15,647	13,659
62,550	62,600	14,920	12,724	15,663	13,673
62,600	62,650	14,936	12,738	15,678	13,687
62,650	62,700	14,951	12,752	15,694	13,701
62,700	62,750	14,967	12,766	15,709	13,715
62,750	62,800	14,982	12,780	15,725	13,729
62,800	62,850	14,998	12,794	15,740	13,743
62,850	62,900	15,013	12,808	15,756	13,757
62,900	62,950	15,029	12,822	15,771	13,771
62,950	63,000	15,044	12,836	15,787	13,785

63,000

At least	But less than	Single	Married filing jointly *	Married filing separately	Head of a household
63,000	63,050	15,060	12,850	15,802	13,799
63,050	63,100	15,075	12,864	15,818	13,813
63,100	63,150	15,091	12,878	15,833	13,827
63,150	63,200	15,106	12,892	15,849	13,841
63,200	63,250	15,122	12,906	15,864	13,855
63,250	63,300	15,137	12,920	15,880	13,869
63,300	63,350	15,153	12,934	15,895	13,883
63,350	63,400	15,168	12,948	15,911	13,897
63,400	63,450	15,184	12,962	15,926	13,911
63,450	63,500	15,199	12,976	15,942	13,925
63,500	63,550	15,215	12,990	15,957	13,939
63,550	63,600	15,230	13,004	15,973	13,953
63,600	63,650	15,246	13,018	15,988	13,967
63,650	63,700	15,261	13,032	16,004	13,981
63,700	63,750	15,277	13,046	16,019	13,995
63,750	63,800	15,292	13,060	16,035	14,009
63,800	63,850	15,308	13,074	16,050	14,023
63,850	63,900	15,323	13,088	16,066	14,037
63,900	63,950	15,339	13,102	16,081	14,051
63,950	64,000	15,354	13,116	16,097	14,065

64,000

At least	But less than	Single	Married filing jointly *	Married filing separately	Head of a household
64,000	64,050	15,370	13,130	16,112	14,079
64,050	64,100	15,385	13,144	16,128	14,093
64,100	64,150	15,401	13,158	16,143	14,107
64,150	64,200	15,416	13,172	16,159	14,121
64,200	64,250	15,432	13,186	16,174	14,135
64,250	64,300	15,447	13,200	16,190	14,149
64,300	64,350	15,463	13,214	16,205	14,163
64,350	64,400	15,478	13,228	16,221	14,177
64,400	64,450	15,494	13,242	16,236	14,191
64,450	64,500	15,509	13,256	16,252	14,205
64,500	64,550	15,525	13,270	16,267	14,219
64,550	64,600	15,540	13,284	16,283	14,233
64,600	64,650	15,556	13,298	16,298	14,247
64,650	64,700	15,571	13,312	16,314	14,261
64,700	64,750	15,587	13,326	16,329	14,275
64,750	64,800	15,602	13,340	16,345	14,289
64,800	64,850	15,618	13,354	16,360	14,303
64,850	64,900	15,633	13,368	16,376	14,317
64,900	64,950	15,649	13,382	16,391	14,331
64,950	65,000	15,664	13,396	16,407	14,345

65,000

At least	But less than	Single	Married filing jointly *	Married filing separately	Head of a household
65,000	65,050	15,680	13,410	16,422	14,359
65,050	65,100	15,695	13,424	16,438	14,373
65,100	65,150	15,711	13,438	16,453	14,387
65,150	65,200	15,726	13,452	16,469	14,401
65,200	65,250	15,742	13,466	16,484	14,415
65,250	65,300	15,757	13,480	16,500	14,429
65,300	65,350	15,773	13,494	16,515	14,443
65,350	65,400	15,788	13,508	16,531	14,457
65,400	65,450	15,804	13,522	16,546	14,471
65,450	65,500	15,819	13,536	16,562	14,485
65,500	65,550	15,835	13,550	16,577	14,499
65,550	65,600	15,850	13,564	16,593	14,513
65,600	65,650	15,866	13,578	16,608	14,527
65,650	65,700	15,881	13,592	16,624	14,541
65,700	65,750	15,897	13,606	16,639	14,555
65,750	65,800	15,912	13,620	16,655	14,569
65,800	65,850	15,928	13,634	16,670	14,583
65,850	65,900	15,943	13,648	16,686	14,597
65,900	65,950	15,959	13,662	16,701	14,611
65,950	66,000	15,974	13,676	16,717	14,625

66,000

At least	But less than	Single	Married filing jointly *	Married filing separately	Head of a household
66,000	66,050	15,990	13,690	16,732	14,639
66,050	66,100	16,005	13,704	16,748	14,653
66,100	66,150	16,021	13,718	16,763	14,667
66,150	66,200	16,036	13,732	16,779	14,681
66,200	66,250	16,052	13,746	16,794	14,695
66,250	66,300	16,067	13,760	16,810	14,709
66,300	66,350	16,083	13,774	16,825	14,723
66,350	66,400	16,098	13,788	16,841	14,737
66,400	66,450	16,114	13,802	16,856	14,751
66,450	66,500	16,129	13,816	16,872	14,765
66,500	66,550	16,145	13,830	16,887	14,779
66,550	66,600	16,160	13,844	16,903	14,793
66,600	66,650	16,176	13,858	16,918	14,807
66,650	66,700	16,191	13,872	16,934	14,821
66,700	66,750	16,207	13,886	16,949	14,835
66,750	66,800	16,222	13,900	16,965	14,849
66,800	66,850	16,238	13,914	16,980	14,863
66,850	66,900	16,253	13,928	16,996	14,877
66,900	66,950	16,269	13,942	17,011	14,891
66,950	67,000	16,284	13,956	17,027	14,905

67,000

At least	But less than	Single	Married filing jointly *	Married filing separately	Head of a household
67,000	67,050	16,300	13,970	17,042	14,919
67,050	67,100	16,315	13,984	17,058	14,933
67,100	67,150	16,331	13,998	17,073	14,947
67,150	67,200	16,346	14,012	17,089	14,961
67,200	67,250	16,362	14,026	17,104	14,975
67,250	67,300	16,377	14,040	17,120	14,989
67,300	67,350	16,393	14,054	17,135	15,003
67,350	67,400	16,408	14,068	17,151	15,017
67,400	67,450	16,424	14,082	17,166	15,031
67,450	67,500	16,439	14,096	17,182	15,045
67,500	67,550	16,455	14,110	17,197	15,059
67,550	67,600	16,470	14,124	17,213	15,073
67,600	67,650	16,486	14,138	17,228	15,087
67,650	67,700	16,501	14,152	17,244	15,101
67,700	67,750	16,517	14,166	17,259	15,115
67,750	67,800	16,532	14,180	17,275	15,129
67,800	67,850	16,548	14,194	17,290	15,143
67,850	67,900	16,563	14,208	17,306	15,157
67,900	67,950	16,579	14,222	17,321	15,171
67,950	68,000	16,594	14,236	17,337	15,185

* This column must also be used by a qualifying widow(er).

Continued on next page

68,000

If line 37 (Form 1040) is— At least	But less than	Single	Married filing jointly*	Married filing separately	Head of a household
68,000	68,050	16,610	14,250	17,352	15,199
68,050	68,100	16,625	14,264	17,368	15,213
68,100	68,150	16,641	14,278	17,383	15,227
68,150	68,200	16,656	14,292	17,399	15,241
68,200	68,250	16,672	14,306	17,414	15,255
68,250	68,300	16,687	14,320	17,430	15,269
68,300	68,350	16,703	14,334	17,445	15,283
68,350	68,400	16,718	14,348	17,461	15,297
68,400	68,450	16,734	14,362	17,476	15,311
68,450	68,500	16,749	14,376	17,492	15,325
68,500	68,550	16,765	14,390	17,507	15,339
68,550	68,600	16,780	14,404	17,523	15,353
68,600	68,650	16,796	14,418	17,538	15,367
68,650	68,700	16,811	14,432	17,554	15,381
68,700	68,750	16,827	14,446	17,569	15,395
68,750	68,800	16,842	14,460	17,585	15,409
68,800	68,850	16,858	14,474	17,600	15,423
68,850	68,900	16,873	14,488	17,616	15,437
68,900	68,950	16,889	14,502	17,631	15,451
68,950	69,000	16,904	14,516	17,647	15,465

69,000

At least	But less than	Single	Married filing jointly*	Married filing separately	Head of a household
69,000	69,050	16,920	14,530	17,662	15,479
69,050	69,100	16,935	14,544	17,678	15,493
69,100	69,150	16,951	14,558	17,693	15,507
69,150	69,200	16,966	14,572	17,709	15,521
69,200	69,250	16,982	14,586	17,724	15,535
69,250	69,300	16,997	14,600	17,740	15,549
69,300	69,350	17,013	14,614	17,755	15,563
69,350	69,400	17,028	14,628	17,771	15,577
69,400	69,450	17,044	14,642	17,786	15,591
69,450	69,500	17,059	14,656	17,802	15,605
69,500	69,550	17,075	14,670	17,817	15,619
69,550	69,600	17,090	14,684	17,833	15,633
69,600	69,650	17,106	14,698	17,848	15,647
69,650	69,700	17,121	14,712	17,864	15,661
69,700	69,750	17,137	14,726	17,879	15,675
69,750	69,800	17,152	14,740	17,895	15,689
69,800	69,850	17,168	14,754	17,910	15,703
69,850	69,900	17,183	14,768	17,926	15,717
69,900	69,950	17,199	14,782	17,941	15,731
69,950	70,000	17,214	14,796	17,957	15,745

70,000

At least	But less than	Single	Married filing jointly*	Married filing separately	Head of a household
70,000	70,050	17,230	14,810	17,973	15,759
70,050	70,100	17,245	14,824	17,991	15,773
70,100	70,150	17,261	14,838	18,009	15,787
70,150	70,200	17,276	14,852	18,027	15,801
70,200	70,250	17,292	14,866	18,045	15,815
70,250	70,300	17,307	14,880	18,063	15,829
70,300	70,350	17,323	14,894	18,081	15,843
70,350	70,400	17,338	14,908	18,099	15,857
70,400	70,450	17,354	14,922	18,117	15,871
70,450	70,500	17,369	14,936	18,135	15,885
70,500	70,550	17,385	14,950	18,153	15,899
70,550	70,600	17,400	14,964	18,171	15,913
70,600	70,650	17,416	14,978	18,189	15,927
70,650	70,700	17,431	14,992	18,207	15,941
70,700	70,750	17,447	15,006	18,225	15,955
70,750	70,800	17,462	15,020	18,243	15,969
70,800	70,850	17,478	15,034	18,261	15,983
70,850	70,900	17,493	15,048	18,279	15,997
70,900	70,950	17,509	15,062	18,297	16,011
70,950	71,000	17,524	15,076	18,315	16,025

71,000

At least	But less than	Single	Married filing jointly*	Married filing separately	Head of a household
71,000	71,050	17,540	15,090	18,333	16,039
71,050	71,100	17,555	15,104	18,351	16,053
71,100	71,150	17,571	15,118	18,369	16,067
71,150	71,200	17,586	15,132	18,387	16,081
71,200	71,250	17,602	15,146	18,405	16,095
71,250	71,300	17,617	15,160	18,423	16,109
71,300	71,350	17,633	15,174	18,441	16,123
71,350	71,400	17,648	15,188	18,459	16,137
71,400	71,450	17,664	15,202	18,477	16,151
71,450	71,500	17,679	15,216	18,495	16,165
71,500	71,550	17,695	15,230	18,513	16,179
71,550	71,600	17,710	15,244	18,531	16,193
71,600	71,650	17,726	15,258	18,549	16,207
71,650	71,700	17,741	15,272	18,567	16,221
71,700	71,750	17,757	15,286	18,585	16,235
71,750	71,800	17,772	15,300	18,603	16,249
71,800	71,850	17,788	15,314	18,621	16,263
71,850	71,900	17,803	15,328	18,639	16,277
71,900	71,950	17,819	15,342	18,657	16,291
71,950	72,000	17,834	15,356	18,675	16,305

72,000

At least	But less than	Single	Married filing jointly*	Married filing separately	Head of a household
72,000	72,050	17,850	15,370	18,693	16,319
72,050	72,100	17,865	15,384	18,711	16,333
72,100	72,150	17,881	15,398	18,729	16,347
72,150	72,200	17,896	15,412	18,747	16,361
72,200	72,250	17,912	15,426	18,765	16,375
72,250	72,300	17,927	15,440	18,783	16,389
72,300	72,350	17,943	15,454	18,801	16,403
72,350	72,400	17,958	15,468	18,819	16,417
72,400	72,450	17,974	15,482	18,837	16,431
72,450	72,500	17,989	15,496	18,855	16,445
72,500	72,550	18,005	15,510	18,873	16,459
72,550	72,600	18,020	15,524	18,891	16,473
72,600	72,650	18,036	15,538	18,909	16,487
72,650	72,700	18,051	15,552	18,927	16,501
72,700	72,750	18,067	15,566	18,945	16,515
72,750	72,800	18,082	15,580	18,963	16,529
72,800	72,850	18,098	15,594	18,981	16,543
72,850	72,900	18,113	15,608	18,999	16,557
72,900	72,950	18,129	15,622	19,017	16,571
72,950	73,000	18,144	15,636	19,035	16,585

73,000

At least	But less than	Single	Married filing jointly*	Married filing separately	Head of a household
73,000	73,050	18,160	15,650	19,053	16,599
73,050	73,100	18,175	15,664	19,071	16,613
73,100	73,150	18,191	15,678	19,089	16,627
73,150	73,200	18,206	15,692	19,107	16,641
73,200	73,250	18,222	15,706	19,125	16,655
73,250	73,300	18,237	15,720	19,143	16,669
73,300	73,350	18,253	15,734	19,161	16,683
73,350	73,400	18,268	15,748	19,179	16,697
73,400	73,450	18,284	15,762	19,197	16,711
73,450	73,500	18,299	15,776	19,215	16,725
73,500	73,550	18,315	15,790	19,233	16,739
73,550	73,600	18,330	15,804	19,251	16,753
73,600	73,650	18,346	15,818	19,269	16,767
73,650	73,700	18,361	15,832	19,287	16,781
73,700	73,750	18,377	15,846	19,305	16,795
73,750	73,800	18,392	15,860	19,323	16,809
73,800	73,850	18,408	15,874	19,341	16,823
73,850	73,900	18,423	15,888	19,359	16,837
73,900	73,950	18,439	15,902	19,377	16,851
73,950	74,000	18,454	15,916	19,395	16,865

74,000

At least	But less than	Single	Married filing jointly*	Married filing separately	Head of a household
74,000	74,050	18,470	15,930	19,413	16,879
74,050	74,100	18,485	15,944	19,431	16,893
74,100	74,150	18,501	15,958	19,449	16,907
74,150	74,200	18,516	15,972	19,467	16,921
74,200	74,250	18,532	15,986	19,485	16,935
74,250	74,300	18,547	16,000	19,503	16,949
74,300	74,350	18,563	16,014	19,521	16,963
74,350	74,400	18,578	16,028	19,539	16,977
74,400	74,450	18,594	16,042	19,557	16,991
74,450	74,500	18,609	16,056	19,575	17,005
74,500	74,550	18,625	16,070	19,593	17,019
74,550	74,600	18,640	16,084	19,611	17,033
74,600	74,650	18,656	16,098	19,629	17,047
74,650	74,700	18,671	16,112	19,647	17,061
74,700	74,750	18,687	16,126	19,665	17,075
74,750	74,800	18,702	16,140	19,683	17,089
74,800	74,850	18,718	16,154	19,701	17,103
74,850	74,900	18,733	16,168	19,719	17,117
74,900	74,950	18,749	16,182	19,737	17,131
74,950	75,000	18,764	16,196	19,755	17,145

75,000

At least	But less than	Single	Married filing jointly*	Married filing separately	Head of a household
75,000	75,050	18,780	16,210	19,773	17,159
75,050	75,100	18,795	16,224	19,791	17,173
75,100	75,150	18,811	16,238	19,809	17,187
75,150	75,200	18,826	16,252	19,827	17,201
75,200	75,250	18,842	16,266	19,845	17,215
75,250	75,300	18,857	16,280	19,863	17,229
75,300	75,350	18,873	16,294	19,881	17,243
75,350	75,400	18,888	16,308	19,899	17,257
75,400	75,450	18,904	16,322	19,917	17,271
75,450	75,500	18,919	16,336	19,935	17,285
75,500	75,550	18,935	16,350	19,953	17,299
75,550	75,600	18,950	16,364	19,971	17,313
75,600	75,650	18,966	16,378	19,989	17,327
75,650	75,700	18,981	16,392	20,007	17,341
75,700	75,750	18,997	16,406	20,025	17,355
75,750	75,800	19,012	16,420	20,043	17,369
75,800	75,850	19,028	16,434	20,061	17,383
75,850	75,900	19,043	16,448	20,079	17,397
75,900	75,950	19,059	16,462	20,097	17,411
75,950	76,000	19,074	16,476	20,115	17,425

76,000

At least	But less than	Single	Married filing jointly*	Married filing separately	Head of a household
76,000	76,050	19,090	16,490	20,133	17,439
76,050	76,100	19,105	16,504	20,151	17,453
76,100	76,150	19,121	16,518	20,169	17,467
76,150	76,200	19,136	16,532	20,187	17,481
76,200	76,250	19,152	16,546	20,205	17,495
76,250	76,300	19,167	16,560	20,223	17,509
76,300	76,350	19,183	16,574	20,241	17,523
76,350	76,400	19,198	16,588	20,259	17,537
76,400	76,450	19,214	16,602	20,277	17,552
76,450	76,500	19,229	16,616	20,295	17,567
76,500	76,550	19,245	16,630	20,313	17,583
76,550	76,600	19,260	16,644	20,331	17,598
76,600	76,650	19,276	16,658	20,349	17,614
76,650	76,700	19,291	16,672	20,367	17,629
76,700	76,750	19,307	16,686	20,385	17,645
76,750	76,800	19,322	16,700	20,403	17,660
76,800	76,850	19,338	16,714	20,421	17,676
76,850	76,900	19,353	16,728	20,439	17,691
76,900	76,950	19,369	16,742	20,457	17,707
76,950	77,000	19,384	16,756	20,475	17,722

* This column must also be used by a qualifying widow(er).

Continued on next page

1993 Tax Table—*Continued*

If line 37 (Form 1040) is—		And you are—			
At least	But less than	Single	Married filing jointly *	Married filing separately	Head of a household
		Your tax is—			

77,000

At least	But less than	Single	Married filing jointly	Married filing separately	Head of a household
77,000	77,050	19,400	16,770	20,493	17,738
77,050	77,100	19,415	16,784	20,511	17,753
77,100	77,150	19,431	16,798	20,529	17,769
77,150	77,200	19,446	16,812	20,547	17,784
77,200	77,250	19,462	16,826	20,565	17,800
77,250	77,300	19,477	16,840	20,583	17,815
77,300	77,350	19,493	16,854	20,601	17,831
77,350	77,400	19,508	16,868	20,619	17,846
77,400	77,450	19,524	16,882	20,637	17,862
77,450	77,500	19,539	16,896	20,655	17,877
77,500	77,550	19,555	16,910	20,673	17,893
77,550	77,600	19,570	16,924	20,691	17,908
77,600	77,650	19,586	16,938	20,709	17,924
77,650	77,700	19,601	16,952	20,727	17,939
77,700	77,750	19,617	16,966	20,745	17,955
77,750	77,800	19,632	16,980	20,763	17,970
77,800	77,850	19,648	16,994	20,781	17,986
77,850	77,900	19,663	17,008	20,799	18,001
77,900	77,950	19,679	17,022	20,817	18,017
77,950	78,000	19,694	17,036	20,835	18,032

78,000

At least	But less than	Single	Married filing jointly	Married filing separately	Head of a household
78,000	78,050	19,710	17,050	20,853	18,048
78,050	78,100	19,725	17,064	20,871	18,063
78,100	78,150	19,741	17,078	20,889	18,079
78,150	78,200	19,756	17,092	20,907	18,094
78,200	78,250	19,772	17,106	20,925	18,110
78,250	78,300	19,787	17,120	20,943	18,125
78,300	78,350	19,803	17,134	20,961	18,141
78,350	78,400	19,818	17,148	20,979	18,156
78,400	78,450	19,834	17,162	20,997	18,172
78,450	78,500	19,849	17,176	21,015	18,187
78,500	78,550	19,865	17,190	21,033	18,203
78,550	78,600	19,880	17,204	21,051	18,218
78,600	78,650	19,896	17,218	21,069	18,234
78,650	78,700	19,911	17,232	21,087	18,249
78,700	78,750	19,927	17,246	21,105	18,265
78,750	78,800	19,942	17,260	21,123	18,280
78,800	78,850	19,958	17,274	21,141	18,296
78,850	78,900	19,973	17,288	21,159	18,311
78,900	78,950	19,989	17,302	21,177	18,327
78,950	79,000	20,004	17,316	21,195	18,342

79,000

At least	But less than	Single	Married filing jointly	Married filing separately	Head of a household
79,000	79,050	20,020	17,330	21,213	18,358
79,050	79,100	20,035	17,344	21,231	18,373
79,100	79,150	20,051	17,358	21,249	18,389
79,150	79,200	20,066	17,372	21,267	18,404
79,200	79,250	20,082	17,386	21,285	18,420
79,250	79,300	20,097	17,400	21,303	18,435
79,300	79,350	20,113	17,414	21,321	18,451
79,350	79,400	20,128	17,428	21,339	18,466
79,400	79,450	20,144	17,442	21,357	18,482
79,450	79,500	20,159	17,456	21,375	18,497
79,500	79,550	20,175	17,470	21,393	18,513
79,550	79,600	20,190	17,484	21,411	18,528
79,600	79,650	20,206	17,498	21,429	18,544
79,650	79,700	20,221	17,512	21,447	18,559
79,700	79,750	20,237	17,526	21,465	18,575
79,750	79,800	20,252	17,540	21,483	18,590
79,800	79,850	20,268	17,554	21,501	18,606
79,850	79,900	20,283	17,568	21,519	18,621
79,900	79,950	20,299	17,582	21,537	18,637
79,950	80,000	20,314	17,596	21,555	18,652

80,000

At least	But less than	Single	Married filing jointly	Married filing separately	Head of a household
80,000	80,050	20,330	17,610	21,573	18,668
80,050	80,100	20,345	17,624	21,591	18,683
80,100	80,150	20,361	17,638	21,609	18,699
80,150	80,200	20,376	17,652	21,627	18,714
80,200	80,250	20,392	17,666	21,645	18,730
80,250	80,300	20,407	17,680	21,663	18,745
80,300	80,350	20,423	17,694	21,681	18,761
80,350	80,400	20,438	17,708	21,699	18,776
80,400	80,450	20,454	17,722	21,717	18,792
80,450	80,500	20,469	17,736	21,735	18,807
80,500	80,550	20,485	17,750	21,753	18,823
80,550	80,600	20,500	17,764	21,771	18,838
80,600	80,650	20,516	17,778	21,789	18,854
80,650	80,700	20,531	17,792	21,807	18,869
80,700	80,750	20,547	17,806	21,825	18,885
80,750	80,800	20,562	17,820	21,843	18,900
80,800	80,850	20,578	17,834	21,861	18,916
80,850	80,900	20,593	17,848	21,879	18,931
80,900	80,950	20,609	17,862	21,897	18,947
80,950	81,000	20,624	17,876	21,915	18,962

81,000

At least	But less than	Single	Married filing jointly	Married filing separately	Head of a household
81,000	81,050	20,640	17,890	21,933	18,978
81,050	81,100	20,655	17,904	21,951	18,993
81,100	81,150	20,671	17,918	21,969	19,009
81,150	81,200	20,686	17,932	21,987	19,024
81,200	81,250	20,702	17,946	22,005	19,040
81,250	81,300	20,717	17,960	22,023	19,055
81,300	81,350	20,733	17,974	22,041	19,071
81,350	81,400	20,748	17,988	22,059	19,086
81,400	81,450	20,764	18,002	22,077	19,102
81,450	81,500	20,779	18,016	22,095	19,117
81,500	81,550	20,795	18,030	22,113	19,133
81,550	81,600	20,810	18,044	22,131	19,148
81,600	81,650	20,826	18,058	22,149	19,164
81,650	81,700	20,841	18,072	22,167	19,179
81,700	81,750	20,857	18,086	22,185	19,195
81,750	81,800	20,872	18,100	22,203	19,210
81,800	81,850	20,888	18,114	22,221	19,226
81,850	81,900	20,903	18,128	22,239	19,241
81,900	81,950	20,919	18,142	22,257	19,257
81,950	82,000	20,934	18,156	22,275	19,272

82,000

At least	But less than	Single	Married filing jointly	Married filing separately	Head of a household
82,000	82,050	20,950	18,170	22,293	19,288
82,050	82,100	20,965	18,184	22,311	19,303
82,100	82,150	20,981	18,198	22,329	19,319
82,150	82,200	20,996	18,212	22,347	19,334
82,200	82,250	21,012	18,226	22,365	19,350
82,250	82,300	21,027	18,240	22,383	19,365
82,300	82,350	21,043	18,254	22,401	19,381
82,350	82,400	21,058	18,268	22,419	19,396
82,400	82,450	21,074	18,282	22,437	19,412
82,450	82,500	21,089	18,296	22,455	19,427
82,500	82,550	21,105	18,310	22,473	19,443
82,550	82,600	21,120	18,324	22,491	19,458
82,600	82,650	21,136	18,338	22,509	19,474
82,650	82,700	21,151	18,352	22,527	19,489
82,700	82,750	21,167	18,366	22,545	19,505
82,750	82,800	21,182	18,380	22,563	19,520
82,800	82,850	21,198	18,394	22,581	19,536
82,850	82,900	21,213	18,408	22,599	19,551
82,900	82,950	21,229	18,422	22,617	19,567
82,950	83,000	21,244	18,436	22,635	19,582

83,000

At least	But less than	Single	Married filing jointly	Married filing separately	Head of a household
83,000	83,050	21,260	18,450	22,653	19,598
83,050	83,100	21,275	18,464	22,671	19,613
83,100	83,150	21,291	18,478	22,689	19,629
83,150	83,200	21,306	18,492	22,707	19,644
83,200	83,250	21,322	18,506	22,725	19,660
83,250	83,300	21,337	18,520	22,743	19,675
83,300	83,350	21,353	18,534	22,761	19,691
83,350	83,400	21,368	18,548	22,779	19,706
83,400	83,450	21,384	18,562	22,797	19,722
83,450	83,500	21,399	18,576	22,815	19,737
83,500	83,550	21,415	18,590	22,833	19,753
83,550	83,600	21,430	18,604	22,851	19,768
83,600	83,650	21,446	18,618	22,869	19,784
83,650	83,700	21,461	18,632	22,887	19,799
83,700	83,750	21,477	18,646	22,905	19,815
83,750	83,800	21,492	18,660	22,923	19,830
83,800	83,850	21,508	18,674	22,941	19,846
83,850	83,900	21,523	18,688	22,959	19,861
83,900	83,950	21,539	18,702	22,977	19,877
83,950	84,000	21,554	18,716	22,995	19,892

84,000

At least	But less than	Single	Married filing jointly	Married filing separately	Head of a household
84,000	84,050	21,570	18,730	23,013	19,908
84,050	84,100	21,585	18,744	23,031	19,923
84,100	84,150	21,601	18,758	23,049	19,939
84,150	84,200	21,616	18,772	23,067	19,954
84,200	84,250	21,632	18,786	23,085	19,970
84,250	84,300	21,647	18,800	23,103	19,985
84,300	84,350	21,663	18,814	23,121	20,001
84,350	84,400	21,678	18,828	23,139	20,016
84,400	84,450	21,694	18,842	23,157	20,032
84,450	84,500	21,709	18,856	23,175	20,047
84,500	84,550	21,725	18,870	23,193	20,063
84,550	84,600	21,740	18,884	23,211	20,078
84,600	84,650	21,756	18,898	23,229	20,094
84,650	84,700	21,771	18,912	23,247	20,109
84,700	84,750	21,787	18,926	23,265	20,125
84,750	84,800	21,802	18,940	23,283	20,140
84,800	84,850	21,818	18,954	23,301	20,156
84,850	84,900	21,833	18,968	23,319	20,171
84,900	84,950	21,849	18,982	23,337	20,187
84,950	85,000	21,864	18,996	23,355	20,202

85,000

At least	But less than	Single	Married filing jointly	Married filing separately	Head of a household
85,000	85,050	21,880	19,010	23,373	20,218
85,050	85,100	21,895	19,024	23,391	20,233
85,100	85,150	21,911	19,038	23,409	20,249
85,150	85,200	21,926	19,052	23,427	20,264
85,200	85,250	21,942	19,066	23,445	20,280
85,250	85,300	21,957	19,080	23,463	20,295
85,300	85,350	21,973	19,094	23,481	20,311
85,350	85,400	21,988	19,108	23,499	20,326
85,400	85,450	22,004	19,122	23,517	20,342
85,450	85,500	22,019	19,136	23,535	20,357
85,500	85,550	22,035	19,150	23,553	20,373
85,550	85,600	22,050	19,164	23,571	20,388
85,600	85,650	22,066	19,178	23,589	20,404
85,650	85,700	22,081	19,192	23,607	20,419
85,700	85,750	22,097	19,206	23,625	20,435
85,750	85,800	22,112	19,220	23,643	20,450
85,800	85,850	22,128	19,234	23,661	20,466
85,850	85,900	22,143	19,248	23,679	20,481
85,900	85,950	22,159	19,262	23,697	20,497
85,950	86,000	22,174	19,276	23,715	20,512

* This column must also be used by a qualifying widow(er).

Continued on next page

86,000

At least	But less than	Single	Married filing jointly *	Married filing separately	Head of a household
86,000	86,050	22,190	19,290	23,733	20,528
86,050	86,100	22,205	19,304	23,751	20,543
86,100	86,150	22,221	19,318	23,769	20,559
86,150	86,200	22,236	19,332	23,787	20,574
86,200	86,250	22,252	19,346	23,805	20,590
86,250	86,300	22,267	19,360	23,823	20,605
86,300	86,350	22,283	19,374	23,841	20,621
86,350	86,400	22,298	19,388	23,859	20,636
86,400	86,450	22,314	19,402	23,877	20,652
86,450	86,500	22,329	19,416	23,895	20,667
86,500	86,550	22,345	19,430	23,913	20,683
86,550	86,600	22,360	19,444	23,931	20,698
86,600	86,650	22,376	19,458	23,949	20,714
86,650	86,700	22,391	19,472	23,967	20,729
86,700	86,750	22,407	19,486	23,985	20,745
86,750	86,800	22,422	19,500	24,003	20,760
86,800	86,850	22,438	19,514	24,021	20,776
86,850	86,900	22,453	19,528	24,039	20,791
86,900	86,950	22,469	19,542	24,057	20,807
86,950	87,000	22,484	19,556	24,075	20,822

87,000

At least	But less than	Single	Married filing jointly *	Married filing separately	Head of a household
87,000	87,050	22,500	19,570	24,093	20,838
87,050	87,100	22,515	19,584	24,111	20,853
87,100	87,150	22,531	19,598	24,129	20,869
87,150	87,200	22,546	19,612	24,147	20,884
87,200	87,250	22,562	19,626	24,165	20,900
87,250	87,300	22,577	19,640	24,183	20,915
87,300	87,350	22,593	19,654	24,201	20,931
87,350	87,400	22,608	19,668	24,219	20,946
87,400	87,450	22,624	19,682	24,237	20,962
87,450	87,500	22,639	19,696	24,255	20,977
87,500	87,550	22,655	19,710	24,273	20,993
87,550	87,600	22,670	19,724	24,291	21,008
87,600	87,650	22,686	19,738	24,309	21,024
87,650	87,700	22,701	19,752	24,327	21,039
87,700	87,750	22,717	19,766	24,345	21,055
87,750	87,800	22,732	19,780	24,363	21,070
87,800	87,850	22,748	19,794	24,381	21,086
87,850	87,900	22,763	19,808	24,399	21,101
87,900	87,950	22,779	19,822	24,417	21,117
87,950	88,000	22,794	19,836	24,435	21,132

88,000

At least	But less than	Single	Married filing jointly *	Married filing separately	Head of a household
88,000	88,050	22,810	19,850	24,453	21,148
88,050	88,100	22,825	19,864	24,471	21,163
88,100	88,150	22,841	19,878	24,489	21,179
88,150	88,200	22,856	19,892	24,507	21,194
88,200	88,250	22,872	19,906	24,525	21,210
88,250	88,300	22,887	19,920	24,543	21,225
88,300	88,350	22,903	19,934	24,561	21,241
88,350	88,400	22,918	19,948	24,579	21,256
88,400	88,450	22,934	19,962	24,597	21,272
88,450	88,500	22,949	19,976	24,615	21,287
88,500	88,550	22,965	19,990	24,633	21,303
88,550	88,600	22,980	20,004	24,651	21,318
88,600	88,650	22,996	20,018	24,669	21,334
88,650	88,700	23,011	20,032	24,687	21,349
88,700	88,750	23,027	20,046	24,705	21,365
88,750	88,800	23,042	20,060	24,723	21,380
88,800	88,850	23,058	20,074	24,741	21,396
88,850	88,900	23,073	20,088	24,759	21,411
88,900	88,950	23,089	20,102	24,777	21,427
88,950	89,000	23,104	20,116	24,795	21,442

89,000

At least	But less than	Single	Married filing jointly *	Married filing separately	Head of a household
89,000	89,050	23,120	20,130	24,813	21,458
89,050	89,100	23,135	20,144	24,831	21,473
89,100	89,150	23,151	20,158	24,849	21,489
89,150	89,200	23,166	20,173	24,867	21,504
89,200	89,250	23,182	20,188	24,885	21,520
89,250	89,300	23,197	20,204	24,903	21,535
89,300	89,350	23,213	20,219	24,921	21,551
89,350	89,400	23,228	20,235	24,939	21,566
89,400	89,450	23,244	20,250	24,957	21,582
89,450	89,500	23,259	20,266	24,975	21,597
89,500	89,550	23,275	20,281	24,993	21,613
89,550	89,600	23,290	20,297	25,011	21,628
89,600	89,650	23,306	20,312	25,029	21,644
89,650	89,700	23,321	20,328	25,047	21,659
89,700	89,750	23,337	20,343	25,065	21,675
89,750	89,800	23,352	20,359	25,083	21,690
89,800	89,850	23,368	20,374	25,101	21,706
89,850	89,900	23,383	20,390	25,119	21,721
89,900	89,950	23,399	20,405	25,137	21,737
89,950	90,000	23,414	20,421	25,155	21,752

90,000

At least	But less than	Single	Married filing jointly *	Married filing separately	Head of a household
90,000	90,050	23,430	20,436	25,173	21,768
90,050	90,100	23,445	20,452	25,191	21,783
90,100	90,150	23,461	20,467	25,209	21,799
90,150	90,200	23,476	20,483	25,227	21,814
90,200	90,250	23,492	20,498	25,245	21,830
90,250	90,300	23,507	20,514	25,263	21,845
90,300	90,350	23,523	20,529	25,281	21,861
90,350	90,400	23,538	20,545	25,299	21,876
90,400	90,450	23,554	20,560	25,317	21,892
90,450	90,500	23,569	20,576	25,335	21,907
90,500	90,550	23,585	20,591	25,353	21,923
90,550	90,600	23,600	20,607	25,371	21,938
90,600	90,650	23,616	20,622	25,389	21,954
90,650	90,700	23,631	20,638	25,407	21,969
90,700	90,750	23,647	20,653	25,425	21,985
90,750	90,800	23,662	20,669	25,443	22,000
90,800	90,850	23,678	20,684	25,461	22,016
90,850	90,900	23,693	20,700	25,479	22,031
90,900	90,950	23,709	20,715	25,497	22,047
90,950	91,000	23,724	20,731	25,515	22,062

91,000

At least	But less than	Single	Married filing jointly *	Married filing separately	Head of a household
91,000	91,050	23,740	20,746	25,533	22,078
91,050	91,100	23,755	20,762	25,551	22,093
91,100	91,150	23,771	20,777	25,569	22,109
91,150	91,200	23,786	20,793	25,587	22,124
91,200	91,250	23,802	20,808	25,605	22,140
91,250	91,300	23,817	20,824	25,623	22,155
91,300	91,350	23,833	20,839	25,641	22,171
91,350	91,400	23,848	20,855	25,659	22,186
91,400	91,450	23,864	20,870	25,677	22,202
91,450	91,500	23,879	20,886	25,695	22,217
91,500	91,550	23,895	20,901	25,713	22,233
91,550	91,600	23,910	20,917	25,731	22,248
91,600	91,650	23,926	20,932	25,749	22,264
91,650	91,700	23,941	20,948	25,767	22,279
91,700	91,750	23,957	20,963	25,785	22,295
91,750	91,800	23,972	20,979	25,803	22,310
91,800	91,850	23,988	20,994	25,821	22,326
91,850	91,900	24,003	21,010	25,839	22,341
91,900	91,950	24,019	21,025	25,857	22,357
91,950	92,000	24,034	21,041	25,875	22,372

92,000

At least	But less than	Single	Married filing jointly *	Married filing separately	Head of a household
92,000	92,050	24,050	21,056	25,893	22,388
92,050	92,100	24,065	21,072	25,911	22,403
92,100	92,150	24,081	21,087	25,929	22,419
92,150	92,200	24,096	21,103	25,947	22,434
92,200	92,250	24,112	21,118	25,965	22,450
92,250	92,300	24,127	21,134	25,983	22,465
92,300	92,350	24,143	21,149	26,001	22,481
92,350	92,400	24,158	21,165	26,019	22,496
92,400	92,450	24,174	21,180	26,037	22,512
92,450	92,500	24,189	21,196	26,055	22,527
92,500	92,550	24,205	21,211	26,073	22,543
92,550	92,600	24,220	21,227	26,091	22,558
92,600	92,650	24,236	21,242	26,109	22,574
92,650	92,700	24,251	21,258	26,127	22,589
92,700	92,750	24,267	21,273	26,145	22,605
92,750	92,800	24,282	21,289	26,163	22,620
92,800	92,850	24,298	21,304	26,181	22,636
92,850	92,900	24,313	21,320	26,199	22,651
92,900	92,950	24,329	21,335	26,217	22,667
92,950	93,000	24,344	21,351	26,235	22,682

93,000

At least	But less than	Single	Married filing jointly *	Married filing separately	Head of a household
93,000	93,050	24,360	21,366	26,253	22,698
93,050	93,100	24,375	21,382	26,271	22,713
93,100	93,150	24,391	21,397	26,289	22,729
93,150	93,200	24,406	21,413	26,307	22,744
93,200	93,250	24,422	21,428	26,325	22,760
93,250	93,300	24,437	21,444	26,343	22,775
93,300	93,350	24,453	21,459	26,361	22,791
93,350	93,400	24,468	21,475	26,379	22,806
93,400	93,450	24,484	21,490	26,397	22,822
93,450	93,500	24,499	21,506	26,415	22,837
93,500	93,550	24,515	21,521	26,433	22,853
93,550	93,600	24,530	21,537	26,451	22,868
93,600	93,650	24,546	21,552	26,469	22,884
93,650	93,700	24,561	21,568	26,487	22,899
93,700	93,750	24,577	21,583	26,505	22,915
93,750	93,800	24,592	21,599	26,523	22,930
93,800	93,850	24,608	21,614	26,541	22,946
93,850	93,900	24,623	21,630	26,559	22,961
93,900	93,950	24,639	21,645	26,577	22,977
93,950	94,000	24,654	21,661	26,595	22,992

94,000

At least	But less than	Single	Married filing jointly *	Married filing separately	Head of a household
94,000	94,050	24,670	21,676	26,613	23,008
94,050	94,100	24,685	21,692	26,631	23,023
94,100	94,150	24,701	21,707	26,649	23,039
94,150	94,200	24,716	21,723	26,667	23,054
94,200	94,250	24,732	21,738	26,685	23,070
94,250	94,300	24,747	21,754	26,703	23,085
94,300	94,350	24,763	21,769	26,721	23,101
94,350	94,400	24,778	21,785	26,739	23,116
94,400	94,450	24,794	21,800	26,757	23,132
94,450	94,500	24,809	21,816	26,775	23,147
94,500	94,550	24,825	21,831	26,793	23,163
94,550	94,600	24,840	21,847	26,811	23,178
94,600	94,650	24,856	21,862	26,829	23,194
94,650	94,700	24,871	21,878	26,847	23,209
94,700	94,750	24,887	21,893	26,865	23,225
94,750	94,800	24,902	21,909	26,883	23,240
94,800	94,850	24,918	21,924	26,901	23,256
94,850	94,900	24,933	21,940	26,919	23,271
94,900	94,950	24,949	21,955	26,937	23,287
94,950	95,000	24,964	21,971	26,955	23,302

* This column must also be used by a qualifying widow(er).

Continued on next page

If line 37 (Form 1040) is—		And you are—				If line 37 (Form 1040) is—		And you are—			
At least	But less than	Single	Married filing jointly *	Married filing separately	Head of a household	At least	But less than	Single	Married filing jointly *	Married filing separately	Head of a household
		Your tax is—						Your tax is—			

95,000

At least	But less than	Single	MFJ	MFS	HoH
95,000	95,050	24,980	21,986	26,973	23,318
95,050	95,100	24,995	22,002	26,991	23,333
95,100	95,150	25,011	22,017	27,009	23,349
95,150	95,200	25,026	22,033	27,027	23,364
95,200	95,250	25,042	22,048	27,045	23,380
95,250	95,300	25,057	22,064	27,063	23,395
95,300	95,350	25,073	22,079	27,081	23,411
95,350	95,400	25,088	22,095	27,099	23,426
95,400	95,450	25,104	22,110	27,117	23,442
95,450	95,500	25,119	22,126	27,135	23,457
95,500	95,550	25,135	22,141	27,153	23,473
95,550	95,600	25,150	22,157	27,171	23,488
95,600	95,650	25,166	22,172	27,189	23,504
95,650	95,700	25,181	22,188	27,207	23,519
95,700	95,750	25,197	22,203	27,225	23,535
95,750	95,800	25,212	22,219	27,243	23,550
95,800	95,850	25,228	22,234	27,261	23,566
95,850	95,900	25,243	22,250	27,279	23,581
95,900	95,950	25,259	22,265	27,297	23,597
95,950	96,000	25,274	22,281	27,315	23,612

96,000

At least	But less than	Single	MFJ	MFS	HoH
96,000	96,050	25,290	22,296	27,333	23,628
96,050	96,100	25,305	22,312	27,351	23,643
96,100	96,150	25,321	22,327	27,369	23,659
96,150	96,200	25,336	22,343	27,387	23,674
96,200	96,250	25,352	22,358	27,405	23,690
96,250	96,300	25,367	22,374	27,423	23,705
96,300	96,350	25,383	22,389	27,441	23,721
96,350	96,400	25,398	22,405	27,459	23,736
96,400	96,450	25,414	22,420	27,477	23,752
96,450	96,500	25,429	22,436	27,495	23,767
96,500	96,550	25,445	22,451	27,513	23,783
96,550	96,600	25,460	22,467	27,531	23,798
96,600	96,650	25,476	22,482	27,549	23,814
96,650	96,700	25,491	22,498	27,567	23,829
96,700	96,750	25,507	22,513	27,585	23,845
96,750	96,800	25,522	22,529	27,603	23,860
96,800	96,850	25,538	22,544	27,621	23,876
96,850	96,900	25,553	22,560	27,639	23,891
96,900	96,950	25,569	22,575	27,657	23,907
96,950	97,000	25,584	22,591	27,675	23,922

97,000

At least	But less than	Single	MFJ	MFS	HoH
97,000	97,050	25,600	22,606	27,693	23,938
97,050	97,100	25,615	22,622	27,711	23,953
97,100	97,150	25,631	22,637	27,729	23,969
97,150	97,200	25,646	22,653	27,747	23,984
97,200	97,250	25,662	22,668	27,765	24,000
97,250	97,300	25,677	22,684	27,783	24,015
97,300	97,350	25,693	22,699	27,801	24,031
97,350	97,400	25,708	22,715	27,819	24,046
97,400	97,450	25,724	22,730	27,837	24,062
97,450	97,500	25,739	22,746	27,855	24,077
97,500	97,550	25,755	22,761	27,873	24,093
97,550	97,600	25,770	22,777	27,891	24,108
97,600	97,650	25,786	22,792	27,909	24,124
97,650	97,700	25,801	22,808	27,927	24,139
97,700	97,750	25,817	22,823	27,945	24,155
97,750	97,800	25,832	22,839	27,963	24,170
97,800	97,850	25,848	22,854	27,981	24,186
97,850	97,900	25,863	22,870	27,999	24,201
97,900	97,950	25,879	22,885	28,017	24,217
97,950	98,000	25,894	22,901	28,035	24,232

98,000

At least	But less than	Single	MFJ	MFS	HoH
98,000	98,050	25,910	22,916	28,053	24,248
98,050	98,100	25,925	22,932	28,071	24,263
98,100	98,150	25,941	22,947	28,089	24,279
98,150	98,200	25,956	22,963	28,107	24,294
98,200	98,250	25,972	22,978	28,125	24,310
98,250	98,300	25,987	22,994	28,143	24,325
98,300	98,350	26,003	23,009	28,161	24,341
98,350	98,400	26,018	23,025	28,179	24,356
98,400	98,450	26,034	23,040	28,197	24,372
98,450	98,500	26,049	23,056	28,215	24,387
98,500	98,550	26,065	23,071	28,233	24,403
98,550	98,600	26,080	23,087	28,251	24,418
98,600	98,650	26,096	23,102	28,269	24,434
98,650	98,700	26,111	23,118	28,287	24,449
98,700	98,750	26,127	23,133	28,305	24,465
98,750	98,800	26,142	23,149	28,323	24,480
98,800	98,850	26,158	23,164	28,341	24,496
98,850	98,900	26,173	23,180	28,359	24,511
98,900	98,950	26,189	23,195	28,377	24,527
98,950	99,000	26,204	23,211	28,395	24,542

99,000

At least	But less than	Single	MFJ	MFS	HoH
99,000	99,050	26,220	23,226	28,413	24,558
99,050	99,100	26,235	23,242	28,431	24,573
99,100	99,150	26,251	23,257	28,449	24,589
99,150	99,200	26,266	23,273	28,467	24,604
99,200	99,250	26,282	23,288	28,485	24,620
99,250	99,300	26,297	23,304	28,503	24,635
99,300	99,350	26,313	23,319	28,521	24,651
99,350	99,400	26,328	23,335	28,539	24,666
99,400	99,450	26,344	23,350	28,557	24,682
99,450	99,500	26,359	23,366	28,575	24,697
99,500	99,550	26,375	23,381	28,593	24,713
99,550	99,600	26,390	23,397	28,611	24,728
99,600	99,650	26,406	23,412	28,629	24,744
99,650	99,700	26,421	23,428	28,647	24,759
99,700	99,750	26,437	23,443	28,665	24,775
99,750	99,800	26,452	23,459	28,683	24,790
99,800	99,850	26,468	23,474	28,701	24,806
99,850	99,900	26,483	23,490	28,719	24,821
99,900	99,950	26,499	23,505	28,737	24,837
99,950	100,000	26,514	23,521	28,755	24,852

$100,000 or over — use Tax Rate Schedules

* This column must also be used by a qualifying widow(er).

1993
Tax Rate
Schedules

Caution: *Use **only** if your taxable income (Form 1040, line 37) is $100,000 or more. If less, use the **Tax Table**. Even though you cannot use the tax rate schedules below if your taxable income is less than $100,000, all levels of taxable income are shown so taxpayers can see the tax rate that applies to each level.*

Schedule X—Use if your filing status is **Single**

If the amount on Form 1040, line 37, is: Over—	But not over—	Enter on Form 1040, line 38		of the amount over—
$0	$22,100	.... 15%		$0
22,100	53,500	$3,315.00 +	28%	22,100
53,500	115,000	12,107.00 +	31%	53,500
115,000	250,000	31,172.00 +	36%	115,000
250,000	....	79,772.00 +	39.6%	250,000

Schedule Y-1—Use if your filing status is **Married filing jointly** or **Qualifying widow(er)**

If the amount on Form 1040, line 37, is: Over—	But not over—	Enter on Form 1040, line 38		of the amount over—
$0	$36,900	.... 15%		$0
36,900	89,150	$5,535.00 +	28%	36,900
89,150	140,000	20,165.00 +	31%	89,150
140,000	250,000	35,928.50 +	36%	140,000
250,000	....	75,528.50 +	39.6%	250,000

Schedule Y-2—Use if your filing status is **Married filing separately**

If the amount on Form 1040, line 37, is: Over—	But not over—	Enter on Form 1040, line 38		of the amount over—
$0	$18,450	.... 15%		$0
18,450	44,575	$2,767.50 +	28%	18,450
44,575	70,000	10,082.50 +	31%	44,575
70,000	125,000	17,964.25 +	36%	70,000
125,000	....	37,764.25 +	39.6%	125,000

Schedule Z—Use if your filing status is **Head of household**

If the amount on Form 1040, line 37, is: Over—	But not over—	Enter on Form 1040, line 38		of the amount over—
$0	$29,600	.... 15%		$0
29,600	76,400	$4,440.00 +	28%	29,600
76,400	127,500	17,544.00 +	31%	76,400
127,500	250,000	33,385.00 +	36%	127,500
250,000	....	77,485.00 +	39.6%	250,000

Where To Report Certain Items From 1993 Forms W-2, 1098, and 1099

Report any Federal income tax withheld from these forms on Form 1040, line 54. If you itemize your deductions, report any state or local income tax withheld from these forms on Schedule A, line 5.

Form	Item and Box in Which It Should Appear	Where To Report if Filing Form 1040
W-2	Wages, salaries, tips, etc. (box 1)	Form 1040, line 7
	Allocated tips (box 8)	See **Tip Income**
	Advance EIC payments (box 9)	Form 1040, line 52
	Dependent care benefits (box 10)	Form 2441, line 11
W-2G	Gambling winnings (box 1)	Form 1040, line 22 (Schedule C or C-EZ for professional gamblers)
1098	Mortgage interest (box 1)	Schedule A, line 9a*
	Points (box 2)	Schedule A, line 9a*
	Refund of overpaid interest (box 3)	See the instructions for Form 1040, line 22*
1099-A	Acquisition or abandonment of secured property	See Pub. 544
1099-B	Stocks, bonds, etc. (box 2)	Schedule D
	Bartering (box 3)	See Pub. 525
	Futures contracts (box 9)	Form 6781
1099-DIV	Ordinary dividends (box 1b)	Form 1040, line 9
	Capital gain distributions (box 1c)	Form 1040, line 14 (or Schedule D)
	Nontaxable distributions (box 1d)	See the instructions for Form 1040, line 9
	Investment expenses (box 1e)	Form 1040, line 9, and Schedule A, line 20
	Foreign tax paid (box 3)	Schedule A, line 7 (or Form 1116)
1099-G	Unemployment compensation (box 1)	Form 1040, line 20. But if you repaid any unemployment compensation in 1993, see the instructions for line 20
	State or local income tax refund (box 2)	See the instructions for Form 1040, line 10*
	Discharge of indebtedness (box 5)	Form 1040, line 22, but first see Pub. 908*
	Taxable grants (box 6)	Form 1040, line 22*
	Agriculture payments (box 7)	See the Schedule F instructions or Pub. 225
1099-INT	Interest income (box 1)	Form 1040, line 8a
	Early withdrawal penalty (box 2)	Form 1040, line 28
	Interest on U.S. savings bonds and Treasury obligations (box 3)	See the instructions for Form 1040, line 8a
	Foreign tax paid (box 5)	Schedule A, line 7 (or Form 1116)
1099-MISC	Rents (box 1)	See the instructions for Schedule E
	Royalties (box 2)	Schedule E, line 4 (timber, coal, iron ore royalties, see Pub. 544)
	Prizes, awards, etc. (box 3)	Form 1040, line 22
	Nonemployee compensation (box 7)	Schedule C, C-EZ, or F (Form 1040, line 7, if you were not self-employed)
	Other income (boxes 5, 6, 8, 9, and 10)	See the instructions on Form 1099-MISC
1099-OID	Original issue discount (box 1)	See the instructions for Form 1040, line 8a
	Other periodic interest (box 2)	See the instructions on Form 1099-OID
	Early withdrawal penalty (box 3)	Form 1040, line 28
1099-PATR	Patronage dividends and other distributions from a cooperative (boxes 1, 2, 3, and 5)	Schedule C, Schedule C-EZ, Schedule F, or Form 4835, but first see the instructions on Form 1099-PATR
	Credits (boxes 6, 7, and 8)	Form 3468 or Form 5884
1099-R	Distributions from IRAs	See the instructions for Form 1040, lines 16a and 16b
	Distributions from pensions, annuities, etc.	See the instructions for Form 1040, lines 17a and 17b
	Capital gain (box 3)	See the instructions on Form 1099-R
1099-S	Gross proceeds from real estate transactions (box 2)	Form 2119 (or Form 4797 or Schedule D if the property was not your home)
	Buyer's part of real estate tax (box 5)	See the instructions for Schedule A, line 6*

* If the item relates to an activity for which you are required to file Schedule C, C-EZ, E, or F, or Form 4835, report the taxable or deductible amount allocable to the activity on that schedule or form instead.

List of IRS Tax Publications

You can use the order blank in this publication to send for any other IRS tax publications you need. Many of these free publications are listed below. A full list can be found in Publication 910, *Guide to Free Tax Services*.

You can also use the order blank to send for any tax forms, schedules, or instructions you need.

You can also call 1–800–TAX–FORM (1–800–829–3676) to order publications and tax forms.

General Guides

1
Your Rights as a Taxpayer

225
Farmer's Tax Guide

334
Tax Guide for Small Business

509
Tax Calendars for 1994

553
Highlights of 1993 Tax Changes

595
Tax Guide for Commercial Fishermen

910
Guide to Free Tax Services

Specialized Publications

3
Tax Information for Military Personnel (Including Reservists Called to Active Duty)

4
Student's Guide to Federal Income Tax

15
Circular E, Employer's Tax Guide

54
Tax Guide for U.S. Citizens and Resident Aliens Abroad

378
Fuel Tax Credits and Refunds

448
Federal Estate and Gift Taxes

463
Travel, Entertainment, and Gift Expenses

501
Exemptions, Standard Deduction, and Filing Information

502
Medical and Dental Expenses

503
Child and Dependent Care Expenses

504
Divorced or Separated Individuals

505
Tax Withholding and Estimated Tax

508
Educational Expenses

510
Excise Taxes for 1994

513
Tax Information for Visitors to the United States

514
Foreign Tax Credit for Individuals

516
Tax Information for U.S. Government Civilian Employees Stationed Abroad

517
Social Security and Other Information for Members of the Clergy and Religious Workers

519
U.S. Tax Guide for Aliens

520
Scholarships and Fellowships

521
Moving Expenses

523
Selling Your Home

524
Credit for the Elderly or the Disabled

525
Taxable and Nontaxable Income

526
Charitable Contributions

527
Residential Rental Property

529
Miscellaneous Deductions

530
Tax Information for First-Time Homeowners

531
Reporting Tip Income

533
Self-Employment Tax

534
Depreciation

535
Business Expenses

536
Net Operating Losses

537
Installment Sales

538
Accounting Periods and Methods

541
Tax Information on Partnerships

542
Tax Information on Corporations

544
Sales and Other Dispositions of Assets

547
Nonbusiness Disasters, Casualties, and Thefts

550
Investment Income and Expenses

551
Basis of Assets

552
Recordkeeping for Individuals

554
Tax Information for Older Americans

555
Federal Tax Information on Community Property

556
Examination of Returns, Appeal Rights, and Claims for Refund

557
Tax-Exempt Status for Your Organization

559
Survivors, Executors, and Administrators

560
Retirement Plans for the Self-Employed

561
Determining the Value of Donated Property

564
Mutual Fund Distributions

570
Tax Guide for Individuals With Income from U.S. Possessions

571
Tax-Sheltered Annuity Programs for Employees of Public Schools and Certain Tax-Exempt Organizations

575
Pension and Annuity Income (Including Simplified General Rule)

583
Taxpayers Starting a Business

584
Nonbusiness Disaster, Casualty, and Theft Loss Workbook

587
Business Use of Your Home

589
Tax Information on S Corporations

590
Individual Retirement Arrangements (IRAs)

593
Tax Highlights for U.S. Citizens and Residents Going Abroad

594
Understanding the Collection Process

596
Earned Income Credit

597
Information on the United States-Canada Income Tax Treaty

721
Tax Guide to U.S. Civil Service Retirement Benefits

901
U.S. Tax Treaties

907
Information for Persons with Disabilities

908
Bankruptcy and Other Debt Cancellation

909
Alternative Minimum Tax for Individuals

911
Tax Information for Direct Sellers

How to Get IRS Forms and Publications

You can visit your local IRS office or order tax forms and publications from the IRS Forms Distribution Center listed for your state at the address below. Or, if you prefer, you can photocopy tax forms from reproducible copies kept at participating public libraries. In addition, many of these libraries have reference sets of IRS publications that you can read or copy.

If you are located in:

Alaska, Arizona, California, Colorado, Hawaii, Idaho, Kansas, Montana, Nevada, New Mexico, Oklahoma, Oregon, Utah, Washington, Wyoming, Guam, Northern Marianas, American Samoa

Alabama, Arkansas, Illinois, Indiana, Iowa, Kentucky, Louisiana, Michigan, Minnesota, Mississippi, Missouri, Nebraska, North Dakota, Ohio, South Dakota, Tennessee, Texas, Wisconsin

Connecticut, Delaware, District of Columbia, Florida, Georgia, Maine, Maryland, Massachusetts, New Hampshire, New Jersey, New York, North Carolina, Pennsylvania, Rhode Island, South Carolina, Vermont, Virginia, West Virginia

Send to "Forms Distribution Center" for your state

Western Area Distribution Center
Rancho Cordova, CA 95743-0001

Central Area Distribution Center
P.O. Box 8903
Bloomington, IL 61702-8903

Eastern Area Distribution Center
P.O. Box 85074
Richmond, VA 23261-5074

Foreign Addresses—Taxpayers with mailing addresses in foreign countries should send their requests for forms and publications to:

Eastern Area Distribution Center
P.O. Box 85074
Richmond, VA 23261-5074
or
Western Area Distribution Center
Rancho Cordova, CA 95743-0001,
whichever is closer.

Puerto Rico
Eastern Area Distribution Center
P.O. Box 85074
Richmond, VA 23261-5074

Virgin Islands
V.I. Bureau of Internal Revenue
Lockharts Garden, No. 1A
Charlotte Amalie, St. Thomas
VI 00802

Detach at This Line

- -

Order Blank

We will send you 2 copies of each form and 1 copy of each publication or set of instructions you circle. Please cut the order blank on the dotted line above and **be sure to print or type your name and address accurately on the bottom portion.**

To help reduce waste, please order only the forms, instructions, and publications you think you will need to prepare your return. Use the blank spaces to order items not listed.

You should either receive your order or notification of the status of your order within 7-15 work days after we receive your request.

1040	Schedule F (1040)	1040EZ	3903 & instructions	8829 & Instructions	Pub. 508	Pub. 575	
Instructions for 1040 & Schedules	Schedule R (1040) & instructions	Instructions for 1040EZ	4562 & instructions	Pub. 1	Pub. 521	Pub. 590	
Schedules A&B (1040)	Schedule SE (1040)	1040-EZ (1994) & Instructions	4868 & Instructions	Pub. 17	Pub. 523	Pub. 596	
Schedule C (1040)	1040A	1040X & Instructions	5329 & Instructions	Pub. 334	Pub. 525	Pub. 910	
Schedule C-EZ (1040)	Instructions for 1040A & Schedules	2106 & Instructions	8283 & Instructions	Pub. 463	Pub. 527	Pub. 917	
Schedule D (1040)	Schedule 1 (1040A)	2119 & Instructions	8582 & Instructions	Pub. 501	Pub. 529	Pub. 929	
Schedule E (1040)	Schedule 2 (1040A)	2210 & Instructions	8606 & Instructions	Pub. 502	Pub. 550	Pub. 936	
Schedule EIC (1040A or 1040)	Schedule 3 (1040A) & Instructions	2441 & Instructions	8822 & Instructions	Pub. 505	Pub. 554		

Name

Number and street

City or town   State   ZIP code

What Is Tele-Tax?

Automated Refund Information allows you to check the status of your refund.

Recorded Tax Information includes about 140 topics that answer many Federal tax questions. You can listen to up to three topics on each call you make.

How Do I Use Tele-Tax?

Choosing The Right Number

Use only the number listed on this page for your area. Use a local city number only if it is not a long distance call for you. **Please do not dial "1-800" when using a local city number.** However, when dialing from an area that does not have a local number, be sure to dial "1-800" before calling the toll-free number.

Automated Refund Information

Be sure to have a copy of your tax return available since you will need to know the first social security number shown on your return, the filing status, and the **exact** whole-dollar amount of your refund. Then, call the appropriate phone number listed on this page and follow the recorded instructions.

The IRS updates refund information every 7 days. If you call to find out about the status of your refund and do not receive a refund mailing date, please wait 7 days before calling back.

Touch-tone service is available Monday through Friday from 7:00 A.M. to 11:30 P.M. (Hours may vary in your area.)

Recorded Tax Information

A complete list of topics is on the next page. Touch-tone service is available 24 hours a day, 7 days a week.

Select, by number, the topic you want to hear. Then, call the appropriate phone number listed on this page. **For the directory of topics, listen to topic 123.** Have paper and pencil handy to take notes.

Toll-Free Tele-Tax Telephone Numbers

Alabama
1-800-829-4477

Alaska
1-800-829-4477

Arizona
Phoenix, 640-3933
Elsewhere, 1-800-829-4477

Arkansas
1-800-829-4477

California
Counties of: Alpine, Amador, Butte, Calaveras, Colusa, Contra Costa, Del Norte, El Dorado, Glenn, Humboldt, Lake, Lassen, Marin, Mendocino, Modoc, Napa, Nevada, Placer, Plumas, Sacramento, San Joaquin, Shasta, Sierra, Siskiyou, Solano, Sonoma, Sutter, Tehama, Trinity, Yolo, and Yuba,
    1-800-829-4032
Oakland, 839-4245
Elsewhere, 1-800-829-4477

Colorado
Denver, 592-1118
Elsewhere, 1-800-829-4477

Connecticut
1-800-829-4477

Delaware
1-800-829-4477

District of Columbia
628-2929

Florida
1-800-829-4477

Georgia
Atlanta, 331-6572
Elsewhere, 1-800-829-4477

Hawaii
1-800-829-4477

Idaho
1-800-829-4477

Illinois
Chicago, 886-9614
In area code 708,
    1-312-886-9614
Springfield, 789-0489
Elsewhere, 1-800-829-4477

Indiana
Indianapolis, 631-1010
Elsewhere, 1-800-829-4477

Iowa
Des Moines, 284-7454
Elsewhere, 1-800-829-4477

Kansas
1-800-829-4477

Kentucky
1-800-829-4477

Louisiana
1-800-829-4477

Maine
1-800-829-4477

Maryland
Baltimore, 244-7306
Elsewhere, 1-800-829-4477

Massachusetts
Boston, 536-0709
Elsewhere, 1-800-829-4477

Michigan
Detroit, 961-4282
Elsewhere, 1-800-829-4477

Minnesota
St. Paul, 644-7748
Elsewhere, 1-800-829-4477

Mississippi
1-800-829-4477

Missouri
St. Louis, 241-4700
Elsewhere, 1-800-829-4477

Montana
1-800-829-4477

Nebraska
Omaha, 221-3324
Elsewhere, 1-800-829-4477

Nevada
1-800-829-4477

New Hampshire
1-800-829-4477

New Jersey
1-800-829-4477

New Mexico
1-800-829-4477

New York
Bronx, 488-8432
Brooklyn, 488-8432
Buffalo, 685-5533
Manhattan, 406-4080
Queens, 488-8432
Staten Island, 488-8432
Elsewhere, 1-800-829-4477

North Carolina
1-800-829-4477

North Dakota
1-800-829-4477

Ohio
Cincinnati, 421-0329
Cleveland, 522-3037
Elsewhere, 1-800-829-4477

Oklahoma
1-800-829-4477

Oregon
Portland, 294-5363
Elsewhere, 1-800-829-4477

Pennsylvania
Philadelphia, 627-1040
Pittsburgh, 261-1040
Elsewhere, 1-800-829-4477

Puerto Rico
1-800-829-4477

Rhode Island
1-800-829-4477

South Carolina
1-800-829-4477

South Dakota
1-800-829-4477

Tennessee
Nashville, 781-5040
Elsewhere, 1-800-829-4477

Texas
Dallas, 767-1792
Houston, 541-3400
Elsewhere, 1-800-829-4477

Utah
1-800-829-4477

Vermont
1-800-829-4477

Virginia
Richmond, 783-1569
Elsewhere, 1-800-829-4477

Washington
Seattle, 343-7221
Elsewhere, 1-800-829-4477

West Virginia
1-800-829-4477

Wisconsin
Milwaukee, 273-8100
Elsewhere, 1-800-829-4477

Wyoming
1-800-829-4477

Tele-Tax Topics

Topic numbers are effective January 1, 1994.

Call the IRS With Your Tax Question

If you cannot answer your tax question by reading the tax form instructions or one of our free tax publications, please call us TOLL FREE. "Toll Free" is a telephone call for which you pay only local charges, if any. This service is generally available Monday through Friday during regular business hours.

If you want to check on the status of your refund, call Tele-Tax. See page 30 for the number.

Choosing The Right Number

Use only the number listed on this page for your area. Use a local city number only if it is not a long distance call for you. **Please do not dial "1-800" when using a local city number.** However, when dialing from an area that does not have a local number, be sure to dial "1-800" before calling the toll-free number.

Before You Call

Remember that good communication is a two-way process. IRS representatives care about the quality of the service we provide to you, our customer. You can help us provide accurate, complete answers to your tax questions by having the following information available:

1. The tax form, schedule, or notice to which your question relates.
2. The facts about your particular situation (the answer to the same question often varies from one taxpayer to another because of differences in their age, income, whether they can be claimed as a dependent, etc.).
3. The name of any IRS publication or other source of information that you used to look for the answer.

Before You Hang Up

If you do not fully understand the answer you receive, or you feel our representative may not fully understand your question, our representative needs to know this. The representative will be happy to take the additional time required to be sure he or she has answered your question fully and in the manner that is most helpful to you.

By law, you are responsible for paying your fair share of Federal income tax. If we should make an error in answering your question, you are still responsible for the payment of the correct tax. Should this occur, however, you will not be charged any penalty. To make sure that IRS representatives give accurate and courteous answers, a second IRS representative sometimes listens in on telephone calls. No record is kept of any taxpayer's identity.

Toll-Free Tax Help Telephone Numbers

Alabama
1-800-829-1040

Alaska
Anchorage, 561-7484
Elsewhere, 1-800-829-1040

Arizona
Phoenix, 640-3900
Elsewhere, 1-800-829-1040

Arkansas
1-800-829-1040

California
Oakland, 839-1040
Elsewhere, 1-800-829-1040

Colorado
Denver, 825-7041
Elsewhere, 1-800-829-1040

Connecticut
1-800-829-1040

Delaware
1-800-829-1040

District of Columbia
1-800-829-1040

Florida
Jacksonville, 354-1760
Elsewhere, 1-800-829-1040

Georgia
Atlanta, 522-0050
Elsewhere, 1-800-829-1040

Hawaii
Oahu, 541-1040
Elsewhere, 1-800-829-1040

Idaho
1-800-829-1040

Illinois
Chicago, 435-1040
In area code 708,
   1-312-435-1040
Elsewhere, 1-800-829-1040

Indiana
Indianapolis, 226-5477
Elsewhere, 1-800-829-1040

Iowa
Des Moines, 283-0523
Elsewhere, 1-800-829-1040

Kansas
1-800-829-1040

Kentucky
1-800-829-1040

Louisiana
1-800-829-1040

Maine
1-800-829-1040

Maryland
Baltimore, 962-2590
Elsewhere, 1-800-829-1040

Massachusetts
Boston, 536-1040
Elsewhere, 1-800-829-1040

Michigan
Detroit, 237-0800
Elsewhere, 1-800-829-1040

Minnesota
Minneapolis, 644-7515
St. Paul, 644-7515
Elsewhere, 1-800-829-1040

Mississippi
1-800-829-1040

Missouri
St. Louis, 342-1040
Elsewhere, 1-800-829-1040

Montana
1-800-829-1040

Nebraska
Omaha, 422-1500
Elsewhere, 1-800-829-1040

Nevada
1-800-829-1040

New Hampshire
1-800-829-1040

New Jersey
1-800-829-1040

New Mexico
1-800-829-1040

New York
Bronx, 488-9150
Brooklyn, 488-9150
Buffalo, 685-5432
Manhattan, 732-0100
Nassau, 222-1131
Queens, 488-9150
Staten Island, 488-9150
Suffolk, 724-5000
Elsewhere, 1-800-829-1040

North Carolina
1-800-829-1040

North Dakota
1-800-829-1040

Ohio
Cincinnati, 621-6281
Cleveland, 522-3000
Elsewhere, 1-800-829-1040

Oklahoma
1-800-829-1040

Oregon
Portland, 221-3960
Elsewhere, 1-800-829-1040

Pennsylvania
Philadelphia, 574-9900
Pittsburgh, 281-0112
Elsewhere, 1-800-829-1040

Puerto Rico
San Juan Metro Area,
766-5040
Elsewhere, 1-800-829-1040

Rhode Island
1-800-829-1040

South Carolina
1-800-829-1040

South Dakota
1-800-829-1040

Tennessee
Nashville, 834-9005
Elsewhere, 1-800-829-1040

Texas
Dallas, 742-2440
Houston, 541-0440
Elsewhere, 1-800-829-1040

Utah
1-800-829-1040

Vermont
1-800-829-1040

Virginia
Richmond, 649-2361
Elsewhere, 1-800-829-1040

Washington
Seattle, 442-1040
Elsewhere, 1-800-829-1040

West Virginia
1-800-829-1040

Wisconsin
Milwaukee, 271-3780
Elsewhere, 1-800-829-1040

Wyoming
1-800-829-1040

Phone Help for People With Impaired Hearing Who Have TDD Equipment

All areas in U.S., including Alaska, Hawaii, Virgin Islands, and Puerto Rico:
1-800-829-4059

Note: *This number is answered by TDD equipment only.*

Hours of TDD Operation:

8:00 A.M. to 6:30 P.M. EST
   (Jan. 1–April 2)

9:00 A.M. to 7:30 P.M. EDT
   (April 3–April 15)

9:00 A.M. to 5:30 P.M. EDT
   (April 16–Oct. 29)

8:00 A.M. to 4:30 P.M. EST
   (Oct. 30–Dec. 31)

A Glossary of Tax and Financial Terms

A

Accelerated Cost Recovery System (ACRS). A method of **depreciation** that, in general, allowed you to deduct the cost of a **capital asset** at a faster rate than was previously possible. ACRS is used for almost all **assets** you began depreciating in the years 1981–1986. See Chapter 10, *Rental Income and Expenses.*

Accelerated depreciation. A method of **depreciation** that allows you to deduct the cost of property more rapidly than **straight-line depreciation.** Accelerated depreciation rates are included in **ACRS** rates and most Modified Accelerated Cost Recovery System **(MACRS)** rates if you want to use them. See Chapter 10, *Rental Income and Expenses.*

Accountable plan. An employer's plan for reimbursing employees for business-related expenses, under which the employees are required to substantiate each business expense to the employer and return any reimbursement in excess of the substantiated expenses. Reimbursements received under an accountable plan are generally excluded from wages and are not subject to employment taxes. See Chapter 28, *Car Expenses and Other Employee Business Expenses.*

Accounting to an employer. Providing an employer with documents (a diary, a statement of expenses, etc.) that support expenses you have incurred.

Accrual method of accounting. A method of accounting in which income is reported in the year in which it is earned and expenses are reported in the year in which they are incurred. See and compare **cash method of accounting.** See Chapter 1, *Filing Information.*

Acquisition debt. Indebtedness (subject to a $1 million ceiling) used to acquire a principal residence or a second home, the interest on which is fully deductible.

ACRS. See **Accelerated Cost Recovery System.**

Adjusted basis. The measure used as a starting point for determining a gain or a loss on the sale or exchange of property. Your **basis** in property is adjusted by certain increases (**capital expenditures,** for example) or decreases (**depreciation**). See Chapter 14, *Basis of Property.*

Adjusted gross income. Your **gross income** reduced by certain adjustments allowed by law. For example, you may reduce your gross income by your deductible **IRA** contribution. See Chapter 31, *How to Figure Your Tax.*

ADS. See **Alternative Depreciation System.**

Alimony. Periodic payments made under (1) a decree of divorce or **separate maintenance,** (2) a written separation agreement, or (3) a decree of **support.** Alimony may be taken as a **deduction** in calculating your **adjusted gross income.** See Chapter 19, *Alimony.*

Alternative Depreciation System (ADS). A way of depreciating assets using the straight-line depreciation method and longer recovery periods than are available under **MACRS.** Mandatory for such items as foreign assets, luxury automobiles, and tax-exempt use property. See Chapter 10, *Rental Income and Expenses.*

Alternative Minimum Tax (AMT). A tax that may apply in lieu of income tax when a taxpayer has **tax preference items** or certain deductions allowed in determining regular taxable income. How to calculate the alternative minimum tax is explained in Chapter 31, *How to Figure Your Tax.*

Amended return. A return (Form 1040X) filed within a 3-year period to correct a mistake on an original income tax return or to claim a refund.

Amortization. A deductible expense allowed as a means of recovering your investment in an intangible asset. Compare with **depreciation.**

Amount realized. The **fair market value** of property, including money (at face value), received in a sale or an exchange.

AMT. See **Alternative Minimum Tax.**

Annuity. A sum of money paid periodically that includes the return of your invested capital plus income generated by it. An annuity is frequently purchased by an individual for investment purposes and is used by retirement plans to pay **pensions.** See Chapter 11, *Retirement Plans, Pensions, and Annuities.*

Annuity trust. A type of **trust** in which one of the beneficiaries is paid a specified amount of income at least annually. See Chapter 11, *Retirement Plans, Pensions, and Annuities.*

Applicable federal rate. Interest rates published by the IRS for use in determining imputed interest on transactions providing for below-market interest.

Asset. Property that has value.

At-risk limitations. Generally, partnership losses are deductible up to the amount you have at risk in the activity. The amount at risk is the cash and property contributed to the activity and any amounts borrowed for use in the activity for which you are personally liable. See Chapter 13, *Other Income*.

Audit. An examination of your financial records. When the **IRS** examines your tax records, it is called an audit. See Chapter 41, *If Your Return Is Examined*.

Away from home overnight. A period substantially longer than an ordinary workday during which you are away from your **tax home.** The period you are away from home must include time for sleep or rest.

B

Bad debt. An amount owed you representing a cash outlay or an item already included in income that you are unable to collect. See Chapter 15, *Sale of Property*.

Basis. Generally, the cost of an **asset.** See Chapter 14, *Basis of Property*.

Boot. The taxable receipt of cash or its equivalent as part of an exchange of properties.

C

Calendar year. A 12-month period ending on December 31. Most individual taxpayers are required to file their returns on the basis of such a year. Compare **fiscal year.**

Capital asset. In general, property held for personal purposes or investment, rather than for business purposes.

Capital expenditures. The costs for additions or improvements that increase the value or **useful life** of your property.

Capital gain dividend (capital gain distribution). A distribution to shareholders in a **mutual fund** of a **capital gain** realized by the fund on the sale of a part of its investment portfolio. See Chapter 9, *Dividends and Other Corporate Distributions*.

Capital gain or loss. A gain or loss arising from the sale or exchange of **capital assets.** You compute your capital gain or loss by comparing the amount you realize on the sale or exchange of an **asset** with the **adjusted basis** of the asset. See Chapter 17, *Reporting Gains and Losses*.

Capital loss carryover. The excess of **capital losses** over **capital gains** that cannot be deducted in a particular year and must be carried over to the succeeding year.

Capitalize. To treat an expenditure as a cost or an additional cost of property that increases the property's **basis**—as opposed to treating the expenditure as a current deduction.

Cash method of accounting. A method of accounting in which income is reported when it is actually or **constructively received** and expenses are reported when they are paid.

Casualty loss. A loss arising from fire, storm, shipwreck, or other similar and unexpected occurrences. See Chapter 26, *Nonbusiness Casualty and Theft Losses*.

Child support. Payments made to support a minor child following a divorce or a separation. The payments cannot be deducted from your **gross income** and are not taxable to the recipient parent. Starting in 1985, the parent with custody of

the child is generally entitled to the dependency **exemption** unless such a right is expressly waived. See Chapter 19, *Alimony*.

Clifford trust. A short-term **trust** in which the beneficiary receives the income from the property placed in the trust. When the trust expires, after 10 years or on the death of the beneficiary, if earlier, the property that remains in the trust is returned to the original donor. Current tax rules have terminated the tax benefits of such trusts.

Community income. Income that is treated as belonging equally to each spouse, no matter which spouse actually earns or receives it. See **community property.**

Community property. Property that belongs equally to husband and wife. This concept of property ownership is used in Arizona, California, Idaho, Louisiana, Nevada, New Mexico, Texas, and Washington.

Condemnation. The seizure of property for compensation by a government agency for a public purpose.

Constructive receipt. Income you are taxed on because it was made available to you to draw on, even if it has not yet been physically transferred to you.

Consumer interest. Interest incurred on personal and consumer purchases. Consumer interest is not deductible in 1991 and thereafter. Also called personal interest.

Corporation. A business entity owned by shareholders that is generally treated as a separate taxpayer.

D

Declining balance depreciation. A method of **accelerated depreciation** by which each year's **depreciation** is a percentage of the reduced **basis** of the **asset.** See Chapter 10, *Rental Income and Expenses*.

Deductions. Expenses allowed by law to reduce your **gross income** to **adjusted gross income** or **taxable income.**

Deferred gain. A gain realized but not recognized as **taxable income** until a later time.

Deficiency. The difference between your correct tax liability and the amount reported on your return.

Dependency exemption. An exemption of $2,350 in 1993 allowed to a taxpayer for a qualifying **dependent.** See Chapter 3, *Personal Exemptions and Dependents*.

Dependent. An individual who is supported by a taxpayer in a manner that entitles the taxpayer to claim an **exemption** allowance on his or her income tax return. See Chapter 3, *Personal Exemptions and Dependents*.

Dependent care credit. A credit to reduce your taxes dollar-for-dollar based on expenses incurred in caring for a **dependent** so that you can be gainfully employed. See Chapter 33, *Child and Dependent Care Credit*.

Depletion. A deductible expense that reflects the decrease of a depletable natural resource, such as oil and gas, as it is extracted. See Chapter 10, *Rental Income and Expenses*.

A GLOSSARY OF TAX AND FINANCIAL TERMS

Depreciable asset. Property used in a trade or a business or held for the production of income with a **useful life** of more than 1 year.

Depreciation. A deductible expense that reflects a reasonable allowance for wear and tear of tangible property. Only property that has a **useful life** of more than 1 year and is used for business or income-producing purposes can be depreciated. Depreciation can be calculated under various prescribed methods. See Chapter 10, *Rental Income and Expenses.*

Direct rollover. An eligible rollover distribution that is paid directly to an eligible retirement plan for the benefit of the distributee. See Chapter 11, *Retirement Plans, Pensions, and Annuitites.*

Discount income. Income on an obligation purchased at a discount and maturing at face value.

Dividend. Generally, a share of a corporation's profits that is distributed to shareholders and is taxable to them.

Domicile. The place that an individual intends to be his or her permanent residence.

Dual-status alien. An individual who is a **nonresident alien** for part of the year and a **resident alien** or U.S. citizen for the rest of the year. See Chapter 39, *Foreign Citizens Living in the United States.*

E

Earned income. Compensation for personal services rendered. Earned income does not include amounts received from an **annuity** or a **pension.**

Earned income credit. A refundable credit, based on **earned income,** available to taxpayers with low income and dependent children.

Eligible retirement plan. A qualified retirement plan, an individual retirement account, or an individual retirement annuity.

Eligible rollover distribution. Any distribution of all or any portion of the balance to the credit of the employee in a qualified retirement plan.

Employee. An individual whose work is performed under the control or direction of an employer.

Estimated tax. A direct quarterly payment of taxes that is required, for example, when the taxes withheld from your wages are inadequate. See Chapter 5, *Tax Withholding and Estimated Tax.*

Exclusion. An amount that is excluded from **gross income.**

Exemption. An amount allowed to a taxpayer as a **deduction** for himself or herself and for each **dependent.** Each exemption is worth $2,350 in 1993.

F

Fair market value. The price a willing buyer would pay and a willing seller would accept, neither of whom is under any compulsion to buy or to sell.

Fiduciary. An individual who has discretionary authority to receive and manage another's income. Also, an individual who

holds **assets** in a **trust** in which another person has an interest.

Finance charges. Interest paid on purchases made on a deferred-payment basis.

Fiscal year. A 12-month period ending on the last day of any month other than December.

Foreign corporation. A corporation organized outside the laws of the United States.

Foreign tax credit. A credit allowed for income taxes paid to a foreign tax jurisdiction (e.g., a foreign country) to mitigate double taxation.

401(k) plan. A tax-favored deferred compensation plan under which a portion of an employee's salary is withheld on a pretax basis and allowed to earn income on a tax-deferred basis until withdrawal is authorized at age 59 1/2, separation from service or other qualifying events.

G

Gross income. All of the **income** of a taxpayer before subtracting any allowable **deductions.**

H

Head of household. A taxpayer who is unmarried and pays more than 50% of the cost of maintaining a residence for the entire year for a qualifying individual. If you are a head of household, you qualify for special tax rates. See Chapter 2, *Filing Status.*

Health insurance credit. A refundable credit claimed for amounts paid for health insurance coverage that includes one or more qualifying children.

High income surtax. A 10% surtax on higher income taxpayers, which results in a 39.6% top tax bracket. The surtax is imposed on taxable income in excess of $250,000 ($125,000 if you are married filing separately).

Holding period. The length of time an **asset** is held. The holding period of a capital asset determines whether a sale or an exchange results in a **long-term** or a **short-term capital gain** or **loss.** See Chapter 17, *Reporting Gains and Losses.*

Home equity debt. Debt secured by a principal residence or a second residence in excess of acquisition debt. Interest on home equity indebtedness not in excess of $100,000 is generally fully deductible.

I

Imputed interest. Interest deemed to have been earned or charged on a debt if the stated interest rate is below the rate set by law.

Incentive stock option (ISO). A type of stock option that can be received and exercised without recognition of income until the option stock is sold, if certain statutory requirements are met, See Chapter 6, *Wages, Salaries, and Other Earnings.*

Income averaging. A method that taxes some of the income in a high-income year as if it were spread over a 4-year period. Income averaging is not available for years after 1986.

Income with respect to a decedent. Income earned by an individual before death but taxed to the survivor who receives it after the earner dies.

Independent contractor. A person whose work hours and procedures (as opposed to end product) are not controlled by another and who is therefore deemed to be self-employed for tax purposes.

Individual Retirement Account. See **Individual Retirement Arrangement.**

Individual Retirement Annuity. See **Individual Retirement Arrangement.**

Individual Retirement Arrangement (IRA). An account under which certain individuals are permitted to establish a retirement plan and to deduct their contributions to the account. The maximum contribution that can be deducted each year is $2,000 per person. See Chapter 18, *Individual Retirement Arrangements (IRAs).*

Inflation adjustment. The adjustment by which, beginning in 1989, the tax rate brackets, standard deduction, and personal exemption amounts are adjusted for inflation.

Installment payment election. Certain taxpayers may elect to pay the additional 1993 taxes they owe because of the tax rate changes in the 1993 Tax Act in three equal annual installments. The installments are due each year on April 15, beginning April 15, 1994. See Chapter 31, *How to Figure Your Tax.*

Installment sale method of accounting. A method of reporting the gain from a sale during the years in which the installment payments of the purchase price are received instead of reporting the entire amount of the gain in the year of sale.

Intangible personal property. Property whose value consists of rights rather than material attributes. Some examples are patents, notes receivable, and accounts receivable.

Internal Revenue Service (IRS). The division of the U.S. Treasury Department that is responsible for the enforcement of the tax laws.

Investment credit. A tax credit (now repealed) based on the cost of **tangible personal property** used for business purposes.

Involuntary conversion. The forced disposition of property as a result of casualty, theft, or **condemnation.** Upon conversion, you usually receive cash through insurance proceeds or condemnation awards.

IRA. See **Individual Retirement Arrangement.**

IRS. See **Internal Revenue Service.**

Itemized deductions. Expenses claimed on your individual tax return that are subtracted from your **adjusted gross income** to arrive at **taxable income**. Some examples are medical expenses, interest, taxes, and charitable contributions. See Part III, *Standard Deduction and Itemized Deductions.*

J

Joint return. A tax return filed by a husband and wife that combines their incomes and **deductions.**

K

Keogh plan. A retirement plan for **self-employed** individuals. Contributions to Keogh plans, within specified limits, are deductible, and income accumulates tax-free until it is withdrawn. The money in the plan is subject to various restrictions. Keogh plans are also sometimes known as HR 10 plans. See Chapter 18, *Individual Retirement Arrangements (IRAs).*

Kiddie tax. The popular name for the tax on the investment income in excess of $1,200 of a dependent child under age 14, based on the parent's marginal tax rate.

L

Legally separated. A husband and wife who are separated and required to live apart under a decree of separate maintenance.

Like-kind exchange. A tax-free exchange of properties held for either productive use in a trade or a business or for investment that are of the same nature or character. The term is also used in connection with **involuntary conversions.**

Long-term capital gain or loss. Gain or loss on the sale or exchange of a **capital asset** that has been held for a legislatively mandated **holding period.** For property purchased after December 31, 1987, the long-term holding period is more than 1 year.

Lump-sum distribution. The distribution or payment within 1 taxable year of the total balance due from an employer-funded qualified **pension** or profit-sharing plan triggered by a specified event (e.g., retirement, separation from service).

Luxury Tax. An excise tax imposed on the excess of the cost of certain luxury items (e.g., cars, boats, aircraft, jewelry, and furs) over threshold amounts. This tax has been repealed on all items, except cars. See Chapter 23, *Taxes.*

M

MACRS. See Modified Accelerated Cost Recovery System.

Marginal tax rate. The tax rate at which each additional dollar of income over a specified ceiling is taxed.

Marital deduction. Provision that allows unlimited transfers to a spouse free of estate and gift tax.

Material participant. A taxpayer who participates in an activity on a regular, continuous, and substantial basis. The term is used in connection with passive activity losses.

Miscellaneous itemized deductions. A class of itemized deductions (e.g., investment expenses, fee for tax advice, union dues) that is deductible only to the extent that the total exceeds 2% of adjusted gross income.

Modified Accelerated Cost Recovery System (MACRS). A method of depreciation generally used for assets acquired after 1986. See Chapter 10, *Rental Income and Expenses.*

Mutual fund. A company that is in the business of investing its shareholders' funds, usually in stocks or bonds; sometimes known as a **regulated investment company.**

N

Net operating loss. Generally, a business loss that exceeds current income. A net operating loss may be carried back 3 years and carried forward for 15 years to reduce taxes in 1 or more of those years.

Nonqualified stock option. A type of stock option that when exercised creates **ordinary income** for the taxpayer.

Nonrecourse financing. A type of debt for which, in the event of forfeiture, the lender may not seek recovery from the borrower personally but must look only to the financed property.

Nonrecovery property. A term that applies to most tangible depreciable property that was in use *prior* to 1981. See Chapter 10, *Rental Income and Expenses*.

Nonresident alien. An individual who is not a citizen or permanent resident of the United States. See Chapter 39, *Foreign Citizens Living in the United States*.

Nontaxable exchange. An exchange of property in which no gain or loss is recognized for tax purposes.

O

OID. See **original issue discount.**

Ordinary gain or loss. A gain or loss other than a **capital gain or loss.**

Ordinary income. Income that does not arise from the sale or exchange of a **capital asset** or a **section 1231 asset** and is not subject to any preferential tax treatment.

Original issue discount (OID). Applies to debt instruments initially sold at prices below their face value. The difference between the face value and the amount paid is OID. Generally, the OID must be included in taxable income over the life of the debt instrument. See Chapter 8, *Interest Income*.

Outside salesperson. An **employee** who engages in selling, principally away from his or her employer's place of business.

Owner-employee. An **employee** who is the **proprietor** of a business. Also, a partner who owns more than 10% of either the capital or the profit interest in a partnership.

P

Passive activity loss. A loss from a trade or a business in which the taxpayer is not a **material participant.** Passive activity losses are subject to deduction limitations. Passive activities include rental activities and investments in limited partnerships. See Tax Shelters and Passive Activity Losses in Chapter 13, *Other Income*.

Patronage dividend. A taxable distribution made by a cooperative to its members or patrons.

Pension. An arrangement under which payments are made to retired employees from an employer-funded retirement plan for past services rendered.

Percentage depletion. A method of calculating **depletion** that applies a fixed percentage to the **gross income** generated by the mineral property. See Chapter 10, *Rental Income and Expenses*.

Personal-use property. Property that is not held for investment or use in a trade or a business.

Points. Certain charges paid by a borrower, calculated as a percentage of the loan proceeds; each point is 1%. They are also called loan origination fees, maximum loan charges, or premium charges. See Chapter 24, *Interest Expense*.

Proprietor. An individual who is the sole owner of his or her trade or business.

Q

QTIP Trust. See **Qualified Terminal Interest Property Trust.**

Qualified charitable organization. A nonprofit philanthropic organization specifically approved by the U.S. Treasury as a recipient of charitable contributions that are deductible for tax purposes. See Chapter 25, *Contributions*.

Qualified plan. An **employee** benefit plan established by an employer that meets certain requirements and therefore qualifies for certain tax benefits. Two examples are **pension** and profit-sharing plans.

Qualified residence interest. Interest paid or accrued during the taxable year on acquisition indebtedness (limited to $1 million) or home equity indebtedness (limited to $100,000). See Chapter 24, *Interest Expense*.

Qualified Retirement Plan. See **Qualified plan.**

Qualified small business stock (QSBS). Certain stock issued after August 10, 1993 and held for more than five years. The gain from the sale of this stock is eligible for a 50% exclusion from gross income.

Qualified Terminal Interest Property Trust (QTIP Trust). A trust that allows you to transfer property to your spouse for life only, while still qualifying for the marital deduction. See Chapter 42, *Planning Ahead for 1994 and Beyond*.

Qualifying widow(er). A filing status for a surviving spouse with dependents that allows the individual to use the same tax rates and tables as if he or she were married filing jointly.

R

Real estate investment trust (REIT). A **trust** that invests principally in **real estate** and mortgages. It is taxed only on the income that it does not distribute to its beneficiaries or shareholders.

Real property (real estate). Physical property that is permanent and nonmovable in nature. Two examples are land and buildings.

Realized gain or loss. The difference between the amount you are entitled to receive on a sale or exchange of property and the **adjusted basis** of the property.

Recognized gain or loss. The amount of gain or loss realized that must be included in your **taxable income.**

Recovery property. A term that applies to most tangible depreciable property placed in use *after* 1980 and *before* 1987.

Regulated investment company. An investment company subject to Security and Exchange Commission regulations. If the investment company distributes its income to its shareholders, it does not pay any taxes.

Reinvested dividends. Dividends that are used to purchase additional shares of stock in the company rather than being distributed in cash. A reinvested dividend is taxable income in the year in which it is **constructively received.**

REIT. See **Real estate investment trust.**

Remainder interest. An interest in property or a **trust** that is left after the income beneficiaries have received their income interest.

Resident alien. An individual who is not a citizen of the United States but is a permanent resident of the United States.

Rollover. A distribution from a qualified plan that is reinvested tax-free in another qualified plan or IRA within 60 days of the date of receipt.

Royalty income. Income received for the use of certain kinds of property (e.g., mineral and literary properties, patents).

S

S corporation. A corporation that meets the requirements of, and elects to be taxed under, Subchapter S of the Internal Revenue Code. Generally, this type of corporation acts as a conduit, passing through to the shareholders its **taxable income** or loss, much like a partnership.

Salvage value. The estimated value of an **asset** at the end of its **useful life.**

Section 179 deduction. A tax rule whereby you can elect to deduct, instead of depreciate, up to $17,500 of certain trade or business property in the year in which the property is placed in service. See Chapter 36, *If You Are Self-Employed: How to File Schedule C.*

Section 1231 assets. Generally, **depreciable assets** used in a trade or a business and held for the required long-term holding period. Net gains from the sale or exchange of section 1231 assets (after recapture of **depreciation**) are treated as **capital gains;** net losses are treated as **ordinary losses.** See Chapter 17, *Reporting Gains and Losses.*

Self-employed. An individual who works in his or her own trade or business.

SEP. See **Simplified Employee Pension.**

Separate maintenance payments. Payments made from one spouse to another when they are living apart. The payments are made in accordance with a court order or an agreement between the parties. See Chapter 19, *Alimony.*

Service business. A business that derives income from providing personal services. Two examples are law and accounting firms.

Short sale. A sale of borrowed securities made either to fix a gain to be reported in a subsequent year or to profit from an expected decline in price.

Short-term capital gain or loss. A gain or loss on the sale or exchange of a **capital asset** that has been held for less than the legislatively mandated **holding period.** For property purchased after December 31, 1987, that holding period is 1 year or less. See Chapter 17, *Reporting Gains and Losses.*

Simplified Employee Pension (SEP). An individual retirement arrangement that permits your employer to contribute up to 15% of your compensation, subject to limitations, to your IRA each year. See Chapter 18, *Individual Retirement Arrangements (IRAs).*

Single. The filing status of an individual who is unmarried on the last day of a calendar year.

Single premium annuity contract. An **annuity** contract with a life insurance company. In exchange for a single premium, the life insurance company agrees to make periodic annuity payments, beginning on a specified date.

Specialized small business investment company (SSBIC). A licensed partnership or corporation under the Small Business Administration's Small Business Investment Act of 1958, § 301(d). Corporations and individuals can elect to roll over, without the payment of any capital gain tax, the capital gain from the sale of publicly traded securities into the purchase of common stock or a partnership interest in a SSBIC.

Standard deduction. A **deduction** used to reduce income by taxpayers who do not itemize their deductions. The amount of the deduction depends on your filing status, whether you are 65 or older or blind, and whether you can be claimed as a **dependent** on another taxpayer's return. Adjusted annually for inflation since 1989. See Chapter 20, *Standard Deduction.*

Standard mileage rate. An IRS-approved optional amount used to claim a **deduction** for business transportation expenses in lieu of deducting actual expenses (not including parking, tolls, interest, and taxes). The standard mileage rate is currently 28 cents for all business miles.

Statute of limitations. The time period within which the IRS can assess and collect taxes and taxpayers can file for refunds.

Stock appreciation right (SAR). A right granted to an **employee** for additional compensation based on the amount of the appreciation in the company's stock between the date on which the right is granted and the date on which the right is exercised.

Stock dividend. A distribution by a corporation of additional shares of its stock to existing shareholders.

Stock option. An option to buy stock at a specified price.

Straddle. Offsetting investment positions.

Straight-line depreciation. A method of **depreciation** in which the cost or other **basis** of the **asset** is deducted in equal amounts over the property's **useful life.** See Chapter 10, *Rental Income and Expenses.*

Sum of the years' digits depreciation. A method of **accelerated depreciation** that is based on a formula developed from the expected **useful life** of the property.

Supplemental young child credits. A supplemental credit that may be added to the basic earned income credit for certain taxpayers with young children.

Support. Payments made for the care and maintenance of a **dependent.** Expenditures for support include payments for food, lodging, medical expenses, and so on.

Surviving Spouse. See **Qualifying widow(er)**.

T

Tangible personal property. Physical property that can be moved. Two examples are machinery and automobiles.

Tax credit carryforward (or carryover). Tax credit that you were unable to use to reduce previous year's tax and that can be applied to offset future tax.

Tax-exempt income. Income that is not subject to federal income tax. An example is income from state and municipal bonds.

Tax home. Generally, a taxpayer's place of business, employment, or post of duty. A tax home's location is used to determine if certain travel expenses are deductible as incurred away from home.

Tax loss carryforward (or carryover). Generally, a **net operating loss** that you were not able to apply against your income during the 3-year carryback period and that may now be applied against future income. The tax benefit of the loss expires if it is not utilized within a 15-year carryover period.

Tax preference items. Items that could subject you to the alternative minimum tax (AMT). Two examples are **accelerated depreciation** of **real property** and **percentage depletion.**

Tax Rate Schedules. Schedules issued by the IRS that must be used in figuring individual income tax for persons who may not use **Tax Tables** (i.e., persons with taxable income of at least $100,000).

Tax-Sheltered Annuities [section 403(b) plans]. A tax-favored, deferred compensation plan only for employees of tax-exempt organizations and public schools, under which a portion of an employee's salary is withheld on a pretax basis and allowed to earn income on a tax-deferred basis until withdrawal is authorized at age 59 1/2, separation from service, or other qualifying events.

Tax Tables. Tables issued by the IRS that must be used in figuring individual income tax for persons with **taxable income** of less than $100,000.

Taxable income. Your **gross income** minus all allowable **deductions** and **exemptions.** (This is the amount on which income tax is computed, before tax credits.)

Tenants by the entirety. Generally, husband and wife who own property jointly. At the death of one, the survivor takes the entire estate.

Tenants in common. Two or more parties, each of whom holds an undivided share of an entire property. After the death of one party, the survivor does not take the entire estate. The decedent's will or state law determines what happens to the decedent's share.

Trade date. The date on which a purchase or sale of securities occurs. The trade date is used in determining the **holding period** of a security.

Trust. An entity to which **assets** are transferred for protection, management, and distribution to others.

U

Unitrust. A charitable remainder **trust** of which there is an income beneficiary who is not a charitable organization. The income beneficiary receives annual payments based on a fixed percentage of the net **fair market value** of the trust's **assets.**

Useful life. The number of years a **depreciable asset** may reasonably be expected to be in use in a trade or a business.

W

Wash sale. A transaction in which you sell stock at a loss and 30 days before or after the sale you buy substantially identical stock. Losses from wash sales are not deductible.

Index

NOTE: Boldface numerals indicate Ernst & Young Explanations, TaxAlerts, TaxPlanners, and TaxSavers

Do You Make These Six Common Mistakes On Your Taxes?

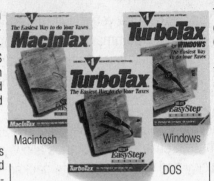

The Ernst & Young Tax Guide Reader Survey

Please complete this questionnaire and return it with your rebate request on the reverse side of this page or mail the survey separately to The E&Y Tax Products Rebate Offer, P.O. Box 1151, Grand Rapids, MN 55745-1151.

1. How do you prepare your taxes? (you may check more than one)
   Book_____ Which one(s)? _____
   Software _____ Which one(s)? _____
   Accountant _____
   Tax Preparer _____

2. Do you itemize your deductions? Yes ____ No ____

3. Have you purchased *The Ernst & Young Tax Guide* before? Yes ____ No ____
   How many years have you purchased it? _____

4. Why did you choose *The Ernst & Young Tax Guide*?
   ___ Ernst & Young brand name   ___ Useable tax forms
   ___ Topics covered   ___ Recommended
   ___ Numerous examples   ___ Special features (TaxAlerts, TaxPlanners, TaxSavers, TaxOrganizers)

5. How could we make *The Ernst & Young Tax Guide* even more useful for you?
   _____
   _____

6. How would you rate your interest in an Ernst & Young electronic product that:
   6a. lets you reference/read the tax guide on your PC?
       ___ Not interested   ___ Interested   ___ Very interested
   6b. helps you prepare your tax return?
       ___ Not interested   ___ Interested   ___ Very interested
   6c. provides interactive tax planning and strategies?
       ___ Not interested   ___ Interested   ___ Very interested

7. How much would you be willing to pay for an Ernst & Young electronic product?
   ___ $19.95   ___ $29.95   ___ $39.95   ___ over $50.00

8. What is your education level?
   ___ High School diploma or less   ___ Some College
   ___ College graduate   ___ Graduate courses or degree

9. Age: 25-34 ___ 35-49 ___ 50-65 ___ Over 65 ___

10. Marital status: Single ___ Married ___ Divorced/Separated ___ Widowed ___

11. Sex: Male _____ Female _____

12. Annual household income: $20,000-$34,999 ___ $35,000-$49,999 ___
    $50,000-$74,999 ___ $75,000-$100,000 ___ $100,000-$199,999 ___ Over$200,000 ___

13. Would you be willing to respond to a follow up survey by phone? Yes ___ No ___
    Telephone number (____) _____

Name _____
Title _____
Company _____
Address _____
City, State, Zip _____

SPECIAL CONSUMER OFFERS!

Get a one dollar rebate on your purchase
of each of the following tax guides. Increase your
dollar value of the rebate (up to $3.00)
if you buy more than one book.

For Year-Round Planning

$1.00 Rebate for The Ernst & Young
Tax-Saving Strategies Guide 1994

For Preparing Federal Tax Returns

$1.00 Rebate for The Ernst & Young
Tax Guide 1994

For Preparing NY, NJ, and CT State Tax Returns

$1.00 Rebate for The Ernst & Young
New York, New Jersey, Connecticut
State Tax Guide 1994

Plus get a free calculator with your rebate!

- -

OFFICIAL REFUND CERTIFICATE

I have purchased the Ernst & Young guides checked below and have enclosed the purchase receipt with the
books' prices circled. Please send me the appropriate refund.

(1 Book)	(2 Books)	(3 Books)
❏ $1 Refund	❏ $2 Refund	❏ $3 Refund

Mail to: The E&Y Tax Products Rebate Offer
P.O. Box 1151
Grand Rapids, MN 55745-1151

_____
Name (Please Print)

_____
Address

_____
City

_____
State   Zip

_____
Signature

_____
Store Where Purchased

Please complete the Reade   y on the reverse side and mail with your rebate request.